D0847421

Contemporary Authors

Contemporary Authors

A Bio-Bibliographical Guide to
Current Writers in Fiction, General Nonfiction,
Poetry, Journalism, Drama, Motion Pictures,
Television, and Other Fields

FRANCES C. LOCHER
Editor

MARTHA G. CONWAY
MARIE EVANS
DAVID VERSICAL
Associate Editors

volume 104

GALE RESEARCH COMPANY • THE BOOK TOWER • DETROIT, MICHIGAN 48226

EDITORIAL STAFF

Christine Nasso, *General Editor, Contemporary Authors*

Frances C. Locher, *Editor, Original Volumes*

Martha G. Conway, Marie Evans,
and David Versical, *Associate Editors*
Anne M. Guerrini, B. Hal May,
and Les Stone, *Senior Assistant Editors*
Tim Connor, Charity Anne Dorgan, Diane L. Dupuis,
Nancy S. Gearhart, Michael L. LaBlanc, Lillian S. Sims,
Mary Sullivan, and Susan M. Trosky, *Assistant Editors*
Denise M. Cloutier, Shirley Kuenz, Christine J. May,
Norma Sawaya, and Shirley Seip, *Editorial Assistants*

Kathryn T. Floch, Adele Sarkissian,
and Barbara A. Welch, *Contributing Editors*
Peter Benjaminson, C. H. Gervais, Jean W. Ross,
and Judith Spiegelman, *Interviewers*
Andrea Geffner, Arlene True,
and Benjamin True, *Sketchwriters*
Eunice Bergin, *Copy Editor*

Special recognition is given to the staff of
Young People's Literature Department, Gale Research Company

Frederick G. Ruffner, *Publisher*   James M. Ethridge, *Editorial Director*

Copyright © 1982 by
GALE RESEARCH COMPANY

Library of Congress Catalog Card Number 62-52046
ISBN 0-8103-1904-7
ISSN 0010-7468

Authors Featured in This Volume

Among the more than 1,600 listings in *Contemporary Authors*, Volume 104,
are full-length sketches on these authors and media people.

Melvin Belli—Well-known American trial lawyer, innovator in the field of civil law, and defense attorney for Lee Harvey Oswald's accused murderer, Jack Ruby; author of an auto-biography, *My Life on Trial,* and more than thirty other popular and scholarly books.

Romulo Betancourt—Late Venezuelan political activist and advocate of a democratic government; served as Venezuela's president; author of nearly twenty books, including *Venezuela: Oil and Politics.*

Andre Brink—Award-winning South African novelist and playwright; author of *Rumours of Rain* and the once-banned *A Dry White Season.* (Sketch includes interview.)

Bryher—British writer, critic, and poet, best known for her historical novels *Gate to the Sea* and *This January Tale* as well as other well-received works, recognized for the quality of their writing and their mastery of history.

John Byrne—British playwright; his plays include "The Slab Boys," "Writer's Cramp," and "Normal Service."

Mary S. Calderone—Award-winning American physician; co-founder of Sex Information Educational Council of the United States (SIECUS); author of books, including *Sexuality and Human Values* and *The Family Book About Sexuality.*

Rod Carew—Professional baseball player; now first baseman for the California Angels; described as "the best damn hitter in baseball"; author of an autobiography.

Arlene Croce—Award-winning American dance critic; now with *New Yorker* magazine; author of well-received collection of her dance columns, *Afterimages.* (Sketch includes interview.)

Salvador Dali—Well-known Spanish painter, illustrator, designer, and etcher; commonly regarded as founder and leader of the surrealist movement; author of several books, including autobiographies and art manifestos; also author of surrealist screenplays.

Elizabeth Drew—Award-winning American journalist; author of books on the American political scene, including *Washington Journal: The Events of 1973-74* and *Portrait of an Election: The 1980 Presidential Campaign.* (Sketch includes interview.)

Linda Du Breuil—Late prolific American author under a variety of pseudonyms and in several genres, including science fiction, historical fiction, murder mysteries, and gothic novels. (Sketch includes interview, obtained four months prior to the author's death.)

Dizzy Gillespie—Award-winning, widely recognized American jazz performer, composer, and arranger; besides his numerous musical compositions, he wrote his autobiography, *To Be or Not to Bop.*

Ellen Goodman—Award-winning American journalist; won 1980 Pulitzer Prize for distinguished commentary; author of books *Turning Points, Close to Home,* and *At Large.* (Sketch includes interview.)

Robert W. Greene—American investigative journalist, currently assistant managing editor of *Newsday;* has received prestigious awards in his field, among them two Pulitzer Prizes; author of books, including *The Heroin Trail* and *The Sting Man: Inside ABSCAM.*

Vaclav Havel—Prize-winning Czech playwright whose plays have been banned from the Czech stage since 1968; he is recognized as one of the most important playwrights in eastern and central Europe; plays known to the West include "The Garden Party," "The Memorandum," and "The Increased Difficulty of Concentration."

Hans Hellmut Kirst—German novelist; described by some as the conscience of his people with regard to the burden of Nazism on postwar Germany; author of internationally known works, including *The Wolves, Revolt of Gunner Asch, The Night of the Generals,* and his trilogy, *Zero Eight Fifteen.*

Kris Kristofferson—Award-winning American songwriter, country singer, and film actor.

A. J. Liebling—Well-known late American reporter and columnist with the *New Yorker* magazine for twenty-eight years; sometimes called "the conscience of American journalism."

Raymond Fernand Loewy—Award-winning French-born American industrial designer; originator of the streamlining concept, calling it "beauty through function and simplification"; author of three books, including an autobiography, *Never Leave Well Enough Alone.*

Henry R. Luce—Late American journalist; founder of the magazine publishing empire Time Inc., including *Time, Fortune, Sports Illustrated,* and *Life* magazines.

Raymond Massey—Canadian-born American actor, director, and producer; best known for stage and screen portrayals of Abraham Lincoln and as the character Dr. Gillespie on the "Dr. Kildare" television series; author of his autobiography in two volumes, *When I Was Young* and *A Hundred Different Lives.* (Sketch includes interview.)

Vladimir Maximov—Soviet novelist and playwright exiled for opposition to the Soviet political system; author of *Farewell From Nowhere, Quarantine, A Man Survives,* and other novels and plays.

David McFadden—Canadian poet and fiction writer; has won awards for his books of poetry *A Knight in Dried Plums* and *A New Romance.* (Sketch includes interview.)

Gian Carlo Menotti—Award-winning composer, librettist, and playwright; his name is associated with well-known operas, including "Amahl and the Night Visitors," "The Consul," "The Saint of Bleecker Street," and his Broadway success, "The Medium"; co-founder of Festival of Two Worlds in Spoleto, Italy.

Marvin M. Mitchelson—American attorney who has been involved in several precedent-setting cases, including *Marvin* v. *Marvin,* which concerned the legal rights of lovers who live together, and the case of the *People* v. *Douglas,* which gave indigents the right to counsel, a principle later adopted in all fifty states.

C. L. Moore—American science fiction writer; author of the genre classic *Judgment Night.* (Sketch includes interview.)

Peter Nichols—Award-winning British playwright; author of black comedies, including "A Day in the Death of Joe Egg," "The National Health," and "The Freeway."

Vijaya Lakshmi Pandit—Well-known Indian nationalist; first woman elected to India's legislature; served India in other governmental capacities; wrote four books, including the recent memoir *The Scope of Happiness.*

Gail Thain Parker—American free-lance writer; policy changes she made while Bennington College's president resulted in her forced resignation; author of four nonfiction books, including *The Writing on the Wall: Inside Higher Education in America.*

Molly Picon—American actress, well known in Yiddish theatre as "the sweetheart of Second Avenue"; elected to Theatre Hall of Fame; author of *So Laugh a Little* and her autobiography, *Molly!*

Abraham Polonsky—American screenwriter and novelist; blacklisted from 1951 to 1967; tells *CA* how blacklisting affected him personally and professionally. (Sketch includes interview.)

V. Sackville-West—British novelist and poet; subject of *Portrait of a Marriage,* a biography by her son Nigel Nicolson; associated with the Bloomsbury group and with Virginia Woolf in particular.

Lee Salk—American columnist, author, and award-winning psychologist in the field of pediatric psychology; *How to Raise a Human Being, What Every Child Would Like His Parents to Know,* and *Fathers and Sons: An Intimate Relationship* are among his books.

Alvin Sapinsley—American writer; author of many teleplays, notably public television's rendition of *The Scarlet Letter,* produced by WGBH-TV (Boston) in 1979.

Siegfried Sassoon—Late British poet and author best known for his poems written during World War I and his autobiographical novels.

Tony Scaduto—American free-lance writer and journalist; well known as author of books on popular musicians, including *Bob Dylan* and *Mick Jagger: Everybody's Lucifer.*

George P. Shultz—American economist and labor relations specialist, who served in several posts during the Nixon administration; author of works in his field, including *Leaders and Followers in an Age of Ambiguity* and *Economic Policy Beyond the Headlines.*

Jerry Sonenblick—American attorney; author of *The Legality of Love,* a paperback guide on "the hottest topic in legal circles these days," the legal rights of lovers living together.

Peter Terson—British regional playwright; his plays include "Mooney and His Caravans," "I'm in Charge of These Ruins," and "Zigger Zagger."

John Kennedy Toole—Late American college teacher whose novel, *A Confederacy of Dunces,* was published eleven years after the author's death; a best-seller, it made the author, posthumously, a success both critically and commercially.

Roy Wilkins—Award-winning late American civil rights activist; long-time director of the NAACP; instrumental in 1954 Supreme Court decision that declared segregation in public schools unconstitutional.

Emlyn Williams—British actor, director, and playwright, best known for his 1930's productions "Night Must Fall" and "The Corn Is Green," and for his one-man shows on the lives of Charles Dickens and Dylan Thomas.

Preface

This volume of *Contemporary Authors* marks the first step in broadening the series' scope to encompass authors deceased since 1900 whose works are still of interest to today's readers. (Previously, *CA* covered only living writers and authors deceased 1960 or later.) Since the great poets, novelists, short story writers, and playwrights of the early twentieth century are popular writers for study in today's high school and college literature courses, and since their writings continue to be analyzed by today's literary critics, these writers are in many ways as contemporary as the authors *CA* has featured up to this point. Students and others, not recognizing the stated scope of *CA*, have often questioned the absence from the series of major writers of the early twentieth century.

Therefore, future volumes of *CA* will contain full-length sketches on important authors who lived and wrote between 1900 and 1959. To begin providing information on authors from this period, most of whom will receive longer treatment later, we are including in this and subsequent *CA* volumes brief, one-paragraph entries on them. These brief entries are further explained in the section of the preface below headed "New Feature: Brief Entries."

The emphasis of *CA* will, of course, continue to be on living and recently deceased authors. A large proportion of the more than 1,600 entries in this volume (which bring to over 67,000 the number of authors now represented in the series) cover current, nontechnical writers in all genres—fiction, nonfiction, poetry, drama, etc.—whose books are issued by commercial, risk publishers or by university presses. Authors of books published only by known vanity or author-subsidized firms are ordinarily not included. Since native language and nationality have no bearing on inclusion in *CA*, authors whose writings are in languages other than English are included in *CA* if their works have been published in the United States or translated into English.

Although *CA* focuses primarily on authors of published books, the series also encompasses prominent persons in communications: newspaper and television reporters and correspondents, columnists, newspaper and magazine editors, photojournalists, syndicated cartoonists, screenwriters, television scriptwriters, and other media people.

No charge or obligation is attached to a *CA* listing. Authors are included in the series solely on the basis of the above criteria and their interest to *CA* users.

Compilation Methods

The editors make every effort to secure information directly from living authors through questionnaires and personal correspondence. If authors of special interest to *CA* users are deceased or fail to reply to requests for information, material is gathered from other reliable sources. Biographical dictionaries are checked (a task made easier through the use of Gale's *Biography and Genealogy Master Index* and other volumes in the "Gale Biographical Index Series"), as are bibliographical sources, such as *Cumulative Book Index* and *The National Union Catalog*. Published interviews, feature stories, and book reviews are examined, and often material is supplied by the authors' publishers. Whether prepared from questionnaires or through extensive research, all sketches on living writers are sent to the authors for review prior to publication. Sketches on recently deceased authors are sent to family members, agents, etc., if possible, for a similar review.

New Feature: Brief Entries

CA users have indicated that having some information, however brief, on authors not yet in the series would be preferable to waiting until full-length sketches can be prepared as outlined above under "Compilation Methods." Beginning with this volume, therefore, *CA* introduces one-paragraph entries on authors, including both early twentieth-century and current writers, who presently do not have sketches in *CA*. These short listings, identified by the heading *BRIEF ENTRY,* highlight the author's career and writings and often provide a few sources where additional information can be found.

Brief entries are not intended to replace sketches. Instead, they are designed to increase *CA*'s comprehensiveness and thus better serve *CA* users by providing pertinent information about a large number of authors, many of whom will be the subjects of full sketches in forthcoming volumes.

This volume, for example, includes brief entries on living authors, such as Hank Aaron, Bella Abzug, and Philip Agee, for whom full-length sketches have not yet been compiled. As noted earlier in the preface, this volume also contains a substantial number of brief entries on authors deceased since 1900 who are still of interest to today's readers. Among the early twentieth-century authors in this volume who are slated for full sketch treatment in the future are Leo Tolstoy, Mark Twain, and Virginia Woolf.

Informative Sidelights

Numerous *CA* sketches contain Sidelights, which provide a personal dimension to the listing, supply information about the critical reception the authors' works have received, or both. Some authors work closely with *CA*'s editors to develop lengthy, incisive Sidelights, as in the case of Hungarian-born Marie de Balkany, who writes under the pen name Marie Balka. She contends, "My life lies more between the covers of my books than in my days, although I don't write about myself." Concerned that her books reflect her commitment to well-expressed writing as well as theme, Balkany remarks that *Le Dieu eparpille,* her latest book, is "my best book, the one that has taken me farthest in toil, meaning, and achievement. More than the others it has been ignored." Speaking in poignant terms about how ultimately important readership is to a writer, Balkany tells *CA:* "A writer's lifespan is a journey . . . . Were I to die tomorrow one could say about me: 'She fought to give life to ghosts, turn them into flesh and blood. She tried to read a pattern into the senseless maze of life. She did it obscurely, without prizes, honors, awards, and yet she lived each day with passion, as if it were the last.' " Nevertheless hopeful, Balkany admits, "I shall, of course, not die tomorrow, nor the day after, and something may yet happen to pull me out from the cold toward recognition."

Journalists, too, report to *CA*'s editors how their concern with communication can be applied in their craft. For many of them, book writing becomes either a natural extension of their work or a compensation for limitations they perceive in the medium. For instance, Leonard Levitt stresses to *CA*'s readers that "writing is hard and unglamorous work." He notes, "I learned my craft writing for newspapers, but after some point newspaper writing and good writing become antithetical." Recently turned full-time writer, Levitt points out that his nonfiction book *The Healer* "grew out of a story I covered for the Long Island *Newsday,* but its scope and point of view surpassed the limits of newspaper journalism."

CA's editors compile equally incisive Sidelights when authors and media people of particular interest to *CA* readers are unable to supply Sidelights material or when demand for information about the critical reception their works have received is especially high. For instance, in his Sidelights on Melvin Belli, assistant editor Tim Connor depicts the flamboyant attorney as a legal innovator, defender of unpopular causes, courtroom actor, and jet-setter, a man who "emerges as Puck, Pan and Gladstone rolled into one." Dance critic Arlene Croce's Sidelights section, by assistant editor Mary Sullivan, acknowledges that "a lot of us have thought for some time that Croce is about the best reviewer writing about any of the arts." Senior assistant editor Anne M. Guerrini writes about Salvador Dali's bizarre surrealism and includes in her Sidelights quotes from the artist's first autobiography, *The Secret Life of Salvador Dali,* in which he admits: "At seven I wanted to be Napoleon. And my ambition has been growing steadily ever since." In her Sidelights about jazz musician Dizzie Gillespie, assistant editor Diane L. Dupuis portrays him as "a great figure in American music, in world music, and perhaps the greatest living musical innovator we have." And stage, screen, and television actor Raymond Massey's Sidelights, written by assistant editor Lillian S. Sims, recall how the theatre was first described to Massey by his mother as a " 'once-upon-a-time' place where people called actors and actresses tell stories." These sketches, as well as others with Sidelights compiled by *CA*'s editors, provide informative and enjoyable reading.

Writers of Special Interest

CA's editors make every effort to include a substantial number of entries in each volume on active authors and media people of special interest to *CA*'s readers. Since *CA* also includes sketches on deceased writers of special interest, a significant amount of work on the part of *CA*'s editors goes into the compilation of full-length entries on important deceased authors. Some of the prominent writers whose sketches are contained in this volume are noted in the list headed "Authors Featured in This Volume" immediately preceding the preface.

Exclusive Interviews

CA provides exclusive, primary information on certain authors in the form of interviews. Prepared specifically for *CA,* the never-before-published conversations presented in the section of the sketch headed *CA INTERVIEW* give *CA* users the opportunity to learn the authors' thoughts, in depth, about their craft. Subjects chosen for interviews are, the editors feel, authors who hold special interest for *CA*'s readers.

Authors and journalists in this volume whose sketches include interviews are Andre Brink, Arlene Croce, Elizabeth Drew, Linda Du Breuil, Ellen Goodman, Raymond Massey, David McFadden, C.L. Moore, and Abraham Polonsky.

Obituary Notices Make *CA* Timely and Comprehensive

To be as timely and comprehensive as possible, *CA* publishes brief, one-paragraph obituary notices on deceased authors within the scope of the series. These notices provide date and place of birth and death, highlight the author's career and writings, and list other sources where additional biographical information and obituaries may be found. To distinguish them from full-length sketches, obituaries are identified with the heading *OBITUARY NOTICE.*

CA includes obituary notices for authors who already have full-length sketches in earlier *CA* volumes, in effect completing their sketches. Fifteen percent of the obituary notices in this volume are for authors with listings already in *CA. CA also* contains obituary notices for authors not yet included in the series. Deceased authors of special interest presently represented only by obituary notices are scheduled for full-length sketch treatment in forthcoming *CA* volumes.

Cumulative Index Should Always Be Consulted

The most recent *CA* cumulative index is the user's guide to the volume in which an author's listing appears. The entire *CA* series consists of original volumes, containing entries on authors new to the series, and revision volumes, containing completely updated entries on authors with earlier sketches in the series. The cumulative index, which lists all original and revision volume entries, should always be consulted to locate the specific volume containing an author's original or most recently revised sketch.

For the convenience of *CA* users, the *CA* cumulative index also includes references to all entries in three related Gale series—*Contemporary Literary Criticism* (CLC), which is devoted entirely to current criticism of today's novelists, poets, playwrights, short story writers, filmmakers, screenwriters, and other creative writers, *Something About the Author* (SATA), a series of heavily illustrated sketches on authors and illustrators of books for young people, and *Authors in the News* (AITN), a compilation of news stories and feature articles from American newspapers and magazines covering writers and other members of the communications media.

Retaining *CA* Volumes

As new volumes in the series are published, users often ask which *CA* volumes in their collections, if any, can be discarded. The chart following the preface is designed to assist users in keeping their collections as complete as possible.

As always, suggestions from users about any aspect of *CA* will be welcomed.

IF YOU HAVE:	YOU MAY DISCARD:
1-4 First Revision (1967)	1 (1962) 2 (1963) 3 (1963) 4 (1963)
5-8 First Revision (1969)	5-6 (1963) 7-8 (1963)
Both 9-12 First Revision (1974) AND *Contemporary Authors Permanent Series,* Volume 1 (1975)	9-10 (1964) 11-12 (1965)
Both 13-16 First Revision (1975) AND *Contemporary Authors Permanent Series,* Volumes 1 and 2 (1975, 1978)	13-14 (1965) 15-16 (1966)
Both 17-20 First Revision (1976) AND *Contemporary Authors Permanent Series,* Volumes 1 and 2 (1975, 1978)	17-18 (1967) 19-20 (1968)
Both 21-24 First Revision (1977) AND *Contemporary Authors Permanent Series,* Volumes 1 and 2 (1975, 1978)	21-22 (1969) 23-24 (1970)
Both 25-28 First Revision (1977) AND *Contemporary Authors Permanent Series,* Volume 2 (1978)	25-28 (1971)
Both 29-32 First Revision (1978) AND *Contemporary Authors Permanent Series,* Volume 2 (1978)	29-32 (1972)
Both 33-36 First Revision (1978) AND *Contemporary Authors Permanent Series,* Volume 2 (1978)	33-36 (1973)
37-40 First Revision (1979)	37-40 (1973)
41-44 First Revision (1979)	41-44 (1974)
45-48 (1974) 49-52 (1975) 53-56 (1975) 57-60 (1976) ↓ ↓ 104 (1982)	NONE: These volumes will not be super-seded by corresponding revised vol-umes. Individual entries from these and all other volumes appearing in the left column of this chart will be revised and included in the *New Revision Series.*
Volumes in the *Contemporary Authors New Revision Series*	NONE: The *New Revision Series* does not replace any single volume of *CA.* All volumes appearing in the left column of this chart must be retained to have in-formation on all authors in the series.

CONTEMPORARY AUTHORS

*Indicates that a listing has been compiled from secondary sources believed to be reliable,
but has not been personally verified for this edition by the author sketched.*

A

AALLYN, Alysse
See CLARK, Melissa

*   *   *

AARON, Hank
See AARON, Henry Louis

*   *   *

AARON, Henry Louis   1934-
(Hank Aaron)

BRIEF ENTRY: Born February 5, 1934, in Mobile, Ala. American professional baseball player. Aaron began his baseball career in the Negro League in 1952, then played with the Atlanta Braves (named Milwaukee Braves until 1966) from 1954 to 1974. He was the National League batting champion in 1956 and 1959 and was named the National League's most valuable player in 1957. Aaron reached the pinnacle of his career in 1974 when he hit his 715th home run, breaking Babe Ruth's career home run record. In 1975 and 1976 Aaron played for the Milwaukee Brewers and before retiring raised his home run total to 755. Aaron was elected to baseball's Hall of Fame in 1982. Aaron's writings include *Aaron, r.f.* (World Publishing, 1968), *How to Hit and Run the Bases* (Grosset, 1971), and *Hitting the Aaron Way* (Prentice-Hall, 1974). *Biographical/critical sources: Current Biography,* Wilson, 1958; *New York Times,* April 30, 1972, July 8, 1973, July 26, 1973, September 11, 1975, April 1, 1976; *Biography News,* Gale, April, 1974.

*   *   *

ABBENSETTS, Michael   1938-

PERSONAL: Born June 8, 1938, in Georgetown, Guyana; became citizen of England, 1974; son of Neville John (a doctor) and Elaine Abbensetts. *Education:* Attended Queens College (Guyana), 1952-56, Stanstead College (Canada), 1956-58, and Sir George Williams University (Canada), 1960-61. *Home:* 4 Caxton Rd., London W12 8AJ, England. *Agent:* Gil Parker, William Morris Agency, 1350 Avenue of the Americas, New York, N.Y. 10019; and Jane Annakin, William Morris Agency Ltd., 147-149 Wardour St., London W1V 3TB, England.

CAREER: Playwright. Tower of London, London, England, security attendant, 1963-67; associated with Sir John Soahe

Museum, 1968-71, Carnegie-Mellon University, Pittsburgh, Pa., professor of drama, 1981—. Resident dramatist at Royal Court Theatre, 1974. *Awards, honors:* George Devine Award from Royal Court Theatre, 1973, for "Sweet Talk"; Afro-Caribbean Award from *Afro-Caribbean Post,* 1979, for "Empire Road."

WRITINGS: Empire Road (novel), Granada, 1979.

Plays: *Sweet Talk* (two-act; first produced in the West End at Royal Court Theatre, 1973), Methuen, 1974; "Alterations" (two-act), first produced in the West End at Theatre at New End, 1978; "Samba" (two-act), first produced in the West End at Tricycle Theatre, 1980; "In the Mood" (two-act), produced in the West End at Hampstead Theatre, October, 1981.

Teleplays: "The Museum Attendant," 1973; "Inner City Blues," 1974; "Crime and Passion," 1975; "Roadrunner," 1977; "Black Christmas," 1977. Also author of scripts for the television series "Empire Road," 1978-79.

Radio plays; broadcast by BBC-Radio, except as noted: "Sweet Talk," 1974; "Home Again," 1975; "The Sunny Side of the Street," 1977; "Brothers of the Sword," 1978; "Alterations," BBC World Service, 1980; "The Fast Lane," Capital Radio, 1980; "The Dark Horse," 1981.

WORK IN PROGRESS: A television play, "Easy Money" (tentative title); a play, "The Caribbean Lady" (tentative title).

SIDELIGHTS: Abbensetts told *CA:* "When I first started to write for the theatre, there were maybe two or three black playwrights living in England. Certainly black novelists wrote plays, but I'm talking about black playwrights. Originally, I too wanted to be a novelist. Then I saw a version of John Osborne's play 'Look Back in Anger.' It changed my life. After that, all I wanted was to be a playwright. This turned out to be slightly more difficult than I imagined. I knew so little about plays, not only did I have to teach myself to *write* plays, I also had to teach myself to *read* them. I loved reading books, but reading a play was foreign to me.

"The first play I ever wrote was a long one-act, not a full-length play. I no longer remember the title, but the play was about a West Indian adolescent and the mother of a Canadian school friend. When I was about sixteen or seventeen I was sent away to a boarding school in Canada. One summer, a school friend and his mother who was divorced invited me down to their summer cottage. The play is loosely based on what happened during that holiday.

"After I wrote the play I did not know what to do with it. I should add that by then I was living in London, having decided England was the best country for a budding playwright. Anyway, I realized the best thing to do was find myself an agent. I know no agents. None. So I bought a copy of a play by David Mercer and looked to see who his agent was. He was represented by Peggy Ramsay. It was not until later that I discovered that Miss Ramsay was one of the most influential and successful agents in England. So not knowing any of this I just turned up on her doorstep with my play, only to be told by her assistant, 'Oh no, Miss Ramsay never, never accepts a script delivered by hand.' One had to write a letter of introduction first. However, luck was with me that day, because Miss Ramsay's assistant did accept my play. Never underestimate the charm of a Gemini!

"Two weeks later I was still waiting for a reply. So I telephoned to see what had happened about my play. Miss Ramsay herself answered the phone. 'What,' she said, 'you just turned up and left a play here. Come and take it away immediately.' The next day I turned up at her office to take my play away. I discovered that Miss Ramsay had gone to Edinburgh and had taken a pile of plays to read on the train. By accident my play happened to be among the pile. The next day my phone rang. This time it was Peggy Ramsay phoning me. She liked my play. She suggested we meet. So I went around to her office yet again. She talked, I listened. She told me that though she had liked the play, she felt I could do better. She advised me to write another play. A full-length play. 'Tell us,' she said, 'what it feels like to be a black man in England today.'

"The next day I quit my job and decided this would be my make-or-break play. I began a play about a sweet-talking young man whose weakness was gambling on the horses. In the interest of research, I began to frequent betting parlours to such an extent that I became hooked on gambling. Every morning I would write from 7:30 to 1:00. Then all afternoon I would spend betting on the horses. I couldn't stop myself. I hated Sundays when there was no racing. Yet when the play was finished I lost all interest in gambling. I have never bet again since. The play took me about six months to write. I called it 'Sweet Talk.'

"'Sweet Talk' was later performed at the Royal Court Theatre, the same theatre where, years before, Osborne's 'Look Back in Anger' started. To date, 'Sweet Talk' has been staged in ten different countries. Perhaps the strangest thing of all is that Peggy Ramsay never did become my agent."

* * *

ABBEY, Lloyd Robert 1943-

BRIEF ENTRY: Born April 4, 1943, in London, Ontario, Canada. Canadian educator and poet. Abbey has taught English at the University of Toronto since 1977. His writings include The Antlered Boy (Fiddlehead Poetry Books, 1970), Flies (Oberon Press, 1973), and Braindances (Oberon Press, 1979). Address: Victoria College, University of Toronto, Toronto, Ontario, Canada M5S 1K7. Biographical/critical sources: Times Literary Supplement, April 10, 1981.

* * *

ABELES, Elvin 1907-
(Kerwin Bowles)

PERSONAL: Surname is pronounced Abb-uh-les; born July 5, 1907, in New York, N.Y.; son of Emanuel (a dentist) and Adele (Cohen) Abeles; married Nadya Morgenstern (a dancer),

September 14, 1929. Education: Cornell University, B.A., 1928; Columbia University, M.A., 1931. Home: 80-04 213th St., Queens Village, N.Y. 11427. Office: Macmillan Publishing Co., Inc., 866 Third Ave., New York, N.Y. 10022.

CAREER: Associated with Civil Works Administration, 1933-34, and Works Progress Administration, 1934-41; Workers Alliance (union), New York City, editor of Work, 1937-40; U.S. Navy Yard, Brooklyn, N.Y., machinist, 1942-44; Unicorn Press, New York City, began as encyclopedia editor, became production manager, 1946-48; free-lance writer and editor, 1948-49; Blanchard Press, New York City, in production department, 1949-50; free-lance writer and editor, 1950-54; P. F. Collier, New York City, associate editor of Collier's Encyclopedia, 1954-59; Grolier Society, New York City, associate editor of Encyclopedia International, 1959-61; P. F. Collier, editor of National Encyclopedia, 1961-65; Stravon Educational Press, New York City, editor of Living History of the World, 1965-70; free-lance writer and editor, 1971-73; Macmillan Education Corp., New York City, associate editor of Collier's Encyclopedia, 1973-74; free-lance writer and editor, 1974-80; Macmillan Publishing Co., Inc., New York City, associate editor of Collier's Encyclopedia and Merit Students Encyclopedia, 1980—. Worked as copy editor for Paris edition of Chicago Tribune and Paris Times. Military service: U.S. Navy, 1944-46.

WRITINGS: The Student and the University, Parents' Magazine Press, 1969.

Children's books; under pseudonym Kerwin Bowles: Mike and the Giant (biography of Michelangelo), Stravon, 1951; The Magic Painter (biography of Rembrandt), Stravon, 1951; The Man Who Painted the Sun (biography of Van Gogh), Stravon, 1951. Contributor to Collier's Encyclopedia, Living History of the World, and Harper Encyclopedia of Science.

SIDELIGHTS: Abeles told CA: "I married in Paris and returned to New York during the Depression. I worked for a master's degree but could get no appropriate job, so I lived on the Works Progress Administration until World War II. I helped organize the unemployed and was editor of the union paper for the Workers Alliance. During World War II I became a machinist. I have been an editor rather than a writer, always writing on assignment.

"In all my encyclopedia work I thoroughly enjoyed what I was doing; when I did not, I resigned and found something better (usually). I never stayed in a job I didn't enjoy; I never applied for a job since leaving the Navy; I never knew where I would work next, or if I would work; and I never made much money or had a prestige job. But I always learned something while I worked, which made working worthwhile. I still enjoy editing, while my youthful colleagues are apparently miserable at it (they certainly cannot live on what we get)."

* * *

ABZUG, Bella (Savitzky) 1920-

BRIEF ENTRY: Born July 24, 1920, in New York, N.Y. American lawyer, politician, and author. Bella Abzug began her law practice in New York City in 1944. She defended victims of Senator Joseph McCarthy's attack on suspected communists and worked as counsel for the American Civil Liberties Union. Abzug was elected United States representative from New York in 1971 and served for three terms. An outspoken Democrat and sought-after public speaker, she worked tirelessly during the Vietnam era to end war and the draft and to promote the amnesty movement. Abzug was a co-founder of Women Strike for Peace in the 1960's and received their woman of the year award in 1975. An advocate of the Equal Rights Amendment, Abzug presided over the National Commission on the Observance of International Women's Year in 1977 and co-chaired the President's National Advisory Committee for Women in 1978. She wrote *Bella!: Ms. Abzug Goes to Washington* (Saturday Review Press, 1972). *Address:* 37 Bank St., New York, N.Y. 10014; and 76 Beaver St., New York, N.Y. 10005. *Biographical/critical sources: Current Biography,* Wilson, 1971; *Christian Science Monitor,* June 28, 1972; *New York Times Book Review,* July 2, 1972; *Biography News,* Gale, January/February, 1975; *New York Times,* August 21, 1977.

* * *

ABZUG, Robert H(enry) 1945-

PERSONAL: Born May 2, 1945, in New York, N.Y.; son of Seymour W. (a business executive) and Frances (Wolff) Abzug; married Penne L. Restad (in legal research), November 16, 1980. *Education:* Harvard University, B.A. (magna cum laude), 1967; University of California, Berkeley, Ph.D., 1977. *Residence:* Austin, Tex. *Office:* Department of History, University of Texas, Austin, Tex. 78712.

CAREER: University of California, Berkeley, instructor in history, 1976-77; University of California, Los Angeles, lecturer in history, 1977-78; University of Texas, Austin, assistant professor of history, 1978—. Member of board of trustees of Carver Museum of Black History, 1981—. *Member:* American Historical Association, Organization of American Historians.

WRITINGS: (Contributor) Nathan I. Huggins, Martin Kilson, and Daniel Fox, editors, *Key Issues in the Afro-American Experience II,* Harcourt, 1971; *Passionate Liberator,* Oxford University Press, 1980. Contributor to history journals.

WORK IN PROGRESS: A book on antebellum reform; a book about America's initial responses to the opening of the concentration camps in 1945.

* * *

ACKERMANN, Paul Kurt 1919-

BRIEF ENTRY: Born September 5, 1919, in Bremen, Germany (now West Germany). American educator, editor, and author. Ackermann joined the staff of Boston University in 1948 and has been professor of German, theology, and religious studies since 1965. His works include editions of Thomas Mann's *Die Bekenntrisse des Hochstaplers* (Houghton, 1958), Friedrich Duerrenmatt's *Der Besuch der alten Dame* (Houghton, 1960), Max Frisch's *Biedermann und die Brandstifter* (Houghton, 1963), and Frisch's *Homo Faber* (Houghton, 1973). *Address:* Department of Modern Languages, Boston University, 718 Commonwealth Ave., Boston, Mass. 02215.

* * *

ADAMS, Glenda 1939-

PERSONAL: Born December 30, 1939, in Sydney, Australia; came to the United States, 1964; daughter of Leonard Henry and Elvira (Wright) Felton. *Education:* University of Sydney, B.A., 1962; Columbia University, M.S., 1965. *Residence:* New York, N.Y. *Agent:* Rhoda Weyr, William Morris Agency, 1350 Avenue of the Americas, New York, N.Y. 10036.

CAREER: Held various writing and editorial jobs in New York, N.Y., and Europe, 1965-72; associate director of Teachers and Writers Collaborative, 1973-76; workshop instructor at Columbia University and Sarah Lawrence College, 1976—. *Awards,*

honors: Fellow of New York State Creative Artist Program Service, 1975-76; senior fellow of Australia Council, 1979.

WRITINGS: Lies and Stories, Inwood Press, 1976; *The Hottest Night of the Century* (stories), Angus & Robertson, 1979; *Games of the Strong* (novel), Angus & Robertson, 1981.

Work represented in anthologies, including *Bitches and Sad Ladies; In the Looking Glass; Statements Two.* Contributor of stories to magazines in the United States, England, Australia, Denmark, and the Netherlands, including *Ms., Mother Jones, Transtlantic Review, Sun,* and *Seattle Review.*

WORK IN PROGRESS: A novel, publication by Angus & Robertson expected in 1983; stories.

* * *

ADAMS, Henry (Brooks) 1838-1918
(Tauraatua i Amo, Frances Compton Snow)

BRIEF ENTRY: Born February 16, 1838, in Boston, Mass.; died March 27, 1918, in Washington, D.C. American historian, philosopher, and author. An eccentric figure in American letters, Adams is best known for his third-person autobiography, *The Education of Henry Adams* (1918). In this Pulitzer Prize-winning work, Adams suppressed personal details to focus on his "dynamic theory of history." He contrasted thirteenth-century man's spiritual aspirations, symbolized by the Virgin in his earlier *Mon Saint Michel and Chartres* (1913), with the chaotic and scientifically oriented twentieth century he dubbed the "Dynamo." Most of Adams's books deal with the conflict between man and nature, man's inability to control the course of the world, and Adams's own search for order in a world he believed was falling apart. His novels and two biographies, like his other works, are noted for their historical and political commentary. His nine-volume study entitled *The History of the United States of America During the Administrations of Thomas Jefferson and James Madison* (1890) is still considered one of the best works on U.S. politics in the early 1800's. Adams's voluminous correspondence has been published in several collections. He was a descendant of presidents John Adams and John Quincy Adams. *Biographical/critical sources: The Oxford Companion to American Literature,* 4th edition, Oxford University Press, 1965; *A Formula of His Own: Henry Adams's Literary Experiment,* University of Chicago Press, 1970; *American Authors and Books, 1640 to the Present Day,* 3rd revised edition, Crown, 1972; *Twentieth-Century Literary Criticism,* Volume 4, Gale, 1981.

* * *

ADAMS, William Yewdale 1927-

BRIEF ENTRY: Born August 6, 1927, in Los Angeles, Calif. American anthropologist, educator, and author. Adams has been a professor of anthropology at the University of Kentucky since 1971. He also worked as an archaeologist for UNESCO in liaison with the Sudan Antiquities Service from 1959 to 1966. He wrote *Survey and Excavations in Lower Glen Canyon, 1952-58* (Northern Arizona Society for Science and Art, 1961), *Shonto: A Study of the Role of the Trader in a Modern Navaho Community* (U.S. Government Printing Office, 1963), and *Nubia: Corridor to Africa* (Princeton University Press, 1977). *Address:* Department of Anthropology, University of Kentucky, Lexington, Ky. 40506. *Biographical/critical sources: Who's Who in the South and Southwest,* 14th edition, Marquis, 1975; *Times Literary Supplement,* December 2, 1977.

ADELMAN, Morris Albert 1917-

BRIEF ENTRY: Born May 31, 1917, in New York, N.Y. American economist, educator, and author. Adelman joined the faculty at Massachusetts Institute of Technology in 1948 and became a professor of economics there in 1961. He was a fellow of the Social Science Research Council, 1947-48, and the Ford Foundation, 1962-63. His writings include *A & P: A Study in Price-Cost Behavior and Public Policy* (Harvard University Press, 1959), *The Supply and Price of Natural Gas* (Basil Blackwell, 1962), *Alaskan Oil: Costs and Supply* (Praeger, 1971), and *The World Petroleum Market* (Johns Hopkins Press, 1972). *Address:* 83 Nehoidan Rd., Waban, Mass. 02168; and Department of Economics, Massachusetts Institute of Technology, E52-354, Cambridge, Mass. 02139. *Biographical/critical sources: American Economic Review,* December, 1960; *Who's Who in World Jewry: A Biographical Dictionary of Outstanding Jews,* Pitman, 1972; *Economist,* May 13, 1972, June 2, 1973.

* * *

ADELMAN, Saul J(oseph) 1944-

PERSONAL: Born November 18, 1944, in Atlantic City, N.J.; son of Benjamin (a writer) and Kitty (Sandler) Adelman; married Carol Jeanne Sugerman (a baker), March 28, 1970; children: Aaron, Barry, David. *Education:* University of Maryland, B.S., 1966; California Institute of Technology, Ph.D., 1972. *Home:* 1434 Fairfield Ave., Charleston, S.C. 29407. *Office:* Department of Physics, The Citadel, Charleston, S.C. 29409.

CAREER: Goddard Space Flight Center, Greenbelt, Md., postdoctoral resident research associate in astronomy, 1972-74; Boston University, Boston, Mass., assistant professor of physics, 1974-78; The Citadel, Charleston, S.C., assistant professor of physics, 1978—. *Member:* International Astronomical Union, American Astronomical Society, Optical Society of America, Royal Astronomical Society, British Interplanetary Society, Astronomical Society of the Pacific, Phi Beta Kappa, Sigma Xi, Sigma Pi Sigma, Phi Kappa Phi.

WRITINGS: Bound for the Stars: Space Travel in Our Solar System and Beyond, Prentice-Hall, 1981. Contributor of more than fifty articles to scientific journals.

WORK IN PROGRESS: A science-fiction novel, with father, Benjamin Adelman.

* * *

ADKINS, A(rthur) W(illiam) H(ope) 1929-

BRIEF ENTRY: Born October 17, 1929, in Leicester, England. British classicist, educator, and author. Adkins has been a professor of Greek, philosophy, and early Christian literature at the University of Chicago since 1974, and Edward Olson Professor of Greek since 1977. He began teaching at Scottish and British universities in 1954 and was a fellow of Exeter College, Oxford, from 1961 to 1965. His scholarly writing includes *Merit and Responsibility: A Study in Greek Values* (Clarendon Press, 1960), *From the Many to the One: A Study of Personality and Views of Human Nature in the Context of Ancient Greek Society, Values, and Beliefs* (Cornell University Press, 1970), and *Moral Values and Political Behavior in Ancient Greece: From Homer to the End of the Fifth Century* (Norton, 1972). *Address:* Department of Classics, University of Chicago, 5801 Ellis Ave., Chicago, Ill. 60637. *Biographical/critical sources: Times Literary Supplement,* January 8, 1971; *Virginia Quarterly Review,* winter, 1974; *Directory of*

American Scholars, Volume III: *Foreign Languages, Linguistics, and Philosophy,* 7th edition, Bowker, 1978.

* * *

A.E.
See RUSSELL, George William

* * *

AGEE, Philip 1935-

BRIEF ENTRY: Born July 19, 1935, in Tacoma Park, Fla. American author. Agee spent twelve years as an operative of the Central Intelligence Agency, including work in Mexico and Ecuador, after which he wrote the exposes *Inside the Company: CIA Diary* (Simon & Schuster, 1975), *Dirty Work: The CIA in Western Europe* (Lyle Stuart, 1978), and *Dirty Work II: The CIA in Africa* (Lyle Stuart, 1980). The U.S. Government has taken legal steps to prevent Agee from receiving profits from these books, which were published without the permission of his former employer. Agee has not resided in the United States in recent years, preferring to live in England and West Germany. *Biographical/critical sources: New York Times,* July 12, 1974, April 3, 1980; *Spectator,* January 11, 1975; *American Political Science Review,* March, 1980.

* * *

ALAIN-FOURNIER
See FOURNIER, Henri Alban

* * *

ALCAYAGA, Lucila Godoy
See GODOY ALCAYAGA, Lucila

* * *

ALEICHEM, Sholom
See RABINOVITCH, Sholem

* * *

ALEXANDER, Josephine 1909-
(Josephine Lora)

PERSONAL: Born July 4, 1909, in Biloxi, Miss.; daughter of Sol (a manufacturer) and Lily (Bien) Brown; married Harry Holmes Alexander, Jr. (divorced, 1948); children: Susan Offaly, David Dean. *Education:* University of California, Berkeley, B.A., 1932. *Home:* 140 Downey St., San Francisco, Calif. 94117. *Agent:* Carol A. Murray, 2427 10th St., Berkeley, Calif. 94710. *Office:* Swords to Plowshares, 944 Market St., San Francisco, Calif. 94102.

CAREER: Rancher and dude rancher in Arizona, 1934-48; worked as secretary in Dillon Beach, Calif., and San Francisco, Calif., 1949-72; Swords to Plowshares, San Francisco, Calif., secretary, 1972—. Associated with The Lamplighters and Norman G. Levine and Associates. Photojournalist. *Member:* Media Alliance.

WRITINGS: American Through the Eye of My Needle: Common Sense for the Eighties, Dial, 1981. Contributor to magazines, including *Pacific Discovery, Nation,* and *Harvest Years,* and newspapers, sometimes under pseudonym Josephine Lora, including *Sacramento Bee* and *Santa Rosa Press Democrat.*

WORK IN PROGRESS: At Sea on the Range, completion expected in 1981; *By the Sea With the Grange; My Grandfather the Rabbi; Democracy's Best Weapon: A Free Press.*

SIDELIGHTS: Josephine Alexander commented: "If writing is your addiction, rejection slips accumulate, and your courage falters, reflect upon my record. After being a writer without portfolio until the age of seventy, my first book was published at the age of seventy-one. I expect in the next decade or two to produce some companion volumes. The first was written with no hope of commercial publication, for it is a harsh look at conglomerates, of which most of our book-publishing and book-selling powers are a part. Yet, an eloquent statement that freedom of speech is alive and well in America, it was published by Dial, an affiliate of Dell, an affiliate of Doubleday, a biggie with book and baseball clubs.

"*At Sea on the Range* is an account of my life as the wife of an impoverished and isolated Arizona homesteader during the Great Depression, while I myself came from a sheltered, middle-class, urban environment.

"*By the Sea With the Grange* is an account of the six years I spent with my teenage children in the California fishing town of Bodega Bay, where, in my capacity as a free-lance photojournalist, I uncovered the public utility's secret plan to build a harbor-destroying atomic energy plant on the San Andreas fault, two years ahead of their schedule.

"*My Grandfather the Rabbi* is a memoir of my maternal grandfather, Rabbi Herman M. Bien, a playwright and newspaper editor of San Francisco in the 1850's. Also a Nevada legislator and a draftsman of the state's constitution, he ended up in Vicksburg, Mississippi, an outspoken supporter of Abraham Lincoln and emancipation in that stronghold of antebellum embitterment. He was the published author of a novel, a book of verse, plays, and essays, as well as a musician and inventor.

"*Democracy's Best Weapon: A Free Press* is a study of our commercial press, its faults, virtues, and ways to use it more effectively."

BIOGRAPHICAL/CRITICAL SOURCES: Los Angeles Times, February 6, 1981.

* * *

ALLARDT, Linda 1926-

BRIEF ENTRY: Born June 9, 1926, in Brecksville, Ohio. American educator and poet. Linda Allardt has been a professor of English at the University of Rochester since 1976. She won Borestone Mountain Poetry Awards in 1969 and 1975 and Hackney Literary Awards in poetry in 1973 and 1974. Her writings include *The Names of the Survivors* (Ithaca House, 1979) and an edition of *Journals and Miscellaneous Notebooks of Ralph Waldo Emerson,* Volume XII: *1835-1862* (Harvard University Press, 1976). *Address:* 2 Ann Lynn Rd., Pittsford, N.Y. 14534; and Department of English, University of Rochester, Rochester, N.Y. 14627.

* * *

ALLEN, Mary
See CLEVELAND, Mary

* * *

AMES, Jennifer
See GREIG, Maysie

* * *

AMO, Tauraatua i
See ADAMS, Henry (Brooks)

ANATOL
See SCHNITZLER, Arthur

* * *

ANDERSDATTER, Karla M(argaret) 1938-
(Karla Margaret)

PERSONAL: Surname is pronounced *On*-ders-dot-ter; surname legally changed, 1979; born April 9, 1938, in San Francisco, Calif.; daughter of Howard Riley (a sailor and painter) and Daphne (a teacher; maiden name, Haugen) Crosier; married Robert Billings (a pilot), September 17, 1960 (divorced November, 1970); children: Jennifer Kathleen Billings, Scott Billings. *Education:* University of California, Los Angeles, B.A., 1958, M.A., 1968. *Politics:* "Humanist." *Home address:* P.O. Box T, Sausalito, Calif. 94965.

CAREER: Elementary school teacher in Santa Rosa County, Fla., 1960-61, San Diego, San Mateo, and Los Angeles, Calif., 1961-65, and Duckwater, Nev., 1976-77; San Francisco State University, San Francisco, Calif., part-time lecturer in education, 1974—. Coordinator of poetry at Mill Valley Book Depot; publisher of Open Reader; exhibitor at San Francisco Book Fair; gives workshops and poetry readings; storyteller; artist-in-residence at Centrum Foundation. Member of Committee of Small Magazine Editors and Publishers. *Member:* American Storytellers, Association for Humanistic Psychology, Poets and Writers.

WRITINGS—Poetry: (Under name Karla Margaret) *Spaces,* In Between Books, 1974; *I Don't Know Whether to Laugh or Cry 'Cause I Lost the Map to Where I Was Going,* Second Coming Press, 1978; *Transparencies: Love Poems for the New Age,* New World Press, 1980.

Fantasies for children: (Under name Karla Margaret) *Witches and Whimsies,* In Between Books, 1975; *Marissa the Tooth Fairy,* In Between Books, 1979; *Follow the Blue Butterfly,* In Between Books, 1980.

Work represented in anthologies, including *Dream Notebook,* edited by Robert Gumpertz and Diane Brewer, San Francisco Book Co., 1976; *San Jose State University's Bicentennial Anthology,* 1976; *A Shout in the Streets,* Queens University, 1981. Contributor of articles, stories, and poems to magazines and newspapers, including *Haight Ashbury Journal, Maybe Mombasa, Nitty Gritty,* and *Room: A Women's Literary Journal.*

WORK IN PROGRESS: The Nevernuff Nasty, a children's fantasy; *Journey of Seven Directions,* a woman's myth; *The Gifts of Aletheia,* a fairy tale; *A Quality of Light,* a novel; *Cranberries and Roses,* Books I-II, poems; *Among Women and Men,* poems; *All Things Possible,* poems; *The Rising of the Flesh,* poems; *Myths for Tomorrow,* prose; fairy tales.

SIDELIGHTS: Andersdatter told *CA:* "Because I write for so many different focuses, it is difficult to categorize my work, and hence difficult to find *one* publisher to deal with quality poetry, fiction, children's fantasy, and prose nonfiction. Basically my work is simply the creation of stories from the internal processes that affect and influence and direct my life. Being a writer is like being a true genie, and true magic is nothing more than true knowledge, harvested from living our destinies in this outer reality we call the world. As Thomas McGrath, one of today's finest poets, once said: 'It begins with the world—not the word.' My work begins with my inner world and takes form in the outer world of words."

ANDERSON, E.W.   1901-1981

OBITUARY NOTICE: Born July 8, 1901; died September, 1981. Psychiatrist and educator. The *London Times* described Anderson as "one of the most learned psychiatrists of his time." He was a professor of psychiatry at Victoria University of Manchester, England, from 1949 to 1965, Lord Chancellor's medical visitor from 1965 to 1973, and a professor emeritus of Manchester University. His university background was subsequent to a wide range of psychiatric experience in mental hospitals, including the Cassel and Maudsley hospitals, and his writings included a widely acclaimed book, *Psychiatry.* A friend and former colleague described Anderson as a man who "may have seemed in some ways the classical absent-minded professor, talking with courteous and elaborate precision as he took snuff (to which he was much addicted), when very late for an appointment. . . . At Manchester he was no empire-builder. As Director of the Psychiatric Department he laid emphasis on quality rather than expansion." Obituaries and other sources: *London Times,* September 7, 1981.

*   *   *

ANDERSON, J(ohn) R(ichard) L(ane)   1911-1981

OBITUARY NOTICE—See index for *CA* sketch: Born June 17, 1911, in Georgetown, British Guiana (now Guyana); died August 21, 1981. Journalist, novelist, and poet. Anderson was a senior member of the *Guardian* for over twenty years. In that time he held various positions, including correspondent at Eisenhower's headquarters, labor correspondent, assistant editor, industrial editor, and leader writer. Before joining the *Guardian* staff, he was associated with the *News Chronicle* and the *Textile Recorder.* Interested in sailing and exploration, in 1966 Anderson recreated Lief Ericson's colonizing voyage, traveling from the Faeroes, Iceland, and Greenland, to Martha's Vineyard on the East Coast of North America in a forty-four-foot cutter. This four thousand-mile trip was recorded in *Vinland Voyage.* He also established radio communication with Sir Francis Chichester, who circumnavigated the world, so the explorer's experiences could be shared by the public. Among his books on exploration, sailing, and topography are *The Upper Thames* and *The Oldest Road.* His other works include children's books, such as *The Discovery of America, The Vikings,* and *Discovering History;* novels, namely *Reckoning in Ice* and *Death in the Thames;* and a book of verse, *The Lost Traveller.* Obituaries and other sources: *London Times,* August 25, 1981.

*   *   *

ANDERSON, Kristin
See Du BREUIL, (Elizabeth) L(or)inda

*   *   *

ANDERSON, Sherwood   1876-1941

BRIEF ENTRY: Born September 13, 1876, in Camden, Ohio; died March 8, 1941, in Cristobal, Canal Zone. American laborer, advertising copywriter, paint manufacturer, novelist, and short story writer. Anderson worked as a house painter, stable groom, and newsboy before serving in Cuba during the Spanish-American War. Returning from the war, he became an advertising copywriter in Chicago and then a manager of a paint manufacturing firm in Elyria, Ohio. In 1913, according to the famous story, Anderson walked out on his job and his

family, and rejecting his materialistic middle-class life, he began a new life as a writer. His first novel, *Windy McPherson's Son* (1916), describes a man's break with conventional middle-class life and values. Among the first American authors to explore the complexities of motivation and the psychological process, Anderson was particularly interested in the psychology of sexuality and the unconscious. These interests are reflected in Anderson's first collection of short stories, *Winesburg, Ohio* (1919), which is considered his best and most important work. The stories also demonstrated a significant break with the traditional short story of his times. Rejecting the development of plot through action, Anderson unified his stories with growing emotional intensity. Among his other works are *Poor White* (1920), *The Triumph of the Egg* (1921), and two autobiographies, *A Story Teller's Story* (1924) and *Tar, A Midwest Boyhood* (1926). *Biographical/critical sources: Current Biography,* Wilson, 1941; *Encyclopedia of World Literature in the Twentieth Century,* updated edition, Ungar, 1967; *Twentieth Century Writing: A Reader's Guide to Contemporary Literature,* Transatlantic, 1969; *Twentieth-Century Literary Criticism,* Volume 1, Gale, 1978.

*   *   *

ANDOUARD
See GIRAUDOUX, (Hippolyte) Jean

*   *   *

ANDREYEV, Leonid (Nikolaevich)   1871-1919
(James Lynch)

BRIEF ENTRY: Born c. June 18, 1871, in Orel, Russia (now U.S.S.R.); died September 12, 1919, in Kuokkala, Finland (now U.S.S.R.). Russian lawyer and author. Andreyev is renowned for his extremely pessimistic writings, which bear the influence of Schopenhauer, Chekhov, and Edgar Allan Poe. His most famous play, *He Who Gets Slapped* (1921), concerns a circus clown whose performance centers on being slapped by others. Eventually, his fellow entertainers learn of his previous occupation as a writer, a position he abandoned when his wife deserted him for another scribe who stole his ideas. In Andreyev's other plays, particularly *To the Stars* (1917) and *Life of Man* (1915), he emphasized the gulf between the intellectual and the worker while bemoaning the unswerving cruelty of life. Andreyev's novels, including *The Red Laugh* (1915) and *The Seven Who Were Hanged* (1909), are often cited for their attention to social issues. However, Andreyev was reproached by Russian critics for his failure to pose solutions to problems such as poverty and capital punishment. In his later years, Andreyev grew increasingly melancholic. After three suicide attempts, he left his homeland for Finland, where he became a vehement critic of Russian social and political policies. Andreyev is credited by scholars with introducing symbolism to Russian drama. *Biographical/critical sources: Twentieth Century Authors: A Biographical Dictionary of Modern Literature,* 1st supplement, H. W. Wilson, 1955; *Longman Companion to Twentieth Century Literature,* Longman, 1970; *McGraw-Hill Encyclopedia of World Drama,* McGraw, 1972; *Twentieth-Century Literary Criticism,* Volume 3, Gale, 1980.

*   *   *

ANNUNZIO, Gabriele D'
See D'ANNUNZIO, Gabriele

ANTELL, Will D.   1935-

PERSONAL: Born October 2, 1935, in White Earth, Minn.; married, 1958; children: three. *Education:* Bemidji State College, B.S., 1959; Mankato State College (now University), M.S., 1964; University of Minnesota, Ed.D., 1973. *Office:* Minnesota Department of Education, 550 Cedar St., St. Paul, Minn. 55101.

CAREER: Teacher at public schools in Janesville, Minn., and Stillwater, Minn., 1959-68; Minnesota Department of Education, St. Paul, human relations consultant, 1968-69, director of Indian education, 1969-73, assistant commissioner of education, beginning in 1974. Regent of Institute of American Indian Art, 1971—; chairman of Special Committee on Indian Education of National Council for Indian Opportunity, 1970-72; visiting professor of educational administration at Harvard University, 1973-74; National Advisory Council on Indian Education, vice-chairman, 1973-74, chairman, beginning in 1974. *Member:* American Association of School Administrators, American Education Research Association, National Indian Education Association (president, 1970-72). *Awards, honors:* National Defense Education Act fellowship, Northern Michigan University, 1965, University of Minnesota, 1968; Bash Foundation fellowship, 1972.

WRITINGS: (Editor) *American Indians: An Annotated Bibliography of Selected Library Resources,* University of Minnesota, 1970; *William Warren* (juvenile biography), Dillon, 1973; *Culture, Psychological Characteristics, and Socioeconomic Status in Educational Program Development for Native Americans,* National Educational Laboratory Publishers, 1974.*

*   *   *

ANTHONY, Inid E.   1925-

PERSONAL: Born May 6, 1925, in England; daughter of William Thomas (a teacher) and Ann Elizabeth (a nurse; maiden name, Jones) Anthony. *Education:* Attended Victoria University of Manchester and Institute of Archaeology, London. *Religion:* Anglican. *Residence:* Cardiff, Wales. *Office:* Welsh Folk Museum, St. Fagan's, Cardiff CF5 6XB, Wales.

CAREER: Roman Baths Museum, Bath, England, assistant curator, 1952-56; Verulamium and St. Albans City Museums, St. Albans, England, director, 1956-70; Welsh Folk Museum, Cardiff, Wales, head of department of domestic and corporate life, 1970—. *Wartime service:* Voluntary Aid Detachment, 1944-46. *Member:* Society of Antiquaries (fellow).

WRITINGS: Roman London, Granada, 1972; *Guide to Archaeological Sites in Wales,* Shire Publications, 1973. Contributor to academic journals.

*   *   *

APOLLINAIRE, Guillaume
See KOSTROWITZKI, Wilhelm Apollinaris de

*   *   *

APPLETON, Lawrence
See LOVECRAFT, H(oward) P(hillips)

*   *   *

APTER, Samson   1910-

PERSONAL: Born May 15, 1910, in Apatow, Poland; came to the United States, 1936, naturalized citizen, 1942; son of Joseph and Malie (Trefler) Apter; married Mina Rasiuk (a dress designer), April, 1935; children: Daniel, David. *Education:* Attended Jewish Teachers Seminary, New York, N.Y., 1936-38. *Religion:* "Jewish traditional." *Home:* 66-66 Thornton Pl., Rego Park, N.Y. 11374. *Office:* Congress for Jewish Culture, 25 East 78th St., New York, N.Y. 10021.

CAREER: Writer. Worked on magazine *Our Hope* in Warsaw, Poland 1925-27; Yiddish P.E.N. Club, New York City, secretary, 1964-78; Yiddish Writers Union, New York City, secretary, 1978—. Assistant to executive director of Congress for Jewish Culture; delegate to international congresses in France, Ireland, and Israel. *Member:* International P.E.N. (vice-president of Yiddish club). *Awards, honors:* Award from Yiddish Culture Federation, 1946, for novel, *In the Roman Ghetto;* Congress for Jewish Culture award, 1977, for novel, *The Preisingers,* and Jacob Gladstone Literary Award, 1977, from Congress for Jewish Culture, for general literary achievements.

WRITINGS: Between Towns (short stories), Wochenblat, 1936; *Der Bunt and Other Stories,* Jewish Culture Federation, 1942; *In the Roman Ghetto* (novel), Jewish Culture Federation, 1946; *In a New World* (historical novel), Central Yiddish Culture Organization, 1956; *The Preisingers* (novel), Cyco & Peretz Publishers, 1964, translation from the Yiddish by Joseph Singer published under same title by A. S. Barnes, 1980; *When the Troopers Will Come* (short stories), Central Yiddish Culture Organization, 1973; *The Marrano Family Da Silva* (historical novel), published serially by Jewish Daily Forward, 1981.

WORK IN PROGRESS: A biographical novel about Jewish immigrant life in the United States and Canada, publication expected in 1984.

BIOGRAPHICAL/CRITICAL SOURCES: Jewish Daily Forward, June 15, 1980; *Detroit Jewish News,* August 22, 1980.

*   *   *

ARCHER, Mildred   1911-

PERSONAL: Born December 28, 1911, in London, England; daughter of Valentine (a schoolmaster) and Agnes (Dodd) Bell; married William George Archer, July 17, 1934 (deceased); children: Michael, Margaret Archer Lecomber. *Education:* St. Hilda's College, Oxford, M.A., 1934. *Home:* 18A Provost Rd., Hampstead, London NW3 4ST, England.

CAREER: Oxford University, Oxford, England, secretary, 1949-54; India Office Library and Records, London, England, in charge of department of prints and drawings, 1954-80; writer, 1980—. *Member:* Royal Asiatic Society (fellow). *Awards, honors:* D.Litt., Oxford University, 1978; Officer of Order of the British Empire, 1979.

WRITINGS: Patna Painting, Royal India Society, 1947; (with husband, William George Archer) *Indian Painting for the British,* Oxford University Press, 1955; *Tippoo's Tiger,* H.M.S.O., 1959; *Natural History Drawings in the India Office Library,* H.M.S.O., 1962; *Indian Architecture and the British,* Royal Institute of British Architects, 1968; *British Drawings in the India Office Library,* H.M.S.O., 1969; *Company Drawings in the India Office Library,* H.M.S.O., 1972; *Indian Popular Painting in the India Office Library,* H.M.S.O., 1977; (editor with John Bastin) *The Raffles Drawings in the India Office Library,* Oxford University Press, 1978; *India and British Portraiture,* Sotheby Parke Bernet Publications, 1979; *Early Views of India,* Thames & Hudson, 1980; (with Toby Falk) *Indian Miniatures in the India Office Library,* Sotheby Parke Bernet

Publications, 1981. Contributor to magazines, including *Connoisseur, Apollo,* and *History Today.*

WORK IN PROGRESS: British Artists in India; Indian Painting for the British; Memoirs of India.

BIOGRAPHICAL/CRITICAL SOURCES: Los Angeles Times Book Review, February 22, 1981.

* * *

ARDEN, Noele
   See DAMBRAUSKAS, Joan Arden

* * *

ARIETI, Silvano   1914-1981

OBITUARY NOTICE—See index for *CA* sketch: Born June 28, 1914, in Pisa, Italy; died of cancer, August 7, 1981, in New York. Psychoanalyst and writer best known for his work on schizophrenia and creativity. A neo-Freudian, Arieti believed that schizophrenia was a psychological, not biological, disorder which should be treated with psychotherapy instead of drugs. His book *Interpretations of Schizophrenia,* which received a National Book Award in 1975, stressed this belief and presented methods by which physicians could better understand the schizophrenic mind. His next book, *Creativity: The Magic Synthesis,* explained Arieti's theory which added a tertiary process to Freud's primary and secondary processes. A professor of clinical psychiatry at the New York Medical College, Arieti was the editor in chief of *The American Handbook of Psychiatry* as well as a training supervisor and the past president of the William Alanson White Psychoanalytic Clinic. He was also a former president of the Society of Medical Psychoanalysts and the American Academy of Psychoanalysis. He wrote many books, including *Intrapsychic Self: Feeling, Cognition and Creativity in Health and Mental Illness, The Will to Live, New Dimensions in Psychiatry: A World View, The Parnas,* and *Abraham.* Obituaries and other sources: *New York Times,* August 10, 1981; *Newsweek,* August 14, 1981.

* * *

ARMERDING, Carl Edwin   1936-

PERSONAL: Born April 30, 1936, in Boston, Mass.; son of Howard Sherman and Grace Stratton (Horsey) Armerding; married Betsy Jane Leonard (a teacher), December 21, 1963; children: John Calvin, Jennifer Ruth, Geoffrey Howard. *Education:* Gordon College, A.B., 1957; Trinity Evangelical Divinity School, B.D., 1965; Brandeis University, M.A., 1966, Ph.D., 1968. *Religion:* Protestant. *Home:* 3861 West 39th Ave., Vancouver, British Columbia, Canada V6N 3A8. *Office:* Regent College, University of British Columbia, 2130 Westbrook Mall, Vancouver, British Columbia, Canada V6T 1W6.

CAREER: Wheaton College, Wheaton, Ill., assistant professor, 1969-70; University of British Columbia, Regent College, Vancouver, professor of Old Testament, 1970—, principal of Regent College, 1977—. Lecturer in South America, 1978. European representative of Officers' Christian Union, 1961-62. Member of board of directors of California Center for Biblical Studies. *Military service:* U.S. Navy, 1957-61; became lieutenant junior grade. U.S. Naval Reserve, 1961—; present rank, commander. *Member:* Evangelical Fellowship of Canada (member of board of directors), Society of Biblical Literature (president of Northwest region, 1975-76), Institute for Biblical Research, Society for Old Testament Studies. *Awards, honors:* National Defense fellow in Arabic Studies,

1965-68; fellow of Hebrew Union Biblical and Archaeological School of Jerusalem, 1968-69; fellow at Hebrew University of Jerusalem, 1969-70.

WRITINGS: (Editor with W. Ward Gasque) *Dreams, Visions, and Oracles,* Baker Book, 1977, revised edition published as *Handbook of Biblical Prophecy,* 1979; (editor) *Evangelicals and Liberation,* Presbyterian & Reformed, 1977. Contributor of articles and reviews to magazines. Editor-at-large of *Christianity Today,* 1970-80.

WORK IN PROGRESS: "Commentary on Exodus," to be included in *The New International Commentary of the Old Testament;* "Commentary on Judges," to be included in *Word Biblical Commentary,* for Word, Inc.

* * *

ARNETT, Caroline
   See COLE, Lois Dwight

* * *

ARTAUD, Antonin   1896-1948
   (Le Reveler)

BRIEF ENTRY: Born September 4, 1896, in Marseilles, France; died of cancer, March 4, 1948, in Paris, France. French actor and author. Artaud's early years were plagued with a variety of illnesses, including meningitis and neurasthenia. Extremely painful headaches caused his premature departure from the university. He convalesced briefly, then joined the French army. He was soon expelled, however, when opium treatments for the severe head pains resulted in a dependency on the drug. Artaud then spent two years in a Swiss institution. He returned to Paris in 1920 and befriended actor Charles Dullin, whom he assisted in productions of plays. Artaud also wrote a few volumes of poetry, including *Backgammon of the Sky* (1923) and *Umbilical Limbo* (1925). His verse dwelled on his many afflictions in a symbolic fashion that recalled the influence of Rimbaud and Nerval. In the mid-1920's, he became involved with Andre Breton's surrealist collective, for which he contributed the story for the motion picture "La Coquille et le clergyman" (1927). Within a year, however, Artaud broke away from the surrealists to develop his own brand of theatre. Dubbed the "theatre of cruelty," Artaud's productions were attempts to immerse the audience in painful experiences resulting in a higher level of consciousness. He tried to accomplish this by focusing his plays around themes of rape, incest, and murder. His ideas were poorly received in France, and after recording his concepts in *Manifestos of the Theatre of Cruelty* (1932) and *The Theatre and Its Double* (1936), he fled to Mexico. There, in a futile attempt to cure his head pains, he became involved with sun worshippers. He returned to Europe in the late 1930's, only to suffer a crippling mental breakdown. Artaud spent the next nine years in institutions. In the interim, though, his theories of the theatre were reconsidered as revolutionary in France. Upon his release in 1947, he was acclaimed as a genius. He died soon afterward of cancer. *Biographical/critical sources: World Authors, 1950-1970,* H. W. Wilson, 1975; *Twentieth-Century Literary Criticism,* Volume 3, Gale, 1980.

* * *

ASHBOLT, Allan Campbell   1921-

PERSONAL: Born November 24, 1921, in Melbourne, Australia; son of Irwin James and Vera (Campbell) Ashbolt; married Jeanne Liddy, June 2, 1944 (died July 16, 1979); married

Anne Schlebaum (a psychiatrist), May 2, 1981; children: (first marriage) Kerry, Anthony. *Education:* University of Melbourne, B.A., 1949. *Home:* 8 Monteith St., Turramurra, New South Wales 2074, Australia.

CAREER: Mercury Theatre, Sydney, Australia, director, 1945-49; Victorian Council of Adult Education, Melbourne, Australia, lecturer and writer, 1949-51; University of Sydney, Sydney, lecturer in tutorial classes and writer, 1951-56; Australian Broadcasting Commission, Sydney, producer of talks and documentaries, 1954-58, North American correspondent, 1958-61, federal supervisor of talks, 1961-67, head of special projects for television, 1967-69, director of special projects for radio, 1969-78; writer, 1978—. Commonwealth education officer, 1951; lecturer for Workers' Educational Association, 1951-56; member of council of Mitchell College of Advanced Education, 1977—, deputy chairman of council, 1981—; visiting fellow at University of New South Wales. Chairman of Australian Mass Communications Council, 1973-74, and National Film Theatre, 1974. Member of Australian Labour party national policy committee on arts and media, 1969-77. *Military service:* Australian Imperial Force, 1942-45.

MEMBER: Australian Society of Authors (member of management committee, 1979—; chairman, 1981—), Ex-Services Human Rights Association (president, 1966-71). *Awards, honors:* Award from International Festival of Sociological and Ethnographic Films, 1966, for "Living on the Fringe"; award from Australian Film Institute, 1968, for "The Drover's Wife"; award from National Book Council, 1975, for *An Australian Experience.*

WRITINGS: An American Experience (nonfiction), Gollancz, 1966, Paul Eriksson, 1967; *An Australian Experience: Words From the Vietnam Years,* Australasian Book Society, 1974.

Television plays: "Living on the Fringe," broadcast by Australian Broadcasting Commission, 1965; "The Drover's Wife," broadcast by Australian Broadcasting Commission, 1968.

Also author of documentaries and current affairs programs, 1957-68. Work represented in anthologies, including *Australian Abroad,* 1968; *Peace, Power, and Politics in Asia,* 1969; *Australians in America,* 1977. Australian correspondent for *New Statesman,* 1969-77. Drama critic for *Sydney Morning Herald,* 1951-56, book reviewer, 1951-58 and 1961-70.

WORK IN PROGRESS: Intersections, a collection of "biographical studies of various Australians with whom my life has intersected at crucial points"; *The Media and Public Consciousness,* a study of the Australian media.

* * *

ASHE, Douglas
   See BARDIN, John Franklin

* * *

ASHE, Penelope
   See GREENE, Robert W.

* * *

ASHLEY, Steven
   See McCAIG, Donald

* * *

ASWAD, Betsy   1939-

PERSONAL: Surname is pronounced Az-wad; born February 10, 1939, in Binghamton, N.Y.; daughter of George Marrinan (a railroad employee) and Jane (a social worker; maiden name, Sprout) Becker; married Richard N. Aswad (an attorney), September 22, 1962; children: Richard, Kristin Dewitt. *Education:* Attended Hood College, 1957-58; Harpur College (now State University of New York at Binghamton), B.A. (with high honors), 1961; State University of New York at Binghamton, M.A., 1965, Ph.D. (with distinction), 1973. *Politics:* "Utopian Socialist." *Religion:* Presbyterian. *Home:* 192 Deyo Hill Rd., Binghamton, N.Y. 13905. *Agent:* Betty Anne Clarke, Clarke Literary Agency, 28 East 95th St., New York, N.Y. 10028. *Office:* State University of New York at Binghamton, Binghamton, N.Y. 13901.

CAREER: WNBF-TV, Binghamton, N.Y., film editor, 1957; *Link Log* (house organ), Hillcrest, N.Y., assistant editor, 1962-63; State University of New York at Binghamton, Binghamton, teaching assistant, 1963-67, instructor in English, 1967-74; member of adjunct faculty, 1974—. Apprentice actress at Southern Tier Playhouse, summers, 1957 and 1958; member of Friends of Binghamton Public Library (secretary, 1977-78). *Awards, honors:* Fellow of College in the Woods, State University of New York at Binghamton, 1973; Mystery Writers of America, nomination for best first novel, 1981, for *Winds of the Old Days.*

WRITINGS: Winds of the Old Days (novel), Dial, 1980.

WORK IN PROGRESS: The Rainbow Sign, an adventure novel, publication expected in 1982; *The Forlorn Hope,* a novel about the Donner party.

SIDELIGHTS: Rosalind, the heroine of Betsy Aswad's first novel, *Winds of the Old Days,* is a literature teacher whose husband was murdered on Super Bowl Sunday, 1971. Seven years later, again on a Super Bowl Sunday, the solution to the murder is revealed. Super Bowl Sundays provide families and friends with opportunities to gather, and Aswad uses these occasions to reveal clues, characters, and motives. She never mentions the specific games or scores, and "because of that, the novel is certain to dissappoint readers looking for a good jock book," observed Jonathan Storm in the *Detroit Free Press.*

Like her heroine, Aswad is a college English teacher. Several critics noted that her literary expertise is evident in *Winds of the Old Days,* and they praised her ambitious writing. "The novel functions at a considerably higher level than most murder mysteries," Storm wrote. While generally impressed with Aswad's style, some reviewers were distracted by, as *Chicago Tribune Book World*'s Alice Cromie put it, "her constant ellipses and obscure references."

Most of the novel's action takes place on a campus—familiar territory to Aswad. "It is a novel rich in humor, much at the expense of College English departments," commented Gene Grey of the *Binghamton Evening Press.* It offers "an almost nostalgic reflection on the days when the youth rebellion, both on campuses and in the streets, made the '60s so vivid."

In addition to using a setting with which she is familiar, Aswad admits that many of her characters are based on people she knows. "A successful writer," she explained to David R. Kocieniewski of *Pipe Dream,* "needs a kind of negative capability. You must be able to absorb everyone and everything around you." Describing the process of writing an early unpublished novel, she told Kocieniewski, "I was just writing when all of a sudden the narrator had a memory I didn't give him."

To illustrate the process of writing her second book, *The Rainbow Sign,* Aswad told *CA:* "Right now I have seven characters sitting in a bar in the Sheraton in La Paz, Bolivia. I've never been to Bolivia. I am faking Bolivia. The reason they're in Bolivia is that one of my characters is doing a book on Che Guevara, and another of my characters decided he wanted to go with her badly enough to hijack a boat. All in league now with the hijacker, these people are sitting in this fictional bar, and three of them are about to go to Vallegrande where Che was laid out. I've never been to Vallegrande, but I have this picture of a tacky little Indian church with a shrine to Che; I can see the laundry where they displayed his body.

"As I write, I've found (almost) that the less one knows of something, the better one does it. For example, in *Winds of the Old Days,* I did some makeshift stuff on the Reimann sphere, a topological heaven. My brother-in-law (a mathemetician) complimented me on it. What I do with English literature, which I do know, only brings down slurs.

"I have this unfinished novel someplace that's based on biochemistry and bondings. I'm also a wide-eyed convert to Christianity. At heart, I guess I'm a phenomenologist."

AVOCATIONAL INTERESTS: History, astrology.

BIOGRAPHICAL/CRITICAL SOURCES: Binghamton Evening Press, December 1, 1980; *Chicago Tribune Book World,* January 18, 1981; *Detroit Free Press,* January 25, 1981; *Pipe Dream* (State University of New York at Binghamton student newspaper), March 6, 1981.

* * *

ATHANS, George (Stanley), Jr.   1952-

PERSONAL: Born July 6, 1952, in Kelowna, British Columbia, Canada; son of George D. (a physician and Olympic diving coach) and Irene (a swimming coach; maiden name, Hartzell) Athans; married Claire Suzanne Sicotte, December 1, 1975; children: Shawn Sacha (daughter). *Education:* Concordia University, B.A. and Certificate in Communications and Public Relations, both 1975; graduate study at McGill University. *Home and office:* 3669 Jeanne Mance, Montreal, Quebec, Canada H2X 2K4.

CAREER: A.W.A. Marketing Ltd., Montreal, Quebec, president, 1971—. Marketing consultant with Sea Gliders, Inc., 1971-75, Saucier, Inc., 1972-74, Montreal Skis, Inc., 1975-78, and Fitzwright Manufacturing Co., 1979; manager of Athans Skiing Enterprises Ltd., 1975—. Assistant to Department of National Health and Welfare and Sports Canada, 1969. Producer of rock music concert in Kelowna, British Columbia, 1969; producer of water sports shows for Montreal International Boat Show, 1972; assistant producer of Montreal's Aqua Show, 1976; producer of Labatt Blue Professional Water Ski Cup, 1980; chairman of World Cup Freestyle Snow Ski Championships, 1981. Member of Canada's National Water Ski Team, 1966-75, and Canadian Pro Snow Ski Tour, 1974. Radio and television sports commentator for Canadian Broadcasting Corp., 1977—. Member of elite development committee of Canadian National Water Ski Team, 1980. Stage manager at Mother Martins, 1970.

MEMBER: International Association of Tournament Water Skiers (charter member; member of board of directors, 1975), Canadian Water Ski Association (honorary life member), Association of Canadian Television and Radio Artists, Montreal Amateur Athletic Association, Club La Cite. *Awards, honors:* Dozens of water skiing awards include Canadian champion water skier, 1965-74, western hemisphere champion water skier, 1968 and 1970, California International Cup, 1970 and 1972, world champion water skier, 1971-74, World Cup, 1971, and

Masters Championship, 1974; modern sculpture award from Loyola University, 1970; named male athlete of the year by University of British Columbia, 1971; member of Canada's Amateur Hall of Fame, 1971—; special merit award from Province of British Columbia, 1971, and British Columbia Sports Federation, 1971; Canadian amateur athlete of the year, 1972-73; Quebec athlete of the year, 1973; member of Canada's Sports Hall of Fame, 1974—; athletic distinction award from Sir George Williams University, 1974; named athlete of the year by National Sporting Goods Associaton of Canada, 1974; member of Order of Canada, 1974; member of First Gallery of Canadian Athletes, 1975—; Canadian Superstars swimming champion, 1976; honorary chairman of World Water Ski Championships, 1979.

WRITINGS: (With Clint Ward) *Water Skiing,* P. Collier, 1975. Contributor to national magazines, including *Better Boating* and *Canadian Consumer.*

SIDELIGHTS: Athans was born into a family of champions. His father was a British Commonwealth and Canadian diving champion and his mother a top-ranked swimmer. He was swimming and water skiing by the time he was six years old and was winning competitions at age nine. He has since competed successfully all over the world, including Mexico, Spain, Columbia, Tahiti, Australia, and throughout Europe.

Athan's last public appearance as a water skier was in 1976, when he was seen in a CBS-TV production, "Challenge of the Sexes," but he has appeared in commercials and as a public speaker, promoting water skiing in Canada. He has produced water sports shows and sports specials for television.

AVOCATIONAL INTERESTS: Squash, swimming, jogging, tennis, photography, interior and graphic design, rock music.

* * *

ATHERTON, Gertrude (Franklin Horn)   1857-1948
(Frank Lin)

BRIEF ENTRY: Born October 30, 1857, in San Francisco, Calif.; died June 14, 1948, in San Francisco, Calif. American author. Atherton wrote several historical novels, including *The Conqueror* (1902), a fictitious biography of Alexander Hamilton, *American Wives and English Husbands* (1898), and *Ancestors* (1907). Because she was critically neglected in America, Atherton moved to England, where she received the acclaim she had been denied at home. Seven years later she returned to San Francisco, the town in which she had once caused a scandal with her erotic serialization "The Randolphs of Redwoods" Atherton also wrote an autobiography, *My San Francisco* (1946), as well as a novel, *The Californians* (1898), and a two-volume history of California that included the short story collection *Before the Gringo Came* (1894), revised as *The Splendid Idle Forests* (1902). *Biographical/critical sources: Twentieth Century Authors: A Biographical Dictionary of Modern Literature,* 1st supplement H. W. Wilson, 1955; *Longman Companion to Twentieth Century Literature,* Longman, 1970; *The Penguin Companion to American Literature,* McGraw, 1971; *American Authors and Books, 1640 to the Present Day,* 3rd revised edition, Crown, 1972; *Cassell's Encyclopaedia of World Literature,* revised edition, Morrow, 1973; *Twentieth-Century Literary Criticism,* Volume 2, Gale, 1979.

* * *

ATHERTON, Lucius
See MASTERS, Edgar Lee

AUGARDE, Steve 1950-

PERSONAL: Given name Stephen Andre Augarde; born October 3, 1950, in Birmingham, England. Education: Attended Yeovil School of Art, Somerset College of Art, and Rolle Teacher Training College. Agent: c/o Andre Deutsch Ltd., 105 Great Russell St., London WC1B 3LJ, England.

CAREER: Author and illustrator of children's books. Worked as a gardener for the National Trust at Montacute House, England.

WRITINGS—All juveniles; all self-illustrated: A Lazy Day, Fabbri & Partners, 1974; Pig, Deutsch, 1976, Bradbury, 1977; Barnaby Shrew Goes to Sea, Deutsch, 1978; Barnaby Shrew, Black Dan, and the Mighty Wedgwood, Deutsch, 1979; Mr. Mick, Deutsch, 1980.*

*   *   *

AUSTIN, Stephen
See STEVENS, Austin N(eil)

*   *   *

AVERY, Lynn
See COLE, Lois Dwight

*   *   *

AXELRAD, Sylvia Brody 1914-
(Sylvia Brody)

PERSONAL: Born October 17, 1914, in New York, N.Y.; daughter of Isidor and Gussie (Sperling) Brody; married Sidney Axelrad, May 11, 1949 (died, 1976). Education: Attended Topeka Institute for Psychoanalysis, 1948-50; New York University, Ph.D., 1954. Religion: Jewish. Home address: Macauley Rd., Katonah, N.Y. 10536. Office: 1148 Fifth Ave., New York, N.Y. 10028.

CAREER: City University of New York, New York City, director of joint child development research project (with Lenox Hill Hospital), 1963-73, adjunct professor of psychology at Graduate Division of Psychology, 1967-73, associate of Center for Social Research at Graduate Center, 1978—. Private practice of clinical psychoanalysis. Visiting professor at Albert Einstein College of Medicine, 1972-73, and New York University, 1979-80. Member: International College of Pediatrics (fellow), American Psychological Association, Association for Child Psychoanalysis, Society for Research in Child Development, American Association for the Advancement of Science, New York Freudian Society, Sigma Xi.

WRITINGS—Under name Sylvia Brody: Patterns of Mothering, International Universities Press, 1956; Passivity, International Universities Press, 1964; (with husband, Sidney Ax-

elrad) Anxiety and Ego Formation in Infancy, International Universities Press, 1970; (with S. Axelrad) Mothers, Fathers, and Children, International Universities Press, 1978. Also author of films for film library of New York University. Contributor of more than one dozen articles to journals in the behavioral sciences.

WORK IN PROGRESS: Research on psychoanalytic studies of infancy, continuities in behavior during early childhood, and comparative studies of consecutive siblings.

SIDELIGHTS: Sylvia Axelrad told CA: "I have a long-standing concern for safeguarding emotional health and intellectual potentials beginning in earliest infancy. Another interest is parent education. Other interests include evolution of character and personality in childhood, as observed in my clinical practice of psychoanalysis with children, and in my research."

*   *   *

AYERS, Rose
See GREENWOOD, Lillian Bethel

*   *   *

AZUELA, Mariano 1873-1952
(Beleno)

BRIEF ENTRY: Born January 1, 1873, in Lagos de Moreno, Jalisco, Mexico; died of a heart attack, March 1, 1952, in Mexico City, Mexico; buried in the Rotonda de Hombres Ilustres, Mexico City, Mexico. Mexican physician, political activist, and author. Azuela was best known for his novels of the Mexican Revolution, which depict various facets of Mexican society set against the political changes of the twentieth century. His 1916 book Los de abajo, translated as The Underdogs (1929), grew out of the author's experiences as a doctor in a revolutionary regiment. This book is considered Mexico's major literary work from that era. While Azuela's early works decry the plight of the poor, his later writings examine corruption in all levels of Mexican society and reveal the author's disillusionment with compromised revolutionary ideals. Azuela practiced medicine among the poor throughout his career while producing short stories, plays, essays, criticism, fictional biographies, and more than twenty novels. His major works in English translation include Marcela: A Mexican Love Story (1932), Two Novels of Mexico: The Flies; The Bosses (1956), and Two Novels of the Mexican Revolution: The Trials of a Respectable Family; The Underdogs (1963). Residence: Mexico City, Mexico. Biographical/critical sources: Cyclopedia of World Authors, Harper, 1958; Encyclopedia of World Literature in the Twentieth Century, updated edition, Ungar, 1967; Luis Leal, Mariano Azuela, Twayne, 1971; World Authors, 1950-1970, H. W. Wilson, 1975; Twentieth-Century Literary Criticism, Volume 3, Gale, 1980.

B

BAATZ, Charles A(lbert)   1916-

PERSONAL: Surname is pronounced Botts; born April 4, 1916, in Port Chester, N.Y.; son of Charles Frederick (in business) and Anna (in business; maiden name, Lenherr) Baatz; married Olga K. Kozoriz (an educator and writer), January 25, 1947; children: Barry and Terrence (twins). *Education:* Georgetown University, B.A., 1942, Ph.L., 1943; Fordham University, Ph.D., 1966. *Politics:* Democrat. *Religion:* Roman Catholic. *Home:* 168 Village Rd., South Orange, N.J. 07079. *Office:* Department of Psychology, Seton Hall University, South Orange, N.J. 07079.

CAREER: Oratory School, Summit, N.J., associate headmaster, 1945-49; Seton Hall University, South Orange, N.J., professor of psychology, 1949—, chairman of department, 1955-62. Adjunct associate professor at Fordham University, 1951-60. Co-founder, vice-president, and member of board of trustees of New Jersey Council for Education Foundation; past president of South Orange Citizens for Responsive Government. *Member:* World Youth Vocational Education Association (co-founder, vice-president, and member of board of trustees), American Catholic Philosophical Association (life member), Kappa Delta Pi (Xi Gamma chapter).

WRITINGS: (Editor) *Philosophy of Education: A Guide to Information Sources,* Gale, 1980; (editor with wife, Olga Baatz) *The Psychological Foundations of Education: A Guide to Information Sources,* Gale, 1981.

WORK IN PROGRESS: Research on philosophical and psychological foundations of education.

SIDELIGHTS: Baatz wrote that his areas of expertise include religious education, philosophy, and the psychology and philosophy of education. He added that he is descended from ancient French nobility.

*   *   *

BAATZ, Olga K.   1921-

PERSONAL: Born in January, 1921; daughter of Vlodimir (a priest) and Anna (Lozenko) Kozoriz; married Charles Albert Baatz (a professor of psychology), January 25, 1947; children: Barry and Terrence (twins). *Education:* D'Youville College, B.S., 1943; graduate study at Fordham University, 1949-52. *Politics:* Democrat. *Religion:* Roman Catholic. *Home:* 168 Village Rd., South Orange, N.J. 07079. *Office:* Our Lady of Sorrows School, South Orange, N.J. 07079.

CAREER: Instructor at Berkeley Secretarial School in East Orange, N.J.; editor-in-chief and feature writer for *Berkeley Briefs,* 1947-60; Our Lady of Sorrows School, South Orange, N.J., director of Learning Center, 1972—.

WRITINGS: (Editor with husband, Charles A. Baatz) *The Psychological Foundations of Education,* Gale, 1981.

WORK IN PROGRESS: Editing another book on the psychological foundations of education.

SIDELIGHTS: Olga Baatz is interested in English and writing, especially in developing thinking, reading, and writing skills. Other interests are religion, educating the gifted, and "establishing peaceful and creative family and social relations."

*   *   *

BAB
   See GILBERT, W(illiam) S(chwenck)

*   *   *

BABEL, Isaac (Emanuilovich)
   See BABEL, Isaak (Emmanuilovich)

*   *   *

BABEL, Isaak (Emmanuilovich)   1894-1941(?)

BRIEF ENTRY: Born in 1894 in Odessa, Russia (now U.S.S.R.); died in a concentration camp in the Soviet Union, c. 1941. Russian short story writer, journalist, dramatist, and screenwriter. Babel grew up in Odessa's Jewish ghetto and during his youth studied Hebrew, the Bible, and the Talmud. He was encouraged in his career by writer Maxim Gorky, who published Babel's first short stories in 1916. Known best for his short stories, which are largely autobiographical, Babel produced most of his work in the 1920's. His most celebrated work, *Konarmiia* (1926; translated as *Red Cavalry,* 1929), presents a series of impressionistic sketches based on the author's service with General Budionni's cavalry on the Polish front. Babel remained in the Soviet Union, writing little throughout the thirties and maintaining what he called a literary "genre of silence." Babel disappeared in 1939, apparently arrested by the Stalinist regime. He is reported to have died in 1941. Numbered among his works in English translation are *Benya Krik, Gangster; and Other Stories* (1948), *Collected Stories* (1955), *Lyubka, the Cossack; and Other Stories* (1963),

Isaac Babel: The Lonely Years, 1925-39 (1964), and *You Must Know Everything: Stories* (1969). *Biographical/critical sources: Encyclopedia of World Literature in the Twentieth Century*, updated edition, Ungar, 1967; *The Penguin Companion to European Literature*, McGraw, 1969; *Twentieth Century Writing: A Reader's Guide to Contemporary Literature*, Transatlantic, 1969; Patricia Carden, *The Art of Isaac Babel*, Cornell University Press, 1972; James E. Falen, *Isaac Babel: Russian Master of the Short Story*, University of Tennessee Press, 1974; *Twentieth-Century Literary Criticism*, Volume 2, Gale, 1979.

* * *

BACH, George Robert 1914-

PERSONAL: Born November 2, 1914, in Riga, Latvia; married Peggy Dahlstrom (an art historian), October 14, 1940; children: five. *Education:* University of Iowa, Ph.D., 1944. *Home:* 8437 Hollywood Blvd., Los Angeles, Calif. 90069.

CAREER: Member of faculty at University of Iowa, Iowa City, Kent State University, Kent, Ohio, Western Reserve University (now Case Western Reserve University), Cleveland, Ohio, University of Southern California, Los Angeles, University of California, Los Angeles, Michigan State University, East Lansing, and St. George Medical School, Granada, Spain, Psychotherapist. *Member:* American Academy of Psychotherapy (president).

WRITINGS: Children's Play Fantasy, American Psychological Association, 1945; *Intensive Group Therapy*, Ronald, 1954; *Intimate Energy*, Morrow, 1968; *Pairing*, Wyden Books, 1970; *Creative Aggression*, Doubleday, 1972; *Stop, You Are Driving Me Crazy*, Putnam, 1980.

WORK IN PROGRESS: The Caring Book.

* * *

BACHMANN, Gideon 1927-

PERSONAL: Born February 18, 1927, in Heilbronn, Germany (now West Germany); son of Ernst and Bella Bachmann; married Deborah Imogen Beer (a photographer), April 27, 1970. *Education:* Attended University of London, 1942-43, Cambridge University, 1944, City College (now of the City University of New York), 1953-54, and New School for Social Research, 1955-57. *Home:* The Manor House Loft, Hurley, Berkshire SL6 5NB, England. *Office:* Via di Sant' Eustachio, 3, I–00186, Rome, Italy.

CAREER: Cinemages, New York, N.Y., editor and publisher, 1954-59; radio broadcaster and film critic in New York and California; documentary filmmaker. Visiting professor of film at Rhode Island School of Design, Rome Campus, and American College, Paris, France; lecturer at more than thirty universities in the United States, Canada, England, Italy, Germany, Australia, and Yugoslavia. U.S. representative at International Union of Film Critics; jurist at several film festivals, including those in Cannes, Moscow, Berlin, and Venice. *Member:* International Federation of Film Press, American Federation of Film Critics (president), British Film Institute. *Awards, honors:* Silver Lion from Venice Film Festival for "Underground New York"; recipient of other prizes for documentary films.

WRITINGS: Bewegte Bilder, published as *Craft and Craftiness of the Movies*, Beltz, 1977. Also author of book *Believe Nothing!* (an introduction to film for youth), 1977, and television features, including "Underground New York," "Ciao, Federico!," "A Camera Is Not a Molotov Cocktail!," "How Israel

Sees Arabs," "Crisis, Movies, and Kibbutz," "A Man Is Many Things," "The Speechless Cinema," and "Jonas." Rome editor of *Film Quarterly*. Contributor of numerous articles to newspapers and magazines throughout the world, including *Sight and Sound, Der Spiegel*, and *Filmcritica*.

SIDELIGHTS: Bachmann's films often examine the use of the camera in cinema, politics, battle, and self-expression. In "A Camera Is Not a Molotov Cocktail!," the anti-Mafia films of Italian director Damiano Damiani are contrasted with the political cinema of young people in Italy who use the camera to demonstrate their opinions on various social issues. Bachmann makes another contrast in "How Israel Sees Arabs," where he juxtaposes the Israeli media representation of Arabs to scenes of actual Arab life in Israel. Another film, "Crisis, Movies and Kibbutz," studies the failing Israeli film industry, while "The Speechless Cinema" examines the industry in black Africa. "Underground New York" investigates avant-garde films of American artists such as Andy Warhol.

Other films by Bachmann are documentaries on such filmmakers as Federico Fellini ("Ciao, Federico!"), Pier Paolo Pasolini ("A Man Is Many Things"), and Jonas Mekas ("Jonas").

Bachmann's films have been shown at numerous festivals, including those in Cannes, Sydney, Krakow, Venice, and San Francisco. He has collaborated with several other filmmakers, including Fellini, Pasolini, Shirley Clarke, and Bernhard Wicki.

* * *

BACON, Martha Sherman 1917-1981

OBITUARY NOTICE—See index for *CA* sketch: Born 1917 in California; died in 1981 in Providence, R.I. Educator, poet, novelist, and author. The daughter of the Pulitzer Prize-winning poet Leonard Bacon, Martha Bacon met with critical acclaim as a poet in 1942. An associate professor of English at Rhode Island College, she published several volumes of poetry, including *Lament for the Chieftains* and *Things Visible and Invisible*, as well as novels, such as *A Star Called Wormwood* and *A Masque of Exile*. In addition to these, she wrote children's books and a book about her travels in Africa, *Sophia Scrooby Preserved*. She also contributed to *The Writer, Atlantic Monthly*, and other magazines. Obituaries and other sources: *AB Bookman's Weekly*, July 13-20, 1981.

* * *

BACON, R(onald) L(eonard) 1924-

PERSONAL: Born in 1924 in New Zealand. *Home:* Unit 3, 16 Turama Rd., Royal Oak, Auckland, New Zealand.

CAREER: Worked as a teacher and as deputy principal of a New Zealand intermediate school. *Awards, honors:* Russell Clark Award from New Zealand Library Association, 1978, for *The House of the People*.

WRITINGS: In the Sticks (novel), illustrated by David More, Collins, 1963; *Along the Road* (novel), illustrated by More, Collins, 1964; (with Gregory Riethmaier) *Auckland: Gateway to New Zealand* (travel), Collins, 1968; (with Riethmaier) *Auckland: Town and Around* (travel), Collins, 1973.

Juveniles: *The Boy and the Taniwha*, illustrated by Para Matchitt, Collins, 1966, International Publications Service, 1976; *Again the Bugles Blow*, illustrated by V. J. Livingston, Collins, 1973, International Publications Service, 1976; *Rua and the Sea People*, illustrated by Matchitt, Collins, 1968, International Publications Service, 1976; *The House of the People,* illustrated by Robert F. Jahnke, Collins, 1977.*

*   *   *

BADDELEY, V.C. Clinton
  See CLINTON-BADDELEY, V.C.

*   *   *

BAER, Edith R(uth)   1920-

PERSONAL: Born April 29, 1920, in Mannheim, Germany (now West Germany). *Education:* Received B.A. from University of London. *Home:* 42 Woodlands, London N.W. 11, England.

CAREER: British Broadcasting Corp. (BBC), member of European services, 1944-53, member of monitoring service, 1953-61, executive radio producer, 1961—. *Member:* Writers Guild of Great Britain, Institute of Linguists (fellow).

WRITINGS—Published by BBC Publications, except as noted: (Editor) *Der Arme Millionar: A BBC Radio Course in Everyday German* (based on Erich Kastner's novel, *Drei Manner im Schnee),* 1967; (with R. M. Oldnall) *Starting German: Reiseburo Atlas,* Volume I, 1968, Volume II, 1968, Volume III, 1969; (with Alexandra Marchlvon Herwarth and Wulf Kunne) *Wiedersehen in Ansburg: A Follow-up Course to "Reiseburo Atlas,"* 1969; (editor) *Teaching Languages: Ideas and Guidance for Teachers Working with Adults,* 1976; *A Frost in the Night* (novel), Pantheon, 1980.

Author of numerous language programs for BBC radio, including "German for Beginners," 1962, "Spanish for Beginners," 1963, and with R. Beckley of "Es Geht Weiter: Everyday German by Radio," 1965.

AVOCATIONAL INTERESTS: Traveling, gardening, swimming.*

*   *   *

BAIN, Kenneth Ray   1942-

PERSONAL: Born January 29, 1942, in Summerville, Ga.; son of Jesse Lee (a teacher; in sales) and Vera D. (a teacher; in real estate; maiden name, Brooks) Bain; married Marsha Faye Marshall (a secretary), July 23, 1966; children: Kenneth Marshall, Tonia Larisa. *Education:* Baylor University, B.A., 1965; North Texas State University, M.A., 1970; University of Texas, Ph.D., 1977. *Home:* 4709 North Seventh, McAllen, Tex. 78501. *Office:* Honors Studies, Pan American University, Edinburg, Tex. 78539.

CAREER: Northeastern State University, Tahlequah, Okla., instructor in history, 1966-67; San Antonio College, San Antonio, Tex., instructor in history, 1967-71; University of Texas, Austin, extension lecturer in history, 1971-74; Oklahoma Heritage Service, Shawnee, writer, 1974-78; Pan American University, Edinburg, Tex., assistant professor, 1978-81, associate professor, 1981—, coordinator of American studies, 1978-81, director of honors program, 1981—. Writer for Southern Heritage Service, 1978-81. *Member:* American Historical Association, Organization of American Historians.

WRITINGS: The March to Zion: United States Policy and the Founding of Israel, Texas A & M University Press, 1979; (with James Gormly) *Student Guide to the Restless Centuries,* Burgess, 1980; (with Harry Middleton) *Lyndon Johnson and the Political Cartoonists,* Lyndon B. Johnson Library, 1981.

Co-author of film scripts: "The American Civil War," released by Oklahoma Heritage Service in 1978; "Life of the Soldier," released by Oklahoma Heritage Service in 1978; "How to Write a Family History," released by Southern Heritage Service in 1980; "Leisure," released by Southern Heritage Service in 1981.

WORK IN PROGRESS: A textbook on U.S. diplomatic history, with James Gormly and Paul D. Travis; a book on Europeans and Indians, with Travis and James McLeod.

SIDELIGHTS: Bain commented: "I have traveled extensively in both the United States and Mexico. I began writing history primarily because of my fascination with people. They are a comic and tragic species. One has to learn to laugh to keep from crying.

"I am most intrigued with why human beings have done all of the stupid and terrible things they have done to each other. Thus, I became interested in the Arab-Israeli dispute and the development of U.S. policy toward that dispute as another example of tragedy begetting tragedy. I am also fascinated with the way people spend their time and in the values reflected by that process, so I have a great interest in the whole history of leisure activities, from small town park picnics to professional sports.

"Writing is both painful and exhilirating. I must work with words, toy with sentences, arrange their parts one way and then another, in order to make them behave. It often takes an hour to write one good paragraph. I usually emerge from the process soaking wet and exhausted and convinced I'll never try it again. I do my best work in the mornings. If I can arrange my schedule (teaching chores), I write for several hours without stopping. Later, I edit. Even if I like what I have written, I keep it for several days, find something else to do in the meantime, and then return to it for another round of cutting words, changing phrases, and shoving clauses hither and yon. God, how I wish I could be like those blokes who exhale perfect prose. They do exist, don't they? I've certainly always believed in them the way some children believe in Santa Claus and the Easter Bunny. But, alas, I'm not one of them."

AVOCATIONAL INTERESTS: Photography, filmmaking.

*   *   *

BAINES, Jocelyn   1925(?)-1973

OBITUARY NOTICE: Born c. 1925; died in 1973 in London, England. Writer and manager of rare bookshops in London. Baines is best known for his book *Joseph Conrad.* Obituaries and other sources: *AB Bookman's Weekly,* March 19, 1973.

*   *   *

BAKER, (Allen) Albert   1910-
  (Jack Kane)

PERSONAL: Born January 18, 1910, in San Francisco, Calif.; son of Eaton and Josephine (Halstead) Baker; married Marceil G. Kolstad (a writer), February 24, 1930; children: Mauvra Nan Baker Osborn. *Education:* St. Mary's College, Moraga, Calif., Junior Certificate in Arts and Letters, 1934. *Religion:* Christian. *Residence:* Fair Oaks, Calif.

CAREER: Stevedore on docks in San Francisco, Calif., 1934; acid treater at refinery in Martinez, Calif., 1935-42; bus driver along the West Coast, 1942-67; writer, 1946—. Union business agent in northern California, 1947-52.

WRITINGS: Trail of Doom, Avalon, 1971; (under pseudonym Jack Kane) *Buzzard Bait* (for young adults), Bouregy, 1975;

Border War, Avalon, 1976; *Ride for Hell,* Major, 1976; *A Noose for the Marshal,* Major, 1977; *Arizona Crossfire,* Major, 1978. Also author of *Mountain Rescue* (juvenile), Scholastic Book Services; *Rebel Guns,* Avalon; *The Raid on the Gila,* Avalon; *Gunfight at Auburn City,* Avalon; *Guns Over the Border,* Avalon; *Renegade Marshal,* Avalon.

Contributor of about two hundred fifty stories to western magazines, including *Famous Western* and *Rio Kid Western,* and *Scholastic.*

WORK IN PROGRESS: A series of western books, publication by Worldwide expected in 1982.

SIDELIGHTS: Baker told *CA:* "Basically my background led me into writing. I was raised in the gold country above Auburn, California. My ancestors arrived during the gold rush of '49. My father mined in California and Alaska during the rush, worked as a cowboy on a cattle spread in Bakersfield, and was picked up and accused of being a Dalton gang member. He lived it, I write about it."

AVOCATIONAL INTERESTS: Travel, collecting old books on the West.

*   *   *

BAKER, John   1901(?)-1971

OBITUARY NOTICE: Born c. 1901; died November 26, 1971, in London, England. Bookseller and publisher. Baker founded the Readers Union in 1937 and the Phoenix House in 1947. Obituaries and other sources: *AB Bookman's Weekly,* December 13, 1971.

*   *   *

BAKER, Richard Terrill   1913-1981

OBITUARY NOTICE—See index for *CA* sketch: Born March 27, 1913, in Coggon, Iowa; died of cancer, September 3, 1981, in Manhattan, N.Y.; cremated. Journalist, educator, clergyman, and author. An ordained Methodist minister, Baker was considered by J. Montgomery Curtis past editor of the American Press Institute and by John Hohenberg, former secretary of the Pulitzer Board, to be "one of the finest, if not the finest, journalism professors in the country." A professor of journalism at Columbia University for thirty-four years, Baker began his teaching career during World War II as a faculty member and the acting dean at a journalism school established in China by the Chinese National Government and Columbia University. He was also a correspondent for the Religious News Service and an adviser on this topic for the State Department. Earlier in his career, Baker received a Pulitzer traveling fellowship. In 1980 he was given a scroll for "conscientious and able representation" from the Pulitzer Board, of which he was the secretary. He wrote several books on Asian studies, and his other writings include *The Seed and the Soil, The Trumpet of a Prophecy, The Christian as a Journalist,* and *A History of the Graduate School of Journalism.* Obituaries and other sources: *New York Times,* September 24, 1981; *AB Bookman's Weekly,* September 14, 1981.

*   *   *

BALDWIN, Monica   1896(?)-1975

OBITUARY NOTICE: Born c. 1896; died November 17, 1975, in England. Author of three books, including *I Leap Over the Wall: Contrasts and Impressions After Twenty-eight Years in a Convent.* Obituaries and other sources: *Time,* January 30, 1950; *AB Bookman's Weekly,* January 5, 1976.

BALDWIN, Rebecca
See CHAPPELL, Helen

*   *   *

BALKA, Marie
See BALKANY, Marie (Romoka Zelinger) de

*   *   *

BALKANY, Marie (Romoka Zelinger) de   1930-
(Marie Balka)

PERSONAL: Born January 27, 1930, in Romania; daughter of Aladar Zelinger (an engineer) and Ilona (a princess; maiden name, Bathory-Vindisgraetz) de Balkany; children: Francesco, Sabina. *Education:* Attended Sorbonne, University of Paris. *Religion:* Roman Catholic. *Home:* 9 rue de Lille, 75007 Paris, France.

CAREER: Free-lance writer. *Member:* P.E.N., European Movement, Table Ronde des Affaires Europeennes.

WRITINGS—Under pseudonym Marie Balka, except as noted: (Under name Marie de Balkany) *Un Air de fete* (novel), Julliard, 1961; *La Rancon du silence,* Gallimard, 1969, translation by the author published as *Outpost,* Delacorte, 1973; *La Nuit,* Gallimard, 1971; *Oratorio,* Gallimard, 1973; *Les Mains nues* (novel), Gallimard, 1975; *Quatre Roses rouges* (novel), A. Michel, 1979; *Le Dieu eparpille* (title means "The Scattered God"), A. Michel, 1980.

WORK IN PROGRESS: La Pluie des mangues; Rouge d'Afrique; Elisabeth la Rouge.

SIDELIGHTS: Balkany told *CA:* "I was born into one of those lunatic families some people esteem—Hungarians with quite a background, power- and money-mad, successful people who hit it big and confused what they were with what they possessed. I have been in revolt against them and their aims from the day I knew my name. They, of course, consider me foolish, useless, quite mad, some kind of a failure—an Artist. They never read a line I've written.

"I live in Paris, in an old house with a small garden, near St.-Germain-des-Pres. I also have a residence in Normandy. I neither drink nor take drugs. I am healthy and sane. When my writing satisfies me, I am cheerful and easygoing; it does not always satisfy me.

"I have always written, although in my younger days I held all kinds of jobs ranging from packing dresses to advertising. I was at one time the only female real-estate broker in France.

"I speak fluent French, English, Italian, German, Spanish, Portuguese, Hungarian, Rumanian. I also write and read Arabic and understand some Tamashek, the Tuareg tribal language. I have sailed a lot around the Mediterranean and have traveled in Chad, Central Africa, and Uganda. For the past eight years I have been spending two months every spring with the Tuareg tribes in the Sahara desert, traveling through Algeria, Niger, and Mali; I can't go to Libya anymore. I live and travel with them, hunt with them, and occasionally I watch them fight. I was the first woman to follow the salt caravan from Agadez to Bilma, though I did not make it to the end—the Niger police stopped me in Fachi.

"My life lies more between the covers of my books than in my days, although I don't write about myself. My books are all, except the last one, about men and women of today, trying to cope with being—love, work, family, money, fame, rejection, failure or success, death or defeat. They are about small-time people and tycoons, soldiers, doctors actresses, lovers, whores, thugs, migrants; about revolted youths, policemen, automobile racers; the struggle for survival or for meaning. They are about women versus family, women versus society, women versus freedom, women versus men. They are about dreams crushed by money, about deserters and people who try to live inside the law, about the tyranny of greed and the tyranny of weakness. I have tried very hard to enclose a whole world between the pages of a book; sometimes I have succeeded.

"In my last book, *Le Dieu eparpille* ("The Scattered God"), I tried to go beyond, using myths and symbols, poetry and legend. It's my best book, the one that has taken me farthest in toil, meaning, and achievement. More than the others it has been ignored.

"A writer's lifespan is a journey, a ceaseless combat with demons or quicksand. Were I to die tomorrow one could say about me: 'She fought to give life to ghosts, turn them into flesh and blood. She tried to read a pattern into the senseless maze of life. She did it obscurely, without prizes, honors, awards, and yet, she lived each day with passion, as if it were the last.' I shall, of course, not die tomorrow, nor the day after, and something may yet happen to pull me out from the cold toward recognition."

* * *

BANKOFF, George Alexis
    See MILKOMANE, George Alexis Milkomanovich

* * *

BARCLAY, Ann
    See GREIG, Maysie

* * *

BARDIN, John Franklin   1916-1981
    (Douglas Ashe, Gregory Tree)

OBITUARY NOTICE—See index for *CA* sketch: Born November 30, 1916, in Cincinnati, Ohio; died July 9, 1981, in New York. Editor and author. Associated with the Edwin Bird Wilson advertising agency for nearly twenty years, Bardin was an instructor at writer's workshops at the New School for Social Research. He edited the publications of the American Bar Association, the American Medical Association, and the United Jewish Appeal of Greater New York as well as the magazines *Coronet* and *Today's Health*. As a writer, Bardin was partial to detective fiction concentrating on abnormal psychology. His better-known novels include *The Deadly Percheron, The Last of Philip Banter, Devil Take the Blue-Tail Fly,* and *The Burning Glass.* Several of his books, such as *A Shroud for Grandmama* and *So Young to Die,* were written under the pseudonyms Douglas Ashe and Gregory Tree. Obituaries and other sources: *New York Times,* July 17, 1981.

* * *

BARKER, A(rthur) J(ames)   1918-1981

OBITUARY NOTICE—See index for *CA* sketch: Born September 20, 1918, in Yorkshire, England; died June 10, 1981, in Cape Town, South Africa. Military officer and author. Commissioned into the British Army in 1936, Barker served in the East African campaign of 1940 and in such places as Ceylon, India, Egypt, Malaya, Burma, and northwestern Europe. After

retiring from the military, Barker worked as an administrator and an editor of scientific reports for the United Kingdom Atomic Energy Authority. Upon his retirement from this position in 1968, he received a fellowship from the North Atlantic Treaty Organization (NATO). His works include *The March on Delhi, The Vainglorious War: 1854-56, Pearl Harbor, The Redcoats Are Coming, Stuka,* and *Arab-Israeli Wars.* Obituaries and other sources: *London Times,* June 23, 1981.

* * *

BARKER, Harley Granville
    See GRANVILLE-BARKER, Harley

* * *

BARNES, Jane
    See CASEY, Jane Barnes

* * *

BARNES, Joseph Fels   1907-1970

OBITUARY NOTICE: Born July 21, 1907, in Montclair, N.J.; died February 28, 1970, in New York, N.Y. Journalist, editor, and translator. Barnes was a correspondent and editor with the *New York Herald Tribune* before becoming senior editor at Simon & Schuster. His translations of Russian works include *The Story of Life,* by Konstantin Paustovsky. Obituaries and other sources: *AB Bookman's Weekly,* March 16, 1970; *Who Was Who in America, With World Notables,* Volume V: *1969-1973,* Marquis, 1973.

* * *

BARNOUW, Adriaan Jacob   1877-1968

OBITUARY NOTICE: Born October 9, 1877, in Amsterdam, Holland; died September 27, 1968, in New York, N.Y. Educator, writer, and journalist. Barnouw began his teaching career in 1902 at The Hague's Municipal Gymnasium; in 1921 he became Queen Wilhelmina Professor of Dutch Language and Literature at Columbia University. As a journalist he worked as a correspondent at The Hague for *New York Nation* and later became associate editor of *Weekly Review.* His many books include *Anglo-Saxon Christian Poetry, Holland Under Queen Wilhelmina, The Dutch: A Portrait Study of the People of Holland,* and *The Fantasy of Pieter Brueghel.* Obituaries and other sources: *Authors of Books for Young People,* 2nd edition, Scarecrow, 1971; *Who Was Who Among North American Authors, 1921-1939,* Gale, 1976; *Who Was Who Among English and European Authors, 1931-1949,* Gale, 1978.

* * *

BARN OWL
    See HOWELLS, Roscoe

* * *

BAROJA (y NESSI), Pio   1872-1956

BRIEF ENTRY: Born December 28, 1872, in San Sebastian, Spain; died October 30, 1956, in Madrid, Spain. Spanish novelist. Baroja was a member of the "Generation of '98," a group concerned with social problems of Spain. He wrote mainly about the poor, working-class people of his country and of the injustice, poverty, and hypocrisy that haunted them. Baroja hated the falseness he found everywhere, but held little hope for improvement in the future. He wrote in a simple style, using the idiomatic language of the working man. Some critics called his writing harsh and clumsy, but others felt these were the very qualities that made it powerful. Baroja's major literary achievements came before 1912. Among his best-known works are *The Struggle for Life* (1904), *Zalacain the Adventurer* (1909), and *The Tree of Knowledge* (1911). Baroja was made a member of the Royal Spanish Academy in the 1930's, but after Franco came to power in Spain in 1939, all but one of Baroja's nearly one hundred books were banned for the negative picture they presented of Spanish life. His work was not widely read until after his death. *Biographical/critical sources: Twentieth Century Authors: A Biographical Dictionary of Modern Literature,* H. W. Wilson, 1942; *Hispania,* September, 1966; *Twentieth Century Writing: A Reader's Guide to Contemporary Literature,* Transatlantic, 1969; *The Oxford Companion to Spanish Literature,* Clarendon Press, 1978.

*   *   *

BARRIE, J(ames) M(atthew)   1860-1937

BRIEF ENTRY: Born May 9, 1860, in Kirriemuir, Forfarshire (now Angus), Scotland; died June 19, 1937, in London, England. Scottish novelist, journalist, short story writer, and playwright best known for his 1904 play *Peter Pan.* Barrie was first noted as a writer of sentimental, nostalgic novels and short stories based on his childhood and hometown in Scotland, including *Auld Licht Idylls* (1888), *A Window in Thrums* (1889), *The Little Minister* (1891), and *An Auld Licht Manse* (1893). After 1900 Barrie concentrated chiefly on writing for the stage and produced several plays, of which *Quality Street* (1901) and *What Every Woman Knows* (1908) number among the best known. Barrie was made a baronet in 1913 and received Britain's Order of Merit in 1922. He served as chancellor of Edinburgh University from 1930 to 1937. *Biographical/critical sources: Cyclopedia of World Authors,* Harper, 1958; *Encyclopedia of World Literature in the Twentieth Century,* updated edition, Ungar, 1967; *Twentieth Century Writing: A Reader's Guide to Contemporary Literature,* Transatlantic, 1969; *The Penguin Companion to English Literature,* McGraw, 1971; Harry M. Geduld, *Sir James Barrie,* Twayne, 1971; *Twentieth-Century Literary Criticism,* Volume 2, Gale, 1979.

*   *   *

BARRINGTON, Thomas Joseph   1916-

PERSONAL: Born May 17, 1916, in Dublin, Ireland,; son of Thomas Joseph (a civil servant) and Eileen (Bracken) Barrington; married Aine Cox (a teacher), July 1, 1942; children: Anthony, Colm, Ruth, Anne, Conor, Paul. *Education:* National University of Ireland, University College, Dublin, B.A., 1940. *Religion:* Roman Catholic. *Home:* Dargleside, Enniskerry, County Wicklow, Ireland, *Office:* Institute of Public Administration, 59 Landsdowne Rd., Dublin 4, Ireland.

CAREER: Lalor Ltd., Dublin, Ireland, management trainee, 1934-37; Capuchin Publications, Dublin, editorial assistant, 1937-41; Department of Finance, Dublin, administrative officer, 1941-44; Department of Local Government (now Department of the Environment), Dublin, private secretary to minister, 1944-46; assistant principal of general local administration, 1946-49, principal of personnel section, 1949-59, principal of town planning section, 1959-60; Institute of Public Administration, Dublin, founding member, 1957, member of executive committee, 1957-59, 1967-77, director, 1960-77, consultant, 1977—. Member of Economic and Social Research Institute, 1960—; member of executive committee of International Institute of Administrative Sciences, 1971-80; member

of Irish Council for the European Movement, 1972—; member of executive committee, 1973—; founding member of Public Agency for Personal Service Overseas, 1973—, member of executive committee, 1973-78, member of council, 1973-80.

MEMBER: Royal Society of Antiquaries of Ireland, Statistical and Social Inquiry Society of Ireland, National Library Society of Ireland, Kerry Archaelogical and Historical Society, Royal Dublin Society, Irish Futures Society, Irish Association, Muckross House Trustees.

WRITINGS: Notes for Interview Boards, Institute of Public Administration (Dublin), 1963; *From Big Government to Local Government,* Institute of Public Administration (Dublin), 1975; *Discovering Kerry,* Blackwater, 1976; *Irish Administrative System,* Institute of Public Administration (Dublin), 1980. General editor of series of cassettes on Irish topography. Founding editor of *Administration,* 1953-76.

WORK IN PROGRESS: The Responsible Society, a book about the problem of modern Irish democracy and government, with particular reference to public administration, publication by Institute of Public Administration, Dublin, expected in 1983; *Introduction to Irish Public Administration; Discovering Wicklow,* a local history and topography.

SIDELIGHTS: Barrington told *CA:* "I became a civil servant because I believed that in Ireland, at least, government has a big role in national development.

"Because I spent most of my civil service career in the Department of Local Government (now the Department of the Environment), I became interested in the 1950's in local government, community and regional development, and in problems of decentralization. These, despite much disappointment, remain an abiding interest.

"It was dissatisfaction with the gap between the potentialities of the Irish public service and its actual performance that led a group of us to found the Irish Institute of Public Administration in 1957. I became its first employee in 1960 to turn it into an effective institute for public service reform. The institution is now healthy, active, and reasonably effective, but reform is as elusive here as elsewhere.

"The 1960's saw the liberation of many African countries. Ireland has had close connections with these countries, especially the English-speaking ones, through missionary and other contacts. The governmental and developmental problems were, and are, daunting, and our institute rapidly became involved in Irish overseas bilateral aid projects in the public administration area, starting with Zambia in 1964. The development of Irish aid generally became a major interest of mine. This involved visits to a very large number of countries, mainly African ones.

"General disappointment with progress in relation to raising the effective level of government at home and abroad led in the 1970's to a deeper interest in the development of the study of public administration. Hence my activity in the International Institute of Administrative Sciences, and its offshoot, the European Group of Public Administration, and in European unification generally. The desire to make some contribution to the development of public administration studies as a whole led me to retire from active work in the Institute of Public Administration in 1977 and to devote my energies to study and writing.

"My interest in topography began as a by-product of holidays spent each year in County Kerry in the southwest of Ireland. Apart from beautiful scenery and fascinating people, the area has an extraordinary jumble of relics of the past, dating back some four or five millenia. The attempt to understand this jumble and put it in some sort of order led, over a period of fourteen years, to my big book on Kerry. It also led, more recently, to my work on a similar book on Wicklow, the very beautiful county south of Dublin where I have lived for some forty years. These interests, in turn, led to our project of descriptive cassettes covering all the counties of Ireland. Our aim is to give motoring tourists a greater understanding of what there is to be seen.''

* * *

BARROWS, Chester L. 1892(?)-1975

OBITUARY NOTICE: Born c. 1892; died October 24, 1975, in Philadelphia, Pa. Historian. Barrows wrote *William M. Evarts: Lawyer, Diplomat, Statesman,* published in 1942. Obituaries and other sources: *AB Bookman's Weekly,* December 22, 1975.

* * *

BARRY, Iris 1895-1969

OBITUARY NOTICE: Born in 1895 in England; died December 22, 1969, in Marseilles, France. Film historian and critic. A founder-member of the London Film Society, Barry was a pioneer in the field of film criticism. She did most of her work in the United States, where she was the director of the New York Museum of Modern Art Film Library and president of the International Federation of Film Archives. Her numerous books on the film include *D.W. Griffith: American Film Master.* Obituaries and other sources: *AB Bookman's Weekly,* February 16, 1970; *The Oxford Companion to Film,* Oxford University Press, 1976; *Filmgoer's Companion,* Granada, 7th edition, 1980.

* * *

BARTH, Alan 1906-1979

OBITUARY NOTICE—See index for *CA* sketch: Born October 21, 1906, in New York, N.Y.; died November 20, 1979, in Washington, D.C. Journalist and author best known for his work promoting civil rights. Espousing liberal politics, Barth wrote to analyze and criticize political phenomena. His book *The Loyalty of Free Men* discussed McCarthyism, and *Government by Investigation* looked at disparities in legislative investigation. For his work, Barth received a Sidney Hillman Award and an Oliver Wendall Holmes Award. His other writings include *The Price of Liberty* and *The Heritage of Liberty.* Obituaries and other sources: *AB Bookman's Weekly,* December 24-31, 1979.

* * *

BARTLETT, Hubert Moyse
   See MOYSE-BARTLETT, Hubert

* * *

BARTLETT, Robert V(irgil) 1953-

PERSONAL: Born May 2, 1953, in Portland, Ind.; son of Clarence William (in business) and Catherine (in business; maiden name, Stueckler) Bartlett; married Sally Marie Witulski (a foods manager), December 29, 1973. *Education:* Indiana University, A.B. (with distinction), 1974, M.P.A., 1976, Ph.D., 1982. *Home:* 3617 Kingsbury Ave., Bloomington, Ind. 47401. *Office:* Program of Advanced Studies in Science, Technology, and Public Policy, Indiana University, 1800 North Fee Lane, Bloomington, Ind. 47405.

CAREER: Indiana University, Bloomington, associate instructor, 1974-75 and 1978, instructor in political science and public administration, 1978-80, research associate in advanced studies in science, technology, and public policy, 1978—. *Member:* American Political Science Association, Policy Studies Association, Phi Beta Kappa, Audubon Society, Nature Conservancy, Theatre Circle.

WRITINGS: The Reserve Mining Controversy: Science, Technology, and Environmental Policy, Indiana University Press, 1980. Contributor to political science journals. Editor of *Neighborhood Organization Research Group News Bulletin,* 1977-79.

WORK IN PROGRESS: Science and Rationality in Public Policy: An Assessment of the National Environmental Policy Act, publication expected in 1983.

SIDELIGHTS: Bartlett wrote: ''I enjoy teaching and have a broad range of teaching interests, all relevant to my research interests. My approach includes a strong emphasis on written and oral presentations in order to encourage development of higher level cognitive skills such as analysis, application, evaluation, criticism, and synthesis.

''My present research is focused on an investigation of the concept of rationality and the use of science in public decision-making as exemplified by the environmental impact statement requirement of the National Environmental Policy Act of 1969. I expect most of my future research to be stimulated by my interests in science and technology as major forces in modern society, and by my intellectual concern about environmental quality.''

* * *

BAUDUC, R.
   See SEGRE, Dan V(ittorio)

* * *

BAYLESS, Kenneth 1913(?)-1972

OBITUARY NOTICE: Born c. 1913; died of a stroke, September 16, 1972. Publisher and editor. Bayless published and edited *Pacific Fish and Game News* from 1943 to 1954. In 1955 he joined Peterson Publishing Company as an editor of technical books and became publisher of the company's Specialty Publications Division. Obituaries and other sources: *Publishers Weekly,* October 30, 1972.

* * *

BAYNES, Cary F. 1873(?)-1977

OBITUARY NOTICE: Born c. 1873; died October 29, 1977, in Ascona, Switzerland. Translator. Baynes was best known for her English translation of Richard Wilhelm's German translation of *I Ching.* The book was especially popular with college students in the 1960's and remains in print as part of the Bollingen Series, published by Princeton University Press. She also co-translated four works by the Swiss psychoanalyst Carl Jung, including *Modern Man in Search of a Soul.* Obituaries and other sources: *Publishers Weekly,* November 21, 1977.

* * *

BAYNES, Dorothy Colston
   See COLSTON-BAYNES, Dorothy

BEAN, Normal
 See BURROUGHS, Edgar Rice

*   *   *

BEASLEY, Maurine   1936-

PERSONAL: Born January 28, 1936, in Sedalia, Mo.; daughter of Dimmitt H. (a judge) and Maurine (Hieronymus) Hoffman; married Henry R. Beasley (an international affairs officer for U.S. Department of Commerce), December 24, 1970; children: Susan Sook. *Education:* University of Missouri, B.J. and B.A., both 1958; Columbia University, M.S., 1963; George Washington University, Ph.D., 1974. *Home:* 4920 Flint Dr., Bethesda, Md. 20016. *Office:* College of Journalism, University of Maryland, College Park, Md. 20742.

CAREER: Kansas City Star, Kansas City, Mo., reporter, 1959-62; *Washington Post,* Washington, D.C., reporter, 1963-73; University of Maryland, College Park, assistant professor, 1975-80, associate professor of journalism, 1980—. *Member:* Women in Communication, Society of Professional Journalists, Phi Beta Kappa. *Awards, honors:* Named outstanding teacher of reporting by Modern Media Institute, 1981.

WRITINGS: (With Sheila Gibbons) *Women in Media: A Documentary Source Book,* Women's Institute for Freedom of the Press, 1977; (with Richard Harlow) *Voices of Change: Southern Pulitzer Winners,* University Press of America, 1979; (with Richard Lowitt) *One Third of a Nation: Lorena Hickok Reports on the Great Depression,* University of Illinois Press, 1981.

SIDELIGHTS: As investigator to Harry Hopkins (federal administrator of emergency relief under President Franklin Roosevelt), Lorena Hickok toured the United States from 1933 to 1935 to discover firsthand how Americans were faring during the Great Depression. *One Third of a Nation,* which Maurine Beasley co-edited, is a collection of Hickok's reports from that tour. "Hickok's U.S.A. is real and sad. Characters are individual people, not faceless statistics," wrote Peter Kovler in the *Washington Post.* "Her work has profound meaning," Kovler continued, for it offers the "needed reminder that there are real people who are 'ill-housed, ill-clad, ill-nourished.'"

Maurine Beasley wrote: "There have been many famous women journalists who surmounted the barriers of sexual prejudice to make an impact on the world around them. Generally they are never mentioned in the history books. I want to hunt them up and make their work available for others to read. They had something to say that still speaks today. One thing they said in every syllable they wrote: Women have minds as well as bodies. Sex should not limit one's capacity to develop oneself."

BIOGRAPHICAL/CRITICAL SOURCES: Washington Post, July 7, 1981.

*   *   *

BEAUCHAMP, Kathleen Mansfield   1888-1923
 (Katherine Mansfield)

BRIEF ENTRY: Born October 14, 1888, in Wellington, New Zealand; died of tuberculosis, January 9, 1923, in Fontainebleau, France. New Zealand short story writer, poet, and critic. Mansfield preferred cosmopolitan London to her native land, but it was her short stories about New Zealand, collected in *Bliss* (1920) and *The Garden Party* (1922), that established her as an important writer of the twentieth century. Her stories, reminiscent of Chekhov's, had a distinctive poetic style that emphasized mood rather than plot. She helped develop the art of the short story with her stream of consciousness style. A friend of D. H. Lawrence and Aldous Huxley, she is said to have been the model for Gudrun in Lawrence's *Women in Love* and Beatrice Gilray in Huxley's *Point Counter Point.* Though her last years were plagued by poor health and restlessness, this period brought forth some of her most masterful and revealing writing, collected in *Letters to J. Middleton Murry* (1951) and *Collected Short Stories* (1945). Mansfield was known for her careful observations and her ability to shift point of view from one character to another within a story. When she died at age thirty-four, many critics felt Mansfield had only begun to explore her full potential as a writer. Her other works include *The Dove's Nest and Other Stories* (1923) and *The Little Girl and Other Stories* (1924). *Biographical/critical sources: Cyclopedia of World Authors,* Harper, 1958; *Everyman's Dictionary of Literary Biography, English and American,* revised edition, Dutton, 1960; *The Reader's Encyclopedia,* 2nd edition, Crowell, 1965; *Encyclopedia of World Literature in the Twentieth Century,* updated edition, Ungar, 1967; *Twentieth-Century Literary Criticism,* Volume 2, Gale, 1979.

*   *   *

BEAUFORT, John (David)   1912-

PERSONAL: Born September 23, 1912, in Edmonton, Alberta, Canada; came to United States in 1922, naturalized citizen, 1943; son of Ernest (a journalist) and Margaret Mary (Crawley) Beaufort; married Francesca Bruning (an actress), June 28, 1940. *Education:* Attended Boston University, 1930-33 and 1935-39, and Rollins College, 1933-35. *Office: Christian Science Monitor,* 220 East 42nd St., Suite 3006, New York, N.Y. 10017.

CAREER/WRITINGS: Christian Science Monitor, copy clerk and junior reporter in Boston, Mass., 1930-35, reporter and assistant reviewer, 1935-39, film and theatre critic in New York City 1939-42, war correspondent in Pacific theater, 1943-45, chief of bureau in New York City, 1946-50, arts and magazine editor in Boston, Mass., 1951, arts editor and theatre and film critic in New York City, 1952-62, chief of bureau of London, England, 1962-65, feature editor in Boston, 1965-70, New York drama critic, 1970-57, contributing New York drama critic and feature writer, 1975—. Contributor to *Funk and Wagnalls Yearbook.* Contributor of articles and reviews to magazines and newspapers, including *Collier's* and *Observer. Member:* Drama Desk (president, 1956-57), New York Drama Critics Circle, New York Drama Forum Association (president, 1976-79), Critics Circle of London (honorary member), Coffee House Club, Players Club. *Awards, honors:* Award from Directors Guild of America, 1961.

*   *   *

BEAUVAIS, Robert   1911-

PERSONAL: Born March 6, 1911, in Paris, France; son of Raoul (a representative) and Laura (Stellman) Beauvais; married Ginette Garcin (an actress), February 16, 1974; children: (from previous marriage) Jean Nicolas, Elisabeth, Marianne. *Education:* Received Diplome de Langue Chinoise from Ecole des Langes Orientales. *Home:* 8 rue de Paris, 92100 Boulogne-Billaucourt, France.

CAREER: Writer. Associated with *Poste Parisien* in Paris, France, Radio Luxembourg, and Radiodiffusion Nationale. *Military service:* French Army; received Croix de Guerre and Medaille de la Resistance. *Member:* Societe de auteurs dramatiques, Societe de gens de lettres, SACEM. *Awards, honors:* Prize from Fondation Daintour de L'Academie Francaise.

WRITINGS—In English translation: *Pigeon Vote*, Hachette, 1971; *Le demi-juif* (novel), Julliard, 1977, translation by Harold J. Salemson published as *The Half Jew*, Taplinger, 1980. Also author of play "Les Derniers Outrages," translation by John Fernald produced as "Hannibal's Way."

In French: *Histoire de France et de s'amuser*, Fayard, 1964; *Quand les Chinois*, Fayard, 1966; *L'Hexagonal tel qu'on le parle*, Hachette, 1970; *Le Francais "Kiskose*," Fayard, 1975, *Nous serons tous des protestants*, Plon, 1976; *Guy Beart: Choix de textes, bibliographie, discographie*, P. Seghers, 1965, 2nd edition, 1960; *Les Tartufes de l'ecologie*, Fayard, 1978; *Et celle-la, vous la connaissez?: Deux cents histoires politiques de "gauche" et de "droite*," Plon, 1978; (with wife, Elisabeth Beauvais) *Mythologie, mythofolies*, Hachette, 1979. Also author of play "Carton Pate."

Contributor to magazines.

WORK IN PROGRESS: Dictionnaire France Hexagonal; Le Baragouin; Le Dernier Tabor; a television adaptation of musical comedy "Pourquoi."

* * *

BECK, Leslie   1907(?)-1978

OBITUARY NOTICE: Born c. 1907; died in 1978 in England. Educator. A scholar and authority on Descartes, Beck served on the faculty of Oxford University. His writings include *The Method of Descartes* and *The Metaphysics of Descartes*. Obituaries and other sources: *AB Bookman's Weekly*, September 11, 1978.

* * *

BECK, Robert Edward   1941-

PERSONAL: Born June 7, 1941, in Denver, Colo.; son of Arthur Walter and Caroline Adelheid (Petrie) Beck; married Barbara Ruth Pennell (a nurse), August 21, 1965; children: Philip Arthur, Christopher William, Jennifer Grove. *Education:* Harvey Mudd College, B.S., 1963; University of Pennsylvania, Ph.D., 1969. *Religion:* Presbyterian. *Home:* 238 Tomstock Rd., Norristown, Pa. 19403. *Office:* Department of Mathematics, Villanova University, Villanova, Pa. 19085.

CAREER: Villanova University, Villanova, Pa., instructor, 1966-69, assistant professor, 1969-73, associate professor, 1973-78, professor of mathematics, 1978—. *Member:* American Mathematical Society, American Association of University Professors, Association for Computing Machinery, Sigma Xi, Phi Kappa Phi, Pi Mu Epsilon.

WRITINGS: (Editor with Bernard Kolman, and contributor) *Computers in Nonassociative Rings and Algebras*, Academic Press, 1977; (with Kolman) *Elementary Linear Programming with Applications*, Academic Press, 1980. Contributor to *Encyclopedia of Economics and Business*. Contributor of more than fifteen articles and reviews to technical journals.

WORK IN PROGRESS: Construction of Nilpotent Lie Algebras Over Arbitrary Fields, with Bernard Kolman; research on computational algebra, especially structure and representation theory of Lie algebras.

BEDOYERE, Michael De La
See De La BEDOYERE, Michael

* * *

BEERBOHM, Henry Maximilian   1872-1956

BRIEF ENTRY: Born August 24, 1872, in London, England; died May 20, 1956, in Rapallo, Italy; buried in St. Paul's Cathedral, London, England. English satirical essayist, caricaturist, short story writer, critic, and novelist. Moving in the same literary circle as Oscar Wilde, Beerbohm established his reputation as a wit and satirical essayist during the 1890's. Directing his attacks at social and aesthetic targets, the author became a contributor to the *Yellow Book* when it first appeared in 1894. In 1896 he published a volume of iconoclastic essays, *The Works of Max Beerbohm*, and in 1898 he succeeded George Bernard Shaw as the drama critic of *Saturday Review*, a position he held for twelve years. After his marriage to American actress Florence Kahn in 1910, the author retired to Rapallo, Italy, where, except for periods during World Wars I and II, he remained until his death. During his retirement, Beerbohm continued publishing his works, including a dozen volumes of prose, a comic novel, *Zuleika Dobson; or, An Oxford Love Story* (1911), and a book of parodies, *A Christmas Garland* (1912). In addition to his writings, Beerbohm published ten collections of caricatures, including about three hundred fifty drawings. In recognition of his work, the author received honorary doctorates from Edinburgh and Oxford Universities and was elected to an honorary fellowship at Merton College, Oxford. He was knighted in 1939. Among his best-known works are *Seven Men* (1919), *And Even Now* (1921), *Things New and Old* (1923), *A Variety of Things* (1928), and *Max's Nineties: Drawings 1892-1899* (1958). *Residence:* Villino Chiaro, Rapallo, Italy. *Biographical/critical sources: Twentieth Century Writing: A Reader's Guide to Contemporary Literature*, Transatlantic, 1969; *Twentieth-Century Literary Criticism*, Volume 1, Gale, 1978.

* * *

BELASCO, David   1853-1931

BRIEF ENTRY: Born July 25, 1853, in San Francisco, Calif.; died May 14, 1931, in New York, N.Y. American actor, theatrical producer, and playwright. For more than forty years Belasco was one of the most powerful figures in American theatre, producing nearly four hundred plays and launching some of the most celebrated actors and actresses of the early twentieth century. He began as an actor himself and, in addition to managing and producing, wrote or co-wrote numerous plays, including *Hearts of Oak* (1879), *The Heart of Maryland* (1895), *The Girl of the Golden West* (1905), and *The Return of Peter Grimm* (1915). His 1900 play *Madame Butterfly*, an adaptation of the story by John Luther Long, was made into a popular opera by Giacomo Puccini. Belasco is credited by some with having established the star system in American theatre and with introducing important innovations in lighting techniques and set design. The theatre he named after himself remains an active Broadway establishment. *Biographical/critical sources:* Craig Timberlake, *The Bishop of Broadway: The Life & Work of David Belasco*, Library Publishers, 1954; *The Reader's Encyclopedia of American Literature*, Crowell, 1962; *Twentieth Century Writing: A Reader's Guide to Contemporary Literature*, Transatlantic, 1969; Lise-Lone Marker, *David Belasco: Naturalism in the American Theatre*, Princeton University Press, 1975; *Twentieth-Century Literary Criticism*, Volume 3, Gale, 1980.

BELDEN, Gail
See BELDEN, Louise Conway

* * *

BELDEN, Louise Conway 1910-
(Gail Belden)

PERSONAL: Born November 1, 1910, in Chicago, Ill.; daughter of Barret (a corporation executive) and Louise (Shoenberger) Conway; married Gail Chester Belden (a corporation executive), June 27, 1936; children: Gail Chester, Jr., Elizabeth (Mrs. Lawrence Iwan), Louise (Mrs. Jonathan Fairbank). *Education:* Wellesley College, B.A., 1931; University of Delaware, M.A., 1958. *Politics:* Republican. *Religion:* Protestant. *Home:* 700 Coverdale Rd., Wilmington, Del. 19805. *Office:* Winterthur Museum, Winterthur, Del. 19735.

CAREER: Worked as a professional voluntarist, 1931-58; Winterthur Museum, Winterthur, Del., assistant curator, 1958-75, research associate, 1975—. *Member:* Decorative Arts Society, Decorative Arts Trust, National Trust for Historic Preservation, Delaware Art Museum, Greenville Country Club, Junior League.

WRITINGS: (Under pseudonym Gail Belden; with Michael Snodin) *Collecting for Tomorrow: Spoons,* Walter Parrish International, 1975; *Marks of American Silversmiths in the Ineson-Bissell Collection,* University Press of Virginia, 1980; *Two Hundred Years of American Party Tables,* Norton, 1982. Contributor to antiques magazines.

SIDELIGHTS: Belden told *CA:* "Always fond of food, fun, and games, I concentrate on the social history of early America, focusing on dining, drinking, and dicing. I lecture and write on table decorations, dessert services, billiard tables, loving cups, cookie molds, and other archeological witnesses to man's best nature."

* * *

BELENO
See AZUELA, Mariano

* * *

BELL, Derrick Albert, Jr. 1930-

PERSONAL: Born November 6, 1930, in Pittsburgh, Pa.; son of Derrick Albert and Ada Elizabeth (Childress) Bell; married Jewel Allison Hairston, June 26, 1960; children: Derrick Albert III, Douglass Dubois, Carter Robeson. *Education:* Duquesne University, A.B., 1952; University of Pittsburgh, LL.B., 1957. *Home:* 2260 Lincoln St., Eugene, Ore. 97405. *Office:* School of Law, University of Oregon, Eugene, Ore. 97403.

CAREER: U.S. Department of Justice, Washington, D.C., member of staff of conscientious objector section and civil rights division, 1957-59; National Association for the Advancement of Colored People, New York, N.Y., staff attorney for Legal Defense and Education Fund, Inc., 1960-66; U.S. Department of Health, Education and Welfare, Washington, D.C., deputy director of Office of Civil Rights, 1966-68; U.S. Office of Economic Opportunity, Western Center of Law and Poverty at University of Southern California, Los Angeles, director, 1968-69; Harvard University, Cambridge, Mass., lecturer, 1969-71, professor of law, 1971-80; University of Oregon, Eugene, professor of law and dean of law school, 1981—. *Military service:* U.S. Air Force, 1952-54; became first lieutenant. *Member:* National Conference of Black Lawyers, Society of American Law Schools, American Bar Association. *Awards, honors:* Ford Foundation grants, 1972 and 1975.

WRITINGS: Race, Racism, and American Law, Little, Brown, 1973, 2nd edition, 1980; *Shades of Brown: New Perspectives on School Desegregation,* Teachers College Press, 1980. Contributor to law journals.

WORK IN PROGRESS: Symbolic Justice, a book on Justice Thurgood Marshall's contribution to the Supreme Court; *Still Looking for the Pony,* a book of autobiographical essays.

SIDELIGHTS: Bell told *CA:* "In my writing, there is little of craft and certainly nothing of art, but it serves as a medium of expression which, while only infrequently effectual, remains a soul-satisfying means of speaking out against racism, poverty, and this society's self-deluding conviction that happiness can be purchased, integrity feigned, and the Lord's judgment forever postponed."

* * *

BELL, Gordon Bennett 1934-

PERSONAL: Born April 15, 1934, in Houston, Tex.; son of Gordon Bennett, Jr., and Jewel Blanche Bell; married MaryLou Mortimer (in public relations), December 24, 1973; children: David Anthony. *Education:* University of Houston, B.B.A., 1959. *Religion:* Scientology. *Residence:* Florida. *Agent:* c/o McGraw-Hill Book Co., 1221 Avenue of the Americas, New York, N.Y. 10020.

CAREER: Church of Scientology, Washington, D.C., secretary, 1959-64; minister, 1971-76; free-lance writer and artist, 1976—.

WRITINGS: The Golden Troubador (novel), McGraw, 1980.

WORK IN PROGRESS: Arie'L, a four-volume sequel to *The Golden Troubador; The Rise and Fall of the Patrician State,* and *The Rim Planet Blues,* two novels about space opera.

SIDELIGHTS: Bell commented: "The spiritual gains achieved through the experiences of the religion of scientology are directly responsible for my inspirations, particularly *The Golden Troubador.* We live on a lost planet in the middle of a third-rate galaxy where the people are constantly hit with the idea we are an 'only one' planet. The universal truths that are covered up here are indeed worth the trouble of defeating the cover-up and those who promote it."

* * *

BELLI, Melvin M(ouron) 1907-

PERSONAL: Born July 29, 1907, in Sonora, Calif.; son of Caesar Arthur and Leonie (Mouron) Belli; married Betty Ballantine, 1933 (marriage ended); married Toni Nichols (marriage ended); married Joy Maybelle Turney, May 3, 1956 (marriage ended); married Pat Montandon, 1966 (annulled); married Lia G. T. Triff, June 3, 1972; children: (first marriage) Richard R., Melvin Mouron, Jean, Susan; (second marriage) Caesar Melvin; (third marriage) Melia. *Education:* University of California, Berkeley, A.B., 1929, LL.B., 1933. *Residence:* San Francisco, Calif. *Office:* Belli & Choulos, Belli Building, 722 Montgomery St., San Francisco, Calif. 95133; and 6330 Wilshire Blvd., Beverly Hills, Calif. 90048.

CAREER: National Recovery Administration (NRA), undercover investigator, 1933; attorney with various law firms, 1933-40; Belli, Ashe & Gerry, San Francisco, Calif., senior partner, 1940—. Senior partner of Belli, Ashe & Gerry, Los Angeles, Calif., 1958-68, Belli, Ashe, Ellison, Choulos & Lieff, 1968—, Belli & Choulos, San Francisco and Los Angeles, and Belli, Weil, & Jacobs, Rockville, Md. Founder and moderator of

Belli Seminars in Law, 1950—; president of Belli Foundation Lecturers, 1960—. Member of California Building Standards Commission; member of board of directors of Disability and Casualty Inter-Insurance Exchange; past member of board of directors of Northwest Affairs Council; member of board of trustees of National Epilepsy Foundation. Lecturer; guest on television and radio programs.

MEMBER: International Bar Association (patron), International Academy of Trial Lawyers (co-founder; fellow; member of board of directors; dean emeritus), International Academy of Law and Science, Association Internationale des Juristes Democrates, International Legal Aid Association, Inter-American Bar Association, American Bar Association, Federal Bar Association, American Trial Lawyers Association (past president of San Francisco chapter and western states chapter; chairman of torts section, 1959), American Judicature Society, Office League of America, American League to Abolish Capital Punishment (member of board of directors), American Academy of Forensic Sciences, National Association of Claimants Compensation Attorneys (chairman of aviation section and torts section), American Institute of Hypnosis, Authors Guild, Asociacion Nacional de Abogados (Mexico; honorary member), Societe de l'Honneur et de la Droit (president), California Bar Association, Municipal Motorcycle Officers of California (honorary member), Northern California Service League, Criminal Trial Lawyers Association of Northern California, Tuolumne County Historical Society, Plaintiffs' Trial Lawyers Association of Los Angeles County, San Francisco Bar Association, Beverly Hills Bar Association, Hollywood Bar Association, Barristers Club of San Francisco (past member of board of directors), Lawyers Club of San Francisco, Phi Delta Phi, Delta Tau Delta, Masons (Shriners), Scribes, Islam Shrine (California commander), San Francisco Press Club, Union Club, Olympic Club, Commonwealth Club, Tuolumne County Reunion Association (past president), E. Clampus Vitus (honorary member). *Awards, honors:* Legion of Honor (Cuba); L.H.D. from Columbia Institute of Chiropractic, 1970; Ph.D. from University of Houston, 1970; J.D. from New England School of Law; named dean emeritus of College of Law, University of California, Riverside; grand collar of Order of St. Brigidia.

WRITINGS: Modern Trials, 1954-1960, six volumes, Bobbs-Merrill, 1954, abridged edition, 1963; *Blood Money: Ready for the Plaintiff,* Grosset, 1956, reprinted as *''Ready for the Plaintiff!'': A Story of Personal Injury Law,* Holt, 1956; (editor) *Trial and Tort Trends Through 1955,* twelve volumes, Central Book Co., 1956; *Modern Damages,* six volumes, Bobbs-Merrill, 1959; (with Danny R. Jones) *Belli Looks at Life and Law in Japan,* Bobbs-Merrill, 1960; (editor with Albert Averbach) *Tort and Medical Yearbook,* Bobbs-Merrill, 1961; (with Jones) *Belli Looks at Life and Law in Russia,* Bobbs-Merrill, 1963; (with Maurice C. Carroll) *Dallas Justice: The Real Story of Jack Ruby and His Trial,* McKay, 1964 (published in England as *Justice in Dallas,* Elek, 1965); *Jack Ruby, Appellant, Versus the State of Texas, Appellee: Amicus Curiae Brief for Jack Ruby, Defendant and Appellant,* American Brief Co., 1965; *Trial Tactics,* Trial Lawyers Service Co., 1967; *Criminal Law,* introduction by Erle Stanley Gardner, Sherbourne, 1968; *The Law Revolt: A Summary of Trends in Modern Criminal and Civil Law,* Volume I: *Criminal Law,* Volume II: *Civil Law,* Trial Lawyers Service Co., 1968; *The Law Revolution,* introduction by Gardner, Sherbourne, 1968; (with Robert Kaiser) *My Life on Trial: An Autobiography,* Morrow, 1976.

Also author of *The Adequate Award,* 1953; *The Use of Demonstrative Evidence in Achieving the More Adequate Award,* 1955; *Medical Malpractice,* 1955; and *The More Adequate Award, Demonstrative Evidence, Belli on Blackstone,* and *String 'em Up With Caution.* Contributor to *Courtroom Champions.*

Correspondent for International News Service and Hearst newspapers. Author of "So That's the Law," a daily column syndicated by *San Francisco Chronicle.* Contributor of articles and reviews to law journals, popular magazines, and newspapers. Associate editor of *Torts, National Association of Claimants Compensation Attorneys Law Journal,* and *American Trial Lawyers Association Journal,* 1950—; advisory editor of *Negligence and Compensation Service,* 1955—; honorary member of editorial advisory board of *Southwestern Law Journal,* 1970.

SIDELIGHTS: One of America's foremost trial lawyers, Belli is known for his colorful personal style as well as his legal ability. His specialty is tort law, the law of civil damage suits, an area in which his innovative techniques have led to important changes in legal practice. His commitment to defending unpopular people and causes, as well as his unusual and often flamboyant courtroom tactics, have frequently placed him in conflict with the American Bar Association (ABA), the American Medical Association (AMA), insurance companies, and other institutions.

Belli has served as counsel in over two hundred cases in which awards exceeded $100 thousand, and settlements won for his clients total more than $100 million. He became famous as "The King of Torts" (a nickname he dislikes) in the 1950's, after he won six-figure awards—virtually unprecedented at that time—in several personal-injury suits. He pioneered the use of demonstrative evidence: photographs, movies, enlarged x-rays, scale models, human skeletons, and other devices to make the nature of injuries graphically clear. In one case involving the loss of his client's leg, he brought into court a package wrapped in butcher's paper; this proved to be an artificial leg, which Belli unwrapped slowly and dropped into a juror's lap. Though his tactics were denounced by insurance companies who were alarmed by the large settlements Belli won for his clients, Belli persistently wrote and lectured on his techniques and on the importance of adequate compensation for injury victims. In large part as a result of his crusade, the use of demonstrative evidence is now commonplace in liability cases, and average awards have risen considerably.

Belli's book *Ready for the Plaintiff* is an account of his experiences as a lawyer in personal-injury cases. It also provides an explanation, in layman's language, of many of the principles of tort law. Charles Raudebaugh of the *San Francisco Chronicle* considered the book very well written: "What might be difficult going on such a subtle subject as the legal concept of *stare decisis,* for instance, is rendered illuminating and entertaining."

Medical malpractice suits are also a Belli specialty, one he has pursued since the 1930's. He has often attacked the professional code that discourages doctors from testifying against each other. "Good old Doc Frebish may have come into the operating room dead drunk, carrying a rusty knife and wearing an old pair of overalls, but as long as he's a member in good standing of the AMA, not one doctor in 10,000 will testify against him," he told *Playboy.* "If you ever do actually get a doctor to take the stand and testify against another doctor's flagrant and perhaps tragic malpractice he's regarded as a 'stoolie' and will be ostracized for life." Belli has long insisted that lawyers should learn about medicine, pointing out that most civil and criminal cases involve some aspect of medical knowledge or practice. "I probably know as much medicine as I do law," he has said.

Belli laid the groundwork for the consumer and environmental court actions of the 1970's. In several cases in the 1940's and

1950's, he expanded consumers' rights by arguing successfully that any product carries an implied warranty and that therefore actual negligence need not be proved if the product is defective. These decisions provided much of the legal basis for class action suits brought by Ralph Nader and other activists. Belli has since sought to extend warranty law to such products as cigarettes, suing tobacco companies on behalf of cancer victims.

Belli has represented many prominent people, including Mae West, Errol Flynn, Lenny Bruce, and Tony Curtis; he has also devoted much of his career to representing unpopular and sometimes indigent clients. In the first years of his practice he took on, for no fee, several "hopeless" criminal cases like that of Frank Avilez, "The Black-Gloved Rapist," whose 440 year sentence Belli got reduced to 220 years. He remains passionate in his conviction that every defendant is entitled to competent counsel. He once said, "Any lawyer worthy of the name has a commitment to defend the pariahed, unpopular defendant." He told *Playboy:* "I will defend *anyone* who comes to me— even the president of the Bar Association. . . . A.B.A. presidents are constantly trumpeting on the majestic subject 'The Defense of Unpopular Causes,' and proclaiming that it's every lawyer's duty to give a courageous representation of his unfortunate brother, however unpopular he is, however heinous his crime. These are the same great vocal defenders who whimper, from behind their corporate desks, when some poor unfortunate's case has to be tried, 'Sure, he's entitled to the best defense, but *you* defend him, I can't afford to!'"

In his most famous and controversial criminal case, Belli defended Jack Ruby in his trial for the murder of Lee Harvey Oswald, the assassin of John F. Kennedy. Belli was offered $100,000 not to defend Ruby, and some accused him of seeking publicity by taking the case, a charge Belli denies. "As far as publicity is concerned," he observed, "I'd had my fill of that long before that travesty of a trial ever came along." When the jury rejected Ruby's insanity defense, finding him guilty and sentencing him to death, Belli leaped up and shouted, "May I thank the jury for a victory of bigotry and injustice!" Calling the verdict "the shotgun justice of a kangaroo court," he was harshly criticized for his outburst and was threatened with expulsion by the ABA, but he continued to denounce the Dallas authorities' treatment of both Ruby and Oswald.

In *Dallas Justice,* Belli presented his view of the Ruby case, appending the medical and psychological reports on Ruby, and arguing that a fair trial was impossible in Dallas. The book, like the case, was controversial. Thomas Szasz, in the *New Republic,* called it "a highly slanted, propagandistic account." But the *New York Times Book Review*'s George Fuermann, who he considered the book dogmatic and one-sided, nevertheless wrote, "One becomes persuaded that Mr. Belli is right, that the trial should have been held someplace other than Dallas."

Belli's courtroom theatrics, his penchant for stylish, scarlet-lined suits, his many marriages, and his jet-set lifestyle have contributed to his notoriety almost as much as have his legal achievements. He shrugs off criticism of his showmanship, pointing to his results, and he freely admits that he enjoys the histrionic side of trial law. "I might have been an actor," he told *Playboy* in 1965; since then he has appeared in two motion pictures, "Wild in the Streets" and "Gimme Shelter," and has guest-starred in an episode of the television series "Star Trek."

In his autobiography, *My Life on Trial,* Belli tells of his taste "for all things bright and beautiful, kinky and flawed, for good wines, great tables, wide travels and beautiful women." He recounts his many romances as well as his legal career, and he takes on his customary antagonists, including the ABA. Critics found the book entertaining and Belli's humor appealing. As John Murray of *Best Sellers* observed, "Belli emerges as Puck, Pan and Gladstone rolled into one."

Belli has written more than thirty books, scholarly as well as popular. His six-volume *Modern Trials,* a study of modern procedures in civil and criminal law, has become a standard textbook in law schools.

BIOGRAPHICAL/CRITICAL SOURCES: Life, October 18, 1954; Robert Wallace, *Life and Limb: An Account of the Career of Melvin M. Belli, Personal Injury Trial Lawyer,* Doubleday, 1956; *San Francisco Chronicle,* December 9, 1956; *Time,* January 26, 1959, December 20, 1963; *Saturday Evening Post,* February 8, 1964; *New York Times Book Review,* November 1, 1964, November 21, 1976; *New Republic,* November 21, 1964; *Playboy,* June, 1965; *Newsweek,* April 17, 1967, September 27, 1976; Digby Diehl, *Supertalk,* Doubleday, 1974; Melvin M. Belli, *My Life on Trial,* Morrow, 1976; Norman Sheresky, *On Trial,* Viking, 1977; *Best Sellers,* January, 1977; *People,* March 3, 1980.

—*Sketch by Tim Connor*

*   *   *

BELOTSERKOVSKY, Vladimir Naumovich Bill
See BILL-BELOTSERKOVSKY, Vladimir Naumovich

*   *   *

BELY, Andrey
See BUGAYEV, Boris Nikolayevich

*   *   *

BELYI, Andrei
See BUGAYEV, Boris Nikolayevich

*   *   *

BENET, Stephen Vincent   1898-1943

BRIEF ENTRY: Born July 22, 1898, in Bethlehem, Pa.; died March 13, 1943, in New York, N.Y. American author. Benet won his first Pulitzer Prize for poetry in 1929 for the book-length poem *John Brown's Body* (1928). Generally considered to be his best work, this verse novel has been cited for its details of Civil War history and its intense American spirit. Benet chose traditional subjects for most of his writing, retelling and popularizing American history, folktales, and legends. His most successful form was the ballad, though he wrote entertaining short stories as well. He won an O. Henry Memorial Prize for "The Devil and Daniel Webster" (1937), later adapting the story for production as a folk opera. When Benet died at age forty-four, he left behind *Western Star* (1943), the first volume of a proposed American history in verse for which he posthumously received his second Pulitzer Prize. *Biographical/critical sources: Cyclopedia of World Authors,* Harper, 1958; *Concise Encyclopedia of Modern World Literature,* Hutchinson, 1963.

*   *   *

BENOIT, Richard   1899(?)-1969

OBITUARY NOTICE: Born c. 1899; died December 30, 1969, in New Hartford, N.Y. Writer and editor of law textbooks for

Matthew Bender & Co., Inc. Benoit's writings include *Personal Injury Actions, Defenses and Damages,* and *Negligence in the New York Courts.* Obituaries and other sources: *Publishers Weekly,* January 12, 1970; *Who Was Who Among North American Authors, 1921-1939,* Gale, 1976.

*   *   *

BENTON, Helen Hemingway   1902(?)-1974

OBITUARY NOTICE: Born c. 1902; died after a brief illness, May 3, 1974, in Phoenix, Ariz. Publisher. After the death of her husband, Senator William Benton, in 1973, Helen Benton succeeded him as publisher and vice-president of Encyclopaedia Brittannica, Inc. Obituaries and other sources: *Who's Who of American Women,* Marquis, 4th edition, 1966; *Publishers Weekly,* June 3, 1974; *AB Bookman's Weekly,* June 17, 1974.

*   *   *

BERCOVITCH, Reuben   1923-

PERSONAL: Born July 18, 1923, in New York, N.Y.; son of Joe and Mary Bercovitch; married Blanche Brodie (an academic counselor), January 26, 1947; children: Stephen, Fred, Saul, Marc. *Education:* Attended Brooklyn College (now is City University of New York), 1946; Columbia University, B.S., 1948. *Religion:* Jewish. *Agent:* Berenice Hoffman Literary Agency, 215 West 75th St., New York, N.Y. 10023.

CAREER: Free-lance writer for films and television, 1956-68; ABC Films, Los Angeles, Calif., producer, 1968; free-lance writer, 1968-73; Lorimar Production, Los Angeles, film producer, 1973-75; Bill Jack Productions, Los Angeles, film producer, 1975-76; free-lance writer, 1976—. *Military service:* U.S. Army, Armoured Divison, 1942-46; served in European theater; became technical sergeant. *Member:* International P.E.N., Authors Guild, Writers Guild of America (West). *Awards, honors:* Ernest Hemingway Fiction Award, 1978, for *Hasen.*

WRITINGS: Odette, Ashley Books, 1973; *Hasen,* Knopf, 1978.

Translations represented in anthologies, including *Yiddish Stories,* edited by Irving Howe and Eliezer Greenberg, Holiday House, 1974, *I. L. Peretz: Selected Stories,* edited by Howe and Greenberg, Schocken, 1974, and *Ashes Out of Hope,* edited by Howe and Greenberg Schocken, 1977. Contributor to *Literary Review.*

*   *   *

BERGREEN, Laurence R.   1950-

PERSONAL: Born February 4, 1950, in New York, N.Y.; son of Morris H. (a lawyer) and Adele (a lawyer; maiden name, Gabel) Bergreen; married Elizabeth Freeman (a musician), June, 1975. *Education:* Harvard University, A.B., 1972. *Office:* 15 East 10th St., New York, N.Y. 10003.

CAREER: Museum of Broadcasting, New York City, assistant to president, 1977-78; New School for Social Research, New York City, faculty member, 1980—.

WRITINGS: Look Now, Pay Later: The Rise of Network Broadcasting, Doubleday, 1980. Contributor to *Academic American Encyclopedia.* Contributor to magazines, including *Newsweek, American Film, TV Guide, Quest,* and *Television Quarterly.*

WORK IN PROGRESS: A novel.

SIDELIGHTS: In his book *Look Now, Pay Later,* Laurence Bergreen provides a history of the broadcasting industry. In addition, his book contains sketches of major journalists and broadcasting executives, including Edward R. Murrow, Eric Sevareid, Edwin Armstrong, and Fred Silverman. Writing for the *Washington Journalism Review,* E. William Henry praised Bergreen for both his "highly readable, perceptive study of the broadcasting industry" and his "compelling portraits of the broadcast pioneers and their successors." Blaik Kirby of the *Toronto Globe and Mail* recommended *Look Now, Pay Later* for "anyone interested in broadcasting," declaring, "It is often an exciting tale and it is so thorough that I have complete faith in its accuracy and fairness."

Bergreen condemns the high-level competition and private-profit motives that dictate television programming in America. They are the cause, he claims, of the increasing inferiority of television fare. As Kirby noted, Bergreen points to the British Broadcasting Corporation as a "shining example of broadcasting as it should be."

Bergreen told *CA:* "Writing has found me, rather than my rushing to embrace it. I first began to write in a more than scatterbrained fashion when living in London from 1972 to 1974. Though most nonfiction is too limited to inspire my deepest responses, the discipline of journalism has contributed a great deal to my fiction, and it is fiction that I regard as the ultimate challenge. When writing my first book, a history of the American broadcasting industry, I found myself becoming more imaginatively engaged in the story of the rise of a business venture than I would have guessed possible at the outset. After a while it struck me that the networks served as a huge metaphor for the craggy face of American enterprise. It was a microcosm of society—at least as it looks to me here in New York—a fascinating, discordant combination of remarkable elements and people."

BIOGRAPHICAL/CRITICAL SOURCES: Toronto Globe and Mail, June 28, 1980; *Washington Journalism Review,* July/August, 1980.

*   *   *

BERKOFF, Steven   1937-

PERSONAL: Born August 3, 1937, in London, England; son of Alfred (a tailor) and Pauline (Hyman) Berkoff; married Shelley Lee (a dancer and choreographer), August 21, 1976. *Education:* Studied acting at Webber-Douglas Academy in London, England, 1958-59, and at Ecole Jacques Le Coq in Paris, France, 1965. *Agent:* Joanna Marston, 4 Hereford Square, London SW7, England.

CAREER: Actor, director, writer, and adapter of plays for London Theatre Group, London England. Actor in motion pictures, including "Barry Lyndon" and "A Clockwork Orange."

WRITINGS: East and Other Plays, J. Calder, 1977; *Gross Intrusion* (short stories), J. Calder, 1977; *The Trial* [and] *Metamorphosis* (plays), Amber Lane, 1981. Also author or adapter of such plays as "Greek," "Agamemnon," "Decadence," and "The Fall of the House of Usher."

SIDELIGHTS: Berkoff told *CA* that "getting up in the morning" has been his motivation and that "the bailiffs" were the circumstances surrounding his writing. Writing to be "notorious," Berkoff hopes to achieve "fame, money, and sex" through his books. His writing habits include "avoiding it," and he advises aspiring writers to "get out of my way." The author revealed that he has no views on his contemporaries, although he sees the current literary scene as "pathetic." Berkoff's books have been translated into other languages, but they have not been adapted to other media.

He commented: "My main motivation is to write well and to create theatrical works that do not send people to sleep. I write for the sheer pleasure of it and as a hobby. Writing should never be work—the closest thing to writing is loving or day-dreaming or eating a salt-beef sandwich with a pickle."

* * *

BERMAN, Emile Zola 1902-1981

OBITUARY NOTICE: Born November 3, 1902, in New York City; died July 3, 1981, in New York City. Trial lawyer and attorney best known for his defense of Senator Robert Kennedy's assassin, Sirhan Sirhan. Berman, named in honor of the French author Emile Zola, specialized in controversial and unpopular cases. A practicing lawyer since 1926, he first won wide public attention in 1956 when he undertook the defense of Marine Corps Staff Sergeant Matthew McKeon. McKeon was charged with causing the deaths of six recruits when he led them on a disciplinary march into a tidal creek. Berman defended McKeon by defending the Marine Corps' training methods, and McKeon was exonerated. His defense of Sirhan Sirhan relied on the argument that the assassin was a "mentally ill youth" who committed the crime while "out of contact with reality, in a trance." Criticized for accepting Sirhan's case, Berman explained, "I'm not defending his crime, only his rights." Obituaries and other sources: *Newsweek*, February 6, 1969; *Time*, January 17, 1969, July 20, 1981; *Current Biography*, Wilson, 1972, August, 1981; *Who's Who in America*, 39th edition, Marquis, 1976; *New York Times*, July 5, 1981.

* * *

BERNAL, Martin Gardiner 1937-

PERSONAL: Born March 10, 1937, in London, England; son of Desmond John (a scientist) and Margaret (a writer; maiden name, Gardiner) Bernal; married Judith Pace Dunn, June 18, 1960 (divorced, 1975); married Leslie Miller (a sociologist), March 10, 1979; children: Sophie Frances, William Magnus, Paul Alexander, Patrick Jacob. *Education:* Received B.A., M.A., and Ph.D., from King's College, Cambridge; postdoctoral study at University of California. Berkeley, 1962-65, and Harvard University, 1964. *Politics:* "Left." *Religion:* None. *Office:* Cornell University, Ithaca, N.Y. 14530.

CAREER: Cambridge University, Cambridge, England, fellow of King's College, 1965-73; Cornell University, Ithaca, N.Y., associate professor, 1972—. *Military service:* Served with Royal Air Force; became senior aircraftsman.

WRITINGS: (Editor) *Minsheng*, Lungmen Dengleang, 1968; *Chinese Socialism*, Cornell University Press, 1975.

WORK IN PROGRESS: A revisionist history of ancient Greece; research on Afro-Asiatic origins.

* * *

BERNANOS, (Paul Louis) Georges 1888-1948

BRIEF ENTRY: Born February 20, 1888, in Paris, France; died of cirrhosis of the liver, July 5, 1948, in Neuilly-sur-Seine, France; buried in Pellevoisin, France. French philosopher, novelist, journalist, and short story and political writer. Best known for his moralistic and visionary theological novels dating from the era between the two world wars, Bernanos presented a Christian faith capable of overcoming the death and despair dominating the modern world. His first novel, *Sous le soleil de satan* (translated as *The Star of Satan*, 1927; *Under the Sun of Satan*, 1949), was published in 1926. A study of mysticism,

satanism, a young girl, and a country priest, the book established the author's reputation within France. In 1936 Bernanos won the French Academy's Grand Prix du Roman for his novel *Journal d'un cure de campagne* (1936; *The Diary of a Country Priest*, 1937). This book, presenting the sufferings of a young priest in his war against sin, brought Bernanos worldwide recognition as a novelist. A passionate political writer as well, Bernanos cared deeply about the disturbing events in his contemporary Europe, finally relocating himself and his family in Brazil in 1938 to protest the Munich Pact. He wrote effectively in support of the de Gaullist Free France movement during World War II, and his work was read throughout free and occupied Europe. He returned to France in 1945, but moved to Tunisia in the last year of his life. Other major works in English translation include *A Diary of My Times* (1938), *Joy* (1946), *Night Is Darkest* (1953), and *Last Essays* (1955). *Biographical/critical sources:* Peter Hebblethwaite, S.J., *Bernanos: An Introduction*, Hillary House Publishers Ltd., 1965; *Encyclopedia of World Literature in the Twentieth Century*, updated edition, Ungar, 1967; William Bush, *Georges Bernanos*, Twayne, 1969; *The Penguin Companion to European Literature*, McGraw, 1971; *Twentieth-Century Literary Criticism*, Volume 3, Gale, 1980.

* * *

BERNSTEIN, Jacob 1946-

PERSONAL: Born September 20, 1946, in Germany; came to America, 1948; naturalized U.S. citizen, 1962; son of Meyer (a tailor) and Sara (Tuvel) Bernstein; married Linda Thorton, July 6, 1978; children: Rebecca, Elliott. *Education:* University of Illinois at Urbana-Champaign, B.A., 1968; graduate study at Roosevelt University, 1976. *Residence:* Winnetka, Ill. *Address:* MBH Commodities, P.O. Box 353, Winnetka, Ill. 60093.

CAREER: MBH Management Corp., Winnetka, Ill., editor of *MBH Weekly Commodity Newsletter*, 1972—, president and conductor of seminars, 1974—. Thorton Management Corp., Winnetka, president, 1978-80; B & B Properties (real estate firm), Chicago, Ill., partner, 1979—. Financial consultant to grain and livestock producers, metal market analysts, and private speculators. *Awards, honors:* The *MBH Commodities Weekly Newsletter* was rated number one commodity newsletter by *Commodities* (magazine), 1980.

WRITINGS: Seasonal Cash Study: Commodity Prices, MBH, 1977; *Seasonal Futures Charts: Commodities*, MBH, 1979; *Commodities: Now Through 1984*, MBH, 1979; *The Investor's Quotient: The Psychology of Successful Investing in Commodities and Stock*, Wiley, 1980; *Commodity Cycles: A Window on Time*, Wiley, 1981; *A Seasonal Study of Commodity Spreads*, Wiley, 1982.

Contributor of articles to magazines and periodicals, including *Commodities, Successful Farming*, and *Hard Money News*. Member of editorial board of *Commodities*, 1980.

WORK IN PROGRESS: The Killer Wave, an economic novel.

SIDELIGHTS: Jacob Bernstein told *CA:* "My writings are designed to enlighten the public about an area too long considered the exclusive domain of professionals. The role of technical and cyclical factors in economics is an important one, and its growth as a new science is inevitable. My work further attempts to bring philosophical considerations into the area of price analysis. All markets are subject to forces of human emotion. These are, in turn, a function of philosophical orientation. Hence, market philosophy is a significant area of investigation.

"The psychology of investing is an area of special interest inasmuch as it combines my two greatest concerns: the market and psychology. My book, *The Investor's Quotient: The Psychology of Successful Investing in Commodities and Stock,* sets forth the theory that most investors are failures in their efforts to multiply capital, because of such emotionally limiting factors as anxiety, frustration, inter-personal conflicts, insecurity, and even feelings of sexual inadequacy. In many respects these behavioral difficulties tend to limit success in any area that requires discipline, organization, and persistence. Hence, one who is generally a 'loser' in other areas of life will also tend to be a 'loser' in the market place. Rather than investigating new and better methods of selecting investments, the average investor who typically suffers from some or all of the above behavioral limitations might be better off working on changes in himself. Note that I have termed these 'behavioral,' since I believe that they are problems in behavior *per se,* and not necessarily emotional limitations (although their symptomatology may be emotional). In other words, I believe that the true domain of the psychologist is behavior. Hence, I provide behavioral guidelines and not psychological assistance. There are many problems best treated by the professional therapist, but there are also many investment related behaviors that can be corrected by some simple and disciplined approaches outlined in my book. A second book on the subject will go into greater detail.''

AVOCATIONAL INTERESTS: Study of past life regression, theories of reincarnation, extrasensory perception, and the occult; organic and French intensive gardening; electronics.

*   *   *

BERNSTEIN, Jane   1949-

PERSONAL: Born June 10, 1949, in Brooklyn, N.Y.; daughter of David (a salesman) and Ruth (an office worker; maiden name, Levinson) Bernstein; married Paul Glynn (a biophysicist), July 20, 1975; children: Charlotte Claire. *Education:* New York University, B.A., 1971; Columbia University, M.F.A., 1977. *Religion:* Jewish. *Home:* 29 Cowperthwaite Place, Westfield, N.J. 07090. *Agent:* Lois Wallace, Wallace & Sheil, 177 East 70th Street, New York, N.Y. 10021. *Office:* 42 Grove St., No. 28, New York, N.Y. 10014.

CAREER: Fillmore East Theatre, New York City, box office treasurer, 1967-71; Ideal Publishing Corp., New York City, editor, 1973-75; Rutgers University, New Brunswick, N.J., instructor in media and fiction, 1977-79; writer. *Member:* Writers Guild of America, East. *Awards, honors:* Harper & Row writing fellowship, 1976.

WRITINGS: Departures (novel), Holt, 1979. Contributor of short stories to *Mademoiselle* and *Prairie Schooner.*

WORK IN PROGRESS: A novel about the son and daughter of concentration camp survivors, publication by Holt expected in 1983.

SIDELIGHTS: Departures is the story of a young woman, Lydia, who struggles to maintain a sense of identity when her personal life is shattered by a series of sudden departures—her father and grandfather die, her lover leaves to pursue a film career—and her mother and sister are unable or unwilling to help Lydia come to grips with her losses. She abandons the writing of her doctoral dissertation to take a job in a factory that makes cigarette lighters and attempts to pull her life back together.

Bernstein told *CA:* "When I was working on my third unpublished novel, a teacher of mine assured me that my life would not change once I was published. In a way, of course, she was right. On an average day, the same things make me happy or

unhappy as they did before my novel was accepted. But now that I have been published, I have overcome the feeling that it is useless to go on writing fiction for my file cabinets, that there was something bizarre about a grown person staying home all day long and telling stories. Now I have a whole series of new worries. I have lost the bravado I once had. But the knowledge that my finished work will reach readers has indeed changed my life. Now what I do is write each day. I may procrastinate, but I no longer question the sanity of my pursuit.''

AVOCATIONAL INTERESTS: Marathon running.

BIOGRAPHICAL/CRITICAL SOURCES: Chicago Tribune Book World, October 14, 1979; *New York Times Book Review,* December 2, 1979; *Observer,* September 21, 1980; *Times Literary Supplement,* January 2, 1981.

*   *   *

BERSSENBRUGGE, Mei-mei   1947-

PERSONAL: Given name is pronounced May-may; born October 5, 1947, in Peking, China; American citizen born abroad; daughter of Robert (an engineer) and Martha (an engineer; maiden name, Wang) Janes. *Education:* Reed College, B.A., 1969; Columbia University, M.F.A., 1974. *Home address:* P.O. Box 685, El Rito, N.M. 87530.

CAREER: Writer. Visiting professor at University of Cincinnati, 1977; artist in Carlsbad, N.M., 1977 and 1980-81. Gives readings at colleges and poetry festivals. Member of board of directors of Segue Foundation, 1977—; member of literature panel of New Mexico Art Commission, 1980-81. *Member:* Rio Grande Writers Association. *Awards, honors:* National Endowment for the Arts grant, 1976; book award from Before Columbus Foundation, 1980.

WRITINGS—Books of poems: *Fish Souls,* Greenwood Press, 1971; *Summits Move With the Tide,* Greenfield Review Press, 1974; *Random Possession,* I. Reed Books, 1979; *The Heat Bird,* Burning Deck, 1982.

Author of "One, Two Cups" (one-act play), first produced in New York, N.Y., at Basement Workshop, May, 1979.

Work represented in anthologies, including *Life and Literature,* Scott, Foresman; *A Geography of Poets,* Bantam; *Third Woman,* Houghton. Contributor to magazines, including *American Rag, East-West Journal, Partisan Review, Yardbird Reader,* and *River Styx.*

WORK IN PROGRESS: A videotape production of own play, "One, Two Cups."

SIDELIGHTS: Mei-mei Berssenbrugge wrote: "I live in rural northern New Mexico when I'm not teaching or traveling."

*   *   *

BERTRAM, Anthony   1897-1978

OBITUARY NOTICE: Born November 19, 1897, in London, England; died August 2, 1978, in England. Writer, editor, and art critic. Bertram was a lecturer on art at Oxford University between 1927 and 1968. He served as art critic to the *Spectator* and *Saturday Review* in the 1920's and as editor of *Design for Today.* His many writings include novels, biographies of Rubens and Michelangelo, and such critical works as *Contemporary Painting* and *A Century of British Painting.* Obituaries and other sources: *Who's Who,* 126th edition, St. Martin's, 1974; *Who Was Who Among English and European Authors,*

1931-1949, Gale, 1978; *AB Bookman's Weekly*, October 16, 1978.

* * *

BETANCOURT, Romulo   1908-1981

PERSONAL: Born February 22, 1908, in Guatire, Miranda, Venezuela; died September 28, 1981, of a stroke, in New York City; son of Luis (an accountant) and Virginia Betancourt; married Carmen Valverde (a teacher); children: Virginia. *Education:* Attended Central University of Venezuela, 1927-28. *Home:* Edif. 4, Calle Los Cedros, La Florida, Caracas, Venezuela.

CAREER: Organizer of Boys of '28 (liberal student movement), Caracas, Venezuela, 1928; leader of unsuccessful rebellion against Venezuelan dictator Juan Vicente Gomez, 1928, and participant in subsequent attempts to overthrow Gomez, 1929-36; founder and editor of *Orve* (newspaper), 1936; ordered to leave Venezuela by dictator Eleazar Lopez Contreras, 1937, but remained in hiding until captured and exiled, 1939; lived in exile in Chile and Argentina, 1939-41; returned to Venezuela and organized Accion Democratica (political party), 1941; founder of *El Pais* (newspaper), 1943; participant in successful coup to overthrow President Isaias Medina Angarita, 1945; provisional president of Venezuela, 1945-47; exiled by dictator Marcos Perez Jimenez, 1948; lived in exile in the United States, Cuba, Costa Rica, and Puerto Rico, 1948-58; president of Venezuela, 1959-64; writer, 1964-81. *Awards, honors:* Honorary doctorates from Harvard University, University of California, and Rutgers University; awarded decorations by Venezuela, Colombia, Peru, Ecuador, Cuba, Guatemala, Mexico, Panama, Chile, and Sweden.

WRITINGS—In English translation: *Venezuela: Politica y petroleo*, Fondo de Cultura Economica, 1956, translation by Everett Bauman published as *Venezuela: Oil and Politics*, foreword by Arthur M. Schlesinger, introduction by Franklin Tugwell, Houghton, 1979; *Venezuela: Duena de su petroleo*, Catala Centauro Editores, 1975, translation by Donald Peck published as *Venezuela's Oil*, Allen & Unwin, 1978.

In Spanish: *Problemas venezolanos*, Editorial Futuro, 1940; *Trayectoria democratica de una revolucion*, Imprenta Nacional, 1948; *Romulo Betancourt: Pensamiento y accion*, [Mexico], 1951; *Venezuela: Factoria petrolera*, [Mexico], 1954; *Romulo Betancourt: Posicion y doctrina*, Editorial Cordillera, 1958; *Por los caminos de sucre: En la entrana de Venezuela*, Imprenta Nacional, 1959; *Dos anos de gobierno democratico, 1959-1961*, Imprenta Nacional, 1961; *Hacia America Latina democratica e integrada*, prologue by Mariano Picon-Salas, Editorial Senderos, 1967; *El petroleo de Venezuela*, Fondo de Cultura Economica, 1976; (author of prologue) *J. M. Siso Martinez, Juan Oropesa, Mariano Picon Salas*, Fundacion Diego Cisneros, 1977; *America Latina: Democracia e integracion*, Seix Barral, 1978; *El dieciocho de octubre de 1945: Genesis y realizaciones de una revolucion democratica*, introduction by Simon Alberto Consalvi, prologue by Diogenes de La Rosa, Seix Barral, 1979. Also author of *Dos meses en las carceles de Gomez*, 1928, and *En las huellas de la pezuna*, 1929.

SIDELIGHTS: Betancourt's political activism began shortly after he entered law school at Central University of Venezuela in Caracas in 1927. In February, 1928, he organized a liberal student movement, the Boys of '28, and was jailed for several weeks for taking part in a demonstration against dictator Juan Vicente Gomez. Upon his release in April, 1928, Betancourt led an unsuccessful rebellion against Gomez and was forced to flee to Colombia.

While traveling throughout Latin America in search of refuge and aid for his efforts to overthrow Gomez, Betancourt was exposed to communist revolutionary philosophy, and in 1930 he joined the Communist party. Betancourt, however, soon became disenchanted with communism, and in his later years he told an American reporter that his association with the Communist party was "a youthful attack of small pox that left me immune to the disease."

Becoming a strong advocate of political democracy during his years in exile, Betancourt joined the anti-communist left when he returned to Venezuela in 1936, shortly after Gomez's death. He continued to press for political reform through *Orve*, a newspaper he founded and edited, but was soon ordered to leave the country by the new dictator, Eleazar Lopez Contreras. Betancourt remained in hiding in Venezuela until 1939, when he was captured and exiled. Permitted to return home shortly before the national elections of 1941, he organized the political party Accion Democratica, whose first presidential candidate was Romulo Gallegos, a well-known novelist and Betancourt's former high school teacher.

The Venezuelan Parliament awarded the 1941 election to General Isaias Medina Angarita, but in 1945 he was overthrown by a group of military officers headed by Betancourt. Serving as provisional president from 1945 to 1947, Betancourt instituted democratic reforms, including rent reductions and profit-sharing arrangements between businesses and employees. Betancourt, later to become one of the architects of the Organization of Petroleum Exporting Countries (OPEC), also implemented the fifty-fifty oil formula, which required oil companies to share half of their profits with the Venezuelan government. Keeping his promise to hold free elections by direct universal suffrage, Betancourt turned the reins of government over to the winner of the 1947 elections, Accion Democratica candidate Romulo Gallegos. Some conservative military groups, however, feared the rapid change promised by Accion Democratica and staged a bloodless coup in November, 1948. The new dictator, Marcos Perez Jimenez, forced Betancourt into an exile that lasted ten years.

After Jimenez was ousted by the military in 1958, Betancourt returned to Venezuela as the Accion Democratica candidate for president. He campaigned and was elected on a platform promising a coalition cabinet and a return to democratic reform. Under Betancourt's rule, labor unions were organized, land reform was instituted, industrialization and road-building were initiated, and Venezuela began its transformation into a wealthy, modernized nation. Despite political unrest and a 1960 bomb attempt on his life, Betancourt continued to enjoy popular support. Prohibited by Venezuelan law from seeking re-election for ten years, Betancourt was succeeded in office in 1964 by Accion Democratica candidate Dr. Raul Leoni. Betancourt traveled to Europe and Asia and lived in Bern, Switzerland, for a time before returning to Venezuela.

Most of Betancourt's early writing was done while he was living in exile. *Dos meses en las carceles de Gomez*, an account of the two months he spent in prison for opposing Gomez, and *En las huellas de la pezuna*, a study of Venezuelan politics, were written while Betancourt was exiled in Colombia. Betancourt's first examination of the economics and politics of oil in Venezuela was *Problemas venezolanos*, written while he was in Chile and Argentina during his second period of exile. When expelled again in 1948, he wrote his two major works on oil, politics, and economics, *Venezuela: Factoria petrolera* and *Venezuela: Politica y petroleo*.

Venezuela: Politica y petroleo is a political and economic history of Venezuela from the 1880's to the mid-1950's. Throughout the book Betancourt argued that a nation can achieve political independence only as a result of economic independence. "National sovereignty is a juridical concept, a legal abstraction," he wrote. "For it to become a reality, a country must be able to have a fair degree of control over its own economic destiny, but this cannot be true in a country where the big economic decisions are completely in the hands of a dozen or so North American and British oil company directors."

Washington Post Book World critic Lisa Peattie described *Venezuela: Oil and Politics* as "a vehicle for the political opinions of Romulo Betancourt." But many of his political theories have become realities: In Venezuela, the world's third leading producer of oil, Betancourt's opinions have been translated into the nationalization of that country's oil fields; on an international scale, his opinions were instrumental in the 1960 formation of the Organization of Petroleum Exporting Countries (OPEC). Indeed, Betancourt's firm belief in democracy resulted in a degree of stability in the Latin American country that enabled Venezuela to develop its natural wealth for the benefit of its people.

BIOGRAPHICAL/CRITICAL SOURCES: Robert Jackson Alexander, *Prophets of the Revolution: Profiles of Latin American Leaders,* Macmillan, 1962, *The Venezuelan Democratic Revolution: A Profile of the Regime of Romulo Betancourt,* Rutgers University Press, 1964; John D. Martz, *Accion Democratica: Evolution of a Modern Political Party in Venezuela,* Princeton University Press, 1966; *U. S. News & World Report,* December 19, 1958; *Times Literary Supplement,* August 6, 1976; *Hispanic American Historical Review,* February, 1977; *Washington Post Book World,* May 6, 1979; *Guardian Weekly,* June 10, 1979; *Booklist,* June 15, 1979; *Virginia Quarterly Review,* autumn, 1979; *Americas: A Quarterly Review of Inter-American History,* October, 1979; *Political Science Quarterly,* spring, 1980.

OBITUARIES: Newsweek, October 12, 1981; *Time,* October 12, 1981.*

—*Sketch by Michael LaBlanc*

*   *   *

BETTI, Ugo   1892-1953

BRIEF ENTRY: Born February 4, 1892, in Camerino, Italy; died June 9, 1953, in Rome, Italy. Italian attorney, poet, and playwright. Betti's international reputation rests on his plays, which were tragic, bizarre, and often violent expressions of the crisis of modern society. He saw man as the epitome of egotism in a wicked world, bereft of tolerance and sanity, stubbornly disregarding God's will. A lawyer and magistrate, Betti described the inadequacy of the court system and human justice in such plays as "Landslide at the North Station" (1932) and "The Fugitive" (1952). The solution he found for man's spiritual predicament involved society's responsibility for the problems of its members as well as compassion and Christian mercy. The alternative he presented was eternal isolation of the individual from his fellowman and from God. Betti's earliest writings were lyrical poems, many composed when he was a German prisoner of war during World War I. He also wrote interpretations of the law, short stories, newspaper articles, comic plays, and the essay "Religion and Theatre" (1957). Most of Betti's plays were produced during his lifetime, but major publication and wide translation came after his death. *Biographical/critical sources: Encyclopedia of World Literature in the Twentieth Century,* updated edition, Ungar, 1967; *Twentieth Century Writing: A Reader's Guide to Contemporary Literature,* Transatlantic, 1969.

BIALOSTOCKI, Jan   1921-

PERSONAL: Born August 14, 1921, in Saratov, Saratov Oblast, U.S.S.R.; son of Jan (a musician) and Valentina (Vereninov) Bialostocki; married Jolanta Maurin (an art historian), August 8, 1955; children: Martha. *Home:* Dluga 30/34, m. 7, Warsaw, Poland 00-238. *Office:* Muzuem Narodowe, al. Jerozolimskie, Warsaw, Poland 3,00-495.

CAREER: Muzeum Narodowe, Warsaw, Poland, curator of foreign art, 1955—; University of Warsaw, Warsaw, extraordinary professor, 1962-1972, professor of modern art history, 1972—. *Member:* Polish Academy of Sciences (chairman of committee for the history of art, 1972—), Royal Academy of Letters and Sciences (Netherlands), Flemish Academy of Sciences and Letters (Belgium), Bavarian Academy of Sciences (West Germany), San Fernando Academy of Fine Arts (Madrid, Spain), Academy of Sciences and Literature (Mainz, West Germany). *Awards, honors:* LL.D. from University of Groningen, 1969; Herder Prize, 1970; Polish State Prize (first class), 1978.

WRITINGS—In English translation: (editor) *Zbiory Muzeum Narodowego w Warszawie,* introduction by Stanislaw Lorentz, Muzeum Narodowe w Warszawa, 1962, translation by Maria Rogoyska published as *The National Museum in Warsaw: Handbook of the Collections,* Muzeum Narodowe w Warszawa, 1963; *The Art of the Renaissance in Eastern Europe: Hungary, Bohemia, and Poland,* Cornell University Press, 1976.

In Polish: *Krajobrazy flamandzkie epoki manieryzmu,* Muzeum Narodowe w Warszawa, 1951; (contributor) Janina Michalkowa, editor, *Galeria Malarstwa Obcego: Przewodnik,* Muzeum Narodowe w Warszawa, 1954; (with Michal Walicki) *Malarstwo europejskie w zbiorach polskich, 1300-1800* (title means "European Paintings in Polish Collections, 1300-1800"), Pantstwowy Instytut Wydawniczy, 1955; *Bruegel, pejzazsta,* Panstwowe Wydawnictwo Naukowe, 1956; *W pracowniach dawnych grafikow,* Arkady, 1957; *Hogarth,* Arkady, 1959; *Piec wiekov mysli o sztuce: Studia i rozprawy z dziejow teorii i historii sztuki,* Panstwowe Wydawnictwo Naukowe, 1959.

(Compiler) Andrzej Chudzikowski, editor, *Malarstwo europejskie: Katalog zbiorow,* Muzeum Narodowe w Warszawa, c. 1960; *Malarstwo Niderlandzkie w zbiorach Polskich, 1450-1550,* Muzeum Narodowe w Warszawa 1960; *Teoria i tworczosc: O tradycji i inwencji w teorii sztuki i ikonografii,* Wydawnictwo Poznanskie, 1961; *Sztuka cenniejsza niz zloto: Opowiesc o sztuce europejskiej naszej ery,* two volumes, Panstwowe Wydawnictwo Naukowe, 1963; *Sztuka czasow Michala Aniola,* Pabianickie Zaklady Graficzne, 1963; *Sztuka i mysl humanistyczna: Studia z dziejow sztuki i mysli o sztuce,* Panstwowy Instytut Wydawniczy, 1966.

Mysil o sztuce i sztuka XVII i XVIII wieku, Panstwowe Wydawnictwo Naukowe, 1970; *O sztuce dawnej Ameryki: Meksyk i Peru,* Wydawnictwa Artystyczne i Filmowe, 1972; (with others) *Narodziny krajobrazu; katalog wystawy ze zbiorow: Ermitazu, Drezdna, Pragi, Budapesztu oraz muzeow polskich,* Muzeum Norodowe w Warszawa, 1972; *Pojecia, problemy, metody, wspolczesnej nauki o sztuce: Qwadziescia szesc artykulow uczonych europejskich i amerykanskich,* Panstwowe Wydawnictwo Naukowe, 1976; *Refleksje i syntezy ze swiata sztuki,* Panstwowe Wydawnictwo Naukowe, 1978; *Mysliciele, kronikarze i artysci o sztuce: Od starozytnosci do 1500 r,* Panstwowe Wydawnictwo Naukowe, 1978; *Historia sztuki wsrod nauk humanistycznych,* Zaklad Narodowy im Ossolinskish, 1980.

Other writings: *Les Musees de Pologne, Gdansk, Krakow, Warszawa* (in French), Centre National de Recherches (Belgium), 1966; *Stil und Ikonographie: Studien zur Kunstwissenschaft* (in German), VEB Verlag der Kunst, 1966; (with Beitraegen von Fedja Anzelewsky) *Spaetmittelalter und beginnende Neuzeit* (in German), Propylaen Verlag, 1972; *Die Eigenart der Kunst Venedigs* (in German), [Mainz-Wiesbaden, West Germany], 1979.

Editor: *Poussin i teoria klasycyzmu*, Zaklad Narodowy im Ossolinskish, 1953; *Albrecht Duerer jako pisarz i teoretyk sztuki*, Zaklad Narodowy im Ossolinskich, 1956; *Rembrandt w oczach wspolczesnych*, Panstwowy Instytut Wydawniczy, 1957; *Dwuglos o Berninim: Baldinucci i Chantelou*, Zaklad Narodowy im Ossolinskich, 1962; *Sztuka i historia: Ksiega pamiatkowa ku czci profesora Michala Walickiego*, Artystyczne i Filmowe, 1966; *Sarmatia artistica*, Panstwowe Wydawnictwo Naukowe, 1968; *Granice sztuki: Z badan nad teoria i historia sztuki, kultura artystyczna oraz sztuka ludowa*, Panstwowe Wydawnictwo Naukowe, 1972; (with Irena Koloszynska) *Polska i Anglia: Stosunki kulturalno-artystyczne*, Muzeum Narodowe w Warszawa, 1974; *Interpretacja dziela sztuki: Studia i dyskusje*, Pantswowe Wydawnictwo Naukowe, 1976.

Contributor of numerous articles to scholarly journals.

WORK IN PROGRESS: L'Arte del quattrocento nel nord di Europa, for UTET (Italy).

SIDELIGHTS: In *The Art of the Renaissance in Eastern Europe: Hungary, Bohemia, and Poland*, Bialostocki discusses the diffusion of the Italian Renaissance artistic style into Eastern European countries where, he concludes, the style ultimately became more "original" and "pure" than it had been in Western Europe. A *Book Forum* reviewer praised the book's illustrations and bibliography and recommended the work as a useful addition to art history collections.

BIOGRAPHICAL/CRITICAL SOURCES: Book Forum, fall, 1976.

* * *

BICKERMAN, Elias J(oseph) 1897-1981

OBITUARY NOTICE—See index for *CA* sketch: Born July 1, 1897, in Russia (now U.S.S.R.); died in 1981 in Tel Aviv, Israel. Educator and author. A former professor of ancient history at Columbia University and an authority on Greek history, Bickerman wrote texts on the history of the Middle East. Because of the theological nature of his research, many of the professor's books are used as textbooks in seminaries. Bickerman received many awards, including the R. Kreglinger Triennal Award from the University of Brussels, two Guggenhiem fellowships, and an award from the Association des Etudes Grecques. In addition, the author earned a Bollingen Foundation fellowship in 1959. His writings include *The Maccabees: An Account of Their History, Der Gott der Makkabaer, From Ezra to the Last of the Maccabees, Greece, Four Strange Books of the Bible*, and *The Ancient History of Western Civilization*. Obituaries and other sources: *AB Bookman's Weekly*, September 14, 1981.

* * *

BICKMAN, Martin 1945-

PERSONAL: Born September 23, 1945, in Boston, Mass.; son of James (a manufacturer) and Sara (Kachinsky) Bickman; married Louise Danny (a psychologist), October 11, 1968; children: Sarah Rachel. *Education:* Amherst College, A.B.

(magna cum laude), 1967; Harvard University, M.A.T., 1969; University of Pennsylvania, M.A., 1973, Ph.D., 1974. *Politics:* "Radical left." *Religion:* "Humanist." *Home:* 709 18th St., Boulder, Colo. 80302. *Office:* Department of English, University of Colorado, Boulder, Colo. 80309.

CAREER: English teacher at public high school in Lexington, Mass., 1967-68; Synectics Educational Systems, Cambridge, Mass., researcher and curriculum developer, 1968-69; English teacher at residential high school for gifted economically disadvantaged students in Simpsonville, Ky., 1969-70; University of Colorado, Boulder, assistant professor, 1974-80, associate professor of English, 1980—. *Member:* Phi Beta Kappa, Phi Delta Kappa. *Awards, honors:* Theodore Christian Hoepfner Prize from *Southern Humanities Review*, 1974, for article, "Flawed Words and Stubborn Sounds: Another Look at Structure and Meaning in *Walden*".

WRITINGS: (Contributor) Luanne Frank, editor, *Literature and the Occult*, UTA Press, 1977; *The Unsounded Centre: Jungian Studies in American Romanticism*, University of North Carolina Press, 1980. Contributor of articles and reviews to academic journals, including *Science-Fiction Studies*. Member of editorial board of *English Language Notes*, 1975—, and *Dickinson Studies*, 1979—; editor of *Higginson Journal*, 1978; member of editorial staff of *Jungian Studies*, 1979—.

WORK IN PROGRESS: Approaches to Teaching Moby Dick, for Modern Language Association, research on the relation of psychological discovery to narrative form in nineteenth-century American fiction.

SIDELIGHTS: Bickman wrote: "*The Unsounded Centre* tries to bring Jungian psychology to bear on the literary texts of American Romanticism in a speculative, undogmatic way. It views Jungian thought as arising from the same intellectual and metaphorical systems that stand behind Romanticism, most importantly the paradigm of unity-division-reintegration as seen in much Romantic philosophy and poetry. Jung conceptualizes and interiorizes this pattern, which makes his work particularly illuminating for American Romanticism."

* * *

BIERCE, Ambrose (Gwinett) 1842-1914(?)

BRIEF ENTRY: Born June 24, 1842, in Chester, Ohio; died c. 1914. American journalist, poet, essayist, and short story writer. After serving as a lieutenant in the Union Army during the Civil War, Bierce went to San Francisco where he became a journalist and earned the reputation as "the wickedest man in San Francisco." Friends and enemies alike referred to him as "bitter Bierce" because of his witty, cynical, and sometimes scathing attacks on the events and personalities of the day. Among his favorite targets were millionaries, women, labor leaders, and dogs. Often compared to Poe, Bierce wrote macabre short stories peopled with misfits and grotesques. Emphasizing the role of blind fate in men's lives, many of his short stories have horrifying surprise endings. His influence is discernible in the writings of Ernest Hemingway, Nathanael West, and William Faulkner. In 1913 Bierce went to Mexico to be close to the action of the Mexican Civil War and was last heard from in 1914. Although he was presumed dead, his actual fate remains a mystery. Among his best-known works are *Tales of Soldiers and Civilians* (1891 [reissued in 1892 as *In the Midst of Life*]), *Black Beetles in Amber* (1892), *Can Such Things Be?* (1893), and *The Cynic's Word Book* (1906 [retitled *The Devil's Dictionary* in 1911]). *Biographical/critical sources: Webster's New World Companion to English and American Literature*, World Publishing, 1973; *Twentieth-Century Literary Criticism*, Volume 1, Gale, 1978.

BILL-BELOTSERKOVSKY, Vladimir Naumovich 1884-1970

OBITUARY NOTICE: Born in 1884; died in March, 1970, in Moscow, U.S.S.R. Playwright best known for his popular, propagandistic plays in the Soviet Union, including "Shtorm," "Shtil," and "Luna sleva." "Shtorm" was the first Bolshevik Party play and served as a model for other socialist playwrights. Obituaries and other sources: *The Oxford Companion to the Theatre,* 3rd edition, Oxford University Press, 1967; *The Penguin Companion to European Literature,* McGraw, 1969; *AB Bookman's Weekly,* April 6, 1970; *Modern World Drama: An Encyclopedia,* Dutton, 1972; *Cassell's Encyclopaedia of World Literature,* revised edition, Morrow, 1973.

* * *

BILLINGS, John Shaw 1898-1975

OBITUARY NOTICE: Born May 11, 1898, in Beech Island, S.C.; died of kidney failure and pneumonia in 1975 in Augusta, Ga.; buried in Hammond Cemetery, Beech Island, S.C. Journalist and editor. Following service as an ammunitions truck driver in World War I, Billings began his journalism career as a reporter with the Bridgeport, Conn., *Telegram* and then as a Washington correspondent for the *Brooklyn Eagle.* In 1928 he joined the staff of *Time* magazine as the periodical's capital stringer. He subsequently became national affairs editor and in 1933 managing editor. Seventeen days before the first issue of *Life* was scheduled to go to press in 1936, Billings, at the request of Henry R. Luce, took over management of the magazine. Under Billings's leadership, *Life* not only made it to the newsstands on time, but it also became what was then the most successful magazine in publishing history. A pioneer in the genre of photojournalism, Billings raised the circulation of *Life* to over four million before leaving the magazine in 1944 to become editorial director of Time, Inc., publications. He retired in 1955 due to illness. Obituaries and other sources: *Time,* September 8, 1975; *Who Was Who in America, With World Notables,* Volume VI: *1974-76,* Marquis, 1976.

* * *

BINGHAM, Jane Marie 1941-

PERSONAL: Born September 21, 1941, in Huntington, W.Va.; daughter of Ferrell Jeff and Nora Lucille (Stephenson) Bingham. *Education:* Flint Junior College, A.A., 1961; Central Michigan University, B.A., 1964; Michigan State University, M.A., 1966, Ph.D., 1970. *Residence:* Rochester, Mich. *Office:* Department of Education, Oakland University, O'Dowd Hall, Rochester, Mich. 48063.

CAREER: Elementary school teacher at public schools in Flint, Mich., 1961-65; Michigan State University, East Lansing, assistant instructor in education, 1965-66; Flint Junior College, Flint, Mich., instructor in children's literature, summer, 1967; Oakland University, Rochester, Mich., instructor, 1969-70, assistant professor, 1970-75, associate professor of children's literature, 1975—. Member of Friends of Flint Public Library, Detroit Public Library, Avon Township Library, Kerlan Collection at University of Minnesota, Osborne Collection at Toronto Public Library, DeGrummond Collection at University of Mississippi, and Detroit Institute of Art.

MEMBER: International Reading Association, International Research Society for Children's Literature, Association for Childhood Education International, National Council of Teachers of English (treasurer of Children's Literature Assembly, 1973-75; chairperson, 1976-78), American Library Association (member of Laura Ingalls Wilder and Caldecott Medal awards committees; chairperson of National Planning for Special Collections Committee), Children's Literature Association (board member, 1975-78; secretary, 1975-76).

WRITINGS: Fifteen Centuries of Children's Literature, Greenwood Press, 1980. Author of "Children's Literature: Views and Reviews," a quarterly column written with Grayce Scholt for *Michigan Reading Journal,* 1971-76. Contributor of articles and reviews to education, library, and women's studies journals. Editor of *Children's Literature in Review* and *The Three R's: Reading, Writing and Radio, a Magazine of the Arts for Children.*

WORK IN PROGRESS: "I am continuing research on the treatment of minorities in children's books and on the history of children's literature. I am also keeping various annotated bibliographies of books for children up to date as well as a "Handbook of Children's Literature," a mimeo which I use in my children's literature courses."

SIDELIGHTS: Jane Bingham wrote: "In 1981 I completed a trip which took me to American Samoa, New Zealand, Australia, Hong Kong, China, Thailand, Bangladesh, India, Kenya, South Africa, and Swaziland. I collected examples of children's books along the way and became acutely aware of the need for books and other teaching resources in many developing countries. I was especially impressed with the variety of India's and Bangladesh's children's books—in spite of the difficulties their creators often encounter in publishing and promoting them. I also found that becoming aware of and enjoying the literature from other countries enriched my appreciation of American children's books. I found myself asking over and over why we, with the plethora we have to choose from, too often opt for the mediocre rather than the 'rarest kind of best.' As educators, creators, and consumers, we all too often forget to think of children's books as real literature because we fail to apply critical literary standards. It is my hope that my teaching and writing will draw attention to the continuing need for quality books in our own country and will also encourage American students and teachers to adopt a wider, world view of children's literature."

* * *

bin ISHAK, Yusof
See ISHAK, Yusof bin

* * *

BINKLEY, William Campbell 1889-1970

OBITUARY NOTICE: Born April 30, 1889, in Newbern, Tenn.; died August 19, 1970, in New Orleans, La. Educator. Binkley was a professor of history at Vanderbilt University from 1930 to 1953. He then joined the faculty of Tulane University, where he taught for the next seventeen years. He was the author of *The Expansionist Movement in Texas,* and his most popular book was *The Texas Revolution.* Obituaries and other sources: *AB Bookman's Weekly,* September 21, 1970; *Who Was Who in America, With World Notables,* Volume V: *1969-1973,* Marquis, 1973.

* * *

BIOSSAT, Bruce 1910(?)-1974

OBITUARY NOTICE: Born c. 1910; died of a heart attack,

May 27, 1974, in Washington, D.C. Journalist. After posts with United Press International and the *Chicago Daily News,* Biossat became a political reporter and columnist for the Newspaper Enterprise Association. His columns and articles appeared in more than four hundred newspapers. Obituaries and other sources: *Time,* June 10, 1974; *Who Was Who in America, With World Notables,* Volume VI: *1974-1976,* Marquis, 1976.

* * *

BISHOP, Susan M.   1921(?)-1970

OBITUARY NOTICE: Born c. 1921; died May 17, 1970, in Evanston, Ill. Editor. After eleven years on the staff of the *Chicago Tribune Magazine of Books,* Bishop joined the *Chicago Sun-Times Book Week* as an editorial assistant in 1968. Obituaries and other sources: *Publishers Weekly,* June 22, 1970.

* * *

BJARME, Brynjolf
See IBSEN, Henrik (Johan)

* * *

BJOERNSON, Bjoernstjerne (Martinius)   1832-1910

BRIEF ENTRY: Born December 8, 1832, in Bjoergan, Norway; died April 26, 1910, in Paris, France. Norwegian playwright, novelist, and poet. Winner of the Nobel Prize for literature in 1903 and composer of Norway's national anthem, Bjoernson is best remembered in his native land for his peasant stories. Works like the novel *Sunny Hill* (1857) reflected his interest in the history and people of Norway. He wrote folktales, lyric poems, and songs, juxtaposing sagas of ancient heroic ancestors with stories of modern Norwegians and their struggles. Bjoernson also wrote many plays concerning social problems. His social plays preceded Ibsen's work on similar issues, and Bjoernson is ranked second only to Ibsen as a major Norwegian writer. His most controversial play may have been "The Gauntlet" (1883), in which he proposed that men and women be judged by identical standards of sexual conduct. To critics, however, the height of Bjoernson's career was achieved with the play "Beyond the Power" (1883). In this and later plays, he showed a shift from an interest in social problems to a concern for spiritual matters. In all his writing, Bjoernson combined realism and poetry to stimulate Norwegian national pride and break the hold of the Danish language and traditions then dominating Norwegian writing. He is remembered as a great patriot, a national poet, and an enemy of inequality and oppression. *Biographical/critical sources: Columbia Dictionary of Modern European Literature,* Columbia University Press, 1947; *McGraw-Hill Encyclopedia of World Drama,* McGraw, 1972.

* * *

BJORNSON, Bjornstjerne (Martinius)
See BJOERNSON, Bjoernstjerne (Martinius)

* * *

BLACK, Douglas M.   1896(?)-1977

OBITUARY NOTICE: Born c. 1896 in Brooklyn, N.Y.; died May 15, 1977, in New York, N.Y. Lawyer and publisher. Black, who had formed his own Wall Street law firm in 1935, was president and publisher of Doubleday & Co. from 1946 to 1963. Holding the view that publishing is "a commerce first and a 'noble calling' second," he led Doubleday through a period of great expansion. During his presidency, the company introduced its Anchor line of paperbacks, built two new printing plants, and expanded its book club and bookstore operations. Black served as publisher for presidents Eisenhower and Truman. A staunch defender of press freedom, Black published such controversial works as *Scottsboro Boy, The Year of the Oath,* and *Memoirs of Hecate County.* Obituaries and other sources: *Publishers Weekly,* May 30, 1977.

* * *

BLACK, Jonathan
See von BLOCK, Bela W(illiam)

* * *

BLAIR, Eric Hugh   1903-1950
(George Orwell)

BRIEF ENTRY: Born January 23, 1903, in Bengal, India; died of tuberculosis, January 21, 1950, in London, England. English essayist, novelist, critic, and journalist. Following his education in England, Orwell took a job in Burma with the Indian Imperial Police. But after five unhappy years, he returned to Europe and lived a life of destitution for several years. *Down and Out In Paris and London* (1933), Orwell's first published work, was based on his years of poverty, as were *A Clergyman's Daughter* (1935), *Keep the Aspidistra Flying* (1936), and *The Road to Wigan Pier* (1937). A staunch believer in human freedom and social justice and an ardent foe of communism, Orwell experienced his greatest success with *Animal Farm: A Fairy Story* (1945), a satiric novel protesting Stalinism and totalitarianism. He also blasted authoritarian theory in his futuristic *Nineteen Eighty-Four* (1949). Inspired by Yevgeny Zamiatin's *We, Nineteen Eighty-Four* offers a terrifying vision of an enslaved, dehumanized, totalitarian planet. *Biographical/critical sources: Twentieth Century Writing: A Reader's Guide to Contemporary Literature,* Transatlantic, 1969; *Webster's New World Companion to English and American Literature,* World Publishing, 1973; *Who's Who in Twentieth Century Literature,* Holt, 1976; *Twentieth-Century Literary Criticism,* Volume 2, Gale, 1979.

* * *

BLAIS, Madeleine   1947-

PERSONAL: Born August 25, 1947, in Chicopee, Mass.; daughter of Raymond Joseph (a doctor) and Maureen (a teacher; maiden name, Shea) Blais; married John Strong Miner Katzenbach (a writer), May 10, 1980. *Education:* College of New Rochelle, B.A., 1969; Columbia University, M.S., 1970. *Office: Tropic* Magazine, *Miami Herald,* 1 Herald Plaza, Miami, Fla. 33101.

CAREER: Worked as reporter for *Trenton Times,* Trenton, N.J., and *Boston Globe,* Boston, Mass.; free-lance writer for *Miami Herald,* Miami, Fla.; *Miami Herald,* feature writer for Sunday magazine, *Tropic,* 1979—. *Awards, honors:* Second place in Ernie Pyle feature competition; Pulitzer Prize in feature writing, 1980.

WRITINGS: They Say You Can't Have a Baby: The Dilemma of Infertility, Norton, 1979. Contributor of articles to newspapers and periodicals including *Chicago Tribune.*

SIDELIGHTS: In her book *They Say You Can't Have a Baby,* Madeleine Blais focuses primarily on the psychological aspects of infertility.

BIOGRAPHICAL/CRITICAL SOURCES: Chicago Tribune, May 27, 1979.

BLAKNEY, Raymond D. 1897(?)-1970

OBITUARY NOTICE: Born c. 1897; died October 24, 1970, in Claremont, Calif. Educator. Blakney was a president of Olivet College and a translator of ancient Chinese manuscripts. Obituaries and other sources: *New York Times,* October 27, 1970; *AB Bookman's Weekly,* January 4, 1971.

* * *

BLANCO, Luis Anado 1903(?)-1975

OBITUARY NOTICE: Born c. 1903; died March 9, 1975, in Rome, Italy. A writer and poet, Blanco was Cuba's ambassador to the Vatican. Obituaries and other sources: *AB Bookman's Weekly,* April 7, 1975.

* * *

BLANE, Gertrude
See BLUMENTHAL, Gertrude

* * *

BLAZER, J.S.
See SCOTT, Justin

* * *

BLEDSOE, William Ambrose 1906-1981

OBITUARY NOTICE: Born July 19, 1906, in Mattoon, Ill.; died July 30, 1981, in San Carlos, Calif. Economist, author, and bookseller. Bledsoe taught economics at the University of Illinois, Beloit College, and Drake University while also serving as a housing economist with the federal government. His writings on economics include *Classical and Neo-Classical Economic Doctrines and Modern Economic Thought.* Following his retirement in 1961, he became an antiquarian bookseller, specializing in scholarly works on political science, social history, and business and economics. He edited *Screen Guild* magazine for two years and contributed to *American Mercury* magazine. Obituaries and other sources: *Who's Who in the West,* 16th edition, Marquis, 1978; *AB Bookman's Weekly,* September 7, 1981.

* * *

BLISS, Corinne Demas 1947-

PERSONAL: Born May 14, 1947, in New York, N.Y.; daughter of Nicholas Constantine and Electra (Guizot) Demas; children: Austin Constantine. *Education:* Tufts University, A.B. (magna cum laude), 1968; Columbia University, M.A. (with highest honors), 1969, M.Phil., 1978, Ph.D., 1980. *Residence:* South Hadley, Mass. *Agent:* Harriet Wasserman, Russell & Volkening, Inc., 551 Fifth Ave., New York, N.Y. 10017. *Office:* Department of English, Mount Holyoke College, South Hadley, Mass. 01075.

CAREER: University of Pittsburgh, Pittsburgh Pa., instructor in English, 1970-78; Mount Holyoke College, South Hadley, Mass., assistant professor of English, 1978—. Lecturer at Chatham College, 1977-78; guest writer at Westfield State College, 1979; visiting writer at Goddard College, spring, 1981; gives readings at colleges. Founder and director of Valley Writers; editor for Author's Registry (literary agency), 1967 and 1968. *Member:* Modern Language Association, Society of

Children's Book Writers. *Awards, honors:* National Endowment for the Arts fellowship, 1978.

WRITINGS: (With son, Austin Bliss) *That Dog Melly!* (juvenile; with own photographs), Hastings House, 1981.

Work represented in anthologies, including *Secrets and Other Stories by Women,* 1979. Contributor of about twenty-five stories and poems to magazines, including *Images, Poetry, Fragments, Transatlantic Review,* and *Esquire.*

WORK IN PROGRESS: The Same River Twice, a novel; *Matthew's Meadow,* a children's book; *The Magic Whistle Tree,* a children's book; *Lifelines,* a collection of stories, publication by University of Missouri Press expected in 1983.

SIDELIGHTS: Corinne Bliss told *CA:* "I am most naturally a short story writer and only recently have turned to the novel. The subject of my doctoral dissertation was the short story— basically it was an inquiry into how writers make readers respond the way they want them to and a study of what makes certain short stories work.

"Certainly writing about literature and teaching it influences my own writing—just as being a writer influences my teaching of literature and writing. My children's books have been written for my own child and his friends, and the age level I write for changes as he does."

AVOCATIONAL INTERESTS: Travel in Greece, music, cross-country skiing.

* * *

BLOCK, Hal 1914(?)-1981

OBITUARY NOTICE: Born c. 1914; died June 16, 1981, in Chicago, Ill. Comedy writer. One of the original panelists on the television game show "What's My Line?," Block wrote comedy routines for such performers as Bob Hope, Milton Berle, and Jerry Lewis. Obituaries and other sources: *Washington Post,* June 19, 1981.

* * *

BLOK, Alexander (Alexandrovich) 1880-1921

BRIEF ENTRY: Born November 28, 1880, in St. Petersburg (now Leningrad), Russia (now U.S.S.R.); died of heart failure, August 7, 1921, in Petrograd (now Leningrad), U.S.S.R.; buried at Smolensk Cemetery in Leningrad. Russian poet and playwright. Blok has been called the greatest Russian lyrical poet of the twentieth century. His early work *Poems About a Beautiful Lady* (1905), in which he created a mystical abstraction of feminity, marked him as a spokesman of Russia's short-lived symbolist movement. Blok was originally enthusiastic about the 1905 revolution and wrote idealistically. He soon became disappointed with the failure of the revolution, however, and began to produce ironic, realist works such as *Unexpected Joy* (1907) and *Snow Mask* (1907). In his later poems Blok wrote mainly of his love for Russia. He embraced the ideals of the Bolsheviks and the 1917 revolution and expressed his messianic vision of Russia in *The Twelve* (1918), which some critics have called his masterpiece. Blok's last major work was *The Scythians* (1918), a challenge to the non-communist West and an unofficial offer of friendship from the Soviet Union. Blok later became destitute, and his health deteriorated rapidly. After his death he left behind voluminous diaries and correspondence, which preserved the pessimism, emotional fanaticism, and despair of his last years. *Biographical/critical sources: Twentieth Century Authors: A Biographical Dictionary of Modern Literature,* H. W. Wilson, 1942;

Franklin D. Reeve, *Aleksandr Blok: Between Image and Idea*, Columbia University Press, 1962; *McGraw-Hill Encyclopedia of World Drama*, McGraw, 1972.

*   *   *

BLOOM, Harry   1913(?)-1981

OBITUARY NOTICE: Born c. 1913 in South Africa; died July 28, 1981, in Canterbury, England. Writer and lawyer best known for his anti-apartheid novel, *Episode*. Following the book's publication, Bloom was arrested and detained by South African authorities for six weeks. *Episode* sold twenty thousand copies in South Africa and was published in seventeen other countries. The American edition was published under the title *Transvaal Episode*. Bloom also wrote the novel *Whittaker's Wife*. Obituaries and other sources: *Twentieth Century Writing: A Reader's Guide to Contemporary Literature*, Transatlantic, 1969; *Publishers Weekly*, September 11, 1981.

*   *   *

BLUE, Martha Ward   1942-

PERSONAL: Surname legally changed in 1973; born January 17, 1942, in Cincinnati, Ohio; daughter of Quentin Kelvin (in automobile business) and Martha (Manning) Craft; married Roy Burton Ward, September 11, 1965 (divorced September, 1975); children: Zoe K. Nara. *Education:* University of Arizona, B.A., 1964, LL.B., 1966. *Agent:* Katinka Matson, John Brockman Associates, Inc., 200 West 57th St., New York, N.Y. 10019. *Office:* Law Office of Ward & Blue, 323 North Leroux, Flagstaff, Ariz. 86001.

CAREER: Dinebeiina Nahiilna Be Agaditahe, Tuba City, Ariz., staff attorney for Navajo legal services program, 1967-70 and 1971-73; Micronesian Legal Services Corp., staff attorney in Saipan, Mariana Islands, and Ponape, Caroline Islands, 1970-71; Law Office of Ward & Blue, Flagstaff, Ariz., private practice of law, 1974—. Member of board of directors of Dinebiina Nahiilna Be Agaditahe, Native Americans for Community Action, and Coconino County Legal Aid (past president); member and chairman of Arizona State Bar Art Law Committee and Unauthorized Practice of Law Bar Section; consultant to Office of Navajo Economic Opportunity and Center on Social Welfare Law and Policy. *Member:* Authors Guild, Handweavers Guild of America, American Arbitration Association, Arizona Women Lawyers Association (member of executive board of directors), Arizona Authors Association, Soroptimist International of Flagstaff.

WRITINGS: (With Sally W. Barlow), *Your Right to Indian Welfare*, U.S. Civil Rights Commission, 1973; (with Barlow) *Handbook on BIA General Assistance for Attorneys and Advocates*, Native American Rights Fund, 1973; (with Marion Davidson) *Making It Legal: A Law Primer for the Craftmaker, Visual Artist, and Writer*, McGraw, 1979. Contributor to law journals.

WORK IN PROGRESS: Tamarisk Springs Trading Post, a novel about a female trader on a Navajo reservation at the turn of the century, publication expected in 1983.

SIDELIGHTS: Blue told *CA:* "My interest in history, archaeology, as well as my attraction to different cultures, has resulted in my legal work centering on or near Indian reservations for the past decade since I left Micronesia. A theory I have developed from my reading, personal experiences, and observations is that the Anglo pioneer women generally strove to reconstruct life as they knew it prior to coming westward. But other women recognized the validity of the local native cultures and incorporated them in their life-styles. These were women of a different mettle: adventurous, curious, and less culture-bound.

"My fascination with Indian trading posts led to research in this area and the conclusion that the traders were the unheralded scouts, frontier persons, whatever you want to call them, on the Indian reservations. Traders were the catalyst to a modern day part-barter, part-cash system. They were the economic facilitators for native Americans in replacing their handmade material goods with manufactured American ones. They were also usually the only alien presence that was *not* concerned with changing religious beliefs, etc.—thus my idea of combining the story of the traders and a turn-of-the-century woman. Native American women, as women elsewhere, form a base, a foundation, a solidarity for the individual and family background. Thus my Anglo character, a woman trader, would have acceptance because of the native American woman's role in her society. As a lawyer starting out over fourteen years ago, I found this natural acceptance refreshing."

*   *   *

BLUMENTHAL, Gertrude   1907-1971
(Gertrude Blane)

OBITUARY NOTICE: Born in 1907; died of a heart attack, December 27, 1971. Publisher and editor. Blumenthal was the publisher and editor in chief of Julian Messner and a vice-president of Simon & Schuster. At Messner she edited the "Messner Biographies for Young People" series and launched two others, "Milestones in History" and "Messner Career Books." Her own writings include, under the pen name Gertrude Blane, *Flower Box Surprise*. Obituaries and other sources: *Foremost Women in Communications*, Bowker, 1970; *New York Times*, December 31, 1971; *Publishers Weekly*, January 10, 1972.

*   *   *

BOGIN, George   1920-

PERSONAL: Born April 28, 1920, in New York, N.Y.; son of Maurice (a retailer) and Sophie (Katz) Bogin; married Ruth Fleischer (a historian), November 6, 1948; children: Meg, Nina. *Education:* Columbia University, B.S., 1939. *Home:* 3 Brook Lane, Great Neck, N.Y. 11023.

CAREER: H. Bogin & Son, Inc. (furniture retailer), Astoria, N.Y., president, 1940-77; writer, 1977—. *Military service:* U.S. Army, 1942-45; served in Europe; received two Bronze Stars. *Member:* Poetry Society of America, Poets and Writers.

WRITINGS: In a Surf of Strangers (poems), University Presses of Florida, 1981. Contributor to magazines, including *Paris Review, American Poetry Review, Chicago Review, Nation, Massachusetts Review*, and *Beloit Poetry Journal*.

WORK IN PROGRESS: A book of poems; editing and translating a collection of poetry by Jules Supervielle.

SIDELIGHTS: Bogin wrote: "I am committed to writing poetry which is accessible (or seemingly so) but which opens up when penetrated to illuminations not immediately guessed. The image, the sound, the illumination are everything to me. My major interests beyond literature are film and languages."

*   *   *

BOND, Raymond T.   1893(?)-1981

OBITUARY NOTICE: Born c. 1893 in Brooklyn, N.Y.; died

July 16, 1981, in Jamaica, N.Y. Bookseller, publisher, and author. Bond was a bookseller in New York and St. Louis before joining the sales division of Dodd, Mead & Co. in 1920. In 1925 he was named head of advertising, publicity, and promotion. He served as the company's president from 1957 to 1964, working with such authors as Roger Tory Peterson, Rutherford Platt, and Allen and Helen Cruickshank. Bond was the author of two books, *A Handbook for Poisoners* and *Codes and Ciphers*. Obituaries and other sources: *New York Times*, July 19, 1981; *Publishers Weekly*, August 7, 1981.

* * *

BOND, Simon 1947-

PERSONAL: Born August 19, 1947, in New York, N.Y.; son of Terence Roy (a civil servant) and Hilda (a civil servant; maiden name, Everett) Bond. *Education:* Attended West Sussex College of Design, 1965-68. *Home address:* c/o 12 Brick Kiln Lane, Shepshed, Leicestershire LE12 9EL, England.

CAREER: Illustrated County Magazine Group, Nottingham, England, assistant art editor, 1968-69; free-lance cartoonist, 1970—. In sale of fine jewelry, 1969-74, 1977.

WRITINGS: One Hundred One Uses for a Dead Cat (cartoons), Clarkson N. Potter, 1981; *Unspeakable Acts* (cartoons), Clarkson N. Potter, 1981. Also author of film script "Shorts." Contributor of cartoons to magazines, including *New Yorker, Esquire, Saturday Evening Post, Lampoon, Punch*, and *Men Only*.

WORK IN PROGRESS: Cartoon projects.

SIDELIGHTS: Bond commented: "Cartooning is primarily intended to make you laugh. Humor is difficult enough, so it is a high goal; however, it should never be taken too seriously or it stops being fun. Though at present I'm known as a cartoonist, I really see myself as a humorist, as drawing is only one area of delivery. In time I hope to do more in film and television. I believe if you have a sense of humor all areas are open.

"I started cartooning seriously in 1970 and spent the next ten years scribbling away and developing a style. The ideas have held up well over that period of time, while the drawings have improved. But like many cartoonists I'm not too keen on my own drawings. We'd all like to be someone else.

"The initial success of my first book has given my career a huge boost, not only the cartooning, but also in the other areas I would like to move into—TV and film. Although I would be very careful and try to keep quality above quantity (since over exposure kills 'comedic' talent with ease), I would be interested in all options. It is up to me to be judicious in choice. Other than that, my plans are hazy; though the overall aim is obviously to try to consolidate and to find nice, new, funny ideas. So I'll end this here, make a cup of tea, and have a think. Quiet please!"

* * *

BONHOMME, Denise 1926-

PERSONAL: Born January 20, 1926, in Paris, France; came to the United States in 1947, naturalized citizen, 1951; daughter of Rene Louis (a banker) and Jeanne Anna (Giroud) Bonhomme; children: Claire Helen Quebedeau-Schreiner, Norman Quebedeau. *Education:* Academie de Lille, Baccalaureat, 1943; attended Sorbonne, University of Paris, 1943-45; University of Oregon, M.A., 1969. *Home:* 1220 Tasman Dr., No. 420, Sunnyvale, Calif. 94086.

CAREER: French-English translator and interpreter for U.S. Forces in Europe, 1945-47; worked as administrative and legal secretary in Austin, Tex., 1947-64; Mount Angel College, Mount Angel, Ore., assistant professor of French, 1964-72; office worker in Monterey, Calif., and teacher in Seaside, Calif., and Monterey, 1972-77; Electric Power Research Institute, Palo Alto, Calif., program secretary, 1977-80; National Semiconductor, Santa Clara, Calif., secretary and word processor, 1981—. Volunteer speaker at Soledad State Prison, 1973-74.

WRITINGS: Le Collier symbolique d'Alfred de Vigny (title means "The Symbolic Necklace of Alfred de Vigny"), privately printed, 1968; *The Esoteric Substance of Voltairian Thought*, Philosophical Library, 1975.

WORK IN PROGRESS: Revision of *Le Collier symbolique d'Alfred de Vigny; Auschwitz, American Style*, "an autobiographically-inspired novel on bare survival in an anti-intellectual environment."

SIDELIGHTS: Denise Bonhomme wrote: "My chief raison d'etre is an attempt to expose the veiled message contained in the works of numerous great writers. The message in question is the same from antiquity to our days.

"The topic of my major work is Voltaire. But the book suggests that similar research can be done on the writings of many other thinkers. The literary 'smugglers' of the past hold a cyclic view of evolution, as do their contemporary brothers. Within that framework they foresaw an era (ours) in which mankind would have spectacular abilities to destroy itself if true wisdom and/or ethics did not prevail.

"My work is controversial. I do not expect it to be recognized during my lifetime. But it has brought ample rewards in the mere fact of its 'doing'; also in student contacts and resulting friendships that will not die. It is my contribution to the collective 'bottle to the sea' cast on the ocean of time by minds and spirits quite superior to my own. I hope their message may 'reach port' before it is too late."

BIOGRAPHICAL/CRITICAL SOURCES: Eclectic Theosophist, July 15, 1975.

* * *

BONI, Albert 1892-1981

OBITUARY NOTICE—See index for *CA* sketch: Born October 12, 1892, in New York, N.Y.; died July 31, 1981, in Ormond Beach, Fla. Publisher and editor. An innovative publisher, Boni revolutionized the industry in the areas of paperbacks, book clubs, and book reproduction techniques. With his brother Charles, Boni embarked on his first business venture, the Washington Square Book Shop, a meeting place for writers. In 1917 he formed a partnership with Horace Liveright which resulted in the publishing firm of Boni & Liveright. The publisher of the Modern Library of the World's Best Classics, the firm also published works by Thornton Wilder, Ford Maddox Ford, Theodore Dreiser, and Leon Trotsky. The partnership, however, was unhappy, so Boni sold his share to Liveright. Boni then returned to a partnership with his brother, this time in the publishing field. With Harry Scherman, the Bonis founded the Little Leather Library, thirty volumes of 3" x 4" imitation leather books that sold nearly one million copies in Woolworth stores in their first year. Eventually, the Little Leather Library became the Book-of-the-Month Club. In 1923, Albert and Charles Boni Publishers printed the works of authors such as Will Rogers, Jim Tully, Marc Van Doren, and Marcel Proust; the company also sponsored a one-dollar book club. Boni began the Paper Books Program in 1929, which allowed consumers to buy twelve soft-cover books per year for five dollars. Boni founded the Readex Microprint Corp., the first endeavor at micropublishing reference material. With Lawrence Land, the publisher founded the Washington Square players, a theatrical group later known as the Theatre Guild. He was the editor of several books, including *Modern Book of French Verse* and *A Guide to the Literature of Photography and Related Subjects.* Obituaries and other sources: *New York Times,* August 1, 1981; *Publishers Weekly,* August 14, 1981; *AB Bookman's Weekly,* September 14, 1981.

*   *   *

BONNER, Brian   1917-

PERSONAL: Surname is pronounced *Bow*-ner; born February 27, 1917, in Culdaff, Ireland; son of Patrick (a farmer) and Margaret (MacQuigg) Bonner. *Education:* Salesian College, Palleskenry, Ireland, Diploma in Scholastic Philosophy, 1937; House of Philosophy, Macclesfield, England, accountant, 1938. *Politics:* "Ireland free of British presence." *Religion:* Roman Catholic. *Home:* Dunaghrianain, Culdaff, Lifford, County Donegal, Ireland. *Office:* Smith Group Ltd., 28 Fitzwilliam Pl., Dublin 2, Ireland.

CAREER: Salesian College, Palleskenry, Ireland, accountant and office manager, 1938-47; Department of Posts and Telegraphs, Dublin, Ireland, member of clerical staff, 1947-57; Smith Group Ltd., Dublin, senior business executive, 1957—. *Member:* Royal Society of Antiquaries of Ireland, La Academia de San Romauldo de Ciencias Letras y Artes of San Fernando, County Donegal Historical Society.

WRITINGS: Our Inis Eoghain Heritage, Foilseachain Naisiunta Teo, 1972; *Where Aileach Guards,* Foilseachain Naisiunta Teo, 1974; *That Audacious Traitor,* Foilseachain Naisiunta Teo, 1975. Contributor to *Donegal Annual* and *Riocht na Midhe.*

WORK IN PROGRESS: Redford-Glebe: The History of an Ulster Townland; a study of the diocese of Derry; research on the origins of Irish surnames.

SIDELIGHTS: Bonner wrote: "Born in an area which has extant evidence of the peoples who lived there four thousand years ago stimulated my desire to find out about the history of the district and some information about the past generations. Years of research gathered a considerable store of data. My curiosity about the past was, at least in part, satisfied.

"Why not convey the story to others? The result was my three books now published, dealing with the history and culture of the peninsula of Inis Eoghain on the extreme northern tip of the island of Ireland. The publisher had no trouble in finding a ready market for the books.

"A matter of absorbing interest to me is the story of the Celtic peoples from the time of their entry on the European stage in the pre-Christian era up to the present. This led to a study of Scotland, Wales, Brittany, and those other areas where the Celts settled.

"The languages I studied were English, Irish, and Latin. Some attention was also given to Scottish Gaelic and Italian.

"I hold that each individual should get a full opportunity to develop in all spheres: artistically, culturally, economically, intellectually, politically, socially, and spiritually. The educational system should be so geared. The community made up of individuals so enriched would be a happy one. Economic success is over-emphasized in most societies.

"One of my dearest wishes is enshrined in the dictum often quoted among the Irish: '*Eire saor, Eire gan roinnt agus Eire Gaolach,*' or 'Ireland free, Ireland one, and Ireland Gaelic.'"

*   *   *

BONNIFIELD, Paul   1937-

PERSONAL: Born January 30, 1937, in Denver, Colo.; son of Charles Mathew (a line worker) and Lauramay (Snead) Bonnifield; married Ellen Heacock, July 11, 1970; children: Heather Marie, Juanita Theresa. *Education:* Attended Western State College of Colorado, 1956-57; Oklahoma Panhandle State College, B.S., 1967; New Mexico Highlands University, M.A., 1969; Oklahoma State University, Ph.D., 1974. *Religion:* Southern Baptist. *Home address:* P.O. Box 243, Yampa, Colo. 80483.

CAREER: High school teacher in Walsh, Colo., 1967-68; Colorado Mountain College, Leadville, assistant professor of history and political science and division chairman, 1969-71; Oklahoma State University, Stillwater, teaching assistant, 1972-74; Panhandle State University, Goodwell, Oklahoma, instructor in American history, 1975-77; Rio Grande Western Railroad, Phippsburg, Colo., brakeman and conductor, 1978—. *Military service:* U.S. Marine Corps, 1958-61.

WRITINGS: (Contributor) LeRoy H. Fisher, editor, *The Civil War Era in Indian Territory,* Lorrin L. Morrison, 1974; *Oklahoma Innovator: The Life of Virgil Browne,* University of Oklahoma Press, 1976; *The Dust Bowl: Men, Dirt, and Depression,* University of New Mexico Press, 1979. Contributor to history journals.

WORK IN PROGRESS: Coal: The Cream of Northwestern Colorado.

SIDELIGHTS: Bonnifield told *CA:* "To write history is to become totally involved with the folks—their loves, their hates, their this, their that. The writer is an intricate part of the epic for his duty is to tell the story. Historians are obligated to be as truthful and honest as possible, but to do this they must master the art of feeling, tasting, seeing, and hearing as well as reasoning with their era.

"To find thrilling subjects does not require a large library, archive, or study grant. History is everywhere and valid topics are always present. It is only necessary for an historian to first search for and become a part of his subject, then record what the experience taught.

"The worst tragedy to afflict our twentieth century is the loss of emphasis on current local history. We can readily read about the pre-twentieth century New England, the South, the Midwest, and the West. But the most exciting century of change and complexity has little time for the local folks—the people—the people who make the century so well spiced and full of flavor and zest."

*   *   *

BOR, Norman   1893(?)-1973

OBITUARY NOTICE: Author of scientific works on botanical subjects. Obituaries and other sources: *AB Bookman's Weekly,* March 19, 1973.

*   *   *

BORCHERT, James   1941-

PERSONAL: Born January 13, 1941, in Cleveland, Ohio; son

of Frank Roy (a certified public accountant) and Miriam (a registered nurse; maiden name, Elson) Borchert; married Sally Rogers, August, 1964 (divorced May, 1974). *Education:* Miami University, Oxford, Ohio, B.A., 1963; Indiana University, M.S.Ed., 1965; University of Cincinnati, M.A., 1966; University of Maryland, Ph.D., 1976; postdoctoral study at University of California, Berkeley, 1978-79. *Politics:* Socialist. *Office:* Merrill College, University of California, Santa Cruz, Calif. 95064.

CAREER: Alabama A & M College, Normal, instructor in social science, 1966-67; University of Maryland, College Park, instructor in education, 1968; University of California, Santa Cruz, lecturer, 1973-74, acting assistant professor, 1974-76, assistant professor, 1976-80, associate professor of community studies and history, 1980—. Member of Housing Advisory Committee of Santa Cruz, 1977-78. *Member:* American Historical Association, American Studies Association, Immigration History Society, Organization of American Historians, Pioneer America Society, Slovak Studies Association, Society for the Anthropology of Visual Communication, Columbia Historical Society. *Awards, honors:* Fellow in American cultural history at Smithsonian Institution, 1974-75; Ralph Henry Gabriel Prize from American Studies Association, 1977, for book manuscript, *American Mini-Ghettoes.*

WRITINGS: Alley Life in Washington: Family, Community, Religion, and Folklife in the City, 1850-1970, University of Illinois Press, 1980. Contributor to history and American studies journals.

WORK IN PROGRESS: An Immigrant Neighborhood in Modernizing America, 1890-1980, publication expected in 1990; research on historical photo-analysis.

SIDELIGHTS: Borchert wrote: "I am interested in how people respond collectively to new environments—how they alter, change, adapt the environment and themselves to 'survive,' given the physical and social limitations they confront. My approach to this is interdisciplinary, drawing on as many sources and methods as possible and utilizing a historical perspective. I find the ethnographic approach most useful and agree that one should seek to view the world as much as possible through the eyes and minds of the people being studied.

"*Alley Life* grew out of an experience teaching in a predominantly black college in Huntsville, Alabama, my close contacts with the poverty program there, and my later residence in the New Deal planned community cooperative of Greenbelt, Maryland. It was written in response to such studies as Daniel P. Moynihan's Labor Department report on the black family, Frank Riesman's *Culturally Deprived Child,* Charles Silberman's *Crisis in Black and White,* and Stanley Elkins's *Slavery.* These studies' portrayal of deprivation, family breakdown, and social pathology in the black experience sharply conflicted with my own study, research, and experience."

* * *

BORCHERT, Wolfgang   1921-1947

BRIEF ENTRY: Born May 20, 1921, in Hamburg, Germany (now West Germany); died November 20, 1947, in Basel, Switzerland. German playwright. Borchert's literary reputation rests on one play, "The Man Outside" (1947), which premiered on stage the day after his death. Paralleling his own life in several ways, Borchert's play describes the efforts of a young infantry soldier to find his place in postwar Germany; it was his protest against the decadent and corrupt society he encountered in his own search. He also wrote some poems,

war sketches, and short stories, collected in *The Dandelion* (1947) and *On That Tuesday* (1947). Borchert's career was interrupted early in World War II when he was imprisoned and condemned to death by the Nazi government for criticizing Nazi leaders in his personal correspondence. His death sentence was commuted to military service on the eastern front, where he became seriously ill. Released from service, Borchert was almost immediately captured by enemy forces and spent several months in a Soviet prisoner of war camp in 1944 and 1945 before escaping on foot to Germany. The last two years of his life, during which he wrote constantly, were marred by illness and intense bitterness toward war and German society. *Biographical/critical sources: McGraw-Hill Encyclopedia of World Drama,* McGraw, 1972; *World Authors, 1950-1970,* H. W. Wilson, 1975.

* * *

BORENSTEIN, Emily   1923-

PERSONAL: Born May 6, 1923, in Elizabeth, N.J.; daughter of Louis (a business owner) and Jennie (a secretary; maiden name, Molowitz) Schwartz; married Morris Borenstein (a professor of music), June 27, 1942; children: Janet Borenstein Brickner, Sandra Borenstein Guskin, Marc. *Education:* Attended Juilliard School of Music, 1941-42; Orange County Community College, A.A.S., 1961; Columbia University, B.S., 1964; New York University, M.A., 1972. *Religion:* Jewish. *Home and office:* 189 Highland Ave., Middletown, N.Y. 10940.

CAREER: Middletown Psychiatric Center, Middletown, N.Y., supervisor of Hospital Volunteer Services, 1958-68; writer, 1972—. Gives poetry readings and workshops; poetry adviser to Orange County Council for the Arts, 1972-76. Piano instructor. *Member:* Poetry Society of America, Poets and Writers, Hadassah (president, 1978-81). *Awards, honors:* Poetry award from *Jewish Currents,* 1978, for "Holocaust."

WRITINGS: Woman Chopping (prose poems), Timberline Books, 1978; *Cancer Queen* (poems), Barlenmir, 1979; *Finding My Face* (prose poems), Thunder City, 1979; *Night of the Broken Glass: Holocaust Poems,* Timberline Books, 1981. Contributor of more than one hundred twenty-five poems to literary magazines. Music, drama, and dance reviewer for *Middletown TH-Record,* 1956-60.

WORK IN PROGRESS: Deep as Job's Faith, a volume of poetry; research on Holocaust literature and Judaica.

SIDELIGHTS: Emily Borenstein commented: "*Cancer Queen* was motivated by the terminal illness and death of my mother from cancer in 1975. *Night of the Broken Glass* is a book of Holocaust poems and poems about Israel and Jerusalem. The Holocaust theme and my Jewish heritage play a large and significant part in my writing. My latest work, like my recent trip to Israel in June, 1981, is a journey back in time and a journey into myself—a pilgrimage, a quest, and the culmination and fulfillment of the meaning and purpose of my book *Night of the Broken Glass.* I know that as a poet and in my soul of souls, 'wherever I go, I am going to Eretz Israel.'"

AVOCATIONAL INTERESTS: Reading, music, theatre, art, national politics, world affairs.

* * *

BORODIN, George
See MILKOMANE, George Alexis Milkomanovich

BOSSERT, Steven T(homas) 1948-

PERSONAL: Born July 22, 1948, in San Diego, Calif.; son of Thomas Richard (a contractor) and Evelyn (Harris) Bossert; married L. Gay Gelvin, October 20, 1978. *Education:* University of California, San Diego, B.A. (with high honors), 1970; University of Chicago, Ph.D., 1975. *Residence:* Concord, Calif. *Office:* Far West Laboratory for Educational Research and Development, 1855 Folsom St., San Francisco, Calif. 94103.

CAREER: University of Michigan, Ann Arbor, assistant professor of sociology, 1974-80; Far West Laboratory for Educational Research and Development, San Francisco, Calif., senior research director, 1980—. Visiting research associate at National Institute of Education, 1977. *Member:* American Sociological Association, American Educational Research Association, Sociology of Education Association (member of board of directors, 1980-82).

WRITINGS: Tasks and Social Relationships in Classrooms: A Study of Instructional Organization and Its Consequences (monograph), Cambridge University Press, 1979; (contributor) John Levine and Margaret Wang, editors, *Teacher and Student Perceptions: Implications for Learning,* Erlbaum, 1982. Contributor to *Handbook of Contemporary Urban Life.* Contributor to education journals.

WORK IN PROGRESS: Instructional Sociology, with James Block; research on the effects of classroom organization on student learning and on the instructional management role of the school principal.

* * *

BOTHAM, Noel 1940-

PERSONAL: Born January 23, 1940, in York, England; son of Frank and Amelia Botham; married Annette Martin (a language teacher), March 19, 1960; children: Tania, Katrina, Guy, Lucinda. *Education:* Attended private boys' school in Dulwich, England. *Religion:* Church of England. *Home:* 34 Park Hill, Carshalton, Surrey, England. *Office:* 72/78 Fleet St., London E.C.4, England.

CAREER: Surrey Mirror, Surrey, England, reporter, 1959-60; *The Star,* London, England, reporter, 1960-61; *Daily Herald,* London, reporter, 1961-62; *France Dimanche,* Paris, feature editor, 1963-65; *Daily Sketch,* London, chief reporter, chief foreign correspondent, and night news editor, 1965-71; *News of the World,* London, investigative reporter, 1972-75; chief of London bureau of *National Enquirer,* 1980—. *Member:* National Union of Journalists.

WRITINGS: (With Wilfred Lester) *Seven Sexual Ages of Woman,* Lymer Publications, 1973; (with Peter Donnelly) *Valentino, the Love God,* Ace Books, 1976; *The Runners* (novel), Everest Books, 1981.

Editor: D. J. Payne, *My Princess,* Fawcett, 1961; Marcel Baron, *A Life of Crime,* Dalmas, 1962; Angel De Velasco, *My Nazi Masters,* Dalmas, 1963; P. Rubirosa, *Rubirosa,* Dalmas, 1963; David Berglas, *David Berglas Biography,* Hopt, 1965; Juan Peron, *Peron,* Dalmas, 1966.

Creator (and co-producer) of "George Brown Asks," a series on Southern Television.

SIDELIGHTS: Botham commented: "Having been based in France and Spain, and having traveled throughout the world as a foreign and war correspondent for national newspapers, have provided the most significant influence on my writing and personal attitudes toward peoples and international politics. I could not conceive abandoning journalism totally.

"My only advice to would-be authors is never to read a single page of any book you write until you have completed the last page. Too many potentially good writers foundered when they read the first page of their work, and being dissatisfied rewrote it endlessly—never completing page two."

* * *

BOTSCH, Robert Emil 1947-

PERSONAL: Born February 22, 1947, in New York, N.Y.; son of Emil Joseph and Margaret (a teacher; maiden name, Matthews) Botsch; married Carol Sears (a college teacher), June 24, 1973; children: David William. *Education:* North Carolina State University, B.S., 1968; received M.A. from University of North Carolina, Ph.D., 1977. *Office:* Department of Political Science, University of South Carolina, 171 University Parkway, Aiken, S.C. 29801.

CAREER: Illinois State University, Normal, assistant professor of political science, 1977-78; University of South Carolina, Aiken, associate professor of political science, 1978—. *Military service:* U.S. Army; assigned to White House Communications Agency, 1968-71. *Member:* American Political Science Association, South Carolina Political Science Association, Sigma Xi.

WRITINGS: We Shall Not Overcome: Populism and Southern Blue-Workers, University of North Carolina Press, 1980; (contributor) Todd Baker, Lawrence Moreland, and Robert Steed, editors, *Studies in Contemporary Southern Political Attitudes and Behavior,* Praeger, 1981. Contributor to political science and social science journals.

WORK IN PROGRESS: A journal article comparing the structure and content of southern workers' political beliefs in the late 1970's with that which existed in the 1930's; collecting background information on "the political battle among interest groups over workman's compensation laws and workplace safety regulations pertaining to byssinosis," including oral histories.

* * *

BOTT, George 1920-

PERSONAL: Born September 21, 1920, in Ashbourne, England; son of George and Harriet (Leason) Bott; married Elizabeth Belshaw, February 5, 1944; children: George Michael Charles, Martin Geoffrey Leason. *Education:* University of Leeds, B.A. (honors), 1942, diploma in education, 1947. *Home:* 16 Penrith Rd., Keswick, Cumbria CA12 4HF, England.

CAREER: High school English teacher in Leeds, England, 1947-48; Cockermouth Grammar School, Cockermouth, England, senior English master and librarian, 1949-79; writer, 1979—. Book editor for Scholastic Publications in the late 1960's and early 1970's. *Military service:* British Army, Royal Corps of Signals, 1942-46; became captain. *Member:* Society for Teachers of English, Fell and Rock Climbing Club, Cumberland and Westmorland Antiquarian and Archaeological Society, Cumbrian Literary Group (president), Keswick Lecture Society (president), Keswick Mountaineering Club (president).

WRITINGS: (Editor) *George Orwell: Selected Readings,* Heinemann, 1958; (editor) *Read and Relate,* Esselte Stadium (Stockholm, Sweden), 1960; (editor) *Shakespeare: Man and Boy,* Faber, 1961; *Sponsored Talk,* Ferguson, 1971; *Read and Respond,* Cornelsen, 1981. Contributor to periodicals.

WORK IN PROGRESS: A History of Keswick.

SIDELIGHTS: Bott wrote: "My main interests now that I have retired are reviewing and local history, and anything connected with the Lake District."

* * *

BOTTRALL, Margaret Florence Saumarez 1909-

PERSONAL: Born June 27, 1909, in Sydney, Australia; daughter of Herbert Saumarez (a minister of the Church of England) and Muriel (Hanbury) Smith; married Ronald Bottrall (a poet), November 21, 1934 (divorced, 1954); children: Anthony. *Education:* Lady Margaret Hall, Oxford, B.A., 1930, M.A., 1935; attended Yale University, 1931-33. *Religion:* Anglican. *Home:* 72 Cavendish Ave., Cambridge, England.

CAREER: Writer. Cambridge University, Cambridge, England, lecturer in education and senior tutor at Hughes Hall, 1960-72, emeritus fellow of Hughes Hall and fellow of Lucy Cavendish College, chairman of board of trustees of Lucy Cavendish College, 1976-80. *Member:* University Women's Club.

WRITINGS: George Herbert, J. Murray, 1954; *Every Man a Phoenix* (stories in seventeenth-century autobiography), J. Murray, 1958; *Personal Records,* Hart-Davis, 1961; (editor) *William Blake: Songs of Innocence and Experience,* Macmillan, 1970; (editor) *Gerard Manley Hopkins: Poems,* Macmillan, 1975. Contributor of reviews to *Economist.*

WORK IN PROGRESS: A history of Hughes Hall, Cambridge, completion expected in 1985; continuing research on Gerard Manley Hopkins and George Herbert.

SIDELIGHTS: Margaret Bottrall wrote: "My professional life started late—after the dissolution of my marriage. Instead of extensive traveling, Cambridge became my center of activity, where summer teaching still keeps me reasonably busy. Herbert and other devotional writers of the seventeenth century remain my closest friends from the past, but Hopkins in many ways resembles the metaphysicals, and continues to exert a strong fascination."

* * *

BOUREGY, Thomas 1909(?)-1978

OBITUARY NOTICE: Born c. 1909 in Paterson, N.J.; died October 7, 1978, in Manhattan, N.Y. Publisher. Bouregy was the president and publisher of Thomas Bouregy & Co., Inc., and its affiliate, Airmont Publishing Co. Bouregy founded his company in 1949, acquiring Airmont Publishing in 1951. Together, the two companies published hardcovers and classics as well as a line of paperbacks. Obituaries and other sources: *Publishers Weekly,* November 13, 1978.

* * *

BOUSQUET, Marie-Louis Valentin 1887(?)-1975

OBITUARY NOTICE: Born c. 1887; died October 13, 1975, in Paris, France. Paris editor for *Harper's Bazaar.* Bousquet was at the center of the French literary world for more than fifty years. Among the authors she introduced to American readers were Colette, Jean Cocteau, and Marcel Proust. Obituaries and other sources: *AB Bookman's Weekly,* November 24, 1975; *World of Fashion: People, Places, Resources,* Bowker, 1976.

BOUTELL, Clarence Burley 1908-1981
   (Clip Boutell)

OBITUARY NOTICE: Born February 8, 1908, in Washington, D.C.; died July 29, 1981, in Norwalk, Conn. Columnist and writer. Boutell held management positions with several New York City publishers until 1943. That year he joined the *New York Post* as a columnist and began writing a literary gossip column, "Authors Are Like People," under the by-line Clip Boutell. Syndicated in numerous newspapers, the column featured interviews with authors, book reviews, and news about the publishing and literary world. He was the organizer and first chairman of the Council on Books in Wartime, which provided literary entertainment for servicemen, and an editor of the Fiction Book Club. In the 1950's, Boutell worked as copy chief at Denhard & Stewart and the *Christian Herald,* concluding his career at the Famous Writers School. He was co-editor of an anthology, *Speak of the Devil,* and author of *The Fat Baron.* Obituaries and other sources: *Current Biography,* Wilson, 1946; *American Authors and Books, 1640 to the Present Day,* 3rd revised edition, Crown, 1972; *Who's Who in America,* 40th edition, Marquis, 1978; *Publishers Weekly,* August 28, 1981; *AB Bookman's Weekly,* September 14, 1981.

* * *

BOUTELL, Clip
   See BOUTELL, Clarence Burley

* * *

BOVEN, William 1887(?)-1970

OBITUARY NOTICE: Born c. 1887; died in February, 1970, in Lausanne, Switzerland. Educator and psychiatrist. Boven was an assistant to Sigmund Freud and a professor of psychiatry at Lausanne University. His writings include *Adam and Eve and the Problem of Sex.* Obituaries and other sources: *AB Bookman's Weekly,* April 6, 1970.

* * *

BOWE, Frank 1947-

PERSONAL: Born March 29, 1947, in Danville, Pa.; son of Frank G. and Katherine (Windsor) Bowe; married Phyllis Schwartz, May 12, 1974; children: Doran, Whitney. *Education:* Western Maryland College, B.A., 1969; Gallaudet College, M.A., 1971; New York University, Ph.D., 1976. *Home:* 651 Peninsula, Woodmere, N.Y. 11598.

CAREER: New York University, New York, N.Y., research scientist, 1972-76; American Coalition of Citizens With Disabilities, Washington, D.C., chief executive officer, 1976-81; Frank Bowe Associates, Inc. (consulting firm on employment), Woodmere, N.Y., founder, 1981, president, 1981—. *Awards, honors:* LL.D. from Gallaudet College, 1981.

WRITINGS: Handicapping America, Harper, 1978; *Rehabilitating America,* Harper, 1980; *Comeback* (biography), Harper, 1981.

WORK IN PROGRESS: A suspense thriller with disability a key motif, for Harper.

SIDELIGHTS: Bowe's specialization is working with programs and policies for the aging, the handicapped, and veterans.

Bowe told *CA:* "My company advises major corporations on affirmative action programs for these populations. Left deaf at age three from measles, I know from personal experience the problems about which I write. During 1981 I served as U.S.

representative to the U.N. for the International Year of Disabled Persons, by appointment of the U.S. secretary of state. This experience led me to write *Comeback*. In regard to this book, I often assert: Coming to know how six severely disabled people led their lives is the best way I know for someone to understand disability—regardless of the reader's nationality.''

* * *

BOWER, Barbara
    See TODD, Barbara Euphan

* * *

BOWLES, Kerwin
    See ABELES, Elvin

* * *

BOYCOTT, Desmond (Lionel) Morse
    See MORSE-BOYCOTT, Desmond (Lionel)

* * *

BOYD, Nancy
    See MILLAY, Edna St. Vincent

* * *

BOYNTON, Peter S.   1920(?)-1971

OBITUARY NOTICE: Born c. 1920; died January 11, 1971, in Honolulu, Hawaii. Educator and author. Boynton was senior tutor and co-chairman of the College of Letters at Wesleyan University. He wrote two novels, *Games in the Darkening Air* and *The Eavesdropper.* Obituaries and other sources: *Publishers Weekly*, February 1, 1971.

* * *

BRABAZON, James
    See SETH-SMITH, Leslie James

* * *

BRADDON, George
    See MILKOMANE, George Alexis Milkomanovich

* * *

BRADFORD, Lois J(ean)   1936-

PERSONAL: Born May 29, 1936, in Griswold, Iowa; daughter of John W. (a farmer) and Marion (Snyder) Siefford; married Guy W. Bradford, Jr. (a consulting engineer), 1968; children: Robin, Dana. *Education:* Omaha School of Commerce, medical secretary, 1955; attended Colorado Women's College, 1969. *Home:* 29 Galston Dr., Robbinsville, N.J. 08691.

CAREER: Worked as secretary, 1956-68; writer. *Member:* International Women's Club, American Society of Engineers Auxiliary.

WRITINGS: Here Come the Racing Ducks (juvenile), Garrard, 1972. Contributor to *Omaha World Herald.*

WORK IN PROGRESS: A children's book about Alaskan Indians; a children's book about ''an Arab boy with goat troubles.''

SIDELIGHTS: Lois Bradford commented: ''My husband's business moves us about every twenty-four to thirty-six months.

We have lived in Alaska and Saudi Arabia, and traveled all the way around the world because of his job. I find interesting stories about children wherever we go.

''I am more of a crafts person than a writer. A story has to intrigue or amuse me a great deal before I leave my sewing or stained glass hobbies to spend the necessary time required to properly 'tell' the story. If I were more disciplined I would be more published!''

* * *

BRADLEY, David (Henry, Jr.)   1950-

PERSONAL: Born September 7, 1950, in Bedford, Pa.; son of David Henry (a minister and historian) and Harriette M. (a historian; maiden name, Jackson) Bradley. *Education:* University of Pennsylvania, B.A. (summa cum laude), 1972; attended Institute for United States Studies, London; King's College, London, M.A., 1974. *Home address:* P.O. Box 146, Bedford, Pa. 15522. *Agent:* Wendy Weil, Julian Bach Literary Agency, Inc., 747 Third Ave., New York, N.Y. 10017. *Office:* Department of English, Temple University, Philadelphia, Pa. 19122.

CAREER: Educational Testing Service, Princeton, N.J., research assistant with Office of Data Analysis and Research, 1971; J.B. Lippincott Co. (publisher), Philadelphia, Pa., assistant editor in Philadelphia and New York, N.Y., 1974-76; Temple University, Philadelphia, visiting instructor, 1976-77, assistant professor of English, 1977—. Guest lecturer at University of Warwick, University of Nottingham, and University of Edinburgh, 1972-73; visiting lecturer at University of Pennsylvania, 1975, and San Diego State University, 1980-81. Member of board of directors of Bradley, Burr & Sherman, 1977-79. *Member:* Associated Writing Programs.

WRITINGS: South Street (novel), Viking, 1975; *The Chaneysville Incident* (novel), Harper, 1981. Contributor of articles, stories, and reviews to magazines and newspapers, including *Signature, Savvy, Tracks, Quest,* and *New York Arts Journal.*

WORK IN PROGRESS: A novel, tentatively about the upheavals of the late 1960's and early 1970's.

SIDELIGHTS: The Chaneysville Incident is based on an event brought to light by Bradley's mother, Harriette. Mrs. Bradley, a local historian in Bedford, Pennsylvania, did research on local blacks for the area's 1970 bicentennial. She learned of thirteen runaway slaves who had been intercepted near Chaneysville, Pennsylvania, on their flight for freedom along the Underground Railroad in the mid-1800's. The slaves, who had told their captors that they would rather die than be sent back into slavery, were taken at their word and murdered. After Mrs. Bradley informed her son that she had discovered the slaves' burial site, he decided to write their story.

David Bradley tried several approaches to telling the story before deciding to write a historical novel. His first inclination had been to present a straightforward historical account of the facts, but he felt that the resulting manuscript was too dry. Attempts to write a traditional novel seemed, in Bradley's estimation, to deny the reader of important historical data. After eleven years of research and writing (during which time Bradley wrote and published another novel, *South Street*) he completed *The Chaneysville Incident.*

The book pleased reviewers, including *Publishers Weekly* critic Patricia Holt, who assesed *The Chaneysville Incident* as ''a complicated book, with long historical passages that are so readable they go down like cream.'' *Los Angeles Times* book editor Art Seidenbaum called *The Chaneysville Incident* "the most important piece of fiction I've read so far this year, perhaps the most significant work by a new male black author since James Baldwin."

Bradley commented: "I think of myself as an 'old-fashioned' writer, primarily because my fictional models are 'old-fashioned.' Like the Victorians, I am interested in the basics of plot and character, less concerned with abstract ideas. It is my belief that writers of novels should have no belief, that the idea of what is true is something that emerges from the writing, rather than being placed into it. Ultimately, I believe that if I cannot create a character who holds an idea, write a conversation (as opposed to a speech) that expresses it, or work out a plot that exemplifies it, there is something wrong either with my understanding of the idea or with the idea itself. In either case it has no place in my writing.

"I must frankly say that I do not love many 'contemporary' novels. For the most part they seem to me self-absorbed, self-indulgent, derivative, and basically lacking truth. Our technique has become an end rather than a means, primarily, I think, because we are writers have been led to believe that truth does not sell. If we would write well, we are told, we will be obscure. Obscurity, then, becomes the measure of writing well. I do not believe this. I have faith in the ability of people to respond to a story that treats them with kindness, honesty, dignity, and understanding. I put my faith not in publishers, and certainly not in reviewers and/or critics, but in those who read."

BIOGRAPHICAL/CRITICAL SOURCES: Los Angeles Times, April 8, 1981, April 24, 1981; *Publishers Weekly,* April 10, 1981; *New York Times,* April 19, 1981, May 12, 1981, *Saturday Review,* July, 1981.

* * *

BRANDT, Yanna Kroyt 1933-

PERSONAL: Born September 6, .1933, in Germany; daughter of Boris (a concert artist) and Sophie (Blumin) Kroyt; married Nathan H. Brandt, Jr. (a writer and editor), April 5, 1955; children: Anthony, Ariane. *Education:* Vassar College, A.B., 1953; Columbia University, M.S., 1954. *Religion:* Jewish. *Residence:* New York, N.Y. *Agent:* McIntosh & Otis, Inc., 475 Fifth Ave., New York, N.Y. 10017. *Office:* 17 West 60th St., New York, N.Y.

CAREER: WNET-TV, New York City, producer, director, and writer, 1961-64, 1970-72; National Broadcasting Co. (NBC-TV), New York City, associate producer and writer, 1963-70; currently president of Kroyt Brandt Productions and Anthar Productions, Inc., New York City. Founder of Neighborhood Improvement Committee; treasurer of 1349 Tenants Association, 1974-76. *Member:* Writers Guild of America, National Academy of Television Arts and Sciences. *Awards, honors:* George Polk Award, 1963, for television program "Cuban Missile Crisis"; Sylvania Award, 1964, for "Astronomy for You"; Ohio State Award from Ohio State University and American Film Festival Award, both 1976, both for television series "Vegetable Soup"; Writers Guild of America Award, 1976, for television drama "Superlative Horse"; Emmy Award from National Academy of Television Arts and Sciences, 1981, for "FYI"; Action for Children's Television Award, 1981, for "High Feather."

WRITINGS—Television scripts: "Sonny Brown and the Fallen Sparrows" (documentary), first broadcast by PBC-TV, April, 1973; "Superlative Horse" (drama), first broadcast by NBC-

TV, December, 1975; "Vegetable Soup" (series), first broadcast by NBC-TV, 1975; "The Nutcracker" (dramatic adaptation of ballet by Peter Tchaikovsky), first broadcast by CBS-TV, December, 1977.

Author of numerous other scripts for NBC-TV, CBS-TV, and NET-TV. Contributor of articles to magazines, including *Redbook, Reader's Digest,* and *New York Times Magazine.*

WORK IN PROGRESS: Screenplays and dramatic television series.

SIDELIGHTS: Yanna Kroyt Brandt told *CA:* "The special joy of writing for film or TV is, for me, collaboration. I don't like working alone. I enjoy the creative pleasure of sharing ideas, comments, and criticisms with others. I have rarely, if ever, been asked to do anything that violated my sense of taste. In that sense I've been very lucky. The kinds of programs I've worked on have allowed for a great deal of freedom."

* * *

BRANYAN, Robert L(ester) 1930-

PERSONAL: Born January 15, 1930, in Philadelphia, Pa.; son of Lester S. and Martha (Border) Branyan; married Helen Baird (a teacher), June 9, 1956; children: Jane Branyan Danner, George R. *Education:* Wisconsin State College, Platteville (now University of Wisconsin—Platteville), B.S., 1955; Iowa University, M.A., 1957; University of Oklahoma, Ph.D., 1961. *Politics:* Democrat. *Religion:* Episcopal. *Home:* 1320 Glen Ave., Mount Pleasant, Mich. 48858. *Office:* Department of History, Central Michigan University, Mount Pleasant, Mich. 48859.

CAREER: High school teacher of history in Iowa City, Iowa, 1955-56; University of Missouri, Kansas City, instructor, 1959-61, assistant professor, 1961-64, associate professor, 1964-67, professor of history, 1967-75; Central Michigan University, Mount Pleasant, professor of history, 1976—, dean of School of Graduate Studies, 1976-81. *Military service:* U.S. Army, 1951-53. *Member:* Phi Alpha Theta, Sigma Iota Epsilon. *Awards, honors:* Danforth associate, 1964—.

WRITINGS: (Editor with A. Theodore Brown) *The Paradox of Plenty: Readings on the Agricultural Surplus Since World War II,* William C. Brown, 1968; (editor with Lawrence Larsen) *Aspects of American History, 1776-1876,* Kendall/Hunt, 1970; (editor with Larsen) *Aspects of American History, 1877-1970,* Kendall/Hunt, 1970; (editor with Larsen) *Urban Crisis in Modern America,* Heath, 1971; (with Larsen) *The Eisenhower Administration, 1953-61: A Documentary History,* Random House, 1971; *Taming the Mighty Missouri: A History of the Kansas City Corps of Engineers, 1907-1971,* U.S. Army Corps of Engineers, 1974. Contributor to history journals.

WORK IN PROGRESS: Research on Eisenhower's trip to the Far East in 1960.

SIDELIGHTS: Branyan commented: "For the last five years my time has been taken up with academic administration and my research activities have been delayed. However, now that I am returning to full-time teaching I hope to get back to my work in progress." *Avocational interests:* Community theatre (acting and administration).

* * *

BRASCH, Charles Orwell 1909-1973

OBITUARY NOTICE: Born July 27, 1909, in Dunedin, New Zealand; died of Hodgkin's disease, May 19, 1973. Poet and

editor. Brasch was a major intellectual and cultural leader in
New Zealand, where he founded and edited the country's most
influential literary periodical, *Landfall.* The quarterly, published between 1947 and 1966, was praised for its scrupulous
and impartial editorial work, its high literary standards, and
its illustrated, analyzed, and indexed contents. Brasch expatriated himself from New Zealand for many years, but his
poetry was centered around the life of his native country. In
his early, lyrical poems, published in *The Land and the People*
and *Disputed Ground,* Brasch explored his ambivalent feelings
about the colonists who settled New Zealand while destroying
the country's native Maori culture. In later works, such as *The
Estate, Ambulando,* and *Not Far Off,* the poet was able to
resolve many of the contradictions that troubled the earlier
poems. *Home Ground,* published posthumously in 1974, contains the most hopeful and mature poems of Brasch's career,
including verses praised for their beauty of cadence. Obituaries
and other sources: *Twentieth Century Writing: A Reader's Guide
to Contemporary Literature,* Transatlantic, 1969; *The Author's
and Writer's Who's Who,* 6th edition, Burke's Peerage, 1971;
Cassell's Encyclopaedia of World Literature, revised edition,
Morrow, 1973; *AB Bookman's Weekly,* June 25, 1973; *World
Authors, 1970-75,* H. W. Wilson, 1980.

* * *

BRASSELLE, Keefe   1923(?)-1981

OBITUARY NOTICE: Born February 7, c.1923, in Elyria, Ohio;
died July 7, 1981, in Downey, Calif. Actor and television
producer. Brasselle was best known for his leading role in
"The Eddie Cantor Story." He was the author of *The Can-
nibals,* a novel about the television industry and behind-the-
scenes intrigue. Obituaries and other sources: *The ASCAP Biographical Dictionary of Composers, Authors, and Publishers,*
3rd edition, American Society of Composers, Authors, and
Publishers, 1966; *International Motion Picture Almanac,*
Quigley, 1979; *Time,* July 27, 1981; *Newsweek,* July 27, 1981.

* * *

BRECHT, Bertolt   1898-1956
(Eugen Berthold Friedrich Brecht)

BRIEF ENTRY: Born February 10, 1898, in Augsburg, Bavaria, Germany (now West Germany); died of a coronary
thrombosis, August 14, 1956, in East Berlin, Germany. German playwright, poet, theatrical producer, and theoretician.
Considered one of the greatest and most influential dramatists
of this century, Brecht originated the concept of "epic theatre." Believing that an audience's emotional involvement in a
play clouded its ability to grasp the play's message, Brecht
attempted to create distance between cast and audience. Using
dance, song, soliloquy, and choral reading, he shattered the
traditional stage illusions of reality in an effort to make the
audience "think rather than feel." Strongly fused with pacifist
and Marxist principles, Brecht's writings tried to show that the
evils of capitalism corrupt the rich and brutalize the poor and
that social forces determine man's nature. Brecht was an outspoken critic of nazism and went into self-imposed exile following the advent of Hitler in 1933. He lived in Denmark,
Finland, and then the United States until 1949 when he returned
to East Berlin. There, as founder and director of the famous
theatre company Berliner Ensemble, he dominated the European theatre until his death. Among his best-known works are
"Trommeln in der Nact" (1922; translated as *Drums in the
Night,* 1966), "Mann ist Mann" (1927; translated as *A Man's
a Man,* 1957), "Die Dreigroschenoper" (1929; translated as
The Threepenny Opera, 1949), "Mutter Courage und Ihre

Kinder: Eine Chronik aus dem Dreissigjaehrigen Krieg" (1949;
translated as *Mother Courage and Her Children,* 1949), and
"Leben des Galilei-II" (1957; translated as *Galileo,* 1952).
Residence: East Berlin, Germany. *Biographical/critical sources:*
*Twentieth Century Authors: A Biographical Dictionary of Mod-
ern Literature,* H. W. Wilson, 1942; *Reader's Encyclopedia
of World Drama,* Crowell, 1969; *Twentieth Century Writing:
A Reader's Guide to Contemporary Literature,* Transatlantic,
1969; *Modern World Drama: An Encyclopedia,* Dutton, 1972;
Twentieth-Century Literary Criticism, Volume 1, Gale, 1978.

* * *

BRECHT, Eugen Berthold Friedrich
See BRECHT, Bertolt

* * *

BRENT OF BIN BIN
See FRANKLIN, (Stella Maraia Sarah) Miles

* * *

BREUER, Marcel   1902-1981

OBITUARY NOTICE—See index for *CA* sketch: Born May 22,
1902, in Pecs, Hungary; died of heart disease, July 1, 1981,
in New York, N.Y. Designer, architect, and author. A Bauhaus
architect who espoused technology in sculpture, Breuer helped
to shape architecture and design in the twentieth century. Renowned for bringing European modernism to the United States,
Breuer began his career as a furniture designer in Germany.
He is responsible for many famous furniture designs, and his
chairs, such as the Wassily and the Cesca, are held to be
classics. In his creations and theory, Breuer emphasized architectural technology and construction, often using prefabricated elements in his buildings. Stylistically the architect was
fond of walls of stone or glass and of repeating a prefabricated
element on a facade. His best known designs of public buildings
include the Paris headquarters of UNESCO, the IBM Research
Center in France, St. John's Abbey in Minnesota, and the
headquarters of the Department of Housing and Urban Development. Around the beginning of the 1960's, a stylistic change
to heavy masonry illicited the architect's most famous work,
the Whitney Museum of Art in Manhattan. Breuer's dream to
construct a new, monumental edifice in New York, a sky-
scraper over the Grand Central Terminal, was foiled in 1978
when the United States Supreme Court ruled that the original
terminal building must be preserved as a landmark. Breuer
received gold medals from the American Institute of Architects
and from the Academie d'Architecture. His work was exhibited
at the Metropolitan Museum of Art. The architect's writings
include *Sun and Shadow* and *Adventure in Architecture.* Obituaries and other sources: *New York Times,* July 13, 1981; *Time,*
July 13, 1981; *Newsweek,* July 13, 1981.

* * *

BRIDGES, Robert (Seymour)   1844-1930

BRIEF ENTRY: Born October 23, 1844, in Walmer, Kent,
England; died April 21, 1930, in Chilswell, Oxford, England.
English physician and poet. Although trained as a medical
doctor, Bridges left his practice in 1882 to devote the remainder
of his life to the creation and study of poetry. Among his
valuable contributions to the literary world is *Poems of Gerard
Manley Hopkins* (1918), the posthumously published works of
Hopkins, with whom Bridges had maintained a friendship and
correspondence. Bridges's poems are concerned with beauty,

truth, and wisdom, which he felt could be gained only through a knowledge of God. His books of poetry include *The Growth of Love* (1876), *The Humours of the Court* (1893), *October and Other Poems, With Occasional Verses on the War* (1920), and *The Testament of Beauty* (1929). Concerned with preserving the purity of the English language, Bridges founded and managed the Society for Pure English. He was named poet laureate in 1913 and received the Order of Merit in 1929. *Residence:* Chilswell, Oxford, England. *Biographical/critical sources: Twentieth Century Authors: A Biographical Dictionary of Modern Literature,* H. W. Wilson, 1942; *Twentieth Century Writing: A Reader's Guide to Contemporary Literature,* Transatlantic, 1969; *Webster's New World Companion to English and American Literature,* World Publishing, 1973; *Twentieth-Century Literary Criticism,* Volume 1, Gale, 1978.

* * *

BRIDIE, James
     See MAVOR, Osborne Henry

* * *

BRIFFAULT, Herma   1898-1981

OBITUARY NOTICE: Born May 4, 1898, in Reedville, Ohio; died August 13, 1981, in New York, N.Y. Writer and translator. Briffault was best known for her English translations of modern French literature. She translated many works by the novelist Colette and won special critical praise for her renditions of *The Illusionist* and *House of Lies,* both by Francoise Mallet-Joris. As a ghostwriter Briffault wrote eighteen books under other people's names, including Marguerite Duras and Francois Mauriac. Obituaries and other sources: *Foremost Women in Communications,* Bowker, 1970; *Who's Who in America,* 40th edition, Marquis, 1978; *New York Times,* August 18, 1981.

* * *

BRIGGS, G. A.   1891(?)-1978

OBITUARY NOTICE: Born c. 1891; died January 11, 1978. Writer. Briggs wrote books for the layperson on high fidelity, acoustics, and musical instruments. He was the author of the first books on high fidelity speakers, beginning with a ninety-page paperback entitled *Loudspeakers: The How and Why of High Fidelity.* His other writings included *Musical Instruments and Audio* and *Audio Biographies.* Obituaries and other sources: *Publishers Weekly,* March 20, 1978.

* * *

BRIGNETTI, Raffaeilo   1922(?)-1978

OBITUARY NOTICE: Born c. 1922; died in February, 1978, in Rome, Italy. Writer. Brignetti was the author of novels about the sea, including *The Golden Beach* and *The Blue Seagull.* Obituaries and other sources: *AB Bookman's Weekly,* April 8, 1978.

* * *

BRINK, Andre (Philippus)   1935-

PERSONAL: Born May 29, 1935, in Vrede, South Africa; son of Daniel (a magistrate) and Aletta (a teacher; maiden name, Wolmarans) Brink; married Estelle Naude (divorced); married Salomi Louw (divorced); married Alta Miller (a potter), July 17, 1970; children: Anton, Gustav, Danie, Sonja. *Education:*

Potchefstroom University, M.A. (Afrikaans), 1958, M.A. (English), 1959; postgraduate study at Sorbonne, University of Paris, 1959-61; Rhodes University, D.Litt., 1975. *Home:* Portsbury Rd., Grahamstown, Cape Province 6140, South Africa. *Office:* Department of Afrikaans and Dutch Literature, Rhodes University, Grahamstown, Cape Province 6140, South Africa.

CAREER: Rhodes University, Grahamstown, South Africa, lecturer, 1961-73, senior lecturer, 1974-75, associate professor, 1976-79, professor of Afrikaans and Dutch literature, 1980—. *Member:* South African P.E.N., Afrikaans Writers' Guild (president, 1978—), Society of Netherlandic Literature. *Awards, honors:* Reina Prinsen Geerlings Prize, 1964; Central News Agency award for Afrikaans literature, 1965, for *Ole;* prize for prose translation from South African Academy, 1970, for *Alice Through the Looking Glass;* Central News Agency award for English literature, 1978, for *Rumours of Rain;* Martin Luther King Memorial Prize and Prix Medicis Etranger, both 1980, both for *A Dry White Season.*

WRITINGS—Novels, except as noted; in English: *Die Ambassadeur,* Human & Rousseau, 1963, translation by Brink published as *File on a Diplomat,* Longmans, Green, 1965; *A Portrait of Woman as a Young Girl,* Buren Publishers, 1973; *Kennis van die aand,* Buren Publishers, 1973, translation by Brink published as *Looking on Darkness,* W. H. Allen, 1974, Morrow, 1975; *'n Oomblik in die wind,* Taurus, 1975, translation published as *An Instant in the Wind,* W. H. Allen, 1976, Morrow, 1977; *Gerugte van reen,* Human & Rousseau, 1978, translation published as *Rumours of Rain,* Morrow, 1978; *'n Droe wit seisoen,* Taurus, 1979, translation published as *A Dry White Season,* W. H. Allen, 1979, Morrow, 1980; *Houd-den-Bek* (title means "Shut Your Trap"), translation published as *A Chain of Voices,* Morrow, 1982.

Other: *Lobola vir die lewe* (novel; title means "Dowry for Life"), Human & Rousseau, 1962; *Bagasie* (three one-act plays), Tafelberg Publishers, 1964; *Ole* (travelogue), Human & Rousseau, 1965; *Aspekte van die nuwe prosa* (criticism; title means "Aspects of the New Fiction"), Academica, 1967, revised edition, 1975; *Midi* (travelogue), Human & Rousseau, 1969; *Afrikaners is plesierig* (two one-act plays; title means "Afrikaners Make Merry"), Buren Publishers, 1973; *Elders mooiweer en warm* (three-act play; title means "Elsewhere Fine and Warm"; first produced in Bloemfontein at Little Theatre, April, 1970), Human & Rousseau, 1974; *Pavane* (three-act play; first produced in Cape Town at Hofmeyr Theatre, 1974), Human & Rousseau, 1974; *Aspekte van die nuwe drama* (criticism; title means "Aspects of the New Drama"), Academia, 1974.

Also translator into Afrikaans of works by other authors, including William Shakespeare, Henry James, Graham Greene, Lewis Carroll, Albert Camus, Marguerite Duras, Georges Simenon, Pavel Kohout, and Cervantes. Author of scenarios for South African films and television series, including "The Settlers." Contributor to periodicals, including *World Literature Today, Asahi Journal, Theatre Quarterly,* and *Standpunte.*

SIDELIGHTS: Brink told *CA:* "My postgraduate study in Paris brought me an explosive awareness of contemporary trends in European literature and resulted in the novel *Lobola vir die lewe,* which has since been termed a breakthrough in the modern Afrikaans novel. I later became involved in the 'Sestiger,' or 'Writers of the Sixties,' movement which brought about a total renewal in Afrikaans fiction by destroying all the existing taboos pertaining to sex, ethics, religion, and politics governing traditional Afrikaans fiction.

"In 1968 I left South Africa to settle in Paris with the exiled poet Breyten Breytenbach, but the nature of the student revolt of that year forced me to reassess my situation as a writer and prompted my return to South Africa in order to accept full responsibility for whatever I wrote, believing that, in a closed society, the writer has a specific social and moral role to fill. This resulted in a more committed form of writing exploring the South African political situation and notably my revulsion of apartheid. My first novel to emerge from this experience was *Kennis van die aand,* which became the first Afrikaans book to be banned by the South African censors. This encouraged me to turn seriously to writing in English in order not to be silenced in my own language. Under the title *Looking on Darkness,* it became international success, with translations into a dozen languages, including Finnish, Turkish, Japanese, Czechoslovakian, and Russian.

"Since that time I write regularly in both Afrikaans and English, usually preparing a first draft in Afrikaans, followed by a complete rewriting of the novel in English, and a final translation back into Afrikaans. I regard this laborious process as an essential part of exploring my material, using English as an aid to see more clearly and to evaluate more objectively. In my latest novel, *A Chain of Voices,* some of the 'voices' were originally written in Afrikaans and two separate versions were then prepared from this mixed text, in which the different languages prompted differences in point of view and style.

"However close my work is to the realities of South Africa today, the political situation remains a starting point only for my attempts to explore the more abiding themes of human loneliness and man's efforts to reach out and touch someone else. My stated conviction is that literature should never descend to the level of politics; it is rather a matter of elevating and refining politics so as to be worthy of literature.

"*Looking on Darkness* elicited much comment because it is one of the first Afrikaans novels openly to confront the apartheid system. This account of an illicit love between a 'Cape Coloured' man and a white woman evoked, on the one hand, one of the fiercest polemics in the history of that country's literature and contributed, on the other, to a groundswell of new awareness among white Afrikaners of the common humanity of all people regardless of color. In numerous letters from readers I was told that 'for the first time in my life I now realize that "they" feel and think and react just like "us."' In France, where publication of the book coincided with the Soweto riots of 1976, it became something of a handbook on the South African situation and sold over one hundred thousand copies. The same thing happened in other European countries.

"In *An Instant in the Wind* I used essentially the same relationship—a black man and a white woman—but placed it in the midst of the eighteenth century in an attempt to probe the origins of the racial tensions of today. An episode from Australian history in which a shipwrecked woman and a convict return to civilization on foot is here transposed to the Cape Colony with so much verisimilitude that many readers have tried to look up the documentation in the Cape Archives.

"*Rumours of Rain,* set on the eve of the Soweto riots, is placed on a much larger stage. The apartheid mind is demonstrated in the account given by a wealthy businessman of the one weekend in which his whole familiar world collapsed through the conviction of his best friend for terrorism, the revolt of his son, the loss of his mistress, and the sale of his family's farm. In spite of his efforts to rigorously separate all the elements of his life, he becomes the victim of his own paradoxes and faces an apocalypse.

"In comparison with the complex structures of this work, *A Dry White Season* has a deceptively simple plot: a black man dies while being detained by the security police. In all good faith his white friend tries to find out what really happened, and as a result the whole infernal machinery of the State is turned against him. An interesting aspect of this novel is that it was begun almost a year before the death in detention of black-consciousness leader Steve Biko in 1976. In fact, the death of Biko came as such a shock to me that for a long time I couldn't go back to writing. I believe that however outraged or disturbed one may be, a state of inner serenity must be obtained before anything meaningful can emerge in writing.

"In *A Chain of Voices* I have tried to extend and expand my field of vision. Using as a point of departure a slave revolt in the Cape colony in 1825, I used a series of thirty different narrators to explore the relationships created by a society shaped by the forces of oppression and suffering. The 'separateness' of the voices haunted me; masters and slaves, all tied by the same chains, are totally unable to communicate because their humanity and their individuality are denied by the system they live by. I tried to broaden and deepen the enquiry by relating the voices, in four successive sections, to the elements of earth, water, wind, and fire.

"Apart from writing, the theatre is my abiding passion, and since 1969 I have regularly directed plays for professional companies. This, in turn, has stimulated my playwriting, which I often explore as a medium of devastating social satire. In this vein my most notable successes have been a satirical adaptation of Shakespeare's *Comedy of Errors* and the irreverent *Afrikaners is plesierig.* In the latter, Afrikanerdom is represented as a circus tent about to be taken over by a communist proprietor but is instead blown down by the 'winds of change.'

"I have written several scenarios for South African-made films and three television series, all of them based on episodes in South African history.

"Since my tastes in literature are catholic, I have never been a disciple of any one school. The most abiding influence on my work, however, has been Camus, notably in his view of man in a state of incessant revolt against the conditions imposed upon him, and reacting creatively to the challenge of meaninglessness. In much of my work this is linked to an element of mysticism derived from the Spanish writers of the seventeenth century. The other most abiding influence on my writing is the study of history. All my work is pervaded with a sense of 'roots,' whether in the collective history of peoples or in the private history of an individual."

CA INTERVIEW

CA interviewed Andre Brink by telephone on September 18, 1980, at his home in Grahamstown, South Africa.

CA: Your latest novel, A Dry White Season, *was initially banned by the South African government censors. Why do you think the ban was later lifted?*

BRINK: That's a rather difficult question because it formed part of an entire new pattern that started emerging towards the end of last year, which also involved the latest book of the well-known author Nadine Gordimer. Her novel was called *Burger's Daughter.* These two bans were lifted within a couple of weeks of each other. A couple of months later another ban was lifted on a novel by a leading Afrikaans novelist, Etienne le Roux. This novel had been banned for several years, in fact, before the ban was later lifted. So one got the impression that after a sort of head-on collision was developing betweeen writers and the government, some liberalization in the censorship system became apparent towards the end of last year.

The trouble is that the books which were unbanned were books very obviously chosen from the works of authors with some sort of an international reputation, and they were all books by white authors. In spite of very heavy pressure from writers' organizations in the country to have certain bans on the books of black South African authors reviewed at the same time, nothing came of that. In other words, one got the impression that this was part of a rather elaborate window dressing to placate some of the most vociferous opponents among writers by letting through their books in the hope that they would tone down their criticism. But obviously, those of us who have had our works unbanned are more adamant than ever before to make sure that if there is liberalization in the new deal, then it must affect everybody, and it certainly must affect black authors as much as it does white authors. A couple of months later, as a result of the pressure—especially from the Afrikaans Writers' Guild—*Forced Landing,* an anthology of black writing edited by Mothobe Mutloatse, was sent on review to the appeal board. That appeal has not yet been heard, so we don't know yet whether it's going to be successful or not. [Note: Brink later commented: "Just after this interview, the ban on *Forced Landing* was, in effect, lifted, which must be seen as a breakthrough. However, one of the most significant works by a black author in recent years, *Call Me Not a Man* by Mtutuzeli Matshoba, remains banned—because the Directorate of Publications declined to take the matter on appeal as it does, as a matter of course, when the work of leading white authors is involved."]

CA: Why were the Afrikaans writers later in producing banned works than English and black writers?

BRINK: That may have been a development which one could approach from two sides. On the one hand, I suppose because Afrikaans writers belonged through their culture and their language to the same group who were and still are in power in the country, many of them felt a certain reluctance about an open confrontation. One should also be reminded that it is a very young literature—because Afrikaans as a language is only a hundred years old. In the nature of things, fiction tends to develop at a rather late stage. Although poetry blossomed in the 1930's, prose developments really came only in the course of the 1960's; before that it tended to be either folksy and humorous, or very heavy Calvinist stuff with a sort of drought-and-poor-white background—the sort of realism one had in the United States in the 1930s and early '40s. There wasn't a very real need to explore those areas which might come up for censorship.

On the other hand, I think from the authorities' side there was also a certain reluctance to clamp down on authors, because for a very long time the literary struggle went hand-in-hand with the political struggle in the country. It took the authorities quite a long time to acknowledge the fact that authors had now moved to the other side of the fence, as it were, and were no longer encouraging the national identity struggle but were beginning to explore more and more profoundly the problems and the agonies and the rebellions of the individual mind. Once a certain invisible line was crossed, once books of a certain nature became published in Afrikaans, and once the authorities got so far as to start banning one of them, then Afrikaans authors found themselves in a more vulnerable position than English authors in the country. My novel *Looking on Darkness* had the dubious distinction of becoming the first Afrikaans

book to be banned—and after seven years the ban is still in force. Nowadays Afrikaans works seem to be in the front line when it comes to bans.

CA: You write almost simultaneously in Afrikaans and English. What are the strengths and weaknesses of Afrikaans?

BRINK: Personally, from my experience in working in both languages, there is a certain virility, a certain earthy, youthful quality about Afrikaans because it is such a young language, and because, although derived from an old European language like Dutch, it has found completely new roots in Africa and become totally Africanized in the process. One writer said a couple of years ago that Afrikaans at this stage seems to resemble the English language in the time of Shakespeare. It is not very firmly and finally formalized yet. One can do almost anything with it. If you haven't got a word for something you want to express, you simply make a word or pluck a word from another language and shape it to fit into yours. Working in this young and virile and very vital language is quite exhilarating, which creates a very special sense of adventure for authors working in it.

And if one works in both languages, there is the wonderful experience of approaching the same subject, the same territory, through two totally different media. One is the more or less rigorous English language, the world language, and although one can still do a hell of a lot of new things in it, so much of it has already become standardized: it's almost as if one looks at the African experience through European eyes when one writes English. Through the Afrikaans language, it is a totally different, a more "immediate," experience. It's a language that can take much more emotionalism, for instance, whereas English tends towards the understatement. Afrikaans is more overt, more externalized, more extroverted in its approach.

I find, for instance, that when I'm working on a novel in which European and African characters appear, I very often tend to think in English terms when I deal with the European characters or the white characters, and to do the reverse when I deal with African characters.

CA: What is the quality and quantity of critical writing in South Africa now?

BRINK: It varies quite a lot in the different literatures. One should bear in mind that, fortunately or unfortunately—I'd rather tend to the latter view—we have at least three distinct literatures in the country. We've had them for a long time. They tend to be converging at the moment. The black African writing, which takes place generally in English (very little is done in the vernacular), English South African writing, and then Afrikaans writing. Up to now, there have really been three different schools, or certainly two different schools, of criticism approaching these different literatures. It's only in very recent times that there has been a development towards the exploration of the African themes, of the whole African experience, in literature, and that is bringing about a convergence in criticism, too. As for the nature and the quality of this criticism, I'm afraid there is very much of an inbreeding atmosphere about it. It can become very suffocating because the scene is so small, everybody tends to know everybody else, and everybody can so easily tread on everybody else's toes. All the writers and critics know each other, and criticism very often becomes simply a vehicle for airing personal vendettas. That has certainly become the case in Afrikaans criticism, which is a totally claustrophobic experience at the moment.

CA: As editor of the book page of the Afrikaaner weekly Rapport, *were you in a position to encourage better critical writing?*

BRINK: Well, I certainly tried my best just to keep things open and to expand the horizon, and in one's approach to indigenous works to try and bring in some sort of reference to what was going on in world criticism as such. I'm fascinated by the world of letters generally. A few of the younger critics fortunately seem to feel the same way about it. The problem seems to be that the majority of critics in Afrikaans are, I suppose for obvious reasons, attached to Afrikaans departments in Afrikaans universities, and so they tend to follow the government line, the apartheid policy, the whole ideology of the authorities in power. That is reflected in their criticism, so any work of a dissident nature is immediately slammed and torn to pieces. Any work encouraging the status quo is praised. I think the situation is very much the same as with state literature and state criticism one finds in Russia—not quite as far advanced, not quite as stifling yet, but there are dangerous trends in that direction.

CA: Isn't it difficult for a writer in South Africa to have some sense of his own place among the other writers in his country?

BRINK: I think that is certainly very possible. It's also quite easy to get a totally distorted view of it if one gets caught up in the local scene only, because it's so small, and it becomes very difficult not only to determine one's worth or one's place in the local scene, but to try and measure and weigh one's work against work that is being done elsewhere in the world. That is where I find it immensely useful and stimulating to write in English as well, and to get some sort of a measure there from criticism on the outside.

CA: Do South African writers find much support from writers, scholars, and institutions of learning abroad?

BRINK: Very little. I think some of the English writers do, certainly. The problem is that so much of black writing is a very recent phenomenon, and I don't think it has sufficiently filtered through to the consciousness of the world outside. Also, because so much of this is so immediately and urgently and directly involved with the black struggle in the country, many of these writers simply aren't concerned with the opinions of writers elsewhere and of critics and readers and students elsewhere. To them writing is an instrument of revolution in the liberation struggle.

On the other hand, about two years ago a new and very vital branch of P.E.N. International was established in Soweto, the black suburb of Johannesburg, and that is proving to be a real magnetic field of activity. Quite a number of writers from all population groups and from all over the country have now joined that group. [In August, 1981, Brink told *CA:* "A most disturbing recent development was the dissolution of the Soviet's P.E.N. center in January, 1981, as a result of pressure exerted on black writers by members of their community to find any association between black and white abhorrent. Politically and historically this is, of course, completely understandable, and in this respect I am in full sympathy with the black writers. But on the level of *writing* as such it is a sad event—and a devastating comment on the deterioration of relationships in South Africa. On the other hand it should be emphasized that personal and private contacts among black and white writers continue as before, and are even more intense than before."] I think it would be of enormous value if black writings of Africa could get more exposure abroad and more encouragement from abroad, because it is so enormously vulnerable to all sorts of prosecution in this country. Not only that, but it's so easy simply to pounce on a black author and silence him by intimidation or detention.

Afrikaans writers have very little exposure abroad because the language is so inaccessible. The only country where it is reasonably well understood—Holland—is so totally against anything white South African that there is almost a boycott of Afrikaans literature in that country, which in some respects is very sad because I think an interesting proportion of Afrikaans literature today is tending towards at least a mild form of dissidence.

CA: Would you comment on the racial situation in South Africa as compared to that in the United States?

BRINK: In some respects the parallels are very obvious and almost overwhelming, but because these things on the surface seem to be so similar, one very often tends to forget the roots may be totally different. First of all, the whole ratio between white and black is totally different, and the whole background of the blacks in the two societies is totally different in that American blacks derived mainly from slavery and have that background which forced them into a certain position of contestation in the twentieth century. In South Africa, there was a fair variety of independent and fiercely self-aware indigenous black tribes who fight and struggle from the awareness of that particular past. I must personally add that I think the impact of slavery on South African society has never been fully evaluated or fully explored yet. I certainly think it contributed an enormous amount to twentieth-century attitudes. In fact, I'm in the process of writing a novel going back to those roots—I suppose that's why I'm so conscious of it right now.

I think the most obvious difference, of course, is that although racism is rampant in both countries, and although, especially in some of the states of the United States, there are enormous new eruptions of racial strife from time to time, at least the basic trend of that society seems to be towards a recognition of human dignity irrespective of color. America seems to be slowly working its way through racism, which I personally regard as a sort of adolescent phase in the history of civilization and society; whereas in South Africa it is entrenched in the whole system and framework of laws on which society has had its base. It is not just a matter of sentiment, of personal resentment, of tradition and custom, but these negative aspects of society are so firmly rooted in the framework of laws that it is very, very difficult to eradicate.

CA: How much black literature is taught in the colleges and universities in South Africa?

BRINK: It is sad, I think, to admit that until pretty recently, almost nothing was done about that. In fact, my university, Rhodes University, was the first, as far as I know, to introduce a full-fledged university course in African writing in English, and less is done about black writing in French. There seems to be a spreading interest in a number of universities, but it remains a very recent phenomenon.

CA: Is there any attempt on the part of the government to control that teaching or is it left up to the universities?

BRINK: So far it has been left mainly up to the universities, but of course there is a very real problem that makes it unnecessary for the government to interfere directly: so much of significant black writing is banned in the country anyway that only a limited amount of it is accessible even to those students who specialize in African literature at a university. One of the saddest aspects of it is that South African black writing is probably one of the worst hit areas. This dates back to the late 1950's and early 1960's, when an entire generation of really important black writers were silenced with a single stroke of the pen. I think that more than forty of them were banned as persons because they had been listed as Communists, which means that nothing ever written by them, even the purest lyrical poem which has nothing to do with politics whatsoever, can be published or disseminated in South Africa. Those are writers like Mazisi Kunene or Dennis Brutus or Lewis Nkosi or Alex La Guma. It means that generation, which represented an incredible creative force and a peak in creative writing in South Africa at the time, was just obliterated. Black writing in the country after that had to start from scratch; because the new generation had no access to those writings, they didn't know what had gone before, had no tradition to rely on. It is only in the past five or six years that black writing is beginning to blossom again.

CA: Is the network of dissidents growing politically stronger?

BRINK: I think inevitably it is, yes. It's difficult to talk about a *network* because another appalling aspect of it is that so many of these people are still working in isolation, really. But I do think that organizations like P.E.N. are beginning to bring together these writers so that more and more of them discover—especially the young, beginning ones—that they are not completely alone, that there are others in different parts of the country who feel the same way, who write the same sort of stuff. I think in that sense certainly it is a growing movement and the influence coming from it is increasing, and these works are becoming more accessible—authors are finding more and more ways of distributing what they have written. That, of course, is the important thing—not only that we keep on working, but that the public gets in touch with our works.

CA: You studied in Paris and at one point considered living there permanently, didn't you?

BRINK: I was a student in Paris from 1959 to 1961. After that I went back for a few shorter spells, and then again at the end of 1967 I went back for a full year. That was when I really had the intention of settling there permanently. Of course 1968 was the year of the student revolt, with all the social issues involved and the stimulating introspection that was going on in Paris at the time about the whole relationship between the individual and his society—one's social responsibility. All of that helped to nudge me towards the acknowledgment of the rather simple fact that if I wanted to go on writing, and if writing meant something vital to me and wasn't just a matter of dabbling, I had to go back to the midst of my own society and assume my responsibilities in it. There are many writers who are not in this position, writers forcibly exiled or unable to return for a variety of other reasons, so it is a totally different matter in their case. But I think if a writer has the choice, he can only choose to come back and be here.

CA: How do you feel about being so frequently and favorably compared to Alan Paton?

BRINK: It's always difficult to stand in somebody's shadow or to feel oneself compared to someone else. I have a tremendously high regard for him, although I know there are many people today who regard him as a sort of passé liberal. The point is that his *Cry, the Beloved Country,* written in 1948, was the first book which interpreted the agony of being black in South Africa, not only to English-speaking South Africans themselves, but to the world at large, and I think Paton belonged to that particular age. The impact of that book has still not receded—I think it still sells tens of thousands of copies every year. Although in many respects I represent a younger,

totally different sort of generation and a different sort of response—a more radicalized sort of response—I personally feel deeply honored by that comparison. I have only the highest regard for that man and what he did in the context of his time.

CA: How did South African audiences react to the experimental work that you published there in the early 1960's?

BRINK: There was a rather ambiguous response. From the authorities there was a sort of paternalistic worry about it—this youngster's now come back from abroad with all sorts of pernicious new ideas like existentialism and God knows what else. They felt threatened by that, but there was still a sense of benevolence. They thought that by patting me on the back and saying that I should get rid of this sickness and come back to my roots and be a good boy again, they could make everything all right.

But there was a tremendous, immediate surge of positive response from the younger generation, the student generation. I think they simply were so fed up, so sick and tired of what was being dished up in Afrikaans fiction and drama at that time, that to get something new and relevant and cosmopolitan, something that put them in touch with what was happening in the world at large at the moment, was breaking through the terrible sense of isolation so many of these young people were experiencing. So there was this wonderfully positive reaction to what I and the whole small group of writers called the "Sestigers," or "Sixtyers," were doing. That has developed over the years, too. It's quite interesting that when earlier dissidents had been ostracized from the Afrikaans community—either symbolically or physically—they were just broken in spirit because that ostracism was total. But when the establishment tried to do that to us, they discovered that we had such a ground swell of sympathy within the white Afrikaans group from the younger generation that ostracism never really worked in our case. Although the establishment turned its back on us and tried to treat us like outcasts and act against us in all possible ways, we have retained these links with the generation which I think is the one that really matters—the younger one, the student population. That is something enormously important to a writer, to know that he's not working in a vacuum, and to have this give-and-take situation that provides feedback all the time. I think from that one can draw the resources one requires to go on.

CA: As a teacher, what kind of advice can you give to students who want to stay in South Africa and write?

BRINK: First of all, not to do what so many of them seem to be doing at the moment. I've been getting a steady stream of manuscripts over the last fifteen or more years, and initially the letters accompanying those manuscripts posed the obvious question, "Do you think this is good enough to be published?" In the last five years or so, the first question in the accompanying letter has invariably become, "Do you think this will get past the censors?" I think that if there's one bit of advice, it's almost a matter of pleading with them to get rid of this anxiety, this sort of cringing even before the ax has fallen. I think that one cannot possibly produce anything worthwhile if one writes with the possibility of a censor in mind. You've got to be absolutely true to your experience and sincere about it. If there's something valid in that, one will find a way to disseminate it and get it across. The main thing, first of all, is to be honest about one's own experience and get it down on paper. After that, one can devise means and schemes to communicate it to others, but first of all it's got to be written, and one can't write with one eye on the censor.

BIOGRAPHICAL/CRITICAL SOURCES: Newsweek, December 2, 1974; *World Literature Today,* autumn, 1977; *New Statesman,* November 17, 1978.

—*Interview by Jean W. Ross*

* * *

BRINK, Carol Ryrie   1895-1981

OBITUARY NOTICE—See index for *CA* sketch: Born December 28, 1895, in Moscow, Idaho; died August 15, 1981, in La Jolla, Calif. Lecturer and author. Predominantly the author of children's books, Brink received recognition for *Caddie Woodlawn.* The story of her grandmother's life on the Wisconsin frontier, the novel earned a Newbury Medal in 1936 as "the most distinguished contribution to American literature for children." Published in 1935, *Caddie Woodlawn* continued to be a best-seller even in the 1980's. *Magical Melons,* a sequel to the Caddie Woodlawn story, appeared in 1944. In 1966 *Snow in the River,* a novel for adults, received the McKnight Family Literature Fund Award, and Brink won prizes from the National League of American Pen Women for her poetry. The author wrote twenty-seven books, including *Anything Can Happen on the River, Two Are Better Than One, Winter Cottage, The Bad Times of Irma Baumlein,* and *Harps in the Wind.* Obituaries and other sources: *Chicago Tribune,* August 19, 1981; *New York Times,* September 1, 1981; *Publishers Weekly,* September 11, 1981; *AB Bookman's Weekly,* September 14, 1981; *School Library Journal,* October, 1981.

* * *

BRISK, Melvin J.   1924-1981

OBITUARY NOTICE: Born August 23, 1924, in Cleveland, Ohio; died of a heart attack, July 2, 1981, in Winnetka, Ill. Journalist, literary agent, and publisher. Brisk was a reporter in Cincinnatti, New York City, and Chicago before becoming president of Quadrangle Books in 1961. During his eleven years at Quadrangle the company published more than two hundred books, including works by historian Alan Nevins, poet Karl Shapiro, and sociologist Morris Janowitz. After the company was sold to the New York Times Co. in 1969, Brisk became the executive director of Crain Books. He later served as associate publisher and part-time consultant to the company. Obituaries and other sources: *New York Times,* July 4, 1981; *Publishers Weekly,* July 17, 1981.

* * *

BROCK, Ben
See HOWELLS, Roscoe

* * *

BRODY, Sylvia
See AXELRAD, Sylvia Brody

* * *

BROGAN, Gerald E(dward)   1924-1981

OBITUARY NOTICE—See index for *CA* sketch: Born August 15, 1924, in Bentonville, Ark.; died in 1981. Librarian and author. Brogan began his career as a reference librarian at the Denver Public Library in Colorado. As a librarian, he was associated with Long Beach City College, the community colleges of Hawaii, and Chico State College, now California State University in Chico. At the time of his death, Brogan was the head librarian at the College of the Redwoods in Eureka, California. He wrote *Using Libraries Effectively* with Jeanne Buck. Obituaries and other sources: *Library Journal,* July, 1981.

* * *

BROOKE, Rupert (Chawner)   1887-1915

BRIEF ENTRY: Born August 3, 1887, in Rugby, England; died of blood poisoning, April 23, 1915, on a French hospital ship in the Aegean Sea; buried on Skyros, Greece. English poet, critic, and playwright. Brooke was an extraordinarily handsome man who was celebrated as the embodiment of English youth, naivete, and idealism. His early poems, among them the oft-quoted "The Old Vicarage at Grantchester" (1912), reflected the pastoral, romantic innocence of the Georgian school of poets, but Brooke later came under the influence of the Decadents and the seventeenth-century metaphysical poets. In the first years of World War I, he was best known for his enormously popular war sonnets, found in *War Sonnets in New Numbers* (1914) and *1914* (1915), which contained a patriotic, sentimental view of battle and lost youth. Brooke's early death and burial on a Greek isle secured for him a legendary, romantic stature, but it also had the effect of limiting his literary reputation. After the war, critics and artists, disillusioned by the horror and destruction of the war, derided Brooke's work, seeing in it many of the false beliefs and values that had led the world to catastrophe. Some scholars, however, argue that had Brooke lived to confront the harsh realities of war his poetry might have taken a sharply modern turn. He had begun to experiment with poetic realism, common dictions, and loose verse forms, but he died before he could fully exploit these new possibilities. In the world of letters he remains a transitional figure, caught between the Victorian and modern ages. His other writings include *The Collected Poems of Rupert Brooke* (1915), *Lithuania: A Drama in One Act* (1915), and *John Webster and the Elizabethan Drama* (1916). *Biographical/critical sources: Encyclopedia of World Literature in the Twentieth Century,* updated edition, Ungar, 1967; *Twentieth Century Writing: A Reader's Guide to Contemporary Literature,* Transatlantic, 1969; *Twentieth-Century Literary Criticism,* Volume 2, Gale, 1979.

* * *

BROOKS, Philip   1899(?)-1975

OBITUARY NOTICE: Born c. 1899; died April 29, 1975, in Manhasset, N.Y. Writer and bookseller. A specialist in the location and acquisition of rare books, Brooks was associated for most of his career with the Brick Row Bookshop and the Argosy Book Shop in New York City. For many years he managed the Wall Street branch of Brick Row, after which time he worked independently, acquiring books for a limited list of clients. In 1927 he began writing a weekly column for the *New York Times Book Review,* called "Notes on Rare Books," and continued his association with the *Times* until 1969. Obituaries and other sources: *New York Times,* May 1, 1975; *AB Bookman's Weekly,* August 4, 1975.

* * *

BROWN, Christy   1932-1981

OBITUARY NOTICE: Born in 1932 in Dublin, Ireland; died of asphyxiation, September 6, 1981, in Parbrook, Somerset, England. Novelist and poet. Brown was born with crippling cerebral palsy, and his only usable limb was his left foot. With the help and support of his mother and Irish pediatrician Dr. Robert Collis, Brown was able to gain remarkable control over the appendage, allowing him to paint and type with his toes. His first book, published in 1954, was an autobiographical account entitled *My Left Foot*. He completed his second book sixteen years later, an enormous autobiographical novel called *Down All the Days*, which became a best-seller in sixteen countries. His other writings include *A Shadow of Summer*, *Wild Grow the Lillies*, *Of Snails and Skylarks*, and the typescript for a new novel, *A Promising Career*, delivered to his publishers shortly before his death. Obituaries and other sources: Christy Brown, *My Left Foot*, Secker & Warburg, 1954; *New York Times*, October 28, 1971; *Newsweek*, October 16, 1972, September 21, 1981; *The Writer's Directory, 1980-82*, St. Martin's, 1979; *London Times*, September 8, 1981; *Detroit News*, September 8, 1981; *Publishers Weekly*, September 18, 1981; *AB Bookman's Weekly*, October 19, 1981.

* * *

BROWN, Croswell 1905(?)-1971

OBITUARY NOTICE: Born c. 1905; died July 15, 1971, in New York, N.Y. Writer and editor. A staff writer and editor for the *New Yorker*, Brown was best known for his books on crime, among them *They Went Wrong*. Obituaries and other sources: *AB Bookman's Weekly*, August 16, 1971.

* * *

BROWN, Eleanor Gertrude 1887-1968

OBITUARY NOTICE: Born August 28, 1887, in Osborn, Ohio; died in 1968. High school teacher and writer. Brown taught in the Dayton Public School System for thirty-five years. She was the first blind person to teach sighted children in a public high school and the first blind woman to receive a Ph.D. from Columbia University. She wrote three books, *Milton's Blindness*, *Into the Light*, and *Corridors of Light*, her autobiography. Obituaries and other sources: Eleanor Gertrude Brown, *Corridors of Light*, Antioch Press, 1958. (Date of death provided by Dean E. Fitzwater.)

* * *

BROWN, John Gracen 1936-

PERSONAL: Born October 8, 1936, in Martinsburg, W.Va.; son of Arthur Yeakley (a secretary) and Virgil Marion (Waters) Brown. *Education:* Attended West Virginia University, 1955-59; Southern Illinois University, B.S. in Ed., 1961, M.S. in Ed., 1962. *Politics:* "Has varied." *Religion:* "Western Christianity." *Home and office:* 430 Virginia Ave., Martinsburg, W.Va. 25401.

CAREER: High school teacher in Phillips, Wis., 1962-63; high school guidance director at Milton-Milton Junction, Wis., 1963-64; National Park Service, Sharpsburg, Md., laborer, 1973-1977 carpenter and mason in Martinsburg, W.Va., 1977—.

WRITINGS: Variation in Verse (poems), Branden Press, 1975; *The Judgment* (four-act play; first produced in Orchard Lake, Mich., at St. Mary's College, 1975), Unitarian Universalist Religious Arts Guild, 1978. Also author of unproduced plays, including "Paul in Rome," "In the Day of Josiah," "The Mission," "The Vineyard," "On Clovis," "Brunhilda," and "Marozia."

WORK IN PROGRESS: A Sojourn of the Spirit, poems; "Catherine II," a play about Catherine the Great of Russia.

SIDELIGHTS: Brown commented: "I come from a background that has maintained something of its rural nature, and includes others who were involved in the arts. My own reading, viewing, listening, and thinking have often centered around the classics: in prose, the works of Tolstoy, Dostoyevski, and Victor Hugo; in drama, Shakespeare and Moliere; poetry of Walt Whitman, T.S. Eliot, and Dylan Thomas; music, Beethoven; painting, the Dutch School in particular. There are many contemporary writers I admire, too: Henry Nelson Wieman on theology, Oswald Spengler on the drama of history, Freud on psychology, and Dewey on philosophy and education. I believe that to find the core today, it is best to return to the countryside. Many are doing this today—some haphazardly and some by direct intent."

* * *

BROWN, Karl 1895(?)-1970

OBITUARY NOTICE: Born c. 1895; died March 6, 1970, in New York, N.Y. Editor. Brown was an editor and bibliographer at the New York Public Library. He also edited the *Library Journal* for ten years. Obituaries and other sources: *AB Bookman's Weekly*, May 5, 1970.

* * *

BROWN, L. J.
See Du BREUIL, (Elizabeth) L(or)inda

* * *

BROWN, Robert D. 1924-

PERSONAL: Born July 1, 1924, in Whiting, Ind.; son of Raymond (a policeman) and Elsie (in sales; maiden name, Wilhite) Brown; children: Susan Brown Cary, Clayton, Sarah *Education:* Attended Magdalen College, Oxford, 1945-46; Indiana University, A.B. (with honors), 1949, M.A., 1950, Ph.D., 1952. *Agent:* George Ziegler, 160 East 97th St., New York, N.Y. 10029. *Office:* Department of English, Western Washington University, Bellingham, Wash. 98225.

CAREER: Oregon State University, Corvallis, instructor, 1952-54, assistant professor, 1955-56, associate professor of English, 1957-65, director of honors program, 1964; Western Washington University, Bellingham, professor of English, 1965—, chairman of department, 1965-67, academic dean, 1967-70. Grader and analyst for Educational Testing Service, 1962—. Lecturer on KOAC-TV and KOAP-TV, 1962-63; host and writer for "What's Happening," on KOAP-TV, 1964-65. Expert witness for State of Washington, 1974—; consultant to Washington State Department of Social and Health Services. *Military service:* U.S. Army, in Intelligence; parachutist and member of war crimes group, 1945-47; became master sergeant. *Member:* Modern Language Association of America, American Association of University Professors (vice-president of Washington State Chapter, 1973-76), Mystery Writers of America.

WRITINGS: (With David G. Spencer) *Exposition and Persuasion*, Appleton, 1956; (with F. G. Norris and Thomas Kranidas) *Oregon Signatures*, Oregon State Press, 1958; *Viewer's Guide: Hebrew, Greek, Roman, and Christian*, Oregon State Press, 1962; *Viewer's Guide: Order and Reason*, Oregon State Press, 1962; *Viewer's Guide: The Heritage of Romanticism*, Oregon State Press, 1963; (with Robert A. Peters) *Guide to Better Themes*, Scott, Foresman, 1970; *Prime Suspect* (mystery novel), Belmont-Tower 1981. Contributor to literature journals and *Ellery Queen's Mystery Magazine*.

WORK IN PROGRESS: Cacy Gage on Penthe, a science-fiction novel.

BROWNING, L. J.
See Du BREUIL, (Elizabeth) L(or)inda

*   *   *

BROWNING, Peter   1928-

PERSONAL: Born December 31, 1928, in Cleveland, Ohio; son of Robert Hamilton (a physician) and Lucy (a pianist and composer; maiden name, Beckett) Browning. *Education:* Attended Oberlin College, U.S. Coast Guard Academy, and Ohio State University. *Home:* P.O. Box 8040, Walnut Creek, Calif. 94569.

CAREER: Thompson Products, Cleveland, Ohio, delivery person, 1946-47; Interlake Steamship Co., Cleveland, ordinary seaman, 1949; new car and truck transporter and convoy leader between Detroit, Mich., and Los Angeles, Calif., 1949-58; Greyhound Corp., Los Angeles, dispatcher, 1959; associated with U.S. Post Office in Huntington Beach, Calif., 1964; writer, 1968—. News writer for Pacifica Radio, Berkeley, Calif., 1966-67. *Military service:* U.S. Navy, 1947-49.

WRITINGS: The Last Wilderness (nonfiction; with own photographs), Chronicle Books, 1975; (with Carol Holleuffer) *Roaming the Back Roads,* Chronicle Books, 1979. Contributor of articles and photographs to *Minority of One, Harper's, Smithsonian,* and *Nation.*

WORK IN PROGRESS: A directory of stamp-auction houses, publication by Fell expected in 1982; a history of Death Valley and the vicinity; a book based on his ten years as a truck transporter.

SIDELIGHTS: Browning commented: "I've made two long canoe trips in the Northwest Territories, one of which became the subject of my first book. I am an inveterate backpacker and wilderness traveler—in the Sierra Nevada, the desert Southwest, and northern Canada. I'm also a photographer.

"The stamp-auction house directory arises from my own stamp collecting and investing activities. The Death Valley book comes from my desert travels and interest in western history. A 1972 article in *Harper's* came from conservationist interests—the article was on Walt Disney's attempt to build a resort in Mineral King Valley in the Sierra."

*   *   *

BROWNSTONE, David M.   1928-

PERSONAL: Born August 7, 1928, in New York, N.Y.; married Irene M. Franck (a writer), January 20, 1969; children: Douglass L., Gregory D. *Education:* Brooklyn College (now of the City University of New York), B.A., 1948. *Agent:* Paul R. Reynolds, Inc., 12 East 41st St., New York, N.Y. 10017. *Office:* Hudson Group, 74 Memorial Plaza, Pleasantville, N.Y. 10514.

CAREER: Commerce Clearing House, New York City, marketing representative, 1957-61; Institutional Publishing Co., New York City, president, 1961-62; Tax Research Institute of America, New York City, vice-president and general manager, 1962-72; Institute for International Research Ltd., New York City, founder, president, and creator of *International Tax Report* and *International Investment Advisor* in New York City and London, England, 1972-74; Hudson Group, Pleasantville, N.Y., principal, 1974—. *Awards, honors: Where to Find Business Information* was named best business and management book of the year by Association of American Publishers, 1979.

WRITINGS: Successful Selling Skills for Small Business, Wiley, 1978; *Sell Your Way to Success,* McKay, 1978; (with Gene R. Haws) *How to Get the Money to Pay for College,* McKay, 1978; (with wife, Irene M. Franck, and son, Douglass L. Brownstone) *Island of Hope, Island of Tears: An Oral History of Ellis Island,* Rawson, Wade, 1979; (with Gorton Carruth) *Where to Find Business Information,* Wiley, 1979, 2nd edition, 1981.

(With Franck and Carruth) *The VNR Dictionary of Business and Finance,* Van Nostrand, 1980; (with Hawes) *The Complete Career Guide,* Simon & Schuster, 1980; (with Franck) *The VNR Investor's Dictionary,* Van Nostrand, 1980; (with Jacques Sartisky) *Personal Financial Survival: Guide for the Eighties and Beyond,* Wiley, 1981; (with Franck) *The VNR Real Estate Dictionary,* Van Nostrand, 1981; (with Franck) *The VNR Dictionary of Publishing,* Van Nostrand, 1982. General editor of "Small Business Series," Wiley. Past co-editor of *Film Review Digest.*

WORK IN PROGRESS: The Historical Encyclopedia of Occupations, with wife, Irene M. Franck, publication by Facts on File expected in 1984; *The Manager's Practical Handbook,* with Franck, publication by Wiley expected in 1984; *The Sales Professional's Practical Handbook,* with Franck, publication by Wiley expected in 1985.

*   *   *

BRUNDAGE, Dorothy J(une)   1930-

PERSONAL: Born June 18, 1930, in Cleveland, Ohio; daughter of William D. (a toolmaker) and Isabelle (Porter) Palmer; married Donald D. Brundage, November 29, 1953; children: David C., Ellen K. *Education:* Case Western Reserve University, B.S.N., 1953; Emory University, M.N., 1968; Walden University, Ph.D., 1980. *Home address:* Route 6, Box 215, Mebane, N.C. 27302. *Office:* 1004 School of Nursing, Duke University, Durham, N.C. 27710.

CAREER: Worked as nurse; Anniston Memorial Hospital, School of Nursing, Anniston, Ala., instructor in nursing, 1965-67; Duke University, Durham, N.C., assistant professor, 1970-79, associate professor of nursing and associate dean of School of Nursing, 1979—. *Member:* American Association of Nephrology Nurses and Technicians (member of advisory board, 1981-83), American Nurses' Association, American Association of University Professors, American Association for Higher Education, American Association for the Advancement of Science, Sigma Theta Tau (secretarty, 1973-74; councellor, of Beta Epsilon chapter, 1976-78). *Awards, honors:* Thelma Ingles Award from Beta Epsilon chapter of Sigma Theta Tau, 1976, for "Assessing Rehabilitation in Home Hemodialysis Patients—a Useful Tool," and 1977, for "Rehabilitation and Home Hemodialysis: Patient-Associated Variables."

WRITINGS: (Contributor) *American Nurses' Association Clinical Sessions,* Appleton, 1970; *Nursing Management of Renal Problems,* Mosby, 1976, 2nd edition, 1980; (contributor) Wilma J. Phipps, Nancy Fugate Woods, and Barbara C. Long, editors, *Medical-Surgical Nursing,* 7th edition (Brundage was not included in earlier editions), Mosby, 1979; (with Katina Strauch) *Guide to Library Resources for Nursing,* Appleton, 1980.

WORK IN PROGRESS: Problems Facing Spouses of Patients With End-Stage Renal Disease Treated by Dialysis.

SIDELIGHTS: Dorothy Brundage wrote: "The nursing elective course I developed and taught at Duke University, 'Nursing in Nephrology,' led directly to my book on renal problems and my current research interests. Clinical research projects involving nursing are needed to help solve major health-care problems such as those faced by patients with renal problems. Nursing has an important role in decreasing the human cost of disability. We also must be involved in the cost-effective delivery of health care that utilizes limited resources.''

* * *

BRUSSEL, Jacob 1900(?)-1979

OBITUARY NOTICE: Born c. 1900 in Poland; died October 6, 1979, in New York, N.Y. Antiquarian bookseller and reprint publisher. Brussel was the proprietor of several bookshops in New York City, including the first store he opened in the 1920's, the Ortelius Bookshop on Astor Place. Later in life, Brussel entered the reprint publishing business, bringing out such works as Henry Miller's *Tropic of Cancer,* a bibliography of erotica entitled *Pisanus Fraxi,* and an edition of the Gutenberg Bible. For publishing such books as Miller's novel, Brussel was attacked by John Sumner's Society for the Prevention of Vice and later imprisoned. ''Absurd though it seems to us now,'' wrote Walter Goldwater in *AB Bookman's Weekly,* ''it was then serious enough, and Jack was imprisoned for publishing and selling books that 20 years later would have made his fortune and established him as an honored member of the publishing world.'' Obituaries and other sources: *AB Bookman's Weekly,* December 10, 1979.

* * *

BRYAN, Christopher 1935-

PERSONAL: Born January 24, 1935, in London, England; son of William Joseph (an engineer) and Amy (May) Bryan; married Wendy Elizabeth Smith (a social worker), July 2, 1972. *Education:* Wadham College, Oxford, B.A. (in English and theology; both with honors), 1958; Ripon Hall Theological College, M.A., 1959. *Politics:* ''Social Democrat/Liberal.'' *Home:* 6 Park Pl., St. Leonard's, Exeter, Devonshire, England. *Office:* School of Education, St. Luke's, University of Exeter, Heavitree, Exeter, Devonshire, England.

CAREER: Ordained Episcopalian deacon, 1960, priest, 1961; St. Mark's Church, Reigate, England, assistant curate, 1960-64; Salisbury Theological College, Salisbury, England, tutor and vice-principal, 1964-70; Virginia Theological Seminary, Alexandria, associate professor and associate director of Center for Continuing Education, 1970-74; Diocese of London, England, senior education officer, 1974-79; University of Exeter, lecturer in religious education and St. Luke's Foundation Chaplain, 1979—. Presenter of ''The Bible for Today'' on Anglia Television.

WRITINGS: Way of Freedom, Seabury, 1974. Contributor to *Perspectives.*

WORK IN PROGRESS: Night of the Wolf, a novel; *In the Beginning,* studies of the book of Genesis; *What Christians Believe.*

SIDELIGHTS: Bryan told *CA:* ''I detect three major phases in my thinking. I was initially influenced deeply by C. S. Lewis, Charles Williams, J.R.R. Tolkein, and the whole of that group known as 'The Inklings.' Secondly, I 'discovered' the theology of the Reformation and without doubt Karl Barth is the name most important to me here. Finally, I have come of late to a deeper concern about the Hebrew origins of Christian faith, and to feel the need for renewed dialogue between Christianity and Judaism. On the emotional and personal side, I owe much to the Human Relationship Training movement, as I have experienced it both in Britain and in the United States.''

BRYHER
See ELLERMAN, Annie Winifred

* * *

BUCK, James H. 1924-

PERSONAL: Born August 8, 1924, in Lima, Ohio; married Virginia Marie Jeffers, December 17, 1947; children: Jan Buck Filler, Julie Buck Thompson, Nancy. *Education:* University of Washington, Seattle, A.B., 1949; Stanford University, A.M., 1953; American University, Ph.D., 1959. *Home:* 248 Moss Side Dr., Athens, Ga. 30606. *Office:* Office of the Vice-President for Academic Affairs, University of Georgia, Athens, Ga. 30602.

CAREER: U.S. Army, career officer, 1942-47, 1949-67, in various troop command, staff, and intelligence assignments in southwest Pacific, Korea, and Japan, retiring as lieutenant colonel; University of Georgia, Athens, associate professor of history, 1967—, associate vice-president for academic affairs, 1980—. Professor at Air War College, 1978-80. *Member:* International Studies Association (regional vice-president, 1974-75), Association for Asian Studies (regional president, 1974-75), Rotary International. *Awards, honors*—Military: Legion of Merit, Bronze Star.

WRITINGS: (Editor) *The Modern Japanese Military System,* Sage Publications Inc., 1975; (with Sam Sarkesian) *Introduction to Comparative Politics,* Alfred Publishing, 1979; (editor) *Military Leadership,* Sage Publications, 1981. Contributor to military and Asian studies journals.

* * *

BUGAYEV, Boris Nikolayevich 1880-1934 (Andrey Bely)

BRIEF ENTRY: Born in October, 1880, in Moscow, Russia (now U.S.S.R.); died January 8, 1934, in U.S.S.R. Russian novelist, poet, and critic. As spokesman for the second generation of Russian symbolist poets, Bely saw his work not only as an aesthetic experience but as a whole way of life. An early novelette in rhythmic prose, *Simfonia* (1902), was so heavily imbued with the structure and sound of musical composition that it was hailed as the start of a new literary genre. In about 1910, Bely's interests shifted toward theosophy and the occult. He traveled in Europe and became aware that the imposed order of the society in which he lived hovered on the brink of chaos. He combined his successful experiments in rhythmic prose, the formal clarity of language, and a background of extensive research on style to produce *St. Petersburg* (1913). This novel has been called a masterpiece of twentieth-century Russian prose. Like many Russian intellectuals, Bely at first welcomed the Bolshevik Revolution, notably in the poem ''First Meeting'' (1921), but his enthusiasm soon waned. In his later years, Bely's best work was concentrated in his memoirs and literary criticism of Russian masters of the past. His analysis of Gogol, *Masterstvo Gogolya* (1929), is considered one of his most important achievements. *Biographical/critical sources: Encyclopedia of World Literature in the Twentieth Century,* updated edition, Ungar, 1967; Konstantin Mochulsky, *Andrei Bely: His Life and Works,* Ardis, 1977.

* * *

BUNDY, William P(utnam) 1917-

PERSONAL: Born September 24, 1917, in Washington, D.C.;

son of Harvey H. and Katharine L.B.; married Mary Acheson, January 30, 1943; children: Michael, Carol, Christopher. *Education:* Yale University, A.B., 1939; Harvard University, M.A., 1940, LL.B., 1947. *Office:* Council on Foreign Relations, 58 East 68th St., New York, N.Y. 10021.

CAREER: Associated with Covington & Burlington (law firm), Washington, D.C., 1947-51; Central Intelligence Agency, Washington, D.C., with Board of National Estimates, 1951-61; deputy assistant secretary of defense for international security affairs in Washington, D.C., 1961-63, assistant secretary, 1963-64; U.S. Department of State, Washington, D.C., assistant secretary of state for East Asian and Pacific affairs, 1964-69; Massachusetts Institute of Technology, Cambridge, visiting professor of international studies and senior research associate at Center for International Studies, 1969-71; Council on Foreign Affairs, New York, N.Y., editor of *Foreign Affairs,* 1972—. Staff director of President Eisenhower's Commission on National Goals, 1960; member of board of trustees of Yale University, 1961-80, and American Assembly. *Military service:* U.S. Army, Signal Corps, 1941-46; served in European theater; became major; received Legion of Merit, member of Order of the British Empire. *Member:* Century Club. *Awards, honors:* Distinguished public service medal from U.S. Department of Defense, 1964; distinguished honor award from U.S. Department of State, 1969.

WRITINGS: (Editor) *Two Hundred Years of American Foreign Policy,* New York University Press, 1977; (editor) *The World Economic Crisis,* Norton, 1975; (editor) *America and the World, 1978,* Pergamon, 1979; (editor) *America and the World, 1979,* Pergamon, 1980; *America and the World, 1980,* Pergamon, 1981. Also contributor to *Goals for Americans,* 1960. Author of a column in *Newsweek,* 1970-72. Contributor to *Foreign Affairs.*

*   *   *

BUNIN, Ivan Alexeyevich   1870-1953

BRIEF ENTRY: Born October 22, 1870 (some sources say October 10), in Voronezh, Russia (now U.S.S.R.); died of a heart attack, November 8, 1953, in Paris, France. Russian author. After beginning his career as a classical poet in the tradition of Pushkin, Bunin won fame in Russia for *The Village* (1910), a pessimistic novel that described the disintegration of rural life at the turn of the century. International acclaim followed publication of the story "The Gentleman From San Francisco" (1915), a satire on the vanity and ultimate uselessness of bourgeois Western society. He won a Nobel Prize for literature for *The Well of Days* (1933), a semi-autobiographical work that cemented his reputation with critics. An anti-Bolshevik, Bunin left Russia in 1919, spending the rest of his life as an expatriate, mainly in France. His gift was for careful observation and clarity of style, and he wrote with a deliberate detachment that enhanced his artistry. He was also a translator into Russian of such English-language poets as Byron and Longfellow, and an outspoken critic, as demonstrated in *Memories and Portraits* (1951). *Biographical/critical sources: Columbia Dictionary of Modern European Literature,* Columbia University Press, 1947; *Twentieth Century Writing: A Reader's Guide to Contemporary Literature,* Transatlantic, 1969; Serge Kryzytski, *The Works of Ivan Bunin,* Mouton, 1971.

*   *   *

BURCH, Mary Lou   1914-

PERSONAL: Born September 21, 1914, in Cedar Falls, Iowa;

daughter of George Hugh and Alice (Brown) Mitze; married Robert L. Burch (a professor and editor), June 3, 1939; children: Barbara Burch Callahan, Sue Burch Wyckoff, Carol Burch Booth, Robert H. *Education:* Iowa State Teachers College (now University of Northern Iowa), B.A., 1935; University of Iowa, M.A., 1939. *Home address:* Route 3, Box 56A, Landrum, S.C. 29356.

CAREER: High school teacher of English in Dinsdale, Iowa, 1935-38; Waverly High School, Waverly, Iowa, teacher of English and speech, 1938-39; writer.

WRITINGS: (With husband, Robert L. Burch) *Effective Studying,* Volumes I-II, Xerox Education Publications, 1973; *Making Leaf Rubbings,* Stephen Greene Press, 1978. Contributor to *Yankee.*

WORK IN PROGRESS: Suddenly You're the Cook; a book on building a solar house, based on her own experience.

SIDELIGHTS: Mary Burch told *CA:* "My writing has always been based on subjects I thought were apt to be of some particular benefit. The study books were motivated by the conviction that something should be done to improve the situation regarding term papers and reports; the cookbook is designed to help non-cooks who are suddenly required to provide meals to do so easily and with satisfaction; our solar-related experiences could be helpful to people contemplating building."

*   *   *

BURNABY, John   1891-1978

OBITUARY NOTICE—See index for *CA* sketch: Born July 28, 1891, in Etton, Beverly, Yorkshire, England; died in March, 1978, in England. Educator, clergyman, and author. An ordained member of the clergy of the Church of England, Burnaby worked as a lecturer in theology and divinity at Trinity College and at Cambridge University. He had been a Regius professor emeritus since 1958. Concerned with the history and theology of early Christianity, his works include *Amor Dei: A Study of the Religion of St. Augustine, Is the Bible Inspired?, Christian Words and Christian Meanings,* and *The Belief of Christendom.* Obituaries and other sources: *AB Bookman's Weekly,* July 10, 1978.

*   *   *

BURROUGHS, Edgar Rice   1875-1950
(Normal Bean)

BRIEF ENTRY: Born in 1875 in Chicago, Ill.; died in 1950. American writer. The creator of Tarzan, Burroughs wrote more than sixty books, most of which recorded bedtime stories that the author told himself. His most famous work, *Tarzan of the Apes* (1914), sold 25 million copies and was printed in fifty-six languages by 1940. The first Tarzan movie was released in 1918. In 1930, a year after the ape-man appeared in a comic strip, the original movie was reproduced as a sound film. In addition to the Tarzan adventures, Burroughs wrote crude science fiction stories, many of which have been published in more than fifty languages. Prior to becoming a writer, Burroughs worked as a soldier, policeman, department store manager, gold miner, cowboy, and storekeeper. His works include *The Princess of Mars* (1917), *Tarzan the Untamed* (1920), *Pellucidar* (1923), *Tanar of Pellucidar* (1930), *The Pirates of Venus* (1934), and *Tarzan and "The Foreign Legion"* (1947). *Biographical/critical sources: Twentieth Century Writings: A Reader's Guide to Contemporary Literature,* Transatlantic, 1969; *The Penguin Companion to American Literature,* McGraw,

1971; *Twentieth-Century Literary Criticism,* Volume 2, Gale, 1979.

* * *

BURSTINER, Irving 1919-

PERSONAL: Born November 7, 1919, in New York, N.Y.; son of Max (a confectionery machine foreman) and Carrie (a millinery retailer; maiden name, Nedowitz) Burstiner; married Rose Friend, November 3, 1940; children: Harry, Ronald, Alan, Stuart (deceased). *Education:* Brooklyn College (now of the City University of New York), B.A., 1940; St. John's University, Jamaica, N.Y., M.S., 1965, Ph.D., 1970. *Politics:* Democrat. *Religion:* Jewish. *Home:* 430 Shore Rd., Long Beach, N.Y. 11561; and 354 Lake Frances Dr., West Palm Beach, Fla. 33411. *Office:* Department of Marketing, Bernard M. Baruch College of the City University of New York, Box 199, 17 Lexington Ave., New York, N.Y. 10010.

CAREER: Barricini Stores, Inc. (confectionary), Long Island, N.Y., director of retail stores, 1946-49; Barricini, Inc., Long Island, vice-president of marketing, 1950-71; Bernard M. Baruch College of the City University of New York, New York, N.Y., assistant professor, 1971-78, associate professor of marketing, 1978—. Owner and director of Creative Management Institute (consultants). Adjunct professor at universities. *Military service:* U.S. Army, 1944-46; became sergeant. *Member:* International Council for Small Business, Mensa, American Collegiate Retailing Association, Creative Education Foundation, Phi Delta Kappa.

WRITINGS: (With W. F. Coventry) *Management: A Basic Handbook,* Prentice-Hall, 1977; *The Small Business Handbook,* Prentice-Hall, 1979; (editor of revision) Marion Kellogg, *Putting Management Theories to Work,* Prentice-Hall, 1979; *Run Your Own Store,* Prentice-Hall, 1981; (editor) *The Essential Guide to Management,* Prentice-Hall, 1981; *Mail Order Selling,* Prentice-Hall, 1982. Contributor to education, business, and management journals.

WORK IN PROGRESS: A retailing textbook, publication by Irwin expected in 1983.

SIDELIGHTS: Burstiner commented: "I am interested in people, places, executive development and training, creative thinking, and all areas of marketing." *Avocational interests:* Science fiction.

* * *

BUSH, Charlie Christmas 1888(?)-1973
(Christopher Bush, Michael Horne)

OBITUARY NOTICE: Born c. 1888 in East Anglia, England; died in 1973 in London, England. Author best known for numerous mysteries written under the pseudonym Chrisopher Bush, including *The Case of the Prodigal Daughter* and *The Plumley Inheritance.* Bush also mined his war experiences for material in mysteries such as *The Case of the Fighting Soldier* and *The Case of the Kidnapped Soldier.* As Michael Horne, he wrote of life in the English countryside. Obituaries and other sources: *AB Bookman's Weekly,* December 3, 1973; *Encyclopedia of Mystery and Detection,* McGraw, 1976.

* * *

BUSH, Christopher
See BUSH, Charlie Christmas

BUSH, Grace A(bhau) 1936-

PERSONAL: Born May 23, 1936, in Philadelphia, Pa.; daughter of Harry Nelson (in sales) and Grace (Humphreys) Abhau; married Edward A. Bush (a certified public accountant), February 9, 1962; children: Elizabeth. *Education:* Kent State University, B.S., 1957, M.S., 1960. *Religion:* Methodist. *Office:* Department of Computer Sciences, Kent State University, Rockwell Hall, Kent, Ohio 44242.

CAREER: Kent State University, Kent, Ohio, instructor, 1957-69, assistant professor, 1969-74, associate professor of mathematics, 1974—, associate director of computer services, 1965—. *Member:* Mathematical Association of America, Association for Computing Machinery, Data Processing Management Association.

WRITINGS: (With John E. Young) *Foundations of Mathematics,* McGraw, 1968, 2nd edition, 1973; (with Young) *Geometry for Elementary Teachers,* Holden-Day, 1971; (with Young) *The Mathematics of Business,* Science Research Associates, 1974; (with Young) *Fundamentos de Matematicas,* McGraw, 1980.

* * *

BUTLER, Margaret Gwendoline

PERSONAL: Born in Nottingham, England; daughter of George and Edith (Puttick) Butler. *Education:* University of London, Certificate for Teaching. *Religion:* Church of England. *Residence:* Clacton-on-Sea, England.

CAREER: St. Osyth's College of Education, Clacton-on-Sea, England, principal lecturer in dress and design, 1956-72; writer, 1972—.

WRITINGS: Clothes, Batsford, 1958, 3rd edition, 1965; (with Beryl S. Greves) *Fabric Furnishings,* Batsford, 1972; (with Greves) *Fashions for the Home,* Drake, 1972.

WORK IN PROGRESS: Dress Pattern Drafting, with Joan Rogers.

SIDELIGHTS: Margaret Butler wrote: "All my books were prepared because I felt there was an urgent need for them by teachers and I wished to share my knowledge of the crafts. I am interested in any subject in any way connected with any form of needlecraft."

* * *

BUTLER, Samuel 1835-1902

BRIEF ENTRY: Born in 1835 in Nottinghamshire, England; died in 1902. English sheep farmer and author. In his writings, Butler combined fact with fantasy to illustrate Victorian society's attitudes on wealth, religion, and the family. His most famous work, *The Way of All Flesh,* a spiritual autobiography published a year after his death, captures the Victorians' reverence for money and the Bible. In the book, which is the story of a child and his cruel, but well-meaning, father, Butler vents his anger and hatred. Heralded by George Bernard Shaw, among others, as a great work, *The Way of All Flesh,* though not widely read, has been imitated by other authors. As a writer, Butler has been criticized for his complacency and for not taking his work seriously. Among his books on evolution are *Life and Habit: An Essay After a Completer View of Evolution* (1878) and *Evolution Old and New; or, The Theories of Buffon, Dr. Erasmus Darwin, and Lamark, as Compared With That of Mr. C. Darwin* (1879). His other works include *A First Year in Canterbury Settlement* (1863), *Erewhon; or,*

Over the Range (1872), *The Fair Haven: A Work in Defence of the Miraculous Element in Our Lord's Ministry Upon Earth, Both as Against Rationalistic Impugners and Certain Orthodox Defenders* (1873), and *Alps and Sanctuaries of Piedmont and the Canton Ticino* (1882). *Residence:* London, England. *Biographical/critical sources: Webster's New World Companion to English and American Literature,* World Publishing, 1973; *Twentieth-Century Literary Criticism,* Volume 1, Gale, 1978.

* * *

BUTTENWIESER, Paul (Arthur) 1938-

PERSONAL: Surname is pronounced *But*-ton-wee-zer; born April 15, 1938, in New York, N.Y.; son of Benjamin Joseph (an investment banker) and Helen (a lawyer; maiden name, Lehman) Buttenwieser; married Catherine Frum (a social worker), August 9, 1963; children: Susan, Stephen, Janet. *Education:* Harvard University, A.B. (cum laude), 1960, M.D., 1964; attended Boston Psychoanalytic Institute, 1970-75.

CAREER: Bronx Municipal Hospital Center, Bronx, N.Y., intern in pediatrics, 1964-65; Massachusetts Mental Health Center, Boston, Mass., psychiatric resident, 1965-67; fellow in child psychiatry, 1967-68; Beth Israel Hospital, Boston, fellow in child psychiatry, 1970-71, assistant psychiatrist, 1971—; Harvard University, Cambridge, Mass., clinical instructor in psychiatry, 1971—; private practice of psychiatry and child psychiatry, 1971—; private practice of psychoanalysis, 1975—. Faculty member of extension program of Boston Psychoanalytical Society, 1976—. *Military service:* U.S. Army, Medical Corps, 1968-70; became major. *Member:* American Psychiatric Association, Massachusetts Psychiatric Society, Boston Psychoanalytic Society.

WRITINGS: Free Association, Little, Brown, 1981.

WORK IN PROGRESS: A novel.

SIDELIGHTS: Buttenwieser told *CA:* "My earliest love was music. As a child I was expected to become a pianist, and I studied for that career until my teenage years. When I decided to become a doctor, I hoped to do something artistic with my life as well. I wanted to combine writing with a career in psychiatry, and to some extent I have been able to do it. The problem has not been a matter of time—I write during evenings and weekends, like many other writers who hold jobs—as much as switching from the world I live in to the world I write about. The world of Roger Liebman, the protagonist of *Free Association,* is very different from mine, although we are both psychiatrists. We are most alike in our concerns: our ambitions, our frustrations, and our insecurities. I wanted to present a psychiatrist as a rounded character, instead of as a caricature or an all-wise seer. The world of psychoanalysis lends itself readily, I think, to comedy, but it is a comedy of people—analysts and patients alike—who often take themselves too seriously.

"I feel that *Free Association* has said substantially what I would like to say about psychoanalysis, and I am moving on to another world in my current novel. I would like to write with as much variety as I am able, while exploring in each work the themes that interest me the most: love and work, to use Freud's deceptively complicated formulation; that is to say, the difficulty of living with someone else, the difficulty of living without someone else, the difficulty of living."

* * *

BUTTI, Ken(neth Michael) 1950-

PERSONAL: Born August 16, 1950, in Carson City, Nev.; son

of Alvin Michael (a public official) and Violet (Hall) Butti. *Education:* Attended Lassen Junior College, 1968-69, Los Angeles Pierce College, 1975-78, and University of California, Los Angeles, 1979. *Residence:* Santa Monica, Calif. *Office:* c/o Cheshire Books, 514 Bryant St., Palo Alto, Calif. 94301.

CAREER: Butti, Perlin Co., Santa Monica, Calif., president, 1975—. *Member:* International Solar Energy Society.

WRITINGS: (With John Perlin) *A Golden Thread: 2,500 Years of Solar Architecture and Technology,* Van Nostrand, 1980; *Terrestrial Uses of Solar,* McGraw, 1981. Contributor to *Solar Age, Chicago,* and *Co-Evolution Quarterly.*

WORK IN PROGRESS: Research on bioclimatic design in housing and solar energy use around the world.

SIDELIGHTS: Butti told *CA:* "Waste and abuse of our energy resources presents a great threat to the continued development of industrialized nations. Co-author John Perlin and I have extensively explored an environmentally benign and renewable alternative to conventional energy—solar energy.

"We have spent over four years researching the practical roots of solar energy use for our book *A Golden Thread: 2500 Years of Solar Architecture and Technology.* As this is a difficult topic to study, we found it necessary to augment formal research with personal correspondence and interviews with key historical figures. We blended quotes, a concise narrative, and numerous illustrations to enliven and make more interesting an essentially complex and dry subject.

"Our writings have helped expand public awareness of the fact that solar energy *does* indeed have a history, thereby placing its current use in an important new perspective. The sun will inevitably be a major energy source for mankind; it is up to each of us as to how long this transition will take."

The *New York Times* called *A Golden Thread* "a clear and evocative account of the 2,500-year history of a technology—solar energy—that many people thought was purely a 20th-century development." Reviewer Bayard Webster added that "it will be an eye-opener to some solar experts, as well as a historical primer for solar enthusiasts."

BIOGRAPHICAL/CRITICAL SOURCES: New York Times, April 1, 1980; *San Francisco Examiner,* May 5, 1980; *Christian Science Monitor,* May 14, 1980; *Los Angeles Times,* June 28, 1980; *Los Angeles Times Book Review,* November 30, 1980; *Technology Review,* November/December, 1980; *New York Times Book Review,* April 5, 1981.

* * *

BUXTON, Anthony 1892(?)-1970

OBITUARY NOTICE: Born c. 1892; died August 9, 1970, in England. Author of books on sports and fishing. Buxton gained notoriety for his participation in the "Dreadnaught Hoax" of 1910, in which, along with Virginia Woolf and a few friends, he penetrated British naval security by posing as foreign royalty. Buxton, Woolf, and the others were given an official tour of the battleship *Dreadnaught.* The infiltration was later revealed to the press by one of the perpetrators. Obituaries and other sources: *AB Bookman's Weekly,* October 5, 1970; *Who Was Who Among English and European Authors, 1931-1949,* Gale, 1978.

* * *

BUXTON, David Roden 1910-

PERSONAL: Born February 26, 1910, in London, England;

son of Charles Roden (a politician) and Dorothy (Jebb) Buxton; married Annelore Gerstl, 1939 (divorced); married Mary Violet Buxton, December 9, 1950; children: Roden, Elizabeth Buxton Waterfield, Richenda, Francesca, Charles Benedict, James. *Education:* Trinity College, Cambridge, B.A., 1931, M.A., 1936. *Home:* Old Ellwoods, 55 Bridleway, Grantchester, Cambridgeshire CB3 9NY, England.

CAREER: Worked for Imperial Institute of Entomology, East Africa, 1933-36; associated with British Colonial Service in West Africa, 1936-42, and Ethiopia, 1942-46; British Council, Overseas Service, London, worked in Addis Ababa, Ethiopia, 1946-49, Graz, Austria, 1949-53, Rome, Italy, 1954-59, and Munich, West Germany, 1959-62; British Council Home Service, Cambridge, England, research fellow of Clare Hall, 1967-73; writer, 1973—. *Member:* Society of Antiquaries of London.

WRITINGS: Russian Mediaeval Architecture, Cambridge University Press, 1934; *Travels in Ethiopia,* Benn, 1949, 2nd edition, 1957; (translator) Emile Male, *The Early Churches of Rome,* Benn, 1960; *The Abyssinians,* Praeger, 1970; *The Wooden Churches of Eastern Europe,* Cambridge University Press, 1981. Contributor to scholarly journals.

SIDELIGHTS: Buxton wrote: "My youthful enthusiasms were equally divided between biology and historical architecture. Entomology became my profession, but architecture 'as an expression, and a mirror, of geography and civilization' remained an absorbing parallel interest which, since my retirement in 1967, has pushed most other interests into the background.

"I have always been a passionate traveler with a taste for the least known parts of Africa and Europe, a love of camping, and a distaste for smart company and prestigious hotels. I have at various times felt identified with several peoples in Africa and eastern Europe, and could once claim a certain gift in languages. I have lost all those I once spoke, except for German and French, both acquired at an early age.

"Politically (and also religiously) I am non-aligned, though to a great extent disenchanted with the left-wing politics I was brought up to believe in. However I retain a detestation of all lethal weapons and a conviction that no arms race (or 'balance of terror') can indefinitely preserve the peace. I am therefore a firm supporter of movements against the use, the threat of use, or the possession of nuclear armaments."

*   *   *

BUXTON, Harold J(ocelyn)   1880-1976

OBITUARY NOTICE: Born in 1880; died March 12, 1976, in England. Clergyman and author. Buxton served as bishop of Gibraltar from 1933 to 1947. He later became rector of Launton, Oxford. His writings include *Transcaucasia, Substitution of Law for War,* and *A Mediterranean Window.* Obituaries and other sources: *Who's Who,* 127th edition, St. Martin's, 1975; *AB Bookman's Weekly,* April 19, 1976.

*   *   *

BUZZELL, Robert (Dow)   1933-

PERSONAL: Born April 18, 1933, in Lincoln, Neb.; son of Dow Alan (an engineer) and Grace (Blomquist) Buzzell; married Edith Moser (a travel agent), June 5, 1953; children: Susan, Robert D., Jr., Barbara, William. *Education:* George Washington University, A.B., 1953; University of Illinois, M.S., 1954; Ohio State University, Ph.D., 1957. *Home:* 15

Swarthmore Rd., Wellesley, Mass. 02181. *Office:* School of Business, Harvard University, Boston, Mass. 02163.

CAREER: Ohio State University, Columbus, assistant professor, 1957-60, associate professor of business, 1960-61; Harvard University, School of Business, Boston, Mass., associate professor, 1961-67, professor of business, 1967—, Sebastian S. Kresge Professor of Marketing, 1980—. Member of board of directors of Lane Bryant, Inc., Chelsea Industries, Inc., and General Nutrition, Inc. Also worked as teacher and consultant in Europe, Japan, and Latin America. *Member:* American Marketing Association, Phi Beta Kappa.

WRITINGS: Wholesaling, Ronald, 1959; *Mathematical Models in Marketing,* School of Business, Harvard University, 1964; *Product Innovation in Food Processing,* School of Business, Harvard University, 1966; *Marketing Research and Information Systems,* McGraw, 1969; *Marketing: A Contemporary Analysis,* McGraw, 1972. Contributor to business and marketing journals.

SIDELIGHTS: Buzzell told *CA:* "Competition in most industries has become 'global' in scope. An important challenge for managers and management scholars during the 1980's will be to investigate and understand how companies can organize and operate effectively in the new atmosphere of worldwide rivalry."

*   *   *

BYRNE, John   1940-

PERSONAL: Born January 6, 1940, in Paisley, Scotland; son of Patrick and Alice (McShane) Byrne; married Alice Simpson (an artist), April 1, 1964; children: John, Cecilia. *Education:* Attended St. Mirin's Academy and Glasgow School of Art. *Home:* Ellenmount, 3 Castle Brae, Newport-on-Tay, Fife, Scotland. *Agent:* Margaret Ramsay, 14A Goodwin Court, St. Martin's Lane, London WC2, England.

CAREER: Worked in graphics for Scottish television, 1964-66; A. F. Stoddard & Co. (carpet manufacturer), Elderslie, Scotland, designer, 1966-68; Borderline Theatre Co., Irvine, Scotland, playwright-in-residence, 1978-79; Duncan of Jordanstone College of Art, Dundee, Scotland, writer-in-residence, 1981—. Held exhibitions of paintings. *Awards, honors:* Named most promising playwright by *London Evening Standard,* 1978.

WRITINGS—Plays: "Writer's Cramp," first produced at Edinburgh Festival in Fringe, 1977, first produced in London at Bush Theatre, 1977; "The Slab Boys," first produced in Traverse, 1978, first produced on the West End at Royal Court Theatre, 1978, first produced in New York City at Hudson Guild, 1980; "Normal Service," first produced in London at Hampstead Theatre Club, 1979; "The Loveliest Night of the Year," first produced in Traverse, 1979, produced as "Threads" at Hampstead Theatre, 1980; "Hooray for Hollywood," first produced in Louisville, Kentucky, 1980; "Cara Coco," first produced in Scotland at Borderline Theatre Co., 1981.

Also author of "The Butterfly's Hoof," a teleplay produced by BBC-TV, 1978.

WORK IN PROGRESS: "Paisley Patterns," a play that concludes a trilogy containing "The Slab Boys" and "Threads"; a novelization of "Writer's Cramp"; a radio series based on "Normal Service"; a play set in America.

SIDELIGHTS: Byrne told *CA:* "Theatre was still very new to me when I started writing at the age of thirty-six, although I had designed several shows before then. I think I really caught the bug when a friend bought me tickets for a West End play in 1969 when I was in London hanging a one-man show of my paintings. The idea that I could write anything for the stage didn't occur to me until some time later.

"'Writer's Cramp' was the first play: a series of letters strung together with short dramatic scenes into a sort of ragbag. The letters were written initially for my own amusement in a sketchbook. It was my wife who said, 'Why don't you turn those into a play?' 'The Slab Boys' followed close on McDade's heels. (McDade is the hero of 'Writer's Cramp.') In contrast to 'Writer's Cramp,' 'The Slab Boys' was seen as a realistic comedy, which, of course, it is nothing of the kind. It pretends to be, certainly. I enjoyed the notion of working in a classic farce device of a character losing his trousers halfway through the action. This farcical element was taken further in 'Threads,' the sequel to 'The Slab Boys,' when the same character attempts suicide in public. Needless to say, the 'suicide' is a totally botched job. However, that's not really what the two plays are about. Well, not all they're about, anyway.

"Having started so late as a dramatist I discovered that I had a whole backlog of incident and episode in my life (no matter that they were of no great significance) to call upon, to cull, for fodder. Up until I started writing I'd found no great use for them. I didn't use them directly in painting. They weren't worth recounting as they stood, but they did provide the springboard for several stage plays. 'Normal Service' is one such play. I enjoy anti-climaxes enormously—they make me laugh. 'Normal Service' was full of anti-climaxes, a whole series built on top of the other, culminating in one great anti-climax where the hated director has his kilt thrust into a guillotine at the office party and faints clean away at what he imagines has happened, only to be brought round some moments later by the office secretary who attempts to revive him by dangling a tiny chipolata sausage doused in tomato ketchup in front of his eyes. Needless to say, he passes into oblivion once again carrying with him the nightmarish vision of his lost manhood. But that is not what the play's about, at least, not all of what it's about. I was trying to look at the characters' attitudes to the opposite sex (seven of the play's eight characters are men). I'm not sure if I managed to get that across fully.

"I do try not to interfere with or influence the people in the plays too much once they get down on paper. (I know that sounds dreadfully twee!) What I really mean is that I try to let them speak. They aren't all my mouthpieces. I don't necessarily approve or disapprove of their attitudes, their outlooks, their behavior. It's really up to them to sort themselves out, and for the audience to sort them out.

"I despise sentiment. I enormously admire writers who can deal with feeling. Chekhov is my great favorite. I could watch and listen to Chekhov till the cows come home. Not all of the plays I intend to write will be based on my own experiences. I do have an imagination. I'm prodding it with a sharp stick at the moment."

C

CABLE, George Washington 1844-1925
(Drop Shot, Felix Lazarus)

BRIEF ENTRY: Born October 12, 1844, in New Orleans, La.; died January 31, 1925, in St. Petersburg, Fla. American novelist, short story writer, and essayist. After service in the Confederate army and a stint as a surveyor, Cable wrote a weekly column of humorous sketches and poems for the *New Orleans Picayune*. Eventually hired as a reporter, he later refused—because of his Calvinist convictions—to write theatre reviews, and the paper fired him. He then went to work as an accountant and began a program of self-education that led to his abiding interest in Louisiana Creoles and civil rights. In *Old Creole Days* (1879), a collection of short stories first published in *Scribner's Monthly*, and *The Grandissimes* (1880), his first novel, Cable created exact descriptions of local New Orleans color and displayed a mastery of Creole and slave dialects. His next book, *Madame Delphine* (1881), contained the same attention to detail and character that distinguished the earlier works and established Cable as a leader of the local-color movement in Southern literature. In 1884 Cable turned historian with a collection of essays on the subject of Creole ancestry, *The Creoles of Louisiana*. Other essays, published in *The Silent South* (1885) and *The Negro Question* (1890), revealed the author's deep concern for civil rights and prison reform. The loud protest of fellow southerners against the first of these two books convinced Cable to leave his home and settle in Northampton, Massachusetts, where he continued to write on issues of social reform. Although he wrote several more novels in later years, critics found them overly sentimental, melodramatic, and generally inferior to his previous work. *Residence:* Northampton, Mass. *Biographical/critical sources:* Lucy Leffingwell Cable Bikle, *George W. Cable: His Life and Letters*, Scribner, 1928; *The Reader's Encyclopedia of American Literature*, Crowell, 1962; *Webster's American Biographies*, Merriam, 1974; *Twentieth-Century Literary Criticism*, Volume 4, Gale, 1981.

*   *   *

CALDERONE, Mary S(teichen) 1904-
(Mary Steichen Martin)

PERSONAL: Born July 1, 1904, in New York, N.Y.; daughter of Edward J. (a photographer) and Clara (Smith) Steichen; married W. Lon Martin (an actor), 1926 (divorced, 1933); married Frank A. Calderone (with U.S. Health Services), November 29, 1941; children: (first marriage) Nell (deceased, 1935), Linda Steichen Hodes; (second marriage) Francesca Calderone Stuart, Maria S. *Education:* Vassar College, B.A., 1925; University of Rochester, M.D., 1939; Columbia University, M.P.H., 1941. *Religion:* Society of Friends (Quakers). *Home:* 230 East 50th St., New York, N.Y. 10022. *Office:* SIECUS, 80 Fifth Ave., Suite 801, New York, N.Y. 10011.

CAREER: Bellevue Hospital, New York City, intern, 1939-40; part-time school physician in Great Neck, N.Y., 1949-53; Planned Parenthood Federation of America, New York City, medical director, 1953-64; Sex Information Educational Council of the United States (SIECUS), New York City, executive director, 1964-75, president, 1975—. Bronfman Lecturer at American Public Health Association, 1967; Lower Lecturer at Academy of Medicine of Cleveland and Cuyahoga County Medical Society, 1970; Isadore Rubin Memorial Lecturer at SIECUS conference, 1971; Samuel D. Gross Lecturer at University of Louisville Phi Delta Epsilon Medical Fraternity, 1973; Hundley Memorial Lecturer in Gynecology at Obstetrical and Gynecological Society of Maryland, 1973; Rufus Jones Lecturer at Friends' General Conference, 1973; Visiting Alpha Omega Alpha Professor at University of Colorado Medical School, 1978; Abraham Weckstein Memorial Lecturer at New York University, 1979. Member of board of directors of American Association for World Health and U.S. Committee for World Health Organization, 1964—; physician-in-residence at Washington University, St. Louis, Mo., 1965; Conroy Fellow at St. Paul's School, 1967; special visiting fellow at Phillips Exeter Academy, 1967; university scholar at Virginia Polytechnic Institute, 1970; rapporteur for World Health Organization committee on training of health professionals in human sexuality, 1975.

MEMBER: American Medical Association (honorary life member), American Public Health Association (fellow), American Association of Marriage and Family Counselors (honorary life member), American Association of World Health (member of board of directors), American College of Sexologists, Society for the Scientific Study of Sex (fellow), Association of Sexologists, Alpha Omega Alpha (honorary alumnus member).

AWARDS, HONORS: Distinguished service award from Mental Health Association of Nassau County, 1958; annual award for distinguished service to humanity from Albert Einstein Medical Center, 1966; Woman of Conscience Award from National Council of Women, 1968; university citation to alumni from University of Rochester, 1968; Life Cycle Center Award from Kimberly-Clark Corp., 1968; Woman of Achievement Award from Albert Einstein College of Medicine of Yeshiva University, 1969; named one of America's seventy-five most important women by *Ladies' Home Journal,* 1971; annual citation from Sex Information Educational Council of the United States, 1971; annual award from Education Foundation for Human Sexuality, 1973; annual award from American Association of Sex Educators, Counselors, and Therapists, 1973; named humanist of the year by American Humanist Association, 1974; named one of fifty most influential women in the United States by Newspaper Enterprises Association, 1975; annual award from Society for Scientific Study of Sex, 1976; Elizabeth Blackwell Award for distinguished service to humanity from Hobart and William Smith Colleges, 1977; Margaret Sanger Award from Planned Parenthood Federation of America, 1980; Edward Browning Award for Prevention of Disease from American Public Health Association, 1980. Honorary degrees: Doctor of Medical Science from Women's Medical College of Pennsylvania, 1967; Doctor of Humane Letters from Newark State College, 1971; Doctor of Science from Adelphi University, 1971, Worcester Foundation for Experimental Biology, 1974, Brandeis University, 1975, and Haverford College, 1978; Doctor of Laws from Kenyon College, 1972; Doctor of Pedagogy from Hofstra University School of Education, 1978; Doctor of Humane Letters from Dickinson College, 1981.

WRITINGS: (Under name Mary Steichen Martin; with father, Edward Steichen) *The First Picture Book: Everyday Things for Babies,* Harcourt, 1930; (under name Mary Steichen Martin; with E. Steichen) *The Second Picture Book,* Harcourt, 1931; (editor) *Abortion in the United States,* Hoeber-Harper, 1958; *Release From Sexual Tensions,* Random House, 1960; (editor) *Manual of Family Planning and Contraceptive Practice,* Williams & Wilkins, 1964, revised edition, 1970; (editor) *Sexuality and Human Values,* Follett, 1974; (author of foreword) Helen Johnson, editor, *Questions and Answers About Sex and Love,* St. Martin's, 1979; (with Eric W. Johnson) *The Family Book About Sexuality,* Harper, 1981. Contributor of articles to professional journals, including *Clinical Pediatrics, Journal of the International College of Surgeons, Postgraduate Medicine,* and *University of Rochester Medical Review.* Contributor of articles to magazines, textbooks, and encyclopedias.

SIDELIGHTS: Mary Calderone's work for the Sex Information Educational Council of the United States (SIECUS) has frequently brought her under attack. Her critics argue that educating children about sex arouses their curiosity and encourages sexual experimentation at an unnecessarily early age. She counters such arguments by providing valid and current research findings, by reminding people that the world is full of sexual stimuli, that children will learn about sex one way or another, and that it is better to give them accurate information than to hope that they will be able to sort out all the misinformation on their own.

Calderone has been working for education about sexuality in the general population since 1953, when she was appointed medical director of the Planned Parenthood Federation of America. She resigned from that position in 1964 because she believed that the organization's focus—contraception—was narrow. While working for Planned Parenthood, she received many letters from people whose ignorance about sexual matters she found disturbing. There were requests for information not only about birth control, but about sexual problems in general. The letters reflected feelings of guilt, fear, and confusion. It became "clear to her that conflicting religious and social attitudes were combining to prevent the kind of free, open discussion of sex that was necessary if we were to achieve sound

and healthy acceptance of a major and God-given part of our human nature," wrote David Mace in *Friends Journal.*

Calderone's concern about the need for sex education led her to help establish SIECUS, which Mace described as "a high-level, cross-disciplinary organization determined to pull human sexuality out of the gutter." The council describes itself as an organization dedicated to dignifying human sexuality "by openness of approach, study, and scientific research . . . to the end that human beings may be aided towards responsible use of the sexual faculty and towards assimilation of sex into their individual life patterns as a creative and re-creative force."

To achieve these goals, SIECUS participates in the sex education training of doctors, clergy members, psychiatrists, and other professionals, and provides information to individuals and organizations on such subjects as premarital sex, masturbation, homosexuality, impotence, and frigidity. The figures attest to the council's success in establishing human sexuality as an acknowledged aspect of both physical and mental health. At the inception of SIECUS, only 1 percent of the medical schools in the United States included sex education in their curricula; ten years later, 95 percent were including it, although the number has dropped in recent years to 60 percent.

The council had not planned to become involved in sex education in the schools until educators, having nowhere else to turn, came to SIECUS for guidance. "We're not out to subvert parents," Calderone assured Laura Berman of the *Detroit Free Press.* "Parents make the best sex educators, but it's so important that it be done in a positive way, one based on information." Children absorb parental attitudes about sex, she asserts. "Parents give a child his basic sex education through what they project as to their feelings about themselves, how they treat each other, how they treat the child. Parents first must accept their own sexuality, then they must accept a child's sexuality," she told Phyllis Stewart of the *Long Island Press.* Calderone also believes that sex education by parents should begin at an early age and continue through adolescence. It should do much more than teach the mechanics of reproduction. "Sex involves something you are, not just something you do," she explained to Stewart. "Children and adults must be taught to understand their sexuality so they can respect it, appreciate it, and use it properly at the right time in life."

Although SIECUS has made great progress in its effort to dignify human sexuality, Calderone is aware that many people cling to irrational fears and "refuse to learn the facts." At various times throughout her career, she has been attacked by groups who oppose sex education. SIECUS, because it encouraged sex education, was accused of being a "Communist plot to overthrow the United States," and Calderone, as the most visible and outspoken member of the council, was "denounced and derided in a hate campaign that recognized no limits," Mace wrote. "At one protest meeting in a church . . . those assembled were enjoined to go home and pray for her death."

Calderone is a devout Quaker, and it was her faith, she explained to Berman, that carried her through those times when "terrible things were said." She believes that "sexuality is a part of God because . . . it is part of being human." "I've been willing to say things people are scared to say," she acknowledged, "but I don't see myself as at all courageous. I was simply in a good position to do this and someone had to."

Calderone told *CA:* "My motivation for writing is simple: to give ordinary people access to the facts scientists now have about the different aspects of human sexuality common to all people everywhere, as well as of the variations that occur as the result of socialization patterns that are specific to different societies and cultures. Such knowledge, when understood, accepted, and applied at appropriate times between birth and death, can undoubtedly serve in positive rather than the negative ways we can now see. It can act to avoid or prevent many of the sexual dysfunctions easily observable in our society and elsewhere. It is this stance of mine, taken twenty-two years ago and persistently developed and maintained, that has slowly but surely enlisted the support and active participation of the scientific world today in many parts of the globe.''

AVOCATIONAL INTERESTS: House plants, cooking.

BIOGRAPHICAL/CRITICAL SOURCES: Friends Journal, March 15, 1971; *Annals of the New York Academy of Sciences,* March 15, 1973; *Long Island Press,* April 28, 1974; *Authors in the News,* Volume 1, Gale, 1976; *University of Rochester Medical Review,* spring, 1976; Thomas C. Hunter, editor, *Beginnings,* Crowell, 1978; *Modern Maturity,* August-September, 1978; Don Gold, editor, *Until the Singing Stops,* Holt, 1979; *People,* January 21, 1980; *Detroit Free Press,* November 18, 1980; *New York Times,* April 20, 1981.

—Sketch by Mary Sullivan

*   *   *

CALDWELL, Bettye (McDonald) 1924-

PERSONAL: Born December 24, 1924, in Smithville, Tex.; daughter of Thomas M. (a railroad engineer) and Juanita (Mayes) McDonald; married Fred T. Caldwell, Jr. (a surgeon), June 8, 1947; children: Paul Frederick, Elizabeth Lanier. *Education:* Baylor University, B.A., 1945; University of Iowa, M.A., 1947; Washington University, St. Louis, Mo., Ph.D., 1951. *Politics:* Democrat. *Religion:* Protestant. *Home:* 187 Pleasant Valley Dr., Little Rock, Ark. 72212. *Office:* Center for Child Development and Education, College of Education, University of Arkansas, 33rd & University, Little Rock, Ark. 72204.

CAREER: Northwestern University, Evanston, Ill., assistant professor of psychology, 1953-55; Washington University, St. Louis, Mo., research associate, 1955-58; State University of New York Upstate Medical Center, Syracuse, research associate, 1959-65; Syracuse University, Syracuse, professor of child development and education, 1965-69; University of Arkansas, Fayetteville, professor of education, 1969-74; University of Arkansas at Little Rock, Little Rock, professor of education, 1974—, Donaghey Distinguished Professor, 1978—. Member of board of directors of First National Bank, Little Rock. *Member:* National Association for the Education of Young Children, American Orthopsychiatric Association (member of governing board), American Educational Research Association, Society for Research in Child Development (member of governing council). *Awards, honors:* Woman of the year award from *Ladies' Home Journal,* 1976, for humanitarian and community service; alumna of the year award from Baylor University, 1980.

WRITINGS: (Editor) *Review of Child Development Research,* Volume III, University of Chicago Press, 1973; (editor with Donald Stedman) *Infant Education,* Walker & Co., 1977; (with Robert H. Bradley) *Assessing the Home Environment,* Dorsey, 1982; (with Bradley) *Child Development and Education,* Dorsey, 1982. Contributor of more than a hundred articles and a story to academic journals. Editor of *Child Development,* 1968-72.

SIDELIGHTS: Bettye Caldwell told *CA:* "The volume of my writing picked up drastically approximately twenty years ago when I first began working in the field of infant education and day care. There were very few people interested in the applied side of infant development during that time, even though a number of distinguished researchers were beginning to explore the mind of the infant in such a way that it seemed obvious that someone needed to be concerned with the application of the exciting theoretical ideas coming from such efforts. Thus, after I began a research project concerned with the way the social environment affects the cognitive and social development of the young infant, I found it necessary to write a great deal about the work. In part this was necessary because so little else was available in the scientific literature at that time, but it was also important because the world had suddenly discovered a field and wanted to learn more about it. In the course of responding to this interest, I developed a writing style that has been helpful in communicating scientific research to the general public. I have worked at learning to 'de-jargonize' all of my writings on infant and child development and feel that I now enjoy writing for the general public more than I enjoy writing for the small group of people whose area of research is identical to my own.

"I think I have been more of a speaker than a writer; thus, much of my writing is 'writ in electronic transfer units,' if not in water. Right now I am in a period during which I want to summarize some of my life, and I'm writing more than ever. I have just developed a new writing interest—translating the materials I have written for scientific journals into a format suitable for television and movie scripts. This is a totally new type of writing for me that I find challenging and satisfying.''

*   *   *

CALHOUN, Donald W(allace) 1917-

PERSONAL: Born June 14, 1917, in Worcester, Mass.; son of Arthur Wallace (a teacher) and Mildred (a teacher; maiden name, Tourtellot) Calhoun; married Lorraine Nauss, November 25, 1947 (died November 6, 1967); children: Lisa Michele. *Education:* Erskine College, A.B., 1937; Furman University, A.M., 1938; attended University of North Carolina, 1940-42; University of Chicago, Ph.D., 1950. *Politics:* "Democratic socialist.'' *Religion:* Society of Friends (Quakers). *Home:* 10321 Southwest 103rd Ter., Miami, Fla. 33176. *Office:* Department of Sociology, University of Miami, Coral Gables, Fla. 33124.

CAREER: Kansas Wesleyan University, Salina, instructor in sociology, 1939-40; Limestone College, Gaffney, S.C., instructor in sociology and history, 1941; American Friends Service Committee, Seattle, Wash., executive secretary of peace section, 1943-45; Illinois Institute of Technology, Chicago, assistant professor of sociology, 1946-48; University of Minnesota, Minneapolis, assistant professor of general studies, 1948-52; writer and teacher, 1952-55; operated organic citrus grove in Fort Pierce, Fla., 1955-57; Bethune-Cookman College, Daytona Beach, Fla., professor of social science, 1958-62; University of Miami, Coral Gables, Fla., assistant professor, 1962-63, professor of social science, 1963-69, professor of anthropology, 1969-79, professor of sociology, 1979—. *Wartime service:* Served with Civilian Public Service, 1942-43. *Member:* American Association of University Professors, American Civil Liberties Union.

WRITINGS: (Editor with Arthur Naftalin, Benjamin Nelson, Andreas Papandreou, and Mulford Sibley) *Personality, Work, Community,* Lippincott, 1953, 3rd edition, 1961; *Social Science in an Age of Change,* Harper, 1971, 2nd edition, 1978; *Persons-in-Groups: A Humanistic Social Psychology,* Harper, 1976; *Sport, Culture, and Personality,* Leisure Press, 1981; (with Donald D. Kirtley) *Physical Disability: A Psychosocial Perspective,* Prentice-Hall, 1981.

WORK IN PROGRESS: The Oceanic Quest: Toward a Religion Beyond Illusion, publication by Prentice-Hall expected in 1983; Physical Disability: A Psychosocial Perspective, with Donald D. Kirtley, publication by Prentice-Hall expected in 1984.

SIDELIGHTS: Calhoun told CA: "The question central to all my works is 'How can human beings be persons rather than things?' The theme of Social Science in an Age of Change appears in the final chapter, 'Beyond Exploitation,' with exploitation defined as the relationship that turns an individual into a thing. Persons-in-Groups: A Humanistic Social Psychology explains its topic in the first sentence: 'The purpose of this book is to examine what it means to be human, how we get to be human, the obstacles that stand in the way, and how we can use our common knowledge to increase our common humanity.' Sport, Culture, and Personality deals with jock liberation (my term) seen as part of a counterculture that has been challenging exploitation over the world since our Declaration of Independence. Physical Disability: A Psychosocial Perspective concerns the humanization of disabled people in a world that has traditionally dehumanized them. The Oceanic Quest is the search to restore the kind of 'oceanic' oneness (Freud's and Piaget's term) with the universe as it is experienced by the infant in its mother's arms by relieving the alienation from nature, fellow humans, and self that originates in an exploitative society. Again the preface of this book treats the countercultural surge of the 1960's as an embodiment of this quest. I see my nonacademic interludes as a conscientious objector, as a peace worker, and as a 'natural foods' farmer as expressing this same theme that runs through all my writing."

*   *   *

CALVIN, Ross   1890(?)-1970

OBITUARY NOTICE: Born c. 1890; died in 1970 in Albuquerque, N.M. Clergyman and author of books on the American Southwest, including Sky Determines. Obituaries and other sources: AB Bookman's Weekly, March 2, 1970.

*   *   *

CAMERON, Kate
    See Du BREUIL, (Elizabeth) L(or)inda

*   *   *

CAMPBELL, Ballard Crooker, Jr.   1940-

PERSONAL: Born November 30, 1940, in Orange, N.J.; son of Ballard C. (in business) and Ruth (Boman) Campbell; married Wendy E. Kent (an artist), December 26, 1965; children: Cynthia Ann, Erica Lynn. Education: Northwestern University, B.A., 1962; Northeastern University, M.A., 1964; University of Wisconsin—Madison, Ph.D., 1970. Office: Department of History, Northeastern University, Boston, Mass. 02115.

CAREER: Northeastern University, Boston, Mass., instructor, 1969-70, assistant professor, 1970-75, associate professor of history, 1975—. Member of Arlington, Mass., town meeting, 1979. Member: American Historical Association, Organization of American Historians, Social Science History Association, Immigration History Society. Awards, honors: Grant from American Philosophical Society, 1971; fellow at Charles Warren Center, Harvard University, 1976-77.

WRITINGS: (Contributor) Stephan Botein and others, editors, Experiments in History Teaching, Danford Center for Teaching

and Learning, Harvard University, 1977; Representative Democracy, Harvard University Press, 1980. Contributor to history journals and newspapers, including Journal of Interdisciplinary History, Historical Methods, Wisconsin Magazine of History, New York Times, Christian Science Monitor, and Boston Evening Globe.

WORK IN PROGRESS: The American State Legislatures and the Transformation of Federalism, 1880-1980, completion expected in 1985.

SIDELIGHTS: Campbell told CA: "The serious study of any dimension of our universe has an infectious quality. Those afflicted with the malady experience the meaning of the aphorism: the more one learns, the less one knows. Paradoxically, the search for the cure only worsens the disease. History in particular embodies this dilemma; the quest to understand the complexities of the human past is never finished. This, I suppose, explains why I had laid plans to write two more books before I had completed my first. This outsider no doubt finds it difficult to comprehend the intellectual perplexities that bedevil scholars."

*   *   *

CAMPBELL, (Ignatius) Roy (Dunnachie)   1901-1957

BRIEF ENTRY: Born October 2, 1901, in Durban, Natal, South Africa; died in an automobile accident, April 22, 1957, near Setubal, Portugal. South African bullfighter, fisherman, broncobuster, horse breeder, journalist, translator, autobiographer, satirist, and poet. Widely recognized as the most important South African poet, Campbell was noted for his interesting character as well as his poetry. Brought up in the wilds of Natal and Rhodesia, he worked as a fisherman, bullfighter, horse breeder, and bronco buster during his twenties and early thirties. A veteran of three wars, Campbell was only fifteen when he joined the Sixth South African Infantry in World War I. Later, a militant convert to Roman Catholicism, he joined the fascist rebels in the Spanish civil war; his long satiric poem, "Flowering Rifle" (1939), is a celebration of Franco's victory. In 1942 Campbell entered the British Army and served in East and North Africa during the Second World War. Before taking up residence in England in 1928, Campbell was active in South African letters, editing Voorslag, a satirical journal, and writing some of his best and most famous poetry, including "The Flaming Terrapin" (1924). His brash and extroverted poetry contrasted sharply the self-searching and socially conscious poetry of the 1930's. Among his best-known works are "The Wayzgoose" (1928), a satire on South African intellectuals, and "The Georgiad" (1931), an attack on the literary figures of the Bloomsbury group. Campbell also translated Spanish, Portuguese, and French authors, and wrote two autobiographical books, Broken Record (1934) and Light on a Dark Horse (1952). Biographical/critical sources: The Concise Encyclopedia of Modern World Literature, Hutchinson, 1963; The Reader's Encyclopedia, 2nd edition, Crowell, 1965; Canadian Writers: A Biographical Dictionary, revised edition, Ryerson Press, 1966; Encyclopedia of World Literature in the Twentieth Century, updated edition, Ungar, 1967; Cassell's Encyclopaedia of World Literature, revised edition, Morrow, 1977.

*   *   *

CANEY, Steven   1941-

PERSONAL: Born May 8, 1941, in Wilmington, Del.; son of Manuel and Sarah Caney; married wife, Rochelle (a family therapist), August 24, 1963; children: Jennifer, Noah. Education: Attended Temple University, 1959-62; Rhode Island

School of Design, B.F.A., 1965. *Home:* 85 Indian Hill, Carlisle, Mass. 01741; and College Rd., Box 209, Center Harbor, N.H. 03226.

CAREER: Creative Playthings, Princeton, N.J., product developer and designer, 1965-67; Steven Caney Design (product development and advertising agency), Carlisle, Mass., president, 1968—. Assistant professor at Rhode Island School of Design, 1981—; lecturer at Harvard University, Princeton University, University of Cincinnati, Xavier University, Seattle Community College, and Philadelphia College of Art. Executive vice-president of Atlas Energy Systems, 1978—. Design director at Boston Children's Museum, 1967-72; chairman of Carlisle Arts Council. Remote-host of talk show on WCVB-TV and "P.M. Magazine" series on KDKA-TV, both 1979—. *Awards, honors:* Prizes from Ford Motor Co., 1956 and 1958, both for product design.

WRITINGS—For children: *Steven Caney's Toybook,* Workman Publishing, 1971; *Steven Caney's Playbook,* Workman Publishing, 1974; *Steven Caney's Kid's America,* Workman Publishing, 1978; *Steven Caney's Inventions and Contraptions,* Workman Publishing, 1981. Feature writer for *Games, Redbook,* and *Home.* Contributing editor of *Learning.*

WORK IN PROGRESS: Children's television series.

SIDELIGHTS: Caney is an independent toy and game inventor, one of few successful independents. He feels that modern society provides less for the young person's imagination than it used to, and his toys are designed specifically to appeal to the child, not necessarily the parent. He tries to use readily-available tools and supplies to minimize cost and works with small manufacturing companies that allow him the freedom he requires.

His books on homemade toys and games have been more successful than he expected. *Kids' America* combines history with projects, crafts, and games.

Steven Caney told *CA:* "Even though I may be a liberal idealist in my attitudes about play and growing children, I am also a staunch capitalist and a good businessman. I get my ideas to the people!"

AVOCATIONAL INTERESTS: Photography, television production.

*   *   *

CANNON, Jimmy   1909-1973

OBITUARY NOTICE: Born April 10, 1909, in New York, N.Y.; died December 15, 1973, in New York, N.Y. Journalist and author. Cannon worked as a war correspondent, homicide reporter, and sportswriter for newspapers, including the *New York Post.* His writings include *The Sgt. Says* and two collections of sports stories, *Nobody Asked Me* and *Who Struck John?* Obituaries and other sources: *The Reader's Encyclopedia of American Literature,* Crowell, 1962; *Time,* December 17, 1973.

*   *   *

CAPEK, Karel   1890-1938

BRIEF ENTRY: Born January 9, 1890, in Male Svatonovice, Bohemia (now Czechoslovakia); died of pneumonia, December 25, 1938, in Prague, Czechoslovakia. Czech playwright, novelist, and travel writer. Capek's international reputation blossomed with his plays about the dangers of modern technology, totalitarian regimentation, greed, and materialism. His play "R.U.R.: Rossum's Universal Robots" (1920, which intro-

duced the word robot into science fiction jargon, used robots to demonstrate the potential of science and technology to destroy mankind, and "The Insect Comedy" (c. 1920) prophesied in parable form the destruction of man through totalitarianism and greed. His plays were immensely popular in Europe and the United States, less so in Czechoslovakia, where his travel writing and scholarly writing about Czech president Masaryk were preferred. During the 1930's Capek turned away from drama to write newspaper articles, short stories, and novels, including *The War With the Newts* (1936). When the Nazis threatened Prague, Capek espoused his nation's right to defend itself and wrote "The White Plague" (1937) and "The Mother" (1938), expressionist plays against facism. Refusing to leave Czechoslovakia, Capek died only months before the German occupation of Prague. Capek's utopian fantasies reflected in sometimes grotesque fashion the world he lived in. He predicted accurately the horrors of totalitarian society and the fate of its victims. Some critics have said that, by creating characters in the form of robots and insects, Capek was able to champion the cause of individual people without ever developing a well-rounded human character. *Biographical/critical sources: The Reader's Encyclopedia of World Drama,* McGraw, 1972.

*   *   *

CAPPON, Lester J(esse)   1900-1981

OBITUARY NOTICE: Born September 18, 1900, in Milwaukee, Wis.; died August 24, 1981, in Chicago, Ill. Archivist and author. Cappon was renowned for his expertise in Virginia history. He was director of the Institute of Early American History and Culture from 1955 to 1969. He compiled several bibliographies, including *Bibliography of Virginia History Since 1865,* and edited the two-volume *Adams-Jefferson Letters.* Obituaries and other sources: *American Authors and Books, 1640 to the Present Day,* 3rd revised edition, Crown, 1972; *Who's Who in America,* 39th edition, Marquis, 1976; *Directory of American Scholars,* Volume I: *History,* 7th edition, Bowker, 1978; *New York Times,* August 27, 1981; *AB Bookman's Weekly,* September 14, 1981.

*   *   *

CARCOPINO, Jerome   1881(?)-1970

OBITUARY NOTICE: Born c. 1881; died March 17, 1970, in Paris, France. Educator, historian specializing in ancient Rome, and author of works in his field. Carcopino taught at the Sorbonne and was French minister of education in 1940. He wrote several volumes on Roman life, including the best-seller *Daily Life in Ancient Rome.* Obituaries and other sources: *The Oxford Companion to French Literature,* corrected edition, Clarendon Press, 1966; *AB Bookman's Weekly,* April 6, 1970; *Publishers Weekly,* May 4, 1970.

*   *   *

CAREW, Rod(ney Cline)   1945-

PERSONAL: Born October 1, 1945, near Gatun, Panama; came to United States in 1962; son of Olga (French) Carew; married Marilynn Levy, October, 1970; children: Charryse, Stephanie, Michelle. *Education:* Attended public school in Manhattan, N.Y. *Religion:* Episcopalian. *Office:* 2000 State College Blvd., Anaheim, Calif. 92806.

CAREER: Professional baseball player. Signed with Minnesota Twins, Bloomington, Minn., 1964; played with teams in Melbourne, Fla., Orlando, Fla., and Wilson, N.C., 1964-66; Minnesota Twins, second baseman, 1967-76, first baseman, 1976-78; California Angels, Anaheim, Calif., first baseman, 1979—. Fund raiser for various charitable causes. *Awards, honors:* American League Rookie of the Year, 1967; American League batting titles, 1969, 1972-75, 1977-78; American League Most Valuable Player, 1977; Major League Player of the Year, 1977; American League All-Star Team, 1967-79; Roberto Clemente Award for community service; Medal of Honor from Panama.

WRITINGS: (With Ira Berkow) *Carew,* Simon & Schuster, 1979.

SIDELIGHTS: Described by some as "the best damn hitter in baseball," Carew was regarded throughout the 1970's as the baseball player most likely to compile a .400 season batting average. Carew's seven American League batting titles, earned from 1969 to 1978, demonstrate his uncontestable supremacy at bat, as does his career .334 batting average.

Carew developed an early interest in baseball, and although his family was poor, his mother always made sure he had baseball shoes and a glove. Coached by his uncle, Carew practiced hitting rag balls bound with tape, and began to develop other baseball skills while playing with little league teams in his native Panama. By the time he was thirteen, he was playing in a senior league as one of the best hitters.

The Carew family moved from Panama to New York City in 1962. Carew's part-time job prevented his participation in high school sports, but on weekends he played sandlot ball in parks near Yankee Stadium. Brought to the attention of a Minnesota Twins scout, Carew was given a chance to try out when the Twins arrived in New York to play a series with the Yankees.

The Twins signed Carew a month later. In Orlando, Florida, Carew was the first black player on the Minnesota farm team, which put him under extreme pressure. After less than three years in the minors, however, Carew became the Twins' starting second baseman. His quick, sharp eye and flexible stance helped him compile impressive batting statistics. Named American League Rookie of the Year in 1967, Carew batted .292 that season. In 1969 he won his first American League batting title, with an average of .332, and tied a major league record by stealing home seven times.

In 1970 a base runner crashed into Carew as he was pivoting at second base to turn a double play. The resulting torn knee cartilage kept him out of enough games to disqualify him for the batting title that year. The injury also left him wary of pivoting, which caused friction between Carew and Twins manager Bill Rigney despite the second baseman's determination to overcome his fear.

After the 1971 season Carew, seeking to strengthen his injured knee, contracted to play winter baseball in Aragua, Venezuela. In November, after sixteen games, he was asked to manage the Aragua team. As a playing manager Carew moved the team from fifth place to a tie for first place and eventually to the circuit championship. He led the circuit with a .355 batting average.

Carew continued to display his consistent hitting talents in the following years, collecting six more batting titles. He also proved to be a leader on and off the baseball field. He became known for playing despite injuries, for his tireless batting practice, and for his work with younger players on the team. He won the Roberto Clemente Award in the seventies for distinguished community service, which recognized both his public roles as fundraiser and his unpublicized visits to patients at the Mayo Clinic. Minnesota Twins manager Gene Mauch commented to *Time:* "As impressed as I am with Rod Carew the

hitter, Rod Carew the baseball player, I am more impressed with Rod Carew the man."

Carew switched to first base for the Twins in 1976 and that year led American League first basemen in double plays with one hundred forty-nine. Although he had previously played with the Minnesota team for a modest salary, he began to have contractual problems with the owner. Despite Carew's interest in remaining with the Twins, in 1978 his contract was about to expire. In September of that year Twins owner Calvin Griffith reportedly made racial slurs and criticized Carew's desire to stay with the Twins during a speech to the local Lion's Club. Soon after, Carew was traded for four players to the team of his choice, the California Angels, who accorded their new first baseman a five-year contract with a salary that marked Carew as a sports star.

The trade to the Angels did not affect Carew's hitting skills. He ended the 1980 season with a .331 batting average, having played in almost every game. Carew's 1981 season was interrupted by the players' strike and, late in the season, by shoulder injuries, yet Carew, for the thirteenth consecutive season, batted a .300 or higher season average. Picked as the starting first baseman for the American League All-Star team, he ended the 1981 season with a lifetime .332 average. In April, 1981, Carew stole home in a dramatic, ninth-inning, game-winning move. In September he stroked his two thousand five hundredth career hit, with career hits totalling twenty-five hundred and five by the end of the season. Carew speculated about his retirement in a 1979 *Sports Illustrated* feature: "I'd like to get 3,000 hits, . . . but if I don't make it in the next five years, I won't hang around chasing after them. I know everybody says it, but I'd like to finish on top. Right now, I just want to go out there and have fun, let baseball be the little boys' game it's supposed to be."

Carew's autobiography, *Carew,* appeared in 1979. A critic in *West Coast Review of Books* found that "Carew conceals nothing about his interracial marriage, his father, his own womanizing, or anything else which belongs in the story of his growth from a poor boy in Panama into a fine ballplayer and a fine man," and credited Carew with "a sensitivity that is both fresh and appealing."

BIOGRAPHICAL/CRITICAL SOURCES: New York Times, June 9, 1974, June 12, 1975; *Newsweek,* July 11, 1977; *Time,* July 18, 1977; *Sports Illustrated,* June 19, 1978, March 12, 1979; Rod Carew and Ira Berkow, *Carew,* Simon & Schuster, 1979; *Fortune,* March 12, 1979; *Chicago Tribune Book World,* July 8, 1979; *West Coast Review of Books,* September, 1979.*

—*Sketch by Diane L. Dupuis*

*   *   *

CAREWE, S. C.
See Du BREUIL, (Elizabeth) L(or)inda

*   *   *

CARLSON, Judith Lee   1952-
(Judy Lee)

PERSONAL: Born July 29, 1952, in Greenport, N.Y.; daughter of Arthur Garrell (a seafood wholesaler) and Shirley (Barton) Carlson. *Education:* Attended State University of New York College at Oswego, 1970-73, and State University of New York at Stony Brook, 1974-75. *Religion:* "Born-again Catholic." *Residence:* Seattle, Wash. *Agent:* George Finger, 317 18th Ave. E., Seattle, Wash. 98112. *Office:* 317 18th Ave. E., Seattle, Wash. 98112.

CAREER: Syracuse Post-Standard, Syracuse, N.Y., copy editor trainee, 1973-74; S. T. Preston & Son (mail order firm), Greenport, N.Y., copywriter, 1974-76; Edward Weiss Advertising, New York, N.Y., account executive, 1977-79; freelance writer, 1979—. *Member:* Authors Guild.

WRITINGS: (Under name Judy Lee) *Save Me!* (nonfiction), Doubleday, 1980.

WORK IN PROGRESS: Empty Spaces, on the relationship between an alcoholic mother and her daughter, examined after the mother's sudden, violent death.

SIDELIGHTS: Judith Carlson wrote: "*Save Me!* was an important first book for several reasons. It was an unsolicited manuscript accepted on speculation and written in three months. Perhaps the greatest motivation came from a close friend and fellow writer who told me that it would be absolutely impossible for me to do this. One of my major reasons for writing the book was to prove him wrong. I was lucky enough to do that and terribly delighted because I'd been planning the book for five years.

"I wasn't one of the few writers who strike it rich from a first book, but the experience changed my life and career goals. I am presently attending nursing school in Seattle, although I plan to continue writing. I don't live to write any more, and before I can complete another book I have to live a little. The book I'm slowly working on now has sprung up from the grief caused by my mother's death and the living through of many changes.

"I was lucky to have *Save Me!* published. At the same time I felt it was a very good book. I am now somewhat disappointed with its simplicity and its pace. Much of this is due to the time limit within which I had to finish the manuscript. In the future I want to work more on style and depth, perhaps doubling the length of *Empty Spaces.*

"First time around I was frightened by the idea of promoting my work and since the publisher wouldn't let me, due to the personal content of the book and the people who could have been hurt, I didn't have to worry about it too much. But I doubt I'll write again under a pseudonym. I would like to experience the pleasure of going on the road and speaking about my book."

*   *   *

CARMAN, (William) Bliss   1861-1929

BRIEF ENTRY: Born April 15, 1861, in Fredericton, New Brunswick, Canada; died June 8, 1929, in New Canaan, Conn.; buried in New Canaan, Conn. Canadian poet. Carman is best remembered for his early nature poems, which displayed his sensitive powers of observation, and his light romantic work, first collected in *Low Tide on the Grand Pre: A Book of Lyrics* (1893). He dedicated himself to poetry as a carefree bohemian in New York City, teaming up with Richard Hovey to produce a three-volume series beginning with *Songs From Vagabondia* (1894). The vagabond series marked a clear departure from the gentle Canadian poetry of the day, and the gypsy flavor of Carman's robust lyrics increased his popularity. In such essay collections as *The Kinship of Nature* (1906), Carman expressed his support of "unitrinianism," or education through the aesthetic forms of poetry, music, and dance. His later work, such as *Pipes of Pan* (1906), showed an increasing fascination with symbolism and musical language. In the year before his death, Carman came to be unofficially known as the poet laureate of Canada. *Biographical/critical sources: Twentieth Century Authors: A Biographical Dictionary of Modern Literature,* H. W.

Wilson, 1942; *The Oxford Companion to Canadian History and Literature,* Oxford University Press, 1967; George Woodcock, editor, *Colony and Confederation: Early Canadian Poets and Their Background,* University of British Columbia Press, 1974.

*   *   *

CARNELL, E. J.
See CARNELL, (Edward) John

*   *   *

CARNELL, (Edward) John   1912-1972
(E. J. Carnell)

OBITUARY NOTICE—See index for *CA* sketch: Born April 8, 1912, in Plumstead, London, England; died March 23, 1972, in London, England. Editor, literary agent, and author. One of the pioneers of British science fiction, Carnell owned and operated a literary agency specializing in the genre. He edited several science fiction anthologies, including *No Place Like Earth, Gateway to Tomorrow,* and *Weird Shadows From Beyond.* As the editor of the magazines *New Worlds in Science Fiction, Science Fantasy,* and *Science Fiction Adventures,* Carnell encouraged aspiring writers to compose science fiction. In 1964 the author began compiling the twenty-one-volume "New Writings in SF" series, which was completed in 1972. Obituaries and other sources: *AB Bookman's Weekly,* May 15, 1972.

*   *   *

CARPENTER, Duffy
See HURLEY, John J(erome)

*   *   *

CARRINGTON, Grant   1938-

PERSONAL: Born June 4, 1938, in New Haven, Conn.; son of Alfred Otis (a laborer) and Margaret Louise (a secretary; maiden name, Frey) Carrington. *Education:* Attended California Institute of Technology, 1956-57, and New Haven State Teachers College, 1957-59; New York University, B.A., 1962; attended George Washington University, 1962-63, and University of Maryland, 1965-68; University of Florida, M.A.T., 1970. *Politics:* "Anarchist." *Religion:* Seventh-Day Adventist. *Residence:* Baltimore, Md. *Agent:* Uto Prop, 56 Wuppertal 2, Werth 62, West Germany. *Office:* Westinghouse Electric Corp., P.O. Box 746, Baltimore, Md. 21203.

CAREER: Goddard Space Flight Center, Greenbelt, Md., aerospace technician, 1962-68; Naval Telecommunications Command, Washington, D.C., computer specialist, 1971-74; Alan's Gator Haus, Gainesville, Fla., delivery boy, 1975-76; University of Florida, Gainesville, computer programmer, 1976; Savannah River Ecology Laboratory, Aiken, S.C., computer programmer, 1977-80; Westinghouse Electric Corp., Baltimore, Md., computer programmer, 1980—. Gives poetry readings. *Member:* Writers Guild of America, Association of Computing Machinery. *Awards, honors:* Short story prize from Sandhills Writers Conference, 1971, for "Andromeda Unchained."

WRITINGS: Time's Fool (novel), Doubleday, 1981; *Down Among the Ipsies* (novel), Berkley Publishing, 1982.

Plays: "A World Not of Mine" (three-act), first produced in New Haven, Conn., at Southern Connecticut State College,

March 12, 1960; (with Thomas F. Montelone) "U.F.O.!" (three-act), first produced in Sandy Spring, Md., at Sandy Spring Community Theatre, March 11, 1977.

Work represented in anthologies, including *One Hundred Great Science Fiction Short Short Stories*, 1978, and *Black Holes*, 1978.

Author of songs, including "Lament for LaFarge," 1966, "Navajo!," 1969, and "And Then There Were None," 1972, all published in *Broadside*. Contributor of stories, poems, articles, and reviews to magazines and newspapers, including *Cavelier, Nickelodeon, Poetry Review, American Muse, Fantastic,* and *Nimrod*. Associate editor of *Amazing/Fantastic*, 1971-74; book review editor of *New Look*, 1975-76; contributing editor of *Eternity*, 1978—.

WORK IN PROGRESS: All the Instruments of War, a novel, publication by Berkley Publishing expected in 1983; "When the Summer's Gone," a play.

*   *   *

CARTER, Janet 1938-

PERSONAL: Born October 7, 1938, in Dallas, Tex.; daughter of John F. (a women's wear manufacturer) and Jean (Greenwood) Henson; married David M. Coker (in sales), 1958 (divorced, 1966); married Richard A. Carter (a singer), 1966 (divorced, 1976); married Micky C. Combs (a recruiter), 1980 (divorced, 1981); children: (second marriage) David Andrew, Christopher Allen and Richard Wesley (twins). *Education:* Attended University of Texas, 1974-75; East Texas State University, B.S., 1976. *Religion:* Methodist. *Home:* 11426 Lanewood Circle, Dallas, Tex. 75218. *Agent:* Ann Elmo Agency, Inc., 62 East 42nd St., New York, N.Y. 10017.

CAREER: Stitchendipity Art Needlework (designer, manufacturer, and merchandiser of needlepoint and crewel embroidery kits), Austin, Tex., owner, 1966-75; Literary Services Unlimited (editorial and word processing agency), Dallas, Tex., owner, 1975—. President of Greenville Jay-Cettes, 1963; founder of Hunt County Mothers of Twins Club, 1975; officer of Dallas Parents Without Partners, 1979. *Member:* Authors Guild, Romance Writers of America, Women in Communications.

WRITINGS: The Other Me (novel), Harcourt, 1976. Contributor of articles, stories, and poems to magazines, including *Seventeen, Creative Crafts, Christian Single, American Girl,* and newspapers. Editor of *Forthcoming*, 1976.

WORK IN PROGRESS: Another novel, "exploring women's searches for identity and self-definition within or outside of traditional role scripting." Research on early history of Dallas.

SIDELIGHTS: Janet Carter told *CA:* "I write to explain things to myself, of course, but further, I write to observe and describe other women's new self-acceptance and self-rejection as they teach themselves to deal with the sometimes overwhelming chaos resulting when they find themselves no longer willing to live with traditionally accepted truths. I hope I have outgrown the early stage of the shocked and strident voice and mellowed into a more direct search for the 'tickle of recognition.'"

BIOGRAPHICAL/CRITICAL SOURCES: Family Circle, June, 1969; Mary Bass Gibson, *The Family Circle Book of Careers at Home,* Regnery, 1971; *Greenville Herald Banner,* December 5, 1976; *Equal Times,* March, 1979.

CARY, (Arthur) Joyce (Lune) 1888-1957

BRIEF ENTRY: Born December 7, 1888, in Londonderry, Ireland; died March 29, 1957, in Oxford, England. Anglo-Irish novelist and critic. Considered one of the major contributors to the trilogy as a literary form, Cary is best known for his three novels of English domestic life; *Herself Surprised* (1948), *To Be a Pilgrim* (1949), and *The Horse's Mouth* (1950) were widely read and critically acclaimed. He also wrote a series of books based on his political and military experiences during his six-year residency in Africa. These novels, describing the cultural rituals and beliefs of Africa, include *Aissa Saved* (1930), *An American Visitor* (1933), *The African Witch* (1936), and *Mister Johnson* (1939). Cary's works are marked by an intense and keen sensitivity to the inner workings of people as they face everyday stresses, surprises, and hardships. *Biographical/critical sources: Current Biography,* Wilson, 1949; *Twentieth Century Writing: A Reader's Guide to Contemporary Literature,* Transatlantic, 1969; *Twentieth-Century Literary Criticism,* Volume 1, Gale, 1978.

*   *   *

CASALE, Ottavio M(ark) 1934-

PERSONAL: Born January 23, 1934, in Cleveland, Ohio; son of Ottavio and Natalina (D'Arienzo) Casale; married Linda L. Lenaway (a realtor), January 27, 1962; children: Laura, Elizabeth. *Education:* Kent State University, B.A., 1955; University of Michigan, M.A., 1959, Ph.D., 1965. *Politics:* Independent. *Home:* 815 Bryce Rd., Kent, Ohio 44240. *Office:* Department of English, Kent State University, Kent, Ohio 44242.

CAREER: Kent State University, Kent, Ohio, assistant professor, 1965-69, associate professor, 1969-79, professor of English, 1979—, dean of Honors College, 1981—. Senior Fulbright lecturer in Italy, 1971-72. *Military service:* U.S. Army, 1955-57. *Member:* Modern Language Association of America, Poe Studies Association. *Awards, honors:* Woodrow Wilson fellow, 1958-59; National Endowment for the Humanities grant, 1978.

WRITINGS: (Editor with Louis Paskoff) *The Kent Affair: Documents and Interpretations,* Houghton, 1971; (editor and translator) *A Leopardi Reader,* University of Illinois Press, 1981; (contributor) Joel Myerson, editor, *The Transcendentalists: A Review of Research and Criticism,* Modern Language Association of America, 1982; (contributor) George Stade, editor, *European Writers: The Romantic Century,* Scribner, 1982. Contributor to literature journals.

WORK IN PROGRESS: A study of Melville and Leopardi.

SIDELIGHTS: Casale wrote: "I am an Italian-American of peasant stock, fortunate enough to have a good education in literature and to be able to write on literary subjects (especially romanticism), which would have been beyond the pale for my people a generation ago. I am grateful."

*   *   *

CASBERG, Melvin Augustus 1909-

PERSONAL: Born July 10, 1909, in Poona, India; came to the United States in 1926; son of Samuel D. (an American missionary) and Jessie (a missionary; maiden name, Lively) Casberg; married Olive Van Valin, June 1, 1932; children: Sylvia Mae, Melvin A., Ronald Van. *Education:* Greenville College, A.B., 1930; St. Louis University, M.D., 1936. *Religion:* Presbyterian. *Home and office:* 955 Elk Grove Lane, Solvang, Calif. 93463.

CAREER: St. Louis City Hospital, St. Louis, Mo., intern, 1936-37, resident in surgery, 1937-40; Umri Mission Hospital, Berar, India, medical missionary of the Free Methodist Church and surgeon-in-chief, 1941-42; Harriman Jones Clinic Hospital, Long Beach, Calif., chief of surgery, 1946-48; St. Louis University, St. Louis, associate professor of surgery and dean of School of Medicine, 1949-52; U.S. Department of Defense, Washington, D.C., chairman of Armed Forces Medical Policy Council, 1952-53, assistant secretary of defense (health and medical), 1953-54; Dugway Proving Ground, Dugway, Utah, consultant to U.S. Army Chemical Corps, 1954-57; University of Texas, Austin, vice-president for medical affairs, 1965-69; Christian Medical College, Ludhiana, India, director and principal, 1959-62; Harriman Jones Medical Clinic, Long Beach, surgeon, 1963-75. Senior attending surgeon at Harbor General Hospital, 1947-48. Visiting professor at Howard University, 1952-54. Member of National Defense Executive Reserves, 1956-59, board of governors of American National Red Cross, 1953-54, California governor's emergency medical advisory committee, 1954-56, and medical advisory council of Medical International Cooperation (MEDICO), 1958, Meals for Millions, 1964-68, and George Russell Carr Foundation, 1963; vice-president of Thomas A. Dooley Foundation, 1962-68, and American Doctors (AMDOC), 1966; consultant to Surgeon General of the U.S. Army. *Military service:* U.S. Army, Medical Corps, 1942-46; served in North Africa and China-Burma-India theater; became lieutenant colonel.

MEMBER: American Board of Surgery (diplomate, 1946), American College of Surgeons (fellow), American Trauma Society (founding member), National Society for Medical Research (member of board of directors, 1950-56), American Medical Association (chairman of section on military medicine, 1952), Society of Medical Consultants to the Armed Forces, Air Force Clinical Surgeons Association, Association of Surgeons in India, Indian Association for the Advancement of Medical Education (member of executive council, 1960-62), Western Surgical Association, District of Columbia Medical Society, Los Angeles Surgical Society, Long Beach Surgical Society, Los Angeles Academy of Medicine (fellow; member of board of directors, 1968-73; president, 1971-72), Long Beach Medical Association (president, 1972), Sigma Xi, Alpha Omega Alpha, Alpha Epsilon Delta. *Awards, honors:* LL.D. from Westminster College, Fulton, Mo., 1951, and Los Angeles Pacific College, 1964; gold medal of honor from Military Medical Service of France, 1953; civilian award from U.S. Department of Defense, 1954; D.Sc. from Greenville College, 1958.

*WRITINGS—*All suspense novels; all published by Strawberry Hill: *Death Stalks the Punjab,* 1981; *Five Rivers to Death,* 1981; *Dowry of Death,* 1982. Contributor to education and scientific journals. Member of editorial board of *Journal of Medical Education,* 1958-60, and *Indian Journal of Medical Education,* 1960-62.

SIDELIGHTS: Casberg wrote: "My professional education culminated in the specialty of surgery. I have been seduced from clinical medicine a number of times into medical education and administration, functioning as the dean of medical colleges in this country and India, and also for a period as the medical alter ego of the secretary of defense at the appointment of President Eisenhower.

"Having spent the greater part of my professional career in the scientific discipline, it might have seemed natural for me on retirement to continue writing within the confines of science. However, at that crucial stage of my life, the right brain mutinied and took over the left brain, insisting (of all things) that two plus two might not equal four. With this release from the practical confines of a mind steeped in science, I am finding a delightfully stimulating and refreshing new vocation, the fantasy of creative fiction.

"Mystery stories have always intrigued me, so I opted for this field of writing, with a setting in the Far East. My childhood, prior to entering college in the United States, had been lived in India where my parents spent some thirty years as missionaries. I knew the people, their language, their customs and geography, having attended grade school in the Himalayas and high school in south India. Often I have been asked about what research is required by my stories. Here is where those of my age, having stored a wealth of information through the years, have certain advantages in writing; practically all preparation for the mysteries is done seated at my desk.

"After reading my first manuscript, the publisher of Strawberry Hill Press asked that I write a trilogy of mysteries, all taking place in the northwestern provinces of India, and all with the same Indian detective. It has been my purpose to write more than just another mystery and to weave into the stories the tapestry of the Indian people, customs, and geography. I have been happy with the correspondence from India, where the readers have complimented me on the authenticity of *Death Stalks the Punjab.*"

* * *

CASE, Jack Gaylord   1918(?)-1970

OBITUARY NOTICE: Born c. 1918; died November 13, 1970, in Scarsdale, N.Y. Editor of collegiate textbooks for Macmillan Co. Obituaries and other sources: *Publishers Weekly,* December 14, 1970.

* * *

CASEY, Jane Barnes   1942-
(Jane Barnes)

PERSONAL: Born September 6, 1942, in New York, N.Y.; daughter of Charles Tracy and Janet (White) Barnes; married John Casey, June 17, 1967 (separated); children: Maud, Eleanor. *Education:* Sarah Lawrence College, B.A., 1964; University of Iowa, M.F.A., 1968. *Home:* 615F Madison Ave., Charlottesville, Va. 22903. *Agent:* Wendy Lipkind Agency, 225 East 57th St., New York, N.Y. 10022.

CAREER: University of Virginia, Charlottesville, part-time lecturer in English, 1980—. *Member:* Authors Guild. *Awards, honors:* Grant from National Endowment for the Arts, 1976-77.

*WRITINGS—*Under name Jane Barnes: *I, Krupskay* (novel), Houghton, 1974; *Double Lives* (novel), Doubleday, 1981. Contributor of articles and stories to magazines, including *Shenandoah, Mademoiselle, Denver Quarterly,* and *Virginia Quarterly Review.*

* * *

CASEY, Patrick
See THURMAN, Wallace

* * *

CASTLE, Edgar Bradshaw   1897-1973

OBITUARY NOTICE: Educator and author of works on education, including *Principles of Education for Teachers in Af-*

rica, Principles of Education for Teachers in India, and *The Teacher.* Obituaries and other sources: *AB Bookman's Weekly,* October 15, 1973.

* * *

CATHER, Willa (Sibert)   1873-1947

BRIEF ENTRY: Born December 7, 1873, in Gore, Va.; died of a cerebral hemorrhage, April 24, 1947, in New York, N.Y. American novelist and poet. Cather was a journalist for several years before leaving that profession to become an English teacher and then managing editor of *McClure's Magazine.* She enjoyed her first literary success with the novel *O Pioneers!* (1913). Cather, who grew up in Nebraska among immigrant farmers, based this first novel and many subsequent works on the farm and prairie scenes of her childhood. Perhaps best known for *My Antonia* (1918), *The Professor's House* (1925), and *Death Comes for the Archbishop* (1927), Cather is recognized as a stoic, moral writer who did not forsake traditional values while writing in an age of changing standards. In 1922 she won the Pulitzer Prize for *One of Ours,* one of her less prominent books. *Residence:* New York, N.Y. *Biographical/critical sources: Twentieth Century Authors: A Biographical Dictionary of Modern Literature,* H. W. Wilson, 1942, 1st supplement, 1955; *Twentieth Century Writing: A Reader's Guide to Contemporary Literature,* Transatlantic, 1969; *Twentieth-Century Literary Criticism,* Volume 1, Gale, 1978.

* * *

CAVAFY, C(onstantine) P(eter)
See KAVAFIS, Konstantinos Petrou

* * *

CAVANAGH, Helen (Carol)   1939-

PERSONAL: Born December 4, 1939, in Quincy, Mass.; daughter of Wapaa Albert and Blanche Holmes (Magnant) Hanninen; married Lawrence Joseph Cavanagh (a corrections officer), June 18, 1960; children: Christopher, Lawrence Joseph, Jr., Patrick, Carin. *Education:* Attended Bay Path Junior College, 1957-58. *Home and office:* 29 Burgess Ave., Spotswood, N.J. 08884. *Agent:* Jay Garon-Brooke Associates, Inc., 415 Central Park W., New York, N.Y. 10025.

CAREER: Writer, Boston, Mass., clerk, 1958-59; WEEI-Radio, Boston, secretary, 1959; *Sentinel,* East Brunswick, N.J., reporter, feature writer, and author of column, "Telling It Like It Is," 1970-78; free-lance writer, 1978—. Member of Spotswood Planning and Zoning Board; town historian; director of local Writer's Workshop. Creative writing teacher at Old Bridge Community School. *Awards, honors:* Award from New Jersey Institute of Technology, 1979, for *Second Best* and *Honey.*

WRITINGS—For young adults; novels, except as noted; all published by Scholastic Book Services: *Second Best,* 1979; *Honey,* 1979; *Superflirt,* 1980; *The Easiest Way,* 1980; *My Day By Day Diary With Special Poems for Me,* 1980; *Angelface,* 1981; *Summer Girl,* 1982. Contributor of stories and poems to magazines and newspapers, including *True Romances, Down East,* and *Co-Ed.*

WORK IN PROGRESS: Driftwood, a novel for contemporary women; *Daughter of the Dawn,* a historical romance for adults; *The Apricot Idea,* psychological suspense novel for adults; *A Place for Me,* a novel for young adults for Scholastic Book Services.

SIDELIGHTS: Helen Cavanagh told *CA:* "It's not just that I remember what it's like to be sixteen years old, or twelve; in

my heart I still am! Just as I can look ahead and be eighty, sometimes I can go way back to when I was a year and a half. I can also be my true age when I have to be.

"Of course, what's true and what feels true gets all mixed together whenever I sit down to write. Who knows why? Maybe because I'm a mixture myself: part Finn, part French, part New England yankee. Perhaps too because I'm left-handed (lefties often take liberties with logic). Very possibly it's because I gazed out the window too much when I should have been paying attention to the teacher.

"Over the years I've had many jobs, including mother's helper, waitress, salesperson, secretary, model, toy store clerk, and newspaper reporter and columnist. I didn't realize it at the time, but these experiences would be valuable when I began to write steadily.

"In *Second Best,* I dealt with Shelly's struggles with jealousy and self-doubt, Honey's problems with her mother and father, and Superflirt Susan's confusion. Also, Abbie in *The Easiest Way* must struggle and suffer, and so does Colleen in a new book. All these girls are me, and I feel their pain, but in my books *we* always win and learn a little more about ourselves, and become better people. If their experiences, the events of their lives are not exactly true when I write them, they eventually become true. Who's to say that's not the same, or even closer to the truth? I think it is, but what do I know? I'm a leftie and I still look out the window too much."

* * *

CAZEAU, Charles J(ay)   1931-

PERSONAL: Born June 25, 1931, in Rochester, N.Y.; son of Floyd A. (a musician) and Nan M. (an artist; maiden name, Barbehenn) Cazeau; married Janet G. Donovan (a therapist), August 11, 1960 (died November, 1971); children: Sharon Lee, Suzanne Carroll. *Education:* University of Notre Dame, B.S., 1954; Florida State University, M.S., 1955; attended Virginia Polytechnic Institute; University of North Carolina, Ph.D., 1962. *Home:* 300 Paradise Rd., East Amherst, N.Y. 14051. *Office:* Department of Geological Sciences, State University of New York at Buffalo, Buffalo, N.Y. 14226.

CAREER: Exxon Corp., Houston, Tex., geologist, 1955-58; Clemson University, Clemson, S.C., assistant professor of geology, 1960-63; State University of New York at Buffalo, associate professor of geology, 1963—. President of CPF Associates. Member of Scientific Committee for Investigating Claims of the Paranormal. *Member:* American Association of Petroleum Geologists, Society of Economic Paleontologists and Mineralogists, National Association of Geology Teachers, Carolina Geological Society, Sigma Xi.

WRITINGS: Physical Geology Laboratory Manual, Kendall-Hunt, 1971, 2nd edition, 1974; *Earthquakes* (juvenile), Follett, 1975; *Physical Geology,* Harper, 1975; *Exploring the Unknown,* Plenum, 1979; *Magic and the Will to Believe,* Plenum, 1982. Author of column "Let's Explore the Unknown." Contributor to scientific journals and museum bulletins.

WORK IN PROGRESS: Science, Reason, and Religion, publication by Plenum expected in 1984.

SIDELIGHTS: "Money is a great inspiration in writing," Cazeau told *CA,* "but I also believe there is a need for scientists to tell the man on the street in simple language just what he does and why, and to answer the pseudoscientists who delude the public with drivel.

"Every man should know how to change diapers. I changed many thousands. Despite this psychological advantage, my kids are still not certain that I am a great man after all. I'm not certain either."

* * *

CHAMBERS, Lenoir 1891-1970

OBITUARY NOTICE: Born December 26, 1891, in Charlotte, N.C.; died January 10, 1970, in Norfolk, Va. Journalist and author of the biography *Stonewall Jackson.* Chambers edited the *Norfolk Ledger-Dispatcher* from 1944 to 1950 and the *Virginian-Pilot* from 1950 to 1962. In 1960 he received a Pulitzer Prize for his editorials on segregation. Obituaries and other sources: *Publishers Weekly,* February 9, 1970; *Who Was Who in America, With World Notables,* Volume V: *1969-1973,* Marquis, 1973.

* * *

CHAMBERTIN, Ilya
See von BLOCK, Bela W(illiam)

* * *

CHAMPERNOWNE, David (Gawen) 1912-

PERSONAL: Born July 9, 1912, in Oxford, England; son of F. G. (bursar of Keble College, Oxford) and Isabel Mary (Rashleigh) Champernowne; married Wilhelmina Dullaert, 1948; children: two sons. *Education:* Attended Winchester College, 1925-31; King's College, Cambridge, M.A. (with first class honors), 1938. *Home:* 25 Worts Causeway, Cambridge CB1 4RJ, England. *Office:* Trinity College, Cambridge University, Cambridge, England.

CAREER: University of London, London School of Economics and Political Science, London, England, assistant lecturer in economics and statistics, 1936-38; Cambridge University, Cambridge, England, lecturer in statistics and fellow of Trinity College, 1938-40; Prime Minister's Statistical Department, London, England, assistant, 1940-41; Ministry of Aircraft Production, London, assistant director of programs, 1941-45; Oxford University, Oxford, England, director of Institute of Statistics, 1945-48, professor of statistics, 1948-59, fellow of Nuffield College, 1945-49; Cambridge University, reader, 1959-70, professor of economics and statistics, 1970-78, professor emeritus, 1978—, fellow of Trinity College. *Member:* British Academy (fellow), Royal Economics Society (fellow), Oxford Political Economy Club.

WRITINGS: Uncertainty and Estimation in Economics, three volumes, Holden-Day, 1969; *The Distribution of Income Between Persons,* Cambridge University Press, 1973. Co-editor of *Economic Journal of the Royal Economic Society,* 1971—.

WORK IN PROGRESS: A book about economic inequality and distribution of income, with F. A. Cowell.

* * *

CHANDLER, Howard 1915(?)-1981

OBITUARY NOTICE: Born c. 1915; died of a heart attack, August 17, 1981, in Sebastopol, Calif. Founder of Chandler Publishing during the 1950's. Chandler was also co-founder of Chandler & Sharp Publishers. Obituaries and other sources: *Publishers Weekly,* September 25, 1981.

* * *

CHANDLER, Raymond 1888-1959

BRIEF ENTRY: Born July 23, 1888, in Chicago, Ill.; died March 26, 1959, in La Jolla, Calif. Often recognized with Dashiel Hammett as one of the best writers of hard-boiled whodunits, Chandler enjoyed instant success with the publication of his first novel, *The Big Sleep,* in 1939. In that work, Chandler introduced the character Philip Marlowe, a tough, witty, and honorable detective who is concerned with saving society from moral corruption. Marlowe is the protagonist of Chandler's subsequent crime novels, including *Farewell, My Lovely* (1940), *The Lady in the Lake* (1943), *The Simple Art of Murder* (1950), and *The Long Goodbye* (1954). *Biographical/critical sources: Current Biography,* Wilson, 1946; *Twentieth Century Authors: A Biographical Dictionary of Modern Literature,* 1st supplement, H. W. Wilson, 1955; *Twentieth Century Writing: A Reader's Guide to Contemporary Literature,* Transatlantic, 1969; *Twentieth-Century Literary Criticism,* Volume 1, Gale, 1978.

* * *

CHAPIN, Harry (Forster) 1942-1981

OBITUARY NOTICE: Born December 7, 1942, in New York, N.Y.; died in an automobile accident, July 16, 1981, in Jericho, Long Island, N.Y. Singer, musician, social activist, composer, and poet. Chapin created a narrative musical style called the "story-song," typified by his first hit recording, "Taxi," in 1972. He enjoyed subsequent successes with songs such as "Cat's in the Cradle," "W.O.L.D.," and "Sequel to Taxi." In addition to his musical compositions, Chapin issued a volume of poetry, *Looking . . . Seeing.* The singer actively worked for various social causes, performing more than one hundred benefit concerts per year for various organizations. Chapin's main concern was world hunger, and he frequently lobbied in Washington, fighting for programs to alleviate starvation in the United States and abroad. Obituaries and other sources: *Rock On: The Illustrated Encyclopedia of Rock n' Roll,* Volume II: *The Modern Years, 1964-Present,* Crowell, 1978; *New York Times,* July 17, 1981; *Time,* July 27, 1981; *Rolling Stone,* September 3, 1981.

* * *

CHAPMAN, John Jay 1862-1933

BRIEF ENTRY: Born March 2, 1862, in New York, N.Y.; died November 4, 1933. American lawyer, poet, playwright, and essayist. Considered one of the best, though often unsung, writers of the turn of the century, Chapman was a lawyer for ten years before leaving law to pursue a literary career. His books of prose and essays express his passionate views on other literary figures, politicians, and American events of his time. Among his works are *Emerson, and Other Essays* (1898), *William Lloyd Garrison* (1913), *Memories and Milestones* (1915), and *Greek Genius, and Other Essays* (1915). In addition Chapman wrote numerous plays, including *The Treason and Death of Benedict Arnold* (1910). *Biographical/critical sources: Concise Dictionary of American Biography,* Scribner, 1964; *Twentieth Century Authors: A Biographical Dictionary of Modern Literature,* H. W. Wilson, 1942.

* * *

CHAPMAN, Ruth 1912(?)-1979

OBITUARY NOTICE: Born c. 1912; died August 28, 1979, in Brattleboro, Vt. Actress and editor for Holt, Rinehart & Winston of works such as *Design and Painting for the Theatre* and *The Professional Journalist.* Obituaries and other sources: *Publishers Weekly,* October 1, 1979.

CHAPPELL, Helen 1947-
(Rebecca Baldwin)

PERSONAL: Born May 1, 1947, in Pennsylvania; daughter of Leslie Edward (a physician) and Helen (Brukart) Chappell; divorced. *Education:* Franconia College, B.A., 1969; attended School of Visual Arts, 1971-73, and New School for Social Research, 1975. *Politics:* Democrat. *Religion:* Episcopalian. *Home address:* P.O. Box 314, Oxford, Md. 21662. *Agent:* Joseph Elder, Joseph Elder Agency, 150 West 87th St., New York, N.Y. 10025. *Office:* Joseph Elder Agency, 150 West 87th St., New York, N.Y. 10025.

CAREER: Associated with the Joseph Elder Agency in New York, N.Y. *Member:* National Organization for Women. *Awards, honors:* Bread Loaf Writers Conference scholar, 1975.

WRITINGS: The Waxing Moon, Links, 1974; *All Things in Their Season,* Delacorte, 1981.

Historical novels; under pseudonym Rebecca Baldwin: *A Gentleman From Philadelphia,* Fawcett, 1977; *The Cassandra Knot,* Fawcett, 1979; *Peerless Theodosia,* Fawcett, 1979; *A Sanditon Quadrille,* Fawcett, 1980; *The Match-Makers,* Fawcett, 1980; *A Season Abroad,* Fawcett, 1981; *The Dollar Duchess,* Fawcett, 1981.

WORK IN PROGRESS: Drawing Blood, a novel, publication expected in 1982; a fantasy novel, publication expected, in 1983; a historical novel, publication expected in 1983; "Basket Cases," a screenplay, completion expected in 1983.

SIDELIGHTS: Helen Chappell commented: "I write fiction because I have no other vocation in life. I tend to concentrate, in my serious work, on the world in microcosm. After a long apprenticeship as a pulp writer of everything from television to science fiction, I feel competent to write, not only 'serious' fiction, but also screenplays. My ultimate fantasy is directing a film I've written."

*   *   *

CHARLES, Gordon H(ull) 1920-
(Charles Hull)

PERSONAL: Born August 23, 1920, in Salisbury, N.C.; son of Earl F. (a railway clerk) and Myrtle C. (a secretary; maiden name, Hull) Charles; married Dorothy V. Hahnenberg (a sales clerk), August 23, 1947; children: Ruthann Charles Kalohn, Donald, William, Janice Charles Vondra. *Education:* Chapin Business School, graduated, 1940. *Politics:* Independent. *Religion:* Methodist. *Home:* 1171 North Pioneer Rd., Honor, Mich. 49640. *Office address:* P.O. Box 295, Honor, Mich. 49640.

CAREER: WTCM-Radio, Traverse City, Mich., announcer, 1945-52; *Traverse City Record-Eagle,* Traverse City, outdoor editor, 1952-61; South Dakota Department of Game, Fish, and Parks, Pierre, information and education chief and editor of *South Dakota Conservation Digest,* 1961-65; *Michigan Out-of-Doors,* Lansing, editor, 1965-70; *Traverse City Record-Eagle,* outdoor editor, 1970—. Owner of Outdoor/Travel Features Syndicate, 1970—. *Military service:* U.S. Army, Radio Intelligence, 1942-45.

MEMBER: Outdoor Writers Association of America, Society of American Travel Writers (member of free-lance council, 1980—), Midwest Travel Writers Association, Association of Great Lakes Outdoor Writers, Michigan Outdoor Writers Association (president, 1960-61). *Awards, honors:* Magazine

awards from American Association for Conservation Information, 1961-65, for excellence of features and layout; conservation writing awards from Michigan Outdoor Writers Association, 1971-73, 1978-80, for best conservation coverage of the year; third place feature writing award from United Press International, 1974, for photo feature on conservation; feature writing award from Safari Club International, 1975, for "Hunters Were the First Conservationists"; feature writing award from Midwest Travel Writers Association, 1975, for "Sugar Island," a photo feature; special citations from Michigan Legislature, 1976, for National Trout King honors, and 1980, for thirty-five years of journalistic excellence; feature photography award from Society of American Travel Writers for "Morocco Dancers."

WRITINGS: Pocket Field Guide to Nature, Stackpole, 1959; *Game Birds and Animals of South Dakota,* South Dakota Department of Game, Fish, and Parks, 1964; *Guide to Sleeping Bear Dunes National Lakeshore,* Gateway Publishing, 1975. Author of "Outdoors With Gordie," a column syndicated by Outdoor/Travel Features Syndicate to about twenty Michigan newspapers. Contributor of more than three thousand articles to more than four hundred magazines and newspapers, sometimes under pseudonym Charles Hull. Editor of *Michigan Sportsman,* 1980—.

WORK IN PROGRESS: History of Pigeon River Country (Michigan), publication expected in 1982.

SIDELIGHTS: Charles commented: "Most of my writing reflects my high interest in conservation subjects, although I am not a strict 'environmentalist,' believing instead in the wise use of all natural resources (there is a vast difference). I also write extensively on nature subjects, wildlife, hunting, fishing, and other outdoor recreation. Stories from travels throughout North America, South America, the Caribbean, Africa, New Zealand, Europe, and Asia will be included in future writings. I prefer my own photography, using it as a vehicle to build on."

*   *   *

CHASE, Naomi Feigelson 1932-
(Naomi Feigelson)

PERSONAL: Born May 26, 1932, in Pittsburgh, Pa.; daughter of Henry (a judge) and Rachel (Savage) Ellenbogen; married Eugene B. Feigelson (a psychoanalyst), August 31, 1959 (divorced January, 1966); married Gordon Chase (died January, 1981); children: (first marriage) Elizabeth, Jonathan. *Education:* Attended Bryn Mawr College, 1950-52; Radcliffe College, B.A. (magna cum laude), 1954; Brandeis University, M.A., 1956; doctoral study at Columbia University, 1958. *Religion:* Jewish. *Home:* 26 Campbell Park, Somerville, Mass. 02144. *Agent:* Joan Daves, 59 East 54th St., New York, N.Y. 10022.

CAREER: McKeesport Daily News, McKeesport, Pa., staff member, summers, 1949-50; Harbridge House, Cambridge, Mass., editor, 1955-56; high school English teacher in Washington, D.C., 1959; American Association of University Women, Washington, D.C., assistant to director of publications, 1959-61; National Broadcasting Co. (NBC-TV), New York City, publicity representative for "Today," "Children's Theater," and news documentaries, 1967; College for Human Services, New York City, special assistant to director, 1968; New York City Department of Consumer Affairs, New York City, director of press and public information, 1969-70; New York City Health Services Administration, New York City, director of press and public information, 1971-72; State of Massachusetts, Boston, member of governor's program and policy staff, 1974-75; Massachusetts Council on the Arts and Humanities, Boston, supervisor of public relations and consultant on press and public information, 1975-77; Harvard University, Cambridge, extension instructor in writing, 1978-79; Massachusetts Department of Social Services, Boston, writer and consultant in program and media for foster care, adoptions, and day care, 1981—. Organizer of (and participant in) poetry and prose readings. *Member:* Poets and Writers. *Awards, honors:* Grants from Ford Foundation, 1972-73 and 1977-78, and Maurice Falk Medical Foundation, 1976-77; fellow of MacDowell Colony, 1979 and 1981.

WRITINGS: (Under name Naomi Feigelson) *The Underground Revolution: Hippies, Yippies, and Others*, Funk, 1970; *A Child Is Being Beaten: Violence Against Children in Public and Private Places*, Holt, 1975; *Listening for Water* (poems), Archival Press, 1980; *The Myth of the Saved Child*, Pantheon, 1981. Reporter for *Village Voice*, 1966-74. Contributor of articles, poems, and stories to magazines, including *New York, Medical World News, Ms., Greenfield Review, Yankee*, and *Dun's Review*, and newspapers.

* * *

CHAYEFSKY, Paddy   1923-1981

OBITUARY NOTICE—See index for *CA* sketch: Born January 29, 1923, in the Bronx, N.Y.; died of cancer, August 1, 1981, in Manhattan, N. Y. Playwright and screenwriter. Chayefsky began writing while recovering from an injury, for which he received a Purple Heart, sustained when he stepped on a land mine during World War II. Named Sidney at birth, Chayefsky was dubbed "Paddy" during the war because, though he was Jewish, he asked to attend Mass rather than serve K. P. duty. Using his ethnic heritage as a background for many of his works, the writer illustrated the ordinary man's search for love and happiness. With a sympathetic and good-humored view of his characters, he wrote about victims unable to express themselves. Often they were portraits of people he knew as a youngster; usually they were realistic characters "caught," he said, "in the decline of their society." Chayefsky's works reflected changing society through a satiric viewpoint. "It's the world that's gone nuts, not me," he wrote. "It's the world that's turned into a satire." He was also known for his naturalistic dialogue, which flowed like a tape recording, and for his use of catch phrases like "I'm mad as hell, and I'm not taking it anymore," from the film "Network." At first a gag writer, Chayefsky became a radio and television scriptwriter. "Marty," possibly his most popular work, was originally the television story of a fat, lonely, unhappy butcher. His other television scripts, such as "The Mother," "Holiday Song," and "The Big Deal," proved that television could be a medium for serious drama. Adapted into a motion picture that won the grand prize at the Cannes Film Festival, "Marty" earned its writer an Academy Award as did the films "The Hospital" and "Network." Chayefsky's other film credits include "As Young as You Feel," "The Bachelor Party," and "Altered States." His plays include "Gideon" and "The Latent Homosexual." Obituaries and other sources: *Washington Post*, August 2, 1981; *New York Times*, August 2, 1981, August 3, 1981; *Chicago Tribune*, August 3, 1981; *London Times*, August 3, 1981; *Time*, August 10, 1981; *Newsweek*, August 10, 1981.

* * *

CHAYEFSKY, Sidney
See CHAYEFSKY, Paddy

CHEKHONTE, Antosha
See CHEKHOV, Anton (Pavlovich)

* * *

CHEKHOV, Anton (Pavlovich)   1860-1904
(A Man Without a Spleen, Antosha Chekhonte, My Brother's Brother)

BRIEF ENTRY: Born January 17, 1860, in Taganrog, Russia (now U.S.S.R.); died of tuberculosis, July 2, 1904, in Badenweiler, Germany (now West Germany); buried in Moscow, U.S.S.R. Russian physician, short story writer, and playwright. He was a trained physician but rarely practiced medicine, preferring instead to pursue the literary career he began while still a student at Moscow University. His first story, "A Letter to a Learned Friend," was published in 1880, and by 1887 he had written more than six hundred stories and humorous sketches. Chekhov dismissed most of these early writings as "thoughtless and frivolous," but the best of them show a writer sensitive to the underlying social and psychological forces of life. Between 1886 and 1889 he undertook an intense search for a world view and adopted Leo Tolstoy's ideas on morality, particularly his doctrine of nonresistance to evil. Among his "Tolstoian stories" are "The Cossack" (1887), "The Meeting" (1887), and "The Shoemaker and the Devil" (1888). In 1890 Chekhov made an arduous journey to the penal colony on Sakhalin Island and concluded that nonresistance was an inadequate response to evil and human misery. The period following his disillusionment with Tolstoian ideals was one of artistic emancipation and maturity for Chekhov. The lost opportunities of life, the isolation of the individual, and the hopeless plight of Russia's peasantry are subjects that dominate his later work, delivered in the sombre, melancholic tones that many critics construe as evidence of the author's pessimistic viewpoint. Such stories as "Ward No. 6" (1892), "The House With the Attic" (1896), "Peasants" (1897), "Gooseberries" (1898), "The Lady With the Lapdog" (1899), and "The Betrothed" (1903) reveal a writer at the height of his powers. Chekhov's great plays also date from this period and include "The Seagull" (1896), "Uncle Vanya" (1897), "The Three Sisters" (1901), and "The Cherry Orchard" (1903). Each of these plays is considered a dramatic masterpiece and contains Chekhov's deepest thoughts on the meaning and values of life. *Biographical/critical sources:* W. H. Bruford, *Anton Chekhov*, Yale University Press, 1957; *Cyclopedia of World Literature*, Harper, 1958; Ronald Hingley, *Chekhov: A Biographical and Critical Study*, revised edition, Allen & Unwin, 1966; *Encyclopedia of World Literature in the Twentieth Century*, updated edition, Ungar, 1967; *Twentieth-Century Literary Criticism*, Volume 3, Gale, 1980.

* * *

CHENG, F.T.
See CHENG, Tien-hsi

* * *

CHENG, Tien-hsi   1884-1970
(F. T. Cheng)

OBITUARY NOTICE: Born in 1884; died January 31, 1970. Diplomat and author of books on the art, civilization, and laws of China. His works include *Civilization and Art of China* and *East and West: Episodes in a Sixty Years' Journey*. Obituaries and other sources: *Asiatic Review,* October 7, 1946; *AB Bookman's Weekly,* March 2, 1970.

* * *

CHESTERTON, G(ilbert) K(eith)   1874-1936

BRIEF ENTRY: Born May 29, 1874, in Campden Hill, London, England; died June 14, 1936, in Beaconsfield, Buckinghamshire, England. English novelist, poet, critic, essayist, journalist, biographer, historian, and short story writer. Attracted to Catholicism from an early age, Chesterton was received into the Roman Catholic Church in 1922, and his writings before and after his conversion tend to reflect Catholic values. As a champion of the orthodoxy, he wrote many essays and books on contemporary religious topics and religious philosophy, as well as biographies of St. Francis of Assisi and St. Thomas Aquinas. Although Chesterton is remembered for his witty and exuberant essays, his fantasy novel, *The Man Who Was Thursday: A Nightmare* (1908), and his two serious long poems, *The Ballad of the White Horse* (1911) and *Lepanto* (1915), his popular reputation rests on the Father Brown stories. This series of detective stories depicts an absent-minded, eccentric, but lovable priest with an analytical mind similar to that of Sherlock Holmes. Originally appearing as five separate volumes between 1911 and 1935, the stories were published in a collected edition, *The Father Brown Stories,* in 1929. Among Chesterton's other works are *Orthodoxy* (1910), *The Victorian Age in Literature* (1913), *Autobiography* (1936), and *The Paradoxes of Mr. Pond* (1936). *Residence:* Top Meadow, Beaconsfield, Buckinghamshire, England. *Biographical/critical sources: The Concise Encyclopedia of Modern World Literature,* Hutchinson, 1963; *Encyclopedia of World Literature in the Twentieth Century,* updated edition, Ungar, 1967; *Twentieth Century Writing: A Reader's Guide to Contemporary Literature,* Transatlantic, 1969; *Webster's New World Companion to English and American Literature,* World Publishing, 1973; *Twentieth-Century Literary Criticism,* Volume 1, Gale, 1978.

* * *

CHIAROMONTE, Nicola   ?-1972

OBITUARY NOTICE: Died January 18, 1972, in Rome, Italy. Editor and author. Chiaromonte was a frequent contributor to periodicals such as *Partisan Review* and *Dissent.* For twelve years he helped edit *Tempo Presente.* He also wrote books on literature. Obituaries and other sources: *AB Bookman's Weekly,* March 6, 1972.

* * *

CHIESA, Francesco   1871(?)-1973

OBITUARY NOTICE: Born c. 1871; died in 1973 in Lugano, Switzerland. Author best known for *Tempo di Marzo,* his semi-autobiographical novel that was praised for its psychological insight. Chiesa also wrote poetry and short stories. Obituaries and other sources: *Columbia Dictionary of Modern European Literature,* Columbia University Press, 1947; *Encyclopedia of World Literature in the Twentieth Century,* updated edition, Ungar, 1967; *Everyman's Dictionary of European Writers,* Dutton, 1968; *Cassell's Encyclopaedia of World Literature,* revised edition, Morrow, 1973; *AB Bookman's Weekly,* October 1, 1973.

* * *

CHINARD, Gilbert   1882(?)-1972

OBITUARY NOTICE: Born c. 1882 in France; died February 8, 1972, in Princeton, N.J. Educator and author. Chinard was known for his expertise on Franco-American cultural relations. He also wrote biographies of Thomas Jefferson, Benjamin Franklin, and John Adams. Obituaries and other sources: *The Oxford Companion to American Literature,* 4th edition, Oxford University Press, 1965; *American Authors and Books, 1640 to the Present Day,* 3rd revised edition, Crown, 1972; *AB Bookman's Weekly,* February 28, 1972.

* * *

CHIPMAN, John S(omerset)   1926-

PERSONAL: Born June 28, 1926, in Montreal, Quebec, Canada; son of Warwick Fielding (a lawyer, diplomat, and poet) and Mary Somerset (Aikins) Chipman; married Margaret Ann Ellefson, June 24, 1960; children: Thomas Noel, Timothy Warwick. *Education:* Attended University of Chile, 1943-44; McGill University, B.A., 1947, M.A., 1948; Johns Hopkins University, Ph.D., 1951. *Home:* 2121 West 49th St., Minneapolis, Minn. 55409. *Office:* Department of Economics, University of Minnesota, 1122 Business Administration Building, 271 19th Ave. S., Minneapolis, Minn. 55455.

CAREER: Harvard University, Cambridge, Mass., assistant professor of economics, 1951-55; University of Minnesota, Minneapolis, associate professor, 1955-60, professor of economics, 1960-81, Regents' Professor of Economics, 1981—. Visiting professor at Harvard University, 1966-67; guest professor at Institute for Advanced Studies, Vienna, Austria, 1970 and 1972. *Member:* American Economic Association, American Statistical Association (fellow), American Academy of Arts and Sciences (fellow), Canadian Economic Association, Royal Economic Society, Institute of Mathematical Statistics, Econometric Society (fellow; member of council, 1971-76 and 1981-83), Phi Beta Kappa. *Awards, honors:* Guggenheim fellow, 1980-81; James Murray Luck Award from National Academy of Sciences, 1981, for scientific reviewing.

WRITINGS: The Theory of Intersectoral Money Flows and Income Formation, Johns Hopkins Press, 1951; (editor with Leonid Hurwicz, Marcel K. Richter, and Hugo F. Sonnenschein) *Preferences, Utility, and Demand,* Harcourt, 1971; (editor with Charles P. Kindleberger) *Flexible Exchange Rates and the Balance of Payments,* North-Holland Publishing, 1980. Contributor to economic and statistical journals. Associate editor of *Econometrica,* 1956-64; co-editor of *Journal of International Economics,* 1971-76, editor, 1977—; associate editor of *Canadian Journal of Statistics,* 1980-83.

WORK IN PROGRESS: Analysis of Welfare Criteria, with James C. Moore; *The Theory of Aggregation.*

* * *

CH'O, Chou
See SHU-JEN, Chou

* * *

CHOPIN, Kate (O'Flaherty)   1851-1904

BRIEF ENTRY: Born February 8, 1851, in St. Louis, Mo.; died of a cerebral hemorrhage, August 22, 1904, in St. Louis, Mo. American author. Chopin, a diligent student of the works of Guy de Maupassant, is best known for her novels and short stories about Acadian and Creole society in Louisiana. Drawing upon her experiences as a plantation owner's wife in Louisiana, Chopin wrote a novel, *At Fault* (1890), and two collections of short stories, *Bayou Folk* (1894), and *A Night in Acadie* (1897),

Although the novel was not considered remarkable, the short story collections established the author's reputation as an important writer of local color. In recent years some critics have also come to regard Chopin as a writer in the realist tradition. Chopin's work was well received until the publication of *The Awakening* (1899). Critics reacted violently to the novel of adultery and miscegenation, causing its author to curtail her writing activities. The book, Chopin's last, has since been described as "a novel of the first rank." Chopin also contributed articles and short stories to magazines, including *Youth's Companion, Harper's,* and *Century. Residence:* St. Louis, Mo. *Biographical/critical sources:* Daniel S. Rankin, *Kate Chopin and Her Creole Stories,* University of Pennsylvania Press, 1932; Per Seyersted, *Kate Chopin: A Critical Biography,* Louisiana State University Press, 1969; *New York Times,* February 8, 1970; *New Republic,* March 15, 1975; *New Statesman,* February 24, 1978.

*   *   *

CHRISTIANS, Clifford Glenn   1939-

PERSONAL: Born December 12, 1939, in Hull, Iowa; son of Arnold (a teacher) and Verbena (Geerdes) Christians; married Priscilla Jean Kreun, June 13, 1961; children: Glenn, Ted, Paul. *Education:* Calvin College, A.B., 1961; Fuller Theological Seminary, Th.M., 1965; University of Southern California, M.A., 1970; University of Illinois, Ph.D., 1974. *Religion:* Protestant. *Home:* 1002 West William, Champaign, Ill. 61820. *Office:* College of Communications, University of Illinois, 119 Gregory Hall, Urbana, Ill. 61801.

CAREER: Christian Reformed Home Missions, Grand Rapids, Mich., director of communications, 1966-70; University of Illinois, Urbana, research assistant professor, 1974-80, research associate professor of communications, 1980—. *Member:* Association for Education in Journalism, Society of Educators and Scholars, Hastings Center Program on Applied and Professional Ethics. *Awards, honors:* Campus Award from University of Illinois, 1978, for excellence in teaching; visiting scholar at Princeton University, 1980.

WRITINGS: (With William Rivers and Wilbur Schramm) *Responsibility in Mass Communications,* Harper, 1957, 3rd edition, 1980; (with Catherine Covert) *Teaching Ethics in Journalism Education* (monograph), Hastings Center, 1980; (editor with Jay Van Hook) *Jacques Ellul: Interpretive Essays,* University of Illinois Press, 1981. Contributing editor of *Journal of Communication;* member of editorial board of *Journalism Monographs;* editor of *Communication,* 1979.

WORK IN PROGRESS: Case Studies in Media Ethics, with Kim Rotzoll and Mark Fackler, publication expected in 1982; a study of ethical decision-making in media professions, for McCormick Foundation; research on humanistic (qualitative) research methodologies, social philosophy (especially Jacques Ellul), and media ethics.

SIDELIGHTS: Christians wrote: "The largest percentage of my time in research and teaching concerns professional ethics. For journalism and advertising, however, that raises a number of problems regarding education (that is, the relationship of professional and liberal arts); therefore, I am interested in curriculum and pedagogy. In the background of media ethics are several epistemological and philosophical questions that need to be addressed in a compelling way. Therefore I usually describe my concerns as the social and moral philosophy of communications."

BIOGRAPHICAL/CRITICAL SOURCES: Mass Communication Review, autumn, 1979; *Communicare: Journal of Communication Sciences,* Volume I, number 1, 1980.

CHUBB, Elmer
See MASTERS, Edgar Lee

*   *   *

CITINO, David   1947-

PERSONAL: Born March 13, 1947, in Cleveland, Ohio; son of John D. (a purchasing agent) and Mildred Rita (a secretary; maiden name, Bunasky) Citino; married Mary Helen Hicks (a medical technologist), July 26, 1969; children: Nathan John, Dominic John. *Education:* Ohio University, B.A., 1969; Ohio State University, M.A., 1972, Ph.D., 1974. *Home:* 283 East Walnut, Marion, Ohio 43302. *Office:* Department of English, Ohio State University at Marion, 1465 Mount Vernon Ave., Marion, Ohio 43302.

CAREER: Ohio State University at Marion, Marion, assistant professor, 1974-80, associate professor of English, 1980—. Judge of poetry competitions; gives readings, lectures, and workshops. *Member:* Modern Language Association of America, Society for the Study of Midwestern Literature, Poets' League of Greater Cleveland. *Awards, honors:* Prize Poems Award from *Poet and Critic* and Iowa State University Press, 1977, for "Hazel" and "Laws of Hospitality"; grants from Ohio Arts Council, 1977-80, 1979; Poetry in Transit Award from Poets' League of Greater Cleveland, 1980, for "One Mouth, Love, and Ache."

WRITINGS: (Editor) *Seventy-Three Ohio Poets,* Ohio Arts Council, 1978; *Last Rites and Other Poems,* Ohio State University Press, 1980.

Work represented in anthologies, including *Best Poems of 1976: Borestone Mountain Poetry Awards, 1977; Anthology of Magazine Verse and Yearbook of American Poetry; Poets in the Gallery: A Chapbook of Columbus Poems,* Columbus Gallery of Fine Arts, 1977. Contributor of poems to over two hundred magazines, including *Literary Review, Great Lakes Review, Kenyon Review, Aspen Anthology, Poet and Critic,* and *Dalhousie Review.* Founder and editor of *Cornfield Review: An Annual of the Creative Arts,* 1975—; editor of *Faculty and Staff Bulletin* (Ohio State University at Marion), 1975—.

WORK IN PROGRESS: Two books of poetry.

SIDELIGHTS: Citino wrote: "I'm a poet, teacher, and critic, with strong interests in folklore, myth, ancient and medieval history, cultural anthropology, the Cleveland Indians, Jung, Whitman, American poetry, the Renaissance in Europe, Ohio rivers, popular songs of the 1950's, Ireland, Italian-Americans, James Joyce, Mario Lanza, and the poet's relationship to the university in America. I feel very fortunate to be able to write and to teach writing. Writing teaches me much about teaching, and teaching teaches me much about writing."

*   *   *

CLABBY, John   1911-

PERSONAL: Born June 11, 1911, in Poona, India; son of William George and Violet (Trevor-Roper) Clabby; married Emily Lancaster, November 9, 1939 (divorced, 1975); married Anne Harries, July 15, 1976; children: Jennifer. *Education:* Royal Veterinary College, London, M.R.C.V.S., 1932. *Religion:* Church of England. *Home:* Coxland Stud, Ewhurst, near Cranleigh, Surrey, England.

CAREER: British Army, Royal Veterinary Corps, served as veterinary officer with Indian Cavalry, 1933-38, with first cavalry division in Palestine, 1939-40, with male pack transport in Eritrea, 1940-41, and with veterinary hospital in Greece, 1941, prisoner of war in Germany, 1941-45, received post-war appointments, 1945-59, assistant director of Army Veterinary and Remount Services in India, the Middle East, and the Far East, 1959-63, retired as colonel commandant, 1976; writer, 1976—. Chief executive officer of Animal Health Trust, London, England, 1963-76. *Member:* British Equine Veterinary Association (president, 1973-74), Worshipful Company of Farriers (master, 1973-74). *Awards, honors*—Military: Member of Order of British Empire, 1941, officer of order, 1958, commander of order, 1964.

WRITINGS: The History of the Royal Army Veterinary Corps, J. A. Allen, 1961; *The Natural History of the Horse,* Taplinger, 1976.

SIDELIGHTS: John Clabby told *CA:* "My motivation for writing *The History of the Royal Army Veterinary Corps* was to set on record the past achievements and present usefulness of the Corps that was in imminent danger of disbandment because the Army had little further need of horses and mules. Fortunately, the military requirement for war dogs, for guard and other purposes, was steadily increasing, and the Royal Army Veterinary Corps was retained in order to see to their care and training. It has never looked back and is now as strong as ever it was.

"I was at the Equine Research Station in England when I undertook the writing of *The Natural History of the Horse,* largely to make myself better informed on the origins of this animal on which we spent so much time and money."

AVOCATIONAL INTERESTS: Breeding racehorses.

*   *   *

CLARK, Evans   1888-1970

OBITUARY NOTICE: Born August 9, 1888, in Orange, N.J.; died August 28, 1970, in Nyon, Switzerland. Economist and author of works in his field, including *How to Budget Health, The Internal Debts of the United States,* and *Stock Market Control.* Obituaries and others sources: *Current Biography,* Wilson, 1947, November, 1970; *New York Times,* August 29, 1970; *AB Bookman's Weekly,* September 21, 1970.

*   *   *

CLARK, Melissa   1949-
(Alysse Aallyn)

PERSONAL: Born December 4, 1949, in Philadelphia, Pa.; daughter of Bronson Pettibone and Eleanor (Meanor) Clark; married David Earl (marriage ended October, 1979); married Thomas Benham Scheffey (an attorney), August 30, 1980. *Education:* Attended Antioch College, Columbia, Md., 1970-72; Brooklyn College of the City University of New York, M.F.A. *Politics:* Independent. *Religion:* Episcopalian. *Home:* 10 North Mill Rd., Cranbury, N.J. 08512. *Agent:* Lisbeth Mark, Lucianne Goldberg Literary Agent, Inc., 255 West 84th St., New York, N.Y. 10024.

CAREER: Secretary, receptionist, and switchboard operator, 1974-76; dancer in Washington, D.C., 1976-79; writer, 1979—. Critic on WPFW-Radio, 1978-79; teacher at Maryland Writers Conference, 1978-79; gives readings.

WRITINGS: "Let's Speak Vietnamese" (one-act play), published in *Dramatika Magazine,* 1974; (under pseudonym Alysse Aallyn) *Devlyn* (novel), Harcourt, 1977. Contributor of about thirty poems to magazines, including *Commonweal, Smith, Seneca Review,* and *Swedenborgian Messenger.*

WORK IN PROGRESS: The Ripening Grave, a suspense novel; *The Perils of Shalott,* a novel; *The Speechless,* a novel.

SIDELIGHTS: Melissa Clark commented: "I am currently conducting a fund-raising effort to establish a new press to publish poetry, short fiction, and anthologies."

*   *   *

CLARKE, Joan (Lorraine)   1920-

PERSONAL: Born August 23, 1920, in ʼnev, Australia; daughter of William Harold (a mental hospital attendant) and Florence (a domestic servant; maiden name, Divall) Willmott; married R. G. Clarke, 1946 (divorced, 1957); children: Jonathon Mayo. *Education:* Metropolitan Secretarial School, Secretarial Diploma, 1938. *Home:* 1/10 Rangers Rd., Cremorne, New South Wales 2090, Australia.

CAREER: Secretary, scriptwriter, and broadcaster with Broadcasting Station 2GB, Sydney, Australia, 1940-45; secretary, 1945-68; Freelance Secretarial Services, founder and manager, 1968-75; free-lance writer, editor, and researcher, 1976—. *Member:* International P.E.N., Australian Society of Authors (foundation member; member of committee of management), Fellowship of Australian Writers, National Book Council, Society of Women Writers, Society of Editors. *Awards, honors:* Co-recipient with Zoe O'Leary of woman of the year award from International Women's Committee, 1969, for *Girl Fridays in Revolt;* senior fellowship grant from Australia's Literature Board, 1978.

WRITINGS: (Editor) *Youth Speaks* (poetry), Broadcasting Station 2GB, 1941; (with Zoe O'Leary) *Girl Fridays in Revolt,* Alpha Books, 1969; *Dr. Max Herz, Surgeon Extraordinary,* Alternative Publishing, 1976; (editor of revision) *Writers Handbook,* 2nd edition, A. H. & A. W. Reed, 1979; (with G. Weller) *Gold!,* Longman Cheshire, 1981; (editor with Jacqueline Kent) Doris Fitton, *Not Without Dust and Heat* (autobiography), Harper, 1981.

Plays: "Home Brew" (three-act), first produced in Sydney, Australia, at New Theatre, 1954; (with John Meredith) "Wild Colonial Boy" (three-act), first produced in Brisbane, Australia, at New Theatre, 1956.

Work represented in anthologies, including *Tracks We Travel,* Overland, 1953; *Australia's Political Milestones,* Thomas Nelson, 1976. Contributor to magazines and newspapers. Past editor of *Australian Author.*

WORK IN PROGRESS: Migrant Doctor, a biography of a Jewish refugee from Germany in the 1930's; research for a fictionalized biography of her mother's grandfather, who was among the first Greeks to arrive in Australia.

SIDELIGHTS: Joan Clarke told *CA:* "I am probably better known here in Australia as an editor than as an author, but it would be nice to imagine posterity changing that status. The problem is that writers from Australia and New Zealand (countries with small populations and no indigenous language) have small editions. Few can live off royalties, so we have to work at something else, like journalism or editing. Under those circumstances, books take a long time to produce.

"At the age of two, one of my legs was paralyzed by polio. Most of my childhood was spent in hospitals, so I had little formal education, but developed a love for books and writing. When other doctors could do nothing for me, Max Herz (ostracized since World War I because he was German) operated and enabled me to walk without calipers. My biography of him was payment-in-part of my great debt to him.

"I have always been interested in biography, the German language, and history (*Gold!* is a history of life on early Australian gold fields). I have a special interest in and concern for people coming to this country with non-Anglo-Saxon backgrounds, and I hate racial discrimination. I am a strong supporter of the charter of International P.E.N., and was Australia's co-delegate to its 1975 congress in Vienna."

BIOGRAPHICAL/CRITICAL SOURCES: North Shore Times, October 8, 1975; *Manly Daily,* January 29, 1977; *Mosman Daily,* February 2, 1977; *Manning River Times,* April 20, 1977.

*   *   *

CLARKE, Mary   1923-

PERSONAL: Born August 23, 1923, in London, England; daughter of Frederick and Ethel Kate (Reynolds) Clarke. *Education:* Attended private girls' school in London, England. *Home:* 11 Danbury St., Islington, London N1 8LD, England. *Office: Dancing Times,* Clerkenwell House, 45-47 Clerkenwell Green, London EC1R 0BE, England.

CAREER: Dance (magazine), New York City, London correspondent, 1943-55; *Dancing Times,* London, England, assistant editor, 1954-63, editor and co-director, 1963—; *Dance News,* New York City, London correspondent, 1955-70. Member of the grand council of the Royal Academy of Dancing. *Member:* Gautier Club.

WRITINGS: Shakespeare at the Old Vic, Volume I (with Roger Wood): *Hamlet, All's Well That Ends Well, King John, Twelfth Night, Coriolanus, The Tempest,* A. & C. Black, 1954, Volume II (with Wood): *1954-55: Macbeth, Love's Labour's Lost, The Taming of the Shrew, King Richard II, As You Like It, King Henry IV (Parts I and II),* Macmillan, 1956, Volume III (with Wood): *1955-56: Julius Caesar, The Merry Wives of Windsor, The Winter's Tale, King Henry V, Othello, Troilus and Cressida,* Hamish Hamilton, 1956, Macmillan, 1957, Volume IV: *1956-57: Timon of Athens, Cymbeline, King of Britain, Much Ado About Nothing, The Two Gentlemen of Verona, The Merchant of Venice, Antony and Cleopatra, Titus Andronicus and The Comedy of Errors, King Richard III,* Macmillan, 1957, Volume V: *1957-58: Hamlet, King Henry VI (Parts I, II, and III), Measure for Measure, A Midsummer Night's Dream, King Lear, Twelfth Night, King Henry VIII,* Macmillan, 1958; *The Sadler's Wells Ballet: A History and an Appreciation,* A. & C. Black, 1955, Macmillan, 1956, reprinted, Da Capo, 1977; *Six Great Dancers: Taglioni, Pavlova, Nijinsky, Karsavina, Ulanova, Fonteyn,* Hamish Hamilton, 1957; (editor with Arnold L. Haskell) *World Ballet,* Hulton, 1958; (editor with Francis Gadan, Robert Maillard, and Ronald Crichton) *A Dictionary of Modern Ballet* (translated from French by John Montague and Peggie Cochrane), Methuen, 1959.

Dancers of Mercury: The Story of Ballet Rambert, A. & C. Black, 1962; *Presenting People Who Dance,* Paul Hamlyn, 1961; (editor) Cyril William Swinson (under pseudonym Hugh Fisher) *Margot Fonteyn,* 3rd edition (Clarke was not associated with earlier editions), A. & C. Black, 1964.

(With Clement Crisp) *Ballet: An Illustrated History,* Universe Books, 1973; (with Crisp) *Making a Ballet,* Studio Vista, 1974, Macmillan, 1975; (with Crisp) *Introducing Ballet,* Studio Vista, 1976; (with Crisp) *Understanding Ballet,* Harmony Books, 1976; (with David Vaughan) *The Encyclopedia of Dance and Ballet,* Putnam, 1977; (with Crisp) *Design for Ballet,* Haw-

thorn, 1978; (with Crisp) *Ballet in Art: From the Renaissance to the Present,* C. N. Potter, 1978.

(With Crisp) *A History of Dance,* Crown, 1981; (with Crisp) *The Ballet-Goer's Guide,* Knopf, 1981. Contributor to *Encyclopaedia Britannica.* Assistant editor of *Ballet Annual,* 1952-63; dance critic for *Guardian,* 1977—.

*   *   *

CLARKE, Peter   1936-

PERSONAL: Born September 19, 1936, in Evanston, Ill.; son of Clarence L. and Dorothy (Whitcombe) Clarke; married Karen Storey, 1962; children: Christopher. *Education:* University of Washington, Seattle, B.A., 1959; University of Minnesota, M.A., 1961, Ph.D., 1963. *Home:* 1525 Harding Rd., Ann Arbor, Mich. 48104. *Office:* Annenberg School of Communications, University of Southern California, University Park, Los Angeles, Calif. 90007.

CAREER: Peter Clarke & Associates Advertising, Seattle, Wash., owner, 1954-59; University of Minnesota, Minneapolis, instructor in mass communication, 1961-63; Univerist of Washington, Seattle, acting assistant professor, 1963-64, assistant professor, 1964-67, associate professor, 1967-72, director of School of Communication, 1971-72, University of Michigan, Ann Arbor, professor of journalism, 1972-79, professor of communication, 1979-81, chairman of department of journalism, 1973-79, and of department of communication, 1979-81; University of Southern California, Los Angeles, dean of Annenberg School of Communications, 1981—. *Member:* Association for Education in Journalism (chairman of research committee), American Statistical Association, American Psychological Association, American Association for Public Opinion Research, American Sociological Association, American Political Science Association.

WRITINGS: (Contributor) Donald L. Shaw, editor, *Decision Points in Mass Communications Research,* North Carolina Journalism Monographs, 1967; *New Models for Communication Research,* Sage Publications, 1973; (contributor) Alex S. Edelstein and other editors, *Information Societies: Comparing the Japanese and American Experiences,* International Communication Center (Seattle, Wash.), 1978. Co-editor of series, "Annual Reviews of Communication Research," Sage Publications, 1972—, and "People and Communication," Sage Publications, 1976—. Contributor of more than forty articles and chapters to academic journals, books, and research reports. Co-editor of *American Behavioral Scientist,* January, 1971.

WORK IN PROGRESS: The Broken Quill: How the Press Covers Elections to Congress, with Susan H. Evory.

SIDELIGHTS: Clarke told *CA:* "My research and writing focus on the political functions of mass media and the social effects of new tele-communication technologies."

*   *   *

CLARKE, William Kendall   1911(?)-1981

OBITUARY NOTICE: Born c. 1911; died June 26, 1981, in Marlborough, Conn. Author of television dramas and novels. Clarke wrote numerous scripts for television serials. His novels include *Tomfool's Pike* and *The Robber Baroness.* Obituaries and other sources: *New York Times,* July 24, 1981.

*   *   *

CLAUDEL, Paul (Louis Charles Marie)   1868-1955

BRIEF ENTRY: Born August 6, 1868, in Villeneuve-sur-

Fere-en Tardenois, France; died of a heart attack, February 23, 1955, in Paris, France. French diplomat, playwright, and poet. Claudel became an ardent follower of Catholicism in 1886 after experiencing a spiritual awakening while attending Christmas Day Mass at Notre Dame Cathedral. In such plays as "The Hostage" (1911), "The Tidings of Mary" (1912), and "The Satin Slipper" (1925), Claudel presented such an elaborate case for the Roman Catholic faith that he was publicly honored by Pope Pius XXI in 1950. A descendant of Symbolist poets and a one-time disciple of Mallarme, Claudel wrote poetic plays that embody the conflict between religious fervor and human passion, his view that love between people is a manifestation of love for God, and the theme of salvation through self-sacrifice. In 1890 he began his career as consul and diplomat, traveling throughout the world. Most of his plays were written during this period and were later collected in thirteen volumes, *Oeuvres completes* (1950-58). Claudel also wrote eloquent essays on metaphysics, sociology, poetics, and religion. All his writing was so heavily influenced by his religious faith that devout Roman Catholic critics were sometimes reluctant to find fault and others, including the nonreligious, could not separate the quality of his writing from his passionate religious views. For the last twenty years of his life, Claudel concentrated on studying and translating the Bible and writing biblical commentary, favoring symbolic interpretation over textual criticism. *Biographical/critical sources:* Richard Griffiths, editor, *Claudel: A Reappraisal,* Rapp & Whiting, 1968; *McGraw-Hill Encyclopedia of World Drama,* McGraw, 1972; *Twentieth-Century Literary Criticism,* Volume 2, Gale, 1979.

* * *

CLEAVER, William J(oseph)   1920-1981

OBITUARY NOTICE: Born March 24, 1920, in Hugo, Okla; died August 20, 1981, in Winter Haven, Fla. Author of numerous children's books with wife, Vera Cleaver. Among their writings are two National Book Award nominees, *The Whys and Wherefores of Littabelle Lee* and *Grover.* Obituaries and other sources: *Who's Who in America,* 41st edition, Marquis, 1980; *Publishers Weekly,* September 18, 1981.

* * *

CLEMENS, Samuel Langhorne   1835-1910
(Thomas Jefferson Snodgrass, Mark Twain)

BRIEF ENTRY: Born November 30, 1835, in Florida, Mo.; died April 21, 1910, in Redding, Conn. American printer, journalist, and author. Twain is best known for his tales of the pre-Civil War South. His most popular novel, *The Adventures of Huckleberry Finn* (1885), concerns a Southern youth who encounters numerous oddball characters and adventures while rafting down the Mississippi River. Though largely prized for its humor and idiomatic dialogue, *The Adventures of Huckleberry Finn* is also viewed by critics as a scathing indictment of Christian hypocrisy, slavery, and materialism. In 1889 Twain wrote *A Connecticut Yankee in King Arthur's Court,* in which he similarly exposed the absurdity of American values by transporting a New England worker to medieval England. Two of his novels satirize classism through role-reversal. In *The Prince and the Pauper* (1882), two identical youths in medieval times agree to exchange identities out of displeasure with their own situations; in *Pudd'nhead Wilson* (1894), master and slave switch roles in a more serious and ultimately devastating tale. Twain's other best-known works are *The Adventures of Tom Sawyer* (1876), a youth-oriented predecessor to *Huckleberry Finn,* and *Life on the Mississippi* (1883), a satiric memoir of the South. Most critics consider Twain's canon to be uneven, but his best

work is often cited for its humor, characterization, and portrayal of the South. In his later years, Twain grew increasingly pessimistic, blaming the world's problems on man's selfish nature. Forced into a lecture tour to overcome his bankruptcy, Twain exhibited his quick wit and keen insight on subjects ranging from slavery to capitalism. *Biographical/critical sources: Everyman's Dictionary of Literary Biography, English and American,* revised edition, Dutton, 1960; *Oxford Companion to American Literature,* 4th edition, Oxford University Press, 1965.

* * *

CLEVELAND, Mary   1917-
(Mary Allen; Mary Twelveponies, a pseudonym)

PERSONAL: Born December 21, 1917, in Knightstown, Ind.; daughter of Reuel L. (a printer) and Ethel (Thornton) Wood; married Bert Allen, 1942 (deceased); married Olie Adkins, 1952 (deceased); married William Cleveland (a welder), June 5, 1963; children: (first marriage) Elizabeth Allen Bevan; (second marriage) Bruce. *Education:* Attended Earlham College, 1937-38. *Politics:* "Looking forward to the Millennium." *Religion:* Society of Friends (Quakers). *Home and office address:* P.O. Box 167, Palo Cedro, Calif. 96073.

CAREER: Rancher (horses, cattle, and milk goats) and horse trainer, 1937—. Instructor at Shasta College, 1972-78.

WRITINGS—Under pseudonym Mary Twelveponies: *Ride and Learn With Mary Twelveponies,* Horse Lover's, 1970, revised edition, privately printed, 1978; *Everyday Training: Backyard Dressage,* A. S. Barnes, 1980; *There Are No Problem Horses, Only Problem Riders,* Houghton, 1982.

Author of "Burrs Under the Saddle," a problem-horse column in *Horse Lover's,* 1967-77, and "Everyday, Training: Backyard Dressage," "There Are No Problem Horses—Only Problem Riders," "Fact and Fiction," "Mary's Twelve Ponies," and "What's Your Problem," columns in *Horse and Horseman,* 1976—.

Contributor to horse magazines (sometimes under name Mary Allen).

WORK IN PROGRESS: Mary's Twelve Ponies; research on Bible doctrine.

SIDELIGHTS: Mary Cleveland wrote: "My first love has always been horses, then my other animals—cattle, milk goats, dogs, and cats. I only went to college because they offered horseback riding twice a week. After that I ran a riding stable and trained horses. In 1942 I moved to California, married a California *vaquero,* and I lived on various California and Nevada ranches where he worked. From Bert I learned a great deal about the training of the legendary California reined stock horse, an offshoot of the Spanish and Portuguese dressage horses.

"From 1947-53 I lived near Covina, California, training horses and successfully showing my own half-Arab mare in trail class. At that time, as Mary Allen, I wrote several articles for *Horse Lover's* magazine because I could see that people needed help with their riding and horse training. I gradually moved north in California, ending up near Palo Cedro, and about to be crowded right out of the state by migratory city escapees. In 1966 my daughter suggested that I write a problem-horse column because of my ability to pinpoint the causes of the problems and prescribe the workable cures. I hesitated because I wouldn't be able to see the horses, but after reading some perfectly horrible and dangerous advice in a similar column, I submitted.

"When I put together the first column, I needed a name. Mary Cleveland didn't sound like anyone who knew horses. When I first met my husband Bill, I owned twelve horses, and he promptly named me Mary Twelveponies, so I have used that name.

"I wrote *Ride and Learn With Mary Twelveponies* to tell beginning horse owners and riders exactly what they needed to know to select, care for, and ride a horse, without burdening them with useless instruction, such as the supposedly proper conformation of the horse (which has nothing to do with his usefulness and ability as a pleasure horse).

"I wrote *Everyday Training* because I am tired of seeing horses unintentionally abused under the heading of training. I had been learning and practising elementary dressage under Hermann Friedlaender and Charles DeKunffy, both internationally known and respected dressage instructors. The basic principles of dressage training lay the best foundation for all types of more advanced training without physical and psychological injury to the horse, yet our all-American horsemen were failing to explore the possibilities of these principles because they felt put down by dressage enthusiasts' unintentional holier-than-thou attitude. My intent—to explain basic dressage training as a member of the put-down group, thus getting them to listen, apply, and save the horses.

"I wrote 'There Are No Problem Horses' for *Horse and Horseman*. Advice-to-problem-horse-owners columns are quite popular now, but invariably the 'experts' fail to consider all aspects of the problems and fail to give comprehensive advice. My success stems from doing just the opposite—exploring the possible causes and offering, not just quickie solutions, but thorough explanations of how to rehabilitate the horses. My ten years of experience with the column had shown me what problems occur most often and how to explain the cures. There is a great need for a book like this because nowadays so many people who shouldn't, own horses. I have to help them join the ranks of those who should—and save the horses.

"While trying to spare horses traumatic training experiences through educating their handlers is of deep concern to me, another area of vital interest is helping people understand animal thought processes, especially those of horses. Most scientists who study animal behavior are so determined to avoid putting human-like interpretations on animal behavior that they often misinterpret the animal's behavior. While there are notable exceptions, most scientists who study animals are just scientists, not animal people.

"*Mary's Twelve Ponies* is a collection of the more interesting things my animals have done. While some of the stories may seem a little out of the ordinary, every time I tell one to an animal person, he can always match or top it with a similar story of his own. These are the behavioral incidents that scientists either miss or ignore because they don't fit into one of their stereotyped categories. While I wrote these primarily to entertain, I also want to put on record true accounts and correct interpretations of specific animal acts. My interpretations aren't humanistic because I have the God-given talent for thinking like the animals.

"Another area of vital concern to me is spreading the Gospel. God has specifically stated that this generation (probably my daughter's, definitely my grandson's) will see one-world government and the Great Tribulation with its anti-Christ dictator who will make Hitler look like a pantywaist. The Lord has also told us that those who are Christians before the rise of the anti-Christ will not have to endure the Tribulation. I wish that all people would see the wisdom of believing God's word."

AVOCATIONAL INTERESTS: Playing the flute.

* * *

CLIGNET, Remi Pierre 1931-

PERSONAL: Born February 28, 1931, in Reims, France; came to the United States in 1963; son of Georges (an engineer) and Genevieve (Wirbel) Clignet; married Arielle de Sainte Marie (a ceramicist), December 27, 1958; children: Sara, Marion. *Education:* University of Paris, Licence es Lettres, 1951, Licence es Droit, 1953, Licence es Psychologie, 1958, Doctorat Recherches Sociologiques, 1963. *Home:* 7515 Radnor, Bethesda, Md. 20034. *Office:* Department of Family Relations and Community Development, University of Maryland, College Park, Md. 20742.

CAREER: National Ministry of Education, Abidjan, Ivory Coast, head of psychology office, 1959-61, psychologist, 1959-61; Center for Science and Technology Building, Paris, France, head of research department in sociology of housing, 1961-62; University of Chicago, Chicago, Ill., research associate in sociology, 1963-64; Northwestern University, Evanston, Ill., assistant professor, 1964-67, associate professor, 1967-70, professor of sociology, 1970-79; University of Maryland, College Park, professor of family relations and community development, 1979—. Consultant to U.S. Agency for International Development and International Bank for Reconstruction and Development. *Military service:* French Navy, 1954-56. *Member:* American Sociological Association.

WRITINGS: The Fortunate Few, Northwestern University Press, 1966; *Many Wives, Many Powers,* Northwestern University Press, 1970; (contributor) P. Foster and A. Zolberg, editors, *Ghana and the Ivory Coast: Perspectives on Modernization,* University of Chicago Press, 1971; (contributor) R. Naroll and R. Cohen, editors, *Handbook of Cultural Anthropology,* Natural History Press, 1971; *Liberty and Equality in the Educational Process,* Wiley, 1974; *The Africanization of the Labor Market,* University of California Press, 1977. Contributor to sociology and education journals.

WORK IN PROGRESS: The Structure of Artistic Revolutions; Between Nature and Culture: The Ordeal of Familial Life.

SIDELIGHTS: Clignet commented: "I am mostly interested in the historical and cultural relativity of human phenomena, and as such, am interested in examining the variability not only of the organizational forms of social life (schools, families, sciences, arts, etc.), but also of the theories elaborated to account for the relevant variations. I am therefore turned toward comparative studies of an interdisciplinary nature."

* * *

CLINTON-BADDELEY, V.C. 1911(?)-1970

OBITUARY NOTICE: Born c. 1911; died August 6, 1970, in London, England. Actor, editor, and author. After quitting his position as an editor of *Encyclopaedia Britannica,* Clinton-Baddeley worked as an actor and playwright. He wrote literary and drama criticism, as well as several mysteries, notably *Death's Bright Dart* and *Only a Matter of Time,* featuring Dr. Davie. Obituaries and other sources: *Publishers Weekly,* November 23, 1970.

* * *

CLYMER, (Joseph) Floyd 1895-1970

OBITUARY NOTICE: Born in 1895; died January 22, 1970, in Los Angeles, Calif. Author and collector of automobiles and motorcycles. Clymer wrote many books on automobiles, including *Those Wonderful Old Automobiles, Treasury of Early American Automobiles, 1877-1925,* and *Treasury of Foreign Cars, Old and New.* Obituaries and other sources: *AB Bookman's Weekly,* February 16, 1970.

* * *

COBB, Geoffrey Belton 1892(?)-1971

OBITUARY NOTICE: Born c. 1892; died August 15, 1971, in Tunbridge Wells, England. Author of mysteries, including *No Alibi* and *Suspicion in Triplicate.* Obituaries and other sources: *AB Bookman's Weekly,* September 27, 1971.

* * *

COBB, Roger W(illiam) 1941-

PERSONAL: Born February 26, 1941, in Port Angeles, Wash.; son of Maurice C. (a customs inspector) and Eunice (Bergman) Cobb; married Gail Marguerite Greaser, June 14, 1973. *Education:* University of Washington, Seattle, B.A., 1962; University of California, Los Angeles, M.A., 1964; Northwestern University, Ph.D., 1967. *Residence:* Providence, R.I. *Office:* Department of Political Science, Brown University, Providence, R.I. 02912.

CAREER: University of Pennsylvania, Philadelphia, assistant professor of political science, 1967-73; Brown University, Providence, R.I., assistant professor, 1973-75, associate professor, 1975-81, professor of political science, 1981—. *Member:* American Political Science Association.

WRITINGS: (With Charles D. Elder) *International Community,* Holt, 1968; (with Elder) *Participation in American Politics: The Dynamics of Agenda-Building,* Johns Hopkins Press, 1972.

WORK IN PROGRESS: A book dealing with political symbols, publication expected in 1982; a monograph on gerontological policy-making in Michigan and area agencies on aging, publication expected in 1982.

SIDELIGHTS: Cobb told *CA:* "My interests are conflict and cooperation and how they intersect. My first book stresses cooperation and the second stresses conflict. Another interest is how language and terms (symbols) become the crucial items of conflict and supersede the conflict itself."

* * *

COBURN, Louis 1915-

PERSONAL: Original name, Louis Cohen; name legally changed in 1937; born August 13, 1915, in New York, N.Y.; son of Benjamin (a tailor) and Bertha (a seamstress; maiden name, Smoradinsky) Cohen; married Selma Spielman (a psychologist), June 25, 1950; children: Barry, Michael. *Education:* City College (now of the City University of New York), B.A., 1936, M.S. in Ed., 1941; Columbia University, B.L.S., 1938; New York University, Ed.D., 1961. *Politics:* Democrat. *Religion:* Jewish. *Home:* 137-01 63rd Ave., Flushing, N.Y. 11367. *Office:* Graduate School of Library and Information Studies, Queens College of the City University of New York, 64-15 Kissena Blvd., Flushing, N.Y. 11367.

CAREER: Library teacher at high schools in Bronx, N.Y., 1938-56, and Jamaica, N.Y., 1956-63; Queens College of the City University of New York, Flushing, N.Y., assistant professor, 1963-73, associate professor of library and information studies, 1974-79. *Military service:* U.S. Army Air Forces, cryptographic security officer, 1942-46; became first lieuten-

ant. *Member:* American Library Association, American Association of University Professors, Common Cause, New York Library Association, New York Technical Services Librarians, New York Library Club, New York City School Librarians Association, New York University Alumni Association, Alumni Association of City College of New York, Queens College Retirees Association, Beta Phi Mu.

WRITINGS: Case Studies in School Library Administration, Queens College Press, 1968; *Library Media Center Problems: Case Studies,* Oceana, 1973; *Classroom and Field: The Internship in American Library Education,* Queens College Press, 1980. Contributor to *Elementary English.*

WORK IN PROGRESS: Research on librarianship and publishing.

SIDELIGHTS: Coburn wrote: "Throughout my professional life, my major interests have centered around the role and functions of librarians serving people's informational needs. Based upon twenty-five years of experience as a high school librarian, I became convinced that libraries are one of the most effective agencies in our society for spreading knowledge through the power of print and audiovisual materials. Sixteen years of subsequent experience as a college teacher brought me into close contact with the problems of library education and contributed to my appreciation of both the practical and theoretical aspects of professional training. This interest stimulated the research and writing of two books of case studies about school library/media center problems, as well as the monograph on the internship in American library education."

* * *

COFFIN, Harold 1905(?)-1981

OBITUARY NOTICE: Born c. 1905; died of a heart attack, September 12, 1981, in Capitola, Calif. Journalist. Coffin worked for the *San Francisco Call-Bulletin, San Francisco Chronicle,* and *Honolulu Star-Bulletin.* For thirteen years he wrote the column "Coffin's Needle." He also contributed articles to *Readers Digest, Look,* and *Saturday Evening Post.* Obituaries and other sources: *Chicago Tribune,* September 16, 1981.

* * *

COHEN, Mortimer J. 1894-1972

OBITUARY NOTICE: Born March 1, 1894, in New York, N.Y.; died January 28, 1972, in Philadelphia, Pa. Rabbi, editor, and author. Cohen was best known for his popular *Pathways Through the Bible.* Obituaries and other sources: *AB Bookman's Weekly,* February 21, 1972; *The National Cyclopaedia of American Biography,* Volume 56, James T. White, 1975.

* * *

COHLER, David Keith 1940-

PERSONAL: Born May 6, 1940, in Chicago, Ill.; son of Charles E. (in sales) and Esther (a purchasing manager; maiden name, Zion) Cohler. *Education:* Northwestern University, B.S.J., 1961; University of Lyon, Certificate of Language Proficiency, 1961; University of Munich, Certificate of Language Proficiency, 1962. *Residence:* Chicago, Ill. *Agent:* Adams, Ray & Rosenberg, 9200 Sunset Blvd., Penthouse 25, Los Angeles, Calif. 90069.

CAREER: Newswriter, producer, and correspondent for Agence France-Presse in Paris, France, 1961-62, for Radio Free Europe in Munich, West Germany, and Paris, 1962-65, for American Broadcasting Co. (ABC) in New York City, 1966-68, for Westinghouse Broadcasting Co., Group W, in London, England, Paris, Washington, D.C., and Chicago, Ill., 1969-72, for United Press International-Television News (UPI-TV) in New York City, 1974-75, for National Broadcasting Co. (NBC) in Saigon, South Vietnam, and Chicago, 1975-78; free-lance writer, 1978—. Adjunct professor at Northwestern University and Herbert H. Lehman College of the City University of New York.

WRITINGS: Gamemaker (novel), Doubleday, 1980; *Freemartin* (novel), Little, Brown, 1981.

WORK IN PROGRESS: A novel dealing with drug smuggling, with screenplay, publication expected in 1982.

SIDELIGHTS: Cohler commented: "What interests me usually holds me just long enough to write a book about it."

*   *   *

COLE, Lois Dwight   1903-1979
(Lois Dwight Cole Taylor; Caroline Arnett, Lynn Avery, Nancy Dudley, Allan Dwight, Anne Eliot, Ann Lattin, pseudonyms)

OBITUARY NOTICE—See index for *CA* sketch: Born in 1903 in New York, N.Y.; died July 20, 1979, in Manhattan, N.Y. Editor and author. Cole worked as an editor with a number of publishing companies, including Harcourt Brace, Macmillan, McGraw-Hill, Whittlesey House, T. Y. Crowell, G. P. Putnam's Son, William Morrow, and Walker & Co. While employed at Macmillan, Cole made an appointment for her friend Margaret Mitchell to talk with editor Harold Latham. The meeting resulted in the publication of the enormously popular novel *Gone With the Wind.* Among her several books for both adults and children, many written under pseudonyms, are *Mystery of the Vanishing Horses, Linda Goes on a Cruise, Soldier and Patriot: The Life of General Israel Putnam,* and *Stephanie.* Obituaries and other sources: *New York Times,* July 29, 1979; *Publishers Weekly,* August 6, 1979; *AB Bookman's Weekly,* September 10, 1979.

*   *   *

COLEMAN, Roy V.   1885-1971

OBITUARY NOTICE: Born July 21, 1885, in Oneida, Kan.; died November 6, 1971, in Westport, Conn. Editor and author. Coleman worked as an editor at Scribner's. He also wrote *The First Frontier* and *Liberty and Property.* Obituaries and other sources: *AB Bookman's Weekly,* December 13, 1971; *American Authors and Books, 1640 to the Present Day,* 3rd revised edition, Crown, 1972.

*   *   *

COLETTE, (Sidonie-Gabrielle)   1873-1954
(Willy, Colette Willy)

BRIEF ENTRY: Born January 28, 1873, in Saint Saveur-en Puisaye, Burgundy, France; died August 3, 1954, in Paris, France. French novelist and journalist. Considered the foremost French woman author of her day, Colette spent the first twenty years of her life in the Burgundy countryside, and her work is noted for its understanding and sensitive descriptions of country life and nature. After her marriage, at age twenty, to Henry Gauthier-Villars, Colette wrote the "Claudine" novels based on her memories of her Burgundian childhood and her mother. The novels, all published under her husband's pen name "Willy," appeared between 1900 and 1903. Divorced in 1906,

the author supported herself for ten years on the music hall stage as a dancer and mime. During this time she produced her first independent works, including *La Vagabond* (1911). After her second marriage in 1912, Colette devoted herself ardently to journalism. Nevertheless, it was in her novels of this period that she introduced Mitsou and Cheri, the characters who made her famous. In 1935 she married for a third time and was elected to membership in the Royal Belgian Academy. Ten years later she became the first woman to be elected to the Goncourt Academy. After her death she was given a state funeral, the highest posthumous honor a French citizen can receive; it was the first time a French woman writer was so honored. In addition to the "Claudine" novels, Colette's best-known works include *Mitsou; ou, Comment l'esprit vient aux filles* (1919; title means "Mitsou; or, How Girls Grow Wise"), *Cheri* (1920), *La Maison de Claudine* (1922; title means "Claudine's House") and *Gigi* (1944). *Residence:* Palais-Royal, Paris, France. *Biographical/critical sources: Twentieth Century Authors: A Biographical Dictionary of Modern Literature,* 1st supplement, 1955; *Twentieth Century Writing: A Reader's Guide to Contemporary Literature,* Transatlantic, 1969; *Twentieth-Century Literary Criticism,* Volume 1, Gale, 1978.

*   *   *

COLLETTA, Nat J(oseph)   1944-

PERSONAL: Born November 19, 1944, in Marlboro, N.Y.; son of Joseph Anthony and Grace (Valone) Colletta; married Nancy Donahue, June 8, 1968; children: Megan. *Education:* State University of New York at Buffalo, B.A., 1966, M.Ed., 1968; Michigan State University, Ph.D., 1972. *Home:* 2853 Brandywine St. N.W., Washington, D.C. 20008. *Office:* Indonesia Country Program Division, World Bank, 1818 H St. N.W., Washington, D.C. 20433.

CAREER: U.S. Peace Corps, Washington, D.C., volunteer worker in Ponape, Eastern Caroline Islands, 1968-70; Michigan State University, East Lansing, instructor in education, 1970-71; University of Missouri, Kansas City, lecturer in educational sociology, summer, 1972; University of Science, Malaysia, Minden, Penang, visiting senior Fulbright-Hays lecturer in sociology and education, 1972-73; State University of New York College at Buffalo, assistant professor of professional studies and applied science, 1973-74; Ministry of Education and Culture, Jakarta, Indonesia, adviser to Research, Planning, and Development Division, 1974-76; World Bank, Washington, D.C., education and training specialist in eastern Africa projects department, 1977-80, program officer and anthropologist in Indonesia Country Program Division of East Asia Pacific programs department, 1980—. Adjunct professor at University of Virginia, American University, and Washington Center of University of Southern California, 1977-80. Organized international conferences; consultant to World Education, Inc., International Bank for Reconstruction and Development, and Institute for International Education.

MEMBER: Comparative and International Education Society, Society for International Development, American Anthropological Association, American Sociological Association, Asian Studies Association, American Council on Anthropology and Education, American Educational Studies Association, Micronesian Anthropological Association. *Awards, honors:* Ford Foundation grant for Micronesia, 1971; Fulbright-Hays fellow, 1972.

WRITINGS: A Series of Bibliographies in Non-Formal Education, Volume I: *Non-Formal Education in Anthropological Perspective: A Select and Annotated Bibliography,* Volume II:

A Select Bibliography and Non-Formal Educational Programs in Different Geographical Regions of the World, Volume III: *A Bibliography of Selected Topics in Non-Formal Education*, Institute for International Studies in Education, Michigan State University, 1972; *Alternative Strategies in Educational Planning: Non-Formal Education*, South East Asian Development Association, 1972; (with T. A. Todd) *Social and Cultural Influences on Poverty-Oriented Human Resource Development Policies and Programs: A Select and Annotated Bibliography*, Regrave Publishers, 1980; *American Schools for the Natives of Ponape: A Study of Education and Culture Change in Micronesia*, University Press of Hawaii, 1980; (with Ross Kidd) *Cultivating Indigenous Structures and Traditional Media for Nonformal Education and Development*, German Foundation for International Development, 1982.

Contributor: John A. Lent, editor, *Cultural Pluralism and Social Class Formation in the Malaysian Context: An Institutional Perspective*, Northern Illinois University Press, 1977; Peter Knight, editor, *Implementing Human Development Programs*, World Bank, 1981. Contributor of about fifteen articles to education, Asian studies, and sociology journals.

*   *   *

COLSTON-BAYNES, Dorothy   1881(?)-1973
(Dormer Creston)

OBITUARY NOTICE: Born c. 1881; died in 1973 in England. Author of books, including biographies, under pseudonym Dormer Creston. Obituaries and other sources: *AB Bookman's Weekly*, July 30, 1973.

*   *   *

COLVIN, Ralph Whitmore   1920-1981

OBITUARY NOTICE: Born July 23, 1920, in Neenah, Wis.; died June 12, 1981, in New York, N.Y. Psychologist, educator, and author of works in his field. Colvin taught at Columbia University and Fordham University and was associated with centers for child care. He was also chief of clinical psychology at the Institute for Basic Research in Mental Retardation. He wrote *Preschool Education: A Handbook for Training Early Childhood Educators*. Obituaries and other sources: *American Men and Women of Science: The Social and Behavioral Sciences*, 12th edition, Bowker, 1973; *New York Times*, June 20, 1981.

*   *   *

CONNELL, Maureen   1931-

PERSONAL: Born August 2, 1931, in Nairobi, Kenya, came to United States, 1967; daughter of Myles Vincent and Nora (Burward) Connell; married John Guillermin (a director of motion pictures), July 20, 1956; children: Michelle, Michael-John. *Education:* Received degree from London Academy of Music and Dramatic Art, 1953. *Agent:* Georges Borchardt, 136 East 57th St., New York, N.Y. 10022.

CAREER: Worked as actress in London, England, 1953-60; writer. Member of board of directors of Neighbors of Watts Organization, 1968-74.

WRITINGS: "Journey to Eddie" (short story), published in *New Yorker*, March 18, 1974; *Mary Lacey* (novel), Harper, 1981.

WORK IN PROGRESS: A novel for Harper, *Pockets*, set in Los Angeles, California; book reviews.

SIDELIGHTS: Connell's novel *Mary Lacey* concerns a woman who, like Connell, grew up in Kenya, moved to England, and became the wife of a man involved in filmmaking. Susan Wood wrote that "Connell's novel is firmly rooted in place and time, and full of believable characters that exist apart from any connection they might have to their creator's life." A reviewer for the *Detroit Free Press* praised *Mary Lacey* as "powerful, compelling reading."

Connell told *CA:* "My father was Irish, my mother was Anglo-Irish, and I was born in a black man's country. That's why I write—to forge out an identity that keeps lurking off into the undergrowth of my unconscious! Writing is my connection; it gives a purpose for all we go through on this planet. I never set out to be a writer. I thought one had to go to Cambridge or Oxford to become one. My writing evolved. Now it seems all my past led to this point, and all there is to do is share it, get on with it. I try to have as much fun as possible in the process!"

BIOGRAPHICAL/CRITICAL SOURCES: Washington Post, June 5, 1981; *Detroit Free Press*, June 14, 1981.

*   *   *

CONNELL, William Fraser   1916-

PERSONAL: Born June 28, 1916, in Lockhart, Australia; son of Henry Gustavus (a civil engineer) and Stella (Barwick) Connell; married Margaret Lloyd Peck, December 20, 1939; children: Patricia Margaret Connell Selkirk, Robert William, Helen Mary. *Education:* University of Melbourne, B.A., 1938, B.Ed., 1939, M.A. and M.Ed., both 1944; University of Illinois, M.A., 1949; University of London, Ph.D., 1948. *Politics:* Labor. *Religion:* Episcopalian. *Home:* 34 Tanti Ave., Mornington, Victoria 3931, Australia. *Office:* Faculty of Education, Monash University, Clayton, Victoria 3168, Australia.

CAREER: Teacher at secondary schools in Sydney, Australia, and Newcastle, Australia, 1939-42; University of Sydney, Sydney, Australia, senior lecturer, 1951-54, reader, 1954-55, professor of education, 1955-76, professor emeritus, 1977—; Monash University, Clayton, Australia, honorary fellow in education, 1978—. Chairman of education seminars for Asian and Pacific Council in Korea, 1969, and Taiwan, 1970; chairman of National Committee on Social Science Teaching, 1970-78, government committee to report on education in Tasmania, 1977-79, and accreditation board for colleges of advanced education in Victoria, 1980—. *Military service:* Royal Australian Navy Volunteer Reserve, active duty, 1942-45; served in Pacific, Atlantic, and Indian Oceans; became lieutenant.

MEMBER: Comparative Education Society of Europe, Australian and New Zealand History of Education Society (president, 1971), Comparative Education Society of Australia, Australian Association for Research in Education (honorary member; president, 1973), Academy of the Social Sciences in Australia (fellow), American History of Education Society, Victorian Institute for Educational Research (honorary member), Phi Delta Kappa, Kappa Delta Pi. *Awards, honors:* Grants from Australian Research Grants Committee, 1970-72, 1975-77; Mackie Medal from Australian and New Zealand Association for the Advancement of Science, 1978; officer of Order of the British Empire, 1979.

WRITINGS: The Educational Thought and Influence of Matthew Arnold, Routledge & Kegan Paul, 1950, reprinted, Greenwood Press, 1971; (contributor) I. S. Turner, editor, *1956 Jubilee Lectures*, Sydney Teachers College, 1956; (with E. E. Skilbeck and E. P. Francis) *Growing up in an Australian City*,

Australian Council for Educational Research, 1957; *The Foundations of Secondary Education,* Australian Council for Educational Research, 1961, 2nd edition, 1964; (editor with W. E. Andersen, W. J. Campbell, R. L. Debus, and others) *The Foundations of Education,* Novak, 1962, 3rd edition, 1974; (with Debus, H. P. Philip, and Vija Veidemanis) *The University and Its Community,* Novak, 1964; (contributor) R.W.T. Cowan, editor, *Education for Australians,* F. W. Cheshire, 1964; (with Debus and W. R. Niblett) *Readings in the Foundations of Education,* Novak, 1967; (with P. H. Partridge and S. W. Cohen) *Teaching Social Science in Secondary Schools,* Novak, 1969; (contributor) W. J. Fenley, editor, *Education in the 1970's and 1980's,* Hicks Smith, 1969.

(Contributor) N. D. Harper, editor, *Pacific Circle Two,* Queensland University Press, 1972; (with R. W. Connell, R. E. Stroobant, and others) *Twelve to Twenty,* Hicks Smith, 1975; (with F. H. Christie, P. W. Jones, and R. Lawson) *China at School,* Novak, 1975; (contributor) Clifford Turney, editor, *Sources on the History of Australian Education,* Angus & Robertson, 1975; (contributor) David Purpel and Kevin Ryan, editors, *Moral Education,* McCutchan, 1976; (contributor) L. Cairns, R. King, and D. Smith, editors, *Living Education,* World Education Fellowship, 1977; (with C. M. Koopman and C. A. Hoban) *Studying the Local Community,* Allen & Unwin, 1978; (with J. K. Edwards, B. E. Mitchell, and others) *Tasmanian Education Next Decade,* Tasmanian Government Printers, 1979; (contributor) A. F. Madden and W. H. Morris-Jones, editors, *Australia and Britain: Studies in a Changing Relationship,* Sydney University Press, 1980; *A History of Education in the Twentieth-Century World,* Teachers College Press, 1980; *The Australian Council for Educational Research, 1930-1980,* Australian Council for Educational Research, 1980.

Contributor to journals. Foundation editor of *Australian Journal of Education,* 1957-73.

WORK IN PROGRESS: A study of three prominent Australian educators, publication by Sydney University Press expected in 1982; a general history of education, from earliest times, publication by Harcourt expected in 1983; a study of the nature of educational change in Australian education in the twentieth century, completion expected in 1983.

SIDELIGHTS: Connell told *CA:* "During my time at University of Sydney I became interested in encouraging members of the department of education to undertake joint research programs and to write up the outcomes. Hence, the large number of cooperative works and the chapters I have written for books. I found it a productive, interesting, and sometimes frustrating procedure.

"In this way we produced within a few months *The Foundations of Education,* as a joint effort of ten members of the staff under my editorship and, over the years, it sold about a hundred-twenty thousand copies. On the other hand, *The University and Its Community* struggled along after the principal researcher left for a job in Thailand. For years we used to give away a copy to every visitor to the department, and we still have stacks of copies we can't get rid of. With *Twelve to Twenty,* which we knew would be a good seller, we selected four publishers and invited them to tender for the contract with our group. One of the more traditional was a little hurt at the thought that the publishers, rather than the authors, should be the beggars and at the prospect of competing openly with other publishers, but eventually did come to the party.

"While wandering off into these joint excursions in educational psychology, educational foundations, and curriculum, I've always been itchy to get back to writing in the history of edu-

cation. Over most of this period, therefore, I've worked on the history of education in the twentieth century, and after about fifteen years of slow accumulation, a large book on the subject has at last appeared. This book and the history of the Australian Council for Educational Research have required a good deal of travel in pursuit of both archival and publisher material, including visits to the United States, Europe, the Soviet Union, and various parts of Asia."

*   *   *

CONNELLY, Philip M(arshal)   1904(?)-1981

OBITUARY NOTICE: Born c. 1904; died May 20, 1981, in Los Angeles, Calif. Journalist. While editor of *People's World* in 1951, Connelly was convicted of attempting to overthrow the American Government. The Supreme Court later overturned the conviction. He had also worked for the *Los Angeles Examiner* and the *Los Angeles Herald-Express.* Obituaries and other sources: *New York Times,* June 3, 1981.

*   *   *

CONRAD, Alfred Borys   1899(?)-1979

OBITUARY NOTICE: Born c. 1899; died in 1979 in England. Author of *My Father: Joseph Conrad.* Conrad also wrote short stories and presided over the Joseph Conrad Society. Obituaries and other sources: *AB Bookman's Weekly,* February 12, 1979.

*   *   *

CONRAD, Joseph   1857-1924

BRIEF ENTRY: Birth-given name Jozef Teodor Konrad Korzeniowski; born December 3 (listed in some sources as December 6), 1857, in Berdyczew, Poland; died of a heart attack, August 3, 1924, in Bishopsbourne, England. English novelist best known for his tales of the sea, including the novella *The Nigger of the "Narcissus"* (1897) and the novel *Lord Jim* (1900). Conrad spent most of his early adult life in the French mercantile marines, where he read the novels of Charles Dickens while working as a seaman. Dickens's novels piqued Conrad's interest in England, and in 1887 he traveled there. For the next twelve years Conrad worked as a commander of British ships in the Orient. Within that time he became a master of the English language, and in 1889 he began his first novel, *Almayer's Folly* (1895). The novel reflected Conrad's interest in the Orient while drawing heavily from his experiences at sea. These experiences are used in several novels, including the masterpieces *Lord Jim* and *Nostromo* (1904). In both novels the characters must overcome emotional limitations to fully realize themselves. This theme is addressed repeatedly in Conrad's fiction, especially in his novella *The Heart of Darkness* (1902), in which a character's megalomania leads to his guiltless destruction of others. Critics generally divide Conrad's career into two periods: the first contains his widely acclaimed stories of the sea and emotional upheaval; the second half includes several commercially successful melodramas that critics consider inferior to the earlier work. Conrad's influence on English literature is immense, and peers such as William Faulkner and Thomas Mann list him among the great novelists. *Biographical/critical sources: Twentieth Century Authors: A Biographical Dictionary of Modern Literature,* H. W. Wilson, 1942; *Encyclopedia of World Literature in the Twentieth Century,* updated edition, Ungar, 1967; *Twentieth-Century Literary Criticism,* Volume 1, Gale, 1978.

CONTOSTA, David R(ichard)   1945-

PERSONAL: Born February 3, 1945, in Lancaster, Ohio; son of Miles R. (a banker) and Betty J. (a teacher) Contosta; married Jessica Hawthorne (a writer), July 29, 1972; children: Nicole, Alexandra, Jessica. *Education:* Miami University, Oxford, Ohio, A.B., 1967, M.A., 1970, Ph.D., 1973. *Politics:* Democrat. *Religion:* Episcopalian. *Home:* 224 West Nippon St., Philadelphia, Pa. 19119. *Office:* Department of History, Chestnut Hill College, Germantown and Northwestern, Philadelphia, Pa. 19118.

CAREER: High school history teacher in Lancaster, Ohio, 1968-70; Miami University, Oxford, Ohio, instructor in history, 1973-74; Chestnut Hill College, Philadelphia, Pa., assistant professor, 1978, associate professor of history, 1978—. *Member:* American Historical Association, American Studies Association, Phi Beta Kappa, Phi Kappa Phi. *Awards, honors:* Fulbright fellow, 1972; grants from Pennsylvania Council for Humanities, 1975, National Endowment for the Humanities, 1979-80, and American Philosophical Society, 1981.

WRITINGS: Henry Adams and the American Experiment, Little, Brown, 1980.

Author (and narrator/producer) of "Nineteenth-Century Architecture in Lancaster, Ohio," first broadcast by Miami University Broadcasting, December, 1971. Contributor to history journals.

WORK IN PROGRESS: A biography of Whitelaw Reid, completion expected in 1985.

SIDELIGHTS: Henry Adams, great-grandson of President John Adams and grandson of President John Quincy Adams, is the subject of David Contosta's biography, *Henry Adams and the American Experiment.* A central figure in American politics, Henry Adams left little record of his troubled personal life, and Contosta is "wisely unwilling to speculate about Adams' psyche," observed Alden Whitman in the *Los Angeles Times.* Contosta examines the development of Adams's increasingly pessimistic political views "as if he were delivering an expository lecture," Whitman noted. "All the known facts are there, but there is not much fire in the belly. Nor was there, for that matter, in Henry Adam."

Contosta told *CA:* "I am intrigued both by the patterns and relics of the past, and by the dramatic or quite casual ways these patterns affect our lives. Recently I have become fascinated by architectural history. As an amateur photographer I find it relaxing to record man's dreams by the buildings he's erected and the materials he's used."

BIOGRAPHICAL/CRITICAL SOURCES: Los Angeles Times, December 17, 1980.

*   *   *

CONWAY, Peter
See MILKOMANE, George Alexis Milkomanovich

*   *   *

CONZELMAN, James Gleason   1898-1970
(Jimmy Conzelman)

OBITUARY NOTICE: Born March 6, 1898, in St. Louis, Mo.; died July 31, 1970. Pianist, actor, football coach, and author. Conzelman coached the Chicago Cardinals to the National Football League championship in 1947. He was also a newspaper publisher, song writer, and writer for the *Saturday Eve-* *ning Post.* Obituaries and other sources: *Time,* August 10, 1970; *Who's Who in Football,* Arlington House, 1974.

*   *   *

CONZELMAN, Jimmy
See CONZELMAN, James Gleason

*   *   *

COOK, William H(arleston)   1931-

PERSONAL: Born January 1, 1931, in Little Rock, Ark.; son of Thomas Lee (in dairy work) and Jamie (Reynolds) Cook; married Rachel Lee, August 29, 1954; children: Camille, William Craig, Pamela Kay. *Education:* Attended Ouachita Baptist University, 1948-50; Hardin-Simmons University, B.A., 1952; Southwestern Baptist Theological Seminary, Th.D., 1960. *Residence:* Bartlesville, Okla. *Office:* First Baptist Church, P.O. Box 1080, Bartlesville, Okla. 74003.

CAREER: Ordained Baptist minister, 1950; pastor of Baptist churches in Gatesville, Tex., 1955-57, Harrison, Ark., 1957-60, and Levelland, Tex., 1960-69; First Baptist Church, Bartlesville, Okla., pastor, 1969—. Instructor at South Plains College, 1969; member of board of trustees of Wayland Baptist College and Oklahoma Baptist University, 1975-79. Past member of Texas Baptist Executive Board; member of board of directors of Baptist General Convention of Oklahoma (first vice-president, 1972). Speaker at seminars in the United States, South Africa, Switzerland, Japan, India, and Brazil.

WRITINGS: Success, Motivation, and the Scriptures, Broadman, 1974. Contributor to *Baptist Standard, Commission, Oklahoma Baptist Messenger,* and *Proclaim.*

*   *   *

COON, Carleton Stevens   1904-1981

OBITUARY NOTICE—See index for *CA* sketch: Born June 23, 1904, in Wakefield, Mass.; died of cancer, June 3, 1981, in Gloucester, Mass. Anthropologist, educator, and author. Considered one of the last great general anthropologists, Coon made contributions to many areas of the science. He studied the social anthropologies of contemporary societies, but his main interest was ancient man. Conducting both archeological and biological studies, the anthropologist traced the development of man from its earliest form to its first agricultural society. In addition, he studied human adaptations to extreme environments, and he fostered a theory of race which purported that the five races of man evolved differently at different times and in different places. Though discounted by scientists, the theory received support from racists, whose views Coon repudiated. Coon conducted studies of primitive tribal groups currently living in the Middle East and in Patagonia, and he led expeditions which unearthed 150,000-year-old bones of a Neanderthal man as well as some bones of a Stone Age Hotu man. A professor at Harvard and at the University of Pennsylvania, Coon became the curator of ethnology at the University Museum in Philadelphia, and he was also associated with the Peabody Museum of Archeology and Ethnology in Massachusetts. He was awarded the Legion of Merit, the Viking Medal in Physical Anthropology, and the Philadelphia Anthenaeum Award. His writings include *The Story of Man, The Seven Caves, A North Africa Story, A Reader in General Anthropology, The Origin of Races,* and *Adventures and Discoveries.* Obituaries and other sources: *New York Times,* June 6, 1981; *Washington Post,* June 7, 1981; *Newsweek,* June 15, 1981; *Time,* June 22, 1981.

COOPER, Paul F(enimore)   1900(?)-1970

OBITUARY NOTICE: Born c. 1900; died January 18, 1970, in Cooperstown, N.Y. Adapter and editor of folk-tale collections. Cooper was the great-grandson of novelist James Fenimore Cooper. Obituaries and other sources: *AB Bookman's Weekly,* February 16, 1970.

*   *   *

CORDELIER, Maurice
See GIRAUDOUX, (Hippolyte) Jean

*   *   *

CORN, Alfred   1943-

PERSONAL: Born August 14, 1943, in Bainbridge, Ga.; son of A. D. and Grace (Lahey) Corn; married Ann Jones, August, 1967 (divorced, June, 1971). *Education:* Emory University, B.A., 1965; Columbia University, M.A., 1970. *Office:* Department of English, Connecticut College, New London, Conn. 06520.

CAREER: University Review, New York City, associate editor, 1970-71; Da Capo Press, Inc., New York City, staff writer, 1971-72; free-lance writer, 1972-74, 1975-76; Yale University, New Haven, Conn., visiting lecturer in English, 1977-78; Connecticut College, New London, visiting associate professor of English, 1978-81. *Member:* International P.E.N., National Book Critics Circle. *Awards, honors:* Award from Ingram-Merrill Foundation, 1974; George Dillon Prize from *Poetry,* 1975; Blumenthal Prize, 1977; National Endowment for the Arts grant, 1979.

WRITINGS—Poetry; all published by Viking: *All Roads at Once,* 1976; *A Call in the Midst of the Crowd,* 1978; *The Various Light,* 1980.

WORK IN PROGRESS: Another book of poems; a novel.

SIDELIGHTS: Corn wrote: "Ever since my older sister taught me, I have loved to read. Around age ten it occurred to me that someone had to *write* the books that were on the shelves: possibly I might myself become a producer and not merely a consumer of literature. No person, no program prompted the desire to write: it seems to have come over me without much fanfare or explanation.

"Now, though, I think I ought to have a clearer notion of why I write, or rather publish, apart from the wish to shine in public, or for money, the lesser motives that all writers share. I hope it isn't too idealistic of me to imagine that books can truly make a difference in our lives, that they can delight us and teach us. I have paid close attention to my own life and the lives of others around me, as well as the lives of others as recorded in books. I have devoted a good part of my life to studying the English (or American) language and to other languages (French, Italian, Latin, German, Spanish, Attic Greek). When I write I try to bring all the resources of experience and language to bear on what I say, in the belief that the result will strike the reader as rare and valuable, beautiful and useful. I think I have written things that allowed readers (without forcing them) to share things I have felt—emotions from terror to sorrow to love to joy, and with a constant reliance on comedy, the funny things in life, and in words that we wouldn't want to miss. It seems to me that a poem, story, or novel as part of its nature ought to be (if only inferentially) a kind of working model for the well-lived life. A book is like a dwelling:

you don't want to live either in a mausoleum, or a prison, or an office, or a bull ring, or a church. It's possible too that you might like to live in *different* sorts of houses over a lifespan: a tent in the woods for a while, then an apartment in Manhattan, then a two-story frame house with lots of acreage.

"I also consider that those writers who actually bother to reflect on that they do (and why) should try to ask themselves what it is they might bring to contemporary literature that isn't already there. Too often everybody just does the same thing everybody else does because approval is forthcoming. I hate duplication of effort—do we need thirty name brands of detergent? It seems to me that over and over again the voices in the mainstream repeat the same battle cries, not acknowledging that the day was long since carried. We hear a lot of pounding in favor of all that is (at least theoretically) instinctual, unreflective, untutored, unconscious, red-hot, brawling; and this is presumably a rebellion launched against an 'Establishment' often described as academic or East Coast. A quick perusal of the academies of the East Coast and then the record of reputations and rewards ought to put a quick end to this myth. I believe that those writers who wish to perform in the useful role of gadfly, a sting to intelligence and conscience, should at this moment in history, urge readers to *think* and not simply to lunge. Who can doubt that the problems we face now, on the societal and personal level, are enormous? Who can then believe that help will come if we all adopt unthinking, 'instinctual' behavior? Love goes better when thought and imagination are expended in the other's behalf, and an analogy at the level of community relationships shouldn't be hard to come up with. Thought beyond the immediate circle of selfish desires takes practice; literature can help us in this by teaching us to pay attention to things outside ourselves, especially other people, and then to think about them, using our imagination and experience, and finally to help us devise actions that promote well-being—ours and others'.

"At the same time, an important role that books play is to console us for irremediable sorrows, of which there are so many kinds. Not all the things we read lead to action; many lead to contemplation and an invisible healing. How this happens isn't explained. It also strikes me that few contemporary authors are concerned with the curative and contemplative aspects of literature; and I'm probably allowing this estimate of the present time to serve as a reinforcement for my own wish to write along these lines. If ever our society should revert to the puritanical restraint and suppression of individuality that was the rule in the nineteenth century, then, gadfly that I am, no doubt I would wish to begin to write in favor of brash self-assertion, and the community be damned; meanwhile, I live in the 1980's and hope to bring in something compensatory to my own day.

"Among the qualities I like, apart from moral or philosophical content, are richness of perception and texture; the sensation of the shaping hand of art (which is its own universe); verbal agility and surprise; the presence of 'voice' and personality; concentration of meaning; light touch; the non-routine, fresh, and unusual; and rhythm. I like poems that have story qualities, and fiction that has poetic qualities. Wit, comedy, satire, 'laughter in the soul,' all of these I like. Also, writing that brings me information (of whatever kind) that I didn't already have: much of what I know I learned by letting my explorations in subject matter teach me.

"As to my own career as a writer, it is still perhaps in the formative stage. I believe my books of poems show a steadily widening scope as to subject matter and verbal power. I have also written a good many critical articles and drafted a couple of novels. My earliest attempts at fiction I've thrown out as unpublishable, but for several years I've been revising and changing a novel that I think is about ready to be published. No more than half of the poems in my first book still seem readable to me, but the good ones are quite good. As for my second book, it is mostly the long sequence on New York that has attracted notice. I put the book together as a single book, and wish more attention were paid to how the lyrics in the first part shape response to the New York poem. My third book, written after I moved to Connecticut, is in a way purgatorial, a pastoral scaling of the craggy mountain of poetry and life. I have begun work on a book-length poem which, if luck is with me, will be in some sense a counterpart to the *Paradiso* of Dante's *Comedy*. (I intend this only as a general model, and no more binding than to the extent that my New York book was my version of *Inferno,* and *The Various Light,* of *Purgatorio*.) Dante is *the* great post-classical writer. He is not to be rivaled, not even by Shakespeare, my other idol.

"First and last, though, I am an American writer. I love Walt Whitman, Melville, Dickinson, James, Pound, Crane. Those American writers for whom the European tradition was available and life-giving stand a better chance, in my view, of continuing to be read (the world over) than those who won't have anything to do with it. It seems to me that American literature (especially if you add Latin America) is now the greatest. It's an honor to belong to that literature."

*   *   *

CORNELL, Felix M.   1896(?)-1970

OBITUARY NOTICE: Born c. 1896; died March 19, 1970, in Cambridge, Md. Founder of Cornell Maritime Press, a publishing house that specialized in books for seamen. Obituaries and other sources: *Publishers Weekly,* April 13, 1970; *AB Bookman's Weekly,* May 4, 1970.

*   *   *

CORNER, George W(ashington)   1889-1981

OBITUARY NOTICE—See index for *CA* sketch: Born December 12, 1889, in Baltimore, Md.; died September 28, 1981, in Huntsville, Ala. Physician, researcher, educator, administrator, and author. With Willard M. Allen, Corner is credited with identifying the hormone progesterone, a key discovery in the development of the birth-control pill. A researcher studying anatomy and embryology, Corner taught at Johns Hopkins University and the University of California before becoming the first anatomy professor at the University of Rochester's School of Medicine. Beginning in 1940, the scientist became the director of the department of embryology at the Carnegie Institution in Washington. He was also the historian at the Rockefeller Institute and an executive officer of the American Philosophical Society. Corner received more than ten honorary degrees, and he won the American Association of Anatomists' Henry Gray Award. His other awards include the Squibb Award from the Society for the Study of Internal Secretions, the Dale Medal from the British Society of Endocrinology, and the Welch Medal from the American Association for the History of Medicine. He wrote several books, including *Attaining Manhood: A Doctor Talks to Boys About Sex, Attaining Womanhood: A Doctor Talks to Girls About Sex, Ourselves Unborn: An Embryologist's Essay on Man, Doctor Kane of the Arctic Seas, Anatomist at Large: An Autobiography and Selected Essays,* and *The Seven Ages of a Medical Scientist.* Obituaries and other sources: *New York Times,* October 1, 1981.

CORNWELL, Bernard   1944-

PERSONAL: Born February 23, 1944, in London, England; came to the United States in 1980; married Judy Acker (a travel agent), October 20, 1980. *Education:* University of London, B.A., 1967. *Residence:* Westfield, N.J. *Agent:* Toby Eady Associates, Inc., 333 West 86th St., Apt. 1801, New York, N.Y. 10024.

CAREER: British Broadcasting Corp. (BBC-TV), London, England, producer, 1969-76; BBC-TV, Belfast, Northern Ireland, head of current affairs, 1976-79; Thames Television, London, editor of television news, 1979-80; free-lance writer, 1980—.

WRITINGS: Sharpe's Eagle (novel), Viking, 1981; *Sharpe's Gold* (novel), Viking, 1982; *Sharpe's Company* (novel), Viking, 1982.

WORK IN PROGRESS: Sharpe's Sword, a novel, publication expected in 1983.

SIDELIGHTS: Cornwell wrote: "Presently my work is devoted entirely to the Richard Sharpe novels, of which ten have been commissioned by Collins in London. They are picaresque adventure stories set during the Peninsular War, 1808-14, and follow the adventures of a British soldier. They are shamelessly modeled on C. S. Forester's 'Hornblower' series. I have always had a fascination with the Duke of Wellington's army, research on it has been a hobby since my youth, and the Sharpe novels come from that research."

*   *   *

CORTNER, Richard C(arroll)   1935-

PERSONAL: Born November 6, 1935, in Duncan, Okla.; son of Clarence Arthur (a mechanic) and Mary Lee (Sigler) Cortner; married Hanna Joan Otteson (a political scientist), November 14, 1970. *Education:* University of Oklahoma, B.A. (with distinction), 1956; Johns Hopkins University, M.A., 1958; University of Wisconsin, Madison, Ph.D., 1961. *Home:* 1425 Calle Tiburon, Tucson, Ariz. 85704. *Office:* Department of Political Science, University of Arizona, 341 Social Science Building, Tucson, Ariz. 85721.

CAREER: Johns Hopkins University, Baltimore, Md., instructor in political science, 1957-58; University of Tennessee, Knoxville, assistant professor, 1961-65, associate professor of political science, 1965-66; University of Arizona, Tucson, associate professor, 1966-70, professor of political science, 1970—. *Member:* American Political Science Association, Supreme Court Historical Society, Western Political Science Association, Phi Beta Kappa, Pi Sigma Alpha. *Awards, honors:* Woodrow Wilson fellow, 1956-57; award of merit from American Association for State and Local History, 1971, for *The Apportionment Cases.*

WRITINGS: The Wagner Act Cases, University of Tennessee Press, 1964; *The Jones and Laughlin Case,* Knopf, 1970; *The Apportionment Cases,* University of Tennessee Press, 1970; *The Arizona Train Limit Case: Southern Pacific Company Versus Arizona* (monograph), University of Arizona Press, 1970; (with Clfford M. Lytle) *Constitutional Law and Politics: Three Arizona Cases* (monograph), University of Arizona Press, 1970; (with Lytle) *Modern Constitutional Law: Commentary and Case Studies,* Free Press, 1971; *The Supreme Court and Civil Liberties Policy,* Mayfield, 1975; *The Supreme Court and the Second Bill of Rights: The Fourteenth Amendment and the Nationalization of Civil Liberties,* University of Wisconsin Press, 1981. Contributor to *Encyclopedia of Southern History.* Contributor of articles and reviews to professional journals, including *Annals of the American Academy of Political and Social Science.*

WORK IN PROGRESS: An analysis of litigation, tentatively titled *Moore Versus Dempsey: The National Association for the Advancement of Colored People and the Phillips County Riot Litigation,* publication expected in 1982.

SIDELIGHTS: Cortner commented: "Throughout all of my writing, I have attempted to analyze constitutional litigation within the context of the political system and to explicate such litigation as a part of the political process in the United States."

* * *

COSGROVE, Richard A(lfred) 1941-

PERSONAL: Born February 26, 1941, in Jersey City, N.J.; son of Robert A. (a physician) and Grace (a teacher; maiden name, Byrnes) Cosgrove; married Loretta Cummings (an assistant to a corporation president), August 24, 1963; children: Rosemary, Joseph, David, Elizabeth Anne. *Education:* College of the Holy Cross, B.S., 1962; University of California, Riverside, M.A., 1963, Ph.D., 1967. *Office:* Department of History, University of Arizona, Tucson, Ariz. 85721.

CAREER: University of Arizona, Tucson, assistant professor, 1967-72, associate professor of history, 1972—. *Member:* American Historical Association, Conference for British Studies.

WRITINGS: The Rule of Law: Albert V. Dicey, Victorian Jurist, University of North Carolina Press, 1980. Contributor to history journals.

WORK IN PROGRESS: Our Lady the Common Law: The Anglo-American Legal Community, 1870-1930.

* * *

COSMAN, Carol

PERSONAL: Married Robert B. Alter (a professor), June 17, 1973; children: Gabriel. *Home:* 123 Tamalpais Rd., Berkeley, Calif. 94708.

CAREER: Educator.

WRITINGS: (Translator) Marthe Robert, *The Old and the New: From Don Quixote to Kafka,* University of California Press, 1977; (editor with Joan Keefe and Kathleen Weaver) *The Penguin Book of Women Poets,* Allen Lane, 1978, Viking, 1979; (with husband, Robert Alter) *A Lion for Love: A Critical Biography of Stendhal,* Basic Books, 1979.

SIDELIGHTS: Cosman's second book, *The Penguin Book of Women Poets,* is a collection of verse written by women from various eras and cultures. In the *New Republic* Joyce Carol Oates described the collection as a "dizzying profusion" in which one moves through time and literature with "the effect being approximately that of a train ride at high speed through an exotic and varied landscape." She noted that the book stimulates one into further reading, "which is perhaps an anthology's primary reason for being."

Several critics commented favorably on Cosman and Alter's *A Lion for Love: A Critical Biography of Stendhal.* V. S. Pritchett wrote in the *New York Review of Books* that this biography of the French novelist is "sensible, fresh, [and]fairly free of academic jargon." A *New Yorker* critic said it is a "worthwhile addition to Stendhal studies" which "puts everything together—life, works, and their interrelations." John Sturrock of the *New York Times Book Review* added, "There

is a wide choice of biographies of Stendhal by now, but I know of none more coherent or civilized than this one."

BIOGRAPHICAL/CRITICAL SOURCES: New Statesman, November 10, 1978; *Modern Language Review,* January, 1979; *New Republic,* April 21, 1979; *New York Review of Books,* September 27, 1979; *New York Times Book Review,* October 11, 1979; *New Yorker,* October 29, 1979; *Commentary,* December, 1979.*

* * *

COULTER, E(llis) Merton 1890-1981

OBITUARY NOTICE—See index for *CA* sketch: Born July 20, 1890, in Newton, N.C.; died July 5, 1981, in Georgia. Educator and author. Coulter began his career teaching history and political science at Marietta College. He joined the history department of the University of Georgia in 1919. Formerly the head of the department, he was a regents' professor emeritus of history and a past chairman of the university's division of social sciences. In 1978 the university created the E. Merton Coulter Professorship of Southern History in his honor. The first president of the Southern Historical Association, Coulter edited the *Georgia Historical Journal* and ten volumes of the *History of the South.* His books include *College Life in the Old South, A Short History of Georgia, The South During Reconstruction, Confederate States of America, 1861-1865,* and *George Walton Williams: The Life of a Southern Banker.* Obituaries and other sources: *New York Times,* July 6, 1981; *Washington Post,* July 8, 1981.

* * *

COULTER, Edwin M(artin) 1937-

PERSONAL: Born July 18, 1937, in Waynesboro, Va.; son of Homer Preston (a landscape architect) and Eileen (Rader) Coulter; married Aleta Holbrooks (a teacher), June 22, 1963; children: John Edwin, David Preston. *Education:* Furman University, B.A., 1962; University of Virginia, Ph.D., 1965. *Politics:* Democrat. *Religion:* Episcopalian. *Home:* 207 Augusta Rd., Clemson, S.C. 29631. *Office:* Department of Political Science, Clemson University, Clemson, S.C. 29631.

CAREER: Arkansas State University, State University, assistant professor, 1965-67, associate professor and chairman of Division of Social Science, both 1967-68; Oklahoma College of Liberal Arts, Chickasha, associate professor of political science and chairman of Division of Social Science, both 1968-71; Clemson University, Clemson, S.C., associate professor of political science, 1971—. Broadcaster on public radio network. *Military service:* U.S. Navy, 1955-58. *Member:* American Political Science Association, Southern Political Science Association, South Carolina Political Science Association, Phi Beta Kappa, Raven Society. *Awards, honors:* Woodrow Wilson fellow.

WRITINGS: Principles of Politics and Government, Allyn & Bacon, 1981. Contributor to academic journals.

WORK IN PROGRESS: A Primer on National Security Policy, publication expected in 1983.

SIDELIGHTS: Coulter told *CA:* "I am attempting to write basic-level textbooks that relate to contemporary undergraduates and their level of preparation. I tend to take a macroanalytical view of national security and a humanistic approach to issues of foreign policy."

COUPEY, Philippe 1937-

PERSONAL: Born November 8, 1937, in New York, N.Y.; son of Eric and Jo (Dalley) Coupey; married Ellen Fields; children: Celine. *Education:* St. Lawrence University, B.A., 1960; Sorbonne, University of Paris, Licence, 1964. *Home:* 18 rue Cels, Paris 14, France. *Agent:* Elaine Markson Literary Agency, Inc., 44 Greenwich Ave., New York, N.Y. 10011.

CAREER: Ordained Zen Buddhist monk, 1980; part-time uranium prospector in New Mexico and Wyoming, 1957—; interpreter for Nigerian ambassador to France, 1978-79.

WRITINGS: The Voice of the Valley (nonfiction), Bobbs-Merrill, 1979; *Requiem for Henry Miller* (nonfiction), Handshake Editions, 1981; (translator) *Book of Sutras,* Editions Zen, 1981.

WORK IN PROGRESS: The Lion's Roar, the Zen teachings of Taisen Deshimaru Rushi; *The Monte Carlo Clan,* fiction based on author's youth in Monte Carlo.

SIDELIGHTS: Coupey has been a Zen disciple to Master T. Deshimara since 1972.

*   *   *

COURT, W(illiam) H(enry) B(assano) 1905(?)-1971

OBITUARY NOTICE: Born c. 1905; died September 29, 1971, in Birmingham, England. Educator, economist, and author. Court's writings include *British Economic History, 1870-1914, A Concise Economic History of Britain,* and *Scarcity and Choice in History.* Obituaries and other sources: *AB Bookman's Weekly,* November 8, 1971.

*   *   *

COUSINS, Peter Edward 1928-

PERSONAL: Born March 28, 1928, in Harrogate, England; son of Edward (a manager) and Lucie Stephanie (Leisser) Cousins; married Pamela Pratt (a teacher). *Education:* King's College, Cambridge, M.A., 1950; King's College, London, B.D., 1964; also studied through London Bible College. *Religion:* Christian. *Home:* 3 Fairpark Rd., Exeter, England. *Office:* Paternoster Press Ltd., Paternoster House, 3 Mount Radford Cres., Exeter, Devonshire EX2 4JW, England.

CAREER: Teacher at grammer schools, 1951-57; teacher at secondary school in Southgate, England, 1958-60; head of religious education at girls' school in Putney, England, 1960-65; Gipsy Hill College, Kingston-upon-Thames, England, senior lecturer, 1966-71, principal lecturer in religious studies, 1971-75; Paternoster Press Ltd., Exeter, England, editorial director, 1975—. *Member:* Philosophical Society of Great Britain (fellow; member of council), Royal Commonwealth Society.

WRITINGS: A Christian's Guide to the Death of Christ, Hodder & Stoughton, 1967; (with Michael Eastman) *The Bible and the Open Approach in Religious Education,* Tyndale Press, 1968; *Education and Christian Parents,* Scripture Union, 1969; (with wife, Pamela Cousins) *The Power of the Air,* Hodder & Stoughton, 1978; *The "Brethren,"* Religious Education Press, 1982. Contributor to magazines and newspapers, including *Crusade.* Editor of *Spectrum,* 1968-74.

WORK IN PROGRESS: Studying an evangelical approach to teaching world religions.

SIDELIGHTS: Cousins wrote: "By temperament and training I'm a communicator and teacher. Almost everything I've written has been undertaken with a view to informing people, encouraging them, or disturbing them. In this context, style matters not at all—or immensely. Getting the right words in the right order is not primarily an aesthetic concern but a functional necessity."

*   *   *

COWAN, Stuart DuBois 1917-

PERSONAL: Born April 30, 1917, in Tarrytown, N.Y.; son of Stuart DuBois (in advertising) and Lucy D. (Coffey) Cowan; married Pauline Horn, November 2, 1940 (died December, 1974); married Grace R. Lombardi, December 28, 1976; children: (first marriage) Stuart A., Robert B.; (second marriage; stepchildren) Jan, Candace. *Education:* Princeton University, B.A., 1939. *Home address:* North St., Box 596, Rye, N.Y. 10580. *Agent:* Willis Kingsley Wing, Crosslands-90, Kennett Square, Pa. 19348; and Curtis Brown Ltd., 575 Madison Ave., New York, N.Y. 10022.

CAREER: Cowan & Dengler, Inc., New York City, advertising copywriter, 1946-54; Donahue & Coe, Inc., New York City, vice-president and advertising copywriter, 1954-59; Raytheon Co., Lexington, Mass., vice-president and in commercial marketing, 1959-63; United Research, Inc., Cambridge, Mass., president and chief executive officer, 1963-68; business consultant, 1968-70; Radio Publications, Inc., Wilton, Conn., executive vice-president and member of board of directors, 1970—. Assistant director of American Radio Relay League; member of board of directors of Greenwood Union Cemetery Corp. *Military service:* U.S. Naval Reserve, active duty on destroyers, 1940-46; served in Atlantic and Pacific theaters; became lieutenant commander. *Member:* Institute of Electrical and Electronic Engineers, U.S. Naval Institute, American Marketing Association, Stage Harbor Yacht Club, Princeton Club.

WRITINGS: (With Samm Sinclair Baker) *Vigor for Men Over Thirty,* Macmillan, 1967; (with William I. Orr) *Better Shortwave Reception,* Radio Publications, 1970; *The Truth About Citizens Band Antennas,* Radio Publications, 1971; *The Radio Amateur Antenna Handbook,* Radio Publications, 1978; (with Edward J. Beattie) *Toward the Conquest of Cancer,* Crown, 1980.

Contributor: *New Products-New Profits,* American Management Association, 1964; *After Business Hours,* Funk, c.1950. Also contributor to electronic, marketing, and health journals.

SIDELIGHTS: Cowan told *CA:* "Writing is a priceless opportunity to touch the lives of people for better or worse—to inform, entertain, and perhaps even inspire. Most of us hope that our efforts are worthwhile because writing is such hard work."

*   *   *

COWART, David (Guyland) 1947-

PERSONAL: Born December 22, 1947, in Tuscaloosa, Ala.; son of Eugene Guyland (in engineering management) and Margaret (a publisher; maiden name, Matthews) Cowart; married Georgia Ann Jackson (an author and a teacher of piano, piano pedagogy, and musicology), September 5, 1970. *Education:* University of Alabama, B.A., 1969; Indiana University, M.A., 1971; Rutgers University, Ph.D., 1977. *Residence:* Columbia, S.C. *Office:* Department of English, University of South Carolina, Columbia, S.C. 29208.

CAREER: U.S. Peace Corps, Washington, D.C., volunteer teacher of English in Ethiopia, 1969-70; University of South

Carolina, Columbia, instructor, 1977-79, assistant professor of English, 1979—. *Military service:* U.S. Army, radio and television broadcaster, 1971-73; served in Panama. *Member:* Modern Language Association of America, South Atlantic Modern Language Association, Philological Association of the Carolinas.

WRITINGS: Thomas Pynchon: The Art of Allusion, Southern Illinois University Press, 1980; (contributor) Robert Morace and Katherine Vanspanckeren, editors, *Critical Perspectives on John Gardner,* Southern Illinois University Press, 1981.

Contributor, except as noted: *Dictionary of Literary Biography,* Gale, Volume 2: *American Novelists Since World War II,* 1978, Volume 4: *American Writers in Paris, 1920-1939,* 1980, Volume 5: *American Poets Since World War II,* 1980, (editor with Thomas Wymer) *Twentieth-Century American Science-Fiction Writers,* 1981.

Contributor of numerous articles and reviews to scholarly journals.

WORK IN PROGRESS: Arches and Light: The Fiction of John Gardner.

SIDELIGHTS: Cowart wrote: "*Arches and Light* is a study of Gardner's impressive craftsmanship as well as an evaluation of his claims for the possibilities of 'moral fiction' in the present literary environment.

"I try to write criticism that is interpretive and pedagogical, and I deplore recent developments in criticism—attempts to make it as 'creative' or as dense as the part it is charged with elucidating. Oscar Wilde said: 'Nowadays, to be intelligible is to be found out'; I wish the Surgeon General would require that statement to appear on the title pages of certain of the more pretentious critical books. My literary interests are catholic but with special interest in fiction and the modern period. I also dabble in fiction.

"As a teacher, I become less and less willing to con students with courses in film, science fiction, and other popular culture subjects. Such courses allow students to dodge the classics, which they desperately need to read. They are sadly lacking in a sense of the cultural continuity of Western civilization— a continuity that ephemeral popular culture can hardly supply."

AVOCATIONAL INTERESTS: Classical music, travel.

* * *

COX, James Anthony   1926-
   (Mark Porter)

PERSONAL: Born April 23, 1926, in Orange, N.J.; son of James Joseph (a butcher) and Emma (Polifka) Cox; married JoAnne Dixon Francis (a word processor), August 9, 1951; children: John, Susan Cox Gleason, James, Laura Cox Michalek, Mary, Catherine, Michael, Elizabeth. *Education:* Attended Seton Hall University, 1946-48; New York University, B.S., 1950. *Religion:* Roman Catholic, *Home and office:* 293 Whitford Ave., Nutley, N.J. 07110.

CAREER: Caltex Petroleum Corp., New York City, assistant editor, 1951-62; National Geographic Society, Washington, D.C., project editor, 1962-63; Time-Life Books, New York City, project editor, 1963; Texas Gulf Sulphur Co., New York City, assistant manager of public relations, 1963-68; Shell Oil Co., New York City, magazine editor, 1969-71; free-lance writer, 1971—. Consultant to Philadelphia Academy of Natural Sciences and National Association of Ocean Industries. *Military service:* U.S. Naval Reserve, active duty, 1944-46; served in American, Pacific, and Chinese theaters.

WRITINGS: (Under pseudonym Mark Porter) *Slashing Blades* (juvenile novel), Simon & Schuster, 1960; *Mollusks,* Grolier, 1970; *The Endangered Ones* (nonfiction), Crown, 1975; *A Century of Light* (history of General Electric Co.), Benjamin Co., 1978; *Shells: Treasures From the Sea,* Larousse, 1979; *Put Your Foot in Your Mouth* . . . (juvenile nonfiction), Random House, 1980; *One Thousand Facts About Sex,* Rutledge Books, 1982. Contributor to magazines, including *Reader's Digest, True, Smithsonian,* and *Sea Frontiers.*

WORK IN PROGRESS: Great Zoos of the World; a book about a woman with multiple personalities; wildlife books for children for Sierra Club.

SIDELIGHTS: Cox told *CA:* "I free-lance full time; therefore I will write anything, or at least give it a good shot. Fiction has always been my first love, but I survive with nonfiction, mostly in the form of assignments from industry."

* * *

CRAIG, Nancy
   See MASLIN, Alice

* * *

CRANE, (Harold) Hart   1899-1932

BRIEF ENTRY: Born July 21, 1899, in Garretsville, Ohio; committed suicide, April 27, 1932, in the Gulf of Mexico. American poet. Scarred by his parents' unsuccessful marriage and horrified by the materialism and insensitivity of modern America, Crane found a spiritual escape from the hatred and despair of the world through poetry. One of America's greatest poets, he was an undisciplined individual who lived among the best and worst of society until, disillusioned that he had lost his creative talent, Crane jumped from the S.S. *Orziba* and drowned himself in the Gulf of Mexico. Crane's creative genius is apparent in his two major poetry collections, *White Buildings* (1926) and *The Bridge* (1930), though some critics have called his works unintelligible owing to his use of private symbolism. In two of his poems, "For the Marriage of Faustus and Helen" and his major work "The Bridge," the poet utilized brilliant visual and tactile imagery plus experimental techniques of time to voice his reaction against the pessimism of T. S. Eliot's "The Waste Land." Though he admired Eliot, he was influenced in technique by Rimbaud and wanted, like Whitman, to create an American myth. A major poem of the twentieth century, "The Bridge" is Crane's "mystical synthesis of 'America'" which connects the country's past, present, and future. An excellent example of the "objective correlative" principle, a theory suggesting that images be arranged and interpreted by their emotional effects so that they catch and communicate a feeling, "The Bridge" is considered the first poem to adequately portray the mechanized twentieth century. The poem was written sporadically over seven years, during which time Crane's reputation degenerated because of his alcoholism, financial problems, and homosexual activities. Like most of his works, "The Bridge" has been criticized for its sensation and abstraction. Nevertheless, because of "The Bridge," Crane received the Helen Haire Levinson Prize in 1931 and later a Guggenheim fellowship. *Residence:* Vera Cruz, Mexico. *Biographical/critical sources: Cyclopedia of World Authors,* Harper, 1958; *Twentieth-Century Literary Criticism,* Volume 2, Gale, 1979.

* * *

CRAWELLS, Carl
   See HERM, Gerhard

CRAWFORD, Jean   1907(?)-1976

OBITUARY NOTICE: Born c. 1907; died October 13, 1976, in New York, N.Y. Editor for Rinehart, Dutton, and Crown publishers. Obituaries and other sources: Publishers Weekly, November 8, 1976.

*   *   *

CRAWFORD, Vaughn Emerson   1917(?)-1981

OBITUARY NOTICE: Born c. 1917; died September 25, 1981, in Port Chester, N.Y. Curator and author of Sumerian Economic Texts From the First Dynasty of Isin (BIN IX). Crawford was considered an expert in Sumerian script. He was associated with the Museum of Modern Art from 1957 to his death. Obituaries and other sources: New York Times, September 27, 1981.

*   *   *

CRAWFORD, William H.   1907(?)-1973

OBITUARY NOTICE: Born c. 1907; died September 20, 1973, in Belgrade, Me. Editor and educator. Crawford worked for Oxford University Press and Seabury Press before accepting a position as headmaster of St. Peter's School in Peekskill, N.Y., in 1971. Obituaries and other sources: Publishers Weekly, October 22, 1973.

*   *   *

CRESTON, Dormer
See COLSTON-BAYNES, Dorothy

*   *   *

CRISLER, Lois (Brown)   ?-1971

OBITUARY NOTICE: Died June 4, 1971, in Seattle, Wash. Educator and author. Crisler taught at the University of Washington. She wrote of her experiences in the wilderness in Arctic Wild and Captive Wild. Obituaries and other sources: Who's Who Among Pacific Northwest Authors, 2nd edition, Pacific Northwest Library Association, 1969; Publishers Weekly, August 2, 1971.

*   *   *

CRISPIN, Edmund
See MONTGOMERY, (Robert) Bruce

*   *   *

CRITCHLEY, Lynne
See RADFORD, Richard F(rancis), Jr.

*   *   *

CROCE, Arlene   1934-

PERSONAL: Born May 5, 1934, in Providence, R.I.; daughter of Michael Daniel and Louise Natalie (Pensa) Croce. Education: Attended University of North Carolina at Greensboro, 1951-53; Barnard College, B.A., 1955. Residence: Brooklyn, N.Y. Agent: Maxine Groffsky, 2 Fifth Ave., New York, N.Y. 10011. Office: New Yorker, 25 West 43rd St., New York, N.Y. 10036.

CAREER: Ballet Review, New York City, founder and editor, 1965-78; New Yorker (magazine), New York City, dance critic,

1973—. Free-lance dance critic. Awards, honors: Hodder fellow, Princeton University, and Guggenheim fellow, both 1971; dance panelist for National Endowment for the Arts (NEA), 1977-80; Afterimages was named one of twenty best books of 1977 by the New York Times Book Review; American Academy of Arts and Letters literature award and mayor's award for Art and Culture from mayor of New York City, both 1979.

WRITINGS: The Fred Astaire & Ginger Rogers Book, Outerbridge & Lazard, 1972; Afterimages, Knopf, 1977. Contributor of reviews to magazines and periodicals, including New York Times Book Review, Film Quarterly, National Review, Sight and Sound, Dancing Times, Atlantic Monthly, Harper's, and Commentary.

WORK IN PROGRESS: A second collection of reviews for Knopf, publication expected in 1982.

SIDELIGHTS: Noting that "theatrical criticism is surely one of the most awkward, slippery, and transient of all observant crafts," Lincoln Kirstein proclaimed in the New York Review of Books that Arlene Croce's Afterimages "can be read as the most reliable chronicle of theatrical dancing in the United States from 1966 to 1977." The book, which contains selections of Croce's dance criticism from the Ballet Review, the Dancing Times, and the New Yorker, consistently delighted its reviewers. When Arlene Croce "does a big historical job on The Sleeping Beauty, it feels fresh because it comes from a writer's instinct for what her audience needs to know," observed Robert Garis in the Hudson Review. "As she moves easily from ballet to modern dance to movies to the World's Professional Dancing Championships, it's not unlike accompanying Shaw through the musical world of the late nineteenth century, and when I call Croce a superb journalist, I have the Shavian standard in mind."

Afterimages also prompted comparisons to the critical work of such writers as James Agee and Randall Jarrell. "The line between reviewing and criticism is a smudged one, but Arlene Croce's dance column in The New Yorker falls into the latter category as easily as Randall Jarrell's poetry chronicle or James Agee's film commentary," declared Martha Duffy in Time. By "bringing Baryshnikov or Balanchine—or Fred Astaire—to life," asserted Newsweek's Jack Kroll, Croce brings "civilization to life, just as Bernard Shaw did when he wrote about Bernhardt or Duse, or James Agee when he wrote about Chaplin or Keaton."

Part of Croce's success can be attributed to her vast knowledge of dance—knowledge that comes, observed Duffy, from "watching every possible performance—every last Giselle, however badly miscast, any tentative choreographer who can get a pickup company together for a few evenings in a church basement." Her criteria for judging dance, noted Richard Poirier in the New York Times Book Review, "are relatively simple—that whatever she sees must live up to the highest standards appropriate to it, whether it's in the State Theatre, on or off Broadway, or in a loft."

Critics seem to agree, however, that what is most impressive about Croce is, as Poirier put it, "her capacity for the most beautifully detailed and exciting descriptions of particular dance movements. No one can more compellingly re-create in language a step or a sequence." In a review of the New York City Ballet's 1975 performance of "The Four Temperaments," which was choreographed by George Balanchine, Croce wrote: "When, in the opening statement of the ballet . . . we see a girl, supported on her points, turning from side to side and transferring her weight from one foot to the other as she turns, we see her do it with a finicky grace: she lifts and lowers the free foot, curls it around the standing leg, and carefully flexes it before arching to full point. We see, in short, a foot becoming a point—nature being touched to artificial life. The detail looms for an instant, then quickly takes its place in the grand scheme of the ballet.'' Another example of Croce's description of dance, which appears in her second collection of reviews, concerns Karole Armitage's solo in choreographer Merce Cunningham's ''Fractions'': ''As she [Armitage] kicks, turns, and strides in huge seconds and fourths, she seems in a very real sense to be breaking ground. Old structures crumble; air rushes up.''

Reviewers of *Afterimages* also enjoyed Croce's comments about New York City and the asides about dance audiences that punctuate her reviews. ''The matinee audience used to wear large hats, which it gladly removed on request,'' Croce wrote in a review that also appears in her second collection. ''Now it wears bangle bracelets. If you ask it to stop jangling, it doesn't know what you mean.'' David Kalston of the *Times Literary Supplement* declared that *Afterimages* is, ''in the tonic manner of Shaw on London, a brilliant and funny book about Manhattan: its appetites and possibilities, its audiences' vulgarities and realized dreams.'' ''A lot of us have thought for some time that Croce is about the best reviewer writing about any of the arts,'' acknowledged Garis. ''Now, after the publication and reviews of *Afterimages,* that opinion can be taken for granted.''

AVOCATIONAL INTERESTS: Old movies.

CA INTERVIEW

CA interviewed Arlene Croce by phone on August 19, 1980, in New York City.

CA: One reviewer of your book Afterimages *wrote, ''What makes [Croce] a critic worth following—in every sense—is the range of her culture and the joy of her conviction that it is possible even in this 'oversold decade' to distinguish the shoddy from the true.'' Is there any way the interested but untutored viewer can distinguish the shoddy from the true in dance?*

CROCE: I think that anybody who is alive to dance as a phenomenon of our nature, as something that people do naturally, can appreciate and distinguish good dancing when it's done by professionals. I don't believe that there is a battery of specialized information you need to have before you go to a performance. But I believe, too, that cultivation of a subject can only enhance one's appreciation and enjoyment of it. As with everything that is really fascinating, you can only gain by knowing more about it. The best way to go about familiarizing yourself with the values of any art form is by steady exposure. Of course that isn't always possible for people who don't live close to the major entertainment centers where ballet is mounted in seasons. But I don't think there is any real substitute for live performance and for the steady exposure to it that you can get when you do live near it, in New York or any city that does have a professional company. Dance is the art, of course, that does not duplicate itself in any other form, and so it has to be live to be enjoyed.

CA: You've mentioned that problem in reviewing ballet. It's the afterimage that you have when you leave—you don't have a film to see over or a book to pick back up.

CROCE: No. We now have documents in the form of videotapes and filmed performances, and sometimes films of specially staged performances. But I think we have to be very careful how we use filmed and taped dance performances, because all we really have there is a record of one performance,

not the text of a ballet, not the *truth* about how something really is. That doesn't exist. Dance only exists in performance, and performance is variable.

CA: Holly Brubach, in her June, 1979, article in Vogue, *described you as ''at once sophisticated and impressionable,'' and said, ''Her mind justifies the ways of her heart.'' Do you feel that those are fair descriptions?*

CROCE: I don't think I would use those terms in talking about myself, but I do know that thinking about what I've seen and writing about what I've seen is the only way I really *know* what I've seen.

CA: Are you able to approach dance criticism in the way you do because you were not formally trained for it?

CROCE: I expect so. I regret that I wasn't formally trained for it, but the age at which I discovered that I wanted to write about dance, I was too old to begin formal dance training. I wish that I had had it, and I wish that I'd had formal musical training as well. But, of course, no one ever sets out to be a critic. It's something that happens. You do the best you can with the equipment that you've got. It's very hard for me to say how I would be writing if I had other methods of approach. All I know is I have to do my best with what I do have.

CA: You've said the writing is the hardest part of your work, and that you learned to write to fill in the gaps when you were editing Ballet Review. *Do you think of the reader when you're writing?*

CROCE: Yes, I do, constantly. I ask myself, ''Am I making sense?'' I have to, because I'm dealing in a subject that is very hard to communicate verbally, so I'm constantly aware of the shortcomings of my tactics as a writer. I think any writer on dance has to be interested in communication almost for its own sake.

CA: Were there any difficulties in researching the production details of the movies you described in The Fred Astaire & Ginger Rogers Book?

CROCE: It was endlessly difficult because the movies were made so long ago. I interviewed people who were associated with the making of those films, but many of them had simply forgotten a lot of what went on, which is quite understandable. I think the book came along too late; but then, of course, if I had tried to write it earlier, there might not have been the interest for it that there was by the time I did write it. And my own experience with those films was delayed—I didn't even get to see most of them until the 1960's, when they were part of a general revival of interest in the 1930's. The first time around, I was too young; I had to wait until I was all grown up and it was all gone. I believe that there is much, much more to be told about what went into the making of the Astaire-Rogers series than I was able to find out in the early 1970's.

CA: I was surprised to read that Astaire had done so much of the cutting and editing and production of those movies.

CROCE: I think he had to be given that kind of absolute control because he was the ultimate authority on those matters, and it was intelligent of RKO [Radio-Keith-Orpheum, a motion picture production and exhibition firm] to recognize that. No one else there, or anywhere else in Hollywood, could have known how important those matters were and how they were interconnected.

CA: Do you think that we've outgrown the state of mind that made those movies so delightful at the time?

CROCE: This is a theory, isn't it? The end of innocence, the end of optimism. There is a lyrical enthusiasm in those films that we only feel the pang of nostalgia for now. Songs are certainly not being written in that mode. At least, I'm not aware of too many songwriters today who share the ebullience of the Gershwins and Irving Berlin and Jerome Kern and Cole Porter. That was really a golden era. We have those movies which are classics, and those songs which are classics, and it's a very tough standard to beat. However, I think that the feelings people have about them today are just the same as the feelings people had then. The human emotions to which those songs appeal haven't changed in the slightest. That's why the films are still popular and why we can call them classics. They transcend the cult of nostalgia.

CA: Do you have any opinion on the social dancing that people are doing now, such as disco?

CROCE: I can't comment on it except as it seems to feed into professional dancing. Recreational dancing is not uninteresting to me, but I can't keep up with it. It's a different kind of interest. I think you have to be younger and plugged into changes and fads in pop music. I'm not. I don't even go dancing.

CA: What kind of effect do you think the Russian defectors and immigrants are having on American dance?

CROCE: They've had an immeasurable effect already, starting with Nureyev and certainly including Baryshnikov, who has now taken over the artistic direction of the American Ballet Theater.

CA: Is there a kind of general explanation for the novice on how Russian and American dancers differ?

CROCE: It depends on which American dancers and even on which Russian dancers you're talking about. The school of ballet from which Nureyev and Makarova and Baryshnikov emerged in Leningrad is the same school that produced most of the great Russian dancers who colonized the West. Even before the post-Diaghilev diaspora there was a certain impact felt in the West from the Maryinsky Ballet, and it is mainly that institution, of course, that has spread itself and proliferated in the major ballet capitals of the West, with the exception of Copenhagen, which has always been Bournonville's laboratory, basically. You could say Western ballet is almost exclusively Russian in root. Now, there are different branches. I think it might be possible to say that, in the school of ballet founded in America by George Balanchine you probably have the purest evocation of the Maryinsky at the time at which he left it. But America has had almost as great an impact on Balanchine as he's had on it. Any differences in Russian and American style come largely from his adaptation of Russian academic technique to the American physique and temperament. We're speedier and slangier. And there are other differences that I don't think the novice would be concerned with. There is certainly the most relevant connection between Russian ballet historically and our own contemporary American ballet, there's no question about it.

CA: Do you think there is a lot of inferior work being done in the field of experimental dance?

CROCE: There is a lot of inferior work being done in that field and in every other field in dance. About 60 to 70 percent of it is not good, wherever you go, wherever you see it, whether it's at Lincoln Center or a Soho loft. You hear a great deal about the dance boom, and I think it's been overplayed. The quality of dance is overpromoted.

CA: You have said in regard to the increased popularity of ballet that you thought it was tied in with our being more aware of our bodies, more concerned with physical fitness, more open about our sexuality. Isn't there more to it than that?

CROCE: What I was trying to say is that I certainly *hope* that there is more than that. There is a certain faddish enthusiasm just now. But the ballet has always been popular—it's been growing in popularity for nearly half a century. I hope that these current fads—sexual liberation, fitness, and all of those things that tend to surround discussion of the ballet—are only temporary considerations.

CA: You wrote about ten years ago in Harper's: *"It isn't mindlessness but the state beyond mind that moves us in perfect dancing. It's what moves the dancer, too." Is that state innate to the well-trained dancer?*

CROCE: I wish I could answer you, but I don't know how a dancer's mind works—I have no idea; I've never been a dancer. What I'm pretty sure of is that the dancer doesn't think. There's no cogitation or ratiocination in a great performance.

CA: Is it a difficult state for the viewer to achieve?

CROCE: The viewer doesn't have to achieve it. If you are susceptible to what dancing is about—and I think a lot of people are—your rational mind has no part, really, in your response. You just simply are gripped without knowing how and sometimes without knowing why. You just get excited. After I've seen a lot of bad stuff for weeks, months—season in, season out, sometimes—and I begin to think I'm jaded and incapable of responding, almost invariably there will come a performance quite out of the blue when that thing happens, that unexpected surge of delight that just simply comes off the stage. It doesn't come from me. I don't have to labor for it; it just comes. And I know that it's real and it's good.

CA: Do you read other dance criticism?

CROCE: Oh, yes. I try to keep up with as much of it as I can. In fact, for years I did have a more than professional interest in doing so because I edited a journal of dance and was constantly trying to find and attract new writers, so the state of dance criticism was always of great concern.

CA: Do you feel that much of it is good?

CROCE: There is certainly much more of it. More intelligent and aware people seem to be interested in writing about dance.

CA: In the past you've faulted critics for glossing over bad individual performances, for being afraid to criticize dancers personally in reviews. Is there still that tendency among critics?

CROCE: To criticize physically is to criticize personally, and as long as dance critics shrink from that they will be failing to do their job. Also there's a tendency in our culture to equalize the accomplishments of talented and untalented individuals in the interest of a democratic reaction. Dancer x may be ever so much less talented and attractive than dancer y, but he works as hard—harder! Why shouldn't he get high marks, too? We're always ready to sentimentalize *effort*. And because everyone knows how hard dancers work, we tend to sentimentalize the whole profession. Yes, it's hard physical work, but as Twyla Tharp has said, physical discipline is the easiest kind there is.

CA: What do you find most exciting about your work?

CROCE: The dancing itself, when it is continually developing and thrilling to watch. And also, of course, there is the whole contest between what is happening and the attempt to *record* what is happening. That will always be a fresh stimulus for me, I hope.

CA: I've read that if you were really having difficulty in starting to write, you would think of a particular writer and imitate his style.

CROCE: That was said lightly, of course. But one of the things that I am conscious of is criticism as the act of the writer. I don't consider myself a part of the dance profession, and I don't write for dancers but for the audience. I hope to interest people who respond to values in writing as well as values in dancing.

CA: If you could, would you change any part of what you've done so far?

CROCE: I would take away all of the mistakes, of course. But even if I did that, I would go on making them as long as I'm unable to erase whatever mechanism in me it is that makes mistakes.

CA: You said in a 1976 Mademoiselle *interview: "You have to accept that you will be involved in some kind of fallacy or other no matter what you write. I don't tell the truth." Do you think that applies to all good critical writing?*

CROCE: Edwin Denby, whose work I hold in great reverence, once said that every critic has blind spots, and you simply have to learn what they are and maneuver around them. But you can't pretend that they don't exist for you.

BIOGRAPHICAL/CRITICAL SOURCES: National Review, December 8, 1972; *Saturday Review,* December 16, 1972; *New York Times Book Review,* December 17, 1972, November 27, 1977; *Time,* January 22, 1973, January 9, 1978; *New York Review of Books,* November 29, 1973, November 24, 1977; *New Yorker,* December 8, 1975, October 23, 1978, December 4, 1978; *Newsweek,* November 14, 1977; *Hudson Review,* summer, 1978; *Commentary,* August, 1978, *Times Literary Supplement,* December 1, 1978.

—*Interview by Jean W. Ross*

* * *

CROWLEY, Aleister
   See CROWLEY, Edward Alexander

* * *

CROWLEY, Edward Alexander   1875-1947
   (Aleister Crowley, Frater Perdurabo, Count Vladimir Svareff)

BRIEF ENTRY: Scottish poet, author, and practitioner of black magic. Crowley was notorious for his black-magic rites, and he established Satanic temples in both England and Italy. Using a number of pseudonyms, he wrote and edited books on magic and the occult, including *Magick in Theory and Practice* (1929). He also wrote several books of verse, including *Snowdrops*

From a Curate's Garden, 1881 A.D. (c. 1904) and *Alexandra* (1909), which, because of their erotic content, were sought out and destroyed whenever possible by British customs officials. It is claimed Crowley served as model for the protagonist of W. Somerset Maugham's novel *The Magician. Biographical/ critical sources: Reader's Encyclopedia,* 2nd edition, Crowell, 1965.

* * *

CULLER, Jonathan   1944-

PERSONAL: Born October 1, 1944, in Cleveland, Ohio; son of A. Dwight (a professor) and Helen (a professor; maiden name, Simpson) Culler; married Veronica Forrest-Thomson, April, 1971 (divorced); married Cynthia Chase (a university teacher), December, 1976. *Education:* Harvard University, B.A., 1966; St. John's College, Oxford, B.Phil., 1968, D.Phil., 1972. *Home address:* P.O. Box 133, Jacksonville, N.Y. 14854. *Office:* Department of English, Cornell University, Rockefeller Hall, Ithaca, N.Y. 14853.

CAREER: Cambridge University, Cambridge, England, fellow of Selwyn College, 1969-74; Oxford University, Oxford, England, lecturer in French and fellow of Brasenose College, 1974-77; Cornell University, Ithaca, N.Y., professor of English and comparative literature, 1977—. Visiting professor at Yale University, 1975. *Awards, honors:* Rhodes scholar, 1966-69; James Russell Lowell Prize from Modern Language Association of America, 1975, for *Structuralist Poetics.*

WRITINGS: Flaubert: The Uses of Uncertainty, Cornell University Press, 1974; *Structuralist Poetics: Structuralism, Linguistics, and the Study of Literature,* Cornell University Press, 1975; *Ferdinand de Saussure,* Fontana, 1976, Viking, 1977; *The Pursuit of Signs,* Cornell University Press, 1981; *On Deconstruction: Literary Theory in the 1970's,* Cornell University Press, 1982; *Roland Barthes,* Oxford University Press, 1982. Member of editorial board of *New Literary History, Diacritics, Publications of the Modern Language Association of America, Poetics Today, Comparative Criticism,* and *Structuralist Review.*

* * *

CULLINAN, Bernice Ellinger   1926-

PERSONAL: Born October 12, 1926, in Hamilton, Ohio; daughter of Lee Alexander and Hazel (Berry) Dees; married George W. Ellinger, June 5, 1948 (marriage ended, January, 1966); married Paul Anthony Cullinan (a professor), June 9, 1967; children: (first marriage) Janie Ellinger Ream, James Webb. *Education:* Ohio State University, B.S., 1948, M.A., 1951, Ph.D., 1964. *Religion:* Episcopalian. *Home address:* Tudor Lane, Sands Point, N.Y. 11050. *Agent:* Sheldon Fogelman, 10 East 40th St., New York, N.Y. 10016. *Office:* Department of Early Childhood and Elementary Education, New York University, Washington Sq., New York, N.Y. 10003.

CAREER: Teacher at public elementary schools in Ohio, 1944-52 and 1957-61; Ohio State University, Columbus, assistant professor, 1964-67; New York University, New York City, associate professor, 1967-72, professor, 1972—. Educational consultant to Viking Penguin, Inc., 1977—. Teacher on "Sunrise Semester," broadcast by Columbia Broadcasting System (CBS-TV), spring, 1978. Member of board of directors of International Reading Association, 1979-82. *Member:* National Conference on Research in English, National Council of Teachers of English (member of literature commission, 1979-82), American Library Association, American Psychological Association, American Educational Research Association.

WRITINGS: *Literature for Children: Its Discipline and Content,* W. C. Brown, 1971; (editor) *Black Dialects and Reading,* National Council of Teachers of English, 1974; (editor with Carolyn Carmichael) *Literature and Young Children,* National Council of Teachers of English, 1977; (editor with M. Jerry Weiss) *Books I Read When I Was Young,* Avon, 1980; *Literature and the Child,* Harcourt, 1981.

Author of videotape series, "Teaching Reading and Literature," New York University, 1981.

WORK IN PROGRESS: Research on developmental factors in children's responses to literature.

SIDELIGHTS: Bernice Cullinan wrote: "The center of my professional interest lies in encouraging teachers and parents to use good books with children. My teaching, writing, and research converge on literary criticism, children's responses to literature, and practical ways to stimulate children's reading. My primary interests lie in identifying good books for children and in helping teachers and librarians find creative ways to share them. My research centers on children's response to literature with the goal of finding out how to help more children become avid readers."

* * *

CULOTTA, Nino
   See O'GRADY, John (Patrick)

* * *

CULVER, Roger B(ruce)   1940-

PERSONAL: Born September 6, 1940, in Brigham City, Utah; son of Theodore G. (a controller for the Federal Aviation Administration) and Louise (Huther) Culver; married Bonnie Korcsok, December 17, 1965; children: Kenneth, Kathleen, Lawrence. *Education:* University of California, Riverside, B.A., 1962; Ohio State University, M.Sc., 1966, Ph.D., 1971. *Home:* 1628 Independence Rd., Fort Collins, Colo. 80526. *Office:* Department of Physics, Colorado State University, Fort Collins, Colo. 80523.

CAREER: Colorado State University, Fort Collins, instructor, 1966-71, assistant professor, 1971-75, associate professor, 1975-81, professor of astronomy, 1981—. Visiting astronomer at Kitt Peak Observatory and Perkins Observatory; fellow at Lowell Observatory. *Member:* International Astronomical Union,

American Astronomical Society, American Physical Society, Astronomical Society of the Pacific. *Awards, honors:* Charles Lory Teacher of the Year Award, 1977, from Colorado State University; National Science Foundation summer fellowship, 1981.

WRITINGS: *An Introduction to Experimental Astronomy,* W. H. Freeman, 1974, revised edition, 1981; *A College Outline in Astronomy,* Harper, 1979; (with Philip A. Ianna) *The Gemini Syndrome,* Pachart, 1979; *Sunsign Sunset,* Pachart, 1982; (editor; with David D. Meisel) *Astronomy Before the Telescope,* Volume I: *The Earth-Moon System,* Pachart, 1982. Author of "Colorado Skies," a column in *Fort Collins Coloradoan.* Contributor to astronomy and physics journals. Editor of *Astronomy Quarterly.*

WORK IN PROGRESS: *Stalking the Ancient Astronauts,* with Philip A. Ianna, on the ancient astronomy theory of von Daniken, completion expected in 1983.

SIDELIGHTS: Culver told *CA:* "At the precise instant in human history when many of our most serious social problems—energy supply, pollution, and control of mass destruction weapons systems—are heavily laden with science and technology, society at large has developed a considerable degree of apprehension and distrust for that same science and technology.

"As a scientific writer and educator, the development of this 'two-culture' gap, as C. P. Snow refers to it, is of considerable concern to me. The primary thrust of my written work in astronomy has therefore been in the direction of making astronomical and scientific concepts more clearly defined and comprehensible to both the student and the general public. One aspect of this effort has been to delineate the differences between the science of astronomy and the medieval semi-science of horoscopic astrology, the latter of which is now enjoying its best days since before the scientific revolution of the seventeenth century. This effort has resulted in two popularly-oriented books on astronomy and astrology, *The Gemini Syndrome* and *Sunsign Sunset.*"

* * *

CUSS, (Theodore Patrick) Camerer   1909(?)-1970

OBITUARY NOTICE: Born c. 1909; died in March, 1970, in Wimbledon, England. Horologist and author of *The Story of Watches.* Cuss chaired the British Horological Institute. Obituaries and other sources: *AB Bookman's Weekly,* April 6, 1970.

D

DACY, Douglas Calvin 1927-

BRIEF ENTRY: Born in 1927 in Austin, Tex. American economist, educator, and author. A member of the research staff of the Institute for Defense Analyses in 1974, Dacy now teaches economics at the University of Texas. His writings include *The Economics of Natural Disasters: Implications for Federal Policy* (Free Press, 1969), *The Fiscal System of Wartime Vietnam* (Program Analysis Division, Institute for Defense Analyses, 1969), *A Shortrun Macroeconomic Model* (1969), and *Approaches to the Treatment of Incommensurables in Cost-Benefit Analysis* (Program Analysis Division, Institute for Defense Analyses, 1973). *Address:* Department of Economics, University of Texas, Austin, Tex. 78712.

*   *   *

DAKIN, Edwin Franden 1898-1976

OBITUARY NOTICE: Born in 1898; died March 26, 1976, in Covington, La. Editor and author. Dakin edited periodicals, including *Commerce and Finance,* and wrote *Mrs. Eddy: The Biography of a Virginal Mind.* Obituaries and other sources: *AB Bookman's Weekly,* June 28, 1976.

*   *   *

DALI, Salvador (Domenech Felipe Jacinto) 1904-

PERSONAL: Born May 11, 1904, in Figueras, Gerona, Catalonia, Spain; son of Salvador (a notary) and Felipa Dome (Domenech) Dali; married Gala Eluard (original name, Elena Deluvina Diaranoff), September, 1935. *Education:* Attended San Fernando Institute of Fine Arts, Madrid, 1921-23 and 1925-26. *Religion:* Roman Catholic. *Home address:* Port Lligat, Cadaques, Spain. *Agent:* c/o Carstairs Gallery, 11 East 57th St., New York, N.Y. 10022; and c/o Hotel St. Regis, Fifth Ave. and 55th St., New York, N.Y. 10022.

CAREER: Painter, illustrator, designer, and etcher. First one-man exhibition of paintings held in Barcelona, Spain, 1925. Set designer for stage productions, including "Mariana Pineda" (play), 1927, "Tannhauser," 1939, "Bacchanale," 1939, "Labyrinth" (ballet), 1941, "El Cafe de Chinitas," 1944, "Sentimental Colloquy" (ballet), 1944, "Tristan fou" (ballet), 1944, "As You Like It," 1948, "Salome," 1948, "William Tell," "Ballet de Gala," 1961, "The Spanish Lady and the Roman Cavalier" (opera), 1961. Designer of "Dali's Dream of Venus" exhibition at New York World's Fair, 1939; designer of dream sequences in motion picture "Spellbound," United Artists, 1944; designer of clothes with Coco Chanel and Schiparelli; designer of jewelry, furniture, perfume, glass china, fabrics, and decorations. Lecturer. Works represented in permanent collections, including Museum of Modern Art, Musee National d'Art Moderne, Paris, Metropolitan Museum of Art, Salvador Dali Museum, Cleveland, Ohio, Teatro Museo Dali, Figueras, Spain, National Museum, Stockholm, Sweden, Art Institute of Chicago, Staatsgalerie Moderner Kunst, Munich, West Germany, Glasgow Art Gallery, National Gallery of Art, Washington, D.C., and Kunstmuseum, Basel, Switzerland. *Awards, honors:* Huntington Hartford Foundation award, 1957; gold medal of the city of Paris, 1958.

WRITINGS—In English translation: *The Declaration of Independence of the Imagination and of the Rights of Man to His Own Madness,* [New York], 1939; *La Vie secrete de Salvador Dali* (autobiography), translation by Haakon M. Chevalier published as *The Secret Life of Salvador Dali,* Dial, 1942, new and enlarged edition, 1961, 5th edition, Vision Press, 1976; *Rostros ocultos* (novel), translation by Chevalier published as *Hidden Faces,* Dial, 1944, Morrow, 1974; (editor and illustrator) Michel Eyquem de Montaigne, *Essays,* translated by Charles Cotton, Doubleday, 1947; (and illustrator) *Fifty Secrets of Magic Craftsmanship,* translation by Chevalier, Dial, 1948; (with Philippe Halsman) *Dali's Mustache: A Photographic Interview,* Simon & Schuster, 1954; *Les Cocus du vieil art moderne,* Fasquelle, 1956, translation by Chevalier published as *Dali on Modern Art: The Cuckolds of Antiquated Modern Art,* Dial, 1957.

Impressions and Private Memoirs of Salvador Dali, January, 1920, translated by Joaquim Cortada i Perez and edited by A. Reynolds Morse, Morse Foundation, 1962; *Journal d'un genie* (autobiography), La Table Ronde, 1964, translation by Richard Howard published as *Diary of a Genius,* Doubleday, 1965; (with Alain Bosquet) *Entretiens avec Salvador Dali,* Editions Pierre Belfond, 1966, translation by Joachim Heugroschel published as *Conversations With Dali,* Dutton, 1969; (and illustrator) *Lettre ouverte a Salvador Dali,* A. Michel, 1966, translation by Harold J. Salemson published as *Open Letter to Salvador Dali,* James Heineman, 1968; (with Luis Bunuel) *L'Age d'or;* [and] *Un chien andalou* (two screenplays; title of former means "The Golden Age," produced in France by Vicomte de Noailles, 1930; title of latter means "An Andalusian Dog," co-produced in France with Bunuel, 1928), translated by Marianne Alexandre from unpublished French manuscripts, Simon & Schuster, 1968.

Dali par Dali, Draeger, 1970, translation by Eleanor R. Morse published as *Dali by Dali*, Abrams, 1970; (with Andre Parinaud, and illustrator) *Comment on Devient Dali: Les Aveux inavouables de Salvador Dali* (autobiography), R. Laffont, 1973, translation by Salemson published as *The Unspeakable Confessions of Salvador Dali as Told to Andre Parinaud*, Morrow, 1976; *Les Diners de Gala*, Draeger, 1973, translation by J. Peter Moore published under same title by Felicie, 1973; *Explosion of the Swan: Salvador Dali on Frederico Garcia Lorca and Three Poems by Gerard Malanga*, Black Sparrow Press, 1975; (with Max Gerard and Louis Orizet, and illustrator) *Les Vins de Gala*, Draeger, 1977, translation by Olivier Bernier published as *Dali: The Wines of Gala*, Abrams, 1978.

In French: *La Femme visible*, Editions surrealistes, 1930; *Babaouo*, [Paris], 1932, reprinted, Editorial Labor, 1978; (with Michel Deon, and illustrator) *Histoire d'un grand livre: Don Quichotte*, J. Foret, 1957; *Le Mythe tragique de l'Angelus de Millet*, J. J. Pauvert, 1963; (with Louis Pauwels) *Les Passions selon Dali*, Denoel, 1968; *Dali de Draeger*, edited by Gerard, Le Soleil Noir, 1968; *Oui: Methode paranoiaque-critique et autres textes*, Denoel-Gonthier, 1971; (contributor) *Proces en diffamation, plaide devant la Conference du Stage*, P. Belfond, 1971; (contributor) Henri-Francois Rey, *Dali dans son labyrinthe: Essai*, B. Grasset, 1974; (with Sarane Alexandrian) *Dali et les poetes*, Filipacchi, 1976.

Illustrator: Andre Breton, *Second Manifeste du surrealisme*, Kra, 1930; Breton, *Le Revolver a cheveux blancs*, Cahiers libres, 1932; Isidore Lucien Ducasse, *Les Chants de Maldoror*, A. Skira, 1934; Tristan Tzara, *Grains et Issues*, Denoel & Steel, 1935; Paul Eluard, *Cours naturel*, Sagittaire, 1938; Maurice Yves Sandoz, *The Maze*, Doubleday, Doran, 1945; Billy Rose, *Wine, Women, and Words*, Simon & Schuster, 1948; Sandoz, *La Labyrinthe*, Mermod, 1949; Sandoz, *La Maison sans fenetres*, P. Seghers, 1949; Sandoz, *La Limite*, La Table Ronde, 1951; Sandoz, *On the Verge*, Doubleday, 1950; Eugenio d'Ors y Rovira, *La Verdadera historia de Lidia de Cadaques*, J. Janes, 1954; Clair Goll and Yvan Goll, *Nouvelles petites fleurs de Saint Francais d'Assise*, Emile-Paul, 1958; Pedro Antonio de Alarcon, *Le Tricorne*, Nouveau Cercle Parisien du Livre, 1958; Dante Alighieri, *La Divine comedie*, Editions d'art Les Heures Claires, 1960; Gerson D. Cohen, *Aliyah*, introduction by David Ben-Gurion, Sherwood, 1968; Lewis Carroll, *Alice's Adventures in Wonderland*, Maecenas, 1969; Alexander Jones, editor, *The Jerusalem Bible*, Doubleday, 1970; Alfred Laepple, *Bilder zur Bibel*, Pattloch, 1974.

Contributor to magazines, including *Le Surrealisme au service de la revolution*, *L'Amic des arts*, *Gaseta de les arts*, *Le Minotaure*, *American Weekly*, and *Cahiers d'art*. Also contributor to sound recording "Dali in Venice: 'The Spanish Lady and the Roman Cavalier,'" Richmond, 1962.

SIDELIGHTS: Soft, dripping watches covered with ants, lobster telephones, decomposed donkeys lying in pianos, ladies with sea urchins under their arms, and old, bald women dressed as toreadors, omelets perched on their heads: these are only a few elements that comprise the bizarre, surrealist world of Salvador Dali. Conjuring strange visions of the unconscious and disturbing views of paranoia, Dali readily admits that "even I don't know what my paintings mean." The artist also claims the theme of his life to be, "The only difference between a madman and myself is that I am not mad!" His pranks and outrageous behavior fill reams of newsprint and prompt critics like Neal Anthony to ask, "Is Dali the Clown Prince of Art?"

Perhaps the best-known surrealist, Dali is often regarded as the founder and leader of that artistic movement. Contrary to this popular belief, Dali did not create surrealism. He joined the surrealists five years after Andre Breton's *Surrealist Manifesto* established the movement in 1924. Dali, however, was the only surrealist who aggressively generated publicity, thus eclipsing many of his colleagues in the public eye. Indeed, Dali cultivated the press to such an extent that the artist's friend and patron, A. Reynolds Morse, observed that Dali's personal fame far exceeds the fame of his paintings, thereby raising a doubt "about his qualifications as a painter." Although Morse pointed out that notoriety "cheapened what is not cheap," Dali continues to court publicity. The artist once remarked: "In America, my secretary brings me all the press comments about my works in sealed envelopes each morning after breakfast. I never open them. But the heavier they weigh the happier I am." In addition to the information written about him, Dali has chronicled his life in several autobiographies.

The boundary between fact and fiction is often indistinct in Dali's life stories. Most of the descriptions of his childhood and early adulthood come from Dali himself, who is prone to exaggeration and exhibitionism. George Orwell called the artist's first autobiography, *The Secret Life of Salvador Dali*, "a strip-tease act conducted in pink limelight." Possessing what Orwell termed "an atrocious egoism," Dali hails himself as the savior of modern art. In *Secret Life* he elaborated his aspirations: "At seven I wanted to be Napoleon. And my ambition has been growing steadily ever since." As a self-appointed genius, the artist regards all aspects of his life, however intimate or trivial, as important and worth noting in his books. This propensity prompted critic Peter Conrad to note that "Dali has no secret life," his "confessions" being "eminently, . . . garrulously speakable."

Dali maintains that he was unusual from birth, due in part to the fact that his parents named him Salvador, after his older brother who had died three years earlier. "My brother and I resembled each other like two drops of water, but we had different reflections," compared Dali. "Like myself he had the unmistakeable [*sic*] facial morphology of a genius. He gave signs of alarming precocity, but his glance was veiled by a melancholy, characterising insurmountable intelligence." He continued: "I, on the other hand, was much less intelligent but reflected everything. I was to become the prototype *par excellence* of the phenomenally retarded 'polymorphous perverse' having kept intact all the reminiscences of the nursling's erogenic paradises; I clutched at pleasure with boundless, selfish eagerness and on the slightest provocation I would become dangerous."

Young Dali was strange and threatening. As the only child until the birth of his sister, he was spoiled by his parents. Dali frequently threw fits of temper and violence and claims to have had hallucinations as early as the age of three. He confesses to pushing a boy off a suspension bridge onto the ground fifteen feet below. He also contends that when his sister was still a toddler he viciously kicked her in the head. The "savage act," Dali remembered, gave him "delirious joy." Showing, too, indications of his later pronounced exhibitionism, the young Dali liked to hurl himself down flights of stairs. The boy deemed the attention he gained far outweighed the pain he felt.

Along with his aberrant behavior, Dali displayed early signs of artistic ability. He began painting in a realistic style before he was ten years old. Although favoring landscapes during this period, the fledgling painted two notable works featuring people. "Portrait of Helen of Troy" and "Joseph Greeting His Brethren" illustrate the influence on Dali of the nineteenth-century academic Spanish artists. His parents, in order to facilitate his work, permitted their son to use the laundry room as his studio. In the little chamber he would paint for hours while bathing in a wash tub.

When Dali was older, he was sent to live with Ramon Pitchot, a family friend. An established artist in the impressionist style, Pitchot provided Dali a milieu in which his creativity flourished. The impressionist paintings adorning the Pitchot house were "visual cocktails" to Dali, and he maintained that the art form "represented my first contact with an anti-academic and revolutionary aesthetic theory." Dali began to experiment with affixing objects to his paintings, as when he added cherry stems and real worms to a bunch of painted cherries, inspiring Pitchot to remark, "That shows genius." Throughout his stay with the elder painter, Dali fantasized more frequently, and it was at this time he developed one of his many famous fetishes. Finding a crutch in the attic of the house, Dali became obsessed with the object. The obsession has endured; crutches have since appeared often in Dali's works, and his house in Port Lligat is decorated with several such props.

Entering the San Fernando Institute of Fine Arts in Madrid in 1921, Dali studied seriously during his early school career. Having no time for friends, he devoted himself entirely to his art and visits to the Prado Art Museum. Dali's style began to change as he fell under the influence of cubist Juan Gris. Leaving behind the pleasant colors of impressionism, Dali started to paint in dark, earthy tones. In time, Dali became disenchanted with his education, complaining, "I was expecting to find limits, rigour, science, I was offered liberty, laziness, approximations."

It was then that Dali discovered dada, a movement which revolted against the notions of art as collectible objects or revered practice. Art historian David Gasconyne explained that "dada spat in the eye of the world." This defiance interested Dali, and he soon joined the small group of dadaists at the institute. With his friends Luis Bunuel, Federico Garcia Lorca, and Rafael Alberti, Dali began to frequent cafes to discuss his new ideas. He took to wearing fancy clothes and make-up, and even plastered his hair down with varnish. The rebellion of dada permeated Dali's life. In 1923 he was accused of inciting a riot after a student demonstration involving the appointment of a professor. As punishment, he was suspended from school for a year.

Having earned his reputation as a rebel, the artist returned home to Figueras and was soon arrested by the government. Although Dali had done nothing revolutionary, ferment was sweeping Spain, and he was detained in prison for a month as a preventive measure. When released, Dali turned to his painting with renewed vigor. Shunning the casual life he led in Madrid, he became "ascetic once more," stating "I literally gave myself over body and soul to painting and to my philosophical research." Dali discovered the metaphysical painting of Italian painter Giorgio de Chirico whose melancholy pictures presented a view of reality that appealed to Dali. Although none of the fantastic dream elements of surrealism appear in his pictures, de Chirico, reported art historian Helen Gardner, "has been considered a source of inspiration for those artists who created the Surrealist movement in the early 1920's." Thus exposed, Dali painted pictures employing the haunted, vacant perspectives of de Chirico.

Resuming his studies at the institute in 1925, Dali quickly found himself in trouble again because he refused to take an art history examination. "I am sorry," he scoffed, "but I am infinitely more intelligent than these . . . professors." He was expelled for "outrageous misconduct" in October, 1926.

During the following year, Dali took a brief trip to Paris, exhibited his canvases in Barcelona, and painted in a variety of styles. He vacillated between cubism, realism, and neoclassicism, and he continued painting his strange visions. The picture "Blood Is Sweeter Than Honey" presaged Dali's surrealist involvement. The strange painting, which features the rotting corpse of a donkey, resulted in an enduring estrangement from his family, already disturbed by reports of Dali's unconventional life-style. By 1928 Dali's reputation had begun to spread beyond the boundaries of Catalonia. He moved to Paris under the patronage of fellow artist Joan Miro. With his help, Dali was introduced into Parisian art circles. He met many of the surrealists, including Tristan Tzara, Breton, and poet Paul Eluard.

Meanwhile, Dali collaborated with his childhood friend Luis Bunuel in writing and producing the surrealist film, "An Andalusian Dog." According to Dali, Bunuel brought him a script that was "extremely mediocre—*avant garde* in an incredibly naive sort of way." Rejecting his friend's idea, Dali proposed that his own scenario be used. He asserted that his script "*had* the touch of genius and went completely counter to the contemporary cinema." Dali reported that Bunuel concurred. Bunuel, however, described the film's conception differently. "It all began with two twin dreams Dali and I had," he related. "He dreamed obsessively of a hand crawling with ants. I dreamed of a slit eyeball. We wrote the script by associating images and eliminating anything that had a political, historical, esthetic or moral connotation."

The resulting film shocked and revolted audiences. A nurse was on duty during screenings to aid any victims of fainting spells or nausea. Opening with a scene in which a woman's eye is slashed by a razor, the picture continues with a bevy of disjointed images. Carlos Fuentes described the film's content in the *New York Times:* "Pianos are stuffed with dead donkeys and with a ballast of struggling Jesuits strangled by horse's reins; pale hermaphrodites are run down by speeding cars on indifferent boulevards; a man erases his lips, and a woman's pubic hair sprouts on his face, and this in turn liberates the following image, which is a black sea urchin; striped boxes contain mutilated hands; hands are full of swarming ants; fourth floor apartment doors open to wintry beaches where the dummies of lovers will rot this coming spring, buried chest-high in the sand."

Within the year, Dali officially joined the surrealists, although Breton later recounted that the artist "insinuated himself into the . . . movement." Dali's first surrealist painting, "The Lugubrious Game," whose title was supplied by Eluard, caused a small furor in the group. The surrealists, distressed to find scatological elements in the picture, wondered if Dali was a coprophagic. "When Breton saw this painting," Dali noted, "he hesitated for a long time before its scatological elements, for in the picture appeared a figure seen from behind, whose drawers were bespattered with excrement." "The involuntary aspect of this element, so characteristic in psychopathological iconography, should have sufficed to enlighten him," Dali continued. "But I was obliged to justify myself by saying that it was merely a simulacrum. No further questions were asked. But had I been pressed, I should certainly have had to answer that it was the simulacrum of the excrement itself."

Although Dali liked the publicity he received while associated with the surrealists, he disliked such surveillance by Breton. "This idealistic narrowness was, from my point of view, the fundamental 'intellectual vice' of the early period of Surrealism," he criticized. "Hierarchies were established where there was no need for any." Bunuel agreed: "Group solidarity was a tremendous thing among the surrealists. Breton would call us in to sit in judgment if we deviated from the group morality." The minor controversy surrounding "The Lugubrious Game" was indicative of Dali's stormy relationship with Breton and the surrealists.

But in 1929 Dali was the toast of the surrealists. His first exhibition under the group's aegis was held in Paris at the Galerie Goemans. The show was successful, and Dali sold several of his works. Breton wrote the introduction to the exhibit catalogue heralding the arrival of the artist: "Dali is like a man who hesitates between talent and genius, or as one might once have said, between vice and virtue. He is one of those who arrive from so far away that one barely has time to see them enter—only enter. He takes his place, without saying a word, in a system of interference. . . . With the coming of Dali, it is perhaps the first time that the mental windows have been opened really wide, so that one can feel oneself gliding up towards the wild sky's trap."

Dali dubbed his style the "paranoiac-critical" method. Like his surrealist colleagues, Dali relied heavily on the psychological tenets advanced by Sigmund Freud. The artist described his technique as "a spontaneous method of irrational knowledge based upon the critical-interpretive association of delirious phenomena." Breton attempted to clarify this definition, explaining: "It is perfectly clear that with Dali we are dealing with a case of latent paranoia of the most benign kind, a paranoia on isolated levels of delirium . . . the evolution of which is immune from all accidents of a confusional nature. Dali's first-rate intelligence excels at reconnecting these levels to each other immediately after the event, and at gradually rationalizing the distance travelled." Painting in his paranoiac-critical style, Dali inevitably depicts his fetishes, irrational fears, and longings. Thus his pictures display his obsessions with such things as watches, shoes, bread, milk, teeth, flies, and crutches. His paintings also often reveal his attraction to death, his fear of grasshoppers, and his love for his wife Gala.

Gala was considered the "Surrealist Muse" among the artists within that movement. She inspired much of the surrealist work but was already married to Eluard when Dali, like many of his colleagues, fell in love with her. Margaret Case Harriman of the *New Yorker* related that "most of the surrealists had been in love with Gala before her marriage to Eluard, and her effect on them was so remarkable that it became the accepted form of criticism among surrealists to say of a colleague's painting, book, or sculpture, if it was good, 'Ah, well, he was in love with Gala then.'" Dali pursued her in spite of her status and initial dislike of him. While Gala and Eluard visited him on his vacation in Cadaques, Spain, Dali attracted her notice by covering his body with a mixture of fish glue and water and wearing ragged clothes. When Eluard returned home, Gala remained with Dali. In his books the artist is very outspoken about his love for Gala and he frequently intertwines her name with his own signature on his paintings.

It was Dali's relationship with Gala that disrupted his friendship with Bunuel. In 1930 the two men collaborated on a second film called "The Golden Age." They wrote the screenplay together, but after the first day of shooting, Dali had nothing more to do with the film of his friend. Fuentes noted that "the Castor-and-Pollux relationship between the two Spaniards seems to have been severely damaged when Dali fell in love with Gala . . . , and Bunuel tried to strangle the lady on a rock at Cadaques because he saw in her a diabolical influence." Despite the conflicts during its production, the film was a success for the surealists. Shocking its viewers, the film sparked fights in the theatre. Mobs threw objects at the screen and ruined

paintings by Yves Tanguy, Man Ray, Max Ernst, Miro, and Dali hanging in the foyer. "The Golden Age," which criticized bourgeois decadence, was banned three months after its release.

Dali's first one-man showing was held in the United States in 1933. A year after this New York introduction, the painter visited America for the first time, calling the trip "his American campaign." He and Gala made international headlines when they attended the first surrealist ball held in the United States. Fleur Cowles described the lavish affair in her book, *The Case of Salvador Dali*. "In the center of the stairs a bathtub filled with water hung precariously over the guests' heads," she reported. "A hundred-pound block of ice dripped over the door. A cow's uncarved carcass, at one end of the ballroom, had a huge horned gramophone perched inside the open ribs—French songs blaring away. The whole monstrous object was propped up by Dali's favorite fetish—crutches." Since a Dali drawing was offered as an award for the best costume, guests came dressed in outlandish outfits. "Some women," continued Cowles, had "their heads in birdcages with frightful Dali-like wounds and mutilations painted on their bodies, 'living mouths' in the center of their stomachs, eyes peering out of cheeks and backs and underarms." Nonetheless, it was Gala's attire that aroused the greatest sensation. Dressed as a baby doll, ants painted by Dali on her face, she was accused of coming as the Lindbergh baby. Reports of this lurid speculation appeared in newspapers around the world.

The artist made headlines soon afterwards with a lecture he gave in London. He arrived at the engagement in a deep-sea diving suit, replete with ornamental dagger and cue stick, and escorted by two Russian wolfhounds. The headgear of his garment, however, could not be removed, and Dali was nearly asphyxiated before being freed. When asked to explain his odd costume, Dali announced, "I just wanted to show that I was plunging deeply into the human mind."

The next several years were occupied with three trips to Italy. There Dali reacquainted himself with Renaissance art. His renewed interest in classical and academic works and his return to Catholicism resulted in a more traditional style. Between excursions to Italy, Dali visited Freud in London. The only thing known about the interview is Freud's parting observation: "I have never seen a more complete example of a Spaniard. What a fanatic."

Back in New York City to execute an exhibit for the U.S. World's Fair in 1939, Dali once again brewed trouble and publicity. Commissioned to create "Dali's Dream of Venus," the artist devised a characteristically bizarre display. "Seventeen live mermaids wearing fins, tails, brassieres, and very little else dived and played inside a tank filled with water," stated Cowles. "These girls were supposed to represent a 'prenatal chateau,' but among other things they were busy at highly surrealist activities inside the tank. . . . Some milked an underwater cow, some played imaginary music on piano keys painted on the body of a rubber woman (who was chained to a grand piano). Some 'liquid ladies' (as Dali called them) were also busy telephoning and typing." "Dream of Venus" did not meet with the approval of its financial backers, but after much haranguing ("I shouted, I lost my temper—all through my secretary.") a compromise was arrived at. The artist, however, felt the solution unsatisfactory. In response he wrote a manifesto entitled *The Declaration of Independence of the Imagination and the Right of Man to His Own Madness*.

Acknowledging Dali's burgeoning popularity in the United States, Bonwit Teller asked him to design a window display for its Fifth Avenue store in 1939. Dali complied with a window that included "a mannequin whose head was roses (her fingernails ermine, her negligee green feathers)," related Cowles. Featured also was "a lobster telephone" and a male mannequin who "wore Dali's 'aphrodisiac' dinner jacket with eighty-one glasses of *creme de menthe* attached to it. . . . Each glass was complete with dead fly and straw." To finish the scene, "an old-fashioned bathtub was lined in Persian lamb [and] filled with water and floating narcissi—with three wax hands holding mirrors about the edge." The store managers soon altered the display. "Dali was so infuriated by [the] changes made without his permission," recounted Cowles, "that he stalked into the shop, walked inside the window, tipped the water out of his bathtub and smashed his way right through the pane of glass into the street amid a stunned sidewalk audience." He was arrested and then freed on the theory that such temperament is allowed an artist.

This notoriety, combined with Dali's shifts in ideology, further eroded the already shaky ties between the artist and the surrealists. Dali had always caused friction in the cohesive group. Apart from the sensation about "The Lugubrious Game," Dali had been chastised by Breton several times. "He had already come very close, on several occasions, to exclusion," Breton disclosed, "once for having proposed, in one of his paintings, a gratuitously indecent representation of Lenin, again for declaring to all around him that railway smashes delighted him so long as the first-class coaches were spared." Another notable confrontation occurred after the artist's New York exhibition. Dali's interest in Catholicism, nazism, and monarchism had resulted in a meeting at Breton's house. Conroy Maddox described the encounter in his book *Dali.* "Dali turned up with a thermometer in his mouth, pretending to have 'flu,'" the writer related. "As the discussion became more heated, he kept checking his temperature, and with each attack on him proceeded to take off one of the numerous shirts he was wearing until, naked to the waist, he threw himself at Breton's feet. Dali's defence was that his obsession with Hitler was purely paranoid and apolitical, and he would probably be one of the first to be done away with as a degenerate, if Europe was conquered." Maddox added that "not all the Surrealists were unanimous in their opposition, and Dali succeeded so well in creating an atmosphere of confusion and hysteria that the affair eventually petered out."

Nevertheless, it was Dali's popularity in America that finally led to his expulsion. Cowles explained that "whatever the political provocations, Breton was shrewd enough not to use them openly to expel Dali." "It was something more humanly frail," she theorized. "Dali's success in the United States was a delicate straw but it broke the camel's back. The surrealists counted up his excessive press attention. Dali had somehow got, overnight, the reputation of being inventor, owner, chief voice and boss of the movement. It looked as if surrealism was the personal hobby of one man." Cowles asserted that "Breton was livid." "Banding together with [the] remaining members of the original club," she continued, they denounced "him as a dilettante, a Franco-ite (which he was, and is), a 'posseur,' and—worst of all insults—too much of an academician to be allowed to remain in their ranks."

After the bitter parting, Breton attacked Dali on several occasions. Soon after the break, Breton declared that "Salvador Dali's influence has declined very rapidly." "This was inevitable," he went on, "in view of the almost pathological desire to please which leads him to improve ceaselessly upon his own paradoxes. . . . I do not see how anyone in independent circles could conceivably pay any further attention to his message. Dali's painting is already being eroded by profound and absolute monotony. His determination to rarify his paranoiac method still further has reduced him to concocting

entertainments on the level of *crossword puzzles.*" Ten years later in 1949, Breton postulated that the artist he had praised had "disappeared about 1935—giving way to the personality known under the name Avida Dollars ["Greedy Dollars"], fashionable portraitist recently converted to the Catholic faith and to the artistic ideals of the Renaissance, who boasts today of the congratulations and encouragements of the Pope."

Dali did in fact become a portraitist for wealthy patrons in the United States. As World War II escalated in Europe, Dali moved to California. He executed several pictures for Helena Rubinstein and Billy Rose while collaborating with designers Coco Chanel and Schiaparelli. Dali also worked in Hollywood on motion pictures, including "Spellbound."

During this period of exile, the artist wrote *The Secret Life of Salvador Dali.* The book met with mixed reviews. Orwell bluntly pronounced, "It is a book that stinks." He elaborated: "Dali's fantasies probably cast useful light on the decay of capitalist civilization. . . . He is a symptom of the world's illness." *New Yorker* critic Clifton Fadiman ventured that "reading 'The Secret Life' is something like spending a night locked up all alone in a waxworks horror show." "The Narcissism which Dali so candidly admits," appraised Howard Devree in the *New York Times,* "seems to me the candor of the spoiled child." The writer continued: "Dali's revelations have been termed shocking, too intimate, sadistic, pornographic, revolting. But it seems to me that his advertising sense is at work here as in his painting. The same formula has been followed, the same academic waxwork has been treated to the same cosmetic decoration. This is not Buddha but a spoiled child contemplating his navel." Apart from these unfavorable opinions, B. D. Wolfe of the *New York Herald Tribune* proclaimed the work "a remarkably skillful piece of writing." "It is impossible not to admire this painter as writer," he contended.

Secret Life was soon followed by Dali's first novel, *Hidden Faces.* Critics were generally not impressed. "Whatever Dali has done has usually been distinguished by some degree of originality," reflected James Stern in *Nation.* "But this book, he continued, "is confused, old-fashioned, derivative, and intensely boring." "One finds in this novel none of the qualities that are good in his pictures, which are certainly not deficient in craftsmanship," faulted the *New Yorker's* Edmund Wilson. "There is no clarity, no sharp-focussed vividness, no delicacy or firmness of line."

After the war Dali returned to his native country, committing himself to classicism and academicism and devoting himself to Catholicism. Explaining his change in philosophy, Dali confessed: "I was atheistic originally, a sacrilegious mystic. In Spain everyone goes to one extreme or the other." He began to paint his first religious works, the Pope himself blessing the 1948 picture "The Madonna of Port Lligat." Dali terms his technique the "mystical nuclear" style or the "critical-paranoiac mystique." In discussing his art he remarked: "Away with negation and retrogression, away with surrealist malaise and existential qualms. Mysticism is the paroxysm of joy in the ultra-individualistic affirmation of all man's heterogeneous tendencies on the absolute unity of ecstasy." Despite this pronouncement, Dali continues to return to his hallucinatory images and the vestiges of his surrealist style. Alongside pictures entitled "The Christ of St. John of the Cross" and "The Sacrament of the Last Supper" exist others bearing baffling captions such as "The Prodigious Story of the Lace Maker and the Rhinocerous," "Galacidalacidesoxyribonucleicacid," and "The Apotheosis of the Dollar."

Dali has slowed down considerably. Between 1950 and 1970, he painted only eighteen major works. Suffering from Parkinson's disease, Dali can no longer paint since his hands shake uncontrollably. Regardless of Gala's announcement in 1980 that "Dali is an indestructible rock," *New York Times* writer James M. Markham conceded that "old age, infirmity, and the long, darkening shadow of financial mismanagement seem to be bringing . . . Dali . . . to a pathetic, sordid end." The painter is once again involved in a scandal. Before his ailment became advanced, Dali, Markham reported, apparently signed thousands of sheets of blank paper with his profitable name. Consequently, "a work of 'art,' with which he had little or nothing to do," explained Markham, would be transformed "into a Dali 'original.'" The possibility of a market flooded with signed fakes could destroy the business in Dali graphics. The journalist quoted one New York art dealer who worried that "people wouldn't even buy the good stuff if they knew of this."

In 1980 Dali was honored in a major retrospective exhibition in Paris. Containing more than one hundred fifty paintings, two hundred drawings, thirty objects, and two thousand documents, the Dali show attracted 1.2 million people in four months. Critics viewed the works spanning a lifetime and ventured to determine Dali's role in modern art. "Almost all the works of art that make up his contribution to modernism, and on which his fame as a serious artist rests," judged a *Time* reviewer, "were painted before his 35th birthday." "In fact they were done in about seven years, from 1929 to 1936," the writer elaborated. "Before, his work is all a pastiche of others. After 1937, it is mostly parody of himself. . . . No modern painter has armored himself more assiduously in mediocrity." *Newsweek*'s Scott Sullivan disclosed that although "much of the vast . . . show is meretricious," it nevertheless "illustrates Dali's impressive work: his haunting psychic landscapes, hard-edged and viscous at the same time, which have become a permanent feature of the century's visual consciousness."

BIOGRAPHICAL/CRITICAL SOURCES—Books: Salvador Dali, *The Secret Life of Salvador Dali*, Dial, 1942; James Thrall Soby, *Salvador Dali*, Museum of Modern Art, 1946; Fleur Cowles, *The Case of Salvador Dali*, Little, Brown, 1959; Robert Descharnes, *World of Salvador Dali*, Harper, 1962; Dali, *Diary of a Genius*, Doubleday, 1965; Albert Reynolds Morse, *Salvador Dali, 1910-1965*, New York Graphic Society, 1965; Carlton Lake, *In Quest of Dali*, Putnam, 1969; Alain Bosquet, *Conversations With Dali*, Dutton, 1969; George Orwell, *Dickens, Dali, and Others*, Harcourt, 1970; Andre Breton, *Surrealism and Painting*, Icon, 1972; David Larkin, *Dali*, Ballantine, 1974; *Biography News*, Volume I, Gale, 1974; Helen Gardner, *Art Through the Ages*, sixth edition, Harcourt, 1975; Dali, *The Unspeakable Confessions of Salvador Dali as Told to Andre Parinaud*, Morrow, 1976; Conroy Maddox, *Dali*, Hamlyn, 1979.

Periodicals: *New Yorker*, July 1, 1939, January 2, 1943, July 1, 1944, December 20, 1952, February 15, 1964; *New York Herald Tribune*, December 27, 1942; *New York Times*, January 17, 1943, June 11, 1944, April 12, 1981; *Time*, June 5, 1944, August 26, 1946, December 8, 1947, July 21, 1952, January 24, 1955, January 5, 1959, December 31, 1965, May 15, 1972, March 3, 1980; *Weekly Book Review*, June 11, 1944; *New Republic*, June 12, 1944; *Book Week*, June 18, 1944, November 21, 1965; *Nation*, July 22, 1944; *Life*, August 9, 1948, January 25, 1963, July 24, 1970; *Newsweek*, June 29, 1959, April 11, 1960, August 22, 1960, December 27, 1965, January 21, 1980; *Saturday Review*, October 14, 1961; *Christianity Today*, January 4, 1974; *Art and Artists*, February, 1970, August, 1975; *New York Times Book Review*, February 29, 1976;

National Review, May 14, 1976; *New Statesman*, June 25, 1976; *Times Literary Supplement*, July 2, 1976; *Art News*, April, 1980, January, 1981; *Detroit Free Press*, October 19, 1980, September 6, 1981.*

—*Sketch by Anne M. Guerrini*

*   *   *

DALY, Cahal Brendan 1917-

PERSONAL: Born October 1, 1917, in Loughguile, Northern Ireland. *Education:* Received M. A. from Queen's University, Belfast, Northern Ireland; received D.D. from St. Patrick's College, Maynooth, Ireland; received L.Ph. from Institut Catholique, Paris, France. *Home:* Bishop's House, St. Michael's, Longford, Ireland.

CAREER: Ordained Roman Catholic priest; classics master at secondary school in Belfast, Northern Ireland, 1945-46; Queen's University, Belfast, lecturer, 1946-63, reader in scholastic philosophy, 1963-67; St. Michael's, Longford, Ireland, bishop of Ardagh and Clonmacnois, 1967—.

WRITINGS: Morals, Law, and Life: An Examination of the Sanctity of Life and the Criminal Law by Granville Llewellyn Williams, Clonmore, 1962; *Violence in Ireland and Christian Conscience*, Veritas Publications, 1973. Also author of *Natural Law: Morality Today*, 1965, and *Peace: The Work of Justice*, 1979. Co-editor of *Ballymascanlow*, 1978.

Contributor: I. T. Ramsey, editor, *Prospect for Metaphysics*, G. Allen, 1961; T. A. Langford and W. H. Poteat, editors, *Intellect and Hope*, Duke University Press, 1968; D. M. High, editor, *New Essays in Religious Language*, Oxford University Press, 1969. Also contributor to *Understanding the Eucharist*, 1969, and to theology and philosophy journals.

*   *   *

DALY, Robert 1943-

PERSONAL: Born June 17, 1943, in Wayne County, Ohio; son of John Ralph (a boilermaker) and Margaret (a clerk; maiden name, Zuefle) Daly; married Sharon Lee Cunert (a clerk), August 20, 1966; children: Laura Kathleen, Susannah Catherine. *Education:* University of Akron, B.A., 1965, M.A., 1967; Cornell University, Ph.D., 1972. *Office:* Department of English, Clemens Hall, State University of New York at Buffalo, Amherst, N.Y. 14260.

CAREER: Iowa State University, Ames, instructor in English, 1967-69; State University of New York at Buffalo, assistant professor, 1973-77, associate professor of English, 1977—. Visiting associate professor at Cornell University, 1980. *Member:* Modern Language Association of America. *Awards, honors:* Leverhulme fellowship for research in England, 1972-73; grants from New York State Research Foundation, 1975, 1977; Guggenheim fellowship, 1979-80.

WRITINGS: God's Altar: The World and the Flesh in Puritan Poetry, University of California Press, 1978. Member of editorial board of *Early American Literature*.

*   *   *

DAMBRAUSKAS, Joan Arden 1933-
(Noele Arden)

PERSONAL: Born October 24, 1933, in Salisbury, England; daughter of Noel Arden and Dorothy Isobel Shepherd; married K. Rigby, March 29, 1959 (marriage ended, 1966); married Leonas Dambrauskas (an engineer), June 26, 1966; children:

one son, one daughter. *Religion:* Church of England. *Home:* 6 Albert Rd., Harlescott, Shrewsbury, Shropshire, England.

CAREER: Writer. *Member:* Conservation Trust, Mind Association, PROPAR.

WRITINGS: (Under pseudonym Noele Arden) *Child of a System,* Quartet, 1977.

*   *   *

DANDY, James Edgar   1903-1976

OBITUARY NOTICE: Born September 24, 1903; died November 10, 1976, in England. Botanist and author of works in his field. Dandy was keeper of botany at the British Museum. He wrote *List of British Vascular Plants* and *Index of Generic Names of Vascular Plants.* Obituaries and other sources: *Who's Who,* 128th edition, St. Martin's, 1976; *AB Bookman's Weekly,* January 10, 1977.

*   *   *

DANIEL, Daniel   1890(?)-1981

OBITUARY NOTICE: Born c. 1890; died July 1, 1981, in Pompano Beach, Fla. Journalist known for his coverage of football and boxing in newspapers such as *New York World Telegram.* Daniel was also associated with *Ring* magazine. Obituaries and other sources: *New York Times,* July 2, 1981; *Newsweek,* July 13, 1981; *Time,* July 13, 1981.

*   *   *

D'ANNUNZIO, Gabriele   1863-1938
(Duca Minimo)

BRIEF ENTRY: Born March 12, 1863, in Pescara, Italy; died of a stroke, March 1, 1938, in Gardone, Italy. Italian poet and playwright. D'Annunzio's writing epitomized the style known as "European decadent." He wrote of passion and sensuality with a mastery of the Italian language, particularly in its archaic form, that marked a peak in Italian poetry. His flamboyant, scandalous lifestyle accented the stimulating nature of his work, eventually causing the entire body of his writing to be placed on the *Index* of the Roman Catholic church. The novels he wrote before 1900 seemed to imitate the gloomy Russian novels of the day, or the sensuous French and romantic German styles, but as a poet D'Annunzio was highly acclaimed as a pioneer of realism. One of his best-known works is the lyric cycle *Praises of the Sky, of the Sea, of the Earth, and of Heroes* (1899), an extravagant, amoral, and unrestrained celebration of the senses and all life's pleasures. During D'Annunzio's notorious affair with celebrated actress Eleonora Duse, he wrote several tragic plays, including "La Giaconda" (1899) and "The Daughter of Jorio" (1904), generally considered to be his most powerful contribution to Italian drama and the last high point of his writing career. Soon after that, D'Annunzio moved to France where he espoused the rising Fascist cause. His colorful military exploits during World War I made him a national hero in Italy. His postwar writing was mainly Fascist propaganda, but his outrageous public and private behavior, coupled with his amoral passion for beauty as expressed in his earlier poetry, made D'Annunzio a popular literary figure throughout his career. *Biographical/critical sources: New York,* December 12, 1964; *Twentieth Century Writing: A Reader's Guide to Contemporary Literature,* Transatlantic, 1969; *Daily Telegraph,* September 5, 1975.

D'ARCY, Margaretta   1934-

PERSONAL: Born in 1934; married John Arden (a writer); children: Francis Gwalchmei (deceased), Finn, Adam, Jacob, Neuss. *Home:* Gort Roe, Corrandulla, County Galway, Ireland. *Agent:* Margaret Ramsay Ltd., 14a Goodwin's Court, London WC2N 4LL, England.

CAREER: Associated with Noman Productions, 1963; Corrandulla Arts and Entertainment Club, Corrandulla, Ireland, artistic director, 1973-74; associated with Galway Theatre Workshop, 1975-77, and Non-Stop Connolly Show Productions, 1975—. *Member:* Society of Irish Playwrights, Irish Council of Civil Liberties, Haringey Irish Society, Theatre Writers Union (England), H-Block/Armagh Action Group. *Awards, honors:* Award from Arts Council, 1974, for *The Island of the Mighty* and *The Ballygombeen Bequest.*

WRITINGS: Tell Them Everything, Pluto, 1981.

Published plays; with husband, John Arden: *The Business of Good Government* (one-act; first produced in Somerset at Brent Knoll Church, 1960), Eyre Methuen, 1960; *Happy Haven* (two-act; first produced at Bristol University, 1960), Penguin, 1960; *Ars Longa Vita Brevis* (one-act; first produced in London at the Royal Shakespeare Co., 1964; title means "Art Is Long, Time Is Short"), Cassell, 1963; *Friday's Hiding* (one-act; first produced in Edinburgh at Lyceum Theatre, 1966) Eyre Methuen, 1965; *The Royal Pardon* (two-act; first produced in Devon at Beaford Arts Centre, 1966), Eyre Methuen, 1966; *The Hero Rises Up* (two-act; first produced in London at The Roundhouse, 1968), Eyre Methuen, 1968; *The Island of the Mighty* (three-act; first produced on the West End at Aldwych Theatre), Eyre Methuen, 1972; *The Ballygombeen Bequest,* Scripts, 1972; *The Non-Stop Connolly Show* (fourteen-act; first produced in Dublin at Liberty Hall, 1975), Pluto, 1978; *Vandaleur's Folly* (two-act; first produced at Lancaster University, 1978), Eyre Methuen, 1981.

Unpublished plays: "A Pinprick of History" (one-act), first produced in London at the Almost Free Theatre, 1977; "Irish Women's Voices" (one-act) first produced in London at Women's Space, 1978; "The Trial and Imprisonment of Countess Markievicz" (one-act), first produced in London at Caxton House, 1979.

Co-author: "Vietnam War Game" (thirteen-hour marathon), first produced in New York at New York University, 1967; "Muggins Is a Martyr" (two-act), first produced in London at Unity Theatre, 1968; "Two Hundred Years of Labour History" (two-act), first produced in London at Alexandra Palace, 1971; "My Old Man's a Tory" (one-act), first produced in London at Wood Green, 1971; "Little Red Riding Hood" (one-act), first produced in London at Haringey, 1971; "The Henry Dubb Show" (eight-hour marathon) first produced at University of California, Los Angeles, 1973; "The Devil and the Parish Pump" (one-act), first produced in Galway, Ireland, at Corrandulla Arts Centre, 1974; "The Crown Strike" (one-act), first produced in Galway, 1975; "Sean O'Scrudu" (one-act), first produced in Galway, 1976; "The Hunting of the Mongrel Fox" (one-act), first produced in Galway, 1976; "No Room at the Inn" (one-act), first produced in Galway, 1976; "Mary's Name" (one-act), first produced in Galway, 1977.

Radio and television scripts; with Arden: "Keep the People Moving" (radio script), British Broadcasting Corp., 1972; "Portrait of a Rebel" (television script), Radio Telefis Eireann, 1973. Also author of television scripts "When Irish Eyes Are . . ." and "Petrifaction."

Contributor to journals, including *New Statesman* and *Dialog.*

SIDELIGHTS: D'Arcy told *CA:* "My creative spark is largely derived from my experience of British imperialism in Ireland, and the suffering and bitterness that it causes. I have been twice in jail in Northern Ireland for speaking out against injustices there. I am against state repression, and all other repressions that impede human development and civil liberties, but I express my feeling chiefly through comedy and satire."

BIOGRAPHICAL/CRITICAL SOURCES: John Arden, *Presenting the Pretence,* Eyre Methuen, 1977; *New Society,* January 18, 1979; Catherine Itzin, *Stages of the Revolution,* Eyre Methuen, 1980; *Other Stages,* spring-summer, 1980.

*   *   *

DARIO, Ruben
    See SARMIENTO, Felix Ruben Garcia

*   *   *

DARLOW, Michael (George)   1934-

PERSONAL: Born June 13, 1934, in Wolverhampton, England; son of George Francis and Dorothy Irene Darlow; married Sophia Sipic (a teacher), February 20, 1964. *Education:* Attended Northern Theatre School, 1951-54. *Politics:* Labour. *Religion:* Humanist. *Home and office:* 28 Furlong Rd., London N.7, England. *Agent:* Andrew Mann Ltd., 1 Old Compton St., London W.1, England.

CAREER: Granada Television, London, England, producer and director, 1965-69; Derby Playhouse, Derby, England, director, 1970; free-lance television producer, director, and writer, 1970—. Controller of drama at Clyde Fair International, 1972; professional actor; committee member of Channel Four Group. *Military service:* Royal Air Force, pilot officer, 1954-56. *Member:* Independent Programme Producers Association (member of council), British Academy of Film and Television Arts. *Awards, honors:* Award from British Academy of Film and Television Arts, 1968, for best factual program, "Cities at War."

WRITINGS: (With Richard Fawkes) *The Last Corner of Arabia,* Namara Publications, 1976; (with Gillian Hodson) *Terence Rattigan: The Man and His Work,* Quartet Books, 1979.

Television scripts: "Francois Truffaut," first broadcast by British Broadcasting Corp., 1974; "The Sun Is God (J. M. Turner)," first broadcast by Thames Television, 1974; "Auschwitz: The Final Solution," first broadcast by Thames Television, 1975.

Contributor to magazines and newspapers, including *Sight and Sound.*

WORK IN PROGRESS: The Past and Future of British Television: Its Structure and Practice.

SIDELIGHTS: Darlow commented: "All my writing has been primarily concerned to correct a false impression, right a wrong, or share an enthusiasm."

BIOGRAPHICAL/CRITICAL SOURCES: Guardian, June 9, 1970.

*   *   *

DAUGHERTY, Sonia Medwedeff   ?-1971

OBITUARY NOTICE: Born in Moscow, U.S.S.R.; died May 4, 1971, in Bedford Hills, N.Y. Author best known for her biographies for children. She also wrote a trilogy for children that included *Mashinka's Secret, The Broken Song,* and *All Things New,* and was a contributor to *New Yorker* and *Christian*

Science Monitor. Obituaries and other sources: *Publishers Weekly,* June 21, 1971; *AB Bookman's Weekly,* August 2, 1971.

*   *   *

DAVENPORT, Walter   1889-1971

OBITUARY NOTICE: Born January 7, 1889, in Talbot County, Md.; died December 9, 1971, in Southern Pines, S.C. Editor and journalist. Davenport was the first editor of *Liberty.* He also edited *Collier's.* Obituaries and other sources: *AB Bookman's Weekly,* January 17, 1972; *Who Was Who in America, With World Notables,* Volume V: *1969-1973,* Marquis, 1973.

*   *   *

DAVIES, W(illiam) H(enry)   1871-1940

BRIEF ENTRY: Born July 3, 1871, in Newport, Monmouthshire, England; died September 26, 1940, in Nailsworth, Gloucestershire, England. British poet and novelist. With his first book of poems, *Soul's Destroyer* (1905), Davies attracted the attention of the major writers of his day. Encouraged by George Bernard Shaw, he wrote *The Autobiography of a Super-Tramp* (1908), which established him as a popular figure in Georgian England. His early career was inauspicious. Almost penniless before 1908, he traveled across the United States and Canada as a hobo and worked by choice in England as a street singer and peddler; these experiences inspired his poetry. Davies wrote about the country and nature, which he loved, and the suffering of the poor, with which he was intimately familiar. Although he encountered public adoration and critical acclaim after 1908, his verse remained unspoiled. After the success of his autobiography, Davies wrote almost constantly. Some critics felt he produced too much and that much of his work was only mediocre, but others believed his prolific output did nothing to diminish the quality and effect of his best poems. *Biographical/critical sources: Twentieth Century Authors: A Biographical Dictionary of Modern Literature,* H. W. Wilson, 1942; R. J. Stonesifer, *W. H. Davies: A Critical Biography,* J. Cape, 1963; *Virginia Quarterly Review,* winter, 1966.

*   *   *

DAVIS, Barbara Kerr   1946-

PERSONAL: Born June 8, 1946, in Passaic, N.J.; daughter of Arthur G. (in sales) and Victoria (a secretary; maiden name, Pawloski) Kerr; married Henry A. Davis (a physician), June 5, 1968; children: Lisa, Peter. *Education:* Pennsylvania State University, B.A., 1967; Temple University, M.A., 1970, Ph.D., 1975. *Home:* 1655 Nautilus St., La Jolla, Calif. 92037.

CAREER: Teacher in elementary school in Philadelphia, Pa., 1967; Temple University, Philadelphia, instructor in English, 1974-75. Instructor at extension division of University of California, San Diego *Member:* Phi Beta Kappa. *Awards, honors:* National Defense Education Act fellowship, 1968-71, Robertson Prize, 1970, and research fellowship, 1971-72, all from Temple University.

WRITINGS: Letters to My Husband's Analyst (novel), Hawthorn, 1979. Contributor to *Hudson Review* and *Twentieth Century Literature.*

WORK IN PROGRESS: Another novel,

SIDELIGHTS: Barbara Davis told *CA:* "I am interested in women's studies—in reading works by women and getting others interested in such reading as well. We were all introduced to literature through works by 'great writers' who, someone decided, were almost all male. I belong to a group of women who meet about once a month to discuss literature by women from Jane Austen and George Eliot to Margaret Drabble, Tille Olsen, and Iris Murdoch.''

*   *   *

DAVIS, Henry P.   1894(?)-1970

OBITUARY NOTICE: Born c. 1894; died November 8, 1970, in Foley, Ala. Editor, authority on dogs, and author. Davis edited *Sports Afield*'s column on dogs and wrote *Modern Dog Encyclopedia*. Obituaries and other sources: *AB Bookman's Weekly,* January 4, 1971.

*   *   *

DAVIS, Rebecca (Blaine) Harding   1831-1910

BRIEF ENTRY: Born June 24, 1831, in Washington, Pa.; died September 29, 1910, in Mt. Kisco, N.Y. American editor, essayist, short story writer, and novelist. One of the earliest American realists, Davis was the first to write about the lives of industrial workers and to include blacks as major characters in her fiction. Her first two published works are also considered her best. ''Life in the Iron Mills'' (1861), her first short story, and *Margaret Howth: A Story of To-day* (1862), her first novel, exposed the conditions endured by iron workers and depicted slum life in a mill town. ''Life in the Iron Mills'' has been called ''the *Uncle Tom's Cabin* of Capitalism.'' Soon after her first works were published, Davis yielded to popular tastes and editorial pressure and began to conclude her novels and stories with cheerful and often inappropriate endings. This, and the fact that she spent much of her time writing trite love stories and Gothic mysteries to supplement her income, adversely affected the quality of her serious writing. From 1869 to the mid-1870's Davis was associate editor of the *New York Tribune*. Among her other notable works are *Waiting for the Verdict* (1868), a novel about racial bias, and *John Andross* (1874), a story about the Whiskey Ring and the effects of political corruption in Pennsylvania. *Biographical/critical sources: The Reader's Encyclopedia of American Literature,* Crowell, 1962; *The Oxford Companion to American Literature,* 4th edition, Oxford University Press, 1965; *The Reader's Encyclopedia,* 2nd edition, Crowell, 1965; *American Authors and Books, 1640 to the Present Day,* 3rd revised edition, Crown, 1972.

*   *   *

DAVIS, Robert Con   1948-

PERSONAL: Born July 4, 1948, in Phoenix, Ariz.; son of Hugh G. and Elva Covene (Wood) Davis. *Education:* California State University, Hayward, B.A., 1972; University of California, Davis, M.A., 1974, Ph.D., 1979. *Home:* 1227 South Berry Rd., Norman, Okla. 73069. *Office:* Department of English, University of Oklahoma, Norman, Okla. 73019.

CAREER: University of Pisa, Pisa, Italy, lecturer in American literature, 1974-75; University of California, Davis, visiting assistant professor of English and comparative literature, 1979-80; University of Oklahoma, Norman, assistant professor of English and director of graduate studies in English, 1980—. *Member:* Modern Language Association of America. *Awards, honors:* Fulbright fellowship for Italy, 1974-75; University of Oklahoma junior faculty summer fellowship, 1981.

WRITINGS: (Editor) *The Fictional Father: Lacanian Readings of the Text,* University of Massachusetts Press, 1981; (editor)

Twentieth-Century Interpretations of ''The Grapes of Wrath,'' Prentice-Hall, 1982. Contributor of articles and reviews to literature journals. Guest editor of *Arizona Quarterly,* spring, 1980; book review editor of *Genre*.

WORK IN PROGRESS: The Paternal Romance: The Father in Fiction, a study of authority and narrative structure in Anglo-American fiction, Lacanian in orientation, publication expected in 1983.

SIDELIGHTS: Davis wrote: ''I am glad to see the study of American literature become more sophisticated in its critical methodology. For too long American critics have worked in isolation from the philosophical and critical developments in the rest of the world. I think a critic should work by all means from intensely personal interests, but then find a means of access to communal and cultural discourse of his/her time. The dialogue between American and French critics in the last fifteen years is a healthy sign that a viable cultural discourse is today taking place. The current generation of American scholar/critics, I think, will build on this work and will continue to reconcile American scholarship with European theoretical speculation. I hope to add to this work—both as an educator and as a critic. The day may come soon when being American will no longer be synonymous with being anti-intellectual and anti-theoretical.''

*   *   *

DAVIS, Winston (Bradley)   1939-

PERSONAL: Born November 5, 1939, in Jamestown, N.Y.; son of Wesley and Judith Eloise (Swanson) Davis; married Linda Joan Peters; children: Colin Brent, Monica Lynn. *Education:* University of Rochester, B.A. (summa cum laude), 1961, graduate study, 1961-62; attended Harvard University, 1961-62; Columbia University, M.A., 1965; Colgate-Rochester Divinity School, B.D., 1967; attended Inter-University Center, Tokyo, Japan, 1971-72; University of Chicago, Ph.D., 1973. *Office:* School of Sociology, Kwansei Gakuin University, Nishinomiya-shi, Uegahara 1-1-155, Japan 662.

CAREER: Colgate-Rochester Divinity School, Rochester, N.Y., lecturer in New Testament Greek, 1965-67; Stanford University, Stanford, Calif., assistant professor of religious studies, 1973-79; Kwansei Gakuin University, Nishinomiya, Japan, professor of sociology of religion, 1979—. Lecturer at Konan University, Illinois Center, 1980; public speaker; conducted field studies in Japan. *Member:* American Academy of Religion, Association for Asian Studies, Phi Beta Kappa. *Awards, honors:* Woodrow Wilson fellowship, 1961-62; grant from Stanford University's Center for Research in International Studies for research in Japan, 1973, 1976-77; National Endowment for the Humanities grant for Japan, 1976-77; grant from Japan Fund, 1977.

WRITINGS: (Contributor) *Great Religions of the World,* National Geographic Society, 1971; (contributor) *Contemporary Christian Trends,* Word, Inc., 1972; *Toward Modernity: A Developmental Typology of Popular Religious Affiliations in Japan* (monograph), East Asian Papers, Cornell University, 1977; (contributor) Frank E. Reynolds and Theodore M. Ludwig, editors, *Transitions and Transformations in the History of Religions: Essays in Honor of Joseph M. Kitagawa,* E. J. Brill, 1980; *Dojo: Magic and Exorcism in Modern Japan,* Stanford University Press, 1980. Contributor of articles, translations, and reviews to scholarly journals.

WORK IN PROGRESS: A book on religion and political rebellion in nineteenth-century Japan; various projects on twentieth-century Japanese religion and society; research on social values of religious communities, especially Buddhist and Christian ones.

SIDELIGHTS: Davis's present teaching interests are religion and society in Asia, social structure and change in world religions, secularization and modernization theories, social teachings of world religions, and religion in classical social theory. He has also taught courses in values, technology, science, and anthropology.

In 1973 he spent the summer in Kyoto, studying new religions, utopian communities, and Pure Land Buddhism. In 1976 his field work was a study of Shinto parish guilds in Wakayama, and since 1979 he has concentrated on religion and social protest movements in Tokugawa.

Davis got the idea for *Dojo* in 1976 when he attended a brief training course offered by the Mahikari cult. It was his initiation into a world of malevolent spirits and exorcism, a world with which he remained in contact for some time afterward. His book is a description of modern Japanese cult practices and an examination of "churches of magic" in modern society.

Davis told *CA:* "My work always falls somewhere between history and sociology of religion. Recently I have moved more in the direction of history. I am dealing with the relationship between religion (especially pilgrimage and other popular movements) and political rebellions among the common folk of Tokugawa, Japan."

BIOGRAPHICAL/CRITICAL SOURCES: Times Literary Supplement, August 22, 1980; *Japan Times,* December 12, 1980.

*   *   *

DAVISON, Jane   1932(?)-1981

OBITUARY NOTICE: Born c. 1932 in Toronto, Ontario, Canada; died July 4, 1981, in Cambridge, Mass. Social historian, editor, and author. Davison was an editor at *Mademoiselle* magazine and at Anchor-Doubleday and New York University Press. Her two books, *The Old House: Restoring, Rehabilitating and Renovating* and *The Fall of a Doll's House: Three Generations of American Women and the Houses They Lived In,* were published in 1980. Obituaries and other sources: *New York Times,* July 8, 1981; *Chicago Tribune,* July 8, 1981; *Publishers Weekly,* August 7, 1981.

*   *   *

DAY, Bradford M(arshall)   1916-

PERSONAL: Born September 20, 1916, in Marblehead, Mass.; son of Bradford M. and B. Edna (Montgomery) Day; married Rita Jezewska, October 6, 1945; children: Bradford M. III, Sharon, Irene, Diana, Richard, Janet. *Education:* Attended Chabot College. *Politics:* "Left of Karl Marx." *Religion:* "Degad." *Home:* 2686 Leeward St., Hayward, Calif. 94545.

CAREER: Worked as a merchant seaman, 1942-44; associated with a machine shop in Brooklyn, N.Y., 1944-45; laboratory worker, 1945-62; bookstore owner in New York and California, 1962-70; real estate broker, 1970—; associated with CALTRANS, 1973-79; writer, 1974—. Also worked as a garbage collector, restaurateur, and landscaper.

WRITINGS: The Supplemental Checklist of Fantastic Literature, Arno, 1974; *The Checklist of Fantastic Literature in Paperbound Books,* Arno, 1974; *Bibliography of Adventure,* Arno, 1978.

WORK IN PROGRESS: A long science-fiction novel, publication expected in 1982; a short science-fiction novel, publication expected in 1982.

SIDELIGHTS: Day told *CA:* "I enjoy using my imagination to develop a system to explain our cosmos. It is one small voice crying in the wilderness of human culture, but we all cry at times.

"I can understand (but have no sympathy for) stupidity. Arrogance, which so often goes with this lack of intelligence, is the mark of one who suspects self-stupidity, but blusters in the attempt to prove his rightness, at least to his own impoverished ego. How can any human have patience with this?

"Failings we all have, foremost of which is greed, arrant lust for possession of tangible goods. Most greed is dictated by fear: fear of not having enough for some vague purpose, or fear of not having as much as (or more than) some other person. Greed is a desire to possess for the sake of possessing or for the power it gives the possessor. Always in the eyes of others, fear/envy reflects the greatness of the owner.

"Humans have another horrid failing: a sick desire to dominate or be dominant over other humans. It runs the gamut from the pecking order among otherwise near equals, to the boss and worker relationship, the neighborhood bully, the vicious attacker, the authority figure in any line of endeavor (priest, professor, village shaman or sage), and lastly (and most devastating) politicians and their unthinking allies.

"I have the (wistful) feeling that power should not be exercised except in emergency, and never for the sake of self-satisfaction. I expect to witness this gladsome event some time during my one thousandth reincarnation. Perhaps it will begin with the third or fourth species after homo sapiens is naught but fossilized bones.

"I attempted to put a *bit* of my 'sharing concept' in my long novel; possibly it is not obnoxiously present. Possibly it is not present in sufficient strength, or presented with sufficient skill, but at least I tried, as others have."

AVOCATIONAL INTERESTS: Conceiving chess in three dimensions, and other board games.

*   *   *

DAY, Gardiner Mumford   1900-1981

OBITUARY NOTICE: Born February 22, 1900, in Staten Island, N.Y.; died July 19, 1981, in Amherst, N.H. Episcopal rector. Day served as rector of Christ Church in Cambridge, Mass., from 1941 until 1965. He was also active in the Massachusetts and New Hampshire Civil Liberties Unions. Among his books on religion is *The Apostles Creed: An Interpretation for Today.* Obituaries and other sources: *Who's Who in America,* 38th edition, Marquis, 1974; *New York Times,* July 21, 1981.

*   *   *

DEKKER, George   1934-

PERSONAL: Born September 8, 1934, in Long Beach, Calif.; son of Gilbert John (a tunnel construction foreman) and Laura (Barnes) Dekker; married Linda Jo Bartholomew (a university lecturer and editor); children: Anne Allegra, Clare Joy, Ruth Siobhan, Laura Daye. *Education:* University of California, Santa Barbara, B.A., 1955, M.A., 1958; Cambridge University, M.Litt., 1961; University of Essex, Ph.D., 1966. *Politics:* "Unaffiliated liberal." *Residence:* Palo Alto, Calif. *Office:*

Department of English, Stanford University, Stanford, Calif. 94305.

CAREER: California Division of Forestry, Weott, Calif., fire control foreman, 1956-57; Convair Astronautics, Vandenberg Air Force Base, Calif., engineering writer, 1958-59; University of Wales, University College, Swansea, lecturer in English, 1962-64; University of Essex, Colchester, England, lecturer, 1964-66, senior lecturer, 1966-70, reader in literature, 1970-72, dean of School of Comparative Studies, 1969-71; Stanford University, Stanford, Calif., associate professor, 1972-74, professor of English, 1974—, chairman of department, 1978-81. Consultant to National Endowment for the Humanities. *Member:* International Association of University Professors of English, Modern Language Association of America. *Awards, honors:* National Endowment for the Humanities fellowship, 1977.

WRITINGS: Sailing After Knowledge: The Cantos of Ezra Pound, Routledge & Kegan Paul, 1963; *James Fenimore Cooper: The Novelist,* Routledge & Kegan Paul, 1967; (editor with Larry Johnston) *Cooper, the American Democrat,* Penguin, 1969; (editor with John McWilliams) *James Fenimore Cooper: The Critical Heritage,* Routledge & Kegan Paul, 1973; *Coleridge and the Literature of Sensibility,* Vision Press, 1978.

WORK IN PROGRESS: A book on American historical romance, completion expected in 1983.

SIDELIGHTS: Dekker wrote: "I had a couple of brief but successful careers before committing myself to an academic career. I come by my own propensities honestly. My dad was a westerner and a rolling stone; my mother was raised on an Idaho ranch and, before her marriage, worked all over the United States, including canning salmon in Alaska and running a telephone switchboard in Utah."

*   *   *

De La BEDOYERE, Michael 1900-1973

OBITUARY NOTICE: Born May 16, 1900; died in 1973. Writer and editor. De La Bedoyere was editor of the *New Catholic Herald* from 1934 to 1962 and the founder and editor of *Search*. He wrote several books on religion, including *Christian Crisis, Living Christianity,* and *Francis: A Biography of the Saint of Assisi.* Obituaries and other sources: *Catholic Authors: Contemporary Biographical Sketches,* Volume I: *1930-1947,* St. Mary's Abbey, 1948; *The Author's and Writer's Who's Who,* 6th edition, Burke's Peerage, 1971; *Who's Who in the World,* 3rd edition, Marquis, 1976; *Who Was Who Among English and European Authors, 1931-1949,* Gale, 1978.

*   *   *

DEMAREST, Phyllis Gordon 1911-1969

OBITUARY NOTICE: Born March 31, 1911, in London, England; died of a heart attack, December 22, 1969, in San Gabriel, Calif. Novelist and author of short stories. Demarest wrote seven novels, including *The Naked Risk, The Wilderness Brigade,* and *The Angelic City.* Obituaries and other sources: *Who's Who of American Women,* Marquis, 1958; *Publishers Weekly,* May 25, 1970.

*   *   *

DeMILLE, Alexandria
See Du BREUIL, (Elizabeth) L(or)inda

DEMPSTER, Stuart 1936-

PERSONAL: Born July 7, 1936, in Berkeley, Calif.; son of Fred Harper (a chemist) and Kathryn (a teacher; maiden name, Shepardson) Dempster; married Renko Ishida (a teacher), December 19, 1964; children: Brian, Loren. *Education:* San Francisco State College (now University), B.A., 1958, M.A., 1967. *Residence:* Seattle, Wash. *Office:* School of Music, University of Washington, Seattle, Wash. 98195.

CAREER: Oakland Symphony, Oakland, Calif., principal trombonist, 1962-66; University of Washington, Seattle, associate professor of music, 1968—. Instructor at San Francisco Conservatory of Music, 1961-66; assistant professor at California State University, Hayward, 1963-66. Member of performing group at Mills College, 1963-66; performer and lecturer on tour in the United States, Europe, and Australia. *Military service:* U.S. Army, bass trombonist with Seventh Army Symphony, 1958-60; served in Europe.

MEMBER: International Trombone Association, Musician's Union, Phi Mu Alpha. *Awards, honors:* Paul Masson Composition Award from Paul Masson Wineries, 1963; grant from Martha Baird Rockefeller Fund for Music, 1971; fellow of Center for Advanced Study, University of Illinois, 1971-72; Fulbright-Hays scholarship for Australia, 1973; National Endowment for the Arts grants, 1978 and 1980; award from International Trombone Association, 1978; United States-United Kingdom Bicentennial fellowship, 1979; Guggenheim fellowship, 1981-82.

WRITINGS: The Modern Trombone: A Definition of Its Idioms, University of California Press, 1979.

Musical compositions: "Quartet Number One for Brass," Ensemble Publications, 1963; (editor) Robert Erickson, "Ricercare a Five for Trombones," Okra Music Corp., 1966; (editor) Luciano Berio, "Sequenza Five for Trombone Solo," Universal, 1968; (editor) Ernst Krenek, "Five Pieces for Trombone and Piano," Baerenreiter, 1969; (editor) Ben Johnston, "One Man for Trombonist and Percussion," Media, 1976; (editor) Erickson, "General Speech for Solo Trombone," Okra Music Corp., 1976; (editor) William Bergsma, "Blatant Hypotheses for Trombone and Percussion," Galaxy Music Corp., 1979; "Ten Grand Hosery" (mixed-media ballet), University of California, 1979. Also author of "Pipedream" (mixed-media presentation), 1972; "Life Begins at Forty" (a series of concerts and musical gallery shows), 1976; "Standing Waves," 1976; "Didjeridivish," 1976.

Recordings: "In C," Columbia Records, 1968; "In No Strange Land for Trombone, Contrabass, and Tape," Nonesuch Records, 1969; "Ricercare a Five for Trombones," AR Records, 1970; "American Sampler," Olympic Records, 1976; "Five Pieces for Trombone and Piano," Orion Records, 1978; "New Music for Virtuosos Two," New World Records, 1978; "Stuart Dempster in the Great Abbey of Clement VI," Arch Records, 1979; "The Modern Trombone," University of California Press, 1979; "Chamber Music III for Trombone and Piano," Columbia Records, 1981; "Concerto for Trombone and Orchestra," Louisville Orchestra Series Recordings, 1981.

WORK IN PROGRESS: Research on the accoustical repertoire of the trombone through mixed media, ethnic studies, and experimentation; research on the Australian aboriginal didgeridoo and other ethnic instruments as they apply to the trombone's acoustical repertoire, and as unique buzzed-lip instruments.

SIDELIGHTS: Dempster told *CA:* "The work that led to my book stems from a personal commission program begun in the early 1960's. The first fruits of that program came in 1966 with solo compositions for trombone from Berio, Erickson, and Oliveros. The collaborations with these composers, along with my research into *everything* the trombone could do, which included investigating groups such as Spike Jones, made it possible for the book to happen. The Australian aboriginal *didgeridoo* research completed the background and put the trombone into a larger perspective.''

BIOGRAPHICAL/CRITICAL SOURCES: David Baker, *Contemporary Techniques for the Trombone*, Charles Colin, 1974; *Instrumentalist*, May, 1974; *Composer*, spring, 1978; *Newsletter of the International Trombone Association*, April, 1979.

*   *   *

DENHAM, Avery Strakosch   ?-1970
(Avery Strakosch)

OBITUARY NOTICE: Died December 8, 1970, in Rosemont, Pa. Journalist and author. Denham contributed articles to many periodicals, including *Saturday Evening Post, Collier's, Cosmopolitan,* and *New York Times Magazine.* She also wrote two books in collaboration with A.S.W. Rosenbach. Obituaries and other sources: *New York Times,* December 10, 1970; *AB Bookman's Weekly,* January 4, 1971.

*   *   *

DENIS, Armand   1896(?)-1971

OBITUARY NOTICE: Born c. 1896 in Brussels, Belgium; died April 15, 1971, near Nairobi, Kenya. Wildlife conservationist, television film director, and author. Denis directed 105 half-hour television films on African wildlife. His ''Filming in Africa'' series was cited as the best television documentary of 1954, and his ''Savage Splendor'' was the first full-length color film to be produced in Africa. Among his books are *On Safari: The Story of a Man's Life in Search of Adventure* and *Cats of the World.* Obituaries and other sources: *New York Times,* April 16, 1971; *Publishers Weekly,* May 10, 1971.

*   *   *

DENIS, Charlotte
See PLIMMER, Charlotte
and PLIMMER, Denis

*   *   *

DENNEY, Diana   1910-
(Diana Ross; Gri, a pseudonym)

PERSONAL: Born July 8, 1910, in Valetta, Malta; daughter of William (a sailor) and Margery (Grenfell) Ross; married Antony Denney, 1939 (divorced, 1948); children: Sarah and Teresa (twins), Timothy. *Education:* Girton College, Cambridge, B.A. (with honors), 1931; attended Central School of Art, London, 1932-34. *Home:* Minster House, Shaw, Melksham, Wiltshire, England.

CAREER: Author and illustrator of books for children. Worked as a junior school general teacher, 1930-34, and intermittently as an art instructor in evening classes.

WRITINGS—Under name Diana Ross: *The World at Work,* Country Life, 1939; *The Story of the Beetle Who Lived Alone,* Faber, 1941; (with Antony Denney) *Uncle Anty's Album,* Faber, 1941; *The Golden Hen and Other Stories,* self-illustrated under pseudonym Gri, Faber, 1942; *The Little Red Engine Gets a Name,* Faber, 1942; *The Wild Cherry,* self-illustrated under

pseudonym Gri, Faber,1943; *Nursery Tales,* Faber, 1944; *The Story of Louisa,* Penguin, 1945; *The Story of the Little Red Engine,* Faber, 1945, reprinted, Harmondsworth, 1976; *The Little Red Engine Goes to Market,* Faber, 1946; *Whoo, Whoo, the Wind Blew,* Faber, 1946.

The Enormous Apple Pie and Other Miss Pussy Stories, Lutterworth Press, 1951; *The Tooter and Other Nursery Tales,* Faber, 1951; *The Bridal Gown and Other Stories,* self-illustrated under pseudonym Gri, Faber, 1952; *The Little Red Engine Goes to Town,* Faber, 1952; *Ebenezer the Big Balloon,* Faber, 1952; *The Bran Tub,* self-illustrated under pseudonym Gri, Lutterworth Press, 1954; *The Little Red Engine Goes Travelling,* Faber, 1955; *The Little Red Engine and the Rocket,* Faber, 1956; *William and the Lorry,* Faber, 1956; *Child of Air,* self-illustrated under pseudonym Gri, Lutterworth Press, 1957; *The Little Red Engine Goes Home,* Faber, 1958; *The Dreadful Boy,* Hamish Hamilton, 1959.

The Merry-Go-Round, Lutterworth Press, 1963; *Old Perisher,* Faber, 1965; *The Little Red Engine Goes to Be Mended,* Faber, 1966; *Nothing to Do,* Hamish Hamilton, 1966; *The Little Red Engine and the Taddlecombe Outing,* Transatlantic, 1969; *The Little Red Engine Goes Carolling,* Transatlantic, 1971; *I Love My Love With an A: Where Is He?,* Merrimack, 1972.

SIDELIGHTS: Diana Ross's ''Little Red Engine'' stories were first created for a nephew who lived near a railroad, and feature tales of a dutiful engine that makes every effort to satisfy its passengers. *Avocational interests:* Painting, pottery, sculpture.

*   *   *

DESCHIN, Celia Spalter   1903-

PERSONAL: Born July 19, 1903, in New York, N.Y.; daughter of Abraham and Yette (Ritoff) Spalter; married Jacob Deschin, April 22, 1929. *Education:* Smith College, B.A. (cum laude), 1924; Columbia University, M.S.W., 1942; New York University, Ph.D., 1958. *Home:* 6 Wyngate Pl., Great Neck, N.Y. 11021.

CAREER: Teacher of Latin and French at high school in Hartford, Conn., 1924-30; Brooklyn Bureau of Social Services, New York City, social worker, 1938-43; Jewish Family Service, New York City, social worker, 1938-43; American Red Cross home service counselor in Ohio, 1943-44; War Relocation Authority, Tule Lake, Calif., welfare counselor, 1944-45; special teaching assignment at McGill University School of Social Work, Montreal, Quebec, 1945-46; State University of New York, Downstate Medical Center, Brooklyn, N.Y., research associate in psychiatry, 1948-52; American Social Health Association, New York City, director of New York Teenage VD Study, 1958-61; Adelphi University, Graduate School of Social Work, Garden City, N.Y., professor of research, 1961-68, professor emeritus, 1968—. Author. Board member of Great Neck Committee for Human Rights, 1962—; member of governing council of American Jewish Congress, 1968—; participant in radio, television interviews, and public information programs. *Member:* National Association of Social Workers, American Public Health Association (fellow), American Sociological Association, American Academy of Arts and Sciences, American Associaton of University Professors, American Orthopsychiatric Association, Society for the Scientific Study of Sex, Council on Social Work Education, Eastern Sociological Society, Royal Society of Health of Great Britain, Phi Beta Kappa.

WRITINGS: The Five Towns: A Community Self-Portrait, As Seen Through the Eyes of Its Adult Residents, Its Adolescents,

Health and Welfare Experts, and Its Community Leaders, Adelphi University Graduate School of Social Work, 1965; *The Teenager and VD: A Social Symptom of Our Times,* Richards Rosen, 1969; *They Can Communicate: Self-Image Evaluation,* Children's Integration Project, 1970; *The Teenager in a Drugged Society: A Symptom of Crisis,* Richards Rosen, 1972. Contributor of articles to periodicals, including *Ladies' Home Journal* and *PTA Magazine.**

* * *

DESSAUER, John H(ans) 1905-

PERSONAL: Born May 13, 1905, in Aschaffenburg, Germany (now West Germany); naturalized U.S. citizen; son of Hans and Bertha Dessauer; married Margaret Lee (a philanthropist), June 29, 1935; children: John P., Margot (Mrs. Gerard Norton), Thomas David. *Education:* Institute of Technology, Munich, Germany (now West Germany), B.S., 1924; Institute of Technology, Aachen, Germany, (now West Germany), M.S., 1927, D.Ing., 1929. *Religion:* Roman Catholic. *Home:* 37 Parker Dr., Pittsford, N.Y. 14534.

CAREER: Ansco, New York, research chemist, 1925-35; research chemist and director for Habloid Co., 1935-51; Xerox Corp., Rochester, N.Y., vice-president in charge of research and product development, and director, 1946-58, executive vice-president of research and engineering, 1959-66, director of Rank Xerox Ltd., 1959-70, vice-chairman of board of directors and executive vice-president of research and advanced engineering, 1966-70, director, 1959-73. Emeritus member of board of trustees of Fordham University; trustee of New York State Science and Technological Foundation, 1972—. *Member:* National Academy of Engineering (past council member), American Chemical Society, American Institute of Chemists (fellow), American Optical Society, American Physical Society, New York Academy of Science (fellow). *Awards, honors:* Philipps Award from Institute of Electrical and Electronics Engineers, 1974; gold medal from Industrial Research Institute; L.H.D. from Le Moyne College, 1963; D.Sc. from Clarkson College, 1975.

WRITINGS: (Editor with Harold E. Clark) *Xerography and Related Processes,* Focal Press, 1965; *My Years With Xerox: The Billions Nobody Wanted,* Doubleday, 1971. Contributor to *Research Management.*

* * *

de TERRA, Helmut 1900-1981

OBITUARY NOTICE: Born July 11, 1900, in Guben, Germany (now East Germany); died July 22, 1981, in Bern, Switzerland. Anthropologist and author. A specialist in the Pleistocene and Cenozoic eras, de Terra took part in the 1956 expedition that uncovered the "Oreopithecus" skeleton. The find challenged Charles Darwin's theory that apes and man descended from a common ancestor. De Terra's books include *Studies on the Ice Age in India and Associated Human Cultures, The Life and Times of Alexander von Humboldt,* and *Man and Mammoth in Mexico.* Obituaries and other sources: *The International Who's Who,* Europa, 1980; *New York Times,* July 24, 1981; *AB Bookman's Weekly,* September 7, 1981.

* * *

DEVARAJA, N(and) K(ishore) 1917-

PERSONAL: Born June 3, 1917, in Rampur, Uttar Pradesh, India; son of Mathura Das (a bullion merchant and jeweler) and Basanti (Devi) Devaraja; married wife, Rajeshwari, May

11, 1937; children: Neerja Devaraja Gupta (daughter), Devakant (son), Shailja Devaraja Kumar (daughter), Deva Mitra (son). *Education:* Banaras Hindu University, B.A., 1936; Allahabad University, M.A., 1938, D.Phil., 1942. *Politics:* "Nil." *Religion:* "Hinduism, more correctly, Humanism." *Home:* 52 Badshah Nagar, Lucknow, Uttar Pradesh, India. *Office:* Centre of Advanced Study in Philosophy, Banaras Hindu University, Varanasi 5, Uttar Pradesh, India.

CAREER: H. D. Jain Degree College, Arrah, Bihar, India, head of department of logic, psychology, and philosophy, 1942-45; Rajendra College, Chapara, Bihar, head of department of logic and philosophy, 1946-48; K.G.K. College, Muradabad, Uttar Pradesh, India, head of department of logic and philosophy, 1948; Lucknow University, Lucknow, Uttar Pradesh, 1948-60, began as lecturer, became assistant professor in department of philosophy; Banaras Hindu University, Varanasi, Uttar Pradesh, Sayaji Rao Gaekwad Professor of Indian Civilization and Culture and head of department of Indian philosophy and religion, 1960-67, professor and head of department of philosophy and director of Centre of Advanced Study in Philosophy, 1967—. University of Calcutta, Brahmanand Keshub Chandra Sen Memorial lecturer, 1967, K. C. Bhattacharya lecturer, 1971. Presided over first Rajasthan philosophy conference, Jaipur, 1962; general president of Akhil Bharatiya Darshan Parishad, Jaipur, 1964; presided over history of philosophy section of Indian Philosophical Congress, Delhi University, 1965; presided over philosophy and religion section of the All India Oriental Conference, Varanasi, 1968.

MEMBER: Indian Philosophical Congress (life member), Akhil-Bharatiya Darshan-Parishad (life member; chairman), Institute of Religion and Social Change (Honolulu). *Awards, honors:* Bengal-Hindi Mandal prize, 1944, for *Purvi aur pashchimi darshan;* prizes from Uttar Pradesh Government for *Adhunik samiksha, Bahar-bhitar,* and *Itihas purusha;* UNESCO grant for regional cultural studies in the United States, 1957-58; Hindustani Academy prize, 1960, for best work on philosophy published between 1950-60, for *Sanskriti ka darshanik vivechan.*

*WRITINGS—*In English: *An Introduction to Sankara's Theory of Knowledge,* Motilal Banarsidass, 1962, 2nd edition, 1972; *The Philosophy of Culture: An Introduction to Creative Humanism,* Kitab Mahal, 1963; *The Mind and Spirit of India,* Motilal Banarsidass, 1967; *Hinduism and Christianity,* Asia Publishing House, 1969; (editor with N. S. Hirematha) *A Source Book of Sankara* (introduction in English and Hindi; text in Sanskrit and Hindi), Banaras Hindu University, 1971; *Philosophy, Religion, and Culture: Essays in Search of Definitions and Directions,* Motilal Banarsidass, 1973; (editor) *Indian Philosophy Today,* Macmillan (India), 1975; *Hinduism and the Modern Age,* Islam and Modern Age Society, 1975.

In Hindi; all published under author's surname only; poetry: *Pranaya-git* (title means "Love Lyrics"), 1939; *Jiwan-rashmi* (title means "Life Rays"), 1948; *Dharti aur Svarga* (title means "This Earth, That Paradise"), 1954; *Urvashi ne kaha* (title means "Thus Spoke Urvashi"), 1960; *Itihas purush* (title means "The Spirit of History"), 1965; *Ila aur Amitabh* (title means "Heloise and Abelard"), 1972; *Subah ke bad* (title means "After Morning Is Over"), 1975; *Ahat atmayen* (title means "Wounded Souls"), 1978.

Novels: *Bahar-bhitar* (title means "Inside and Outside"), 1954, published as *Bhitar ka ghav* (title means "The Hidden Wound"), 1970; *Rodey aur patthar* (title means "Brick Pieces and Stones"), 1958; *Ajaya ki dayari* (title means "The Diary of Ajaya"), 1960; *Main, ve aur apa* (title means "Me, They, and You"),

1969; *Dohri aga ki lapat* (title means "The Double Blaze"), 1973; *Doosra sutra* (title means "The Alternative"), 1978.

Other: *Purvi aur pashchimi darshan* (title means "Eastern and Western Philosophy"), 1944, 3rd edition, 1979; *Chhayavad ka patan* (title means "The Decline of Hindi Romantic Poetry"), 1948, 2nd edition published as *Chhayavad: Utthan, patan, punarmulyankan* (title means "The Rise, Fall, and Assessment of Hindi Romantic Poetry"), 1975; *Sahity a chinta* (title means "Thinking of Literature"), 1950; *Adhunik samiksha* (title means "Modern Criticism"), 1954; *Pratikryayen* (title means "Reactions"), 1966; *Bhartiya Sanskriti, mahakavyon ke alok men* (title means "Indian Culture in the Light of Epic Literature"), 1960, 3rd edition, 1966; (editor) *Bhartiya barshan* (title means "Indian Philosophy"), 1975, 2nd edition, 1979; *sahitya, samiksha aur Sanskritibodh* (title means "Literature, Criticism, and Cultural Awareness"), 1977. Also author of *Sanskriti ka darshanik vivechan.*

Contributor of articles to periodicals.

SIDELIGHTS: Devaraja told *CA:* "Though by profession a teacher of philosophy, I have been preoccupied with literature, both as a connoisseur and as a writer, throughout my career as writer and thinker. My earliest verses were written probably at the age of twelve; first allegorical novel (unpublished) at the age of fourteen; another novel (unpublished) on school life at the age of eighteen. I studied Sanskrit for about eight years, which developed a liking for classics and the classical style of clear, concise statement and expression. Later, my respect for the classics was strengthened under the influence of T. S. Eliot, whose critical ideas, together with the classical theory of Rasa, have largely shaped my thinking about literature. However, as a philosopher, I happen to be a confirmed atheist and a humanist. I have designated my philosophical outlook—and I take philosophizing as seriously as writing literature—'creative humanism,' which has far-reaching implications for both the theory of knowledge and the theory of values as developed by me.

"The beauty and pathos of man's life on the earth and in the universe, and moral imbalances of the socio-political scene, constitute perennial sources of inspiration to literary writers. In any case the author has to relive and reconstruct the perceptions and emotions that make up the mind and spirit of his times. While remaining an interested observer of the changing literary scene, I have not yet found it possible to identify myself with any movement (experimental, Marxist-progressivism, anti-romanticism); nor have I had the time and inclination to originate a new movement. To me, it is more important that a literary tradition, not attaching too much importance to slogans and catch-words, should produce works that may endure. Such works, I am persuaded, can be produced only by authors with a *distinctive* moral and metaphysical outlook. I am constrained to observe that contemporary Indian literature frequently fails to attain maturity embedded in such an outlook. (This was a factor in Tolstoy's dissatisfaction with Guy de Maupassant's fiction.)

"At various stages in my writing I have been influenced by Sumitra Nandan Pant, Tagore, Kalidasa, and Paul Valery (in poetry); and Jainendre Kumar, Ajheya, Dostoevsky, Henry James, and Marcel Proust (in fiction). In philosophy the major influences have probably been Advaita Vedanta, Immanuel Kant and Wilhelm Dilthey."

*   *   *

DEVERSON, Harry   1909(?)-1972

OBITUARY NOTICE: Born c. 1909; died September 18, 1972,

in London, England. Editor and author. Deverson was a managing editor at Wolfe Publishing in London. Among his many books is *The London Walkabout.* Obituaries and other sources: *AB Bookman's Weekly,* October 16, 1972.

*   *   *

de VILMORIN, Louise Leveque
     See VILMORIN, Louise Leveque de

*   *   *

DEW, Joan King   1932-

PERSONAL: Born June 24, 1932, in Columbus, Ga.; daughter of H. Grady (in sales) and Vivian (a registered nurse; maiden name, Cook) King; married Clifford Dew (marriage ended); married Albert Schmitt (marriage ended); children: (first marriage) Clifford, Jr., David; (second marriage) Christopher. *Education:* Attended Florida State University, 1949-50. *Home:* 179 Woodmont Blvd., Nashville, Tenn. 37205. *Agent:* Lynn Nesbit, International Creative Management, 43 West 57th St., New York, N.Y. 10019. *Office address:* P.O. Box 15904, Nashville, Tenn. 37215.

CAREER: Fort Lauderdale Daily News, Fort Lauderdale, Fla., reporter and feature writer, 1950-56; *Nassau Guardian,* Nassau, Bahamas, editor, 1956-58; Art and Publicity Ltd., Kingston, Jamaica, copy chief, 1958-60; *Valley Times Today,* North Hollywood, Calif., feature writer, author of column "Male Call," and editor, 1960-66; free-lance writer in Hollywood, Calif., 1966-77, and Nashville, Tenn., 1977—. Stringer for United Press International in the Bahamas, 1956-58.

WRITINGS: Singers and Sweethearts: The Women in Country Music, Doubleday, 1977; (with Tammy Wynette) *Stand by Your Man: The Autobiography of Tammy Wynette,* Simon & Schuster, 1978; (with Minnie Pearl) *Minnie Pearl: Autobiography,* Simon & Schuster, 1980; *Ruby Dawn* (novel), Simon & Schuster, 1982. Author of "Gleeful Gourmand," a column in *Nashville.* Contributor to national magazines, including *Redbook, Cosmopolitan, Coronet,* and *McCall's.*

SIDELIGHTS: "I've come to believe writing is more a compulsion than a career," Joan Dew commented. "It is the loneliest work imaginable, and even when a project is finished and in print there is always the feeling that it could have been better . . . if only I'd had more time, if only I could have escaped the distracting responsibilities of home and children . . . if, if, *if.* The most fun, the *only* fun, I've ever had as a writer was working on newspapers because there's that wonderful camaraderie of the newsroom, the sense of purpose, the respect for ethical journalism. But even there I don't remember ever having fun at the typewriter.

"Yet, I've never considered any work other than writing—and a good thing, too, since I'm unemployable in any other field. I did try clerking in a store once during college and got fired because I couldn't make change.

"I hope to spend the rest of my life writing fiction (the license to tell lies in print is heady freedom after thirty years of devotion to facts, facts, facts), and I will undoubtedly continue to read authors like Camus, John Fowles, and Frederic Exley and wonder where the hell I come off calling myself a writer, all the while knowing I'd sell my soul for a best-seller, no matter what the reviews."

AVOCATIONAL INTERESTS: "I love to travel (have visited Europe, most of the West Indies, all the Hawaiian islands, and forty-two states) but deadlines rarely allow more than short trips, and I like to settle in and get to know my surroundings to get the feel of a new place. I love to cook and am quite good at it, but unfortunately wear what I eat the next day, so I try not to make gourmet meals often.''

*   *   *

DEW, Robb Forman 1946-

PERSONAL: Born October 26, 1946, in Mt. Vernon, Ohio; daughter of Oliver Duane (a neurosurgeon) and Helen (Ransom) Forman; married Charles B. Dew (a professor of history), January 26, 1968; children: Charles Stephen, John Forman. *Education:* Attended Louisiana State University. *Agent:* Elizabeth McKee, c/o Harold Matson Co., Inc., 22 East 40th St., New York, N.Y. 10016.

CAREER: Writer.

WRITINGS: Dale Loves Sophie to Death (novel), Farrar, 1981. Contributor of stories to periodicals and magazines, including *Mississippi Quarterly, Southern Review, Virginia Quarterly,* and *New Yorker.*

WORK IN PROGRESS: "A novel about the ordinary violence of domestic life," tentatively titled *Jacob Bean.*

SIDELIGHTS: Dew told *CA:* "I grew up as a Southerner and I believe that background is the source of my interest in the intricacies of family life. My grandfather, with whom I lived for a portion of my adolescence, was the poet and critic John Crowe Ransom, and his voice has certainly shaped my style."

Dew deals with the "intricacies of family life" in *Dale Loves Sophie to Death.* This first novel focuses on Dinah Howells, a happily married, thirty-six-year-old mother of three children. Every summer, Dinah and her offspring vacation in Enfield, Ohio, where Dinah grew up, and where her divorced parents and brother still live. Dinah's perennial return to Enfield is an attempt to capture some of the love that she was denied by her parents and brother; in essence, Dinah is still a child seeking comfort from a familiar place, which is "essential to the very stability of her being."

As Dinah and the kids swim, sun, and socialize, Dinah's husband, Martin, is at home, lonely. To escape his depression, he has an affair, while Dinah, in the meantime, considers having an affair herself with her former high school boyfriend. The Howells's relationship is reaffirmed and strengthened, however, when their son Toby becomes ill and is hospitalized.

Critics have warmly received Dew's story of familial love. Katha Pollitt of the *New York Times Book Review* wrote: "It takes a certain artistic courage to write the traditional novel of domestic feeling today, a novel with no violence, no million-dollar deals, no weird sex—and perhaps as much editorial courage to print it. The rewards of 'Dale Loves Sophie to Death' are quiet but rich, and prove once again that in fiction there are no automatically compelling subjects. There are only compelling writers." Robert Wilson of the *Washington Post Book World* commented: "*Dale Loves Sophie to Death* deserves to be among those few novels published this year that will be read again in other years."

BIOGRAPHICAL/CRITICAL SOURCES: New York Times Book Review, April 26, 1981; *Newsweek,* May 4, 1981; *Washington Post Book World,* June 7, 1981.

*   *   *

de WET, Hugh Oloff 1912(?)-1976(?)

OBITUARY NOTICE: Born c. 1912; died c. 1976 in England.

Sculptor and author. De Wet's subjects as a sculptor included Dylan Thomas, Ezra Pound, and Robert Graves. In his book *The Valley of the Shadow* he wrote of the years he spent under a death sentence in a Gestapo prison during World War II. Obituaries and other sources: *AB Bookman's Weekly,* February 9, 1976.

*   *   *

di BASSETTO, Corno
See SHAW, George Bernard

*   *   *

DICHTER, Harry 1900(?)-1978(?)

OBITUARY NOTICE: Born c. 1900 in Russia (now U.S.S.R.); died c. 1978 in Atlantic City, N.J. Publisher, music collector, and author. Dichter was a music curator for the Free Library of Philadelphia and the founder of the Musical Americana publishing company. He wrote *American Music: Its Lure and Lore.* Obituaries and other sources: *AB Bookman's Weekly,* June 19, 1978.

*   *   *

DICKINSON, Lois Stice 1898(?)-1970

OBITUARY NOTICE: Born c. 1898; died December 26, 1970, in Summit, N.J. Medical writer and editor. Obituaries and other sources: *New York Times,* December 28, 1970; *AB Bookman's Weekly,* January 18, 1971.

*   *   *

DIEFENDORF, Jeffry M(indlin) 1945-

PERSONAL: Born October 19, 1945, in Pasadena, Calif.; son of William Morris and Sonia (Mindlin) Diefendorf; married Barbara Boonstoppel (a professor of history), December 19, 1972. *Education:* Stanford University, B.A., 1967; University of California, Berkeley, M.A., 1968, Ph.D., 1975. *Residence:* Portsmouth, N.H. *Office:* Department of History, University of New Hampshire, Durham, N.H. 03824.

CAREER: Stanford University, Stanford, Calif., lecturer in history, 1973-76; University of New Hampshire, Durham, assistant professor, 1976-81; associate professor of history, 1981—. *Member:* American Historical Association, Council for European Studies, Conference Group for German Politics, New England Historical Association, Western Association for German Studies, Phi Beta Kappa, Phi Kappa Phi, Phi Alpha Theta. *Awards, honors:* American Council of Learned Societies grant, 1977; National Endowment for the Humanities fellowship, 1981-82.

WRITINGS: Businessmen and Politics in the Rhineland, 1789-1834, Princeton University Press, 1980.

WORK IN PROGRESS: A book on the reconstruction of German cities after 1945, completion expected in 1984.

SIDELIGHTS: Diefendorf told *CA:* "German history is intriguing because it is full of puzzles. We often associate Germany with nationalism, but in fact a German nation-state was created relatively late and only with great difficulty. The Germans have shown they can develop liberal, democratic institutions; why did it take so long to do so, and what role did the middle class play in the process? How did Prussia come to dominate Germany? How did residents of outlying cities become Prussians and then Germans? These are the questions that led to my first book. My current project is one that any tourist could formulate. How did Germany manage to build new and apparently functional cities out of the devastation of World War II—especially when other countries seem unable to cope with routine urban renewal? Who made the decisions? Where did the money and materials come from? Given the magnitude of the task, physical reconstruction has received surprisingly little attention.

"Since I have jumped from the early nineteenth to the mid-twentieth century, and from a kind of prosopography to a broader urban history, I have had to educate myself in new fields, such as urban planning. But this is the challenge and pleasure of writing history. It is not just the setting down in order of facts from the past."

* * *

DiMONA, Joseph

CAREER: Writer.

WRITINGS: (With Ann Corio) *This Was Burlesque* (nonfiction), Grosset, 1968; *Seventy Sutton Place* (novel), Dodd, 1972; *Great Court-Martial Cases* (nonfiction), introduction by Birch Bayh, Grosset, 1972; *Last Man at Arlington* (novel), A. Fields, 1973; (with George Wolf) *Frank Costello: Prime Minister of the Underworld* (biography), Morrow, 1974; *The Benedict Arnold Connection* (novel), Morrow, 1977; (with H. R. Haldeman) *The Ends of Power* (nonfiction), G. K. Hall, 1978; *To the Eagle's Nest* (novel), Morrow, 1980.

SIDELIGHTS: Intrigue, terror, and suspense are critical elements in Joseph DiMona's novels. His second, *The Benedict Arnold Connection*, is the story of a government investigator's search for a demented nuclear scientist who plans to detonate a bomb off the eastern U.S. coast. His third novel, *To the Eagle's Nest*, is set in Germany where a movie crew is filming a picture about Adolf Hitler. The stars of the film are taken hostage by German terrorists and face a threat of execution.

DiMona has also collaborated on several books. He worked with George Wolf on a biography of underworld mobster Frank Costello, with burlesque queen Ann Corio on a history of burlesque, and with former White House Chief of Staff H. R. Haldeman on *The Ends of Power*. An account of Haldeman's views on the Nixon administration and Watergate scandal, *The Ends of Power* has been described as an interesting but poorly written book. "[This book] is stylistically and even grammatically poor, many of its statements are mere assertions or speculations, and much of its reasoning is simplistic," commented T. J. Seess in *Best Sellers*. Another critic, Elizabeth Drew of *New York Times Book Review*, complained that the book was "bewilderingly organized" and had a "wooden narrative."

BIOGRAPHICAL/CRITICAL SOURCES: New York Times Book Review, November 4, 1973, September 25, 1977, March 12, 1978; *Best Sellers*, July 15, 1974, October, 1977; *New York Review of Books*, April 6, 1978; *National Review*, April 14, 1978; *Times Literary Supplement*, April 21, 1978.*

* * *

DIPLOMATICUS
See GUERRA y SANCHEZ, Ramiro

* * *

DOBSON, Dennis   1919(?)-1979(?)

OBITUARY NOTICE: Publisher. Dobson was known for publishing unusual and difficult works, including those of George Padmore, Daniel Halevy, and B. Rajan. His Dobson Books Ltd. also reprinted Edith Sitwell's *English Eccentrics*. Obituaries and other sources: *AB Bookman's Weekly*, February 12, 1979.

* * *

DODGE, Daniel
See Du BREUIL, (Elizabeth) L(or)inda

* * *

DOENECKE, Justus Drew   1938-

PERSONAL: Surname is pronounced *Don*-a-key; born March 5, 1938, in Brooklyn, N.Y.; son of Justus Christian (a building estimator) and Eleanor (an elementary school teacher; maiden name, Smith) Doenecke; married Carol Anne Soukup (an artist), March 21, 1970. *Education:* Colgate University, A.B., 1960; Princeton University, M.A., 1962, Ph.D., 1966. *Religion:* Episcopal. *Office:* Division of Social Science, New College, University of South Florida, Sarasota, Fla. 33580.

CAREER: Colgate University, Hamilton, N.Y., instructor in history, 1963-64; Ohio Wesleyan University, Delaware, Ohio, instructor, 1965-66, assistant professor of history, 1966-69; University of South Florida, New College, Sarasota, assistant professor, 1969-71; associate professor, 1971-77, professor of history, 1977—.

MEMBER: American Historical Association, Organization of American Historians, Conference on Peace Research in History (member of council, 1975—), Society for the History of American Foreign Relations, Society for History Education, Phi Beta Kappa. *Awards, honors:* Woodrow Wilson fellowship, 1960-61; Danforth fellowship, 1960-65; fellow of Institute for Humane Studies, Menlo Park, Calif., summers, 1970-71, 1975-76, 1981, senior research fellow, 1977-78; National Endowment for the Humanities fellow, summer, 1971; grants from John Anson Kittredge Educational Fund, 1973, 1980, Harry S Truman Library Institute, 1973, and Shell Oil Co., 1975.

WRITINGS: The Literature of Isolationism: A Guide to Non-Interventionist Scholarship, 1930-1972, Ralph Myles, 1972; *Not to the Swift: The Old Isolationists in the Cold War Era*, Bucknell University Press, 1978; *The Presidencies of James A. Garfield and Chester A. Arthur*, Regents Press of Kansas, 1981; *The Diplomacy of Frustration: The Manchurian Crisis of 1931-1933 as Revealed in the Papers of Stanley K. Hornbeck*, Hoover Institution 1981. Contributor to *Dictionary of the History of American Foreign Policy* and *Dictionary of American Biography*. Contributor to history journals.

WORK IN PROGRESS: American Isolationism, 1939-41; American Public Opinion and the Manchurian Crisis, 1931-1933.

SIDELIGHTS: Doenecke told *CA:* "Much of my work has focused on alternatives to the foreign policies of Franklin D. Roosevelt, Truman, and Eisenhower. In venturing into such topics as isolationism, pacifism, and anti-interventionism, I hope to put anti-interventionist thought in the context of its own time and thereby reveal the hopes and fears of its proponents. My interpretation is revisionist only in the sense that I see the anti-interventionist heritage, like that of the administrations they so passionately criticized, containing wisdom as well as folly. The warnings of anti-interventionists against presidential duplicity remain timely. So does their critique of messianic foreign policy pronoucements. It is never the purpose of my work to plead their case or to justify their beliefs and behavior. It is very much my purpose to delineate who the isolationists were, what they believed, and what they did, and—so far as possible—to correct the one-sided and unequivocally negative picture that has come down in so much of our popular rhetoric and culture.''

*   *   *

DOLGUN, Alexander Michael   1926-

PERSONAL: Born September 29, 1926, in New York, N.Y.; son of Michael Steven and Ann (Katrynick) Dolgun; married Irene Knysh, January 23, 1965; children: Andrew. *Education:* Attended law school in Moscow, Soviet Union, 1940-43; Moscow Publishing and Printing Institute, B.S., 1961; Institute of Postgraduate Training for Workers of the Media, M.A., 1965. *Religion:* Roman Catholic. *Home:* 12704 Deep Spring Dr., Potomac, Md. 20854. *Office:* National Institutes of Health, Bethesda, Md. 20205.

CAREER: Associated with the U.S. Department of State, 1943-56, imprisoned in Lubyanka, Lefortovo, and Sukhanovka prisons, and in Dzhezhazgan Labor Camp in Soviet Union, 1948-56; international health program officer with National Institutes of Health, Bethesda, Md.

WRITINGS: (With Patrick Watson) *Alexander Dolgun's Story: An American in the Gulag,* Knopf, 1975.

SIDELIGHTS: After leaving his U.S. embassy office in Moscow on December 13, 1948, Dolgun was abducted by Soviet secret police and imprisoned for eight years. His experiences and the treatment he endured are unique because Dolgun is, and was at the time, an American citizen. Charged with espionage and anti-Soviet activity, Dolgun said he was told that his arrest was part of a Soviet plan to stage an anti-American trial. No one was informed of his arrest, and it was some time before his embassy or his family learned what had happened to him. Eventually his parents, who had moved from New York to the Soviet Union in the 1930's, were also arrested, and his mother went insane under torture and died. In 1951 authorities lost interest in staging a trial, and Dolgun was sentenced to twenty-five years in a labor camp. Released in 1956 under a general amnesty for political prisoners, he was not allowed to return to the United States until 1971. During the 1960's Dolgun was interviewed by Aleksandr I. Solzhenitsyn, and his experiences are described in detail in *The Gulag Archipelago, 1918-1956.*

BIOGRAPHICAL/CRITICAL SOURCES: New York Times, December 29, 1973; Aleksandr Solzhenitsyn, *The Gulag Archipelago,* 1918-1956, Volume I, Harper, 1974.

*   *   *

DOMINIAN, Jack   1929-

PERSONAL: Born August 25, 1929, in Athens, Greece; son of Charles (a bank cashier) and Mary (Scarlatou) Dominian; married Edith Mary Smith, June 23, 1955; children: Suzanne, Louise, Elise, Catherine. *Education:* Cambridge University, B.A., 1952, M.B., B.Chir., 1955, M.A., 1956. *Religion:* Roman Catholic. *Home:* Pefka, The Green, Croxley Green, Rickmansworth, Hertfordshire, England. *Office:* Central Middlesex Hospital, Park Royal, London N.W.10, England.

CAREER: Stoke Mandeville Hospital, Aylesbury, England, house officer, 1955-56; Radcliffe Infirmary, Oxford, England, house officer, 1957-58; Maudsley Hospital, London, England, registrar, 1958-61, senior registrar, 1961-64; Central Middlesex Hospital, London, consulting physician, 1965—. *Military service:* British Army, 1948-49. *Member:* Royal College of

Psychiatry (fellow), Royal Society of Medicine, Royal College of Edinburgh, Royal College of Physicians (Edinburgh; fellow). *Awards, honors:* D.Sc. from University of Lancaster, 1976.

WRITINGS: Psychiatry and the Christian, Burns & Oates, 1962; *Christian Marriage,* Darton, Longman & Todd, 1967; *Marital Breakdown,* Darton, Longman & Todd, 1968; *The Church and the Sexual Revolution,* Darton, Longman & Todd, 1971; *The Marriage Relationship Today,* Union of Christian Mothers, 1974; *Cycle of Affirmation,* Darton, Longman & Todd, 1975; *Authority: A Christian Interpretation,* Burns & Oates, 1976; *Depression,* Fontana, 1976; (with A. R. Peacocke) *From Cosmos to Love,* Darton, Longman & Todd, 1976; *Proposals for a New Sexual Ethic,* Darton, Longman & Todd, 1977; *Marriage, Faith, and Love,* Darton, Longman & Todd, 1981. Contributor to theology and medical journals.

WORK IN PROGRESS: A book on pastoral counseling in marriage.

SIDELIGHTS: Dominian wrote: ''My interests are centered on marriage and its future, Christian marriage, love, and the relationship between psychology and Christianity. I consider marriage to be in a stage of transition as a result of the emancipation of women and therefore a fundamental change in the man-woman relationship. The enfolding relationship is egalitarian and emphasizes feelings, emotions, and sexuality. There will be an increase in marital breakdown until societies are ready to educate and support this new development, which is likely to become a global one in due course. I see my task as preparing the ground for this change in European and Christian thought.''

*   *   *

DONIGER, Lester (Laurence)   1909-1971

OBITUARY NOTICE: Born October 15, 1909, in Raczi, Poland; died April 26, 1971, in Great Neck, Long Island, N.Y. Editor, publisher, and business executive. Doniger founded the journals *Pulpit Digest* and *Pastoral Psychology,* and he co-founded and later served as president of Channel Press. He was also president and director of Doniger & Raughley publishers. Obituaries and other sources: *New York Times,* April 28, 1971; *Publishers Weekly,* May 10, 1971; *Who's Who in World Jewry: A Biographical Dictionary of Outstanding Jews,* Pitman, 1972.

*   *   *

DONNAN, Marcia Jeanne   1932-

PERSONAL: Born February 20, 1932, in San Jose, Calif.; daughter of Eugene L. Wilcox and Delphine Wilcox Hawkins; married John A. Donnan (a research meteorologist); children: two. *Education:* Attended San Jose State College (now University) and Colorado State University. *Office:* South Dakota State Department of Labor, State Capitol, Pierre, S.D. 57501.

CAREER: Editor of *Rapid City Journal,* Rapid City, S.D.; South Dakota State Department of Labor, Pierre, began as special assistant to secretary of labor, became secretary of labor, 1975. National trustee of Status of Women Research and Education Fund, 1974—; member of Regional Manpower Advisory Council, 1975—. *Member:* Zonta International, National Press Women (committee chairperson, 1967—), National Association of the Community of Women (national secretary, 1974—). *Awards, honors:* First place press award from Associated Press of South Dakota, 1970-74; first place, National Press Honors, 1970 and 1973; Golden Press Award, 1971, for America's best feature series on youth.

WRITINGS: Cosmetics From the Kitchen, Holt, 1972; (with husband, John A. Donnan) *Rain Dance to Research* (juvenile), McKay, 1977. Author of numerous news stories and feature articles.

AVOCATIONAL INTERESTS: Skiing, swimming, horseback riding.*

*   *   *

DORIAN, Nancy C(urrier)   1936-

PERSONAL: Born November 5, 1936, in New Brunswick, N.J.; daughter of Donald Clayton (a professor) and Edith (a professor and writer; maiden name, McEwen) Dorian. *Education:* Connecticut College, B.A., 1958; attended University of Bonn and Free University of Berlin, 1958-59, and Yale University, 1959-60; University of Michigan, M.A., 1961, Ph.D., 1965. *Religion:* Unitarian-Universalist. *Office:* Departments of German and Anthropology, Bryn Mawr College, Bryn Mawr, Pa. 19010.

CAREER: Bryn Mawr College, Bryn Mawr, Pa., lecturer, 1965-66, assistant professor, 1966-72, associate professor, 1972-78, professor of linguistics in German and anthropology, 1978—, Kenan Professor, 1980-85. Visiting lecturer at University of Pennsylvania, autumn, 1966, spring, 1970; departmental assistant of linguistics seminar at University of Kiel, 1967-68. *Member:* International Linguistic Association, International Association for the Study of Child Language, Linguistic Society of America, Celtic Studies Association, Scottish Oral History Group, An Comunn Gaidhealach, Northeast Folklore Society. *Awards, honors:* Fulbright scholar, 1958-59; grants from American Council of Learned Societies, 1963-64, and National Science Foundation, 1978-79; summer grants from American Council of Learned Societies, 1970, American Philosophical Society, 1976, and National Endowment for Humanities, 1980.

WRITINGS: East Sutherland Gaelic, Dublin Institute for Advanced Studies, 1978; *Language Death,* University of Pennsylvania Press, 1981. Contributor to linguistics, folklore, and anthropology journals.

WORK IN PROGRESS: Ebb and Flow: Recollections of Fisherfolk Life in Golspie (East Sutherland), an oral history of the East Sutherland fisherfolk in Scotland, publication expected in 1983; research on language death among the secular Pennsylvania Dutch.

SIDELIGHTS: Nancy Dorian told *CA:* "Working with a vanishing language and way of life leads quite naturally to a desire to preserve some record of them, at least in print. So many splendid little communities have passed out of existence and are unremembered. If East Sutherland Gaelic life must disappear, at least there will be a few works which celebrate it.

"Language death (extinction) is a great deal more common worldwide than many people suppose. Small groups everywhere, especially indigenous minority groups like those of the aboriginal peoples of parts of the Soviet Union, Australia, North and South America, and Formosa, are giving up their languages and adopting those of the larger and politically dominant groups in their countries. Some observers would say that this is a positive development, because it reduces communication difficulties and represents the assimilation of 'less advanced' peoples into mainstream life. I disagree. I doubt that it ever represents an advance for the human race to eliminate the lifeways of people native to an area, people who have spent thousands of years adapting culturally and linguistically to their environment. Nearly always the people giving up their language and culture suffer various forms of maladaptation under the stress of losing their cultural heritage: Alcoholism, mental illness, suicide, and crime tend to rise under such conditions. The cost even to individuals who adapt successfully is high, as they are forced to choose between their traditional culture and a new one and also, usually, between their own people and another group which will only half accept them in any case.

"Apart from this immediate human cost, which is severe enough, there is the loss to us all in the sense of a diminution of the rich possibilities of human expression, linguistic and cultural. Each language (and each society) has its own genius; even unwritten folk languages preserve a vast amount of lore and oral literature, song and proverbial wisdom. We learn not only about the range of linguistic and cultural behaviors that are humanly possible, but infinitely more about ourselves by setting other varieties of linguistic and cultural organization beside our own.

"Since it is already the norm in many parts of India and Africa and certain parts of aboriginal South America, there seems no inherent reason why all people everywhere cannot become bilingual or multilingual by adding a second, internationally useful (even artificially designed) language to their mother tongue. This is very different from putting pressure on smaller peoples to give up their own native tongues altogether and adopt the politically dominant language of their area instead. We have learned slowly and painfully that the elimination of just one plant or insect species can have a serious effect on the whole local ecology. We seem even slower to learn to value human variation and to realize that the loss of a language and the culture it represents is both irreversible and of far-reaching consequences for people and for a region.

"If I am granted a normal life span, I will one day be one of the last fluent speakers of East Sutherland Gaelic. Although it is not my mother tongue, I feel even now, with under a hundred fluent speakers left, how sad it is that a language so rich in expression, in proverbial lore, and in the terminology of a specialized seafaring life can be savored by so few. Humorous turns of speech or pithy sayings that are peculiar to East Sutherland Gaelic will be lost forever, and the last few of us who are able to converse in the dialect will perhaps sometimes remember an unusual phrase or saying used by a long-dead person and realize how long it is since we have heard it. Who will the last speaker be? How will she or he feel when there is no one left at all to share a joke with, or enjoy a witty saying or an expressive curse? My comfort, when this time comes, will be to have left a record of the fisherfolk language and way of life, both on the technical level that specialists require and on a more popular level accessible to everyone, including the English-speaking descendants of the next century who will come sooner or later in search of their lost heritage. *Cha till e gu brath*—'it will never return.'"

*   *   *

DORN, Frank   1901-1981

OBITUARY NOTICE—See index for *CA* sketch: Born June 25, 1901, in San Francisco, Calif.; died of cancer, July 26, 1981. Military officer and author. Dorn began his military career when he graduated from West Point in 1923. As an assistant military attache serving with Joseph W. Stilwell in Peking, Dorn came in contact with notable figures such as Chou Enlai and Chaing Kai-shek. After World War II, Dorn worked at the Army Information School at Carlisle Barraks, Pennsylvania. In 1953 he retired as a brigadier general from his position as the deputy chief of information in the Department of the Army. An accomplished painter, Dorn exhibited his work in Paris, Madrid, Majorca, Mexico City, and Washington, D.C. His books on China include *The Forbidden City: The Biography of a Palace* and *The Sino-Japanese War, 1937-1941.* Among his other works are a novel, *Forest Twilight,* and two cookbooks, *The Dorn Cookbook: A Treasury of Fine Recipes From All Around the World* and *Good Cooking With Herbs and Spices.* Obituaries and other sources: *Washington Post,* July 28, 1981.

* * *

DOWNING, Paul B(utler) 1938-

PERSONAL: Born November 26, 1938, in Milwaukee, Wis.; son of Earle B. (an engineer) and Marion (an artist; maiden name, Bannon) Downing; married Barbara Wenzel (a word processor), December 1, 1979. *Education:* University of Wisconsin—Milwaukee, B.S., 1963; University of Wisconsin (now University of Wisconsin—Madison), M.S. (economics), 1966, Ph.D. and M.S. (water resources management), both 1967. *Home:* 3412 Monitor Lane, Tallahassee, Fla. 32312. *Office:* Policy Sciences Program, Florida State University, 332 Bellamy, Tallahassee, Fla. 32306.

CAREER: University of California, Riverside, assistant professor, 1969-72, associate professor of economics, 1972-74; Virginia Polytechnic Institute and State University, Blacksburg, associate professor of economics, 1973-80; Florida State University, Tallahassee, professor of economics and policy sciences, 1980—. Economist with Implementation Research Division of U.S. Environmental Protection Agency, 1972-73; fellow of International Institute for the Environment and Society, Berlin, West Germany, 1979; consultant to U.S. Department of Commerce. *Military service:* U.S. Army, economist for Office of the Assistant Secretary of Defense at the Pentagon, 1967-69; became captain.

MEMBER: American Economic Association, Public Choice Society, Association for Public Policy Analysis and Management, Southern Economic Association. *Awards, honors:* Grants from Project Clean Air, 1970, Urban Crisis Program, 1970-72, National Science Foundation and Ford Foundation, 1974, Environmental Law Institute and Resources for the Future, 1977, and U.S. Department of Commerce, 1978; economic policy fellow of Brookings Institution, 1972-73.

WRITINGS: The Economics of Urban Sewage Disposal, Praeger, 1969; (editor and contributor) *Air Pollution and the Social Sciences: Formulating and Implementing Control Programs,* Praeger, 1971; (editor and contributor) *Local Service Pricing Policies and Their Effect on Urban Spatial Structure,* University of British Columbia Press, 1977.

Contributor: Daniel Holland, editor, *The Assessment of Land Value,* University of Wisconsin Press, 1970; James N. Pitts and Robert L. Metcalf, editors, *Advances in Environmental Science and Technology,* Wiley, Volume III, 1974, Volume VII (Downing was not included in other volumes), 1977; *The Application of Multiple Regression Analysis in Assessment Administration: Studies in Property Taxation,* International Association of Assessing Officers, 1975; Edwin M. Rams, editor, *Analysis and Valuation of Retail Locations,* Reston, 1976; J. Thomas Black, editor, *Urban Land Markets: Price Indices, Supply Measures, and Public Efforts,* Urban Land Institute, 1980; J. Richard Aranson and Eli Schwarts, editors, *Management Policies in Local Government Finance,* International City Managers Association, 1981.

Contributor of about thirty articles and reviews to economic and natural resources journals. Member of editorial board of *Policy Studies Journal.*

WORK IN PROGRESS: Implementing Pollution Laws in the United States and Europe; The Political Economy of Pollution Control; User Charges in Local Government Finance; research on frequently cited works in public finance, resource, and environmental economics, and on the law and economics of pollution control.

SIDELIGHTS: Downing wrote: "I believe in applying economics to real circumstances rather than theorizing. Economics is of most interest when applied. Correct application requires that one pay particular attention to the political and institutional setting of the problem at hand." *Avocational interests:* Automobile racing, musical theatre.

* * *

DOYLE, Arthur Conan 1859-1930

BRIEF ENTRY: Born May 22, 1859, in Edinburgh, Scotland; died of a heart attack, July 7, 1930, in Crowborough, England. Scottish physician and writer. Sir Arthur Conan Doyle's immortality as a writer was established, to his own dismay, when he introduced that master of deductive logic, arch-detective Sherlock Holmes, in "A Study in Scarlet" (1887). Doyle produced four novels and more than fifty stories based on Holmes, each one full of adventure and mystery. His work elevated the detective story to a literary genre in its own right. He also wrote such science fiction as *The Lost World* (1912). But Doyle would have preferred to base his literary reputation on his other writings: historical novels, like the popular and critically acclaimed *The White Company* (1890), or masterful scholarly works, including *The British Campaigns in Europe* (1912). In about 1915, Doyle's interest in spiritualism led to an apparent conversion, and with the exception of a few Sherlock Holmes tales to appease his fans, most of his later writing was devoted to propagation of the "psychic religion." *Biographical/critical sources: Twentieth Century Authors: A Biographical Dictionary of Modern Literature,* H. W. Wilson, 1942; Pierre Nordon, *Conan Doyle,* J. Murray,1966; *The McGraw-Hill Encyclopedia of World Biography,* McGraw, 1973; Ronald Pearsall, *Conan Doyle: A Biographical Solution,* St. Martin's, 1977.

* * *

DRAGON, Caroline
See Du BREUIL, (Elizabeth) L(or)inda

* * *

DRAKE, Francis Vivian 1894-1971

OBITUARY NOTICE: Born in 1894 in London, England; died July 4, 1971, in Stonington, Conn. Educator on aviation fighting techniques and author. Drake began his career as an investment banker but turned to full-time writing after the stock market collapse of 1929. Much of his work appeared in *Reader's Digest,* where he worked as a roving editor beginning in 1943. Drake collaborated with his wife to write the novel *Big Flight;* he also wrote a book on strategic bombing, *Vertical Warfare,* and an autobiography, *Above the Battle.* Obituaries and other sources: *New York Times,* July 7, 1971; *AB Bookman's Weekly,* July 19, 1971.

* * *

DREW, Elizabeth 1935-

PERSONAL: Born November 16, 1935, in Cincinnati, Ohio;

daughter of William J. (in business) and Estelle (Jacobs) Brenner; married J. Patterson Drew, April 11, 1964 (died September 2, 1970); married David Webster, September 26, 1981. *Education:* Wellesley College, B.A., 1957. *Residence:* Washington, D.C. *Agent:* Morton Janklow, 375 Park Ave., New York, N.Y. 10022. *Office:* Room 405, 1300 19th St. N.W., Washington, D.C. 20036.

CAREER: Writer magazine, Boston, Mass., editorial assistant, 1957-59; *Congressional Quarterly,* Washington, D.C., writer and editor, 1959-64; free-lance writer, 1964-67; *Atlantic Monthly,* Washington, D.C., Washington editor, 1967-73; host of television program "30 Minutes With," Public Broadcasting System (PBS), Washington, D.C., 1971-73; *New Yorker* magazine, New York, N.Y., writer, 1973—; commentator for *Washington Post-Newsweek* stations in Washington, D.C., and various other cities, 1973—. *Member:* Phi Beta Kappa. *Awards, honors:* Society of Magazine Writers award for excellence, 1970; Wellesley College Alumnae Achievement Award and Dupont Columbia Award for broadcast journalism, both 1973; D.H.L. from Hood College and Yale University, both 1976, Trinity College, 1978, Reed College, 1979, and Williams College, 1981; *Ladies' Home Journal* Woman of the Year in Communications award, 1977; Missouri Medal for distinguished service in journalism, 1979; LL.D. from Georgetown University Law Center, 1981.

WRITINGS: Washington Journal: The Events of 1973-74, Random House, 1975; *American Journal: The Events of 1976,* Random House, 1977; *Senator,* Simon & Schuster, 1979; *Portrait of an Election: The 1980 Presidential Campaign,* Simon & Schuster, 1981.

SIDELIGHTS: "All my writing in some form or another is meant to illuminate the political process," Elizabeth Drew told Stella Dong of *Publishers Weekly.* Drew's books, which were originally serialized in the *New Yorker,* all focus on aspects of modern American politics. Explaining what motivated her to write about politics and politicians, Drew related: "Those people in Washington are deciding matters which mean a great deal to us, which is why we have a stake in understanding how they do it, what they're like—and in raising their standards as high as we possibly can. My job, as I see it, is to explain how it works and why it works as best I can."

Drew's first volume, *Washington Journal: The Events of 1973-74,* chronicles the Watergate incident from Spiro Agnew's resignation in September, 1973, to Richard Nixon's exit from office in August of the following year. According to critics, Drew presents an objective, accurate account of the events of the episode. "Her journal is unique among Watergate books in the author's refusal to pass judgments, argue a thesis, or proffer any 'inside story,'" commented William V. Shannon of the *New York Times Book Review.* "Rather, it is a sober, thorough and sensitive report of what is known to have been said and done by the many participants in the Watergate drama during its final year. The book's distinctive value lies in its careful rendering of the whole scene and of each event." Greil Marcus of *Rolling Stone* concurred: "Unquestionably the best book yet on Watergate, and conceivably, the best we will ever get." *Chicago Sun Times* reviewer Peggy Constantine proclaimed: "This is one Watergate book—of some 200—that surely will last."

In her second work, Drew recorded her impressions of the 1976 election against the backdrop of the American bicentennial and the issues before the nation. Similar in format to *Washington Journal, American Journal* also was warmly received. Godfrey Hodgson of the *Washington Post Book Review* assessed it as "thoroughly successful" and "one of the more

intelligent and readable books I have read about an American presidential election, written by a reporter who combines in a way that is sadly rare, access to accurate information about what is going on with some sense of what this means to those who are not insiders." The *Houston Post*'s Arthur Wiese commented: "Drew's work is consistently thoughtful, witty, perceptive and reassuringly free from bias. *American Journal* is grand reading, entertaining, enlightening, and strangely poignant." And Alyn Brodsky, in a *Miami Herald* review, remarked that Drew offers "both delicious reading (no other cliche will do) and an awareness of how much we missed by concentrating on the overall picture." However, Richard Reeves, who also wrote a book on the election and bicentennial, noted in the *New York Times Book Review* that "although the book is marked by a clear intelligence . . . 'American Journal' just doesn't work. It is without passion; chances are not taken; it is edited as if readers had no other sources of information, sometimes reducing copy to a style reminiscent of 'see Spot run.'"

In writing *Senator,* Drew followed one senator's activities, interviewed other senators, and used her years of experience covering Capitol Hill to show how the Senate functions. In the process she revealed that "there are a lot more good ones [politicians] out there than we think." For ten days she trailed Senator John C. Culver of Iowa as he worked with his colleagues and aides, met with constituents, and spent time relaxing with his family. Her observations illustrate the pressured, hectic life of a senator, especially an active one who is concerned with a broad range of issues.

Senator elicited praise from critics such as Bruce Dexter of the *Los Angeles Times* who wrote: "Drew brings to the work the same narrative gifts and meticulous prose along with an objectivity so rare in the era of 'involved' journalism." Eric Redman of the *Washington Post Book World* felt Drew successfully portrayed the "demand and tedium of Senate life," and recommended: "This is the book to read if you're wondering why so many members of Congress are declining to seek reelection."

Portrait of an Election: The 1980 Presidential Campaign, Drew's fourth book, reviews the political scene from November, 1979, to November, 1980. Drew begins her chronicle by discussing the candidates' decisions to run in the presidential race, including Senator Edward Kennedy's reluctance to throw his hat into the ring. In more than three hundred fifty pages, the author characterizes and appraises the major candidates—Anderson, Bush, Carter, Kennedy, and Reagan—and describes both the Republican and Democratic conventions, highlighting the particularly tense moments, such as the premature announcement of Gerald Ford, instead of George Bush, as Ronald Reagan's running mate. Drew also outlines the campaign strategies used by the office seekers, including memos on strategy from Carter and Reagan advisers. To the events she documents, Drew adds commentary and personal interviews with the candidates, making *Portrait of an Election* a record of the pre-election year as seen by a Washington insider.

CA INTERVIEW

CA interviewed Elizabeth Drew by phone on July 10, 1980, at her home in Washington, D.C., where she was preparing to leave for Detroit to cover the Republican Convention.

CA: You have said you didn't start out with the intention of being a writer or anything so definite as that. What ideas did you have about a career when you were a student at Wellesley?

DREW: I didn't have any ideas about it. I was there in the mid-1950's, when one didn't think about that kind of thing very much. The motto of Wellesley was *Non ministrari sed ministrare.* Our joke used to be that the translation of that was "Not to be ministers, but ministers' wives." That wasn't far off from the ethic of that period. A few of our classmates did go on to law school and medical school, but they were the unusual ones. Most either married right out of college or took just any old job until they got married. I suppose the latter was the category I was in.

CA: Did the ambition evolve from the work you got into?

DREW: I don't know that there was any ambition that evolved. I would say that the work evolved. It was really very serendipitous and a series of happenings. One thing just led to another, and a lot of accidents were involved, but there was never any plan. There still isn't. People find this hard to believe, and particularly younger women who are now coming out of college, because there has been such an enormous cultural change. It's hard for them to imagine; they think that you must be putting them on. It's just not the case.

I sometimes give commencement addresses, and I'll talk about it in that context—to soothe them, among other things, to say, "Look, you can't have a life plan. If you have one, you're likely not to make it anyway in the terms that you think. Life is too unpredictable and accidental. Be open to the unpredictabilities of it. You don't know where they're going to take you. Relax a little bit; don't sit there and think that if you don't see how you're going to reach fulfillment in three years, you will go crazy." So somewhere between what was going on in my day and what is going on now is probably the happier medium. What I mean by what is going on now is that young women are feeling so much pressure to know exactly what they're going to do and have a plan for doing it. I think it's very hard on them, and it doesn't conform to reality anyway.

CA: When you started working, did you run into any sexual discrimination?

DREW: No, considering my first job was as a secretary, so that was as it should have been in those days. I was a secretary to some architects in Cambridge, and they really didn't have enough business to keep me employed fulltime, so I went to work for the *Writer* magazine in Boston. Again, that wasn't because I wanted to be a writer; I really hadn't thought about it. As a matter of fact, I had deliberately not majored in English in college because I didn't want to take writing courses. I suppose the shrinks might have something to say about that, but I don't really think there *is* anything to say about it. That's just the way it was. I majored in government. In any event, I went to the *Writer* magazine and again, there were a couple of jobs for editorial assistants, and those were jobs that women were expected to hold. My work just evolved out of that.

No, I didn't meet with discrimination at first. The only time I met with it was later, after I had been at *Congressional Quarterly* for a while and was thinking about going into newspaper work. That was still at the time when bureau chiefs looked you in the eye and said, "Sorry, we don't hire women." It's hard to believe, but it wasn't really that long ago. We tend to forget how quickly and dramatically things have changed. The only other time was in television. Certain people in television haven't gotten used to women being on the air. I don't have that kind of problem now at all, but I did run into it once or twice in public television.

CA: One of the strengths of your work is very thorough research. Do you employ a staff for a large part of that?

DREW: No, I do it myself. Once in a while I can have my assistant look something up, check a figure, that sort of thing, but it's all my own reading and reporting. You can't delegate that; you have to absorb it and burrow into the material so that you really understand it—that isn't anything anyone else can do for you.

CA: Are there any research problems peculiar to political journalism?

DREW: No, I would think maybe on the contrary, there is so much material. In Washington, there is so much that you're doing that is in documents, in hearings, legislative records, background reports. So the thing is to fight your way out of being inundated with that kind of thing. But it's mainly doing whatever is the necessary reading and then doing very extensive and thorough reporting, talking to a lot of people, and getting immersed in the material so that you feel you've mastered it and you can sort out what really matters and is interesting. The trick is to learn all that, to get the feel of it, and to cull what matters and what would interest the reader—not to throw it all back at them, because you can't.

CA: An editor once said to you that you research too much, which seems a strange criticism to make of someone in your field.

DREW: At first I thought it was a terribly worrisome thing, but then I thought, well, of course you do—you have to. You have to know more than you're going to end up telling the reader so that you have a feel for the subject. Also, when you go for your interview, you know what to ask; you don't take their time—or your own, frankly—in having somebody recite the ABCs of an issue. You should know those going in and take the interview to the next step. You want to be able to go in there and say, in effect, "Yes, I know about this." What you want to do in your interviews is take it to the next frontier of information.

CA: You've won a number of awards, and you hold honorary degrees from Yale, Trinity College, Hood, and Reed. Is there a single honor that has meant more to you than the others?

DREW: No, they've all been lovely. The institutions treat you nicely and they really are lovely occasions.

CA: You've done television interviews with many prominent political figures. Have you had any very awkward moments doing that?

DREW: Oh, sure, lots. Three that come to mind. One was the second interview I ever did; I was quite green, coming out and getting on the air for a half hour. The interviews were either live or taped, but there were no changes involved. That was part of the understanding. The second television interview I did in the whole world was with Senator Muskie. This was early in 1971 and it was clear that he was getting ready to run for the presidency. I had made it clear to everyone, the interviewees included, that I wasn't going to use the program in the same way that the Sunday panel programs worked. They serve their purpose, but I wanted mine to be different; I certainly was aware that politicians didn't announce their presidential plans on interview programs, and it was a waste of time to dance around that subject. I wanted to explore how the subjects' minds worked, what they really thought about things.

Well, on came Senator Muskie and I noticed that he wasn't in a very good mood; he was tired—he had been traveling in the

Middle East and Moscow, I think. I did have a question that I asked a number of people, which was, "If *you* were president, what would *you* do about these things?" so they wouldn't get on there and just complain. Instead of saying how terrible everything was, they would have to say what they would do about it. I did that with Muskie, and he didn't take to that very kindly. At that point, nobody much knew about his towering temper. His last major public appearance had been the 1970 election-eve appearance: he was in the wing chair and he looked like Abe Lincoln and was calming everybody down, and that was everybody's vision of Muskie. Now here was this enormous man going into a rage, accusing me of trying to get him to announce his candidacy. I told him that I didn't ask him if he were running for president, and I didn't expect him to tell me here, but I thought it was fair to ask him what he would do about these things. Then he stormed and raged some more. That was pretty awkward.

Then I remember in Israel, finding that Golda Meir was not exactly the jolly Gertrude Berg figure that was her widespread image. She was very difficult to interview. It was the end of the day and she was tired and the batteries kept blowing out. It was my first foreign interview and there were a lot of technical problems that we just didn't know about. That was pretty hard.

Then of course there were several interviews during Watergate—not that they were so awkward, it's just that they were difficult. Research had to be brought to bear so that you knew an awful lot and could take the questions to the next level. We did make news on that. In fact, one of the scenes from my interview with Richard Kleindienst was in the movie "All the President's Men." Part of the interview verified a point that Woodward and Bernstein were trying to make, so there's a little filmstrip of that in the movie, and that is the full extent of my movie career.

CA: You covered Watergate in your first book, Washington Journal, *which was highly commended by critics for your perceptive coverage and your commentary on the events. Has your perspective on Watergate grown or changed in any way since those events?*

DREW: No, not particularly. What I was trying to do was to chronicle at the time what was going on in a way that would sort out the wheat from the chaff and capture the mood of the time. This is the kind of thing that you can't go back and recreate. It began as a magazine assignment for the *New Yorker* and it kept growing; we didn't know how long I would do it or what would happen. I had said to William Shawn, editor of the *New Yorker,* towards the end of the summer of '73, "I have this feeling that we might be changing presidents." That was when Agnew had gotten in trouble; and whoever was picked to succeed him might end up as president. The country had never been through anything like that. We talked about what I might do, and we arrived at the idea of keeping a chronicle of what happened as the nation went through this unprecedented experience. One of my gurus took me to lunch and said, "Write it so that fifty years from now, people will look back and say, 'That's what it was like.'" That was very, very valuable advice.

CA: In American Journal *you covered the presidential race of 1976, and you commented on the concerns of that bicentennial year. How do you approach political coverage?*

DREW: What I try to do is capture what is going on—again, sort out what in my own judgment is more important. There is so much material, there is so much going on, and there is so much concern with daily events—who's going to do what, and who's going to win that primary, and who's he going to pick as a running mate. I try to get outside that and capture what is going on at the period: Who are the principal people involved? How do they think? How do they address the issues that affect the public? They are human beings, and I think so much of that is always lost in journalism. I try to portray their human beingness whether I'm writing about a political race or a person in Washington or an issue. I try to show the interaction of processes and people to get across why things happen the way they do. When I'm doing the political coverage, it's that, and it's also a time to capture things that are going on at the time in a way that will make it stand up, so people can go back and say, "Well, that's how that person was dealing with that kind of situation, and that's how it looked and that's how it came across, and that's how it smelled and that's how it felt." I think that there is a real place for that kind of journalism.

CA: You did a great deal of that in your third book, Senator, *in following the daily activities of Senator Culver from Iowa and presenting a realistic picture of his work. It must have been very difficult for you to follow him so closely in preparation for writing the book.*

DREW: I said to him at the end of that ten-day period, "I don't know about you, Senator, but I'm not running for reelection." He is, but that's his problem!

CA: Was he pleased with the image of him that emerged in the book?

DREW: I don't know. We never talked about it in those terms. He understood what I was doing, that he was the vehicle for my description of what a senator really does all day every day. I proposed the idea to William Shawn [editor of the *New Yorker*], and it began as a much less ambitious magazine piece; then we could tell that the scale was changing, just because Culver himself was dealing with so many different kinds of issues. That was one of the reasons I chose him. His range of issues was broad and also terribly interesting and important, whether it was environment or defense or judiciary committee kinds of issues. It was a good range of issues. And when I went to Iowa, what I was looking for there was, how did he relate to different constituent groups? It turned out that it was just so much richer even than I had imagined, so the scale of it grew. Culver understood that I wasn't profiling him. I was writing about a senator and what senators do.

I went into it having spent a fair amount of time on Capitol Hill, and I had a vague idea about it. I certainly was aware of how pressured these people are, and I knew from having to go interview them and having spent time talking with them that they live under enormous pressures. While I had mentioned that in other pieces, I suddenly realized that nobody had any idea of what they do all day every day and how they relate to their colleagues, how they relate to their different constituents, how they get a piece of legislation through, really. So when I proposed this idea to William Shawn—and he is a genius, I believe; he knows an awful lot—he said, "Well, that's true; we don't have any idea of what these people do, and so that would be a good piece to do."

One of the nice things about that is that so many of the other senators came up and said, "You made a good choice in picking him [Culver]," but then also, after they saw the book, they said, "This really gets across what goes on here." They'd all like to say that they work that hard and that well; I'm not claiming that for a minute. I deliberately picked one of the good ones also to get across a subsidiary message, which is that there are good, hardworking people in our political system and we'd better value them, because that's what makes the difference in whether this system can work at all or not. It wasn't a terribly fashionable thing to say, but I noticed that most of the reader reaction was, you made us feel better by showing us that such people exist.

CA: Are you happy with political coverage in the news media? Do you think it's good generally?

DREW: That's sort of a broad subject to comment on. I try to do what I do the best I can. I think there are roles for different kinds of journalism, different forms and formats. Some of it is better than others, but I try to mind my own business and do my own work as well as I can, to serve a certain kind of purpose that there seems to be room for.

CA: Do you think it's possible for the average person to find balanced, thorough political coverage?

DREW: Oh, it's possible, but it's hard, particularly if they live in a city that doesn't have good newspapers, and that's most cities. They have to work at it. One of my points is that there are a lot of people in this country who do care about the political system. They may not be happy with it, but I always tell them when I make speeches that it's not as good as they want it to be, but it isn't going to be any better than they demand that it be. And the more informed the citizen is, the better the system of government is going to be. The worst things go on when citizens are apathetic or in the dark. There are an awful lot of them out there who really do care, and, as a matter of fact, I have a theory that even the apathy and disgust are the other side of caring. People wouldn't be upset if they didn't care. They haven't given up; they're just unhappy. There are a lot of people out there who want information, who want to know how it works, and I think that's one of the ways you try to keep the democratic system vital and alive.

CA: Your work is more demanding than that of many other writers. Do you ever think of hiding away for a year and writing a gothic novel—something completely different?

DREW: No, I don't. What you have to do is keep your balance and keep your sanity by taking breaks, getting out of Washington, traveling out of the country, to the extent that's possible. I can't all that often, and this year [1980], an election year, it's very, very hard. But changing the subject, so to speak, worrying about which beach to go to does wonders for clearing the head, particularly when everyone else is talking about who so-and-so is going to pick for vice-president and how many states Anderson is going to carry—I mean, you can go mad. I have friends who are not involved in the political world, which really helps. I play tennis, I go out; it is very important to me and I make it a point to lead as normal a life as I can. Now there will be periods when some things have to get shorter shrift, particularly in a political year, but your friends understand. And you very determinedly find a period when you can just take a break and get away and change the subject or worry about your backhand. I think it's more a question of trying to keep your perspective while you're doing it, both within the subject matter and in terms of life, and also take some breaks from it.

But I've never thought of taking a year away. I guess I'm too interested in what I'm doing. I'm in a very fortunate situation in which people actually pay me to learn about government, to meet interesting people—whether they are admirable or not—

who are affecting our country, well or horrendously, to try to figure it out, and then to put it down on paper. That's the hard part. I really don't like to write. But it is my full-time work to try to understand what's going on, and that's interesting.

BIOGRAPHICAL/CRITICAL SOURCES: New York Times Book Review, September 14, 1975, September 11, 1977, May 13, 1979; *Newsweek,* October 13, 1975; *Rolling Stone,* December 4, 1975; *Chicago Sun Times,* August 15, 1977; *Miami Herald,* September 18, 1977; *Washington Post Book World,* September 25, 1977, May 27, 1979; *Christian Science Monitor,* November 9, 1977; *Houston Post,* November 13, 1977; *Boston Globe,* December 13, 1977, June 3, 1979; *Publishers Weekly,* May 7, 1979; *Los Angeles Times,* June 3, 1979; *Seattle Times,* July 22, 1979.

—*Sketch by Nancy S. Gearhart*
—*Interview by Jean W. Ross*

* * *

DRIBERG, Thomas Edward Neil 1905-1976 (Tom Driberg, William Hickey)

OBITUARY NOTICE—See index for *CA* sketch: Born May 22, 1905, in Crowborough, Sussex, England; died of a heart attack, 1976, in London, England. Politician, journalist, and author. Driberg served as a member of the British Parliament for over thirty years. Prior to his political career, he wrote a gossip column in the *Daily Express* under the pseudonym William Hickey. A left-wing Laborite, Driberg criticized the "imperialists" in Washington and Wall Street. His writings include *The Best of Both Worlds: A Personal Diary, "Swaff": The Life and Times of Hannen Swaffen, Colonnade, 1937-1947,* and *Mosely? No!* Obituaries and other sources: *Time,* August 23, 1976.

* * *

DRIBERG, Tom See DRIBERG, Thomas Edward Neil

* * *

DROP SHOT See CABLE, George Washington

* * *

DROZ, Eugenie 1893(?)-1976

OBITUARY NOTICE: Born c. 1893; died September 19, 1976, in Geneva, Switzerland. Bookseller, publisher, and author. A specialist in sixteenth-century French culture, Droz founded the periodical *Humanisme et Renaissance* in 1934. Her books and other writings reflect her interest in early French printing. Obituaries and other sources: *AB Bookman's Weekly,* November 1, 1976; *Gazette des Beaux-Arts,* December, 1976.

* * *

DRUMMOND, (James) Roscoe 1902-

PERSONAL: Born January 13, 1902, in Theresa, N.Y.; son of John Henry and Georgia Estella (Peppers) Drummond; married Charlotte Bruner (a journalist and editor), September 11, 1926 (marriage ended, 1977); married Carol Cramer (a singer); children: Geoffrey (deceased). *Education:* Syracuse University, B.S.J., 1924; attended Ricker College, 1962. *Religion:* Church of Christ, Scientist. *Home and office:* 6637 McLean

Dr., Olde Dominion Sq., Mclean, Va. 22101. *Agent:* Joseph Newman, 3204 Highland Pl. N.W., Washington, D.C. 20003.

CAREER: Christian Science Monitor, Boston, Mass., reporter, 1924, assistant city editor, assistant to executive editor, and chief editorial writer, c. 1924-30, European editorial manager, 1930-33, general news editor and member of editorial board, 1933-34, executive editor, 1934-40, chief of bureau in Washington, D.C., 1940-53, creator and author of column "State of the Nation"; *New York Herald Tribune,* New York, N.Y., chief of bureau in Washington, D.C., 1953-55; author of Washington column for Los Angeles Times Syndicate in Los Angeles, Calif. Director of information for Marshall Plan with Economic Cooperation Administration (ECA) in Paris, France, 1949-51; member of board of trustees of Freedom House, 1962-67, vice-chairman of board.

MEMBER: American Society of Newspaper Editors, National Press Club, Overseas Writers, Alpha Kappa Psi, Sigma Phi Epsilon, Beta Gamma Sigma, Sigma Delta Chi, Gridiron Club, Cosmos Club. *Awards, honors:* Award, 1928, for editorial on the significance of the International Press Exhibition in Cologne, Germany; George Arents Award, 1946, for excellence in journalism; Litt.D. from Dartmouth College, 1947; D.H.L. from Principia College; LL.D. from Syracuse University, 1955.

WRITINGS: (With Gaston Coblentz) *Duel at the Brink,* Putnam, 1960. Contributor to magazines, including *Saturday Evening Post, Collier's,* and *Saturday Review.*

WORK IN PROGRESS: A book of reminiscences of his dealings with people in public life, including all the U.S. presidents from Franklin D. Roosevelt to Jimmy Carter.

SIDELIGHTS: Drummond wrote: "I never recall using a single fact I acquired in college, but from two special professors I acquired respect for scholarship and the desire to understand why other people think as they do."

*   *   *

Du BREUIL, (Elizabeth) L(or)inda   1924-1980
(Kristin Anderson, L. J. Brown, L. J. Browning,
Kate Cameron, S. C. Carewe, Alexandria DeMille,
Daniel Dodge, Caroline Dragon, Ellen Evans,
Emerald Evans, Edmund Griffen, Lorinda Hagen,
Elizabeth Hanley, D. Berry Lindner, Margaret
Maitland, Jon Mark, Catherine Power, D. Royal,
Brian Summer, Toni Vaughn)

PERSONAL: Born October 20, 1924, in LeRoy, Ill.; died December 9, 1980; daughter of John F. (a carpenter) and Eva (a practical nurse; maiden name, Emmons) Hagen; married Marshall O'Brien (divorced); married Gene Poling (divorced); married Frank Du Breuil (deceased); children: (first marriage) Carolyn O'Brien Belew; (second marriage) John Eric. *Education:* Attended University of Cincinnati, c. 1945. *Politics:* "Democrat, primarily." *Home and office:* P.O. Box 169 French Lick, Ind. 47432.

CAREER: Writer. Worked as reporter, florist, photographer, singer, and dancer. President of local Community Theatre and Little Theatre. *Member:* Mental Health Association, Orange County Historical Society, Kappa Kappa Kappa.

WRITINGS: Nightmare Baby, Belmont, 1970; *Evil, Evil,* Belmont-Tower, 1973; *The Girl Who Writes Dirty Books,* Nordon, 1975; *Sex Clinic,* Nordon, 1975; *The Sunday Seducer,* Nordon, 1975; *The Trial,* Nordon, 1975; *Without a Man of Her Own,* Nordon, 1975; *Divorce Las Vegas Style,* Nordon, 1976; *Kept Men,* Nordon, 1976; *Poppy,* Nordon, 1976; *Ulti-*

mate Sex, Nordon, 1976; *Housewife Hustlers,* Nordon, 1976; *Only on Sunday,* Nordon, 1976; *Heyday,* Manor, 1978; *Crooked Letter,* Belmont-Tower, 1979; *Deadly Party,* Belmont-Tower, 1979; *Follow the Leader,* Belmont-Tower, 1979; *Mirror Image,* Belmont-Tower, 1979; *So Dear, So Deadly,* Belmont-Tower, 1979; *Some Call It Perjury,* Nordon, 1979; *Break a Leg,* Kensington, 1980; *Double Standard,* Nordon, 1980; *The Telephone Murders,* Kensington, 1981; *Nevada,* Nordon, in press; *Winter Roses,* Nordon, in press.

Under pseudonym Kristin Anderson: *The Wholesome Hooker,* Belmont-Tower, 1978.

Under pseudonym L. J. Brown: *Satan's Daughter,* Corinth, 1969.

Under pseudonym L. J. Browning: *Passion in White Corridors,* Greenleaf, 1972.

Under pseudonym Kate Cameron; all published by Nordon, except as noted: *Evil at Whispering Hills,* 1973; *The Curse of Whispering Hills,* 1974; *Shadows on the Moon,* 1974; *The Awakening Dream,* 1974; *Legacy of Terror,* 1974; *The Legend of Holderly Hall,* 1974; *Shadows of the Past,* 1974; *Deadly Nightshade,* 1975; *Portraits of the Past,* 1975; *Music From the Past,* 1975; *Voices in the Fog,* 1975; *Kiss Me, Kill Me,* Belmont-Tower, 1979.

Under pseudonyms Daniel Dodge and Edmund Griffen: *Washington Playground,* Nordon, 1976.

Under pseudonym Ellen Evans: *Alternate Entries,* Seamark Press, 1975; *Teenage Street Girls,* Tower, 1975; *Teenage Hookers,* Tower, 1976.

Under pseudonym Emerald Evans: *Sex School Mistress,* Midwood, 1973.

Under name Lorinda Hagen: *Amy Jean,* Tower, 1977; *Lacey,* Tower, 1977; *Banners of Desire,* Leisure Books, 1978; *Sister of the Queen,* Leisure Books, 1978; *Letitia,* Tower, 1978; *Corrie,* Tower, 1978; *Summer of '32,* Nordon, 1979; *Bold Blades Flashing,* Nordon, 1979; *Sweet Sinner,* 1979; *The Eye of the Law,* Tower, 1979; *In Love and War,* Nordon, 1980; *Alabama Brown,* Tower, 1980; *Somebody's Daughter, Somebody's Wife,* Nordon, 1980.

Under pseudonym Elizabeth Hanley: *The Surrogate,* Nordon, 1977; *Life After Death,* Nordon, 1977; *Ms. President,* Nordon, 1977; *The Flame and the Fire,* Belmont-Tower, 1978; *Guilty as Charged,* Belmont-Tower, 1979.

Under pseudonym Margaret Maitland: *Sacred and Profane,* Tower, 1978.

Under pseudonyms Jon Mark and Toni Vaughn: *The New Triangle,* Manor, 1975.

Under pseudonym Catherine Power: *Bride of the Beast,* Greenleaf, 1972.

Under pseudonym Brian Summer: *Cherry Pink,* Midwood, 1971.

Also author of *Loving Heir* under pseudonym Alexandria DeMille, and more than three hundred fifty other works, including *Doctor Proctor, Libido 23,* and *The Hat,* under pseudonyms including S. C. Carewe, Caroline Dragon, D. Berry Lindner, and D. Royal.

WORK IN PROGRESS: A novel about the daughter of an Illinois farm family; a nonfiction book tentatively titled *Grace Errors,* about doctor's errors; a fiction-biography of the first female president of the United States.

SIDELIGHTS: Du Breuil told *CA:* "I'm undoubtedly a compulsive writer and am only completely happy when I'm writing or doing research. Most of the time I'm almost completely happy, though. My writing reflects my impatience with hypocrisy and prejudice. Maybe I'm a natural soap-box orator and I would like to help change the world for the better. I'm people-oriented and like almost everyone, even despicable characters inside books or outside them, and I think my writing shows this. I'll begin to show a person as downright mean and nasty, but they often become sympathetic characters, probably because I understand that we all do the very best we can at any given moment.

"Of all the books I've written, *Guilty as Charged* is my favorite. I'm sure it will make me rich and famous instead of poor and infamous, or notorious. It's probably going to be referred to as a plea against the death sentence."

CA INTERVIEW

CA interviewed Linda Du Breuil by telephone on August 5, 1980.

CA: You've written more than four hundred books. How do you do it?

Du BREUIL: I write like it's the way I make my living. I consider it a job, and I don't have to be inspired—I'm *always* inspired, if there is any such thing. When I sit down at the typewriter, I just naturally write. I love to write. I'll probably never live long enough to write all the things I want to write. I like to write almost as much as I like to read. All my characters seem so real to me. Even though I always write with a plan, I don't always adhere to it because it doesn't seem logical or reasonable that those people could behave in the way I'd originally planned. They're very interesting to watch as they progress.

CA: Are you always writing, or do you rest between books?

Du BREUIL: I sometimes rest two or three days, sometimes two or three weeks.

CA: Do childhood experiences have any influence on your writing?

Du BREUIL: Definitely. I grew up in an atmosphere that was very good for a budding writer—of course I didn't know it at the time. I did have a happy childhood. I had a lot of love: the people in the little town loved me, my mother loved me, my sister loved me. I didn't have a father; he left. Many people came to my mother's house. She was a practical nurse. She had people who would come to the house terminally ill and baby cases that she would take me out on. She took care of people in the home; there was no nursing homes at that time—no place to put people when they were old—and my mother never did turn away anyone. I don't either. I've often had people in my home until they could get on their feet—you know, strangers passing through and young people. I like having young people because it keeps me in contact with what's going on.

CA: What points have you wanted to make to your readers?

Du BREUIL: Well, I'm very much for equal rights for everyone. I've always deplored the prejudice of people against people of different color. I'm a foaming-at-the-mouth, equal-rights-for-women worker.

CA: These are things that you wanted to get across in your books?

Du BREUIL: Oh yes, even when I was writing sex books, which I did a lot. That's why I have so many books—I have at least a hundred of those. Of course, they wouldn't ever be considered pornography now. Really, the stuff on television is much worse than what I was writing then, and everybody was shocked, except my mother, sister, and relatives. I did that then, and those editors fussed about it. They went ahead and printed it, but they fussed about it. My most recent editor has mentioned a couple of times that she'd just as soon I didn't put all my heroines on a soap box. I don't pattern them after me, but I do pattern them after someone; usually they're a composite. She said that I had better lay off of that for a while because she thinks my readers might get tired of it. I had these women back at the turn of the century and during the Civil War doing things that most women didn't do at that time. But there were some that did, and they fought hard to be whole people. Of course, I like those people once I start writing about them, and I let them do what they seem to be wanting to do.

CA: How did your interest in the occult develop?

Du BREUIL: I grew up in LeRoy, Illinois, during the Depression. It cost ten cents to get to the show and it didn't cost anything to get to church. If you had a nickel once in a while you put it in the collection box and it salved your conscience. We attended all the churches, including the spiritualist church. Our local library was endowed by a spiritualist with the provision that they build a spiritualist church in conjunction with it. So we had a spiritualist church, and I saw all these people coming and going. I attended seances when I was growing up, and I got so I could tell the fakes from the those who were sincere, but maybe sincerely wrong. Of course there are crazy people, but there are also people who are sincere believers. That's how I got my experience, and I still attend those meetings every now and then to keep my hand in it.

CA: Do you attend the science fiction conventions?

Du BREUIL: No. I didn't really want to write science fiction and didn't even know I was doing it when I was. I only wrote four or five of those. I think I just got tired of writing the same kind of thing. In some of them, I combined a lot of humor with the science fiction and the sex. At the time those were very popular. A lot of the stuff I wrote is pure schlock. I mean *pure*—really awful. I wouldn't let my great-niece read them—not because of the four-letter words and things, but because it's poor writing. You turn out something for five hundred dollars, maybe two hundred pages; it's just really dumb writing for dumb little old ladies, some of it. Some of those dumb gothics are pretty bad, too. But at least I would get my heroines in a situation where they couldn't get out. I'd break their legs or their arms or give them some horrible sickness where they couldn't move when the bullets started flying. I haven't done any gothics for a long time now.

CA: Do you have to do much research for the historical novels?

Du BREUIL: Yes, intensive, and I love writing them. They're very, very interesting to me. I like the research.

CA: Is historical fiction your favorite genre?

Du BREUIL: Yes, I think it is. It might be a toss-up between historical novels and contemporary funny books about people in small towns. I enjoy putting the men down. I like men; I get along fine with them. But I like to show them up as ignorant bastards whenever I can, and at the same time make them very funny. I especially did that just recently in *Double Standard*.

It was funny to me when I read it over, because I did such an excellent job of portraying the characters of a couple of these people. One's a sheriff.

CA: French Lick, Illinois, is something of an artists' colony. Are there many writers there as well?

Du BREUIL: I kind of started a writers' colony. I've been here ten years. My sister lives next door, and she does all my typing for me. She has started writing now; she's published three books. She said she couldn't, but she did. My niece has had an article published, and my son has done about twelve books. I recently helped a girl get a book sold, and another one does articles. Then there's another girl who's had three short stories published. I do a couple of writing classes a month in the fall when I have time. It helps me, too.

CA: You like the contact with other writers?

Du BREUIL: Yes. I like contact with anybody, even the most stupid people. Sometimes they drop the greatest jewels, and I use them. I'm always writing, even when I don't have the pencil and paper—that inhibits people. But I'll write funny little things down, and I'll always use them.

CA: Do you get a lot of mail from your readers?

Du BREUIL: Yes, quite a bit.

CA: Do your correspondents ever ask for help in any way?

Du BREUIL: Most all of them are asking for help. There are a few men who thought I had done all of those things in my books. I wrote them right back and assured them that I had never even committed murder, and God knows how many murder mysteries I've written. I'm a very sensitive person when it comes to murder. But I do tell the men that I didn't do any of that, I just have a good imagination. God, the things people tell me, things they probably wouldn't even tell their psychiatrists.

Most people want help writing. I received a letter from a woman who asked me to give her some pointers. She had just read a book of mine called *Crooked Letter,* a murder mystery—I like to write those—so I wrote her about five pages to help her to the best of my ability. Quite often I heard from these people again. If people care enough about writing to bother writing a letter, then they're usually serious. I receive a lot of letters from youngsters and high school students wanting to write. I do everything to encourage them. There was a class in California that read an occult book of mine, and one girl wrote to me. I wrote back to her and she sent me something she had written, and I edited it and sent it back to her. Then she wrote back and said that she was taking typing with an eye to becoming a writer. I think that's wonderful.

CA: Why have you often used pseudonyms? Was it your choice or an editorial decision?

Du BREUIL: I never did make the choice. I preferred not to use the pseudonyms. The editors of those adult books felt that the books should never be under my own name. I didn't mind. I wasn't ashamed of them.

CA: Is there any genre you haven't tried yet but would like to do?

Du BREUIL: Yes. I have one started, and I'm about one hundred pages into it. It doesn't go back far enough to be called a history, but it's like a family epic of many generations, and I'm fascinated with the characters. The only thing I can think of that would be vaguely like it is James Michener's *Centennial.*

CA: Is there any advice you'd give to people who want to write?

Du BREUIL: I would say, short and sweet, and I'm not a religious person, but I do believe in loving your neighbor. And if you love your neighbor, and you want to write, it helps.

CA: Do you think that without compassion a writer can't produce good work?

Du BREUIL: I don't think so. Of all the reading I've done in my life, I can see where portions of it were done without love, because you have to express hatred and bitterness and so forth. But I think that, on the whole, people who write want to show love more than they want to show hatred.

AVOCATIONAL INTERESTS: Flower gardening, house plants, baking bread, carpentry.

[Sketch verified by sister, Mrs. E. H. Wilson]

—*Interview by Jean W. Ross*

*   *   *

DUBY, Georges (Michel Claude) 1919-

PERSONAL: Born October 7, 1919, in Paris, France; son of Louis and Marguerite (Dimanche) Duby; married Andree Combier, September 15, 1942; children: Jean, Catherine Duby Pouillon, Martine Duby Piovesan. *Education:* University of Lyons, agrege des lettres, 1942, docteur es lettres, 1953. *Home:* Beaurecueil, 13100 Le Tholonet, France. *Office:* College de France, 11 place Marcelin Berthelot, 75231 Paris, Cedex 5, France.

CAREER: Universite de Lyon, Lyons, France, assistant in faculty of letters, 1944-49; Universite de Besancon, Besancon, France, professor of medieval history, 1950-51; Universite d'Aix-Marscille, Aix-en-Provence, France, professor of medieval history, 1951-69; College de France, Paris, professor of history of medieval societies, 1970—. Lecturer at numerous colleges and universities in Europe, England, North Africa, Canada, and the United States. Director of Centre d'Etudes des Societies Mediterraneennes. *Military service:* French Army, 8th Artillery Regiment, 1940-41. *Member:* Institut de France, American Philosophical Society (foreign member), Medieval Academy of America (associate member), British Academy (associate member), Royal Historical Society (associate member), Academie Royale de Belgique (associate member), Accademia Nazionale dei Lincei (foreign member), Haut Comite de la Langue Francaise.

AWARDS, HONORS: Premier Prix Gobert, Academie Francaise, 1953, for *La Societe aux XIe et XIIe siecles dan la region maconnaise,* and 1962, for *L'Economie rurale et la vie des compagnes dan l'Occident medieval;* Fondation de France prize, 1973; Prix des Ambassadeurs, 1973, for *Le Dimanche de Bouvines;* Prix des Critiques, 1979, for *Les Trois Ordres; ou, L'Imaginaire du feodalisme;* Docteur honoris causa, Universite de Louvain and Vrije Universiteit Amsterdam; chevalier de l'Ordre du Merite Agricole.

WRITINGS: La Societe aux XIe et XIIe siecles dans la region maconnaise, A. Colin, 1953, reprinted, Services d'Edition et de Vente des Productions de l'Education Nationale, 1971; *Re-*

cueil des pancartes de l'abbaye de la Ferte-sur-Grosne, 1113-1178, Editions Ophrys, 1953; (with others) *Le Moyen Age: L'Expansion de l'orient et la naissance de la civilisation occidentale*, Presses Universitaires de France, 1955; (with R. Mandrou) *Histoire de la civilisation francaise*, A. Colin, 1958, revised edition, 1968, translation by James Blakely Atkinson published as *A History of French Civilization*, Random House, 1964; *L'Economie rurale et la vie des campagnes dans l'occident medieval: France, Angleterre, Empire, IXe-XVe siecles*, Aubier (Paris), 1962, translation by Cynthia Postan published as *Rural Economy and Country Life in the Medieval West*, University of South Carolina Press, 1968; *Fondements d'un nouvel humanisme, 1280-1440* (also see below), Skira, 1966, translation by Peter Price published as *Foundations of a New Humanism, 1280-1440*, World Publishing, 1966; *L'Europe des cathedrales, 1140-1280* (also see below), Skira, 1966, translation by Stuart Gilbert published as *The Europe of the Cathedrals, 1140-1280*, Skira, 1966; *Adolescence de la chretiente occidentale, 980-1140* (also see below), Skira, 1967, translation by Gilbert published as *The Making of the Christian West, 980-1140*, Skira, 1967; *L'An mil*, Julliard, 1967; (contributor) *Medieval Agriculture, 900-1500*, translated by Roger Greaves, Collins, 1969; (editor and author of preface) Edouard Baratier, *Atlas historique*, A. Colin, 1969.

(Editor) *Histoire de la France*, Larousse, 1970-72, Volume I: *Naissance d'une nation, des origines a 1348*, Volume II: *Dynasties et revolutions, de 1852 a nos jours: Guerriers et paysans, VII-XIIe siecle; Premier Essor de l'economie europeenne*, Gallimard (Paris), 1973, translation by Howard B. Clarke published as *The Early Growth of the European Economy: Warriors and Peasants From the Seventh to the Twelfth Century*, Cornell University Press, 1974; *Le Dimanche de Bouvines: 27 juillet 1214*, Gallimard, 1973; *Hommes et structures du moyen age*, Mouton, 1973; (with wife, Andree Duby) *Les Proces de Jeanne d'Arc*, Gallimard, 1973; *Merveilleuse Notre-Dame de Lausanne: Cathedrale bourguignonne*, Editions du Grand-Pont, 1975; *Saint Bernard: L'Art cistercien*, Arts et Metiers Graphiques, 1976; *Le Temps des cathedrales: L'Art et la societe, 980-1420* (contains *Adolescence de la chretiente occidentale, 980-1140*, *L'Europe des cathedrales, 1140-1280*, and *Fondements d'un nouvel humanisme, 1280-1440*), Gallimard, 1976, translation by Eleanor Levieux and Barbara Thompson published as *The Age of the Cathedrals: Art and Society, 980-1420*, University of Chicago Press, 1981. *The Chivalrous Society* (articles), translated by Postan, University of California Press, 1977; (editor with Jacques Le Goff) *Famille et parente dans l'occident medieval*, Ecole Francaise de Rome, 1977; (editor) *Atlas historique Larousse*, Larousse, 1978; *Medieval Marriage: Two Models From Twelfth-Century France* (lectures), translated by Elborg Forster, Johns Hopkins Press, 1978; *Les Trois Ordres; ou, L'Imaginaire du feodalisme*, Gallimard, 1978, translation by Arthur Goldhammer published as *The Three Orders: Feudal Society Imagined*, University of Chicago Press, 1980; *L'Europe au moyen age: Art roman, art gothique*, Arts et Metiers Graphiques, 1979; *Dialogues: Georges Duby—Guy Lardreau*, Flammarion, 1980; *Le Chevalier, la femme et le pretre*, Hachette, 1981.

Also editor of books in the "Histoire de la France rurale" series, Editions de Seuil. Editor of *Etudes Rurales*.

WORK IN PROGRESS: Research on family structures and historical memory in Europe during the Middle Ages; editing three books, *Histoire de la France urbaine, Histoire de la vie privee*, and, with M. Duverger and E. Le Roy Ladurie, a history of political systems.

SIDELIGHTS: Duby told *CA:* "One of my goals is to make accessible to a wide audience the findings of extensive research

on the feudal society's operational structures and cultural horizons. Thus, toward this aim, I have produced a series of nine television films, entitled 'Le Temps des cathedrales,' that met with success in France and in several other European countries."

The English translation of Duby's book *Le Temps des cathedrales* was published as *The Age of the Cathedrals: Art and Society, 980-1420*, in 1981. A comprehensive study of the early Gothic cathedrals of France, *The Age of the Cathedrals* discusses the various building plans of the churches and explains the social and religious milieu that gave rise to their construction. *New York Times Book Review* art critic John Russell was impressed with the thoroughness of Duby's scholarship. "If 'The Age of the Cathedrals' has a fault," the reviewer assessed, "it is that Professor Duby knows too much, has too many new ideas and takes such a delight in setting them out. . . . In time, as in place, our author darts back and forth. And as he races along we become aware of questions that had never entered our heads before." This volume in which "an exceptional intelligence marches to the beat of a kettledrum," Russell noted, "can be read with pleasure even by those who would not normally be drawn to the subject."

BIOGRAPHICAL/CRITICAL SOURCES: New Yorker, November 14, 1964; *New York Review of Books*, January 28, 1965, November 21, 1968; *Best Sellers*, July 15, 1966, August 1, 1967; *Virginia Quarterly Review*, winter, 1968; *Yale Review*, winter, 1969; *Economist*, March 9, 1974; *Times Literary Supplement*, April 14, 1978, April 24, 1981; *American Historical Review*, April, 1979; *English Historical Review*, July, 1979; *New York Times Book Review*, August 23, 1981.

*   *   *

DUCA MINIMO
See D'ANNUNZIO, Gabriele

*   *   *

DUDLEY, Nancy
See COLE, Lois Dwight

*   *   *

DUELL, Charles Halliwell   1905-1970

OBITUARY NOTICE: Born July 20, 1905, in New Rochelle, N.Y.; died July 10, 1970, in Sherman, Conn. Publisher. Duell worked at Doubleday Doran & Co. and as vice-president of William Morrow & Co. before forming Duell, Sloan & Pearce in 1939. When that company was purchased by Meredith Publishing in 1961, Duell became executive director of the book division of Meredith Press. He retired from Meredith in 1966 to publish *Cook Book Digest* magazine. Obituaries and other sources: *Publishers Weekly*, August 3, 1970; *AB Bookman's Weekly*, September 21, 1970; *Who Was Who in America, With World Notables*, Volume V: *1969-73*, Marquis, 1973.

*   *   *

DUFFEE, David E(ugene)   1946-

PERSONAL: Born May 9, 1946, in New Haven, Conn.; son of F. Eugene (an insurance executive) and Dorothy (a professor; maiden name, Cantfil) Duffee; married Barbara Warner (a researcher), October 7, 1978; children: (previous marriage) Jennifer, Tracy, Derek. *Education:* St. Lawrence University, A.B., 1968; State University of New York at Albany, M.A., 1971, Ph.D., 1973. *Home address:* R.D.3, Box 179A, Troy, N.Y.

12180. *Office:* Graduate School of Criminal Justice, State University of New York at Albany, Albany, N.Y. 12222.

CAREER: Pennsylvania State University, University Park, assistant professor, 1971-75, associate professor of criminal justice, 1975-77; independent researcher in the area of criminal justice, 1977-78; State University of New York at Albany, visiting associate professor, 1978-79, associate professor of criminal justice, 1979—. *Member:* Phi Beta Kappa. *Awards, honors:* Woodrow Wilson fellowship, 1968-69.

WRITINGS: Correctional Policy and Prison Organization, Sage-Halsted, 1975; (with Robert Fitch) *An Introduction to Corrections: A Policy and Systems Approach,* Goodyear Publishing, 1976; (with Frederick Hussey and John Kramer) *Criminal Justice: Organizational Structure and Analysis,* Prentice-Hall, 1978; *Correctional Management,* Prentice-Hall, 1980; (with Hussey) *Probation, Parole, and Community Field Services,* Harper, 1980; *Explaining Criminal Justice: Community Theory and Criminal Justice Reform,* Oelgeschlager, Gunn & Hain, 1980; (with Peter B. Meyer and Kevin N. Wright) *Outcomes of a Pre-Release System,* Oelgeschlager, Gunn & Hain, in press; (with Wright) *Dilemmas of Centralization in a Community Penal Program,* Oelgeschlager, Gunn & Hain, in press; (with Fitch and Meyer) *Offender Needs and Service Provision in a Penal Pre-Release System,* Oelgeschlager, Gunn & Hain, in press.

Contributor: Frederick L. Faust and Paul Brantingham, editors, *Juvenile Justice Philosophy,* West Publishing, 1974; Edward Eldefonso, editor, *Issues in Corrections,* Glencoe, 1974; George S. Killinger, Paul F. Cromwell, and Bonnie J. Cromwell, editors, *Corrections and Administration,* West Publishing, 1976; Wright, editor, *Crime and Criminal Justice in a Declining Economy,* Oelgeschlager, Gunn & Hain, 1981. Contributor of about one dozen articles to journals.

SIDELIGHTS: Duffee wrote: "I am concerned with the relationship between changes in the political and economic structure of society and the operation of public institutions, from which people usually do not receive the services expected. I am also a serious writer of fiction, but have yet to be taken seriously."

* * *

DUFFY, Charles 1940-

PERSONAL: Born May 9, 1940, in Boston, Mass.; son of Charles F. and Margaret (O'Leary) Duffy; married Ivy Lyew (an artist), August 28, 1966; children: Ariane, Tara. *Education:* Boston College, B.A., 1961, M.A., 1964; Tufts University, Ph.D., 1973. *Office:* Department of English, Providence College, Providence, R.I. 02918.

CAREER: Providence College, Providence, R.I., 1965—, began as instructor, became associate professor of English. *Member:* Modern Language Association of America, American Committee for Irish Studies.

WRITINGS: Kidds Cave (novel), Tower, 1981. Contributor to *Renascence, Concerning Poetry,* and *James Joyce Quarterly.*

WORK IN PROGRESS: An espionage novel set in Jamaica.

* * *

DUHAMEL, Marcel 1900(?)-1977

OBITUARY NOTICE: Born c. 1900; died March 6, 1977, near Cannes, France. Translator and founder of the Serie Noire crime series of Gallimard publishers. Under Duhamel's su-

pervision, close to two thousand titles were published in the Serie Noire. The series brought the works of many American writers to French readers and introduced to France the Dashiell Hammett style of detective fiction. In addition to his Serie Noire translations, Duhamel also translated the works of American fiction writers, including Ernest Hemingway, John Steinbeck, and Henry Miller. Obituaries and other sources: *Publishers Weekly,* April 4, 1977.

* * *

du HAULT, Jean
See GRINDEL, Eugene

* * *

DUNBAR, Paul Laurence 1872-1906

BRIEF ENTRY: Born June 27, 1872, in Dayton, Ohio; died of tuberculosis, February 9, 1906, in Dayton, Ohio. American poet, playwright, and author. Considered America's first major black poet, Dunbar was born of Kentucky slaves who escaped to the North. He was educated in Dayton public schools and had visions of being a lawyer, but, unable to afford law school, he was forced to take a job as an elevator operator. In 1893, at his own expense, Dunbar published his first volume of poetry, *Oak and Ivy,* and sold copies to passengers in his elevator. He gained national recognition when William Dean Howells reviewed his second work, *Majors and Minors* (1895), in *Harper's Weekly.* With the appearance of *Lyrics of Lowly Life* (1896), Dunbar was established as a popular poet among both blacks and whites who read his poems of the black experience. Dunbar is noted as a leading figure of Harlem's Renaissance. His other works, some written in dialect, the rest in standard English, include *The Love of Landry* (1900), *In Old Plantation Days* (1903), and *Lyrics of Sunshine and Shadow* (1905). *Residence:* Dayton, Ohio. *Biographical/critical sources: The Penguin Companion to American Literature,* McGraw, 1971; *Twentieth-Century Literary Criticism,* Volume 2, Gale, 1979.

* * *

DUNHILL, Alfred H(enry) 1896(?)-1971

OBITUARY NOTICE: Born c. 1896; died July 8, 1971, in Hove, Sussex, England. Tobacco executive and author. The son of the founder of Alfred Dunhill Ltd., Dunhill served as chairman of the tobacco and pipe-making firm for thirty-three years. He revised his father's *The Pipe Book* and wrote *The Gentle Art of Smoking.* Obituaries and other sources: *New York Times,* July 9, 1971; *AB Bookman's Weekly,* August 2, 1971.

* * *

DUNNING, John H(arry) 1927-

PERSONAL: Born June 26, 1927, in Sandy, Bedfordshire, England; son of John Murray (a Baptist minister) and Anne Florence (Baxter) Dunning; married Christine Mary Brown, August 4, 1975; children: (previous marriage) one son. *Education:* University of London, degree (with first class honors), 1951; University of Southampton, Ph.D., 1957. *Office:* Department of Economics, University of Reading, Reading RG6 2AH, England.

CAREER: University of Southampton, Southampton, England, lecturer and senior lecturer in economics, 1952-64; University of Reading, Reading, England, Foundation Professor of Economics, 1964-74, head of department, 1964—, Esmee Fairbairn Professor of International Investment and Business Studies, 1975—. Visiting professor at University of Western Ontario and University of California, Berkeley, 1968-69, Boston University, 1976, Stockholm School of Economics, 1978, and University of Montreal, 1980; Walker Ames Professor of Economics at University of Washington, Seattle, 1981. Director of Economists Advisory Group Ltd. Member of South East Economic Planning Council, 1965-69; member of Chemical Economic Development Committee, 1970-77; adviser to Committee on Invisible Exports; consultant to international agencies, national governments, and business enterprises, including United Nations, World Bank, and Department of Trade and Industry (United Kingdom). *Member:* Academy of International Business (fellow), Royal Economic Society (member of council, 1969-73). *Awards, honors:* D.Phil. from University of Uppsala, 1975.

WRITINGS: American Investment in British Manufacturing Industry, Allen & Unwin, 1958, Arno, 1976; (with C. J. Thomas) *British Industry: Change and Development in the Twentieth Century,* Hutchinson, 1961, 2nd edition, 1963; *Economic Planning and Town Expansion: A Case Study of Basingstoke,* Workers Education Association, 1963; (with P. G. Hall and others) *A New Town in Mid Wales,* H.M.S.O., 1966; (with D. Lees and others) *The Economics of Advertising,* Hutchinson, 1967; *The Role of American Investment in the United Kingdom Economy,* Political and Economic Planning, 1969.

Studies in International Investment, Allen & Unwin, 1970; (with E. V. Morgan) *The City of London: An Economic Study,* Allen & Unwin, 1971; (editor) *The Multinational Enterprise,* Allen & Unwin, 1971; *Problems of the Small Firm in Raising External Finance,* H.M.S.O., 1971; *Insurance and the Economy,* Institute of Economic Affairs, 1971; (editor) *Readings in International Investment,* Penguin, 1972; (editor) *Economic Analysis and the Multinational Enterprise,* Allen & Unwin, 1974; (with R. D. Pearce) *Profitability and Performance of the World's Leading Companies,* Financial Times, 1975; *U.S. Industry in Britain,* Wilton House, 1976; (with T. Houston) *British Industry Abroad,* Financial Times, 1976; *United Kingdom Enterprises in Manufacturing Industry in LDC's and Their Effect on Trade Flows,* United Nations Conference on Trade and Development, 1977; (with G. Norman) *Factors Influencing the Location of Offices of Multinational Enterprises,* Location of Offices Bureau, 1979; (with J. Stopford and K. Haverich) *The World Directory of Multinational Enterprises,* Macmillan, 1980; *International Production and the Multinational Enterprise,* Allen & Unwin, 1981; (with Pearce) *The World's Largest Industrial Companies,* Gower Press, 1981; (with M. Burstall and A. Lake) *The Impact of Multinational Enterprises on National Scientific and Technological Capacity: The Pharmaceutical Industry,* Organization for Economic Cooperation and Development, 1981; (with M. McQueen) *Transnational Corporations in the International Tourist Industry,* United Nations Center on Transnational Corporations, 1981.

Contributor: G. R. Denton, editor, *Economic Integration in Europe,* Weidenfeld & Nicolson, 1969; I. A. Litvak and C. J. Maule, editors, *Foreign Investment: The Experience of Host Countries,* Praeger, 1970; A. Shonfield and C. P. Kindleberger, editors, *North American and Western European Policies,* Macmillan, 1970; *Contribution to a Foreign Economic Policy for the 1970's,* Part IV: *The Multinational Corporation and International Investment,* U.S. Government Printing Office, 1970; Kindleberger, editor, *The International Corporation,* M.I.T. Press, 1970; P. P. Streeten, editor, *Trade Strategies for Development,* Macmillan, 1973; J.S.G. Wilson and C. F. Scheffer, editors, *Multinational Enterprises: Financial and Monetary Aspects,* Sijthoff, 1974; Gerard Curzon and others, editors, *The Multinational Enterprise in a Hostile World,*

Macmillan, 1976; B. Ohlin, P. O. Hesselborn, and P. M. Wiskman, editors, *The International Allocation of Economic Activity,* Macmillan, 1977; B. Balassa, editor, *Changing Patterns in Foreign Trade and Payments,* Norton, 1978; L. G. Mattson and F. Wiedersheim-Paul, editors, *Recent Research on the Internationalisation of Business,* Almqvist & Wiksell, 1979; F. A. Grassini and B. S. Yamey, editors, *Stato e Industria in Europa: Il Regno Unito,* Mulino, 1979; B. Hindley, editor, *Commercial Policy and International Diplomacy,* Macmillan, 1981; T. Sagafi-nejad, R. W. Moxon, and H. V. Perlmutter, editors, *Technology Transfer Control Systems: Issues, Perspectives, and Policy Implications,* Pergamon, 1981. Also contributor to *Third World Multinational Corporations,* edited by K. Kumar, 1981.

Contributor to *Collier's Encyclopedia.* Contributor of more than eighty articles to business and economic journals. Founding editor of *Business Ratios;* member of editorial board of *Journal of International Business Studies* and *Journal of Business Research.*

WORK IN PROGRESS: Research on "the theory of the international production and the interaction between multinational enterprises and patterns of economic development"; a study of alternative forms of international resource transfer.

SIDELIGHTS: Dunning told *CA:* "I am one of the pioneers in the study of international direct investment and the multinational enterprise. I have maintained a lively interest in the subject since the mid 1950's. I am equally at home with theoretical issues as policy oriented research, and am currently advising both the Organization for Economic Cooperation and Development (OECD) and the United Nations Center on Transnational Corporations on matters relating to multinational enterprise. I describe myself as a 'moderate,' in my political attitude to multinational enterprises: I believe strongly that they can make an important contribution to economic development, particularly those of advanced developing countries, but that it is the responsibility of governments to manage their own affairs so that the net benefits of foreign direct investment can be maximized. I believe also that governments and multinational enterprises are learning to live with each other and that this augurs well for international economic relations in the 1980's and 1990's."

*   *   *

DUNSANY, Edward John Moreton Drax Plunkett 1878-1957
(Lord Dunsany)

BRIEF ENTRY: Born July 24, 1878, in London, England; died October 25, 1957. Irish dramatist, poet, and short story writer. Considered an influential writer of fantasy in the twentieth century, Dunsany was the eighteenth baron in his line, succeeding his father in 1899. Though Dunsany thought himself to be chiefly a poet, he was best known as a playwright. His first play, *The Glittering Gate* (1909), was written at the request of William Butler Yeats for production at Dublin's Abbey Theatre. Like his subsequent works, Dunsany's first production demonstrated his vivid imagination and polished prose style. As popular in the United States as in his Irish homeland, Dunsany once had five of his plays running at the same time in New York. His writings include *The Gods of Pegana* (1905), *A Night at an Inn: A Play in One Act* (1916), *Plays for Earth and Air* (1937), and *Mirage Water* (1938). He also wrote an autobiography, *Patches of Sunlight* (1938). *Biographical/critical sources: Modern World Drama: An Encyclopedia,* Dutton, 1972; *Who Was Who in the Theatre, 1912-1976,* Gale, 1978; *Twentieth-Century Literary Criticism,* Volume 2, Gale, 1979.

DURANT, Stuart 1932-

PERSONAL: Born January 2, 1932, in London, England; son of Cyril Evelyn (a consulting engineer) and Mary Elizabeth Morfydd (a teacher; maiden name, Lewis) Durant; married Ruth Maia Doniach, December 19, 1970; children: Miriam Bronwen, Owen Gabriel, Galia Megan. *Education:* Attended Architectural Association School of Architecture, 1953-56, and Brera (Milan), 1961; Royal College of Art, M.A., 1973. *Home:* 140 Petersham Rd., Richmond, Surrey TW10 6UX, England.

CAREER: British Broadcasting Corp. (BBC), London, England, painter, 1958-59, television set designer, 1959-64; freelance television designer, 1965-69; antiquarian bookseller, 1969-74; Kingston Polytechnic, Kingston upon Thames, England, lecturer in history of design, 1974—. Member of advisory committee of Royal College of Art's Colour Library. *Military service:* British Army, Royal Army Education Corps and Royal Fusiliers, 1951-53. *Member:* William Morris Society.

WRITINGS: Victorian Decorative Design, St. Martin's, 1972; *The Theory of Colour,* B. Weinreb, Weilred, 1972; (contributor) Martin Shuttleworth, editor, *William Morris and Victo-rian Decorative Art,* Design Council, 1981; *Christopher Dresser, 1834-1904,* Academy Editions, 1982. Also contributor to *Phaidon Encyclopaedia of Decorative Art, 1890-1904,* edited by Philippe Garner, Design Council. Contributor of articles and reviews to architecture journals.

WORK IN PROGRESS: Nineteenth-Century Sources of Islamic Design, for Academy Editions.

SIDELIGHTS: Durant told *CA:* "I am particularly interested in the role of ornament in nineteenth- and twentieth-century architectural and design theory and practice. The subject has long been a neglected one, but the relationship between ornament and abstractionism is currently being explored. I am hoping to teach the 'syntax' of ornament at the post-graduate level. I developed an interest in the subject apparently serendipitously, since I am a compulsive purchaser of books."

*   *   *

DWIGHT, Allan
See COLE, Lois Dwight

E

EADIE, John W(illiam) 1935-

PERSONAL: Born December 18, 1935, in Fort Smith, Ark.; son of William Robert and Helen (Montgomery) Eadie; married Joan Holt, August 18, 1957; children: Robin, Christopher. *Education:* University of Arkansas, B.A., 1957; University of Chicago, M.A., 1959; University of London, Ph.D., 1962. *Home:* 5 Westbury Court, Ann Arbor, Mich. 48105. *Office:* Department of History, University of Michigan, Ann Arbor, Mich. 48109.

CAREER: Ripon College, Ripon, Wis., assistant professor of history, 1962-63; University of Michigan, Ann Arbor, assistant professor, 1963-67, associate professor, 1967-73, professor of history, 1973—, Richard Hudson Professor of History, 1981-82, director of Summer Institute in Ancient History, 1977, member of executive committee of Center for Coordination of Ancient and Modern Studies, 1969-76, associate director of center, 1972-74, humanities and arts adviser to vice-president for research, 1974—. Conducted archaeological field studies in Yugoslavia, 1968-72, 1976, Syria, 1971, Carthage, 1976, and Jordan, 1980—. Visiting fellow at Clare Hall, Cambridge, 1968-69. Member of Michigan Council for the Humanities, 1976-80, chairman, 1977-80; consultant to Encyclopaedia Britannica Films, 1963-66.

MEMBER: American Historical Association, Association of Ancient Historians, Society for the Promotion of Roman Studies, Archaeological Institute of America, Cambridge Philological Society. *Awards, honors:* Marshall scholar at University of London, 1960-62; Ford Foundation grant, 1968-69; grant from National Endowment for the Humanities, 1973, fellowship, 1974; American Council of Learned Societies grants, 1974, 1979; distinguished service award from Michigan Council for the Humanities, 1980.

WRITINGS: The Breviarium of Festus: A Critical Edition With Historical Commentary, Athlone Press, 1967; *The Conversion of Constantine,* Holt, 1971; (with Deno Geanakopolos, J. H. Hexter, and Richard Pipes) *Western Civilization,* Harper, 1975; (editor) *Classical Traditions in Early America,* Center for Coordination of Ancient and Modern Studies, University of Michigan, 1976; (editor with John D'Arms, and contributor) *Ancient and Modern: Essays in Honor of Gerald F. Else,* Center for Coordination of Ancient and Modern Studies, University of Michigan, 1977.

Contributor: Vladislav Papovic and Edward Ochsenschtager, editors, *Sirmium Reports,* Volume V, Archaeological Institute of Boegred, 1971; John H. Humphrey, editor, *Excavations at Carthage, 1976,* Volume III, Kelsey Museum, 1977; D. H. Miller and Jerome O. Steffen, editors, *The Frontier: Comparative Studies,* University of Oklahoma Press, 1977. Also contributor to *City, Town, and Countryside in the Early Byzantine Era,* edited by Robert Hohlfelder, 1982. Contributor to encyclopedias. Contributor of about twenty-five articles and reviews to history, philology, and archaeology journals.

WORK IN PROGRESS: First Among Equals: Usurpation and the Loss of Authority in the Later Roman Empire, A.D. 235-284.

* * *

ECHEGARAY (y EIZAGUIRRE), Jose (Maria Waldo) 1832-1916
(Jorge Hayaseca y Eizaguirre)

BRIEF ENTRY: Born in 1832 in Madrid, Spain; died in 1916 in Madrid, Spain. Spanish mathematician, engineer, statesman, and playwright. Echegaray began his career as a professor of hydraulics at the School of Civil Engineering in Madrid. During that time he published works on thermodynamics and geometry. He also became interested in economics, was a proponent of free enterprise, and, during the revolutionary period in Spain (1868-74), held several governmental posts. Under the pseudonym Jorge Hayaseca y Eizaguirre, Echegaray wrote his first play, "El libro talonario" (1874). During the next thirty years, he wrote sixty-four plays, many of which reflected his social concerns. They include: "O locura o santidad" (1877), "El gran galeoto" (1881), "El hijo de Don Juan" (1892), and "El loco dios" (1902). Written in both verse and prose, his plays are typically romantic melodramas in the tradition of Castilian chivalry. Echegaray was also heavily influenced by the naturalistic mode of playwrights such as Henrik Ibsen. His characters were intense people driven by their passions and ideals. Though immensely popular during the author's lifetime, his plays are now considered obsolete. However, Echegaray continues to be recognized as a major link between nineteenth-century and twentieth-century Spanish drama. He shared the 1904 Nobel Prize for literature with Frederic Mistral. *Biographical/critical sources: Cyclopedia of World Authors,* Harper, 1958; *Everyman's Dictionary of European Writers,* Dutton, 1968; *Penguin Companion to European Literature,* McGraw, 1969; *Modern World Drama: An Encyclopedia,* Dutton, 1972; *Twentieth-Century Literary Criticism,* Volume 4, Gale, 1981.

ECKSTEIN, Gustav 1890-1981

OBITUARY NOTICE—See index for *CA* sketch: Born October 26, 1890, in Cincinnati, Ohio; died September 23, 1981, in Cincinnati, Ohio. Educator, physician, scientist, and author. An expert on animal behavior, Eckstein taught physiology and psychiatry at the University of Cincinnati since 1917. Though he retired from teaching in 1961, Eckstein remained an active researcher and writer. His main interests were birds, animals, and philosophy. In 1935 he studied conditioned reflexes with Ivan Pavlov. Eckstein was the model for the character of the scientist in George S. Kaufman's play "The Man Who Came to Dinner." Capable of writing in many genres, the professor published *The Body Has a Head,* a best-seller and a Book-of-the-Month Club selection. He also wrote plays, such as "Christmas Eve" and "The Pet Shop," and a book of animal biographies called *Lives.* Eckstein's other works include *Noguchi, Canary: The History of a Family, Everyday Miracles,* and a biography of Pavlov left incomplete at the time of his death. Obituaries and other sources: *New York Times,* September 25, 1981.

* * *

EDWARDS, Eli
See McKAY, Claude

* * *

EFRON, Marina Ivanovna Tsvetaeva
See TSVETAEVA (EFRON), Marina Ivanovna

* * *

EFROS, Susan Elyse 1947-

PERSONAL: Born February 19, 1947, in New York, N.Y.; daughter of George (a vacuum cleaner repairman and world champion bowler) and Jerry (an artist; maiden name, Wasserman) Efros. *Education:* University of California, Berkeley, B.A. (with honors), 1968, M.A., 1971; doctoral study at Columbia University, 1968-70. *Home and office:* 1357 Hopkins St., Berkeley, Calif. 94702.

CAREER: High school teacher of English, drama, and journalism in Richmond, Calif., 1971-73; Mount Zion Hospital, San Francisco, Calif., teacher of creative writing to schizophrenic patients, 1973-75; *California Living,* San Francisco, journalist, 1975; Merritt College, Oakland, Calif., instructor in English literature and creative writing, 1976—. Actress in the play "Voices," 1976. Hostess of "Connections," on KPFA-Radio; drama coach. Gives readings at schools and poetry centers and on radio and television. *Awards, honors:* Grant from National Endowment for the Arts, 1978; second prize from International Gay Theatre Alliance, 1980, for play, "Interior Mirrors."

WRITINGS: Coming Together (poems), Albion, 1969; (editor) *This Is Women's Work,* Panjandrum, 1974, 2nd edition, 1975; *Two-Way Streets* (poems), Jungle Garden Press, 1975; *Walking Vanilla* (novel), Waterfall, 1978; *Moving In* (poems), Waterfall, 1981; *Hair Shots* (novel), Waterfall, 1982; *Winchester Mackenzie* (novel), Waterfall, 1982.

Plays: "Interior Mirrors" (three-act), first produced in New York, N.Y., at Shandol Theatre, April, 1981.

Contributor to magazines and newspapers, including *Feminist Art Journal of New York, Female Psychology,* and *Emerging Self.*

SIDELIGHTS: Susan Efros wrote: "Movement is important, vital to me, all kinds of movement of the heart and of the feet. *Walking Vanilla* is a novel about getting unstuck and moving on past fear, depression, and doubt. I find that health is movement, taking chances, risking being totally honest, totally oneself. My writing is my vehicle to get the closest to myself, my essence, and give the reader my inside insights. I also swim, dance, run, and ride a bicycle.

"I believe in the integration of body and mind; they can be friends and help each other out. I have a lover and several close friends. I love to hike and get a good tan in the summer. Sometimes I think I'm a fish (Pisces). I swim a mile or more a day. I write best when my body is clear and I've taken the time to look around me—at people in cafes (I adore cafes!), at flowers and trees and birds and bees on the mountain (Tilden Park is a hiking area near my home I visit several times a week). I also go to the ocean frequently; the power and endlessness of the sea's waves inspire me to create. I like to laugh, read crazy novels, cook gourmet meals, and drink champagne.

"I think love is the best thing we can give each other, and if I can give that in my work, I'm happy. My work with clients (writers and artists) is about love. I try to be a good mirror for them, showing them their best selves, giving them their own faith and power back to go on with their work when doubt creeps in. I go for the total release of madness inside for health and creativity. I'm a lover of life and movement. I dance across the page of my writing. I hope you do, too, whoever you are."

BIOGRAPHICAL/CRITICAL SOURCES: Feminist Review, October, 1977; *Women Emerging,* St. Martin's, 1979.

* * *

EHRENREICH, Herman 1900(?)-1970

OBITUARY NOTICE: Born c. 1900; died March 31, 1970, in New York, N.Y. Poet and drama critic. Ehrenreich wrote *A World Without Jews.* Obituaries and other sources: *AB Bookman's Weekly,* May 25, 1970.

* * *

EIDESHEIM, Julie 1884-1972

OBITUARY NOTICE: Born in 1884 in Buffalo, N.Y.; died February 5, 1972, in New York, N.Y. Free-lance copyeditor and author. Known as the dean of free-lance copyeditors, Eidesheim worked for nearly every major U.S. publishing firm. She wrote an editing manual, *Editor at Work,* in 1939. Obituaries and other sources: *Publishers Weekly,* March 13, 1972; *AB Bookman's Weekly,* May 15, 1972.

* * *

EINHORN, Virginia Hilu
See HILU, Virginia

* * *

EISENBERG, Hershey H. 1927-

PERSONAL: Born March 2, 1927, in Los Angeles, Calif.; son of Sam (a tailor) and Lucille (Pine) Eisenberg; married Phyllis Silberman, February 2, 1952; children: Marci, Linda Mary, Julie. *Education:* California State University, Los Angeles, B.A., 1952; also attended University of Southern California and University of California, Los Angeles. *Agent:* Joan Stewart, William Morris Agency, 1350 Avenue of the Americas,

New York, N.Y. 10019. *Office address:* P.O. Box 245, Van Nuys, Calif. 91401.

CAREER: Teacher at public schools in Los Angeles, Calif., 1953-58; membership director for B'nai B'rith, 1958-61; Pan American Life Insurance, Van Nuys, Calif., producing general agent, 1961—. Taught life underwriting course. Member of Speaker's Bureau of Anti-Defamation League. *Military service:* U.S. Coast Guard.

WRITINGS: The Reinhard Action, Morrow, 1980. Author of a restaurant column.

WORK IN PROGRESS: The Armenian, a saga of an Armenian family from the Turkish holocaust in 1915 to the present.

AVOCATIONAL INTERESTS: Travel (Europe), cooking, wine tasting, playing tennis, jogging.

*   *   *

ELGIN, Mary
See STEWART, Dorothy Mary

*   *   *

ELIOT, Anne
See COLE, Lois Dwight

*   *   *

ELLENBOGEN, Eileen 1917-

PERSONAL: Born April 13, 1917, in Cairo, Egypt; daughter of Aaron (a barrister) and Victoria (Mosseri) Alexander; married Gershon Ellenbogen (a barrister), March 26, 1944; children: Katherine Ruth Ellenbogen Whiteman. *Education:* Girton College, Cambridge, M.A., 1940. *Politics:* "Mildly liberal, but largely apolitical." *Religion:* "Jewish by birth, agnostic by inclination." *Residence:* London, England.

CAREER: Air Ministry, London, England, assistant principal, 1941-44; writer, 1944—; translator. Occasional scriptwriter and broadcaster for British Broadcasting Corp. (BBC-Radio); examiner in English literature for the entrance examination of Oxford and Cambridge universities, c. 1961—.

WRITINGS—Translator; novels by Georges Simenon: The Iron Staircase, Hamish Hamilton, 1963; *The Blue Room,* Hamish Hamilton, 1965, Harcourt, 1978; *Maigret and the Headless Corpse,* Hamish Hamilton, 1967; *Maigret Takes the Waters,* Hamish Hamilton, 1969; *Maigret's Boyhood Friend,* Hamish Hamilton, 1969; *Maigret and the Wine Merchant,* Curtis Books, 1971; *Maigret and the Madwomen,* Hamish Hamilton, 1972, Harcourt, 1979; *Sixth Simenon Omnibus,* Hamish Hamilton, 1973; *The Innocents,* Hamish Hamilton, 1973; *Maigret and the Man on the Boulevard,* Hamish Hamilton, 1975; *Maigret and the Loner,* Hamish Hamilton, 1975; *Maigret and the Apparition,* Harcourt, 1976 (published in England as *Maigret and the Ghost,* Hamish Hamilton, 1976), *Maigret and the Spinster,* Hamish Hamilton, 1977; *Maigret in Exile,* Hamish Hamilton, 1978, Harcourt, 1979; *Maigret and the Toy Village,* Hamish Hamilton, 1978, Harcourt, 1979; *Maigret and the Man on the Bench,* Harcourt, 1979.

Other translations: Line Jaque, *Sew the French Way,* Mills & Boon, 1961; Marguerite Duras, *The Rapture of Lol V. Stein,* Hamish Hamilton, 1967; Duras, *The Vice-Consul,* Hamish Hamilton, 1968; Girogio Scerbanenco, *Duca and the Milan Murders,* Cassell, 1970; Christine de Rivoyre, *Boy,* M. Evans, 1974; B. Philippe, *The Jockey,* Hamish Hamilton,

1975; Marcel Pagnol, *The Time of Love,* Hamish Hamilton, 1979.

Author of pamphlets. Contributor of articles to fine arts journals, including *Encyclopaedia of Antiques* and *Changing World.*

SIDELIGHTS: Eileen Ellenbogen commented: "I am a dilettante by temperament. I take equal pleasure in using my mind and my hands. Until the high price of gold made it impossible for me to continue, I designed and made precious jewelry for family, friends, and myself, having undergone training at two distinguished colleges of art in London.

"I had originally intended to pursue an academic career at Cambridge, but the war intervened, and by the time it was over I was already married and had a young child. As it turned out, I have much relished the freedom to pursue a wide variety of unrelated interests. Whatever I do I like to do well, but beyond that I am not in the least ambitious, and although I like to excel if I can, should hate to do so at anyone else's expense.

"I am unable to drive a car, as all machines are my mortal enemies, unless they require no human intervention more complex than the pressing of a knob. I am, however, a wizard with a needle (though, needless to say, sewing machines utterly defeat me), and no slouch in the kitchen.

"I am so fast and voracious a reader in three languages that our flat contains more books than space. I devour about five detective stories a week, and apart from those, I read mainly serious novels, poetry, and drama of all periods.

"Far from considering television a debasing medium, at least as it exists in Great Britain, I am an enthusiastic admirer of many of the available programs, particularly in the spheres of drama, art in all its forms, and natural history. I am addicted to American television, some of which is rebroadcast in England, combining as it does superlative technical skills with compulsive though totally meretricious content. I positively experience withdrawal symptoms when such programs as 'Dallas' are in recess!"

*   *   *

ELLERMAN, Annie Winifred 1894-
(Bryher)

PERSONAL: Name legally changed to Bryher; born September 2, 1894, in Margate, Kent, England; daughter of Sir John Reeves (an industrialist and financier) and Hannah (Glover) Ellerman; married Robert McAlmon (a writer and publisher), 1921 (divorced, 1927); married Kenneth Macpherson (a writer and editor), 1927 (divorced, 1947). *Education:* Educated in Eastbourne, Sussex, England, and by private tutor. *Home:* Kenwin, Burier, Vaud, Switzerland.

CAREER: Writer, critic, and poet. *Close-Up* (film magazine), Territet, Switzerland, and London, England, co-founder and co-editor, 1927-33. *Member:* Interplanetary Association.

*WRITINGS—*Under name Bryher, except as noted; novels, except as noted: (Under name Annie Winifred Ellerman) *Region of Lutany and Other Poems* (poems), Chapman & Hall, 1914; *Development,* preface by Amy Lowell, Macmillan, 1920; (with others) *Arrow Music* (poems), J. & E. Bumpus, 1922; *Two Selves,* Contact Press, 1923, Chaucer Head, c. 1927; *Civilians,* Pool (Territet, Switzerland), 1927; (with Trude Weiss) *The Lighthearted Student,* Pool (London), 1930; *The Fourteenth of October,* Pantheon, 1952; *The Player's Boy,* Pantheon, 1953; *The Roman Wall,* Pantheon, 1954; *Beowulf: Roman d'une maison de the dans Londres bombarde,* Mercure de France, 1948, translation from the French published as *Beowulf*, Pantheon, 1956; *Gate to the Sea*, Pantheon, 1958; *Ruan*, Pantheon, 1960; *The Coin of Carthage*, Harcourt, 1963; *Visa for Avalon*, Harcourt, 1965; *This January Tale*, Harcourt, 1966; *The Colors of Vaud*, Harcourt, 1969.

Other: *Amy Lowell: A Critical Appreciation*, Eyre & Spottiswoode, 1918; (translator) Bion of Smyrna, *The Lament for Adonis*, A. L. Humphreys, 1918; *A Picture Geography for Little Children, Part One: Asia*, J. Cape, 1925; *West* (travel), J. Cape, 1925; *Film Problems of Soviet Russia*, Pool (London), 1929; (with Robert Herring and Dallas Bower) *Cinema Survey*, Brendin, 1937; *Paris 1900*, translated by Sylvia Beach and Adrienne Monnier, La Maison des Amis Livres, 1938; *The Heart to Artemis: A Writer's Memoirs*, Harcourt, 1962; (editor with husband, Kenneth Macpherson) *Close-Up: A Magazine Devoted to the Art of Films*, ten volumes, Arno, 1970; *The Days of Mars: A Memoir, 1940-46*, Harcourt, 1972.

Regular contributor of reviews and articles to *Saturday Review* and *Sphere*, 1917-18. Contributor of poetry, articles, and reviews to numerous periodicals, including *Bookman, North American Review, Poetry, Contact, Transatlantic Review, Transition, Seed, Life and Letters Today, Fortnightly Review, Little Review*, and *This Quarter*.

SIDELIGHTS: The daughter of wealthy parents, Bryher traveled extensively in her youth. The Ellermans' journeys often prevented Bryher from going to regular schools, so she was privately tutored. The author feels she was fortunate not to have been sent to school. "Fate was kind and I did few formal lessons in my childhood, with the result that my mind developed freely and was ravenous for knowledge." During the family's meanderings through Egypt, Europe, the Middle East, and the Mediterranean, Bryher acquired a lifelong fascination with history and archaeology, and participated in archaeological expeditions until the onset of World War I. She used her knowledge of these subjects to fuel her historical novels.

Bryher began contributing articles and reviews to the *Saturday Review* and *Sphere* in 1917. She attributes much of her maturation as a writer to the influence of the editors of these magazines, A. A. Baumann and Clement Shorter, respectively. Also influential were her friend Havelock Ellis and Sigmund Freud's work in psychoanalysis. When she began to write, the author legally changed her name to Bryher so as not to take advantage of her father's powerful influence in British publishing firms. Bryher, the name of one of the Scilly Isles off the coast of England, was an island she often visited as a child.

Eventually, Bryher met Hilda Doolittle (H.D.), who became a close friend. Sylvia Beach noted in her book *Shakespeare and Company* that H. D. introduced Bryher into her literary circle. "H.D. was one of the most admired of the so-called Imagists," asserted Beach, "a group that included Ezra Pound, John Gould Fletcher, and others." Bryher gradually numbered among her acquaintances such luminaries as James Joyce, Andre Gide, Ernest Hemingway, and Gertrude Stein. With H.D., the author visited the United States in 1920 and 1921. On this trip Bryher met her first husband. A writer from Minnesota, Robert McAlmon also published avant-garde literature at the Contact Press. The two married the day after they met.

In 1927 Bryher and McAlmon divorced, and later that year she married Kenneth Macpherson, an authority on the cinema. Together they founded and edited the magazine *Close-Up*. This publication is often praised as the finest periodical on the art of silent films. Bryher and Macpherson divorced in 1947.

Although she has also written poetry and nonfiction, Bryher's historical novels have received the greatest recognition. Many critics are impressed with her mastery of history and her ability to write as if she were an actual spectator of events she describes. Shelby Martin observed in the *Bulletin of the New York Public Library*: "Bryher's novels deal with a wide variety of periods—from Switzerland of the Roman outposts to England of the Norman Conquest—and yet the documentation for each period is accurate and unobtrusive. All of the novel focus upon periods of chaos when the old foundations of cultures are destroyed and new foundations must be developed. Her characters are ordinary people forced by circumstances to deal with the collapse of the world as they have known it. The problem of loyalty to culture, religion, and/or friendship under the new conditions is developed both realistically for that moment in time and metaphorically for twentieth-century crises. Her prose is spare and yet her images convey haunting beauty." Writing in the *Observer Review*, Susanna Eliot described Bryher's novel *This January Tale* as a picture of "the past without the comforts of romance, and for all its starkness gives you the uneasy feeling that the author was somehow there when it happened."

Eleventh-century England is the setting of Bryher's first historical novel, and the event described is the Battle of Hastings. "Her attention to detail, ability to recreate the terrain of Cornwall and the countryside around Hastings, her . . . knowledge of the age and history of the period—all are superbly realized" in *The Fourteenth of October*, complimented P. J. Driscoll of *Commonweal*. "One stands in admiration of her achievement, and particularly of the verbal beauty with which she colors her descriptive writing." J. H. Jackson agreed in the *San Francisco Chronicle*. "Bryher tells the story with all the warmth and spirit of one long soaked in the atmosphere of the period," he remarked. "Her narrative is convincing, pulsing with life."

The author's next effort, *The Player's Boy*, takes place in England after the death of Elizabeth I. Horace Gregory of the *New York Times* asserted that it "is written with the intensity and sharpness of a dramatic poem." *The Roman Wall* tells the story of an outpost of the Roman Empire about to be invaded by Germanic tribes. In the *New York Herald Tribune Book Review*, Geoffrey Bruun disclosed: "She can banish time and make the past as real and credible as the present. This is her special secret and her special charm."

Returning to her own time in *Beowulf*, Bryher depicts London during World War II and the Battle of Britain. Again she received favorable reviews. *Commonweal*'s R. T. Horchler appraised the novel as "intelligent, ingenious, beautifully and subtly written, and completely without pretension," while David Daiches took note of its realism. "This is no romantic story of heroism, no flamboyant demonstration that 'Britain can take it,'" he contended, "but a quiet, perceptive, authentic account of the worries, the discomforts and the almost casual endurance of a small number of representative characters."

In *Poetry*, Marianne Moore named *Gate to the Sea* the best of Bryher's novels. "Of them all," she reflected, *Gate to the Sea* "is the most compactly vivid and expertly absorbing—a masterpiece." Other reviewers were similarly taken with this story of fourth-century Poseidonia's defeat at the hands of an Italic tribe. Geoffrey Bruun declared that Bryher's "mastery of mood owes something to her zest for archaeology, but her art is concentrated in her flawless prose." Horace Gregory elaborated: "No one living today writes prose with more quiet, unstressed authority than Bryher's."

Ruan evokes a view of sixth-century Britain, which, as the *Chicago Sunday Tribune*'s W. J. Igoe mused, "has something of the formal perfection of the Grecian friezes one sees perpetuated in Wedgewood china and yet . . . [it has] a remote ghostly vitality that is strangely moving." *The Coin of Car-*

thage takes place in Italy and Carthaginian North Africa after the second Punic War. "This is the most accomplished of Bryher's . . . books," heralded W. G. Rogers in the *New York Times Book Review*. "Her novel serves Rome and Carthage as handsomely as Edith Hamilton's essays serve Greece."

This January Tale introduces a different view of the Norman conquest of the Saxons in 1066. Brhyer claims in this historical novel that contrary to the popular theory, the invasion did not bring a greater civilization to the Anglo-Saxons. She maintained: "Art and learning virtually disappeared. A magnificent language was destroyed." *Book Week*'s Richard Winston applauded the work: "Like all of Bryher's fiction, it vibrates with a kind of frozen music: it is both swiftly moving and perfectly static, full of action and yet fixed in time and space, slight yet comprehensive. It is a mysterious effect, and I do not pretend to understand how it is achieved; but it is there all the same."

In addition to her writing, Bryher is involved in a number of philanthropic activities. Beach revealed in her book that the author maneuvered the rescue of dozens of Nazi victims during World War II and helped them establish new lives in the United States. She also has "done more than anyone knows to maintain international contacts throughout wars, and to keep together her large family of intellectuals, who are dispersed in many countries. She looked after them in war and peace, and her correspondence is vast." In her memior, *The Days of Mars*, Bryher upheld that "it is friendship that counts in the long dreary days that are full of hardships rather than valor."

BIOGRAPHICAL/CRITICAL SOURCES: Boston Transcript, November 20, 1920; *Commonweal*, May 30, 1952, August 20, 1954, October 12, 1956, October 10, 1958, December 2, 1960; *San Francisco Chronicle*, June 10, 1952; *New York Times*, May 17, 1953, August 26, 1956, September 14, 1958, November 6, 1960; *New York Herald Tribune Book Review*, May 24, 1953, May 16, 1954, September 14, 1958, November 13, 1960; *Saturday Review*, September 1, 1956, November 12, 1960; Sylvia Beach, *Shakespeare and Company*, Harcourt, 1959; *Poetry*, February, 1959; *Chicago Sunday Tribune*, December 18, 1960; *Springfield Republican*, December 18, 1960; Bryher, *The Heart to Artemis: A Writer's Memoirs*, Harcourt, 1962; *New York Herald Tribune Books*, June 2, 1963; *New York Times Book Review*, June 2, 1963, April 25, 1965, November 27, 1966, February 8, 1970; *Time*, June 21, 1963; *Book Week*, November 6, 1966; *New Republican*, January 14, 1967; *Observer Review*, January 7, 1968; *Listener*, February 1, 1968; *Christian Science Monitor*, February 18, 1970; Bryher, *The Days of Mars: A Memoir, 1940-46*, Harcourt, 1972; *Bulletin of the New York Public Library*, summer, 1976.*

—*Sketch by Andrea Geffner and Anne M. Guerrini*

*   *   *

ELLIOTT, Susan (Anthony) 1947-

PERSONAL: Born June 20, 1947, in New York, N.Y.; daughter of Robert Hare Egerton and Mary (Turnbull) Elliott. *Education:* Chatham College, B.A., 1969; graduate study at Fordham University, 1979-80. *Politics:* Independent. *Home:* 444 East 84th St., New York, N.Y. 10028. *Office:* High Fidelity, 825 Seventh Ave., New York, N.Y. 10019.

CAREER: Boston Symphony Orchestra, Boston, Mass., press secretary, 1969-70; Holt, Rinehart & Winston, Inc., New York City, textbook editor, 1970-72; *Musical America*, New York City, managing editor, 1972-76; free-lance editor, 1972-78; *High Fidelity*, New York City, editor of "Backbeat,"

1976—. Chief editorial and design consultant for *ASCAP in Action*. *Member:* American Society of Composers, Authors and Publishers, American Guild of Authors and Composers (member of council, 1978), Dramatists Guild, Blue Hill Troupe. *Awards, honors:* Popular music award from American Society of Composers, Authors and Publishers, 1979, for "Love Thy Elf."

WRITINGS: (Editor) *1980 Songwriter's Market*, Writer's Digest, 1979. Also editor of *Scriabin: Enigmas and Answers*, St. Martin's. Composer of music for *Gospelanimals*, Triune/Triangel Music, 1980. Contributor of articles and reviews to magazines.

WORK IN PROGRESS: An adaptation of *From the Mixed-up Files of Mrs. Basil E. Frankweiler;* a musical revue; animation scripts; researching and writing material for children's television.

*   *   *

ELLIS, Richard 1938-

PERSONAL: Born April 2, 1938, in New York, N.Y.; son of Robert Butler and Sylvia (Levy) Ellis; married Anne Kneeland (a photographer), September 25, 1963; children: Elizabeth Tiffany, Timothy Kneeland. *Education:* University of Pennsylvania, B.A., 1959. *Home:* 1185 Park Ave., New York, N.Y. 10028. *Agent:* Carl Brandt, Brandt & Brandt Literary Agents, Inc., 1501 Broadway, New York, N.Y. 10036.

CAREER: Academy of Natural Sciences, Philadelphia, Pa., exhibit designer, 1962-64; Philadelphia Zoological Gardens and Aquarama, Philadelphia, free-lance designer, 1962-64; American Museum of Natural History, New York City, worked in exhibition department, 1964-65; Museum Planning, Inc., New York City, consultant in museum design, 1965-72; painter, writer, and illustrator, 1972—. Paintings and drawings exhibited at museums and galleries, including Mystic Seaport, Los Angeles County Museum of Natural History, and American Museum of Natural History; member of U.S. delegation to International Whaling Commission, 1980 and 1981; public speaker. Member of board of trustees of Rare Animal Relief Effort. *Military service:* U.S. Army, 1959-61. *Member:* Society of Animal Artists (vice-president), American Cetacean Society (member of board of directors), Society of Vertebrate Paleontologists, American Society of Mammalogists, Authors Guild, New York Academy of Sciences, Explorers Club.

WRITINGS—Self-illustrated: *The Book of Sharks*, Grosset, 1976; *The Book of Whales*, Knopf, 1980; *Porpoises and Dolphins*, Knopf, 1982.

Author of "Richard Ellis," a column in *Sport Diver*. Contributor of articles and illustrations to magazines, including *American Artist, Science Digest, Scientific American, New York, Audubon, Oceans, Science/80, Explorers Journal*, and *National Wildlife*.

WORK IN PROGRESS: Magazine articles.

SIDELIGHTS: Ellis is recognized as a painter of marine natural history. Often asked to advise on museum installations, in 1978 he completed a thirty-five-foot whale mural for the Denver Museum of Natural History, and he has recently completed a major series of paintings of whales and dolphins for the National Geographic Society. His research has taken him to Baja California, Quebec, Newfoundland, Hawaii, Bermuda, Puget Sound, Nantucket, southern California, Patagonia, and Japan. His paintings of whales have been employed successfully in campaigns to name four whales as state mammals: the sperm whale in Connecticut, the gray whale in California, the humpback in Hawaii, and the right whale in Massachusetts.

Ellis's *Book of Whales* has been praised in both the *New York Times* and *Washington Post*. Bayard Webster of the *Times* reported: "Mr Ellis is an artist, and the superb reproductions of his paintings and drawings show whales as man can rarely see them. And, when such art is combined with enlightening nonpolemic prose about how whales are born, live and die, the uniqueness of their niche in nature becomes obvious."

Colman McCarthy of the *Washington Post* also admired Ellis's work, calling it "a thorough, well written and finely illustrated account of the creatures described by Melville as living in the 'unshored, harborless immensities' of the deep. . . . For the general reader, Ellis is the careful educator who wants to share his joy that 'we are now caught up in a period of whale consciousness, as conservation groups the world over campaign to protect great whales . . . We are on the threshold of an understanding of some of the world's most interesting creatures. But the secrets of cetaceans are not readily revealed, and we approach some species as if they were created to be captured and trained for our amusement.'"

BIOGRAPHICAL/CRITICAL SOURCES: American Artist, August, 1979; *Sport Diver,* fall, 1978, winter, 1978, spring, 1979, summer, 1979; *New York Times,* November 4, 1980; *Washington Post,* June 1, 1981.

*   *   *

ELLISON, Jerome   1907-1981
(N. Emorey)

OBITUARY NOTICE—See index for *CA* sketch: Born October 29, 1907, in Maywood, Ill.; died June 9, 1981, in Branford, Conn. Editor and author. Formerly the editor of *Collier's,* Ellison also contributed and edited works for *Life, Reader's Digest, Liberty, Magazine of the Year, Saturday Evening Post,* and *Best Articles and Stories* in addition to writing articles and short stories for *McCall's, Nation,* and *New Republic.* In 1946 he began the *Associated Magazine Contributors,* a publication he owned with Pearl S. Buck, Roger Butterfield, John Dos Passos, and John Steinbeck. Ellison also worked as the editorial director of the Bureau of Overseas Publications of the Office of War Information. His works include novels, such as *The Prisoner Ate a Hearty Breakfast, The Dam,* and *John Brown's Soul,* his autobiography *Report to the Creator,* and other works like *A Serious Call to an American (R)Evolution* and *The Last Third of Life Club.* Obituaries and other sources: *New York Times,* June 10, 1981; *AB Bookman's Weekly,* July 13-20, 1981.

*   *   *

ELUARD, Paul
See GRINDEL, Eugene

*   *   *

EMBERLEY, Michael   1960-

PERSONAL: Born June 2, 1960, in Boston, Mass.; son of Edward R. (an artist and writer) and Barbara (a craftsperson; maiden name, Collins) Emberley. *Education:* Attended Rhode Island School of Design, 1979-80. *Home:* 6 Water St., Ipswich, Mass. 01938.

CAREER: Writer and illustrator, 1980—.

WRITINGS: Dinosaurs! (self-illustrated children's book), Little, Brown, 1980.

WORK IN PROGRESS: A self-illustrated book on sports equipment around the world, publication by Little, Brown expected in 1982.

SIDELIGHTS: Emberley wrote: "It was my father, a writer and illustrator of children's books, who encouraged me to publish a book at the age of nineteen, although I had little formal art training. I had worked on similar books he had written, so the drawing book was a familiar style for me.

"For a first book it was a natural form and subject. When I was younger I was fascinated by dinosaurs, as I am today, and it seems that just about all kids share this interest, so it contained the best combination of features to produce a commercially successful book. A book that will not sell, no matter how noble, unique, or insightful, is occupational suicide.

"The commercial aspect of writing may seem a creative hindrance to some, but to me it is an extra challenge that makes the business more interesting and stimulating.

"My second book is about the variety of highly specialized pieces of sports equipment, a subject in which I am very interested. Many sports, never even heard of by the average American, hold international championships every year, and all have equipment and clothing that have developed for each sport's special demands.

"My own passion is for bicycle racing, in all its complexity. I have competed at the national level and enjoy the company of other people involved in the sport. I hope to do a book about cycle racing in the future.

"Books like these require much research, which can only be interesting to me if the subject is one I thoroughly enjoy."

*   *   *

EMERY, Allan C(omstock), Jr.   1919-

PERSONAL: Born May 14, 1919, in Weymouth, Mass.; son of Allan Comstock (a wool merchant) and Elsie Davis (Conant) Emery; married Marian Hancock Smith, September 16, 1941; children: Allan Comstock III, Arthur H., Annetta Emery Thurber. *Education:* Attended Wheaton College, Wheaton, Ill., 1937-38, and U.S. Coast Guard Academy, 1943. *Office:* 790 Commercial St., P.O. Box 90, East Weymouth, Mass. 02189.

CAREER: Emery & Conant, Inc. (wool merchants), Boston, Mass., in sales, 1938-60; Emery Wool Co., Boston, owner, president, and treasurer, 1960-65; ServiceMaster Hospital Corp., Boston, president and founder, 1965-73, president of Hospital Northeast Division, 1974-76; independent business consultant in East Weymouth, Mass., 1977—. In sales, treasurer, and member of board of directors of Emery, Russell & Goodrich, Inc.; member of board of directors of ServiceMaster Industries, Inc., 1977—. Member of board of trustees of Wheaton College, Wheaton, Ill., and Gordon-Conwell Theological Seminary. *Military service:* U.S. Coast Guard, 1941-45; became lieutenant junior grade. *Member:* Evangelistic Association of New England (president), Billy Graham Evangelistic Association (president and member of board of directors), Union Club of Boston. *Awards, honors:* Named business and professional leader in business services by Religious Heritage of America, 1975.

WRITINGS: A Turtle on a Fencepost (nonfiction), Word, Inc., 1979. Contributor to *Christianity Today.*

BIOGRAPHICAL/CRITICAL SOURCES: Eternity, February, 1980; *Family Life,* May, 1981.

EMOREY, N.
See ELLISON, Jerome

* * *

ENDFIELD, Mercedes
See von Block, Bela W(illiam)

* * *

ENGLAND, George W(illiam) 1927-

PERSONAL: Born June 19, 1927, in Pierre, S.D.; son of James Forrest and Ellen (Hebbert) England; married Josephine Levitt, August 1, 1948; children: Paula S., Mark W., Brad F., Julie M. *Education:* University of Minnesota, B.A., 1951, M.A., 1952, Ph.D., 1956. *Home:* 1980 Riverside Dr., Norman, Okla. 73069. *Office:* Center for Economic and Management Research, College of Business Administration, University of Oklahoma, 307 West Brooks, Norman, Okla. 73019.

CAREER: Radio Corporation of America, Camden, N.J., associate in personnel research department, 1952-53; University of Minnesota, Minneapolis, assistant professor, 1956-59, associate professor, 1959-62, professor of psychology and industrial relations, 1962-79, principal investigator at Work Adjustment Center, 1959-67; University of Oklahoma, Norman, professor of management and director of Center for Economic and Management Research, 1979—. Visiting professor at University of North Carolina, Stanford University, Macalester College, Colorado State University, and University of Western Australia; lecturer at Banff School of Advanced Management, 1957-73; graduate lecturer at Kyushu University; member of faculty of Minnesota Executive Program. Senior researcher at Shri Ram Centre for Industrial Relations, New Delhi, India, and Korea Development Institute; senior research fellow at International Institute of Management, Berlin, West Germany. Speaker at academic, business, and government meetings; arbitrator in private and public employment sectors; consultant to President's Committee on Manpower. *Military service:* U.S. Navy, 1945-56.

MEMBER: American Psychological Association (fellow), American Association for the Advancement of Science, American Association of University Professors, Academy of Management, American Arbitration Association, Midwest Psychological Association, Minnesota Psychological Association. *Awards, honors:* Ford Foundation fellow, 1965-66; senior research specialist grant from East-West Center at University of Hawaii, 1965-66, summer, 1967; awards from American Personnel and Guidance Association, 1960, 1965, and 1967 for *Work Adjustment* series of monographs.

WRITINGS: (With L. H. Lofquist) *Problems in Vocational Counseling,* W. C. Brown, 1960; *The Development and Use of Weighted Application Blanks,* W. C. Brown, 1961, revised edition, Industrial Relations Center, University of Minnesota, 1971; (with N. C. Agarwal and O. P. Dhingra) *The Manager and the Man,* Kent State University Press, 1974; *The Manager and His Values: An International Perspective,* Ballinger, 1975; (section editor) M. D. Dunnette, editor, *Handbook of Industrial and Organizational Psychology,* Rand McNally, 1976; (with Anant Negandhi and Bernhard Wilpert) *Organizational Functioning in a Cross-Cultural Perspective,* Kent State University Press, 1979; (with Negandhi and Wilpert) *The Functioning of Complex Organizations,* Gunn & Hain, 1980.

Contributor: H. G. Heneman and other editors, *Employment Relations Research,* Harper, 1960; L. H. Lofquist, editor, *Psychological Research and Rehabilitation,* American Psycholog-

ical Association, 1960; *Ethics and Employment,* Graduate School of Business Administration, University of Minnesota, 1967; Desmond Graves, editor, *Management Research: A Cross-Cultural Perspective,* Elsevier Scientific Publishing, 1973; P. E. Jacob, editor, *Automation and Industrial Workers,* Pergamon, 1979. Contributor of about thirty-five articles to psychology and business journals. Member of editorial board of *Organization and Administrative Sciences* and *Academy of Management Journal.*

WORK IN PROGRESS: The Meaning of Working: A Ten-Country Study; Worker Motivation, Satisfaction, and Effectiveness; Behavioral Outcomes of Worker Dissatisfaction; A Study of U.S. Managerial Value Systems and Behavior; A Comparative Analysis of Personal Value Systems in the United States, Korea, Japan, India, and Australia; A Fifteen-Country Study of the Impact of Automation on Working Conditions, Work Content, and Worker Reactions; research on value systems and behavior of naval officers.

* * *

ENGLAND, Maurice Derrick 1908-1980

PERSONAL: Born August 17, 1908, in Sutton, England; died February 24, 1980; son of Maurice (a master mariner) and Emily (Antill) England; married Florence Elizabeth Joan; children: Alasdair Maurice, Gillean Elizabeth England White. *Education:* London Foot Hospital, M.S.C.H. and F.S.C.H. *Agent:* (Photographs) Ardea London Ltd., 35 Brodrich Rd., Wandsworth Common, London SW17 4DX, England.

CAREER: Senior lecturer at London Foot Hospital. Natural history photographer. *Awards, honors:* Officer of Order of the British Empire.

WRITINGS: Birds of the Tropics (with own photographs), Hamlyn, 1974.

SIDELIGHTS: England made ornithological/photographic trips all over the world, but particularly eastern Africa and Trinidad and Tobago.

* * *

ENSTROM, Robert (William) 1946-

PERSONAL: Born October 18, 1946, in Los Angeles County, Calif.; son of Elmer Melvin, Jr. (a lawyer) and Klea Elizabeth (Bissell) Enstrom. *Education:* Attended University of California, San Diego, 1964-69. *Home address:* P.O. Box 723, Julian, Calif. 92036. *Agent:* P. Sutherland, 2612 Burgener Blvd., San Diego, Calif. 92110.

CAREER: Advanced Tests and Inspections, San Diego, Calif., chemist, 1969-70; *Prospector and Mountaineer* (newspaper), Julian, Calif., reporter and writer, 1975-76; writer, 1976—.

WRITINGS: (Editor) *Glimpses of the Civil War,* Franson Publications, 1976; *Encounter Program* (science fiction novel), Doubleday, 1977; *Beta Colony* (science fiction novel), Doubleday, 1980.

WORK IN PROGRESS: Science fiction novels, tentatively titled *Star Fire,* publication expected in 1982, *Hollenglen,* 1983, and *Shamilian,* 1984.

SIDELIGHTS: Enstrom commented: "One of my major interests is exploring the uses and limitations of language. There are various important problems associated with the use of any language as a means of communication. For example: How do you communicate the complete subjective sensations of any experience to another person who has not lived through a similar experience? As a foundation for any language and its associated civilization is an unstated (but understood) body of shared experience. Failure to appreciate this leads to difficulties, especially when communication is attempted between civilizations with vastly different bases of experience. Color has little meaning to a person who has never experienced it. Justice has little meaning to the people of a civilization where it does not exist. The word 'revolution' has different meanings for different peoples, based on separate historical experiences, all of which are unique but given the common label 'revolution.'

"Another problem with language communications is the fact that events undergo several translations in passing from one person to another. I experience the sensation of touching a warm rock, then I translate the sensation of this experience into words/symbols to communicate the event to another person. This other person, in turn, must *un*translate the words/symbols and construct from them some semblance of an experience—which will almost certainly be different from the experience I tried to communicate or which any third person would construct from the same set of words/symbols.

"To be successful as a writer of fiction, it is important to communicate more than mere information with the words you use—you've got to communicate an experience."

*   *   *

ERRINGTON, Frederick (Karl)   1940-

PERSONAL: Born September 28, 1940, in Ames, Iowa; son of Paul L. (a professor of zoology) and Carolyn (a professor of English; maiden name, Storm) Errington. *Education:* Wesleyan University, Middletown, Conn., B.A. (with high honors), 1962; attended Harvard University, 1962-63; Cornell University, Ph.D., 1970. *Home address:* P.O. Box 536, West Swanzey, N.H. 03469. *Office:* Department of Anthropology and Sociology, Keene State College, Keene, N.H. 03431.

CAREER: Amherst College, Amherst, Mass., assistant professor of anthropology, 1970-77; University of Western Ontario, London, visiting associate professor of anthropology, 1977-78; Keene State College, Keene, N.H., assistant professor of anthropology, 1978—. Conducted anthropological field work in Papua New Guinea and Indonesia. *Member:* American Anthropologic Association, Phi Beta Kappa, Phi Kappa Phi. *Awards, honors:* Wesleyan Alumni fellowship, 1958-62; Woodrow Wilson fellowship, 1962-63; Herbert Lehman fellowship, 1966-67; Minar D. Crary fellowship from Amherst College, 1972.

WRITINGS: Karavar: Masks and Power in a Melanesian Ritual, Cornell University Press, 1974.

WORK IN PROGRESS: Minangkabau Consciousness: Interpretation of Person and Social Form in a Sumatran Society.

SIDELIGHTS: Errington studied cargo cults, men's ritual in Dukduk-Tuban society, and political change on Karavar, in the Duke of York Islands; he has also worked among the Minangkabau in West Sumatra. He wrote: "For my next fieldwork, I plan to examine the way that politics and experience are interpreted in a small Montana ranching community. I am particularly interested in the images of both self-reliance and mutual dependence that are expressed in cultural performances such as the annual rodeo, in the editorials and letters of the county newspaper, and in the male presentation of self."

ESENIN, Sergei (Alexandrovich)   1895-1925
(Sergei Alexandrovich Yesenin)

BRIEF ENTRY: Born in 1895 in Konstaninovo, Russia (now U.S.S.R.); committed suicide, December 28, 1925, in Leningrad, U.S.S.R. Russian poet. During his brief, unstable lifetime, Sergei Esenin gained recognition as one of the great poetic voices of the revolutionary period in Russia. Born of peasant parents, he received very little formal education, and although he later traveled quite extensively, it was the pre-revolution countryside of his youth that served as inspiration for most of his poetry. Although Esenin initially supported the Bolshevik revolution, thinking that it would prove beneficial to the peasant class, he became disenchanted when he saw that it would lead only to the industrialization of Russia. A longing for a return to the simplicity of the peasant lifestyle characterizes his work, as does his innovative use of images drawn from village lore. He is credited with having helped to establish the imaginist movement in Russian literature, a movement that was distantly related to the imagist movement associated with American-born poet Ezra Pound. Esenin, who was married briefly to American dancer Isadora Duncan and later to a granddaughter of Leo Tolstoy, led an erratic, unconventional life that was punctuated by bouts of drunkenness and insanity. Before hanging himself in a Leningrad hotel, Esenin slit his wrists, and, using his own blood, wrote a farewell poem. Among his numerous collections of poetry are *Radunitsa* (1916), *Inoniya* (1918), *Ispoved' khuligana* (1920), and *Moskva kabatskaia* (1924). *Biographical/critical sources: Concise Encyclopedia of Modern World Literature,* Hutchinson, 1963; *Who's Who in Twentieth Century Literature,* Holt, 1976; *Twentieth-Century Literary Criticism,* Volume 4, Gale, 1981.

*   *   *

ESSE, James
See STEPHENS, James

*   *   *

ESTES, J(oseph) Worth   1934-

PERSONAL: Born May 10, 1934, in Lexington, Ky.; son of Joseph Alvie (a magazine editor) and Betsy (a professor of psychology; maiden name, Worth) Estes; married Cynthia Waggoner (a teacher), June 20, 1959. *Education:* Harvard University, A.B., 1955; Boston University, M.A., 1963, M.D., 1964. *Home:* 68 Greenacre Rd., Westwood, Mass. 02090. *Office:* School of Medicine, Boston University, 80 East Concord St., Boston, Mass. 02118.

CAREER: Massachusetts General Hospital, Boston, intern, 1964-65; University Hospital, Boston, research fellow in medicine, 1965-66; Institute of Child Health, London, England, research fellow, 1966-67; Boston University, Boston, assistant professor, 1967-72, associate professor, 1972-81, professor of history of pharmacology, 1981—. Member of board of trustees of Westwood Public Library, 1970-76, and Boston Medical Library, 1974-77, 1980-83; vice-chairman of Massachusetts Governor's Conference on Libraries, 1973-81. *Military service:* U.S. Army, 1955-57.

MEMBER: American Association for the Advancement of Science, American Association for the History of Medicine, Society for Ancient Medicine, American Antiquarian Society, American Society for Pharmacology and Experimental Therapeutics, Massachusetts Library Trustees Association (president, 1973-77), Massachusetts Medical Society, Colonial Society of Massachusetts, Sigma Xi (chapter president, 1979-81).

WRITINGS: Hall Jackson and the Purple Foxglove: Medical Practice and Research in Revolutionary America, 1760-1820, University Press of New England, 1979; (editor with Philip Cash and Eric H. Christianson) *Medicine in Colonial Massachusetts, 1620-1820,* Colonial Society of Massachusetts, 1980. Associate editor of *Journal of the History of Medicine and Allied Sciences,* 1981-83.

WORK IN PROGRESS: Imhotep and the Medical Skills of Ancient Egypt, publication expected in 1982; *Naval Medicine in the Age of Sail: The Voyage of the "New York," 1802-1803,* 1983; a history of drug usage, completion expected in 1985.

SIDELIGHTS: J. Worth Estes wrote: "My interest in the written roots of medicine began during a summer I spent with Dr. Paul Dudley White, whose collection of books on the early history of cardiology provided a do-it-yourself introduction to the subject. A few years later he and I collaborated on a paper about the introduction of digitalis to medicine, but I would have lost interest in the subject had not serendipity brought to my attention the 1785 correspondence with which the new drug was first sent to America. Those documents made me attempt to write a brief description of them for one of the journals of medical history, but so many ancillary questions arose during the study that, after ten years, I could expand those answers into my first book.

"My training in investigative pharmacology has, in the meantime, catapulted my explorations into studies of protopharmacological (i.e., drug usage before the first pharmacology laboratory was established in 1849) therapy, relying on modern statistical and even laboratory techniques to enhance our understanding of what my professional ancestors did for their patients, and why. Further serendipitous discoveries—the log of a naval surgeon in the otherwise forgettable Barbary Wars, for instance—continue to modify my earlier views of medical practice before the modern era. It comes as rather a shock to find that it remained firmly based on a relatively immutable set of false premises until well into the nineteenth century, and that the continually evolving inquisition into human physiology that now characterizes medicine is a relatively new development in human thinking.

"Some day I hope to be able to determine what factors enter into physicians' therapeutic decisions, both now and in the past. The study of the past, when most drugs *could* not have provided much in the way of specific therapeutic value, is critically important to understanding how physicians choose drugs today, when all are *expected* to be of value."

* * *

EUPHAN
    See TODD, Barbara Euphan

* * *

EVANS, Ellen
    See Du BREUIL, (Elizabeth) L(or)inda

* * *

EVANS, Emerald
    See Du BREUIL, (Elizabeth) L(or)inda

* * *

EVERTON, Macduff   1947-

PERSONAL: Born August 13, 1947; son of Clyde (a priest)

and Frances (Pickard) Everton; children: Ricky. *Education:* Attended University of California, Santa Barbara, 1981. *Home address:* P.O. Box 709, Summerland, Calif. 93067.

CAREER: Free-lance photographer in Latin America, 1967-75; artist-in-residence for the state of Washington, 1976-78; Quaking Aspen Pack Station, Sequoia National Forest, Calif., mule skinner and station manager, 1977—. Knife thrower and *commandante de carburo* with Circo Magico Modelo, Yucatan and Mexico, 1971-75.

WRITINGS: El Circo Magico Modelo: Finding the Magic Circus (juvenile), Carolrhoda, 1979.

Illustrator: *Birdmen of Papantla,* Ward, Ritchie, 1972.

WORK IN PROGRESS: Research and photographs on the changing culture of the Maya of Yucatan.

* * *

EWART, Charles
    See LYTE, Charles

* * *

EYRE, Katherine Wigmore   1901-1970

OBITUARY NOTICE: Born September 23, 1901, in Los Angeles, Calif.; died February 27, 1970, in San Francisco, Calif. Novelist and author of short stories. Eyre published her first book, *Lottie's Valentine,* in 1941 and in the next two years followed with two other juvenile works, *Susan's Safe Harbor* and the popular *Spurs for Antonia.* After writing several juveniles about life on American ranches, Eyre changed the focus of her writing to English history with such works as *The Song of a Thrush,* about the niece and nephew of Richard III. Eyre's first adult novel, the best-selling mystery *The Lute and the Glove,* was also set in England. Her later mysteries include *The Chinese Box, Amy,* and *Monk's Court.* Obituaries and other sources: *Current Biography,* Wilson, 1957; *Who's Who of American Women,* 2nd edition, Marquis, 1961; *Publishers Weekly,* May 4, 1970; *American Authors and Books, 1640 to the Present Day,* 3rd revised edition, Crown, 1972.

* * *

EYRE, Ronald   1929-

PERSONAL: Born April 13, 1929, in Mapplewell, England; son of Christopher and Mabel (Smith) Eyre. *Education:* Received M.A. from Oxford University. *Agent:* Larry Dalzell, Dalzell Durbridge Authors Ltd., 3 Goodwin's Court, St. Martin's Lane, London W.C.2, England.

CAREER: Worked as a teacher; director of television plays, 1957—; theatrical producer and director, 1963—; actor. Has worked with Royal Shakespeare Company and National Theatre.

WRITINGS: Ronald Eyre on the Long Search, Collins & World, 1979.

Plays: "Something's Burning," first produced in 1974; (adapter) "The Marquis of Keith," first produced in 1974. Also author of television plays, including "A Crack in the Ice," "Bruno," and "Are You There?"

Also author of scripts for "The Long Search," BBC-TV, 1974-77.

SIDELIGHTS: Eyre commented: "My book is an account of a three-year project, between 1974 and 1977, when I wrote and presented 'The Long Search,' a thirteen-part film series for the British Broadcasting Corp. and Time-Life, dealing with contemporary manifestations of religion.''

BIOGRAPHICAL/CRITICAL SOURCES: Ronald Hayman, *Playback,* Davis-Poynter, 1973; Judith Cook, *Directors' Theatre,* Harrap, 1974; *Observer,* September 25, 1977.

*   *   *

EYSMAN, Harvey (Allen) 1939-

PERSONAL: Born November 16, 1939, in New York, N.Y.; son of Mouritz (a certified public accountant) and Etta (Schwartz) Eysman; married Donna O'Hara (a writer), September 28, 1969; children: Regan Tara. *Education:* Attended Massachusetts Institute of Technology, 1957-61; Brooklyn Law School, J.D., 1964, LL.M., 1966. *Religion:* Jewish. *Residence:* Great Neck, N.Y. *Office:* 15 Park Row, New York, N.Y. 10038.

CAREER: Private practice of law in Manhattan and Great Neck, N.Y., 1965—. Village attorney, Village of Russell Gardens, N.Y., 1976—. Member of Atomic Energy Committee, Association of the Bar of the City of New York, 1966-67; member of board of hearing examiners, Judicial Conference of the State of New York, 1967-69; Great Neck United Community Fund, member of board of directors, 1974-77, and executive vice-president, 1976. *Member:* Mystery Writers of America, New York State Bar Association, Masons (district deputy grand master, 1977-78).

WRITINGS: Courier's Fist (novel), Beaufort Book Co., 1981. Contributor to magazines, including *Sky and Telescope.*

WORK IN PROGRESS: A science fiction novel; a suspense novel; research on the origin of certain Masonic myths.

SIDELIGHTS: Eysman wrote: ''*Courier's Fist* was submitted unsolicited and accepted by the publisher to which it was first sent. In an interview in *Library Journal,* I said: 'I try to write as I would tell a story to friends, and to sound in writing as I sound in speaking. My aim is to entertain; my hope is to impel the reader to turn pages, to read even faster. I want him to be sorry when the book is done.'

''My desire to write arose more than ten years ago, but the pressures of my professional life and the spectrum of my interests postponed any attempt seriously to pursue a writing career. During a period of relative inactivity, I outlined a story that subsequently became my first novel. The experience was fully enjoyable, and the hours of rewriting and editing became a soothing respite from the pace of my usual activities.

''After completion of my studies at Massachusetts Institute of Technology, including a year of research in high energy particle physics, I studied law in New York City. At present I operate a law practice in the New York metropolitan area. I have traveled extensively throughout northern Europe as counsel to several quasi-governmental and private European agencies. In France and the Netherlands, where I have taught both French and Dutch, I have lectured on comparative legal systems. I frequently speak to community groups and fraternal organizations on a broad range of subjects, including law, photography, anthropology, and mythology.

''I have acted in and directed amateur Shakespearean productions, musical and farce comedy, and have performed professionally as a concert and jazz musician. I have also free-lanced semi-professionally as a photographer in New York advertising agency markets.''

AVOCATIONAL INTERESTS: Distance running.

F

FABIAN, Ruth
    See QUIGLEY, Aileen

*   *   *

FAGLES, Robert 1933-

BRIEF ENTRY: Born September 11, 1933, in Philadelphia, Pa. American educator and author. Fagles has been a member of the faculty at Princeton University since 1960 and a professor of English and comparative literature since 1970. His books include a translation of *Complete Poems*, by Bacchylides (Yale University Press, 1961), a translation of *The Oresteia*, by Aeschylus (Viking, 1975), *Pope's Iliad and Odyssey* (Yale University Press, 1967), and *I, Vincent: Poems From the Pictures of Van Gogh* (Princeton University Press, 1978). *Address:* Program in Comparative Literature, Princeton University, 333 East Pyne, Princeton, N.J. 08540. *Biographical/critical sources: Directory of American Scholars*, Volume II: *English, Speech, and Drama*, 7th edition, Bowker, 1978.

*   *   *

FAIN, Tyrus Gerard 1933-

PERSONAL: Born April 18, 1933, in San Antonio, Tex.; son of Clarence B. and Louise (Foster) Fain; married Katharine Plant (an editor), 1978; children: Tanya, Keneth, Paul. *Education:* Attended University of Texas, 1952-56, and Yale University, 1956-60. *Politics:* Democrat. *Office:* Gerard International, 1629 K St. N.W., Washington, D.C. 20006.

CAREER: U.S. Department of State, Washington, D.C., 1961-68; U.S. Senate, Washington, D.C., staff member, 1969-71; *Congressional Record Abstracts*, Washington, D.C., publisher, 1972-77; Gerard International, Washington, D.C., president, 1977—.

WRITINGS—Editor with Katherine C. Plant and Ross Milloy: *The Intelligence Community: History, Organization, and Issues*, introduction by Frank Church, Bowker, 1977; *Federal Reorganization: The Executive Branch*, foreword by Bert Lance, Bowker, 1977; *National Health Insurance*, introduction by Edward M. Kennedy, Bowker, 1977.

Editor of Bowker's "Public Documents" series, and *Congressional Record Abstracts*.

WORK IN PROGRESS: *The American Oil Industry Abroad* and *OPEC: A Documentary History*.

FAIRLIE, Henry (Jones) 1924-

PERSONAL: Born January 13, 1924, in London, England; son of James and Rita (Vernon) Fairlie; married Elisabeth Todd Phillips, 1949; children: Simon, Charlotte, Emma. *Education:* Corpus Christi College, Oxford, B.A., 1945. *Politics:* "Tory Socialist." *Religion:* Church of England. *Office: New Republic*, 1220 19th St. N.W., Washington, D.C. 20036.

CAREER: *Observer*, London, England, feature writer, 1948-50; *London Times*, London, political editorial writer, 1950-54; free-lance writer, 1954—.

WRITINGS: *The Life of Politics*, Methuen, 1969; *The Kennedy Promise*, Doubleday, 1973; *The Spoiled Child of the Western World: The Miscarriage of the American Idea in Our Time*, Doubleday, 1976; *The Parties: Republicans and Democrats in This Century*, St. Martin's, 1978; *The Seven Deadly Sins Today*, New Republic Books, 1978. Contributor to British and American journals, including *New Republic*.

SIDELIGHTS: Fairlie has written several books that explore contemporary American politics. In *The Kennedy Promise*, for example, Fairlie analyzes the presidential campaign and administration of John F. Kennedy. A *New Yorker* reviewer pointed out that Fairlie criticizes Kennedy on several counts, most notably for raising "hopes in the American people that no one could fulfill." In addition, Fairlie criticized Kennedy for pursuing a policy of "brinkmanship," deliberately allowing such situations as the Cuban missile crisis to escalate into serious emergencies in order to exaggerate their importance. Kennedy's responses to them would appear more dramatic, Fairlie argued, and thus increase his prestige. According to *Books and Bookmen* critic Frank Lipsius, Fairlie concludes that "'low-profile' presidents function better than Kennedy-type rabble rousers." R. D. Novak of *National Review* commented that although Fairlie "badly exaggerates Kennedy's neglect of domestic affairs," his "overriding insight of what was wrong with Kennedy is worth considering."

In his next book, *The Spoiled Child of the Western World*, Fairlie discusses the need for the United States to "recover its morale and equilibrium." *Time*'s Lance Morrow said that "much of Fairlie's book is a rich and occasionally cranky meditation on the ways in which Americans have retreated into self-gratification and a kind of infantilism." *New Statesman* critic Godfrey Hodgson observed that Fairlie blames this situation on the undue influence that men such as Darwin, Freud, Marx, and Einstein have on American values. The result of this influence, says Fairlie, has been a rejection of the uniquely American idea of egalitarian democracy on which the nation was founded. *Commentary*'s Suzanne Weaver reported that the "book is often a delight, full of the eclectic learning and acute observation that we have come to expect of Fairlie."

In *The Parties: Republicans and Democrats in This Century* Fairlie continues his probe into the American political system with an analysis of the roles of the country's two major political parties. *Best Sellers*'s Norman Lederer observed that, although Fairlie criticizes both the "articulate intellectuals" within the Democratic party and the "aimless" political philosphy of the Republican party, he nevertheless strongly supports the political party system and urges that it be maintained "as a meaningful entity in the American political process." Lederer described Fairlie's analysis of the American party system as "penetrating and witty."

BIOGRAPHICAL/CRITICAL SOURCES: New York Times Book Review, January 21, 1973, January 18, 1976, March 19, 1978, May 28, 1978; *National Review,* March 2, 1973, June 23, 1978, August 4, 1978; *New Statesman,* May 25, 1973, January 21, 1977; *Commentary,* June, 1973, July, 1976, October, 1978; *Books and Bookmen,* September, 1973; *Time,* March 15, 1976; *Best Sellers,* July, 1978.

* * *

FALCONER, Alun ?-1973

OBITUARY NOTICE: Died September 27, 1973, in England. Novelist and television scriptwriter. Falconer wrote the novel *The Liberators.* Obituaries and other sources: *AB Bookman's Weekly,* December 3, 1973.

* * *

FARMER, Bertram Hughes 1916-

PERSONAL: Born March 18, 1916, in Malmesbury, England; son of Seymour and Mary Martha (Hughes) Farmer; married Anne Allison Stewart, April 5, 1947; children: David Seymour, Pauline Mary Farmer Cranfield, Hugh John, John Walter Robert. *Education:* St. John's College, Cambridge, B.A., 1937, M.A., 1941. *Office:* St. John's College, Cambridge University, Cambridge CB2 1TP, England.

CAREER: University of Wales, University College of Swansea, lecturer in geography, 1946-47; Cambridge University, Cambridge, England, fellow of St. John's College, 1948—, president of college, 1967-71, lecturer, 1952-67, reader in South Asian geography, 1967—, director of Centre of South Asian Studies, 1964—. *Military service:* British Army, Royal Tank Regiment and Royal Engineers, 1940-46; became major; mentioned in dispatches. *Member:* Institute of British Geographers (vice-president, 1970-71). *Awards, honors:* Gill Memorial Prize from Royal Geographical Society, 1953; Prix Christian Garner from Societe de Geographie de Paris, 1955; D.Litt. from University of Peradeniya, 1981.

WRITINGS: Pioneer Peasant Colonization in Ceylon, Oxford University Press, 1957; *Ceylon: A Divided Nation,* Oxford University Press, 1963; *Agricultural Colonization in India Since Independence,* Oxford University Press, 1974; (editor) *Green Revolution?: Technology and Change in Rice-Growing Areas of Tamil Nada and Sri Lanka,* Macmillan, 1977. Contributor to learned journals. Editor of *Transactions of the Institute of*

British Geographers, 1961-66, and *Geographical Journal,* 1980—.

WORK IN PROGRESS: Research on South Asian geography and affairs, especially agrarian affairs.

* * *

FARQUHARSON, Charlie
See HARRON, Don(ald)

* * *

FAST, Barbara 1924-

PERSONAL: Born December 19, 1924, in Minneapolis, Minn.; daughter of John J. (in business) and Blanche (Hewitt) Sher; married Julius Fast (a writer), June 8, 1946; children: Jennifer Fast Gelfand, Melissa Fast Boguslauska, Timothy. *Education:* Attended University of Minnesota, 1941-42, and New York University, 1942. *Home and office:* 45 East 85th St., New York, N.Y. 10028; and Peter Rd., Southbury, Conn. *Agent:* Robert P. Mills Ltd., 156 East 52nd St., New York, N.Y. 10022.

CAREER: Writer. *Military service:* U.S. Army, Women's Army Corps, 1944-46; received two battle stars. *Member:* Authors Guild.

WRITINGS: Getting Close (nonfiction), Putnam, 1978; *Talking Between the Lines* (nonfiction), Viking, 1979.

WORK IN PROGRESS: Tag Sale, a novel of three generations of American woman.

SIDELIGHTS: Barbara Fast wrote: "I have written books that deal with intimacy and communication, two subjects that are deep problems in today's world. My novel in progress combines these two problems as they occur in three generations of a family."

* * *

FAVERTY, Frederic Everett 1902-1981

OBITUARY NOTICE—See index for *CA* sketch: Born September 29, 1902, in Chester, Ill.; died August 9, 1981, in Evanston, Ill. Educator and author. Faverty began his career at Northwestern University in 1930, where he later served as Morrison Professor of English and chairman of the department. He was also a literary columnist and a book reviewer for the *Chicago Tribune,* a member of the advisory board of *Victorian Poetry,* and a member of the Journalists of Victorian Studies' editorial board. A specialist in Victorian literature, he was a consultant for several literary and educational institutions, including the Publishers Modern Language Association. In 1957 the author won a Friend of Literature Award. His books include *Legends of Joseph in Old Middle English; Matthew Arnold, the Ethnologist; The Victorian Poets: A Guide to Research;* and *Your Literary Heritage.* Obituaries and other sources: *Chicago Tribune,* August 14, 1981.

* * *

FAWCETT, Ken(neth Richard) 1944-

PERSONAL: Born May 22, 1944, in Berkeley, Calif.; son of Richard G. and Gertrude (Dade) Fawcett; married Lana Linser (a speech pathologist), August 8, 1970. *Education:* University of California, Berkeley, B.S., 1967. *Home:* 3186 La Mesa Dr., San Carlos, Calif. 94070.

CAREER: High school mathematics teacher in Concord, Calif., 1968-70; senior systems analyst and major systems project manager for Bank of America, 1970—. Boy Scouts of America post adviser, 1970-78, and troop leader, 1979—.

WRITINGS: *Tower Peak,* Wilderness Press, 1975.

WORK IN PROGRESS: Magazine articles about hiking in Alaska.

SIDELIGHTS: Fawcett has been hiking in the Sierras since he was about fifteen years old. At eighteen he completed a fifty-mile Sierra hike in one day. In 1964 he opened a food store for backpackers in San Carlos.

*   *   *

FEDERBUSH, Arnold   1935-

PERSONAL: Born March 16, 1935, in New York, N.Y.; son of Isaac (a landlord) and Sarah (Kirschenbaum) Federbush. *Education:* New York University, B.A., 1956; University of California, Los Angeles, M.A., 1962. *Religion:* Jewish. *Home:* 840 South Serrano Ave., Los Angeles, Calif. 90005. *Agent:* Stu Robinson, 556 South San Vicente Blvd., Los Angeles, Calif. 90048.

CAREER: Writer and film editor. Worked for Rastar Productions and Jacoby Storm Productions, 1970. *Member:* Screen Writers Guild (West), Mensa. *Awards, honors:* Golden Eagle from Council on International Nontheatrical Events, 1963, for writing, producing, and directing documentary film, "111th Street"; gold medal for best paperback fantasy from *West Coast Review of Books,* 1979, for *Ice!*

WRITINGS: *The Man Who Lived in Inner Space* (novel), Houghton, 1973; *Ice!* (novel), Bantam, 1978.

Films: "111th Street," Macmillan Films, 1963; "The Man Who Lived in Inner Space"; "Ice!"; "Manchild in the Promised Land" (based on the book by Claude Brown).

WORK IN PROGRESS: *Fault,* a novel.

SIDELIGHTS: Federbush wrote: "I began my professional life as a documentary filmmaker, but now, when would-be writers are becoming would-be filmmakers, I have gone in the opposite direction. Filmmaking involves too many attributes I don't seem to have, such as raising money, and remembering to focus. My published novels both grew out of unproduced screenplays, and I have been gradually learning that the abilities to dream, cogitate, and procrastinate seem to carry minimal harm in novels. One may destroy the world, and star an Eskimo, without worries of budget and 'bankable' stars. My first novel was carried on the shelf alphabetically next to William Faulkner, so I've already come close to greatness.

"I regard my novels much in the same way I regarded the dramatic documentary film, as attempts to educate and entertain simultaneously, as if someone devoted to a particular field had written the one novel he or she had dreamed of, the single experience that summed up that person's excitement and love.

"In that connection, the nicest words a reviewer could use were on my first novel: 'It leaves behind a feeling for the sea so real that closing the book one feels as if he has just climbed out of the waves and is shucking mash and flippers at the water's edge.' It was particularly gratifying considering all my experience was in the local library."

*   *   *

FEIG, Barbara Krane   1937-

PERSONAL: Born November 8, 1937, in Mitchell, S.D.;

daughter of Peter A. and Sally (Gorchow) Krane; married Jerome Feig (a Chicago Board of Options executive), June 8, 1963; children: Patricia Lynn, Lizabeth Ann. *Education:* Attended Washington University, St. Louis, Mo., 1955, 1956, and Roosevelt University, 1957; Pestalozzi Teachers College, B.E., 1960. *Religion:* Jewish. *Home:* 904 Castlewood Ter., Chicago, Ill. 60640.

CAREER: Elementary school teacher in Chicago, Ill., 1960-68; Media Merchandising, Inc., Chicago, vice-president and member of board of directors, 1974—. President of J. B. Pal & Co., Inc., 1975—; member of board of trustees of Chicago Institute for Psychoanalysis and women's board of Francis Parker School; consultant to Barclee Cosmetics, Inc. *Member:* Chicago Art Institute, Chicago Council on Foreign Relations, Chicago Symphony Orchestra, Field Museum of Natural History.

WRITINGS: *Now You're Cooking: A Guide to Cooking for Boys and Girls,* J. B. Pal, 1975; *The Parents' Guide to Weight Control for Children,* C. C Thomas, 1980.

SIDELIGHTS: Barbara Feig told *CA:* "I gained my understanding of children, and their delight in creating, from several years of elementary school teaching. Children need to be aware of their own accomplishments, and I hope that my books will help them achieve this.

"In 1975 I wrote *Now You're Cooking.* This put me in contact by mail as well as in person with many children and their parents who enjoyed my approach to the subject and had ideas they wanted to share with me. I was surprised, however, at the number of parents who told me that as much as they liked my book, their children tended to be overweight, and they didn't want to encourage a kitchen-based hobby. My curiosity aroused, I investigated this situation more systematically. I learned that the battle for weight control does not begin in middle age, as we tend to think, but in the nursery. I also found that there is much that has already been learned about the scientific management of the overweight child, but that the communication between the professional and those in need of help is lacking.

"In the next few years, I interviewed many parents and children to get their ideas about food habits and weight problems. I talked to parents who were struggling with the problem of excess poundage in their children, to some who had lost the battle and to others who had won it. Often I found that adults and children had serious misconceptions about their weight difficulties and were doing things that would worsen the situation rather than help it. Many gave up without ever really trying to improve their condition because they thought it would be too complicated. Other parents and children had developed some very good ideas from which many others could benefit. This book grew out of my search and research."

AVOCATIONAL INTERESTS: Skiing, riding, tennis.

*   *   *

FEIGELSON, Naomi
See CHASE, Naomi Feigelson

*   *   *

FEINSTEIN, Otto   1930-

PERSONAL: Born May 18, 1930, in Vienna, Austria; came to the United States in 1940, naturalized citizen, 1947; son of Abraham (a lawyer; in business) and Bella (Silber) Feinstein; married Nicolette Marget Cecelia Carey (an editor), December

3, 1961; children: Sarah, Tamara. *Education:* University of Chicago, A.B., 1950, Ph.D., 1965; University of Geneva, License in Political and Economic Science, 1955. *Religion:* Jewish. *Home:* 679 West Hancock, Detroit, Mich. 48201. *Office:* Department of Political Science, Wayne State University, Detroit, Mich. 48202.

CAREER: Wayne State University, Detroit, Mich., assistant professor, 1960-65, associate professor, 1965-69, professor of political science, 1978—, associate vice-president for urban affairs, 1976-79. Education director at WTVS-TV, 1980—. Member of Michigan Ethnic Heritage Studies Center, Michigan Quality of Work Life Council, Detroit City/University Consortium, and To Educate the People Consortium. *Member:* International Studies Association, American Political Science Association, American Association of University Professors, National Center for Urban Ethnic Affairs. *Awards, honors:* Awards from Michigan Senate, 1975, for founding University Studies and Weekend College, and Detroit City Council, 1981, for telethon on unemployment.

WRITINGS: (Editor) *Two Worlds of Change,* Doubleday, 1965; *Higher Education in the United States,* Heath, 1970; (editor) *Ethnic Groups in the City,* Heath, 1970; (with Eric Beckstael) *Higher Education in Europe,* Heath, 1970; (with Frank Angelo) *To Educate the People,* Center for Urban Studies, Wayne State University, 1976; *Humanities-Based Curriculum for Working Adults,* Center for Urban Studies, Wayne State University, 1979. Writer for "Ethnic Studies," and "International and Domestic Conflict," both series on ABC-TV in Detroit. Editor of *New University Thought,* a journal, and "Latin American Series" for Anchor Press.

WORK IN PROGRESS: "Ethnicity—U.S.A.," a series for WTVS-TV in Detroit; chief writer of "Telecurriculum"; research on the future of the social sciences in the United States.

* * *

FELD, Bernard T(aub) 1919-

PERSONAL: Born December 21, 1919, in New York, N.Y.; son of Abraham Louis (a dress cutter) and Helen (Taub) Feld; married Eliza McCormick (a writer), June 6, 1947; children: Elizabeth T., Ellen D. *Education:* City College (now of City University of New York), B.S., 1939; Columbia University, Ph.D., 1945. *Politics:* None. *Religion:* None. *Home:* 42 Arlington St., Cambridge, Mass. 02140. *Office:* Department of Physics, Massachusetts Institute of Technology, Cambridge, Mass. 02139.

CAREER: Manhattan Project, research associate in New York, N.Y., 1941-42, group leader in Chicago, Ill., 1942-44, and Los Alamos, N.M., 1944-45; Massachusetts Institute of Technology, Cambridge, instructor, 1946-57, professor of physics, 1957—, director of laboratory for nuclear science, 1969-71, head of division of nuclear and high-energy physics, 1975—. Visiting professor at University of Rome and University of Padua, 1953-54, Ecole Polytechnique, 1966-67, and Imperial College, 1973-75. Visiting scientist at European Center for Nuclear Research, 1960-61. Trustee of Associated Universities, 1958-60; president of Council for a Livable World, 1963-74; Pugwash Conference on Science and World Affairs, member of international continuing committee, 1963—, secretary-general and chairman of executive committee, 1973—. Consultant for Brookhaven National Laboratory and member of the executive committee of Cambridge Electron Accelerator.

MEMBER: American Academy of Arts and Sciences (fellow; vice-president for mathematics and physical sciences, 1972-

75), American Physical Society (fellow), Federation of American Scientists, Council on Foreign Relations, Phi Beta Kappa, Sigma Xi. *Awards, honors:* Townsend Harris Medal from alumni of City College of City University of New York, 1969; Leo Sziland award from American Physical Society, 1975; public service award from Federation of American Scientists, 1975.

WRITINGS: The Neutron: Experimental Handbook, Volume II: *Physics,* Wiley, 1953; *Models of Elementary Particles,* Ginn, 1969; *The Impact of New Technology on the Arms Race,* M.I.T. Press, 1970; *The Future of the Sea-Based Deterrent,* M.I.T. Press, 1972; *A Voice Crying in the Wilderness* (essays), Pergamon, 1979. Associate editor of *Annals of Physics,* 1957—; consulting editor of Blaisdell-Ginn-Xerox Publishing Co., 1959-72; editor-in-chief of *Bulletin of the Atomic Scientists,* 1976—.

BIOGRAPHICAL/CRITICAL SOURCES: Scientific American, June, 1971; *Bulletin of the Atomic Scientists,* January, 1972.

* * *

FELDMANN, Susan Judith 1928-1969
(Susan Taubes)

OBITUARY NOTICE: Born in 1928; committed suicide, November 6, 1969. Educator and author of *Divorcing.* Obituaries and other sources: *Publishers Weekly,* January 5, 1970.

* * *

FENTRESS, John Simmons 1925(?)-1981

OBITUARY NOTICE: Born c. 1925 in Maribel, N.C.; died of cancer, August 11, 1981, in Chevy Chase, Md. Journalist. Fentress was an editorial writer for the *Charlotte Observer* after beginning his career at the *Raleigh News and Observer.* He joined *Time* magazine in 1961, serving first as its Atlanta bureau chief and later as head of its Saigon bureau. He covered the 1968 and 1972 presidential elections for the magazine and was named its chief political correspondent in 1972. Obituaries and other sources: *Washington Post,* August 12, 1981.

* * *

FERGUSSON, James 1904-1973

OBITUARY NOTICE: Born in 1904 in London, England; died October 25, 1973. Journalist, historian, and author. Fergusson worked for the British Broadcasting Corporation (BBC-Radio) from 1934 to 1944, producing "BBC Talks" programs and commenting on Nazi propaganda during World War II. After the war he served on the staff of the *Glasgow Herald* for five years before beginning a twenty-year career as keeper of the records of Scotland. Among his books are *Alexander the Third,* *The Sixteen Peers of Scotland,* and *The Man Behind Macbeth.* Obituaries and other sources: *The Author's and Writer's Who's Who,* 6th edition, Burke's Peerage, 1971; *AB Bookman's Weekly,* December 3, 1973; *Who Was Who Among English and European Authors, 1931-1949,* Gale, 1978.

* * *

FERMAN, Joseph W(olfe) 1906-1975

OBITUARY NOTICE: Born June 8, 1906, in Lida, Lithuania (some sources say New York, N.Y.); died December 29, 1975. Publisher. Ferman worked for the *American Mercury* for many years before becoming vice-president of Mercury Press. He bought the press in the mid 1950's, and as president he published *Ellery Queen's Mystery Magazine, The Magazine of*

Fantasy and Science Fiction, and a number of lines of mystery paperbacks. His publications won five Hugo Awards for best professional magazines. Ferman edited the book *No Limits* in 1964. Obituaries and other sources: *American Authors and Books, 1640 to the Present Day,* 3rd revised edition, Crown, 1972; *New York Times,* December 30, 1974; *Publishers Weekly,* January 27, 1975; *Contemporary Science Fiction Authors,* Arno, 1975; *Who Was Who in America, With World Notables,* Volume VI: *1974-1976,* Marquis, 1976; *Science Fiction and Fantasy Literature,* Volume II: *Contemporary Science Fiction Authors II,* Gale, 1979.

* * *

FERRER, Gabriel (Francisco Victor) Miro
   See MIRO (FERRER), Gabriel (Francisco Victor)

* * *

FEUCHTWANGER, Lion   1884-1958
   (J. L. Wetcheek)

BRIEF ENTRY: Born July 7, 1884, in Munich, Germany (now West Germany); came to the United States, 1940; died December 21, 1958, in Los Angeles, Calif. German novelist, playwright, and poet. Lion Feuchtwanger, a member of the literary avant-garde in Berlin during the 1920's and 1930's, is credited with having discovered and promoted the work of playwright Bertolt Brecht. In fact, the two collaborated on several plays, including *Das Leben Eduard des zweiten von England* (1928), an adaptation of Christopher Marlowe's *Edward II.* After achieving substantial recognition as a playwright, Feuchtwanger turned to writing historical novels, depicting such characters as Marie Antoinette, the Spanish painter Goya, Benjamin Franklin, and Cotton Mather. His innovative application of modern psychological analysis to the historical novel is considered to be his major contribution to that genre. Because Feuchtwanger's writing reflected his liberal, pacifist views, several of his works were suppressed by the Nazi regime. He was interned in a French concentration camp in 1940, but he later escaped and fled to the United States. Under the pseudonym J. L. Wetcheek he wrote *Pep* (1928), a book of satirical poems about America. Numbered among his novels are *Jud Suess* (1925), *Der juedische Krieg* (1932), *Die soehne* (1935), and *Der Tag wird kommen* (1945). *Residence:* Pacific Palisades, Calif. *Biographical/critical sources: Twentieth Century Authors: A Biographical Dictionary of Modern Literature,* H. W. Wilson, 1942, 1st supplement, 1955; *Columbia Dictionary of Modern European Literature,* Columbia University Press, 1947; *McGraw-Hill Encyclopedia of World Drama,* McGraw, 1972; *Twentieth-Century Literary Criticism,* Volume 3, Gale, 1980.

* * *

FEUERWERGER, Marvin C(harles)   1950-

PERSONAL: Born October 16, 1950, in Cleveland, Ohio; son of Henry and Gita (Berkowitz) Feuerwerger; married Debra Lichtman (an attorney), December 1, 1974; children: David. *Education:* Attended Hebrew University of Jerusalem, 1969-70; Columbia University, B.A., 1971; Harvard University, Ph.D., 1977. *Politics:* Democrat. *Religion:* Jewish. *Home:* 3100 Connecticut Ave. N.W., Apt. 337, Washington, D.C. 20008. *Office:* Office of the Secretary of Defense, International Security Affairs, Pentagon, Room 4B868, Washington, D.C. 20301.

CAREER: Legislative assistant to U.S. Representative Christopher J. Dodd, 1977, and U.S. Representative Stephen J.

Solarz, 1978; White House, Washington, D.C., deputy adviser, 1978-80; Office of the Secretary of Defense, International Security Affairs, Washington, D.C., assistant policy planner, 1980—. *Member:* American Political Science Association.

WRITINGS: Congress and Israel: Foreign Aid Decision-Making in the House of Representatives, 1969-1971, Greenwood Press, 1979. Contributor to political science journals.

SIDELIGHTS: Feuerwerger told *CA:* "*Congress and Israel* utilizes interviews with over seventy-five congressmen and key executive branch officials to analyze congressional activity concerning Israel during the Nixon and Ford administrations. The book examines Congress's behavior in the areas of foreign assistance, arms sales, and diplomacy and analyzes the motives and processes that underlie that behavior. It explains why the overwhelming majority of congressmen has strongly supported Israel and why a small majority has not. It also provides an incisive and detailed analysis of the Israel-related activity of the House Affairs Committee during the Ninety-fourth Congress.

"*Congress and Israel* also sheds considerable light on broader issues, including the limits of Congress's influence on foreign policy formation and the importance of domestic considerations in Congress's foreign policy deliberations."

* * *

FIFER, Ken   1947-

PERSONAL: Born October 6, 1947, in New York, N.Y.; son of William and Shirley (Zlatkin) Fifer; married Elizabeth Nusbaum (a professor of English), December 26, 1970. *Education:* City College of the City University of New York, B.A., 1968; University of Michigan, M.A., 1969, Ph.D., 1972. *Home:* 1724 Maple St., Bethlehem, Pa. 18017.

CAREER: Poet, editor, critic, and educator. Artist-in-the-Schools, Pennsylvania Council on the Arts, 1975—. Member of board of directors of Lehigh Valley Arts Council, 1979—. Poetry consultant for Arts in Special Education Project of Pennsylvania, 1980—.

WRITINGS: Falling Man (poems), Ithaca House, 1979; (editor) *Staring at the Word Mexico* (poems), Pennsylvania Council on the Arts, 1979; (editor) *Frog Theory* (poems), Pennsylvania Council on the Arts, 1980; (editor) *Big Numbers* (poems) Pennsylvania Council on the Arts, 1981. Contributor to literary magazines. Editor of *Anon,* 1968-72, and *Forms,* 1979-80.

WORK IN PROGRESS: After Fire, poems.

SIDELIGHTS: Ken Fifer told *CA:* "I give poetry readings and conduct poetry workshops at elementary schools, high schools, community colleges, universities, community centers, hospitals, and prisons throughout Pennsylvania. For the most part, I tell my students that all theories concerning writing are lies. Sometimes those lies are amazingly useful to a writer. Sometimes they have to be swept aside by the urgency of the task at hand. I find it useful presently to think of my own writing as a sort of meditative and intense listening. I am a poet because I do not know what to say."

* * *

FINE, S(eymour) Morton   1930-

PERSONAL: Born April 5, 1930, in Bronx, N.Y.; son of Morris J. (a butcher) and Bertha (Low) Fine; married Lillian R. Shapiro (an office adminstrator), July 15, 1962; children: Lisa Beth, Michael Zachary. *Education:* City College (now of the City University of New York), B.S., 1952; Columbia University, M.A., 1957, Ed.D., 1974. *Religion:* Jewish. *Home:* 121 Ferndale Rd., Scarsdale, N.Y. 10583. *Office:* Department of Health and Physical Education, York College of the City University of New York, Jamaica, N.Y. 11451.

CAREER: Recreation teacher at vacation playgrounds of public schools in New York City, 1950-51; high school teacher of health and physical education in New York City, 1954-55; junior high school teacher of health and physical education and coach of basketball and track in New York City, 1955-56; high school teacher of health and physical education in New York City, 1956-70, coach of track, cross-country running, and gymnastics, 1956-65, chairman of department of health and physical education, 1965-70; York College of the City University of New York, Jamaica, N.Y., assistant professor, 1970-74, associate professor of health and physical education, 1974—. Program director and director of aquatic activities at children's day camps, 1952-68; teacher in charge of New York City Board of Education Evening Community Center, 1954-57, coordinator of narcotics planning project for board of education's Bureau for Health and Physical Education, 1970; public speaker. *Military service:* U.S. Army, Special Services, 1952-54.

MEMBER: American School Health Association, Association for the Advancement of Health Education, Association for City University Health Educators (vice-president, 1972-73), New York State Federation of Professional Health Educators, New York City Association for Teachers of Health and Physical Education (member of executive committee, 1965-70; vice-president, 1970-71). *Awards, honors:* Citation from New York City Public Schools Coaches Association, 1960, for coaching New York City cross country championship team; annual award from New York City Association for Teachers of Health and Physical Education, 1969, for outstanding contributions to the profession.

WRITINGS: (With Ivan Kusinitz) *Love, Sex, and the Family: A Guide for Young Adults,* New American Library, 1971; *Physical Fitness Laboratory Teachers Manual,* Physical Fitness Laboratory (Westport, Conn.), 1970; (with Kusinitz) *The Fitness Challenge,* Physical Fitness Laboratory, 1970; (with Kusinitz) *Exercise and Physical Fitness for Almost Everyone,* Consumers Report Books, 1981.

Filmstrips: (And consultant) "The Fitness Challenge," released by Physical Fitness Laboratory, 1970; "Drugs and Your Body," released by Viewlex Corp., 1971; "Drugs and Your World," released by Viewlex Corp., 1971. Contributor to magazines, including *School Health Journal.*

SIDELIGHTS: Fine told *CA:* "In the past I have been interested in youth and their quest for accurate and appropriate information to assist in decision making. My current effort at patient education is in response to the 'wellness' and 'health promotion' movements and their efforts to control skyrocketing medical costs via the use of more effective prevention approaches."

*   *   *

FINGER, Seymour Maxwell   1915-

PERSONAL: Born April 30, 1915, in New York, N.Y.; son of Samuel Isaac (in business) and Bella (Spiegel) Finger; married Helen Kotcher, April 5, 1956; children: Mark P. *Education:* Ohio University, B.S., 1935; graduate study at University of Cincinnati, 1942, and Harvard University, 1953-54. *Politics:* Democrat. *Religion:* Jewish. *Home:* 476 Morris Ave., Rockville Centre, N.Y. 11570. *Agent:* Bertha Klausner Inter-

national Literary Agency, Inc., 71 Park Ave., New York, N.Y. 10016. *Office:* 33 West 42nd St., New York, N.Y. 10036.

CAREER: Photo Reflex Studios, Inc., New York, N.Y., branch manager, 1935-37; teacher of English at junior high school in Atlanta, Ga., 1937-38; Photo Reflex Studios, Inc., branch manager, 1938-40, regional supervisor, 1940-43, assistant to vice-president, 1945-46; American Foreign Service, Washington, D.C., vice-consul at American embassy in Stuttgart, Germany, 1946-49, third secretary at American embassy in Paris, France, 1949-51, second secretary and economic officer at American legation in Budapest, Hungary, 1951-53, second secretary and economic defense officer at American embassy in Rome, 1954-55, first secretary at American embassy in Vientiane, Laos, 1955-56, senior U.S. adviser on economic and social affairs at United Nations in New York City, 1956, senior economic adviser to U.S. mission to the United Nations, 1956-65, deputy counselor to U.S. mission, 1964, counselor, 1966, ambassador and senior adviser to permanent U.S. representative to the United Nations, 1967-71; Staten Island College of the City University of New York, Staten Island, N.Y., professor of government and international organization, 1971—.

Director of Ralph Bunche Institute on the United Nations of the City University of New York and professor at Graduate School of the City University of New York, both 1973—. Member of U.S. delegation to the United Nations General Assembly, 1956-71, chairman of Security Council committee on sanctions in Rhodesia; U.S. representative to governing council of United Nations Development Program; member of Task Force for a Nuclear Test Ban; member of board of directors of National Committee on American Foreign Policy, Travel Program for Foreign Diplomats, Commission to Study the Organization of Peace, and South Nassau Communities Hospital, 1973-74; consultant to World Jewish Congress and Brookings Institution. *Military service:* U.S. Army, 1943-46; served in European theater; became staff sergeant; received five battle stars.

MEMBER: International Peace Academy (member of North American council), Society for International Development (New York President), American Society of International Law, American Foreign Service Association, American Academy of Political and Social Science, United Nations Association of the United States of America, Institute for Mediterranean Affairs (president, 1971—), Council on Foreign Relations, Diplomatic and Consular Office Retirees, Phi Beta Kappa, Kappa Delta Pi, Oceanside Country Club, American Club (Paris, France), American Club (Rome, Italy), *Awards, honors:* Certificate of merit from Ohio University, 1967; citation from B'nai B'rith, 1970; humanitarian award from American Committee for the Rescue and Rehabilitation of Iraqi Jews, 1971; Rockefeller Foundation fellowship, 1977-78.

WRITINGS: (Editor and contributor) *The New World Balance and Peace in the Middle East: Mirage or Reality?,* Associated Universities Press 1975; (editor with Yonah Alexander) *Terrorism: Interdisciplinary Perspectives,* John Jay, 1977; (editor with Joseph R. Harbert, and contributor) *U.S. Policies in International Institutions,* Westview, 1978; *Your Man at the U.N.: People, Policies, and Bureaucracy in the Making of American Foreign Policy,* New York University Press, 1980.

Contributor: Sam Merlin, editor, *The Big Powers and the Present Crisis in the Middle East,* Fairleigh Dickinson University Press, 1968; Yonah Alexander, editor, *International Terrorism,* Praeger, 1976; David A. Kay, editor, *The Changing United Nations: Options for the United States,* New York Academy of Political Science, 1977; Alexander and Robert A. Kilmarx, editors, *Political Terrorism and Business: The Threat and Re-*

sponse, Holt, 1978; Alexander, editor, *Self-Determination,* Westview, 1979. Contributor to academic journals, popular magazines, and newspapers, including *Newsday.*

WORK IN PROGRESS: A study of the United Nations Secretariat and the role of the secretary-general, publication by Orbis expected in 1981; *Ilona,* a novella, publication expected in 1981; a study of actions and attitudes of American Jews during the Holocaust, completion expected in 1983.

SIDELIGHTS: Finger told *CA:* "My careers—in business, war, diplomacy, and at the university—have involved doing things; writing has been the result rather than the goal. In listing my publications, I have been truly surprised at their quantity and variety. Though I admire creative writing and enjoy reading it, my own writing has generally been expository: to convey ideas, analyze issues, and recount events.

"I have been impelled to write about the U.N. because I have been involved with it for fifteen years as a diplomat and for ten years as an academic. For all its faults, serious faults, I believe the U.N. is important for world peace and human survival. Its peace-keeping activities in the Middle East and the Congo (Zaire) prevented dangerous Soviet-U.S. military confrontations. The U.N. is also important in dealing with serious global problems: the race between rapid population growth and food production; the pressure of growing demands on other finite resources, especially non-renewable resources like petroleum; the arms race; nuclear proliferation; the uses of outer space and the seabeds; and threats to global ecology.

"But, one must be realistic in expectations about the U.N. It has no power except that which governments are willing to give it. Consequently it has been unable to stop wars where nations are determined to fight. It works only when its members can agree to cooperate. Such agreements have brought about significant achievements in food production, population policy, economic development, nuclear non-proliferation, outer space, de-colonization, and protection of the environment.

"The adoption, by the U.N. General Assembly, of resolutions blatantly biased against Israel, while not enforceable, has diminished the U.N.'s standing in the United States and among other Western governments. Consequently, the United Nations' ability to assist in a negotiated settlement of the Arab-Israel dispute has been weakened, along with its overall influence.

"I became interested in international terrorism because of U.N. negotiations leading to the adoption of conventions against hijacking and other interference with civil aviation, and against the taking of hostages. These conventions are binding only on governments that ratify them; consequently, they have been helpful but only partially effective. The effort must continue to get more governments to ratify these conventions and to ensure full compliance with them.

"The Holocaust, my current research interest, represents a threat to human survival comparable to nuclear weapons. It was the first systematic program to exterminate an entire people, the Jews of Europe. Six million Jews were slaughtered in the Holocaust. The vicious ideology behind it is not dead and could threaten Jews and other peoples again. I am now involved in research into the actions and attitudes of American Jews during the Holocaust. The goal is to learn from the failures of that period and to spread the findings widely as a defense against future genocidal efforts."

AVOCATIONAL INTERESTS: Running, swimming.

FINIFTER, Ada W(eintraub)   1938-

PERSONAL: Born June 6, 1938, in New York, N.Y.; daughter of Isaac and Stella (Colchamiro) Weintraub; married Bernard M. Finifter, 1960. *Education:* Brooklyn College (now of City University of New York), B.A. (cum laude), 1959; University of Michigan, M.A., 1961; University of Wisconsin (now University of Wisconsin—Madison), Ph.D., 1967. *Home:* 1743 Old Mill Rd., East Lansing, Mich. 48823. *Office:* Department of Political Science, Michigan State University, East Lansing, Mich. 48824.

CAREER: University of Michigan, Ann Arbor, assistant study director of political behavior program at Survey Research Center, 1961-62; Catholic University, Caracas, Venezuela, professor of social science, 1963-64; Michigan State University, East Lansing, assistant professor, 1967-72, associate professor, 1972-81, professor of political science, 1981—. Congressional fellow, 1973-74; visiting fellow at Australian National University, 1978. Chairman of conferences and workshops.

MEMBER: American Association of University Professors, American Political Science Association (member of council, 1973-75; chairperson of Woodrow Wilson award committee, 1977; program chairman, 1982) Midwest Political Science Association (member of executive council, 1971-74), Inter-University Consortium for Political and Social Research (member of council, 1971-74; chairman of advisory committee on American politics). *Awards, honors:* National Science Foundation grant, 1973 (for study in Budapest, Hungary), 1977-79; senior Fulbright scholar in Australia 1978; grant from Russell Sage Foundation, 1979-81.

WRITINGS: Alienation and the Social System, Wiley, 1972. Contributor and member of editorial board of *American Journal of Political Science,* 1971-75, *Sex Roles: A Journal of Research,* 1975-79, *American Political Science Review,* 1976—, *American Politics Quarterly,* 1978—, and *Political Behavior,* 1979—.

WORK IN PROGRESS: A survey study of American migrants to Australia, with husband, Bernard M. Finifter; continuing research on alienation from the American political system, and its consequences.

SIDELIGHTS: Finifter told *CA:* "My major research interest is in the interaction between individuals and the social systems in which they live, particularly in democratic political systems. To this end, I have studied people's attitudes toward their political systems and the conditions under which they freely choose to live in other societies. These studies are designed to illuminate the nature of the bonds that tie individuals to their social and political systems."

*   *   *

FIRBANK, (Arthur Annesley) Ronald   1886-1926

BRIEF ENTRY: Born January 17, 1886, in London, England; died May 21, 1926, in Rome, Italy. English novelist, playwright, and short story writer. Born to a wealthy family, Firbank was educated by private tutors until past the age of fourteen. He attended Cambridge beginning in 1906, and there adopted the lifestyle of a leisured aesthete. In 1908 Firbank converted to Catholicism, and after leaving Cambridge without a degree in 1909, he toyed with the idea of seeking a post with the Vatican. Instead he settled in London, adopting the pose of a literary and artistic man-about-town. Noted as a personality as much as a writer, Firbank is often compared to his contemporary Frederick Rolfe because the two men shared certain interests, including Catholicism, medievalism, and homosexuality. Although concerned with the dilemma of the hypersensitive individual isolated and destroyed by a depraved world, Firbank treated his dreary themes with wit and satiric gaiety. Having little in the way of plot development, his novels often feature exotic settings and are filled with quotes from imaginary sources and history. His best-known works include *Vainglory* (1915), *Inclinations* (1916), *The Flower Beneath the Foot* (1924), and *Sorrow in Sunlight* (1924; published as *Prancing Nigger* in 1925). *Biographical/critical sources: Twentieth Century Authors: A Biographical Dictionary of Modern Literature*, H. W. Wilson, 1942; *Encyclopedia of World Literature in the Twentieth Century*, updated edition, Ungar, 1967; *Twentieth Century Writing: A Reader's Guide to Contemporary Literature*, Transatlantic, 1969; *Twentieth-Century Literary Criticism*, Volume 1, Gale, 1978.

* * *

FISHER, A(rnold) Garth   1933-

PERSONAL: Born May 18, 1933, in Orem, Utah; son of Byron P. and Cecil (Mann) Fisher; married Geraldine Rollo, December 29, 1953; children: Charlene Fisher Pelton, Randy, Clark, Karin, Jamie (deceased). *Education:* College of Southern Utah, A.S., 1953; Brigham Young University, B.S., 1955; Sacramento State College, M.A., 1965; University of New Mexico, Ph.D., 1969. *Religion:* Church of Jesus Christ of Latter-day Saints (Mormons). *Home:* 549E 3750 N., Provo, Utah 84601. *Office:* Department of Physical Education, Brigham Young University, RB116, Provo, Utah 84602.

CAREER: Brigham Young University, Provo, Utah, assistant professor, 1969-71, associate professor, 1971-76, professor of physical education, 1976—. *Military service:* U.S. Air Force, 1956-65; served in Vietnam; received Air Medal. *Member:* American Association for Health, Physical Education, Recreation, and Dance (research chairman of southwest district), American College of Sports Medicine (fellow). *Awards, honors:* Maeser Award from Brigham Young University, 1981.

WRITINGS: (With Wayne R. Jensen) *The Scientific Basis of Athletic Conditioning*, Lea & Febiger, 1972, 2nd edition, 1979; *Your Heart Rate: The Key to Real Fitness*, Brigham Young University Press, 1976; (with Robert K. Conlee) *The Complete Book of Physical Fitness*, Brigham Young University Press, 1979; (with Phillip E. Allsen) *Jogging*, W. C. Brown, 1980. Author of "Stay Fit for Life." a weekly column in *Deseret News*. Contributor to scientific journals.

WORK IN PROGRESS: Research on exercise and cardiovascular function as evaluated by echo cardiography and on weight control and exercise.

SIDELIGHTS: Fisher told *CA:* "With regard to writing, I find that organizing throughout on a sheet of paper helps me tie the whole thing together. I am surely a better teacher because of my writing. With regard to exercise, I am more and more convinced that everyone needs it. Our research has shown positive effects in almost every aspect of health. In fact, weight control seems almost impossible without exercise."

* * *

FISHER, Ameel J(oseph)   1909-

PERSONAL: Born June 16, 1909, in Wilmington, N.C.; son of A.K. and Selma (Malouf) Fisher; married Ann McCormack, November 29, 1942. *Education:* Attended University of North Carolina, 1927-28, University of State of New York (now State University of New York), 1933-34. *Politics:* Independent. *Home and office:* 6 Stuyvesant Oval, New York, N.Y. 10009.

CAREER: Jacksonville Journal, Jacksonville, Fla., reporter, 1929-30; *Brooklyn Eagle,* Brooklyn, N.Y. reporter, 1931-32; *Commerce & Industry,* New York City, writer, 1933; Gags, Inc., New York City, managing editor, 1933-34; radio dramatist and free-lance writer, 1935-42; United Press International, New York City, writer and editor, 1945-51; correspondent for United Press Movietone (now United Press International Television News), 1952-74. Notable assignments include coverage of national political conventions, racial disturbances and riots, the influx of Cubans into Miami, and the space program. *Military service:* U.S. Army Air Force, 1942-45; served in aviation engineer command; became sergeant; received Bronze Star. *Member:* Writers Guild of America, American Federation of Television and Radio Artists. *Awards, honors:* Award from New York Press Club, 1968, for distinguished television news coverage.

WRITINGS—Television plays: "Stage of the Dead," 1978; "Buried Treasure," 1979.

Contributor of radio plays to numerous programs, including "That Strange Mr. Pertwee," "Tonight's Best Story," "Great Men in History," "Lives of Great Composers," "Gang Busters," and "Famous Jury Trials." Contributor to periodicals, including *National Enquirer, Eagle,* and *Cavalier.*

WORK IN PROGRESS: Mr. Pertwee—the Reluctant Thaumaturge, a fantasy adapted from the radio plays; a second volume featuring Wilbur Pertwee; research for a book on the Middle East, "with emphasis on the biased reporting by the American press and the incredible attitude of the U.S. Government and Washington politicians in bowing to the strongest pressure group in the nation."

SIDELIGHTS: Fisher told *CA:* "Two distinct feelings, literally a world apart, dominate my thinking as regards writing. One is the crushing reality of the times—persistent and ever recurring wars, the hatreds, the hypocrisy of governments, the attempted and successful 255 assassinations—witness the string from John F. Kennedy, George Wallace, and Gerald Ford, to President Reagan and Pope John Paul II; and the inability of virtually every country to cope with crime and the breakdown of the social fabric. And at the other end of the spectrum is the world of make-believe, or fantasy. For me, each of these opposites—realism and fantasy—hold a fascination that is reflected in my past and projected writings. Thus, the two are combined in the person of Wilbur Pertwee, the protagonist of a dramatized series I wrote and which is now adapted in story form. Though Will Pertwee himself is a down-to-earth no nonsense, withal timid type, he becomes involved in a succession of incredible events that bring him an unwanted notoriety. As the title implies, these flights of fancy are not of his own making, and in many instances represent his attempt to escape from the world of reality."

BIOGRAPHICAL/CRITICAL SOURCES: Frank Buxton, *Radio's Golden Age,* Viking, 1966.

* * *

FISHER, Barbara   1940-
(Barbara Fisher Perry)

PERSONAL: Born December 10, 1940, in New York, N.Y.; daughter of David (an attorney) and Regina (Mandel) Fisher; married Ernest Perry, September 23, 1967 (divorced, 1980); children: Athelantis. *Education:* Hunter College of the City University of New York, B.A., 1962. *Home and office:* 799 Greenwich St., New York, N.Y. 10014. *Agent:* Philip G. Spitzer Literary Agency, 111-25 76th Ave., Forest Hills, N.Y. 11375.

CAREER: Dauntless Books, Inc., New York City, editorial assistant, 1962-63; Academic Press, Inc., New York City, writer in promotion department, 1963-64; Chelsea Theater Center, New York City, director of research and development, 1966-68; Ten Penny Players, New York City, co-director and editor of publications, 1967—. Manager and fiscal director of 799 Greenwich Street Tenants Corp., 1972—; fundraiser for Institutes for the Achievement of Human Potential, 1974-76; fiscal director of New York Book Fair, 1978—; co-director of Waterways Project. Instructor at workshops; consultant to New York State Narcotics Control Commission. *Awards, honors:* Grants from New York State Council on the Arts, 1970, Rockefeller Brothers Fund, 1970, International Business Machines, 1971, and William C. Whitney Fund, 1972.

WRITINGS: (Under name Barbara Fisher Perry) *Care Without Care,* Avon, 1970; (contributor) *More Than a Gathering of Dreamers,* Coordinating Council of Literary Magazines, 1981.

Author of "Noisy City Sam" (one-act play for children), first produced in New York City, at Clinton Park, July, 1970.

Contributor to magazines. Co-editor with Richard Spiegel of *Foreward Face,* Cranio-Facial Unit of University Hospital, New York. Also co-editor of "Nutrition Awareness Program," a series of books and materials; a newsletter for Active New York City Committee on the Handicapped Parent, Educational Advocacy, with Spiegel; and *Waterways,* 1979—.

WORK IN PROGRESS: Adah Isaacs Menken; revised edition of *Care Without Care,* with supplement on educational advocacy; a resource book for parents and professionals.

SIDELIGHTS: Barbara Fisher commented: "I am a patients' rights and educational rights advocate and resource person for people who need help in these areas. When possible we do our own letterpress printing and are active in the small press movement and the populist poetry movement, believing books and poetry should be accessible to all. I am animal, child, and people oriented.

"Given education, training, and support systems people can exercise more control over their lives. Educational and health care decisions must be shared by the persons directly affected *and* by the professionals. Literature and the arts similarly can be experienced by the laymen. The arts don't have to be elitist, almost mystical experiences removed from the everyday experience of 'ordinary' people. As an educational and health care advocate I help train, initiate programs for, and advocate for, when necessary, people who have yet to find their personal voice. As a publisher involved in the Populist Poetry movement I want to share with the reading public the dissimilar voices of people who care about extending themselves and their ideas through the printed and performed word. In my own writing (fiction, nonfiction, poetry or drama), I try to use English clearly and with rhythm and beauty so that the reader can understand what I am saying and empathize as well."

BIOGRAPHICAL/CRITICAL SOURCES: Human Behavior, May, 1978; *Tub,* Volume II, number 1, 1978.

*   *   *

FISHER, Wesley Andrew 1944-

PERSONAL: Born October 23, 1944, in New York, N.Y.; son of Mitchell Salem (an attorney) and Esther (a marriage and divorce counselor; maiden name, Oshiver) Fisher; married Regine Rayevsky (an interpreter), September 15, 1979; children: Maxim. *Education:* Harvard University, A.B. (magna cum laude), 1966; attended Moscow State University, 1970-71; Columbia University, Certificate of the Russian Institute, 1976,

M.Phil., 1976, Ph.D. (with distinction), 1976. *Religion:* Jewish. *Office:* 1206 International Affairs, Columbia University, New York, N.Y. 10027.

CAREER: Columbia University, New York City, instructor, 1972-76, assistant professor of sociology, 1976—, associate chairman of sociology department, 1980—, representative to the International Research and Exchanges Board, 1971—. Guest lecturer at Foreign Service Institute, U.S. Department of State, 1976; visiting scholar at Center for the Study of Population Problems, Moscow State University, 1976-77; guest lecturer at Tartu University, 1978; visiting lecturer at New School for Social Research, 1978-79. Interpreter and translator for American Council of Learned Societies and U.S.S.R. Academy of Sciences joint commission in the social sciences and humanities, 1975—; consultant and translator for W. W. Norton & Co. and Random House, 1977; interpreter and escort for U.S. Department of State; interpreter and administrator for visiting Soviet scholars, writers, and officials. Managing editor for sociology and education for *Soviet Union,* 1979—. Member of the admissions committee for the Leningrad University semester program for the Council on International Education, 1975; member of the selection committee of the International Research and Exchanges Board, 1979. Organizer of symposia.

MEMBER: New York Association for New Americans (member of board of directors, 1979—), Phi Beta Kappa, Harvard Club. *Awards, honors:* Grants from International Research and Exchanges Board, 1970-71, 1976-77, and 1978; Fulbright fellow, 1970-71, research grant, 1976-77.

WRITINGS: (Editor with Murray Yanowitch, and translator) *Social Stratification and Mobility in the U.S.S.R.,* International Arts and Sciences Press, 1973; (with Lynn Fisher) *The Moscow Gourmet: Dining Out in the Capital of the U.S.S.R.,* Ardis, 1974; *The Soviet Marriage Market: Mate Selection in Russia and the U.S.S.R.,* Praeger, 1980.

Contributor: *Russian and Soviet Studies: A Handbook for Graduate Students,* American Association for the Advancement of Slavic Studies, 1973; Joachim Baer and Norman Ingham, editors, *Studia litteraria russica in honorem V. Setchkarev,* Wilhelm Fink Verlag, 1974; William Welsh, editor, *Survey Research and Public Attitudes in the U.S.S.R. and Eastern Europe,* Pergamon, 1981. Editor of restaurant section of *Information Moscow.* Contributor of articles, translations, and reviews to scholarly journals and newspapers, including *Opera News, Slavic Review,* and *Social Science Quarterly.*

WORK IN PROGRESS: Research on Soviet society and on family life in the Soviet Union.

*   *   *

FitzGERALD, Brian Seymour Vesey
See VESEY-FitzGERALD, Brian Seymour

*   *   *

FITZHUGH, Robert Tyson 1906-1981

OBITUARY NOTICE: Born August 15, 1906, in Baltimore, Md.; died September 22, 1981, in Hudson, N.Y. Educator and author. Fitzhugh was a professor of English at the University of Maryland, Lehigh University, and Brooklyn College of the City University of New York. He wrote a handbook on writing and two books on Robert Burns, including *Robert Burns: The Man and the Poet.* Obituaries and other sources: *Directory of American Scholars: Volume II: English, Speech, and Drama,* 7th edition, Bowker, 1978; *New York Times,* September 24, 1981.

FLANAGAN, Dorothy Belle
See HUGHES, Dorothy B(elle)

*   *   *

FLANNERY, Peter   1951-

PERSONAL: Born October 12, 1951, in Jarrow, England; son of Andrew and Anne Flannery. *Education:* University of Manchester, B.A., 1973. *Home:* 10 Main Rd., Langley, Cheshire, England. *Agent:* Harvey Unna and Stephen Durbridge, 14 Beaumont Mews, London W1N 4HE, England.

CAREER: Worked as actor, stage manager, singer, and director, 1974-76; resident dramatist at Royal Shakespeare Co., 1979-80; playwright. Member of drama panel of North West Arts Association, 1980——. *Member:* Theatre Writers Union. *Awards, honors:* Award for best new play from *London Times,* 1978, for "Savage Amusement"; Thames Television Playwright Award, 1979; Writer's Bursary from Arts Council, 1980.

WRITINGS—Published plays: *Savage Amusement* (two-act; first produced in London by Royal Shakespeare Co., 1978), Rex Collings, 1978; *Heartbreak Hotel* (two-act; first produced in Manchester at Contact Theatre, 1975), Woodhouse Books, 1979; (with Mick Ford) *The Adventures of Awful Knawful* (two-act; first produced in London by Royal Shakespeare Co., 1978), Methuen, 1980.

Unpublished plays: "Last Resort" (one-act), first produced in London at Sidewalk Theatre, 1976; "Are You With Me?" (one-act), first produced in Nottingham by Nottingham Playhouse Roundabout Co., 1977; "The Boy's Own Story" (one-act), first produced in Manchester at RAT Theatre, 1978; "Jungle Music" (two-act), first produced in Manchester at Contract Theatre, 1979; "Our Friends in the North" (five-act), first produced in Stratford-upon-Avon by Royal Shakespeare Co., 1982.

Also author of television film "Joy Ride," broadcast by Granada Television, 1980.

WORK IN PROGRESS: A play about political extremism; a play about the destruction of culture.

*   *   *

FLETCHER, Angus (John Stewart)   1930-

PERSONAL: Born June 23, 1930, in New York, N.Y. *Education:* Yale University, B.A., 1950, M.A., 1952; University of Grenoble, diploma, 1951; Harvard University, Ph.D., 1958. *Home:* 20 West 64th St., New York, N.Y. 10023. *Office:* Herbert H. Lehman College of the City University of New York, Bronx, N.Y. 10468.

CAREER: Cornell University, Ithaca, N.Y., instructor in English literature, 1958-62; Columbia University, New York City, 1962-68, began as assistant professor became associate professor; State University of New York at Buffalo, professor, 1968-74; Herbert H. Lehman College of the City University of New York, New York City, distinguished professor of English and comparative literature, 1974——. Visiting professor at University of California, Los Angeles, 1973-74; distinguished professor at Graduate Center of the City University of New York, 1974——; Dreyfuss Visiting Professor of Humanities at California Institute of Technology, 1977-78. *Member:* Renaissance Society of America, English Institute, Modern Language Association of America.

WRITINGS: Allegory: The Theory of a Symbolic Mode, Cornell University Press, 1964; *The Transcendental Masque: An Essay on Milton's Comus,* Cornell University Press, 1971; *The Prophetic Moment: An Essay on Spenser,* University of Chicago Press, 1971; *Positive Negation: Threshold, Sequence, and Personification in Coleridge,* English Institute, 1972; *I. Richards and the Art of Critical Balance,* Oxford University Press, 1973; *Allegory: Dictionary of the History of Ideas,* Scribner, 1973; (editor and author of foreword) *The Literature of Fact: Selected Papers From the English Institute,* Columbia University Press, 1976. Contributor to literature journals.*

*   *   *

FLORIT, Eugenio   1903-

PERSONAL: Birth-given name, Eugenio Florit y Sanchez de Fuentes; born October 15, 1903, in Madrid, Spain; came to the United States in 1940, naturalized citizen, 1960; son of Ricardo (a law clerk) and Maria (a poet; maiden name, Sanchez de Fuentes) Florit. *Education:* Instituto La Habana, B.A., 1922; University of Havana, LL.D., 1926. *Home:* 440 Riverside Dr., New York, N.Y. 10027.

CAREER: Official in Cuban Exterior Ministry, 1927-40; Cuban Consular Service, New York City, consular official, 1940-45; Columbia University, New York City, instructor, 1942-45, professor at Barnard College, 1945-69, professor emeritus of Spanish, 1969. Taught at Spanish summer school of Middlebury College, Vermont, 1944-64. *Member:* Academia Norteamericana de la Lengua Espanola, Hispanic Society of America, Modern Language Association. *Awards, honors:* Mitre Medal from Hispanic Society of America, 1969; Prize of Literature from Institute of Puerto Rico, New York City, 1972.

WRITINGS—In English: (Editor) *Invitation to Spanish Poetry,* Dover, 1965; (editor and translator) *Spanish Poetry: A Selection From the Cantar de Mio Cid to Miguel Hernandez,* Dover, 1971.

In Spanish; all poetry: *Treinta y dos poemas breves* (title means "Thirty-two Short Poems"), [Havana], 1927; *Tropico* (title means "Tropic"), Revista de Avance, 1930; *Doble acento* (title means "Double Accent"), Editorial Ucacia, 1937; *Reino* (title means "Kingdom"), Ucar, Garcia, 1938; *Cuatro poemas de Eugenio Florit* (title means "Four Poems by Eugenio Florit"), Ucar, Garcia, 1940; *Poema mio* (title means "My Poems"), Letras de Mexico, 1947; (editor and translator) *Antologia de la poesia norteamericana contemporanea* (title means "Anthology of Contemporary North American Poetry"), Union Panamericana, 1955; *Asonante final, y otros poemas* (title means "Last Assonant, and Other Poems"), Origenes, 1955; *Alfonso Reyes: La poesia* (title means "The Poetry of Alfonso Reyes"), Hispanic Institute in the United States, 1956; *Antologia poetica (1930-1955)* (title means "An Anthology of My Poems"), prologue by Andres Iduarte, Instituto Internacional de Literatura Ibero-Americana, 1956.

(With Enrique Anderson Imbert) *Literatura hispanoamericana: Antologia e introduccion historica* (title means "Spanish American Literature: Anthology and Historical Introduction"), Holt, 1960; *Siete poemas* (title means "Seven Poems"), Cuadernos Julio Herrera y Reissig, 1960; *Tres autos religiosos* (title means "Three Religious Short Plays"), Palma de Mallorca, 1960; (with Beatrice P. Patt) *Retratos de Hispanoamerica* (title means "Portraits of Spanish America"), Holt, 1962; (editor) *Cien de las mejores poesias espanolas* (title means "One Hundred of the Best Spanish Poems"), Las Americas, 1965; *Habito de esperanza: poemas, 1936-1964* (title means "A Cloak of Hope, 1936-1964"), Insula, 1965; (editor and author of introduction and notes) Federico Garcia Lorca, *Obras escogidas* (title means "Selected Works"), Dell, 1965; *Concordancias de la obra poetica de Eugenio Florit* (title means "Concordancias of the Poetical Works of Eugenio Florit"), edited by Alice M. Pollin, New York University Press, 1967; (compiler with Jose Olivio Jimenez) *La poesia hispanoamericana desde el modernismo* (title means "Spanish American Poetry Since Modernism"), Appleton-Century-Crofts, 1968.

Antologia penultima (title means "Penultimate Anthology"), Editorial Plenitude, 1970; (editor) *Antologia poetica (1898-1953)* (title means "An Anthology of Poems (1898-1953)"), Editorial Biblioteca Nueva, 1971; *De tiempo y agonia* (title means "Of Time and Agony"), introduction by Amelia Agostini de del Rio, Roberto Esquenazi-Mayo, and Jose Olivio Jimenez, Ediciones de la Revista de Occidente, 1974; *Poesia casi siempre: Ensayos literarios* (title means "Mostly Poetry: Literary Essays"), Mensaje, 1978; *Poesia en Jose Marti, Juan Ramon Jimenez, Alfonso Reyes, Federico Garcia Lorca y Pablo Neruda: Cinco ensayos* (title means "The Poetry of Jose Marti, Juan Ramon Jimenez, Alfonso Reyes, Federico Garcia Lorca, and Pablo Neruda: Five Essays"), Ediciones Universal, 1978; *Versos pequenos (1938-1975)* [title means "Short Poems (1938-1975)"], El Marco, 1979. Editor of *Revista Hispanica Moderna*, 1960-69.

AVOCATIONAL INTERESTS: Music, painting.

BIOGRAPHICAL/CRITICAL SOURCES: Stanley Burnshaw, *The Poem Itself*, Holt, 1960; *Hispania*, May, 1969, May, 1972, September, 1972; Eugenio Florit, *Antologia Penultima*, prologue by Jose Olivio Jimenez, Editorial Plenitude, 1970.

*   *   *

FOISIE, Jack 1919-

PERSONAL: Born April 21, 1919, in Seattle, Wash.; son of Francis Patrick (a labor relations negotiator) and Winifred Amanda (Shaw) Foisie; married Florence Mildred McTighe (an artist), April 8, 1944; children: Kathleen Florence, Franklin Sean, Patricia Abbie. *Education:* Attended University of Washington, 1938-39, and University of California, Berkeley, 1940-41. *Address:* P.O. Box 5660, Johannesburg 2000, South Africa. *Office:* Los Angeles Times, Foreign Bureau, Times Mirror Square, Los Angeles, Calif. 90053.

CAREER/WRITINGS: San Francisco Chronicle, San Francisco, Calif., reporter, 1940, and 1945-64; Los Angeles Times, Los Angeles, Calif., bureau chief in Saigon, South Vietnam, 1964-66, Bangkok, Thailand, 1966-74, Cairo, Egypt, 1974-76, and Johannesburg, South Africa, 1976—. Notable assignments include coverage of Korean War and Vietnam War. Contributor to periodicals, including *Saturday Evening Post*. Technical advisor on motion picture "The Story of G. I. Joe," 1944. *Military service:* U.S. Army, 1941-45; received Legion of Merit. *Awards, honors:* Nieman fellowship, 1946-47; award from Overseas Press Club, 1966.

SIDELIGHTS: Foisie told *CA:* "How did I become involved in war coverage? After being part of a disastrous defeat of the U.S. First Armoured Division at Kasserine Pass on the Algerian-Tunisia border in the first large-scale action between American and German forces in World War II, I enlarged on my pre-draft copyboy experience on the *San Francisco Chronicle,* and so gained a transfer to the military paper, *Stars and Stripes,* then publishing in Algiers. I was a combat correspondent for the rest of the war. Although I am no war lover, as I hasten to assure my wife and children, I seem to spend considerable time (first for the *Chronicle* and now the *Los Angeles Times*), reporting conflicts."

FONSTAD, Karen Wynn 1945-

PERSONAL: Born April 18, 1945, in Oklahoma City, Okla.; daughter of James E. (a painting contractor) and Estis (a secretary; maiden name, Wampler) Wynn; married Todd A. Fonstad (an associate professor of geography), March 21, 1970; children: Mark, Kristina. *Education:* University of Oklahoma, B.S., 1967, M.A., 1971. *Home:* 737 Wright St., Oshkosh, Wis. 54901.

CAREER: University of Oklahoma, Norman, staff therapist at infirmary, 1967-68, senior therapist at Medical Center, 1969-71; Mercy Medical Center, Oshkosh, Wis., staff therapist, 1971; University of Wisconsin—Oshkosh, instructor in geography, 1972; Mercy Medical Center staff therapist, 1974; University of Wisconsin—Oshkosh, instructor in geography, 1977. Member of Oshkosh City Plan Commission, 1974—, vice-chairman, 1978—. *Member:* National Council for Geographic Education, Association of American Geographers, Wisconsin Council for Geographic Education (publications editor, 1972-74, 1980-82).

WRITINGS: The Atlas of Middle-earth, Houghton, 1981.

WORK IN PROGRESS: Research on alternatives for financing central business district "free-to-the-customer" parking.

SIDELIGHTS: Karen Fonstad wrote: "The marvelous thing about being a housewife who is 'unemployed' (and likes being so) is the possibility to pursue whatever strikes me as interesting at the moment. I do not consider myself an author. I did not write *The Atlas of Middle-earth* for the sake of royalties (nice as they are), but rather to satisfy my own wish to do it. Most of my projects are like that; hence, my civic involvement in an unpaid and unsung position. One fellow who interviewed me interpreted my position as a 'free-lance cartographer with emphasis on the *free!*'—a most appropriate description of my attitude. Some of my most rewarding time has been spent doing paintings for my church and research for committees."

BIOGRAPHICAL/CRITICAL SOURCES: St. Louis Post-Gazette, May 31, 1981; *Christian Science Monitor,* June 10, 1981; *Milwaukee Sentinel,* June 29, 1981; *Los Angeles,* July 5, 1981.

*   *   *

FORD, Ford Madox 1873-1939

BRIEF ENTRY: Birth-given name, Ford Madox Hueffer; name legally changed in 1919; born December 17, 1873, in Merton, Surrey, England; died June 26, 1939, in Deauville, France. English novelist, poet, critic, and editor. Noted as much for his literary associations as for his contributions to the development of technique in the novel, Ford was born into a pre-Raphaelite family of artists and writers and began writing before he was twenty. A friend of Joseph Conrad, Ford helped the author master English while learning from him the technique of impressionism. The two authors eventually collaborated on three novels, *The Inheritors* (1901), *Romance* (1903), and *The Nature of Crime* (1924). In 1908 Ford founded and edited *The English Review,* a journal whose contributors included James Wells, D. H. Lawrence, John Galsworthy, and Thomas Hardy. Unfortunate marital circumstances and service in World War I provided Ford with the material for his best and most famous works. *The Good Soldier: A Tale of Passion* (1915) and a tetralogy of novels, eventually published as *Parade's End* (1950), demonstrate Ford's innovative techniques in the areas of point-of-view and timeshift. In 1924 he founded the *transatlantic review* in Paris and introduced the work of

James Joyce and Ernest Hemingway. He also became the center of a literary group that included Gertrude Stein and Ezra Pound. In 1927 he became professor of comparative literature at Olivet College in Michigan and spent the rest of his life in the United States and France. Among his other works are *Joseph Conrad: A Personal Remembrance* (1924) and *Portraits From Life: Memories and Criticisms* (1937). *Biographical/critical sources: Encyclopedia of World Literature in the Twentieth Century,* updated edition, Ungar, 1967; *Twentieth Century Writing: A Reader's Guide to Contemporary Literature,* Transatlantic, 1969; *Webster's New World Companion to English and American Literature,* World Publishing, 1973; *Twentieth-Century Literary Criticism,* Volume 1, Gale, 1978.

*   *   *

FORD, Webster
   See MASTERS, Edgar Lee

*   *   *

FORTNUM, Peggy
   See NUTTALL-SMITH, Margaret Emily Noel

*   *   *

FORZANO, Giovacchino   1884-1970

OBITUARY NOTICE: Born in 1884 in Borgo San Lorenzo, Italy; died in October, 1970, in Rome, Italy. Playwright, librettist, newspaper editor, and stage and screen director. Forzano achieved popular acclaim with his witty, varied, and inventive stage successes of the 1920's. Among his works of this period are "Sly," based on Shakespeare's character Christopher Sly, and "Gutlibi," about a Senegalese boxer involved in Bolshevik politics. In addition to his light comedies, Forzano wrote several historical dramas based on the French Revolution, including "Il conte de Brechard" and "Campo di Maggio" (adapted as "Napoleon, the Hundred Days"). Despite such plays, however, Forzano was often criticized for the lack of seriousness in his work. He was also active in opera, writing librettos for Puccini, Mascagni, Lehar, and other composers. Forzano is remembered, too, for his collaborations on several plays with Mussolini. Obituaries and other sources: *Columbia Dictionary of Modern European Literature,* Columbia University Press, 1947; *The Concise Encyclopedia of Modern Drama,* Horizon Press, 1964; *New York Times,* October 29, 1970; *Time,* November 9, 1970; *Opera,* December 5, 1970.

*   *   *

FOSS, Dennis C(arleton)   1947-

PERSONAL: Born April 27, 1947, in Boston, Mass.; son of George W. (a manufacturer) and Jean Foss. *Education:* Bates College, B.A. (with honors), 1970; University of New Hampshire, M.A., 1972, Ph.D., 1976. *Home:* 3233 South Third St., Springfield, Ill. 62703. *Office:* Office of the Vice-President for Academic Affairs, Sangamon State University, Springfield, Ill. 62708.

CAREER: Sangamon State University, Springfield, Ill., assistant professor, 1975-81, associate professor of sociology, 1981—, vice-president for academic affairs and dean of faculty, 1981—. *Member:* American Sociological Association, Eastern Sociological Society.

WRITINGS: (With Richard G. Dumont) *The American View of Death: Acceptance or Denial?,* Schenkman, 1972; (contributor) Luis Lenero-Otero, editor, *Beyond the Nuclear Family*

Model, Sage Publications, 1977; *The Value Controversy in Sociology: A New Orientation for the Profession,* Jossey-Bass, 1977. Contributor to sociology journals.

WORK IN PROGRESS: Research on social psychology of loneliness, cybernetics systems theory, and educational administration.

SIDELIGHTS: Foss wrote: "*The American View of Death* was motivated by the fact that little social psychological research had been done on death; this was a comparatively unexplored area. *The Value Controversy in Sociology* is a central issue within the field that any sociologist needs to grapple with, and one systematic way of doing it is presented in the book. One should think early about value choices one makes, so as not to end up disappointed with achievements or accomplishments. I am interested in areas of inquiry where there is heavy debate or controversy, for out of this creativity arises."

*   *   *

FOSTER, Jeanne Robert (Ollivier)   1884-1970

OBITUARY NOTICE: Born March 10, 1884, in Johnsburgh, N.Y.; died September 23, 1970, in Schenectady, N.Y. Poet and editor. Foster was literary editor of the *Review of Reviews* from 1910 to 1922 and American editor of the *Transatlantic Review.* Her books of poems include *Wild Apples, Neighbors of Yesterday,* and *Rock Flower.* She edited *The John Quinn Letters* in 1925. Obituaries and other sources: *New York Times,* September 25, 1970; *AB Bookman's Weekly,* October 26, 1970; *American Authors and Books, 1640 to the Present Day,* 3rd revised edition, Crown, 1972; *Who Was Who in America, With World Notables,* Volume V: *1969-1973,* Marquis, 1973.

*   *   *

FOSTER-HARRIS, William   1903(?)-1978

OBITUARY NOTICE: Born c. 1903; died May 19, 1978, in Norman, Okla. Educator and author. Foster-Harris was a professor and director of the Oklahoma University School of Professional Writing. He wrote *The Look of the Old West, Basic Formulas of Fiction, Patterns of Plot,* and more than nine hundred short stories. Foster-Harris received the Golden Saddleman Award from the Western Writers of America in 1974. Obituaries and other sources: *AB Bookman's Weekly,* July 10, 1978.

*   *   *

FOURNIER, Henri Alban   1886-1914
   (Alain-Fournier)

BRIEF ENTRY: Born October 3, 1886, in La Chapelle-d'Angillon, France; killed in action, September 22, 1914, in Bois Saint-Remy, France. French journalist, poet, and novelist. Alain-Fournier's fame is due to the one novel the author published before he was killed early in World War I. This novel, *Le Grand Meaulnes* (1913; translation published as *The Wanderer,* 1928, and as *The Lost Domain,* 1959), presents a nostalgic quest on the part of the central character, who tries to recapture the lost love and lost dreams of his youth. The dream-like, wistful novel is based upon a romantic episode in the author's own life. The novel is characterized by a simple, uncomplicated style and an intense, lyrical tone. By 1920 the novel had gained critical attention and had become immensely popular, influencing fiction written between the two world wars. A collection of Alain-Fournier's poems and prose poems, *Miracles,* was published posthumously in 1924. Several volumes of his correspondence were also published, allowing critics insight into an author whose untimely death, it is believed, cut short a life of great literary promise. *Biographical/critical sources: Twentieth Century Authors: A Biographical Dictionary of Modern Literature,* H. W. Wilson, 1942; *Cyclopedia of World Authors,* Harper, 1958; *The Oxford Companion to French Literature,* corrected edition, Clarendon Press, 1966; *Encyclopedia of World Literature in the Twentieth Century,* updated edition, Ungar, 1967; *Cassell's Encyclopaedia of World Literature,* revised edition, Morrow, 1973.

*   *   *

FOWLER, James W(iley) III 1940-
(Jim Fowler)

PERSONAL: Born October 12, 1940, in Reidsville, N.C.; son of James W., Jr. (a Methodist minister) and Lucille (Haworth) Fowler; married Lurline P. Locklair (a minister of education), July 7, 1962; children: Joan, Margaret. *Education:* Duke University, B.A., 1962; Drew Theological Seminary, B.D. (magna cum laude), 1965; Harvard University, Ph.D., 1971, postdoctoral study, 1973. *Home:* 2740 Janellen Dr. N.E., Atlanta, Ga. 30345. *Office:* Candler School of Theology, Emory University, Atlanta, Ga. 30322.

CAREER: Interpreters' House, Lake Junaluska, N.C., associate director, 1968-69; Harvard University, Divinity School, Cambridge, Mass., director of continuing education and lecturer in the department of the church, 1969-71, assistant professor and chairperson, 1971-74, associate professor of applied theology and director of research project on faith and moral development, 1974-76; Boston College, Chestnut Hill, Mass., associate professor of theology and human development, 1976-77; Emory University, Atlanta, Ga., professor and director of Center for Faith Development, 1977—. Associate in education at Harvard University, 1977—; coordinator of International Symposium on Moral and Faith Development, Abbye de Senanque, France, 1979; lecturer at conferences and institutions in the United States and abroad. Member of Town Meeting, Arlington, Mass., 1972-77, chairman of park and recreation commissions, 1974-77.

MEMBER: American Academy of Religion, Religious Education Association, Phi Beta Kappa. *Awards, honors:* Joseph P. Kennedy, Jr., Foundation grant, 1974-76; distinguished teaching award from Associated Alumni of Harvard Divinity School, 1976.

WRITINGS: To See the Kingdom: The Theological Vision of H. Richard Niebuhr, Abingdon, 1974; (under name Jim Fowler; with Sam Keen) *Life Maps: Conversations on the Journey of Faith,* Word, Inc., 1978; (with Robin Lovin and others) *Trajectories in Faith: Five Life Studies,* Abingdon, 1979; (with Antoine Vergote and others) *Toward Moral and Religious Maturity,* Silver Burdett, 1980; *Stages of Faith: The Psychology of Human Development and the Quest for Meaning,* Harper, 1981.

Contributor: Thomas Hennessey, editor, *Values and Moral Education,* Paulist Press, 1976; G. Durka and A. Smith, editors, *Emerging Issues in Religious Education,* Paulist Press, 1976; Francis Eigo, editor, *From Alienation to At-Oneness,* Villanova University Press, 1977; M. Sawicki and B. Marthaler, editors, *Catechesis: Realities and Visions,* U.S. Catholic Conference, 1977; J. Moltman and others, *Hope for the Church,* Abingdon, 1979; (author of foreword) Carlyle Marney, *The Recovery of the Person,* 2nd edition, Abingdon, 1979; Brenda Munnsell, editor, *Kohlberg and Moral Education: Basic Issues in Philosophy, Psychology, Religion, and Education,* Religious Education Press, 1980.

Contributor of articles and reviews to various religious magazines and journals, including *Religious Education, Journal of Religion, Christian Century, Religion in Life,* and *Perkins Journal.*

WORK IN PROGRESS: Becoming Adult, Becoming Christian; Carlyle Marney, Giant Pilgrim.

SIDELIGHTS: Fowler told *CA:* "My academic career unfolded as I sought to pursue issues that concerned and interested me most. It should not be surprising that interdisciplinary pursuits have claimed me; I was fated by commitment and interest to live in interaction between university and church, and I was inclined by my time, place, and circumstances of birth and early childhood to be one who lives on boundaries.

"My chief satisfaction as a teacher and writer has come from the way some early work I did on faith development, based on listening to some two hundred life stories at Interpreters' House, ignited the interests of a wide range of religious and non-religious folk. With some splendid associates across eight years, I have pursued research in this area. To my surprise, the resulting body of theory shows signs of becoming a field of inquiry itself. At Emory University we are founding the Center for Faith Development where this research will continue and where we will expand our work in the direction of experimentation—on behalf of church, education and counseling—with modes of formation and transformation in faith.

"My family is a key commitment and major source of joy in my life. Our two daughters continually pull me out of books and writing, reminding me of the vitality of music, dance, and horseback riding. My wife pursues a career that parallels mine and works with me at the challenging adventure of finding vitality in a lasting marriage. We have a retreat in the mountains of western North Carolina where, with friends, family, and in solitude, we periodically recover the rootedness in Spirit which gives purpose and power to our demanding lives."

BIOGRAPHICAL/CRITICAL SOURCES: Moral Education Forum, June, 1978.

*   *   *

FOWLER, Jim
See FOWLER, James W(iley) III

*   *   *

FOX, Fred 1903(?)-1981

OBITUARY NOTICE: Born c. 1903; died August 27, 1981, in Pasadena, Calif. Comic-strip artist and author. Fox entertained readers for more than thirty years with his comic strip "Freckles and His Friend." At the height of its popularity the syndicated cartoon, which never displayed Fox's byline, appeared in more than seven hundred newspapers. Fox also wrote for radio, television, motion pictures, and such entertainers as Groucho Marx. Obituaries and other sources: *Chicago Tribune,* September 2, 1981.

*   *   *

FRADDLE, Farragut
See MEARNS, David Chambers

*   *   *

FRANCK, Irene M(ary) 1941-

PERSONAL: Born March 14, 1941, in Albany, N.Y.; daughter

of Otto Charles (a postal clerk) and Pauline (an insurance agent; maiden name, Zuk) Franck; married David M. Brownstone (a writer), January 20, 1969. *Education:* State University of New York at Binghamton, B.A., 1962. *Agent:* Paul R. Reynolds, Inc., 12 East 41st St., New York, N.Y. 10017. *Office:* Hudson Group, Inc., 74 Memorial Plaza, Pleasantville, N.Y. 10570.

CAREER: Worked as English teacher in high schools in New York, 1962-63; L. W. Hayes Real Estate and Insurance, Binghamton, N.Y., office manager, 1963-65; New York Telephone Co., Albany, N.Y., chief operator, 1966-67; English teacher in high schools in New York, 1967-70; John Wiley & Sons, Inc., New York, N.Y., editor, 1970-79; Hudson Group, Inc. (independent group of writers and editors), Pleasantville, N.Y., principal and president, 1979—; writer. Folksinger in New York state, 1963-65. Member board of directors of Temeraire Enterprises, Inc. *Member:* Authors Guild, Organization of American Historians, Oral History Association.

WRITINGS: (With husband, David Brownstone, and Douglass Brownstone) *Island of Hope, Island of Tears* (oral history of Ellis Island), Rawson, Wade, 1979; (with David Brownstone) *The Van Nostrand Reinhold Investor's Dictionary*, Van Nostrand, 1980; (with David Brownstone) *The Van Nostrand Reinhold Real Estate Dictionary*, Van Nostrand, 1980; (with David Brownstone and Gorton Carruth) *The Van Nostrand Reinhold Dictionary of Business and Finance*, Van Nostrand, 1980; (with David Brownstone) *The Van Nostrand Reinhold Dictionary of Publishing*, Van Nostrand, 1981. Co-editor of *Film Review Digest*, 1975-77.

WORK IN PROGRESS: The Streets Were Paved With Dreams; Historical Encyclopedia of Occupations, publication by Facts on File expected in 1984.

* * *

FRANKENSTEIN, Alfred Victor   1906-1981

OBITUARY NOTICE—See index for *CA* sketch: Born October 5, 1906, in Chicago, Ill.; died of a heart attack, June 22, 1981, in San Francisco, Calif. Critic, educator, and author. Interested in American culture, Frankenstein concentrated on contemporary art and music criticism. He began his career as the assistant music critic of the *Chicago American* and then moved to the position of music critic for the *San Francisco Chronicle*, a post he held for thirty years. Frankenstein contributed criticism to many magazines, including *High Fidelity* and *Music America*, and he served as the program annotator for the San Francisco Symphony Orchestra. Often Frankenstein became involved in controversy when he would champion the local performers of San Francisco over internationally known talent. As a teacher and lecturer, Frankenstein was affiliated with Mills College, Stanford University, and the University of California in Berkeley. He also served as the curator of American art at the M. H. de Young Museum and at the University of California. His books include *After the Hunt, The Royal Visitors, A Modern Guide to Symphonic Literature, American Self-Portraits, Shirl Goedike*, and *Our Land, Our Sky, Our Water*. Obituaries and other sources: *New York Times*, June 24, 1981; *Time*, July 6, 1981.

* * *

FRANKLIN, Benjamin
See HASEK, Jaroslav (Matej Frantisek)

* * *

FRANKLIN, Jon Daniel   1942-

PERSONAL: Born January 13, 1942, in Enid, Okla.; son of Bejamin Max and Wilma (a copyreader; maiden name, Winburn) Franklin; married Nancy Creevan, December 12, 1959 (divorced, 1975); children: Teresa June, Catherine Cay. *Education:* University of Maryland, B.S. (with high honors), 1970. *Home and office address:* P.O. Box 814, Baltimore, Md. 21203. *Agent:* Greenburger-Acton Rights Associates, 17 Grove St., New York, N.Y. 10014.

CAREER: U.S. Navy, journalist in the Far East, 1959-67; *Prince Georges Post*, Hyattsville, Md., editor and reporter, 1967-70; *Baltimore Evening Sun*, Baltimore, Md., science writer, 1970-80. Visiting associate professor at Towson State University. Member of unit council of Newspaper Guild at Baltimore Sunpapers. *Member:* National Association of Science Writers, National Press Club, Maryland Press Club, Newspaper Guild. *Awards, honors:* James T. Grady Medal from American Chemical Society, 1975, for popularizing science; Pulitzer Prize for feature writing, 1979.

WRITINGS: (With Alan Doelp) *Shocktrauma* (nonfiction; Book-of-the-Month Club alternate selection), St. Martin's, 1980.

WORK IN PROGRESS: A book on brain surgery.

SIDELIGHTS: Shocktrauma describes the life-saving work performed by the Maryland Institute for Emergency Medical Services. The clinic specializes in treating accident victims suffering from shock, a deadly condition involving failure of the circulatory system.

* * *

FRANKLIN, (Stella Maraia Sarah) Miles   1879-1954
(Brent of Bin Bin)

BRIEF ENTRY: Born October 14, 1879, in Talbingo, Australia; died September 19, 1954, in Sydney, Australia. Australian novelist. Miles Franklin won widest acclaim for *All That Swagger* (1936), a novel exposing the isolation and emptiness of people in the Australian bush country. Her first successful book was *My Brilliant Career* (1901), which was hailed as the first truly Australian novel, compelling, sensitive, and true to life. It described pioneer life in the bush, depicting the gloomy atmosphere and discontented, often unlikable settlers so realistically that she alienated many readers. While visiting the United States, Franklin wrote *Some Everyday Folk and Dawn* (1909), dealing with the issue of women's suffrage. Critics contended that this book lacked the powerful sweep of her earlier writing; at the same time, though, they felt that this less depressing and more humorous work showed her increasing maturity as a writer. *Biographical/critical sources:* Ray Mathew, *Miles Franklin*, Lansdowne, 1963; Marjorie Barnard, *Miles Franklin*, Twayne, 1967; *The McGraw-Hill Encyclopedia of World Biography*, McGraw, 1973.

* * *

FRATER PERDURABO
See CROWLEY, Edward Alexander

* * *

FRAZETTA, Frank   1928-

PERSONAL: Born February 9, 1928, in Brooklyn, N.Y.; son of Alfred Frank and Mary (Prinz) Frazetta; married Eleanor Doris Kelly (manager of Frazetta Prints, Inc.); children: Frank, Bill, Holly Heidi. *Education:* Attended Brooklyn Academy of Fine Art. *Home and office address:* P.O. Box R, Marshalls Creek, Pa. 18335.

CAREER: Artist. Illustrator of comic strips, including "Johnny Comet" (title changed to "Ace McCoy"), 1952-53, "Flash Gordon," 1953, and "L'il Abner." Also illustrator of numerous covers of books, periodicals, and albums. Formerly associated with comic-book publishers, including Baily, Pines, Fawcett, and National. Founded Frazetta Prints, Inc. *Member:* National Cartoonists Association. *Awards, honors:* Two Hugo awards; four awards from Warren Publishers; and awards from other organizations and periodicals, including *Playboy*.

WRITINGS—Illustrator: *The Fantastic Art of Frank Frazetta*, Rufus Publications, 1975; *Frank Frazetta*, Bantam, 1977; *Frank Frazetta: Book Three*, Bantam, 1978; *Frank Frazetta: Book Four*, Bantam, 1980.

SIDELIGHTS: Frazetta's renditions of fantastic demons, bloodied warriors, and shapely females adorn hundreds of book covers and posters. As the illustrator of paperback copies of Robert E. Howard's mythic warrior Conan, he helped spark a revived interest in the late Texas storyteller's work. And his recreations of the fantastic worlds and characters of Edgar Rice Burroughs in paintings and book covers have lured countless readers to the worlds of Tarzan, the jungle warrior; David Innes, explorer of the Earth's inner world, Pellucidar; and John Carter, Prince of Mars. "Those covers gripped the fancy," Donald Newlove wrote in *Esquire*, "not just their eroticism but often their compelling sense of composition, of a picture that delivered fantasy with a looming hammerblow." He added: "There is never anything ghoulish in [Frazetta's] work, no bleeding cuts, only a bit of blood on the swords; there's no love of decay and fetidness—his swamps and jungles are soft green, lush, aswirl and gently vivid, germinal . . . , a perfect setting for the erotic."

Frazetta disdains the overly ponderous and intellectual air of modern art. "I can't do what Andrew Wyeth does," he told Newlove. "I want feelings." He prizes his commercial success and the durability of his style. "The impact of my best work never lessens," he declared, "it only looks better. And better! I'm my own worst critic and I know what the competition has done. But mine holds up, design, color, movement, no gimmicks, plenty of solidity, and form. You don't tire of it. I'm talking about my best work." Frazetta also told Newlove that flexibility was a key to his longevity. "When I become a bore, I change," he contended. "I have the freedom now to do what I want. No profound message. Just some fine art." He told *CA:* "Unlike some artists, my goal was to captivate a larger audience without any sacrifice in artistic quality."

AVOCATIONAL INTERESTS: Baseball.

BIOGRAPHICAL/CRITICAL SOURCES: American Artist, May, 1976; *Esquire*, June, 1977.

*   *   *

FRENCH, R(obert) B(utler) D(igby)   1904-1981

OBITUARY NOTICE—See index for *CA* sketch: Born May 26, 1904, in Londonderry, Ireland; died September 19, 1981. Educator and author. Prior to World War II, French worked as a leader writer for the *Irish Times*. From 1942 to 1945 he was stationed in South America as a member of the Overseas Division of the British Broadcasting Corp. French began his teaching career at the Royal Belfast Academical Institution, but most of his teaching days were spent as a senior lecturer at Trinity University. Besides his teaching duties, French served the university as the editor of *Trinity*, as the school's public relations and press officer, as a tutor, and as the secretary of the university council. The educator wrote reviews and pantomimes for the Dublin University Players, and he was a cor-

respondent for the *London Times* as well as a contributor to magazines. He wrote the book *P. G. Wodehouse*. Obituaries and other sources: *London Times*, September 25, 1981.

*   *   *

FRIEDMANN, Georges   1902(?)-1977

OBITUARY NOTICE: Born c. 1902; died in November, 1977, in Paris, France. President of the International Sociology Association and author. Friedmann wrote *The End of the Jewish People?* and *The Problems of Latin America*. Obituaries and other sources: *AB Bookman's Weekly*, March 20, 1978.

*   *   *

FRY, P(atricia) Eileen   1947-

PERSONAL: Born May 27, 1947. *Home:* 201 South Bryan, Bloomington, Ind. 47401. *Office:* Fine Arts Slide Library, Indiana University, Fine Arts 415, Bloomington, Ind. 47405.

CAREER: Writer. Fine arts slide librarian at Indiana University, Bloomington.

WRITINGS: (With Betty Jo Irvine) *Slide Libraries: A Guide for Academic Institutions, Museums, and Special Collections*, Libraries Unlimited, 1974, 2nd edition, 1979.

*   *   *

FRY, Plantagenet Somerset
See SOMERSET FRY, (Peter George Robin) Plantagenet

*   *   *

FUCHS, Vivian (Ernest)   1908-

PERSONAL: Born February 11, 1908, in Isle of Wight; son of Ernest and Violet Anne (Watson) Fuchs; married Joyce Connell, 1933; children: Hilary Brooks, Peter E.K. *Education:* St. John's College, Cambridge, M.A., 1932, Ph.D., 1936. *Home:* 78 Barton Rd., Cambridge CB3 9LH, England.

CAREER: Worked as geologist for expeditions organized by Cambridge University to East Greenland, 1929, and eastern African lakes, 1930-31, and for expedition to eastern Africa, 1931-32; leader of expeditions to Lake Rudolf Valley in Kenya, 1933-34, Lake Rukwa, Tanzania 1937-38, and Falkland Islands Dependencies in Antarctica, 1947-50; director of Falkland Islands Dependencies Scientific Bureau, 1950-55; leader of Commonwealth Trans-Antarctic expedition, 1955-58; British Antarctic Survey, London, England, director, 1958-73; writer, 1973—. *Military service:* British Army, 1939-46; served in Africa and Europe; became major; mentioned in dispatches.

MEMBER: International Glaciological Society (president, 1963-66), Royal Society (fellow), British Association for the Advancement of Science (president, 1972), Royal Geographical Society (fellow), Geological Society (fellow), Athenaeum Club. *Awards, honors:* Cuthbert Peek grant from Royal Geographical Society, 1936, founders' gold medal, 1951, special gold medal, 1958; silver medal from Royal Society of Arts, 1952, polar medal, 1953, clasp, 1958; honorary degrees include LL.D. from University of Edinburgh, 1958, and University of Birmingham, 1974, D.Sc. from University of Durham, 1958, Cambridge University, 1959, and University of Leicester, and Sc.D. from University of Wales, University College of Swansea, 1971; knighted, 1958; gold medals from Royal Scottish Geographical Society, 1958, Geographical Society (Paris,

France), 1958, and Geographical Society (Chicago, Ill.) 1959; Richthofen Medal from Berlin Geographical Society, 1958; Kirchenpauer Medal from Hamburg Geographical Society, 1958; Plancius Medal from Amsterdam Geographical Society, 1959; Hans Egede Medal from Copenhagen Geographical Society, 1959; Hubbard Medal from National Geographical Society (Washington, D.C.), 1959; medal from Explorers Club, 1959; Prestwich Medal from Geographical Society (London, England), 1960; honorary fellow of Wolfson College, Cambridge, 1970.

WRITINGS: (With Edmund Hillary) *The Crossing of Antarctica: The Commonwealth Trans-Antarctic Expedition, 1955-58*, Cassell, 1958, Little, Brown, 1959; *Antarctic Adventure: The Commonwealth Trans-Antarctic Expedition, 1955-58*, Cassell, 1959, Dutton, 1961; (author of introduction) Robert Falcon Scott, *Scott's Last Expedition: The Personal Journals of Captain R. F. Scott on His Journey to the South Pole*, Folio Society, 1964; (editor) *Forces of Nature*, Holt, 1977. Contributor to scientific journals. Also author of forewords to books, including *Antarctic Adventure* by Raymond Priestley, Hurst.

SIDELIGHTS: Traveling twenty-five hundred miles in ninety-nine days under conditions of extreme hardship, Sir Vivian Fuchs led the Commonwealth Trans-Antarctic Expedition which completed the first land journey across the Antarctic continent. Scientific studies conducted by the Fuchs expedition and a companion New Zealand expedition led by Sir Edmund Hillary corroborated that there is a single continent beneath the Antarctic polar ice cap and also that the expeditionary route included land above sea level. During the course of their explorations, the New Zealanders discovered a nine thousand-foot mountain range, and the British expedition discovered a seven thousand-foot range.

Fuchs's books have been translated into seventeen languages, including Polish, German, French, Hungarian, Japanese, and Norwegian.

BIOGRAPHICAL/CRITICAL SOURCES: Illustrated London News, January 18, 1958, February 15, 1958, May 17, 1958; *Time*, February 3, 1958; Gerald Bowman, *Men of Antarctica*, Fleet, 1959; *New York Times: Men in the News, 1958*, Lippincott, 1959; *Senior Scholastic*, November 18, 1959; Egon Lehrburger (under pseudonym Egon Larsen) *Sir Vivian Fuchs*, Roy, 1959; Douglas Mackenzie, *Opposite Poles: On the Relationship Between Sir Vivian Fuchs and Sir Edmund Hillary in the British Commonwealth Transantarctic Expedition, 1957-1958*, R. Hale, 1963; D. Newton and D. Smith, *Fuchs, Anderson*, Oliver, 1971.

FUKA, Vladimir   1926-1977

OBITUARY NOTICE: Born February 25, 1926, in Pisek, Czechoslovakia; died March 29, 1977, in Rhinebeck, N.Y. Book designer and illustrator, painter, and author. Fuka was known for his illustrations for children's books, but his specialty was book design. His artwork was displayed at the 1958 Brussels World Fair and at the 1965 International Illustrators Exhibition in Bologna, where he won first prize. In 1966 he defected from Czechoslovakia. In addition to the hundreds of books he designed and illustrated, Fuka wrote *Imaginary Portraits*. Obituaries and other sources: *Who's Who in Graphic Art*, Amstutz & Herdeg Graphis, 1962; *New York Times*, March 31, 1977; *AB Bookman's Weekly*, May 9, 1977.

*   *   *

FULTZ, Walter J.   1924(?)-1971

OBITUARY NOTICE: Born c. 1924; died August 6, 1971, in Maine. Editor. Fultz was chief editor of Gold Medal Books, where he had served as executive editor until 1970. He had previously worked for Scott Meredith Literary Agency and Lion Books. Obituaries and other sources: *New York Times*, August 8, 1971; *Publishers Weekly*, September 13, 1971.

*   *   *

FURMAN, Laura

CAREER: Writer.

WRITINGS: The Glass House (stories; includes "The Glass House," "The Smallest Loss," "Last Winter," "My Father's Car," and "Eldorado"), Viking, 1980. Contributor of stories to *New Yorker*.

WORK IN PROGRESS: A suspense story set in Texas.

SIDELIGHTS: Furman's *Glass House* is a collection of five short stories and a novella. According to *New York Times Book Review*'s Lynne Sharon Schwartz, the book's title symbolizes the "fragile" lives of the stories' central characters. "Furman plays out her glass-house metaphor with delicate composure, like a musician dallying with a motif, and leaves the reader entranced. . . . Despite their sadness, [Furman's] stories glow with youth, hope, and a future." A *Chicago Tribune Book World* critic noted that "these are deftly done, interesting stories—an excellent read."

BIOGRAPHICAL/CRITICAL SOURCES: Washington Post Book World, October 19, 1980; *New York Times Book Review*, November 9, 1980; *Chicago Tribune Book World*, November 16, 1980; *Los Angeles Times Book Review*, November 23, 1980.*

G

GABRIEL, Richard Alan 1942-

BRIEF ENTRY: Born December 16, 1942, in Providence, R.I. American political scientist, educator, and author. Gabriel's writings include *The Ethnic Factor in the Urban Polity* (Mss Information, 1973), *The Environment: Critical Factors in Strategy Development* (Mss Information, 1973), *Program Evaluation: A Social Science Approach* (Mss Information, 1975), *Crisis in Command: Mismanagement in the Army* (Hill & Wang, 1978), and *The New Red Legions: An Attitudinal Portrait of the Soviet Soldier* (Greenwood Press, 1980). *Address:* 100 Allen St., Manchester, N.H. 03102; and Department of Politics, St. Anselm's College, Manchester, N.H. 03102. *Biographical/critical sources: New Republic,* June 10, 1978; *Washington Post Book World,* June 25, 1978; *New York Times Book Review,* July 23, 1978, July 15, 1979; *National Review,* September 29, 1978.

* * *

GAESS, Roger 1943-

PERSONAL: Surname rhymes with "lace"; born March 13, 1943, in Waterbury, Conn.; son of Roger (a metalworker) and Yvonne (Petraitis) Gaess; married Jacquie Reing (a photographer), September 10, 1966. *Education:* University of Connecticut, B.A., 1966; Syracuse University, M.A., 1970; Columbia University, M.F.A., 1973. *Politics:* "Left." *Religion:* Unitarian-Universalist; Jain; agnostic. *Home address:* P.O. Box 250, Washington, Conn. 06793.

CAREER: Dover Publications, Inc., New York, N.Y., editor, 1969-71; free-lance writer and editor, 1972—. *Member:* Poets and Writers.

WRITINGS: (Editor) *Leaving the Bough: Fifty American Poets of the Eighties,* International Publishers, 1982. Contributor of poems and articles to magazines and newspapers, including *Ambit, Urthkin, Poetry,* and *New York Times.* Editor of *Expatriate Review,* 1971-74; guest editor of *Small Press Review.*

WORK IN PROGRESS: Research for a novel set in Zurich during World War 1.

SIDELIGHTS: Gaess wrote: "Because it's been my impression that the overwhelming majority of published poetry in America is beside the point, written by various sorts of careerists for whom poetry is in essence merely another business, I attempted to assemble a collection of active poetry of involvement and commitment, where imagination was grounded both in need and experience. The result was *Leaving the Bough.* 'Early Words, Early Warnings,' the preface of the anthology, is my clearest statement of what is of value to me in poetry. I occasionally do journalism, as well, and my favorite form is travel writing."

* * *

GAG, Flavia 1907-1979

OBITUARY NOTICE—See index for *CA* sketch: Born May 24, 1907, in New Ulm, Minn.; died October 12, 1979, in Crescent City, Fla. Illustrator and author. The author and illustrator of children's books, Gag began writing and drawing as a child with her brothers and sisters. Both she and her sister Wanda, whose biography Gag began, went on to achieve recognition as artists and writers. Her works include *The Melon Patch Mystery, Four Legs and a Tail, Tweeter of Prairie Dog Town, Florida Snow Party,* and *Chubby's First Year.* She also contributed stories to magazines for children, including *St. Nicholas, Child Life,* and *Jack and Jill.* Obituaries and other sources: *School Library Journal,* December, 1979.

* * *

GAGER, John Goodrich, Jr. 1937-

BRIEF ENTRY: Born November 21, 1937, in Boston, Mass. American educator, religious scholar, and author. Gager has taught religion at Princeton University since 1968. He wrote *Moses in Greco-Roman Paganism* (Abingdon, 1972) and *Kingdom and Community: The Social World of Early Christianity* (Prentice-Hall, 1975). *Address:* Department of Religion, Princeton University, 613 1879 Hall, Princeton, N.J. 08540. *Biographical/critical sources: Directory of American Scholars,* Volume IV: *Philosophy, Religion, and Law,* 7th edition, Bowker, 1978.

* * *

GAGLIARDO, Ruth Garver 1895(?)-1980

OBITUARY NOTICE: Born c. 1895 in Hastings, Neb.; died January 5, 1980, in Wichita, Kan. Librarian, educator, and author. Gagliardo served as director of library services for the Kansas Teachers Association from 1942 to 1966, and she also wrote for and edited *Children's Book Shelf.* Active in numerous other areas as well, Gagliardo founded the William Allen White

Children's Book Award in 1952 and originated the children's Traveling Book Exhibit. Early in her career Gagliardo wrote one of the first book review columns to feature children's books; she later contributed to *Wonderful World of Books* and compiled *Let's Read Aloud.* The Association of School Librarian established a scholarship in her name in 1965. Obituaries and other sources:*Who's Who of American Women,* 5th edition, Marquis, 1968; *Authors of Books for Young People,* 2nd edition, Scarecrow, 1971; *Publishers Weekly,* February 8, 1980; *School Library Journal,* February, 1980.

* * *

GAGNON, Paul Adelard   1925-

BRIEF ENTRY: Born January 6, 1925, in Springfield, Mass. American historian, educator, and author. Gagnon began teaching history at the University of Massachusetts in 1952 and became a professor and dean of faculty about 1966. He was a Fulbright scholar at University of Paris, 1951-52, and has been a founding member of the editorial staff of *Massachusetts Review* since 1959. He wrote *France Since 1789* (Harper, 1964) and *Encablures* (Seminaire de Sherbrooke, 1977). *Address:* 14 Rutland St., Cambridge, Mass. 02138; and Department of History, University of Massachusetts, Harbor Campus, Boston, Mass. 02125. *Biographical/critical sources: Who's Who in America,* 130th edition, St. Martin's, 1978.

* * *

GAILMOR, William S.   1910(?)-1970

OBITUARY NOTICE: Born c. 1910; died November 13, 1970, in Norwalk, Conn. Medical writer and journalist. Gailmor was noted for his radio news analyses and commentary. Obituaries and other sources: *AB Bookman's Weekly,* January 4, 1971.

* * *

GALSWORTHY, John   1867-1933
(John Sinjohn)

BRIEF ENTRY: Born August 14, 1867, in Kingston Hill, Surrey, England; died January 31, 1933, in London, England. English novelist, playwright, and short story writer. Galsworthy is considered the last great Victorian novelist. Born to wealth, he studied law and was called to the Bar in 1890, but did not take up the practice. Instead he traveled extensively, and while on a trip to the Far East he met Joseph Conrad, who encouraged him to become a writer. Noted for his relatively objective observations of the society of his times, Galsworthy captured the spirit of his age while revealing its shortcomings. His success as a writer began with his first play, "The Silver Box," produced in 1906. Its subject, "one law for the rich and one law for the poor," brought a new sense of social responsibility to English drama. Galsworthy's later plays also dealt with social and ethical issues. For example, "Strife" (1909) deals with the war between capital and labor, and "Justice" (1910), depicts the severity of solitary confinement and actually led to reforms in the British penal system. The author's first successful novel, *A Man of Property* (1906), initiated a series of novels collectively called the *Forsyte Saga.* Centering the series around the character of Soames Forsyte, Galsworthy portrayed a declining upper middle-class society from the 1880's to the years following World War I. A trilogy with two interludes, the saga analyzes the conflict between idealism and materialism. Founder of the P.E.N. club, Galsworthy was offered a knighthood for his literary achievements, but refused. He did, however, accept the Order of Merit in 1929 and the

Nobel Prize in 1932. Among his other works are *Fraternity* (1909), *Loyalties* (1922), and *Caravan* (1925). *Biographical/critical sources: Twentieth Century Writing: A Reader's Guide to Contemporary Literature,* Transatlantic, 1969; *Webster's New World Companion to English and American Literature,* World Publishing, 1973; *Twentieth-Century Literary Criticism,* Volume 1, Gale, 1978.

* * *

GANTNER, Neilma   1922-
(Neilma Sidney)

PERSONAL: Born November 7, 1922; daughter of Sidney B. (a department store founder) and Merlyn (Baillieu) Myer; married Vallejo Gantner (divorced); children: Vallejo B. (deceased), Carrillo B. *Education:* Attended University of Melbourne, 1940; Stanford University, A.B., 1954. *Address:* P.O. Box 497, South Yarra, Victoria 3141, Australia; and "Isola" Barragga Bay, Bermagui South, New South Wales 2547, Australia.

CAREER: International Social Service, member of Australian executive board, 1955—, member of international executive board, 1965-69. Member of executive committee of Sidney Myer Music Bowl, 1959-80. *Member:* Fellowship of Australian Writers, Australian Society of Authors, Catalyst Club of Lyceum Club.

WRITINGS—Under pseudonym Neilma Sidney: *Saturday Afternoon,* F. W. Cheshire, 1959; *Beyond the Bay,* F. W. Cheshire, 1966; *The Eye of the Needle,* Lloyd O'Neil, 1970; *The Return,* Thomas Nelson, 1976.

Work represented in anthologies, including *Australian Signposts* and *Modern Australian Humour.*

WORK IN PROGRESS: A novel.

SIDELIGHTS: Sidney commented: "I am engaged in my first attempt at a comic-fantastic novel, a magical car journey across Australia with four characters aboard. The book has a serious purpose, the welcoming of the Vietnamese boat people in Darwin. It is a difficult book because of the mixture of comedy and contemporary problems, but worth pursuing."

* * *

GARCIA LORCA, Federico   1898-1936

BRIEF ENTRY: Born June 5, 1898, in Fuentevaqueros, Granada, Spain; murdered August 19, 1936, in Viznar, Granada. Spanish poet and playwright. Garcia Lorca's reputation rests on his folk-oriented poems written between 1920 and 1930. In his first important work, *Libro de poemas* (1921), Garcia Lorca skillfully intertwined his childhood experiences and Spanish folklore in modern, yet accessible, verse. In *Poema del Cante Jondo* (1931), he restricted his imagery to the Andalusian landscape and villagers in a series of poems on passion and death. His finest work is probably *Romancero gitano* (1928), a collection of poetic ballads mixing traditional and contemporary Spanish elements in highly readable form. Garcia Lorca was dismayed by his reputation as a "gypsy poet" following publication of these volumes, however, and in 1929 he fled to America. His verse from that period, *Poet in New York* (1940), contrasts sharply with the earthiness of its predecessors. The poems focus on the monotony and despair of industrial life and portray civilization as a vast wasteland. After returning to Spain, Garcia Lorca began writing plays—an occupation he had left in 1920 to concentrate on poetry. Although the dramas were well received, especially *Yerma* (1934), they are not ranked with his finer works. The following year, however, he wrote another collection of poetry, *Llanto por Ignacio Sanchez Majias* (1935), which is often said to contain his most lyrical poetry. Unfortunately, Garcia Lorca's works were found offensive by the Spanish Government, and in 1936 he was murdered by supporters of General Franco. *Biographical/critical sources: The Oxford Companion to the Theatre*, 3rd edition, Oxford University Press, 1967; *Twentieth Century Writing: A Reader's Guide to Contemporary Literature*, Transatlantic, 1969; *Penguin Companion to European Literature*, McGraw, 1969; *Twentieth-Century Literary Criticism*, Volume 1, Gale, 1978.

* * *

GARDNER, Isabella (Stewart) 1915-1981

OBITUARY NOTICE—See index for *CA* sketch: Born September 7, 1915, in Newton, Mass.; died July 7, 1981, in Manhattan, N.Y. Poet, actress, and author. Gardner was an actress from 1939 to 1943 and later the associate editor of *Poetry*. She contributed poems to that magazine as well as to other periodicals, including *Nation* and *Atlantic Monthly*, and she gave poetry readings in the United States, England, Ireland, and Italy. Two of her books, *Birthdays From the Ocean* and *The Looking Glass*, were nominated for National Book Awards; her most recent work, *That Was Then*, was nominated for an American Book Award. Her other works include *Un'Altra Infazia* and *West of Childhood: Poems, 1950-1965*. Obituaries and other sources: New York Times, July 10, 1981; *Publishers Weekly*, July 24, 1981.

* * *

GARDNER, Sheldon 1934-

PERSONAL: Born April 20, 1934, in Chelsea, Mass.; son of Philip (a shopkeeper) and Goldie (Stepansky) Gardner; married Ann E. Cofield, December 15, 1957 (divorced, 1969); married Gwendolyn Stevens (a psychologist), October 27, 1972; children: David V., Loren Ann Gardner Anderson, Stephen Forest, Pamela F., A. Beth. *Education:* Harvard University, A.B., 1956; University of Southern California, Ph.D., 1963. *Politics:* Libertarian. *Home:* 2006 Bend Rd., Cape Girardeau, Mo. 63701. *Office:* St. Francis Mental Health Center, Cape Girardeau, Mo. 63701.

CAREER: Mental Health Center of Western North Carolina, Asheville, psychologist, 1963-65; Pasadena Child Guidance Clinic, Pasadena, Calif., training director, 1965-69; California State College, Los Angeles (now California State University, Los Angeles), associate professor, 1969-71; Hyperkinesis Clinic, Pasadena, executive director, 1971-73; Psychiatric Clinic for Children, Long Beach, Calif., chief psychologist, 1973-76; Voorman Clinic, Upland, Calif., clinical director, 1977-78; St. Francis Mental Health Center, Cape Girardeau, Mo., clinical psychologist, 1978—. Private practice of clinical psychology, 1964-76.

WRITINGS: (With wife, Gwendolyn Stevens) *Care and Cultivation of Parents*, Simon & Schuster, 1979; (with Stevens) *Women of Psychology: Pioneers and Innovators*, Schenkman, 1981; (with Stevens) *Women of Psychology: Expansion and Refinement*, Schenkman, 1981. Author of "In My Opinion," a column in *Southeast Missourian*. Contributor to psychology journals.

WORK IN PROGRESS: Psychology of Women, with wife, Gwendolyn Stevens, completion expected in 1982.

SIDELIGHTS: Gardner commented: "My interest is in making psychological data and theories available and comprehensible to the lay public, especially children. Because my wife is an active feminist, she has influenced my work and attitudes in the direction of a greater understanding and acceptance of the women's movement.

"It is ironic, in light of my long history of male chauvinism, that most of my publications of the past few years have been quasi-militant feminist in orientation. Our research on the lives of three hundred eminent psychologists who happened to be women and who have been totally ignored by historians of psychology has, more than any single event, convinced me that female intellectuals and professionals have suffered from serious injustice. Not only do the biographies show gender discrimination in the careers of these women, but the important contributions these women made to our science have been subsequently depreciated or ignored. I have, in short, become belatedly a feminist."

* * *

GARLAND, (Hannibal) Hamlin 1860-1940

BRIEF ENTRY: Born September 14, 1860, in West Salem, Wis.; died March 4, 1940, in Los Angeles, Calif. American novelist, short story writer, essayist, and memoirist. The son of pioneers, Hamlin Garland spent his youth in Wisconsin, Iowa, and South Dakota. As a young man he traveled to Boston, where he taught for a time at the Boston School of Oratory and was encouraged by novelist William Dean Howells to pursue a writing career. Garland's early exposure to the poverty and drudgery of agrarian life directed much of his writing, in which he sought to shatter the myth of utopian rural America. His *Main Travelled Roads: Six Mississippi Valley Stories* (1891) continues to be recognized as a major contribution to American literary history. In *Crumbling Idols: Twelve Essays on Art, Dealing Chiefly With Literature, Painting and the Drama* (1894), Garland set forth his theory of "veritism," a form of literary realism that protested the social and economic forces contributing to the hardship of rural life. During the early 1900's Garland strayed from his commitment to realism and produced several romantic novels set in the Rocky Mountains. Such books as *The Captain of The Gray-Horse Troop* (1902) and *Cavanagh, Forest Ranger: A Romance of the Mountain West* (1910) were commercially successful but did not earn critical respect. In his later years Garland wrote his highly acclaimed *Middle Border* autobiographical series. He won a Pulitzer Prize for *A Daughter of the Middle Border* (1921). *Residence:* Los Angeles, Calif. *Biographical/critical sources: Cyclopedia of World Authors*, Harper, 1958; *The Reader's Encyclopedia of American Literature*, Crowell, 1962; *Webster's American Biographies*, Merriam, 1974; *Twentieth-Century Literary Criticism*, Volume 3, Gale, 1980.

* * *

GARMENT, Grace R. 1927(?)-1976

OBITUARY NOTICE: Born c. 1927; committed suicide, December 3, 1976, in Boston, Mass. Television scriptwriter. For more than a year Garment contributed two scripts each week for the ABC-TV serial "The Edge of Night." A few months before her death she gave up her writing and volunteered herself for psychiatric treatment. Her husband was Leonard Garment, a former aide to President Nixon. Obituaries and other sources: *New York Times*, January 27, 1977; *Time*, February 7, 1977.

* * *

GARZA, Roberto J(esus) 1934-

PERSONAL: Born April 10, 1934, in Hargill, Tex.; son of

Andres (a horse trainer) and Nazaria (de la Fuente) Garza; married Idolina Alaniz (an educator), August 24, 1957; children: Roberto J., Jr., Sylvia Lynn. *Education:* Texas A & I University, B.A., 1959, M.A., 1964; Oklahoma State University, Ed.D., 1975; graduate study at University of Kansas, University of Arizona, and University of Washington, Seattle. *Politics:* Democrat. *Religion:* Roman Catholic. *Home:* 254 Palo Verde Dr., Brownsville, Tex. 78520. *Office:* Division of Education, Pan American University, 80 Fort Brown, Brownsville, Tex. 78520.

CAREER: High school Spanish teacher and counselor in Premont, Agua Dulce, and Alice, Tex., 1959-63, Alton, Ill., 1960-61, and Rawlins, Wyo., 1963-64; St. Joseph Junior College, St. Joseph, Mo., instructor in Spanish and chairman of department of Spanish, French, and German, 1964-65; Southwest Texas Junior College, Uvalde, instructor in Spanish and chairman of Division of Fine Arts, 1966-68; Sul Ross State University, Alpine, Tex., assistant professor of Spanish language and literature, 1968-70; Oklahoma State University, Stillwater, instructor in Spanish, 1971-72; Pan American University, Brownsville Center, Brownsville, Tex., assistant professor, 1973-76, professor of secondary education and head of Division of Education, 1977—. Psychometrist and Spanish language specialist with U.S. Peace Corps, summer, 1966; guidance counselor at Gary Job Corps, summer, 1967; administrative assistant and researcher at Associated City-County Economic Development Corp. of Hidalgo County, 1970-71; member of faculty at University of Notre Dame, 1972-73; member of Texas Education Agency Accreditation Team, 1979—. *Military service:* U.S Army, 1954-56. *Member:* American Association of University Professors, American Association for Higher Education, Smithsonian Associates, Texas Association of College Teachers, Sigma Iota, Phi Delta Kappa.

WRITINGS: Chicano Theatre: An Anthology, University of Notre Dame Press, 1975. Contributor to *La Luz.*

WORK IN PROGRESS: Contemporary Chicano Short Stories: An Anthology, publication by University of Notre Dame Press expected in 1983; writing on Chicano drama; research on comparative higher education systems.

SIDELIGHTS: Garza told *CA:* "Every piece of literary work is an attempt to further find understanding and meaning to our existence in this labyrinth called life."

* * *

GATHORNE-HARDY, Jonathan G.   1933-

PERSONAL: Born May 17, 1933, in Edinburgh, Scotland; son of Anthony (a doctor) and Ruth (Thorowgood) Gathorne-Hardy; married Sabrina Tennant (a restorer), October, 1962 (divorced); children: Jenny, Benjamin. *Education:* Trinity College, Cambridge, B.A., 1957. *Home:* West Lodge, Compton Bassett, Calne, Wiltshire, England. *Agent:* Curtis Brown, 1 Craven Hill, London W2 3EP, England; and Laura Cecil, 10 Exeter Mansions, 106 Shaftesbury Ave., London W.1, England.

CAREER: Writer. Worked as advertising copywriter, publisher, bookseller, book reviewer, and free-lance journalist. *Military service:* British Army, 1952-53; became lieutenant.

WRITINGS: One Foot in the Clouds (novel), Hamish Hamilton, 1961; *Jane's Adventures In and Out of the Book* (juvenile), Alan Ross, 1966; *Chameleon* (novel), Hamish Hamilton, 1967; *Jane's Adventures on the Island of Peeg* (juvenile), Alan Ross, 1968, published as *Operation Peeg,* Lippincott, 1974; *The Office* (novel), Dial, 1971; *The Rise and Fall of the British*

Nanny (nonfiction), Hodder & Stoughton, 1972, published as *The Unnatural History of the Nanny,* Dial, 1973; *Jane's Adventures in a Balloon* (juvenile), Gollancz, 1975, published as *The Airship Ladyship Adventure,* Lippincott, 1977; *The Public School Phenomenon, 597-1977* (nonfiction), Hodder & Stoughton, 1977, published as *The Old School Tie: The Phenomenon of the English Public School,* Viking, 1978; *The Terrible Kidnapping of Cyril Bonhamy* (juvenile), Evans Brothers, 1978; *Cyril Bonhamy and the Great Father Christmas Robbery* (juvenile), Evans Brothers, 1981; *Marriage: What It Was, What It Is, What It Will Be,* Summit Books, in press, published in England as *The Way We Love Now,* J. Cape, in press.

SIDELIGHTS: In addition to being a noted social historian, Jonathan Gathorne-Hardy is a writer of fanciful tales for adults and children. As a creator of fiction for adolescents, Gathorne-Hardy's most notable characters are Jane, who resides in an old English castle, and the castle's fastidious housekeeper, Mrs. Deal. Together they find themselves in outrageous predicaments, such as in *Jane's Adventures In and Out of the Book* when Jane discovers a bizarre world as she walks into the illustrations of an ancient book. And as world travelers in *Jane's Adventures on the Island of Peeg* and *Jane's Adventures in a Balloon,* they find themselves on a Scottish isle and in the midst of deepest Africa.

In writing his adult nonfiction, Gathorne-Hardy closely studied the social and historical roots of two British institutions: the public school and the nanny. His research resulted in *The Public School Phenomenon* and *The Rise and Fall of the British Nanny.* Both books are written in an informal tone and have been praised for their completeness.

BIOGRAPHICAL/CRITICAL SOURCES: Times Literary Supplement, September 1, 1972; *Christian Science Monitor,* January 3, 1973; *New York Times Book Review,* July 1, 1973, November 26, 1978; *Time,* August 13, 1973, August 21, 1978; *New Republic,* June 10, 1978; *Washington Post Book World,* October 29, 1978.

* * *

GAY, A. Nolder
See KOELSCH, William Alvin

* * *

GAZDANOV, Gaito   1903-1971
(Georgii Gazdanov)

OBITUARY NOTICE: Born in 1903; died December 5, 1971, in Munich, West Germany. Novelist. An expatriate Russian author of psychological novels, Gazdanov wrote *Buddha's Return* and the autobiographical *Night Roads,* among other works. Obituaries and other sources: *AB Bookman's Weekly,* December 20, 1971.

* * *

GAZDANOV, Georgii
See GAZDANOV, Gaito

* * *

GEARY, Frederick Charles   1886(?)-1975(?)

OBITUARY NOTICE: Born c. 1886; died c. January, 1975, in Shoreham-by-Sea, Sussex, England. Educator and author. Geary was a tutor at Oxford University's Corpus Christi College. He wrote a book of verses in Latin and co-wrote a volume of Latin prayers. Obituaries and other sources: *AB Bookman's Weekly,* January 20, 1975.

*   *   *

GEARY, Patrick J(oseph)   1948-

PERSONAL: Born September 26, 1948, in Jackson, Miss.; son of Walter Thomas (in business) and Celine (a health statistician; maiden name, McGinn) Geary; married Mary Carroll (a nursing supervisor), August 29, 1970; children: Catherine Celine, Anne Irene. *Education:* Spring Hill College, A.B., 1970; attended Catholic University of Louvain, 1968-69; Yale University, M.Phil., 1973, Ph.D., 1974. *Religion:* Roman Catholic. *Home and office:* 10 Southwest 23rd Dr., Gainesville, Fla. 32607.

CAREER: Princeton University, Princeton, N.J., assistant professor of history, 1974-80; University of Florida, Gainesville, associate professor of history, 1980—. *Military service:* U.S. Army Reserve, 1973—; captain. *Member:* Mediaeval Academy of America, American Historical Association, American Association for the Advancement of the Humanities. *Awards, honors:* Woodrow Wilson fellowship, 1970; grants from governments of Austria, 1976, and West Germany, 1981, and from American Philosophical Society, 1981.

WRITINGS: "Furta Sacra": Thefts of Relics in the Central Middle Ages, Princeton University Press, 1978. Contributor to history and archaeology journals.

WORK IN PROGRESS: A book on the sense of self and community identity in the Rhone Valley, 700-1100, in order to understand the social and perceptional evolution of European society, completion expected in 1983.

SIDELIGHTS: Geary told *CA:* "In my writing I attempt to examine the relationships between social and material conditions on the one hand, and religion, ideology, and memory on the other. I am interested in the way past societies have creatively perceived their past, themselves, and their relationships with other individuals, groups, and divinities. Besides the obvious influence on my work of modern French historians, particularly Georges Duby, I suspect that my interest in time, perception, and creation of a past develops from my own very strong self identity as a Southerner, and more particularly as a Louisianian, and from the work of phenomenological existentialists such as Maurice Merleau-Ponty. I see myself as one of a minority of American historians attempting to revolutionize the positivistic, uncritical, and myopic tradition of medieval historiography which dominates work in this field done in North America."

*   *   *

GEDO, Mary M(athews)   1925-

PERSONAL: Born June 13, 1925, in Belleville, Ill.; daughter of Lloyd William and Anna (McGuigan) Mathews; married John Emeric Gedo (a psychoanalyst), April 17, 1953; children: Paul, Andrew, Nicholas. *Education:* University of Illinois, B.S., 1948; Wellesley College, M.A., 1950; Northwestern University, Ph.D., 1972. *Politics:* Democrat. *Religion:* None. *Home:* 736 Tenth St., Wilmette, Ill. 60091.

CAREER: Institute for Juvenile Research, Chicago, Ill., staff psychologist, 1951-55; Northwestern University, Evanston, Ill., teaching assistant, 1968-69; Loyola University, Chicago, part-time instructor, 1969-70; De Paul University, Chicago, assistant professor of psychology, 1973-77; writer, 1977—. Adult lecturer at Art Institute of Chicago, 1967—. *Member:* College

Art Association, Wilmette Historical Society (member of board of directors), Hyde Park Improvement Society (member of board of directors).

WRITINGS: Picasso: Art as Autobiography, University of Chicago Press, 1980. Author of museum catalogs. Contributor to journals, including *Arts, Art Journal, American Art Review,* and *Art Quarterly.* Editor of newsletter of Wilmette Historical Society.

WORK IN PROGRESS: A monograph, tentatively titled *The Prophet in His Own Country: The Art of Manierre Dawson,* publication by Illinois State Museum expected in 1983 or 1984; a chapter for a book tentatively titled *Empathy,* edited by Joseph Lichtenberg, publication by International Universities Press expected in 1983; a chapter for a book tentatively titled *Proceedings of the Fiftieth Anniversary Celebration of the Chicago Psychoanalytic Society and the Institute for Psychoanalysis,* edited by George Pollock and John E. Gedo, for International Universities Press.

SIDELIGHTS: Mary Gedo wrote: "Before I began my study of art history, I trained and functioned as a clinical psychologist. My dual background has made me particularly attuned to the psychological sources of artistic motivation and expression, and I have developed a different type of methodology for the study of an artist's *oeuvre,* one more suited to my interests than the standard approach. In utilizing my method, I try to combine standard formal and iconographical studies with the type of in-depth approach to the work which people trained, as I was, to give projective tests (such as the Rorschach Ink Blots) utilize to analyze patient protocols."

AVOCATIONAL INTERESTS: "Music, especially opera, and ballet. I am totally unathletic and uninterested in all sports. I love to travel and have made numerous trips to Europe, especially France and Italy. I am a Romanesque cathedral buff, and enjoy visiting small French and Italian cities with important Romanesque churches."

*   *   *

GEEN, Russell Glenn   1932-

PERSONAL: Born May 3, 1932, in Ironwood, Mich.; son of William and Minnie Jane Geen; married Barbara Kimmel (a teacher), September 9, 1960; children: Thomas, William. *Education:* Michigan State University, B.A., 1954; University of Wisconsin (now University of Wisconsin—Madison), M.S., 1964, Ph.D., 1967. *Politics:* Independent. *Home:* 601 Stewart Rd., Columbia, Mo. 65201. *Office:* Department of Psychology, University of Missouri, Columbia, Mo. 65201.

CAREER: University of Missouri, Columbia, 1967—, began as assistant professor, became professor of psychology. *Member:* American Psychological Association, Psychonomic Society, Society of Experimental Social Psychology, Society for Psychophysiological Research, Midwestern Psychological Association.

WRITINGS: Personality, Mosby, 1976; (with E. C. O'Neal) *Perspectives on Aggression,* Academic Press, 1976. Editor of *Journal of Research in Personality,* 1977—.

WORK IN PROGRESS: Human Motivation, for Allyn & Bacon; *Human Aggression,* with E. Donnerstein, for Academic Press.

*   *   *

GEER, William D.   1906(?)-1976

OBITUARY NOTICE: Born c. 1906; died of a stroke, August

20, 1976, in Gilsum, N.H. Publishing executive. After graduating from Yale University, Geer worked for Time Inc. until he retired for health reasons in 1954. While with the company he collaborated on the ''March of Time'' radio programs, published *Fortune* magazine from 1942 until 1948, and produced the television series ''Crusade in Europe.'' Geer moved to New Hampshire in 1969, where he co-edited a local recipe cookbook, *Gilsum Vittles.* Obituaries and other sources: *New York Times,* August 23, 1976; *Time,* August 30, 1976; *Advertising Age,* August 30, 1976.

* * *

GEISMAR, Maxwell (David)   1909-1979

OBITUARY NOTICE—See index for *CA* sketch: Born August 1, 1909, in New York, N.Y.; died of a heart attack, July 24, 1979, in Harrison, N.Y. Critic, editor, and author. Known as a ''radical'' literary critic, Geismar contributed reviews on most major American authors to many newspapers and periodicals, including the *New York Times,* the *New York Herald Tribune, Nation, Atlantic Monthly,* and *American Scholar.* He is best known for his book *Writers in Crisis,* of the ''Novel in America'' series. Geismar also served as the senior editor of *Ramparts.* Obituaries and other sources: *Publishers Weekly,* August 6, 1979.

* * *

GELLER, Evelyn
See GOTTESFELD, Evelyn

* * *

GELMAN, Woodrow   1915(?)-1978
(Woody Gelman)

OBITUARY NOTICE: Born c. 1915; died February 9, 1978, in Valley Stream, N.Y. Publisher, comic-strip artist, and collector of popular art. Gelman was the publisher of Nostalgia Press. His collection of magazines, posters, photographs and other examples of popular art have been displayed at the Metropolitan Museum of Art in New York and the Louvre in Paris. Obituaries and other sources: *New York Times,* February 11, 1978; *Publishers Weekly,* April 3, 1978.

* * *

GELMAN, Woody
See GELMAN, Woodrow

* * *

GENDEL, Evelyn W.   1916(?)-1977

OBITUARY NOTICE: Born c. 1916; died December 18, 1977, in New York, N.Y. Editor and author. Gendel was a senior editor at Arbor House and Simon & Schuster before she became a senior editor at Bobbs-Merrill publishers. While at Simon & Schuster she was the editor of Jacqueline Susann's *The Love Machine.* She wrote a number of cookbooks and children's books, including the popular *The Tortoise and the Turtle.* Obituaries and other sources: *New York Times,* December 20, 1977; *Publishers Weekly,* December 26, 1977.

* * *

GEORGE, Richard R(obert)   1943-

PERSONAL: Born September 6, 1943, in Buffalo, N.Y.; son

of Robert Herbert and Doris Kathleen George; married Susan Marie Williams, March 18, 1967; children: Jamie, Jodi, Jineen. *Education:* State University of New York College at Buffalo, B.S., 1965, M.S. (elementary education), 1975; Niagara University, M.S. (counseling), 1978. *Religion:* Protestant. *Home:* 291 West Klein, Williamsville, N.Y. 14221. *Agent:* Murray Pollinger, 4 Garrick St., London WC2E 9BH, England. *Office:* The Chapel, 895 North Forest Rd., Buffalo, N.Y. 14221.

CAREER: Teacher at public schools in Lockport, N.Y., 1965-67, 1969-78; The Chapel on North Forest Road, Buffalo, N.Y., minister of education, 1978—. Principal of private Christian elementary school in Williamsville, N.Y., 1980-81. *Military service:* U.S. Army, clerk, 1967-69.

WRITINGS: Charlie and the Chocolate Factory: A Play (for children; adapted from the novel by Roald Dahl), Random House, 1976.

WORK IN PROGRESS: James and the Giant Peach: A Play, an adaptation of the children's novel by Dahl; *How to Write a Children's Play; Practical Strategies in Biblical Counseling;* inspirational poems.

SIDELIGHTS: George told *CA:* ''I am (with my obedience) who God (with His patience) would have me to be. I am old-fashioned, traditional, conservative, and most of all committed to Jesus Christ. My life and my writing, to be of any value, must be for Him. I am deeply concerned about the incredible apathy that permeates our self-centered humanistic world. I care that the world in which we live scoffs at the very moral fiber of true biblical Christianity in its hell-bent pursuit of self-destruction.

''The 1980's are to be a time of counseling urgency, due to the tragic inability of frustrated individuals to handle their personal lives. While Christ is 'the Answer,' the present is a fearful reflection of our immediate past, as clergyman after clergyman—not knowing how to energize Christ's teachings—has abdicated his God-given mandate to meet people's needs. He has done this by referring to and turning to secular psychological hoopla. This in turn tells people that God is *not* the answer, and the so-called esoteric knowledge of cold-hearted theorists is to be deemed as 'truth.'

''When in the course of human events shall we start dealing with man's problems and not his symptoms? When shall mankind relearn that happiness is not a product but a by-product and is only attainable by a personal relationship and submissive obedience to God through Jesus Christ?

''I would like to direct my efforts to dissuade others from 'majoring on the minors.' It is more than my ambition; it is more than my craving; it is even more than my obligation—it is my love for God that compels me to press on.

''There is for others—a way. There is for all—a truth. There is for you (as well as I)—a life.''

* * *

GEORGE, Stefan (Anton)   1868-1933

BRIEF ENTRY: Born July 12, 1868, in Buedesheim, Germany (now West Germany); died December 4, 1933, in Minusio, Switzerland. German poet and translator. Stefan George created a concern for the precision of language that revitalized German poetry in the 1890's. He believed that poetry should express mood, not thought, and chose each word for its ability to evoke the desired mood. His poetry was difficult to translate, and to many English-speaking readers it seemed stark, even flat. But critics believed his perfection of form, regular rhythms, and purity of style achieved heights previously considered impossible in the German language. He traveled and studied all over Europe, and his early books, like *Hymnen* (1890), show the influence of the French symbolist poet Mallarme. In *Pilgrimages* (1891), George saw the poet as a sacred isolated wanderer with an exalted mission. He established the George Group, dedicated against materialism, naturalism, and, above all, debasement of the German language. Much of his writing during this time was intended only for members of his elite group, and its private nature tended to discourage outsiders. When he finally permitted wide distribution of his poetry, George encountered critical and public controversy. *The Seventh Ring* (1907) established a somewhat mystical and godlike image of youth, which disturbed many German readers. It also attracted the approval of Nazi worshippers of youth, who saw it as an eloquent propaganda tool. George refused their honors, went into self-imposed exile in Switzerland in 1933, and died there the same year. *Biographical/critical sources:* Ulrich K. Goldsmith, *Stefan George: A Study of His Early Work,* University of Colorado Press, 1959; *Encyclopedia of World Literature in the Twentieth Century,* updated edition, Ungar, 1967; *Twentieth-Century Literary Criticism,* Volume 2, Gale, 1979.

*   *   *

GERARD, Louise   1878(?)-1970

OBITUARY NOTICE: Born c. 1878; died November 5, 1970, in Nottingham, England. Novelist and traveler. Gerard wrote twenty-three novels, including *The Flower of the Flame, Fruit of Eden,* and *Strange Paths.* Obituaries and other sources: *AB Bookman's Weekly,* January 4, 1971.

*   *   *

GERDEN, Friedrich Carl
   See GREVE, Felix Paul (Berthold Friedrich)

*   *   *

GERIN, Winifred   1901(?)-1981

OBITUARY NOTICE—See index for *CA* sketch: Born c. 1901; died June 28, 1981, in London, England. Author. Acclaimed for her biographies of the Brontes, Gerin received the James Tait Black Memorial Prize, the British Academy's Rose Mary Crawshay Prize for English Literature, and a Heinemann Award for her book on the life of Charlotte Bronte. For the author's services to literature, she was made an officer of the Order of the British Empire in 1975. Besides *Charlotte Bronte: The Evolution of Genius,* she wrote *Horatia Nelson,* the life of Viscount Horatio Nelson's daughter, and most recently the biography of Anne Thackeray Ritche, William Makepeace Thackeray's child. Her other Bronte biographies include *Anne Bronte, Branwell Bronte: A Biography, Emily Bronte,* and a two-volume work, *The Brontes.* Obituaries and other sources: *Chicago Tribune,* July 1, 1981; *AB Bookman's Weekly,* July 27, 1981.

*   *   *

GERMANN, Richard Wolf   1930-

PERSONAL: Born May 14, 1930, in Berlin, Germany; came to the United States in 1949, naturalized citizen, 1955; son of Walter (an electronics engineer) and Katharina (a music teacher; maiden name, Klein) Germann; married Sheridan Biays (a writer and specialist in musical instrument decoration), December 27, 1958. *Education:* Studied in Germany and at Boston University; California Pacific College, M.A., 1977. *Home:* 32 Chest-

nut St., Boston, Mass. 02108. *Agent:* Max Gartenberg, 331 Madison Ave., New York, N.Y. 10017. *Office:* Bernard Haldane Associates, 545 Boylston St., Boston, Mass. 02116.

CAREER: Bernard Haldane Associates (international career counselors), Boston, Mass., executive vice-president and director of client services, 1965—. Photographer. Member of board of directors of Lander-Brown Group, Ltd. (corporate and psychological services firm).

WRITINGS: (Editor with Peter Arnold, and contributor) *Bernard Haldane Associates: Job and Career Building,* Harper, 1980; *Reflections of Nature* (photographs), Allen Co., 1977. *Photographs,* Quark Press, 1979. Author of "Job Success," a column in *Boston Herald American.* Contributor to periodicals.

WORK IN PROGRESS: Working and Liking It, with Diane Blumenson and Peter Arnold.

SIDELIGHTS: Germann told *CA:* "My major reason for writing about job finding and career building is the need for educating the public on this vital subject. People spend thousands of dollars on getting an education, and are not taught how to use that education in a fulfilling and remunerative way. My hope is that in years to come, the subject of careers will become equivalent in our educational institutions with reading and writing.

"To me photography is not a hobby, but a necessary counterpart to my work in career education. It's a way to use my creative talent and exercise my visual sense. My philosophy of making photographs is that they are made in the mind and not in the camera. The camera is simply a tool for communicating what I see to others. My favorite subjects are the cathedrals of Europe, and aspects of nature that parallel those great buildings."

*   *   *

GIACOSA, Giuseppe   1847-1906

BRIEF ENTRY: Born October 21, 1847, in Colleretto Parella (now Pedanea), Italy; died September 1, 1906, in Colleretto Parella, Italy. Italian playwright, poet, and short story writer. Giacosa is considered one of Italy's most important realistic playwrights. He first gained popularity, however, with his romantic verse comedies set in the Middle Ages. The first of these plays, "The Wager; or, A Game of Chess" (1873), was so successful that he was able to abandon his law practice and write full time. About 1890 he fell under the influence of the French naturalists and became a leader of the *verismo* movement in Italy. He began writing dramas in prose, concentrating on serious social topics and seeking to reassert the moral values of middle-class society. Of these plays, "Unhappy Love" (1887) is considered by some critics to be his best work. Later work, including his last play, "The Stronger" (1904), showed the influence of Ibsen and some of the European writers of psychological novels. Giacosa is also remembered for his librettos for Puccini operas, including "La Boheme" (1896), "Tosca" (1899), and "Madame Butterfly" (1903). *Biographical/critical sources: McGraw-Hill Encyclopedia of World Drama,* McGraw, 1972.

*   *   *

GIBBON, Lewis Grassic
   See MITCHELL, James Leslie

GIBBS, (Cecilia) May   1877-1969
(C.M.O. Kelly)

OBITUARY NOTICE: Born in 1877 in Surrey, England; died November 27, 1969, in Sydney, Australia. Artist, illustrator, and author. In many of her works for children, Gibbs wrote of the Australian landscape, helping her readers identify with their own land. During World War I Gibbs used her talents as an artist to produce calendars, postcards, and booklets; her success in this work gave her the encouragement to write her best-known book, *Snugglepot and Cuddlepie.* She also wrote a popular comic strip that ran for more than forty years in Australian newspapers. Gibbs's other works include the fiction volumes *Wattle Babies* and *Prince Dande Lion: A Garden Whim-Wham* as well as the verse volume *Bib and Bub: Their Adventures.* Obituaries and other sources: *AB Bookman's Weekly,* January 19, 1970; *Twentieth-Century Children's Writers,* St. Martin's, 1978.

* * *

GIBRAN, Kahlil   1883-1931

BRIEF ENTRY: Born January 6, 1883, in Bechari, Lebanon; died April 10, 1931, in New York, N.Y. Lebanese-American painter, novelist, poet, and essayist. Often called "the Blake of the twentieth century," Gibran, espousing a religion of love, beauty, and redemption, influenced youths in America and in Arabic countries. His plays contained "mystical vision" and "metrical beauty," while his novels were vehicles for stating his personal views. His best work, the novel *The Prophet,* has been translated into thirteen languages and is the first part of a trilogy that teaches men the mastery of life. *The Prophet* deals with man's relation to his fellow man; *The Garden of the Prophet* explores the state of affairs between man and nature; and *The Death of the Prophet* looks at man's relationship with God. Gibran also wrote *The Forerunners* (1920), *Sand and Foam* (1926), *Jesus the Son of Man* (1928), *The Earth Gods* (1931), *Tears and Laughter* (1947), and *Nymphs of the Valley* (1948). *Biographical/critical sources: Twentieth Century Authors: A Biographical Dictionary of Modern Literature,* H. W. Wilson, 1942, 1st supplement, 1955; *Cassell's Encyclopaedia of World Literature,* revised edition, Morrow, 1973; *Twentieth-Century Literary Criticism,* Volume 1, Gale, 1978.

* * *

GIBSON, Gerald Don   1938-

PERSONAL: Born November 22, 1938, in Marshall, Tex.; son of Felix and Lucy Viola (Webb) Gibson; married Emily Ann Cooper (an organist), August 25, 1965. *Education:* Attended University of Texas, 1958-59; Eastman School of Music, B.A., 1962, M.A., 1975; Syracuse University, M.S.L.S., 1968. *Residence:* Rockville, Md. *Office:* Department of Motion Pictures, Broadcasting, and Recorded Sound, Library of Congress, Washington, D.C. 20540.

CAREER: Professional bassoonist, 1958-68; Sibley Music Library, Eastman School of Music, Rochester, N.Y., record librarian, 1963-72; Library of Congress, Washington, D.C., cataloger in music section, 1972-74, assistant head of recorded sound in music division, 1974-79, head of curatorial section of motion picture, broadcasting, and recorded sound division, 1979—. *Member:* International Association of Music Libraries, International Association of Sound Archives, American National Standards Institute, Association of Recorded Sound Collections (president, 1976-78), Association of Audio Ar-

chives (chairman, 1978—), Music Library Association (member of board of directors, 1979-81).

WRITINGS: (Contributor) Pearce Grove, editor, *Nonprint Media in Academic Libraries,* American Library Association, 1975; *Bibliography of Discographies,* Volume I: *Classical Music,* Bowker, 1977. Author of "Annual Cumulation of Bibliography of Discographies," a column in *Association of Recorded Sound Collections Journal,* 1972-75. Editor of *Association of Recorded Sound Collections Journal,* 1972—.

WORK IN PROGRESS: Bibliography of Discographies, Volumes II-V; a discography of organ recordings.

* * *

GIDE, Andre (Paul Guillaume)   1869-1951

BRIEF ENTRY: Born November 22, 1869, in Paris, France; died February 19, 1951, in Paris, France; buried in Cuverville, France. French novelist, essayist, translator, playwright, diarist, and critic. Gide's extensive body of work reveals many of the transformations and transitions in the author's life as he confronted and struggled with personal conflicts. Originally associated with the symbolist school of the turn of the century, Gide later assumed the stance of a moralist in the tradition of Montaigne and Rousseau and dealt controversially with the subjects of sex, religion, and politics. He was torn between the demands of spiritual and physical life and wrote *Les Nourritures Terrestres* (1897; translated as *Fruits of the Earth,* 1949) as a celebration of desire and the senses. His ambivalence over Catholicism and Protestantism is evident in *La Symphonie Pastorale* (1919; translated as *Pastoral Symphony,* 1931). Gide caused great scandal over revelations of his homosexuality in *Corydon* (1924; translated as *Corydon,* 1950) and in *Si Le Grain ne meurt* (1926; translated as *If It Die,* 1935). Among Gide's most widely read and critically acclaimed works are *Les Caves du Vatican* (1914; translated as *The Vatican Swindle,* 1925), an ironic and surrealist tale of crime, and *Les Faux Monnayeurs* (1926; translated as *The Counterfeiters,* 1927), an examination of the French bourgeoisie noted for its subtle psychological characterization. As an essayist Gide spoke against colonialism, fascism, and war, and he defended homosexuality and communism. A trip to Soviet Russia in 1936, however, disillusioned Gide, and he withdrew from political activity soon after. Gide's journals, which span fifty years, are considered by some to contain the author's finest work. He was awarded the Nobel Prize for literature in 1947. *Biographical/critical sources: Cyclopedia of World Authors,* Harper, 1958; *The Concise Encyclopedia of Modern World Literature,* Hutchinson, 1963; Wallace Fowlie, *Andre Gide: His Life and Art,* Macmillan, 1965; *Encyclopedia of World Literature in the Twentieth Century,* updated edition, Ungar, 1967; *Twentieth-Century Writing: A Reader's Guide to Contemporary Literature,* Transatlantic, 1969.

* * *

GIGGAL, Kenneth   1927-
(Henry Marlin, Angus Ross)

PERSONAL: Surname is pronounced Jig-*gawl;* born March 19, 1927, in Dewsbury, England; son of Stanley (a laborer) and Emma (Kirkham) Giggal; married Alice Drummond, 1947; children: Anne Gail. *Education:* Attended grammar school in Dewsbury, England. *Politics:* "Non-partisan." *Religion:* Agnostic. *Home:* The Old Granary, Bishop Monkton, Harrogate, North Yorkshire, England. *Agent:* Andrew Mann Ltd., 1 Old Compton St., London W.1, England.

CAREER: D.C. Thomson (publisher of magazines and newspapers), sales manager in Dundee, Scotland, 1952-59, and London, England, 1959-71; writer, 1971—. *Military service:* Royal Navy, Fleet Air Arm, telegraphist/air gunner, 1944-52; served in Korea. *Member:* Writers Guild of Great Britain, Crime Writers Association, London Arms and Armour Society, Savage Club. *Awards, honors:* Truth Prize from *Truth* magazine, 1952, for story "All On a Summer's Day."

WRITINGS—Espionage novels; under pseudonym Angus Ross: *The Manchester Thing,* John Long, 1970; *The Huddersfield Job,* John Long, 1971; *The London Assignment,* John Long, 1972; *The Dunfermline Affair,* John Long, 1973; *The Bradford Business,* John Long, 1974; *The Amsterdam Diversion,* John Long, 1974; *The Leeds Fiasco,* John Long, 1975; *The Edinburgh Exercise,* John Long, 1975; *The Ampurias Exchange,* John Long, 1976, Walker & Co., 1977; *The Aberdeen Conundrum,* John Long, 1977; *The Burgos Contract,* John Long, 1978, Walker & Co., 1979; *The Congleton Lark,* John Long, 1979; *The Hamburg Switch,* Walker & Co., 1980; *The Deep Purple Fall,* Wahlstrom, 1981; *Sagarro,* Wahlstrom, 1981.

Also author, under pseudonym Angus Ross, of *Sad City Blues,* a collection of short stories which form the basis for a television series, and *The Gentle Art of Murder,* a collection of television plays. Author, under pseudonym Henry Marlin, of numerous Western novels. Contributor of more than two hundred stories and reviews to magazines, including *Geographical.*

WORK IN PROGRESS: The Great American Tragedy (tentative title), a major work to demonstrate his view that the wrong side won the American Civil War; *The Edelman Fund* and *A Bad April,* both novels.

SIDELIGHTS: Giggal's books have been published in Italy, Norway, Sweden, Denmark, Finland, France, and Germany.

He commented: "I was the eldest of thirteen children in a desperately poor family and believe me, anyone who did not actually live through the Hungry Thirties can have no conception of what it was really like. We lacked all but the very basic means of survival, and we *never* had enough to eat.

"This is not gratuitous information. That which happened to me in my childhood should help explain the attitudes of some of the characters in some of my books and plays.

"I escaped into the Royal Navy at the earliest possible age and so began my real education, in the seaports of the world. I cannot ever remember not wanting to be a writer, and my first short story appeared in *Sea Cadet* in 1946. I continued to write short stories and articles throughout the rest of my years in the Navy—and, indeed, still do.

"The history of the American West had always fascinated me, and I began in about 1950 to write a series of novels mostly based on actual incidents and set in accurate locations. All fifteen were published by the then-mighty but now-defunct Amalgamated Press of London.

"During the sixties, the ever-burgeoning responsibilities of my newspapers and magazines career precluded the writing of any other than short works, but my experience in Fleet Street, and the knowledge that many hot news stories were either heavily censored or suppressed by the Home Office, opened my eyes to the fact that espionage doesn't happen only in Washington and London and Bonn; it happens everywhere, and often in the most unlikely (to the uninitiated) places.

"An almost-forgotten incident in Manchester began to assume entirely new dimensions, and speculation as to what might *really* have happened set me off on a trail of research which led compulsively to my first espionage thriller, *The Manchester Thing.*

"This led, in turn, to the embracing of a long-subjugated ideal: I made the traumatic decision to resign my lucrative position, and devote the whole of my time to writing.

"Every title in the 'Towns' series is based very firmly on eminently credible acts of espionage, the subjects of which are meticulously researched. Locations especially so. If I do not already know a place extremely well, I go and live in it until I do. This makes for slow production, and I wish it didn't, but that's the way it is.

"Now, after having written more than thirty novels, most of my work over the past eighteen months has been for television. I find the medium exciting, and one in which—after years of hard-slog research—it is very easy to operate, mainly, I suppose, because the writing of dialogue was always my strongest point. However, and in spite of television's rich rewards, I remain at heart a writer of books.

"Aside from the odd day off for shooting in winter and fishing in summer, I work every day for an average nine hours. I have to. Like Chandler—who remains so far ahead of us all as to be practically out of sight—I write everything at least three times, and so quite agree with whoever it was who said, 'That which is easiest to read is always hardest to write.' Those lucky authors who lay blythe claim to produce a book a month will always be a source of wonder.

"My own novels have been reviewed in every major newspaper in the United Kingdom, and in many others abroad, but that which I found most gratifying was a review of *The Amsterdam Diversion* which appeared, following the book's publication in 1974, in Scotland's prestigious *Glasgow Herald:* 'Hard, fast, efficient prose style, much rarer than one realises, and much more difficult to effect than its simplicity and unpretentiousness suggests.' This, for me, is what it's all about."

BIOGRAPHICAL/CRITICAL SOURCES: Dast, volume X, number 4, 1977.

*   *   *

GILBERT, Doug   1938-1979

OBITUARY NOTICE: Born in 1938; died July 10, 1979, of injuries received in an automobile accident. Journalist and author. Doug Gilbert, who in 1978 was named Canadian sportswriter of the year, served for eighteen years as sports columnist for Canadian and American newspapers. He was an authority on the East German sports system and produced a book on that subject entitled *The Miracle Machine.* Obituaries and other sources: *Publishers Weekly,* August 6, 1979.

*   *   *

GILBERT, W(illiam) S(chwenck)   1836-1911
(Bab)

BRIEF ENTRY: Born November 18, 1836, in London, England; died of a heart attack, May 29, 1911, in Harrow Weald, Middlesex, England. English playwright, librettist, poet, humorist, attorney, and author. Gilbert began his career as a clerk in the Privy Council Office. When a small inheritance enabled him to quit his job, he studied law and practiced that profession for four years until his growing literary success prompted him to write full time. Gilbert contributed regularly to *Fun* magazine under his childhood nickname Bab. His humorous sketches and poems were collected in two volumes entitled *Bab Ballads* (1869) and *More Bab Ballads* (1872). "Dulcamara" was his first produced play, scoring a success for its author in 1866. Gilbert met Arthur Sullivan in 1870, and by the following year the two began their famous partnership. In the first collaboration of its kind, Gilbert wrote the librettos to accompany Sullivan's music. Their comic operas were witty, clever parodies of Victorian society. With such works as "Trial by Jury" (1875), "H.M.S. Pinafore" (1878), and "The Pirates of Penzance" (1880), both attained a popularity that neither equaled in their separate careers. Gilbert is credited as being one of the first modern directors in that he supervised the rehearsals of his plays, finalized all stage directions, and critiqued the actors. He brought to the English theatre a degree of professionalism not previously achieved. His autocracy, however, caused friction with Sullivan, and their stormy twenty-five year collaboration ended in 1896. His other writings include *Engaged* (1878), *Patience; or, Bunthorne's Bride* (1902), and *Iolanthe and Other Operas* (1910). *Residence:* Harrow Weald, Middlesex, England. *Biographical/critical sources: The New Century Handbook of English Literature,* revised edition, Appleton, 1967; *The Reader's Encyclopedia of World Drama,* Crowell, 1969; *The Penguin Companion to English Literature,* McGraw, 1971; *Twentieth-Century Literary Criticism,* Volume 3, Gale, 1980.

*   *   *

GILES, John 1921-

PERSONAL: Born February 1, 1921, in London, England; son of John Samuel and Ellen (Little) Giles; married Margery Lilian MacLeod (a receptionist), December 14, 1946; children: Howard Martin. *Education:* Attended technical school in London, England. *Politics:* Conservative. *Religion:* Church of England. *Home:* Guilton Mill, Poulton Lane, Ash, near Canterbury, Kent CT3 2HN, England.

CAREER: Charles Page & Co. Ltd., London, England, assistant manager of chemical department, 1947-56; Chemical and Feeds Ltd., London, England, manager of chemical department, 1956-66; Air Products Ltd., New Malden, England, senior contracts negotiator, 1966-72; writer, 1972—. Partner and director of Western Front Audio Tours Ltd.; tour consultant and guide to World War I battlefields. Member of Nottingham Rate Payers Association, 1962-63; member of London borough of Bromley council, 1963-66, chairman of civil defense committee, 1965; chairman of Chislehurst political education committee, 1964-66. Member of Conservative Political Centre, London, 1963-65; Conservative candidate for Parliament, 1965. *Military service:* British Army, Royal Artillery and Royal Fusiliers, 1939-47; served in Africa; became lieutenant. Royal Auxiliary Air Force, 1949-59; became flight lieutenant. Royal Air Force Officer Reserve, 1959; *Member:* International Institute of Strategic Studies, Royal British Legion, Military Historical Society, Western Front Association (founder; chairman), King's African Rifles Officers Dinner Club.

WRITINGS: The Ypres Salient, Leo Cooper, 1970, revised edition published as *The Ypres Salient: Flanders Then and Now,* I.E. Picardy, 1979; *The Somme: Then and Now,* Bailey Brothers & Swinfen, 1977. Contributor to newspapers.

WORK IN PROGRESS: A two-volume book on the western front in World War I, one volume on the British sectors, the other on the American sectors, publication expected in 1983-84.

SIDELIGHTS: Giles is considered an authority on World War I battlefields. His first book, *The Ypres Salient,* presents the story of Ypres and the battles of Flanders during 1914-18. His second book, *The Somme: Then and Now,* provides an account

of the military campaign at Somme and the battles which claimed more than one million Allied casualties. Both books include eyewitness reports of battle and photographs contrasting war time scenes with pictures of the same locations as they appear today.

Giles commented: "I concentrate specifically on the subject of World War I, my motivation stemming from the experiences of my father, a regular soldier who was seriously wounded during the retreat from Mons in 1914. I am deeply moved by the subject and have been since I was a small boy. I have visited the old western front battlefields every year for the past twenty years, sometimes three or four times a year.

"A serious health problem forced my early retirement from business, and although this has interfered considerably with my general activities, it has enabled me to pursue my writing on a limited basis.

"I have traveled widely, mainly during my business days, and spent some years in East Africa, where I learned Swahili. European travels included regular visits to Germany, France, Belgium, Denmark, the Netherlands, Spain, Switzerland, Norway, and Sweden."

BIOGRAPHICAL/CRITICAL SOURCES: Kent Life, April, 1974, November, 1978; *East Kent Mercury,* October 6, 1977, October 27, 1977, October 4, 1979; *Kentish Gazette,* October 7, 1977, November 24, 1978; *Bookseller,* November 24, 1979.

*   *   *

GILLESPIE, Dizzy
See GILLESPIE, John Birks

*   *   *

GILLESPIE, John Birks 1917-
(Dizzy Gillespie)

PERSONAL: Born October 21, 1917, in Cheraw, S.C.; son of James (a brickmason) and Lottie (Powe) Gillespie; married Lorraine Willis (a dancer at time of marriage), May 9, 1940. *Education:* Attended Laurinburg Institute, 1933-35. *Religion:* Baha'i. *Home:* 477 North Woodland, Englewood, N.J. 07631. *Office:* c/o Sutton Artists, 505 Park Ave., New York, N.Y. 10022.

CAREER: Jazz trumpet player, 1930—; jazz arranger, 1935—; jazz composer, 1940—. Member of Teddy Hill Orchestra, 1937 and 1938, Cab Calloway Orchestra, 1939-41, Earl Hines Orchestra, 1942-43, Billy Eckstine Orchestra, 1943-44; leader of Dizzy Gillespie Orchestra, 1945-50, Dizzy Gillespie Sextet/Quintet, 1950-56, and Dizzy Gillespie Orchestra, 1956; member or leader of various other big bands and combos. Founder of Dee Gee Record Company, 1951. Appointed cultural emissary of U.S. State Department, 1956 and 1973. Candidate for U.S. presidency, 1964.

Appeared in films, including "Case of the Blues," 1942, "Jivin' in Bebop," 1947, "A Date With Dizzy," 1956, "The Hole," 1962, "The Cool World," 1963, "Youth Wants to Know," 1963, "Jazz Casual," 1964, "Dizzy Gillespie," 1964, "The Hat," 1964, "Jazz All the Way," 1964, "Duke Ellington—I Love You Madly," 1966, "Monterey Jazz Festival," 1967, "It Don't Mean a Thing," 1967, "Monterey Jazz," 1968, "Duke Ellington at the White House," 1969, "Legacy of the Drum," 1970, "Till the Butcher Cuts Him Down," 1971, "Singer Bowl Renamed," 1973, "Dizzy in Brazil," 1973, "Voyage to Next," 1974, "Newport Jazz Festival," 1975,

"Second Chance Sea," 1976, "Everybody Rides the Carousel," 1976, "Whither Whether," 1977.

Appeared on television shows, including "Stage Entrance," 1952, "Person to Person," 1956, "This Is New York," 1957, "Timex All-Star Jazz Show," 1959, "The Lively Ones," 1962, "Bell Telephone Hour: Jazz the Intimate Art," 1968, "Contemporary Memorial," 1968, "Fourth Bill Cosby Special," 1971, "Just Dizzy," 1971, "Timex All-Star Swing Festival," 1972, "Jazz Is Our Religion," 1972, "Jazz the American Art Form," 1972, "Profile: Dizzy Gillespie," 1975, "In Performance at Wolf Trap," 1976, "The Rompin', Stompin', Hot and Heavy, Cool and Groovy All-Star Jazz Show," 1976, "Like It Is," 1976, "Soundstage: Dizzy Gillespie's Be Bop Reunion," 1976, "Like It Is," 1978, "Big Band Bash," 1978, "Soundstage: David Amram and His Friends," 1978, and "The Gulf Road Show," "The Three Flames Show," "Tonight Show," "Today Show," "Ed Sullivan Show," "Al Hirt Show," and "Merv Griffin Show."

AWARDS, HONORS: Jazzmobile Incorporated, Jazzmobile Award, 1967, Grand Master of Jazz Award, 1976; National Academy of Recording Arts and Sciences, nomination for best jazz performance by a group for "Giants" album, 1971, nomination for best jazz performance by a soloist for "Portrait of Jenny," 1971, Grammy Award for best jazz performance for "Oscar Peterson and Dizzy Gillespie" album, 1975, nomination for best jazz performance by a big band for "Afro-Cuban Jazz Moods" album, 1976; Handel Medallion from city of New York, 1972; Ph.D. from Rutgers University and Paul Robeson Award from Institute of Jazz Studies, both 1972; named Duke Ellington fellow of Branford College, Yale University, 1972; citation from mayor of New York City, 1975; Grand Master Award from Jazz Heritage Society, 1976; citation from Joint Session of the South Carolina Legislature, 1976; award from Tau Nu chapter of Omega Psi Phi fraternity, 1976; named Honorary Associate of Mather House, Harvard University, 1977; Ph.D. from Chicago Conservatory of Music, 1978; winner of Bill Sears Heavenly Horn Award. Honored at numerous jazz festivals and workshops and at several colleges and universities. Received keys to cities, including Telluride, Colo., Hamden, Conn., and Annapolis, Md.

Magazine awards: New Star Award from *Esquire,* 1944; more than thirteen awards from *Downbeat,* 1956—, including election to *Downbeat* Music Hall of Fame, 1960; more than ten awards from *Playboy* Readers' Poll, 1957-67, and winner of *Playboy* Musician's Poll for best trumpet, 1960-71; nearly twenty awards from *Metronome,* 1947-60; more than twenty awards from *Jazz Hot,* 1948-68.

WRITINGS—Under name Dizzy Gillespie: *Trumpet Styles: Trumpet Solos With Piano Accompaniment,* transcribed and with piano scores by Frank Paparelli, Leeds Music Corp., 1945; (with Al Fraser) *To Be or Not to Bop: Memoirs* (autobiography), Doubleday, 1979. Also author of *The Dizzy Gillespie Big Bands,* c. 1960.

Composer of songs, instrumentals, and film scores: "Pickin' the Cabbage," 1940; "Paradiddle," 1940; "A Night in Tunisia," 1942; "Salt Peanuts," 1942; "Woody'n You," 1944; "Bebop," 1944; "Dizzy Atmosphere," 1945; "Groovin' High," 1945; "Oop Bop Sh'Bam," 1946; "Things to Come," 1946; "Cool Breeze," 1946; "Diggin' for Diz," 1946; "One Bass Hit," 1947; "Two Bass Hit," 1947; "Oop-Pop-A-Da," 1947; "Ool-Ya-Koo," 1947; "Good Bait," 1947; "Ow," 1947; "Manteca," 1948; "Cubana Be Cubana Bop," 1948; "Tin Tin Deo," 1948; "Afro-Cubano Suite," 1948.

"Blue 'n' Boogie," 1951; "Anthropology," 1951; "Birks Works," 1951; "Swing Low, Sweet Cadillac," 1953; "Oop-Shoo-Bee-Doo," 1953; "Con Alma," 1954; "Hey Pete," 1956; "Dizzy's Business," 1956; "Kush," 1961; "Cool World," 1964; "The Hat," 1965; "Brother K," 1973; "Dizzy's Party," 1976. Also composer of "Something Old, Something New,"; "Lorraine," "Interlude," "Bye," "Blue Mood," "Sugar Hips," "Devil and the Fish," "Rails," "Rumbola," "Fais Gaffe," "This Is the Way," and "Double Six of Paris."

Recordings: "The Men From Minton's," Esoteric, 1941; "Dizzy Gillespie Sextet," Manor, 1945; "Dizzy Gillespie Sextet," Guild/Musicraft, 1945; "Dizzy Gillespie All-Star Quintet," Guild, 1945; "Dizzy Gillespie Jazzmen," Dial, 1946; "Dizzy Gillespie With Johnny Richards' Orchestra," Paramount, 1946; "Dizzy Gillespie Sextet," Musicraft, 1946; "Dizzy Gillespie and His Orchestra," Victor, 1947; "Dizzy Gillespie's Band," Black Deuce, 1947; "Dizzy Gillespie and His Orchestra," Arco, 1947; "Dizzy Gillespie and His Orchestra," Victor, 1947; "Dizzy Gillespie and His Orchestra," Swing, 1948; "Dizzy Gillespie and His Orchestra," Gene Norman Presents, 1948; "Dizzy Gillespie and His Orchestra," Victor, 1949; "Dizzy Gillespie and His Orchestra," Capitol, 1949.

"Dizzy Gillespie Sextet," Dee Gee, 1951; "Dizzy Gillespie and His Sextet," Dee Gee, 1951; "Dizzy Gillespie and the Cool Jazz Stars," MGM, 1952; "Dizzy Gillespie Quintet," Vogue, 1953; "Quintet of the Year—Jazz at Massey Hall," Debut, 1953; "Jam Session," Clef, 1953; "Dizzy Gillespie—Stan Getz," Norgran, 1953; "Dizzy Gillespie and His Orchestra," Norgran, 1954; "Dizzy Gillespie and His Latin-American Rhythm," Norgran, 1954; "Dizzy Gillespie and Roy Eldridge," Clef, 1954; "Dizzy Gillespie and His Orchestra," Norgran, 1956; "Dizzy Gillespie's All-Stars (For Musicians Only)," Verve, 1956; "Dizzy Gillespie and His Orchestra," Verve, 1957; "Dizzy Gillespie—Stuff Smith," Verve, 1957; "Dizzy Gillespie and His Orchestra," Verve, 1957; "Dizzy Gillespie With Sonny Stitt and Sonny Rollins," Verve, 1957.

"Katie Bell Nubin With Dizzy Gillespie and His Orchestra," Verve, 1960; "Dizzy Gillespie Quintet," Verve, 1961; "The Dizzy Gillespie Quintet," Philips, 1962; "Dizzy on the Riviera," Philips, 1962; "Dizzy Gillespie and His Orchestra," Limelight, 1962; "The Dizzy Gillespie Quintet," Philips, 1963; "Dizzy Gillespie and Les Doubles Six," Philips, 1963; "The Dizzy Gillespie Sextet," Philips, 1964; "Dizzy Gillespie Quintet (Jambo Caribe)," Limelight, 1964; "Jazz on a Sunday Afternoon," Solid State, 1967; "Dizzy Gillespie Reunion Big Band," SABA, 1968.

"The Real Thing," Perception, 1970; "A Portrait of Jenny," Perception, 1971; "Giants," Perception, 1971; "Dizzy Gillespie/Mitchell—Ruff Duo," Mainstream, 1971; "The Giant," Prestige, 1973; "Dizzy Gillespie's Big Four," Pablo, 1974; "Oscar Peterson and Dizzy Gillespie," Pablo, 1974; "Dizzy Gillespie y Machito: Afro-Cuban Jazz Moods," Pablo, 1975; "Dizzy's Party," Pablo, 1976; "Carter, Gillespie Inc.: Benny Carter and Dizzy Gillespie," Pablo, 1976; "Free Ride," Pablo, 1977; "Dizzy Gillespie Jam—Montreux '77," Pablo, 1977.

Numerous other recordings include recordings as member of the bands of Teddy Hill, Lionel Hampton, Cab Calloway, Lucky Millinder, Duke Ellington, Coleman Hawkins, Billy Eckstine, Sarah Vaughan, Charlie Parker, and others.

SIDELIGHTS: A widely recognized performer, composer, and arranger, Gillespie is considered a key figure in American musical and social history. As *New York Times* writer Gary Giddins declared, Gillespie is "the man whose bulging cheeks and upturned trumpet bell symbolize jazz." Gillespie is known as one of the creators of bebop, a jazz form that revolutionized the sound of American popular music. This new style of music heralded social change as well; Gillespie and his fellow musicians became leaders in promoting racial pride among American blacks.

Although Gillespie is essentially a jazz musician, he has earned the admiration of leaders in other musical genres. "That man!," exclaimed the late conductor Dimitri Mitropoulous. "When I heard him I was thrilled to death!" Conductor Andre Previn called Gillespie "inventive," "a great trumpet player," and "the perfect jazz musician." Producer and music critic Martin Williams asserted that "John Birks 'Dizzy' Gillespie is a great figure in American music, in world music, and perhaps the greatest living musical innovator we have."

Gillespie's musical talents emerged at an early age: when he was fifteen he won a scholarship to Laurinburg Institute, a technical college in North Carolina, where he studied music theory and harmony for the next two years. While at Laurinburg he began to sit in with touring southern dance bands. "Once, when King Oliver's band came to Cheraw I got an offer [for a job]," Gillespie related. "But at that time, I'd just turned sixteen and was too damned scared to leave home. I'd never ever heard of King Oliver. . . . I didn't know he was so famous. I wasn't hip to King Oliver and knew very little about Louis Armstrong."

The aspiring Gillespie's knowledge of the jazz greats of the early thirties was gained mainly through a neighbor's radio, and this exposure shaped the young trumpeter's hopes for the future. He dreamed of playing with Teddy Hill's Orchestra, which broadcast from New York's Savoy Ballroom. "The whole band gassed me," Gillespie recalled, but he gave special status to the band's lead trumpeter, Roy Eldridge: "Roy was the messiah of our age. . . . We tried to play just like him."

In 1937 Roy Eldrige left Teddy Hill's Orchestra and Gillespie realized a dream: the orchestra asked Gillespie to play lead trumpet for its European tour. Although he had been playing professionally for two years, for Gillespie this tour was the true start of his career. "The real reason Teddy hired me, I believe, was because I sounded so much like Roy," Gillespie mused. "He wanted to keep . . . someone who could play high, fast, and with fire. I had been practicing Roy's solos for almost three years; they were like second nature to me."

Though initially derivative of Eldridge's style, Gillespie's own trumpet style had already begun to develop and distinguish itself at the time he joined Teddy Hill's Orchestra. By 1939 Gillespie, in addition to playing in various big bands, was experimenting with totally new sounds in after-hours jam sessions at New York's Minton's Playhouse. With drummer Kenny Clarke, pianist Thelonious Monk, and bassist Oscar Pettiford, Gillespie began to define a new musical form now known as bebop. Differing greatly from the swing jazz of the thirties and forties, bebop is characterized by great technical facility and speed, rapidly changing modern harmonies, and asymmetrical, syncopated rhythmic phrasing over a fluid drum pulse. "In addition to what it did rhythmically," explained jazz critic Ralph J. Gleason in 1974, "the bebop revolution worked out in small group playing the exploration of all the musical devices of classical music, the use of intervals as surprise, the harmonies and tempos which were excluded almost totally from the big band style."

In *To Be or Not to Bop* Gillespie commented on the development of bebop: "What we were doing at Minton's was playing, seriously, creating a new style of music. . . . We had some fundamental background training in European harmony and music theory superimposed on our own knowledge from Afro-American musical atradition. . . . Musically, we were changing the way that we spoke, to reflect the way that we felt. New phrasing came in with the new accent. Our music had a new accent." Gillespie told *New York Times* writer Gary Giddins about the other instrumentalists in the group at Minton's: "Harmonically, [our pianist] Monk played different from anybody. He was the most original. If you played with him and didn't know the chords, it was shame on you, because he'd embellish and you wouldn't be able to follow." In *To Be or Not to Bop* Gillespie added: "Monk's contribution to the new style of music was mostly harmonic and also spiritual, but [drummer] Kenny Clarke set the stage for the rhythmic content of our music."

Another major innovator in the development of bebop was saxophonist Charlie "Bird" Parker. Gillespie first met Parker in 1940 at a Kansas City hotel. "The moment I heard Charlie Parker, I said, there is *my* colleague," Gillespie recalled in his autobiography. "I never heard anything like that before. The way that he assembled notes together. . . . Charlie Parker and I were moving in practically the same direction too, but neither of us knew it." Parker moved to New York City in 1942, and began playing with the Minton's crowd, influencing the evolution of bebop. Gillespie wrote, "Charlie Parker's contribution to our music was mostly melody, accents, and bluesy interpretation." He further commented to Giddins: "Charlie Parker was the architect of the new sound. He knew how to get from one note to another, the style of the thing. Most of what I did was in the area of harmony and rhythm. . . . When I found out how Charlie Parker played, it was just what I needed to put with my contribution." Thus Gillespie and Parker created a form of music that, according to jazz critic Ralph Gleason, "literally changed the sounds of America." Gleason observed that musicians were "forced to reconsider all their assumptions about playing once they heard Dizzy and Bird."

Although bebop initially caused outrage among musicians, critics, and the public, the music eventually gained in popularity and became a social influence, with Gillespie as its leader. A sort of bebop cult arose, patterning its unique vocabulary and dress after the speech and appearance of bop musicians, principally Gillespie. The "hip" talk and bop uniform—beret, horn-rimmed sunglasses, and goatee—were later adopted by the beatnik movement. Bebop heralded social change on a deeper level as well. Black bebop musicians were conscious of their important contribution to the national culture, and helped awaken racial pride in other American blacks. Bop drummer Kenny Clarke explained this aspect of the bebop contribution: "These young guys that were coming up under us, we were teaching them that whatever you do, get an education. Then you can do whatever you wanna do. . . . The idea was to wake up, look around you, there's something to do."

Gillespie's position as a socio-cultural figure was evident in many activities. In the late fifties he was the first jazz musician appointed cultural ambassador by the U.S. State Department. On tours the Dizzy Gillespie Orchestra represented the U.S. in Africa, Asia, the Near East, Eastern Europe, and South America. In 1972 Gillespie was a guest of the government of Kenya, and in 1977 he performed in Cuba to signal the end of the U.S. trade embargo. He has made films acclaimed for their social message, and he even campaigned for president of the United States in 1964. Gillespie affirmed the social aspect of his music: "The role of music goes hand in hand with social reformation—the changing of society to make things right. . . . Music must reflect society, world society, and the way society is moving because musicians depend upon the society to sustain them; at the same time, music and musicians must help to set things right."

The trumpeter's interest in world cultures has influenced his music in ways that have, in turn, influenced American music as a whole. In 1947 he initiated and made popular a synthesis of jazz and Afro-Cuban rhythms that still thrives. And as a result of Gillespie's first tour of South America the samba and bossa nova were introduced to North American listeners. These innovations have remained important elements in American musical development.

Gillespie has continued to shape the direction of American music. In the early sixties Gleason claimed: "Gillespie is one of the great musicians in jazz history, a trumpet virtuoso without peer and an experimenter and innovator who, after twenty years at the picket point of jazz's development, still is searching and exploring." Throughout the seventies and into the eighties bebop enjoyed a revival, during which Gillespie appeared at workshops and festivals, performed for three presidents at the White House, toured in the U.S. and abroad, and contracted a new series of recordings with Pablo Records. "With the new interest in be-bop, a new vigor has entered Gillespie's playing, and at the age of 60 he is enjoying a renaissance," announced Giddins. In the spring of 1981 Gillespie launched "Jazz-America," a public television project that will present the history of jazz and will include excerpts from two Gillespie concerts performed at New York's Avery Fisher Hall. In a review of these concerts, which featured Gillespie at the head of a bebop quintet and a seventeen-piece big band, *Downbeat*'s Lee Jeske noted that Gillespie has been "at the forefront of jazz for over 40 years. . . . Even at age 63, Gillespie is a true master of improvisation and inspiration."

After more than four decades in the public arena, Gillespie's music and personality have carried undeniable impact. "Dizzy . . . made his mark with such strength that those who came after, no matter who they are, or who they ever will be, must take him into account," declared Gleason. Tenor saxophonist Illinois Jacquet explained that Gillespie has contributed his own style to the world of music. "I saw him developing a style from the early forties up until now. And he has not changed, spiritually, from the time I met him up until now. . . . He has maintained dignity and discipline as a jazz musician, as a trumpet player, and as a man."

The sense of humor and playfulness that earned him the nickname "Dizzy," and the compassion for his fellow man evident in Gillespie's humanitarian activities reveal a personality as dynamic and impressive as the trumpeter's music. This personality emerges clearly in Gillespie's 1979 autobiography, *To Be or Not to Bop: Memoirs*. Jazz scholar Leonard Feather said in his review of the book: "Gillespie is one of the jazz world's noblest and most astonishing survivors . . . and is at once one of the most brilliant, creative, funny and liked innovators in the history of jazz. In these pages, more often by accident than design, he shows us why."

The book contains not only Gillespie's memories but the stories and comments of friends, family, and fellow musicians. "What we learn about," observed Feather, "is the experience of being young, brilliant and black in an America that was more likely to stifle than succor a talent such as Gillespie's." Through Gillespie's account, a vivid picture develops of a nation rapidly, sometimes violently, changing, both musically and socially. Critic Amiri Baraka (Leroi Jones) predicted that *To Be or Not to Bop* "will be a standard reference—musically, historically, socially. It tells us something about America North, and about some of everybody in it." Author and critic Claude Brown summarized, "*To Be or Not to Bop*, a joyous, boisterous chronicle, is also a desperately needed history that will endure as a testament to a giant of modern jazz."

BIOGRAPHICAL/CRITICAL SOURCES: George T. Simon, *The Big Bands*, Macmillan, 1967; Rudi Blesh, *Combo: U.S.A.*, Chilton, 1971; Nicholas Slonimsky, *Music Since 1900*, 4th edition, Scribner's, 1971; Ralph J. Gleason, *Celebrating the Duke, and Louis, Bessie, Billie, Bird, Carmen, Miles, Dizzy, and Other Heroes*, Little, Brown, 1975; Leonard Feather, *The Pleasures of Jazz*, Horizon, 1976; *New York Times*, June 25, 1978, May 23, 1980; Dizzy Gillespie and Al Fraser, *To Be or Not to Bop: Memoirs*, Doubleday, 1979; *Detroit News*, September 2, 1979; *Washington Post Book World*, September 30, 1979; *New York Times Book Review*, February 3, 1980; *Downbeat*, June, 1981.*

—*Sketch by Diane L. Dupuis*

*   *   *

GILROY, Harry   1908(?)-1981

OBITUARY NOTICE: Born c. 1908 in Newark, N.J.; died June 16, 1981, in Browns Mills, N.J. Journalist. In his twenty-one-year career as a writer for the *New York Times*, Harry Gilroy served variously as feature writer, foreign correspondent, and cultural news reporter. During the mid-1950's he covered the Arab-Israeli conflict from Egypt and Israel, and during the early 1960's he reported from Holland and Belgium on the developing Common Market. Obituaries and other sources: *New York Times*, June 18, 1981.

*   *   *

GINGELL, Benjamin Broughton   1924-

PERSONAL: Born in 1924 in Devon, England; son of Walter Craven (an architect) and Mary Inez (Chambers) Gingell; married Jennifer Hamilton Barry, October 4, 1976. *Education:* Corpus Christi College, Oxford, B.A., received M.A., 1950; attended University of Arkansas, 1950. *Politics:* Liberal. *Religion:* Church of England. *Home:* Illyria, 1 Addington Lane, Borrowdale, Salisbury, Zimbabwe. *Office:* P.O. Box ST 125, Southerton, Salisbury, Zimbabwe.

CAREER: Macmillan Publishing Co., Inc., New York, N.Y., educational adviser in New York and England, 1953-57; educational adviser in the Far East for Longmans, Green, & Co., 1957-59; manager and director of Longman Rhodesia, 1959-74, managing director, 1974-79; managing director of Longman Zimbabwe, 1980—. *Military service:* British Army, 1943-47; served in India; became captain. Rhodesian Police Reserve, 1975-80; received Zimbabwe Service Medal and Zimbabwe Independence Medal. *Member:* International P.E.N. (chairman of Rhodesian Centre, 1972-74; vice-chairman, 1974-77), Institute of Directors. *Awards, honors:* Keats Literary Award, 1972 and 1974.

WRITINGS: The Queen's Prayer, Longman Rhodesia, 1977. Also author of *Human and All Human*, 1946, and *Boy of God*, 1972.

WORK IN PROGRESS: Africa Agonistes.

*   *   *

GIRAUDOUX, (Hippolyte) Jean   1882-1944
(Andouard, Maurice Cordelier, J.-E. Maniere)

BRIEF ENTRY: Born October 29, 1882, in Bellac, France; died January 31, 1944, in Paris, France. French novelist and playwright. Though known primarily for his plays, Giraudoux was a prolific writer of novels, essays, and short stories long before he began writing scripts for the stage. His novels, which include *Suzanne et le Pacifique* (1921; translated as *Suzanne and the Pacific*, 1923), *Bella* (1926), and *Choix des elues* (1939), are recognized for their humor, whimsy, fantasy, and impressionism. Those elements are also evident in his plays, many of which starred the French actor Louis Jouvet. During the 1930's Jouvet and Giraudoux worked closely, producing a new play nearly every year. Among Giraudoux's dramas are *Judith: Tragedie en trois actes* (1932), *La Guerre de Troie n'aura pas lieu: Piece en deux actes* (1935; translated as *Tiger of the Gates*, 1955), and *Ondine: Piece en trois actes* (1939; translated as *Ondine*, 1954). *Biographical/critical sources: Cyclopedia of World Authors*, Harper, 1958; *Encyclopedia of World Literature in the Twentieth Century*, updated edition, Ungar, 1967; *The Penguin Companion to European Literature*, McGraw, 1969; *Twentieth-Century Literary Criticism*, Volume 2, Gale, 1979.

* * *

GLAISTER, John   1892-1971

OBITUARY NOTICE: Born in 1892 in Glasgow, Scotland; died October 4, 1971, in Glasgow, Scotland. Physician, lawyer, educator, and author. John Glaister, a professor of forensic medicine at Glasgow University, wrote numerous textbooks in his field, including *Medical Jurisprudence and Toxicology, Hairs and Wools of Mammalia*, and *The Power of Poison*. He also published an autobiography entitled *Final Diagnosis*, and he contributed articles to many scientific journals. Obituaries and other sources: *The Author's and Writer's Who's Who*, 6th edition, Burke's Peerage, 1971; *AB Bookman's Weekly*, November 8, 1971; *Who Was Who Among English and European Authors, 1931-1949*, Gale, 1978.

* * *

GLASGOW, Ellen (Anderson Gholson)   1873(?)-1945

BRIEF ENTRY: Born April 22, 1873 (some sources say 1874), in Richmond, Va.; died November 21, 1945, in Richmond, Va. American author. Glasgow was among the first post-Civil War writers to realistically address social issues in the South. Her early novels, such as *The Voice of the People* (1900) and *The Battle-Ground* (1902), portray the South's contemporary values as ludicrous and idealistic. Though Glasgow continued to expose the folly of Southern values in dramatic novels such as *Virginia* (1913), her career peaked with a series of comedies in the 1920's. In both *The Romantic Comedians* (1926) and *They Stooped to Conquer* (1929) she incisively exposed the absurdity of conventional Southern morality. Many readers were particularly shocked by *They Stooped to Conquer*, in which an unwed mother defies social custom by refusing to ostracize herself while pregnant. Glasgow's penchants for irony and humor merged in *The Sheltered Life* (1926), a novel concerning a woman whose perception of morality prevents her from dealing with her husband's carousing. In addition to her novels, Glasgow also wrote collections of poems, short stories, and essays. She received the Pulitzer Prize in 1942. *Biographical/critical sources:* Ellen Glasgow, *The Woman Within*, Harcourt, 1954; *Cyclopedia of World Authors*, Harper, 1958; *Encyclopedia of World Literature in the Twentieth Century*, updated edition, Ungar, 1967; *Twentieth Century Writing: A Reader's Guide to Contemporary Literature*, Transatlantic, 1969; *Twentieth-Century Literary Criticism*, Volume 2, Gale, 1979.

* * *

GLASS, Malcolm (Sanford)   1936-

PERSONAL: Born December 11, 1936, in Winter Park, Fla.; son of Nelson Sanford (an educator) and Jane (a legal secretary; maiden name, Roberts) Glass; married Anne Davis (a professor of music), July 23, 1959; children: Laurens Elizabeth, Lucinda Anne, Malcolm Brian. *Education:* Stetson University, A.B., 1958; Vanderbilt University, M.A., 1961, doctoral study, 1961. *Politics:* Independent. *Religion:* Independent. *Home:* 166 West Glenwood Dr., Clarksville, Tenn. 37040. *Office:* Department of Languages and Literature, Austin Peay State University, Clarksville, Tenn. 37040.

CAREER: Florida Symphony Orchestra, Orlando, percussionist, 1957-58; Orlando Junior College, Orlando, instructor in English, 1961-62; Austin Peay State University, Clarksville, Tenn., assistant professor, 1962-67, associate professor of English, 1967—. Director and participant in workshops and readings; poetry and photography exhibited in group shows. Director of Kentucky poets-in-the-schools program, 1971-73. Member of Tennessee Arts Commission literary arts panel; member of Clarksville mayor's Council on the Arts and Clarksville Committee on the Humanities; judge of poetry contests.

MEMBER: Associated Writing Programs, Conference on College Composition and Communication, National Council of Teachers of English, Southeastern Conference on English in the Two-Year College, Tennessee Council of Teachers of English, Tennessee Literary Arts Association (vice-president). *Awards, honors:* Grant from Rotary International for Australia, 1967; grants from National Endowment for the Arts and Kentucky Arts Commission, 1971-73; grant from National Endowment for the Arts and Tennessee Art Commission, 1976; fellowship from Southern Federation of State Arts Agencies, 1977; National Endowment for the Humanities fellowship, 1978; distinguished professor award from Austin Peay State University, 1981.

WRITINGS: (Contributor) Richard Langford and William Taylor, editors, *The Twenties: Poetry and Prose*, Everett/Edwards, 1966; (editor with M. Joe Eaton) *Grab Me a Bus* (poems), Scholastic Book Services, 1974; (with Eaton and Stephen Dunning) *Poetry Two*, Scholastic Book Services, 1975; *Bone Love* (poems), University Presses of Florida, 1978; (with Dunning and others) *Writing*, three volumes, Scholastic Book Services, 1978.

Scripts: "A Poem Like Me," first broadcast by Kentucky Educational Television, September, 1972; "What Is a Poet?," first broadcast by WKPC-TV, December, 1975; "The Rehearsal Dinner" (two-act play), unproduced.

Work represented in anthologies, including *An Anthology: The Green River Review, 1968-1973*, edited by Angus Wilson, Green River Press, 1974; *Barbeque Planet Sampler*, edited by Bob Millard, Brevity Press, 1977; *Poets on Photography*, edited by Mark Melnicove, College of the Atlantic, 1979; *Brand X Anthology of Poetry: A Parody Anthology*, edited by William Zaranka, Applewood Books, 1981. Member of editorial board of "Contemporary Poetry Series," Associated Writing Programs. Contributor of poems and articles to magazines, including *Appalachian Journal, Cimarron Review, New Letters, Poetry Northwest, Prairie Schooner*, and *Southern Voices*.

WORK IN PROGRESS: Two novels.

SIDELIGHTS: Glass told *CA:* "As a writer I am primarily known as a poet, but I have written and published fiction, and recently finished a full-length play. I write for readers, not for critics or other writers. As a teacher I specialize in teaching writing—in all genres, and my methods can best be described as inductive. Writing is neither a vocation nor an avocation for me: it is too pleasurable to be considered work, and I take it too seriously for it to be considered a hobby.

"I can't think of any events or experiences which have influenced my thinking or my work. That is, I can't think of any specific incidents that stand out particularly. I suppose I would have to say that *all* events or experiences influence my writing and my views, although it is hard sometimes to see how events affect me. Experience builds and accumulates, and all of it plays a part in shaping what we think and do. Writers are not alone in this; what sets them apart, perhaps, is that they may be more aware of this process than some people and that they like to talk about it more than most people."

*   *   *

GLAZNER, Joseph Mark   1945-

PERSONAL: Born February 25, 1945, in Plainfield, N.J.; son of Louis (a manufacturer) and Sophie (an artist and musician; maiden name, Brody) Glazner. *Education:* University of Southern California, B.A. (magna cum laude), 1967. *Residence:* Toronto, Ontario, Canada. *Agent:* Georges Borchardt, Inc., 136 East 57th St., New York, N.Y. 10022.

CAREER: Free-lance journalist, filmwriter, and photographer, 1967-70; Orba Information Ltd., Montreal, Quebec, partner and editor-in-chief, 1970-74; Southam Communications Ltd., Toronto, Ontario, associate editor of *Executive*, 1974-76; Northern Telecom Ltd., Toronto, manager of corporate communications in Toronto and Montreal, 1976-79; free-lance writer, 1979—. *Member:* Phi Beta Kappa.

WRITINGS—Novels: *Smart Money Doesn't Sing or Dance,* Warner Books, 1979; *Fast Money Shoots From the Hip,* Warner Books, 1980; *Dirty Money Can't Wash Both Hands at Once,* Warner Books, 1980; *Big Apple Money Is Rotten to the Core,* Warner Books, 1981; *Hot Money Can Cook Your Goose,* Warner Books, 1981.

WORK IN PROGRESS: Death in Gomorrah, a novel.

*   *   *

GLEASON, Abbott   1938-

PERSONAL: Born July 21, 1938, in Cambridge, Mass.; son of S. Everett (a historian and public official) and Mary Eleanor (a painter and writer; maiden name, Abbott) Gleason; married Sarah Fischer (a specialist in historic preservation), 1966; children: Nicholas Abbott, Margaret Holliday. *Education:* Attended University of Heidelberg, 1960-61; Harvard University, B.A., 1961, Ph.D., 1969; Brown University, M.A., 1973. *Office:* Kennan Institute for Advanced Russian Studies, Woodrow Wilson International Center for Scholars, Smithsonian Institution Bldg., Washington, D.C. 20560.

CAREER: Brown University, Providence, R.I., assistant professor, 1968-73, associate professor, 1973-78, professor of history, 1978—. Research associate at Russian Research Center, Harvard University, 1968-79; secretary of Kennan Institute for Advanced Russian Studies, Woodrow Wilson International Center for Scholars, 1980—. *Member:* American Historical Association, American Association for the Advancement of Slavic Studies, National Council for Soviet and East European Research (member of board of trustees, 1980—). *Awards, honors:* American Philosophical Society grant, 1971; Howard Foundation fellow, 1973-74; Rockefeller Foundation fellow at Aspen Institute for Humanistic Studies, 1977.

WRITINGS: European and Muscovite: Ivan Kireevsky and the Origins of Slavophilism, Harvard University Press, 1972; *Young Russia: The Genesis of Russian Radicalism in the 1860's,* Viking, 1980. Contributor to *Modern Encyclopedia of Russian*

and Soviet History. Contributor of articles and reviews to scholarly journals.

WORK IN PROGRESS: Editing a book tentatively titled *The Formative Years of Soviet Culture.*

SIDELIGHTS: Gleason told *CA:* "As I suspect a good many historians do, I have something of a double nature. Although I'm a lifelong and card-carrying liberal, the conservative and socially romantic part of my nature manifests itself in a deep interest in conservative and nationalist political movements, which have been central to almost everything I have ever written."

*   *   *

GLOAG, John (Edwards)   1896-1981

OBITUARY NOTICE—See index for *CA* sketch: Born August 10, 1896, in London, England; died July 17, 1981. Advertising executive and author. A director at the Pritchard Wood & Partners advertising agency, Gloag wrote novels, poems, short stories, and books on advertising, as well as works on architecture, industrial design, and other technical subjects. He was a member of the board of trustees of Sir John Soane's Museum for ten years and president of the Society of Architectural Historians of Great Britain. Gloag received a silver medal and a bicentenary gold medal from the Royal Society of Arts, an organization for which he was a council member and a vice-president. Among Gloag's nonfiction works are *Simple Schemes for Decoration, The American Nation: A Short History of the United States,* and *Victorian Comfort: A Social History of Design From 1830-1900.* His fiction includes *Sacred Edifice, Mr. Buckley Is Not at Home,* and *The Eagles Depart.* Obituaries and other sources: *London Times,* July 18, 1981; *AB Bookman's Weekly,* September 14, 1981.

*   *   *

GLUSS, Brian   1930-
(Brian Gluzman)

PERSONAL: Born August 23, 1930, in London, England; came to the United States in 1955, naturalized citizen, 1964; son of Joseph Mordechai (a fur and skin merchant) and Otilie (Tenenhaus) Gluss. *Education:* Cambridge University, B.A., 1952, diploma in mathematical statistics, 1953, M.A., 1956; University of California, Berkeley, Ph.D., 1965. *Politics:* "Eclectic, imaginative, and undogmatic." *Home address:* c/o Chodorow, 1821 La Coronilla Dr., Santa Barbara, Calif. 93109.

CAREER: London School of Economics and Political Science, London, England, research assistant, 1953-54; Prudential Assurance Co., London, actuarial clerk, 1954-55; University of Chicago, Chicago, Ill., statistician for law school's jury project, 1955-56; Dominion Bureau of Statistics, Ottawa, Ontario, assistant to senior research statistician, 1956-58; Illinois Institute of Technology, Research Institute, Chicago, computing and engineering researcher, 1958-63; RAND Corp., Santa Monica, Calif., member of mathematical staff, 1964-66; GE/TEMPO, Santa Barbara, Calif., member of professional staff, 1966-68; University of Illinois at Chicago Circle, Chicago, associate professor, 1968-70, professor of business administration, 1970—. *Awards, honors:* Foundation scholar at Pembroke College, Cambridge, 1952.

WRITINGS: An Elementary Introduction to Dynamic Programming, Allyn & Bacon, 1972.

Author of screenplay "Casanostra" (under pseudonym Brian Gluzman). Contributor to numerous scientific journals and newspapers.

WORK IN PROGRESS: A novel, completion expected in 1984; *Memoirs of a Mediocre, Middle-Aged, Manic-Depressive Mathematician,* completion expected in 1985; research on handgun abolition, on nuclear arms, and on energy stocks in the West and Northwest.

SIDELIGHTS: Gluss commented: "My major interests include writing, teaching, and psychology, with active involvement in politics, national and international affairs, improvisational theatre, stand-up comedy, humanity. In life and in fiction, in reality and fantasy (which is which?), I have found three things to be of paramount import: the will to doubt, the active imagination, and a compulsion for quixotic adventurousness. I don't accept the world as it is, and certainly not the programmed unthinking idiocies of most political and military leaders. If, for example, *they* cannot escape from a language they have wrought that impedes thought and the will for constructive change, then we must not meekly or lazily enter with them into their fantasy-world. I am thinking particularly of the language and logic of nuclear arms and the handgun war, for I think I understand the realities of both far better than the policymakers do: I have had two families, and both have been devastated by war in the home, one by a bomb from an enemy plane, the other by a handgun wielded by the son of a judge.

"Once a headtripper, I do not discount the power of logic; I still value it highly, but I believe the evolution of policies that possess sanity depends also on understanding with one's heart, the ability to feel with one's guts what happens to other human beings in times of war, in times of violence. The impersonal 'objective' approach to policymaking on such issues is, I believe, psychotic and therefore dangerous. The 'we-have-ten-thousand-warheads-the-Russians-have-six-thousand-but-theirs-are-bigger' loses all meaning when merely four hundred warheads would wipe out the Soviet Union, and when our DEW detection system would enable us to send ours off as soon as theirs were on the way. Indeed, about the only missiles we would *not* be able to send off would be any of the new MX's that happened to be racing along their silly racetracks at the time. Yet the paranoid and meaningless phrase 'First Strike Capability' comes up at budget time every year. It is spoken by unthinking zombies to other unthinking zombies, who nod profoundly for the television cameras and for the voters, who assume the zombies must know what they're talking about because they themselves don't understand it. The time must come when the voters realize there is nothing there to understand.

"We must not accept the world as it is, and certainly not the world as such leaders see it. However quixotically, we must try to change things ourselves, and before we can do that we must develop the will to doubt. Despite our pride in our First Amendment rights, there is yet to be meaningful public debate on such issues in the media, which parrots the Alice-in-Wonderland absurdities cited above: just listen carefully and critically to 'Meet the Press,' and you'll realize quickly that at best we get thirty minutes of doublethink, at worst thirty minutes of intentional misinformation.

"As for writing fiction, I guess watching 'Meet the Press' is as good an education for it as anything. I referred earlier to the active imagination. For me, writing fiction suddenly became easy and 'real' when I developed the ability to build my characters in my mind and guts, using all my senses; when I began to see my characters, hear their voices, see the rooms they were in, the view through the windows, get into their guts and feel their feelings and think their thoughts, and feel their pain, their warmth, their love, their anger, their hate, their hope and despair. Once one can do this, the characters take over and write the story themselves, providing their own surprising turns, the most joyful moments in writing. Dialogue is no longer now-he-said-this-what-does-she-say-in-response; the characters simply talk to each other, the writer listens, then records what they say.

"I don't know how one develops this ability. For me, I think it was a coming together of improvisation onstage and in lecturing, and of my life's quest for feeling not only with my mind but also with my heart. In other words, becoming human."

* * *

GLUZMAN, Brian
 See GLUSS, Brian

* * *

GOACHER, Denis   1925-

PERSONAL: Surname is pronounced *Goash*-er; born September 6, 1925, in London, England; children: Kore, Fabrice, Orlando, Columbine. *Education:* Attended secondary school. *Politics:* "Royalist." *Religion:* "Believer." *Home:* Dione House, Wembworthy, Chulmleigh, North Devonshire, England.

CAREER: Free-lance writer, commentator, and actor.

WRITINGS: (Editor with Peter Whigham) Sophocles, *Women of Trachis* (translated by Ezra Pound), Neville Spearman, 1956; (with Whigham) *Clear Lake Comes From Enjoyment* (poems), Neville Spearman, 1959; (with Whigham) *The Marriage Rite* (poems), Ditchling Press, 1960; (translator) Dante Alighieri, *Inferno: Cantos 29-31,* BBC Publications, 1965; *Logbook* (poems), Grosseteste Review Books, 1972; *Night of the Twelfth, Thirteenth* (poems), Sceptre Press, 1973; (editor) Mike Ansell, *Soldier On* (autobiography), P. Davies, 1973; *Transversions* (poems), Gr/Ew Books, 1974; *Three Songs From the Romany King of Wembworthy, to the Accompaniment of a Jew's Harp and Bones,* Sceptre Press, 1976. Also editor of *Riding High,* 1974, and *Leopard,* 1980.

WORK IN PROGRESS: Translating a part of *Carmina Burana.*

SIDELIGHTS: Goacher wrote: "With no money at all except what I've earned or what well-wishers have sometimes thrown me, I have dedicated myself absolutely to poetry for the last thirty years. I have never written a line, for gain, that I have not wanted to write."

* * *

GODOY ALCAYAGA, Lucila   1889-1957
 (Gabriela Mistral)

BRIEF ENTRY: Born April 7, 1889, in Vicuna, Chile; died January 10, 1957, in Hempstead, N.Y. Chilean educator, stateswoman, and poet. Gabriela Mistral began her career as a teacher in rural Chile. She worked diligently for school reform and eventually served as director of elementary and secondary schools throughout Chile. In 1914 she was awarded first prize in Juegos Florales, a Santiago literary contest, for her poems "Sonetos de la muerte." The suicide of her fiance, after his involvement in embezzlement was discovered, had a profound effect on Mistral and was the motivating force behind much of her writing. Her despair over that event, as well as her concern for the world's oppressed people, is evident in her poetry. Named honorary consul by the Chilean Government, Mistral represented her country in Brazil, Spain, Portugal, and the United States. In 1945 she became the first South American to receive a Nobel Prize for literature. Included among her collections of poetry are *Desolacion* (1922), *Ternura* (1924), *Tala* (1938), and *Lagar* (1954). *Biographical/critical sources: Encyclopedia of World Literature in the Twentieth Century,* updated edition, Ungar, 1967; *Twentieth Century Writing: A Reader's Guide to Contemporary Literature,* Transatlantic, 1969; *The Penguin Companion to American Literature,* McGraw, 1971; *Twentieth-Century Literary Criticism,* Volume 2, Gale, 1979.

* * *

GODWIN, Anthony Richard James Wylie 1920(?)-1976
(Tony Godwin)

OBITUARY NOTICE: Born c. 1920 in Bosbury, Herefordshire, England; died of a heart attack, March 15, 1976, in New York, N.Y. Editor and publisher. At the time of his death, Tony Godwin was an editor and co-publisher with Harcourt Brace Jovanovich, Inc. During his lifetime involvement with books, he worked in and managed bookstores, including his own innovative Better Books store in London, which served as a center of literary and artistic activity for twenty years after World War II. Prior to joining Harcourt, he worked as a fiction editor at Penguin Books and later as joint managing director of Weidenfeld & Nicolson. Among the works he published are Edna O'Brien's *The Girl With the Green Eyes,* Lady Antonia Fraser's *Cromwell,* Len Deighton's *The Ipcress File,* and Mordecai Richler's *St. Urbain's Horseman.* He also published numerous books by best-selling author Irwin Shaw. Obituaries and other sources: *New York Times,* March 17, 1976; *Publishers Weekly,* March 29, 1976; *AB Bookman's Weekly,* April 5, 1976.

* * *

GODWIN, Tony
See GODWIN, Anthony Richard James Wylie

* * *

GOLAN, Aviezer 1922-

PERSONAL: Born July 17, 1922, in Jerusalem, Palestine (now Israel); son of Uri Armin (a merchant) and Dvora Ilona (Szmuk) Goldstein; married Zipora Blumstein, June 15, 1946; children: Amnon. *Education:* Attended secondary school in Tel Aviv, Israel. *Religion:* Jewish. *Home:* 5 Israels St., Tel Aviv, Israel. *Agent:* Mirna Pollak, 14 Stand St., Tel Aviv, Israel. *Office:* Yediot Ahronot, Petach Tikva Rd., Tel Aviv, Israel.

CAREER: Reporter for *Haboker* in Palestine and Israel; *Hamashkif,* Jerusalem, Palestine and Israel, correspondent, 1946-49; *Yediot Ahronot,* Tel Aviv, Israel, city editor, 1949-52, chief reporter, 1952-59, correspondent from London, England, 1959-60, chief reporter, 1960—. *Military service:* British Army, 1939-46; became sergeant. Irgun Zvai Leumi, 1946-48. Israel Defense Force, 1949-50. *Member:* Israel Journalists Association. *Awards, honors:* Rotenstreich Prize for Journalism from Israel Journalists Association; Meretz Prize for Journalism.

WRITINGS—In English translation; nonfiction: *Milhemet ha'atsma'ut,* I.D.F. Publications, 1968, translation published as *The War of Independence,* Israel Ministry of Defense, 1974; *The Commanders,* Moses Publishing, 1968; (with Marcelle Ninio) *Operation Susannah,* translated by Peretz Kidron, Harper, 1978; *Code Name: The Pearl,* Delacorte, 1980.

In Hebrew: *Medin'im ve'anshe-tsava* (title means "Statesmen and Military Leaders"; biographies), Moked, 1953; *Ma'arekhet Sinai* (title means "Operation Sinai"), I.D.F. Publications, 1960; *Shishah yeme tehilah* (title means "Six Days of Glory"), Dekel, 1967; (with Shelomo Nakdimon) *Begin* (biography), Idanim, 1978. Also author of *ha-Mizrah ha-tikhon,* 1966, *ha'Etsba' ba-tsafon,* 1967, *Lihyot hayal,* 1968, and *Anshe hapeladah,* 1969.

In Hebrew; titles in translation: *The First Thousand,* Mitzpeh, 1944; *Flames Over Jerusalem,* Ofakim, 1950; *Fighters for Freedom,* Friedman, 1954; *The Middle East,* I.D.F. Publications, 1966; *Men of Steel,* Otpaz, 1969; *To Be a Soldier,* I.D.F. Publications, 1969; *Albert* (biography), I.D.F. Publications, 1976; *Let Dawn Never Come,* Zmora, Bitan, Modan, 1978.

WORK IN PROGRESS: A novel set in Jerusalem in 1948.

BIOGRAPHICAL/CRITICAL SOURCES: Israel Book World, September, 1977.

* * *

GOLDBERG, Hyman 1908(?)-1970
(Prudence Penny)

OBITUARY NOTICE: Born c. 1908; died September 19, 1970, in Stamford, Conn. Journalist and author. Under the pseudonym Prudence Penny, Hyman Goldberg was the author of a newspaper column on cooking. Under his own name he wrote *Man in the Kitchen.* Obituaries and other sources: *New York Times,* September 20, 1970; *AB Bookman's Weekly,* October 5, 1970.

* * *

GOLDEN, Harry (Lewis) 1902-1981

OBITUARY NOTICE—See index for *CA* sketch: Born May 6, 1902, in New York; died after a long illness, October 2, 1981, in Charlotte, N.C. Publisher, editor, and author. Raised in New York, Golden left for the South, working as an advertising salesman and as a reporter for the *Charlotte Observer.* In 1941 he became the founder and publisher of the *Carolina Israelite,* a one-man newspaper which voiced his opinions on civil rights in a humorous manner and fought against racial bigotry in the South. His best-known theory to end segregation, the "Vertical Negro Plan," came in defense of the 1954 Supreme Court decision in *Brown* v. *Board of Education.* Commenting that Southern whites never objected to standing with blacks in supermarkets, elevators, or banks, Golden suggested that abolishing seats in public places and installing stand-up desks in schools would solve the problem of segregation "since no one in the South pays the slightest attention to a Vertical Negro." Writing when segregated facilities were the norm, Golden also observed that Southern whites would use black water fountains, for example, when theirs were out of commission. So the editor urged placing out-of-order signs on white facilities until their users adjusted to sharing with blacks. Golden was also known for his "White Baby Plan." At that time, only blacks accompanying white children to theatres could sit with whites, so Golden put forth that blacks should borrow white children if they wanted to attend the theatre. Prior to founding the *Carolina Israelite,* Golden was a stock brokerage operator who pleaded guilty in 1929 to mail fraud charges and served a four-year prison sentence. When the incident was made public, Golden, who changed his name from Goldhurst upon his release from prison, saw his popularity increase. In 1973 President Richard M. Nixon granted him a full presidential pardon. Golden wrote three best-sellers, *Only in America, For 2¢ Plain,* and

Enjoy! Enjoy!, the biography of his friend Carl Sandburg. Obituaries and other sources: *New York Times*, October 3, 1981; *Chicago Tribune*, October 3, 1981; *Washington Post*, October 3, 1981; *Time*, October 12, 1981; *Newsweek*, October 12, 1981; *AB Bookman's Weekly*, October 19, 1981.

*   *   *

GOLDFARB, Sally F(ay)   1957-

PERSONAL: Born March 31, 1957, in Morristown, N.J.; daughter of Samuel (an engineer) and Irene (a personnel administrator; maiden name, Dale) Goldfarb. *Education:* Yale University, B.A. (summa cum laude), 1978, J.D., 1982. *Residence:* New Haven, Conn. *Office:* c/o E. P. Dutton, 2 Park Ave., New York, N.Y. 10016.

CAREER: Writer, lawyer. *Member:* Phi Beta Kappa.

WRITINGS: (With David Leffell) *The Insider's Guide to the Colleges*, 7th edition (Goldfarb was not associated with earlier editions), Berkley Publishing, 1978; (with Joan Barrett) *The Insider's Guide to Prep Schools*, Dutton, 1979; *Inside the Law Schools*, Dutton, 1980. Contributor to *American Lawyer* and *Student Lawyer*.

WORK IN PROGRESS: Research on legal education.

SIDELIGHTS: Sally Goldfarb commented: ''American private educational institutions function largely in the absence of public scrutiny. My motivation in writing has been a desire to examine the facts that lie behind facades of prestige and selectivity, and to share students' views of their schools with prospective applicants.''

*   *   *

GOLDSMITH, Edward

PERSONAL—Office: Ecologist, 73 Molesworth St., Wadebridge, Cornwall PL27 7DS, England.

CAREER: Associated with *Ecologist* (magazine), Cornwall, England.

WRITINGS: (Editor and contributor) *Can Britain Survive?*, Tom Stacey, 1971; (with Robert Allen) *A Blueprint for Survival*, Houghton, 1972; *The Epistemological and Behavioural Basis of Culturalism: A General Systems Approach*, Wadebridge Ecological Centre, 1974; *The Stable Society*, Wadebridge Ecological Centre, 1977; (editor and contributor) *La Medecine en Question*, Fernand Nathan, 1981.

Contributor: (Author of introduction) Michael Allaby, *Who Will Eat?*, Tom Stacey, 1971; (author of introduction) John Milton and Taghi Farvar, *The Careless Technology*, Tom Stacey, 1971; *Can We Survive Our Future?*, Bodley Head, 1972; *Peace and the Sciences*, International Institute for Peace (Vienna, Austria), 1973; Dennis Meadows, editor, *Alternatives to Growth*, Ballinger, 1977; (author of introduction) Robert van den Bosch, *The Pesticide Conspiracy*, Prism Press, 1980. Contributor to *General Systems Yearbook*. Contributor to scholarly journals and popular magazines, including *Ecologist, Now!, Forum for a Better World, Manas,* and *Zygon*.

BIOGRAPHICAL/CRITICAL SOURCES: Teilhard Review, Volume VII, number 2, 1972; *Teach-In for Survival*, Robinson & Watkins, 1973.

*   *   *

GOMEZ, Joseph A(nthony)   1942-

PERSONAL: Born November 15, 1942, in Albany, N.Y.; son of Joseph A. (in business) and Mary (Van Wagenen) Gomez; married Mary C. Paolucci, September 7, 1963 (divorced); married Andrea Sharf (a filmmaker), March 20, 1976; children: Jodi, Jason, Sasha. *Education:* State University of New York at Albany, B.A., 1964; University of Rochester, M.A., 1967, Ph.D., 1975. *Office:* Department of English, Wayne State University, State Hall, Detroit, Mich. 48202.

CAREER: Temple University, Philadelphia, Pa., instructor in English, 1967-71; Mohawk Valley Community College, Utica, N.Y., assistant professor of English, 1971-76; Wayne State University, Detroit, Mich., associate professor of English, 1976—. *Awards, honors:* Woodrow Wilson fellowship, 1964-65; summer research grants from State University of New York, 1976, and Wayne State University, 1977 and 1980; American Council of Learned Societies fellowship, 1978.

WRITINGS: Ken Russell: The Adaptor as Creator, F. Muller, 1976, Pergamon, 1977; *Peter Watkins*, Twayne, 1979. Contributor of articles and film reviews to film journals, including *Film Heritage, Film Quarterly, Literature/Film Quarterly, Film Criticism, American Classic,* and *Screen*, and of book reviews to *Detroit Free Press*. Contributing editor of *Literature/Film Quarterly;* member of editorial board of *Film Criticism*.

WORK IN PROGRESS: A book on British film directors since World War II, publication by F. Muller expected in 1983.

SIDELIGHTS: Gomez told *CA:* ''I am especially attracted to writing about filmmakers whose work excites me but who have been unfairly ignored (Peter Watkins) or unjustly attacked (Ken Russell and Nicolas Roeg). Contrary to Francois Truffaut's claim that there is 'a certain incompatibility between the terms ''cinema'' and ''Britain,''' I believe that the study of British film can be rewarding and important. Perhaps the excellence of post-World War II British filmmakers has been largely ignored because of misguided critical attitudes which fail to recognize what is unique about their accomplishments. Those critics who identify the genius of British cinema chiefly with documentary realism mourn the manifestation of what might be called the neo-baroque style of Michael Powell, Ken Russell, and Nicolas Roeg. I hope that my work challenges the 'realist hegemony' of much British film criticism.''

BIOGRAPHICAL/CRITICAL SOURCES: Movie Maker, December, 1977; *Cineaste*, summer, 1980; *Film Quarterly*, summer, 1980.

*   *   *

GONGORA, Maria Eugenia   1948-

PERSONAL: Born October 15, 1948, in Seville, Spain; daughter of Mario (a historian) and Maria Helena (a teacher of English; maiden name, Diaz) Gongora. *Education:* University of Chile, teaching certificate, 1970; University of Madrid, Ph.D., 1974. *Home:* Seminario 395, Santiago, Chile. *Office:* Faculty of Philosophy, University of Chile, Larrain 9960, Santiago, Chile.

CAREER: University of Chile, Santiago, lecturer in medieval literature, 1975—. Lecturer at University of Valparaiso, 1975-76, and Technical University, Santiago, 1980. *Member:* French Institute, British Institute. *Awards, honors:* Scholar of Instituto de Cultura Hispanica, 1971-72, and British Council, 1977-79.

WRITINGS: (Translator and author of introduction and notes) *Poems de la Gran Guerra* (bilingual anthology in Spanish, German, English, and French; title means ''Poems of the Great War''), Ediciones Universitarias de Valparisao, 1980. Author of translation and revision of Tennyson's *Battle of Brunanburh*, Revista de Santiago, 1981. Contributor to literature journals.

WORK IN PROGRESS: Research on Chaucer's "former age," publication by Revista Chilena de Literatura, 1981.

SIDELIGHTS: Maria Gongora commented: "My main interests are medieval and modern literature (medieval lyrics, epic poetry, nineteenth- and twentieth-century poetry and novels), folk song, art, and architecture. I have lived in Spain and England for long periods and know the other European countries as well.

"I was brought up in a home where medieval art and history were known and loved. I went over to Europe twice with my parents as a child; I remember loving a few paintings and old Spanish castles at first sight. My first interest in medieval things was therefore in the field of art and architecture.

"I came to be interested in literature when I was reading French literature at the University. The rhythm of the *Chanson de Roland* impressed me strongly. My thesis on epic songs was born of that first rhythmic impression. Present-time folk song interests me in much the same way that medieval lyrics and epic songs do.

"I also find modern novels (Russian, English, and French) fascinating for their plots and characters; they are entertaining and interesting in a very direct way. Dostoevski I find more than interesting, and as I was very young when I read his work, it left quite an unforgettable impression. I was particularly touched by *Crime and Punishment* and *The Brothers Karamasov*. On the other hand, I am terribly fond of Dickens—especially of his comic or semi-comic novels. When I lived in Oxford in 1974 I went to lectures on Edward Lear and Lewis Carroll, and they are now favorites."

AVOCATIONAL INTERESTS: Travel, music, films, art, excursions in the country.

* * *

GOODKIN, Sanford R(onald)   1929-

PERSONAL: Born February 8, 1929, in Passaic, N.J.; son of Robert and Lillian (Ellman) Goodkin; married Frances Elizabeth Aist, July 9, 1950; children: Steven, Mark, Debra. *Home:* 501 Pine Needles Dr., Del Mar, Calif. 92014. *Office:* Sanford R. Goodkin Research Corp., 2190 Carmel Valley Rd., Del Mar, Calif. 92014.

CAREER: Sanford R. Goodkin Research Corp., Del Mar, Calif., founder and chairman of board of directors, 1958—. Member of board of governors of Ben Gurion University, visiting scholar, 1979, and senior fellow of Hubert Humphrey Center for Social Ecology. Adviser to Solar Energy Research Institute; past member of Urban Land Institute's committee on governmental regulations. Member of Town Hall of California, La Jolla Museum of Contemporary Art, Anti-Defamation League (regional chairman), and Bonds for Israel (chairman). Consultant to developers, investors, and city governments.

MEMBER: World Congress of Engineers and Architects (member of executive committee), National Association of Real Estate Editors, Institute of Residential Marketing, Lambda Alpha (founder of San Diego chapter; charter member; historian, 1979), San Diegans. *Awards, honors:* Max C. Tipton Memorial Award for Marketing Excellence, 1974; medal of honor from State of Israel, 1975.

WRITINGS: The Goodkin Guide to Winning in Real Estate, McKay, 1977. Author of columns in *Washington Post, Los Angeles Times,* and *California Builder.* Contributor to newspapers. Editor and publisher of *Goodkin Report, Web Apartment Reporter,* and *Energy Letter.* Contributing editor of

Professional Builder, California Business, San Diego Home and Garden, and *Building News.*

WORK IN PROGRESS: Second edition of *The Goodkin Guide to Winning in Real Estate;* a consumer self-help investment book.

SIDELIGHTS: Goodkin informed *CA* that he is one of the real estate industry's pioneers in the fields of research and strategic planning. He founded his company to offer a wide variety of services to developers, builders, investors, lenders, and government agencies, services that include assistance in all aspects of real estate, market analysis, physical planning, financial projections, marketing plans and systems, and investment/development strategies.

In a 1964 newspaper article, Goodkin predicted the condominium boom that occurred in the late 1960's and early 1970's. During a television interview in 1973, he predicted the housing price crisis of 1974-75. He is an authority on real estate analysis and is in demand as an instructor, lecturer, and commentator on the health and future of real estate. His columns appear in more than thirty publications across the United States.

Goodkin wrote: "I am tired of negative books, so my new investment book will be up-beat on all areas of investment. I believe implicitly in the power of the individual to create change. Real estate has been important because of its impact on the total environment of many families. I am especially interested in urban revitalization, and counsel many professional people.

"I represented the World Congress of Engineers and Architects in Egypt; I was the only American with the first Israeli group to attend.

"I believe success is a totality of marriage, family, business, and community service. I rise at 4:30 each morning to study religion and philosophy and to write. Celebrating the Sabbath, reading, and family life have been sanity-building experiences.

"I will continue to travel widely and do more and more writing, including a book on conversations between Moses and God from the human perspective—I am very excited about this."

* * *

GOODKIND, Henry M.   1904(?)-1970

OBITUARY NOTICE: Born c. 1904; died August 9, 1970, in New York, N.Y. Philatelist, editor, and author. Henry Goodkind wrote numerous articles and books on the history of airmail stamps, including *United States: The 5 Cent Beacon Air Mail Stamp of 1928.* Obituaries and other sources: *New York Times,* August 10, 1970; *AB Bookman's Weekly,* September 21, 1970.

* * *

GOODMAN, Ellen (Holtz)   1941-

PERSONAL: Born April 11, 1941, in Newton, Mass.; daughter of Jackson Jacob (a lawyer and politician) and Edith (Weinstein) Holtz; married, 1963 (divorced, 1971); children: Katherine Anne. *Education:* Radcliffe College, B.A. (cum laude), 1963. *Home:* 66 Stanton Rd., Brookline, Mass. 02146. *Office: Boston Globe,* 135 Morrissey Blvd., Boston, Mass. 02102.

CAREER: Newsweek (magazine), New York, N.Y., researcher and reporter, 1963-65; *Detroit Free Press,* Detroit, Mich., feature writer, 1965-67; *Boston Globe,* Boston, Mass., feature writer and columnist of "At Large," 1967—; syndicated columnist with Washington Post Writers Group, 1976—. Commentator on "Spectrum" show for Columbia Broadcasting

System (CBS-Radio), 1978; weekly guest commentator on "Today" show for National Broadcasting Co. (NBC-TV), 1979. *Awards, honors:* Named New England newspaper woman of the year by New England Press Association, 1968; Catherine O'Brien Award from Stanley Home Products, 1971; Nieman fellow at Harvard University, 1973-74; media award from Massachusetts Commission on the Status of Women, 1974; named columnist of the year by New England Women's Press Association, 1975; Pulitzer Prize, 1980, for commentary; distinguished writing awards from American Society of Newspaper Editors, 1980, for distinguished commentary.

WRITINGS: *Turning Points* (nonfiction), Doubleday, 1979; *Close to Home* (collection of newspaper columns), Simon & Schuster, 1979; *At Large* (collection of newspaper columns), Summit, 1981.

SIDELIGHTS: Called "a serious writer about soft subjects" by Katherine Winton Evans in the *Washington Journalism Review,* Goodman deals in her newspaper columns with such topics as parenting, changing values, divorce, alternative lifestyles, feminism, and gardening. The columnist, however, does not regard the issues she concentrates on as trivial. "I write about different things than other columnists. But I do it out of a sense of news judgment," she explained. "The major stories today are the family and what I call life-and-death issues." Apparently the Washington Post Writers Group agreed, for it syndicated her column in 1976 and sold it to three-fourths of its interested clients as an item for the editorial or op-ed (the page opposite the editorial page) pages. Diane McWhorter of the *Washington Journalism Review,* summarizing the views of William Dickinson, the editorial director of the Washington Post Writers Group, stated "that there was initially some resistance to . . . [Goodman's] gust of real life across the exclusively political plain of the editorial pages," but "editors also saw that [she] would attract women readers to the section."

Indeed, Goodman attracted readers of both sexes. Her column now appears in more than two hundred fifty newspapers and has become the Washington Post Writers Group's fastest-selling article. She appeals to readers across the nation. An editor from a small town in Minnesota observed that "people here like her because she never pulls any punches with highfalutin' language," while a *Los Angeles Times* newspaperman remarked that "what she says hits people in the gut." Critics also react favorably to Goodman's work. Evans appraised her as being "both witty and sensible, entertaining and thoughtful." The writer continued: "You could call her an egghead's Erma Bombeck or a less hilarious Nora Ephron or a steadier John Leonard but still not have her pegged exactly right." McWhorter asserted that Goodman "seems unflaggingly conscientious, even formidable, as she attacks controversies from abortion to housework to Alexander Solzhenitsyn with the combined grace and grit of a paratrooper."

In April, 1980, Goodman won the Pulitzer Prize for distinguished commentary. Regardless of the popularity of her column, the location of Goodman's articles on the editorial page was deemed by Dickinson as a major reason she won the coveted journalism award. "Position made the difference in the way that Goodman was perceived by the reader," he maintained. "By putting her on the editorial page instead of the women's pages, editors were saying 'Attention should be paid.'" Dickinson concluded that "if it had not been for 'the perception of seriousness,' I don't think she could have gotten the Pulitzer." McWhorter allowed that Goodman's "work is indeed a U-turn from the usual direction of hard-news-oriented punditry that the commentary Pulitzer normally honors."

The columnist published her first book in 1979. Begun while Goodman was a Nieman fellow at Harvard University, *Turning Points* explores how people have coped with the changes sparked by the feminist movement. The book incorporates interviews with more than one hundred fifty men and women on how these changes altered their values and lifestyles. In a *Washington Post Book World* review of *Turning Points,* Evans reflected that "the value of . . . [Goodman's] book lies less in the calibration of change than in the raw research, the vivid anecdotes with which these women and men describe their lives." "There's enough front-line reporting of the sexual revolution here," she elaborated, "to keep you thinking a long time about who is winning, who is losing and who the casualties are." Doris Grumbach of the *New York Times Book Review,* however, confessed that "most of the life stories seem commonplace, perhaps because change, especially in the lives of women, has been described so often of late." She added, "there seems little new in what they have to report about their lives." Critics also missed Goodman's sense of humor, which is so apparent in her columns but largely missing in *Turning Points.* "Clearly Goodman did not yet feel enough at ease with the book form to indulge in the humor and occasional recklessness that keep her columns from being heavy," McWhorter speculated. Evans warned that "Ellen Goodman fans will miss the light touch of her newspaper columns in this rather solemn treatise."

Close to Home, a compilation of more than one hundred Goodman columns, elicited the praise her commentary often receives, while drawing criticism for its lack of impact as a collection. Evans found that Goodman "is consistently fun to read, but not all at once." The reviewer further related: "These . . . pieces are like peanuts, very good, small and similar in form. If downed at one sitting, they could start delicious but end up bilious—like anything taken in excess." Molly Ivins theorized in the *New York Times Book Review* that she "suspect[s] it is the form." "Few columnists stand up well to being collected," she noted. "Humor seems to wear better than profundity in collections." Although citing some "obligatory quibbles" about *Close to Home,* John Leonard of the *New York Times* also praised the book. "One finishes . . . [it]," he reflected, "full of gratitude for having been introduced to a witty and civilized human being in a vulgar and self-pitying decade."

CA INTERVIEW

CA interviewed Ellen Goodman on August 4, 1980, in the newsroom of the *Boston Globe.*

CA: You worked as a researcher and reporter at Newsweek. *Did you move from researcher to reporter?*

GOODMAN: No. It was only because I was in the back-of-the-book feature sections that I got to do some reporting. Basically, I was a checker of facts.

CA: Was it mostly women who were researchers at Newsweek?

GOODMAN: It was exclusively women who were researchers and exclusively men who were writers.

CA: You must have had some feelings about that.

GOODMAN: I thought it was horrible! Horrible! But there was no recourse at that point. I was certainly aware that it wasn't fair.

CA: Did you get any flack when you worked as a reporter instead of as a researcher?

GOODMAN: It was sort of informal. I was in the television department for a year and when I did reporting it was quite informal.

CA: Do you know if the researcher/reporter system still exists at Newsweek?

GOODMAN: The system still exists but it's much more integrated than it was, in terms of the sexes.

CA: What did you do at the Detroit Free Press *and the* Boston Globe *before you became a columnist at the* Globe?

GOODMAN: At the *Free Press* I worked in the city room, so I did whatever they gave me to do, and I did a little of everything. I started out on the *Globe* on the Women's Pages, as they were then called, which is where the opening was. It was not my first choice at that time although I was subsequently glad I started on those pages.

CA: Do any of the stories you wrote at the Free Press *stand out in your memory?*

GOODMAN: You're talking to somebody with a lousy memory for these things. I liked doing the daily features. I always liked doing the things that were funny. I preferred the more light-hearted features to the very mundane, workaday fire stuff. You have more of a chance to write when you do features than you do when covering fires.

CA: Do any of the stories you wrote at the Globe, *before you started writing your column, stand out in your memory?*

GOODMAN: I remember several pieces I did then, many, but I couldn't single out one piece that changed American journalism.

CA: I did read about one piece you wrote for the Globe. *It was about a woman who had had an abortion. You interviewed the woman but then wrote the story without using any quotes from her.*

GOODMAN: That was very radical. I did it very much as a narrative and I didn't use one quote from her, which is very unusual. In a lot of papers, I wouldn't have been able to get that through.

CA: What was the reaction at the Globe? *Did they protest?*

GOODMAN: No, in fact they liked the story a lot, and ran it. I've been very lucky being at the *Globe.* They've been very supportive in that sense. They're interested in new forms. It was noted that the article was unusual but the reaction was, "Hey, that was an interesting thing to have tried." Also, I don't think I would have gotten that reaction in the city room. The Women's Pages were very experimental.

CA: How did you start writing a column? Was it an outgrowth of your Nieman fellowship?

GOODMAN: I started writing a column about 1970 when the *Globe* first opened up its op-ed page to inside columns. I wrote about six the first year and after that I was asked if I could do it once a week and I said yes. Then I went on my Nieman and when I came back I wrote columns full time.

CA: What was your original idea in writing a column? What inspired you to do it?

GOODMAN: I had a lot of opinions and I had to keep them out of the news hole.

CA: Did the Nieman fellowship change your column at all? Or was it just an unconnected event?

GOODMAN: It was all part of a process. I mean, why do you want to go on a Nieman? You probably want to go because you want to get out of daily journalism and think about what you're doing. That's one of the reasons why you apply. When I came back, I had solidified those feelings. I definitely wanted to try something new.

CA: Your column is no longer running three times a week, is it?

GOODMAN: Now I do two a week.

CA: Was it a problem doing columns full time?

GOODMAN: I think three columns a week is tough. You're always throwing away the third one. I think most people do. There are very few exceptions to that. If there are exceptions, Mary McGrory is one of them. She does four; she's extraordinary. Of course, she's doing a reporting column, too. You don't have to start from ground zero all the time.

CA: You've mentioned that you're able to put your opinions in your column. But are there any other advantages or disadvantages to writing a column as opposed to feature reporting?

GOODMAN: You're totally self-starting, totally dependent on your own ideas, when you write a column. You're constantly having to think and figure out what you think. It involves much more pressure than doing feature stories. With feature stories very often you wait until someone gives you the idea, and you're not putting yourself on the line all the time, either. Whenever I write something, that's me out there, in a way it isn't when you're a feature story writer.

CA: At what point did your column start being syndicated?

GOODMAN: In March, 1976.

CA: Was that for some particular reason? Were you writing about subjects people considered particularly interesting?

GOODMAN: It was part of a development. I had looked into a couple of ways of moving out, of having greater impact. I had been asked to go with one particular syndicate, but before that happened the Washington Post Writers Group took it.

CA: Has that caused you any problems? That is, do the papers your column is syndicated in censor you at all?

GOODMAN: I would be surprised if there were some papers that didn't run the abortion column. But on the whole, they run it pretty much as is and pretty much on schedule.

CA: Some papers carry your column on the editorial or op-ed pages and some on the women's or life-style pages. What are your feelings about that? Does that bother you at all?

GOODMAN: No, but that's kind of interesting to me. I get funny responses on that. I'm told that when it runs on the women's pages more men read it than usual and more women read it when it runs on the op-ed pages. I have no idea, though, what that means.

CA: Do any papers shift you back and forth depending on the subject?

GOODMAN: I don't think so. There's some sort of a structural purchase thing: you belong to one page or the other.

CA: Do you think it's fair to say you write about cozy subjects or questions, as opposed to larger or what some people might consider more important questions?

GOODMAN: I think I write about much more important questions than the average columnist. It is, in fact, much more important how we raise our children, much more important how we deal with moral and ethical issues, with underlying values, than it is whether Jimmy Carter can control his brother or not. I think an awful lot of columnists engage in trivia, the trivia of what is "important"; politics, for instance, is basically a game men play like any other sport, although not quite that, since the president is also ruling the country. But I think it is much more important to look at the underlying values by which this country exists. It is certainly not cozy to be talking about abortion, the vast social changes in the way men and women lead their lives and deal with each other, about children, about the whole category of subjects I deal with. Those subjects are certainly not cozy; they are pretty uncomfortable.

CA: Do you think that's the reason your column is one of the fastest-growing in the country, or are there other reasons?

GOODMAN: The issues people think are important are the things they're talking about, and these subjects aren't usually visible in the paper. So they're very pleased and relieved to find someone addressing them.

CA: Some people have compared you to Erma Bombeck. Do you think you two are comparable at all?

GOODMAN: We had a funny experience with that, actually, when the ads came out for my first book. The ads, which I had nothing to do with, identified me as "a thinking man's Erma Bombeck." Dumping on Erma Bombeck, you might say. As soon as I saw those ads I told the advertisers to change them. Then I wrote a letter to Erma Bombeck, whom I know only vaguely but like a lot, which said, "I didn't do it; forgive me." And she wrote me back a lovely note, because she is such a wonderfully nice human being, with the response: "Don't worry. When my first book came out, I ripped open the carton containing the paperback books, and written indelibly right across the front of the books was 'Jean Kerr, look to your daisies.'" You see what people do. You can't exist on your own. You can only be compared to other women. I think she's wonderful. But we're nothing alike.

CA: I noticed you do radio commentary, too.

GOODMAN: I did, but I haven't done it in a long time.

CA: Was that very different to do than writing a column?

GOODMAN: It involves a somewhat different style. It is a little more direct. And, of course, you have to deliver it.

CA: Did you find that a problem?

GOODMAN: No, I thought it was great.

CA: Has the Pulitzer Prize changed your life at all?

GOODMAN: No. I enjoyed it. I loved getting it, needless to say. But you know, in our business, you've got to get up the next morning and write the next column.

CA: I thought there might have been some adverse reaction from other people at the Globe.

GOODMAN: Well, I don't know that this is why there wasn't, but that same day the *Globe* got two other Pulitzers. So it was very much a family party. Everybody was extremely nice. It was a very, very nice day.

BIOGRAPHICAL/CRITICAL SOURCES: Newsweek, July 17, 1978; *New Republic,* March 10, 1979; *New York Times Book Review,* March 18, 1979, December 23, 1979, September 20, 1981; *Washington Post Book World,* March 25, 1979; *Chicago Tribune,* May 27, 1979; *New York Times,* November 11, 1979; *Washington Journalism Review,* January/February, 1980, September, 1980; *Washington Post,* September 21, 1981.

—Sketch by Anne M. Guerrini

—Interview by Peter Benjaminson

*   *   *

GOPAL, Sarvepalli   1923-

PERSONAL: Born April 23, 1923, in Madras, India; son of Radhakrishnan and Sivaramamma Sarvepalli. *Education:* Madras University, M.A., 1942, B.L., 1944; Oxford University, M.A., 1947, D.Phil., 1957. *Politics:* Liberal. *Religion:* Hindu. *Home:* 97 Radhakrishnan Salai, Madras 4, India.

CAREER: Andhra University, Waltair, India, lecturer, 1948-49, reader in history, 1949-52; National Archives, Delhi, India, assistant director, 1952-54; Ministry of External Affairs, Delhi, director of Historical Division, 1954-66; Oxford University, Oxford, England, reader in South Asian history, 1966-71; Jawaharlal Nehru University, New Delhi, India, professor of history, 1971—. Past chairman of National Book Trust of India. Fellow of St. Antony's College, Oxford, 1966—. President of Indian History Congress, 1978. *Member:* Royal Historical Society (corresponding fellow).

WRITINGS: The Permanent Settlement in Bengal, Allen & Unwin, 1949; *The Vice Royalty of Lord Ripon,* Oxford University Press, 1953; *The Vice Royalty of Lord Irwin,* Clarendon Press, 1957; *British Policy in India, 1858-1905,* Cambridge University Press, 1965; *Modern India,* Historical Association (London), 1967; *Jawaharlal Nehru,* J. Cape, Volume I: *1889-1947,* 1975, Volume II: *1947-1956,* 1980.

WORK IN PROGRESS: Editing *Selected Works of Jawaharlal Nehru;* writing the third and final volume of the biography of Jawaharlal Nehru, completion expected in 1983.

SIDELIGHTS: Gopal is recognized as an eminent scholar of Indian history. He is the son of a former president of India and maintained a personal friendship with Jawaharlal Nehru, India's prime minister from 1948 to 1964. Through India's current prime minister, Indira Gandhi, Nehru's daughter, Gopal gained access to private papers for use in the preparation of his three-volume biography of Jawaharlal Nehru.

The first volume of this biography examines the early and middle-age years of Nehru and provides "a vivid chronology of the Indian independence movement," stated *New York Times* critic Pranay Gupte. Eric Stokes of the *Times Literary Supplement* declared that the biography's second volume "leaves a forcible impression of how much the international stance of India since independence was fashioned by Nehru in the first critical decade.'' In comparing the second volume to the first, Stokes found that Gopal's ''handling of the subject displays a growing mastery. There is much greater sureness of construction about this second volume.'' Nonetheless, Stokes voiced some reservations about Gopal's approach. ''For a historian given access to a remarkable cache of papers,'' the critic contended, ''[Gopal] turns up little to startle or confound. While this is in no sense an official biography, Gopal inherits a feeling for official restraint.'' Indeed, while reviewer Gupte praised Gopal's objectivity, Stokes argued that Gopal is ''too sensitive to the fragility of the democratic tradition in India to write history without ulterior purpose. Behind the quiet tone of his writing burns a passionate faith that Nehru, even in his weaknesses, embodied that tradition.''

Gopal told *CA:* ''My work in historical studies for the last twenty-five years seeks to examine the impact of Western thought and institutions on India and the efforts of an under-developed society to attain economic and social progress while adapting the democratic system to Indian conditions. It is an unprecedented experiment closely associated with the name and work of Jawaharlal Nehru and its hopes of success are of vital interest to the whole world.''

BIOGRAPHICAL/CRITICAL SOURCES: New York Times, July 21, 1976; *Times Literary Supplement,* January 25, 1980.

* * *

GORDON, (Charles) Harry (Clinton) Pirie
   See PIRIE-GORDON, (Charles) Harry (Clinton)

* * *

GORDON, John (Rutherford)   1890-1974

OBITUARY NOTICE: Born December 8, 1890, in Dundee, Scotland; died December 9, 1974, in London, England. Editor and journalist. At the time of his death, John Gordon was editor in chief of the *London Sunday Express.* He had served as that newspaper's editor since 1928, and beginning in 1940 he wrote a weekly column for the paper entitled ''Current Affairs,'' which was characterized by his outspoken and ironic comments on British life and events. Obituaries and other sources: *The Author's and Writer's Who's Who,* 6th edition, Burke's Peerage, 1971; *New York Times,* December 11, 1974; *Time* December 23, 1974.

* * *

GORST, Elliot Marcet   1885-1973

OBITUARY NOTICE: Born December 18, 1885; died November 28, 1973. Lawyer and author of legal works on railway statutes. Gorst wrote *Guide to Railway Rates Tribunal* and *Title on Railways and Canals in Halsbury's Statutes.* Obituaries and other sources: *Who's Who,* 126th edition, St. Martin's, 1974; *AB Bookman's Weekly,* January 14, 1974.

* * *

GOTFURT, Frederick   1902(?)-1973

OBITUARY NOTICE: Born c. 1902; died February 22, 1973, in London, England. Editor and author. Frederick Gotfurt was the author of novels and plays. Obituaries and other sources: *AB Bookman's Weekly,* March 19, 1973.

GOTTESFELD, Evelyn   1948-
   (Evelyn Geller)

PERSONAL: Born February 5, 1948, in New York, N.Y.; daughter of Harry and Pearl (an office manager; maiden name, Feldman) Gottesfeld. *Education:* Brooklyn College of the City University of New York, B.A. (magna cum laude), 1968; Columbia University, M.L.S., 1972, Ph.D., 1980. *Religion:* Jewish. *Home and office:* 784 Columbus Ave., New York, N.Y. 10025.

CAREER: D. H. Blair, New York City, research assistant, 1968-69; *Library Journal,* New York City, associate editor, 1969-72; free-lance writer, editor, and consultant, 1973-80; D. H. Blair, research associate and consultant, 1980—. Research assistant at Bureau of Applied Social Research, Columbia University, 1974-75. *Member:* American Sociological Association. *Awards, honors:* President's fellow at Columbia University, 1975-76.

WRITINGS—Under pseudonym Evelyn Geller: (Editor) *Communism: End of a Monolith?,* H. W. Wilson, 1978; (editor) *Saving America's Cities,* H. W. Wilson, 1979; *Ideals and Ideology: The Freedom to Read in American Public Libraries, 1876-1939,* MIT Press, 1982. Contributor to library journals and popular magazines, including *Current Biography* and *Stereo and Hi-Fi Times.*

WORK IN PROGRESS: A book with J. Morton Davis, tentatively titled *Incentive Economics.*

SIDELIGHTS: Gottesfeld told *CA:* ''Although I have written poetry, essays, and stories as far back as I can remember, I have never thought of myself as a writer in the truly artistic sense. Nor did I ever single-mindedly focus on that risky career, rather than, say, music (my childhood penchant), psychiatry (my adolescent ambition), or teaching college.

''What I have always loved is intellectual discovery—the joy of finding new ideas and reporting on them, whether in school examinations or in college term papers. Even in creative writing courses, I was reluctant to spoil a real character or story for some artistic design; the original seemed better than the composite. I was lucky enough to stumble onto work that let me carry out and expand these proclivities, since I doubt that I could have braved writing unsolicited manuscripts and would certainly not have survived the first rejection slip.

''My free-lance work has grown out of my work assignments and academic interests, first in the area of libraries and literature, then in sociology. *Ideals and Ideology,* which is based on my Ph.D. thesis, combines these interests. Centering on library censorship in the nineteenth and twentieth centuries, it traces the route by which librarians moved from seeing themselves as censors to defending their role as guardians of the freedom to read. On the small stage of that profession is enacted a drama that embraced a major literary and social revolution.

''*Incentive Economics,* which I have researched and coauthored, was written in 1980 and 1981, at the height of the Carter-Reagan controversies. It explores the issues and tensions of the long-reigning Democratic ideology and policies that were challenged by Reagan, examines the rationale of the new administration, and proposes policy courses that in some cases converge with, in other cases challenge, those of Reagan and his supply-side theorists.

''In both these works, I have sought to resolve a tension that I have experienced in my own career, that between the superficiality of the average journalist and the isolation of the average scholar. My main motivation in writing has been to share ideas in which I am passionately interested and to communicate them clearly without sacrificing the exacting standards of long and rigorous academic training. Journalism has taken quite another route, has become a haven for novelists *manques,* and has even encouraged the feature formulae and rhetoric whose acme were the stories that produced the scandals of the Pulitzer Prize and the *Daily News,* when alternatives like Victor Navasky's *Naming Names* exist, which respect history and illuminate it with sociological insights. Only through modesty, through deference to reality without the ambition to transform it (for transformation and creativity enough exist in the choice, structure, and interpretation of detail) can nonfiction writing legitimately aspire to art."

* * *

GRADY, James 1949-

PERSONAL: Born April 30, 1949, in Shelby, Mont.; son of Thomas W. (a theatre manager) and Donna (a librarian; maiden name, Martin) Grady. *Education:* University of Montana, B.A., 1971. *Politics:* "Too complex to label, but crucial." *Religion:* "Call it reverence." *Home:* 315 F St., Northeast, Washington, D.C. 20002. *Agent:* William Morris Agency, 1350 Avenue of the Americas, New York, N.Y. 10019.

CAREER: Montana Constitutional Convention, Helena, research analyst, 1971-72; Youth Development Bureau, Helena, analyst and bureaucrat, 1972-73; aide to Senator Lee Metcalf in Washington, D.C., 1974; investigative reporter in Washington, D.C., for columnist Jack Anderson, 1975-79; writer. *Member:* Authors Guild, Writers Guild, Mystery Writers of America, Fraternal Order of Police.

WRITINGS: Six Days of the Condor (novel), Norton, 1975; *Shadow of the Condor* (novel), Putnam, 1976; (contributor) Brian Garfield, editor, *I, Witness* (nonfiction), New York Times Press, 1978; *Catch the Wind* (novel), Coward, 1980.

WORK IN PROGRESS: Another novel; several screenplays.

SIDELIGHTS: Grady is best known for his two espionage thrillers, *Six Days of the Condor* and *Shadow of the Condor.* In the first novel, Ronald Malcolm arrives at his CIA office and discovers everyone has been killed. Throughout the book, he dodges fellow agents and hired killers while slowly piecing together the action resulting in the office slaughter. In *Shadow of the Condor,* Malcolm becomes involved in another CIA affair. *New York Times Book Review* reported that the action "includes the C.I.A., Air Force Intelligence, the Russians, the Chinese, you name it. Everything but the Wobblies."

Grady told *CA:* "Perhaps I became a writer looking for answers to questions I couldn't avoid, for control I couldn't otherwise possess, for intrinsic joy/pain relief I couldn't find elsewhere. At this point the why's are immaterial. I'm a writer because I have no other choice.

"I was attracted to the espionage genre primarily because I knew something about it, because those type of stories are entertaining, and, when told properly, contain all the elements of good stories. And, in *Six Days of the Condor,* I knew I had a good story.

"As for writers who influenced me, in the early days I couldn't say. Now, perhaps the biggest influence is the best American novelist, John Steinbeck, and, strange as it may see, one of America's better poets, Bruce Springsteen.

"The best fiction is fiction that tells important stories of real life and tells them well. If 'social comment' includes portrayal of reality, since all portrayals require a perspective, making social comment is unavoidable in good fiction."

BIOGRAPHICAL/CRITICAL SOURCES: Christian Science Monitor, June 19, 1974; *New York Times Book Review,* June 23, 1974, March 30, 1975, December 21, 1975; *Best Sellers,* November, 1975.

* * *

GRAEBNER, William Sievers 1943-

PERSONAL: Born September 16, 1943, in Chicago, Ill.; son of Elmer Robert (in business) and Dorothy (Zilisch) Graebner; married Dianne Bennett (an attorney), August 27, 1966; children: Bennett Sievers, Riley James Bennett. *Education:* Stanford University, B.A., 1965; University of Illinois, M.A., 1966, Ph.D., 1970. *Politics:* "Radical." *Religion:* None. *Home:* 185 Chapin Parkway, Buffalo, N.Y. 14209. *Office:* Department of History, State University of New York College at Fredonia, Fredonia, N.Y. 14063.

CAREER: State University of New York College at Fredonia, assistant professor, 1971-76, associate professor, 1976-80, professor of history, 1980—, Kasling Lecturer, 1981. *Member:* Organization of American Historians, Labor Historians. *Awards, honors:* Frederick Jackson Turner Prize from Organization of American Historians, 1975, for *Coal-Mining Safety in the Progressive Period;* American Council of Learned Societies fellow, 1977-78.

WRITINGS: Coal-Mining Safety in the Progressive Period: The Political Economy of Reform, University Press of Kentucky, 1976; *A History of Retirement: The Meaning and Function of an American Institution, 1885-1978,* Yale University Press, 1980; (editor with Leonard Richards) *The American Record,* two volumes, Knopf, 1981.

WORK IN PROGRESS: A book on democracy as a mechanism of social engineering in twentieth-century America, publication expected in 1982; a book on Buffalo disc jockey George (Hound Dog) Lorenz.

SIDELIGHTS: Graebner commented: "I became a historian because the alternative was military service; only later did I learn to love it. I benefited enormously from the superior library at University of Illinois and from association with Marilee Sargent and Jerry Clore in the late 1960's. I was radicalized sometime in 1968 and remain so. Running through my work (increasingly so) is a strong anti-authoritarian streak. We need to know much more about how authority is organized and exercised, especially in 'democratic' environments and systems. Subtle mechanisms of control and coercion exist both in institutions and processes that are represented as non-coercive and democratic, such as our child-rearing processes, the clubs and social organizations created for juveniles and the aged, and non-directive, 'progressive' education."

AVOCATIONAL INTERESTS: Camping, skiing, hiking, soccer, collecting modernist furniture and other objects.

BIOGRAPHICAL/CRITICAL SOURCES: Los Angeles Times Book Review, November 16, 1980.

* * *

GRAFE, Felix
See GREVE, Felix Paul (Berthold Friedrich)

* * *

GRAHAM, A(lexander) S(teel) 1917-

PERSONAL: Born March 2, 1917, in Glasgow, Scotland; son

of James Macleod (a marine engineer) and Henrietta (Steel) Graham; married Winnifred Margaret Bird, November 9, 1944; children: James Neilson, Arran Steel. *Education:* Glasgow School of Art, Diploma in Drawing and Painting, 1938. *Home:* Huntleys, Ticehurst, East Sussex, England.

CAREER: Free-lance cartoonist, 1945—; *Daily Mail,* London, England, creator of cartoon feature, "Fred Basset" (syndicated worldwide, in the United States by Field Newspaper Syndicate), 1964—. *Military service:* British Army, Argyll and Sutherland Highlanders, 1940-45.

WRITINGS—Self-illustrated: *Please Sir, I've Broken My Arm: A Sporting Commentary in Cartoons by Graham,* N. Vane, 1959; *The Eavesdropper* (cartoons from *New Yorker*), Dial, 1961; *The Doctor and the Eavesdropper,* Museum Press, 1964; *Fred Basset: The Hound That's Almost Human!,* thirty-four volumes, Associated Newspapers, 1964-80; *Graham's Golf Club,* Stanley Paul, 1965; *Oh Sidney—Not the Walnut Tree: People in Cartoons by Graham,* Bles, 1966; *To the Office and Back: More People in Cartoons,* Bles, 1967; *Normally I Never Touch It: People at Parties* (cartoons), Bles, 1968; *Daughter in the House; and, People at Home* (cartoons), Bles, 1969, published in the United States as *Daughter in the House,* Stephen Greene Press, 1971; *I Do Like to Be . . . : People at Leisure* (cartoons), Bles, 1970; *It's Spring, Arthur, Spring* (cartoons), Bles, 1973; *At Least, I'm Practically Alone* (cartoons), Bles, 1973; *All the Other Men Have Mellowed,* Bles, 1975; *A Lively Retirement,* Queen Anne Press, 1975; *Wurzel's neueste Abenteuer* (selections from cartoon feature, "Fred Basset"), Goldmann, 1976; *Augustus and His Faithful Hound,* Mirror Books, 1978.

Illustrator: Michael Parkinson, *Football Daft,* Stanley Paul, 1968; L. G. Alexander, *Practice and Progress: An Integrated Course for Pre-Intermediate Students,* two volumes, 2nd edition, Longman, 1971; Charles Ewart Eckersley, *English Commercial Practice and Correspondence: A First Course for Foreign Students,* 3rd edition, Longman, 1973; Norman W. Schur, *British Self-Taught: With Comments in American,* Johnston & Bacon, 1974; Betty Bendell, *Home and Dry: Confessions of an Unliberated Housewife,* Ebury Press, 1974; Nielson Graham, *Fred Basset and the Spaghetti,* Associated Newspapers Group, 1977; David Noel Burghes, *Introduction to Control Theory, and Applications,* Ellis Horwood, 1980.

Work represented in anthologies, including *The New Yorker 1972-75 Collection.* Contributor to *Punch.*

SIDELIGHTS: Graham reported that about twenty television films based on "Fred Basset" have been sold in England and abroad. He added: "I enjoy visiting the countries in which I am syndicated—particularly if they have good golf courses! I find the most rewarding aspect of being widely syndicated is the great number of letters I get from all over the world, from *all* types of readers."

BIOGRAPHICAL/CRITICAL SOURCES: Cartoonist Profiles, June, 1976.

*   *   *

GRAHAM, Joseph M.   1911(?)-1971

OBITUARY NOTICE: Born c. 1911; died of a heart attack, October 21, 1971, in Queens, N.Y. Editor and writer. Joseph Graham worked as a writer for both the *New York Times* and *Newsweek* before joining Equitable Life Assurance Society, where he served for twenty years as editor of that company's house organ. Graham is credited with reviving general interest in the works of novelist Frank Merriwell, and in 1946 he

established the Society of the Friends of Frank Merriwell. Obituaries and other sources: *New York Times,* October 23, 1971; *AB Bookman's Weekly,* November 8, 1971.

*   *   *

GRAHAM, Michael   1898-1972

OBITUARY NOTICE: Born in 1898 in Manchester, England; died in January, 1972, in Salford, England. Ecologist and author. Michael Graham, a former director of Fishery Research, wrote numerous books, including *Soil and Sense, The Fish Gate, Human Needs,* and *Sea Fisheries.* He also contributed articles to *Riding* and *Spectator.* Obituaries and other sources: *The Author's and Writer's Who's Who,* 6th edition, Burke's Peerage, 1971; *AB Bookman's Weekly,* February 7, 1972.

*   *   *

GRAHAM, Tom
   See LEWIS, (Harry) Sinclair

*   *   *

GRANGER, Margaret Jane   1925(?)-1977
   (Peggy Granger)

OBITUARY NOTICE: Born c. 1925 in Vallejo, Calif.; died of a heart attack, May 12, 1977, in San Anselmo, Calif. Editor and author. Margaret Granger, a former chief editor of Behavior Books, wrote several books for young people, including *Canyon of Decision,* for which she received a Literary Guild award in 1968. She also wrote *After the Picnic* and *Everywoman's Guide to a New Image.* Obituaries and other sources: *Publishers Weekly,* May 30, 1977; *Authors of Books for Young People,* 2nd edition supplement, Scarecrow, 1979.

*   *   *

GRANGER, Peggy
   See GRANGER, Margaret Jane

*   *   *

GRANT, Cynthia D.   1950-

PERSONAL: Born November 23, 1950, in Brockton, Mass.; daughter of Robert C. and Jacqueline (Ford) Grant; married Daniel Heatley; children: Morgan. *Education:* Attended high school in Palo Alto, Calif. *Home:* 26505 Dutcher Creek, Cloverdale, Calif. 95425.

CAREER: Writer, 1974—. *Awards, honors:* Annual book award from Woodward Park School, 1981, for *Joshua Fortune.*

WRITINGS: Joshua Fortune (juvenile), Atheneum, 1980; *Summer Home* (juvenile), Atheneum, 1981; *Big Time* (young adult), Atheneum, 1982.

WORK IN PROGRESS: Hard Love, a young adult novel; *Little Eden,* a novel.

SIDELIGHTS: Cynthia Grant commented: "I have always written. I have to write. Sometimes it's the most fun in the world; other times I feel like chucking my typewriter out the window. As a feminist, it is important to me that my books deal with individuals, not stereotypes. I try to use humor to make my points, as the best time to communicate with people is when they're enjoying themselves, with their defenses down. The object of writing is communication, and that's a two-way street.

"In *Hard Love,* my narrator says that people and time are the two things he thinks most important—loving people and valuing life. I think that says it for me."

GRANT, Evva H.   1913-1977

OBITUARY NOTICE: Born February 22, 1913, in Rock Island, Ill.; died September 29, 1977, in Chicago, Ill. Editor and author. Evva Grant served as editor of PTA Magazine for more than thirty years. She also served as editor in chief of the National Congress of Parents and Teachers. Grant was the author of Parents and Teachers as Partners, and she edited books, including Guiding Children as They Grow and P.T.A. Guide to What's Happening in Education. Obituaries and other sources: Foremost Women in Communications, Bowker, 1970; Publishers Weekly, October 31, 1977; Who's Who of American Women, 11th edition, Marquis, 1979.

* * *

GRANVILLE-BARKER, Harley   1877-1946

BRIEF ENTRY: Born November 25, 1877, in London, England; died August 31, 1946, in Paris, France. American actor, producer of plays, and author. Granville-Barker began acting in his early teens. By the mid-1900's, he became dissatisfied with the melodrama and romantic comedy of popular theatre, so he quit acting and founded the "New Drama" movement. He began producing plays by George Bernard Shaw, John Galsworthy, and Henrik Ibsen and lured other adventurous actors into appearing in his productions. He also began writing plays. Critical praise for these works, including Waste (1909) and The Madras House (1910), centered on his skill at reiterating a single idea through a variety of characters and situations. After producing several plays by William Shakespeare, Granville-Barker retired to work as a critic. He is probably best known for his collected essays, including Prefaces to Shakespeare (1927) and Associating With Shakespeare (1932), which critics noted for their illuminating insight into the bard's works. Biographical/critical sources: Cyclopedia of World Authors, Harper, 1958; Twentieth Century Writing: A Reader's Guide to Contemporary Literature, Transatlantic, 1969; Twentieth-Century Literary Criticism, Volume 2, Gale, 1969.

* * *

GRAY, Jeffrey A(lan)   1934-

PERSONAL: Born May 26, 1934, in London, England; son of Maurice (a tailor) and Dora (a milliner; maiden name, Sack) Gray; married Venus Mostafavi-Rejali, March 29, 1961; children: Ramin Daniel Rejali, Babak Alexis Rejali, Leila Katherine Fatima Rejali. Education: Magdalen College, Oxford, B.A. (modern languages), 1957, B.A. (psychology and philosophy), 1959; Institute of Psychiatry, London, Diploma in Psychology, 1960, Ph.D., 1964. Politics: Social Democrat. Religion: Atheist. Home: 223 Woodstock Rd., Oxford OX2 7AD, England. Office: Department of Experimental Psychology, Oxford University, South Parks Rd., Oxford OX1 3UD, England.

CAREER: Oxford University, Oxford, England, lecturer in psychology, 1964—, fellow of University College, 1965—. Lister Lecturer of British Association for the Advancement of Science, 1967; Myers Lecturer of British Psychological Society, 1975. Member of scientific committees of Medical Research Council and European Science Foundation. Military service: British Army, 1957; became sergeant. Member: European Brain and Behaviour Society, European Neuroscience Association, British Psychological Society, Experimental Psychology Society.

WRITINGS: (Editor) Pavlov's Typology, Pergamon, 1964; The Psychology of Fear and Stress, McGraw, 1971; (editor with V. D. Nebylitsyn) The Biological Bases of Individual Behavior, Academic Press, 1972; Elements of a Two-Process Theory of Learning, Academic Press, 1975; Pavlov, Fontana, 1979, published in the United States as Ivan Pavlov, Viking, 1980; The Neuropsychology of Anxiety: An Enquiry Into the Functions of the Septo-Hippocampal System, Oxford University Press, 1981. General editor of series, "Problems in the Behavioral Sciences," Cambridge University Press. Contributor of more than a hundred articles to scientific journals.

WORK IN PROGRESS: Revision of The Psychology of Fear and Stress, publication by Cambridge University Press; research on neural bases of anxiety.

SIDELIGHTS: Gray commented: "My writing is secondary to my work as an experimental psychologist. My main interest is the neural basis of anxiety, the action of anti-anxiety drugs, and the neural basis of personality traits associated with susceptibility to anxiety. My main research is therefore on the brain in animals (rats).

"I have described a neural system in the brains of animals that underlies, I believe, the experience of anxiety in people. This system continually checks the environment for, and responds to, threats of pain, disappointment, failure, or uncertainty. When these occur, it brings all current behavior to a halt, allowing the animal to seek better alternative behavior strategies. Under conditions of repeated stress, this same system is responsible for the development of behavioral tolerance for stress (a kind of 'toughening up'). Anti-anxiety drugs, such as valium or alcohol, reduce anxiety by damping down activity in this system, but they also appear to block the development of tolerance for stress.

"My work also indicates that individual differences in the activity of the brain system described above underlie the human personality traits associated with psychiatric conditions in which anxiety predominates (e.g. phobias, obsessive-compulsive neuroses). The relevant personality traits are those of neuroticism and introversion described by H. J. Eysenck. I am in the process of constructing an alternative to Eysenck's account of the biological basis of these traits."

* * *

GRAY, Mayo Loiseau   1938-

PERSONAL: Born November 12, 1938, in New York, N.Y.; daughter of Henry and Marion (Doyle) Loizeaux; married Richard T. M. Gray, May 19, 1965 (divorced July, 1978). Education: Attended Immaculate Heart College, 1957-58. Residence: New York, N.Y. Agent: Paul R. Reynolds, Inc., 12 East 41st St., New York, N.Y. 10017.

CAREER: Stage and film actress under name Mayo Loiseau, 1955-60; Gray-Loiseau Productions (theatrical producers), Los Angeles, Calif. and New York City, actress, writer, and producer, 1959-71; Cinnamon Hill and Beach Club Hotel, Grenada, West Indies, architect and designer, 1971-75; Chanticleer Press, New York City, secretary to editor-in-chief, 1976-77; Audubon Magazine, New York City, assistant to editor, 1978-79; writer, 1979—. Director of Sutherland Investments Ltd. (resort developers), 1968-75. Artist-in-residence at Duke University, 1966. Member: Authors Guild, Poets and Writers. Awards, honors: First prize from literary congress of National Federation of Catholic College Students, 1955, for play, "Confetti Fortress."

WRITINGS: The Savage Season (novel), Fawcett, 1978.

Plays: "Confetti Fortress" (one-act), first produced in Los Angeles, Calif., at Loyola University, November 6, 1955; (co-author) "A Wilde Evening With Shaw" (three-act), first produced in Charlottesville, Va., at the University of Virginia, March 29, 1962, (co-author) "Coward Calling" (two-act), first produced in Charlotte, N.C., at the University of North Carolina, November 16, 1966; (co-author) "The Years of the Locust" (two-act), first produced in Durham, N.C., at Duke University, December 7, 1966; (co-author) "The World of Anton Chekhov" (two-act), first produced in Geneva, N.Y., at Hobart College, October 12, 1969.

Work represented in anthologies, including *The Poet Anthology,* 1981. Contributor of poems to *Scimitar and Song* and *Crosscurrents.*

WORK IN PROGRESS: Woman on the Run (tentative title), a contemporary novel of intrigue and romance; *Siege of the Heart,* poems written in Grenada, 1968-75; *Tracks in My Life,* poems, 1976—.

SIDELIGHTS: Mayo Gray told *CA:* "I have toured through every state in the United States, except Hawaii and Alaska. The Caribbean islands were my backyard while living in Grenada. Pursuing design research and product purchasing for Cinnamon Hill, I traveled to Canada, England, France and Spain. Research for the second novel led me to Margarita Island and on a trek across the whole of Venezuela to the border town of Puerto Ayacucho on the banks of the Orinoco. It was an exhilarating experience for a woman traveling alone. I have a need and an affinity for traveling to foreign places and I inevitably combine travel with work.

"In Grenada, West Indies, I had my first experience in living and working in a foreign culture. In order to build a hotel there, we had to merge into the fabric of society. At the most basic level I worked with the carpenters, masons and craftsmen, and, being the architect/designer, I was their boss—a delicate feat in a male chauvinist culture. My co-workers gradually became my allies as we pursued goals of craftsmanship and excellence.

"More subtle and complex was the relationship with the political powers. Before the coup there was no black power hostility in Grenada. Black and white worked and socialized together. The divisive conflict was political, and the politics were not ideological but economic. As foreigners we walked a tightrope. We tippled champagne with West Indian prime ministers, attended government functions, huddled in private meetings with members of the British High Commission *and* with the leaders of the New Jewel, an emerging radical opposition. You could smell the winds of change. You knew the revolution would come when the schism widened and the government, with its secret police and 'mongoose' gang of thugs, became flagrantly oppressive. I had never lived in a country where I could not speak my thoughts, where even at my own dinner table some guest or my own maid might be an informer. I had to learn how to live in a muzzled society, how to talk out of both sides of my mouth, and how to control my distress and outrage over the increasing violations of freedom and the rapid erosion of law and order. The price for speaking out could be immediate eviction from the island as an 'undesirable' with loss of property or perhaps only the hotel burning down in the night; such things were happening all the time. When the middle class did speak out in protest, the outside world did not listen, did not care. The transgressions were considered 'mickey mouse' encroachments, hardly comparable to the situation in certain South American countries. This indifference forged a bond in Grenada between unlikely bedfellows: the idealists, the conservative business community, the peasants, and the unscrupulous seekers of power. In March, 1979, when

Maurice Bishop, with a mandate of approval from the majority, led the New Jewel in a bloodless coup, ousting Eric Gairy, the prime minister, I was living in New York and watching what I had written come true.

"My interest in human rights springs from my compassion for the disadvantaged and my anger against tyranny. As a woman I identify deeply with the struggle of oppressed peoples. Every human being possesses a vigorous instinct to fulfill his or her unique potential. To thwart or stunt this growth is a sin against life. To enslave people, to turn them into puppets, to repress that fundamental right to think, speak, and act as themselves, to destroy the essence of life—communication—is the greatest evil on earth.

"But the odds are always stacked against the achievement of autonomy. It comes hard won because the tyrant wields formidable weapons: lies, intimidation, the throttling of the free exchange of ideas, and, most important, economic power. Bogged down by ignorance and entropy, the subjugated must find the will to fight. Regrettably, the profound urge toward freedom, so naked and vulnerable when it appears, is supremely exploitable. In Grenada I watched repression breed total rebellion and when it all came down, the baby went out with the bath water.

"If you travel through the Caribbean, you will feel the astonishing time warp. Only recently freed from colonial status, the islands seem to lag half a century behind the sophisticated culture of the United States. If you love them, as I do, you will feel exasperation, concern over their growing pains, and the political convolutions in which one charismatic dictator is replaced by another. The set of shackles is exchanged, the pernicious cycle of controller and controlled is perpetuated.

"They share the monumental problems of their larger, wealthier neighbors. Malnutrition, disease, illiteracy, and abysmal poverty hobble progress and spawn a plethora of dictatorships, oligarchies, military juntas, and communist-backed regimes. The remedies are money, education, greater communication, and time. Certainly not guns. If the United States can resist the desire to make these countries its satellites, if our government understands that neither democracy as we practice it nor Marxist communism but some new form of government is required to lift the people from their almost feudal state, then we have the power to help.

"I am no expert, but I would commit my energies to any area in which I could help in this struggle for basic human rights. I confess my apprehension as I watch the fingers of two super powers digging in, seeking domination. The southern hemisphere is turbulent with the winds of change. If those people are once again manipulated, exploited, used as pawns, and denied their rightful autonomy, will they not rise up in violence and rage to burst the chains of a new bondage? We would be wise to read their poets and novelists, listen acutely to their words, grasp their images, and understand that the giant is no longer sleeping."

AVOCATIONAL INTERESTS: Fishing, travel.

*   *   *

GREEN, Deborah   1948-
(Deborah Zook)

PERSONAL: Born October 3, 1948, in Mount Union, Pa.; daughter of Leroy A. (a minister) and Mary (Yordi) Zook; married Bruce Green (a rehabilitation counselor), April 12, 1975. *Education:* Attended Juniata College, 1966-71; received certificate from Greater Pittsburgh Guild for the Blind, 1971;

also attended Morehead State University. *Religion:* "Raised Mennonite, currently Episcopal." *Home address:* P.O. Box 845, Hazard, Ky. 41701. *Office:* Kentucky Bureau for the Blind, P.O. Box 840, Hazard, Ky. 41701.

CAREER: Hazard Vocational School, Hazard, Ky., instructor in Braille, 1971-76; Kentucky Bureau for the Blind, Hazard, rehabilitation counselor, 1976-80, rehabilitation supervisor, 1980—. Member of state advisory council for vocational education and regional advisory committee for vocational education. *Member:* National Rehabilitation Association, Kentucky Rehabilitation Association.

WRITINGS: (Under name Deborah Zook) *Debby* (autobiography), Herald Press, 1974.

SIDELIGHTS: Green told *CA:* "My job brings me in contact with visually handicapped individuals, many of whom have had few opportunities to achieve any kind of independence. My blindness often is, in this situation, an asset. I enjoy relative independence—running a home, working at crafts, and making and writing music. I feel that blindness is more of a nuisance than a handicap."

*   *   *

GREEN, J(ames) C. R.   1949-

PERSONAL: Born September 19, 1949, in Glasgow, Scotland; son of James Gatherer (a statistician) and Jeannie Black (Thomson) Green; married Anne Johnston (a nursing officer), October 11, 1969. *Education:* University of Coimbra, B.A., 1970; University of Nebraska, Ph.D., 1980. *Home:* 3 Achnahaniad, by Portree, Isle of Skye IV51 9HL, Scotland. *Agent:* Anne Johnston, 11 Novi Lane, Leek, Staffordshire ST13 6NS, England. *Office:* J.C.R. Green Ltd., P.O. Box 1, Portree, Isle of Skye IV51 9BT, Scotland.

CAREER: Aquila Publishing Co. Ltd., director, 1970—. Director of J.C.R. Green Ltd. (publisher), 1980—; managing editor of *Prospice;* editor of Paethon Press and Helius Designs; publisher of Skye Island Publishers and Johnston Green & Co. Ltd. Publications director of Birmingham Poetry Centre, 1970-71, chairman, 1971-72; vice-chairman of poetry committee of Birmingham and Midland Institute of Management, 1971-72; producer of poetry programs for BBC-Radio, Birmingham, 1971-73. *Member:* Writers Guild of Great Britain (member of council, 1979-80), Scottish Publishers Association (member of council, 1979).

WRITINGS: (With A. Jackson and C. Lewis) *Go Dig Your Own Grave,* Aertis, 1968; *Notes for Glider Pilots,* H.M.S.O., 1968; *By Weight of Reason* (poems and translations), Aquila, 1974; *A Beaten Image: Poems for Several Places, 1968-1976,* Aquila Publishing, 1977. Also author of *The Vegetarian Diet,* 1968, *Into the Darkness,* 1971, *The Death of Bishop Bowie,* 1971, and *Fernando Pessoa,* 1975.

Translator: Fernando Pessoa, *The Ancient Rhythm,* Aquila Publishing, 1977; Pessoa, *The Tobacconist,* Aquila Publishing, 1977; Pessoa, *The Keeper of the Flocks,* Aquila Publishing, 1978; Pessoa, *Stations of the Cross,* Aquils Publishing, 1978. Also translator of Pessoa's *Lisbon Revisited,* 1975, and Alvaro di Campos's *The Maritime Ode,* 1975.

Editor: (With Michael Edwards and Martin Booth) *Prospice One,* Aquila Publishing, 1973; (with Edwards and Booth) *Prospice Two,* Aquila Publishing, 1974; (with Edwards) *Prospice Five,* Aquila Publishing, 1976; (with Edwards) *Prospice Seven,* Aquila Publishing, 1977. Also co-editor of *Come Together: Poetry for International Youth Year,* 1970, and *Ecology,*

1972.Editor of *Muse,* 1970-73, *Poetry News,* 1970-73, *ALP Newsletter,* 1972-73, and *Printers Pie.*

WORK IN PROGRESS: Aphorisms and Other Words; The Garlic Cookbook; We Who Walk the Night, for Aquila Publishing; *The Book of Boobs,* for Johnston Green & Co.; translating *Lisbon Revisited,* by Fernando Pessoa, for Aquila Publishing; a biography of Pessoa.

SIDELIGHTS: Green wrote: "I have always felt the need to write. Since leaving school and going to live in Portugal, I have felt an overriding passion for the work of Fernando Pessoa, the twentieth-century Portuguese writer. I have published many translations, both in print and on radio and television. I was expelled from Portugal, and returned to Scotland to live in the peace and quiet of Skye. My other interest is in my native language, Gaelic, and I publish several Gaelic books, though not of my own writing."

*   *   *

GREENBERG, Bradley S(ander)   1934-

PERSONAL: Born August 3, 1934, in Toledo, Ohio; son of Abraham and Florence (Cohen) Greenberg; married Delight Thompson, June 5, 1959; children: Beth, Shawn, Debbie. *Education:* Bowling Green State University, B.S., 1956; University of Wisconsin, Madison, M.S., 1957, Ph.D., 1961. *Home:* 2049 Ashland, Okemos, Mich. 48864. *Office:* Department of Communication, Michigan State University, Communication Arts Building, East Lansing, Mich. 48824.

CAREER: Michigan State University, East Lansing, assistant professor, 1964-66, associate professor, 1966-71, professor of communication and chairman of department, 1977—. Senior fellow at East-West Center Communication Institute, 1978-79; visiting professor at University of Southern California, 1979. *Military service:* U.S. Army Reserve, 1956-73; became major. *Member:* International Communication Association, Association for Education in Journalism.

WRITINGS: The Kennedy Assassination and the American Public: Social Communication in Crisis, Stanford University Press, 1965; *Use of the Mass Media by the Urban Poor,* Praeger, 1970; *Life on Television: Content Analyses of U.S. Television Drama,* Ablex Publishing, 1980.

WORK IN PROGRESS: Mass Communication and Mexican-Americans, publication expected in 1982.

*   *   *

GREENBERG, Jae W.   1894(?)-1974

OBITUARY NOTICE: Born c. 1894; died November 26, 1974, in Fairfield, Conn. Publisher. As founder and president of Greenberg Publishers, Jae Greenberg published the works of such authors as Alfred Adler, Betty Smith, Jack London, and Robert Graves. After selling Greenberg Publishers to the Chilton Book Co. in 1958, Greenberg established Sports Car Press, where he published books on cars and airplanes. Obituaries and other sources: *New York Times,* November 27, 1974; *AB Bookman's Weekly,* December 16, 1974; *Publishers Weekly,* January 6, 1975.

*   *   *

GREENBURGER, Ingrid Elisabeth   1913-
(George Rainer)

PERSONAL: Born July 14, 1913, in Berlin, Germany; daughter of Gustav Felix and Elisabeth Gruettefien; married Sanford J.

CONTEMPORARY AUTHORS • *Volume 104*

Greenburger (a literary agent), 1947 (marriage ended, 1971); children: Patrick-Andre, Francis Jerome. *Education:* Attended University of Freiburg. *Home:* 30 Park Ave., New York, N.Y. 10016. *Office:* Sanford J. Greenburger Associates, 825 Third Ave., New York, N.Y. 10022.

CAREER: Sanford J. Greenburger Associates, New York, N.Y., literary agent, 1955—.

WRITINGS: (Under pseudonym George Rainer) *Murkel,* Frick Verlag, 1938; *Die Unschuldigen* (novel), Rowohlt Verlag, 1969; *A Private Treason* (nonfiction), Little, Brown, 1973.

WORK IN PROGRESS: The Van Laerhoven Ways, a novel.

* * *

GREENE, Robert W. 1929-
(Penelope Ashe, a joint pseudonym)

PERSONAL: Born July 12, 1929, in Jamaica, N.Y.; son of Francis M. (an attorney) and Molly (a teacher; maiden name, Clancy) Greene; married Kathleen Liquari, January 28, 1951; children: Robert W., Jr., Lea Marie. *Education:* Attended Fordham University, 1947-50 *Politics:* Republican. *Religion:* Roman Catholic. *Home:* 4 Ardmore Pl., Kings Park, N.Y. 11754. *Agent:* Sterling Lord Agency, Inc., 660 Madison Ave., New York, N.Y. 10021. *Office: Newsday,* Melville, N.Y. 11747.

CAREER: Reporter for *Jersey Journal,* 1949-50; New York City Anti-crime Commision, New York City, senior investigator, 1950-55; *Newsday,* Melville, N.Y., reporter, beginning 1955, leader of investigative team, 1967-73, senior editor, beginning 1970, currently assistant managing editor. Staff investigator for U.S. Senate Select Committee on Unfair Practices in Labor/Management Field, 1957-58. Chairman of publicity for Smithtown Tercentary Committee, 1967. President, 1976-77, and chairman of executive committee of Investigative Reporters and Editors Group. Founding member of board of directors of Suffolk County Happy Landings Fund at C. W. Post College of Long Island University.

MEMBER: Long Island Press Club (president, 1974), Sigma Delta Psi, St. Anthony's Gridiron Club (director). *Awards, honors:* George Polk Award from Long Island University, 1956; Gold Medal Pulitzer Prizes, 1970 and 1974; Peter Zenger Freedom of the Press Award from University of Arizona, 1978; Penny-Missouri Newspaper Award, 1980; James Wright Brown Award; public service awards from Sigma Delta Psi.

WRITINGS: (Co-author under joint pseudonym, Penelope Ashe) *Naked Came the Stranger* (novel), Lyle Stuart, 1970; (co-author) *The Heroine Trail,* New American Library, 1974; *The Sting Man: Inside ABSCAM,* Dutton, 1981.

WORK IN PROGRESS: Vagrant.

SIDELIGHTS: The Sting Man is Greene's analysis of the ABSCAM controversy, in which the FBI entrapped congressional figures into compromising their positions in exchange for financial rewards. Greene refers to the plan as "a massive confidence game," and in the book he concentrates on the actions of Melvin R. Weinberg, a swindler who sought to salvage his reputation by cooperating with the FBI. Weinberg enticed political leaders by promising them Arab funds in exchange for special considerations. Greene also documents ABSCAM's development, fueled partially by Weinberg's enthusiasm, from an investigation of white-collar crime to a trap for congressmen. *Washington Post*'s Kenneth Wooden called *The Sting Man* "a memorable study of conflicts of interest, sordid business deals, dishonest lawyers, the mob and an array of char-

acters who, in the words of the author, are 'equalized by greed.'" He deemed the work "an absorbing and at times hilarious book." John Leonard, in the *New York Times,* agreed, calling it "excellent." Leonard also praised Greene as "a superb investigative reporter."

Greene told *CA:* "I am politically centrist with a strong interest in processes of motivation. My own motivation is to make enough money to support my expensive tastes comfortably."

BIOGRAPHICAL/CRITICAL SOURCES: New York Times, May 1, 1981; *Washington Post,* May 29, 1981.

AVOCATIONAL INTERESTS: European travel, food and cooking, wine, birds, history, public speaking, media, swimming, fishing, languages, reading about organized crime, nature, economics.

GREENWOOD, Lillian Bethel 1932-
(Rose Ayers)

PERSONAL: Born July 24, 1932, in Tisdale, Saskatchewan, Canada; daughter of Terence (a lumber executive) and Lillian Maude (Manton) Greenwood. *Education:* Attended Provincial Normal School, Vancouver, British Columbia, 1952-53; University of British Columbia, B.A., 1965, M.A., 1968. *Home:* 1815 Maple St., Kelowna, British Columbia, Canada V1Y 1H4. *Agent:* Knox Burger Associates Ltd., 39 Washington Sq. S., New York, N.Y. 10012.

CAREER: University of British Columbia, Vancouver, teaching assistant and associate teacher of English, 1966-70; high school English teacher in Kelowna, British Columbia, 1969; University of California, teaching assistant in English, 1974-76; Okanagan College, Kelowna, instructor in creative writing, 1980; Penticton Summer School of the Arts, instructor in creative writing, 1981. *Member:* Canadian Authors Association.

WRITINGS: (Under pseudonym Rose Ayers) *The Street Sparrows* (novel), Coward, 1978.

SIDELIGHTS: Lillian Greenwood wrote: "A minor but annoying health problem kept me from attending school regularly as a child, and much of my early education had to be by correspondence. I found early that I loved reading, and soon discovered there was also pleasure in writing. That this was not a common sensation I encountered repeatedly in my intermittent contact with other children, and it puzzled me greatly. I could be thrilled with a well-placed shot in hockey; why couldn't my peers be excited by an adjective nicely placed? But apparently they could not, so while they learned to skate I read Dickens.

"As an undergraduate at university, I took a couple of creative writing courses, all that was then available, but I don't think either had any particular effect on me. More important was my selling a couple of short stories for use on a Canadian Broadcasting Corp. radio program. I always knew I could write fiction; now I knew that what I wrote might be marketable.

"Years later, having some spare time on my hands, I started another course in writing. This was soon cancelled, but I finished the manuscript I had started, and packed off samples to half a dozen agents. I received not only encouragement, but an offer of representation from an agent, Knox Burger, and though that story was not published, my next was and has been generously reviewed."

* * *

GREGORY, Isabella Augusta (Persse) 1852-1932
(Lady Gregory)

BRIEF ENTRY: Born March 5, 1852, in Roxborough, County

Galway, Ireland; died May 22, 1932. Irish playwright, folklorist, and translator. A proponent of Irish independence, Gregory was an integral part of Ireland's literary renaissance, and she was instrumental in reviving the Irish theatre. She is often called "the godmother of the Abbey Theatre," which she founded with W. B. Yeats and directed. The theatre's "charwoman," as George Bernard Shaw referred to her, Gregory wrote a chronicle of the Irish Theatre movement, *Our Irish Theatre* (1913), as well as plays that combine peasant idiom, poetry, laughter, and irony. "The Workhouse Ward," "The Rising Moon," and "Spreading the News" are considered among her best dramatic productions. To awaken the national consciousness, the author used her knowledge of Irish history and folklore, especially legends, to write personal, rather than historical, folk histories. Her translations of folk literature, such as *Cuchulain of Muirthemne* and *Gods and Fighting Men,* prompted Yeats to label the author "the founder of modern Irish dialect literature." Besides collaborating with Yeats, whom she met in 1898, Gregory also inspired the poet, and her home was a meeting place for Yeats and other writers of the Celtic revival. Her works include *A Book of Saints and Wonders* (1906), *Hyacinth Halvey* (1906), *The Kiltartan History Book* (1909), *The Kiltartan Poetry Book* (1919), *The Story Brought by Brigit* (1924), and *Coole* (1931). *Residence:* Coole Park, Ireland. *Biographical/critical sources: Twentieth Century Authors: A Biographical Dictionary of Modern Literature,* H. W. Wilson, 1942, 1st supplement, 1955; *Everyman's Dictionary of Literary Biography, English and American,* revised edition, Dutton, 1960; *Penguin Companion to English Literature,* McGraw, 1971; *Newsweek,* February 23, 1976; *Twentieth-Century Literary Criticism,* Volume 1, Gale, 1978.

*   *   *

GREIG, Maysie 1902-1971
(Jennifer Ames, Ann Barclay, Mary Douglas Warren)

OBITUARY NOTICE—See index for *CA* sketch: Born in 1902 in Sydney, Australia; died June 10, 1971, in London, England. Popular with audiences, Greig wrote over two hundred romantic novels, including *A Nice Girl Comes to Town, She Walked Into His Parlour,* and *Never the Same.* She wrote *Pandora Lifts the Lid* and *Shadow Across My Heart* under the pseudonym Jennifer Ames, *Men as Her Stepping Stones* under the name Ann Barclay, and *Reunion in Reno* under the pseudonym Mary Douglas Warren. Obituaries and other sources: *AB Bookman's Weekly,* July 19, 1971.

*   *   *

GREVE, Elsa
See GREVE, Felix Paul (Berthold Friedrich)

*   *   *

GREVE, Felix Paul (Berthold Friedrich) 1879-1948
(Friedrich Carl Gerden, Felix Grafe, Elsa Greve, Frederick Philip Grove, Konrad Thorer, Edouard Thorne)

BRIEF ENTRY: Born February 14, 1879, in Rodomno, Prussia (now U.S.S.R.; some sources list year of birth as 1871 or 1872); died August 19, 1948, in Simcoe, Ontario, Canada. Canadian educator, novelist, editor, poet, translator, and short story writer. Greve is best known as Frederick Philip Grove, the name under which the author lived and wrote from approximately 1912 until his death. The son of a tram conductor,

Greve attended Bonn University until 1898, when the death of his mother prompted him to abandon his studies. He then traveled and supported himself by writing and translating, but he lived beyond his means. Incurring large debts, he was jailed in 1903 for fraud. Released after a year, the author endeavored to pay his accounts by writing such books as *Fanny Essler* (1905) and *The Master Mason's House* (1906). Ultimately he fled his obligations by faking a suicide on a ship bound for Sweden in 1909. Biographers speculate he spent the following four years wandering around the United States. In 1912 he surfaced in Manitoba as a schoolteacher named Frederick Philip Grove. Spending the rest of his life in Canada, Grove engaged in a variety of occupations. He worked as an editor at the Graphic Press and later farmed in Simcoe, Ontario. The author of several books, Grove chronicled the harsh pioneer life of the Canadian frontier. His works are grimly realistic, and his 1925 book, *Settlers of the Marsh,* is regarded as the first naturalistic novel written in Canada. Grove never revealed his true identity during his lifetime and perpetrated the fiction in an autobiography entitled *In Search of Myself.* The author received the Yorne Pierce Medal and the Governor General's Award for his works. Grove's books include *Our Prairie Trails* (1922), *A Search for America* (1927), *Two Generations* (1939), and *The Master of the Mill* (1944). *Residence:* Simcoe, Ontario, Canada. *Biographical/critical sources: The Oxford Companion to Canadian History and Literature,* Oxford University Press, 1967; *The Penguin Companion to English Literature,* McGraw, 1971; Douglas O. Spettigue, *FPG: The European Years,* Oberon Press, 1973; *Twentieth-Century Literary Criticism,* Volume 4, Gale, 1981.

*   *   *

GREY, Marian Powys 1883(?)-1972

OBITUARY NOTICE: Born c. 1883 in England; died March 1, 1972, in Sneden's Landing, N.Y. Expert on lace-making and author. Marian Powys Grey, a member of a distinguished literary family that included novelist, poet, and philosopher John Cowper Powys, essayist and critic Llewellyn Powys, and novelist Theodore F. Powys, was a respected authority on handmade lace. From 1950 to 1964 she served as consultant to the textile section of the Metropolitan Museum of Art in New York City, and in 1934 she received a gold medal for her lacework at the Panama Exposition. Her book, *Lace and Lace-Making,* was published in 1953. Obituaries and other sources: *New York Times,* March 2, 1972; *AB Bookman's Weekly,* May 15, 1972.

*   *   *

GREY, Zane 1872(?)-1939

BRIEF ENTRY: Born January 31, c. 1872, in Zanesville, Ohio; died of a heart attack, October 23, 1939, in Altadena, Calif.; cremated. American dentist and author of more than sixty books. In 1904, bored with his dental practice, Grey began writing colorful novels about the American West. His first popular success was *Riders of the Purple Sage* (1912), which established Grey as a pioneer of the Western novel. Grey's books, including *The Border Legion* (1916), *The Call of the Canyon* (1924), and *West of the Pecos* (1937), sold more than thirteen million copies during the author's lifetime, and most are still in print. Although some reviewers have pointed out that the moral principles espoused in Grey's novels are overly simplistic, most critics have noted that his settings are authentically and vividly drawn. His early novel, *Last of the Plainsmen* (1908), which was based upon a trip Grey made with frontiersman C. J. "Buffalo" Jones across the Arizona desert, is considered by many critics to be Grey's best effort. *An American Angler in Australia* (1937) and *Adventures in Fishing* (1952) are among Grey's nonfiction works. *Biographical/critical sources: Saturday Review of Literature,* November 11, 1939; Jean Kerr, *Zane Grey: Man of the West,* Greenburg, 1949; *New Yorker,* July 19, 1952; J. G. Cawelti, editor, *Adventure, Mystery, and Romance,* University of Chicago Press, 1976.

*   *   *

GRI
   See DENNEY, Diana

*   *   *

GRIDZEWSKI, Mieczylawski   1895(?)-1970

OBITUARY NOTICE: Born c. 1895; died January 9, 1970, in London, England. Mieczylawski Gridzewski, founder of the Polish literary journal *Wiadomosci,* was editor of that journal for fifty years. Obituaries and other sources: *AB Bookman's Weekly,* February 16, 1970.

*   *   *

GRIER, Frances Belle Powner   1886(?)-1980(?)

OBITUARY NOTICE: Born c. 1886 in Harristown, Ill.; died c. 1980 in Pomona, Calif. Editor, translator, and author. With her father, publisher Charles T. Powner, Frances Powner Grier established an antiquarian bookstore. She also edited books published by her father's company, and she translated *The Life and Adventures of Joaquin Murrieta* from the original Spanish. She is the author of *California Cook Book.* Obituaries and other sources: *Who's Who of American Women,* 9th edition, Marquis, 1975; *AB Bookman's Weekly,* February 11, 1980.

*   *   *

GRIERSON, Francis Durham   1888-1972

OBITUARY NOTICE: Born in 1888; died September 24, 1972, in London, England. Author. Francis Grierson wrote numerous crime novels as well as nonfiction books on crime detection. Included among his works are *Secret Judges, Heart of the Moon, The Green Diamond Mystery,* and *Murder in Mortimer Square.* He was a contributor to magazines such as *Punch* and *Tatler.* Obituaries and other sources: *AB Bookman's Weekly,* October 16, 1972.

*   *   *

GRIFFEN, Edmund
   See Du BREUIL, (Elizabeth) L(or)inda

*   *   *

GRIGG, John (Edward Poynder)   1924-
   (Lord Altrincham)

PERSONAL: Born April 15, 1924, in London, England; son of Edward William MacClay (first Lord Altrincham; a politician and administrator) and Joan Alice Catherine (Dickson-Poynder) Grigg; married Marion Patricia Campbell (a justice of the peace), December 3, 1958; children: Alexander Henry Campbell, Edward William Jonathan. *Education:* New College, Oxford, M.A., 1948. *Politics:* Conservative. *Religion:* Church of England. *Home:* 32 Dartmouth Row, London SE10 8AW, England *Agent:* A. D. Peters & Co. Ltd., 10 Buckingham St., London WC2N 6BU, England.

CAREER: Free-lance writer, 1948—. Presented television documentary programs for British Broadcasting Corp. *Military service:* British Army, Grenadier Guards, 1943-45. *Member:* Royal Society of Literature (fellow). *Awards, honors:* Whitbread Prize, 1978, for *Lloyd George: The People's Champion.*

WRITINGS—Under name Lord Altrincham: *Two Anglican Essays,* Secker & Warburg, 1958; (co-author) *Is the Monarchy Perfect?,* J. Calder, 1958; *The Young Lloyd George,* Eyre Methuen, 1973; *Lloyd George: The People's Champion,* Eyre Methuen, 1978; *1943: The Victory That Never Was,* Eyre Methuen, 1980; *Nancy Astor: Portrait of a Pioneer,* Sidgwick, 1980, published as *Nancy Astor: A Lady Unashamed,* Little, Brown, 1981. Author of a column in *Guardian,* 1960-69. Associate editor and editor of *National and English Review,* 1948-60.

BIOGRAPHICAL/CRITICAL SOURCES: Spectator, April 26, 1980, June 28, 1980; *Los Angeles Times,* May 12, 1981; *New York Times,* August 26, 1981.

*   *   *

GRIMSDITCH, Herbert Borthwick   1898-1971

OBITUARY NOTICE: Born in 1898 in Liverpool, England; died October 9, 1971, in London, England. Editor and author. Herbert Grimsditch was a contributor to numerous reference works, including *Dictionary of National Biography, Cambridge Bibliography of English Literature,* and *Twentieth Century Authors.* He wrote *Character and Environment in the Novels of Thomas Hardy,* and he contributed articles to such periodicals as the *Manchester Guardian,* the *Nation,* and the *Observer.* Obituaries and other sources: *AB Bookman's Weekly,* November 8, 1971; *Who Was Who Among English and European Authors, 1931-1949,* Gale, 1978.

*   *   *

GRINDEL, Eugene   1895-1952
   (Jean du Hault, Paul Eluard, Maurice Hervent)

BRIEF ENTRY: Born December 14, 1895, in Saint-Denis, France; died November 18, 1952, in Charenton-le-Pont, France. French poet. Grindel, popularly known as Paul Eluard, is best remembered for the love poems he wrote in the middle of his career, beginning with *Capitale de la douleur* (1926). A co-founder of the surrealist movement, he was one of its most authentic poets. In *Necessites d'une vie et les consequences des reves* (1921), he explored the surrealist ideas of free expression and the relationship between dream and reality. Eluard's view of love as the best way to escape from the world, and simultaneously as the truest way to come to know the world, runs through his earlier work. His awareness of human poverty and suffering is more eloquently expressed in later writing. Moved by the effects of the Spanish civil war, Eluard came to believe that the poet must be involved in society. Political and social poetry, tending toward communism in *Donner a voir* (1939), replaced the love poems of earlier years. Regardless of subject matter and theme, however, all of Eluard's work is noted for its colorful images and rhythmic, simple language. *Biographical/critical sources: Twentieth Century Authors: A Biographical Dictionary of Modern Literature,* H. W. Wilson, 1st supplement, 1955; *Encyclopedia of World Literature in the Twentieth Century,* updated edition, Ungar, 1967.

*   *   *

GROVE, Frederick Philip
   See GREVE, Felix Paul (Berthold Friedrich)

GROVE, Lee E(dmonds) ?-1971

OBITUARY NOTICE: Died December 17, 1971, in Washington, D.C. Journalist and author. For fourteen years, Lee Grove was the director of publications of the Council on Library Resources. Obituaries and other sources: *AB Bookman's Weekly*, January 31, 1972.

* * *

GROVER, Philip 1929-

PERSONAL: Born February 25, 1929, in Lima, Ohio; son of William James and Mabel (Kent) Grover; married twice; children: two. *Education:* University of Chicago, B.A., 1949; attended University of Paris, 1950-52; Cambridge University, B.A., 1955, Ph.D., 1969. *Office:* Department of English, University of Sheffield, Sheffield S10 2TN, England.

CAREER: Teacher at secondary school in Soham, England, 1961-63; Cambridgeshire College of Arts and Technology, Cambridge, England, lecturer in English, 1963-69; University of Sheffield, Sheffield, England, lecturer, 1969-74, senior lecturer in English, 1974—. *Member:* British Association for American Studies, National Trust. *Awards, honors:* Overseas grant from British Academy, 1974.

WRITINGS: *Henry James and the French Novel*, Elek, 1973; (with Omar Pound) *Wyndham Lewis: A Descriptive Bibliography*, Dawson, 1978; (editor) *Ezra Pound: The London Years*, AMS Press, 1978. Contributor to language and philology journals.

WORK IN PROGRESS: Research on Olivia Shakespear, nineteenth-century realism, the novel, and literary theory.

SIDELIGHTS: Grover told *CA:* "As an expatriated American, now a naturalized British subject who has also lived and studied in France, I find that I belong not to two cultures but to three. This is reflected in my teaching, research, and writing."

* * *

GRUBIAN, Motel 1909(?)-1972

OBITUARY NOTICE: Born c. 1909; died in March, 1972, in Moscow, U.S.S.R. Poet. Motel Grubian was associated with *Heimland*, an anti-Zionist, Soviet-sponsored magazine. Obituaries and other sources: *AB Bookman's Weekly*, May 15, 1972.

* * *

GRUFFYDD, Peter 1935-

PERSONAL: Born April 12, 1935, in Liverpool, England. *Education:* University College of North Wales, University of Wales, B.A. (with honors), 1960. *Home:* Grosvenor Hotel, Llanberis, Carnarvonshire, Wales.

CAREER: Writer. Rochdale College of Art, England, lecturer in liberal studies, 1965-67; professional actor, 1967; Volkhochschule, Munich, West Germany, teacher, 1970-72. *Military service:* British Army, 1955-57. *Awards, honors:* E. C. Gregory Award, 1963; award from Welsh Arts Council, 1968; award from Arts Council of Great Britain, 1972.

WRITINGS: (With Harri Webb and Meic Stephens) *Triad: Thirty-Three Poems*, Triskel Press, 1963; "The Cuckoo" (radio play), first broadcast in 1968; *The Shivering Seed* (poems), Wesleyan University Press, 1972. Work represented in anthologies, including *Welsh Voices*, 1967, *Poetry 69*, 1969; *Lilting House*, 1969. Contributor to literary journals, including *Poetry Wales*, *Anglo-Welsh Review, Critical Quarterly, Observer*, and *London Welshman.**

* * *

GRUMICH, Charles A. 1905(?)-1981

OBITUARY NOTICE: Born c. 1905; died of a heart attack, June 21, 1981, in New York, N.Y. Journalist. During his forty-three-year career as an Associated Press (AP) news reporter, Charles Grumich covered such stories as the capture of Red Burke, the alleged machine-gunner in Chicago's 1929 St. Valentine's Day massacre, and the 1931 airplane crash that killed Notre Dame football coach Knute Rockne. He also served in AP's New York City bureau as sports feature editor and later as night city editor. Obituaries and other sources: *Chicago Tribune*, June 22, 1981.

* * *

GUEHENNE, Jean
See GUEHENNO, Jean Marcel Jules Marie

* * *

GUEHENNO, Jean Marcel Jules Marie 1890-1978
(Jean Guehenne)

OBITUARY NOTICE: Born March 25, 1890, in Fougeres, France; died in 1978 in Paris, France. Educator and author. In much of his writing, Jean Guehenno extolled the virtues of the working class. Numbered among his many books are *Caliban parle, Journal d'une revolution*, and *La Mort des autres*. Guehenno served as editor of the journal *L'Europe*, and he was the recipient of numerous literary awards, including the Cino del Duca. Obituaries and other sources: *Cassell's Encyclopaedia of World Literature*, revised edition, Morrow, 1973; *Who's Who in the World*, 2nd edition, Marquis, 1973; *International Who's Who*, Europa, 1978; *AB Bookman's Weekly*, December 4, 1978.

* * *

GUERRA y SANCHEZ, Ramiro 1880-1970
(Diplomaticus)

OBITUARY NOTICE: Born in 1880; died October 30, 1970, in Miami, Fla. Educator and author. Formerly a professor at the University of Havana, Guerra y Sanchez was a Cuban exile. Among his writings, which often center on international relations and economics, are *Historia de Cuba, La expansion territorial de los Estados Unidos a espensas de Espana y do los paises hispanoamericanos*, and *Cuba en la vida internacional*. Under the pen name Diplomaticus, the author wrote several volumes, including *The Czechs and Their Minorities* and *No Small Stir: What the Pope Really Said About the Great War*. Obituaries and other sources: *AB Bookman's Weekly*, January 4, 1971.

* * *

GUGGENHEIM, Edward Armand 1901-1970

OBITUARY NOTICE: Born in 1901; died August 9, 1970, in Reading, England. Educator and author. Edward Guggenheim, a professor of chemistry, was the author of *Modern Thermodynamics* and other works on physical chemistry. He also contributed articles to scientific journals. Obituaries and other sources: *AB Bookman's Weekly*, October 26, 1970; *Who Was Who Among English and European Authors, 1931-1949*, Gale, 1978.

*   *   *

GUILLOUX, Louis   1899-1980

OBITUARY NOTICE: Born in 1899 in Saint-Brieuc, Brittany, France; died October 14, 1980, in Saint-Brieuc. Novelist. The son of a leading member of the Socialist party in France, Louis Guilloux was a Socialist himself, and his writings reflect his Socialist concerns. Numbered among his novels are *La Maison du peuple, Compagnons,* and *Angelina.* His *Le Sang noir* was translated into English and published as *Bitter Victory.* In 1967 Guilloux won the Grand Prix National des Lettres, and in 1978 he won the Renaudot Prix. Obituaries and other sources: *Twentieth Century Authors: A Biographical Dictionary of Modern Literature,* H. W. Wilson, 1942; *Columbia Dictionary of Modern European Literature,* Columbia University Press, 1947; *Cassell's Encyclopaedia of World Literature,* revised edition, Morrow, 1973; *AB Bookman's Weekly,* March 9, 1981.

*   *   *

GUNTERMAN, Bertha Lisette   1886(?)-1975

OBITUARY NOTICE: Born c. 1886; died October 3, 1975. Editor. Bertha Gunterman served for forty-five years as editor of juvenile books for Longmans, Green. Obituaries and other sources: *Publishers Weekly,* October 27, 1975.

*   *   *

GYFTOPOULOS, Elias Panayiotis   1927-

PERSONAL: Born July 4, 1927, in Athens, Greece; came to the United States in 1953, naturalized citizen, 1963; son of Panayiotis Elias and Despina (Louvaris) Gyftopoulos; married Artemis Steven Scafferis, 1962; children: Vasso, Maro, Rena (daughters). *Education:* National Technical University of Athens, Mechanical and Electrical Engineer's Diploma, 1953;

Massachusetts Institute of Technology, Sc.D., 1958. *Residence:* Lincoln, Mass. *Office:* Departments of Nuclear Engineering and Mechanical Engineering, Massachusetts Institute of Technology, Cambridge, Mass. 02139.

CAREER: Massachusetts Institute of Technology, Cambridge, research assistant, 1953-55, instructor, 1955-58, assistant professor, 1958-61, associate professor, 1961-65, professor of engineering, 1965-70, Ford Professor of Engineering, 1970—, chairman of university faculty, 1973-75. Member of board of directors of Thermo Electron and New England Nuclear Corps. Chairman of National Energy Council of Greece, 1975-78; U.S. delegate to international conferences on peaceful uses of atomic energy and thermionic electrical power generation; testified as expert witness before U.S. Congress; member of board of trustees of Anatolia College and American Farm School, both in Greece; consultant to Government of Greece.

MEMBER: American Academy of Arts and Sciences (fellow), American Nuclear Society (fellow; chairman of national program committee, 1962-64; member of board of directors, 1966-69; chairman of Aerospace Division, 1968-70), National Academy of Engineering (fellow), American Society of Mechanical Engineers, American Physical Society, American Association for the Advancement of Science, Academy of Athens (fellow).

WRITINGS: (With G.N. Hatsopoulos) *Thermionic Energy Conversion,* M.I.T. Press, Volume I: *Processes and Devices,* 1973, Volume II: *Theory and Applications,* 1979; (with L. J. Lazaridis and T. F. Widmer) *Potential Fuel Effectiveness in Industry,* Ballinger, 1974; (with Hatsopoulos) *A Unified Quantum Theory of Mechanics and Thermodynamics,* Part I: *Postulates,* Part IIa: *Available Energy,* Part IIb: *Stable Equilibrium States,* Part III: *Irreducible Quantal Dispersions,* Plenum, 1976. Contributor to scientific journals and popular magazines, including *Forbes.*

WORK IN PROGRESS: A textbook on thermodynamics.

SIDELIGHTS: Gyftopoulos told *CA:* "Good writing is not only a matter of literary style. It reflects clarity of ideas and the ability to communicate with others. It is essential to advancing scientific knowledge and engineering applications."

H

HABER, Eitan 1940-

PERSONAL: Born March 12, 1940, in Tel-Aviv, Palestine (now Israel); son of Juda and Tova Haber; married Gila Ruth Noll (a medical technician, May 25, 1969; children: Michal, Ilan. *Education:* Attended secondary school in Tel Aviv, Israel. *Religion:* Jewish. *Home:* 19 Ben-Zvi Blvd., Ramat-Gan, Israel. *Office: Yedioth Achrondt,* 138 Derech Petach-Tiqua, Tel-Aviv, Israel.

CAREER: Yedioth Achrondt, Tel-Aviv, Israel, journalist, 1958—. *Military service:* Israel Defense Forces, military correspondent, 1961—; became lieutenant.

WRITINGS: Kippur, Hachette, 1974; (with Yeshayahu Ben Porat and Zeev Schiff) *Entebbe Rescue,* Delacorte, 1977; *Menachem Begin: The Legend and the Man,* Delacorte, 1978; (with Schiff and Ehud Yaari) *The Year of the Dove,* Bantam, 1979; (editor) *The Battle for Peace,* Bantam, 1981; (with Michael Bar-Zohar) *The Quest for the Red Prince,* Morrow, 1981. Writer for Israeli television programs, including "This Is Your Life."

In Hebrew; titles in translation: (With Michael Bar-Zohar) *The Paratroopers Book,* Levin-Epstein, 1969; *The Diary of the First Fighters Squadron,* Israeli Air Force, 1973; (editor with Zeev Schiff) *Israel, Army and Defense: A Dictionary,* Zmora, Bitan, Modan, 1976; (editor with Schiff) *Military Aspects of the Israeli-Arab Conflict,* University Publishing Projects, 1976.

* * *

HACKER, Frederick J. 1914-

BRIEF ENTRY: Born January 19, 1914, in Vienna, Austria. Psychiatrist, educator, and author. Hacker has had a private practice in psychiatry since 1958 and been a professor of legal psychiatry at the University of Southern California since 1970. His early experience, including residency, was at the Menninger Clinic, and he has also worked and studied in Austria. He has written *Aggression* (Verlag Fritz Molden, 1971), *Materials to Aggression* (Verlag Fritz Molden, 1972), *Terror and Terrorism* (Verlag Fritz Molden, 1973), and *Crusaders, Criminals, and Crazies: Terror and Terrorism in Our Time* (Norton, 1977). *Address:* 160 Lasky Dr., Beverly Hills, Calif. 90212; and Department of Psychiatry, University of Southern California, 2025 Zonal Ave., Los Angeles, Calif. 90033. *Biographical/critical sources: Biographical Directory of the Fellows and Members of the American Psychiatric Association,* Bowker, 1977; *Time,* January 31, 1977; *Saturday Review,* February 5, 1977; *New Republic,* May 14, 1977; *National Review,* December 23, 1977.

* * *

HADHAM, John
See PARKES, James William

* * *

HAGBRINK, Bodil 1936-

PERSONAL: Born September 4, 1936, in Stockholm, Sweden; daughter of Eric (a financial director of a newspaper) and Lore (Kaulbach) Hagbrink. *Education:* Attended Ohio University, 1956-57, and Art Academy, Karlsruhe, West Germany, 1959-66. *Home:* Vesslevaegen 40, 16140 Bromma, Stockholm, Sweden.

CAREER: Artist (painter), 1958—. *Member:* Association of Swedish Illustrators, Swedish Union of Authors. *Awards, honors:* Award from Litteraturfraemjandet, 1975, for book *Barnen i Vernette;* certificate of honor from International Board on Books for Young Children, 1980, for *Children of Lapland.*

WRITINGS—Self-illustrated children's books: *Barnen i Vernette,* Bonniers, 1975, translation by Alan Blackwood published as *Children of Vernette,* Thomas Nelson, 1975 (also see below); *Den langa rajden,* Bonniers, 1978, translation by George Simpson published as *Children of Lapland,* Tundra Books, 1980 (also see below).

Television films: "Barnen i Vernette" (adapted from her book), first broadcast by Swedish television in 1975; "Barna i Kautokeino" (adapted from her book *Den langa rajden*), first broadcast by NRK-TV (Norway) in 1981.

WORK IN PROGRESS: Research on Kautokeino Lapps in northern Norway.

SIDELIGHTS: Bodil Hagbrink commented: "Painting is my main field, including painting for children. Trained in painting and graphics by Professor G. Meyer, I began working mostly in oils and had an exhibition in Stockholm in 1968, showing paintings, drawings, and graphics. I also made stained glass windows for two small chapels in France and decorated a wall in Stockholm.

"In my books I have described the lives of some children in the south of France and in Lapland. Far apart geographically, these children are similar in the ways in which they participate in the lives and work of adults, in harmony with and dependence on nature.

"In 1975, 1976, 1977, and 1980 I stayed with Lapp families to sketch and gather material about their way of life and especially their migrations during the year. I have also traveled in Mexico, Europe, and India, and have lived in France (mostly) since 1966."

* * *

HAGEN, Lorinda
See Du BREUIL, (Elizabeth) L(or)inda

* * *

HALL, Helen 1892-

PERSONAL: Born January 4, 1892, in Kansas City, Mo.; daughter of Wilfred and Beatrice (Daika) Hall; married Paul Underwood Kellogg (a writer, editor, and social reformer) February, 1935 (deceased). *Education:* Attended Columbia University and New York School for Social Work, 1912-15. *Home:* 165 East 60th St., New York, N.Y. 10022. *Office:* c/o Keith, 33 East 60th St., New York, N.Y. 10022.

CAREER: Neighborhood House, Eastchester, N.Y., organizer, 1916; associate with Westchester County Children's Department; worked as director of Red Cross work for American Expeditionary Force base hospitals in France and organizer of Young Women's Christian Association girls' clubs; U.S. War Department, Washington, D.C., supervisor of women's relations and organizer of recreational services for enlisted men in China and the Philippines, 1920-22; University Settlement, Philadelphia, Pa., director, 1922-33; Henry Street Settlement, New York, N.Y., director, 1933-67; writer, 1967—. Chairman of unemployment committee of National Federation of Settlements, 1928, president of federation, 1934-40; member of advisory council of Committee on Economic Security, 1934; organized service clubs and rest homes for Red Cross in Australia and the South Pacific during World War II; co-organizer and chairman of Consumers National Federation, 1936-41; member of board of directors and adviser to Consumers Union, 1952—; co-founder of Lower Eastside Neighborhoods Association, 1955, and Mobilization for Youth, 1957. *Awards, honors:* LL.D. from Bates College, 1947; D.H.L. from Smith College, 1969.

WRITINGS: Unfinished Business: In Neighborhood and Nation (autobiography), Macmillan, 1971. Contributor to journals.

* * *

HALL, Ruth 1933(?)-1981

OBITUARY NOTICE: Born c. 1933 in Yorkshire, England; died after a short illness, June 14, 1981, in London, England. Musician, journalist, and author. Ruth Hall, herself an accomplished amateur harpsichordist, reviewed early and baroque keyboard music for the *London Sunday Times.* During her career in journalism, she wrote for many of England's leading newspapers. *Marie Stopes,* Hall's highly acclaimed biography of one of the pioneers of birth control, was published in 1977. She also edited a volume of Marie Stopes's letters entitled *Dear Dr. Stopes: Sex in the 1920's.* Obituaries and other sources: *London Times,* June 15, 1981.

* * *

HALLMAN, Frank Curtis 1943(?)-1975

OBITUARY NOTICE: Born c. 1943; died of an aneurysm, November 26, 1975, in New York, N.Y. Publisher. As founder of Frank Hallman (formerly Aloe Editions), Hallman published limited editions of books by such authors as Joyce Carol Oates, Virginia Woolf, Vanessa Bell, and John Updike. Obituaries and other sources: *Publishers Weekly,* December 29, 1975.

* * *

HAMER, Philip (May) 1891-1971

OBITUARY NOTICE: Born November 7, 1891, in Marion, S.C.; died April 10, 1971, in Washington, D.C. Historian and author. At the time of his death, Philip Hamer was executive director emeritus of the U.S. National Historical Publications Commission. He had previously been associated with the National Archives, and he was the author of *A Guide to Archives and Manuscripts in the United States.* He also edited the *Papers of Henry Laurens.* Obituaries and other sources: *AB Bookman's Weekly,* May 17, 1971; *American Authors and Books, 1640 to the Present Day,* 3rd revised edition, Crown, 1972.

* * *

HAMMAR, Russell A(lfred) 1920-

PERSONAL: Born February 18, 1920, in St. Paul, Minn.; son of Roy J. (a machinist) and Mabel (Nelson) Hammar; married Mildred Peters, June 11, 1943; children: David, Peter. *Education:* Attended San Jose State University, 1941; Hamline University, B.A., 1942; attended Union Theological Seminary, 1946-47; Columbia University, M.A., 1957, Ed.D., 1961. *Politics:* Independent. *Religion:* Protestant. *Home:* 4122 East Hillandale Dr., Kalamazoo, Mich. 49008. *Office:* Department of Music, Kalamazoo College, Kalamazoo, Mich. 49007.

CAREER: Emmanuel Baptist Church, Ridgewood, N.J., director of youth activities and music, 1946-50; singer and conductor in and around New York City, 1946-61; Columbia Artists Management, Inc., New York City, concert tenor, 1950-54; American Broadcasting Co., New York City, staff singer and soloist for "Voice of Firestone," 1954-57; Southern Baptist Theological Seminary, Louisville, Ky., assistant professor of music, 1957-59; Columbia University, New York City, instructor in music, 1959-61; Kalamazoo College, Kalamazoo, Mich., associate professor, 1961-68, professor of music, 1968—, conductor of Bach Festival Orchestra and Chorus, College Singers, Concert Choir, Collegium Musicum, Motet Choir, and Madrigalists. Tenor soloist for television, radio, festivals, symphonies, operas, and Robert Shaw Chorale; musical director and conductor of Kalamazoo Bach Festival Society; recording artist for Decca, Columbia, and RCA; adjudicator and conductor of choral festivals and oratorios in the United States and Europe; vocal and choral clinician; director of workshops.

MEMBER: International Association of Torch Clubs, International Bach Festival Society (director of workshop at Lincoln Center), National Association of Teachers of Singing (state governor and member of state board of governors), American Choral Directors Association (chairman of choral editing standards committee), Association of American Choral Directors, College Music Society, Music Educators National Conference, Michigan School Vocal Association, Phi Mu Alpha Sinfonia. *Awards, honors:* Grant from Great Lakes Colleges Association, 1969, for research in music of Bach family of musicians.

WRITINGS: Singing: An Extension of Speech, Scarecrow, 1978. Contributor to music and education journals, including *Choral Journal, Music Journal,* and *Kalamazoo College Magazine.*

WORK IN PROGRESS: Pragmatic Choral Procedures, publication expected in 1982.

SIDELIGHTS: Russell Hammar told *CA:* "When teaching in the area of musical performance, my most important objective is that of sensitive interpretation of the score over and above its technical demands. Whether in solo singing or choral performance, I find the greatest need is to go beyond the requisite technical demands and seek the intrinsic values which lie inherent in the score. So many people (professional and amateurs alike) involved in 'making music' are satisfied with perfecting notes and rhythm, never truly re-creating the more subtle values awaiting to be 'resurrected' into sound from the abstract, printed page. All too often singers and instrumentalists fail to recognize that the phrase lines of a musical composition rise and fall; that this contour of musical notation must have 'horizontal drive.' In speech we do not accept monotone delivery, so why should music lack intensity, variety, and excitement? This need is especially significant for vocal music in which the words provide added emotional content and meaning to the musical notation."

A reviewer of *Singing: An Extension of Speech* wrote in the *American Music Teacher:* "We welcome an especially fine 'how to' book to the vocal pedagogy shelves. Dr. Hammar . . . has skillfully outlined his pragmatic approach to the complexities of singing. It is based on the relationship of singing to clearly enunciated speech. . . . According to Dr. Hammar, the fundamental truth in learning to sing is to recognize the importance of vowel purity resulting from proper shaping of the oral pharynx. . . . I find his common-sense approach reassuring, his straight-forward style of writing refreshing."

BIOGRAPHICAL/CRITICAL SOURCES: *American Music Teacher,* April-May, 1980.

* * *

HAMMOND, Laurence

PERSONAL: Born in Cincinnati, Ohio; son of Laurence William and Lillian (a secretary; maiden name, Macbrair) Hammond; married Margaret Montague, 1939 (died, 1945); married Merikay Howard, September 13, 1950 (died June, 1974); married Etoile Valdois (a television producer), December 31, 1975; children: Laurence Christopher. *Education:* University of Cincinnati, B.A., 1930; Geneva School of International Studies, Ph.D., 1930; postdoctoral study at Stanford University, 1930-31, and Seabury Western Theological Seminary, 1965-66. *Politics:* "Conservative—Christian." *Religion:* Episcopalian. *Home and office:* 757 Anchor Rode Dr., Naples, Fla. 33940.

CAREER: Worked as miner. Associated with WNEW-Radio, New York City, 1931-33, and Blackett-Sample-Hummert, New York City, 1934-39; NBC-NAM, New York City, producer, 1940; associated with Young & Rubicam, New York City, 1940-41; War Manpower Commission, Washington, D.C., chief of radio, television, and motion pictures, 1941-42; coordinator of information and producer of "News From Home" on all shortwave radio programs to U.S. troops overseas, New York City, 1942; Inter-American Affairs, Washington, D.C., chief of special events and communications, 1943-44; Bendix Radio, Towson, Md., executive vice-president of labor-management committee and editor of *Bendix Beacon,* 1944; United War Fund, Newark, N.J., director of radio programs and motion pictures, 1945; Laurence Hammond Productions, Inc., New York City, president and producer of programs for New Jersey State Teachers' College, 1945-52; Florida Manganese, Inc., Deming, N.M., executive vice-president, 1952-57; associated with Meissner Engineers, Chicago, Ill., 1957-61; free-lance writer, 1967-75; currently host of "Acts Twenty-nine Plus," a syndicated television series distributed three times a week

by National Christian Network to two thousand cable television stations. Member of New York Southern District Grand Jury, 1946-48; member of board of directors of Episcopal Charismatic Fellowship, 1974-78. *Member:* Authors Guild (member of board of directors, 1939-41), Radio-Television Directors-Writers Guild (founding member), Lambda Chi Alpha (president, 1930), Sigma Sigma, Cincinnatus Society.

WRITINGS: *Cavalcade of America,* Milton Bradley, 1937; (with Mirard C. Faught) *Care and Feeding of Executives* (humorous nonfiction), Wormwood Press, 1945; *Beyond Love,* Creation House, 1976; *Never Too Old* (biography of Clyde Clayton Downing), Chosen Books, 1982; *A Piece of Time* (history of radio and television), Doubleday, in press. Also author of *The Story of Rubber* (based on radio series), 1937, and *P. T. Barnum* (based on radio series), 1937. Writer for television and radio programs, including "Gangbusters," "Mr. District Attorney," "Defense for America," "Backstage Wife," "Young Widder Brown," "Driftwood," "Your Family and Mine," "John's Other Wife," and "We the People." Contributor to magazines, including *Reader's Digest, Forbes,* and *Voice of Healing.*

WORK IN PROGRESS: A semi-biographical novel, publication by Creation House.

SIDELIGHTS: Hammond wrote: "I have traveled to more than fifty nations, spending much time on 'spiritual airlifts' to spread Christian witness to universities, business, and government leaders such as Nehru, Indira Gandhi, Nasser, and Prince Philip. I have operated mines in Mexico, Haiti, the southwestern and northwestern United States and Canada.

"Ten years ago I was nearly cut in half by a propeller (a story told in *Beyond Love*), have been miraculously healed, and witness everywhere. I am presently host of a television series, interviewing leaders in politics and sports about what God means in their lives."

* * *

HAMPL, Patricia 1946-

PERSONAL: Born March 12, 1946, in St. Paul, Minn.; daughter of Stanley R. (a florist) and Mary (a librarian; maiden name, Marum) Hampl. *Education:* University of Minnesota, B.A., 1968; University of Iowa, M.F.A., 1970. *Residence:* St. Paul, Minn. *Agent:* Rhoda Weyr, William Morris Agency, 1350 Avenue of the Americas, New York, N.Y. 10019. *Office:* Department of English, University of Minnesota, 207 Lind Hall, Minneapolis, Minn. 55455.

CAREER: KSJN-Radio, St. Paul, Minn., editor of *Minnesota Monthly,* 1973-75; free-lance editor and writer, 1975-79; University of Minnesota, Minneapolis, visiting assistant professor of English, 1979—. Founding member of Loft (for literature and the arts); lecturer; presents workshops. *Awards, honors:* Grant from National Endowment for the Arts, 1976; Grant from Bush Foundation, 1979; Houghton Mifflin literary fellowship, 1981, for *A Romantic Education.*

WRITINGS: *Woman Before an Aquarium* (poetry), University of Pittsburgh Press, 1978; *A Romantic Education* (prose memoir), Houghton, 1981. Contributor to magazines, including *American Poetry Review, New Yorker, Paris Review,* and *Iowa Review.* Co-editor of *Lamp in the Spine,* 1971-74.

WORK IN PROGRESS: A novel; research for a university textbook on memoirs.

SIDELIGHTS: Patricia Hampl wrote: "I am a poet who has been writing more prose in recent years, drawn first by informal prose forms (journals and diaries) to more formal projects. Poetry remains a vital source for me. The encouragement and boost the women's movement of the 1970's gave to women writers and artists was a great gift to me. I suppose I write about all the things I intended to leave behind, to grow out of, or deny: being a Midwesterner, a Catholic, a woman. It is May, lilac time, as I write this in St. Paul, my home town, and it still seems I should describe the lilacs in the alleys one more time.''

BIOGRAPHICAL/CRITICAL SOURCES: *New York Times Book Review*, March 29, 1981; *Chicago Tribune Book World*, May 3, 1981; *Los Angeles Times*, May 29, 1981.

*   *   *

HAMSUN, Knut
    See PEDERSEN, Knut

*   *   *

HANBURY-TENISON, Marika   1938-

PERSONAL: Born September 9,1938, in London, England; daughter of John Montgomerie and Alexander (Stiernstedt) Hopkinson; married Robin Hanbury-Tenison (an explorer, writer, and farmer), January 14, 1959; children: Lucy Antonia, Rupert, Thomas, Trevedoe. *Education:* Attended private schools in London, England. *Politics:* Conservative. *Religion:* Church of England. *Home:* Maidenwell, Cardinham, Bodmin, Cornwall, England. *Agent:* A. D. Peters & Co. Ltd., 10 Buckingham St., London WC2N 6BU, England.

CAREER: Free-lance writer, 1968. Member of board of directors of A.B.M. Ltd.; consultant to Radio Avon. *Member:* National Union of Journalists, Society of Authors. *Awards, honors:* Andre Simon Award from Andre Simon Foundation, 1980, for *Cooking With Vegetables.*

WRITINGS: Soups and Hors D'Oeuvres, Penguin, 1969; *Deep-Freeze Cookery,* Hart-Davis, 1970; *Left Over for Tomorrow,* Penguin, 1971; *Marika Hanbury-Tenison's Menus for Each Month of the Year,* Cabilla Designs, 1972; *For Better, For Worse: To the Brazilian Jungles and Back Again,* Hutchinson, 1972; *Tagging Along,* Coward, 1972; *Eat Well and Be Slim,* Pan Books, 1974; *A Slice of Spice: Travels to Indonesian Islands,* Hutchinson, 1974; *The Best of British Cooking,* Hart-Davis, 1976; *Recipes From a Country Kitchen,* Granada, 1978; *Magimix and Food Processor Cookery Book,* Hutchinson, 1978; *New Fish Cookery,* Granada, 1979; *Deep Freeze Cookery,* Granada, 1979; *Teach Yourself Deep Freezing,* Hodder & Stoughton, 1979; *The Cook's Handbook,* Hodder & Stoughton, 1979; *West Country Cooking,* Granada, 1979; *Book of Afternoon Tea,* David & Charles, 1980; *Cooking With Vegetables,* J. Cape, 1980; *Sunday Telegraph Cook Book,* Granada, 1980; *Soups and Starters,* Granada, 1980; *Marika Hanbury-Tenison's Freezer Cook Book,* Pan Books, 1981; *The Princess and the Unicorn,* Granada, 1981.

Writer for British radio and televison programs. Contributor to magazines, including *Vogue* and *Observer,* and newspapers. Cookery editor of *Sunday Telegraph,* 1968—, and *Spectator,* 1977-79.

WORK IN PROGRESS: Encyclopedia of Cookery, for Granada; a book on cooking with food processors; a children's book; a travel book about Borneo.

SIDELIGHTS: Marika Hanbury-Tenison told *CA:* ''Being married to an explorer, I have had the opportunity to travel to some of the more remote areas of the world and to study the gas-

tronomy of many varied peoples. I believe in creating a perfect cuisine that combines the food and cookery practices of the best cuisines in the world.

''I am in love with my husband and children, my home in the wilder part of Cornwall, and my garden. I also love writing and find it compulsive; when I am well into the swing of a book I find it easy to work for up to twelve hours a day. Although I am mainly known as a food writer I would like very much to extend my work towards writing children's books and general fiction.

''With my husband I have traveled on expeditions to Brazil, Indonesia, and Borneo, and in 1979 I cooked for forty-five scientists for three months in a 'long house' in the Borneo jungle under extremely difficult conditions. Traveling in this way has taught me a lot about food and one's attitude toward food (being without it for sometimes five days at a time tends to make you think quite hard about the subject). During this time I also became an ardent conservationist, and I am directly involved with Survival International, a charity founded by my husband for the protection of isolated tribal minorities.

''With regard to my cookery writing, I feel very strongly that cooking should be *fun* and not a chore, and that if you go into the kitchen expecting to be bored at the idea of cooking *another* meal that meal will reflect your boredom. Home cooking should be imaginative, an excitement to prepare, and a pleasure to eat. I also feel that in this day and age, with inflation and rising food prices, it is time for us to cut down on the amount of meat, fish, and poultry we eat and supplement smaller amounts of these protein ingredients with more and imaginatively cooked vegetables. The time has come to forget about having 'meat with two vegetables,' and to have vegetables with meat instead. It is this theory that I used for the 250 original recipes in my book *Cooking With Vegetables.*''

*   *   *

HANKINS, Frank Hamilton   1877-1970

OBITUARY NOTICE: Born September 27, 1877, in Wilshire, Ohio; died January 23, 1970, in New York, N.Y. Educator and author. A professor of sociology at Smith College, Frank Hankins was the author of books, including *The Racial Basis of Civilization: A Critique of the Nordic Doctrine* and *An Introduction to the Study of Society.* He was also a contributor to reference works and professional journals. Obituaries and other sources: *AB Bookman's Weekly,* February 16, 1970; *Who Was Who in America, With World Notables,* Volume V: *1969-1973,* Marquis, 1973; *Who Was Who Among English and European Authors, 1931-1949,* Gale, 1978.

*   *   *

HANLEY, Elizabeth
    See Du BREUIL, (Elizabeth) L(or)inda

*   *   *

HANNAY, Margaret Patterson   1944-

PERSONAL: Born December 20, 1944, in Rochester, N.H.; daughter of Ralph E. (a Baptist minister) and Lois (a research biologist) Patterson; married David Hannay (a professor of computer science), August 14, 1965; children: Deborah, Catharine. *Education:* Wheaton College, Wheaton, Ill., B.A. (summa cum laude), 1966; College of St. Rose, M.A., 1970; State University of New York at Albany, Ph.D., 1976. *Religion:* Episcopalian. *Residence:* Westerlo, N.Y. *Office:* Department of English, Siena College, Loudonville, N.Y. 12211.

CAREER: State University of New York at Albany, lecturer in English, 1975-80; Siena College, Loudonville, N.Y., assistant professor of English, 1980—. Member of faculty at Russell Sage College, 1974, and College of St. Rose, 1977-78. *Member:* Conference on Christianity and Literature (member of board of directors, 1976-79; national vice-president, 1980-83), Milton Society of America, Modern Language Association of America, Spenser Society, Northeast Modern Language Association.

WRITINGS: (Contributor) Peter Schakel, editor, *Looking for a Form,* Kent State University Press, 1977; (editor) *As Her Wimsey Took Her: Critical Essays on Dorothy L. Sayers,* Kent State University Press, 1979; *C. S. Lewis,* Ungar, 1981. Contributor to *Dictionary of the Bible and the Biblical Tradition in English Literature.* Contributor of articles and reviews to journals, including *Mythlore, Free Indeed, Sayers Review, Christian Scholar's Review, Tolkien Journal,* and *Daughters of Sarah.* Advisory editor of *Christianity and Literature.*

WORK IN PROGRESS: A literary biography of Mary Sidney, Countess of Pembroke.

SIDELIGHTS: Margaret Hannay commented: "I am intrigued by that brief period in sixteenth-century England when women such as Lady Jane Grey, Queen Elizabeth, Catherine Parr, Margaret Roper, Mildred and Anne Cooke—and of course Mary Sidney—were esteemed for their learning. Education for women apparently flourished in the early days of the Protestant Reformation but was given less attention as the Puritans rose to power in England. As I study Mary Sidney I plan to put her life into this context of changing expectations for women."

*   *   *

HANSEN, Emmanuel   1937-

PERSONAL: Born July 27, 1937, in Accra, Ghana; son of James Walter (a pharmacist) and Susuanah (a trader; maiden name, Tetteh) Hansen; married Margaret Elaine Farmer (a librarian), August, 1968; children: Kate, Jane. *Education:* University of Ghana, B.A., 1964; Makerere University, M.A., 1969; Indiana University, M.A., 1971, Ph.D., 1973. *Home:* 3 Glenkerry House, Burcham St., London E.14, England.

CAREER: University of Dar-es-Salaam, Dar-es-Salaam, Tanzania, assistant lecturer in political science, 1967-68; Indiana University, Bloomington, associate instructor in political science, 1970-72; Ohio State University, Columbus, assistant professor of Afro-American studies, 1972-73; University of Ghana, Legon, lecturer, 1973-77, senior lecturer in political science, 1977-79; University of Sussex, Brighton, England, visiting lecturer in development studies, 1979-80; University of Durham, Durham, England, lecturer in political science, 1980—. *Member:* Association of African Political Scientists (vice-president for West Africa).

WRITINGS: *Frantz Fanon: Social and Political Thought,* Ohio State University Press, 1977; (contributor) *Uganda District Government and Politics, 1947-1967,* University of Wisconsin, Madison, 1978. Contributor to political science and African studies journals.

WORK IN PROGRESS: *Praxis and Revolution: The Case of Amilcar Cabral; The Politics of Food and Development in Africa.*

*   *   *

HANSON, Joseph E.   1894(?)-1971

OBITUARY NOTICE: Born c. 1894; died March 15, 1971, in South Orange, N.J. Broadcaster and author. Hanson wrote books for children, including *Hong Kong Altar Boy.* Obituaries and other sources: *AB Bookman's Weekly,* May 17, 1971.

*   *   *

HARAP, Henry   1893-1981

OBITUARY NOTICE: Born November 29, 1893, in Austria; died of cardiopulmonary arrest, September 24, 1981, in Sandy Springs, Md. Educator, editor, and author. A leader in the field of curriculum development, Henry Harap began his career as a professor of education. He later became the associate director of the surveys and field services division of George Peabody College for Teachers in Nashville, Tenn. Among his numerous works on education are *The Education of the Consumer, The Core Curriculum,* and *Preparation of Teachers in the Area of Curriculum and Instruction.* From 1929 to 1943 Harap served as editor of the *Curriculum Journal.* He also edited books, including *The Changing Curriculum* and *Curriculum Trends at Mid-Century.* Obituaries and other sources: *Biographical Dictionary of American Educators,* Greenwood Press, 1978; *Washington Post,* September 26, 1981.

*   *   *

HARDING, Davis P.   1915(?)-1970

OBITUARY NOTICE: Born c. 1915; died February 24, 1970, in New Haven, Conn. Educator and author. Davis Harding, associate professor of English at Yale University, was an authority on the works of John Milton and other writers of the English Renaissance period in literature. He wrote *The Club of Hercules* and *Milton and Ovid.* Obituaries and other sources: *New York Times,* February 27, 1970; *AB Bookman's Weekly,* March 16, 1970; *Publishers Weekly,* May 18, 1970.

*   *   *

HARDY, Jonathan G. Gathorne
See GATHORNE-HARDY, Jonathan G.

*   *   *

HARDY, Thomas   1840-1928

BRIEF ENTRY: Born June 2, 1840, in Higher Bockhampton, Dorsetshire, England; died January 11, 1928, in Dorchester, Dorsetshire, England; buried in Westminster Abbey in London, England. Novelist, poet, short story writer, playwright, and essayist. Dubbed the "Wessex novelist," Hardy set all his novels in the fictional area of Wessex, which closely resembled his beloved native region of Dorsetshire, England. The author published his first novel in 1871 after George Meredith advised him to employ less satire and more plot in his writing. The resulting work, *Desperate Remedies,* was followed by the novels *Under the Greenwood Tree* (1872), *Far From the Madding Crowd* (1874), and *Tess of the D'Urbervilles* (1891). In his writings Hardy advanced his theory that man is affected by forces not within his realm of control. Thus Hardy's novels are largely tragic tales in which the characters are driven by destructive personalities or labor under the strictures of an uncompromising society. Hardy's world view often ran contrary to the prevailing Victorian tastes of his day. Many of his novels were censured for their pessimism and frank treatment of taboo subjects. After receiving particularly harsh criticism for *Jude the Obscure* (1895), Hardy abandoned the novel entirely and turned to writing poetry. The author also wrote an epic drama entitled *The Dynasts* (1904-08), which chronicles the Napoleonic Wars. Hardy, who attended school for only eight years, began his career as an architect before turning to writing. On his death, the residents of Dorsetshire felt that although Hardy's body was to be buried in the Poet's Corner of Westminster Abbey, his heart should rest in the countryside he so loved and immortalized. As a result, Hardy's heart is buried in Stinsford, Dorsetshire, England. His other works include *The Return of the Native* (1878), *The Mayor of Casterbridge* (1886), and *Life's Little Ironies* (1894). *Residence:* Max Gate, Dorchester, Dorsetshire, England. *Biographical/critical sources: Cyclopedia of World Authors,* Harper, 1958; *The Concise Encyclopedia of Modern World Literature,* Hutchinson, 1963; *Twentieth Century Writing: A Reader's Guide to Contemporary Literature,* Transatlantic, 1969; *Twentieth-Century Literary Criticism,* Volume 4, Gale, 1981.

*   *   *

HARRIS, Beulah   ?-1970

OBITUARY NOTICE: Died of cancer, January 8, 1970, in Manhasset, N.Y. Editor and author. During her career in editing, Beulah Harris was associated with E. P. Dutton and McGraw-Hill. She served as editor at Funk & Wagnalls and at Holt, Rinehart & Winston. Harris wrote a cookbook series that includes titles such as *Classic Sauces of France, Provencale Earthenware Cookery,* and *Sausage Making in the Home.* She also wrote *The Four Winds Cookbook.* Obituaries and other sources: *Publishers Weekly,* January 26, 1970.

*   *   *

HARRIS, Joel Chandler   1848-1908

BRIEF ENTRY: Born December 9, 1848, in Eatonton, Ga.; died July 3, 1908, in Atlanta, Ga. American journalist and author. Harris is best known as the creator of Uncle Remus, the narrator of the popular tales featuring Brer Rabbit and Tar-Baby. The stories, written in various black dialects, were collected in several volumes, including *Uncle Remus: His Songs and Sayings* (1881), *Nights With Uncle Remus* (1883), *The Tar-Baby* (1904), and *Uncle Remus and Brer Rabbit* (1907). Most of the tales are constructed as fables in which various anthropomorphic characters must overcome aggressors or devilish odds. The stories are particularly favored by critics for the black dialects Harris incorporated, and several writers have credited him with preserving otherwise forgotten syntax and speech patterns. Harris was also a reporter for the *Atlanta Constitution* and a contributor of humorous essays to the *Savannah Morning News.* From 1907 until his death he edited *Uncle Remus's Magazine. Biographical/critical sources: Cyclopedia of World Authors,* Harper, 1958; *Twentieth-Century Literary Criticism,* Volume 2, Gale, 1979.

*   *   *

HARRIS, Marie   1943-

PERSONAL: Born November 7, 1943, in New York, N.Y.; daughter of Basil (a physician) and Marie (Murray) Harris; married William Matthews (a poet), May 4, 1963 (divorced, 1972); married Charter Weeks (a photographer), November 4, 1977; children: (first marriage) William, Sebastian. *Education:* Attended Georgetown University, 1961-63, and University of North Carolina, 1967-68; Goddard College, B.A., 1971. *Office:* Isinglass Studio, P.O. Box 203, Barrington, N.H. 03825.

CAREER: Alice James Books, Cambridge, Mass., publisher, 1974—; Maximus Advertising, Exeter, N.H., copywriter, 1977—; Isinglass Studio (advertising and marketing firm), Barrington, N.H., partner, 1979—. Administrator of New Hampshire Commission on the Arts Poet-in-the-Schools Program, 1972-76; administrative assistant at Theatre-by-the-Sea, Portsmouth, N.H., 1976-77; poet-in-residence at Hopkins Center, Dartmouth College, 1977-78; gives readings at college and universities and on radio programs. *Member:* Poetry Society of America. *Awards, honors:* Fellow of National Endowment for the Arts, 1976-77.

WRITINGS: Raw Honey (poems), Alice James Books, 1975; *Interstate* (poems), Slow Loris Press, 1980.

Work represented in anthologies, including *But Is It Poetry?,* Dragonfly Press; *Blacksmith Anthology,* Volumes I-II, Blacksmith Press; *Mountain Moving Day,* Crossing Press. Contributor of articles and poems to magazines, including *Parnassus: Poetry in Review, Country Journal, Poetry Now, Epoch, Southern Poetry Review,* and *Penumbra.*

WORK IN PROGRESS: Low Mass (tentative title), poems; editing a collection of critical articles on poetics.

SIDELIGHTS: Marie Harris has described herself as a feminist and farmer as well as a poet.

*   *   *

HARRIS, Mark Jonathan   1941-

PERSONAL: Born October 28, 1941, in Scranton, Pa.; son of Norman (a lawyer) and Ruth (Bialosky) Harris; married Susan Popky (a clinical psychologist), June 9, 1963; children: Laura, Jordan. *Education:* Harvard University, B.A., 1963. *Home and office:* 1043 Point View St., Los Angeles, Calif. 90035. *Agent:* Barbara Lowenstein, 250 West 57th St., New York, N.Y. 10019.

CAREER: Associated Press, Chicago, Ill., reporter, 1963-64; documentary and educational filmmaker, 1964-75; University of Southern California, Los Angeles, senior lecturer in cinema, 1975—. Professor at California Institute of Arts, 1976—. *Member:* Writers Guild of America, Society of Children's Book Writers, Southern California Council on Literature for Children and Young People. *Awards, honors:* Regional Emmy Award from Academy of Television Arts and Sciences, 1965, for "The Golden Calf"; Academy Award for short documentary film from Motion Picture Academy of Arts and Sciences, 1968, for "The Redwoods"; Golden Eagle from Council on International Nontheatrical Events, 1968, for "The Redwoods"; special award from Leipzig International Film Festival, 1968, for "Huelga!"; *With a Wave of the Wand* was a children's choice selection of International Reading Association, 1981.

WRITINGS: With a Wave of the Wand (juvenile), Lothrop, 1980; *The Last Run* (juvenile), Lothrop, 1981.

Films: "The Golden Calf," KGW-TV (Portland, Ore.), 1965; "Huelga!," King Screen Productions, 1967; "The Redwoods," King Screen Productions, 1968; "The Foreigners," King Screen Productions, 1969.

Contributor to magazines and newspapers, including *Prime Time, TV Guide, Washington Post,* and *Newsday.* Past contributing editor of *New West.*

WORK IN PROGRESS: An adult novel, *The Messiah of Palm Springs;* "The American Homefront," a documentary film on the social and economic effects of World War II on the United States.

SIDELIGHTS: Harris wrote: "I began my career as a wire service reporter, then switched to making educational and documentary films during the political turbulent 1960's. 'Huelga!' documented the first year of the Delano grape strike. 'The

Redwoods' was made to help the Sierra Club establish a Redwood National Park. 'The Foreigners' examined a group of Peace Corps volunteers battling poverty and powerlessness in Colombia. In the 1970's, when the money for political films began running out, I turned to teaching and journalism.

"As I've grown older I've found I'm much more interested in creating my own characters than in reporting about real ones. I began with a twelve-year-old protagonist in *With a Wave of the Wand* and moved up to a fourteen-year-old hero in *The Last Run,* reliving my own childhood and gradually working my way up to adulthood. Soon I expect to be able to write about thirty-year-olds.

"If there has been a common concern in all my work, it is how people respond to the critical social problems of our society. Whether it is an impoverished farm worker striking for the right to unionize, or a confused twelve-year-old trying to cope with the turmoil of middle-class divorce, I have tried to explore the struggle that occurs when individuals confront the crucial social forces that shape their lives."

*　　*　　*

HARRIS, P(eter) B(ernard) 1929-

PERSONAL: Born January 31, 1929, in Cardiff, Wales; son of Thomas (a civil servant) and Sarah (Morgan) Harris; married Mary Rosemary Davies (a teacher), July 25, 1953; children: Richard, Julian, Daniel. *Education:* University of Wales, B.A., 1950; University of London, B.Sc., 1953, Ph.D., 1962; University of Natal, D.Litt., 1967. *Politics:* Social Democrat. *Religion:* Roman Catholic. *Office:* Department of Political Science, University of Hong Kong, Hong Kong.

CAREER: Associated with University of Wales, University College, Cardiff, 1947-50, and University of East Africa (now Makerere University), Makerere, Uganda, 1953-56; University of London, London School of Economics and Political Science and Institute of Education, London, England, senior lecturer in government, 1956-62; University of Natal, Durban, South Africa, senior lecturer in political science, 1963-67; University College of Rhodesia and Nyasaland (now University of Rhodesia), Salisbury, professor of political science and head of department, 1967-70; University of Hong Kong, Hong Kong, professor of political science and head of department, 1970—, public orator. *Military service:* Royal Air Force, flying officer, 1950-52. *Member:* St. David's Society of Hong Kong (president, 1981). *Awards, honors:* Gold medals from Hong Kong University, 1976, 1977, 1978, 1979, and 1980, for public oratory.

WRITINGS: Interest Groups in South African Politics, University College of Rhodesia, 1968; *The Withdrawal of the Major European Powers From Africa,* University College of Rhodesia, 1969; *Studies in African Politics,* Hutchinson, 1970; *South African Government and Politics* (edited by D. W. Worrall), Van Schaik, 1971; *The Commonwealth: Political Realities,* Longman, 1975; *Foundations of Political Science,* Hutchinson, 1976; *Hong Kong: A Study of Bureaucratic Politics,* Heinemann, 1978; *Political China Observed,* Croom Helm, 1980; *Hong Kong: Life, Work, and Politics,* Heinemann, 1981; *The Political Economy of the People's Republic of China,* Croom Helm, 1982.

Author of weekly columns. Contributor of about thirty articles to political science journals.

HARRIS, (William) Stewart 1922-

PERSONAL: Born December 13, 1922, in Woking, England; son of Henry (a banker) and Kate (Hay) Harris; married Mary Orr Deas (a welfare officer), October 8, 1955; children: Nicholas, Karina, Alastair, Iona. *Education:* Cambridge University, M.A. (with honors), 1945. *Politics:* Labour. *Home:* 77 Wybalena Grove, Cook, Australian Capital Territory 2614, Australia. *Office: Canberra Times,* Mort St., Braddon, Australian Capital Territory 2600, Australia.

CAREER: Yorkshire Post, Leeds, England, reporter, 1949; *Times,* London, England, sub-editor, 1949-51; *Courier-Mail,* Brisbane, Australia, special writer, 1951-52; *Morning Herald,* Sydney, Australia, special writer, 1952-53; *Courier-Mail,* Brisbane, sub-editor, 1953-54; *Times,* London, assistant to chief correspondent, 1955-57, staff correspondent in Canberra, 1957-63; Australian National University, Canberra, senior research fellow at Research School of Pacific Studies, 1973-77; Library of Parliament, Canberra, foreign affairs research specialist, 1977-80; *Canberra Times,* Braddon, Australia, editorial writer, 1980—. *Military service:* Royal Naval Volunteer Reserve, 1944-46; became lieutenant. *Member:* Australian Society of Authors, Australian Journalists Association, Institute of Journalists (England).

WRITINGS: Political Football, Gold Star, 1972; *This Our Land,* Australian National University Press, 1972; *It's Coming Yet,* Angus & Robertson, 1979. Also author of quarterly *Aboriginal Treaty News.*

SIDELIGHTS: Harris wrote: "I have always been interested in politics and especially in how politics affects ordinary people. I became interested in the Australian Aborigines in the early 1970's, and my last two books covered their situation. It has much improved in the last ten years but differs far too much from state to state. The federal government has not taken charge as it should under the constitution. I am now working with a national independent committee whose aim is to get the federal government to negotiate a treaty with Aboriginal Australians, which will at last give them justice in their own country."

*　　*　　*

HARRIS, William Bliss 1901(?)-1981
(Amos Pettingill)

OBITUARY NOTICE: Born c. 1901 in Denver, Colo.; died June 22, 1981, in Falmouth, Mass. Horticulturist, editor, and author. William Harris, a senior editor for *Fortune,* wrote primarily on the automotive industry for that magazine. In 1949, with his wife, Jane Grant, he established the White Flower Farm, a horticulture business. Under the pseudonym Amos Pettingill, Harris published a popular periodical entitled *The White Flower Farm Garden Book.* Obituaries and other sources: *New York Times,* June 26, 1981; *Newsweek,* July 6, 1981.

*　　*　　*

HARRIS, William Foster
See FOSTER-HARRIS, William

*　　*　　*

HARRISON, Joan (Mary) 1909-

PERSONAL: Born June 20, 1909, in Guildford, Surrey, England; daughter of Walter (a newspaper publisher) and Amelia (Muir) Harrison; married Eric Ambler (an author), October 11,

1958. *Education:* Attended Sorbonne, University of Paris; received B.A. from St. Hugh's College, Oxford. *Home:* 10640 Taranto Way, Los Angeles, Calif. 90024. *Office:* Tarantula Productions, Box 1065, Studio City, Calif. 91604.

CAREER: Copywriter for London Press Exchange (advertising agency), London, England; worked as a clerk in dress shop, a free-lance writer for magazines, and a secretary for several writers; secretary, script reader, and story-conference assistant for film director Alfred Hitchcock, 1933-41; screenwriter, 1937-1951; associate producer of films, 1944, including "Phantom Lady" and "Dark Waters" (also see below); producer of films, 1945-51, including "The Strange Affair of Uncle Harry," Universal, 1945, "Nocturne," RKO,1946, "They Won't Believe Me," RKO, 1947, "Ride the Pink Horse," Universal, 1948, "Once More, My Darling", Universal, 1949 , "Eyewitness," Eagle Lion, 1950, and "Circle of Danger," United Artists, 1951; producer of television series "Alfred Hitchcock Presents," 1953-64; Tarantula Productions, Studio City, Calif., owner, 1964—; executive producer of television series "Journey to the Unknown," beginning 1968. *Awards, honors:* Academy Award nominations for best screenplay from Academy of Motion Picture Arts and Sciences for "Rebecca" and "Foreign Correspondent," both 1940.

WRITINGS—Screenplays: (With Charles Bennett, Edwin Greenwood, Anthony Armstrong, and Gerald Savory) "The Girl Was Young" (adapted from story "A Shilling for Candles" by Josephine Tey), Gaumont, 1937, also released as "Young and Innocent"; (with Sidney Gilliat and J. B. Priestly) "Jamaica Inn" (adapted from the novel by Daphne du Maurier), Paramount, 1939; (with Robert E. Sherwood, Philip MacDonald, and Michael Hogan) "Rebecca" (adapted from the novel by du Maurier), United Artists, 1940; (with Bennett) "Foreign Correspondent" (adapted from autobiography *In Search of History* by Vincent Sheean), United Artists, 1940; (with Samson Raphaelson) "Suspicion" (adapted from novel *Before the Fact* by Francis Iles), RKO, 1941; (with Peter Viertel and Dorothy Parker) "Saboteur," Universal, 1942; (with Bernard C. Schoenfeld) "Phantom Lady" (adapted from the novel by William Irish), Universal, 1944; (with Marian Cockrell) "Dark Waters" (adapted from the novel by Frank Cockrell and Marian Cockrell), United Artists, 1944.

SIDELIGHTS: Harrison began writing screenplays while employed as an assistant to famed film director Alfred Hitchcock. Her screenplays for the Hitchcock films "Rebecca" and "Foreign Correspondent" received Academy Award nominations in 1940. Although neither screenplay won an award, "Rebecca" was chosen by the Academy of Motion Picture Arts and Sciences as the best picture of the year. Both "Rebecca" and "Foreign Correspodent" were also on the *Film Daily* and the National Board of Review of Motion Pictures lists of the ten best pictures of the year.

BIOGRAPHICAL/CRITICAL SOURCES: New York Times, October 12, 1939, March 29, 1940, August 28, 1940, November 21, 1941, May 8, 1942, June 27, 1943, November 22, 1944, August 24, 1945, November 11, 1946, July 17, 1947, October 9, 1947, September 26, 1949, August 28, 1950, July 12, 1951; *Time,* February 28, 1944; *New York Times Magazine,* July 21, 1957.*

*   *   *

HARRON, Don(ald)   1924-
(Charlie Farquharson, Valerie Rosedale)

PERSONAL: Born September 19, 1924, in Toronto, Ontario, Canada; son of Lionel William and Delsia Ada (Hunter) Har-

ron; married second wife, Catherine McKinnon, March 12, 1969; children: (first marriage) Martha, Mary; (second marriage) Kelley. *Education:* University of Toronto, B.A. (with honors), 1948. *Home and office:* 23 Lowther Ave., Toronto 5, Ontario, Canada.

CAREER: Professional actor, 1936—. Host of "Morningside," a public affairs program on CBC-Radio, 1977—. Appeared on television program "Hee-Haw" as Charlie Farquharson; also performs as Valerie Rosedale. *Military service:* Royal Canadian Air Force, pilot officer, 1943-45. *Member:* Cricket Club. *Awards, honors:* Best musical award from *Plays and Players,* 1969, for "Anne of Green Gables"; officer of Order of Canada, 1980.

WRITINGS: (With Norman Campbell) *Anne of Green Gables* (two-act musical comedy; first produced in Charlottetown, Prince Edward Island, at Confederation Theatre, July, 1965), Samuel French, 1970; *Charlie Farquharson's Histry of Canada,* McGraw, 1972; *Charlie Farquharson's Jog Free of Canada, the Whirld, and Other Places,* Gage, 1974; *Charlie Farquharson's KORN Filled Allmynack,* Gage, 1976; *Old Charlie Farquharson's Testymint,* Vanguard, 1978; *Harronside* (autobiography), Macmillan, 1982. Also author of *Charlie Farquharson's Town and Country Appointment Book 1982,* 1981.

Plays: "Here Lies Sarah Binks" (two-act musical comedy), first produced in Toronto, Ontario, at Library Theatre, March, 1968; "Broken Jug" (three-act farce), first produced in New York, N.Y., at Phoenix Theatre, 1969; "Private Turvey's War" (two-act musical comedy), first produced in Charlottetown, Prince Edward Island, at Confederation Theatre, 1970; "The Wonder of It All" (musical), first produced in Victoria, British Columbia, at Four Seasons Theatre, June, 1980.

For television: "And That's the News Good Night," first broadcast in 1969; "Wring Out the Old," first broadcast in 1970; "The Let's Save Canada Hour," first broadcast in 1977; "Once," first broadcast by CBC-TV, October 23, 1980. Created satire series "Shhh! It's the News!' on Global Television, 1974-75. Writer for BBC-TV and BBC-Radio, including "Bedtime With Braden," 1950, and "Spring Thaw."

WORK IN PROGRESS: Screenplay adaptation of play "Anne of Green Gables."

SIDELIGHTS: Harron wrote: "I have been in the entertainment business since 1936, when I started as a child actor in radio. I didn't really take it seriously until 1945, after I returned from the Air Force. I worked in radio, then five years of theatre with Toronto's New Play Society, then went to England, where I ended up writing for radio and appearing in West End theatre. I got cast in a Christopher Fry play, opened on Broadway in 1951, toured the United States for six months, then returned to Canada in time for television in 1952. I appeared in the first three Stratford festivals, did a season with the Bristol Old Vic, six plays on Broadway, three seasons at the American Shakespeare Festival, one for Joe Papp's Shakespeare in the Park, and one for John Houseman at University of California, Los Angeles. I worked for network television in the United States for four or five years, then did 'Mary, Mary' in London for fourteen months with Maggie Smith. Then I returned to Canada with the success of the musical, 'Anne of the Green Gables,' which has played every season in Charlottetown since 1965.

"I have written the screenplay of 'Anne' and the director and composer Norman Campbell is working on it. We also wrote a musical about Canadian painter Emily Carr, which was performed on CBC-TV in 1972. I write one book every two years, based on my 'Hee-Haw' character, Charlie Farquharson. I am still active on stage and in television, despite the fact that eight hours a day, five days a week go into presenting three hours of network radio daily. This has been the most satisfying achievement, linking up the whole country every morning and talking internationally wherever the news happens. People call me a workaholic.''

He added: ''The female Valerie Rosedale is an upper-class WASP (White Anti-Sexual Protestant) character I created during International Women's Year to compete with Toronto's CN Tower, which was erected that year, I believe, to teach Canadian men humility.''

AVOCATIONAL INTERESTS: Football, tennis.

BIOGRAPHICAL/CRITICAL SOURCES: Maclean's, October, 1976; *Today,* May, 1981; Don Harron, *Harronside* (autobiography), Macmillan, 1982.

* * *

HARROW, Benjamin 1888-1970

OBITUARY NOTICE: Born August 25, 1888, in London, England; died December 9, 1970, in New York, N.Y. Chemist, educator, and author. A professor of chemistry, Harrow was the co-author of textbooks on chemistry, including *Laboratory Manual of Biochemistry* and *A Textbook of Biochemistry*. In addition, he contributed articles to research publications in his field. Obituaries and other sources: *New York Times,* December 11, 1970; *AB Bookman's Weekly,* January 4, 1971; *Who Was Who in America, With World Notables,* Volume V: *1969-1973,* Marquis, 1973; *Who Was Who Among English and European Authors, 1931-1949,* Gale, 1978.

* * *

HARTE, (Francis) Bret(t) 1836(?)-1902

BRIEF ENTRY: Born August 25, c. 1836, in Albany, N.Y.; died May 5, 1902. American short story writer. Harte's reputation as a writer was established early in his career with such stories as ''The Outcasts of Poker Flat'' and ''The Luck of Roaring Camp.'' He went west as a young man, settling in San Francisco and working at times as a gold miner, a teacher, and a guard for Wells Fargo. He also edited the *Overland Monthly* in the late 1860's. Harte used his western experiences to weave colorful, romantic tales of the American West. His best work was published in such collections as *The Luck of Roaring Camp and Other Sketches* (1869), *The Outcasts of Poker Flat* (1869), and *Tales of the Argonaut* (1875). After nearly twenty years in California, Harte returned to the East Coast, where he was a popular lecturer, but his writings seemed to have lost their original picturesque charm and regional flavor. His popularity waned and Harte went to Europe, where he served as U.S. consul in Germany and Switzerland. He died abroad. *Biographical/critical sources: The Reader's Encyclopedia of American Literature,* Crowell, 1962; Richard O'Connor, *Bret Harte: A Biography,* Little, Brown, 1966; *Time,* March 18, 1966; *Saturday Review,* April 2, 1966; Patrick Morrow, *Bret Harte,* Boise State College Press, 1972; *Twentieth-Century Literary Criticism,* Volume 1, Gale, 1978.

* * *

HARTMAN, Carl 1928-

PERSONAL: Born August 12, 1928, in New York, N.Y.; son of Ben and Rose (Zucker) Hartman; married Harriet Feldheim (a reading consultant), January 24, 1960; children: Andrew, Jonathan. *Education:* City College (now of the City University of New York), B.S., 1951, M.A., 1952; Columbia University,

M.S.W., 1958. *Politics:* ''Eclectic.'' *Religion:* ''Jewish humanist.'' *Home:* 19031 Green Spruce, Southfield, Mich. 48076. *Office:* Department of Social Work, Wayne State University, Cass Ave., Detroit, Mich. 48202.

CAREER: Worked as director of Camp Tamarack (children's camp), 1960-64; Wayne State University, Detroit, Mich., assistant professor, 1964-70, associate professor of social work, 1970—. Owner and director of Pioneer Camp (for children), 1964-70; clinical director of Family Development Service, Pontiac, Mich., 1971—. *Military service:* U.S. Army, director of military school, 1952-54. *Awards, honors:* National Institute of Mental Health grant, 1978; Wayne State University Educational Development grant, 1981, for audio tapes of physically handicapped about their sexuality.

WRITINGS: Sexual Expression: A Manual for Trainers, Human Sciences Press, 1981.

WORK IN PROGRESS: Client Self-Determination, publication expected in 1982; research on rapists and elderly rape victims; research on spouses of physically handicapped.

SIDELIGHTS: Hartman commented: ''Professionals must become comfortable with their own sexuality before they can work on sexual issues with others. The physically handicapped are humans and sexual people first. They then have special problems in their daily living and relating. People have more control over their lives than they realize. Recognition of choice, options, and priorities help individuals feel free and more powerful.''

* * *

HARTMANN, Heinz 1894-1970

OBITUARY NOTICE: Born November 4, 1894, in Vienna, Austria; died of a heart attack, May 17, 1970, in Stony Point, N.Y. Psychoanalyst, educator, and author. A pupil of Sigmund Freud, Heinz Hartmann expanded on many of Freud's theories. He was managing editor and co-founder with Anna Freud and Ernst Kris of an annual publication entitled *The Psychoanalytic Study of the Child.* He wrote numerous monographs, papers, and essays, and he was the author of *Die Grundlagen der Psychoanalyse.* From 1951 to 1957 Hartmann served as president of the International Psycho-Analytical Association, and in 1958 he received the Charles Frederick Menninger Award from the American Psychoanalytical Association. Obituaries and other sources: *Time,* June 1, 1970; *AB Bookman's Weekly,* June 1, 1970; *The National Cyclopedia of American Biography,* Volume 55, James T. White, 1974.

* * *

HARVEY, Edith 1908(?)-1972

OBITUARY NOTICE: Born c. 1908; died after a long illness, February 12, 1972. Publisher and editor. As vice-president and co-founder with her husband, Zola E. Harvey, of Harvey House, Inc., Edith Harvey worked with children's book authors to promote books on science and the arts. Obituaries and other sources: *Publishers Weekly,* March 27, 1972.

* * *

HARWOOD, (Henry) David 1938-

PERSONAL: Born May 14, 1938, in London, England; son of Frank Courtney (a chemist) and Marguerite Mary (a physician; maiden name, Fenn) Harwood; married Frieda Mary Finnie (a secretary), June, 1968; children: Simon James, Alastair David. *Education:* University of Exeter, B.A. (with honors), 1960;

Newton Park College, Certificate in Education, 1974. *Religion:* United Reform. *Home:* 136 Watleys End Rd., Winterbourne, Bristol BS17 1QG, England.

CAREER: Medical Research Council, London, England, administrative officer, 1960-66; free-lance writer, photographer, and typographical designer, 1966-70; Wiltshire County Council, Melksham, England, youth and community service officer, 1970-74; Filton Technical College, Bristol, England, lecturer in charge of general studies, 1974—.

WRITINGS: Scouts in Action, G. Bell, 1963; *Scouts on Safari,* G. Bell, 1965; *The Scout Handbook,* Scout Association, 1967; *Scouts Indeed!,* G. Bell, 1967; *Alert to Danger!,* G. Bell, 1969.

Exploring Your Neighbourhood, Wolfe, 1970; *How to Read Maps,* Wolfe, 1970; *Cub Scouts,* Ladybird Books, 1971; *Extension Activities Handbook,* Scout Association, 1972; (editor with Valerie Peters) *The Bronze Arrow,* Scout Association, 1973; (editor with Peters) *The Silver Arrow,* Scout Association, 1973; (editor with Peters) *The Gold Arrow,* Scout Association, 1973; *Learnabout Camping,* Ladybird Books, 1977; *Car Games,* Ladybird Books, 1978.

(Editor) *The International Cub Scout Book,* World International, 1980. Editor of *Cub Scout Annual,* 1977—.

SIDELIGHTS: David Harwood wrote: "I have written stories, articles, and features for young people (mainly with a link with scouting or girl guiding) since I was at school. I got a lot out of scouting as a boy, and many of the adventures I had not only provided material for my pen, but also provided inspiration to pass on some of the 'magic' of scouting to the younger generation. Scouting has much to offer young people—fun, training, a sense of purpose, boundaries of behavior, and much more. Through my writing and the books of which I am/have been editor, I like to try and offer some practical inspiration to the youngsters, to set high standards of content and presentation by using the top writers, artists, photographers, and designers.

*   *   *

HASEK, Jaroslav (Matej Frantisek) 1883-1923
(Benjamin Franklin, Vojtech Kapristian z Hellenhofferu, M. Ruffian)

BRIEF ENTRY: Born April 24, 1883 (some sources say April 30, 1883), in Prague, Czechoslovakia; died January 3, 1923, in Lipnice, Czechoslovakia. Czechoslovakian novelist, short story writer, poet, and essayist. Hasek worked as a bank clerk before serving in the Austrian Army in World War I. Captured at the Russian front, he was held prisoner for many years. After his release, Hasek joined the Czechoslovakian forces in the U.S.S.R. and later became a Communist. Returning to his native country in 1920, he began the four-volume work on which his literary reputation rests. *The Good Soldier Schweik* (1920-23) tells the story of Schweik, an overweight Czech dogcatcher who is drafted by the Austrian Army. While a lazy practical joker, Schweik also exhibits a craftiness that enables him to avoid danger and the wrath of officials during the destruction of the Austro-Hungarian empire. Alternately considered by critics as a pacifist tract, a devastating attack on middle-class values, a slight to the Czech national character, and a crude, bawdy story, *The Good Soldier Schweik* was left unfinished at Hasek's death in 1923. The work is frequently autobiographical, as Hasek's military experiences and drunken antics are mirrored in his character Schweik. An alcoholic, Hasek died at the age of forty. In addition to his magnum opus, he wrote numerous short stories and articles under more than

eighty pseudonyms. Hasek's other works, which remain untranslated, include a volume of short stories entitled *Velitelem mesta Bugul'my* (1976). *Biographical/critical sources: Twentieth Century Authors: A Biographical Dictionary of Modern Literature,* H. W. Wilson, 1942; *Columbia Dictionary of Modern European Literature,* Columbia University Press, 1947; *Encyclopedia of World Literature in the Twentieth Century,* updated edition, Ungar, 1967; *The Penguin Companion to European Literature,* McGraw, 1969; *Twentieth Century Writing: A Reader's Guide to Contemporary Literature,* Transatlantic, 1969; *Twentieth-Century Literary Criticism,* Volume 4, Gale, 1981.

*   *   *

HASSLER, William T(homas) 1954-

PERSONAL: Born November 17, 1954, in Raleigh, N.C.; son of William W. (a professor) and Helen T. (a teacher) Hassler. *Education:* University of North Carolina, B.A., 1977; Yale University, J.D., 1980.

CAREER: Office of Robert R. Merhige, Jr., Richmond, Va., law clerk, 1980—.

WRITINGS: (With Bruce A. Ackerman) *Clean Air/Dirty Coal,* Yale University Press, 1981.

*   *   *

HAUPTMANN, Gerhart (Johann Robert) 1862-1946

BRIEF ENTRY: Born November 15, 1862, in Obersalzbrunn, Silesia, Germany (now Poland); died of pneumonia, June 8, 1946 (some sources say June 6, 1946), in Agneterdorf, Silesia, Poland. German playwright, poet, and novelist. The winner of the Nobel Prize for literature in 1912, Hauptmann is regarded as one of Germany's major literary figures. As author of the first naturalistic play "Vor Sonnenaufgang" (1889; title means "Before Dawn"), Hauptmann is best known for his early plays written in that vein. However, he wrote in several styles, including realism, romanticism, symbolic fantasy, and classicism. He is credited with creating the first collective hero for the stage in his most enduring play "Die Weber" (1893; title means "The Weavers"). Of the more than seventy characters featured in this work, none are distinguished, thus making the group of peasant weavers a collective proletarian hero. In the drama "Hanneles Himmelfahrt" (1893), the author also became one of the first playwrights to use a child as a heroine. Despite his eventual literary successes, Hauptmann came to his profession after vacillating between a number of occupations. An indifferent pupil, he alternately studied agriculture, history, and sculpture. When marriage to a wealthy woman freed him from financial worries, Hauptmann pursued a literary career. A prolific writer, he produced more than forty-five plays and sixty books. Among his works number *Promethidenlos* (1885), a book of poetry, the novels *Der Nar in Christo Emanuel Quint* (1910; title means "The Fool in Christ, Emanuel Quint"), *Atlantis* (1912), and *Der Ketzer von Soana* (1918; title means "The Heretic of Soana"), and a travel diary entitled *Griechischer Fruehling* (1908). *Biographical/critical sources: Columbia Dictionary of Modern European Literature,* Columbia University Press, 1947; *Twentieth Century Authors: A Biographical Dictionary of Modern Literature,* 1st supplement, H. W. Wilson, 1955; *Encyclopedia of World Literature in the Twentieth Century,* updated edition, Ungar, 1967; *McGraw-Hill Encyclopedia of World Drama,* McGraw, 1972; *Twentieth-Century Literary Criticism,* Volume 4, Gale, 1981.

HAVEL, Vaclav   1936-

PERSONAL: Born October 5, 1936, in Prague, Czechoslovakia; son of Vaclav M. (a property owner) and Bozena (Vavreckova) Havel; married Olga Splichalova. *Education:* Attended technical college, 1955-57, and Academy of Art, Prague, 1962-67. *Home:* Udejvickeho rybnicku 4, 1600 Prague 6, Czechoslovakia.

CAREER: Playwright. ABC Theatre, Prague, Czechoslovakia, stagehand, 1959-60; Theatre on the Balustrade, Prague, stagehand, 1960-61, assistant to artistic director, 1961-63, literary manager, 1963-68, resident playwright, 1968. *Member:* P.E.N., Union of Writers (Czechoslovakia). *Awards, honors:* Austrian State Prize for European Literature, 1969; *Village Voice* Off-Broadway award, 1970, for "The Increased Difficulty of Concentration."

WRITINGS—In English translation; plays: *Zahradni slavnost* (first produced in Prague, Czechoslovakia, at Theatre on the Balustrade, 1963), [Czechoslovakia], 1964, translation by Vera Blackwell published as *The Garden Party*, J. Cape, 1969 (also see below); *Vyrozumeni* (first produced in Prague at Theatre on the Balustrade, 1965; produced Off-Broadway at Anspacher Theatre, April 23, 1968), Dilia, 1965, translation by Blackwell published as *The Memorandum*, J. Cape, 1967; *Ztizena noznost soustredeni* (first produced in Prague at Theatre on the Balustrade, April, 1968; produced in New York City at Lincoln Center, December 4, 1969), Dilia, 1968, translation by Blackwell published as *The Increased Difficulty of Concentration*, J. Cape, 1972; "Audience" and "Vernisaz," translations by Blackwell Published in *Sorry*, Methuen, 1978 (also see below).

Other writings: (With Ivan Vyskocil) "Autostop" (play; title means "Hitchhike"), first produced in Prague in 1961; *Protokoly* (title means "Protocols"; contains "Zahradni slavnost," "Vyrozumeni," two essays, and selected poems), Mlanda Fronta, 1966; *Hry 1970-1976* (contains "Spiklenci," "Zebracka opera," "Horsky hotel," "Audience," and "Vernisaz"), Sixty-Eight Publishing House (Toronto), 1977.

Work represented in anthologies, including *Three Eastern European Plays*, Penguin, 1970. Contributor to *New York Review of Books*.

SIDELIGHTS: Havel, whom Horace Judson described in *Time* as "one of the most fearless Czech playwrights," is also considered one of the most important playwrights of eastern and central Europe. Writing in *Tulane Drama Review*, Henry Popkin ranked Havel as "the leading Czech dramatist since Karel Capek." Since 1968, however, following the Russian invasion of Czechoslovakia, Havel's works have been banned from the Czech stage. Despite harassment and arrest, Havel remains active in the political reform movement that began in the spring of 1968. He also continues to write plays, even though he now lives under police surveillance.

Denied a higher education because his father had been a wealthy landowner before the Communist takeover in Czechoslovakia, Havel began to support himself by working in a chemical factory. He was able to complete his secondary education, however, by attending night classes and was permitted to attend a technical college, during which time he wrote and published his first essays on poetry and drama. In 1963, while attending the Academy of Arts in Prague, he published a monograph on the writer and painter Joseph Capek.

After his military service, Havel began his successful association with the Theatre on the Balustrade, an avant-garde acting ensemble. Under the leadership of Jan Grossman, who served as producer from 1962 to 1968, the Balustrade became the leading dramatic ensemble in Prague. Grossman, a renowned drama critic and translator, was considered a nonconformist and was officially barred from public theatrical work. But his productions were highly successful with the public despite the criticism and condemnation by both the Czech Communist party and the Soviet cultural attache in Prague.

Some of Havel's own difficulties with the authorities were described by Popkin in "Theatre in Eastern Europe": "Vaclav Havel, the leading Czech dramatist, was expected at the New York meeting of PEN in 1966, but he did not get there. It was charged that his passport had been withdrawn; official sources replied that no Czech citizen is normally in possession of his passport and that Havel was free to travel abroad. And yet, later in the year, Havel did not turn up at an Austrian conference at which he was expected." Havel was permitted to visit the United States in 1968, but his passport was again confiscated in the summer of 1969. On August 26, 1969, as reported by the *New York Times,* Havel made a radio appeal "from an underground station in Liberec, a town in northern Bohemia, monitored by Radio Free Europe in Munich, begging Western intellectuals to raise their voices in condemnation of the Russian occupation of his country."

After the Soviet invasion of Czechoslovakia, Havel and Grossman were forbidden to work in the Czech theatre. Havel received many invitations to continue his work in the West, but he chose to remain in Czechoslovakia, where he continued his fight for freedom. In 1969, for example, he visited the steel mills in Ostrava and spoke to the unions about workers and intellectuals cooperating to defend the freedoms gained in 1968. As *Time* reported, "The meeting was banned by the police and locked out by management, but was held anyway out of doors." Havel remarked at the time: "They haven't arrested me—not yet. As long as I am invited to these meetings, I will go."

Havel was later arrested many times, however, and was continually harrassed. When his adaptation of "The Beggar's Opera" was produced by amateurs in 1975, even members of the audience became victims of police reprisals. In 1977 he became one of the three principal spokesmen for the Charter 77 manifesto, which charged the Czech Government with human and civil rights violations and called for compliance with the provisions of the Helsinki agreement. Since joining with the artists, writers, intellectuals, and working people of the Charter 77 movement, Havel has been arrested three times and imprisoned twice. In March, 1979, the *New York Review of Books* reported that he "has recently been kept under tight surveillance by the political police."

Critics have noted the universality of Havel's plays. E. J. Czerwinski observed in *Books Abroad* that "Havel rarely refers to his country in his works." Havel explains this quality in terms of the political climate in which he wrote his early plays: "They might not have been directly political, but they confronted everyday realities and were a manifestation of freedom where there was no freedom." Because his plays deal with the dehumanization of man within the increasing mechanization of society, he has been labeled an absurdist and, in fact, credited with bringing the absurdist method to Czechoslovakia. But, as the critic for *Plays and Players* noted, out of "the need to deal with current issues through allegory," Havel uses absurdist technique not, like Western absurdists, to explore mental states, but "to disguise public social issues."

Jan Grossman considered Havel's drama not absurd but "appellative." In the introduction to a 1965 collection of Havel's work, Grossman wrote: "I do not know whether Havel's theatre belongs to the 'absurd'. . . . His plays are inventive, artificial; but this quality has nothing to do with romantic fantasies or . . . unbridled insanity. . . . Havel's artificial structuring of the world is made up of real, even commonplace and banal, components, joined most reasonably into a whole.''

Thus grounded in reality, Havel's plays remain decidedly allegorical, and, as noted in both *Plays and Players* and *Time,* for the Czech audience the allusions are immediately recognizable. The protagonist of a Havel play is political bureaucracy itself, or a mechanism of bureaucracy which controls not only the characters, but also the plot and action of the play. For Havel, Grossman maintained, the mechanization of man is not just a theme, ''but the central subject, from which his technique derived and on which it is focused.''

According to Popkin, Havel's first play, ''The Garden Party,'' ''touches upon the discomforts endured by political bureaucracy as it makes its transition from Stalinism to an awkward and severely limited liberalism.'' It concerns the career of Hugo Pludek who, continually mouthing platitudes and political slogans, rises rapidly to control of the Office of Liquidation and the Office of Inauguration. The central problem involves the attempt to dissolve the Office of Liquidation, which, however, can only dissolve itself—an impossible accomplishment since, once the process were begun, the Office would no longer exist to finish the job. Grossman described ''The Garden Party'' as dominated by cliche: ''Man does not use cliche, cliche uses man. Cliche is the hero, it causes, advances, and complicates the plot, determining human action, and deviating further and further from our given reality, creates its own.''

''The Memorandum'' also concerned the political power of language, the distortion of language by bureaucracy. A writer for the *Times Literary Supplement* commented: ''In *The Garden Party* Havel showed us words dominating human beings: the phrase is the real hero of the piece, creating the situations and complicating them, directing human destinies instead of being their tool. In *Vyrozumeni*—to use the original Czech title of *The Memorandum*—man finds himself enmeshed not merely in a succession of phrases but in a whole language.'' The play revolves around an artificial and incomprehensible language aimed at making all office communication precise and unemotional; the fall and rise of the office manager, as a result of his inability to use the new language, constitute the play's main action.

Clive Barnes, in the *New York Times,* called ''The Memorandum'' a ''witty, funny and timely'' political satire, while Robert Hatch, in the *Nation,* considered it a ''bureaucratic burlesque.'' The critic for *Prompt,* however, wrote: ''I would prefer to describe *The Memorandum* as a comedy of hypothesis. The world Havel creates in the play, is a hypothetical one, and therefore possible. Yet, our awareness of the comic, is an awareness of deviations from a concrete normality, either of physical behavior, or vested in certain general ideas: truth, honesty, charity. Thus, in the play there is established a tension between the opposing poles of hypothesis and actuality, possibility and accepted normality, into which the audience is thrust.''

After Havel was silenced by the Czech authorities, ''The Increased Difficulty of Concentration'' was produced in New York City by the Lincoln Center Repertory Theatre. Jules Irving, director of the theatre, described the play as ''an abrasive satire which couples bureaucratic farce, involving an effeminate computer called Puzuk, with an unorthodox structure where events are played back like a film rewinding.'' The play depicts the attempts of an intellectual to establish a viable way of living within his mechanized and meaningless environment. It consists of a day in the life of Dr. Edouard Huml, a social scientist, for whom romantic excesses have become a last refuge.

Marilyn Stasio, in *Cue,* called the work a ''potent satiric drama'' that, ''for all its ominous undertones, [is] an inescapably funny play.'' Mell Gussow, of the *New York Times,* found the play ''gentler'' than ''The Memorandum,'' and *Variety* considered it ''a better play than Havel's earlier work, . . . with application beyond the border of eastern Europe.'' In his review for the *Nation,* Harold Clurman noted the play's importance for the Czech audience: ''The speech that seems almost embarrassingly out of place with us, a speech in which the central character declares his conviction that the truth of life cannot be measured by computers or bureaucratic dictates but only by the motivations of the human heart, is what Havel meant his play to say. That is what gave it social force in his country. . . . Thus the play, a farce of no great subtlety, becomes something vital to the Czech citizen forever under the vigilant and evil eye of—who can say just what.''

In the 1970's Havel managed to get some of his work out of Czechoslovakia, and a few pieces have been broadcast in Great Britain and published in Canada. Before he was silenced, the *Times Literary Supplement* praised him as a playwright of great promise: ''In his preoccupation with the logical and the illogical Havel is a second Lewis Carroll, except that many people in Prague who saw his plays came out laughing 'with a chill up their spine.' His theatre could be the theatre of the absurd but it is not: his central theme is mechanization and what it makes a man, but mechanization is a gimmick rather than an inescapable factor in progress (as Capek might have seen it). It is clear that Havel's master in ideas was Kafka and in expression Ionesco. His is something of a genius whose promise is even greater than his performance. We look forward to his next play.''

BIOGRAPHICAL/CRITICAL SOURCES: Tulane Drama Review, spring, 1967; *Observer Review,* December 17, 1967; *Times Literary Supplement,* March 7, 1968, March 10, 1972; *New York Times,* May 6, 1968, October 22, 1969, December 5, 1969, December 14, 1969; *New Yorker,* May 18, 1968; *Nation,* May 27, 1968, December 22, 1969; *Time,* June 14, 1968, July 25, 1969; *Prompt,* number 12, 1968; *Cue,* December 13, 1969; *Variety,* December 17, 1969; *Books Abroad,* spring, 1971; *Plays and Players,* August, 1971; *New York Review of Books,* August 4, 1977, March 22, 1979.*

—*Sketch by Andrea Geffner*

* * *

HAWGOOD, John Arkas 1905-1971

OBITUARY NOTICE: Born in 1905 in Brighton, Sussex, England; died September 16, 1971, in California. Before becoming a professor of American history at the University of Birmingham, John Hawgood served as a professor of modern history at University College, London. A highly regarded authority on the American West, Hawgood received the Alfred A. Knopf Prize in western American history for his book *The American West.* His other works include *Political and Economic Relations Between the United States and the Provisional German Central Government* and *The Citizen and Government.* Obituaries and other sources: *The Author's and Writer's Who's Who,* 6th edition, Burke's Peerage, 1971; *AB Bookman's Weekly,* November 8, 1971; *Who Was Who Among English and European Authors, 1931-1949,* Gale, 1978.

* * *

HAYASECA y EIZAGUIRRE, Jorge
See ECHEGARAY (y EIZAGUIRRE), Jose (Maria Waldo)

HAYCOCK, Ken(neth) Roy 1948-

PERSONAL: Born February 15, 1948, in Hamilton, Ontario, Canada; son of Bruce F. T. (an administrator) and Doris (a manager; maiden name, Downham) Haycock; married Carol-Ann Low (a teacher), July 31, 1979. Education: University of Western Ontario, B.A., 1968, diploma in education, 1969; University of Toronto, specialist certificate in school librarianship, 1971; University of Ottawa, M.Ed., 1973; University of Michigan, A.M.L.S., 1974. Home: 6871 Shawnigan Pl., Richmond, British Columbia, Canada V7E 4W9. Office: Vancouver School Board, 1595 West 10th, Vancouver, British Columbia, Canada V6J 1Z8.

CAREER: History teacher and head librarian at collegiate institute in Ottawa, Ontario, 1969-70; head of high school learning media center in Ottawa-Carleton, Ontario, 1970-72; educational media consultant for elementary and secondary schools in Wellington County, Ontario, 1972-76; Vancouver School Board, Vancouver, British Columbia, coordinator of library services, 1976—. Associate member of faculty at Queen's University, Kingston, Ontario, 1970-72; instructor at University of Toronto, summer, 1975; lecturer at University of British Columbia, summers, 1976-78, associate professor, 1979 and 1980, member of council of School of Librarianship, 1978—. Local president of Ontario Secondary School Teachers Federation, 1972-76; member of board of trustees of Guelph Public Library, 1975-76; member of British Columbia Ministry of Provincial Secretary and Government Services cultural services branch publishing assistance committee, 1979—; member of national advisory board of centre for Research in Librarianship, University of Toronto, 1977-79; member of Canada Council Advisory Panel on the Promotion of Canadian Books and Periodicals, 1979—; member of British Columbia Council for Leadership in Educational Administration. Educational consultant to Methuen Publishers, 1975-77.

MEMBER: International Association of School Librarianship, World Conference of Organizations of the Teaching Profession, Canadian College of Teachers, Canadian Library Association (member of board of directors, 1974-75 and 1976-79; vice-president, 1976-77; member of council, 1976—; president, 1977-78), Canadian Association of Children's Librarians, Canadian Association of Public Libraries, Canadian Library Trustees' Association, Canadian School Library Association (vice-president, 1973-74; president, 1974-75; chairman of Canadian materials committee, 1974-78; chairman of awards jury, 1975-76), Association for Media and Technology in Education in Canada, American Library Association, American Association of School Librarians (Canadian member of board of directors, 1973-75), British Columbia Library Association, British Columbia Teachers Federation, British Columbia Primary Teachers Association, British Columbia School Librarians' Association, British Columbia School Supervisors of Instruction Association, Manitoba Teachers Society, Manitoba School Library Audio-Visual Association, Ontario Library Association (chairman of legislative action group, 1975-76), Ontario School Library Association, Pacific Instructional Media Association, Vancouver Schools Coordinators Association (president, 1979-80), Phi Delta Kappa, Beta Phi Mu. Awards, honors: Queen Elizabeth II Silver Jubilee Medal, 1977, for contributions to Canadian society; Margaret B. Scott Award of Merit from Canadian School Library Association, 1979, for contributions to school librarianship in Canada; member of British Council study tour, 1980; young leader award from Phi Delta Kappa, 1981.

WRITINGS: Index to the Contents of Moccasin Telegraph, Canadian School Library Association, 1975; (with Ted Monkhouse, Marilyn Crooks, and Brian Reynolds) Security: Secondary School Resource Centres, Ontario Library Association, 1975; Free Magazines for Teachers and Libraries, Ontario Library Association, 1974, revised edition, 1977, supplement, 1978; (contributor) F. R. Branswinke and H. Newsom, Resource Services for Canadian Schools, McGraw, 1977; (with Lynne Isberg) Sears List of Subject Headings: Canadian Companion, H. W. Wilson, 1978; (contributor) L. Amey, editor, The Canadian School-Housed Public Library, Dalhousie University, 1979. Contributor to library and education journals and newspapers. Co-editor of Emergency Librarian; member of editorial board of Moccasin Telegraph, 1974-75, Canadian Materials, 1974-78, and Index to Free Periodicals, 1976—.

WORK IN PROGRESS: Two books in the field of school librarianship and education.

SIDELIGHTS: Haycock wrote: "The Wilson Library Bulletin stated in 1974 that I had the energy of ten Canadian mounties. While I dispute this, my professional life does involve an enormous commitment and element of drive. When Canada had no national journal to review Canadian learning materials, Don Hamilton and I founded Canadian Materials, which is still the only national journal devoted to this purpose. When the country had no national journal for librarians working with children and young adults in school and public libraries, Carol-Ann Haycock and I acquired the only national independent journal and Emergency Librarian has since developed into the country's only refereed journal with strong editing and an international advisory board.

"I've never considered myself a writer, but I am devoted to creative expression with the support of strong editing. My main activity has not been writing, but has been related to writing, creating the kind of environment that is conducive to a flourishing creative community and the expression of ideas, concepts, and proposals that reflect the Canadian context. I do not consider myself a strict nationalist, but we do have something special here that must be preserved, enhanced, and made known. If I can help to provide that support, as well as participate in the process of writing and editing, I feel that I will have not only made a small contribution, but enjoyed it too.

"My main interests are developing in youngsters the skills of lifelong learning and a commitment to informed decision making. As a consequence, my professional life revolves around the improvement of school library resource centers and personnel, and educational change. I hope to devote more time to research and writing as I pursue doctoral studies in England."

BIOGRAPHICAL/CRITICAL SOURCES: Wilson Library Bulletin, November, 1974; Quill and Quire, June, 1977, October, 1979; Moccasin Telegraph, autumn, 1979; Phi Delta Kappan, January, 1981.

*   *   *

HAYDEN, Julia Elizabeth 1939(?)-1981
(Julie Hayden)

OBITUARY NOTICE: Born c. 1939 in Larchmont, N.Y.; died after a short illness, September 14, 1981, in New York, N.Y. Journalist and author. A member of the staff of the New Yorker for fifteen years, Julie Hayden was the author of a collection of short stories entitled Lists of the Past. Obituaries and other sources: New York Times, September 15, 1981.

HAYDEN, Julie
See HAYDEN, Julia Elizabeth

* * *

HEATON, Peter 1919-

PERSONAL: Born May 27, 1919, in Yorkshire, England; son of Stuart and Audrey Arabin (Hart-Davis) Heaton. *Education:* Attended private boys' school in Godalming, England. *Office:* Trade Counter Ltd., Fulham Wharf, Townmead Rd., London S.W.6, England.

CAREER: Writer and illustrator of children's books, 1944—; House of Lords, London, England, clerk in Parliament Office, 1946-59, principal clerk of private bills, 1959-61; Trade Counter (book distributors), London, co-owner, 1961—. *Military service:* Royal Naval Volunteer Reserve, 1938-46, active duty, 1939-46; became lieutenant. *Awards, honors:* Silver medal from London Boat Show, 1973, for *History of Yachting in Pictures.*

WRITINGS: The Holiday Train (self-illustrated juvenile), Penguin, 1945; *Dobbish the Paper Horse* (self-illustrated juvenile), Penguin, 1946; *The Holiday Train Goes to America* (self-illustrated juvenile), Penguin, 1946; *Sailing* (self-illustrated), Penguin, 1949, 5th edition, 1978.

Cruising, Penguin, 1952; *Yachting: A History,* Batsford, 1955, Scribner, 1956.

The Yachtsman's Vade Mecum, A. & C. Black, 1961, 4th edition, 1978, Dodd, 1970, 4th edition, 1978; *Boatcraft: The Understanding and Care of Yachts,* A. & C. Black, 1963; *Songs Under Sail: A Book of Sailor Shanties* (self-illustrated; music by Maria Bird), Burke Publishing, 1963; *Jazz* (self-illustrated), Burke Publishing, 1964; (editor) *The Sea Gets Bluer: Some Small Boat Wanderers and Their Writings,* A. & C. Black, 1965, Duell, Sloan & Pearce, 1966; (editor) *The Sea Gets Greyer: More Small Boat Wanderers and Their Writings,* A. & C. Black, 1966; *So They Want to Learn Sailing,* (self-illustrated), Dufour, 1966; *Peter Heaton on Sailing,* A. & C. Black, 1967; (editor) *Boat* (with own photographs), A. S. Barnes, 1969.

Cruising: Sail or Power, Kaye & Ward, 1970; *A History of Yachting in Pictures,* Tom Stacey, 1972; *Make Sail: Build and Sail Your Own Boat,* Pelham, 1972; *Yachting: A Pictorial History,* Viking, 1972; *Motor Yachting and Boating,* Pelham, 1973, revised edition, Penguin, 1976; *The Singlehanders,* Hastings House, 1976.

Contributor to magazines and newspapers. Past member of editorial board of *Helmsman.*

WORK IN PROGRESS: Painting; literary research.

SIDELIGHTS: Heaton told *CA:* "I have been an artist all my life, doing mainly ships and seascapes. I have exhibited regularly in England and France, and continue to paint and draw vigorously, mostly on commission nowadays.

"I became a sailing author through writing and illustrating children's books. After the 1939-45 war had ended I was demobilized from the Navy and got a job as a clerk in the Parliament Office of the House of Lords. After about a year, I received a call from the late Sir Allen Lane, founder and chairman of Penguin Books. He wanted to do a 'Penguin' on sailing. It seemed a daunting task for a young man with limited experience of the sea. 'You want an expert,' I said to Lane. 'No indeed I do not!' he replied. 'I want an enthusiast!' When I later became involved in publishing myself I remembered those significant words.

"The book was hard going as it had to be done in my spare time but, luckily for me, was a success. I did not expect it would remain in print for over thirty years. It has made me friends all over the world and I could not ask for more. From it I moved into other aspects of sailing and ships generally, wrote for the yachting press, reviewed books, and kept up my drawing and painting, exhibiting, and painting to order. I have painted many famous yachts for their owners and a most pleasurable task that is!

"In 1961 I retired from my job and was able to concentrate on my publishing. I acquired an interest in a small firm which warehoused books for publishers. The Trade Counter has grown into a very large and successful distribution company.

"In 1963 I collaborated with musician Maria Bird on a book of sea shanties, which resulted in my being asked to write a television program for British Broadcasting Corp. They must have had a lot of courage! However, it seemed to go off well and was a hilarious as well as a fascinating experience.

"Today, the boat world has changed, and yet has not. Electronic aids to navigation abound, yachts are built in fiberglass reinforced plastic (and in concrete, too). Sails and ropes are synthetic. And yet, the old enthusiasm for boats is just the same. The freemasonry of the sea speaks across oceans, across frontiers, and across the so-called age gap. But perhaps the biggest difference is the enormous increase in the numbers of men and women who sail, whether in creeks, on lakes, or over the seas, and right round our boisterous old world. That has surely been a fine development. I may even have helped it on a bit myself!"

BIOGRAPHICAL/CRITICAL SOURCES: Patricia Moyes, *Down Among the Dead Men,* Holt, 1961.

* * *

HEGI, Ursula 1946-

PERSONAL: Born May 23, 1946, in West Germany; came to the United States in 1965, naturalized citizen, 1970; daughter of Heinrich and Johanna (Maas) Koch; married Ernest Hegi (a management consultant), October 21, 1967; children: Eric, Adam. *Education:* University of New Hampshire, B.A., 1978, M.A., 1979. *Home address:* Foxborough Dr., Gilford, N.H. 03246. *Agent:* Gail Hochman, Paul R. Reynolds, Inc., 12 East 41st St., New York, N.Y. 10017. *Office:* Department of English, University of New Hampshire, Durham, N.H. 03824.

CAREER: University of New Hampshire, Durham, lecturer in English, 1978—. Participates in writing conferences; gives poetry and fiction readings. *Member:* Associated Writing Programs.

WRITINGS: Intrusions (novel), Viking, 1981. Contributor to magazines, including *McCall's, Feminist Studies, Ms., Blue Buildings, Bradford Review,* and *Kayak.*

WORK IN PROGRESS: The Understudy (tentative title), a novel about the theatre.

* * *

HEIDENSTAM, (Carl Gustaf) Verner von 1859-1940

BRIEF ENTRY: Born July 6, 1859, in Olshammar, Sweden; died May 20, 1940, in Oevralid, Sweden. Swedish poet and novelist. As a youth Heidenstam traveled extensively throughout Europe and the Near East. These travels inspired him to write his first book of poetry, *Vallfart och vandringsaar* (1888;

title means ''Pilgrimage and Wanderyears''), which brought him national attention in Sweden. Several autobiographical works followed before Heidenstam wrote *Renaessans* (1889), which along with the satirical *Pepitas broellop* (1890; title means ''Pepita's Wedding'') began the Swedish literary renaissance, influencing many writers to turn from decadent realism to historical, national, and moralistic themes. *Dikter* (1895) and *Nya Dikter* (1915) are considered Heidenstam's best volumes of lyrical poetry, expressing the poet's love for his homeland. Among Heidenstam's novels are *Karolinerna* (1898; translated as *The Charles Men*, 1920) and *Folkunga-traedet* (1905; translated as *The Tree of the Folkungs*, 1925). In 1916 Heidenstam won the Nobel Prize and in 1938 received the Henrik Steffens Prize. *Biographical/critical sources: Twentieth Century Authors: A Biographical Dictionary of Modern Literature*, H. W. Wilson, 1942; *Columbia Dictionary of Modern European Literature*, Columbia University Press, 1947; *The Penguin Companion to European Literature*, McGraw, 1969.

* * *

HELLENHOFFERU, Vojtech Kapristian z
See HASEK, Jaroslav (Matej Frantisek)

* * *

HENCKEN, Hugh O'Neill   1902-1981

OBITUARY NOTICE: Born January 8, 1902, in New York, N.Y.; died August 31, 1981, in Cape Cod, Mass. Archaeologist and author. A former president of the Archaeological Institute of America, Hugh Hencken served as curator of European archaeology at Harvard University's Peabody Museum. During his career he conducted a number of archaeological digs, including one in Ireland from 1932 to 1936, where he supervised a team of American and Irish archaeologists, anthropologists, and ethnologists. In addition to *The Archaeology of Cornwall, Indo-European Languages and Archaeology,* and *Tarquinia, Villanovans, and Early Etruscans,* Hencken wrote *Tarquinia and Etruscan Origins.* Obituaries and other sources: *The International Who's Who,* Europa, 1978; *Who's Who in America,* 40th edition, Marquis, 1978; *New York Times,* September 4, 1981.

* * *

HENDELSON, William H.   1904-1975

OBITUARY NOTICE: Born July 26, 1904, in Berlin, Germany; died May 28, 1975, in New York, N.Y. Publisher and editor. Prior to coming to the United States from Germany in 1938, William Hendelson was a partner in Knaur Nachfolger, a Berlin publishing firm. He served as editor in chief of numerous reference works, including *Standard International Encyclopedia, Encyclopedia Yearbook,* and *Funk & Wagnalls New Encyclopedia.* He was editor of *The Music Lovers' Almanac* and co-editor of *Practical English for Germans.* Obituaries and other sources: *AB Bookman's Weekly,* August 25, 1975; *Who's Who in America,* 39th edition, Marquis, 1976.

* * *

HENDERSON, Mary
See MAVOR, Osborne Henry

* * *

HENDERSON, Philip (Prichard)   1906-1977

OBITUARY NOTICE—See index for *CA* sketch: Born February 17, 1906, in Barnes, Surrey, England; died in September, 1977, in Hampstead, England. Editor, critic, and author. Henderson worked as an editor at Everyman's Library, at the *British Book News,* for the British Council, and at Chatto & Windus. In 1967 he received an Arts Council Award. A biographer, Henderson is known for *And Morning in His Eyes: A Book About Christopher Marlowe* and for *Christopher Marlowe.* He also wrote *William Morris, Samuel Butler: The Incarnate Bachelor,* and *The Life of Lawrence Oliphant, Traveller, Diplomat and Mystic.* His poetry was collected in *A Wind in the Sand.* Obituaries and other sources: *AB Bookman's Weekly,* March 20, 1978.

* * *

HENNACY, Ammon   1893-1970

OBITUARY NOTICE: Born in 1893; died January 14, 1970, in Salt Lake City, Utah. Editor and author. In 1961 Ammon Hennacy retired from his position as associate editor of the *Catholic Worker* and became director of the Joe Hill House of Hospitality for Migrants and Migrant Workers in Salt Lake City. He was the author of *The Book of Ammon* and *The Autobiography of a Catholic Anarchist.* Obituaries and other sources: *Publishers Weekly,* February 2, 1970; *AB Bookman's Weekly,* February 16, 1970; Joan Thomas, *Years of Grief and Laughter: A Biography of Ammon Hennacy,* Hennacy Press, 1974.

* * *

HENNESSEY, Caroline
See von BLOCK, Bela W(illiam)

* * *

HENRY, James P(aget)   1914-

PERSONAL: Born July 12, 1914, in Leipzig, Germany (now East Germany); came to the United States in 1939, naturalized citizen, 1948; son of Oscar John (an orthodontist) and Winifred Minnie (Paget) Henry; married Isabelle Johnston-McDonald Jardine (a registered nurse), December 3, 1938; children: John Andrew, Peter Howarth, Mark Patrick. *Education:* Sidney Sussex College, Cambridge, B.A., 1935; Cambridge University, M.A., M.B., B.Ch., 1938, M.D., 1952; McGill University, M.Sc., 1942, Ph.D., 1955. *Home:* 528 North Crescent Heights Blvd., Los Angeles, Calif. 90048. *Office:* Department of Physiology and Biophysics, School of Medicine, University of Southern California, Centrifuge Building, 815 West 37th St., Los Angeles, Calif. 90007.

CAREER: Guy's Hospital, London, England, house physician, 1938-39; Vancouver General Hospital, Vancouver, British Columbia, rotating intern, 1939-40; Children's Memorial Hospital, Montreal, Quebec, resident in medicine, 1940-41; California Institute of Technology, Pasadena, fellow in biology, 1943; University of Southern California, Los Angeles, assistant professor, 1943-47, associate professor of physiology, 1947-48; U.S. Air Force, chief of acceleration and stress section of Aero Medical Laboratory at Wright-Patterson Air Force Base, Dayton, Ohio, 1947-56, director of bioscience branch of European office of U.S. Air Research and Development Command in Brussels, Belgium, 1956-59, animal flight specialist for ''Project Mercury'' for National Aeronautics and Space Administration (NASA), Langley Field, Va., 1961, member of headquarters staff of Aerospace Medical Division at Brooks Air Force Base, San Antonio, Tex., 1962-65, retiring as colonel; University of Southern California, visiting professor, 1963-

65, professor of physiology, 1965—, fellow of Andrew Norman Institute for Advanced Study in Gerontology and Geriatrics, 1981—. Civilian member of staff of Air Force Office of Scientific Research and Development, 1944; chairman of working group sixty-seven of the committee on hearing, bioacoustics, and biomechanics of the National Academy of Sciences-National Research Council, 1971-72; participant in seminars, workshops, and symposia in the United States and abroad; consultant to National Institute of Mental Health. *Military service:* U.S. Air Force Reserve, 1952-74.

MEMBER: International Society of Hypertension, International College of Psychosomatic Medicine (fellow), International Academy of Astronautics, Aerospace Medical Association (fellow), American Psychosomatic Society (member of council), American Physiological Society, Academy of Behavioral Medicine Research, Royal College of Surgeons, Royal College of Physicians (licenciate). *Awards, honors:* Arnold D. Tuttle Award from Aerospace Medical Association, 1953, for animal rocket studies; John Jeffries Award from American Institute of Aeronautics and Astronautics, 1955, for work in aviation medicine; shared award from National Aeronautics and Space Administration, 1974, for computerized magnetic mouse detector device; shared Carl-Ludwig Medal from German Heart Association, 1976, for work on blood volume control and circulatory physiology; distinguished scientific achievement award from American Heart Association, 1976; Docteur Honoris Causa from Universite de Bordeaux II, 1981; grants from National Heart, Lung, and Blood Institute and the National Institute of Arthritis, Diabetes, and Digestive and Kidney Diseases.

WRITINGS: Biomedical Aspects of Space Flight, Holt, 1966; (with John P. Meehan) *The Circulation: An Integrative Physiologic Study,* Year Book Medical Publishers, 1971; (with P. M. Stephens) *Stress, Health, and the Social Environment: A Sociobiologic Approach to Medicine,* Springer-Verlag, 1977; (with Irwin L. Kutash, Louis B. Schlesinger, and others) *Handbook on Stress and Anxiety: Contemporary Knowledge, Theory, and Treatment,* Jossey-Bass, 1980.

Contributor: Clayton S. White and Otis O. Benson, Jr., editors, *Physics and Medicine of the Upper Atmosphere: A Study of the Aeropause,* University of New Mexico Press, 1952; Alberto Zanchetti, editor, *Neural and Psychological Mechanisms in Cardiovascular Disease,* Casa Editrice Il Ponte, 1972; Ruth Porter and Julie Knight, editors, *Physiology, Emotion, and Psychosomatic Illness,* Associated Scientific Publishers, 1972; Levi Lennart, editor, *Emotions: Their Parameters and Measurement,* Raven Press, 1975; Goeran Berglund, Lennart Hansson, and Lars Werkoe, editors, *Pathophysiology and Management of Arterial Hypertension,* A. Lindgren & Soner, 1975; Robert G. Grenell and Sabit Gabay, editors, *Biological Foundations of Psychiatry,* Volume II, Raven Press, 1976; Arthur C. Guyton and Allen W. Cowley, Jr., editors, *International Review of Physiology,* Volume IX: *Cardiovascular Physiology II,* University Park Press, 1976.

Lennart Levi, editor, *Society, Stress, and Disease,* Volume III: *The Productive and Reproductive Age: Male/Female Roles and Relationships,* Volume IV: *Working Life,* Oxford University Press, 1980; Herman Van Praag, Malcolm H. Lader, and others, editors, *Handbook of Biological Psychiatry,* Part II: *Brain Mechanisms and Abnormal Behavior: Psychophysiology,* Dekker, 1980; Earl Usdin, Richard Kvetnansky, and Irwin L. Kopin, editors, *Catecholamines and Stress: Recent Advances,* Elsevier-North Holland, 1980; Herbert Weiner, M.A. Hofer, and A.J. Stunkard, editors, *Brain, Behavior, and Bodily Disease,* Raven Press, 1981; Paul F. Brain and David Benton, editors, *A Multidisciplinary Approach to Aggression Research,* Elsev-

ier/North Holland Biomedical Press, 1981; David Krantz, Jerome E. Singer, and Andrew Baum, editors, *Handbook of Medical Psychology,* Lawrence Erlbaum Associates, 1981; (with W.P. Meehan and P.M. Stephens) Jan Brod, H. Liebau, and J.O. Bahlmann, editors, *Stress and Hypertension: Contributions to Nephrology,* Karger, Basel, 1981. Contributor of nearly two hundred articles to scientific journals in the United States, Canada, and Europe.

WORK IN PROGRESS: Medical research and writing.

SIDELIGHTS: Henry told *CA:* "My interest is in psychosomatic medicine, especially in a biosociological approach to the problems of cardiovascular disease. We are looking at the role of chronic psychosocial stimulation in the development of high blood pressure and eventual heart and kidney failure in months-long observation of colonies of socially interacting mice, which, at best, have a two-year lifespan. We are studying the role of caffeine in accelerating these changes and the role of sodium restriction and drugs, such as beta blockers, in preventing them. We are also concerned with the mechanisms by which mental stress affects the neuroendocrine system in different ways according to the predominant emotions. Thus the role of anger in the development of high blood pressure is contrasted with that of depression in disturbing immune response mechanisms. The relation between stress and aging is a major aspect of this work. My current research project is on salt restriction, antihypertensive drugs, and stress."

AVOCATIONAL INTERESTS: Sports, growing flowers.

BIOGRAPHICAL/CRITICAL SOURCES: Lloyd Mallan, *Men, Rockets, and Space Rats,* Messner, 1955; Shirley Thomas, *Men of Space: Profiles of the Leaders in Space Research, Development, and Exploration,* Volume VII, Chilton, 1965; *Journal of the American Medical Association,* May 11, 1970; *Los Angeles Times,* September 6, 1970; *Psychiatric News,* December 16, 1970; Mallan, *Suiting Up for Space: The Evolution of the Space Suit,* John Day, 1971; *Today's Health,* April, 1971; "New Directions in Hypertension, Volume III" (audio cassette), Bristol Laboratories, 1973; *Plastic and Reconstructive Surgery,* January, 1973; *Laboratory Animal,* May-June, 1973; *Hospital Tribune,* August 13, 1973; *New Times,* October 3, 1975; "Stress, Personality, and Cardiovascular Disease" (documentary film), CIBA Laboratories, 1976; *Pasadena Star-News,* February 26, 1978; *Los Angeles Reporter,* March 1, 1978.

*   *   *

HENRY, O.
  See PORTER, William Sydney

*   *   *

HENRY, Oliver
  See PORTER, William Sydney

*   *   *

HERBERT, Thomas Walter, Jr. 1938-

PERSONAL: Born September 7, 1938, in Rome, Ga.; son of Thomas Walter (a professor) and Jean Elizabeth (Linton) Herbert; married Marjorie Millard (an attorney), July 13, 1963; children: Thomas Walter III, Elizabeth Crate. *Education:* Harvard University, B.A., 1960; Union Theological Seminary, New York, N.Y., M.Div., 1963; Princeton University, Ph.D., 1969. *Office:* Department of English, Southwestern University, Georgetown, Tex. 78626.

CAREER: University of California, Berkeley, director of experimental program in ministry, 1963-66; University of Kentucky, Lexington, assistant professor of English, 1969-75; Southwestern University, Georgetown, Tex., Herman Brown Professor of English and chairman of department, 1975—, university scholar, 1981—. *Member:* Modern Language Association of America, Society for Religion in Higher Education, South Atlantic Modern Language Association. *Awards, honors:* Younger humanist fellowship from National Endowment for the Humanities, 1973-74; Guggenheim fellowship, 1981-82.

WRITINGS: Moby Dick and Calvinism: A World Dismantled, Rutgers University Press, 1977; *Marquesan Encounters,* Harvard University Press, 1980. Contributor to theology and language journals.

WORK IN PROGRESS: Nathaniel Hawthorne and the Nuclear Family.

*   *   *

HERBRUCK, Christine Comstock   1942-

PERSONAL: Born October 14, 1942, in Detroit, Mich.; daughter of Clyde Nelson (a lawyer) and Adelaide (a social worker; maiden name, Mason) Comstock; married Peter C. Herbruck, June 16, 1961 (divorced, 1981); children: Jonathan, Katherine, Thomas. *Education:* Attended Northwestern University, 1960-62, and Hamilton College, 1964; Columbia Pacific University, M.A. and Ph.D., 1981. *Religion:* Presbyterian. *Home:* 2184 Cottage Grove, Cleveland Heights, Ohio 44118. *Office:* Parents Anonymous of Northeastern Ohio, 1001 Huron Rd., Cleveland, Ohio 44115.

CAREER: Creative Communication Center, Cleveland, Ohio, partner, 1974-76; Parents Anonymous of Northeastern Ohio, Cleveland, executive vice-president, 1976—. Member of national board of trustees of Parents Anonymous, 1978—; president of board of trustees of Ohio chapter of National Committee for the Prevention of Child Abuse, 1979—. *Awards, honors:* Named outstanding volunteer of the year by local Junior League, 1979.

WRITINGS: Breaking the Cycle of Child Abuse, Winston Press, 1978. Contributor to *Journal of Prevention* and *Frontiers.*

WORK IN PROGRESS: A skills-development approach to nurturing for persons with deprived childhoods, publication expected in 1981; *Staff/Board Partnership: Dream or Nightmare?,* publication expected in 1982; a comparison of group process in a self-help group and a community volunteer group, 1982.

SIDELIGHTS: Christine Herbruck wrote: "Parents Anonymous (PA) is a partnership between parents and professionals to enable parents to discover alternative behaviors to those they consider abusive. Each PA group has a 'sponsor,' a volunteer social worker or psychologist who works with a group of people who fear they are abusing their children. In a group setting the professional volunteers his or her knowledge and the parents volunteer their intimate experience so that together they may discover ways to prevent child abuse.

"It was as a sponsor of a PA group that my interest in the prevention of child abuse became vitally important to me as I saw parents learn to stop abusing and to begin positive, loving parenting. I have learned about child abuse from the people who know it best—those people who experienced it as children, swore they would never do it as adults, and then found themselves in the tragic situation of doing what they had always sworn they would never do. It is also in PA that I have seen these parents learn NOT to do it, learn to be nurturing and

supportive parents, and learn to take pride in their ability to relate well to both children and adults."

*   *   *

HERKEN, Gregg Franklin   1947-

PERSONAL: Born May 23, 1947, in Richmond, Calif.; son of Bernard (a lawyer) and Marguerite (an executive secretary) Herken. *Education:* University of California, Santa Cruz, A.B. (history) and A.B. (government), both 1969; Princeton University, M.A., 1971, Ph.D., 1974. *Home:* 640 Edna Way, San Mateo, Calif. 94402. *Office:* Department of History, Yale University, New Haven, Conn. 06520.

CAREER: University of California, Berkeley, research associate in U.S. history at Institute of International Studies, 1973-74; University of California, Santa Cruz, lecturer in history, 1974-75; California State University, San Luis Obispo, lecturer in history, 1975-77; Oberlin College, Oberlin, Ohio, assistant professor of history, 1978; Yale University, New Haven, Conn., assistant professor of U.S. history, 1978—. *Member:* American Historical Association, Organization of American Historians, Society for Historians of American Foreign Relations. *Awards, honors:* Grant from Harry S Truman Library Institute, 1976; Fulbright-Hays fellowship for Sweden, 1978.

WRITINGS: (Contributor) Barton Bernstein, editor, *The Atomic Bomb: The Critical Issues,* Little, Brown, 1976; (contributor) Michael Hamilton, editor, *To Avoid Catastrophe: A Study in Future Nuclear Weapons Policy,* Eerdmans, 1978; *The Winning Weapon: The Atomic Bomb in the Cold War, 1945-1950,* Knopf, 1981. Contributor to history journals.

WORK IN PROGRESS: The Nuclear Gnostics: Strategists of the Apocalypse, publication by Knopf expected in 1983.

SIDELIGHTS: Herken wrote: "The relationship between technology and foreign policy is the subject of my most recent interest. *The Nuclear Gnostics* is meant to be both an intellectual history and a collective biography of those whose profession has been thinking about the unthinkable. The common wisdom has been that the subject of nuclear weapons policy is too complex and too technical for the citizen to understand. What's been a revelation to me is that the debate is not about numbers—indeed, has never been about numbers—but is really about politics and perceptions, especially perceptions of will. The departure point for my second book is the same as that of the first—what Joseph Conrad called the 'fascination of the abomination.'"

BIOGRAPHICAL/CRITICAL SOURCES: Los Angeles Times, June 5, 1981.

*   *   *

HERM, Gerhard   1931-
(Carl Crawells)

PERSONAL: Born April 26, 1931, in Crailsheim, Germany; son of Eugen (a public servant) and Emma (Wieser) Herm; married Christina Erb (an assistant television director), August 5, 1968. *Education:* Attended University of Kansas, 1951-52, and University of Munich, 1952-55. *Religion:* Protestant. *Home:* Egerweg 6, Ottobrun, West Germany D-8012. *Agent:* Reinhold Stecher, Seeblickstrasse 46, Breitbrunn, West Germany D-8031.

CAREER: Deutsche Studentenzeitung, Bonn, West Germany, editor-in-chief, 1956-58; editor at television station in Hamburg, West Germany, 1958-60; *Muenchner Illurtrierte,* Munich, West Germany, editor, 1960-61; chief of department of local television station in Cologne, West Germany, 1962-66; free-lance writer, 1966—. *Awards, honors:* Ernst Schneider Preis from German Chamber of Commerce, 1971, for television documentary, and 1973, for second best radio documentary.

WRITINGS—In English translation: *Die Phoenizier: Das Pupurreich der Antike,* Econ-Verlag, 1973, translation by Caroline Hillier published as *The Phoenicians: The Purple Empire of the Ancient World,* Morrow, 1975; *Die Kelten: Das Volk, das aus die Dunkel kam,* Econ-Verlag, 1975, translation published as *The Celts: The People Who Came Out of the Darkness,* Weidenfeld & Nicolson, 1976, St. Martin's, 1977.

In German: *Amerika erobert Europa* (title means "America Conquers Europe"), Econ-Verlag, 1964; *Das zweite Rom: Konstantinopel, drehscheibe zwischen Ost und West* (title means "The Second Rome: Constantinople, Turning Point of East and West"), Econ-Verlag, 1968; *Auf der Suche nach dem Erbe: Von Karl dem Grossen bis Friedrich Krupp* (title means "Looking for the Heritage: From Charlemagne to Friedrich Krupp"), Claassen, 1977; *Der Diadochen: Alexanders Erben kaempfen und die Weltherrschaft* (title means "The Diadochs: Alexander's Heirs Fight for World Power"), Bertelsmann, 1978; (under pseudonym Carl Crawells) *Ein feiner alter Herr* (novel; title means "A Nice Old Gentleman"), mvs-Verlag, 1978; *Strahlend in Purpur und Gold: Die heilige Reich von Konstantinopel* (title means "Shining in Gold and Purple: The Holy Empire of Constantinople"), 2nd edition, Econ-Verlag, 1979; *Des Reiches herrlichkeit* (title means "The Glory of the Empire"), Bertelsmann, 1980; *Die Eule ruft im Kaiserpalast* (title means "The Owl Is Howling in the Emperor's Palace"), C. Bertelemann-Verlag, 1982.

Author of "Bauernbarock," a play, first broadcast by Second German Television, March 26, 1976. Author of nearly fifty television documentaries and more than eighty radio scripts.

SIDELIGHTS: Herm commented: "I am fascinated by reality, and am led from the present to the past." *Avocational interests:* Travel (Europe, the Near East, the United States), "the world around me."

*   *   *

HERMAN, Ben 1927-

PERSONAL: Born April 16, 1927, in Dundalk, Md.; son of Morris (in sales) and Lena (Land) Herman. *Education:* Johns Hopkins University, B.A., 1950. *Religion:* Jewish. *Home:* 71 Kinship Rd., Dundalk, Md. 21222.

CAREER: English teacher at public schools in Dundalk, Md., 1950-69; Maryland State Department of Education, Baltimore, editor, 1969-78; writer, 1978—. *Military service:* U.S. Army, medic, 1945-47; served in Italy; became staff sergeant.

WRITINGS: Sunday After Sunday (short stories), Gamaron Press, 1972; *How High Up Is Heaven?* (short stories), Gamaron Press, 1974; *The Rhapsody in Blue of Mickey Klein* (novel), Stemmer House, 1981. Contributor of more than one hundred articles and essays to periodicals, including *Baltimore Sun.*

WORK IN PROGRESS: Green Dust of the Milky Way, short stories for children; *Icarus Victory* (tentative title), a novel about a young soldier in the army of occupation in northern Italy, completion expected in 1984.

SIDELIGHTS: Herman told *CA:* "Isaac Bashevis Singer wrote that 'the aim of literature is to keep time from vanishing.' In my novel and in my stories I have attempted to keep alive a time, a place, and a people I cherished as a boy—old Jewish East Baltimore and the village of Dundalk.

"One of my great pleasures in life is reading my stories and sections of my novel to the children and young people in the schools, for I feel very strongly that the future rests with them. A lovely line from the Talmud says it all: 'The world is saved by the breath of school children.'

"I have been to Europe, Russia, Africa, the Far East, and South America. I enjoy traveling but always keep coming back to Dundalk, where I was born."

*   *   *

HERMES, Patricia 1936-

PERSONAL: Born February 21, 1936, in Brooklyn, N.Y.; daughter of Frederick Joseph (a bank's trust officer) and Jessie (Gould) Martin; married Matthew E. Hermes (a research and development director for a chemical company), August 24, 1957; children: Paul, Mark, Timothy, Matthew, Jr., Jennifer. *Education:* St. John's University, Jamaica, N.Y., B.A., 1957. *Home and office:* 3036 Princess Anne Cres., Chesapeake, Va. 23321. *Agent:* Dorothy Markinko (juvenile books) and Julie Fallowfield (adult books), McIntosh & Otis, Inc., 475 Fifth Ave., New York, N.Y. 10017.

CAREER: Teacher of English and social studies at junior high school in Takoma Park, Md., 1957-58; Delcastle Technical High School, Delcastle, Del., teacher of home-bound children, 1972-73; writer. *Member:* Authors Guild, Society of Children's Book Writers.

WRITINGS—All juveniles; all published by Harcourt: *What If They Knew,* 1980; *Nobody's Fault?,* 1981; *Who Will Take Care of Me?,* 1982; *You Shouldn't Have to Say Goodbye* (novel), 1982. Contributor to magazines, including *Woman's Day, Life and Health, Connecticut, County, American Baby,* and *Mother's Day,* and newspapers.

WORK IN PROGRESS: Interruptions, nonfiction for adults.

SIDELIGHTS: Patricia Hermes told *CA:* "Although I have done many nonfiction articles and essays for adults, I write primarily for children and young adults. I think I have chosen writing for young people because I remember what it was like to be a child, and remember more than anything how painful it was. As adults, we often try to deceive ourselves that childhood is a safe, pleasant place to be. It isn't—at least, not much of the time. For me, it is important to say this to young people, to let them know they are not alone and that others share their feelings, their dreams and fears and hopes. It is important for them to know that things aren't so great in other children's lives either, because I have long believed that anything is bearable when we know that we are not alone. This does not mean that my books must be sad—not at all. What it means is that I need to tell young people that there are tough things going on in their lives but other kids share those problems, and that there is HOPE. Hope is the most important thing I can hold out to them. The pleasure and joy that I find in writing is in expressing how I feel in a way with which young readers can identify.

"Most of the subjects of my books come, in some small way at least, from my own background. Jeremy, in my first book, has epilepsy. When I was a child, I too had epilepsy, and it was a very painful thing emotionally. I wanted to write about it to tell children today what it's like, to help young people who might have the disease, or children who might know someone who has it. But that is not all. One does not have to have epilepsy to have the feelings that Jeremy had, to feel lonely, frightened, rejected. All children feel that way at times, so in writing about those feelings, I hope I can help them cope with their feelings. It is up to my readers to decide if I achieve that goal.

"In *Nobody's Fault?*, a young child dies in an accident. That accident did not really happen, not to my children nor to anyone I know. But many years ago, one of my children did die from a disease when she was just an infant. In some ways then, I am talking about my own feelings in that book, my feelings about losing a child in death. These are feelings I believe a child can identify with, because children have strong feelings. They know about death and separation and loneliness.

"My nonfiction book for adults is also a result of my own feelings. I am writing about what it is like to be a woman today, brought up for roles that no longer exist, in a society that bears little resemblance to the one for which we were traditionally prepared. I write about this because I believe not enough writers are addressing the issue today and women, as well as children (and men), need to be told that they are not alone."

* * *

HERRIDGE, Robert   1914(?)-1981

OBITUARY NOTICE: Born c. 1914; died of a heart attack in 1981 in Woodstock, N.Y. Television producer and writer. Herridge wrote and produced television programs for "Studio One," "Camera Three," and "The Robert Herridge Theatre." Obituaries and other sources: *Time*, July 18, 1960, August 31, 1981; *New York Times*, August 17, 1981.

* * *

HERSHEY, Lenore

PERSONAL: daughter of Max and France (Grombecker) Oppenheimer; married Solomon G. Hershey, December 21, 1942; children: Jane. *Education:* Hunter College (now of the City University of New York), B.A., 1938. *Home:* 750 Ladd Rd., New York, N.Y. 10471. *Office:* 641 Lexington Ave., New York, N.Y. 10022.

CAREER/WRITINGS: McCall's magazine, New York City, senior editor, 1952-68; *Ladies' Home Journal* magazine, New York City, managing editor, 1968—, editor-in-chief, 1973—, author of column "Editor's Diary," 1974—; vice-president of Charter Publications, Inc., New York City. Author of short stories and magazine articles. Secretary of the Committee for Gracie Mansion, 1964-67; lecturer, Radcliffe College, 1968-69; member of President's Advisory Council on the Economic Role of Women, 1972; member of President's Commission for the observance of International Women's Year, 1975; member of media committee of the board of directors of the National Center for Volunteer Action. *Member:* Women's Forum (New York City). *Awards, honors:* Extraordinary Woman of Achievement award from National Conference of Christians and Jews; named one of the twenty-five most influential women in the United States by the National Education Association and World Alumnae, 1977 and 1978; named Mother of the Year, 1978; named to the Hunter College Hall of Fame.*

* * *

HERVENT, Maurice
See GRINDEL, Eugene

HERZOG, Gerard   1920-

PERSONAL: Born December 19, 1920, in Paris, France; son of Robert (an engineer) and Germaine (Beaume) Herzog; married second wife, Josee de Neuville (a writer, composer, and actress under name Marie-Josee Neuville), 1959; children: (first marriage) Carine Herzog Greiner, Frederic; (second marriage) Valerie, Rafaele, Lionel. *Education:* Attended Ecole des Hautes Etudes Sociales, University of Paris. *Politics:* Liberal. *Religion:* "Catholic by education." *Home:* Moulin de l'Abbaye, 91190 Gif-sur-Yvette, France.

CAREER: Director and scriptwriter for numerous dramatic, literary, musical, and political programs on the French television network, 1945—. Official organizer and director of government press conferences and meetings between the French president and visiting heads of state and of various trade and peace talks, including the Vietnam cease-fire negotiations and the Gerald Ford-Valery Giscard d'Estaing summit in Martinique. *Military service:* Served in the French Resistance with the Francis Tireurs et Partisans and in the Service du Travail Obligatoire (forced labor in German factories) during World War II. *Member:* Groupe de Haute Montagne. *Awards, honors:* Chevalier of French Legion of Honor, 1978.

WRITINGS: (With Louis Lachenal) *Les Carnets du vertige* (biography), P. Horay, 1956; *La Voie Jackson* (novel), Athaud, 1976, translation by Hilary Davies published as *Jackson's Way*, Farrar, Straus, 1978.

WORK IN PROGRESS: Expressions, a study of artistic and political expression; *Je, uniformement*, a novel; *Surfina*, a tragedy.

SIDELIGHTS: Herzog told *CA:* "Beginning in my childhood I must have had writing abilities that I couldn't define in any way other than by the effect that these qualities produced on others, teachers or parents. I simply stated things. At the same time I experienced pressure from those around me who took me for such a genius that I was paralyzed. Stifled by the ambition that they maintained for me, through me, I launched myself into a frantic examination of great literary undertakings in the hope of attaining the height at which I'd been placed.

"Then, World War II over, a new form of expression was born before my eyes: radio. I abandoned all literary ambition to throw myself into this new and very satisfying means of expression which was radio, then cinema, then television. I became a director who filmed, with the era's greatest actors, his own screenplays.

"It's taken me twenty-five years to feel natural when confronted with the literary act. After twenty-five years of cinema and television, having professionally mastered image and sound, I have finally returned to my first vocation: writing. But I link these two modes of expression together in my style; I cannot do otherwise. In effect, in a novel, to realize an event is to construct a decor, describe some characters, translate their feelings, relate their actions, report their dialogues, note down the resonant universe in which everything unfolds. In writing a screenplay the work is exactly the same. It is so difficult for me to differentiate one mode of expression from the other that for me, film and novel are one and the same thing.

"My novel *Jackson's Way* has been made into a film and the remarks and compliments of the novel's readers and of the film's viewers use the same arguments and the same words. It's a singular situation and, I think, a privileged one."

Gerard Herzog is the brother of noted mountaineer Maurice Herzog. Together the brothers have completed some of the most rigorous Alpine ascents. *Les Carnets du vertige* tells the story of Louis Lachenal, one of the climbers who accompanied Maurice Herzog to the top of Annapurna in the Himalaya Mountains in 1950.

AVOCATIONAL INTERESTS: Mountain climbing, classical and contemporary music.

* * *

HEYSE, Paul (Johann Ludwig von)   1830-1914

BRIEF ENTRY: Born March 15, 1830, in Berlin, Germany; died April 2, 1914, in Munich, Germany (now West Germany). German author. Heyse is considered a master of the novella. Of his nearly one hundred twenty novellas, "The Angry Girl" (1855) is thought to be his best. His psychological stories were balanced and carefully styled; many reveal his fondness for Italy and Italian culture. In his introduction to the twenty-four volume *Deutscher Novellenschatz* (beginning in 1871), Heyse expounded the "falcon theory" of the novella, urging clarity, simplicity, and an inward struggle producing a crisis symbolized by a concrete object. He was at the center of the Munich traditionalists, writing only about the pleasanter side of life, raising even the humblest characters to positions of dignity and inner nobility. His intense dislike for seeing the sordid side of life in literature placed him opposite the fashionable writers of the emerging naturalist and impressionist schools. Although after some thirty years of popularity Heyse's reputation as a fiction writer waned, he was awarded the Nobel Prize for literature in 1910. Toward the end of his writing career Heyse won lasting critical acclaim for the translations of Italian poets he included in the scholarly five-volume *Italienische Dichter seit der mitte des 18. Jahrhunderts* (1889-1905). *Biographical/critical sources: The McGraw-Hill Encyclopedia of World Biography,* McGraw, 1973; *The Oxford Companion to German Literature,* Clarendon Press, 1976.

* * *

HIBBS, Ben   1901-1975

*OBITUARY NOTICE—*See index for *CA* sketch: Born July 23, 1901, in Fontana, Kan.; died of leukemia, 1975, in Penn Valley, Pa. Journalist, editor, educator, and author. Hibbs began his career as an editor with the *Fort Morgan Times.* From there he took on various editing positions at other periodicals, including the *Pratt Tribune,* the *Goodland News-Republic,* the *Arkansas City Traveler,* the *Country Gentleman,* and the *Reader's Digest.* Best remembered as the editor of the *Saturday Evening Post,* Hibbs was a member of the U.S. Advisory Commission on Information from 1951 to 1954. His writings include *Two Men on a Job: A Behind-the-Scenes Story of a Rowdy Genius and His Mentor, Some Thoughts on Magazine Editing,* and *A Michener Miscellany, 1950-1970.* Obituaries and other sources: *Time,* April 14, 1975.

* * *

HICKEY, William
See DRIBERG, Thomas Edward Neil

* * *

HICKS, John Edward   1890(?)-1971

OBITUARY NOTICE: Born c. 1890; died December 31, 1971, in Kansas City. Historian, journalist, and author. John Hicks, former head of proofreading for the *Kansas City Star,* was the author of *The Adventures of a Tramp Printer* and *Themes From the Old West.* He also wrote numerous articles about the Old

West. Obituaries and other sources: *AB Bookman's Weekly,* January 17, 1972.

* * *

HILDEBRANDT, Greg   1939-

PERSONAL: Born January 23, 1939, in Detroit, Mich.; son of George J. (an executive) and Germaine (Lajack) Hildebrandt; married Diana F. Stankowski, June 8, 1963; children: Mary, Laura, Gregory. *Education:* Attended Mienzinger's Art School. *Home:* 12 Rock Spring Rd., West Orange, N.J. 07052. *Agent:* Jean L. Gruder, 90 Park Ave., Verona, N.J. 07044. *Office:* 90 Park Ave., Verona, N.J. 07044.

CAREER: Free-lance illustrator and writer, 1958—. Consultant to Columbia Pictures. *Military service:* U.S. Army, 1959-63. *Awards, honors:* Gold medal from Society of Illustrators, 1976, for *Clive.*

WRITINGS—Written and illustrated with brother, Tim Hildebrandt: *How Do They Build It?,* Platt, 1974; (with Jerry Nichols) *Urshurak* (fantasy novel), Bantam, 1979.

Illustrator: (With T. Hildebrandt) Audrey Hirsch and Harvey Hirsch, *A Home for Tandy,* Platt, 1971; (with T. Hildebrandt) Watty Piper, editor, *Mother Goose: A Treasury of Best-Loved Rhymes,* Platt, 1972; Aileen Lucia Fisher, *Animal Disguises,* Bowmar/Noble, 1973; Barbara Shook Hazen, *A Nose for Trouble,* Golden Press, 1973; Anthony Hiss, *The Giant Panda Book,* Golden Press, 1973; Gloria Skurzynski, *The Remarkable Journey of Gustavus Bell,* Abingdon, 1973; Simone Zapun, *Games Animals Play,* Platt, 1974; Annie Ingle, *The Big City Book,* Platt, 1975; Winifred Rosen Casey, *The Hippopotamus Book,* Golden Press, 1975; Kathleen N. Daly, *The Wonder of Animals,* Golden Press, 1976; Daly, *Dinosaurs,* Golden Press, 1977; Daly, *Today's Biggest Animals,* Golden Press, 1977; Terry Brooks, *The Sword of Shannara,* Random House, 1977; Ruthanna Long, *The Great Monster Contest,* Golden Press, 1977; Daly, *Hide and Defend,* Golden Press, 1977; Daly, *Unusual Animals,* Golden Press, 1977; *Here Come the Builders!,* Platt, 1978; *Who Runs the City?,* Platt, 1978. Also illustrator of *Clive.*

WORK IN PROGRESS: Research on the lost continent of Atlantis.

SIDELIGHTS: Hildebrandt commented: "I feel that the field of fantasy is just beginning to be appreciated by people. It is now and has always been my first love. Fantasy enables people to escape into a world of pure joy and imagination. I am fortunate to have spent my entire life working with my imagination and I certainly hope I have managed to bring some joy to others through my art and writing."

BIOGRAPHICAL/CRITICAL SOURCES: Ian Summers, *The Art of the Brothers Hildebrandt,* Ballantine, 1979.

* * *

HILL, Napoleon   1883(?)-1970

OBITUARY NOTICE: Born c. 1883 in Virginia; died November 9, 1970, in Greenville, S.C. Journalist and author. Napoleon Hill wrote numerous books on success, including *Grow Rich With Peace of Mind* and *Success Through a Positive Mental Attitude.* His best-selling *Think and Grow Rich* was published in 1937. Obituaries and other sources: *Publishers Weekly,* November 30, 1970; *AB Bookman's Weekly,* January 4, 1971.

HILU, Virginia   1929(?)-1976
  (Virginia Hilu Einhorn)

OBITUARY NOTICE: Born c. 1929; died after a long illness, September 13, 1976, in New York, N.Y. Editor of books in many fields, including psychology, economics, business, and sociology. An editor at Harper & Row for more than twenty years, Hilu arranged and edited the love letters of Kahlil Gibran and Mary Haskell for the 1972 book *Beloved Prophet.* Obituaries and other sources: *New York Times,* September 14, 1976; *Publishers Weekly,* September 27, 1976.

*   *   *

HINKSON, Katharine Tynan
  See TYNAN, Katharine

*   *   *

HINSHAW, H(orton) Corwin   1902-

PERSONAL: Born August 1, 1902, in Iowa Falls, Iowa; son of Milas C. (a horticulturist) and Ida (Bushong) Hinshaw; married Dorothy Youmans (an artist), August 6, 1924; children: Horton Corwin, Jr., Barbara Hinshaw Baird, William E., Dorothy Hinshaw Patent. *Education:* College of Idaho, B.S., 1923; attended University of Pittsburgh, 1923-24; University of California, Berkeley, M.S., 1926, Ph.D., 1927; University of Pennsylvania, M.D., 1933. *Politics:* Republican. *Religion:* Society of Friends (Quakers). *Home:* 512 San Rafael Ave., Belvedere, Calif. 94920. *Office:* 450 Sutter St., San Francisco, Calif. 94108.

CAREER: University of California, Berkeley, instructor, 1926-27, assistant professor of zoology, 1927-28; American University, Beirut, Lebanon, adjunct professor of parasitology, 1928-31; University of Pennsylvania, Philadelphia, instructor in bacteriology, 1931-33; University of Minnesota, Minneapolis, fellow and first assistant in medicine at Mayo Foundation, 1933-36, instructor, 1936-40, assistant professor, 1940-45, associate professor of medicine, 1945-49; Stanford University, Stanford, Calif., clinical professor of medicine, 1949-59, head of Division of Diseases of the Chest; University of California, San Francisco, clinical professor of medicine, 1959—, chief of staff at Medical Center, 1972-74. Diplomate of National Board of Medical Examiners. Visiting physician at Southern Pacific Hospital, 1958-75; director of medical services at Harkness Community Hospital, 1967-75, member of board of trustees, 1970-74, chief of staff, 1972-74; director of health operations and member of board of directors for Health Maintenance, Inc. of Northern California, 1972-74. Member of California Interagency Council of Tuberculosis, 1968-71, and California Committee on Regional Medical Programs, 1969-76; consultant to U.S. Veterans Administration and Weimar Chest Center.

MEMBER: American Broncho-Esophagological Association, American Society for Clinical Investigation, American Clinical and Climatological Association, American College of Physicians (fellow), American Thoracic Society (honorary life member; president, 1948-49), National Tuberculosis Association (vice-president, 1946-47, 1956-60, 1960-61, and 1967-68), American Medical Association, American Lung Association (honorary life member), American College of Chest Physicians (fellow), Argentine Society of Phthisiology (honorary member), Society for Experimental Biology and Medicine, Central Society for Clinical Research, Mississippi Valley Medical Association (honorary member), California Tuberculosis and Health Association (member of board of directors, 1949-54), Min-

nesota Trudeau Society (president, 1947), California Academy of Medicine, San Francisco County Medical Society, San Francisco Tuberculosis and Health Association (member of board of directors, 1950-59). *Awards, honors:* California Medal from California Tuberculosis and Health Association, 1955; D.Sc. from College of Idaho, 1957; Trudeau Medal from American Thoracic Society, 1958; hall of fame award from American Lung Association, 1980; pioneer award from American Chest Physicians.

WRITINGS: (With H. McLeod Riggins) *Streptomycin and Dihydrostreptomycin in Treatment of Tuberculosis,* National Tuberculosis Association, 1949; (with L. Henry Garland) *Diseases of the Chest,* Saunders, 1956, 4th edition (with John F. Murray), 1980.

Contributor: J. Arthur Myers and C. A. McKinley, editors, *The Chest and the Heart,* C. C Thomas, 1948; William Dark and I. Snapper, editors, *Advances in Internal Medicine,* Volume 3, Interscience, 1949; S. A. Waksman, editor, *Streptomycin,* Williams & Wilkins, 1949; John M. Musser and Michael G. Wohl, editors, *Internal Medicine,* Lea & Febiger, 1951; Austin Smith and Paul Werner, editors, *Modern Treatment,* Paul Heober, 1953; Henry Welch, editor, *Principles and Practice of Antibiotic Therapy,* Blakison, 1954; Howard F. Conn, editor, *Current Therapy 1958,* Saunders, 1959; Wohl, editor, *Long Term Illness,* Saunders, 1959; Myers, editor, *Diseases of the Chest, Including the Heart,* C. C Thomas, 1959; Conn, editor, *Current Therapy 1959,* Saunders, 1960; Waksman, editor, *Treatment of Tuberculosis,* Rutgers University Press, 1964; Thomas P. Lowry, editor, *Hyperventilation and Hysteria,* C. C Thomas, 1967; G. P. Youmans, editor, *Tuberculosis,* Saunders, 1979.

Contributor to *Encyclopaedia Britannica.* Contributor of more than two hundred articles to medical and scientific journals. Member of editorial board of *Excerpta Medica,* 1956—; member of editorial advisory board of *Consultant,* 1974—.

SIDELIGHTS: In the preface to the fourth edition of *Diseases of the Chest,* Hinshaw wrote: "Successful physicians look upon their occupation, not as a means of livelihood alone nor as a mission to suffering humanity exclusively, but as a quest—a contest of wits—a solution of mysteries and control over events. It is not exactly a sport—a demeaning word—but still a contest; more like chess than tennis. It is frustrating at times but on other occasions, especially when dealing with chest diseases, it is profoundly satisfying. And that satisfaction is most lasting, more real, when the patient shares in the triumph.

"It has been my rare privilege to play an active role in the development of present-day curative remedies for tuberculosis and leprosy, to have known and worked with some of the greatest scientists of this century, to have traveled and lectured on every continent for nearly fifty years. Medical science has progressed much, much more during this interval than during all preceding history and I have had a 'ring-side seat.'"

*   *   *

HIRSCH, Edward   1950-

PERSONAL: Born January 20, 1950, in Chicago, Ill.; son of Kurt and Irma (Ginsburg) Hirsch; married Janet Landay (an assistant art museum curator), May 29, 1977. *Education:* Grinnell College, B.A., 1972; University of Pennsylvania, Ph.D., 1979. *Home:* 20058 Renfrew Rd., Detroit, Mich. 48221. *Office:* Department of English, Wayne State University, Detroit, Mich. 48202.

CAREER: Wayne State University, Detroit, Mich., assistant professor of English, 1979—. *Member:* Modern Language Association of America, American Folklore Society, American Committee for Irish Studies, Phi Beta Kappa. *Awards, honors:* Watson fellow, 1972-73; awards from Academy of American Poets, 1975-77; Amy Lowell traveling fellow, 1978-79; Ingram Merrill Award from Ingram Merrill Foundation, 1978-79, for poetry; fellow of American Council of Learned Societies, 1981.

WRITINGS: For the Sleepwalkers (poems), Knopf, 1981. Contributor of articles, stories, poems, and reviews to magazines, including *North American Review, New Yorker, Partisan Review, Commentary, Poetry, American Poetry Review, Nation,* and *New Republic.*

WORK IN PROGRESS: The Imaginary Peasant, on modern Irish literature and folklore; another book of poems.

SIDELIGHTS: Hirsch commented: "My goal is to write a few poems that are unforgettable. I love enchanted stories, magical realism, secret signs, and the great modern artists of childhood—Archille Gorky and Paul Klee. Jean Cocteau once said that the goal of every artist should be his own extremity. I want to write poems that are imaginative, astonishing, playful, mysterious, and extreme."

BIOGRAPHICAL/CRITICAL SOURCES: New York Times Book Review, September 13, 1981.

* * *

HIRST, Paul Quentin 1946-

PERSONAL: Born May 20, 1946, in Plymouth, England; *Education:* University of Leicester, B.A., 1968; University of Sussex, M.A., 1969. *Politics:* "Socialist—Labour party." *Religion:* None. *Office:* Department of Politics and Sociology, Birkbeck College, University of London, Malet St., London W.C.1, England.

CAREER: University of London, Birkbeck College, London, England, lecturer, 1969-78, reader in social theory, 1978—.

WRITINGS: Durkheim, Bernard, and Epistemology, Routledge & Kegan Paul, 1975; (with Barry Hindess) *Pre-Capitalist Modes of Production,* Routledge & Kegan Paul, 1975; *Social Evolution and Sociological Categories,* Allen & Unwin, 1976; (with Hindess) *Mode of Production and Social Formation,* Macmillan, 1977; (with Hindess, A.J. Cutler, and S.A. Hussain) *Marx's Capital and Capitalism Today,* Routledge & Kegan Paul, Volume I, 1977, Volume II, 1978; *On Law and Ideology,* Macmillan, 1979; (with Penelope Woolley) *Social Relations and Human Attributes,* Tavistock Publications, 1981. Editor of *Economy and Society,* 1972-74, and *Politics and Power,* 1981—.

* * *

HODGINS, Eric 1899-1971

PERSONAL: Born March 2, 1899, in Detroit, Mich.; died January 7, 1971, in New York, N.Y.; son of Frederic Brinkley (a clergyman) and Edith Gertrude (Bull) Hodgins; married Catherine Cornforth Carlson, July 5, 1930 (died, 1933); married Eleanor Treacy, October 31, 1936; children: (first marriage) Roderic Carlson; (second marriage) Eleanor Patricia. *Education:* Attended Cornell University, 1917; Massachusetts Institute of Technology, S.B., 1922; graduate study at Harvard University, 1923-24. *Religion:* Episcopalian. *Home:* 150 East 50th St., New York, N.Y.

CAREER: Technology Review, Boston, Mass., editor, 1922-27; *Youth's Companion,* Boston, editor, 1927-29; *Redbook,* New York City, advertising salesman, promotion manager, and

associate editor, 1929-33; Time, Inc., New York City, *Fortune* magazine associate managing editor, 1933-35, managing editor, 1935-37, publisher, 1937-41, vice-president of parent company, 1938-46; free-lance writer, 1946-71. Supervising editor for President's Materials Policy Commission, 1950-52; member of committee on public information of the American Heart Association, 1965-67. *Member:* University Club (Boston, Mass.). *Awards, honors:* Litt.D. from Bates College, 1939; George Westinghouse Award from American Association for the Advancement of Science, 1953; Blakeslee Award from American Heart Association, 1964, for *Episode: Report On the Accident Inside My Skull.*

WRITINGS: (With Frederick Alexander Magoun) *Sky High: The Story of Aviation,* Little, Brown, 1929, revised edition, 1935; (with Magoun) *A History of Aircraft,* McGraw, 1931, reprinted, Arno, 1972; (with Magoun) *Behemoth: The Story of Power,* Doubleday, Doran, 1932; *Ocean Express: The Story of the Bremen and the Europa,* North German Lloyd, 1932; *Mr. Blandings Builds His Dream House* (novel), illustrations by William Steig, Simon & Schuster, 1946; *Blandings' Way* (novel), Simon & Schuster, 1950; *Enough Time?: The Pattern of Executive Life,* illustrations by Alan Dunn, Doubleday, 1959; *Episode: Report On the Accident Inside My Skull,* Atheneum, 1964; *Trolley to the Moon: An Autobiography,* Simon & Schuster, 1973. Contributor of articles to periodicals, including *Fortune, New York Herald-Tribune Magazine,* and *New Yorker.*

SIDELIGHTS: Hodgins was a successful magazine editor, who is best remembered as the author of *Mr. Blandings Builds His Dream House,* a humorous novel based upon his own home-building experiences. Originally the story had been published as an article in the April, 1946, issue of *Fortune* magazine. "The book," Hodgins later reflected, "almost wrote itself. . . . After all, I *was* Mr. Blandings and I *had* built a dream house." The book was a best-seller in 1946 and was made into a popular motion picture starring Cary Grant and Myrna Loy. It was also published as a three-act play, dramatized by Reginald Lawrence. Hodgins followed *Mr. Blandings Builds His Dream House* with a sequel, *Blandings' Way,* a satiric commentary on liberal politics and advertising agencies. Hodgins believed it to be the better of the Blandings novels but years later regretfully pointed out that *Dream House* was the book most people remembered.

Both books received favorable reviews. *Saturday Review*'s G. G. Bates especially admired the skillful construction and balanced humor of *Mr. Blandings Builds His Dream House.* "The humor," he said, "lies in the warp and woof of the thing and can't be lifted out in neat little excerpts or indicated by a series of anecdotes." Although many reviewers noted the humor in *Blandings' Way,* several critics pointed out that there is also a sober aspect to the novel. J. W. Jackson of the *San Francisco Chronicle* labeled the book "sad-funny" and *Commonweal*'s William Pfaff said: "This novel is certainly funny. . . . But it is fundamentally an incisive and rather serious book, and I am sure that Mr. Hodgins intends it seriously."

Hodgins's later book, *Episode: Report On the Accident Inside My Skull,* describes the pain, depression, poor medical treatment, and monumental costs that he confronted during his lengthy convalescence from a massive stroke. In spite of its serious subject matter, Marya Mannes of *Book Week* found the book "as funny . . . as it is frightening." F. G. Slaughter said in the *New York Times Book Review* that Hodgins "writes of his CVA [cerebro-vascular accident] with intense feeling, acute perception, flashing humor—and entertaining irascibility."

Hodgins's last book, an autobiography, was published posthumously under the title *Trolley to the Moon.* Unfinished at the time of his death, the book covers Hodgins's life through the mid-1930's, describing his career as a magazine editor and his friendship with his boss at Time, Inc., Henry Luce. According to *Atlantic*'s Edward Weeks, Hodgins's autobiography "would have been his best book" if it had been completed. R. B. Nordberg of *Best Sellers* commented that although *Trolley to the Moon* contains "some language and some incidents that make the book unsuitable except for very mature readers," Hodgins's autobiography is nevertheless "engrossing and endlessly entertaining."

AVOCATIONAL INTERESTS: Printing, typography.

BIOGRAPHICAL/CRITICAL SOURCES: New York Times, April 10, 1932, December 29, 1946, October 8, 1950; *Saturday Review,* January 4, 1947; *New Republic,* January 27, 1947, June 10, 1972; *San Francisco Chronicle,* October 5, 1950; *Commonweal,* November 24, 1950; *Best Sellers,* February 15, 1964, June 1, 1973; *Book Week,* March 1, 1964; *Time,* March 6, 1964; *Atlantic Monthly,* June, 1964, May, 1973; *Newsweek,* May 28, 1973.

OBITUARIES: New York Times, January 8, 1971; *Washington Post,* January 9, 1971; *Newsweek,* January 18, 1971; *Publishers Weekly,* January 18, 1971.*

* * *

HOGARTH, Emmett
  See POLONSKY, Abraham (Lincoln)

* * *

HOGG, Clayton L(eRoy) 1924-

PERSONAL: Born August 5, 1924, near Delphos, Kan.; son of Rolla A. (a farmer) and Vida (Brown) Hogg; married Frances Hine (a bookkeeper), April 18, 1946; children: Mary Elizabeth Hogg Chalk, Margaret Louise, Christine Anne, David Clayton, James Alvin. *Education:* Emporia State College, B.S., 1949, M.S., 1952; attended University of Washington, Seattle, 1952-53. *Home address:* P.O. Box 34, Delphos, Kan. 67436.

CAREER: High school mathematics and science teacher in Erie, Kan., 1949-52; U.S. Air Force, meteorologist in Kansas, Maryland, Tennessee, Japan, Greenland, and the Ryukyu Islands, 1952-70, retiring as major; teacher of English at Kokusai University, Okinawa University, and Shuri English Language Center, all in Okinawa, Japan, 1970-76; wheat farmer, 1976—. *Military service:* U.S. Army Air Forces, 1943-46; became second lieutenant.

WRITINGS: Okinawa (with own photographs), Kodansha, 1973.

WORK IN PROGRESS: A novel, tentatively titled *The Meridian,* set in Kansas in the middle 1930's.

SIDELIGHTS: Hogg told *CA:* "Organizing scientific ideas into some kind of order almost became a way of life for me while I was working on my Master's thesis. Several years later when I read that art, like science, is organized confusion, I was surprised and also pleased. Somehow, understanding that similarity between art and science removed some of my awe from what I thought was creativity in the arts. It gave me a foundation on which I could use art in communication. I agree with the person who said that there is no such thing as creativity; it is just putting ideas together in a different way.

"My interest in photography also falls in line with trying to organize ideas in meaningful relationships. My colored photographs became an important part of my book, *Okinawa.* My purpose in writing the book was to provide a source for understanding the inhabitants and environment of the Ryukyu Islands for us foreigners living there temporarily.

"The book developed from a series of articles I had written for local magazines in Okinawa, covering such subjects as folkcrafts, festivals, the Battle of Okinawa in World War II, Commodore Perry's use of Okinawa while opening the doors of Japan, and others. Like Gibraltar, Okinawa's strategic location has made it a desired possession of powerful countries for centuries. It was through those visits by invaders that Okinawa took on elements of the cultures of China, Japan, and the United States. Somehow through the hardships that came from those invasions and their own feudal system the people have emerged as the most charming in the world, in my opinion. It was a joy to learn about them and their islands."

* * *

HOLBORN, Mark 1949-

PERSONAL: Born July 31, 1949, in London, England; son of Phillip Robert (a financier) and Elizabeth (Keevil) Holborn; married Denise Evans, November 25, 1971; children: Jesse. *Education:* Attended Portsmouth Polytechnic, 1967-70; University of London, B.A., 1970. *Home:* 22 Dalby Rd., London S.W.18, England.

CAREER: Gardener in Regents Park, London, England, 1970-71; teacher of English in Tokyo, Japan, 1972; teacher of English studies in London, 1973-74; farmer in County Kilkenny, Ireland, 1974; teacher of history in London, 1975-79; *Creative Camera,* London, editor, 1981—. Free-lance Japanese affairs commentator for BBC-Radio 3, 1972-74.

WRITINGS: The Ocean in the Sand: Japan From Landscape to Garden, Shambhala, 1978; "Finding Out About Japan" (television script), first broadcast by Thames Television, 1978. Also contributor to and member of editorial board of *Contemporary Photographers,* 1972. Contributor to *London Magazine* and *Aperture.*

WORK IN PROGRESS: A book on post-war Japanese photography, which connects photography with dance, cinema, graphics, and prose, especially the work of Yukio Mishima.

SIDELIGHTS: Holborn told *CA:* "I spent my early childhood in British Guiana, where my father had work with the bauxite mines on the Demarara River. My earliest memory is of jungle. He was a restless man. I traveled in the Soviet Union between the ages of eighteen and twenty-one. I went to Siberia in December, 1971, then on to Japan under the influence of the writing of Gary Snyder. Gropius once said that Japan was a basic design course, and it did provide me with a sense of focus and structure. I witnessed the worst devastation of landscape and pure harmony. This contradiction was the source of my fascination. I wrote about gardens as a bridge to understanding an attitude to landscape. It is an attitude that emerges in architecture, painting, cha-no-yu (tea ceremony), haiku, and even swordsmanship. It goes beyond Japan. Japan occupied the secret pages in the atlas of my imagination, much like Armenia for Osip Mandelstam or Patagonia for Bruce Chatwin. At that time I was not concerned with gardens as such or with Japan as geography. Now I see a different nation and I am studying a darker history of modern Japan, the contradiction of which is most evident in the writing of Yukio Mishima.

"I am learning about photographs; it is a discipline that teaches me about writing and observation. I am repeatedly learning about language through the great Russian poets. My favorite spot is now in Andalusia. My favorite living novelist is Paul Bowles."

BIOGRAPHICAL/CRITICAL SOURCES: *Smithsonian*, February, 1979.

* * *

HOLLISTER, Herbert A(llen) 1933-

PERSONAL: Born December 11, 1933, in North East, Pa.; son of Carleton A. (a merchant) and Esther (Fuller) Hollister; married Carolyn Homer (a cook), July 2, 1956; children: Carleton, John, Lynda, William. *Education:* Attended Pennsylvania State University, 1951-53, and Gannon College, 1953-54; Allegheny College, A.B., 1955; University of Michigan, M.A., 1962, Ph.D., 1965. *Home address:* 2071 State Route 105, Pemberville, Ohio 43450. *Office:* Department of Mathematics and Statistics, Bowling Green State University, Bowling Green, Ohio 43403.

CAREER: Watt Agency, North East, Pa., realtor, 1956-61; high school mathematics teacher in North East, 1959-61; Bowling Green State University, Bowling Green, Ohio, assistant professor, 1965-69, associate professor, 1969-77, professor of mathematics and statistics, 1977—; realtor with John Newlane Real Estate, 1980-81. Member of Wood County Board of Realtors. *Member:* Mathematical Association of America, National Association of Realtors.

WRITINGS: *Modern Algebra: A First Course*, Harper, 1972; *Algebra and Trigonometry*, Harper, 1976; *Techniques of Algebra*, Harper, 1977; *Fundamentals of Real Estate Mathematics*, Prentice-Hall, 1982.

WORK IN PROGRESS: *Basic Mathematics*, publication expected in 1982; *Mathematics of Finance*, publication expected in 1982 or 1983; *Basic Algebra*, publication expected in 1982 or 1983.

SIDELIGHTS: Hollister told *CA:* "I write because I like to teach and, to me, writing a text is just writing what I would say in class. In each book my primary objective is to make complicated ideas seem simple and understandable."

* * *

HOLMES, John 1913-

PERSONAL: Born May 12, 1913, in Bishopton, Renfrewshire, Scotland; son of John (a farmer) and Jeannie (Stewart) Holmes; married Kathleen Mary Trevethick (an animal trainer), December 12, 1955. *Education:* Attended Edinburgh and East of Scotland College of Agriculture, 1932-33. *Politics:* Conservative. *Religion:* Presbyterian. *Office:* Formakin Animal Centre, Cranborne, Dorsetshire BH21 5QW, England.

CAREER: Farmer; dogbreeder, trainer and judge. Associated with Formakin Animal Centre, Cranborne, England. *Member:* International Sheepdog Society, Society of Authors, British Actors Equity Association, Royal Agricultural Society, British Horse Society, British Show Jumping Association.

WRITINGS: (With MacDonald Daly) *Obedient Dogs and How to Have One*, Chambers, 1954; *The Family Dog: Its Choice and Training*, Popular Dogs, 1957; *The Farmer's Dog*, Popular Dogs, 1960; *Obedience Training for Dogs*, Chambers, 1961; *The Obedient Dog for Obedience Classes and Working Trials*, Popular Dogs, 1975. Also author of *The Colourful World of Dogs*, with wife, Mary Holmes, 1976, *The Pedigree Chum Guide to Dog Care*, 1980, and an educational film, "Living With a Dog." Contributor to magazines, including *Dog World, Our Dogs, Field*, and *Horse*.

WORK IN PROGRESS: An autobiography.

SIDELIGHTS: Holmes wrote: "My wife and I are professional animal trainers who have specialized for the last thirty years in training and handling animals (mostly domestic) for films and television. This work has taken me to Germany, Italy, Austria, Israel, and Canada. In 1979 we went to Australia on a sponsored lecture tour, speaking to dog training clubs in Melbourne, Sydney, Canberra, Adelaide, and Tasmania.

"Probably because my first successes as a trainer were with dogs, most of my writing has been about them. The books have sold very well at home and abroad; *The Family Dog* has been published in German and *The Obedient Dog* in Dutch.

"I am particularly interested in working dogs of all sorts, although I have also exhibited dogs successfully in 'beauty' classes, am on the Kennel Club's list of championship show judges, and have judged at Crofts and other important shows.

"I am no intellectual, but appear to have the ability to describe on paper the things I know about or have seen, and to give instruction on animal training. My subjects are mainly animals, but also the countryside and those who live in it, and the film and television business and those who work in it—quite contrasting material!"

* * *

HOLSKE, Katherine ?-1973

OBITUARY NOTICE: Died July 7, 1973, in Greenvale, N.Y. Editor. Holske worked as an editor for Doubleday and E. P. Dutton before joining in 1954 the staff of Walter J. Black, Inc., publishers of the Detective Book Club. She served as editor in chief there from 1960 to 1973, retiring as editor emeritus. Obituaries and other sources: *Publishers Weekly*, July 23, 1973.

* * *

HOMANS, Abigail Adams 1879-1974

OBITUARY NOTICE: Born September 6, 1879; died February 4, 1974, in Boston, Mass. Society matriarch, philanthropist, and author of her memoirs. Homans was the great-great-granddaughter of John Adams, second president of the United States, and the great-granddaughter of John Quincy Adams, the sixth U.S. president. The acknowledged grande dame of Boston's elite Beacon Hill society, she nonetheless maintained a spunky irreverence for her Brahmin milieu. She worked ten hours per day for philanthropic and cultural institutions, and was for sixteen years a trustee of Massachusetts General Hospital. Her frank, best-selling autobiography, *Education by Uncles*, appeared in 1966 and features the author's recollections of formative relationships with her two uncles, Henry Adams and Brooks Adams. Obituaries and other sources: *New York Times*, February 6, 1974; *Newsweek*, February 18, 1974; *Time*, February 18, 1974.

* * *

HOORNIK, Ed(uard Jozef Antonie Marie) 1910-1970

OBITUARY NOTICE: Born March 9, 1910, in The Hague, Netherlands; died March 1, 1970, in Amsterdam, Netherlands. Poet, critic, novelist, and playwright. Hoornik's experiences in a German concentration camp during World War II influenced his postwar writing, which focuses upon mankind's flaws. He edited several literary magazines and encouraged young poets in the 1940's. Among his plays are "The Seeker," "The Seawolf," "The Sin of Cain," and "The Water." Obituaries and other sources: *The Concise Encyclopedia of Modern Drama*, Horizon Press, 1964; *AB Bookman's Weekly*, March 23, 1970; *Cassell's Encyclopaedia of World Literature*, revised edition, Morrow, 1973.

* * *

HORDER, Mervyn 1910-

PERSONAL: Born in 1910 in London, England. *Education:* Trinity College, Cambridge, M.A., 1932. *Address:* c/o Gerald Duckworth & Co. Ltd., 43 Gloucester Cres., London NW1 7DY, England.

CAREER: Duckworth & Co. Ltd. (publisher), London, England, editor, 1938-72; composer, 1960—; writer, 1966—. *Military service:* Royal Air Force, Fighter Command, 1940-46; served in India.

WRITINGS: (Editor) *In Praise of Cambridge*, Muller, 1952; (editor) *In Praise of Oxford*, Muller, 1955; (editor) *The Orange Carol Book*, Constable, 1962, 2nd edition, Schott, 1973; *The Little Genius*, Duckworth, 1966; (with John Betjeman) *Six Betjeman Songs*, Duckworth, 1967; (editor) *A Book of Love Songs*, Duckworth, 1969; *On Christmas Day*, Longmans, Green, 1969; (editor) *Ronald Firbank: Memoirs and Critiques*, Duckworth, 1977; *A Shropshire Lad* (songs by A. E. Housman), Lengnick, 1980. Contributor to magazines, including *Bookseller* and *Folio Society Quarterly*.

WORK IN PROGRESS: Stories about historic British booksellers; stories about Englishmen marooned abroad by accident.

* * *

HORN, Vivi 1878(?)-1971

OBITUARY NOTICE: Born c. 1878; died March 24, 1971, in Stockholm, Sweden. Author, best known for her best-seller, *The Life of Jenny Lind*. Her writings were popular with the Swedish public. Obituaries and other sources: *AB Bookman's Weekly*, May 17, 1971.

* * *

HORNE, Bernard Shea 1905-1970

OBITUARY NOTICE: Born in 1905; died of a stroke, January 4, 1970, in Hyannis, Mass. Businessman, book collector, and bibliographer. Horne served as board chairman of the Joseph Horne Co. department store while building his collection of Izaak Walton editions. Upon retirement he compiled the definitive bibliography of the 385 editions of Walton's *The Compleat Angler*. He is reported to have died two hours after completing the bibliography, which is entitled *The Compleat Angler, 1653-1967: A New Bibliography*. Obituaries and other sources: *AB Bookman's Weekly*, January 19, 1970.

* * *

HORNE, Michael
See BUSH, Charlie Christmas

* * *

HORNSBY, Albert Sidney 1898(?)-1978

OBITUARY NOTICE: Born c. 1898; died September 13, 1978. Educator, lexicographer, and author of numerous dictionaries and guides to English-language usage. Hornsby's *Oxford Advanced Learner's Dictionary* defined grammar, idiom, and context, and resulted from the author's work with foreign stu-

dents. Hornsby was honored by Oxford University and University College, London, for his achievement in the writing of usage guides and dictionaries. Obituaries and other sources: *AB Bookman's Weekly*, October 23, 1978.

* * *

HOTCHKISS, Bill 1936-

PERSONAL: Born October 17, 1936, in New London, Conn.; son of Bill Henry (a sailor, miner, and farmer) and Merle Bertha (Stambaugh) Hotchkiss; married Judith Shears (a writer), April 10, 1976. *Education:* University of California, Berkeley, B.A., 1959; San Francisco State University, M.A., 1960; University of Oregon, M.F.A., 1964, D.A., 1971, Ph.D., 1974; graduate study at University of California, Davis, and California State University, Sacramento. *Politics:* "Libertarian/Republican." *Religion:* "Isakawuatean." *Home:* 14005 Meadow Dr., Grass Valley, Calif. 95945. *Agent:* Scott Meredith Literary Agency, Inc., 845 Third Ave., New York, N.Y. 10022.

CAREER: Fire crew member, mineral supply crew member, and T.S.I. crew foreman for U.S. Forest Service, summers, 1954-58; high school English teacher in Colfax, Calif., 1960-62; University of Oregon, Eugene, instructor in English, 1962-63; Sierra College, Rocklin, Calif., instructor in English and creative writing, 1963-79; Shasta College, Redding, Calif., instructor in English, 1980-81; writer, 1981—. Co-founder, editor, and printer for Blue Oak Press, 1968—. *Member:* Poetry Society of America, Modern Poetry Association, Authors Guild, Range of Light: Poets (director).

WRITINGS: Steephollow Poems, Ponderosa Press, 1966; *To Christ, Dionysus, Odin* (poems), Blue Oak Press, 1969; *The Graces of Fire and Other Poems*, Blue Oak Press, 1974; *Jeffers: The Sivaistic Vision* (criticism), Blue Oak Press, 1975; (editor) Robinson Jeffers, *The Women at Point Sun*, Blue Oak Press, 1975; (editor) Edith Snow, *Hold Your Hands to the Earth*, Blue Oak Press, 1976; (editor with D. A. Carpenter) Cornel Lengyel, *Four Dozen Songs*, Blue Oak Press, 1976; (editor with William Everson) Jeffers, *The Double Axe*, Norton, 1977; *Fever in the Earth* (poem), Blue Oak Press, 1977; *Climb to the High Country* (poems), Norton, 1978; (with Allan Campo and Carpenter) *William Everson: Poet From San Joaquin*, Blue Oak Press, 1978; *Middle Fork Canyon and Other Poems*, Blue Oak Press, 1979; *The Medicine Calf* (novel), Norton, 1981; *Crow Warriors* (novel), Dell, 1981; *Soldier Wolf* (novel), Bantam, 1981; *Ammahabas* (novel), Norton, 1982; *Klamat* (novel), Bantam, 1982.

Contributor: (Author of foreword) Randy White, *Motherlode/La Veta Madre*, Blue Oak Press, 1977; (author of afterword) John Berutti, *Dreams Don't Make Noise When They Die*, Blue Oak Press, 1978; (author of foreword) Marlan Beilke, *Shining Clarity: Man and God in the Work of Robinson Jeffers*, Quintessence, 1978; (author of afterword) Gary Elder, *Arnulfsaga*, Dustbooks, 1979.

Work represented in anthologies, including *From These Hills*, edited by D. A. Carpenter, Blue Oak Press, 1978; *California Heartland*, edited by Gerald Haslam and James Houston, Capra, 1978. Contributor of poems and reviews to literature journals and poetry magazines. Editor of *Sierra Journal*, 1965-78.

WORK IN PROGRESS: A novel based on the life of Kit Carson tentatively titled *The Soup Dance*, publication by Bantam expected in 1983; revising *Too Few the Grave Witnesses*, poems, 1960-80; continuing research on the literature and history of the American West.

SIDELIGHTS: Bill Hotchkiss's *The Medicine Calf* is set in the early nineteenth century in the plains of Nebraska. The hero of the book, Jim Beckwourth, leaves his home in St. Louis, Missouri, and heads West with a team of trappers. He is eventually adopted by a tribe of Crow Indians, and their enemies become his own. "The carnage is fierce," observed Carolyn See in the *Los Angeles Times*. "One unspoken message of *The Medicine Calf* is that if the Indian tribes had been able to give up their preoccupations with destroying each other, the predatory whites might not have had such a comparatively easy time taking over the Great Plains and the rest of the West." See called *The Medicine Calf* elegant, praising the "low-key prose style [that] allows the events, the absolutely amazing events of the book to sneak up, Indian style, on the reader."

"I am a westerner," Hotchkiss told *CA*. "I have climbed into the stillnesses of the great mountains, I have swum in the rivers of this land, I have camped by the shores of lakes and have walked through the sagebrush and sands of the deserts, have slept through foggy nights close by the crashing waves of the Pacific, I have heard the screams of the mountain lion and the squeals of the marmot. I have seen the eagle and the heron take wing, I have listened to the snows fall in the mountains, and I have seen rain fall over the desert and evaporate before it touched the earth. I have seen a mother bear playing with her cubs, I have watched antelope and deer and mountain goat, I have stood on canyon rims and have fallen into vast spaces of wonder. I have set traps for wild animals and have caught myself, have chewed off my own foot in order to make my escape, and I have climbed up into the golden autumn trees to where the swarming blackbirds riot.

"Anterior to the human world of asphalt and glass and electronic communication exists a realm of wildness, and that realm communicates to the wildness inside of us. It suggests but never defines a oneness with all of the forms of life and all of the forms that we think of as non-life. I sometimes believe the Earth itself is a single organism, a single living thing, a vast single being, intelligent being, drifting through suns and tides.

"Where wildness remains, it remains both beautiful and dangerous. It is equally indifferent to the specific needs of kingfisher or human being. I have several times been nearly drowned because I cannot resist swimming in flooding rivers. I've been chased by a bear (somewhere I've read that one should never run from a bear). I've gotten myself stuck half-way up a rock face with no one around for twenty miles. I have stepped on rattlesnakes, slid down mountainsides, nearly breaking my neck, and have gotten lost in caves. Ocean waves are also dangerous. And beware of the kissing bug and the poison oak."

BIOGRAPHICAL/CRITICAL SOURCES: *Los Angeles Times*, February 19, 1981.

*   *   *

HOUDINI
See LOVECRAFT, H(oward) P(hillips)

*   *   *

HOUSE, Kurt D(uane)   1947-

PERSONAL: Born Feburary 27, 1947, in Three Rivers, Tex.; son of Harold D. (a rancher) and Mildred (a teacher; maiden name, Clayton) House. *Education:* Texas Christian University, B.A., 1969; Southern Methodist University, M.A., 1975, doctoral study, 1975—. *Politics:* Republican. *Religion:* Baptist. *Office:* Fan Man, 4606 Travis, Dallas, Tex. 75205.

CAREER: Trade Routes Antiques, Dallas, Tex., owner, 1975—. Fan Man, Dallas, owner, 1979—; real estate agent. *Military service:* U.S. Army Reserve, 1970-76; became first lieutenant. *Member:* National Rifle Association (life member), Texas Archeological Society, Texas Gun Collectors Association (life member), Texas Folklore Society, Southern Texas Archeological Society. *Awards, honors:* Grants from National Aeronautics and Space Administration (NASA), 1973, and Winchester Museum, 1979.

WRITINGS: *Texas Archeology: Essays Honoring R. K. Harris*, Southern Methodist University Press, 1978; *The Henry Rifle*, Winchester Press, in press; "Be Sure to Take Your Winchester" (three-act play), first produced in 1980. Editor of *Fan Collector*.

WORK IN PROGRESS: *The History of Live Oak County, Texas*, publication by Taylor Publishing expected in 1985.

SIDELIGHTS: House commented: "The writings of J. Frank Dobie, who was born in my home county, have influenced me greatly. Conservation, energy management and production, hunting, backpacking, antique collecting, and cooking are some of my major interests. I have done anthropological field work in Alaska, Florida, southern Texas, and New Mexico. I detest labor unions, think most television is the scourge of America, and deplore the lack of ability of most Americans in simple creative arts such as the art of conversation."

*   *   *

HOUSMAN, A(lfred) E(dward)   1859-1936

BRIEF ENTRY: Born March 26, 1859, in Fockbury, Worcestershire, England; died April 30, 1936, in Cambridge, England. English scholar, educator, and poet. Although considered one of the most brilliant and meticulous classical scholars of his time, Housman remains best known as a poet. With a melancholy and hopeless air, the author concentrated on such subjects as the inevitability of death, the aching losses of youth, and the destruction of beauty, love, and friendship. Biographers speculate that Housman's pessimism was caused by his experiences at school. The poet's failure at St. John's College, Oxford, despite his expertise in the classics, and his passionate, unhappy love for his friend Moses Jackson irrevocably altered his life. Though previously spirited and gregarious, Housman became shy and withdrawn and reflected his disappointment in his poetry. He worked as a clerk in the British Patent Office for ten years but continued his studies at night. Gradually establishing a scholarly reputation by publishing articles in academic journals, he was appointed to the chair of Latin at the University College, London, in 1892. Nine years later he moved to Trinity College, Cambridge, becoming the Kennedy Professor of Latin. During his career, Housman executed careful studies of the Latin works of Juvenal, Lucan, Manilius, and Propertius. Critics conjecture that the author's sparse poetry was influenced by his interest in Latin. As Housman only wrote his poetry when feeling ill, he left only three volumes at his death. His books of poetry are *A Shropshire Lad* (1896), *Last Poems* (1922), and *More Poems* (1936). Housman also wrote criticism, including *The Name and Nature of Poetry* (1933). *Residence:* Cambridge, England. *Biographical/critical sources: Cyclopedia of World Authors*, Harper, 1958; *Longman Companion to Twentieth Century Literature*, Longman, 1970; *The Reader's Companion to World Literature*, 2nd edition, New American Library, 1973; *Twentieth-Century Literary Criticism*, Volume 1, Gale, 1978.

HOWARD, Edward G(arfield)   1918(?)-1972

OBITUARY NOTICE: Born c. 1918; died of a heart attack, September 1, 1972, in Washington, D.C. Attorney, historian, book collector, bibliographer, and author. Howard was an expert on Maryland history and served as vice-president and rare book consultant of the Maryland Historical Society. His own collection of rare items on Maryland totalled more than twelve hundred and formed the basis for the author's 1968 book *Marylandia.* He also co-wrote and compiled *Star Spangled Books,* which appeared in 1972. Obituaries and other sources: *AB Bookman's Weekly,* October 9, 1972.

*   *   *

HOWARD, Leigh
See LEE HOWARD, Leon Alexander

*   *   *

HOWARD, Leon Alexander Lee
See LEE HOWARD, Leon Alexander

*   *   *

HOWELLS, Roscoe   1919-
(Barn Owl, Ben Brock)

PERSONAL: Born October 27, 1919, in Saundersfoot, Wales; son of Bertie John (a builder) and Elinor Maud (a nursemaid; maiden name, Jones) Howells; married Lucie Winifred Taylor, June 28, 1943 (died February 21, 1979); married Margaret Olive James (a nurse), October 1, 1979; children: Kevin Roscoe John. *Education:* Attended Cardiff Technical College, 1937-38. *Politics:* "Anti-Communist." *Religion:* United Reformed Church. *Home:* Cwmbrwyn, St. Clears, Carmarthen SA33 4HY, Wales.

CAREER: Farmer, 1943-75; writer, 1954——. Past chairman of Amroth Parish Council; member of Pembrokeshire executive committee of National Farmers Union, past chairman of its milk committee and parliamentary committee. *Member:* Guild of Agricultural Journalists, Institute of Journalists, English Guernsey Cattle Society (member of council), Llanwenog Sheep Society (past president), Pembrokshire Agricultural Society (president, 1977), Glamorgan County Cricket Club (vice-president), Marylebone Cricket Club, Farmers Club.

WRITINGS: Cliffs of Freedom, Gomer Press, 1961; *Farming in Wales* (juvenile), Gomer Press, 1965; *The Sounds Between* (nonfiction), Gomer Press, 1968; *Across the Sounds* (nonfiction), Gomer Press, 1972; *What Price Abortion?,* Gomer Press, 1973; *Total Community,* Five Arches Press, 1975; *Old Saundersfoot,* Gomer Press, 1977; *Heron's Mill* (fiction), Hutchinson, 1979, St. Martin's, 1980; *Tenby Old and New,* Gomer Press, 1981. Contributor to magazines, sometimes under pseudonyms Barn Owl and Ben Brock. Staff writer of *Farm News,* 1957-69.

WORK IN PROGRESS: The Bracelet, a children's book; *There 'Tis Then,* an autobiography; *Crickdam,* a novel.

SIDELIGHTS: Howells told *CA:* "I really went into writing to spell out the problems of the farming community when the government of the day began its usual postwar betrayal of this basic industry. This writing took the form of pseudonymous columns and eventually led to books about the countryside. I have little time for the professional countrymen who set themselves up as country people to write about country things because it is fashionable. I do, though, have tremendous sympathy with country people whose problems have never been properly understood by those who do not live by the land. My books have all been set in Pembrokeshire and concerned with its people.

"As a writer I am only impressed by the favorable comments of literary critics. I learned this long ago from my old friend, the late Howell Glynne, who was for years a principal bass at Covent Garden and Sadlers Wells Opera. Howell only read the reviews of those who wrote well of his performances. The others didn't know what they were talking about. Certainly they could not have shown him how to do it. The common sense of this attitude struck me forcibly when one of my early books, *Farming in Wales,* was reviewed. A highly intelligent reviewer in the *Times Educational Supplement* said it was refreshing that the author had been able to write a book for young people without once being guilty of talking down to the reader. On the same day a silly little twit in our provincial paper said that having written a book for young people the author had inevitably fallen into the trap of talking down to the reader. I am unable to produce cuttings of these reviews because I cannot be bothered to save them.

"I must emphasize that I am very conscious of the fact that reviews sell books and can be most helpful. My friends in the business have been marvelously kind and encouraging over the years. But we must retain our own private assessment of the competence of some reviewers to be entrusted with the task. As far as I can see, the bad reviews usually seem to come from would-be writers. And as often as not they are to be found in the avant-garde ranks of those who turn out the trash supported by the Arts Council or its offshoot, the Welsh Arts Council. This is not to suggest that I cannot accept criticism. Indeed, although I am not conscious of having been influenced by any other writer's work, I have certainly benefited from the harshly critical but constructive advice of Alexander Cordell. My debt to him can neither be expressed nor repaid.

"Having spent most of my life in farming and much of it writing, I would go so far as to say that, if the farming industry in the United Kingdom were not at least one hundred times more efficient than the publishing industry, the country would have been starving years ago. Further comment would only have me arrested on a charge of indecency."

AVOCATIONAL INTERESTS: Rugby, cricket.

*   *   *

HOWELLS, William Dean   1837-1920

BRIEF ENTRY: Born March 1, 1837, in Martin's Ferry, Ohio; died May 11, 1920, in New York, N.Y. American critic and novelist. Howells was respected for the accuracy of his criticism and for the encouragement he provided, as editor of *Atlantic Monthly,* for such promising writers as Mark Twain, Henry James, and Emily Dickinson. In *Criticism and Fiction* (1891), Howells said the writer's task is to present his own honest impressions, to write action without personal comment, to create perspective, to describe motive in all its complexity, and particularly to make the reader question and examine his own beliefs. He felt the purpose of fiction was not primarily to entertain, but to teach. Howells followed these tenets in his own novels. The first were international romances, soon followed by specifically American works. *A Modern Instance* (1882), sometimes considered his strongest novel, dealt with love turned to indifference and finally to hatred. *The Rise of Silas Lapham* (1885), his most popular, showed Howells's developing interest in social conflict, with Lapham's entry into society, his subsequent ruin, and his successful attempt to preserve his integrity. Later novels, like *The Traveler From Al-*

truria (1894), contained more explicit economic and social views, blaming man for the poverty and misery of his fellow men. Believing in the common man of America, Howells wrote about people from all walks of life, as in *A Hazard of New Fortunes* (1890). *Biographical/critical sources:* Clara M. Kirk and Rudolf Kirk, *William Dean Howells*, Twayne, 1962; William M. Gibson, *William Dean Howells*, University of Minnesota Press, 1967; Kermit Vanderbilt, *The Achievement of William Dean Howells*, Princeton University Press, 1968; *The McGraw-Hill Encyclopedia of World Biography*, McGraw, 1973.

* * *

HOWES, Wright   1882-1978

OBITUARY NOTICE: Born December 1, 1882, in Macon, Ga.; died March 22, 1978, in Augusta, Ga. Rare book dealer and bibliographer. For more than fifty years Howes was Chicago's leading rare book dealer. With the support of the Newberry Library he compiled an enthusiastically received descriptive checklist of rare and valuable Americana. The 1954 book was expanded in 1962 to list 11,620 titles and appeared as *U.S.-iana (1650-1950)*. Obituaries and other sources: *Library Quarterly*, July, 1953; *AB Bookman's Weekly*, April 10, 1978.

* * *

HSUN, Lu
See SHU-JEN, Chou

* * *

HUGHES, Alice   1899(?)-1977

OBITUARY NOTICE: Born c. 1899; died June 20, 1977, in White Plains, N.Y. Journalist and syndicated columnist. Hughes's columns, "A Woman's New York" and "You Can Be Beautiful," were syndicated by King Features. She wrote on fashion and traveled widely to report on the lives of women in other cultures. Obituaries and other sources: Ishbel Ross, *Ladies of the Press*, Arno Press, 1974; *New York Times*, June 21, 1977; *Time*, July 4, 1977.

* * *

HUGHES, Dorothy B(elle)   1904-
(Dorothy Belle Flanagan)

PERSONAL: Born August 10, 1904, in Kansas City, Mo.; daughter of Frank Sylvester and Calla (Haley) Flanagan; married Levi Allen Hughes, 1932 (died, 1975); children: Holly Hughes Morelli, Antony Allen, Suzy Amanda Hughes Mackinnon. *Education:* University of Missouri, B.J., 1924; graduate study at University of New Mexico; also attended Columbia University. *Religion:* Roman Catholic. *Home:* 113 Zia Rd. W., Santa Fe, N.M. 87501. *Agent:* Blanche C. Gregory, Inc., 2 Tudor City Pl., New York, N.Y. 10017.

CAREER: Crime reviewer, 1940-79, with *Albuquerque Tribune*, Albuquerque, N.M., *Los Angeles News and Mirror,* Los Angeles, Calif., *New York Herald Tribune,* New York, N.Y., and *Los Angeles Times,* Los Angeles. Member of Museum of New Mexico Foundation; past member of faculty at University of California, Los Angeles. *Member:* Mystery Writers of America, Crime Writers Association (England), Old Santa Fe Association. *Awards, honors:* Edgar Allan Poe Award, 1950, for mystery criticism and grand master award, 1978, for body of work, both from Mystery Writers of America; regents' medal from University of New Mexico, 1979, for recognition of literary work with particular mention of *Pueblo on the Mesa*.

WRITINGS—Crime novels; published by Duell, Sloan & Pearce, except as noted: *The So Blue Marble*, 1940; *The Cross-Eyed Bear*, 1940; *The Bamboo Blonde*, 1941; *The Fallen Sparrow*, 1942; *The Blackbirder*, 1943; *The Delicate Ape*, 1944; *Johnnie*, 1944; *Dread Journey*, 1945; *Ride the Pink Horse*, 1946; *The Scarlet Imperial*, Mystery Book, 1946, reprinted as *Kiss for a Killer*, Spivak, 1954; *In a Lonely Place*, 1947; *The Big Barbecue*, Random House, 1949; *The Candy Kid*, 1950; *The Davidian Report*, 1952, reprinted as *The Body on the Bench*, Dell, 1955; *The Expendable Man*, Random House, 1963.

Nonfiction: *Pueblo on the Mesa: The First Fifty Years of the University of New Mexico*, University of New Mexico Press, 1939; *Erle Stanley Gardner: The Case of the Real Perry Mason*, Morrow, 1978.

Under name Dorothy Belle Flanagan: *Dark Certainty* (poems), Yale University Press, 1931.

Contributor of stories to magazines, including *Saint, Gamma, Ellery Queen's Mystery Magazine,* and *Cosmopolitan*.

WORK IN PROGRESS: Research for a book on Los Alamos, N.M.

SIDELIGHTS: Three of Hughes's books were adapted as motion pictures: "The Fallen Sparrow" starring John Garfield, released by RKO, 1943; "Ride The Pink Horse" starring Robert Montgomery, released by Universal, 1947; and "In a Lonely Place" starring Humphrey Bogart, released by Columbia, 1950.

Hughes told *CA:* "I have written since I was six years old and have published since I was in high school. Book reviewing is more fun than book writing, as you get to both read and write. But my family has always been the most fun. I have ten grandchildren and two great-grandchildren. The older ones now travel with me (in turns) to Europe and Hawaii and New York."

* * *

HULL, Charles
See CHARLES, Gordon H(ull)

* * *

HULME, Kathryn   1900-1981

OBITUARY NOTICE—See index for *CA* sketch: Born January 6, 1900, in San Francisco, Calif.; died August 25, 1981, in Lihue, Hawaii. Administrator and author. Hulme was known for her best-selling book *The Nun's Story*, which sold seven hundred thousand copies and was adapted into a movie starring Audrey Hepburn and Peter Finch. *The Nun's Story* was about Marie Louise Habets, Hulme's friend and business partner. A nurse and a nun, Habets worked in a mental institution in Belgium and in a Congo bush hospital before asking to be released from her vows in order to fight with the Resistance underground against the Nazis. Habets met Hulme while the author was serving with the United Nations Relief and Rehabilitation Administration and with the International Refugees Organization as the deputy director of relocation camps in Bavaria. Like Hemingway and Fitzgerald, Hulme was an expatriate living in Paris before World War II. During the war, however, she worked as a welder in a California shipyard. She wrote nine books, most based on her own experiences. One of her books, *The Wild Place*, won the *Atlantic Monthly*'s first prize for nonfiction in 1953. Her other works include *How's the Road, Annie's Captain, We Lived as Children, Desert Night,* and *Undiscovered Country: A Spiritual Adventure*. Obituaries and other sources: *New York Times*, August 28, 1981; *Chicago Tribune*, August 29, 1981; *Publishers Weekly*, September 11, 1981; *AB Bookman's Weekly*, September 14, 1981.

HULSE, Erroll 1931-

PERSONAL: Born March 3, 1931, in Fort Beaufort, South Africa; son of Edward Vernon (an architect) and Marie (a company director; maiden name, Leibbrandt) Hulse; married Lynette Hendry (a director of a publishing company), February 6, 1954; children: Sharon Ann, Michelle Clare, Neil Andrew, Joanne Sarah. Education: University of Pretoria, M.I.A., 1953; attended London Bible College, 1954-57. Home and office: Cuckfield Baptist Church, 5 Fairford Close, Haywards Heath, West Sussex RH16 3EF, England.

CAREER: Ordained Baptist minister, 1962; Banner of Truth Trust, London, England, manager, 1957-67; Cuckfield Baptist Church, Haywards Heath, England, pastor, 1962—. Director of Carey Publications, 1971—, and Evangelical Press, 1977—. Co-organizer of Carey Conference for Ministers and Family Conference, 1970—; co-organizer of Annual Evangelical and Reformed Studies Conference (interdenominational and multiracial) in South Africa, 1971—. Member: Royal Institute of British Architects (associate).

WRITINGS: Billy Graham: The Pastor's Dilemma, Ian Allan, 1966, Reiner Publications, 1979; The Restoration of Israel, Henry Walter, 1968; An Introduction to the Baptists, Carey Publications, 1972; Baptism and Church Membership, Carey Publications, 1972; The Free Offer of the Gospel, Carey Publications, 1973; (editor and contributor) The Way Ahead, Carey Publications, 1975; (editor and contributor) Local Church Practice, Carey Publications, 1978; The Believer's Experience, Zondervan, 1980; Unity: The Covenant and Baptism, Carey Publications, 1981. Editor of Reformation Today, 1970—.

SIDELIGHTS: Hulse told CA: "I am vitally concerned with the advance of worldwide growth of Reformed Baptists, the planting of churches, and in this connection I travel to Australia, New Zealand, South Africa, Israel, France, the Netherlands, the United States and Canada, and all over England. I sustain correspondence with many in these and other countries.

"My ambition is to write in an edifying way for ordinary people, to interpret the Gospel for those who would designate themselves non-Christians. In this particular area, I have enjoyed very little encouragement having better facilities and increasing success in writing for ordinary Christians. In this I aim to keep abreast with scholarship. I buy and avidly read innumerable books on my subject of expositing the Bible. But I also read secular books not only for enjoyment but to learn from the writing style of others.

"My view is that authors emerge late in life. If you reflect on this, you will see that it is true. It was certainly true of Winston Churchill. But take Alexander Solzhenitsyn as an example. He lived through agonizing experiences. He assimilated materials by eye-gate and ear-gate, analyzed them and studied ways in which these experiences could be best described in words. Finally, after surviving a violent war, labor camps, and cancer wards, he obtained the longed-for opportunity to fulfil his ambition to write. It was those many years of suffering that equipped him with astonishing perseverence, hard work, and sheer grit that is essential for success as an author.

"I constantly pray for long life combined with good health. Some believe it is pious to wear out for God. I believe that is basically noble and correct, but prefer to combine wearing out with lasting out because writing takes so long to accomplish—that is, writing of quality. Very often we are at work (as I am now) when everyone else is asleep.

"Now in 1981 when I am at the half-century mark, I find much fulfillment in writing. In earlier years I threw a lot of my work into the garbage can in disgust. Now I spend much more time thinking and trying to project the particular work into a complete perspective before getting down to paper.

"Being a pastor and preacher, I have a tremendous advantage in having to depend always on the power of the Holy Spirit for success. Failure drives me straight back to the Paraclete. Of course finding adequate time is a problem but to me it would be fatal to be removed from an intimate and constant experience of a wide diversity of people. It is that vital factor which encourages me to write in a relevant, lively, and interesting way. I do not agree with those who steal time from their families. A happy home is dependent on fellowship with wife and children.

"Preparing work for the printer is like sculpture—you carve, chip, and refine a work into shape. As an architect I learned early from my perfectionist architect father to wield a soft pencil. Three instruments and lots of A4 paper form my armory. The three instruments: a 2B pencil (with lots in reserve), a soft rubber eraser, and a handy little pencil sharpener which collects the shavings which soon pile up as I get under way.

"My inflexible ambition is constant improvement and that eventual goal to write so well for unbelievers that they will be persuaded."

AVOCATIONAL INTERESTS: Squash, jogging.

*   *   *

HUNT, Geoffrey 1915(?)-1974

OBITUARY NOTICE: Editor. Hunt was in charge of books on naval history and religion at Oxford University Press and figured importantly in the publication of the New English Bible. Obituaries and other sources: AB Bookman's Weekly, October 7, 1974.

*   *   *

HUNT, Kenneth E(dward) 1917(?)-1978

OBITUARY NOTICE: Born c. 1917; died January 4, 1978. Agriculturist, educator, and author of books in his field. Among Hunt's books are The State of British Agriculture, 1959-60 and Poultry and Eggs in Britain, 1961-62. Obituaries and other sources: AB Bookman's Weekly, March 20, 1978.

*   *   *

HUNTER, Michael (Cyril William) 1949-

PERSONAL: Born April 22, 1949, in Sussex, England; son of Francis (a priest) and Olive (an artist; maiden name, Williams) Hunter. Education: Jesus College, Cambridge, B.A., 1971, M.A., 1975; Worcester College, Oxford, M.A., 1975, D.Phil., 1975. Home: 106 Colvestone Cres., Hackney, London E8 2LJ, England. Office: Department of History, Birkbeck College, University of London, Malet St., London WC1E 7HX, England.

CAREER: Oxford University, Worcester College, Oxford, England, research fellow, 1972-75; University of Reading, Reading, England, research fellow, 1975-76; University of London, Birkbeck College, London, England, lecturer in history, 1976—. Member: Society of Antiquaries (fellow).

WRITINGS: John Aubrey and the Realm of Learning, Duckworth, 1975; Science and Society in Restoration England,

Cambridge University Press, 1981. Contributor to scholarly journals. Member of editorial board of *Book Collector*.

WORK IN PROGRESS: Research on atheism in early modern England and on the thought and writing of John Evelyn, 1620-1706.

* * *

HUNTER, Milton R(eed)   1902-1975

OBITUARY NOTICE: Born October 25, 1902, in Holden, Utah; died in 1975. Educator, church official, and author. Hunter began as a teacher and school administrator in Utah, then became a professor at the Church of Jesus Christ of Latter-day Saints Institute at Utah State University. He served for three decades as a member of the Latter-day Saints First Council of Seventy. Recognized as a leading authority on Mormon and Utah history, he was a member of the Utah Historical Society, the Archeological Society of Utah, and the Sons of Utah Pioneers. Hunter wrote more than twenty books in his field, including *The Gospel Through the Ages, Utah in Her Western Setting, The Utah Story, Archeology and the Book of Mormon,* and *Brigham Young the Colonizer*. Obituaries and other sources: *Who's Who in America,* 39th edition, Marquis, 1976. (Date of death provided by wife, Ferne Gardner Hunter.)

* * *

HURLEY, John J(erome)   1930-
(Duffy Carpenter, S. S. Rafferty)

PERSONAL: Born August 4, 1930, in New Haven, Conn.; son of William J. and Helen (McNierney) Hurley; married Catherine Tinker; children: one son, one daughter. *Education:* Attended Columbia University and University of Bridgeport. *Home:* 231 East 76th St., New York, N.Y. 10021.

CAREER: Bridgeport Post Telegram, Bridgeport, Conn., reporter, 1955-57; Rozene Advertising, Bridgeport and Boston, Mass., senior vice-president, 1957-61; Gaynor & Ducas Advertising, New York, N.Y., vice-president, 1961-70; writer. *Military service:* U.S. Marine Corps, 1951-54; served in Korea. *Member:* Authors Guild.

WRITINGS: (Under pseudonym S. S. Rafferty) *Fatal Flourishes* (stories), Avon, 1979. Work represented in anthologies, including *Ellery Queen's Crime Wave,* Putnam, 1976. Contributor of stories to magazines (under pseudonyms Duffy Carpenter and S. S. Rafferty), including *Alfred Hitchcock's Mystery Magazine, Mystery Monthly,* and *Ellery Queen's Mystery Magazine*.

* * *

HUTTNER, Matthew   1915-1975

OBITUARY NOTICE: Born July 15, 1915, in Baltimore, Md.; died July 13, 1975, in Greenwich, Conn. Publisher. A former chairman of the Overseas Press Club, Huttner founded Pyramid Books in 1949 and served as publisher of Pyramid Books and president of Pyramid Communications, Inc. Obituaries and other sources: *Who's Who in World Jewry: A Biographical Dictionary of Outstanding Jews,* Pitman, 1972; *New York Times,* July 14, 1975; *AB Bookman's Weekly,* July 28, 1975; *Publishers Weekly,* August 4, 1975.

* * *

HUYSMANS, Charles Marie Georges   1848-1907
(Joris-Karl Huysmans)

BRIEF ENTRY: Born February 5, 1848, in Paris, France; died of cancer, May 12, 1907, in Paris, France; buried at Montparnasse Cemetery in Paris. French novelist and art critic. Huysmans has been called a leader of the French decadents and a founder of the naturalist school, but his independence led him away from both. His work of the early 1870's was influenced by Baudelaire and showed a preoccupation with the fantastic and grotesque. Later, as a member of Zola's naturalist group, he wrote the story "Sac au dos" (1880), which is considered one of the best examples of that group's writing. Though Huysmans used naturalist ideals as a base, his novels were too violent and individualistic to be classified as naturalist. Most of his books concerned events of his day: *Down the Stream* (1882) showed the spiritual and intellectual pessimism of the postwar years; *Against the Grain* (1884), his most important and best-known novel, reflected the decadent style of contemporary writers and artists; *La-Bas* (1891) described the revival of the occult in the 1880's; and *En Route* (1895) told of the Roman Catholic revival of the 1890's. Huysmans was also respected as a perceptive art critic, one of the first of his time to appreciate the impressionist movement. *Biographical/critical sources: Encyclopedia of World Literature in the Twentieth Century,* updated edition, Ungar, 1967; George R. Ridge, *Joris Karl Huysmans,* Twayne, 1968; *The McGraw-Hill Encyclopedia of World Biography,* McGraw, 1973.

* * *

HUYSMANS, Joris-Karl
See HUYSMANS, Charles Marie Georges

* * *

HYDE, Fillmore   1896(?)-1970

OBITUARY NOTICE: Born c. 1896; died January 25, 1970, in Madeira. In the 1950's Hyde was director of New York University Press. His book, *The Ritz Carltons,* appeared in 1927. Obituaries and other sources: *AB Bookman's Weekly,* March 2, 1970.

* * *

HYDE, W. Lewis   1945-

PERSONAL: Born October 16, 1945, in Boston, Mass.; son of Walter Lewis (a physicist) and Elizabeth Lee (a librarian; maiden name, Sanford) Hyde; married Patricia Auster Vigderman (an editor), June, 1974. *Education:* University of Minnesota, B.A., 1967; University of Iowa, M.A., 1972. *Home:* 122 Winsor Ave., Watertown, Mass. 02172. *Agent:* Georges Borchardt, Inc., 136 East 57th St., New York, N.Y. 10022.

CAREER: University of Iowa, Iowa City, instructor in literature, 1969-71; free-lance writer, 1971-74; Cambridge Hospital, Cambridge, Mass., alcoholism counselor, 1974-76; writer, 1977—. Visiting lecturer at Tufts University, 1977. *Member:* Lepidopterist Society. *Awards, honors:* Prize from Academy of American Poets, 1966; National Endowment for the Arts fellowship, 1976-77; award from Translation Center at Columbia University, 1978, for translation of Vincente Aleixandre's *Mundo a solas;* National Endowment for the Humanities fellowship, 1979; fellow of Massachusetts Council on the Arts and Humanities, 1980.

WRITINGS: This Error Is the Sign of Love (poetry broadside), Applewood Press, 1978; (translator with Robert Bly, and editor) *Twenty Poems of Vicente Aleixandre,* Harper, 1979; (editor and contributor of translations) *A Longing for the Light: Selected Poems of Vicente Aleixandre,* Harper, 1979; (translator with David Unger) *Vicente Aleixandre, World Alone (1932-*

34), Penmaen Press, 1981; *The Gift: Poetry and the Erotic Life of Property*, Random House, 1982.

Work represented in anthologies, including *The Pushcart Prize, 1976: Best of the Small Presses*, edited by Bill Henderson, Avon, 1976; *Roots and Wings: Poetry From Spain, 1900-1975*, edited by Hardie St. Martin, Harper, 1976. Contributor of about seventy translations, poems, articles, and reviews to magazines and newspapers, including *Kenyon Review, American Poetry Review, Paris Review, New Letters, Lamp in the Spine*, and *Ironwood*.

WORK IN PROGRESS: Hotel With Birds, poems.

*   *   *

HYER, Paul Van 1926-

PERSONAL: Born June 2, 1926, in Ogden, Utah; son of Ariel C. and Johanna (Van Woerkom) Hyer; married Harriet Jones, December 15, 1948; children: Paulette Hyer Patterson, Scott, Eric, Luanne Hyer Olsen, Jana Hyer Davies, Carol Hyer Toone, Annette, David. *Education:* Brigham Young University, B.A., 1951; University of California, Berkeley, M.A., 1953, Ph.D., 1960. *Politics:* "Independent, with democratic leanings." *Religion:* Church of Jesus Christ of Latter-day Saints (Mormons). *Home:* 55 North 900 E., Provo, Utah 84602. *Office:* Department of History, Brigham Young University, Provo, Utah 84602.

CAREER: Brigham Young University, Provo, Utah, assistant professor, 1958-63, associate professor, 1963-66, professor of history and Asian studies, 1966—, coordinator of Asian studies program, 1961-67. Visiting professor at University of Michigan, 1961, and Cheng-chih University, 1971-72. Researcher at Toyo Bunko, 1963-64, and Academia Sinica, 1966-67. Member of screening committee of Institute of International Education. *Military service:* U.S. Navy, aviation electrician, 1944-46. *Member:* Permanent International Altaistic Conference (PIAC), Association for Asian Studies (president of western conference, 1974-75; executive secretary, 1980—), Mongolia Society, Royal Central Asian Society. *Awards, honors:* Maeser Award from Brigham Young University Alumni Association, 1973, for creative research.

WRITINGS: Papers of the CIC Far Eastern Language Institute, University of Michigan, 1963; (contributor) Richard D. Burns, editor, *The Diplomats in Crisis*, American Bibliographical Center-Clio Press, 1974; (contributor) W. A. Veenhoven, editor, *Case Studies on Human Rights and Fundamental Freedoms*, Volume I, Nijhoff, 1975; (contributor) Harry Halen, editor, *Altaica: Memmoirs de la Societe Finno-Ougrienne*, [Helsinki], 1977; (with Sechin Jagchid) *Mongolia's Culture and Society*, Westview Press, 1980. Contributor to *Encyclopedia Americana*. Contributor to Asian studies journals. Editor of *Mongolia Society Bulletin*, 1969—.

WORK IN PROGRESS: A History of Mongolia, publication expected in 1983.

SIDELIGHTS: Hyer commented: "My family was intimately involved in the westward movement into the American frontier, and I have had a great continuing interest in comparative frontier development studies in general and the China frontiers of Mongolia and Tibet in particular. This includes a concern for minority peoples and their frequent tragic fates."

I

IBSEN, Henrik (Johan) 1828-1906
(Brynjolf Bjarme)

BRIEF ENTRY: Born March 20, 1828, in Skien, Norway; died May 23, 1906, in Oslo, Norway. Norwegian poet, playwright, and essayist. One of the most influential playwrights of his time, Ibsen broke away from the romantic tradition of nineteenth-century drama with his realistic portrayals of individuals in the modern world. Ibsen worked as a theatrical adviser and director in Norway during the 1850's while staging many of his own plays. These early works, written in the Scandinavian romantic-historical tradition, brought him little attention; so, frustrated as a playwright, Ibsen left Norway in 1865 for Europe, where he spent most of the next thirty years. During that time he began writing the "social plays" that gained him worldwide attention while shocking audiences with their realism. "A Doll's House" (1879) treated the theme of women's emancipation; "Ghosts" (1881), a psychological drama, discussed venereal disease; and "Hedda Gabler" (1890), Ibsen's last social play, concerned a frustrated aristocratic woman and the vengeance she takes on herself and those around her. Among Ibsen's other well-known plays are "Peer Gynt" (1867) and the realistic dramas "The Pillars of Society" (1877), "The Wild Duck" (1884), and "Rosmersholm" (1886). Ibsen's later plays, including "The Master Builder" (1897) and "When We Dead Waken" (1900), were predominantly symbolic dramas. *Biographical/critical sources:* George Bernard Shaw, *The Quintessence of Ibsenism,* Dramabooks, 1957; Herman Weigand, *The Modern Ibsen,* Dutton, 1960; Rolf Fjelde, editor, *Ibsen: A Collection of Critical Essays,* Prentice-Hall, 1965; Muriel C. Bradbrook, *Ibsen, the Norwegian,* Shoe String Press, 1966; Alex Bolckmans and others, *The International Ibsen: Contemporary Approaches to Ibsen,* Humanities Press, 1967; *Twentieth-Century Literary Criticism,* Volume 2, Gale, 1979.

* * *

IERARDI, Francis B. 1886-1970

OBITUARY NOTICE: Born in 1886; died September 14, 1970, in Somerville, Mass. Newspaper editor. In 1927 Ierardi founded the *Weekly News,* the Western Hemisphere's first Braille newspaper. Ierardi had been blinded at twelve years of age. Obituaries and other sources: *New York Times,* September 17, 1970; *AB Bookman's Weekly,* October 26, 1970.

IGLEHART, Louis Tillman 1915-1981

OBITUARY NOTICE: Born March 2, 1915, in Dawson Springs, Ky.; died May 29, 1981, in Knoxville, Tenn. Journalist and publishing executive. Prior to and following his five-year service with the U.S. Army Air Force during World War II, Iglehart worked as reporter and editor for various newspapers in Kentucky and Tennessee. He served as editor at the University of Tennessee's news bureau beginning in 1949, and in 1957 he became the first director of the University of Tennessee Press. Following his retirement from this position, Iglehart served on the board of directors of the Association of American University Presses and on the advisory board of the Appalachian Consortium. Obituaries and other sources: *Who's Who in America,* 40th edition, Marquis, 1978; *Publishers Weekly,* June 19, 1981.

* * *

IKEDA, Kiyoshi 1928-

BRIEF ENTRY: Born April 5, 1928, in Ewa, Hawaii. American social psychologist, educator, and author. Ikeda began teaching at Oberlin College in 1958, becoming a professor of sociology in 1967. He has been a fellow of the Social Security Administration and Russell Sage Foundation. His writings include *Equilibrium Models and Social Mobility* (University Press of Hawaii, 1965) and *Social Process in Hawaii. Address:* Department of Sociology and Anthropology, Oberlin College, Oberlin, Ohio 44074. *Biographical/critical sources: American Men and Women of Science: The Social and Behavioral Sciences,* 12th edition, Bowker, 1973.

* * *

ILG, Frances L(illian) 1902-1981

OBITUARY NOTICE: Born October 11, 1902, in Oak Park, Ill.; died July 26, 1981, in Manitowish Waters, Wis. Physician, educator, columnist, and author. A recognized authority on child behavior and development, Ilg began her career as a pediatrician associated with Dr. Arnold Gesell, a pioneer in the study of infant and child behavior. Ilg was co-founder of the Gesell Institute of Child Development, later called the Gesell Institute of Human Development. With fellow physician Louise B. Ames, Ilg wrote a syndicated question-and-answer column, "Child Behavior," that was popular with American parents. Ilg co-wrote more than twenty books, many of them best-sellers, detailing human development and behavior from infancy through adolescence. Among these works are *The First Five Years of Life, The Child From Five to Ten, Youth: The Years From Ten to Sixteen, School Readiness,* and *Parents Ask.* Obituaries and other sources: *American Authors and Books, 1640 to the Present Day,* 3rd revised edition, Crown, 1972; *Who's Who of American Women,* 8th edition, Marquis, 1974; *New York Times,* July 28, 1981; *Time,* August 10, 1981.

* * *

IMBRIE, Katherine P(almer) 1952-

PERSONAL: Born September 30, 1952, in New London, Conn.; daughter of John (a professor of geology) and Barbara (Zeller) Imbrie. *Education:* Attended Mount Holyoke College, 1970-72; Wheaton College, Norton, Mass., B.A., 1974. *Home:* 155 Benefit St., Providence, R.I. 02903.

CAREER: Museum of Science, Boston, Mass., assistant editor of publications, 1976-78; Wheaton College, Norton, Mass., assistant director of admissions, 1978-79; Rhode Island School of Design, Providence, assistant director of news bureau, 1979—. *Awards, honors:* Science book award from Phi Beta Kappa, 1979, for *Ice Ages: Solving the Mystery.*

WRITINGS: (With father, John Imbrie) *Ice Ages: Solving the Mystery,* Ridley Enslow, 1979. Contributor to *Providence Journal, George Street Journal,* and *Artcraft.*

WORK IN PROGRESS: The Queen's Fort, a historical novel of nineteenth-century New England.

* * *

IMRIE, Richard
See PRESSBURGER, Emeric

* * *

INGERSOLL, Robert Franklin 1933-

PERSONAL: Born May 28, 1933, in Siloam Springs, Ark.; son of Darrell Leon and Lucille Ella (Henry) Ingersoll; married Sue Southgate Smith, 1953 (divorced, 1954); married Carolyn Jane Adams, 1957 (divorced, 1960); married Inge Hochscheid, 1963 (divorced, 1971); children: Mark Steven. *Education:* Attended University of New Mexico and University of California, Los Angeles; received B.A. from University of California, Santa Barbara; received German language certificate from Heidelberg University. *Religion:* Agnostic. *Home:* 2695 Foothill Rd., Santa Barbara, Calif. 93105; and Rolandstrasse 74, Cologne, West Germany 5. *Office:* McGraw-Hill World News, Bonn Bureau, Pressehaus 1. Heussallee 2-10, Bonn, West Germany 53.

CAREER/WRITINGS: Overseas Weekly and *Overseas Family,* Munich, West Germany, reporter, 1962-65; free-lance foreign correspondent in Bonn, West Germany, for *Toronto Star, Jerusalem Post,* and *Medical Tribune,* 1965-67; McGraw-Hill World News, Bonn, Bonn bureau chief, 1967—. Regular contributor of articles to McGraw-Hill publications, including *Business Week, Engineering News-Record, Medical World News, Scientific Research,* and *American Machinist.* Artist. *Military service:* U.S. Army, 1957-59; received U.S. Armed Forces media award.

* * *

INGHAM, Richard Arnison 1935-

PERSONAL: Born November 15, 1935, in Halifax, England;

son of Gerald Bryan (in business; a master dyer) and Nancy Charlton (Arnison) Ingham; married Aureole Merle Price (divorced, 1977); children: Joyana Mary, William Rupert, Flavia Elizabeth. *Education:* Peterhouse, Cambridge, B.A., 1957, M.A., 1961. *Religion:* Church of England. *Home:* 26 Devonshire Buildings, Bath, Avon, England. *Agent:* Sheri Safran, 21 Ladbroke Gardens, London W.11, England.

CAREER: Worked as trainee and then manager of Elland Finishing Co., 1959-61; writer, 1961-63; teacher at school in Suffolk, England, 1963-65, and at school in Mbabane, Swaziland, 1965-68; writer in Greece, 1968-69; salesman with Hobbs Padgett Group, 1969-70; associated with Ipswich Civic College, 1970-75, and Lewes Technical College, 1975-76; lecturer in English and technical/management communications at Chippenham Technological College, 1977—. Free-lance producer and writer for Swaziland Broadcasting Service, 1965-68; lecturer in programming for International Computers, 1970. *Military service:* Royal Air Force, Education Corps, 1957-59. *Member:* Institute of Scientific and Technical Communication.

WRITINGS: Yoris (novel), Allison & Busby, 1974; (with J. M. Buffton) *Making Contact,* Holt, Volume I, 1979, Volume II, 1981, workbook for Volume II, 1979; *Fifteen From Twenty-Two: Poems, 1955-1976,* privately printed, 1979.

Plays: "Love and War" (three-act), first produced in Mbabane, Swaziland, at Theatre Club, December, 1969; "Fruitie Pie" (one-act), first produced in Bath, England, at Metro Theatre, August, 1980.

WORK IN PROGRESS: Faking, a novel; *Just Holding On,* a comic novel; "Passion," a one-act play.

SIDELIGHTS: Ingham wrote: "I write because I need to do so. I always hoped to live as a writer and nothing else, but good luck has prevented me from doing so. However, I have plans. . . .''

* * *

IPPOLITO, Donna 1945-

PERSONAL: Born May 31, 1945, in Chicago, Ill.; daughter of Charles (a machinist) and Mary (Spicci) Trankina; married Vincent Ippolito, August, 1968 (divorced, 1973). *Education:* Northern Illinois University, B.A. (summa cum laude), 1968; attended Roosevelt University, University of Chicago, Alliance Francaise, and Cuahnahuac Institute. *Residence:* Chicago, Ill.

CAREER: Swallow Press, Chicago, Ill., began as associate editor, became senior editor, 1968—. Editor for Consumer Guide Publications, 1981—. Workshop instructor; lecturer; gives readings from her works. *Member:* Poets and Writers.

WRITINGS: Erotica (prose poem), Artists and Alchemists, 1975; *Uprising of the Twenty Thousand* (monograph on women's history), Motheroot Publications, 1979.

Work represented in anthologies, including *Sprays of Rubies: An Anthology of Women's Writing,* edited by Rochelle Holt, Ragnarok, 1975; *Women in Writing Anthology,* United Sisters, 1975; *Networks: An Anthology,* Ragnarok, 1978. Contributor of stories, poems, articles, and reviews to magazines, including *Womanspirit, Oyez Review, Primavera, East West Journal, Small Press Review,* and *Sunday Clothes.* Founding editor of *Black Maria,* 1967-73.

WORK IN PROGRESS: The Man Who Loved Women, a novel; research on mythology and on travel in Mexico.

SIDELIGHTS: Donna Ippolito wrote: "Though fiction is my major interest, language probably interests me more even than character and plot. Language is one of the means we have for discovering what is yet unknown. Because of this particular interest in language, my narratives are often more condensed than some other kinds of fiction, and there is a greater emphasis on image, word rhythms, and the mythic dimensions of experience. My life and my writing have been much influenced by the ideas of C. G. Jung. For this reason, I believe the artist has the function of entering the unknown and bringing back to the collective the values it needs to remain vital.

"The writer (or artist) can provide much needed spiritual nourishment by presenting a version of reality that includes image, imagination. All thought and action have their origins in image. Only through imaginative activity can we uncover possibilities for change and meaning. The writers I most admire are Frank Waters, Colette, Pablo Neruda, and D. H. Lawrence.''

*　　　*　　　*

ISHAK, Yusof bin   1910(?)-1970

OBITUARY NOTICE: Born c. 1910; died of a heart attack, 1970, in Singapore. Public official, journalist, and editor. In 1963 Ishek became Singapore's first president following the city-state's independence from Britain. Ishak's newspaper, *Utusan Melayu,* was instrumental in forwarding Singapore's fight for independence. Obituaries and other sources: *Time,* December 7, 1970.

J

JABLONSKI, Ronald E. 1929-

BRIEF ENTRY: Born January 16, 1929, in Chicago, Ill. American educator and author. Jablonski worked as an electronics scientist at the Naval Research Laboratory and in industry before turning to teaching. He has been a member of the management faculty at University of Illinois since 1969 and an associate of Columbia University's Seminar on Technology and Social Change since 1964. He wrote *Production Management*, 3rd edition (McGraw, 1969) and *Management of Operational Systems*. *Address:* College of Business Administration, University of Illinois at Chicago Circle, Box 4348, Chicago, Ill. 60680. *Biographical/critical sources: American Men and Women of Science: The Social and Behavioral Sciences,* 12th edition, Bowker, 1973.

*   *   *

JACKSON, A(lexander) B(rooks) 1925-

PERSONAL: Born April 18, 1925, in New Haven, Conn.; son of Alexander Brooks and Maybelle West (Whittaker) Jackson. *Education:* Yale University, B.F.A., 1953, M.F.A., 1955. *Religion:* Episcopal. *Home:* 700 A Raleigh Sq., Norfolk, Va. 23507. *Office:* Department of Art, Old Dominion University, Hampton Blvd., Norfolk, Va. 23508.

CAREER: Southern University, Baton Rouge, La., instructor in art, 1955-56; Norfolk State College, Norfolk, Va., assistant professor of art, 1956-67; Old Dominion University, Norfolk, professor of art, 1967—. Artist-in-residence at Living Arts Center, Dayton, Ohio, summer, 1969, and Dartmouth College, Hanover, N.H., 1971; lecturer. Vice-chairman of Norfolk Fine Arts Committee, 1968-72.

WRITINGS: *As I See Ghent: A Visual Essay,* Donning, 1979.

WORK IN PROGRESS: A visual essay entitled *As I See Rockbridge County; Porch People: Paintings, Drawings, Photographs.*

SIDELIGHTS: Jackson commented: "Each painting or drawing begins as a technical puzzle, most often coupled with something I've seen that makes me want to make one of those! Painting is in part a way of sharing, as teaching is sharing."

BIOGRAPHICAL/CRITICAL SOURCES: *National Republic,* October, 1963; *American Artist,* February, 1968.

JACKSON, Arthur 1921-

BRIEF ENTRY: Born December 19, 1921, in South Shields, England. British publisher's manager and author. Jackson has written for music recording magazines. His books include *The Hollywood Musical* (Secker & Warburg, 1971), *Sinatra and the Great Song Stylists* (1972), *The World of the Big Bands: The Sweet and Singing Years* (Arco, 1977), and *The Book of Musicals: From "Show Boat" to "A Chorus Line"—Broadway, Off-Broadway, London* (Mitchell Beazley, 1977). *Address:* Whiteoaks, 80 Beach Rd., Carlyon Bay, Austell, Cornwall, England. *Biographical/critical sources: New York Times Book Review,* December 4, 1977.

*   *   *

JACKSON, Carole

PERSONAL: Born in Los Angeles, Calif.; daughter of G. Arnold Stevens (a surgeon) and Jean E. Halliburton (a writer and editor); divorced; children: Alexander Bartsch, Megan Elizabeth Bartsch. *Education:* Stanford University, B.A., 1963; State University of New York at New Paltz, M.S., 1965. *Home and office:* 6817 Tennyson Dr., McLean, Va. 22101.

CAREER: Color Me Beautiful, Inc. (color consulting firm), McLean, Va., president, 1980—. Public speaker; guest on television and radio programs. *Member:* Executive Link, Junior League.

WRITINGS: *Color Me Beautiful,* Acropolis Books, 1980.

WORK IN PROGRESS: Two books.

SIDELIGHTS: Jackson told *CA:* "*Color Me Beautiful* is a self-help book for women, giving information on how to analyze your own coloring and determine which palette of colors is most flattering for clothing, makeup, and hair. There are four categories of coloring and a person is either a 'winter,' 'summer,' 'spring,' or 'autumn.' The book is an outcropping of my consulting business. We train Color Me Beautiful consultants all over the United States."

BIOGRAPHICAL/CRITICAL SOURCES: *People,* August 31, 1981.

*   *   *

JACKSON, Gordon 1934-

PERSONAL: Born April 14, 1934, in Cleethorpes, England;

225

son of Herbert James and Doris (Schofield) Jackson; married Hazel L. Kirk, 1959; children: Helen, Nicholas, Adrian. *Education:* University of London, B.A. (with honors), 1955; University of Hull, diploma in education, 1959, Ph.D., 1960. *Politics:* Socialist. *Religion:* Methodist. *Home:* 331 Albert Dr., Glasgow G41 5EA, Scotland. *Office:* Department of History, University of Strathclyde, McCance Building, 16 Richmond St., Glasgow G1 1XQ, Scotland.

CAREER: University of Strathclyde, Glasgow, Scotland, lecturer, 1965-76, senior lecturer in history, 1976-81, reader, 1981—. *Member:* Economic History Society (member of council, 1979—).

WRITINGS: Grimsby and the Haven Company, Corporation of Grimsby, 1970; *Hull in the Eighteenth Century,* Oxford University Press 1971; *The British Whaling Trade,* A. & C. Black, 1978; *The British Ports: A Historical Survey,* World's Work, 1982.

WORK IN PROGRESS: R. T. Wilson and Sons: A History of Animal Processing and By-Products, publication expected in 1982 or 1983.

SIDELIGHTS: Jackson told *CA:* "For the last twenty-five years my principal research interests have been within the general field of trade, shipping, and ports, to which I was introduced as a postgraduate by Ralph Davis, who was the most important influence on my work. In particular I have been interested in the interrelationship between changes in the volume and composition of trade and the provision of post facilities. Each step forward in trade since the eighteenth century has required a reshaping of the major ports, and trade in industrial goods and foodstuffs has required advances in engineering skills that are rarely if ever mentioned in books on 'industrialization.' The book that I am currently finishing emphasizes this relationship.

"I was sidetracked into whaling because it was a trade that has not been written about in Britain for many years. I soon found it a dismal tale of man's inability to organize the sensible exploitation of a dwindling resource. The amount of waste involved was very considerable and led me to question the value of competition in whaling (and in fishing in general). It was with relief that I turned to the study of the processing of animal waste products in a commissioned history of Robert Wilson and sons, who were among the British pioneers following the 'everything but the squeal' processing system developed in Chicago. They made their fortune eventually out of canned dog and cat food. Both whaling and animal processing depend upon scientific and technical initiatives for their advancement, and again I have tried to bring out this element of growth which, I think, probably receives too little attention in many books on economic and business history.

"One of the saddest aspects of whaling was the failure to use the meat effectively, and it is to this aspect that I hope to turn when I have finished the research in hand."

*   *   *

JACOB, (Cyprien-)Max   1876-1944

BRIEF ENTRY: Born July 11, 1876, in Quimper, France; died March 5, 1944, in Drancy, France. French painter and poet. Jacob's importance as a poet lies in the unacknowledged groundwork he set down for the Surrealists who followed. Jacob, an avant-garde cubist painter and associate of Picasso and Apollinaire, described his nightmares, hallucinations, and everyday activities in such volumes as *Le Cornet a des* (1917). This early work was characterized by verbal clowning, puns, irony, and deliberate lack of emotional depth. He experimented

with many literary forms, but since he was less concerned with content than with words for their own sake, it is the poetry for which he is best remembered. Some commentators felt, however, that his voluminous correspondence may be more important to understanding the man and his work. Although he was born a Jew, Jacob experienced strong visions which led to his conversion to Roman Catholicism in 1915 and subsequent retirement to a monastery. His conversion was described in *La Defense de Tartuffe* (1919). He spent most of his retirement in poverty and penitence; his poetry, growing in depth and power, inclined toward mysticism, as in *Saint Matorel* (1936). Despite his conversion, to the Nazis he was still a Jew, and Jacob died in a concentration camp near Paris. *Biographical/critical sources: Columbia Dictionary of Modern European Literature,* Columbia University Press, 1947; *Modern Language Notes,* May, 1963; *Times Literary Supplement,* April 27, 1967; Annette Thau, *Poetry and Antipoetry: A Study of Selected Aspects of Max Jacob's Poetic Style,* University of North Carolina Press, 1976.

*   *   *

JACOT, Michael   1924-

PERSONAL: Born July 8, 1924, in London, England; son of Bernard Louis and Joy Kathleen (Bird) Jacot; married first wife, Stella Maria, October 29, 1947 (divorced, 1975); married Margaret Elizabeth Leggett (an airline executive), April 10, 1975; children: Anne, Paul, Mark, Tim, Matthew, Maria, Dominic, Leo, Andrew, Danielle, Michele. *Education:* Attended London School of Oriental and African Studies, London, 1943; St. John's College, Oxford, B.A. (with honors), 1950, M.A., 1951; attended University of Toronto, 1954-55. *Religion:* Roman Catholic. *Home and office:* 61 Bernard Ave., Toronto, Ontario, Canada M5R 1R4. *Agent:* James Brown Associates, Inc., 25 West 43rd St., New York, N.Y. 10036.

CAREER: British Broadcasting Corp., London, news editor, 1950-52; producer of children's programs for Canadian Broadcasting Corp., 1952-53; films and public relations executive for Imperial Oil Co., 1954-59; Michael Jacot Productions Ltd., Toronto, Ontario, owner, 1959—. *Military service:* Royal Air Force, Intelligence, 1942-45; served in Burma, the Far East, and Europe; received Burma Star. *Member:* Writers Guild of America (East). *Awards, honors:* Grants from British Council, Canada Council, and Ontario Council, 1973-75.

WRITINGS: Sun Is Naked, Methuen, 1960; *Time of My Beginning,* Bronwin, 1960; *The Last Butterfly* (novel), Bobbs-Merrill, 1974. Also author of *Five Faces,* 1974, and *Dark Side of Day,* 1975.

Plays: "The Man With the Red Hat," first produced in Toronto, Ontario, at Hart House; "Honour Thy Father," first produced in Toronto at Crest Theatre. Author of television and radio scripts.

*   *   *

JAHODA, Gloria (Adelaide Love)   1926-1980

OBITUARY NOTICE—See index for *CA* sketch: Born October 6, 1926, in Chicago, Ill.; died of pneumonia, January 13, 1980, in Tallahassee, Fla. Historian and author. Jahoda was a president of the Tallahassee Historical Society, an elected registrar of the Creek Indian nation, and an instructor at Farleigh Dickinson University. The Society of Midland Authors of Florida recognized her *River of the Golden Ibis* as the best history book of 1973. Her other books include *Annie, Delilah's Mountain, The Trail of Tears, The Other Florida,* and *The Road to Sam-*

arkand. Obituaries and other sources: *Publishers Weekly*, February 22, 1980.

* * *

JAMES, Alan Geoffrey 1943-

PERSONAL: Born November 25, 1943, in Guildford, England; son of Geoffrey Frederick and Muriel Bertha (North) James. *Education:* Balliol College, Oxford, M.A., 1965; University of Wales, Bangor, diploma in education, 1966; further graduate study at University of Birmingham, 1967—. *Home:* 3 Glen Ave., Holbrook, Derbyshire DE5 OUE, England. *Office:* Derby Lonsdale College of Higher Education, Mickleover, Derbyshire DE3 5GX, England.

CAREER: Teacher in multi-cultural primary schools in Huddersfield, England, 1966-72; Derby Lonsdale College of Higher Education, Mickleover, England, senior lecturer in education, 1972—. *Member:* National Association for Multiracial Education, National Association for the Teaching of English, National Association of Teachers in Further and Higher Education. *Awards, honors:* Fellowship from Winston Churchill Memorial Trust, for India, 1970.

WRITINGS: Sikh Children in Britain, Oxford University Press, 1974; (editor with Robert Jeffcoate) *School in the Multiracial Society*, Harper, 1982. Contributor to education journals and *New Community*. Editor of *Multiracial School*, 1972-75.

WORK IN PROGRESS: Research on language use of junior school children in collaborative learning, "aimed at a definition of the characteristics of discourse that contribute to learning."

SIDELIGHTS: James wrote: "My main professional interests are all aspects of linguistic and cultural diversity, especially ways in which the forms and uses of language maintain, transmit, and modify cultural assumptions. *Sikh Children in Britain* was an outcome of my teaching experience and my study of upbringing and education in rural Punjab.

"This book was intended as a tribute to the strengths of an ethnic group with whom I had enjoyed a long friendly association. I hope it has made English-speaking teachers a little more sensitive to the way in which the Sikh interpret the world and in particular to the way in which young Sikhs in Britain are developing the meaning of their parent culture in response to the impact of life in Britain. My writing since 1974 has generally been prompted by issues raised in discussion with teachers and students and by listening to children using language. My fascination with so-called 'Dark Age' and medieval culture may seem irrelevant, but the ways in which people of those times interpreted the world in terms of linguistic and visual symbols teach me a great deal about our own conceptions of the human situation and about the inherent logic of unfamiliar cultural systems, ancient and contemporary. My influences include Raymond Williams as the most humane, radical critic of culture, Basil Bernstein and Michael Halliday as interpreters of the role of language in cultural transmission, and Douglas Barnes as a critic of insensitive use of language in teaching."

AVOCATIONAL INTERESTS: English place names, the social, cultural, and intellectual history of medieval Europe, twentieth-century poetry, gardening (ericaceous plants).

* * *

JAMES, Henry 1843-1916

BRIEF ENTRY: Born April 15, 1843, in New York, N.Y.; died February 28, 1916, in London, England; ashes buried in Cambridge, Mass. American novelist and playwright. James was educated in Europe at the request of his father, who wanted him to become a "citizen of the world." In 1876, believing that America did not provide a suitable environment for writers and artists, James moved permanently to England. Many of his novels, particularly his early works *The American* (1877) and *The Portrait of a Lady* (1881), pitted European sophistication against American innocence. In 1897 he put his novels aside and attempted to write for the theatre. His plays were not successful, but they allowed him to develop the dramatic flair that permeated much of his later writing. In *The Spoils of Poynton* (1897) and the novels that followed, James introduced a new concept to the art of the novel. He developed stories through the point of view of one central character in what he called "scenic progression," which later evolved into stream of consciousness. *The Ambassadors* (1903) is considered one of the best examples of this technique. James's contributions to fiction writing have earned him a place as one of the greatest novelists in the English language. He was also a noted critic and essayist. At the outbreak of World War I James renounced his American citizenship and became a British subject to protest the United States' delay in entering the war. The British Government bestowed on him the Order of Merit the year before he died. *Biographical/critical sources:* Joseph Conrad, *Notes on Life and Letters*, J. M. Dent, 1905; Ezra Pound, *Literary Essays of Ezra Pound*, edited by T. S. Eliot, New Directions, 1918; Graham Greene, *Collected Essays*, Viking, 1969; *Webster's New World Companion to English and American Literature*, World Publishing, 1973; *Twentieth-Century Literary Criticism*, Volume 2, Gale, 1979.

* * *

JAMES, Michael 1922(?)-1981

OBITUARY NOTICE: Born c. 1922 in Paris, France; died of cancer, July 12, 1981, in San Diego, Calif. Journalist. Following distinguished service in the U.S. Army Air Corps during World War II, James worked for the Associated Press and *Time* magazine. He joined the *New York Times* staff in 1948, covering stories in Europe and the Far East. He left the *New York Times* in 1963 and served as a reporter and columnist for the *El Centro Imperial Valley Free Press and Morning Post* in California from 1965 to 1977. Obituaries and other sources: *New York Times*, July 13, 1981.

* * *

JAMES, Montague (Rhodes) 1862-1936

BRIEF ENTRY: Born August 1, 1862, in Goodnestone, England; died June 12, 1936, in Eton, England. British medieval scholar and author. As a writer, James is admired most for his ghost stories, collected in *Ghost Stories of an Antiquary* (1905) and *Collected Ghost Stories* (1931). Critics have agreed that his stories, of consistently good quality, surpassed those of most other writers in the genre. His settings were unusually eerie, his ghosts remarkably evil and vindictive, and his plots chillingly plausible. James was also an eminent and highly respected scholar and authority on Christian art. While serving as provost at King's College, Cambridge, and later at Eton College, he edited numerous scholarly collections, including his own translation of *The Apocryphal New Testament* (1924). *Biographical/critical sources: Twentieth Century Authors: A Biographical Dictionary of Modern Literature*, H. W. Wilson, 1942.

JANECZKO, Paul B(ryan) 1945-
(P. Wolny)

PERSONAL: Born July 27, 1945, in Passaic, N.J.; son of Frank John and Verna (Smolak) Janeczko. *Education:* St. Francis College, Biddeford, Maine, A.B., 1967; John Carroll University, M.A., 1970. *Home:* 44 Mary Carroll St., New Auburn, Maine 04210. *Office:* Language Arts Department, Gray-New Gloucester High School, Gray, Maine 04039.

CAREER: High school English teacher in Parma, Ohio, 1968-72, and Topsfield, Mass., 1972-77; Gray-New Gloucester High School, Gray, Maine, teacher of language arts, 1977—. *Member:* National Council of Teachers of English, Maine Reading Association, Maine Teachers of Language Arts.

WRITINGS—Young adult: (Editor) *The Crystal Image* (poems), Dell, 1977; (editor) *Postcard Poems*, Bradbury, 1979; (editor) *It's Elementary* (detective stories), Bantam, 1981; *Loads of Codes and Secret Ciphers*, Simon & Schuster, 1981; (editor) *Dont Forget to Fly* (poems), Bradbury, 1981.

Contributor: Lou Willett Stanek, editor, *Censorship: A Guide for Teachers, Librarians, and Others Concerned With Intellectual Freedom*, Dell, 1976; Jana Varlejs, editor, *Young Adult Literature in the Seventies*, Scarecrow, 1978; Gerard J. Senick, editor, *Children's Literature Review*, Volume III, Gale, 1978. Author of "Back Pages," a review column in *Leaflet*, 1973-76. Author of about fifty articles, stories, poems (under pseudonym P. Wolny), and reviews to newspapers, professional journals, and popular magazines, including *Armchair Detective, New Hampshire Profiles, Modern Haiku, Dragonfly, Friend, Child Life*, and *Highlights For Children*. Guest editor of *Leaflet*, spring, 1977.

WORK IN PROGRESS: A novel for young adults; short stories for children; an activity book on codes and ciphers for Simon & Schuster's "Puzzleback" series.

SIDELIGHTS: Janeczko told *CA:* "I started teaching because I wanted to be the teacher I never had. I've been teaching since 1968 and have found it to be a demanding profession, yet satisfying because I enjoy working with young people and their language.

"Although I wrote some poetry and short stories for my college literary magazine, I started writing for wider publication when, after I'd been teaching for a few years, I began writing for educational journals. About this time I met Jerry Weiss who encouraged me to put together an anthology of the poems I'd been teaching. That collection turned out to be *The Crystal Image*. That book gave me the confidence to develop other anthologies. I'm especially pleased with my latest poetry anthologies because they are unique. *Postcard Poems* contains poems for sharing; poems short enough to fit on a postcard. *Dont Forget to Fly* breaks away from the traditional anthology arrangement and provides a wider poetic experience for the reader, and I'm delighted with the humorous poetry I was able to include in that book.

"When I'm developing an anthology I keep my ears open for a poem that moves me. That's the first rule for developing a good anthology: The material must move you. It can anger you, delight you, make you cry, but you must be moved by it.

"I've always been fascinated by cloaks, daggers, spies, and secrets, so I wrote *Loads of Codes and Secret Ciphers*, a handbook for young people interested in secret writing. I'm also working on an activity book on codes and ciphers.

"Even though I teach full time, I usually manage to write for an hour or two each day. This is not nearly as much time as I would like to spend writing, but for the time being I will have to be satisfied with that.

"Maine is a beautiful place to live and work. But like many beautiful places, it is threatened by the insanity of nuclear power. I work with people who are committed to putting an end to this threat to our planet."

AVOCATIONAL INTERESTS: Running, cooking vegetarian meals, playing five-string banjo, biking, working with wood, tending to his cat, Macduff.

* * *

JAQUES, Florence Page 1890-1972

OBITUARY NOTICE: Born in 1890; died January 1, 1972, in North Oaks, Minn. Author of books on travel and nature. Jaques's books, including *The Geese Fly High* and *As Far as the Yukon*, feature illustrations by her husband, Francis Lee Jaques. Her tribute to her husband, *Francis Lee Jaques: Artist of the Wilderness World*, appeared in 1973. Obituaries and other sources: *New York Times*, January 4, 1972; *AB Bookman's Weekly*, January 17, 1972.

* * *

JARRY, Alfred 1873-1907

BRIEF ENTRY: Born September 8, 1873, in Laval, France; died of tuberculosis compounded by alcoholism, November 1, 1907, in Paris, France. French playwright, poet, and essayist. Jarry's ventures into experimental drama foreshadowed a departure from the realism of conventional approaches to the theatre and influenced the symbolists, the surrealists, and the theatre of the absurd. He is best known for creating the grotesque character Ubu, who began as a parody of one of Jarry's teachers in a school play presented by Jarry and some of his friends. Jarry later rewrote the play as *Ubu roi* (1896; translated as *King Turd*, 1953), in which Ubu is the epitome of cowardly greed and cruelty. The play was outrageous, with scatological language and savage ferocity adding to its *succes de scandale*. Jarry gradually began to affect the mannerisms of Ubu, speaking in a monotone drone and walking in a jerky, robot-like fashion. The Ubu saga continued with *Ubu enchaine* (1900; translated as *King Turd Enslaved*, 1953) and *Ubu cocu* (1944; translated as *Turd Cuckolded*, 1953). Jarry also wrote two novels, *Le Surmale: Roman moderne* (1902; translated as *The Supermale: A Modern Novel*, 1968), the story of a man who has a love-making contest with a machine, and *Gestes et opinions du Docteur Faustroll, pataphysicien* (1911; translated as *Exploits and Opinions of Doctor Faustroll, Pataphysician*, 1965), which defined "pataphysics" as the science of imaginary solutions. Jarry's behavior became increasingly bizarre as his use of ether and alcohol distorted his ability to distinguish himself from his characters. He died in a charity hospital at the age of thirty-four. *Biographical/critical sources: The Romantic Review*, October-December, 1935; Martin Esslin, *The Theatre of the Absurd*, Overlook Press, 1961; *Criticism*, winter, 1962; *Encyclopedia of World Literature in the Twentieth Century*, Ungar, 1967; *Twentieth-Century Literary Criticism*, Volume 2, Gale, 1980.

* * *

JAY, Marion
See SPALDING, Ruth

JENKINS, Hugh (Gater) 1908-

PERSONAL: Born July 27, 1908, in London, England; son of Joseph Walter (in dairy work) and Emily Florence (Gater) Jenkins; married Ethel Marie Crosbie, July 18, 1936. *Education:* Attended secondary school in Enfield, England. *Religion:* Agnostic. *Home:* 75 Kenilworth Court, Lower Richmond Rd., London S.W.15, England. *Office:* Theatres Trust, 10 St. Martin's Court, London SW15 1EN, England.

CAREER: Associated with Prudential Assurance Co., 1939-40; Rangoon Radio, Rangoon, Burma, head of English programs, 1946; publicity officer, editor, and bank officer for National Union of Bank Employees, 1947-50; British Actors Equity, London, England, assistant general secretary, 1950-64; Parliament, London, England, Labour member for Putney, 1964-79, minister for the arts, 1974-76; Theatres Trust, London, director, 1979—. Member of board of directors of National Theatre, 1977-80; past chairman of Theatres Advisory Council; chairman of Battersea Community Arts Centre and Campaign for Nuclear Disarmament. *Military service:* Royal Air Force, 1941-45; became flight lieutenant. *Awards, honors:* Created life peer, 1981.

WRITINGS: The Culture Gap, Marion Boyars, 1979; *Rank and File,* Croom Helm, 1980.

Author of "Solo Boy," first broadcast by BBC-Radio, 1982. Contributor to magazines and newspapers, including *New Statesman.*

WORK IN PROGRESS: Lectures and articles on peace and the arts.

SIDELIGHTS: Lord Jenkins wrote: "I am concerned with peace and the arts. We have to hope that humanity will survive. *The Culture Gap* is concerned with government and the arts. *Rank and File* is about Labour party democracy.

"My radio play 'Solo Boy' is my first work of fiction and is based on my early life. If it is successful it may be followed by further episodes in the life of Paul Williams, who is not Hugh Jenkins but whose experiences run parallel to mine. 'Solo Boy' was commissioned by the BBC, and it would not have been written but for the two-year gap between my ceasing to be a member of Parliament and my becoming a peer.

"During 1981 I made two lecture tours of the U.S.A., speaking on government and the arts to university audiences and branches of the English Speaking Union. I find American audiences very receptive—they laugh at my jokes!

"My main concern is that unless there is a change of course, European civilization is doomed to nuclear destruction. This preoccupation takes first priority in my time."

*   *   *

JESSEL, Camilla (Ruth) 1937-

PERSONAL: Born December 7, 1937, in Bearsted, England; daughter of Richard Frederick (a naval officer) and Winifred May (Levy) Jessel; married Andrzej Panufnik (a symphonic composer), November 27, 1963; children: Roxanna Anna, Jeremy James. *Education:* Sorbonne, University of Paris, degre superieure, 1959. *Home:* Riverside House, Twickenham TW1 3DJ, England. *Agent:* David Higham Associates Ltd., 5-8 Lower John St., London W1R 4HA, England.

CAREER: Free-lance photographer and writer. Work shown in group and one-man photographic exhibitions at Royal Festival Hall, Arts Theatre Club, and Photographers Gallery. Vice-chairman of Home Welfare Committee; member of United Kingdom Child Care Committee and Save the Children. *Member:* Pre-School Playgroups Association (patron), Royal Photographic Society (fellow), Performing Rights Society, Society of Authors. *Awards, honors:* Grant from Nuffield Foundation, 1972; Royal Photographic Society fellowship, 1980.

WRITINGS—Juveniles; all with own photographs, except as noted: *Manuela Lives in Portugal,* Hastings House, 1967; *Thames Pageant* (lyrics for cantata; no photographs), Boosey & Hawkes, 1969; *Paul in Hospital,* Methuen, 1972; *Winter Solstice* (lyrics for cantata; no photographs), Boosey & Hawkes, 1972; *Mark's Wheelchair Adventures,* Methuen, 1975; *Life at the Royal Ballet School,* Methuen, 1979; *The Puppy Book,* Methuen, 1980; *The New Baby,* Methuen, 1981; *Moving House,* Methuen, 1981; *Going to the Doctor,* Methuen, 1981; *Away for the Night,* Methuen, 1981; *The Joy of Birth,* Methuen, 1982.

Photographer: Dorothy Shuttlesworth, *Tower of London,* Hastings House, 1970; Susan Harvey, *Play in Hospital,* Faber, 1972; David Watkins, *Complete Method for the Harp,* Boosey & Hawkes, 1972; Penelope Leach, *Baby and Child,* Knopf, 1978; Sheila Kitzinger, *Pregnancy and Childbirth,* Knopf, 1980; David Moore, *Multi-Cultural Britain* (booklet), Save the Children, 1980. Contributor of photographs to newspapers.

WORK IN PROGRESS: A music book for children, publication by Methuen expected in 1983; a book for parents on child development, publication by Dorling & Kindersley, 1983.

SIDELIGHTS: Camilla Jessel told *CA:* "As a teenager I lived for eighteen months with my parents in a community in South India. I lived a year in Paris, studying French literature and civilization. At the age of twenty I went to America with about one hundred dollars and had twenty-six different temporary secretarial jobs in six cities in one year (Princeton, Washington, New York, New Orleans, Dallas, and San Francisco). I have traveled extensively as a photographer (Africa and Europe) and as the wife of an internationally known conductor and composer (including South America, but not Eastern Europe as my husband is a political refugee).

"I bring up a family and work as my husband's business manager. I enjoy being domestic, cooking, dressmaking, as well as having a career. I believe it's possible to be both liberated and a dedicated wife and mother.

"My motivation is my interest in children and my wish to use photography to combat prejudice and fear, such as the prejudice against the disabled or members of other races; I also want to use photography to educate children and to educate adults to be of more use to children. There is also my sheer enjoyment of photography and an attempt to heighten my own aesthetic standards.

"I started by working with children and was pushed into photography by the press officer of Save the Children, who liked the amateur shots I'd done of the organization's work. That was followed by lots of hard work and lucky breaks. I worked free-lance, including photographing articles for the *Times Educational Supplement.* My first book was commissioned on the strength of two photographs that appeared in the *Guardian.* Doing color slides for a lecture on the psychology of play of children in the hospital, I got the idea of doing a photographic book to overcome children's fears of the hospital. Then I received a grant for a similar book about disabled children. I continued over the years to work with disadvantaged children, but also worked on other subjects, including the book on birth and the facts of life for children."

AVOCATIONAL INTERESTS: Music, theatre, art, ballet, literature, international politics.

BIOGRAPHICAL/CRITICAL SOURCES: Guardian, August 24, 1979; *Daily Telegraph,* August 24, 1979.

*   *   *

JIMENEZ (MANTECON), Juan Ramon   1881-1958

BRIEF ENTRY: Born December 24, 1881, in Moguer, Spain; died May 29, 1958, in San Juan, Puerto Rico. Spanish educator and poet. Considered one of Spain's finest contemporary poets, Jimenez published his first poetry at the age of seventeen and attracted the attention of modernist poets Ruben Dario and Francis Villaespesa. Moving to Madrid, Jimenez became a protege of Dario, but he eventually grew beyond modernism to become a principal figure in the Spanish poetic renaissance of the 1920's, influencing the work of poets such as Garcia Lorca and Rafael Alberti. Jimenez made his home in Madrid until 1936 when civil war drove him into exile. He spent the next fourteen years traveling and lecturing in Latin America and the United States, finally settling in Puerto Rico, where he joined the faculty of the University of Puerto Rico. A prolific writer, Jimenez produced more than thirty volumes of poetry, and in 1956 he was awarded the Nobel Prize for literature. Among his best-known works are *Almas de Violeta* (1900), *Patero y yo* (1914), *Diario de un poeta recien casado* (1917), and *Animal de Fondo* (1949). *Biographical/critical sources: Cyclopedia of World Authors,* Harper, 1958; *Encyclopedia of World Literature in the Twentieth Century,* updated edition, Ungar, 1967; *Twentieth Century Writing: A Reader's Guide to Contemporary Literature,* Transatlantic, 1969; *World Authors, 1950-1970,* H. W. Wilson, 1975; *Twentieth-Century Literary Criticism,* Volume 4, Gale, 1981.

*   *   *

JOHANNINGMEIER, E(rwin) V(irgil)   1937-

PERSONAL: Born December 18, 1937, in St. Louis, Mo.; son of Erwin F. and Estelle (Bulejeska) Johanningmeier; children: Christina B. *Education:* Washington University, A.B., 1960, M.A.Ed., 1964; University of Illinois, Ph.D., 1967. *Home:* 502 D Richlyne, Temple Terrace, Fla. 33617. *Office:* College of Education, University of South Florida, FAO 278, Tampa, Fla. 33620.

CAREER: High school English teacher in St. Louis, Mo., 1960-63; Hofstra University, Hempstead, N.Y., assistant professor of education, 1967-68; University of South Florida, Tampa, assistant professor, 1968-71, associate professor, 1971-76, professor of education, 1976—, chairman of social and psychological foundations of education, 1976-78. *Member:* American Educational Research Association, American Educational Studies Association, National Council of University Research Administrators, History of Education Society, Philosophy of Education Society, Society of Professors of Education, Southern History of Education Society, Phi Delta Kappa.

WRITINGS: (With Henry C. Johnson) *Teachers for the Prairie: The University of Illinois and the Schools,* University of Illinois Press, 1972; (contributor) Ayers Bagley, editor, *The Professor of Education: An Assessment of Conditions,* Society of Professors of Education, 1975; (editor) *Science of Education and the Education Professoriate,* Society of Professors of Education, 1978; *The Americans and Their Schools,* Rand McNally, 1980; (contributor) J. V. Smith and David Hamilton, editors, *The Meritocratic Intellect: Studies in the History of Educational Research,* University of Aberdeen Press, 1980. Contributor to *Encyclopedia of Education* and *American Academic Encyclopedia.* Contributor of articles and reviews to education journals.

WORK IN PROGRESS: The American Dream and the American School, an analysis of American education and culture since World War II, publication expected in 1983 or 1984.

SIDELIGHTS: Johanningmeier told *CA:* "I try to show how developments in post World War II society reshaped our social expectations and the purpose of the school."

*   *   *

JOHNSON, Alden Porter   1914-1972

OBITUARY NOTICE: Born March 24, 1914, in Worcester, Mass.; died September 8, 1972, in Worcester, Mass. Editor and publisher. Johnson published *The Barre Gazette* and expanded his interests to develop Barre Publishing Co., a leading trade and regional book publisher. Obituaries and other sources: *AB Bookman's Weekly,* October 9, 1972; *Who Was Who in America, With World Notables,* Volume V: *1969-1973,* Marquis, 1973.

*   *   *

JOHNSON, E(mil) Richard   1937-

PERSONAL: Born April 23, 1937, in Printice, Wis.; son of Emil Frank (a laborer) and Erna (Leben) Johnson; married Joan Balie, August 16, 1959 (divorced April, 1961); married Kathy Ann Heldt, August 25, 1979; children: Susan. *Address:* State Prison, Stillwater, Minn.

CAREER: Worked as logger, ranch hand, and well digger; worked as forester for U.S. Department of Agriculture, 1962-64; State Prison, Stillwater, Minn., chief clerk at Orientation and Receiving Unit, 1964—, member of Inmate Advisory Council, 1975-82, president of council, 1976-77. *Military service:* U.S. Army, Combat Intelligence, 1956-60; became sergeant. *Member:* Star of the North Jaycees. *Awards, honors:* Edgar Allan Poe Award from Mystery Writers of America, 1968, for *Silver Street.*

WRITINGS—Crime novels: *Silver Street,* Harper, 1968 (published in England as *The Silver Street Killer,* R. Hale, 1969); *The Inside Man,* Harper, 1969; *Mongo's Back in Town,* Harper, 1969; *Cage Five Is Going to Break,* Harper, 1970; *The God Keepers,* Harper, 1970; *Case Load—Maximum,* Harper, 1971; *The Judas,* Harper, 1971; *The Cardinalli Contract,* Pyramid Publications, 1975.

WORK IN PROGRESS: Two crime novels, *The McQuillan Contract* and *The Sleeping Dragon.*

SIDELIGHTS: Johnson commented: "I began writing in prison because I realized that if I were to do anything with my life I would have to do it from those circumstances, and I did not want to waste those years. I write about crime and criminals, of course, because that is what I know best, and I have an endless supply of story material around me. I write now because I know that writing is what I want to do with my life, and I plan my future career around that. I hope someday to write a book on crime and prisons that tells the truth about both without any whitewashing. I'd like to write a tips-on-crime column someday also and suggest to the public how to avoid becoming victims."

*   *   *

JOHNSON, James Weldon   1871-1938

BRIEF ENTRY: Born June 17, 1871, in Jacksonville, Fla.; died in an automobile accident, June 26, 1938, in Wiscasset, Me. American lawyer, educator, social reformer, songwriter, essayist, and novelist. Considered one of the most prominent black leaders of his time, Johnson is primarily known for his novel, *The Autobiography of an Ex-Colored Man*. First published anonymously in 1912 and reissued under the author's name in 1927, the novel was a forerunner of the Harlem Renaissance, a 1920's cultural movement. The first black person ever admitted to the Florida Bar, Johnson also served as executive secretary to the National Association for the Advancement of Colored People (NAACP) from 1920 to 1930 and as consul to Venezuela and Nicaragua during Theodore Roosevelt's administration. In 1925 Johnson received the NAACP's Spingarn Medal. A successful songwriter as well, Johnson wrote "Lift Every Voice and Sing," often called the Negro national anthem. From 1930 until his death he was professor of creative literature at Fisk University. Johnson is the author of poetry, social criticism, history, and autobiography, in addition to popular songs and fiction. His works include *Fifty Years and Other Poems* (1917), *The Book of American Negro Poetry* (1931), *Black Manhattan* (1930) and *Along This Way* (1933). *Biographical/critical sources: Readers Encyclopedia of American Literature*, Crowell, 1962; *Oxford Companion to American Literature*, 4th edition, Oxford University Press, 1965; *Webster's New World Companion to English and American Literature*, World Publishing, 1973; *Webster's American Biographies*, Merriam, 1974; *Twentieth-Century Literary Criticism*, Volume 3, Gale, 1980.

* * *

JOHNSON, Mary Frances K. 1929(?)-1979

OBITUARY NOTICE: Born c. 1929; died of cancer, July 11, 1979. Librarian, educator, editor, and author. Johnson was a professor at the University of North Carolina, Greensboro, and served for one year on the staff of the American Library Association. Editor from 1970 to 1973 of *School Libraries*, she co-wrote *School Media Programs and Networking: A Position Paper* in 1977. *Obituaries and other sources: School Library Journal*, September, 1979.

* * *

JOHNSON, Pamela Hansford 1912-1981
(Nap Lombard, a joint pseudonym)

OBITUARY NOTICE—See index for *CA* sketch: Born May 29, 1912, in London, England; died June 18, 1981, in London, England. Author. The wife of the late novelist and scientist C. P. Snow, Johnson published her first novel, *This Bed Thy Center*, at the age of twenty-two. As a writer, she concentrated on social and human concerns of contemporary society as well as on her characters and their relation to society. Most of her novels have love as a central theme, though Johnson was strongly opposed to permissiveness. Critically, she was known for her use of wit and deft malice. She wrote over twenty novels, including *A Bonfire*, published just prior to her death, *Catherine Carter, The Good Husband, Night and Silence, Who Is Here?, An Impossible Marriage*, and *The Honors Board*. Besides two plays, "Corinth House" and "The Rehearsal," she wrote acclaimed critical studies of Thomas Wolfe, Charles Dickens, Marcel Proust, and Ivy Compton-Burnett. Johnson contributed stories, articles, and reviews to the *Liverpool Post, John O'London's Weekly*, the *Sunday Chronicle*, and the *Washington Post*. Also a poet, she won the *Sunday Referee*'s first award for poetry. Obituaries and other sources: *London Times*, June 20, 1981; *New York Times*, June 20, 1981; *Washington Post*, June 21, 1981; *Newsweek*, June 29, 1981; *Time*, June 29, 1981; *Publishers Weekly*, July 3, 1981; *AB Bookman's Weekly*, July 13-20, 1981.

JOHNSON, Richard N(ewhall) 1900-1971

OBITUARY NOTICE: Born February 13, 1900, in Colorado Springs, Colo.; died of cancer, November 21, 1971, in Annapolis, Md. Entrepreneur, presidential adviser, and publisher. Johnson served as foreign trade policy adviser to the White House staff in 1950 and as assistant director for Mutual Security in the Executive Office of the President from 1951 to 1953. In 1955 he founded LogEtronics, Inc., a successful electronics manufacturing firm, where he served as president until his retirement in 1967. He was president and publisher of the bankrupt *Boston Evening Transcript* from 1939 to 1942, but his attempts to rescue the newspaper from insolvency were not successful. Obituaries and other sources: *New York Times*, November 25, 1971; *AB Bookman's Weekly*, December 20, 1971; *Who Was Who in America, With World Notables*, Volume V: *1969-1973*, Marquis, 1973.

* * *

JOHNSTON, Richard W(yckoff) 1915-1981

OBITUARY NOTICE: Born March 21, 1915, in Eugene, Ore.; died of cancer, August 4, 1981, in Honolulu, Hawaii. Journalist, editor, and author. Johnston joined the United Press in 1939 and served as war correspondent in the Pacific and Far East from 1943 to 1945. In 1946 he became a foreign correspondent and newswriter for *Time* magazine and then joined the staff of *Life* magazine in 1947. When Time, Inc., introduced *Sports Illustrated*, Johnston served first as the new magazine's assistant managing editor and later as its executive editor. His 1948 book, *Follow Me*, is a history of the Second Marine Division. Johnston also wrote *The Airport and Its Neighbors*, edited the text for *Life*'s *Picture History of World War II*, and collaborated with his wife, Laurie Johnston, on a young people's biography of Queen Elizabeth II, *Elizabeth Enters*. Obituaries and other sources: *Who's Who in America*, 40th edition, Marquis, 1978; *New York Times*, August 5, 1981.

* * *

JOHNSTON, Robert Kent 1945-

PERSONAL: Born June 9, 1945, in Pasadena, Calif.; son of Roy G. (a structural engineer) and Naomi (Harmon) Johnston; married Anne Roosevelt (a museum public information officer), December 14, 1968; children: Elizabeth, Margaret. *Education:* Stanford University, A.B., 1967; Fuller Theological Seminary, B.D., 1970; attended North Park Theological Seminary, 1970-71; Duke University, Ph.D., 1974. *Politics:* Democrat. *Home:* 833 Wakefield, Bowling Green, Ky. 42101. *Office:* Department of Philosophy and Religion, Western Kentucky University, Bowling Green, Ky. 42101.

CAREER: Ordained minister of Evangelical Covenant church, 1975; youth minister at Evangelical Covenant church in Pasadena, Calif., 1967-69; assistant minister at Evangelical Covenant church in Chicago, Ill., 1970-71; Western Kentucky University, Bowling Green, assistant professor, 1974-78, associate professor of religion, 1978—. Professor at St. Mark's Seminary, Auburn, Ky., 1979-80; visiting professor at New College, Berkeley, Calif., 1980-81. Interim minister at Presbyterian church in Franklin, Ky., 1977-78. *Member:* American Academy of Religion, Deitrich Bonhoeffer Society, Karl Barth Society, Conference on Christianity and Literature, Phi Beta Kappa.

WRITINGS: (Contributor) W. Ward Gasque and William Sanford LaSor, editors, *Scripture, Tradition, and Interpretation,*

Eerdmans, 1978; *Evangelicals at an Impasse: Biblical Authority in Practice*, John Knox Press, 1979; *Psalms*, Regal Books, 1982; *The Christian at Play*, Eerdmans, in press. Contributor of about fifty articles and reviews to theology journals.

WORK IN PROGRESS: The Good News Bible Commentary: Ecclesiastes, Song of Songs, publication by Harper expected in 1984.

SIDELIGHTS: Johnston worked in Japan for the Evangelical Convent Church in 1965 and in Geneva, Switzerland, as a financial analyst trainee in 1969. He has studied in Belgium and participated in an archaeological expedition in Meiron, Israel.

He wrote that his vocational interests include "the relationship of Christian theology and culture. This includes particular interests in the changing shape of evangelical theology, the relationship of literature to religion, and the relevance of Old Testament wisdom literature for the contemporary individual."

*   *   *

JOHNSTON, Thomas   1945-

PERSONAL: Born August 29, 1945, in Belfast, Northern Ireland; son of Thomas and Elizabeth Johnston; married Patricia Richards (a teacher), August 7, 1967; children: Matthew, Catherine. *Education:* Stranmillis College, certificate of education; Birkbeck College, London, B.Sc.; University of Sheffield, M.A. *Politics:* Socialist. *Home:* 2 Woodside Ave., Nab Wood, Shipley, West Yorkshire, England. *Office:* Bradford College, Bradford, West Yorkshire, England.

CAREER: Mathematics teacher at primary school in London, England, 1966-69; Hereford College of Education, Hereford, England, lecturer in psychology, 1970-72; Bradford College, Bradford, England, lecturer in psychology, 1972—. *Member:* British Psychological Society.

WRITINGS: The Fight for Arkenvald, Doubleday, 1970; "A Game of Murder" (radio play), first broadcast by British Broadcasting Corp. (BBC-Radio), 1976.

WORK IN PROGRESS: A novel.

SIDELIGHTS: Johnston commented: "I don't attempt to write enough. My full-time teaching post prevents any useful work, and my doctoral thesis occupies most of my time. It is a pity; I really ought to do some more creative writing."

*   *   *

JOHNSTONE, D(onald) Bruce   1909-

PERSONAL: Surname legally changed in 1934; born September 18, 1909, in Minneapolis, Minn.; son of D. Bruff (in sales) and Maude (a pianist; maiden name, Howard) Johnson; married Florence Elliott, December 14, 1935; children: Mary Johnstone Hardman, D. Bruce II, David Elliott. *Education:* University of Minnesota, B.A., 1960, and Ph.D.; Harvard University, B.A., 1963, M.S., 1964; Hamline University, B.A., 1970. *Home:* 6920 Rolling Acres Rd., Excelsior, Minn. 55331.

CAREER: Northrup King Seed Co., Minneapolis, Minn., chief horticulturist, 1935-73; writer, 1973—. President and judge of All America Selections of American Seed Trade Association; lecturer for garden and horticulture groups; member of board of Kids, Inc.; consultant. *Military service:* U.S. Navy, 1944-46; became lieutenant senior grade. *Member:* Minnetonka Men's Garden Club (president), Minneapolis Men's Garden Club. *Awards, honors:* Horticultural achievement award from American Seed Trade Association, 1973.

WRITINGS: Vegetable Gardening From the Ground Up, Burgess, 1976; *Garden to Table*, Nature Life of McGill Jensen, 1977; (contributor) *Gardening for Food and Fun*, U.S. Department of Agriculture, 1977; *America's Best Garden Flowers*, Burgess, 1978; *Guide to Canoe Camping*, American Camping Association, 1980. Contributor to *U.S. Department of Agriculture Yearbook*. Contributor to magazines, including *Family Food Garden* and *Minnesota Horticulturist*.

*   *   *

JONES, Arthur Glyn Prys
  See PRYS-JONES, Arthur Glyn

*   *   *

JONES, Arthur Llewellyn   1863-1947
  (Arthur Machen, Leolinus Siluriensis)

BRIEF ENTRY: Born March 3, 1863, in Caerleon, Wales; died December 15, 1947, in Beaconsfield, England. Welsh actor, journalist, and author. In his numerous short stories and novels, Machen wove tales touched with the macabre and the supernatural. Although he never earned his living as a writer, Machen experienced success with several of his works, particularly his novel *The Hill of Dreams* (1907) and his short story collection *The Angel of Mons* (1915). Included in the latter was "The Bowmen, and Other Legends," which was considered Machen's greatest short story. It deals with the World War I battle by the English at Mons. Though the plot is fictitious, many believed Machen's story about divine intervention at the battle to be true. Machen became an actor in 1902, touring with the Benson Shakespearean Repertoire, and at age fifty began a journalistic career with the *London Evening News*. His other writings include *The Anatomy of Tobacco* (written under the psuedonym Leolinus Siluriensis; 1884), *The Chronicle of Clemendy* (1888), *The House of Souls* (1906), and *Things Near and Far* (1923). *Biographical/critical sources: Twentieth Century Authors: A Biographical Dictionary of Modern Literature*, 1st supplement, H. W. Wilson, 1955; *Cyclopedia of World Authors*, Harper, 1958; *Twentieth Century Literary Criticism*, Volume 4, Gale, 1981.

*   *   *

JONES, Eric Lionel   1936-

PERSONAL: Born September 21, 1936, in Andover, England; son of L.A.W. and Beatrice Maud (Taylor) Jones; married Sylvia Bower (a teacher and librarian), August 7, 1958; children: Deborah Jane Bower, Christopher John Bower. *Education:* University of Nottingham, B.A. (with honors), 1958; Oxford University, D.Phil., 1962, M.A., 1964. *Office:* Department of Economics, La Trobe University, Bundoora, Victoria 3083, Australia.

CAREER: Oxford University, Oxford, England, acting lecturer in history of agriculture, 1963, fellow of Nuffield College, 1963-67; University of Reading, Reading, England, lecturer in economic history and founding research director of Institute of Agricultural History, 1967-70; Northwestern University, Evanston, Ill., professor of economics, 1970-75; La Trobe University, Bundoora, Australia, professor of economics, 1975—. Visiting associate professor at Purdue University, 1965-66; visiting professor at Northwestern University, 1968, La Trobe University, 1973, and University of Exeter, 1979-80. President of board of directors of Northwestern University Press, 1973-75. *Member:* Economic History Society of Australia and New Zealand, Economic History Society (United Kingdom),

British Agricultural History Society, Economic History Association (United States).

WRITINGS: Seasons and Prices, Allen & Unwin, 1964; (editor and contributor) Agriculture and Economic Growth in England, 1650-1815, Methuen, 1967; (editor with G. E. Mingay, and contributor) Land, Labour, and Population in the Industrial Revolution, Edward Arnold, 1967; The Development of English Agriculture, Macmillan, 1968; (editor with S. J. Woolf, and contributor) Agrarian Change and Economic Development: The Historical Problems, Methuen, 1969; Agriculture and the Industrial Revolution, Basil Blackwell, 1974; (editor with W. N. Parker, and contributor) European Peasants and Their Markets, Princeton University Press, 1975; The European Miracle, Cambridge University Press, 1981; Storia Dell'Agricoltura e lo Sviluppo Industriale Dell Economie Avanzate (title means "The History of Agriculture and the Industrial Development of the Advanced Economies"; collection of previously published papers with new introduction), Editori Riuniti, 1982.

Contributor: Edwin Cohen, editor, Birds of Hampshire and the Isle of Wight, Oliver & Boyd, 1963; M. C. Radford, editor, The Birds of Berkshire and Oxfordshire, Longmans, 1966; W. E. Minchinton, editor, Essays in Agrarian History, two volumes, David & Charles, 1968; R. M. Hartwell, editor, The Industrial Revolution, Basil Blackwell, 1970; L. P. Cain and P. J. Uselding, editors, Business Enterprise and Economic Change, Kent State University Press, 1973; Mauro Ambrosoli, editor, Le campagne inglesi tra '600 e '800 (title means "Rural England From the Seventeenth Through Nineteenth Centuries"), Rosenberg & Sellier, 1976; Antoni Maczak and William N. Parker, editors, Natural Resources in European History, Resources for the Future, 1978; Peter Burke, editor, The New Cambridge Modern History of Europe, XIII, Companion Volume, Cambridge University Press, 1979; R. C. Floud and D. N. McCloskey, editors, The Economic History of Britain Since 1700, Cambridge University Press, 1981. Contributor of about fifty articles to economic history and ornithology journals.

WORK IN PROGRESS: The Fire Gap: Conflagrations and the History of Towns.

SIDELIGHTS: Jones wrote: "I am interested in very long-term economic change in Europe and Asia; late pre-industrial economies, including colonial America and the early United States; the economic history of agriculture; the economic history of the environment; the history of science, natural history, technology, and education; and regional economic history.

"I have also been a birdwatcher from boyhood; that is, before it became fashionable. I have a passion for the countryside, market towns, and villages, mainly in southern England but also in the Midwest and northeastern seaboard of the United States, in Gippsland, Australia, as well as some parts of western Europe, and for marshland and lowland coasts. I am deeply interested in the biographies of individuals who have worked on topics or in places that appeal to me, and I would like to write a book on rural England that could stand with Margaret Halsey's With Malice Toward Some or John Moore's Portrait of Elmbury. My book would be about Hampshire."

*   *   *

JONES, Helen L(ouise)   1903-1973

OBITUARY NOTICE: Born in 1903 in Billerica, Mass.; died January 6, 1973. Editor, publishing executive, and author. Jones worked at Riverside Press before joining the staff of Little, Brown & Co., where she was editor of the children's

book program. She served as president and director of the Children's Book Council. Her book, Robert Lawson: Illustrator, appeared in 1972. Obituaries and other sources: Publishers Weekly, October 22, 1955, January 22, 1973.

*   *   *

JONES, John J.
   See LOVECRAFT, H(oward) P(hillips)

*   *   *

JONES, Karen Midkiff   1948-

PERSONAL: Born November 29, 1948, in Miami, Fla.; daughter of Carl Merlin and Florence (Barton) Midkiff. Education: Tulane University, B.A. Home: 20 West 84th St., New York, N.Y. 10024. Office: Antiques, 551 Fifth Ave., New York, N.Y. 10176.

CAREER: Author.

WRITINGS: From A to Z: A Folk Art Alphabet, Main Street, 1978. Author of "Museum Accessions" and "Collectors' Notes," columns in Antiques.

*   *   *

JONES, Michael (Christopher Emlyn)   1940-

PERSONAL: Born December 5, 1940, in Wrexham, Wales; son of Reginald Luther and Megan Bevan (Edwards) Jones; married Elizabeth Marjorie Smith (a teacher), July 9, 1966; children: Richard Luther Caradoc. Education: Attended University of Leicester, 1959-60; Trinity College, Oxford, B.A., 1963, D.Phil., 1966, M.A., 1967. Religion: Christian. Home: 3 Florence Boot Close, University Park, Nottingham NG7 2QF, England. Office: Department of History, University of Nottingham, Nottingham NG7 2RD, England.

CAREER: University of Exeter, Exeter, England, tutor in medieval history, 1966-67; University of Nottingham, Nottingham, England, assistant lecturer, 1967-69, lecturer in European history, 1969-80, senior lecturer, 1980—. Member: Royal Historical Society (fellow), Society of Antiquaries (fellow).

WRITINGS: Ducal Britanny, 1364-1399, Oxford University Press, 1970; (translator) Philippe de Commynes, Memoirs, 1461-83, Penguin, 1972; Recueil des actes de Jean IV, duc de Bretagne (title means "Collection of the Letters of John IV, Duke of Brittany"), Volume I: 1357-1382, Klincksieck, 1980. Contributor to history journals.

WORK IN PROGRESS: Recueil des actes de Jean IV, duc de Bretagne, Volume II: 1383-1399, publication by Klincksieck expected in 1983; Noble Britanny, a study of the Breton nobility from the Carolingian period to the sixteeenth century, publication expected in 1986.

SIDELIGHTS: Jones told CA: "My first experience of Brittany was a childhood holiday there shortly after World War II. Interest in its history was sparked by a desire not simply to do research in medieval history but particularly to study a region which formed both then and now part of another society, the development of which paralleled and contrasted with my own. I am still exploring these differences."

BIOGRAPHICAL/CRITICAL SOURCES: Memoires de la societe d'histoire et d'archeologie de Bretagne, Volume LVI, 1979.

JONES, Seaborn (Gustavus), Jr. 1942-

PERSONAL: Born October 10, 1942, in Macon, Ga.; son of Seaborn G., Sr. (an attorney) and Anne (a real estate broker; maiden name, Reynolds) Jones; married Susan Hoagland, September 27, 1978; children: Bronwyn Price. *Education:* Attended Mercer University, 1961-64. *Home:* 22 Skylark Dr., No. 320, Larkspur, Calif. 94939.

CAREER: Writer. WGTV-TV, Athens, Ga., studio manager, 1965-71; WQED-TV, Pittsburgh, Pa., lighting director, 1971-73. Gives readings. *Military service:* U.S. Marine Corps Reserve, 1961-66.

WRITINGS: Drowning From the Inside Out (poetry), Cherry Valley, 1981. Contributor to magazines, including *Coldspring Journal, Artaud's Elbow, Xanadu, Yellow Brick Road,* and *Big Moon.*

WORK IN PROGRESS: In Search of Little Richard, a novel; *From This High,* poems.

SIDELIGHTS: Jones commented: "When I'm at my best I have the patience to wade through the bad poems to catch the good ones. It becomes a matter of quantity breeding quality. I keep a journal of my dreams and write from them. Reading poems by others, especially current poetry, helps me to get in the mood to write. When I'm at my worst I don't have the ability to defer judgment, and I'm usually not reading."

*　　*　　*

JONES, William R(onald) 1933-

PERSONAL: Born July 17, 1933, in Louisville, Ky.; son of Henry Wise (a mail carrier) and Lannie (Brogsdale) Jones; married Lauretta A. Hicks (a social worker), August 25, 1958; children: Jeffrey David, Darrell Roger. *Education:* Howard University, B.A. (magna cum laude), 1955; Harvard University, B.D., 1958; Brown University, Ph.D., 1969. *Politics:* Independent. *Religion:* Humanist. *Home:* 2410 Limerick Dr., Tallahassee, Fla. 32308. *Office:* Department of Religion, Florida State University, 633 Bellamy Building, Tallahassee, Fla. 32306.

CAREER: First Unitarian-Universalist Church, Providence, R.I., assistant minister and director of religious education, 1958-60; Howard University, Washington, D.C., visiting lecturer in philosophy, 1963-69; Yale University, New Haven, Conn., associate professor of religion, 1969-76, coordinator of black studies, 1974-76; Florida State University, Tallahassee, professor of religion and director of Afro-American studies program, 1977—, member of advisory board of Horizons Unlimited. Visiting professor at Union Theological Seminary, spring, 1973, Florida A & M University, 1973, Princeton Theological Seminary, spring, 1974, Brown University, autumn, 1975, and Central State College, 1977; Caldwell Lecturer at Louisville Presbyterian Seminary, 1974; Gates Lecturer at Grinnell College, 1975; Marshall Wood Lecturer at Brown University, 1975; Russell Lecturer at Tufts University, 1975; Goodspeed Lecturer at Denison University, 1975; Martin Luther King Lecturer at Wesley Theological Seminary, 1978. Member of board of directors of National Council of Black Studies and Southeast regional coordinator; presents conferences; guest on television and radio programs.

MEMBER: Society for the Study of Black Religion (charter member), American Academy of Religion, American Humanist Association, American Philosophical Association (chairperson of committee on blacks, 1974-76), Educators to Africa Association, Religious Education Association, Society for the Study of Christian Ethics, Unitarian-Universalist Ministers Association (chairperson of Council on Education for Professional Religious Leadership, 1974-77), Unitarian Historical Society, Collegium: Association for Liberal Religious Studies (charter member), Phi Beta Kappa (vice-president, 1978-79; president, 1979-80). *Awards, honors:* Richard Allen Award, 1972; A. Whitney Griswold Award, 1974.

WRITINGS: Is God a White Racist?: Prolegomenon to Black Theology, Doubleday, 1973; (contributor) C. Eric Lincoln, editor, *The Black Experience in Religion,* Doubleday, 1974; (editor with Calvin E. Bruce, and contributor) *Black Theology II,* Bucknell University Press, 1978; (contributor) Rosino Gibellini, editor, *Perspectives of Black Theology,* Queriniana, 1978. Contributor of about fifteen articles to theology and philosophy journals. Member of editorial board of *Uniquest, Journal of Metaphilosophy,* and *Journal of Religious Humanism;* member of board of governors of *Kairos.*

WORK IN PROGRESS: Anatomy of Racism, completion expected in 1983; *Black Religious Humanism: The Invisible Religion.*

*　　*　　*

JORDAN-SMITH, Paul 1885(?)-1971

OBITUARY NOTICE: Born c. 1885; died June 17, 1971, in Santa Monica, Calif. Journalist, editor, bibliophile, and author of books on literary and bibliophilic subjects. For more than twenty years Jordan-Smith's book column, "I'll Be the Judge, You Be the Jury," appeared in the *Los Angeles Times.* Among his writings are a complete editing and translation, with Floyd Dell, of Robert Burton's *Anatomy of Melancholy,* published in 1927, and a novel, *Nomad,* published in 1925. Obituaries and other sources: *AB Bookman's Weekly,* July 5, 1971.

*　　*　　*

JOSEPH, Bertram L(eon) 1915-1981

OBITUARY NOTICE—See index for *CA* sketch: Born July 1, 1915, in Maesteg, South Wales; died of a heart attack, September 3, 1981, in Glen Cove, Long Island, N.Y. Educator and author best known as an authority on Elizabethan drama. Joseph held a number of positions at several universities, including the University of Wales, the University of Bristol, the University of Washington in Seattle, the London Academy of Music and Dramatic Art, and the Bristol Old Vic School. He was credited with founding and chairing the department of drama and theatre at Queen's College in 1970. Joseph was also associated with productions and Shakespearean readings at the Mermaid Theatre and at the American Museum of Natural History. His works include *Elizabethan Acting, The Tragic Actor, Acting Shakespeare, The Spanish Tragedy,* and his most recent publication, *Shakespeare: An Actor's Workbook.* Obituaries and other sources: *New York Times,* September 5, 1981; *AB Bookman's Weekly,* October 19, 1981.

*　　*　　*

JOYCE, James (Augustus Aloysius) 1882-1941

BRIEF ENTRY: Born February 2, 1882, in Dublin, Ireland; died of a perforated ulcer, January 13, 1941, in Zurich, Switzerland. Irish novelist, short story writer, poet, and dramatist. Considered one of the most influential novelists of the first half of the twentieth century, Joyce developed the stream of consciousness novel using interior monologue to reveal the conscious and unconscious feelings of his characters. An Irish expatriate disillusioned with his country's religion, politics, and literature, Joyce left Dublin in 1904. Nevertheless, Ireland and the Irish people are the subjects of all of his fiction. His most celebrated work, the epic-novel *Ulysses,* parallels the twenty-year journey of Homer's Ulysses with twenty-four hours in the life of his protagonist, Dubliner Leopold Bloom. Published in Paris in 1922, *Ulysses* was banned from the United States until 1933 because it was considered obscene. Among Joyce's best-known works are *Dubliners* (1914), *A Portrait of the Artist as a Young Man* (1916), *Ulysses* (1922), and *Finnegan's Wake* (1939). *Residence:* Zurich, Switzerland. *Biographical/critical sources: Cyclopedia of World Authors,* Harper, 1958; *Twentieth Century Writing: A Reader's Guide to Contemporary Literature,* Transatlantic, 1969; *Webster's New World Companion to English and American Literature,* World Publishing, 1973; *Twentieth-Century Literary Criticism,* Volume 3, Gale, 1980.

K

KABAPHE, Konstantinos Petrou
See KAVAFIS, Konstantinos Petrou

* * *

KABAPHES, Konstantinos Petrou
See KAVAFIS, Konstantinos Petrou

* * *

KAIKO, Takeshi 1930-

PERSONAL: Surname is pronounced *K-eye*-ko; born December 30, 1930, in Osaka, Japan; son of a school principal; married Yoko Maki (a poet and writer), 1949; children: Michilco. *Education:* Osaka Municipal University, B.A., 1953. *Home:* 4-8-14 Igusa, Suginami-ku, Tokyo, Japan. *Office:* 6-6-64 Higashi Kaigon Minanu, Chigosaki-shi, Kanagawa-ken, Japan.

CAREER: Writer. Suntory (Kotobukiya) Ltd., Tokyo, Japan, writer and editor, 1953-64. *Member:* P.E.N., Japan Writers' Association. *Awards, honors:* Akutagawa Prize, 1957; Mainichi Cultural Award for literature, 1968; Kawabata Prize for short stories.

WRITINGS—In English translation: *Kagayakeru yami* (fiction), [Japan], 1968, translation by Cecilia Segawa Seigle published as *Into a Black Sun,* Kodansha, 1980; *Natsu no yami* (fiction), [Japan], 1972, translation by Seigle published as *Darkness in Summer,* Knopf, 1973; *"Panic" and "The Runaway": Two Stories,* translated by Charles Dunn, University of Tokyo Press, 1977.

In Japanese; all published in Japan: *Nihon sammon opera,* 1961; *Kaiko Takeshi shu* (short stories), 1961; *Koe no Karyudo,* 1962; *Katasumi no meiro* (fiction), 1963; *Nihonjin no asobiba,* 1963; *Zubari Tokyo* (addresses, essays, and lectures), two volumes, 1964; *Betonamu senki* (history), 1965; (with Makoto Oda) *Heiwa o yobu koe* (nonfiction), 1967; (with Sakyo Komatsu) *Mokei no jidai* (short stories), 1968; *Nanatsu no mijikai shosetsu* (short stories), 1969; *Watashi no chogyo taizen* (addresses, essays, and lectures), 1969; *Aoi getsuyobi* (fiction), 1969.

Hito to kono sekai (nonfiction), 1970; (with Oda) *Mondai no naka de shaberu* (addresses, essays, and lectures), 1970; (with Shintaro Ishihara) *Ishihara Shintaro, Kaiko Takeshi Shu,* 1970; *Kishibe no matsuri* (short stories), 1971; *Fisshu on* (nonfiction), 1971; *Hadaka no osama* (short stories), 1971; *Kami no*

naka no senso (addresses, essays, and lectures), 1972; *Robinson no matsuei* (fiction), 1973; *Saigon no jujika* (addresses, essays, and lectures), 1973; (with Shiro Hasegawa) *Hasegawa Shiro, Kaiko Takeshi* (fiction), 1973; (with Hasegawa) *Hasegawa Shiro, Kaiko Takeshi* (fiction), 1973; *Kaiko ichiban* (essays), 1974; *Gogo no tanoshimi,* 1974; *Atarashii tentai* (fiction), 1974; (editor with Kiichi Sasaki) *Waga uchi to soto naru Hitora* (nonfiction), 1974; *Mita yureta warawareta* (short stories), 1974.

Manako aru hanabana (essays), 1975; *Shirio peji* (essays), 1975, 2nd edition published as *Kampon Shiroi peji* (essays), 1978; *Kaido Takeshi no zenryaku taidan* (nonfiction), 1976; *Kaiko heiko* (essays), Volume I, 1976, Volume II, 1977; *Kaiko Takeshi zennonfikushon* (essays), Volume I: *Kawa wa nemuranai,* 1977, Volume II: *Sakebi to sasayaki,* 1977, Volume III: *Rojo ni te,* 1977, Volume IV: *Kujaku no shita,* 1976, Volume V: *Kotobaaru koya,* 1977; *Jisen sakka no tabi* (nonfiction), 1977; *Yuyu to shite isoge* (nonfiction), 1977; (with Noboru Takahashi) *Opa* (history and travel), 1978; *Hakuchu no hakuso* (essays), 1979; *Aruku kagetachi* (short stories), 1979; *Shokugo no hanataba* (essays), 1979; *Saigo no bansan* (addresses, essays, and lectures), 1979; (with Tadao Umesao) *Wisuki hakubutsukan* (title means "The Whisky Museum"), 1979.

WORK IN PROGRESS: The third volume of his Vietnam trilogy, which was begun with *Darkness in Summer* and continued in *Into a Black Sun;* a collection of his essays about a nine-month fishing trip to Alaska and South America.

SIDELIGHTS: Kaiko's books have been translated into Russian, German, Dutch, Polish, and Finnish.

* * *

KAIN, Saul
See SASSOON, Siegfried (Lorraine)

* * *

KALEMKERIAN, Zarouhi 1874(?)-1971

OBITUARY NOTICE: Born c. 1874 in Istanbul, Turkey; died July 20, 1971, in Ridgewood, N.J. Poet and author. For fifty years the leading literary figure in New York City's Armenian-American community, Kalemkerian published her first book of poems at age sixteen. Her three prose works are *A Book for My Grandson, My Life's Journey,* and *Days and Profiles.* Obituaries and other sources: *New York Times,* July 21, 1971; *AB Bookman's Weekly,* August 2, 1971.

* * *

KALLET, Marilyn 1946-

PERSONAL: Born December 28, 1946, in Montgomery, Ala.; daughter of Harold (in advertising) and Cecelia (a teacher; maiden name, Sachs) Zimmerman; married Steven Kallet, July 19, 1970 (separated). *Education:* Sorbonne, University of Paris, Diplome Superieur, 1967; Tufts University, B.A. (summa cum laude), 1968; Rutgers University, M.A., 1976, Ph.D., 1978. *Politics:* "Feminist." *Religion:* Jewish. *Office:* Department of English, University of Tennessee, Knoxville, Tenn. 37916.

CAREER: Hobart and William Smith Colleges, Geneva, N.Y., assistant professor of English and comparative literature, 1976-81, coordinator of women's studies program, 1979-81; University of Tennessee, Knoxville, assistant professor of English, 1981—. Co-director of Women's Writing Co-Operative, 1973; resident at Virginia Colony for the Arts, 1980; seminar leader; gives readings. *Member:* Phi Beta Kappa. *Awards, honors:* Woodrow Wilson fellowship, 1968.

WRITINGS: Devils Live So Near (poems), Ithaca House, 1977; (translator) Paul Eluard, *Last Love Poems,* Louisiana State University Press, 1980.

Work represented in anthologies, including *I Take My Real Body: Poems by Six Women,* Rutgers University Press, 1975. Contributor of poems and translations to magazines, including *New Letters, Greenfield Review, Primer, Dream Helmet, Slow Loris Reader,* and *Mag City.* Editor of *Salamander,* 1972 and 1976; contributing editor of *Seneca Review,* 1978—.

WORK IN PROGRESS: In the Great Night, poems; *How to Get Heat Without Fire,* poems; a critical study of the love poems of William Carlos Williams.

SIDELIGHTS: Marilyn Kallet wrote: "Poetry is a form of survival. Singing lets us breathe when the circumstances around us constrict and bind us. My writing taught me to be my own person; words teach me about myself and the world; the poem lets me be active toward my existence. For women in particular, developing a voice is the beginning of a new life—not muffled; not suppressed."

* * *

KAMPOV, Boris Nikolayevich 1908-1981
(Boris Polevoi)

OBITUARY NOTICE: Born March 17, 1908, in Moscow, Russia (now U.S.S.R.); died July 12, 1981, in Moscow, U.S.S.R. Journalist, editor, and author. Known by his pseudonym, Boris Polevoi was a journalist, serving in World War II as a war correspondent on the Russo-German front for *Pravda.* He is remembered for his morale-boosting articles that focused on the bravery and tenacity of the soldiers at the front. Polevoi's most popular book, *The Story of a Real Man,* is based on the true story of a Soviet pilot who lost both legs in combat, but learned to fly again despite his artificial limbs. The story was later made into a successful motion picture. The secretary of the Union of Soviet Writers, Polevoi received numerous awards from his homeland, including the Order of Lenin, which he won twice, and the Hero of Socialist Labor. Among his other writings are *The Hot Shop, Blood-Stained Stone, All Men Are Brothers,* and *Nuremberg Diaries.* Obituaries and other sources: *The International Who's Who,* Europa, 1975; *Who's Who in the Socialist Countries,* K. G. Saur, 1978; *London Times,* July 22, 1981.

KANE, Jack
See BAKER, (Allen) Albert

* * *

KARDINER, Abram 1891-1981

OBITUARY NOTICE: Born August 17, 1891, in New York, N.Y.; died July 20, 1981, in Easton, Conn. Psychiatrist, psychoanalyst, educator, and author. In 1930 Kardiner co-founded the New York Psychiatric Institute, the first school of its kind in the United States. From 1955 to 1957 he directed Columbia University's Psychoanalytic Clinic. A student of Sigmund Freud, Kardiner studied social and cultural anthropology in order to interpret psychological patterns and development in the context of the individual's environment. His books *The Individual and His Society* and *The Psychological Frontiers of Society* grew out of this study. Among his other works are *Sex and Morality* and *The Mark of Oppression: Explorations in the Personality of the American Negro.* Kardiner was one of the last living persons to have been analyzed by Freud and in 1977 published a popular memoir of his sessions in Vienna, *My Analysis With Freud.* Obituaries and other sources: *American Authors and Books, 1640 to the Present Day,* 3rd revised edition, Crown, 1972; *New York Times,* July 22, 1981; *Time,* August 3, 1981.

* * *

KARU, Baruch 1899-1972
(Baruch Krupnik)

OBITUARY NOTICE: Born in 1899 in Chernevtsy, Russia (now U.S.S.R.); died c. May 14, 1972, in Tel Aviv, Israel. Editor, critic, lexicographer, and translator. Karu compiled *A Practical Dictionary of the Talmud* and *A Dictionary of Living Aramaic.* His translations include the works of Charles Dickens, D. H. Lawrence, and other English authors, as well as French, Russian, German, and Yiddish works. For his translation of the ten-volume *History of the Jewish People* Karu won the Tchernichowsky Prize. Obituaries and other sources: *Who's Who in World Jewry: A Biographical Dictionary of Outstanding Jews,* Pitman, 1972; *AB Bookman's Weekly,* May 15, 1972.

* * *

KASER, Paul 1944-

PERSONAL: Born October 25, 1944, in Millersburg, Ohio; son of Paul (a hydrologist) and Hariette (a teacher; maiden name, Anderson) Kaser; married Norma A. Haggberg, October 8, 1971; children: David William, Michael Albert. *Education:* Kent State University, B.A., 1966; California State University, Hayward, M.A., 1975. *Home:* 148 East Peralta, Fresno, Calif. 93704. *Agent:* Ellen Levine, Ellen Levine Literary Agency, 370 Lexington Ave., New York, N.Y. 10017. *Office:* Department of English, Kings River Community College, 995 Reed Ave., Reedley, Calif. 93654.

CAREER: Painesville Telegraph, Painesville, Ohio, reporter, 1965; *Geneva Free Press,* Geneva, Ohio, reporter and photographer, 1965; Chabot College, Hayward, Calif., instructor in English, 1973-74; Ohlone College, Fremont, Calif., assistant instructor, 1974-75; Kings River Community College, Reedley, Calif., instructor in English, 1975—; writer, 1970—. Teacher in city and village public and orphanage schools in Vietnam; assistant instructor at California State University, Hayward, 1973-74. President of board of directors of Hayward Family Tutorial Program, 1974; member of Fresno Adult Literacy Council, 1975-81. *Military service:* U.S. Air Force, 1965-70; served in Vietnam; became captain; received Bronze Star. *Member:* Sigma Delta Chi.

WRITINGS: How Jerem Came Home (novel), Scribner, 1980.

Work represented in anthologies, including *Best American Short Stories, 1975,* edited by Martha Foley, Houghton. Contributor of stories to magazines, including *Panache, Denver Quarterly, Colorado Quarterly,* and *North American Mentor.*

WORK IN PROGRESS: A novel set in a Malaysian leper colony, publication expected in 1982.

SIDELIGHTS: "John Gardner's *On Moral Fiction* was a challenge to American writers," Kaser told *CA.* "In writing fiction, I try to keep Gardner's standards in mind. I don't achieve the goal, but I hope that in an effort to 'teach and delight' I come closer to the impossible mark each time. The risk, of course, is being accused of moral pomposity. The risk is being accused of battening on a set of moral principles to which the prevailing literary elite, in the security of its political, often geographical, province does not adhere. The risk is also of being accused of putting too narrow, too didactic an interpretation on Gardner's assertions, of rearranging reality in order to press it into one's own personal teleological imperative. But the writer intensely interested in creating moral fiction will shun dogmatic responses to the manifold problems of his characters, shun the kind of simplistic, fashionable, cause-and-effect analyses that mark many ephemeral, popular writers in America today. The apprentice writer in America, if she or he intends to do anything but be the cause of destruction of pulp trees, must constantly fight off the seductiveness of the latest sociological, psychological, theological, biological, talk-show and advice-column theory of human motivation and select from the multi-cultural wisdom that has become (by virtue of its survival through a hundred shifts of religion and government) classical. This breadth of view, this refusal to be restricted by the superficial and temporary, should be the goal of the fictionalist. Gardner and Bellow are among those few living American authors who provide us with examples. And those examples are often so impressive as to be discouraging.

"Having lived in four distinctly different cultures (Anglo-American, Mexican, Swedish, and Vietnamese), having seen cultures in the chaos of war and revolution, I know that I have set my goal recklessly. To suppose that I can write the truth about any given set of characters in any given environment suggests self-delusion on a dangerous scale. But there is nothing to write about without that risk. And I will certainly judge my own efforts more critically than any other reader of my work can.

"If all this sounds rather too grandly defensive, I would hasten to add that the moral fictionalist in America today does not stand in stormy exile and aloofness. There are still editors and publishers willing to risk taking on a 'non-commercial' work out of a belief that it has value beyond the profit column. And there are many young writers willing to risk the loneliness if they remain 'undiscovered.'"

AVOCATIONAL INTERESTS: Travel (Malaysia, Japan, Thailand, Hong Kong, Macao, Taiwan, Australia, Western Europe, Egypt, Peru, Bolivia, U.S.S.R., Ukraine, Mexico, Canada).

BIOGRAPHICAL/CRITICAL SOURCES: Los Angeles Times, October 9, 1980; *Library Journal,* November, 1980.

*   *   *

KASS, Jerome   1923(?)-1973

OBITUARY NOTICE: Born c. 1923; died November 11, 1973.

Publishing executive and technical editor and writer. Kass was managing editor and vice-president of J. F. Rider Publishing, Inc. He also helped form A. F. Michael Publishing Service, Inc., and co-founded Baywood Publishing Co., Inc. He served as president of Baywood Publishing beginning in 1967. Kass was a technical editor for *Radio News* and wrote technical articles for encyclopedias. Obituaries and other sources: *Publishers Weekly,* January 21, 1974.

*   *   *

KATONA, George   1901-1981

OBITUARY NOTICE: Born November 6, 1901, in Budapest, Hungary; died June 18, 1981, in West Berlin, West Germany. Psychologist, economist, educator, and author. An American citizen since 1939, Katona was generally regarded as the dean of behavioral economics. As professor of economics and psychology at the University of Michigan from 1946 to 1972, and as founder and director of the economic behavior program at the university's Survey Research Center, Katona originated the regular survey of consumer attitudes. He viewed the consumer as a complex personality and maintained that the consumer's psychological state is an important factor in economic trends. Katona wrote more than a dozen books, including *Psychological Analysis of Economic Behavior, Consumer Expectations, The Mass Consumption Society,* and *Aspirations and Affluence.* He was in West Berlin to receive an honorary doctorate from the Free University of Berlin at the time of his death. Obituaries and other sources: *American Men and Women of Science: The Social and Behavioral Sciences,* 12th edition, Bowker, 1973; *Who's Who in America,* 40th edition, Marquis, 1978; *New York Times,* June 19, 1981; *Time,* June 29, 1981; *Newsweek,* June 29, 1981.

*   *   *

KAVAFIS, Konstantinos Petrou   1863-1933

BRIEF ENTRY: Born April 17, 1863, in Alexandria, Egypt; died April 29, 1933, in Alexandria, Egypt. Greek poet. Despite limited publication during his lifetime, Kavafis is generally considered one of the Mediterranean's finest modern poets. His small canon, including the posthumously published *Complete Poems of C. P. Cavafy* (1961) and *Passions and Ancient Days* (1971), focuses on art and passion. The city of Alexandria is frequently the setting for these poems of homosexual love and the Mediterranean's Hellenist past. Many of the poems contained in the collections, particularly those verses written before 1910, were later renounced by the poet as unacceptable in light of his other works. Kavafis is also well known as the "poet of the city" in Lawrence Durrell's *Alexandria Quartet. Biographical/critical sources: The Reader's Encyclopedia,* 2nd edition, Dutton, 1965; *Everyman's Dictionary of European Writers,* Dutton, 1968; *Cassell's Encyclopaedia of World Literature,* revised edition, Morrow, 1973; *Twentieth-Century Literary Criticism,* Volume 2, Gale, 1979.

*   *   *

KAVIFIS, Konstantinos Petrou
   See KAVAFIS, Konstantinos Petrou

*   *   *

KAZDIN, Alan E(dward)   1945-

PERSONAL: Born January 24, 1945, in Cincinnati, Ohio; son of Leon N. and Eve (Cappello) Kazdin; married Joann M. DiDonato; children: Nicole Marie, Michelle Jeanette. *Educa-*

tion: San Jose State University, B.A., 1967; Northwestern University, M.A., 1968, Ph.D., 1970. *Office:* School of Medicine, Western Psychiatric Institute and Clinic, University of Pittsburgh, 3811 O'Hara St., Pittsburgh, Pa. 15261.

CAREER: Pennsylvania State University, University Park, assistant professor, 1971-74, associate professor, 1974-77, professor of psychology, 1977-80; University of Pittsburgh, Pittsburgh, Pa., professor of psychiatry and psychology, 1980—. Fellow at Center for Advanced Study in the Behavioral Sciences, Palo Alto, Calif. *Member:* Association for the Advancement of Behavior Therapy (past president). *Awards, honors:* Research scientist development award from National Institute of Mental Health, 1981, for research on the treatment and assessment of childhood psychopathology.

WRITINGS: Behavior Modification in Applied Settings, Dorsey, 1975; *The Token Economy: A Review and Evaluation,* Plenum, 1977; *History of Behavior Modification,* University Park Press, 1978; (with B.B. Lahey) *Advances in Clinical Child Psychology,* Plenum, Volume I, 1977, Volume II, 1978, Volume III, 1980; (with G. T. Wilson) *Evaluation of Behavior Therapy,* Ballinger, 1978; (with Wilson and W. S. Argas) *Behavior Therapy: Toward an Applied Clinical Science,* W. H. Feeman, 1979; (with others) *New Perspectives in Abnormal Psychology,* Oxford University Press, 1980; *Research Design in Clinical Psychology,* Harper, 1980. Editor of *Behavior Therapy.*

WORK IN PROGRESS: Research on disorders of severely disturbed children and on their psychological and psychiatric treatment.

* * *

KECK, Leander Earl   1928-

PERSONAL: Born March 3, 1928, in Washburn, N.D.; son of Jacob J. and Elizabeth (Klein) Keck; married Janice Osburn (a minister), September 7, 1956; children: Stephen, David. *Education:* Linfield College, B.A., 1949; Andover Newton Theological School, B.D., 1953; attended University of Kiel, 1955, and University of Goettingen, 1956; Yale University, Ph.D., 1957. *Religion:* Protestant. *Home:* 348 Canner St., New Haven, Conn. 06511. *Office:* Divinity School, Yale University, 409 Prospect St., New Haven, Conn. 06510.

CAREER: Wellesley College, Wellesley, Mass., instructor in biblical history, 1957-59; Vanderbilt University, Nashville, Tenn., 1959-72, began as assistant professor, became professor; Emory University, Atlanta, Ga., professor of New Testament and chairman of Division of Religion, 1972-77; Yale University, New Haven, Conn., Winkley Professor of Biblical Theology and dean of Divinity School, 1979—, Shaffer Lecturer, 1980. Kepler Lecturer at Oberlin College, 1965; Hayward Lecturer at Acadia University, 1967; Bailey Lecturer at Berkeley Baptist Divinity School and lecturer at University of Winnipeg, both 1969; Caleb Davies Lecturer at Phillips University and visiting professor at Emory University and Iliff School of Theology, all 1970; visiting professor at Union Theological Seminary, Manila, Philippines, 1971; Alumni Lecturer at Columbia School of Theology, 1972; Hester Lecturer at Midwestern Baptist Theological Seminary, 1973; Shumate Lecturer at Lynchburg College and Gheens Lecturer at Southern Baptist Theological Seminary, both 1975; Wolford Lecturer at Hartwick College, 1976; Fall Lecturer at Southeastern Baptist Theological Seminary, 1977; Jackson Lecturer at Perkins School of Theology, 1978; Cato Lecturer at University of Melbourne and Gray Lecturer at Duke University, both 1979; Sizemore Lecturer at Midwestern Baptist Theological Seminary,

1980; Sprinkle Lecturer at Atlantic Christian College, 1981; Denio Lecturer at Bangor Theological Seminary, 1982. Conducted research at University of Tuebingen, 1964-65, and Cambridge University, 1971 and 1976.

MEMBER: American Academy of Religion, Society of Biblical Literature (vice-president of Southeastern section, 1972-73; president, 1973-74; chairman of research and publications committee, 1979—), Studiorum Novi Testamenti Societas, Association of Theological Schools (member of executive committee, 1980-86). *Awards, honors:* S.T.D. from Bethany College, 1975; D.D. from Texas Christian University, 1980; D.H.L. from Atlantic Christian College, 1980; D. Litt. from Linfield College, 1980.

WRITINGS: Taking the Bible Seriously, Association Press, 1962; *Mandate to Witness,* Judson, 1964; (editor with J. Louis Martyn) *Studies in Luke-Acts,* Abingdon, 1966; *A Future for the Historical Jesus,* Abingdon, 1971; (with Fred Craddock) *Proclamation: Series B, Pentecost 3,* Fortress, 1976; *The New Testament Experience of Faith,* Bethany Press, 1977; (translator and author of introduction and notes) D. F. Strauss, *The Christ of Faith and the Jesus of History,* Fortress, 1977; *The Bible in the Pulpit,* Abingdon, 1978; *Paul and His Letters,* Fortress, 1979.

Editor of eight volume "Lives of Jesus" series, Fortress, 1971-77. Editor of monograph series for Society of Biblical Literature, 1973-78. Contributor of about seventy-five articles and reviews to scholarly journals. Member of editorial board of *Journal of Biblical Literature,* 1970-73, and *Quarterly Review,* 1980—; review editor of *Religious Studies Review,* 1975—; member of editorial council of *Interpretation,* 1977-80.

WORK IN PROGRESS: Romans for the "Anchor Bible" series, publication expected by Doubleday; *Jesus in New Testament Christology,* publication expected by Fortress.

* * *

KELEMEN, Pal   1894-

PERSONAL: Born April 24, 1894, in Budapest, Hungary; came to the United States in 1932, naturalized citizen, 1939; son of Joseph and Jenny (Gratt) Kelemen; married Elisabeth Hutchings Zulauf, May 2, 1932. *Education:* Attended universities of Budapest, Munich, and Paris. *Religion:* Magyar Reformed. *Home address:* Loon Meadow Dr., Norfolk, Conn. 06058; and P.O. Box 447, Norfolk, Conn. 06058.

CAREER: Conducted independent research at museums in Budapest, Hungary, Vienna, Austria, Florence, Italy, London, England, Madrid, Spain, and Seville, Spain. Visiting professor at University of Texas, 1953, and Columbia University, 1968; lecturer at universities and museums, including National Gallery of Art and Metropolitan Museum of Art. Member of Commission for the Protection and Salvage of Artistic and Historic Monuments in War Areas, 1943-44; conducted surveys and lecture tours for U.S. Department of State in Mexico, Guatemala, Honduras, El Salvador, Nicaragua, Panama, Colombia, Ecuador, Peru, and Bolivia, 1933—, and Portugal, Spain, Switzerland, Hungary, Czechoslovakia, and Belgium, 1948; specialist for International Educational Exchange Service in Portugal, Spain, Italy, Turkey, Greece, and England, 1956; conducted additional research in Sicily. Member of board of trustees of Kodaly Center of America. *Member:* Royal Anthropological Institute (fellow). *Awards, honors:* L.H.D. from University of Arizona, 1976; commander of Order of Merit of Ecuador.

WRITINGS: Battlefield of the Gods: Aspects of Mexican History, Art, and Exploration, Allen & Unwin, 1937; *Medieval*

American Art, two volumes, Macmillan, 1943; *Baroque and Rococo in Latin America,* Macmillan, 1951, 2nd edition, two volumes, Dover, 1967; *Medieval American Art: Masterpieces of the New World Before Columbus,* Macmillan, 1956, 3rd edition, two volumes, Dover, 1969; *El Greco Revisited: Candia, Venice, Toledo,* Macmillan, 1961; *Art of the Americas: Ancient and Hispanic, With a Comparative Chapter on the Philippines,* Crowell, 1969; *Peruvian Colonial Painting, a Special Exhibition: The Collection of the Stern Fund and Mr. and Mrs. Arthur Q. Davis, With an Additional Collection From the Brooklyn Museum,* privately printed, 1971; *Hussar's Picture Book: From the Diary of a Hungarian Cavalry Officer in World War I,* Indiana University, 1972; *Folk Baroque in Mexico: Exhibition of Mestizo Architecture Through the Centuries,* Brewton Co., 1974; *The Painter in Europe and in Viceregal Spanish America,* Kunsthalle, 1976; *Vanishing Art of the Americas,* Walker & Co., 1977. Also author of *El Greco Revisited: His Byzantine Heritage,* 1962, *Stepchild of the Humanities: Art of the Americas Observed,* 1979, and *Colonial Organs of Latin America,* 1980.

Other: (with Paul Westheim) *Die Kunst Alt-Mexikos,* Ullstein, 1964; *L'art precolombien hors du Mexique: L'art colonial ibero-Americain* (bound with *L'art du Mexique precolombien* by Westheim), edited by Eugen Theodor Rimli, Payot, 1966.

Contributor to *Encyclopaedia Britannica* and *Stauffer's World Art History.* Contributor to journals in the United States, Latin America, and Europe.

SIDELIGHTS: Kelemen's encyclopedic work, *Medieval American Art,* received rave reviews from critics. *Nation's* Elizabeth Wilder commented that "for the most part it is so astonishingly good that one is tempted to leave criticism for praise." Covering pre-Columbian art, including that of the Mayan, Toltec, and Aztec cultures, *Medieval American Art* was heralded by P.A. Means of the *New York Times* as "the most complete and penetrating general survey of native American art ever published in English or in any other language." The *Weekly Book Review's* Royal Cortissoz similarly noted that the book "is a fascinating and exceptionally useful work."

Baroque and Rococo in Latin America also met with an enthusiastic reception. Dorothy Adlow asserted in the *Christian Science Monitor* that the book "expands a fascinating subject in an illuminating way." The *New York Times's* Bernard Beven was more fulsome in his praise: "I have no hesitation in saying this is far and away the best, the most informative—and the most readable book in any language on the architecture, sculpture and painting of Latin America and the unique conditions under which these flourished."

BIOGRAPHICAL/CRITICAL SOURCES: New York Times, May 30, 1943, July 1, 1951, April 1, 1962; *Christian Science Monitor,* July 24, 1943, September 27, 1951; *Yale Review,* autumn, 1943; *Nation,* November 6, 1943, July 28, 1951; *New Republic,* December 13, 1943; *Weekly Book Review,* January 2, 1944.*

*   *   *

KELLER, Dolores Elaine   1926-

PERSONAL: Born October 29, 1926, in New York, N.Y.; daughter of Louis and Ada Betsy (Ross) Greene; married Martin Edward Keller, July 27, 1946; children: Steven Edward, Kevin Edward, Wendy Anne. *Education:* Northwestern University, certificate, 1942; Long Island University, B.S. (magna cum laude), 1945; New York University, M.A., 1947, Ph.D., 1956; postdoctoral study at Columbia University, 1961, University of Hawaii, 1964, University of North Carolina, 1969,

and University of California, Davis, 1971; University of California, Berkeley, certificate in electron microscopy, 1966. *Home:* 96 Cypress St., Woodcliff Lake, N.J. 07680. *Office:* Department of Biology, Pace University, New York, N.Y. 10038.

CAREER: High school biology teacher and department head in Prospect Heights and Brooklyn, N.Y., 1949-52, and New York City, 1952-54; Long Island University, Brooklyn, instructor in Romance languages, 1954-56; Fairleigh Dickinson University, Teaneck, N.J., associate professor of science and chairman of department, 1956-66; Pace University, New York City, director of allied health programs, 1965—, professor of biology, 1966—, chairman of department, 1966-68. Private practice in sex therapy, 1974—; senior therapist at Payne Whitney Sexual Dysfunction Clinic, Yale-New Haven Hospital, 1974—; director of Center for Sex Education. Lecturer in adult education program in Union, N.J., 1952—; clinical assistant professor at Cornell University, 1974—; curriculum chairman at Bergen County Community College, 1964—. Research associate at Haskins Laboratories, 1965—, and Columbia University, 1967—. Member of executive committee of Project Hope; member of Bergen County Juvenile Delinquency Commission; executive director of New Jersey Junior Academy of Science; member of national committee of Future Scientists of America; delegate to United Nations International Oceanographic Congress, 1959.

MEMBER: International Society for Clinical and Experimental Hypnosis, American Association for the Advancement of Science (fellow), Electron Microscope Society of America, American Zoological Society, National Science Teachers Association, American Institute of Biological Sciences, American Association for Sex Educators, Counselors, and Therapists, Society of Protozoologists, Society for Clinical and Experimental Hypnosis, Society for the Scientific Study of Sex, Animal Behavior Society, Eastern Association of Sex Therapists, New York Academy of Sciences. *Awards, honors:* National Science Foundation grants and Allied Health grants.

WRITINGS: Sex and the Single Cell, Pegasus, 1972. Also author of *Applied Sex Therapy,* 1974. Contributor to professional journals.*

*   *   *

KELLEY, Allen C(harles)   1937-

PERSONAL: Born September 5, 1937, in Everett, Wash.; son of Charles Edward and Velma L. (Allen) Kelley; married Patty Ann Cochran, June 20, 1959; children: Brian Allen, Michael Charles, Mark Andrew. *Education:* Attended Linfield College, 1955-57; Stanford University, A.B., 1959, Ph.D., 1964. *Home:* 4607 Chicopee Trail, Durham, N.C. 27707. *Office:* Department of Economics, Duke University, Durham, N.C. 27706.

CAREER: Australian National University, Canberra, visiting research fellow, 1962-63; Stanford University, Stanford, Calif., acting assistant professor of economics, 1963-64; University of Wisconsin, Madison, assistant professor, 1964-67, associate professor, 1967-71, professor of economics, 1971-72; Duke University, Durham, N.C., professor of economics, 1972—, chairman of department, 1973-80, associate director of Center for Demographic Studies, 1973—. Visiting professor at Monash University, 1970-71; Esmee Fairbairn Research Professor at Harriet-Watt University of Edinburgh, 1978; research scholar at International Institute for Applied Systems Analysis, Laxenburg, Austria, 1979. Member of board of trustees and executive committee of Joint Council on Economic Education.

MEMBER: International Union for the Scientific Study of Population, American Economic Association (chairman of committee of economic education), Population Association of America, Southern Economic Association, Phi Beta Kappa. *Awards, honors:* Grants from Carnegie Foundation, 1967-69, National Science Foundation, 1969-71; Rockefeller Foundation, 1970-71; Exxon Education Foundation, 1969-72, 1972-74, 1975-78, Ford Foundation, 1973-80, National Institute of Education, 1975-76, and Sloan Foundation, 1979-82; Kazanzian Award from Joint Council on Economic Education, 1972; Arthur Cole Prize in Economic History from Economic History Association, 1972, for most outstanding article in economic history, written with Jeffrey G. Williamson.

WRITINGS—All with Jeffrey G. Williamson: (With R. J. Cheetham) *Dualistic Economic Development: Theory and History,* University of Chicago Press, 1972; *Lessons From Japanese Development: An Analytical Economic History,* University of Chicago Press, 1974; *Modeling Urbanization and Economic Growth,* International Institute for Applied Systems Analysis, 1980; (with Warren G. Sanderson) *General Equilibrium Modeling and development,* Pergamon, 1982.

Contributor: Keith G. Lumsden, editor, *Recent Research in Economic Education,* Prentice-Hall, 1970; Elliot R. Morse and Ritchie H. Reed, editors, *Economic Aspects of Population Change,* U.S. Government Printing Office, 1972; Burton A. Weisbrod and others, editors, *Disease and Economic Development,* University of Wisconsin Press, 1973; Paul A. David and Melvin W. Reder, editors, *Nations and Households in Economic Growth: Essays in Honor of Moses Abramowitz,* Academic Press, 1974; Kazushi Ohkawa and Yujiro Hayami, editors, *Long-Term Analysis of the Japanese Economy,* Nihon Keizai Shimbunsha, 1974; Richard A. Easterlin, editor, *Population and Economic Change in Less Developed Countries,* University of Chicago Press, 1979. Contributor of more than thirty-five articles and reviews to economic journals. Member of editorial board of *Journal of Economic Education,* 1973—.

WORK IN PROGRESS: *Urbanization and Economic Development,* with Jeffrey G. Williamson; *Demographic Change and Development in Rural Egypt,* with Atef Khalifa and Nabil El-Khorazaty, publication expected in 1982.

*   *   *

KELLOCK, Archibald P.
See MAVOR, Osborne Henry

*   *   *

KELLY, C.M.O.
See GIBBS, (Cecilia) May

*   *   *

KELLY, Stephen E(ugene)   1919-1978

OBITUARY NOTICE: Born May 13, 1919, in Brooklyn, N.Y.; died of cancer, April 6, 1978, in Manhattan, N.Y. Publishing executive. Kelly began his career at Time Inc. and worked on *Life* and *Sports Illustrated* magazines. He later served as publisher of *McCall's* and was also the last publisher of the *Saturday Evening Post.* In 1969 he became president of the Magazine Publishers Association and promoted magazines as an advertising medium while fighting rising postal rates. Obituaries and other sources: *Who's Who in America,* 40th edition, Marquis, 1978; *New York Times,* April 7, 1978; *Time,* April 17, 1978.

KEMPER, Robert V(an)   1945-

PERSONAL: Born November 21, 1945, in San Diego, Calif.; son of Ivan L. (in quality control) and Roberta (King) Kemper; married Sandra Lee Kraft (a teacher), September 9, 1967. *Education:* University of California, Riverside, A.B. (with highest honors), 1966; University of California, Berkeley, M.A. (with distinction), 1969, Ph.D., 1971. *Home:* 10617 Cromwell, Dallas, Tex. 75229. *Office:* Department of Anthropology, Southern Methodist University, Dallas, Tex. 75275.

CAREER: Southern Methodist University, Dallas, Tex., assistant professor, 1972-77, associate professor of anthropology, 1977—, member of Urban Studies Council, 1973-75, and Ibero-American Studies Council, 1973—. Visiting professor at Universidad Ibero-Americana, 1970, 1979-80; adjunct associate professor of Health Science Center, University of Texas, Dallas, 1979; research associate at Institute for Mesoamerican Studies, State University of New York at Albany, 1979—. Fellow at Institute of Latin American Studies, University of Texas, 1976-77. Field researcher in Latin America, 1967—. Member of Dallas Municipal Library advisory board, 1975-79; member of library services task force of Inter-University Council of the North Texas Area, 1978-79.

MEMBER: American Anthropological Association (fellow), American Association for the Advancement of Science (fellow), American Ethnological Society, Society for Applied Anthropology (fellow), Current Anthropology (associate), Latin American Studies Association, Rural Sociological Society (associate member), Kroeber Anthropological Society, Cibola Anthropological Association, Society for Urban Anthropology, Latin American Anthropology Group (co-chairman, 1979-81), Association of Borderland Scholars, Sociedad Mexicana de Antropologia, Phi Beta Kappa. *Awards, honors:* Woodrow Wilson fellow, 1966-67; grants from National Institute of General Medical Sciences, 1966-71, National Endowment for the Humanities, 1971-72, Wenner-Green Foundation for Anthropological Research, 1974, 1976, 1979-80, National Science Foundation, 1974-76, Lilly Foundation, 1977, Smithsonian Institution and American Anthropological Association (for India), 1978, Texas State Department of Human Resources, 1978, 1979, National Institute on Drug Abuse, 1979-82, and Ford Foundation, 1980; Fulbright-Hays fellow in Mexico, 1980.

WRITINGS: (Editor with George M. Foster, and contributor) *Anthropologists in Cities,* Little, Brown, 1974; *Campesinos en la ciudad: Gente de Tzintzuntzan* (title means "Peasants in the City: The People of Tzintzuntzan"), Secretaria de Educacion Publica, 1976; *Migration and Adaptation: Tzintzuntzan Peasants in Mexico City,* Sage Publications, 1977; (with John F. S. Phinney) *The History of Anthropology: A Research Bibliography,* Garland Publishing, 1977; (editor with Wayne A. Cornelius) *Metropolitan Latin America: The Challenge and the Response,* Sage Publications, 1978; (editor with Foster, Thayer Scudder, and Elizabeth Colson, and contributor) *Long-Term Field Research in Social Anthropology,* Academic Press, 1979; (editor with Fernando Camara, and contributor) *Migration Across Frontiers: Mexico and the United States,* Institute for Mesoamerican Studies, State University of New York at Albany, 1979; (editor with Margaret Clark and Cynthia Nelson, and contributor) *From Tzintzuntzan to the "Image of Limited Good": Essays in Honor of George M. Foster,* Kroeber Anthropological Society, 1979.

Contributor: Wayne A. Cornelius and Felicity M. Trueblood, editors, *Anthropological Perspectives on Latin American Ur-*

banization, Sage Publications, 1974; Brian M. DuToit and Helen I. Safa, editors, *Migration and Urbanization: Models and Adaptive Strategies,* Mouton, 1975; Jorge E. Hardoy and Richard P. Schaedel, editors, *Las ciudades de America Latina y sus areas de influencia a traves de la historia* (title means "Latin American Cities and Their Areas of Influence Through History"), Ediciones S.I.A.P., 1975; Cornelius and True-blood, editors, *Urbanization and Inequality: The Political Economy of Urban and Rural Development in Latin America,* Sage Publications, 1975; John Hunter, Robert Thomas, and Scott Whiteford, editors, *Urbanization and Population Growth in Latin America: The Rural-Urban Interface,* Schenkman, 1981.

Co-editor of "Latin American Urban Research," a series, Sage Publications, 1976-77. Contributor to *Americana Annual.* Contributor of more than sixty articles and reviews to anthropology journals. Assistant editor of *El Mensajero,* 1974; associate editor of *Urban Anthropology,* 1975-80, and *Comparative Urban Research,* 1975—; editor of *Papers of Kroeber Anthropological Society,* 1968-70, and *Anthropology Newsletter,* 1972-74; member of editorial board of *Urban Anthropology,* 1980—, and international advisory board of *Latin American Urban Research,* 1975-78.

WORK IN PROGRESS: Tzintzuntzan Migrant Project, completion expected in 1983; *History of Anthropology in Mexico,* 1984; *History of Applied Anthropology in the United States, 1940-1955,* 1984.

SIDELIGHTS: Kemper told *CA:* "As an anthropologist, I am interested in diverse aspects of the human situation, throughout the contemporary world and the historical past. My writing on a wide range of topics—migration, urbanization, tourism, Mexico, the United States, the history of anthropology, and research methods—reflects the diversity of my search for understanding cultural change processes. Writing, research, and teaching combine to remind me how fragile is our knowledge of the world in which we live. For me, doing fieldwork is only valuable to the extent that the research results are written up and published in ways useful both to the international community of scholars (not all of whom read English as a first language) and to the community of people who permit my research to go forward. Without the support and encouragement of both communities, there would be no research, no writing, no teaching."

*   *   *

KENNEDY, Edward R(idgway)   1923(?)-1975

OBITUARY NOTICE: Born c. 1923; died of a heart attack, June 16, 1975, in Cleveland, Ohio. Journalist and publisher. Kennedy began his career as a reporter for the *Indianapolis Times* and then spent most of the 1950's in Asia, becoming managing editor of the English-language *Japan Times* in Tokyo. He was publisher of *The World Almanac* and vice-president for publications of the Newspaper Enterprise Association at the time of his death. Obituaries and other sources: *New York Times,* June 18, 1975; *Publishers Weekly,* July 14, 1975; *AB Bookman's Weekly,* August 25, 1975.

*   *   *

KENRICK, Tony   1935-

PERSONAL: Born August 23, 1935, in Sydney, Australia; son of Arthur Francis (an engineer) and Freda (a mind reader; maiden name, Kenrick) Kenrick; married Joan May Wells (a painter), April 13, 1960; children: Melanie, Tim. *Education:*

Attended high school in Sydney, Australia. *Home:* 37 Godfrey Rd. W., Weston, Conn. 06883; and home in London, England. *Agent:* Bill Berger Associates, Inc., 444 East 58th St., New York, N.Y. 10022.

CAREER: Associated with Farmer's advertising department, 1953-56; Notley's, London, England, copywriter, 1956-57; McClaren's, Toronto, Ontario, advertising copywriter, 1957-60; Doyle Dane Bernbach, New York, N.Y., advertising copywriter, 1960-62; Johnson & Lewis, San Francisco, Calif., advertising copywriter, 1962-65; worked for Manhoff, New York, 1965-68; C.D.P., London, England, advertising copywriter, 1968-72; free-lance writer, 1972—. *Military service:* Royal Australian Navy, 1953. *Member:* Authors Guild, Authors League of America, Writers Guild of America (West).

WRITINGS—Crime novels: *The Only Good Body's a Dead One,* J. Cape, 1970, Simon & Schuster, 1971; *A Tough One to Lose,* Bobbs-Merrill, 1972; *Two for the Price of One,* Bobbs-Merrill, 1974; *Stealing Lillian,* McKay, 1975 (published in England as *The Kidnap Kid,* M. Joseph, 1976); *The Seven Day Soldiers,* Regnery, 1976; *The Chicago Girl,* Putnam, 1976; *Two Lucky People,* M. Joseph, 1978; *The Nighttime Guy,* Morrow, 1979; *The Eighty-First Site,* New American Library, 1980.

Screenplays: "Nobody's Perfect," Columbia Pictures, 1981; "Chattanooga Choo Choo," Phil Borack Enterprises, 1982; "Heaven Help Us," Phil Borack Enterprises, 1983.

WORK IN PROGRESS: "Nothing But the Worst," a screenplay for Columbia Pictures; *Faraday's Flowers,* a novel.

SIDELIGHTS: Kenrick wrote: "I made the decision to become a writer after reading three works in the same day: Dante's *Inferno,* Goethe's *Faust,* and *Hamlet.* I said to myself, 'Hell, I can do better than this junk.'"

*   *   *

KENT, Ernest W(illiam)   1940-

PERSONAL: Born December 27, 1940, in Rockford, Ill.; son of Ernest W., Sr. (a bakery manager) and Virginia (Lower) Kent; married Darlene Jaspersen, June 5, 1964 (divorced); married Laura Borchard (a marketing executive), June 3, 1972 (divorced). *Education:* University of Chicago, B.S., 1963, Ph.D., 1970. *Politics:* "Self-interested independent." *Religion:* None. *Home:* 3950 Lake Shore Dr., Apt. 503, Chicago, Ill. 60613. *Office:* Department of Psychology/Pharmacology, University of Illinois at Chicago Circle, P.O. Box 4348, Chicago, Ill. 60680.

CAREER: University of Illinois at Chicago Circle, Chicago, assistant professor, 1969-73, associate professor of psychology, 1974—. *Member:* Society for Neurosciences, American Association for the Advancement of Science.

WRITINGS: The Brains of Men and Machines, McGraw, 1981. Contributor of about forty articles to professional journals, including *Byte.*

WORK IN PROGRESS: Research on cognitive machines and artificial consciousness.

SIDELIGHTS: Kent told *CA:* "I am interested in the development of cognitive machines; that is, machines which perform brain-like functions. As a specialist in both brains and computers, I have become convinced that traditional computers will not suffice, but that such machines are possible (perhaps by using contemporary-type computers as functional parts). My popular writings to date have been an attempt to introduce some of these ideas to a technically-minded audience. Beginning in the fall, 1981, I will be moving to Washington, D.C., to begin work with the National Bureau of Standards on the development of robot brains for industrial automation.''

* * *

KERBY, Bill 1937-

PERSONAL: Born December 13, 1937, in Buffalo, N.Y.; son of Joseph Daniels (in business) and Lucy (a bookseller; maiden name, Chamberlain) Kerby; married Julie Aldrich, 1969 (divorced, 1971); married Elaine Pearsons (a designer and photographer), May 16, 1981. Education: Attended Wofford College, 1957, and Mexico City College, 1959; Kent State University, B.A., 1962; University of California, Los Angeles, M.F.A., 1968. Politics: ''Ex-liberal, ex-hippie, current Hun.'' Religion: Syda Yoga (Baba Muktananda). Agent: Adams, Ray, Rosenberg, 9200 Sunset Blvd., Los Angeles, Calif. 90069.

CAREER: Worked as actor, peach packer, lifeguard, and driving instructor; investigator for welfare department in New York, N.Y., 1962-63; New Communicators, Los Angeles, teacher, 1968; California Institute of Arts, Los Angeles, instructor, 1969; writer. Military service: U.S. Marine Corps, 1956-58. Member: Writers Guild, West.

WRITINGS—Screenplays: (Uncredited; with William S. Roberts) ''The Last American Hero,'' Twentieth Century-Fox, 1973; (with David Whitney) ''Gravy Train,'' Columbia, 1974, re-released as ''The Dion Brothers,'' 1974; (with Tom Rickman) ''Hooper,'' Warner Bros., 1977; (with Bo Goldman) ''The Rose,'' Twentieth Century-Fox, 1979; (co-story only) ''Firepower,'' I.T.C., 1979.

Co-author of teleplay ''Steel Cowboy'' with Doug Wheeler, NBC-TV, 1978. Contributor to periodicals, including Eye, World Countdown, and Los Angeles Free Press.

WORK IN PROGRESS: ''The End of the Line,'' a screenplay for Warner Bros.; ''Dance You Devils,'' a screenplay; The Bottom of the Ninth, a novel.

SIDELIGHTS: Kerby was involved in credit disputes on two of his screenplays, ''The Last American Hero'' and ''The Rose.'' Dispute over the writing credit for ''The Last American Hero'' began when Kerby learned that producer William S. Roberts was being acknowledged as sole author of the script. Unfortunately for Kerby, he neglected to notify the Writers Guild of the discrepancy. ''I didn't even file a statement of my case with the guild,'' he said. ''Without my statement, not only did I get no credit, but the other guy . . . got elevated.'' Lamont Johnson, director of ''The Last American Hero,'' sympathized with Kerby, and began notifying critics, including Pauline Kael, that Kerby's work was going unrecognized. ''I was a grade-C minor celebrity for 32 minutes,'' Kerby declared. Finally, the screenwriter of credit, producer William S. Roberts, demanded arbitration to settle authorship. Kerby lost. ''Remember the old credit 'additional dialogue by,''' Roberts asked. ''If they still gave it out, that's what Kerby should have had.'' Kerby, however, contends that ''it must gall Bill Roberts that I lay claim to his work when my name isn't on the screen, but that's the way it goes.''

A similar dispute developed over authorship of ''The Rose,'' the popular rock music film which featured Bette Midler in the Janis Joplin-like role. Producer Marvin Worth hired Kerby to write the script, then called in director Michael Cimino to work with Kerby on the second draft. ''Worth, myself and Cimino took apart the first draft,'' Kerby noted. ''It was a solid week of brain busting, a solid week of meetings five hours a day. I thought, Gee, this is what show business is all about.'' Cimino

was later dismissed as director, but only after he'd co-written a second draft with Worth. Then another screenwriter, Bo Goldman, was hired to revise the script. In 1979, two years after the writing was completed and the film was made and prepared for release, Kerby learned that credit for the story was shared by Worth and Cimino, and that credit for the screenplay was to be shared by Goldman, Cimino, and himself. Kerby then demanded arbitration from the Writers Guild. ''I knew I had a real good shot at lots of credit,'' he told Los Angeles. But the arbitration proceedings tried Kerby's patience. ''I became vicious and old before my time,'' he revealed. The Writers Guild ruled in Kerby's favor, however. He received sole story credit, and shared the screenwriter's credit with Goldman.

Kerby told CA: ''It might seem as if I spend most of my time worrying about credit. This is not true, fortunately. I while away most of my hours with my wife and cats on Cape Cod (bootie from 'The Rose') or, like most writers I know, reading magazines with large print. Occasionally, I actually write; a process I love. I am virtually unemployable except for writing movies. It's an odd and not very important talent but I am proud to be able to do it. When I grew up in the 1950's in the South, my heroes were either movie stars or writers, due probably in some part to the fact that the ancient couple that owned the Lake Lanier Drive-In were friends of mine and my mother owned the only bookstore in town. Consorting with heroes is a dream come true.''

BIOGRAPHICAL/CRITICAL SOURCES: Film Comment, January-February, 1980; Los Angeles, March, 1980; Village Broadsider, May 6, 1981.

* * *

KERNS, J(ames) Alexander 1894-1975

OBITUARY NOTICE: Born January 17, 1894, in Mason, Mich.; died October 11, 1975, in Staten Island, N.Y. Educator, linguist, and author. An expert in comparative linguistics, Kerns taught at New York University for six years before joining the faculty of Washington Square College in 1937. He taught classics there for more than three decades. Kerns was vice-president of the Linguistic Society of America in 1953. With co-author Benjamin Schwartz he wrote A Sketch of the Indo-European Finite Verb. Obituaries and other sources: Directory of American Scholars, Volume III: Foreign Languages, Linguistics, and Philosophy, 6th edition, Bowker, 1974; AB Bookman's Weekly, December 1, 1975.

* * *

KERSH, Cyril 1925-

PERSONAL: Born February 24, 1925, in London, England; son of Hyman (a master tailor) and Leah (Miller) Kersh; married Suzanne Fajner, June 25, 1956. Education: Attended high school in Essex, England. Religion: Jewish. Home: 14 Ossington St., London W2 4LZ, England. Office: Mirror Group Newspapers, 33 Holborn, London EC1 PDQ, England.

CAREER: Editor of Men Only; editor of Reveille, 1976-79; Mirror Newspapers, London, England, assistant editor, 1979—. Military service: Royal Navy, 1943-47. Member: Our Society, Scribes, Paternosters.

WRITINGS—Novels: The Aggravations of Minnie Ashe, M. Joseph, 1970; The Diabolical Liberties of Uncle Max, M. Joseph, 1973; The Soho Summer of Mr. Green, W. H. Allen, 1974; The Shepherds Bush Connection, W. H. Allen, 1975; Minnie Ashe at War, W. H. Allen, 1979. Contributor to magazines.

WORK IN PROGRESS: Adapting his novels for a television series; memoirs of Fleet Street.

SIDELIGHTS: Kersh told *CA:* "I am the brother of Gerald Kersh (an infinitely finer writer). I was encouraged by a piece I wrote in *Queen* magazine about my mother. It had enough material in it for five short stories, so I wrote five. Then I realized nobody (more or less) prints short stories, so I started a novel. Offered a generous advance, I finished it. It topped the British best-seller lists for several weeks. Since I didn't want to be known as a one-novel author, others followed."

* * *

KEYLOR, Arthur (W.) 1920(?)-1981

OBITUARY NOTICE: Born c. 1920 in Natick, Mass.; died of a heart attack, August 17, 1981, in Manchester, Vt. Publishing executive. Keylor was made vice-president in charge of Time Inc.'s magazine group in 1972. He moved to produce *Fortune* as a biweekly magazine, brought back *Life* in 1978, and introduced *People* and *Discover* magazines. Obituaries and other sources: *Who's Who in Finance and Industry,* 18th edition, Marquis, 1974; *New York Times,* August 18, 1981, *Time,* August 31, 1981.

* * *

KHARITONOV, Yevgeny 1941(?)-1981

OBITUARY NOTICE: Born c. 1941; died of a heart attack, June 29, 1981, in Moscow, U.S.S.R. Poet, novelist, playwright, and short story writer. Kharitonov began his career as a filmmaker but devoted the final twelve years of his life to writing, shunning both official sanction and underground affiliation. His free-form, stream of consciousness style combined with his exploration of unusual themes to form a new trend in Russian experimental fiction. Staged in Moscow, Kharitonov's play "Enchanted Island" was written for actors who can neither hear nor speak. A manuscript of Kharitonov's collected works, "Under House Arrest," is believed to have been seized in the 1980 raids on seven young Soviet writers, among them Kharitonov, who were trying to form a literary club and publish an experimental periodical. Obituaries and other sources: *New York Times,* July 6, 1981; *Time,* July 20, 1981.

* * *

KIELLAND, Alexander Lange 1849-1906

BRIEF ENTRY: Born February 18, 1849, in Stavanger, Norway; died April 6, 1906, in Bergen, Norway. Norwegian novelist and playwright. Kielland's work was full of social protest and campaigns for reform. His purpose became evident in the short story collection *Novelleter* (1879), and his clear narrative and portrayal of the landscape of western Norway attracted much attention. Later work became more indignant: he spoke out against Norwegian bureaucracy in *Arbeidsfolk* (1881), the educational system of the day in *Gift* (1883), and the clergy in *Sankt Hans Fest* (1887). Ironically, Kielland's criticism was directed toward the very class from which he had emerged— the Norwegian aristocracy. Some critics felt his best writing was embodied in the novel *Garman og Worse* (1880), which recollected his childhood in the ancestral home near Stavanger. As he grew older, Kielland seemed disappointed at the failure of his attempts at social reform. That disappointment was expressed in *Jacob* (1891), his last novel. *Biographical/critical sources: Cassell's Encyclopaedia of World Literature,* revised edition, Morrow, 1973.

KIESEL, Stanley 1925-

PERSONAL: Born July 16, 1925, in Los Angeles, Calif.; son of Harry (a retail food clerk) and Lila (Barasch) Kiesel; married Ruth Price (a nursery school teacher), September 15, 1955; children: Polly, Emily. *Education:* Attended Los Angeles City College, 1944-47; California State University at Los Angeles, B.A., 1954; California State University at Northridge, M.A., 1970. *Home:* 1771 Girard Ave. S., Minneapolis, Minn. 55403. *Agent:* c/o Unicorn Books, 306 Dartmouth St., Boston, Mass. 02116. *Office:* Minneapolis Public Schools, Department of Language Arts.

CAREER: Los Angeles City Schools, Los Angeles, Calif., kindergarten teacher, 1954-71; Minneapolis Public Schools, Minneapolis, Minn., poet-in-residence, 1971—. Associated with Poets in the Schools in Illinois, South Dakota, and Minnesota. *Member:* Authors Guild. *Awards, honors: The War Between the Pitiful Teachers and the Splendid Kids* was chosen as one of the best books of 1980 by the editors of the *New York Times.*

WRITINGS: The Pearl Is a Hardened Sinner (poems), Scribner, 1968, enlarged edition, Nodin, 1976; *The War Between the Pitiful Teachers and the Splendid Kids* (juvenile), Dutton/Unicorn, 1980.

Plays: "The Family" (one-act), first produced in Hollywood, Calif., at The Theatre, 1970; "The Ceiling" (one-act), first produced in Hollywood, Calif., at The Theatre, 1970, produced in Minneapolis, Minn., at Minnesota Ensemble Theatre and Walker Art Center, May, 1975; "The Post" (one-act), first produced in Minneapolis, Minn., at Minnesota Ensemble Theatre, June, 1975.

Also composer of songs.

WORK IN PROGRESS: A play about old pirates; a book of rock songs; a trilogy continuing the story of *The War Between the Pitiful Teachers and the Splendid Kids;* a book of poems.

SIDELIGHTS: Kiesel's book for children, *The War Between the Pitiful Teachers and the Splendid Kids,* is about the adventures of Skinny Malinky at Scratchland School. A precocious five-and-a-half-year-old boy, Skinny is determined to evade the school's Status Quo Solidifier, which is described by Peter Andrews in the *New York Times Book Review* as "a dreadful device that can take a rat-faced malingerer and instantly turn him into a 'young person' with slicked-down hair whose first thought is to wonder what he can do for extra credit." Kiesel describes the teachers at Scratchland with "devastating satire" and gives them such names as Mr. Bullotad and Mrs. Solemnsides. Noting that the book would probably appeal to the "natural rebelliousness" of a youngster, Andrews also warned that within three days of finishing it, "the kid will be up before the principal."

Kiesel told *CA:* "I write for pleasure and to please myself. Artists don't need to choose sides; they are the sides."

BIOGRAPHICAL/CRITICAL SOURCES: Los Angeles Times, June 2, 1970; *After Dark,* July, 1970; *Christian Science Monitor,* August 22, 1970; *Minneapolis Tribune/Picture,* December 5, 1971; *Minneapolis Tribune,* June 13, 1975, September 1, 1975; *New York Times,* December 5, 1980; *New York Times Book Review,* January 11, 1981.

* * *

KIEV, I. Edward 1905-1975

OBITUARY NOTICE: Born in 1905; died of a heart attack,

November 3, 1975, in New York, N.Y. Rabbi, librarian, editor, and author. An expert on Judaic and Hebraic literature and chief librarian at the Hebrew Union College-Jewish Institute of Religion for more than thirty years, Kiev was instrumental in building the library's 105,000-volume collection. He edited *Library Trends, The Jewish Book Annual,* and *Studies in Bibliography and Booklore.* Obituaries and other sources: *New York Times,* November 5, 1975; *AB Bookman's Weekly,* December 22, 1975.

* * *

KIM, Samuel S(oonki)   1935-

PERSONAL: Born June 12, 1935, in Hamhung, Korea; came to the United States in 1958, naturalized citizen, 1969; son of Dugun (a principal) and Changkuk Lee Kim; married Helen W. Benham (a professor), June 12, 1965; children: Sonya Wheaton. *Education:* Southwestern at Memphis, B.A., 1960; Columbia University, M.I.A., 1962, Ph.D., 1966. *Politics:* Independent. *Religion:* Presbyterian. *Home:* 960 Elberon Ave., Elberon, N.J. 07740. *Office:* Department of Political Science, Monmouth College, West Long Branch, N.J. 07764.

CAREER: Monmouth College, West Long Branch, N.J., assistant professor, 1966-69, associate professor, 1969-73, professor of political science, 1973—. Visiting professor at Princeton University, 1979-81; adjunct professor at New York University, 1980; senior fellow at Institute for World Order, 1980—. *Member:* International Studies Association, American Political Science Association, American Society of International Law.

WRITINGS: China, the United Nations, and World Order, Princeton University Press, 1979; (co-editor) *The War System: An Interdisciplinary Approach,* Westview, 1980; (co-editor) *China in the Global Community,* Praeger, 1980; (co-editor) *Toward a Just World,* Westview, 1981.

WORK IN PROGRESS: The Quest for a Just World Order, completion expected in 1982.

SIDELIGHTS: In an interview with *Macroscope,* Kim explained the purposes behind his writing of *The Quest for a New World Order.* He stated: "This work will be an attempt to describe, explain, and prescribe responses to current and evolving global crises within the heuristic framework of a normative theory of world order studies. I will be conscious of giving due attention to the attitudinal, normative, institutional, and behavioral problems involved in the struggle of the global citizens to establish a more just and humane world order. An alternative approach to the study of world politics, this study is also designed to remedy what I regard as the main shortcomings and weaknesses of traditional and contemporary mainstream approaches that still dominate the establishment of international studies in the West."

BIOGRAPHICAL/CRITICAL SOURCES: Macroscope, spring, 1981.

* * *

KINDER, Kathleen
    See POTTER, Kathleen Jill

* * *

KING, (David) Clive   1924-

PERSONAL: Born April 24, 1924, in Richmond, Surrey, England; married Jane Tuke, 1949 (divorced, 1974); married Pe-

nelope Timmins, 1974; children: one daughter, one son. *Education:* Downing College, Cambridge, B.A., 1948; attended School of Oriental and African Studies, London, 1966-67. *Home:* 65A St. Augustine's Rd., London NW1 9RR, England. *Agent:* Murray Pollinger, 4 Garrick St., London W.C.2, England.

CAREER: British Council, administrative officer in Amsterdam, Netherlands, 1948-50, student welfare officer in Belfast, Northern Ireland, 1950-51, lecturer in Aleppo, Syria, 1951-54, and visiting professor in Damascus, Syria, 1954-55; East Sussex County Council, Rye, England, warden, 1955-60; British Council, Beirut, Lebanon, lecturer and director of studies, 1960-66; East Pakistan Education Centre, Dacca, education adviser, 1967-71; British Council, Madras, India, education officer, 1971-73. *Military service:* Royal Navy Volunteer Reserve, 1943-46; became sub-lieutenant.

WRITINGS—All for children: *Hamid of Aleppo,* Macmillan, 1958; *The Town That Went South,* Macmillan, 1959; *Stig of the Dump,* Penguin (London), 1963; *The Twenty-Two Letters,* Hamish Hamilton, 1966, Coward, 1967; *The Night the Water Came,* Longman, 1973; *Snakes and Snakes,* Kestrel Books, 1975; *The Secret,* Benn, 1976; *Accident,* Benn, 1976; *First Day Out,* Benn, 1976; *High Jacks, Low Jacks,* Benn, 1976; *Me and My Million,* Kestrel Books, 1976; *The Devil's Cut,* Hodder & Stoughton, 1978; *Ninny's Boat,* Kestrel Books, 1980.

Plays: "Poles Apart," first produced in London, 1975; "The World of Light," first produced in London, 1976; "Good Snakes, Bad Snakes" (television play), first produced 1977.

SIDELIGHTS: Clive King's extensive travels are reflected in the diversity of locations in which his children's stories are set. Critics have frequently commended King for both the authenticity of his settings and the diversity of his themes. In *The Town That Went South,* King describes the reactions of the people of Ramsly when their town comes adrift from the mainland and carries them off to various adventures. A *Times Literary Supplement* reviewer called the book "a brilliantly ingenious piece of escapism for intelligent readers between ten and 100."

Me and My Million concerns Ringo, a resourceful, amoral, and illiterate youngster, who aids his brother in stealing a valuable painting. Ringo's inability to read such things as street signs leads him into a series of misadventures in the course of the caper. Several critics found King's account of Ringo's exploits lively and entertaining, including *Times Literary Supplement* reviewer Jane Powell, who noted that the book is "written in a very colloquial style with . . . zip and verve."

BIOGRAPHICAL/CRITICAL SOURCES: New York Herald Tribune Book Review, June 8, 1958; *Times Literary Supplement,* May 20, 1960, April 2, 1976, September 19, 1980; *Young Reader's Review,* June, 1967.*

* * *

KIRKLAND, Edward Chase   1894-1975

OBITUARY NOTICE—See index for *CA* sketch: Born May 24, 1894, in Bellows Falls, Vt.; died May 24, 1975, in Hanover, N.H. Historian, economist, educator, and author. Kirkland taught at Bowdoin College for three decades before retiring in 1959 to devote himself full time to writing. Among his books is *A History of American Economic Life.* Obituaries and other sources: *AB Bookman's Weekly,* August 25, 1975.

KIRSCH, Herbert 1924(?)-1978

OBITUARY NOTICE: Born c. 1924; died in March, 1978. Educator, economist, and author. Kirsch was a professor of economics at Michigan State University. His numerous writings explore German economic history. Obituaries and other sources: *AB Bookman's Weekly*, July 10, 1978.

* * *

KIRST, Hans Hellmut 1914-

PERSONAL: Born December 5, 1914, in Osterode, East Prussia (now Poland); son of Johannes (a policeman) and Gertrud (Golldack) Kirst; married Ruth Mueller, December 14, 1962; children: one daughter. *Education:* Educated in Osterode, East Prussia. *Politics:* Social-Liberal. *Religion:* Roman Catholic. *Home:* D 8133 Feldating, Moorweg 3/5, b Munich, West Germany. *Agent:* Stecher, Reinhold, D 8081 Breitbruun/Ammeiree, Seebliderstrape 46, West Germany. *Office:* 8000 Munich, Portdamer Ste., Munich 40, West Germany.

CAREER: Writer, 1947—. Worked as gardener, bricklayer, and road builder; writer for *Muendnner Meikuer*. *Military service:* German Army, 1933-45; served in Poland, France, and Russia; became first lieutenant. *Member:* P.E.N., Authors Guild, Mark Twain Society (honorary member). *Awards, honors:* Edgar Allen Poe Award, 1965, for *The Night of the Generals*.

WRITINGS—Novels; all German editions published by K. Desch, except as noted: *Wir nannten ihn Galgenstrick*, 1950, translation by Richard Winston and Clara Winston published as *The Lieutenant Must Be Mad*, Harcourt, 1951; *Sagten Sie Gerechtigkeit, Captain?*, 1952, revised edition published as *Letzte Station Camp 7*, 1966, translation by J. Maxwell Brownjohn published as *Last Stop Camp Seven*, Coward, 1969; *Aufruhr in einer kleinen Stadt*, 1953; *Die letzte karte spielt der Tod*, 1955, translation by Brownjohn published as *The Last Card*, Pyramid Publications, 1967 (published in England as *Death Plays the Last Card*, Fontana, 1968); *Null-acht fuenfzehn*, three volumes, 1954-55, translation by Robert Kee published as *Zero Eight Fifteen*, Weidenfeld & Nicolson, 1955-57, Volume I: *Null-act fuenfzehn in der Kaserne*, 1954, translation published as *The Strange Mutiny of Gunner Asch*, 1955, published as *The Revolt of Gunner Asch*, Little, Brown, 1956, Volume II: *Null-acht fuenfzehn im Krieg*, 1954, translation published as *Forward, Gunner Asch!*, Little, Brown, 1956 (published in England as *Gunner Asch Goes to War*, 1956), Volume III: *Null-acht fuenfzehn bis zum Ende*, 1955, translation published as *The Return of Gunner Asch*, Little, Brown, 1957.

Gott schlaeft in Masuren, 1956; *Keiner kommt davon*, 1957, translation by Richard Graves published as *The Seventh Day*, Doubleday, 1959 (published in England as *No One Will Escape*, Weidenfeld & Nicolson, 1959); *Mit diesen meinen Haenden*, 1957; *Kultura 5 und der Rote Morgen*, 1958; *Glueck laesst sich nicht kaufen*, 1959; *Fabrik der Offiziere*, 1960 (also see below), translation by Kee published as *The Officer Factory*, Collins, 1962, Doubleday, 1963; *Kameraden*, 1961, translation by Brownjohn published as *Brothers in Arms*, Collins, 1965, Harper, 1967; *Null-acht fuenfzehn heute*, 1963, translation by Brownjohn published as *What Became of Gunner Asch*, Harper, 1964; *Die Nacht der Generale*, 1962 (also see below), translation by Brownjohn published as *The Night of the Generals*, Harper, 1963; *Aufstand der Soldaten: Roman des 20 Juli 1944*, 1965 (also see below), translation by Brownjohn published as *Soldiers' Revolt*, Harper, 1966 (published in England as *The Twentieth of July*, Collins, 1966).

Die Woelfe, 1967, translation by Brownjohn published as *The Wolves*, Coward, 1968 (published in England as *The Fox of Maulen*, Collins, 1968); *Kein Vaterland*, 1968, translation by Brownjohn published as *No Fatherland*, Coward, 1970 (published in England as *Undercover Man*, Collins, 1970); *Faustrecht*, 1969, translation by Brownjohn published as *The Adventures of Private Faust*, Coward, 1971 (published in England as *Who's in Charge Here?*, Collins, 1971); *Soldaten, Offiziere, Generale* (contains *Aufstand der Soldaten*, *Fabrik der Offiziere*, and *Die Nacht der Generale*), 1969; *Held im Turm*, 1970, translation by Brownjohn published as *Hero in the Tower*, Coward, 1972; *Verdammt zum Erfolg*, 1971, translation by Brownjohn published as *Damned to Success*, Coward, 1973 (published in England as *A Time for Scandal*, Collins, 1973); *Verurteilt zur Wahrheit*, 1972, translation by Brownjohn published as *A Time for Truth*, Coward, 1974; *Verfolgt vom Schicksal*, 1973; *Alles hat seinen Preis*, Hoffmann & Campe, 1974, translation by Brownjohn published as *Everything Has Its Price*, Coward, 1976 (published in England as *A Time for Payment*, Collins, 1976); *Die Naechte der langen Messer*, Hoffmann & Campe, 1975, translation by Brownjohn published as *The Nights of the Long Knives*, Coward, 1976; *Generals-Affaeren*, Bertelsmann, 1977, translation by Brownjohn published as *The Affairs of the Generals*, Coward, 1979; *Null-acht fuenfzehn in der Partei*, Bertelsmann, 1978, translation by Brownjohn published as *Party Games*, Simon & Schuster, 1980.

Other writings: *Bilanz der Traumfabrik*, Bruckmann, 1963; *Deutschland, deine Ostpreussen: Ein Buch voller Vorurteile*, Hoffmann & Campe, 1968; *Heinz Ruehmann: Ein biographischer Report*, Kindler, 1969; (with David Hamilton and Heinz Edelmann) *Das Udo-Juergens-Songbuch*, Juncker, 1970; *Gespraeche mit meimen Hund Anton*, K. Desch, 1972; *Die Katzen von Caslano*, Hoffmann & Campe, 1977; *Ende '45*, Bertelsmann, 1982.

SIDELIGHTS: Hans Hellmut Kirst is considered by some to be an analyst of the burden of Nazism on postwar Germany, delving into and retelling the stories of the not-too-distant past. He writes from a position of knowledge in this respect, having served for many years in the German Army both before and during World War II. As one who reminds his countrymen of things they would just as soon forget, Kirst has been described as a conscience for his people. Other critics, however, view him more as a skillful storyteller, adept at writing tightly-constructed, suspenseful, adventure-filled novels.

Much of Kirst's fiction is based on fact. Born in the village of Osterode in East Prussia (now part of Poland), he felt early the impact of war. His father was a prisoner of war in Russia during World War I, and Kirst was five when he saw him for the first time. Kirst grew up in a highly nationalistic part of Germany where young men were encouraged to enter military service. At age eighteen he enlisted in the German Army and eventually became a first lieutenant. The author once remarked: "During all those years people acted like idiots. One had to do one's duty as 'a good German.' One did not really know one was in a club of murderers. You have to pay for being involved with criminals." While training officer candidates during World War II, Kirst was captured by American troops and imprisoned for eight months. Following his release, he began writing books and movie reviews, becoming a full-time writer in 1947.

Kirst first gained international prominence for his trilogy *Zero Eight Fifteen*. The title refers to the serial number of a German machine gun, and the story follows the life of Gunner Asch, a low-ranking soldier, in his resistance to the military machine. This is a basic motif that recurs in many of his novels: the lowly soldier, the common man, in conflict with the generals, the representatives of the establishment. In the first volume of the trilogy, which is generally considered to be the best, Kirst presents a picture of barrack and army life before the onset of World War II. In the second and third volumes the scenes shift variously from the Russian front to a German base during the war and then recount the military occupation of Germany.

Reviewers have praised Kirst most highly for his craftsmanship and his skills as a storyteller and satirist. Other critics, however, have described his books as escape literature and charged him with over-simplifying the events surrounding the Third Reich. A reviewer for *New Statesman and Nation,* for instance, called *Revolt of Gunner Asch* a "sparkling little satire. It is a closed story, carefully written and shaped round a few characters. . . . It is all very lively and spry, done with a nice, light, dry touch." But in his review for the *New York Times,* Frederic Morton stated his reservations about the book: The character Asch "jousts entertainingly with the absurdities of the Nazi military code but somehow fails to really grapple with its malevolence. His warfare against 08-15 toilet-kit inspections is shrewd and funny, but for all his unusual discernment, he remains unaware of the concentration camps and the storm troopers' nightsticks among which he must have grown up. Hidden away among the comic riches of this novel are things that call for more bite and less jest, that are fit for brooding, not for laughter."

Similar comments were made about another novel, *The Wolves.* The story presents the rivalry between German nationalists and an independent man of high principles, Materna. He joins the Nazis, seeming to conform, but as William Hill observed in *Best Sellers,* "every concession he makes to the regime somehow turns into a joke against it. . . . There is about the story an aura of unreality because it does not seem to take into account the thoroughness and brutality of the Nazi regime and does not recognize the totality of the second world war." Gertrud Bauer Pickar, in her remarks for *Books Abroad,* praised Kirst for his quick-moving adventure story, but contended that "there is a singular lack of concern with the broader implications. The superficial treatment of the political aspects arises in part from the emphasis on the regional elements, which localize both the roots and impact of the political activity and preclude universal treatment." Kirst disagreed with this critique. He commented in a *Publishers Weekly* interview, "If you look at a drop of water under the microscope you see the structure of the universe, and if you look at what the local Nazis were saying and doing in Osterode, you can see what was going to happen later."

Whether or not the critics approve of his books, the general public has been accepting. Kirst's books have been translated into twenty-eight languages, and *The Night of the Generals* was made into a movie in 1967. A Columbia Pictures release, it starred Peter O'Toole, Omar Sharif, Christopher Plummer, and Joanna Pettet. The *New York Times* remarked that it was "efficiently constructed and played," but that it was also melodramatic and not very "sophisticated and articulate about the crime of war."

Kirst once reflected on the reception of his novels in Germany: "Here the right thinks my view of the Third Reich is erroneous; the left thinks I don't feel enough guilt. In fact, 98% of the Germans stood behind the Nazis, and the young read me to find out why their parents did it. . . . I wanted to show the human tragedy, to show what history can do to men."

BIOGRAPHICAL/CRITICAL SOURCES: New Statesman and Nation, July 9, 1955; *New York Times,* March 4, 1956, February 3, 1967; *Time,* April 28, 1967; *Books Abroad,* spring, 1968; *Publishers Weekly,* June 10, 1968, September 2, 1977; *Best Sellers,* July 15, 1968; *Saturday Review,* August 2, 1969.

—*Sketch by Kathryn T. Floch*

*   *   *

KIRSTEN, Grace   1900-

PERSONAL: Born May 3, 1900, in New York, N.Y.; daughter of Maurice M. (a merchant) and Annie (Matlin) Elish; married Harry Sherman (deceased); married Everett Kirsten, March 5, 1945; children: (first marriage) Maurice. *Education:* Syracuse University, B.A., 1924; Columbia University, M.A., 1952. *Religion:* Jewish. *Home and office:* 1726 Cortelyou Rd., Brooklyn, N.Y. 11226. *Agent:* Don Congdon, Harold Matson Co., Inc., 22 East 40th St., New York, N.Y. 10016.

CAREER: High school English teacher in New York, N.Y., 1924-31; public speaking, voice and diction, and special speech problems teacher, 1931-45; private practice of psychotherapy, 1946—. Lecturer, 1941. Member of staff at Community Guidance Service, Inc. *Member:* Hebrew Education Society (member of board of directors; president of Women's Association). *Awards, honors:* Award from National Conference of Christians and Jews, 1978.

WRITINGS: (With Richard Robertiello) *Big You, Little You: A Separation Therapy,* Dial, 1975. Contributor to *Cosmopolitan.*

WORK IN PROGRESS: Several magazine articles.

SIDELIGHTS: Kirsten told *CA:* "Separation therapy is based on the concept that there is within each individual the little child he or she was up to the age of six. There is also within the individual an adult with potential for great growth. The adult in each of us is the problem solver. The little child in each of us is the seat of all our emotions: joy, anger, fear, love, sadness, and all other feelings.

"The child and the adult have specified roles in the growth of the individual. When the child, who has an overpowering amount of energy, and the adult, who is cerebral, are within the individual, the little child takes over and overwhelms the adult so that the adult is unable to function well. The role of the child is to keep the energy free-flowing and joyful. Only then will the adult part of the individual be free to think clearly and to solve problems.

"The ultimate goal of separation therapy is to help the individual become more efficient, more capable, more creative, and more successful in whatever areas he chooses. How can this be accomplished? My co-author and I have devised the separation technique, documented in *Big You, Little You,* in which we visualize both the child and the potential adult being taken out of the individual and separated from each other by a six foot isosceles triangle. Then Big and Little carry on a dialogue.

"The purpose of the dialogue is to encourage the child part to express all feelings of anger, hostility, inferiority, insecurity, frustration, inadequacy, joylessness, and other feelings that make one unable to function productively and happily. The adult part functions like the good parent who understands the child's feelings and is supportive and loving in every way. The adult also puts limits on the child who has never been properly disciplined and who is often unable to take the frustrations of life that come to each of us.

"When the child part empties his unconscious of all anger, he is then able to function on a happy, zestful level. And the adult, who is no longer overwhelmed by the destructive energy of the child, at this point is free to solve problems and make productive decisions.''

BIOGRAPHICAL/CRITICAL SOURCES: Richie Herink, *The Psychotherapy Handbook,* NAL, 1980.

* * *

KITCHIN, Laurence 1913-

PERSONAL: Born July 21, 1913, in Bradford, England; son of James Tyson (a physician) and Eliza (Hopps) Kitchin; married Hilary Owen (an artist), November 4, 1955. *Education:* King's College, London, B.A., 1934. *Office:* c/o National Westminster Bank, 33 St. James's Sq., London W.1, England.

CAREER: Professional actor, 1936-41; correspondent and theater critic for *Times,* 1956-62; University of Bristol, Bristol, England, lecturer in drama, 1966-70; Stanford University, Stanford, Calif., visiting professor of drama, 1970-72; Brooklyn College of the City University of New York, Brooklyn, N.Y., visiting professor, 1972-73, professor of liberal arts, 1973-76; Simon Fraser University, Burnaby, British Columbia, visiting professor of Shakespeare, 1976-77; writer, 1977—. Associated with British Broadcasting Corp. (BBC-Radio), 1948—. Broadcaster and lecturer. British representative on editorial committee of United Nations Educational, Scientific and Cultural Organization's "World Theatre," 1960-65; member of International Shakespeare Conference, 1980—. *Military service:* British Army, 1941-46. *Member:* Athenaeum Club.

WRITINGS: Mid-Century Drama, Faber, 1960, 2nd edition, 1962; *Drama in the Sixties,* Faber, 1966.

Radio scripts: "The Trial of Lord Byron," first broadcast by BBC-Radio, September 27, 1948, rebroadcast by CBC-Radio, February 26, 1978; "The Elizabethan," first broadcast by CBC-Radio, February 26, 1978; "Court Lady" (translation of work by Castiglione), first broadcast by BBC-Radio, November, 1954, rebroadcast, November, 1978; "Petrarch and His Followers" (verse translations), first broadcast by BBC-Radio, December 18 and December 28, 1978.

WORK IN PROGRESS: Verse translations of sixteenth-century sonnets from Italian, French, and Spanish.

SIDELIGHTS: Kitchin wrote: "I have a special interest in and experience of the Mediterranean for the sake of tradition and in the Bay Area of California as a growth point for the future, which is greatly dependent on microelectronics.

"But these areas are less remote from one another in time and space than they seem. Poets such as Petrarch and Garcilaso have insight into personal relationships which remain valid and enlightening in the late twentieth century. This is why I do my best to turn them into English without archaisms and make them accessible to us.''

* * *

KLAUBER, John 1917-1981

OBITUARY NOTICE: Born January 1, 1917, in Hampstead, England; died August 11, 1981, in France. Historian, psychoanalyst, educator, and author of essays in his field. Klauber initially studied history, but following his military service in World War II he turned to psychology. He began practicing as a Freudian psychoanalyst in 1953. Klauber emphasized realism and common sense, as well as the analyst-patient relationship, in his approach to the mentally disturbed. He was active in England's Institute of Psychoanalysis, was named a fellow of the British Psychological Society in 1971 and a foun-

dation fellow of the Royal College of Psychiatrists in 1972, and was appointed Freud Memorial Professor at University College, London, in 1981. A collection of Klauber's writings, *Difficulties in the Analytic Encounter,* appeared in 1981. Obituaries and other sources: *London Times,* August 17, 1981.

* * *

KNITTEL, John (Herman Emanuel) 1891-1970

OBITUARY NOTICE: Born March 24, 1891, in Darwar, India; died April 26, 1970, in Grisons, Switzerland. Archaeologist, linguist, novelist, and playwright. Recipient of Switzerland's Schiller Prize for literature, Knittel was also Switzerland's golf champion three times. He traveled extensively and sometimes chose exotic settings for his novels, of which the best known is *Into the Abyss.* His novel *Nile Gold* is set in Egypt, while *Midnight People* portrays characters in French Morocco. He adapted his novel *The Torch* for the stage in 1921. Many of Knittel's other books have been filmed or dramatized, and his works have been translated into nineteen languages. Obituaries and other sources: *Twentieth Century Authors: A Biographical Dictionary of Modern Literature,* H. W. Wilson, 1942; *Variety,* May 13, 1970; *AB Bookman's Weekly,* June 1, 1970; *The Author's and Writer's Who's Who,* 6th edition, Burke's Peerage, 1971.

* * *

KNUDSON, Richard L(ewis) 1930-

PERSONAL: Born June 4, 1930, in Newton, Me.; son of Henry Spurgeon (a mariner) and Magda (Olesen) Knudson; married Ann Rankin (a teacher), June 23, 1956; children: Leesa M., Erik S. *Education:* Gorham State College, B.S., 1957; University of Maine, M.S., 1960; Boston University, D.Ed., 1970. *Home:* 21 Franklin St., Oneonta, N.Y. 13820. *Office:* Department of English, State University of New York College at Oneonta, Oneonta, N.Y. 13820.

CAREER: State Department of Education, Augusta, Me., supervisor of English, 1964-66; School Department, South Paris, Me., project director, 1966-70; State University of New York College at Oneonta, associate professor of English, 1970—. *Military service:* U.S. Navy, sonar operator, 1948-52. *Member:* International Motor Press Association, National Council of Teachers of English, Society of Automotive Historians. *Awards, honors:* Fulbright fellowship for the Netherlands, 1962-63.

WRITINGS: MG: The Sports Car America Loved First, Motorcars Unlimited, 1975; *MG International,* Motor Racing Publications, 1977; *Classic Sports Cars* (juvenile), Lerner, 1980; *Rallying* (juvenile), Lerner, 1981; *Land Speed Record Cars* (juvenile), Lerner, 1981; *Model Cars* (juvenile), Lerner, 1981; *The T Series Handbook,* MG International, 1981. Editor of *English Record,* 1973-76.

WORK IN PROGRESS: A definitive work on Frank Kurtis and his cars.

SIDELIGHTS: Knudson wrote: "A fifty-year fascination with automobiles and racing led me to write about cars. As a classroom teacher I saw the appeal that cars had for children, thus many of my books have been slanted to that audience. England is probably my favorite place: civilized people plus plenty of motoring events make it special.

"English sports cars reflect the traditional mood of the country; that is, they look and handle properly, just as they always have. English cars have an appealing honesty about them, and they never pretend to be something they're not.''

AVOCATIONAL INTERESTS: Motorcycles, bow hunting, knife making, travel.

* * *

KOBRAK, Peter 1936-

PERSONAL: Born December 1, 1936, in New York, N.Y.; son of Gerhart Ludwig (in business) and Ruth (Ullman) Kobrak; married Barbara Bennich, December 28, 1964; children: George, Mark, Harold. *Education:* Oberlin College, B.A. (with honors), 1959; University of Wisconsin, Madison, M.S., 1962; Yale University, M.A., 1965; Johns Hopkins University, Ph.D., 1971. *Home:* 1304 West Maple St., Kalamazoo, Mich. 49008. *Office:* Center for Public Administration Programs, Western Michigan University, Kalamazoo, Mich. 49008.

CAREER: Encampment for Citizenship, New York, N.Y., member of staff, 1965; Executive Office of the Governor, Albany, N.Y., program assistant, 1966; U.S. Department of Labor, Washington, D.C., policy analyst in Office of Policy Planning and Research, 1966-67; Johns Hopkins University, Baltimore, Md., lecturer in American government, 1968-69; University of Wisconsin, Milwaukee, instructor, 1969-71, assistant professor of political science, 1971-73, member of Institute of Governmental Affairs, 1969-71; Western Michigan University, Kalamazoo, associate professor of political science, 1974-78, deputy director of Center for Public Administration Programs, 1974-78, director, 1979—, member of board of directors of Institute of Public Affairs, 1975-78, associate director, 1977—. Testified before U.S. Senate; guest on television and radio programs. *Military service:* U.S. Army, 1966. *Member:* American Political Science Association, American Society for Public Administration, National Association of Schools of Public Affairs and Administration.

WRITINGS: Private Assumption of Public Responsibilities: The Role of American Business in Urban Manpower Programs, Praeger, 1973; (with Richard Perlman) *Toward a Comprehensive Manpower Plan: Milwaukee Needs, Program, and Strategies,* Milwaukee Urban Observatory, 1974; (with Robert Kaufman and Alan Leader) *Modernizing Local Government: The Case of Calhoun County,* New Issues Press, 1975.

Contributor: Sar Levitan and Robert Taggart, editors, *Emergency Employment Act: The PEP Generation,* Olympus, 1974; *The Unfolding Youth Initiatives,* Office of Program Evaluation, U.S. Department of Labor, 1978; Levitan and Gregory Wurzburg, editors, *Youth and the Local Employment Agenda,* National Council on Unemployment Policy, 1980. Contributor to academic journals.

WORK IN PROGRESS: Evaluating the Targeted Jobs Demonstration Program, a program of U.S. Department of Housing and Urban Development designed to integrate economic development and manpower efforts more closely.

SIDELIGHTS: Kobrak told *CA:* "My writings have dealt with a series of employment and training programs intended to improve the lot of the economically disadvantaged. These evaluations have included job creation and interagency coordination efforts that preceded CETA as well as youth programs and several other studies since CETA's inception.

"I am interested in opportunity programs designed to help disadvantaged individuals rather than income maintenance programs that too often have the unintended consequence of perpetuating poverty. Employment and training programs are directed at individuals who have the interest and potential to help themselves in spite of disadvantages that they may have encountered earlier in their lives. But the federal government must create incentives that do *not* make it rational for these individuals either to choose to remain on the dole or to give up because the government in their view 'does not care.' As a government and a society we seem to have diffuclty striking this vital balance.''

* * *

KOELSCH, William Alvin 1933-
(A. Nolder Gay)

PERSONAL: Surname is pronounced Kelsh; born May 16, 1933, in Morristown, N.J.; son of Alvin Charles (an industrial executive) and Alice Boniface (Smith) Koelsch. *Education:* Bucknell University, Sc.B. (summa cum laude), 1955; Clark University, A.M., 1959; University of Chicago, Ph.D., 1966. *Politics:* Independent. *Religion:* Episcopalian. *Home:* 81 Waltham St., Boston, Mass. 02118. *Office:* University Archives, Clark University, 950 Main St., Worcester, Mass. 01610.

CAREER: Clark University, Worcester, Mass., visiting assistant professor of geography, 1963; Florida Presbyterian College (now Eckerd College), St. Petersburg, instructor, 1963-65, assistant professor of history, 1965-67; Clark University, assistant professor, 1967-69, associate professor, 1969-81, professor of history and geography, 1981—, university archivist, 1972—. Member of board of trustees of Michael P. Quinn Scholarship Fund, 1969—; member of Massachusetts Archives Advisory Commission, 1974—; member of national finance committee for John B. Anderson's national unity campaign, 1980; archival consultant to National Historical Publications and Records Commission, Alabama Space and Rocket Center, and McClean Hospital. *Military service:* U.S. Army, Transportation Corps, 1955-57; became first lieutenant.

MEMBER: International Geographical Union (corresponding member), American Geographical Society (life fellow), Organization of American Historians (life member), Society of American Archivists, History of Education Society, Society for the Preservation of New England Antiquities, Phi Beta Kappa. *Awards, honors:* Grants from National Science Foundation, 1970 and 1972; grant from Penrose Fund of American Philosophical Society, 1971.

WRITINGS: (Editor) *Lectures on the Historical Geography of the United States,* University of Chicago Press, 1962; (editor with Barbara G. Rosenkrantz, and contributor) *American Habitat,* Macmillan, 1973; (contributor) David Lowenthal and Martin J. Bowden, editors, *Geographies of the Mind,* Oxford University Press, 1976; (contributor) Brian W. Blouet, editor, *Origins of Academic Geography in the United States,* Shoe String, 1981.

Under pseudonym A. Nolder Gay: *The View From the Closet: Essays on Gay Life and Liberation,* Union Park Press, 1978.

Author of "The View From the Closet," a column in *Gay Community News* (under pseudonym A. Nolder Gay), 1973-76. Contributor of articles and reviews to magazines, including *Motive, Virginia Quarterly Review, Soundings, Esplanade, Integrity Forum,* and *Ripon Forum.*

WORK IN PROGRESS: Another anthology of gay essays, publication by Union Park Press expected in 1982; research for a book on the early history of Clark University, completion expected in 1987; research on professionalization in the environmental sciences in the late nineteenth and early twentieth centuries.

SIDELIGHTS: Koelsch wrote: "I am a rather private Bostonian who, like many New Englanders of my generation and earlier, leads a somewhat retired, if intellectually and civically concerned, life-style and who would rather be known for character than personality.

"My writings have stemmed primarily from two identities, academic and gay, both arrived at somewhat by accident, but the first rather more easily assumed than the second. From my graduate days I have been interested in the behavior of people within academic environments, as students, teachers, researchers, administrators, and entrepreneurs. In recent years I have looked at academics as professional scholars as they begin to carve out scientific careers and assemble bases of support in American universities, disciplinary associations, journals, and a research-dominated ethos emerging in the late nineteenth century. I have also been a participant in and have taught, consulted, and written about the conservation of environmental and cultural/historical resources, particularly the understanding and preservation of the built environment and of the documentary record of human activity, especially in the university, the church, medicine, and science.

"Since 1973, growing out of my experience and observation of the gay movement in Boston and nationally, I have written a long series of familiar essays for a heterogeneous audience of gays and their friends, and I revised about fifty of the articles for publication in book form in 1978. My current writing in this genre appears regularly in *Integrity Forum*, an international journal for gay Anglicans and those who support them. I am also active in various projects of the American Library Association's Gay Task Force, especially as a contributor to its periodically revised *A Gay Bibliography*."

According to Koelsch, his book *The View From the Closet: Essays on Gay Life and Liberation* was described by Randy Larsen of *Gay Life* as "charming, intelligently written and in many respects a refreshing departure from other tracts on gay life and liberation." *The Advocate*'s James Saslow, said Koelsch, noted the "wide-ranging scholarship and down-to-earth 'reasonability'" of the book. "M. Nungesser in *Impact*," Koelsch continued, "praised the lucidity and warmth of the writing." Koelsch also pointed out that Nungesser was impressed by his "ability to raise questions without preachiness."

"Most of the foregoing statements, to a degree, reflect the visceral surprise of younger gay persons that someone of another generation may have something fresh to say about matters of concern to them. In part that's because I've always enjoyed the adventure of learning new things myself, and although I do a lot of listening, I have also always felt free to state my own views with directness, clarity, and a kind of cranky independence which is perhaps rather more praised than accepted among bright young activists of whatever persuasion.

"I enjoy defining new questions and directions, reading and thinking about them, and sharing both the process and the conclusions with others, whether friends, students, fellow scholars, gay or general audiences. I like to make connections among diverse things in ways which may seem reasonable at the time. I suppose in the last analysis I write for myself, to clarify and concretize my own explorations, and if nobody else happens to be listening, I just savor the experience on my own."

BIOGRAPHICAL/CRITICAL SOURCES: Advocate, November 29, 1978.

*   *   *

KOENIG, Walter 1936-

PERSONAL: Born September 14, 1936, in Chicago, Ill.; son of Isidore (in business) and Sarah (Strauss) Koenig; married Judith Levitt (a designer and actress), July 11, 1965; children: Joshua Andrew, Danielle Beth. *Education:* Attended Grinnell College, 1954-56; University of California, Los Angeles, B.A., 1958; studied at Neighborhood Playhouse School of the Arts, 1958-60. *Religion:* Jewish. *Home address:* P.O. Box 4395, North Hollywood, Calif. 91607. *Agent:* William Morris Agency, 1350 Avenue of the Americas, New York, N.Y. 10019.

CAREER: Professional actor, 1960—; appeared on television series "Star Trek." Instructor at University of California, Los Angeles, 1972-78, California School of Professional Psychology, 1973, and Sherwood Oaks Film College, 1978—.

WRITINGS: Chekov's Enterprise (nonfiction), Pocket Books, 1980. Writer for television programs, including "Family," "Class of '65," "Incredible Hulk," and "Face to Face."

WORK IN PROGRESS: The Twilight Hour, a psychological suspense novel.

SIDELIGHTS: Koenig appeared as Mr. Chekov on the television series "Star Trek." His book *Chekov's Enterprise* is a journal of the making of "Star Trek: The Motion Picture." Koenig told *CA:* "If one can liken the happy experience of working as a regular in a prestigious television series—with its philosophical dignity, its aesthetic good taste, and its bountiful coffers—to an ideal, albeit, imaginary existence several fathoms deep in the fabled lost city of Atlantis, then, the cancellation of that program has its concomitant parallel in the ruination of that aquamarine mecca, the violent ascension to a gray surface world and a miserable case of the bends. When the series ended, the phone stopped ringing. Faced with the the prospect of life in a decompression chamber, I began to write. So far I've been able to keep the bad nitrogen bubbles away. I think I can write. I've decided to spend the next several years determining whether or not I can think accurately."

*   *   *

KOHN, John S. (Van E.) 1906-1976

OBITUARY NOTICE: Born in 1906; died December 18, 1976, in White Plains, N.Y. Rare book dealer and collector and author of scholarly rare book catalogues. Kohn began his career in the collector's book trade in 1931 and owned his own bookshop from 1935 to 1943. He co-founded the Seven Gables Bookshop in 1946, where he dedicated the next three decades to compiling his highly acclaimed catalogues, including *First Books by American Authors* and *More First Books by American Authors*. Obituaries and other sources: *New York Times,* December 20, 1976; *AB Bookman's Weekly,* January 10, 1977.

*   *   *

KOKYSHEV, Lazor 1933(?)-1975

OBITUARY NOTICE: Born c. 1933; died from injuries suffered in a beating, 1975, in the Altai region of Siberia, U.S.S.R. Poet and novelist. Kokyshev's novel *Arina* appeared in 1959. Obituaries and other sources: *AB Bookman's Weekly,* December 1, 1975.

*   *   *

KOLINS, William 1926(?)-1973

OBITUARY NOTICE: Born c. 1926; died of a heart attack, April, 1973, in England. Kolins worked for publishers in New York and London. He edited *Best Sellers,* served as a contributing editor to *Publishers Weekly,* and at the time of his death was publicity director for Macmillan in London. Obituaries and other sources: *Publishers Weekly,* May 14, 1973.

* * *

KORNFELD, Robert J(onathan) 1919-

PERSONAL: Born March 3, 1919, in Newton, Mass.; son of Lewis F. (a broker) and Lillian S. (an actress) Kornfeld; married Celia Seiferth (a writer and arts administrator), August 23, 1945; children: Robert J., Jr. *Education:* Harvard University, A.B., 1941; graduate study at Harvard University, Tulane University, New York University, Columbia University, College of Mount Saint Vincent, and Circle in the Square School of Drama, 1946-77. *Home:* 5286 Sycamore Ave., Riverdale, N.Y. 10471. *Agent:* Curtis Brown Ltd., 575 Madison Ave., New York, N.Y. 10022; and APA, 9000 Sunset Blvd., Los Angeles, Calif. 90069.

CAREER: XEQ-Radio, Mexico City, Mexico, writer, 1941; *San Francisco Examiner,* San Francisco, Calif., reporter, 1942-43; writer and photographer. Work represented in exhibitions at museums and galleries, including Addison Gallery of Art and Metropolitan Museum of Art. Member of board of Riverdale Contemporary Theatre; chairman of Toscanini Collection; honorary board member of Bronx Arts Ensemble. *Member:* National Arts Club, Dramatists Guild, Writers League, Harvard Club of New York. *Awards, honors:* Awards for best new play for "Passage in Purgatory," 1962, and "Minutes of the Meeting,' 1963, both from Norfolk Little Theatre; second place from New York Writers Conference, 1963, for "Queen of Crags"; award for best play from Broadway Drama Guild, 1979, for "The Art of Love."

WRITINGS: Great Southern Mansions (travelogue), Walker, 1979.

Plays: "Je suis homme" (title means "I Am Man"), first produced in Paris, 1953; "Passage in Purgatory" (one-act), first produced in Norfolk, Va., at Little Theatre, 1962, produced Off-Broadway at Circle in the Square Theatre, 1962; "Kicking the Castle Down" (two-act), first produced Off-Broadway at Gramercy Arts Theatre, 1962; "Clementina" (one-act), first produced at Riverdale Contemporary Theatre, 1963; "Tell the Stars" (two-act), first produced in Waterford, Conn., at Eugene O'Neill Memorial Theatre, 1969; "Reunion" (two-act), first produced in New York City at Cubiculo Theatre, 1978; "An Hour With Poe: Out of Space, Out of Time," first produced in New York City at Lincoln Center for the Performing Arts, 1979; "Glory Hallelujah!" (two-act), first produced in New York City at Eighteenth Street Playhouse, 1979; "The Passion of Frankenstein" (two-act), first produced in New York City at Stage Fifteen, 1980.

Also author of unproduced plays, including "Minutes of the Meeting," "Queen of Crags," "Playing Ludwig," "The Bridge," and "The Art of Love." Author of unproduced screenplay "The Diplomat." Contributor to periodicals, including *New York Times, Il Tempo, San Francisco Examiner,* and *Botteghe Oscure.*

WORK IN PROGRESS: Two plays.

SIDELIGHTS: Kornfeld told *CA:* "I have traveled much. I speak good French, Italian, Spanish, and some other languages. I specialize in Italian travels. The subjects of my plays are philosophical-political, stressing the need for humanism and liberty of thought and action." *Avocational interests:* Skiing.

KOSMALA, Hans 1904(?)-1981

OBITUARY NOTICE: Born c. 1904 in Breslau, Germany (now part of Poland); died in 1981 in Gloucestershire, England. Theologian, Presbyterian minister, and author. Kosmala was one of the world's leading Christian experts on Judaism. He studied and taught at the Institutum Judaicum Delitzschianum in Leipzig from 1926 until it was closed by the Nazis in 1935. In 1939 he fled to England, where he helped found the Christian Institute for Jewish Studies. For twenty years Kosmala served as director of the Swedish Theological Institute in Jerusalem, and for ten years was editor of the *Annual of the Swedish Theological Institute.* His books include *The Jew in the Christian World* and *Studies, Essays and Reviews.* Obituaries and other sources: *London Times,* June 8, 1981.

* * *

KOSTROWITZKI, Wilhelm Apollinaris de 1880-1918
(Guillaume Apollinaire)

BRIEF ENTRY: Born August 26, 1880, in Rome, Italy; died of Spanish influenza, November 9, 1918, in Paris, France. Author. Apollinaire's early writings are generally considered the bridge between French symbolism and surrealism. The short story collections *L'Enchanger pourrissant* (1909) and *Le Bestiaire* (1911) particularly reveal Apollinaire's interests in both the realistic and the fantastic. While writing these early works, Apollinaire met several painters, including Raoul Dufy, Henri Rousseau, and Picasso. He helped popularize Rousseau's work and assisted Picasso in establishing criteria for the Cubist movement. Apollinaire's favorite subject, though, was himself. In his best-known collection of poetry, *Alcools* (1913), he related key events of his past in a melange of styles. He later devoted many poems to his experiences in prison, where he was held while wrongly suspected of stealing Da Vinci's "Mona Lisa." Apollinaire's final works dealt with the violence of the times. Serving in the French military during World War I, he received a head wound and was discharged. He then wrote a novel, *The Poet Assassinated* (1918), and a collection of poems, *Calligrammes: Poems of Peace and War* (1918), in which he contrasted the bliss of love with the despair of war. He died just days before World War I ended. *Biographical/critical sources: Twentieth Century Authors: A Biographical Dictionary of Modern Literature,* H. W. Wilson, 1942; *The Oxford Companion to French Literature,* corrected edition, Clarendon Press, 1966; *Encyclopedia of World Literature in the Twentieth Century,* updated edition, Ungar, 1967; *Twentieth Century Writing: A Reader's Guide to Contemporary Literature,* Transatlantic, 1969; *Twentieth-Century Literary Criticism,* Volume 3, Gale, 1980.

* * *

KOTZ, Mary Lynn 1936-

PERSONAL: Born August 12, 1936, in Mathiston, Miss.; daughter of Joseph E. (a rural mail carrier) and Myrtle (a music teacher; maiden name, Haynes) Booth; married Nick Kotz (a writer), August 7, 1961; children: Jack. *Education:* Attended Sophia University, 1952-53; University of Mississippi, B.A., 1956; graduate study at University of Iowa, 1957. *Home:* 5508 Montgomery St., Chevy Chase, Md. 20015. *Agent:* Sterling Lord Agency, Inc., 660 Madison Ave., New York, N.Y. 10021. *Office:* 1211 Connecticut Ave. N.W., Washington, D.C. 20036.

CAREER: View, Tokyo, Japan, assistant editor, 1952-53; *McComb Enterprise Journal,* McBomb, Miss., in advertising,

1955; United Press International, Memphis, Tenn., reporter, 1956; Meredith Corp. (publisher), Des Moines, Iowa, publicity manager and editor in news bureau, 1957-60; free-lance writer, 1960—; Washington correspondent for *Art News*. Creator of White House Film Library, 1965-67. *Member:* National Association of Mental Health, Women in Communications, District of Columbia Mental Health Association (chairman of publicity, 1969; member of board of directors, 1980), Washington Independent Writers. *Awards, honors:* Named woman of the year by Mississippi Women in Communications, 1974, for *Upstairs at the White House;* Silver EM Award from University of Mississippi, 1980, for outstanding contribution to the field of journalism.

WRITINGS: (Editor) *Let Them Eat Promises,* Prentice-Hall, 1970; *Upstairs at the White House,* Coward, 1973; (with husband, Nick Kotz) *A Passion for Equality: George Wiley and the Movement,* Norton, 1977; (with Marvella Bayh) *Marvella: A Personal Journey,* Harcourt, 1979.

SIDELIGHTS: Mary Lynn Kotz's specialties are the White House, the presidency, first ladies, homes and families, personality features (especially on members of Congress), mental health, art, and artists.

Kotz told *CA:* "To come to know another human being through the interview process is a source of constant renewal of my own connectedness to the human race. To learn that person's joys, fears, motivations, ambitions, history, and way of life and then to communicate all that to a reader gives me a grand sense of pleasure and accomplishment."

AVOCATIONL INTERESTS: Theatre, music.

* * *

KRAUS, Joanna Halpert 1937-

PERSONAL: Born December 7, 1937, in Portland, Me.; daughter of Harold (a merchant) and Florence Halpert; married Ted M. Kraus (an editor and publisher), 1966; children: Timothy Yang Kun. *Education:* Attended Westfield College, London, 1957-58; Sarah Lawrence College, A.B., 1959; University of California, Los Angeles, M.A., 1963; Columbia University, Ed.D., 1972. *Home:* 86 Willowbrooke Dr., Brockport, N.Y. 14420. *Agent:* Patricia Hale Whitton, New Plays, Inc., P.O. Box 273, Rowayton, Conn. 06853. *Office:* State University of New York College at Brockport, Brockport, N.Y. 14420.

CAREER: Children's Theatre Association, Baltimore, Md., associate director and creative drama teacher, 1960-61; Strathmere School of the Arts, North Gower, Ontario, Canada, drama director, summers, 1961-63; New Rochelle Academy, New Rochelle, N.Y., director of drama program, 1962-63; Clark Center for the Performing Arts, New York City, assistant director and supervisor of performance program, 1963-65; Young Men's and Young Women's Hebrew Association (YM-YWHA), New York City, creative drama teacher, 1965-70; New York City Community College, New York City, instructor in public speaking and oral interpretation, 1966-69; Columbia University, Teacher's College, New York City, supervisor of student teachers in speech and theatre, 1970-71; State University of New York College at Purchase, instructor in theatre and drama, 1970-72; State University of New York College at New Paltz, lecturer, 1972-73, assistant professor of theatre and education, 1973-79; State University of New York College at Brockport, associate professor of children's drama, 1979—. Chairperson of Children's Theatre Showcase, 1963-65. Guest storyteller on WEVD-Radio show "Let's Tell Tales," 1973-75. Guest lec-

turer at Western Washington University Institute for Drama and the Child, summer, 1978. Director of plays, including "The Indian Captive," 1973, four original participation plays, 1973-79, and four theatre programs, 1974-76. Coordinator of Arts for Children program, 1980.

MEMBER: International Association of Theatre for Young People, Children's Theatre Association of America, American Theatre Association, Dramatists Guild, United University Professions. *Awards, honors:* Charlotte B. Chorpenning Cup from American Theatre Association, 1971, for achievement in playwrighting; Creative Artists Public Service fellowship in playwrighting, 1976-77.

WRITINGS—All plays, except as noted: *The Ice Wolf* (three-act; first produced in New York City at Equity Library Theatre, 1964), New Plays, 1967; *Mean to Be Free* (two-act; first produced in New York City at Hunter Theatre, 1968), New Plays, 1968; *Seven Sound and Motion Stories* (fiction), New Plays, 1971, revised edition, 1980; *Vasalisa* (three-act; first produced in Davidson, N.C., at Davidson College Theatre, 1972), New Plays, 1973; *The Great American Train Ride, Using Creative Dramatics for Multi-Disciplinary Classroom Project* (nonfiction), New Plays, 1975; *Two Plays From the Far East* (includes "The Dragon Hammer" and "The Tale of Oniroku"), New Plays, 1977; *The Dragon Hammer* (three-act; first produced in Rowayton, Conn., at Trolley Place Theatre, 1977), New Plays, 1978; *Circus Home* (two-act; first produced in Seattle, Wash., at Poncho Theatre, 1977), New Plays, 1979; (contributor of essay) Nellie McCaslin, editor, *Children and Drama,* 2nd edition, Longmans, 1980.

Work represented in anthology *New Women's Theatre,* edited by Honor Moore, Vintage Books, 1977. Contributor of reviews and articles to periodicals, including *Times Herald Record, Children and Drama, Children's Theatre Review,* and *Critical Digest.*

WORK IN PROGRESS: A play on adoption.

SIDELIGHTS: Kraus told *CA:* "When I was thirteen, my life was changed by a marvelous director of children's theatre, Margaret Dutton. We toured towns in Maine where no live theatre for young audiences had ever appeared. The children were spellbound, but no more so than we, the players. I vowed then to pass on that touch of magic. Accuracy and artistry were our goals, and now, as a writer, they are still the same for me. Children should have stories to grow on and should never have anything less than the best. Young people are a wonderful audience, for they listen with their hearts as well as their minds."

* * *

KRAUS, Karl 1874-1936

BRIEF ENTRY: Born April 28, 1874, in Jicin, Czechoslovakia; died June 12, 1936, in Vienna, Austria. Austrian poet, playwright, and essayist. Kraus was a master of satire, aiming his bitter comedy savagely against the disintegration of Western society. He attacked journalists with a special venom, castigating their careless use of language so vindictively and effectively that few critics commented on his work during his lifetime. Kraus's major work was "The Last Days of Mankind" (1919), a play so massive that only its epilogue could be produced. It was an evocation of the horrors of World War I, concluding with a vision of humanity's pending doom. Kraus's plays were styled after the German cabarets of the late nineteenth century, and they often attempted to incite the audience to action against the world's decline in values. His poems, published in the nine-volume *Worte in Versen* (1916-

30), were mellowed by the strength of their lyrical quality. Some critics felt his best satire was embodied in collections of essays, such as *Sittlichkeit und Kriminalitaet* (1908). All of Kraus's writings were published originally in *Die Fackel,* a periodical he founded in 1899 and edited until his death. *Biographical/critical sources: The Concise Encyclopedia of Modern World Literature,* Hutchinson, 1963; Wilma Abeles Iggers, *Karl Kraus: A Viennese Critic of the Twentieth Century,* Nijhoff, 1967; *Encyclopedia of World Literature in the Twentieth Century,* updated edition, Ungar, 1967.

*   *   *

KRAUSE, Frank H(arold) 1942-

PERSONAL: Born June 12, 1942, in Indianapolis, Ind.; son of Frank H. (a civil servant) and Evelyn A. (Greene) Krause; married Billye Michelle Groves, September 16, 1966; children: Justin Christopher, Ryan Michael. *Education:* Butler University, B.S., 1964; Indiana University, M.A., 1967, Ed.D., 1969; further graduate study at Harvard University, 1968. *Home address:* R.R. 12, Box 29, Finnlandia Addition, Muncie, Ind. 47302. *Office:* Counseling and Psychological Services Center, Ball State University, Muncie, Ind. 47306.

CAREER: Butler University, Indianapolis, Ind., assistant football coach, 1964; Indiana National Bank, Indianapolis, assistant to personnel director and recruiter, 1964-66; Indiana University, Bloomington, intern at University Counseling Center, 1968-69; Ball State University, Muncie, Ind., assistant professor, 1969-73, associate professor, 1974-78, professor of psychology, 1978—, counseling psychologist, 1974—, supervisor of graduate programs in England, West Germany, and Spain, 1969-78, director of Counseling Practicum Clinic, 1972-73, director of European Center for Advanced Graduate Studies in Counseling, Sembach, West Germany, 1975-77. Director of Correctional Psychological Associates, Inc., 1973-75. Athletic coach at Sembach Air Base, 1975-78. Member of board of directors of local Young Men's Christian Association, 1979—. Consultant to Indiana Soldiers and Sailors Children's Home, Indiana Women's Prison, and Westinghouse Corp.

MEMBER: National Society for the Study of Education, American Personnel and Guidance Association, Counselor Educators and Supervisors, Indiana Counselor Educators and Supervisors (president, 1971-72), Phi Delta Kappa (faculty sponsor, 1970-75). *Awards, honors:* Community service award from Indiana governor's Voluntary Action Program, 1979; certificate from Indiana chapter of National Committe for the Prevention of Child Abuse, 1979.

WRITINGS: (With Donald E. Hendrickson) *Counseling Techniques With Youth,* C.E. Merrill, 1972; (with Hendrickson) *Counseling and Psychotherapy: Training and Supervision,* C. E. Merrill, 1972; (with Kenneth M. Dimick) *Student Manual for Counseling Practicum,* Ball State University Press, 1972, revised edition, 1974; (with Roger L. Hutchinson) *A Handbook for Houseparents and Other Childcare Workers,* Indiana Soldiers and Sailors Children's Home, 1974; (with Dimick) *Practicum Manual for Counseling and Psychotherapy,* Accelerated Development, 1975, revised edition, 1980. Contributor to counseling, psychology, and education journals. Contributor to periodicals, including *Indiana Law Enforcement* and *Army Administrator.*

WORK IN PROGRESS: Revising *Counseling Techniques With Youth.*

KRAUSZ, Ernest 1931-

PERSONAL: Born August 13, 1931, in Satu-Mare, Romania; son of Maurice (a rabbi) and Bertha Gottlieb; married Gillian Rachel Collins, December 18, 1962; children: Sarah Chayah, Miriam, David Zvi, Benjamin. *Education:* University of London, B.Sc. (with honors), 1955; London School of Economics and Political Science, London, M.Sc., 1960, Ph.D., 1965. *Office:* Department of Sociology, Bar-Ilan University, Ramat-Gan, Israel.

CAREER: Central London Polytechnic, London, England, lecturer in sociology, 1959-64; North-East London Polytechnic, London, principal lecturer in sociology, 1964-67; City University, London, lecturer, 1967-70, senior lecturer, 1970-72, reader in sociology, 1971-72; Bar-Ilan University, Ramat-Gan, Israel, associate professor, 1972-73, professor of sociology, 1973—, dean of faculty of social science, 1974-76. Visiting professor at University of Newcastle, 1976-77. *Member:* National Council of Higher Education, Israel Sociological Association. *Awards, honors:* Senior fellow of Nuffield Foundation, 1961-64.

WRITINGS: Sociology in Britain, Columbia University Press, 1969; *Ethnic Minorities in Britain,* Paladin Press, 1971; (with S. H. Miller) *Social Research Design,* Longman, 1974. Editor of *Studies of Israeli Society,* 1978—.

WORK IN PROGRESS: Research on philosophy of social science and sociological methodology.

*   *   *

KRIEGEL, Harriet

PERSONAL: Born in New York, N.Y.; daughter of Samuel (a podiatrist) and Sally (Grobois) Bernzweig; married Leonard Kriegel (a professor of English and writer); children: Mark Benjamin, Eric Bruce. *Education:* Received B.A. and M.A. from Hunter College (now of the City University of New York). *Home:* 355 Eighth Ave., New York, N.Y. 10001.

CAREER: Public relations director of Cavitron Corp. (medical electronics firm) in New York City; business manager of Economist Intelligence Unit Ltd. (market research firm) in New York City; teacher of English and drama at Walton High School in New York City. Vice-president of board of directors of IRT Theater. *Member:* International Association of Business Communicators.

WRITINGS: Women in Drama, New American Library, 1975. Author and director of film "Domestic Tranquillity." Contributor to *Nation, Commonweal,* and newspapers.

WORK IN PROGRESS: A novel tentatively titled *Working Woman* and a play tentatively titled "She Who Would Play Hamlet."

*   *   *

KRIMSKY, Joseph (Hayylm) 1883(?)-1971

OBITUARY NOTICE: Born c. 1883; died July 31, 1971, in Daytona, Fla. Surgeon and author. Krimsky practiced in New York City and in West Virginia, and during World War I headed a Zionist medical unit in Palestine. He was president of the Federation of Ukrainian Jews and the National Jewish Fund. He wrote several books on philosophical and religious subjects, including *A Doctor's Soliloquy* and *The Wonder of Man. Obituaries and other sources: New York Times,* August 2, 1971; *AB Bookman's Weekly,* August 16, 1971.

KRISLOV, Alexander
See LEE HOWARD, Leon Alexander

* * *

KRISTOFFERSON, Kris 1936-

PERSONAL: Born June 22, 1936, in Brownsville, Tex.; son of a military officer; married Fran Beir (divorced, c. 1972); married Rita Coolidge (a singer), August 19, 1973 (divorced, 1980); children: (first marriage) Tracy, Kris; (second marriage) Casey. *Education:* Attended Pomona College; Oxford University, B.A., 1960. *Office:* c/o Block-Kewley Management, 11 Bailey Ave., Ridgefield, Conn. 06877.

CAREER: Lyricist and composer of songs, 1965—; recording artist and performer in nightclubs, concerts, and on television, 1969—; actor in films, including "Cisco Pike," 1971, "The Last Movie," 1971, "Pat Garrett and Billy the Kid," 1973, "Blume in Love," 1973, "Bring Me the Head of Alfredo Garcia," 1974, "Alice Doesn't Live Here Anymore," 1975, "The Sailor Who Fell From Grace With the Sea," 1976, "A Star Is Born," 1976, "Vigilante Force," 1976, "Semi-Tough," 1978, "Convoy," 1978, "Freedom Road," 1979, "Heaven's Gate," 1981, "Rollover," 1981. Worked as ditch digger, bartender, and janitor in Nashville, Tenn., 1965-68, and as helicopter pilot in New Orleans, La., 1968-70. *Military service:* U.S. Army, 1960-65, served as helicopter pilot in West Germany; became captain. *Member:* Phi Beta Kappa.

AWARDS, HONORS: Four national collegiate awards from *Atlantic Monthly* for short stories; Rhodes scholar; honorary doctorate from Pomona College, 1974; Song of the Year award from Country Music Association, 1970, for "Sunday Mornin' Comin' Down"; Songwriter of the Year award from Nashville Songwriter's Association, 1971; Grammy Award from the National Association of Recording Arts and Sciences, 1971, for "Help Me Make It Through the Night"; Robert J. Burton Awards for most performed country song, 1972, for "Help Me Make It Through the Night," and for best country vocal performance by a duo or group, 1974, for "From the Bottle to the Bottom" with wife, Rita Coolidge, both from Broadcast Music, Inc.; sixteen platinum and thirteen gold LPs worldwide.

WRITINGS: Lyricist and composer of songs, including: "Viet Nam Blues," "Sunday Mornin' Comin Down," "Me and Bobby McGee," "The Pilgrim: Chapter Thirty-three," "Why Me, Lord," "Help Me Make It Through the Night," "For the Good Times," "Jody and the Kid," "When I Loved Her," "The Law Is for the Protection of the People," "Blame It on the Stones," "From the Bottle to the Bottom," "Just the Other Side of Nowhere," "The Silver-Tongued Devil," "Enough for You," (with Donnie Frith) "Give It Time to Be Tender", "Please Don't Tell Me How the Story Ends," "Stranger," "Lovin' Her Was Easier."

Recordings: "Kristofferson," Monument, 1970, later released as "Me and Bobby McGee," Columbia; "The Silver-Tongued Devil and I," Monument, 1972; "Border Lord," Monument, 1972; "Jesus Was a Capricorn," Monument, 1973; (with wife, Rita Coolidge) "Full Moon,' A&M, 1973; "Spooky Lady's Sideshow," 1974; "It's Surreal Things," Monument, 1976; "Easter Island," 1978; "Shake Hands With the Devil,' 1979; "To the Bone," Columbia, 1981. Other recordings include "Songs of Kristofferson," "Who's to Bless and Who's to Blame," (with Coolidge) "Breakaway," and "Big Sur Festival," Columbia.

SIDELIGHTS: Kristofferson is a well-known songwriter, country singer, and film actor whose work has been widely ac-

claimed by both performers and critics. Country music stars Johnny Cash and Willie Nelson, for example, regard Kristofferson as "the most gifted lyric writer working today," and *New Orleans Times-Picayune* critic Paul Lentz appraised Kristofferson as "one of the best songwriters of the decade."

Although Kristofferson is described today as a "hard-drinking, hard-loving man-of-the-road" who cultivates the image of a country boy by wearing nothing but "cowboy boots, disintegrating Levi's and faded western shirts," during his college years his image was that of an ambitious young scholar. Kristofferson had been a talented athlete, an active participant in student activities, and an academically gifted student who was awarded a Rhodes scholarship to attend Oxford University.

While attending Oxford, Kristofferson worked on two novels and began writing lyrics for country songs. He left Oxford during his second year, discouraged about not having his novels published, and enlisted in the U.S. Army. His continuing interest in writing country music led him to resign his military commission several years later in order to pursue a songwriting career.

Kristofferson spent several difficult years working at a variety of odd jobs in order to support himself while seeking a market for his songs. During the late 1960's Kristofferson began singing primarily in an effort to promote his own music. By 1970 Kristofferson was performing on Johnny Cash's television show and was becoming one of the country's top songwriters, largely as a result of the phenomenal success of Janis Joplin's recording of Kristofferson's song "Me and Bobby McGee." This song is considered by some critics to be one of Kristofferson's finest songs; it is certainly among his most popular, having been recorded by more than fifty artists within two years of its initial release. (In fact, other Kristofferson songs have been recorded by more than four hundred fifty artists, earning him almost $500,000 in royalties each year.)

Many of Kristofferson's other lyrics are about loneliness and love, and some critics have observed an autobiographical quality about them. Reviewers have pointed out, for example, that "For the Good Times," a song about a failed marriage, was written following the disintegration of Kristofferson's first marriage and that "The Pilgrim: Chapter 33" appears to describe Kristofferson's own "circuitous course to success." Although several critics have contended that Kristofferson writes his best songs "out of pain," Kristofferson disagreed, saying "Usually . . . it's passion recalled during a period of tranquility." He has admitted, though, that "I've never been good at analyzing what I write in any detail. Once a song's written, the umbilical cord's cut."

Esquire's Tom Burke, however, has analyzed Kristofferson's work and admires "its consistent, undercutting self-satire, its variety, and the verbal mileage he has milked from the notion that things, for all of us, have already been as good as they're ever going to get." Television producer Robert Considine reported that he also admires Kristofferson's songs because Kristofferson writes about "life for ordinary people."

After Kristofferson had emerged a a major singer and songwriter, he was soon asked to audition for motion picture roles. In 1972 he made his acting debut in the film "Cisco Pike." Since then, Kristofferson has appeared in more than fifteen films and has acted in a variety of roles, including that of a trucker in "Convoy," a rancher in "Alice Doesn't Live Here Anymore," a sailor in "The Sailor Who Fell From Grace With the Sea," a motorcyclist in "Bring Me the Head of Alfredo Garcia," and a banker in "Rollover." Kristofferson has also portrayed musicians in several other films, including "Cisco Pike," "Blume in Love," and "A Star Is Born."

Kristofferson claimed that some of these roles did not really require that he act because he had only to portray himself. Of his role in "A Star Is Born" he said, "If I can't play the guy in 'Star' what can I play? A self-destructive musician! I play that every day. No big accomplishment." Tom Burke disagreed, noting that although many of Kristofferson's early roles required that he merely "purvey his ambling, grinning self," his later performances, including that of John Norman Howard in "A Star Is Born" and that of the rancher in "Alice Doesn't Live Here Anymore," demonstrated that Kristofferson has genuine acting ability.

In addition to acting talent, observed a *Time* reporter, Kristofferson possesses "both a searing sexuality and a boyish vulnerability" that have contributed to his movie success. Film star Dyan Cannon also noted Kristofferson's charisma, commenting: "I knew for years he was one of our finest writers—those lyrics, the heartbreak in them—but then I saw him on the screen! Incredible! I've never seen a presence like his."

BIOGRAPHICAL/CRITICAL SOURCES: New York Times, July 26, 1970; *New York Times Magazine,* December 6, 1970; *Newsday,* September 11, 1971; *Saturday Review of the Arts,* February 3, 1973; New Orleans Times-Picayune, January 13, 1974; *Biography News,* Gale, February, 1974; *Esquire,* December, 1976; *Mademoiselle,* January, 1977; *Time,* August 15, 1977; *Rolling Stone,* February 23, 1978.*

—*Sketch by Susan M. Trosky*

*   *   *

KRONENBERG, Maria Elizabeth 1881(?)-1970

OBITUARY NOTICE: Born c. 1881; died in August, 1970, in The Hague, Netherlands. Historian, editor, and author. Kronenberg was best known for her research into the history of Dutch printing, especially as compiler of the *Bibliography of Dutch Printing, 1500-1540.* She was also the author of *Banned Books and Mutinous Printers,* which she wrote during the German occupation of the Netherlands in World War II. Obituaries and other sources: *AB Bookman's Weekly,* October 5, 1970.

*   *   *

KRUPNIK, Baruch
See KARU, Baruch

*   *   *

KUBEK, Anthony 1920-

PERSONAL: Born June 10, 1920, in Ambridge, Pa.; married Naomi Dugan, June, 1948 (deceased); children: David, Joseph, Nora, Margaret. *Education:* Attended Geneva College, 1940-43, and LaSalle University, 1944; Georgetown University, B.S. (with honors), 1948, M.A., 1950, Ph.D., 1956; attended George Washington University, 1949. *Politics:* Independent. *Religion:* Roman Catholic. *Home:* 122 Sherwood Ave., Troy, Ala. 36081. *Agent:* Allan Prigge, Inc., 350 Madison Ave., Suite 200, Cresskill, N.J. 07626. *Office:* Department of Political Science, Troy State University, Troy, Ala. 36081.

CAREER: High school social studies teacher in Arlington, Va., 1950-55; Slippery Rock State Teachers College (now Slippery Rock State College), Slippery Rock, Pa., assistant professor of political science, 1956-58; University of Dallas, Dallas, Tex., 1959-73, began as associate professor, became professor of political science, then research professor; University of Plano, Plano, Tex., dean and chief academic adviser, 1974-75; Troy State University, Troy, Ala., professor of political science,

1975—, curator of General Claire L. Chennault Library. Lecturer at colleges and universities all over the United States; guest lecturer for Catholic Relief System, 1966; distinguished lecturer for *China Times,* 1970; visiting professor at National Taiwan University, National Cheng-chi University, and Fu-Jen Catholic University, 1971; touring lecturer for Overseas Chinese Association in Hong Kong, the Philippines, Malaysia, Singapore, Australia, and New Zealand, 1972; lecturer at Institute of International Relations, Taipei, Taiwan, 1977. Member of American Security Council, Asian Speakers Bureau, Congress of Freedom, Sino-American Amity Fund, and Western Goals; member of advisory board of Young Americans for Freedom. Participant in international conferences; member of joint fact-finding mission of American Security Council and South Vietnam Council on Foreign Relations, 1974; consultant to U.S. Senate. *Military service:* U.S. Navy, pharmacist's mate in Medical Corps, 1943-46; served in the South Pacific.

MEMBER: American Historical Association, American Association for Chinese Studies, American Political Science Association, Association for Asian Studies, China Academy, China Institute, College of Chinese Culture (U.S. representative), University Professors for Academic Order. *Awards, honors:* Grants from Volker Foundation, 1960, O'Donnell Foundation, 1961, Institute for Humane Studies, 1965, Relm Foundation, 1968, Earhart Foundation, 1970, China Institute, 1976, and Pacific Cultural Foundation, 1977; distinguished service award from Armed Forces of the Republic of China, 1968; citation from Military Order of the World Wars, 1971; Order of the Brilliant Star from Republic of China, 1972; award from Shanghai-Tiffin Club, 1980.

WRITINGS: How the Far East Was Lost: American Policy and the Creation of Communist China, 1941-49, Regnery, 1963; (editor) *The Amerasia Papers,* two volumes, Government Printing Office, 1970; *The Red China Papers: What Americans Deserve to Know About U.S.-Chinese Relations,* Arlington House, 1975. Contributor to magazines and newspapers, including *Human Events, Christian Economics, Asian Outlook,* and *Ambassador.* Also author of *Communism at Pearl Harbor* and *The Amerasia Papers: A Clue to the Catastrophe of China,* 1971. Also editor of *The Morgenthau Diary on China,* two volumes, 1965, and author of introduction and epilogue to *The Communist Conquest of Shanghai: A Warning to the West,* by Paolo A. Fossi, 1970.

SIDELIGHTS: Kubek wrote: "I tried to be as objective as possible in my interpretation of recent American foreign policy. I studied under the late Dr. Charles D. Tansill, a diplomatic historian at Georgetown University, who taught me the mechanics of research. I have been interested in modern China, with emphasis on American policy toward it. I can speak Chinese and Russian."

*   *   *

KUEHL, Linda 1939(?)-1978

OBITUARY NOTICE: Born c. 1939; died February 6, 1978, in Washington, D.C. Editor, critic, and author. Kuehl was best known for her interviews with literary figures such as Alfred A. Knopf, Eudora Welty, and Joan Didion, and for her book reviews, which appeared in numerous periodicals. An expert on the history of jazz, she was working on a biography of Billie Holiday at the time of her death. Obituaries and other sources: *Publishers Weekly,* March 6, 1978.

KUP, Karl 1903-1981

OBITUARY NOTICE: Born May 7, 1903, in Haarlem, Netherlands (some sources list birthplace as Berlin, Germany [now East Germany]); died of a stroke, June 25, 1981, in Ridgewood, N.J. Art historian and author. Kup was head of the Art and Architecture Division of the New York Public Library, and for more than thirty years was curator of the library's Spencer Collection of illustrated books and manuscripts. Under his direction, the collection became one of the world's finest, especially noted for its Japanese and Siamese manuscripts, books, and scrolls. After Kup's retirement from the library in 1968, he lectured on art history, book production, and graphic arts at universities in the United States and Japan. His writings include *The Council of Constance, 1414-1418; Books and Printing,* and *The Christmas Story in Medieval and Renaissance Manuscripts From the Spencer Collection.* Obituaries and other sources: *American Artist,* June, 1946, June, 1954, March, 1956; *New York Times,* July 7, 1981; *Publishers Weekly,* July 17, 1981; *AB Bookman's Weekly,* September 7, 1981.

* * *

KUPRIN, Aleksandr Ivanovich 1870-1938

BRIEF ENTRY: Born September 7, 1870, in Narovkhat, Russia (now U.S.S.R.); died August 25, 1938, in Leningrad, U.S.S.R. Russian novelist and short story writer. Kuprin was a popular and critically acclaimed storyteller. His first successful story was "Molokh" (1896), an attack on capitalism. Much of his writing drew on his brief career as a military cadet and officer. The novel *The Duel* (1905), for example, was a realistic and graphic revelation of mismanagement and brutality in army life. Some of his better short stories are those he wrote about adventurers and risk-takers, praising the simple life and depicting love and beauty without the moralizing tone present in other contemporary writing. Kuprin was essentially a traditionalist in the spirit of such nineteenth-century writers as Chekhov, Tolstoy, and Gorky. Among his best-known works are *The Pit* (1915), a shocking novel of prostitution in Odessa, and his short story collections *The River of Life* (1916), *A Slav Soul* (1916), and *Sasha* (1920). Kuprin was opposed to Bolshevism and left Russia for France after 1917, returning to his homeland only a year before his death. *Biographical/critical sources: Twentieth Century Authors: A Biographical Dictionary of Modern Literature,* H. W. Wilson, 1942.

* * *

KURZ, Otto 1908-1975

OBITUARY NOTICE: Born May 26, 1908, in Vienna, Austria; died September 3, 1975, in London, England. Educator, librarian, and author. Kurz was a classical historian whose specialty was the Near East. He was the author of several books on art history. His works include *Fakes* and *European Clocks and Watches in the Near East.* Obituaries and other sources: *Who's Who,* 126th edition, St. Martin's, 1974; *AB Bookman's Weekly,* December 1, 1975.

* * *

KURZER, Siegmund F. 1907(?)-1973

OBITUARY NOTICE: Born c. 1907 in Vienna, Austria; died in an automobile accident, April 22, 1973, in New Zealand. Publishing executive and editor. Kurzer's special interest as an editor was the education of handicapped children. Textbooks published under his supervision include *Learning Disabilities* and *The Exceptional Child in the Family.* Obituaries and other sources: *Publishers Weekly,* June 4, 1973.

L

La BARR, Creighton
  See von BLOCK, Bela W(illiam)

*   *   *

LACAN, Jacques Marie Emile   1901-1981

OBITUARY NOTICE: Born April 13, 1901, in Paris, France; died of cancer, September 9, 1981, in Paris, France. Psychoanalyst and author. A controversial figure, Lacan was considered the most influential thinker in French psychiatry. He brought about a revival of interest in Freudian ideas among French intellectuals with his theories, which drew upon structuralist linguistics as well as Freud's thought. Lacan's unusual practices, such as his use of analytic sessions shorter than the standard fifty minutes, caused him and his followers to be expelled from the International Psychoanalytic Association in 1953. Lacan considered himself a strict Freudian, however, and in 1964 he founded the Freudian School of Paris, which he dissolved in 1980 because of its deviations from Freudianism. Lacan's books include *Ecrits* and *The Four Fundamental Concepts of Psycho-Analysis.* Obituaries and other sources: *New York Review of Books,* January 25, 1979; *New York Times,* September 11, 1981; *Newsweek,* September 21, 1981; *Time,* September 21, 1981.

*   *   *

LADY GREGORY
  See GREGORY, Isabella Augusta (Persse)

*   *   *

LAIKEN, Deirdre S(usan)   1948-

PERSONAL: Born January 21, 1948, in New York, N.Y.; daughter of David and Shirley (Lewis) Laiken; married Alan Schneider (a psychotherapist), June 21, 1978. *Education:* State University of New York College at Buffalo, B.S.Ed., 1969, M.S.Ed., 1970. *Religion:* Jewish. *Home and office:* 1036 Garden St., Hoboken, N.J. 07030. *Agent:* Berenice Hoffman Literary Agency, 215 West 75th St., New York, N.Y. 10023.

CAREER: Buffalo Public Schools, Buffalo, N.Y., teacher of English, 1970-74; Scholastic Magazine, editor, 1974—; writer, 1976—. Part-time creative writing teacher.

WRITINGS: Mind/Body/Spirit (young adult), Messner, 1978; *Beautiful Body Building,* New American Library, 1979; (with

husband, Alan Schneider) *Listen to Me, I'm Angry* (young adult), Lothrop, 1980; (with Lilian Rowen) *Speedwalking,* Putnam, 1981; *Daughters of Divorce* (nonfiction), Morrow, 1981.

WORK IN PROGRESS: A novel; a book for young adults, written with husband Alan Schneider, that explains the dynamics of love and love relationships, tentatively titled *The Love Book.*

SIDELIGHTS: Laiken told *CA:* "*Daughters of Divorce* is a result of five years of research and interviews. It is a study of how parental divorce affects women's attitudes, expectations, and perceptions. To write *Daughters of Divorce,* I spent many hours researching, interviewing women whose parents had divorced, and talking with psychoanalysts. I also included in the book many personal moments in my own life and insights I developed about my own parents' divorce and how that event shaped my attitudes."

AVOCATIONAL INTERESTS: Travel (including residence in Portugal), athletics.

*   *   *

LALIBERTE, Norman   1925-

PERSONAL: Born November 24, 1925, in Worcester, Mass.; son of Romeo and Rosemarie (Lambert) Laliberte; married Rory Sawicki, January 23, 1952; children: Veronique, Jacques, Jesse, Michele, Nicholas. *Education:* Illinois Institute of Technology, B.S., 1951, M.S., 1954; attended Cranbrook Academy of Art, 1952, and Museum of Fine Arts, Montreal, Quebec. *Agent:* Arras Gallery, 29 West 57th St., New York, N.Y. 10019.

CAREER: Professional artist. Member of faculty at Kansas City Art Institute, 1960-61; lecturer at Webster College, 1964; associate professor at Rhode Island School of Design, 1965; artist-in-residence at St. Mary's College, Notre Dame, Ind., 1960-62, and Newton College of the Sacred Heart, 1967-74. Work represented in private and permanent collections and exhibited all over the United States and Canada in group and solo shows, including Art Institute of Chicago, Museum of Contemporary Crafts, Montreal Museum of Fine Arts, and International Festival of Arts; consultant to Vatican Exhibit at New York World's Fair and Sol Productions.

WRITINGS: (With Edward N. West) *The History of the Cross,* Macmillan, 1960; (with Sterling McIlhany) *Banners and Hang-*

ings: Design and Construction, Reinhold, 1966; (with Maureen Jones) *Wooden Images*, Reinhold, 1966; (with Alex Mogelon) *Painting With Crayons: History and Modern Techniques*, Reinhold, 1967; (with Jean M. Morman) *Art: Of Wonder and a World*, Art Education, 1967; (with Mogelon) *Silhouettes, Shadows, and Cutouts: History and Modern Use*, Reinhold, 1968; (with Morman) *Art: Tempo of Today*, Art Education, 1969; (with Mogelon) *Drawing With Pencils: History and Modern Techniques*, Van Nostrand, 1969; (with Mogelon and Richey Kehl) *One Hundred Ways to Have Fun With an Alligator and One Hundred Other Involving Art Projects*, Art Education, 1969.

(With Mogelon) *The Book of Posters*, Art Education, 1970; (with Mogelon) *Drawing With Ink: History and Modern Techniques*, Van Nostrand, 1970; (with Morman) *Limits of Defiance: Strikes, Rights, and Government* (juvenile), F. Watts, 1971; (with Mogelon) *The Art Stencil: History and Modern Uses*, Van Nostrand, 1971; (with Mogelon) *Collage, Montage, Assemblage: History and Contemporary Techniques*, Van Nostrand, 1971; (with Mogelon) *Twentieth-Century Woodcuts: History and Modern Techniques*, Van Nostrand, 1971; (with Mogelon) *Masks, Face Coverings, and Headgear*, Van Nostrand, 1973; (with Mogelon and Beatrice Thompson) *Pastel, Charcoal, and Chalk Drawing: History, Classical and Contemporary Techniques*, Van Nostrand, 1973; (with Mogelon) *The Art of Monoprint: History and Modern Techniques*, Van Nostrand, 1974; (with Mogelon) *The Reinhold Book of Art Ideas: History and Techniques*, Van Nostrand, 1976.

Illustrator: Joseph Pintauro, *The Rainbow Box: A Book for Each Season and a Peace Poster*, Volume I: *The Peace Box: Winter*, Volume II: *The Rabbit Box: Spring*, Volume III: *A Box of Sun: Summer*, Volume IV: *The Magic Box: Autumn*, Harper, 1970; Constance B. Hieatt, *The Castle of Ladies*, Crowell, 1973. Also illustrator of *My Sweet Lord*, Hallmark, 1972.

Contributor to art journals.

BIOGRAPHICAL/CRITICAL SOURCES: American Artist, February, 1970.*

* * *

LAMPL, Paul 1915-

BRIEF ENTRY: Born March 6, 1915, in Vienna, Austria. Architect and author. Lampl joined the architectural firm Eggers Partnership in 1934 and has been a design coordinator there since 1965. His designs include churches and office buildings. He wrote *Cities and Planning in the Ancient Near East* (Braziller, 1968), and illustrated *The Art of Ancient Iran* (Crown, 1965) and *Early Christian and Byzantine Architecture* (Penguin). *Address:* 22 Riverside Dr., New York, N.Y. 10023; and Eggers Partnership, 100 Park Ave., New York, N.Y. 10017. *Biographical/critical sources: American Architects Directory*, 3rd edition, Bowker, 1970.

* * *

LA MURE, Pierre 1909-1976

OBITUARY NOTICE: Born June 15, 1909, in Nice, France; died December 28, 1976, in Los Angeles, Calif. Author. La Mure came to the United States as a correspondent for a French newspaper, and was naturalized in 1937. His biographies of Thomas Edison and John D. Rockefeller, written in French, won him the Strassburger Prize in 1939. His first book in English was *Moulin Rouge*, a novel based on the life of Henri Toulouse-Lautrec, which became an international best-seller. He wrote two other biographical novels, *Beyond Desire* and

Claire de Lune. Obituaries and other sources: *Who's Who in the West*, 15th edition, Marquis, 1976; *Publishers Weekly*, January 31, 1977.

* * *

LANDE, Nathaniel 1939-

PERSONAL: Born May 26, 1939, in Canada; son of Robert (a physician) and Gwendolyn (Lande) Greenblatt; married Linda Hope (divorced, 1975); children: Andrew. *Education:* Oxford University, B.A., 1956; attended Duke University; Antioch College, M.A., 1970. *Residence:* Los Angeles, Calif. *Agent:* Sterling Lord Agency, Inc., 660 Madison Ave., New York, N.Y. 10021.

CAREER: Worked as aide to Presidents John F. Kennedy and Lyndon B. Johnson, White House, Washington, D.C.; executive producer for CBS-TV, New York City, and NBC-TV, Los Angeles, Calif.; director of creative projects for Time-Life Books, New York City; editorial director for Editorial Francisco Alver, Rio de Janeiro, Brazil. Consultant to Technicolor Corp. *Member:* Writers Guild of America, Directors Guild of America, Overseas Press Club of America, Players Club, Annabells, Royal Danish Yacht Club. *Awards, honors:* Gold medals from New York International Film Festival, Cannes Film Festival, and San Francisco Film Festival; silver medal from Chicago Film Festival; Golden Eagle from Council on International Nontheatrical Events.

WRITINGS: Mindstyles, Lifestyles, Price, Stern, 1976; *The Emotional Maintenance Manual*, Rawson, Wade, 1978; *Stages*, Harper, 1978; *Self-Health: The Lifelong Fitness Book*, Holt, 1980; *Cricket* (novel), New American Library, 1981. Contributor to magazines, including *Life* and *Harper's Bazaar*.

WORK IN PROGRESS: A novel; research on social development in children and on relationships.

SIDELIGHTS: Lande commented: "I continue to travel around the world, with homes in Los Angeles and London, and I lecture a great deal about my books on clinical psychology. I have been involved with making 'movies of the week' for television and will probably continue working from time to time in motion picture production."

BIOGRAPHICAL/CRITICAL SOURCES: Chicago Daily News, December 10, 1976; *Publishers Weekly*, December 27, 1976; *Washington Star*, December 13, 1976.

* * *

LANDES, Sonia 1925-

PERSONAL: Born February 21, 1925, in New York, N.Y.; daughter of William Tarnopol (in business); married David S. Landes (a professor of economics); children: Jane Landes Foster, Alison Landes Fiekowsky, Richard. *Education:* George Washington University, received B.A.; Boston University, received M.A.; Sorbonne, University of Paris, received Certificate for Preparation for Teachers of French in Foreign Countries. *Religion:* Jewish. *Residence:* Cambridge, Mass. *Office:* Buckingham Browne & Nichols School, 10 Buckingham St., Cambridge, Mass. 02138.

CAREER: Co-founder and teacher at elementary school in Oakland, Calif., 1961; Buckingham Browne & Nichols School, Cambridge, Mass., high school English teacher and curriculum consultant, 1964— . Lecturer at Simmons College, Brandeis University, and Lesley College; member of board of directors of Ecole Bilingue, 1964-70; conductor of workshops and seminars; reading consultant at open school in Grantchester, England, 1968-69. *Awards, honors:* National Endowment for the Humanities grant, 1976-78.

WRITINGS: (With daughter, Alison Landes) *Pariswalks: Close-ups of the Left Bank of Paris,* New Republic Books, 1975, 2nd edition, 1979. Also author with A. Landes of *Londonwalks* and *Jerusalemwalks.*

WORK IN PROGRESS: "Beyond Literacy," a literature curriculum for elementary school children.

SIDELIGHTS: Sonia Landes wrote: "The two subjects of my work are France, Paris in particular, and children's literature and how to teach it."

BIOGRAPHICAL/CRITICAL SOURCES: "Max Made Mischief," a film released by Documentaries for Learning.

* * *

LANGDON, Robert Adrian   1924-

PERSONAL: Born September 3, 1924, in Adelaide, Australia; son of Arthur Louis (a carpenter) and Doris (a dressmaker; maiden name, McFarling) Langdon; married Iva Louise Layton, December 6, 1959; children: Louise. *Education:* Attended high school in Adelaide, Australia. *Home:* 15 Darambal St., Aranda, Australian Capital Territory 2614, Australia. *Office:* Pacific Manuscripts Bureau, Australian National University, Canberra, Australian Capital Territory 2600, Australia.

CAREER: South Australian Public Service, Adelaide, clerk, 1941-42; worked as free-lance journalist, ships fireman, dock laborer, and secretary in Australia and England, 1946-48; Grace and Co., La Paz, Bolivia, managerial secretary, 1948-51; Canadian National Railways, Toronto, Ontario, Canada, clerk, 1952-53; Advertiser Newspapers Ltd., Adelaide, journalist, 1953-61; Pacific Publications Pty. Ltd., Sydney, Australia, journalist, 1962-63, assistant editor, 1964-68; *Pacific Islands Monthly,* Sydney, assistant editor, 1964-68; Australian National University, Canberra, executive officer of Pacific Manuscripts Bureau, 1968—. *Military service:* Royal Australian Navy, 1942-46. *Member:* Australian Journalists Association, Polynesian Society (New Zealand), Societe des Oceanistes (France), Societe d'Etudes Oceaniennes (Tahiti), Hakluyt Society (England). *Awards, honors:* Australian National University research fellowship, 1977-79; Caballero of Orden de Isabela la Catolica, 1980.

WRITINGS: Tahiti: Island of Love, Cassell, 1959, 5th edition, Pacific Publications, 1979; (editor) *Cumulative Index to Pacific Islands Monthly, 1930-1945,* Pacific Publications, 1968; *The Lost Caravel,* Pacific Publications, 1975; (editor) *American Whalers and Traders in the Pacific: A Guide to Records on Microfilm,* Pacific Manuscripts Bureau, 1978; (editor) *Thar She Went: An Interim Index to the Pacific Ports and Islands Visited by American Whalers and Traders in the 19th Century,* Pacific Manuscripts Bureau, 1979.

Contributor: Peter Hastings, editor, *Papua New Guinea: Prospero's Other Island,* Angus & Robertson, 1971; Noel Rutherford, editor, *Friendly Islands: A History of Tonga,* Oxford University Press, 1977; Niel Gunson, editor, *The Changing Pacific: Essays in Honour of H. E. Maude,* Oxford University Press, 1978. Also contributor to *World Book Encyclopedia, World Book Year Book, Encyclopedia of Papua and New Guinea, Australian Dictionary of Biography,* and *Pacific Islands Year Book.* Contributor to many magazines, newspapers, and learned journals.

WORK IN PROGRESS: Research on the genetic and cultural influence of sixteenth-century Spanish castaways in the Pacific islands.

SIDELIGHTS: Langdon worked his way around the world from 1947 to 1953. He visited Fiji, New Guinea, Malaysia, India, England, the United States and Canada, Bolivia, Peru, Chile, Uruguay, Brazil, Spain, Morocco, Tahiti, and New Zealand. Since 1962 he has made frequent visits to the Pacific islands from New Guinea eastward to Easter Island.

He wrote: "I decided before I was ten that I would be a historian when I grew up, and almost everything I did before I began writing professionally was with that end in view. I have always read omnivorously, but three writers have especially influenced me. George Borrow, the nineteenth-century English writer, aroused my interest in things Spanish with his book *The Bible in Spain.* Somerset Maugham turned my thoughts toward the South Seas and taught me the virtue of telling a story well. The sixteenth-century writer, Francois Rabelais, inspired me to adopt an encyclopedic approach to learning. Borrow and Rabelais also encouraged me to study languages, and all three moved me to travel widely, especially to the more exotic parts of the globe.

"I wrote my first book, a popular history of Tahiti, because that was the most fascinating place I visited during six years of wandering round the world, and because I found that no one had written such a book before.

"My research on Tahiti's history, combined with my knowledge of Spanish and things Spanish, made me uniquely qualified to write *The Lost Caravel,* which sets out to elucidate the fate of the crew of the Spanish caravel, *San Lesmes,* that disappeared on a voyage from the Strait of Magellan to the East Indies in 1526. The book puts forward the theory that the crew of the *San Lesmes* played an important but previously unsuspected role in the prehistory of a number of Polynesian islands from Eastern Island to New Zealand; that some aspects of Polynesian culture that had long been attributed to the genius of the Polynesians were, in fact, derived from Europe.

"Research on the fate of the *San Lesmes* and other Spanish ships lost in the Pacific Ocean in the sixteenth century has opened up so many new lines of inquiry that I see myself preoccupied with them for several years yet. In the process it seems to me that a good deal of the prehistory of Polynesia will have to be reinterpreted and that some interesting discoveries will be made of value to science."

* * *

LANGER, Walter Charles   1899-1981

OBITUARY NOTICE—See index for *CA* sketch: Born February 5 (some sources say February 9), 1899, in Boston, Mass.; died July 4, 1981, in Sarasota, Fla. Psychoanalyst and author. Langer was the director of schools in Silver City, N.M., and Newton, Mass., before briefly joining the Harvard Psychological Clinic. For the rest of his career, he worked as a psychoanalyst in private practice. During World War II, Langer devised a psychological profile of Hitler for the Office of Strategic Services (OSS). After interviewing many acquaintances of Hitler, Langer determined that the Nazi leader was "probably a neurotic psychopath bordering on schizophrenia." The psychoanalyst also predicted that as the Nazis lost an increasing number of battles towards the end of the war, Hitler would "become more and more neurotic" and eventually commit suicide. The Allies used Langer's work in planning their military campaigns. The study was published as *The Mind of Hitler* in 1972. Before the war, Langer studied in Vienna with Anna Freud, the daughter of the "father of psychoanalysis," and in 1938 accompanied Sigmund Freud himself on his journey from Vienna to London to escape the Nazis. Langer's other work includes *Psychology and Human Living.* Obituaries and other sources: *New York Times,* July 10, 1981; *Washington Post,* July 11, 1981; *Newsweek,* July 20, 1981; *Time,* July 20, 1981.

* * *

LARA, Agustin   1900-1970

OBITUARY NOTICE: Born October 14, 1900, in Tlacotalpan; died of heart and lung disease, November 4 or 5, 1970, in Mexico City. Songwriter. A self-taught musician, Lara was one of Mexico's foremost popular composers. His best-known songs include "You Belong to My Heart," "Granada," and "Madrid." Obituaries and other sources: *Baker's Biographical Dictionary of Musicians,* 6th edition, Schirmer, 1978; *New York Times,* November 7, 1970; *Newsweek,* November 16, 1970; *Time,* November 16, 1970.

* * *

LARDNER, Ring(gold Wilmer)   1885-1933

BRIEF ENTRY: Born March 6, 1885, in Niles, Mich.; died September 25, 1933, in East Hampton, N.Y. American short story writer, journalist, and playwright. Lardner is best known as a humorist and a writer of sports stories, but many critics also regard him as an important author of social satire. Lardner began his career as a sportswriter, and many of his most famous stories, like those collected in *You Know Me, Al* (1916), concern baseball, boxing, and other sports. Published in such magazines as the *Saturday Evening Post,* they made him one of America's most popular writers. Edmund Wilson, Virginia Woolf, H. L. Mencken, and other critics praised his sharp perceptions of middle-class society and his accurate rendering of colloquial American speech. Lardner often wrote in the first person; his characters reveal their selfishness, conceit, and hypocrisy through their own words. He wrote of unpleasant people, and some critics have seen his work as motivated by misanthropy, a view that remains controversial. Although some of Lardner's stories, such as "Haircut" and "Golden Honeymoon," have been judged masterpieces of satire, it is widely felt that Lardner—perhaps because he refused to take his talent seriously—never fulfilled his potential as an author. He remained essentially a popular humorist, disavowing serious literary intentions. His other works include *Gullible's Travels* (1917), *Own Your Own Home* (1919), *How to Write Short Stories (With Samples)* (1924), *Round Up: the Stories of Ring W. Lardner* (1929), and (with George S. Kaufman) *June Moon: A Comedy in a Prologue and Three Acts* (1930). *Residence:* East Hampton, N.Y. *Biographical/critical sources: Nation,* March 22, 1933; F. Scott Fitzgerald, *The Crack-Up,* New Directions, 1945; Virginia Woolf, *The Moment and Other Essays,* Harcourt, 1948; *Cyclopedia of World Authors,* Harper, 1958; John Berryman, *The Freedom of the Poet,* Farrar, Straus, 1976; *Twentieth-Century Literary Criticism,* Volume 2, Gale, 1979.

* * *

LARRY
See PARKES, Terence

* * *

LARSON, Janet Karsten   1945-

PERSONAL: Born June 9, 1945, in South Bend, Ind.; daughter of Walter John (a mechanical engineer in aeronautics) and Virginia (a musician; maiden name, Ahlbrand) Karsten; married John David Larson (a Lutheran minister), June 14, 1970.

Education Valparaiso University, B.A., 1967; Northwestern University, M.A., 1968, Ph.D., 1975. *Politics:* Democrat. *Religion:* Lutheran. *Residence:* Highland Park, N.J. *Office:* Department of English, University College, Rutgers University, Newark, N.J. 07102.

CAREER/WRITINGS: Christian Century Magazine, Chicago, Ill., associate editor, 1975-78, editor-at-large, 1978—; Rutgers University, Newark, N.J. assistant professor of English and director of composition, 1978—. Contributor of numerous articles and reviews to periodicals, including *Christian Century* and *Lutheran Women. Member:* National Council of Teachers of English, National Women's Studies Association, Modern Language Association, Dickens Society (member of auditing committee), Conference on Christianity and Literature, Lutheran Academy for Scholarship (member of honorary board), Associated Church Press. *Awards, honors:* Associated Church Press Award for best feature article on a social issue in religious journalism, 1977, for "Redeeming the Time and the Land," a *Christian Century* article about the Indian land rights controversy in Maine.

WORK IN PROGRESS: A book on Charles Dickens; several articles, including "*The Elephant Man* as Dramatic Parable" and "The Dickens in T. S. Eliot: Generating *Prufrock.*"

* * *

LASS, William M.   1910(?)-1975

OBITUARY NOTICE: Born c. 1910; died October 6, 1975. Journalist and author. Lass worked as a newspaperman for many years and was the author of several books, including *I. W. Harper Hospitality Tour of the United States, The Water in Your Life,* and *The Official YMCA Physical Fitness Handbook.* Obituaries and other sources: *Publishers Weekly,* October 27, 1975.

* * *

LASSWELL, Harold D.   1902-1978

OBITUARY NOTICE: Born February 13, 1902, in Donnellson, Ill.; died December 18, 1978, in New York, N.Y. Political scientist, educator, and author. Lasswell was best known for his use of psychological theory in the study of politics. He emphasized the importance of personality in political behavior, believing that politics is primarily the expression of individuals' drives for income, safety, and deference. This theory was propounded in his most widely read book, *Politics: Who Gets What, When, How.* Though Lasswell's ideas quickly found favor with psychiatrists, they were not widely accepted by political scientists until the 1950's. In 1955 he was elected president of the American Political Science Association. His other books include *Psychopathology and Politics, Power and Personality,* and *The Signature of Power: Buildings, Communication, and Policy.* Obituaries and other sources: *Current Biography,* Wilson, 1947; *Twentieth Century Authors: A Biographical Dictionary of Modern Literature,* 1st supplement, H. W. Wilson, 1955; *McGraw-Hill Encyclopedia of World Biography,* McGraw, 1973; *Webster's American Biographies,* Merriam, 1974; *New York Times,* December 20, 1978; *Time,* January 1, 1979.

* * *

LATTIN, Ann
See COLE, Lois Dwight

LAUER, Jeanette C. 1935-

PERSONAL: Born July 14, 1935, in St. Louis, Mo.; daughter of Clinton J. (an automobile worker) and Blanche A. (a book-keeper; maiden name, Gideon) Pentecost; married Robert H. Lauer (a professor), July 2, 1954; children: Jon, Julie, Jeffrey. Education: University of Missouri, St. Louis, B.S. (summa cum laude), 1970; Washington University, St. Louis, Mo., M.A., 1972, Ph.D., 1975. Religion: Presbyterian. Home: 2545 Guildford Dr., Florissant, Mo. 63033. Office: Department of History, St. Louis Community College at Florissant Valley, 3400 Pershall Rd., Florissant, Mo. 63135.

CAREER: Washington University, St. Louis, Mo., instructor in history, 1972-73; St. Louis Community College at Florissant Valley, Florissant, Mo., assistant professor of history, 1974—. Member: American Historical Association, Organization of American Historians, American Studies Association. Awards, honors: Woodrow Wilson fellowship, 1970-71.

WRITINGS: (Contributor) George K. Zollschan and Walter Hirsh, editors, Social Change: Conjectures, Explorations, and Diagnoses, Schenkman, 1976; (with husband, Robert H. Lauer) Fashion Power: The Meaning of Fashion in American Society, 1800-1979, Prentice-Hall, 1981. Co-editor of "Teaching History Today," a column in American Historical Association Newsletter, 1980—. Contributor to history journals.

WORK IN PROGRESS: Research on the human consequences of social change in St. Louis, Mo., 1870-1929, and on intimate relationships in nineteenth- and twentieth-century communitarian groups.

SIDELIGHTS: Lauer told CA: "My research and writing have led me into diverse areas of study. For example, Fashion Power examines the meaning of fashion in America over the past two centuries. This meaning is explored by looking at clothing as nonverbal communication and at the perceived causes of fashion. It also looks at what fashion is believed to say about human nature and the nature of society, at how fashion relates to national identity, and at the consequences of fashion for health, the economy, family life, and personal growth. Fashion plays a vital role in our lives; this study furnishes insight into the nature of its role.

"Stress and change, like fashion, are constants of everyday experience. My current research centers on a sociohistorical examination of the relationship of stress and change in St. Louis from 1870 to 1929. I am examining numerous indicators of change and stress and considering their relationship to each other. Hopefully, this study will provide a better understanding of the impact change has on individuals and society as a whole."

*   *   *

LAURE, Jason 1940-

PERSONAL: Born October 15, 1940, in Chehalis, Wash.; son of James and Lisa (Lawry) Braly. Education: Attended Los Angeles City College, Columbia University, and Sorbonne, University of Paris. Home: 8 West 13th St., New York, N.Y. 10011.

CAREER: Copywriter for New York Times, New York, N.Y.; free-lance photojournalist, 1968—. Photographer for presidential mission of Nelson Rockefeller to Latin America, 1969; accompanied UNICEF's mission among the nomads of the African Sahara, 1970-71; official correspondent in Bangladesh; work exhibited in one-man shows, including Institute of Contemporary Art, London, England, and group shows. Member: African-American Institute.

AWARDS, HONORS: Grant from International Center of Photography, 1972; nominated for Pulitzer Prize for photography, c. 1972, and nominated for award from Overseas Press Club of America, c. 1972, both for pictures of Bangladesh published in New York Times; award from National Educational Association, 1973; for filmstrip, "Bangladesh: Birth of a Nation"; best of the year awards for filmstrips from National Educational Association, 1973, for "Shifting Sands of the Sahel," 1975, for "Zero Population Growth," and "The Dogon of Mali"; Robert Gordon Sproul Award; National Book Award nomination, 1975, for Joi Bangla: The Children of Bangladesh; South Africa: Coming of Age Under Apartheid was named notable book by American Library Association, 1980.

WRITINGS—With own photographs: (With Ettagale Laure) Joi Bangla: The Children of Bangladesh (for young adults), Farrar, Straus, 1974; (with E. Laure) Jovem Portugal: After the Revolution (juvenile), Farrar, Straus, 1977; (with E. Laure) South Aftrica: Coming of Age Under Apartheid (juvenile), Farrar, Straus, 1980.

Filmstrips: "Bangladesh: Birth of a Nation, " Current Affairs Filmstrips, c. 1973; "Shifting Sands of the Sahel," Current Affairs Filmstrips, 1975. Also author of "Zero Population Growth," Current Affairs Filmstrips, and "The Dogon of Mali," Current Affairs Filmstrips. Correspondent for Pace. Contributor to magazines, including National Geographic, Newsweek, Time, Africa Report, and Junior Scholastic, and newspapers.

WORK IN PROGRESS: Africatrek, a photographic odyssey ("This work portrays the vast continent of Africa as I have seen it during my ten years of working and traveling there as a photojournalist and author").

SIDELIGHTS: Laure commented: "I like to say that I specialize in new countries. I was in Bangladesh when it became a new nation and participated in the excitement. When I was in Angola to work on a book, I witnessed that country's change from colonial status, tied to Portugal, to independence. I also saw the civil war that was going on in the country and knew that true independence would be slow in coming. In Portugal I witnessed demonstrations in the street as people tried to find a new kind of government.

"The most difficult aspect of my work is finding the subjects, finding someone whose story I want to tell and then convincing him that he should become part of my work. We can spend so much time with subjects, and at the end find they have changed their minds. This occurs with people at both ends of the financial spectrum, the very poor and the very rich. In Portugal it resulted in having my interview tapes confiscated one time."

BIOGRAPHICAL/CRITICAL SOURCES: Los Angeles Times Book Review, August 3, 1980; Washington Post Book World, September 7, 1980; Chicago Tribune Book World, November 9, 1980.

*   *   *

LAUWERYS, Joseph (Albert) 1902-1981

OBITUARY NOTICE—See index for CA sketch: Born November 7, 1902, in Brussels, Belgium; died June 29, 1981. Educator, editor, and author. A faculty member at the London University Institute of Education for more than thirty-five years, Lauwerys held the positions of lecturer, reader, and professor. As an authority on education, he helped establish UNESCO. In 1970 Lauwerys left the London University Institute of Education to become the director of the Atlantic Institute of Education in Nova Scotia. He also edited the World Year Book of Education. Lauwerys's works include The Content of Education, *Education in Human Relations, A Handbook of British Educational Terms*, and *The Film in the School*. Obituaries and other sources: *London Times*, July 3, 1981.

*   *   *

LAVERS, Norman   1935-

PERSONAL: Born April 21, 1935, in Berkeley, Calif.; son of Cecil N. (an attorney) and Mary (a tax consultant; maiden name, Parker) Lavers; married Cheryl Dicks (a painter), July 20, 1967; children: Gawain. *Education:* San Francisco State College, B.A., 1960, M.A., 1963; University of Iowa, Ph.D., 1969. *Home address:* Route 5, Box 203, Jonesboro, Ark. 72401. *Agent:* Nat Sobel Associates, Inc., 128 East 56th St., New York, N.Y. 10022. *Office:* Department of English, Arkansas State University, State University, Ark. 72467.

CAREER: Northern Illinois University, Dekalb, instructor in English, 1963-65; University of Iowa, Iowa City, instructor in fiction writing, 1967-69; Western Washington State College (now Western Washington University), Bellingham, assistant professor of English, 1970-75; Arkansas State University, State University, assistant professor, 1976-79, associate professor of English, 1979—. *Military service:* U.S. Army, Chinese linguist with Security Agency, 1956-59. *Member:* Poets and Writers, Arkansas Academy of Science. *Awards, honors:* Fellow of Iowa Writers Workshop, 1967-69.

WRITINGS: Mark Harris, Twayne, 1978; *Selected Short Stories*, Juniper Press, 1979; *Jerzy Kosinski*, Twayne, 1982; *Northwest Passage* (novel), Braziller, 1982. Contributor to *Encyclopedia of Short Fiction*. Contributor of stories and articles to magazines, including *Western Birds, Auk, South Atlantic Quarterly, Fiction International, American Poetry Review*, and *Missouri Review*. Editor of newsletter of Arkansas State Audubon Society.

WORK IN PROGRESS: The White Robin, a novel; another novel; a critical study of novelist John Hawkes.

SIDELIGHTS: Lavers commented: "Natural history is my first love, and if I had not been illiterate in mathematics, I probably would have become a professional scientist. Instead, I have taken to literature as a second choice. I am nonetheless a competent amateur naturalist who has traveled all over the world observing and studying birds and, more recently, dragonflies. Whatever I do I write about, so my interests in natural history have resulted in technical papers in scientific journals or more popular travel and birdwatching articles in magazines.

"Natural history often figures in my fiction as well. My novel, *Northwest Passage*, deals in part with the journals of some eighteenth-century English scientific explorers sailing along the west coast of the Americas. *The White Robin* is about a late seventeenth-century Welsh schoolteacher who is working out a theory of evolution based on natural selection—against steadily increasing opposition from the local vicar.

"Though I like working in the long form of the novel, and my book-length critical studies have been about novelists, I also have a strong interest in the short story, which I feel to be the supreme—and most underrated—American literary form. Most of my critical articles are discussions of the recent short story. I have devoted myself for the past several years to trying to learn the very exacting form of the short story.

"I feel that craft and style are very important in writing. In my own writing these have become, through long practice, more or less automatic. Most of my writing takes place in my unconscious, so that when I sit at my typewriter, the writing seems to come of itself, and I write as fast as I can type (a hundred words a minute) and scarcely change a word of the first draft. I am able to write a novel chapter, or a long story, at only two or three morning sessions. When I am not actually writing, I try to avoid thinking about the project I am at work on, in order to give my unconscious maximum scope to work on it."

*   *   *

LAWHORNE, Clifton O.   1927-

PERSONAL: Born August 6, 1927, in Pine Bluff, Ark.; son of Clement B. (in business) and Priscilla (Spann) Lawhorne; married Claudetta Branch, December 7, 1959; children: Kelly Lynn, Jeffry Jack. *Education:* Attended Texas A & M University, 1944-45; Hardin-Simmons University, B.A., 1951; University of Texas, M.J., 1952; Southern Illinois University, Ph.D., 1968. *Politics:* Independent. *Religion:* Presbyterian. *Home:* 1420 Breckenridge, No. 27, Little Rock, Ark. 72207. *Office:* Department of Journalism, University of Arkansas, Little Rock, Ark. 72204.

CAREER: Craine Office Supply Co., Abilene, Tex., offset printer's apprentice, 1942-44; *Kilgore News-Herald*, Kilgore, Tex., reporter intern, summer, 1949; *Marshall News-Messenger*, Marshall, Tex., reporter intern, summer, 1950; Miller Publishing Co., Minneapolis, Minn., printer's apprentice, summer, 1951; *South Austin News*, Austin, Tex., managing editor, 1951-52; *Big Spring Daily Herald*, Big Spring, Tex., oil editor and reporter, 1952-55; *Corpus Christi Caller-Times*, Corpus Christi, Tex., reporter and copy editor, 1955-62; Del Mar College, Corpus Christi, assistant professor of journalism and director of public information, 1962-65; Southern Illinois University, Carbondale, instructor, 1967-68, assistant professor of journalism, 1968-69; Texas Christian University, Fort Worth, professor of journalism and chairman of department, 1969-71; Southern Illinois University, associate professor of journalism, 1971-73, chairman of news editorial faculty, 1971-72; University of Arkansas, Little Rock, professor of journalism, 1973—, chairman of department, 1973-76. Professor at American University in Cairo, 1978-80. *Military service:* U.S. Army Air Forces, cryptographic technician for Airways and Air Communication Service, 1945-48; served in Europe; became staff sergeant. *Member:* Society of Professional Journalists, Association for Education in Journalism (head of Law Division, 1978-79), Sigma Delta Chi, Kappa Tau Alpha.

WRITINGS: Defamation and Public Officials, Southern Illinois University Press, 1971; *The Supreme Court and Libel*, Southern Illinois University Press, 1981. Editor of *Grassroots Editor*, 1970-74.

WORK IN PROGRESS: Research on mass communication law, the press in America, and First Amendment freedoms.

SIDELIGHTS: Lawhorne commented: "My motivating interests are people, the press, and government, and these interests coalesce in my writing. As a youth, I delivered papers and worked in a printing shop; in the Air Force I worked in a communication center; in college I majored in journalism and government. I worked as a newsman, covering government, for about fourteen years before becoming an educator. Through it all I dealt with people, and still do. I am concerned about their freedoms, and I come very close to those concerns while teaching mass communication law and the freedom of people to communicate. The combination of my teaching career, my reporting career, my education and training, then, have dictated my interests in people, government, and the press. My work has become me, and my interests dictate what I will research and what I will write."

* * *

LAWRENCE, Ann (Margaret) 1942-

PERSONAL: Born December 18, 1942, in Tring, Hertford-shire, England; married Alan Smith, 1971. *Education:* University of Southampton, B.A., 1964. *Agent:* Laura Cecil, 10 Exeter Mansions, 106 Shaftesbury Ave., London W1V 7DH, England.

CAREER: Writer of children's fiction. Worked at British Trust for Ornithology, 1964-66; teacher at schools in Aylesbury, Buckinghamshire, England, 1966-71, and Tring, Hertford-shire, England, 1969-71.

WRITINGS—All for children: Tom Ass; or, The Second Gift, Macmillan (London), 1972, Walck, 1973; *The Half-Brothers,* Walck, 1973; *The Travels of Oggy,* Gollancz, 1973; *The Conjuror's Box,* Kestrel Books, 1974; *Mr. Robertson's Hundred Pounds,* Kestrel Books, 1976; *Between the Forest and the Hills,* Kestrel Books, 1977; *Oggy at Home,* Gollancz, 1977; *The Good Little Devil,* Macmillan, 1978; *Mr. Fox,* Macmillan, 1979; *Oggy and the Holiday,* Gollancz, 1979.

SIDELIGHTS: Ann Lawrence's "Oggy" books are tales of the life of a hedgehog. Gentle creatures abound in these children's stories and include such characters as a staid toad, a pretentious fox, and Tiggy the kitty. Humans play a small part in the background of these tales, in which young readers are able to learn much about country animals.

Some of Lawrence's other publications have a historical back-ground. *Mr. Robertson's Hundred Pounds* relates the adven-tures of a sixteenth-century Gloucester merchant who follows a robber all the way to Spain. A Roman town from the Dark Ages is the setting of *Between the Forest and the Hills. The Half-Brothers* is set in the imaginary sixteenth-century king-dom of Evernia. This tale concerns the development of self-awareness and self identity in a young duchess courted by four half-brothers. In *The Conjuror's Box,* young readers are carried across worlds and centuries.*

* * *

LAWRENCE, D(avid) H(erbert) 1885-1930

BRIEF ENTRY: Born September 11, 1885, in Eastwood, Not-tinghamshire, England; died of tuberculosis, March 2, 1930, in Vence, France. English novelist, essayist, and poet. Al-though his first major novel, *Sons and Lovers* (1913), is re-garded as an important event in the development of the modern psychological novel, Lawrence is best known for *Lady Chat-terley's Lover* (1928). That book's explicit treatment of sex caused it to be banned in England and the United States for many years. But sexuality was only one of the many symbols Lawrence used to represent the mystical life force of instinct and emotion that he contrasted with the sterile, dehumanizing rationality he found in modern society. After *Sons and Lovers,* Lawrence moved away from psychological realism to a more symbolic understanding of human relationships in *The Rainbow* (1915) and *Women in Love* (1920). The characters in those books are, wrote Nathan Scott, not "recognizably living per-sonal entities," but "larger-than-life embodiments of a poetic mood." Persecuted for his treatment of sex in *The Rainbow* and for his elopement with his wife Frieda (who was then married to another man), Lawrence left England in 1919 and spent the rest of his life in exile. He lived in Italy, Australia, and New Mexico and wrote many travel essays during this period. His later fiction is usually considered inferior to his work up to 1920, marred by his tendency to preach, but critics

have praised the descriptive writing even in his lesser novels. His other works include *Look! We Have Come Through* (1917), *Sea and Sardinia* (1921), and *The Plumed Serpent* (1926). *Biographical/critical sources:* Anais Nin, *D. H. Lawrence: An Unprofessional Study,* Swallow Press, 1964; Nathan A. Scott, Jr., *Rehearsals of Discomposure: Alienation and Reconcilia-tion in Modern Literature,* King's Crown Press, 1952; F. R. Leavis, *D. H. Lawrence: Novelist,* Chatto & Windus, 1955; *Twentieth Century Writing: A Reader's Guide to Contemporary Literature,* Transatlantic, 1969; Harry T. Moore, *The Priest of Love: A Life of D. H. Lawrence,* Southern Illinois University Press, 1977; *Twentieth-Century Literary Criticism,* Volume 2, Gale, 1979.

* * *

LAWRENCE, Steven C.
See MURPHY, Lawrence A(ugustus)

* * *

LAWSON, Kay 1933-

PERSONAL: Born April 21, 1933, in Salem, Ore.; daughter of Arlo C. (in business) and Ethel L. (a teacher; maiden name, Jones) Davis; married William V. Lawson (a teacher and writer), April 30, 1952; children: Kevin, Marta. *Education:* University of California, Berkeley, B.A., 1959, M.A., 1962, Ph.D., 1971. *Politics:* Democrat. *Home:* 389 Gravatt Dr., Berkeley, Calif. 94705. *Office:* Department of Political Science, San Francisco State University, San Francisco, Calif. 94132.

CAREER: San Francisco State University, San Francisco, Calif., assistant professor, 1968-71, associate professor, 1971-75, professor of political science, 1975—. Extension instructor at University of California, Berkeley, 1963 and 1964; research political scientist at Institute of International Studies, 1963-66. *Member:* International Political Science Association, American Political Science Association, African Studies Association (member of executive council, 1976-78), Western Political Sci-ence Association (member of executive council, 1978-80), Cal-ifornia Committee for Party Renewal (co-founder; member of executive council, 1980—). *Awards, honors:* Social Science Research Council grant, 1974.

WRITINGS: Political Parties and Democracy in the United States, Scribner, 1968; *The Comparative Study of Polical Par-ties,* St. Martin's, 1976; (editor) *Political Parties and Linkage,* Yale University Press, 1980; *The Human Polity: An Introduc-tion to Political Science,* Houghton, in press. Contributor of articles and reviews to scholarly journals.

WORK IN PROGRESS: Editing *When Parties Fail: Emerging Forms of Political Organization,* a volume of essays on alter-native political organizations, with Peter Merkl, publication expected in 1984; *Political Parties and Change,* a study of the Rassemblement pour la Republique (the Gaullist party in France), publication expected in 1985.

SIDELIGHTS: Lawson told *CA:* "I became a political scientist because I am interested in how (if ever) governments can be made to function in the interests of the citizens they control and, going a step further, whether there is any possibility that government by the people could be made a reality rather than a dream. Political organizations, especially political parties, usually claim to serve as intermediary agencies between citizen and state, effecting a linkage between the two which will guar-antee that the interests of the former will be reflected in policy and practice. All of my writing is devoted to studying whether or not this is true, whether and under what conditions it ever could be true. I am interested in considering the answers to these questions all over the world, but particularly in Europe and Africa (I have done field work in France and Nigeria) and in the United States. Until we see how such organizations are not working well as linkage agencies, we have little hope of knowing how to improve their performance.''

AVOCATIONAL INTERESTS: Travel (including Europe and Africa), theatre.

* * *

LAZAR, Wendy 1939-

PERSONAL: Born April 8, 1939, in Rochester, N.Y.; daughter of Sam (a social worker) and Anne (a secretary; maiden name, Koren) Phillips; married Martin Lazar (a psychotherapist and psychiatric social worker), June 3, 1967; children: Jodi Alissa, Kim Sheryl. *Education:* Syracuse University, B.S., 1961. *Home and office:* Women Working Home, Inc., 760 Blanch Ave., Norwood, N.J. 07648.

CAREER: WRVR-FM Radio, New York, N.Y., writer, producer, director, and entertainer, 1962-65; NHK-Radio, Kyoto, Japan, writer and entertainer, 1965-66; WNYE-TV, Brooklyn, N.Y., producer and entertainer, 1967-70; free-lance writer, 1970-80; Amerika Yorozu Sodango (American-Japanese information service), owner, 1979-1980; free-lance writer, publisher, and career consultant for home businesses, 1980—. *Member:* National Federation of Business and Professional Women's Clubs, National Alliance of Homebased Businesswomen (founder; vice-president), League of Women Voters, Committee of Small Magazine Editors and Publishers. *Awards, honors:* Award from Institute for Educational Radio and Television, 1964, for radio program ''Children's World.''

WRITINGS: The Jewish Holiday Book, Doubleday, 1977; (editor with Marion Behr, and contributor) *Women Working Home: The Homebased Business Guide and Directory,* Women Working Home Press, 1981.

Author of radio and television scripts for educational programs in the United States and Japan, including ''Children's World'' and ''Listen!,'' 1963-64, ''Orient-ation,'' 1965, ''You and Your Health,'' 1968, and ''Community Report,'' 1969-70.

WORK IN PROGRESS: Statistical research on women with home-based businesses.

SIDELIGHTS: Wendy Lazar commented: ''There was a time, about twenty years ago, when teachers could always get a job. To my parents, teaching certainly was a more promising profession than broadcast journalism. To satisfy my parents' requirements and my own personal interests, I took a combined major of radio-television and elementary education. It was a decision that was to affect my total career. I never did go into teaching, but headed right for a career in educational broadcasting.

''With an insatiable curiosity about life and people, it was natural for me to have a career that allowed me to write for adults and children and on any subject that appealed to me. Travel has always been important and necessary—I've criss-crossed the United States several times and have spent time in both Asia and Europe, once taking a year to travel around the world. I believe that though one may travel the world over, one hasn't really budged a step until one takes up residence in someone else's point of view. I've taken giant steps! I've forgotten the French I knew but am still able to carry on a conversation in Japanese!

''I've been in touch with thousands of home-based business-women over the last two years and am excited and encouraged

by the growing home-based work force of inventive, energetic, and talented women. They are making changes and making money while restructuring the spirit of free enterprise! Working from home gives us that rare opportunity to coordinate all the activities of our lives into a unified whole. There is total integration of family, work, and leisure. It is joyous to have the flexibility of scheduling, a work setting that reflects one's own personality, and all the comforts of home. It isn't what everyone chooses, but for those of us who have it by choice, it is enormously interesting, stimulating, and rewarding. (I didn't say it was easy, but it's well worth the effort!)''

AVOCATIONAL INTERESTS: Hiking, cross-country skiing, skating, swimming, camping, public speaking, folk singing.

* * *

LAZARUS, Felix
See CABLE, George Washington

* * *

LEACHMAN, Robert Briggs 1921-

PERSONAL: Born June 11, 1921, in Lakewood, Ohio; son of Milton G. (a merchant) and Wilma (Rothenbecker) Leachman; married Lenore Collins (an administrative assistant), June 16, 1945; children: Elaine Leachman Gust, Mark, Gregg. *Education:* Case Western Reserve University, B.S.E.E., 1942; Iowa State University, Ph.D., 1950. *Politics:* Republican. *Religion:* Unitarian Universalist. *Home:* 929 Sixth St. S.W., Washington, D.C. 20024. *Office:* Space Telescope Science Institute, Johns Hopkins University, Baltimore, Md. 21218.

CAREER: Massachusetts Institute of Technology, Cambridge, electronics researcher at Radiation Laboratory, 1942-45; Los Alamos Scientific Laboratory, Los Alamos, N.M., supervisor of research reactors, operator of reactor, and participant in reactor disassembly, 1950-55, researcher in nuclear fission process and nuclear reactions, 1950-67, group leader supervising cyclotron and cyclotron research, 1956-67; Kansas State University, Manhattan, professor of physics, head of department, and director of Nuclear Sciences Laboratory, 1967-72; U.S. Department of Defense, Defense Nuclear Agency, Washington, D.C., special assistant to deputy director for science and technology, 1972-74; Nuclear Regulatory Commission, Washington, D.C., special assistant to deputy director, 1974-78; U.S. Congress, Office of Technology Assessment, Washington, D.C., in nuclear wastes assessment, 1978-79; U.S. House of Representatives, Washington, D.C., member of staff of science and technology committee, 1979-81; Johns Hopkins University, Baltimore, Md., management consultant to Space Telescope Science Institute, 1981—.

Adjunct professor at University of New Mexico, 1964, and Southeastern University, Washington, D.C., 1980—; lecturer at Montgomery Community College, 1978. Conducted research at Nobel Institute, Stockholm, Sweden, 1955-56, and Niels Bohr Institute, Copenhagen, Denmark, 1962-63; member of annual review panel for National Bureau of Standards Center for Radiation Research, 1968-71; member of planning group for U.S. National Heavy-Ion Laboratory at Oak Ridge National Laboratory, 1971-72; foreign expert for International Atomic Energy Agency at conference in Rio de Janeiro, Brazil, 1971; member of Arms Control and Disarmament Agency, summer, 1974.

MEMBER: American Physical Society (fellow), American Nuclear Society, Philosophical Society of Washington (vice-president, 1981), Sigma Xi, Tau Beta Pi, Theta Tau. *Awards, honors:* Guggenheim fellowship for Sweden, 1955-56; Fulbright fellowship for Denmark, 1962-63.

WRITINGS: (With Phillip Althoff) *Preventing Nuclear Theft: Guidelines for Industry and Government,* Praeger, 1972. Contributor of about thirty-five articles to scientific journals and other magazines, including *World Federalist* and *Scientific American.*

*   *   *

LEACOCK, Stephen (Butler)   1869-1944

BRIEF ENTRY: Born December 30, 1869, in Swanmoor, Hampshire, England; died March 28, 1944, in Canada. Canadian humorist, essayist, and biographer. Leacock was a distinguished political scientist and economist, for many years head of his department at McGill University in Montreal, but he is best known as Canada's foremost humorist. He has often been compared with Mark Twain, whom he admired, but the distinctive national and individual characteristics of Leacock's work are also recognized. Leacock was less of a satirist than Twain, for he believed that humor should be gentle, never wounding or distressing anyone. Nevertheless, *Sunshine Sketches of a Little Town* (1912), which made fun of the foibles of the citizens of a small Ontario town and is widely regarded as Leacock's best book, deeply offended the inhabitants of Orillia, Ontario, who had provided Leacock with much of his inspiration. Leacock also wrote several books of literary parodies, including *Literary Lapses* (1911) and *Nonsense Novels* (1911), serious essays on politics, education, and writing, and biographies of Twain and Dickens. His books include *Arcadian Adventures With the Idle Rich* (1914), *My Discovery of England* (1924), and *My Remarkable Uncle and Other Sketches* (1942). *Residence:* Montreal, Quebec, Canada. *Biographical/critical sources: Twentieth Century Authors: A Biographical Dictionary of Modern Literature,* H. W. Wilson, 1942; Stephen Leacock, *The Boy I Left Behind Me,* Doubleday, 1946; Robertson Davies, *Our Living Tradition: Seven Canadians,* University of Toronto Press, 1957; *Canadian Literature,* summer, 1960; David Legate, *Stephen Leacock,* Doubleday, 1971; *Twentieth-Century Literary Criticism,* Volume 2, Gale, 1979.

*   *   *

LEADBETTER, Eric   1892(?)-1971

OBITUARY NOTICE: Born c. 1892; died March 2, 1971, in England. Government official and author. Leadbetter wrote several novels, including *The Evil That Men Do.* Obituaries and other sources: *AB Bookman's Weekly,* May 17, 1971.

*   *   *

LEARNED, Edmund Philip   1900-

PERSONAL: Born December 24, 1900, in Lawrence, Kan.; son of Samuel Stanley and Alice (Preisach) Learned; married Zella M. Rankin, August 30, 1922; children: Betty Lucile, Don Rankin. *Education:* University of Kansas, A.B., 1922, A.M., 1925; Harvard University, M.B.A., 1927, D.C.S., 1930; attended U.S. Army Command and General Staff School, 1941. *Politics:* Democrat. *Religion:* Unitarian-Universalist. *Home:* 1117 Avenida Sevilla, No. 1A Walnut Creek, Calif. 94595.

CAREER: University of Kansas, Lawrence, lecturer in economics, 1922-25; Harvard University, Cambridge, Mass., instructor, 1927-29, assistant professor, 1929-34, associate professor, 1934-39, professor of marketing, 1939-45, and business administration, 1945-60, Charles Edward Wilson Professor of Business Policy, 1960-67, Charles Edward Wilson Professor

emeritus, 1967—. Lecturer at Simmons College, 1928-33; professor at Management Development Institute, Lausanne, Switzerland, 1961-62; director of Cambridge Research Institute, 1967-69; business and economic consultant to U.S. Army and Federal Aviation Agency. *Military service:* U.S. Army Air Forces, director of instruction at statistics school, 1942-43; special consultant to commanding general, 1943-47, and to chief of staff, 1947-66; received distinguished service medal. *Member:* American Economic Association, Academy of Management (fellow), Phi Beta Kappa, Phi Delta Kappa, Pi Sigma Alpha. *Awards, honors:* Exceptional civilian service medal from U.S. Air Force, 1952, meritorious civilian service medal, 1966; medal of extraordinary service from Federal Aviation Agency, 1968.

WRITINGS: State Gasoline Taxes, University of Kansas, 1925; (with M. T. Copeland) *Merchandising of Cotton Textiles,* Harvard University Bureau of Business Research, 1933; (with Malcolm Perrine McNair and Stanley F. Teele) *Problems in Marketing,* McGraw, 1936; (with David N. Ulrich and Donald R. Booz) *Executive Action,* Division of Research, Graduate School of Business Administration, Harvard University, 1951; (with Catherine G. Ellsworth) *Gasoline Pricing in Ohio,* Division of Research, Graduate School of Business Administration, Harvard University, 1959; (with C. Roland Christensen and Kenneth R. Andrews) *Problems of General Management, Business Policy: A Series Casebook,* Irwin, 1961; (with Francis J. Aguilar and Robert C. K. Valtz) *European Problems in General Management,* Irwin, 1963; (with Christensen, Andrews, and W. D. Guth) *Business Policy: Text and Cases,* Irwin, 1965, 4th edition (with Christensen, Andrews, and Joseph L. Bower), 1978; (with Audrey T. Sproat) *Organization Theory and Policy: Notes for Analysis,* Irwin, 1966. Contributor to business journals.

WORK IN PROGRESS: "A write-up of my twenty-four years as consultant to the Air Force for filing in the archives of the Harvard Business School."

SIDELIGHTS: Learned told *CA:* "In forty-four years of teaching at the University of Kansas, at Harvard University, in management programs in Hawaii, Switzerland, and Japan, and at the Headquarters Air Staff and Statistical Officer Candidate School, I have had over sixteen thousand students. Many of these rose to high executive positions in business or government. Some became governors, congressmen, senators, or full generals.

"In all my work, I have found it necessary to enlist the support of all colleagues in defining and accomplishing goals. I believe in bottoms-up as well as top-down management efforts. Great leaders must be aware of the demands imposed by the external environment and the internal personal and organizational demands of their people. Great leaders must also recognize the limitations on their leadership imposed by their own personality. Helping students, members of advanced management programs, and military personnel understand the importance of their roles in dealing with the foregoing complex interrelationships was truly rewarding. I felt I could make a greater contribution to business, government, and society through teaching, research, and some consulting than I could by accepting several outstanding offers from major corporations."

*   *   *

LeBLANC, Rena Dictor   1938-

PERSONAL: Born November 14, 1938, in Chicago, Ill.; daughter of Morris and Rose Pearl Dictor; married Jerry LeBlanc (a free-lance writer), November 27, 1964; children: Mia Therese,

Marisa Lauren. *Education:* Los Angeles City College, A.A., 1958. *Politics:* Democrat. *Religion:* Jewish. *Residence:* Woodland Hills, Calif. *Agent:* Julian Bach Literary Agency, Inc., 747 Third Ave., New York, N.Y. 10017.

CAREER: Free-lance photojournalist and writer. *Member:* American Society of Journalists and Authors. *Awards, honors:* Awards from Los Angeles Press Club, Associated Press, and San Fernando Valley Press Club.

WRITINGS: (With husband, Jerry LeBlanc) *Suddenly Rich,* Prentice-Hall, 1978. Contributing editor of *Los Angeles.*

*   *   *

LEE, Benjamin 1921-

PERSONAL: Born April 29, 1921, in London, England; married wife, Josephine, 1944; children: two daughters. *Education:* Guy's Hospital Medical School, M.D. *Address:* c/o Bodley Head, 9 Bow St., London WC2E 7AL, England.

CAREER: Licensed to practice medicine, 1944; family doctor in London, England, 1944—; writer. *Military service:* Royal Naval Volunteer Reserve; became surgeon lieutenant.

WRITINGS: Paganini Strikes Again (juvenile), Hutchinson, 1970; *The Man in Fifteen* (juvenile), Hutchinson, 1972; *The Frog Report* (juvenile), Hutchinson, 1974; *It Can't Be Helped* (young adult), Bodley Head, 1976, Farrar, Straus, 1979. Also author of screenplays, including "Paganini Strikes Again" (adapted from own novel), 1972, and "Newsboy," 1975.

SIDELIGHTS: Humor in Lee's novels develops from broad comedy in his first book to subtle, off-beat characterization in *It Can't Be Helped. Paganini Strikes Again* is a mystery adventure with two serious lads chasing crooks through London. The adults in the book are characterized as absurd and confused; the children, however, enjoy the adventure. *The Man in Fifteen* is an equally frenzied story involving its heroes in numerous adventures throughout Italy. Again the parents are ineffectual and disordered in the midst of chaos, and the humor emerges through improbable situations and eccentric characters. *The Frog Report* relies more on humor through characterization than does either of its predecessors. The main character is a writer using his story within the story as a means of making sense of the world. Finally, in *It Can't Be Helped,* Lee seems to completely reject slapstick humor in favor of more realistic situations. The story tells of Max and his reactions to his father's death, his mother's madness, and his girlfriend's delusions of pregnancy. Lee sometimes equates humor with childhood, for as Max becomes an adult he develops a sharper perspective of the tragic aspects of life.

BIOGRAPHICAL/CRITICAL SOURCES: Times Literary Supplement, December 10, 1976; *Junior Bookshelf,* April, 1977.*

*   *   *

LEE, Bill
See LEE, William Saul

*   *   *

LEE, G. Avery 1916-

PERSONAL: Born March 3, 1916, in Oklahoma City, Okla.; son of Elisha Vernon (a chef) and Mary A. (Story) Lee; married Ann Rader, September 8, 1940 (died August 1, 1973); married Gladys Salassi (a teacher of French), November 22, 1974; children: (first marriage) Jeni-Su Lee Lacoste, G. Avery, Jr., Gregory. *Education:* Hardin-Simmons University, B.A., 1939;

Yale University, M.Div., 1944. *Politics:* Democrat. *Home:* 5412 Chatham Dr., New Orleans, La. 70122. *Office:* St. Charles Avenue Baptist Church, 7100 St. Charles Ave., New Orleans, La. 70118.

CAREER: Ordained Baptist minister; Louisiana State University, Baton Rouge, director of Baptist student work, 1941-43; associate pastor of Baptist church in Baton Rouge, 1944-47; pastor of Baptist churches in Champaign, Ill., 1947-48, and Ruston, La., 1948-61; St. Charles Avenue Baptist Church, New Orleans, La., pastor, 1961—. Member of executive board of Louisiana Baptist Convention; Louisiana member of Southern Baptist Convention's Christian Life Commission, 1956-69, chairman of commision, 1960-61; president of Greater New Orleans Federation of Churches, 1965. Member of faculty at Baptist Theological Seminary, Bangkok, Thailand, summer, 1979. Active with local charitable organizations. *Member:* Kiwanis International (president; lieutenant governor). *Awards, honors:* D.Litt. from Hardin-Simmons University, 1958.

WRITINGS: Life's Everyday Questions, Broadman, 1953; *Preaching From Ecclesiastes,* Broadman, 1958; *What's Right With the Church,* Broadman, 1967; *Great Men of the Bible and the Women in Their Lives,* Word Books, 1968; *The Reputation of a Church,* Broadman, 1969; *The Roads to God,* Broadman, 1970; *I Want That Mountain,* Thomas Nelson, 1974. Contributor to religious journals.

*   *   *

LEE, Judy
See CARLSON, Judith Lee

*   *   *

LEE, Manning de Villeneuve 1894-1980

OBITUARY NOTICE: Born March 15, 1894, in Summerville, S.C.; died March 31, 1980, in Chestnut Hill, Pa. Artist and illustrator. Lee studied at the Academy of Fine Arts in Philadelphia. His paintings can be found in many private and public collections in the United States and abroad. Lee's work often appeared in magazines, and he illustrated more than two hundred books. He specialized in historical subjects and books for young people, including Robert Louis Stevenson's *Kidnapped,* Rupert S. Holland's *Historic Ships,* and Andrew Lang's *Blue Fairy Book.* Obituaries and other sources: *Illustrators of Children's Books, 1744-1945,* Horn Book, 1947; *Illustrators of Books for Young People,* 2nd edition, Scarecrow, 1975; *Contemporary Illustrators of Children's Books,* Gale, 1978; *Publishers Weekly,* May 30, 1980.

*   *   *

LEE, Vernon
See PAGET, Violet

*   *   *

LEE, William Saul 1938-
(Bill Lee)

PERSONAL: Born November 15, 1938, in Brooklyn, N.Y.; married Dona Johnson (a psychotherapist), April 14, 1979; children: Jennifer Catherine. *Education:* Attended School of Visual Arts, New York, N.Y., 1960-64. *Residence:* Sharon, Conn. *Office:* Penthouse International Ltd., 909 Third Ave., New York, N.Y. 10022.

CAREER: Cartoonist, 1974—, with cartoons nationally syndicated by *Chicago Tribune/New York News* organization, 1975;

Penthouse International Ltd., New York City, humor editor of *Penthouse* and *Omni*, 1976—. Illustrator, with exhibitions in Castelli Gallery, New York City, 1974, Van Gogh Museum, Holland, 1975, Kew Gardens, London, 1975, and Hansen Gallery, New York City, 1975; painter and sculptor, with group show at Montreal Fair, 1973, and one-man show at Visual Arts Center, New York City, 1974; poster artist, with touring group-show exhibition in Europe, 1970-71. *Member:* Television Academy of Arts and Sciences, Motion Picture Institute, National Cartoonists Society, Writers Guild. *Awards, honors:* International Humour Award from Expo '71, Montreal, 1971.

WRITINGS—All under name Bill Lee: (Editor) *No U.S. Personnel Beyond This Point* (drawings), Dell, 1972. Creator and writer of "Town and Country" (comedy series), Columbia Broadcasting System (CBS-TV), 1978. Has published six folios of own drawings; contributor of drawings to over fifty books; contributor of cartoons to periodicals in Europe, South America, and the United States, including *Penthouse, Playboy, Esquire, New Yorker, Cosmopolitan,* and *National Lampoon.*

WORK IN PROGRESS: Investigative Cartooning, a book of drawing and writing.

SIDELIGHTS: Lee wrote: "My motivation is love! Love of the drawn line!"

* * *

LEE HOWARD, Leon Alexander   1914-1979(?)
(Leigh Howard, Alexander Krislov)

OBITUARY NOTICE: Born June 18, 1914; died c. 1979 in London, England. Journalist, editor, and novelist. Editor from 1961 to 1971 of the *London Daily Mirror,* Lee Howard was also a novelist. Under the pseudonym Leigh Howard he wrote *Crispin's Day, Johnny's Sister,* and *Blind Date.* His fictionalized biography of the ancient Greek lyric poet Sappho, *No Man Sings,* appeared in 1956 under the pseudonym Alexander Krislov. Obituaries and other sources: *Who's Who,* 125th edition, St. Martin's, 1973; *AB Bookman's Weekly,* February 12, 1979.

* * *

LEFCOWITZ, Barbara F(reedgood)   1935-

PERSONAL: Born January 15, 1935, in New York, N.Y.; married Allan B. Lefcowitz (a professor and writer), March 25, 1956; children: Marjorie, Eric. *Education:* Smith College, B.A., 1956; State University of New York at Buffalo, M.A., 1964; University of Maryland, Ph.D., 1970. *Home:* 7803 Custer Rd., Bethesda, Md. 20814.

CAREER: Held various teaching and editing positions, including lectureships and fellowships, 1956-71; Anne Arundel Community College, Arnold, Md., assistant professor, 1971-74, associate professor, 1975-80, professor of English, 1980—. Painter and printmaker. Co-founder and director of public events of Writer's Center, Glen Echo, Md. *Member:* Modern Language Association of America. *Awards, honors:* Fiction prize from *Webster Review,* 1979, for "The Mirror of Jerusalem"; poetry prize from *Kansas Quarterly,* 1980, for "Winter Solstice."

WRITINGS: A Risk of Green (poems), Gallimaufry, 1978; *The Wild Piano* (poems), Dryad, 1981. Contributor of more than one hundred articles, stories, poems, and reviews to magazines, including *Chicago Review, New Letters,* and *Prairie Schooner.*

WORK IN PROGRESS: A collection of poems, tentatively titled *The Memoirs of an Amnesiac.*

SIDELIGHTS: Lefcowitz told *CA:* "I began to write seriously quite late in life, around the age of thirty-five (excluding academic articles). Writing, particularly poetry, is a continuing dialogue between self and other, self and nature, self and entropy, history, time. Perhaps, like many poets, I write because I have a memory like swiss cheese (or very loosely-woven lace). My work always involves a struggle between craft and indulgence; experimenting with different voices is one of the greatest challenges. I guess I'm often looking around the corners of things—the seasons, people, music, the rituals of ordinary life. Imagery is crucial; I don't fancy flat, prosey poetry, but I am fond of poetic prose. I'm currently attracted to poets with a magic-realist bent, such as Charles Simic, and to consummate craftsmen, such as Maxine Kumin and Richard Hugo."

AVOCATIONAL INTERESTS: European travel, painting, printmaking.

* * *

LEIGH, Johanna
See SAYERS, Dorothy L(eigh)

* * *

LEISTRITZ, F(redrick) Larry   1945-

PERSONAL: Born September 25, 1945, in Alliance, Neb.; son of Kenneth E. (a rancher) and Elsie (Ray) Leistritz; married Linda K. Nilson, November 24, 1965; children: Lori Jean, Leslie Diane. *Education:* University of Nebraska, B.S. (with high distinction), 1967, M.S., 1968, Ph.D., 1970; attended Oklahoma State University, 1969. *Home:* 226 22nd Ave. N., Fargo, N.D. 58102. *Office:* Department of Agricultural Economics, North Dakota State University, Fargo, N.D. 58105.

CAREER: North Dakota State University, Fargo, assistant professor, 1970-73, associate professor, 1973-77, professor of agricultural economics, 1977—. Visiting professor at Texas A & M University, 1978-79. Member of Upper Midwest Council coal study advisory board, 1974-76; chairman of Great Plains Regional Research Committee, 1974-76; associate director of North Dakota Regional Environmental Assessment Program, 1975-78; member of project review committee of North Dakota Water Resources Research Institute, 1976-80; vice-chairman of research coordinating committee of Great Plains Agricultural Council, 1978-79, chairman, 1979-80; member of National Research Council committee on soil as a resource in relation to surface mining for coal, 1979-80; member of advisory committee of Rocky Mountain Center on the Environment, 1980—. Guest on television programs; lecturer on resource development. Consultant to Argonne National Laboratory, Arthur D. Little, and U.S. Department of Agriculture.

MEMBER: American Agricultural Economics Association, Western Agricultural Economics Association (member of council, 1979-81), Midcontinent Regional Science Association, Gamma Sigma Delta, Alpha Zeta, Omicron Delta Epsilon, Phi Eta Sigma. *Awards, honors:* Grants from U.S. Forest Service, 1971-74, U.S. Department of the Interior, 1973-74, Environmental Protection Agency, 1975-76, Office of Water Research and Technology, 1975-77, and U.S. Energy Research and Development Administration, 1977-78.

WRITINGS: (Contributor) Wilson F. Clark, editor, *Proceedings of the Fort Union Coal Field Symposium,* Volume IV: *Social Impact Section,* Hagen Printing Co., 1975; (with Steven H. Murdock) *Energy Development in the Western United States: Impacts on Rural Areas,* Praeger, 1979; (contributor) G. F. Summers and Arne Selvik, editors, *Nonmetropolitan*

Economic Growth and Community Change, Heath, 1979; (contributor) M. K. Wali, editor, *Ecology and Coal Resource Development,* Pergamon, 1979; (contributor) *Workshop Proceedings: Integration of Environmental Considerations Into Energy-Economic System Models,* Electric Power Research Institute, 1980; (contributor) J. M. Wardwell and D. L. Brown, editors, *New Directions in Urban-Rural Migration,* Academic Press, 1980; (contributor) M. P. Lawson and M. E. Baker, editors, *The Great Plains: Perspectives and Prospects,* University of Nebraska Press, 1980; (with Murdock) *Socioeconomic Impact of Resource Development: Methods for Assessment,* Westview Press, 1981; (editor with L. D. Bender) *Problems of Modeling Local Impacts of Energy Development,* Great Plains Agricultural Council and U.S. Environmental Protection Agency, 1981. Contributor of articles and reviews to professional journals. Member of editorial council of *Western Journal of Agricultural Economics,* 1976-78.

SIDELIGHTS: Leistritz commented to *CA:* "My main interest has been and continues to be in applying economic analysis techniques to natural resource policy issues."

* * *

LENBURG, Jeff 1956-

PERSONAL: Born March 5, 1956, in Gary, Ind.; son of John LeRoy (a retail clerk) and Catherine (Galich) Lenburg. *Education:* Fullerton College, A.A., 1977; California State University, Fullerton, B.A., 1981. *Residence:* Orange, Calif. *Agent:* Dominick Abel, 498 West End Ave., No. 12-C, New York, N.Y. 10024. *Office:* Muscular Dystrophy Association, 1823 East 17th St., Santa Ana, Calif. 92701.

CAREER: Disneyland, Anaheim, Calif., technical writer in costume division, 1974-80; Muscular Dystrophy Association, Santa Ana, Calif., program coordinator, 1980—. News writer for KEZY (AM-FM radio station), 1979-80. Press agent for comic Joe Besser, 1975—.

WRITINGS: (With brother, Greg Lenburg, and Randy Skretvedt) *Steve Martin: The Unauthorized Biography,* St. Martin's, 1980; *The Encyclopedia of Animated Cartoon Series,* Arlington House, 1981; *The Official Three Stooges Scrapbook,* Citadel, 1982; *The Great Movie Cartoon Directors,* McFarland Publications, 1982. Contributor to film magazines.

SIDELIGHTS: Lenburg wrote: "To be a good writer you have to be totally motivated and confident in your own abilities. Maintaining a positive attitude provides me with the essential day-to-day drive to complete my tasks, and I keep writing as a fun vehicle. Like life itself, writing should be taken seriously, but not too seriously."

* * *

Le PATOUREL, John Herbert 1909-1981

OBITUARY NOTICE—See index for *CA* sketch: Born July 29, 1909, in Guernsey, Channel Islands; died July 22, 1981. Educator, editor, and author. Le Patourel taught at University College, London, as a lecturer and reader before moving to the University of Leeds, where he held the chair of medieval history. At Leeds he helped establish the Graduate Centre for Medieval Studies and later served as the center's director. A scholar on the relationship between England and France in the middle ages, Le Patourel was the archivist to the Royal Court of Guernsey and edited the medieval records of Leeds. In 1966 he founded the journal *Northern History.* Le Patourel's works include *The Medieval Administration of the Channel Islands, 1199-1399, Documents Relating to the Manor and Borough of*

Leeds, 1066-1400, and *Ilkley Parish Church.* Obituaries and other sources: *London Times,* August 1, 1981.

* * *

LE REVELER
    See ARTAUD, Antonin

* * *

LESLAU, Wolf 1906-

PERSONAL: Born November 14, 1906, in Krzepice, Poland; came to the United States in 1942, naturalized citizen, 1948; son of Henoch and Ita (Goldreich) Leslau; married Charlotte Halpern, October 29, 1938; children: Elaine, Sylvia. *Education:* Sorbonne, University of Paris, lic. es lett., 1934, Ph.D., 1953; Ecole des Hautes Etudes, diploma, 1934; Ecole Nationale des Langues Orientales, diploma, 1935. *Home:* 1662 Fairburn Ave., Los Angeles, Calif. 90024.

CAREER: Ecole des Hautes Etudes, Paris, France, lecturer in southern Arabic, 1936-39; Ecole Libre des Hautes Etudes, New York City, professor of Semitic studies, 1942-46; Asia Institute, New York City, associate professor, 1946-51; Brandeis University, Waltham, Mass., associate professor of Near Eastern languages, 1951-55; University of California, Los Angeles, professor of Hebrew and Semitic linguistics, 1955-76, professor emeritus, 1976—. Visiting lecturer at Ecole Nationale des Langues Orientales, 1937-39, and Indiana University, 1953; visiting professor at New School for Social Research, 1949-51, and National University, Addis Ababa, Ethiopia, 1954, 1959; made study tours of Ethiopia, 1946-47, 1950-54, 1959, 1962.

MEMBER: American Academy of Arts and Sciences (fellow), American Association of University Professors, American Oriental Society (vice-president), Linguistic Society of America, American Folklore Society, American Anthropological Association, American Academy for Jewish Research (fellow), Academic Council of Friends of Hebrew University, Societe de linguistique de Paris, Societe de Asiatique, Linguistic Circle of New York (member of executive board). *Awards, honors:* American Philosophical Society fellow, 1943, 1948, 1954; Guggenheim fellow, 1946-48; Social Science Research Council fellow, 1950; D.H.L. from University of Judaism, 1962, and Hebrew Union College, 1963; Haile Selassie Award in Ethiopian Studies, 1965; fellow at Caisse Centre national de la recherche scientifique.

WRITINGS—In English: (With Harold Courlander) *The Fire on the Mountain and Other Ethiopian Stories,* Holt, 1950; *Ethiopian Documents: Gurage,* Viking Fund, 1950; (translator and author of introduction) *Falasha Anthology: Translated From Ethiopian Sources,* Yale University Press, 1951, reprinted as *Falasha Anthology: The Black Jews of Ethiopia,* Schocken, 1969; *The Verb in Harari (South Ethiopic),* University of California Press, 1958; *Ethiopic and South Arabic Contributions to the Hebrew Lexicon,* University of California Press, 1958; *A Dictionary of Moca: Southwestern Ethiopia,* University of California Press, 1959.

(Editor with wife, Charlotte Leslau) *African Proverbs,* Peter Pauper, 1962; *Amharic-English and English-Amharic Vocabulary,* University of California, Los Angeles, 1963; (with C. Leslau) *African Folk Tales,* Peter Pauper, 1963; *Etymological Dictionary of Harari,* University of California Press, 1963; (translator) Sahle Sellassie, *Shinega's Village: Scenes of Ethiopian Life,* University of California Press, 1964; *Ethiopian Argots,* Mouton, 1964; (editor) *Bibliographies on the Near*

East, Mouton, 1965; *An Annotated Bibliography of the Semitic Languages of Ethiopia,* Mouton, 1965; *An Amharic Conversation Book,* Harrassowitz, 1965; *Harari,* University of California Press, 1965; *Chaha,* University of California Press, 1966; *Soddo,* University of California Press, 1968; *Amharic Textbook,* University of California Press, 1968; *Hebrew Cognates in Amharic,* Harrassowitz, 1969.

(Editor with C. Leslau) *African Poems and Love Songs,* Peter Pauper, 1970; *English-Amharic Context Dictionary,* Harrassowitz, 1973; *Concise Amharic Dictionary: Amharic-English, English-Amharic,* Harrassowitz, 1976. Editor of *Ethiopians Speak: Studies in Cultural Background,* three volumes, University of California Press.

In French: (Translator) *Lexique soqotri sudarabique moderne,* Collection Societe de linguistique de Paris, 1938; *Documents tigrigna (ethiopien septentrional): Grammaire et textes,* Klincksieck, 1941; *Etude descriptive et comparative du gafat: Ethiopien meridionale,* Klincksieck, 1956; *Coutumes et croyances des Falachas: Juifs d'Abyssinie,* Institut d'ethnologie, 1957.

Contributor to magazines.

AVOCATIONAL INTERESTS: Nature study, theatre.*

* * *

LESSARD, Michel 1942-

PERSONAL: Born June 4, 1942, in Sorel, Quebec, Canada; son of Claude (an electrician) and Maria (a teacher; maiden name, Poulin) Lessard; married Huguette Marquis, May 30, 1969 (divorced); children: Louis Frederic. *Education:* College de Levis, B.A., 1963; Laval University licence es lettres, 1963, D.E.S. 1964, M.A., 1978, Ph.D., 1981. *Agent:* c/o Les Editions de L'Homme, 955 Amherst St., Montreal, Quebec, Canada H2L 3K4. *Office:* Department of Art History, Universite du Quebec a Montreal, Case Postale 8888, Succursale "A," Montreal, Quebec, Canada H3C 3P8.

CAREER: Laval University, Quebec City, Quebec, visiting instructor, 1970-78; Moncton University, Moncton, New Brunswick, visiting instructor, 1970-78; Universite du Quebec, Montreal, Quebec, instructor, 1978—, director of research on traditional architecture and furniture. Collaborator with Gilles Vilandre on conservation of old buildings, 1972-76. Creator and director of films on art for Radio Canada and National Film Board of Canada, 1976-81. *Member:* Association for Preservation Technology, Conseil des monuments et sites du Quebec.

WRITINGS: (With wife, Huguette Marquis) *Encyclopedie des antiquites du Quebec: Trois Siecles de production artisanale,* Editions de l'Homme, 1971; (with Marquis) *Encyclopedie de la maison quebecoise: Trois Siecles d'habitations,* Editions de l'Homme, 1972; (with Gilles Vilandre) *La Maison traditionnelle au Quebec,* Editions de l'Homme, 1974; *Complete Guide to French-Canadian Antiques,* illustrated by Marquis, translation from original French by Elisabeth Abbot, Hart Publishing, 1974; (with Marquis) *L'Art traditionnel au Quebec,* preface by Cyril Simard, Editions de l'Homme, 1975; *Les Granges anciennes du Quebec,* Editions de l'Homme, 1982.

SIDELIGHTS: Lessard told *CA:* "For the past ten years I have been working on the ethno-history and art history of the Quebecois. My purpose is to reveal to this French community of Canada that their ancestors brought to America the French taste and the French manner. An additional intention is to show that this small people had to reinvent the traditions to shape them to the conditions of their new country. My lectures, films, and

books are designed to reveal the particular language of the objects created on the banks of the Saint Lawrence River over the past three centuries."

* * *

LESSER, Robert C. 1933-

PERSONAL: Born October 23, 1933, in New York, N.Y.; son of Frank and Myra Lesser. *Education:* University of Chicago, B.A., 1950, M.A., 1953. *Politics:* "Left-wing liberal." *Religion:* None. *Home and office:* 533 Third Ave., New York, N.Y.

CAREER: Sales representative and writer. *Military service:* U.S. Air Force.

WRITINGS: "A Terror Since September" (play), first produced in Danville, Ky., at Pioneer Playhouse, July 23, 1962; *A Celebration of Comic Art and Memorabilia,* Hawthorn, 1975. Also author of a novel, short stories, and numerous other plays, including "The White King of the Black Canaries." Contributor to *Time-Life Encyclopedia of Collectibles.*

WORK IN PROGRESS: Plays; stories.

* * *

LEVIN, Meyer 1905-1981

OBITUARY NOTICE—See index for *CA* sketch: Born October 8, 1905, in Chicago, Ill.; died of a stroke, July 9, 1981, in Jerusalem, Israel. Journalist, educator, novelist, playwright, screenwriter, film critic, translator, and editor. Levin began his writing career as a reporter with the *Chicago Daily News.* After leaving the newspaper, he ran a marionette theatre, taught puppetry at the New School for Social Research, and worked as an editor and film critic with *Esquire* magazine. Levin was best known as the author of *Compulsion,* a novel about the 1924 Leopold-Loeb murder case. His stage adaptation of this work appeared on Broadway in 1957. His other novels include *The New Bridge, The Old Bunch,* and *My Father's House.* A Zionist, Levin wrote many books on Judaism. His novel *Yehuda* depicts life on a kibbutz in Palestine. He also edited anthologies of Jewish writings and translated Yiddish works into English. Among these books are *Selections From the Kibbutz Buchenwald Diary* and *The Rise of American Jewish Literature.* He also translated the French novels of his wife, Tereska Torres, into English. Levin's several film documentaries include "The Illegals," "The Falashas," and "Bus to Sinai." Obituaries and other sources: *New York Times,* July 11, 1981; *Washington Post,* July 11, 1981; *Time,* July 20, 1981; *Publishers Weekly,* August 7, 1981; *AB Bookman's Weekly,* September 14, 1981.

* * *

LEVINE, Solomon B. 1920-

PERSONAL: Born August 10, 1920, in Boston, Mass.; son of Isaac William (in business) and Sybil (Mannis) Levine; married Elizabeth Jane Billett (a university administrator), December 24, 1943; children: Janet R. Levine Thal, Samuel B., Michael A., Elliott M. *Education:* Harvard University, A.B. (magna cum laude), 1942, M.B.A. (with honors), 1947; Massachusetts Institute of Technology, Ph.D., 1951. *Home:* 916 Van Buren, Madison, Wis. 53711. *Office:* Department of Economics and Business, University of Wisconsin—Madison, 87 Bascom Hall, Madison, Wis. 53706.

CAREER: University of Illinois, Champaign-Urbana, research assistant at Institute of Labor and Industrial Relations, 1949-

50, research associate, 1950-51, assistant professor, 1951-56, associate professor, 1956-60, professor of labor and industrial relations, 1960-69, professor of Asian studies, 1964-69, chairman of Center for International Comparative Studies, 1964-67, director of Center for Asian Studies, 1964-69, coordinator of Keio University research and exchange program in industrial relations, 1963-69; Universtiy of Wisconsin—Madison, professor of business and economics, 1969—, member of Industrial Relations Research Institute, 1969—(member of executive committee, 1970—), chairman of publications committee, 1976-79, chairman of East Asian studies program, 1968-77, and department of international business, 1975—. Fulbright professor at Keio University, 1959; visiting professor at Pennsylvania State University, summer, 1960, Massachusetts Institute of Technology, 1962-63, and University of Singapore, summer, 1968; visiting lecturer in Indonesia, Australia, and New Zealand, 1973.

Member of Japanese Labor History Documentary Group, 1954—, and Japan-Wisconsin Committee on Science, Technology, and Public Policy, 1972—; member of Social Science Research Council and American Council of Learned Societies joint committee on Japanese studies, 1968-72, and Japan Economics Seminar, 1968—; member of executive committee of Midwest Japan Seminar, 1970-77, national screening committee (for the Far East) of Institute of International Education, 1973-75 (chairman of screening committee, 1974-75), and senior advisory panel of University of Mid-America of the Air, 1974-77; member of Public Employment Dispute Settlement Panel and panel of arbitrators of Wisconsin Employment Relations Commission, 1974—; member of international affairs advisory board of International Union of United Automobile, Aerospace, and Agricultural Implement Workers of America, 1978—; consultant to Ford Foundation and Asian Foundation. *Military service:* U.S. Navy, 1942-46; became lieutenant.

MEMBER: Industrial Relations Research Association, American Economic Association, Association for Asian Studies (chairman of Northeast Asian Regional Council, 1973-76; member of executive committee, 1974-75; chairman of finance committee, 1974-77), Japan Society, Academy of International Business, American Arbitration Association, International House of Japan, Midwest Conference of Asian Studies, Midwest Conference on Asian Affairs (president, 1962-63; member of executive committee, 1970-71), Phi Beta Kappa, Japan Illini Club (honorary life member).

AWARDS, HONORS: Fulbright scholarship and Ford Foundation fellowship, both for Hitotsubashi University, 1953-54; Social Science Research Council fellowship, 1957; Foundation fellow of Keio University, 1961—; Fulbright scholarships for Japan and Singapore, 1968, 1973, and for Singapore, Australia, New Zealand, and Japan, 1978; grant from Japan Foundation, 1976, scholarship, 1978.

WRITINGS: Industrial Relations in Postwar Japan, University of Illinois Press, 1958; (editor with Kazuo Okochi and Bernard Karsh, and contributor) *Workers and Employers in Japan: The Japanese Employment Relations System,* Princeton University Press, 1973; (with Hisashi Kawada) *Human Resources in Japanese Industrial Development,* Princeton University Press, 1980.

Contributor: Everett M. Kassalow, editor, *National Labor Movements in the Postwar World,* Northwestern University, Press, 1963; William W. Lockwood, editor, *The State and Economic Enterprise in Japan,* Princeton University Press, 1965; Adolf Sturmthal, editor, *White-Collar Trade Unions,* University of Illinois Press, 1966; R. P. Dore, editor, *Aspects of Social Change in Modern Japan,* Princeton University Press, 1967; Albert A. Blum, editor, *Teacher Unions and Associa-*

tions: A Comparative Study, University of Illinois Press, 1969; Stanley M. Jacks, editor, *Issues in Labor Policy: Papers in Honor of Professor Douglass V. Brown,* M.I.T. Press, 1971; Joe Moore and Felicia Oldfather, editors, *The Japan Readers,* Random House, 1974; Hugh Patrick, editor, *Industrialization and Its Social Consequences in Japan,* University of California Press, 1976; Kassalow and Benjamin Martin, editors, *Labor Relations in Advanced Industrial Societies: Issues and Problems,* Carnegie Endowment for International Peace, 1980.

Contributor to *Encyclopedia Americana.* Contributor of more than fifty articles and reviews to academic journals, including *Annals of the American Academy of Political and Social Science.* Member of editorial board of *Asian Survey,* 1965—.

*   *   *

LEVITAN, Donald   1928-

PERSONAL: Born January 11, 1928, in Boston, Mass.; son of Nathan (a podiatrist) and Sally (Alman) Levitan; married Evelyn Messer (an administrative assistant), June 21, 1965; children: Julie, Neal, David, Ben. *Education:* Boston College, S.B., 1951; Syracuse University, M.A., 1953; New York University, D.P.A., 1972. *Home:* 249 Homer St., Newton, Mass. 02159. *Office:* School of Management, Suffolk University, 47 Mount Vernon St., Boston, Mass. 02108.

CAREER: In real estate and construction industry in New York and New Jersey, 1953-64; U.S. Department of Housing and Urban Development (HUD), Washington, D.C., coordinator of urban renewal rehabilitation for state of New York, 1965-70, community planning and management representative in Boston, Mass., member of federal executive board and special assistant to the regional administrator, 1970-72, co-chairperson of housing and urban development task force, 1971-72; director of intergovernmental relations in Newton, Mass., 1972-74; Suffolk University, Boston, associate professor, 1974-77, professor of public management and administration, 1977—, chairman of department, 1974-76, director of Center of Public Management, 1974-77.

President of Grants Advisory Service, Inc., 1977—; member of board of directors of Continuum, Inc., 1974-79. Member of executive faculty at Boston Architectural Center, 1968-76; lecturer at Boston University, 1973-76, Boston State College, 1973-74, and New England Municipal Clerk's Institute, 1975—; guest lecturer at Brandeis University, Cornell University, Harvard University, Mount Wachusett Community College, New York University, Northeastern University, Simmons College, Syracuse University, Hebrew University of Jerusalem, University of London, University of Massachusetts, and Worcester Polytechnic Institute. Member of Rhode Island Governor's Council on Youth Opportunities, 1970-71; consultant to National Council on Aging, U.S. Civil Service Commission, Chinese Cultural Alliance, and Arthur D. Little. *Military service:* U.S. Navy, 1945-47. *Member:* American Planning Association, American Society for Public Administration, Governmental Research Association, National Municipal League, Municipal Finance Officers Association, Pi Gamma Mu.

WRITINGS: A Citizen's Guide to the Housing and Community Development Act of 1974, Low Income Planning Associates, 1974; *General Revenue Sharing Checklist and Calendar,* National Planning Association, 1974; *Basic Informational Sources and Tools for the Grantsman,* Low Income Planning Aid, 1975; (editor) *The Community Grants Resource Catalog: A Directory for Philanthropic Foundations in the Commonwealth of Massachusetts,* Low Income Planning Aid, 1976; *The Grant Application: Basic Elements and Preparation,* Massachusetts Se-*

lectman's Association, 1976; *Selected Sources and Resources for Grantsmanship in Massachusetts,* Action, 1976; *Selected Sources and Resources for Grantsmanship in Connecticut,* Action, 1976; (with others) *The Federal Granting System: A Guide for Local Governments in Massachusetts,* University of Massachusetts Press, 1978; (with Frank Earley) *Growth and Development in the Boston Metropolis: The Union of Government and Economics, a Marriage of Convenience* (bibliography), Boston Public Library, 1978; (with F. J. Early) *A Guide for Grants-in-Aid in New Mexico,* New Mexico Municipal League, 1978; (with Daniel F. Donahue) *Selected Sources and Resources for Grantsmanship in Pennsylvania,* Pennsylvania League of Cities, 1978; (with Donahue) *Selected Bibliography of Grants Management for State and Local Governments,* New Mexico Municipal League, 1979; (with Donahue) *The Grants Resource Manual,* Government Research Publications, 1980; *A Guide to Grants: Governmental and Nongovernmental,* Government Research Publications, 1980; *Your Massachusetts Government,* Government Research Publications, 9th edition (Levitan was not associated with earlier editions), 1980; *Doing Business on the Hill,* Government Research Publications, 1982.

Contributor: *Housing Innovations,* Boston University, 1969; *1970 Sierra Annual,* Sierra Books, 1970. Also contributor to *La Route 128 et les nouvelles entreprises technologiques: Rapport au Ministere du Development Industriel et Scientifique* (title means "Route 128: A Study of Technological Enterprises"), 1971, and to management, planning, and housing journals.

WORK IN PROGRESS: A Business Guide to Taxes in Massachusetts, publication expected in 1982.

SIDELIGHTS: Levitan wrote: "I have changed areas several times—from business to government to academe—no doubt I will move back and forth. As a consultant and lecturer I have traveled all over the world; these experiences have contributed more to my education than did my formal education."

*   *   *

LEVITT, Leonard   1941-

PERSONAL: Born April 27, 1941, in New York, N.Y.; son of B. B. (in importing business) and Celia (a teacher; maiden name, Kosovsky) Levitt; married Susan Elizabeth Gina (an artist and sculptor), July 20, 1974. *Education:* Dartmouth College, A.B., 1963; Columbia University, M.S., 1967. *Residence:* Sea Cliff, N.Y. 11579. *Agent:* Sterling Lord Agency, Inc., 660 Madison Ave., New York, N.Y. 10021.

CAREER: U.S. Peace Corps, Washington, D.C., volunteer teacher in Tanzania, East Africa, 1963-65; Associated Press (AP), New York City, reporter, 1967; *Detroit News,* Detroit, Mich., reporter, 1968-69; *Time,* New York City, correspondent, 1969-73; free-lance writer, 1973-75; *Newsday,* Garden City, N.Y., reporter, 1975-79; *New York Post,* New York City, investigation editor, 1979-80; writer, 1980—. Adjunct professor at Columbia University, 1971-77. *Awards, honors:* Rockefeller Foundation for the Humanities grant, 1981.

WRITINGS: An African Season (nonfiction), Simon & Schuster, 1967; *The Long Way Round* (novel), Saturday Review Press, 1972; (editor) Richard Clark, *The Brothers of Attica* (nonfiction), Links Books, 1973; *The Healer* (nonfiction), Viking, 1980; *In Shangri-la* (novel), Viking, 1982; "The King at Hastings Street" (play), produced in 1982.

SIDELIGHTS: "Writing is hard and unglamorous work," Levitt commented. "The older I become, the more I demand of myself so that, at least for me, writing does not become any easier.

"I learned my craft writing for newspapers, but after some point newspaper writing and good writing become antithetical. *The Healer* grew out of a story I covered for the Long Island *Newsday,* but its scope and point of view surpassed the limits of newspaper journalism. The story began with the murder of a wealthy suburban mother by her surgeon husband. One of their daughters helped him dispose of the evidence. Another daughter turned him in as he attempted to leave the country with his wife's securities to join his mistress in Denmark. Yet the book became more than this family story. It documented the medical history of this surgeon, showing how an unscrupulous and dangerous man was permitted to practice for twenty-five years by the medical profession, which refused to take disciplinary action against him.

"The play I wrote—which grew out of material during my free-lancing period in the mid-1970's—is about two former gangsters. In their sixties, they own a store in the middle of a black ghetto and spend their days reminiscing about their past glories, and who now, it turns out, are being harassed and shaken down by the young black punks of the neighborhood, just as they themselves shook down honest merchants forty and fifty years before. The play centers on how these two old men come to terms with their present, their past, and their illusions.

"In the summer of 1981 I embarked on a project made possible by a grant from the Rockefeller Foundation for the Humanities, which will take me back to Tanzania, East Africa, where I taught in a rural school as a member of the Peace Corps more than fifteen years ago. My plan is to find my students, who were teenagers then, and to discover what has happened to them. My experiences will become a book, though what form the book will take I do not know at this time."

BIOGRAPHICAL/CRITICAL SOURCES: Los Angeles Times Book Review, November 16, 1980.

*   *   *

LEWALSKI, Barbara Kiefer   1931-

PERSONAL: Born February 22, 1931, in Chicago, Ill.; daughter of John Peter and Vivo (Hutton) Kiefer; married Kenneth Lewalski, June 23, 1956; children: David John. *Education:* Kansas State Teachers College (now Emporia Kansas State College), B.S.Ed., 1950; University of Chicago, A.M., 1951, Ph.D., 1956. *Home:* 157 University Ave., Providence, R.I. 02906. *Office:* Department of English, Brown University, Providence, R.I. 02912.

CAREER: Wellesley College, Wellesley, Mass., instructor in English literature, 1954-56; Brown University, Providence, R.I., began as instructor, 1956, associate professor, 1962-67, professor of English, 1967—, alumni-alumnae university professor of English, 1976—, director of graduate studies in English, 1968-72. Lecturer at Hebrew University of Jerusalem and Bar-Ilan University, 1968; visiting professor at Princeton University, 1974.

MEMBER: Milton Society of America (president, 1970), American Association of University Professors (vice-president), Modern Language Association of America, Renaissance Society of America, Academy for Literature Studies (president, 1976-77). *Awards, honors:* Fulbright scholarship, 1953-54; American Association of University Women fellowship, 1961-62; Guggenheim fellowship, 1967-68; Explicator Prize, 1973; National Endowment for the Humanities senior fellowship,

1974-75; honored scholar of Milton Society of America, 1977; James Russell Lowell Prize, 1980, for *Protestant Poetics and the Seventeenth-Century Religious Lyric.*

WRITINGS: Milton's Brief Epic: The Genre, Meaning, and Art of Paradise Regained, Brown University Press, 1966; (editor) William Shakespeare, *Much Ado About Nothing,* W. C. Brown, 1969; (Contributor) *New Essays on Paradise Lost,* University of California Press, 1969; *Donne's "Anniversaries" and the Poetry of Praise: The Creation of a Symbolic Mode,* Princeton University Press, 1973; (editor with Andrew J. Sabol) *Major Poets of the Earlier Seventeenth Century: Donne, Herbert, Vaughan, Crashaw, Jonson, Herrick, Marvell,* Odyssey, 1973; *Typology and Poetry: A Consideration of Herbert, Vaughan, and Marvell,* University of California Press, 1973; *Protestant Poetics and the Seventeenth-Century Religious Lyric,* Princeton University Press, 1979. Contributor to literature Journals.

BIOGRAPHICAL/CRITICAL SOURCES: Times Literary Supplement, March 7, 1980.*

*   *   *

LEWELS, Francisco J(ose), Jr. 1944-

PERSONAL: Born April 10, 1944, in El Paso, Tex.; son of Francisco Jose and Aurora (Cisneros) Lewels; married Hilda Stockmeyer, March 8, 1974; children: Nicholas, Christopher, Marisa. *Education:* Texas Western College, B.A., 1966; Troy State University, M.S., 1971; University of Missouri, Ph.D., 1973. *Home:* 704 La Mancha Court, El Paso, Tex. 79922. *Office:* Department of Mass Communication, University of Texas, El Paso, Tex. 79968.

CAREER: De Bruyn Advertising Agency, El Paso, Tex., writer, 1963-64; Bill Lynde/Public Relations, El Paso, writer, 1965-66; *Aviation Digest,* Fort Rucker, Ala., writer and editor, 1968-70; *Freedom of Information Digest,* Columbia, Mo., editor, 1970-72; University of Texas, El Paso, assistant professor, 1972-76, associate professor of mass communication, 1976—. Free-lance writer. Communication specialist for U.S. Department of Justice, summer, 1972. *Military service:* U.S. Army, 1966-68; served in Vietnam; became captain; received Air Medal and Bronze Star. *Member:* Society of Professional Journalists, Association for Education in Journalism, Kappa Tau Alpha. *Awards, honors:* Prize from Reader's Digest Workshop, 1981.

WRITINGS: Uses of the Media by the Chicano Movement, Praeger, 1974. Contributor to communication journals.

WORK IN PROGRESS: Research on attitudes of Mexican Americans toward the media and on minority access to broadcasting.

SIDELIGHTS: Lewels wrote: "As the first Mexican American to earn a Ph.D. in journalism in the United States, I feel like a pioneer in the area—particularly in journalism education. I am dedicated to the cause of getting more Hispanic Americans involved in the mass media so that this important minority group might be better represented to the American public."

*   *   *

LEWIN, Betsy 1937-

PERSONAL: Born May 12, 1937, in Pennsylvania; daughter of John K. (in insurance sales) and Winifred (a teacher; maiden name, Dowler) Reilly; married Ted B. Lewin (a writer and illustrator), 1963. *Education:* Prattt Institute of Art, B.F.A., 1959. *Home and office:* 152 Willoughby Ave., Brooklyn, N.Y. 11025.

CAREER: Free-lance writer and illustrator.

WRITINGS—Self-illustrated: Animal Snackers, Dodd, 1980, *Cat Count,* Dodd, 1981.

WORK IN PROGRESS: Hip Hippo, Hooray, a self-illustrated children's book.

SIDELIGHTS: Betsy Lewin wrote: "My books combine my love of drawing, the sounds of words, and the touching humor in much animal behavior. I observe and draw animals and wildlife and paint flowers in watercolors. I have viewed game in East Africa, backpacked in Hawaii's Haleakala Crater, canoed in the Everglades, watched whales off the coast of Baja California, and visited the Pribilof Islands and Alaska."

*   *   *

LEWIS, Alun 1915-1944

BRIEF ENTRY: Born July 1, 1915, in Aberdare, South Wales; died in a shooting accident in 1944 in Arakan, Burma. Welsh educator, military officer, poet, and short story writer. Best known as a war poet, Lewis was a student of history and a grammar school teacher before enlisting in the British Army in 1940. Serving as a lieutenant, he spent two years stationed in England and was transferred to India in 1942. Refusing a staff-officer's position, Lewis insisted on going into action with his unit and was killed in an accident while on active duty. The details surrounding his death have remained a mystery. Dealing with themes such as the anonymity of the soldier, isolation, separation, and death, Lewis's work is noted for its compassion. *Raider's Dawn* (1942), his first book of poetry, and *The Last Inspection* (1942), a collection of short stories, express the frustration and monotony felt by the enlisted soldier waiting to be called to active duty. *Ha! Ha! Among the Trumpets* (1945) contains several poems inspired by Lewis's experiences in India. Among his other works are *Letters From India* (1946) and *In the Green Tree* (1949). *Biographical/critical sources: Twentieth Century Authors: A Biographical Dictionary of Modern Literature,* H. W. Wilson, 1st supplement, 1955; *Encyclopedia of World Literature in the Twentieth Century,* updated edition, Ungar, 1967; *Twentieth Century Writing: A Reader's Guide to Contemporary Literature,* Transatlantic, 1969; *Webster's New World Companion to English and American Literature,* World Publishing, 1973; *Twentieth-Century Literary Criticism,* Volume 3, Gale, 1980.

*   *   *

LEWIS, David 1909-1981

PERSONAL: Born June 23, 1909, in Svisloch, Russia (now U.S.S.R.); died May 23, 1981; son of Morris (a factory worker) and Rose (Lazarus) Lewis; married Sophie Carson, August 15, 1935; children: Stephen Henry, Michael Edward, Janet Lewis Solberg and Nina Lewis Libeskind (twins). *Education:* McGill University, B.A., 1931; Oxford University, B.A., 1935. *Religion:* Jewish. *Home:* 138 Rodney Crescent, Ottawa, Ontario, Canada K1H 5J9. *Office:* Institute of Canadian Studies, Carleton University, Ottawa, Ontario, Canada K1S 5B6.

CAREER: Called to the Bar of Quebec, 1936, appointed Queen's Counsel, 1959; private practice as labor lawyer, 1950-62 and 1963-65; Cooperative Commonwealth Federation, Ottawa, Ontario, national secretary, 1936-50, national vice-chairman, 1950-54, national chairman, 1954-58, national president, 1958-61; Canadian Parliament, Ottawa, New Democrat member of Parliament for York South, Ontario, 1962-63, deputy leader of New Democratic party, 1965-71, leader of party, 1971-75; Carleton University, Ottawa, visiting fellow at Institute of Canadian Studies, 1975-81. Partner of Joliffe, Lewis & Osler (law firm), Toronto, Ontario, 1950-69.

MEMBER: Bar Association of Canada, Canadian Civil Liberties Association (member of board of directors), Canadian Council of Christians and Jews, Canadian Institute of International Affairs, Canadian Jewish Congress, Law Society of Upper Canada, Staff Association of Carleton University. *Awards, honors:* Rhodes scholar at Oxford University, 1932; silver plate of honor from Socialist International, 1976; companion of Order of Canada, 1976.

WRITINGS: (With Frank R. Scott) *Make This Your Canada,* foreword by M. J. Coldwell, Central Canada Publishing Co., 1943; *Louder Voices: The Corporate Welfare Bums,* Lorimer, 1972; *The Good Fight* (memoirs), Macmillan, 1981. Contributor to periodicals.

SIDELIGHTS: Lewis wrote: "I have given my adult life, from my undergraduate days onward, to building the social democratic movement in Canada. My detestation of the inequalities, injustices, and crass materialism of the capitalist system and deep commitment to democratic rights and freedoms have always been my guiding philosophical belief."

AVOCATIONAL INTERESTS: Reading poetry, listening to classical music.

[Date of death provided by daughter Janet Solberg]

*   *   *

LEWIS, Elliott (Bruce)   1917-

PERSONAL: Born November 28, 1917, in New York, N.Y.; son of Julius A. (a printer) and Anne (a journalist; maiden name, Rabinowitz) Lewis; married Cathy Lewis, April 30, 1942 (divorced, 1958); married Mary Jane Croft (an actress), May 9, 1959. *Education:* Attended Los Angeles City College, 1936-37. *Agent:* Robinson/Weintraub, 554 South San Vicente, Los Angeles, Calif. 90048.

CAREER: Actor, producer, director, and novelist. *Military service:* U.S. Army, 1941-44; became master sergeant; received Legion of Merit.

WRITINGS—Novels; all published by Pinnacle Books: *Two Heads Are Better,* 1980; *Dirty Linen,* 1980; *People in Glass Houses,* 1981; *Double Trouble,* 1981.

WORK IN PROGRESS: Three novels, *Death Mask, Cataclysm at Carbon River,* and *Here Today, Dead Tomorrow.*

SIDELIGHTS: Lewis told *CA:* "I have worked in the entertainment business since I was in my teens, as an actor, writer, producer, director, and now mystery novelist. It's a business I love, and I feel fortunate that I've been able to make my living at it. With my current novel series, I'm enjoying myself as much or more than I ever have, I suppose because the writer is the actor, director, producer, wardrobe person, weatherman, location director, stunt and second unit director, crowd handler, transportation gaffer, and everything else I've ever been around, all rolled up into one person."

*   *   *

LEWIS, (Harry) Sinclair   1885-1951
(Tom Graham)

BRIEF ENTRY: Born February 7, 1885, in Sauk Centre, Minn.; died of paralysis of the heart, January 10, 1951, in Rome, Italy; cremated, and ashes returned to birthplace. American novelist, short story writer, journalist, dramatist, and poet.

Considered one of the foremost American writers of the 1920's, Lewis gained international acclaim for his novels attacking the weaknesses of American society. A social critic from an early age, Lewis lived briefly at Helicon Hall, an experimental socialist community founded by Upton Sinclair. Graduated from Yale University in 1908, he spent several years doing editorial and newspaper work. In 1912 he published his first novel, *Hike and the Aeroplane,* under the pseudonym Tom Graham. During the next eight years Lewis wrote five more minor novels, achieving only moderate success. Then, in 1920 he published *Main Street,* a satirical expose of the dull provincialism and rigidity of smalltown U.S.A. The novel was an immediate success, and for the next ten years Lewis continued examining the inadequacies of the American way of life. *Babbitt* (1922) focuses on the confining, sterile life of businessman, solid citizen, and club joiner George F. Babbitt; *Arrowsmith* (1925) portrays the frustrations of a dedicated young doctor in conflict with pettiness and corruption; *Elmer Gantry* (1927) caricatures religious hypocrisy and bigotry; and *Dodsworth* (1929) contrasts the manners and values of Europe and the United States. In 1926 Lewis won a Pulitzer Prize for *Arrowsmith,* but he declined the award. In 1930 he was awarded the Nobel Prize for literature, the first American novelist so honored. His other notable works include *It Can't Happen Here* (1935), *Cass Timberlane* (1945), and *Kingsblood Royal* (1947). *Biographical/critical sources: Twentieth Century Authors: A Biographical Dictionary of Modern Literature,* H. W. Wilson, 1955; *Cyclopedia of World Authors,* Harper, 1958; *Reader's Encyclopedia of American Literature,* Crowell, 1962; *Webster's New World Companion to English and American Literature,* World Publishing, 1973; *Twentieth-Century Literary Criticism,* Volume 4, Gale, 1981.

*   *   *

LEWIS, (Percy) Wyndham   1884(?)-1957

BRIEF ENTRY: Born c. 1884 in a yacht off the coast of Maine; died March 7, 1957, in London, England. English painter, novelist, critic, and essayist. Lewis first became known as a pioneer of modernist abstract painting. He became a spokesman for the vorticist movement and with Ezra Pound edited the short-lived periodical *Blast: Review of the Great English Vortex* in 1914 and 1915. After World War I he became a professional writer with his first novel, *Tarr* (1918), and many critical essays. Lewis disapproved of many literary trends of the time and in his essays attacked Joyce, Lawrence, Hemingway, and other prominent writers. He also satirized English literary society in his novel *The Apes of God* (1930). His aesthetic theories and aggressive polemical style made him a controversial figure, as did his flirtation with fascism in the 1930's. Lewis believed that the proper concern of art was the "outside," the external aspects of things and people; he disliked the subjective, "inside" writing that came to dominate twentieth-century fiction. Many critics consider Lewis among the most important authors of the twentieth century, especially for his trilogy of novels *The Human Age* (1955). His other works include *Time and Western Man* (1927), *The Childermass* (1928), and *Rotting Hill* (1951). *Residence:* London, England. *Biographical/critical sources: Twentieth Century Authors: A Biographical Dictionary of Modern Literature,* H. W. Wilson, 1942; Wyndham Lewis, *Rude Assignment: A Narrative of My Career Up-to-Date,* Hutchinson, 1950; V. S. Pritchett, *Books in General,* Chatto & Windus, 1953; Geoffrey Wagner, *Wyndham Lewis: A Portrait of the Artist as the Enemy,* Routledge & Kegan Paul, 1957; *Cyclopedia of World Literature,* Harper, 1958; *Twentieth-Century Literary Criticism,* Volume 2, Gale, 1979.

LEWONTIN, Richard Charles 1929-

PERSONAL: Born March 29, 1929, in New York, N.Y.; son of Max and Lillian (Wilson) Lewontin; married Mary Jane Christianson, April 10, 1947; children: David John, Stephen Paul, James Peter, Timothy Andrew. *Education:* Harvard University, A.B., (magna cum laude), 1951; Columbia University, M.A., 1952, Ph.D., 1954. *Residence:* Marlboro, Vt. *Office:* Museum of Comparative Zoology, Harvard University, Cambridge, Mass. 02138.

CAREER: North Carolina State University, Raleigh, assistant professor of genetics, 1954-58; University of Rochester, Rochester, N.Y., 1958-64, began as assistant professor, became professor of biology; University of Chicago, Chicago, Ill., professor of zoology and mathematical biology, 1964-73, Louis Block Professor of Biological Sciences, 1969-73, associate dean of biological sciences, 1966-69; Harvard University, Cambridge, Mass., Alexander Agassiz Professor of Zoology, 1973—. Lecturer at Columbia University, 1959, associate of Seminar on Human Evolution, 1959-61.

MEMBER: American Academy of Arts and Sciences (fellow), American Association for the Advancement of Science (fellow), American Eugenic Society (member of board of directors, 1966—), Society for the Study of Evolution (president, 1970), Genetics Society of America, Biometric Society, National Academy of Sciences. *Awards, honors:* National Science Foundation fellowship, 1954-55, senior fellowships, 1961-62, 1971-72; grants from National Science Foundation, 1958-59 and 1963—, Office of Naval Research, 1958-59, U.S. Public Health Service, 1958-63, and Atomic Energy Commission, 1960—; Fulbright fellowship, 1961-62.

WRITINGS: (With Hans Ris and Herschel L. Roman) *Topics in Cell Biology, Inheritance, and Evolution,* Harper, 1971; *The Genetic Basis of Evolutionary Change,* Columbia University Press, 1974; (with Arthur Stanley Goldberger) *Jensen's Twin Fantasy,* University of Wisconsin—Madison, 1976. Also author of *Quantitative Zoology* and editor of *Population Biology and Evolution: Proceedings of the International Symposium, June 7-9, 1967, Syracuse University.* Associate editor of *Evolution,* 1959-63, and *Der Zuchter,* 1965—; co-editor of *American Naturalist,* 1964-70.*

* * *

LIBBY, William C(harles)

PERSONAL: Born in Pittsburgh, Pa. *Education:* Attended University of Pittsburgh; received B.A. from Carnegie-Mellon University; also attended University of Texas, Colorado Springs Fine Arts Center, and Academie Grande Chaumiere. *Office:* Carnegie-Mellon University, P.O. Box 135, Pittsburgh, Pa. 15213.

CAREER: Carnegie-Mellon University, Pittsburgh, Pa., professor of drawing and painting, 1945—. Art work represented in permanent collections, including Library of Congress, Brooklyn Museum, and Metropolitan Museum of Art; work commissioned and exhibited in the United States, Yugoslavia, and Poland, including National Academy of Design and U.S. Information Agency Overseas Exhibition of American Graphic Art. *Member:* Society of American Graphic Artists, National Academy of Design, Associated Artists of Pittsburgh (president, 1955-57). *Awards, honors:* Purchase awards from National Print Exhibition, 1952, 1966; jury award of distinction from Associated Artists of Pittsburgh, 1966.

WRITINGS: Color and the Structural Sense, Prentice-Hall, 1974. Also illustrator of *The Story of an American City* and contributor to art journals.*

* * *

LICHTY, George M. 1905-

PERSONAL: Born May 16, 1905, in Chicago, Ill.; son of Julius and Ella (Hirsch) Lichtenstein; married Eleanor Louise Fretter, January 5, 1931; children: Linda Louise Richardson, Susan Emory Trejo. *Education:* Attended Art Institute of Chicago; University of Michigan, A.B., 1929. *Politics:* Democrat. *Home:* 6519 Meadowridge Dr., Santa Rosa, Calif. 95405. *Office:* Field Newspaper Syndicate, 401 North Wabash Ave., Chicago, Ill. 60611.

CAREER: Chicago Daily Times, Chicago, Ill., sports cartoonist, 1930-32, creator of "Grin and Bear It," 1932-34; United Features Syndicate, New York City, creator of "Grin and Bear It," 1934-40; Chicago Sun-Times Syndicate, Chicago, creator of "Grin and Bear It," 1947-67; Field Newspaper Syndicate, Chicago, creator of "Grin and Bear It," 1967—. *Member:* National Cartoonists Society, San Francisco Press Club, Bohemian Club, Union League Club. *Awards, honors*—All for "Grin and Bear It": Best newspaper panel awards, 1956, 1959, 1963, 1966, 1969; best syndicated panel awards from National Cartoonists Society, 1959, 1963, 1965, 1973.

WRITINGS: Grin and Bear It; Being a Collection of One Hundred Twenty-Four Very Funny and Recognition-Provoking Pictures of the Human Animal in Action, McGraw, 1954; *Is Party Line, Comrade!,* Public Affairs Press, 1965; *Grin and Bear It,* Pocket Books, 1970.

* * *

LIEBLING, A(bbott) J(oseph) 1904-1963

PERSONAL: Born October 18, 1904, in New York, N.Y.; died December 28, 1963, in New York, N.Y.; buried in Green River Cemetery, East Hampton, N.Y.; son of Joseph (a furrier) and Anna (Slone) Liebling; married Anne Beatrice McGinn, July 28, 1934 (divorced, 1949); married Lucille Hille Spectorsky, 1949 (divorced, 1959); married Jean Stafford (a novelist), 1959. *Education:* Attended Dartmouth College, 1920-23; Columbia University, B.Lit., 1925; attended Sorbonne, University of Paris, 1926-27.

CAREER: New York Times, New York City, sports reporter, 1925-26; *Providence Journal* and *Evening Bulletin,* Providence, R.I., staff writer, 1926-30; *New York World,* New York City, staff writer, 1930-31; *New York World-Telegram* and *Journal,* New York City, feature writer, 1931-35; *New Yorker,* New York City, 1935-63, staff writer beginning in 1935, correspondent in France, England, and North Africa, 1939-44, author of column "Wayward Press," 1946-63, contributing author of column "Notes and Comments." *Awards, honors:* Knight of the French Legion of Honor.

WRITINGS: (With Edward B. Marks) *They All Sang,* Viking, 1934; *Back Where I Came From,* Sheridan, 1938; *The Telephone Booth Indian,* Doubleday, Doran, 1942; *The Road Back to Paris* Doubleday, Doran, 1944; (editor with Eugene Jay Sheffer) *La Republique du silence,* Harcourt, 1946, translation by Ramon Guthrie and others published as *The Republic of Silence,* 1947; *The Wayward Pressman,* Doubleday, 1947; *Mink and Red Herring: The Wayward Pressman's Casebook,* Doubleday, 1949.

Chicago: Second City, drawings by Saul Steinberg, Knopf, 1952; *The Honest Rainmaker: The Life and Times of Colonel*

John R. Stingo, Doubleday, 1953; *The Sweet Science: A Ringside View of Boxing,* Viking, 1956; *Normandy Revisited,* Simon & Schuster, 1958; *The Earl of Louisiana,* Simon & Schuster, 1961; *The Press,* Ballantine, 1961, revised edition, 1964, 2nd revised edition, 1975; *Between Meals: An Appetite for Paris,* Simon & Schuster, 1962; *The Jollity Building,* Ballantine, 1962; *The Most of A. J. Liebling,* selected by William Cole, Simon & Schuster, 1963 (published in England as *The Best of A. J. Liebling,* Methuen, 1965); *Molly and Other War Pieces,* Ballantine, 1964.

SIDELIGHTS: A. J. Liebling spent twenty-eight of his years in journalism as a reporter and columnist with the *New Yorker* magazine. His column, "Wayward Press," earned him the reputation as the conscience of American journalism, and his hundreds of articles on subjects as diverse as politics, boxing, and French cuisine made him, according to the *London Times,* "one of the best known figures in the New York literary world."

Liebling joined the *New Yorker* as a staff writer in 1935, achieving prominence as the magazine's Paris correspondent just prior to the Second World War. "During the war," noted the *London Times,* Liebling "frequently accompanied combat patrols in spite of being handicapped with gout, nearsightedness, and a degree of plumpness." He crossed the channel with the first Allied troops, landed under fire at Normandy on D day, and participated in the liberation of Paris. His dispatches were, in the opinion of his biographer Raymond Sokolov, "full of small revealing, all-important details that the wire services and other battle reporters left out," and his writing bridged the gap between objective journalism and fiction. "Joe Liebling was always there on the page, a vivid presence," wrote Sokolov. "He insisted on the personal note, on the importance and relevance of his, the reporter's, reaction to the event he was covering." Liebling was one of the first important writers to work in the literary genre of New Journalism, and Tom Wolfe, a leading writer of this group, looked upon Liebling as his master.

Soon after the war, Liebling began writing the column "Wayward Press," originally the province of Robert Benchley. With a characteristic biting humor, Liebling fought to preserve the integrity of his profession by lampooning and lambasting the shortcomings of editors, publishers, politicians, the public, and reporters alike. In his column, Liebling disdained editors who could not write: "The reign of these non-writers makes our newspapers read like the food in the *New York Times* cafeteria tastes," he once commented. "It is as if, in football, only bad players were allowed to become coaches." He was known also for his barbed pronouncements upon publishers, such as "Freedom of the press is guaranteed only to those who own one." Nothing in the world of journalism was sacred to Liebling. He once observed that the Pulitzer School of Journalism of Columbia University "had all the intellectual status of a training school for future employees of the A & P," and he called the *New York Times* "colorless, odorless, and tasteless." Nevertheless, he had enough confidence in newsmen to have once written that "newspapermen as a class have a yearning for truth as involuntary as a hophead's addiction to junk. . . . A few newspapermen lie to get on in the world, but it outrages them, too, and I never knew a dishonest journalist who wasn't patently an unhappy bastard."

In addition to writing his regular column, Liebling was a leading contributor to the *New Yorker,* producing articles in such prodigious numbers that he once remarked that he could "write better than anyone who could write faster, and faster than anyone who could writer better." His friend and colleague James Thurber, "who had some fantasies about physiques and productivity, insisted that 'Liebling is the only fast-writing fat man I know,'" quoted Nora Sayre in *Nation.* And, according to the *New Yorker,* the quantity of his writing was almost matched by the range of his subject matter. A summary of Liebling's "passionate interests" included "New York, Paris, North Africa, England, boxing, military theory, medieval history, Broadway life, Stendhal, Camus, Colonel Stingo, Pierce Egan, Stephen Crane, and Ibn Khaldun."

Most of Liebling's books are collections of articles and sketches that originally appeared in the *New Yorker,* and they typify the scope of his interests: *The Wayward Pressman* and *The Press* document the press and its shortcomings as well as Liebling's long-standing feud with publisher Colonel Robert R. McCormick and the *Chicago Tribune; The Road Back to Paris* and *Normandy Revisited* are collections of war sketches; *The Sweet Science* is a series of sketches on boxers and boxing; and *The Earl of Louisiana* is a series on Govenor Earl Long. *Between Meals: An Appetite for Paris* spotlights two of Liebling's favorite subjects—food and France—and in it the author describes his gargantuan eating habits with the same zest that he uses to describe the sights and sounds of his favorite foreign city, Paris. New York City, clearly Liebling's first love, is the subject of *Back Where I Came From, The Telephone Booth Indian,* and some of his most famous sketches and articles.

Liebling was considered one of New York City's foremost historians. "His love for the city was not something abstract or general; he knew it and loved it in detail," stated the *New Yorker.* "He liked the sound of Broadway speech, and of the city's sporting talk, and of what he called 'the side-street New York language,' and he preserved it faultlessly in his pieces." Jay Jacobs in the *Reporter* called Liebling "a peerless chronicler of his native New York's demi-monde," a mantle that has led to comparisons of Liebling with Damon Runyan and Emile Zola. Liebling devoted his nonfiction novel, *The Honest Rainmaker: The Life and Time of Colonel John R. Stingo,* to capturing what Sokolov has since called "the pluperfect Broadway type."

Regardless of his subject matter, Liebling prided himself on the accuracy and thoroughness of his work. *Commonweal* critic William James Smith pointed out that Liebling always referred to himself as a reporter, rather than as a writer, and that he was proud that he only reported what he saw without attempting to interpret it as an expert. In describing Liebling's famous interviewing technique, Nora Sayre wrote that the author "was contemptuous of the reporters 'who go out and impress their powerful personalities on their subjects and then come back and make up what they think he would have said if he had had a chance to say anything.'" Sayre summarized Liebling's methods, explaining, "he would unnerve his subjects by staring at them asking almost nothing, so that they soon began to babble, revealing far more than they intended."

In 1963, at the age of fifty-nine, A. J. Liebling died from complications of viral pneumonia. Speaking at the funeral, a friend of Liebling's from the *New Yorker,* Joseph Mitchell, recalled a conversation with the proprietor of a second-hand bookstore: "He said that every few days all through the year someone . . . came in and asked if he had 'Back Where I Came From' or 'The Telephone Indian' or some other book by A. J. Liebling. . . . The man went on to say that he and other veteran second-hand book dealers felt this was a sure and certain sign that a book would endure. 'Literary critics don't know which books will last,' he said, 'and literary historians don't know. *We* are the ones who know. We know which books can be read only once, if that, and we know the ones that can be read and reread and reread.'"

In the years since his death, Liebling has in fact become somewhat of a legend among journalists, especially the young. In 1972, the editors of *More,* the New York journalism review, celebrated their first year of publication with a meeting they called the Liebling Convention in honor of the man they felt epitomized the art and spirit of journalism. Several of Liebling's admirers still lament that he died before he was able to cover some of the century's biggest news events. Sayre commented, "Liebling would have luxuriated in every Nixon tape as though it had been a gourmet meal, a festival of pleasure. . . . If only he'd lived to interview John Mitchell and Howard Hunt and the Rabbi known as Barf." Sokolov also speculated: "If only he had lasted ten more years, he could have written press criticism about Vietnam and Watergate. When the Six-Day War broke out, he might have dusted off his First Division fatigues and revisited Egypt and Israel. He did not make it to ringside for the antic championship defenses of Cassius Clay after he turned Muslim and called himself Ali. Liebling missed out on dozens of big stories, stories he would have written better than anyone else could or did. No one has replaced him at *The New Yorker* or elsewhere as press critic, ring writer or guide to telephone booth Indians."

BIOGRAPHICAL/CRITICAL SOURCES: New Yorker, December 3, 1938, January 11, 1964; *New York Times Book Review,* December 4, 1938, April 27, 1947, November 30, 1947, June 22, 1952, November 11, 1962, December 1, 1963; *Saturday Review,* January 7, 1939, May 17, 1947, November 8, 1947, June 21, 1952; *Time,* November 10, 1947; *New Republic,* November 17, 1947, August 4, 1952; *Editor and Publisher,* August 14, 1948; *Atlantic,* January, 1963; *Harper,* December, 1963; Roy Newquist, *Counterpoint,* Simon & Schuster, 1964; *Commonweal,* January 10, 1964; *Reporter,* February 13, 1964; Edmund M. Midura, *A. J. Liebling: The Wayward Pressman as Critic,* Association for Education in Journalism, 1974; *Nation,* October 7, 1978; Raymond Sokolov, *The Wayward Reporter: The Life of A. J. Liebling,* Harper, 1980.

Obituaries: *New York Times,* December 29, 1963; *London Times,* December 30, 1963, *Publishers Weekly,* January 6, 1964; *Newsweek,* January 13, 1964.*

—Sketch by Lillian S. Sims

*   *   *

LIESNER, Hans Hubertus (Karl Kurt Otto)   1929-

PERSONAL: Born March 30, 1929, in Naumburg, Germany; son of Curt (a lawyer) and Edith L. (Neumann) Liesner; married Thelma Seward, 1968; children: one son, one daughter. *Education:* University of Bristol, B.A.; Nuffield College, Oxford, M.A. *Home:* 32 The Grove, Brookmans Park, Hertfordshire AL9 7RN, England.

CAREER: University of London, London School of Economics and Political Science, London, England, 1955-59, began as assistant lecturer, became lecturer in economics and political science; Cambridge University, Cambridge, England, lecturer in economics, 1959-70, fellow of Emmanuel College, director of studies in economics, bursar of Emmanuel College; Her Majesty's Treasury, London, under-secretary (economics), 1970-76; Departments of Trade, Industry and Prices, and Consumer Protection, London, chief economic adviser, 1976—. *Member:* Reform Club.

WRITINGS: The Import Dependence of Britain and Western Germany: A Comparative Study, International Finance Section, Department of Economics and Sociology, Princeton University, 1957; (with James Edward Meade and S. J. Wells) *Case Studies in European Economic Union: The Mechanics of In-*

tegration, Oxford University Press, 1962; *Atlantic Harmonisation: Making Free Trade Work,* Atlantic Trade Study, 1968; (with S. S. Han) *Britain and the Common Market: The Effect of Entry on the Pattern of Manufacturing Production,* Cambridge University Press, 1971. Contributor to economic journals.

AVOCATIONAL INTERESTS: Skiing, cine-photography, gardening, walking.*

*   *   *

LIGHTBOWN, Ronald William   1932-

PERSONAL: Born June 2, 1932, in England; son of Vincent and Helen (Anderson) Lightbown; married Mary Dorothy Webster (an art historian), September 8, 1962; children: Mark. *Education:* Cambridge University, M.A. *Politics:* None. *Religion:* Anglican. *Office:* Victoria and Albert Museum, London S.W.7, England.

CAREER: Victoria and Albert Museum, London, England, assistant keeper, 1958-73, deputy keeper, 1973-76, keeper of the library, 1976—. Visiting fellow at Institute for Research in the Humanities at University of Wisconsin—Madison, 1974. *Member:* Society of Antiquaries (fellow; secretary, 1979—), Royal Asiatic Society (fellow).

WRITINGS: Sandro Boticelli, Elek, 1978; *Secular French Goldsmiths' Work of the Middle Ages,* Thames & Hudson, 1978; (with M. Corbett) *The Comely Frontspiece,* Routledge & Kegan Paul, 1979; *Donatello and Michelozzo,* Harvey Miller, 1980; (editor and translator, with A. Caiger-Smith) Cipriano Piccolpasso, The Three Books of the Potter's Art, Scolar Press, 1980. Contributor to learned journals.

SIDELIGHTS: Lightbown commented: "I am a Latinist, interested in literature, art history, history, and travel, including two visits to the United States."

*   *   *

LIHN, Enrique   1929-

PERSONAL: Born September 3, 1929, in Santiago, Chile; son of Enrique and Maria (Carrasco) Lihn; married Yvette Mingram, November 10, 1957 (divorced January 14, 1960); children: Andrea. *Education:* Attended University of Chile. *Home:* Marcel Duhaut 2935, Santiago, Chile. *Agent:* Carmen Barcells, Diagonal, 580, Barcelona 21, Spain. *Office:* Department of Humanistic Studies, University of Chile, Ejercito 333, Santiago, Chile.

CAREER: Poet and novelist, 1949—; University of Chile, Santiago, professor and researcher of literature, 1973—. *Awards, honors:* Atenea Prize from Universidad de Concepcion, 1964; municipal prize for narrative, 1965, for *Agua de arroz;* Casa de las Americas prize for poetry, 1966, for "Poesia de Paso"; Pedro de Ona prize and municipal prize for poetry, both for "La musiquilla de las pobres esferas."

WRITINGS—In English translation: *The Endless Malice: Twenty-five Poems of Enrique Lihn,* translated by William Witherup and Serge Echeverria, Lillabulero, 1969; *If Poetry Is to Be Written Right,* translated by Dave Oliphant, Texas Portfolio, 1977; *The Dark Room and Other Poems,* translated by Jonathan Cohen, John Felstiner, and David Unger, New Directions, 1978.

Other writings; poems: *Poemas de este tiempo y de otro, 1949-54,* Ediciones Renovacion (Santiago), 1955; *La pieza oscura,* Editorial Universitaria (Santiago), 1963; *Poesia de paso,* Casa de las Americas (Havana), 1966; *Escrito en Cuba,* Era (Mexico), 1969; *La musiquilla de las pobres esferas,* Editorial Universitaria, 1969; *Algunos poemas,* Ocnos (Barcelona), 1972; *Por fuerza mayor,* Barral Editores (Barcelona), 1975; *Paris, situacion irregular,* Ediciones Aconcagua (Santiago), 1977. Also author of *Nada se escurre,* 1949, and *A partir de Manhattan,* 1979.

Fiction: *Agua de arroz: Cuentos,* Centro Editor (Buenos Aires), 1969; (editor and author of prologue) *Diez cuentos de bandidos,* Quimantu (Santiago), 1972; *Batman en Chile; o, El ocaso de un idolo; o, Solo contra el desierto rojo,* Ediciones de la Flor (Buenos Aires), 1973; *La orquesta de cristal* (novel), Editorial Sudamerica (Buenos Aires), 1976; *El arte de la palabra* (novel), Pomaire (Barcelona), 1980.

WORK IN PROGRESS: El senor Miserda, a novel; *El circo en llamas,* writings on Chile during the years 1973 to 1980; study of cultural survival under dictatorship and the "decay" of the New World.

SIDELIGHTS: Lihn has been a popular poet in Chile for many years and is gaining recognition in the United States as his works are translated to English. His poetry often expresses sadness about death, loss of love, and other tragedies in life. Reviewing *La musiquilla de las pobres esferas,* F. A. Butler of *Books Abroad* wrote, "This is poetry to be read with care and disquiet, for its beauty lies in its aberration." Hayden Carruth of *Nation* predicted, "Lihn's poems . . . are certain to become better known in this country before long."

BIOGRAPHICAL/CRITICAL SOURCES: Books Abroad, winter, 1971; *Nation,* December 23, 1978.

* * *

LIN, Frank
    See ATHERTON, Gertrude (Franklin Horn)

* * *

LINCOLN, Victoria   1904-1981
    (Victoria Lincoln Lowe)

OBITUARY NOTICE—See index for *CA* sketch: Born October 23, 1904, in Fall River, Mass.; died of bone cancer, May 9, 1981, in Baltimore, Md. Educator and novelist. Lincoln won the Edgar Allen Poe Award in 1967 for her book *A Private Disgrace: Lizzie Borden by Daylight.* Lincoln had grown up with Lizzie Borden in Fall River, Mass., and wrote the book in an effort to find out the truth about the Borden murders. The author also taught classes at Johns Hopkins University. Her other works include *Swan Island Murders, February Hill,* and *The Wind at My Back.* Obituaries and other sources: *Chicago Tribune,* May 16, 1981; *AB Bookman's Weekly,* July 27, 1981.

* * *

LINDLEY, Erica
    See QUIGLEY, Aileen

* * *

LINDNER, D. Berry
    See Du BREUIL, (Elizabeth) L(or)inda

* * *

LINDSAY, Frank Whiteman   1909-

PERSONAL: Born October 14, 1909, in Philadelphia, Pa.;

married, 1942; children: three. *Education:* Haverford College, B.A., 1930; Columbia University, M.A., 1932, Ph.D., 1946. *Home:* 1139 Morningside Ave., Schenectady, N.Y. 12309.

CAREER: Haverford College, Haverford, Pa., instructor in Romance languages, 1937-38; teacher at private schools, 1938-46; State University of New York Maritime College, Bronx, assistant professor of Romance languages, 1946-47; Princeton University, Princeton, N.J., instructor in French, 1947-50; Russell Sage College, Troy, N.Y., associate professor, 1950-64, professor of French, 1964-75, professor emeritus, 1975—, chairman of department, 1950-71. *Member:* American Association of Teachers of French.

WRITINGS: (Editor) Georges Simenon, *Trois nouvelles* (title means "Three Novels"), Appleton, 1966; (editor with Anthony M. Nazzaro) *Realite et fantasie: Neuf nouvelles modernes,* Xerox College Publishing, 1971; (editor with Nazzaro) Simenon, *Choix de Simenon,* Appleton, 1972. Contributor to language journals.*

* * *

LINDSEY, Hal

PERSONAL: Born in United States.

CAREER: Writer on religion.

WRITINGS: (With Carole C. Carlson) *The Late Great Planet Earth,* with study guide, Zondervan, 1970; (with Carlson) *Satan Is Alive and Well on Planet Earth,* Zondervan, 1972; *There's a New World Coming: "A Prophetic Odyssey,"* Vision House, 1973; *The Liberation of Planet Earth,* with study guide, Zondervan, 1974; *The Promise,* Harvest House, 1974; *When Is Jesus Coming Again?,* Creation House, 1974; (with Carlson) *The Terminal Generation,* Revell, 1976; *The World's Final Hour: Evacuation or Extinction?,* reprint of *Homo Sapiens,* Zondervan, 1976; *The Events That Changed My Life,* Vision House, 1977. Also author of *The 1980's: Countdown to Armageddon.**

* * *

LINK, Theodore Carl   1905(?)-1974

OBITUARY NOTICE: Born c. 1905; died of an apparent heart attack, February 14, 1974, in University City, Mo. Journalist. As a reporter for the *St. Louis Post-Dispatch,* Link investigated corruption in the Internal Revenue Bureau in 1951, writing a series of articles that won a Pulitzer Prize and led to the resignation of the Democratic Party's national chairman. He was also noted for his investigative reporting on organized crime and the Ku Klux Klan during the 1920's and 1930's. Obituaries and other sources: *New York Times,* February 15, 1974; *Time,* February 25, 1974.

* * *

LINKER, Robert White   1905-

PERSONAL: Born October 22, 1905, in Salisbury, N.C.; son of William M. and Camilla C. (Earnhardt) Linker; married Dorothy L. Insley, September 3, 1935; children: Dorothy Waddell (Mrs. Christian Sander), Thomas Polk. *Education:* University of North Carolina, A.B., 1925, A.M., 1928, Ph.D., 1933. *Religion:* Episcopalian. *Home:* 480 West Lake Dr., Athens, Ga. 30601.

CAREER: High school teacher in North Carolina, 1925-26; Gordon College, Wenham, Mass., professor of languages, 1926-27; Superior Court of Rowan County, N.C., deputy clerk and acting clerk, 1927; University of North Carolina, Chapel Hill, instructor, 1927-37, assistant professor, 1937-46, associate professor, 1946-51, professor of Romance languages, 1951-65, professor emeritus, 1965—; University of Georgia, Athens, professor of Romance philology, 1965-73, head of department of Romance languages, 1968-69. Member of faculty at Linguistic Institute, 1941, member of administrative committee, 1941-42. *Military service:* U.S. Army Air Forces, 1942-46; became major. *Member:* Mediaeval Academy of America, American Musicological Society, South Atlantic Modern Language Association (president, 1972). *Awards, honors:* Chevalier of L'Ordre des Palmes Academiques, 1965, officier, 1974.

WRITINGS: (With Urban Tigner Holmes, Jr., and John Coriden Lyons) *The Works of Guillaume de Salluste, Sieur du Bartas,* three volumes, University of North Carolina Press, 1935-40; (editor) *A Provencal Anthology,* O.H.L. Hedrick, 1940; (editor) *Aucassin et Nicolete,* University of North Carolina Press, 1948; (editor with Urban T. Holmes, Jr.) *French Secular Music of the Late Fourteenth Century,* Mediaeval Academy of America, 1950; (editor) Pierre Pathelin, *Maistre Pierre Pathelin,* Book Exchange (Chapel Hill, N.C.), 1950; (translator) Chrestien de Troyes, *The Story of the Grail,* Book Exchange, 1952, 2nd edition, 1960; *Music of the Minnesinger and Early Meistersinger: A Bibliography,* University of North Carolina Press, 1962; (editor with George Bernard Daniel) *Contes de plusieurs siecles,* Odyssey, 1964; (editor with John E. Keller) *Bidpa'i, Arabic Version: Kalilah wa-Dimnah, Spanish—El libro de Calila e Digna,* Consejo Superior de Investigaciones Cientificas, 1967; (editor with Lindsey Swanson Rogers) *Siegfried,* University Stores, 1967; (with Nathan Womack) Ambroise Pare, *Ten Books of Surgery With the Magazine of the Instruments Necessary for It,* University of Georgia Press, 1969; *Middle French Literature,* [Athens, Ga.], 1973; *A Bibliography of Old French Lyrics,* Romance Monographs, 1979.

BIOGRAPHICAL/CRITICAL SOURCES: Brian Dutton, J. Woodrow Hassell, Jr., and John E. Keller, *Medieval Studies in Honor of Robert White Linker,* Castalia, 1973.*

*   *   *

LINTNER, John (Virgil)   1916-

PERSONAL: Born February 9, 1916, in Lone Elm, Kan.; son of John Virgil and Pearl (Daily) Lintner; married Sylvia Chance, June 17, 1944 (deceased); married Eleanor J. Hodges, June 8, 1963; children: (first marriage) John Howland, Nancy Chance Lintner Molvig; (second marriage) Allan Hodges (stepson). *Education:* University of Kansas, A.B., 1939, M.A., 1940; Harvard University, M.A., 1942, Ph.D., 1946. *Home:* 50 Tyler Rd., Belmont, Mass. 02178. *Office:* Graduate School of Business Administration, Harvard University, Boston, Mass. 02163.

CAREER: University of Kansas, Lawrence, instructor in business administration, 1939-40; National Bureau of Economic Research, New York, N.Y., member of research staff on fiscal policy, 1941; Harvard University, Graduate School of Business Administration, Boston, Mass., assistant professor, 1946-51, associate professor, 1951-56, professor of business administration, 1956-64, George Gund Professor of Economics and Business Administration, 1964—. Member of board of trustees of Cambridge Savings Bank, 1950—, and board of directors of U.S. and Foreign Securities Corp. and Chase of Boston Mutual Funds (also member of board of trustees), 1975—; consultant to business and government, including U.S. Secretary of the Treasury and U.S. Bureau of the Census.

MEMBER: American Academy of Arts and Sciences (fellow), American Economic Association, American Statistical Association, American Finance Association (president, 1974), American Association for the Advancement of Science, Econometric Society (fellow), Society of Fellows of Harvard University, Phi Beta Kappa.

WRITINGS: (With John Keith Butters) *The Effects of Federal Taxes on Growing Enterprises,* Division of Research, Harvard University, 1945; *Mutual Savings Banks in the Savings and Mortgage Markets,* Division of Research, Harvard University, 1948; *Corporate Profits in Perspective,* American Enterprise, 1949; (with Butters and William Lucius Carey) *Effects of Taxation: Corporate Mergers,* Division of Research, Harvard University, 1952; *Security Market Equilibrium, Price or Risk and Size of Market: A Generalization,* Institute of Economic Research, Harvard University, 1972; *Finance and Capital Markets,* National Bureau of Economic Research, 1972. Contributor to economic and business journals. Associate editor and member of executive committee of *Review of Economics and Statistics,* 1950—; associate editor of *Journal of Finance and Economics,* 1973-79.*

*   *   *

LIPSON, Leon Samuel   1921-

PERSONAL: Born August 4, 1921, in Chelsea, Mass.; son of Max and Cecilia (Zetzel) Lipson; married Dorothy Ann Rapoport, June 28, 1949; children: James Ezra, Abigail, Michael Aaron. *Education:* Harvard University, A.B., 1941, M.A., 1943, LL.B., 1950. *Home:* 8 St. Ronan Terrace, New Haven, Conn. 06511. *Office:* School of Law, Yale University, New Haven, Conn. 06520.

CAREER: WCOP-Radio, Boston, Mass., announcer and news editor, 1943-44; Foreign Economic Administration, Washington, D.C., analyst of East European politics and economics, 1944-45; Office of the Military Government of the United States, Berlin, Germany, policy and liaison officer in Restitution Branch of Economic Division, 1946-47; admitted to the Bar of New York State and the Bar of Washington, D.C., 1951; Cleary, Gottlieb, Friendly & Ball (law firm), New York City, associate in New York City and Washington, D.C., 1950-56; Yale University, New Haven, Conn., associate professor, 1957-60, professor of law, 1960—, Townsend Professor, 1972-77, Henry R. Luce Professor of Law, 1977—, associate provost, 1965-68, fellow of Trumbull College. Fellow of Center for Advanced Study in the Behavioral Sciences, Palo Alto, Calif., 1968-69. Director of Institute on Socialist Law, 1975—; adviser to U.S. mission to the United Nations, 1959; member of board of directors of Social Science Research Council, 1970-78, member of executive committee, 1971-78, chairman of board of directors, 1974-76, chairman of executive committee, 1976-78; member of International Research and Exchanges Board, 1973-74; member of advisory board of Rand Graduate Institute, 1977—. Member of American Council of Learned Societies-Social Science Research Council joint committee on Slavic studies, 1977—; consultant to Rand Corp.

MEMBER: International Law Association (chairman of air and space law committee of American branch, 1961-65), American Bar Association (chairman of committee on Soviet law, 1957-59), American Society of International Law, American Association for the Advancement of Slavic Studies (vice-president, 1967-70), American Society of Political and Legal Philosophy. *Awards, honors:* M.A. from Yale University, 1960; Rockefeller Foundation fellow in Italy, 1978.

WRITINGS: (With Nicholas de Belleville Katzenbach) *Report to the National Aeronautics and Space Administration on the*

Law of Outer Space, American Bar Foundation, 1961; (contributor) Donald W. Treadgold, editor, *Soviet and Chinese Communism: Similarities and Differences*, University of Washington Press, 1967; (contributor) A. H. Kassof, editor, *Prospects for Soviet Society*, Praeger, 1968; (editor with Valery Chalidze) *Dokumenty sovetskogo ugolovnogo protsessa: Documents on Soviet Criminal Procedure*, Institute on Socialist Law, 1969; (editor with Chalidze) *Papers on Soviet Law*, Institute on Socialist Law, 1977; (translator with Marco Carynnyk) August Stern, *The U.S.S.R. Versus Dr. Mikhail Stern: Soviet Justice Versus Human Rights*, Urizen Books, 1978. Contributor to law journals.

SIDELIGHTS: Lipson's cassette recording of his lecture "A Lawyer's View of Soviet-American Trade" was released by Westshore in 1977.*

*   *   *

LISKA, George   1922-

PERSONAL: Born June 30, 1922, in Pardubice, Czechoslovakia; came to the United States in 1949, naturalized citizen, 1957; son of Bedrich and Karla (Slezakova) Liska; married Suzy Colombier, June 30, 1962; children: Ian Pierre, Anne Fernande. *Education:* Charles University, Dr.Jr., 1948; Harvard University, Ph.D., 1955. *Office:* School of Advanced International Studies, Johns Hopkins University, 1740 Massachusetts Ave. N.W., Washington, D.C. 20036.

CAREER: Czechoslovak Ministry of Foreign Affairs, secretary to secretary-general, 1946-48; Council for Free Czechoslovakia, Washington, D.C., executive assistant, 1949-52; University of Washington, Seattle, acting assistant professor of political science, 1956-57; Michigan State University, East Lansing, assistant professor of political science, 1957-58; University of Chicago, Chicago, Ill., assistant professor of political science, 1958-61; Johns Hopkins University, Baltimore, Md., research associate at Washington Center for Foreign Policy Research, 1960-63; Wesleyan University, Middletown, Conn., professor of political science, 1963-64; Johns Hopkins University, professor of political science, 1964—, professor at School of Advanced International Studies, Washington, D.C., 1967—, research associate at Washington Center of Foreign Policy Research, 1971—. *Member:* American Political Science Association. *Awards, honors:* Sumner prize from Harvard University, 1955.

WRITINGS—Published by Johns Hopkins University Press, except as noted: *International Equilibrium: A Theoretical Essay on the Politics and Organization of Security*, Harvard University Press, 1957; *The New Statecraft: Foreign Aid in American Foreign Policy*, University of Chicago Press, 1960; *Nations in Alliance: The Limits of Interdependence*, 1962; *The Greater Maghreb: From Independence to Unity?*, Washington Center of Foreign Policy Research, Johns Hopkins University, 1963; *Europe Ascendant: The International Politics of Unification*, 1964; *Imperial America: The International Politics of Primacy*, 1967; *Alliances and the Third World*, 1968; *War and Order: Reflections on Vietnam and History*, 1968.

(With Robert E. Osgood and others) *America and the World: From the Truman Doctrine to Vietnam*, 1970; (with Osgood and others) *Retreat From Empire? The First Nixon Administration*, 1973; *States in Evolution: Changing Societies and Traditional Systems in World Politics*, 1973; *Beyond Kissinger: Ways of Conservative Statecraft*, 1975; *Quest for Equilibrium: America and the Balance of Power on Land and Sea*, 1977; *Career of Empire: America and Imperial Expansion Over Land and Sea*, 1978; *Russia and World Order: Strategic Choices and the Laws of Power in History*, 1980.

SIDELIGHTS: In his books Liska analyzes various aspects of American foreign policy, including Henry Kissinger's promotion of American-Soviet relations in *Beyond Kissinger: Ways of Conservative Statecraft*, and U.S. imperialism in *Career of Empire: America and Imperial Expansion Over Land and Sea*.

BIOGRAPHICAL/CRITICAL SOURCES: Commentary, March, 1976; *Virginia Quarterly Review*, autumn, 1976, summer, 1978; *Choice*, March, 1978; *American Political Science Review*, September, 1978; *American Historical Review*, April, 1979.*

*   *   *

LITTLE, Bryan (Desmond Greenaway)   1913-

PERSONAL: Born February 22, 1913, in Deal, England; son of Arthur Greenaway (a Royal Marines officer) and Phyllis Dorothy (Beloe) Little; married Margaret Maud Stratford, July 3, 1965. *Education:* Jesus College, Cambridge, B.A. (with first class honors), 1935, M.A., 1948. *Religion:* Roman Catholic. *Home:* 3 Burlington Rd., Bristol 6, England.

CAREER: British Admiralty, London and Bath, England, civil servant (administrative grade), 1936-46; University of Bristol, Bristol, England, part-time tutor in extra-mural department, 1950—. *Member:* West Country Writers Association (chairman, 1978-80), Bristol Civic Society (chairman, 1969-72), Bristol and Gloucestershire Archaeological Society (president, 1979-80).

WRITINGS: The Building of Bath, Collins, 1947; *Cheltenham*, Batsford, 1952; *The Three Choirs Cities*, Batsford, 1952; *Exeter*, Batsford, 1953; *The City and County of Bristol*, Laurie, 1954; *The Life and Work of James Gibbs*, Batsford, 1955; *Portrait of Cambridge*, Batsford, 1955; *The Monmouth Episode*, Laurie, 1956; *Crusoe's Captain*, Odhams, 1960; *Cambridge Discovered*, Heffer, 1960; *Bath Portrait*, Burleigh, 1961; *English Historic Architecture*, Batsford, 1964; *Catholic Churches Since 1623*, R. Hale, 1964.

Cheltenham in Pictures, David & Charles, 1967; *Portrait of Somerset*, R. Hale, 1969, 4th edition, 1976; *Birmingham Buildings*, David & Charles, 1971; *English Cathedrals*, Batsford, 1972; *The Colleges of Cambridge*, Arco, 1973; *St. Ives in Huntingdonshire*, Adams & Dart, 1974; *Sir Christopher Wren*, R. Hale, 1975; *Abbeys and Priories in England and Wales*, Batsford, 1979; (with Michael Jeaner and Andor Gomme) *Bristol: An Architectural History*, Lund, Humphries, 1979.

Contributor to magazines and newspapers in England and the United States, including *Virginia Historical Magazine, William and Mary Quarterly, Contemporary Review*, and *Country Life*.

WORK IN PROGRESS: A book on public buildings and statues in Bristol, publication by Redcliffe expected in 1981; a book about Exeter, publication by R. Hale expected in 1982; research on Highgrove and Jetbury.

SIDELIGHTS: Little wrote: "I am essentially a factual writer, with the scholastic background of a Cambridge classical scholar. Careful research and accuracy are most important to me, though good style and readability are also essential. As much research and inquiry go into small works (articles and booklets on houses and churches) as the full-scale books."

*   *   *

LITTLEWIT, Humphrey, Gent.
   See LOVECRAFT, H(oward) P(hillips)

LITWOS
See SIENKIEWICZ, Henryk (Adam Aleksander Pius)

*   *   *

LIVERANI, Mary Rose   1939-

PERSONAL: Born March 9, 1939, in Glasgow, Scotland; daughter of Robert (a ship rigger and miner) and Rose (Bygroves) Lavery; children: Alessandra and Petra (twins). *Education:* Attended University of Sydney, 1957-59; University of New South Wales, B.A., 1968. *Office:* 72 Dumfries Ave., Mount Ousley, Wollongong, New South Wales 2519, Australia.

CAREER: Daily Telegraph, Sydney, Australia, cadet journalist, 1959; teacher of English and history at school in Wollongong, Australia, 1960-68; teacher of English to migrant children in Australia, 1969-70, and in Florence, Italy, 1971; Australian Census Bureau, graduate clerk, 1972; writer, 1973; Wollongong Public Library, Wollongong, librarian assistant, 1974-75; Institute of Advanced Education, Wollongong, library officer, 1975-76, technical services librarian, 1976-80; Wollongong City Library, Wollongong, Commonwealth film censor, 1980—. *Member:* Australian Society of Authors, Library Association of New South Wales. *Awards, honors:* Commonwealth Literary fellowship, from Australian Literature Board, 1973; Barbara Ramsden Award from Fellowship of Australian Writers, 1975; braille book of the year award, from Braille and Talking Book Society, 1977, for *The Winter Sparrows.*

WRITINGS: The Winter Sparrows (nonfiction), Thomas Nelson, 1975. Contributor of articles and reviews to magazines, including *Overland.*

WORK IN PROGRESS: Another nonfiction book (see comments in *SIDELIGHTS*).

SIDELIGHTS: Mary Rose Liverani told *CA:* "I wrote *The Winter Sparrows* after some lengthy nagging from my English lecturer at university. It did quite well because it was freakish, at least in the Australian environment, being a confession of a person who was the unlikely combination of migrant, working class, and female. There is very little migrant literature in Australia. There is even less working class material and less again from women.

"Having completed this opus I felt obliged, pressured rather, into starting something else which I undertook with even less enthusiasm than the first book, and that sorry story, a comparison of teaching in a posh private school with teaching in a rundown school for migrant kids, didn't come off. The publisher told me that with some revisions the book could be turned into a readable novel, but did I want merely to be the author of a readable novel?

"I felt I ought *not* want that, so I started again on something in which I did have some interest and with which I am still wrestling: the story of two Italian engineers who came to Australia as flag carriers for an Italian multinational firm, and who broke away from the parent company to form their own, ending up with millions of dollars. What interested me was the problems the men had in getting capital from an anti-wog capital market, withstanding below-the-belt attacks from Australian competitors, fighting off the labor unions, and creating a fairly singular management style which I thought had something to teach Anglo-Saxons. I spent a year researching the book, and it isn't going very well. What holds me back, in addition, is the feeling of being swamped by all the other books that are already around. I wish there could be an international moratorium on print for ten years so that I could make some headway in my reading.

"I suppose the thing I'm most concerned about in daily life and in my writing is surviving the Great Australian Niceness, which is a kind of spiritual blight that overlies the land. It forces people to hide their feelings, to abort their thoughts so that all anyone has to deal with are inanities and a fixed smile or a state of permanent sulks if one tries to engage in any kind of intellectual intimacy. Europeans usually resign themselves to Australian 'coldness.' I can't, so I live in a state of war with most of them. I scorn them for being 'nice.' They deplore the fact that I'm not 'nice.' We have lived together for thirty years and are more strange to each other than ever."

*   *   *

LLEO, Manuel Urrutia
See URRUTIA LLEO, Manuel

*   *   *

LLEWELLYN, Edward
See LLEWELLYN-THOMAS, Edward

*   *   *

LLEWELLYN-THOMAS, Edward   1917-
(Edward Llewellyn)

PERSONAL: Born December 15, 1917, in Salisbury, England; married Ellen Wise; children: Caroline, Roland, Edward. *Education:* University of London, B.S.; McGill University, M.D., C.M. *Home:* 67 Balliol St., Toronto, Ontario, Canada M4S 1C2. *Office:* Faculty of Medicine, University of Toronto, Toronto, Ontario, Canada.

CAREER: Ocean Steamship Co., Liverpool, England, radio officer, 1935-38; British Broadcasting Corp. (BBC), London, England, junior engineer, 1938-39; Controller Telecoms, Malaya, controller, 1945-51; private practice of medicine in Nova Scotia, 1956-58; Defence Research Medical Labs, Toronto, Ontario, scientist, 1958-61; University of Toronto, Toronto, professor and associate dean, 1961—. *Military service:* Royal Navy, Tenth Cruiser Squadron, 1939-40; radio officer, British Army, 1940-45; became captain. *Member:* Royal Society of Canada (fellow), Science Fiction Writers of America, Royal Society of Arts (fellow), Institution of Electrical Engineers (fellow). *Awards, honors:* Medal from Association of Professional Engineers.

WRITINGS—Under name Edward Llewellyn: *The Douglas Convolution* (science fiction novel), DAW Books, 1979; *The Bright Companion* (science fiction novel), DAW Books, 1980. Author of over seventy scientific papers.

WORK IN PROGRESS: Prelude to Chaos, a science fiction novel.

*   *   *

LOEB, William   1905-1981

OBITUARY NOTICE—See index for *CA* sketch: Born December 26, 1905, in Washington, D.C.; died of cancer, September 13, 1981, in Burlington, Mass. Publisher, journalist, and writer best known for his opinionated editorials on politics and politicians. As publisher of the *Manchester Union Leader,* the only statewide newspaper in New Hampshire, Loeb strongly influenced public opinion. Particularly powerful during presidential election years because of New Hampshire's role as the first state in the nation to hold its primary, Loeb is generally held responsible for derailing Senator Edmund S. Muskie's 1972 bid for the chief executive's office. Loeb called the senator "Moscow Muskie" in one of his editorials and in a later column criticized the politician's wife. Muskie's tearful rebuttal of the publisher's contentions severely damaged his presidential campaign. Loeb began his career working as a reporter on a number of newspapers, including the *Springfield Republican* and the *New York World*. In 1941 he acquired his first newspaper, the *St. Albans Daily Messenger,* and five years later became the publisher of the *Manchester Union Leader*. A promoter of profit-sharing, Loeb served as the chairman of the Council of Profit-Sharing Industries. Obituaries and other sources: Kevin Cash, *Who the Hell is William Loeb?*, Amoskeag Press, 1975; *New York Times*, September 14, 1981; *Chicago Tribune*, September 14, 1981; *Newsweek*, September 28, 1981; *Time*, September 28, 1981.

* * *

LOEWY, Raymond Fernand   1893-

PERSONAL: Born November 5, 1893, in Paris, France; came to the United States in 1919; naturalized U.S. citizen in 1938; son of Maximilian (a journalist) and Marie (Labalme) Loewy; married Jean Tomson, 1931 (divorced, 1945); married Viola Erickson (a public relations director), December 22, 1948; children: (second marriage) Laurence. *Education:* Attended University of Paris; received degree from Ecole de Lanneau, 1918. *Religion:* Catholic. *Home:* 600 Panorama Rd., Palm Springs, Calif.; and Manoir de la Cense, Rochefort-en-Yvelines 78, France; and 20 rue Boissiere, Paris 16 France; and 16 avenue Montaigne, Paris, France. *Agent:* Barthold Fles Literary Agency, 507 Fifth Ave., New York, N.Y. 10017. *Offices:* 25 Burton St., Berkeley Sq., London, England; 39 avenue d'Iena, Paris 16, France; and 91 rue de Lausanne, Fribourg, Switzerland.

CAREER: Free-lance fashion illustrator for magazines, including *Vogue* and *Harper's Bazaar,* beginning in 1919; free-lance window designer for stores in New York City, including Saks Fifth Avenue and Macy's; Westinghouse Electric Co., New York City, art director, 1929; Raymond Loewy International (formerly Raymond Loewy Associates, then Raymond Loewy, William Snaith, Inc., [New York City]), founder, chairman, and chief executive officer, 1929—. Compagnie de l'Esthetique Industrielle, Paris, France, founder, 1952—. Consultant to over two hundred corporations, including Hupp Motor Co., Coca-Cola, United Airlines, Shell International, IBM, and Exxon, 1929—; consultant to National Aeronautics and Space Administration (NASA) on Apollo application program, and on *Saturn I, Saturn V,* and *Skylab* habitability study, 1967-73. Lecturer at colleges and universities, including Harvard Graduate School of Business Administration, Massachusetts Institute of Technology, Columbia University, University of Leningrad. Chairman of the board of Market Concepts; member of the executive board of Art Center College, Los Angeles, Calif.; member of the President's Committee on Employment of the Handicapped, 1965; member of the advisory committee of Industrial Designers College of Architecture, University of California, Los Angeles; member of New York City Board of Education advisory board of vocational education. *Military service:* French Army, American Expeditionary Force, 1914-1918, Fifth Army Corp of Engineers, 1917-1918; became captain; decorated commander of French Legion of Honor; received four Croix de Guerre citations and Interallied Medal.

MEMBER: American Society of Industrial Designers (founder; fellow; president, 1946), American Society of Mechanical Engineers, American Society of Interior Designers (fellow), American Academy of Achievement (fellow), American Society of Space Medicine, British Royal Society of Arts (fellow), French Chamber of Commerce of the United States (vice-president), Society of Automotive Engineers, Society of Naval Architects and Marine Engineers, Racquet and Tennis Club (Palm Springs, Calif.), New York Athletic Club.

AWARDS, HONORS: J. Gordon Bennett Medal, 1906, for model airplane design; elected Royal Designer to Industry by British Royal Society of Arts, 1937; gold medal in transportation from the Paris Fair, 1937, for the GG-1 electric locomotive design; first prize from Paris International Exposition, 1937, and American Design Award from Lord & Taylor, 1938, both for Coldspot refrigerator design; first prize in All-American Package Competition from Paris International Exposition, 1939; Branger Cup for speedboat design; D.F.A. from University of Cincinnati, 1956, Art Center College, and U.S. Academy of Achievement; named citizen of honor of New York City, Palm Springs, Calif., and Rochefort-en-Yveslines, France; named citizen of France by decree of the prime minister; named "One of the Thousand Makers of the Twentieth Century" by *London Sunday Times* 1969; included in "The One Hundred Events That Shaped America," *Life* (bicentennial issue), 1976; elected to hall of fame of American Academy of Achievement; Distinguished Achievement Award from American Society of Industrial Designers, 1978.

WRITINGS: The Locomotive, Its Aesthetics, Studio Publications, 1937; *Never Leave Well Enough Alone* (autobiography), Simon & Schuster, 1951; *Industrial Design,* Overlook Press, 1979.

SIDELIGHTS; Raymond Loewy began his career in industrial design in 1929 when Sigmund Gestetner, a British manufacturer of duplicating machines, commissioned him to improve the appearance of a mimeograph machine, In three days Loewy designed the shell that was to encase Gestetner duplicators for the next forty years, and in the process he helped launch a profession that has changed the look of America.

The Gestetner duplicator was the first of countless items transformed by a technique that Loewy is credited with originating: streamlining. Calling the concept "beauty through function and simplification," Loewy has streamlined everything from postage stamps to spacecrafts for over fifty years. His more famous creations include the Lucky Strike cigarette package, the GG-1 welded locomotive, the Studebaker Avanti, Champion, and Starliner, the Coca-Cola bottle, the John F. Kennedy memorial postage stamp, the interior of *Saturn I, Saturn V,* and *Skylab,* the Greyhound bus and logo, the Shell International logo, the Exxon logo, the U.S. Postal Service emblem, and a line of Frigidaire refrigerators, ranges, and freezers. Raymond Loewy introduced slanted windshields, built-in headlights, and wheel covers for automobiles, and rustproof aluminum shelves for refrigerators. By 1951 his industrial design firm was so prolific that he was able to claim that "the average person, leading a normal life, whether in the country, a village, a city, or a metropolis, is bound to be in daily contact with some of the things, services, or structures in which R.L.A. [Raymond Loewy Associates] was a party during the design or planning stage." In a *New York Times Magazine* article, reporter Susan Heller commented, "One can hardly open a beer or a soft drink, fix breakfast, board a plane, buy gas, mail a letter or shop for an appliance without encountering a Loewy creation."

While Loewy established his reputation as a designer, he boosted his profession by showing the practical benefits to be derived from the application of functional styling. In his book *Industrial Design,* Loewy notes, "Success finally came when we were able to convince some creative men that good appearance was a salable commodity, that it often cut costs, enhanced a product's prestige, raised corporate profits, benefited the customer, and increased employment.''

One of Loewy's first major successes, a Coldspot refrigerator he designed for Sears, Roebuck & Company in 1934, served as a testimonial to creative packaging. Loewy's streamlined Coldspot, with its rustproof aluminum shelves, sent Sears refrigerator sales from 60,000 units to 275,000 units in just two years. Another Loewy design, the GG-1 electric locomotive built by the Pennsylvania Railroad in 1936, demonstrated on an even larger scale the efficacy of industrial design. The welded shell of the GG-1 eliminated tens of thousands of rivets, resulting in improved appearance, simplified maintenance, and reduced manufacturing costs. The first welded locomotive ever built, the GG-1 led to the universal adoption of the welding technique in the construction of locomotives.

In 1930 Loewy became a consultant to the Hupp Motor Company. He calls the Hupp contract ''the beginning of industrial design as a legitimate profession,'' explaining that it was ''the first time a large corporation accepted the idea of getting outside advice in the development of their products.'' The Hupp contract also marked the beginning of Loewy's long and often frustrating association with American automobile manufacturers. ''He waged a long war against the worst extravagances of Detroit styling,'' commented Edward Lucie-Smith in the *Times Literary Supplement*. ''He could take a production-line monster and make it an infinitely better-looking 'special,' with comparatively minor rebuilding. What he could not do was to alter the industry's fundamental attitudes. Gas-guzzlers remained gas-guzzlers, and no fancy-pants designer was going to be allowed to change that.''

Loewy advocated lower, leaner, and more fuel efficient automobiles long before fuel economy became a concern among car buyers. He once admitted, ''I alienated the automotive industry by saying that cars should be lightweight and compact,'' adding, ''I'd also kill chrome forever, or any other applied junk.'' In 1961 while designing the Avanti, Loewy posted a sign saying ''Weight is the enemy.'' The Avanti design eliminated the grill, and Loewy still argues, ''In this age of fuel shortages you must eliminate weight. Who needs grills? Grills I always associate with sewers.''

In spite of the differences that Loewy has had with Detroit stylists, several of his designs are now considered automobile classics, including the 1953 Studebaker Starliner and the 1963 Avanti. Reporting the results of a 1972 poll of stylists representing the Big Four automakers, *Automotive News* announced, ''The 1953 Studebaker, a long-nosed coupe, with little trim and an air of motion about it, was acclaimed the top car of all time.''

In addition to his achievements in the transportation field, Raymond Loewy is, according to Lucie-Smith, ''a great inventor of memorable images (perhaps the world's most skillful creator of company logos and commercial packaging).'' He began designing packaging and logos in 1940 when George Washington Hill, then president of the American Tobacco Company, wagered him fifty thousand dollars that he could not improve the appearance of the already familiar green and red Lucky Strike cigarette package. Accepting the challenge, Loewy began by changing the package background from green to white, thereby reducing printing costs by eliminating the need for green dye. Next he placed the red Lucky Strike target on both sides of the package, increasing product visibility and ultimately product sales. A satisfied Hill paid off the bet, and for over forty years the Lucky Strike pack has remained unchanged.

In designing logos, ''I'm looking for a very high index of visual retention,'' Loewy explains. ''We want anyone who has seen the logotype even fleetingly to never forget it.'' Among Loewy's highly visible logotype designs are the Shell Oil Company pecten, the Exxon double ''*x*'', the Greyhound silhouette, and the Nabisco logo of the National Biscuit Company.

Loewy has also left his mark on the area of store design. One of his early innovations, the first fully climate-controlled, windowless department store, was so well received that the Loewy organization formed a separate division, under the leadership of Loewy's partner, William Snaith, devoted entirely to store design. The company's clients included Saks Fifth Avenue, J. L. Hudson, Macy's, J.C. Penney, Bloomingdale's, and Lord & Taylor.

By the 1970's Loewy's New York office engaged almost exclusively in store design. As a result, Loewy decided to sell the American company and to transfer the base of his design activities to Europe, because, as he said, store design ''has never been my particular field.'' Retaining the name Raymond Loewy International, he started a new firm in Friebourg, Switzerland, and he accelerated existing operations in London and Paris. Finding the continent fertile ground for his interests, Loewy told Susan Heller that ''industrial design in Europe is where it was in the United States 25 years ago.'' His Compagnie de l'Esthetique Industrielle is now the largest firm of its kind in Europe.

In 1975 the Smithsonian Institution mounted a four-month exposition: ''The Designs of Raymond Loewy.'' ''While working closely with the Smithsonian,'' Loewy comments, ''I was provided with the opportunity to reassess the past,'' and he cites his work for the National Aeronautics and Space Administration (NASA) as his most important and gratifying assignment. From 1967 to 1973 Loewy was retained by NASA as a habitability consultant for the Saturn-Apollo and Skylab projects, ''to help insure the psycho-physiological safety and comfort of the astronauts'' under the ''exotic conditions of zero-gravity.'' His innovations, including simulating conditions of gravity and a porthole for vision contact with earth, made it possible for three men to inhabit a space capsule for three months. George Mueller, NASA's deputy administrator for manned space flight, wrote in a letter of appreciation: ''I do not believe that it would have been possible for the Skylab crews to have lived in relative comfort, excellent spirits, and outstanding efficiency had it not been for your creative design, based on a deep understanding of human needs.''

A *New York Times Book Review* critic once commented that ''Mr. Loewy has indeed changed the shape of the modern world.'' Yet it is possible that Loewy's work for NASA has extended his range of influence even further. In Mueller's estimation, Raymond Loewy ''has provided the foundation for man's next great step—an expedition to the planets.''

AVOCATIONAL INTERESTS: Deep-sea diving, race car driving.

BIOGRAPHICAL/CRITICAL SOURCES: Life, May 2, 1949; *Time,* October 31, 1949; Raymond Loewy, *Never Leave Well Enough Alone,* Simon & Schuster, 1951; *Commonweal,* April 13, 1951; Annie E. S. Beard, *Our Foreign-Born Citizens,* Cromwell, 1968; Raymond Loewy, *Industrial Design,* Overlook Press, 1979; *New York Times Magazine,* November 4, 1979; *Publishers Weekly,* November 12, 1979; *Saturday Review,* December, 1979; *New York Times Book Review,* December 2, 1979; *Times Literary Supplement,* February 8, 1980.

—*Sketch by Lillian S. Sims*

LOMBARD, Nap
See JOHNSON, Pamela Hansford

* * *

LONG, Lois 1901-1974

OBITUARY NOTICE: Born December 5, 1901, in Stamford, Conn.; died July 29, 1974, in Saratoga, N.Y. Journalist and editor. Long began her journalism career as a copywriter with *Vogue* magazine in 1922, moving to *Vanity Fair* as a drama critic in 1924. She joined the *New Yorker* in 1925 as "Lipstick," the nightclub columnist. After two years with the magazine she became fashion editor, a position she held for over four decades. Her column "On and Off the Avenue," helped to establish the field of fashion writing and criticism. Although Long retired in 1970, she remained a fashion consultant to the *New Yorker* until her death. Obituaries and other sources: *Who's Who of American Women,* 8th edition, Marquis, 1973; *New York Times,* July 31, 1974; *New Yorker,* August 12, 1974; *Time,* August 12, 1974.

* * *

LONG, Luman Harrison 1907-1971

OBITUARY NOTICE: Born January 20, 1907; died September 12, 1971, in Summit, N.J. Journalist and editor. A newspaper reporter and editor for many years, Long was best known as the editor of the *World Almanac.* Obituaries and other sources: *New York Times,* September 13, 1971; *Who Was Who in America, With World Notables,* Volume V: *1969-1973,* Marquis, 1973.

* * *

LONSDALE, Gordon Arnold 1923(?)-1970
(Konan Trofimovich Molody)

OBITUARY NOTICE: Born c. 1923; died of a heart attack, October 9, 1970, in a suburb of Moscow, U.S.S.R. Spy and author. Lonsdale was the central figure in a celebrated spy case in the early 1960's. He was arrested in London in 1961 and charged with passing naval secrets, including details of Britain's first nuclear submarine, to the Soviet Union. Lonsdale claimed to be a Canadian businessman and possessed a genuine Canadian passport, but some Western security experts believe he was a Soviet submarine officer and that the real Lonsdale died sometime before 1954. Lonsdale's real name was believed to be Konan Trofimovich Molody. Lonsdale served three years in prison and was exchanged in 1964 for a British businessman arrested by the Soviets. In 1965 Lonsdale wrote a book about his activities, *Spy,* in which he claimed to have been a communications aide to Colonel Rudolf Abel, a Soviet spy in the United States in the early 1950's. Obituaries and other sources: *New York Times,* October 14, 1970; Ronald Seth, *The Encyclopedia of Espionage,* New English Library, 1972.

* * *

LOONEY, Robert E(dward) 1941-

PERSONAL: Born June 16, 1941, in San Jose, Calif.; married in 1965; children: one. *Education:* University of California, Davis, B.S., 1963, Ph.D., 1969. *Office:* Department of Business Economics, University of Santa Clara, Santa Clara, Calif. 95053.

CAREER: Stanford Research Institute, Menlo Park, Calif., development economist, 1969-71; Louis Berger, Inc., East Orange, N.J., regional economist, 1971-72; University of Santa Clara, Santa Clara, Calif., assistant professor of economics, 1972—. *Member:* American Economic Association, Society for International Development, Royal Economic Society, Econometric Society.

WRITINGS: The Economic Development of Iran: A Recent Survey With Projections to 1981, Praeger, 1973; *Income Distribution Policies and Economic Growth in Semi-Industrialized Countries: A Comparative Study of Iran, Mexico, Brazil, and South Korea,* Praeger, 1975; *The Economic Development of Panama: The Impact of World Inflation on an Open Economy,* Praeger, 1976; *A Development Strategy for Iran Through the 1980's,* Praeger, 1977; *Iran at the End of the Century: A Hegelian Forecast,* Lexington Books, 1977; *Mexico's Economy: A Policy Analysis With Forecasts to 1990,* Westview Press, 1978; *The Economic Consequences of World Inflation on Semi-Dependent Countries,* University Press of America, 1978. Contributor to business and economic journals.

BIOGRAPHICAL/CRITICAL SOURCES: Journal of Economic Literature, December, 1976; *International Labor Review,* March, 1977, May, 1979.*

* * *

LOOS, Anita 1893-1981

OBITUARY NOTICE—See index for *CA* sketch: Born April 26, 1893, in Sissons (now Mt. Shasta), Calif.; died of a heart attack, August 18, 1981, in New York, N.Y. Playwright, screenwriter, and novelist best known for her lighthearted satire of love and sex, *Gentlemen Prefer Blondes.* A spoof of a romance between intellectual H. L. Mencken and a gold-digging blond, *Gentlemen Prefer Blondes* was later adapted into a play, two motion pictures, and two musical comedies. Although the novel firmly established Loos's reputation, she once commented, "I had no thought of its ever being printed. My only purpose was to make Henry Mencken laugh—which it did." Loos began publishing her work at the age of thirteen and in 1912 wrote her first movie scenario for D. W. Griffith. She created the art of writing silent film captions, and when talking pictures arrived, she wrote more than two hundred screenplays for films, including "The Whole Town's Talking," "The Women," and "San Francisco." Loos also wrote several plays, among which are "Happy Birthday," "Gigi," and "Cheri." Loos chronicled her life in her autobiographies *Twice Over Lightly: New York Then and Now, Kiss Hollywood Goodby,* and *The Talmadge Girls.* Obituaries and other sources: *New York Times,* August 19, 1981; *Chicago Tribune,* August 20, 1981; *Detroit News,* August 30, 1981; *Newsweek,* August 31, 1981; *Time,* August 31, 1981; *Publishers Weekly,* September 4, 1981; *AB Bookman's Weekly,* September 14, 1981.

* * *

LOPATA, Helena Znaniecka 1925-

PERSONAL: Born October 1, 1925, in Poznan, Poland; came to the United States in 1940, naturalized citizen, 1946; daughter of Florian Witold and Eileen (Markley) Znaniecki; married Richard Stefan Lopata, February 8, 1946; children: Theodora Karen Lopata Horvath, Stefan Richard. *Education:* University of Illinois, B.A., 1946, M.A., 1947; University of Chicago, Ph.D., 1965. *Home:* 1017 Grove, Evanston, Ill. 60201. *Office:* Department of Sociology, Loyola University, 6525 North Sheridan Rd., Chicago, Ill. 60626.

CAREER: University of Virginia, Langley Air Force Base Extension, lecturer in social psychology, 1951-52; DePaul University, Chicago, Ill., lecturer in sociology, 1956-60; Roosevelt University, Chicago, lecturer, 1960-64, assistant professor, 1964-67, associate professor of sociology, 1967-69; Loyola University, Chicago, professor of sociology, 1969—, chairman of department, 1970-72, director of Center for Comparative Study of Social Roles, 1972—. Member of advisory board of St. Leonard's Home, 1966-68; member of executive board of Cana Conference, 1971-75; delegate to World Congress on Gerontology, Kiev, Soviet Union, 1972; member of local mayor's council on manpower and economic development, 1974—, and council for senior citizens and the handicapped, 1975—; member of National Commission on Families and Public Policies, 1977—; member of National Institute of Mental Health Review Board, 1977-79; member of advisory council of National Institute on Aging, 1978—.

MEMBER: International Gerontological Association, International Sociological Society, Polish Academy of Arts and Sciences in America (member of Midwest board of directors, 1965-70, and national board of directors, 1978—), American Sociological Association (fellow; member of council, 1978—; chairman of section on sex roles, 1975, and section on the family, 1976), National Council on Family Relations, Society for the Study of Social Problems (fellow; chairman of special problems committee, 1971; vice-president, 1975; member of council, 1978—), Gerontological Society, Polish Academy, Sociologists for Women in Society, Midwest Sociological Association (member of state board of directors, 1972-74; president, 1975-76), Midwest Council for Social Research on Aging (president, 1969-70; postdoctoral training director, 1971-77), Illinois Sociological Association (president, 1969-70). *Awards, honors:* Grants from *Chicago Tribune*, 1956, Administration on Aging, 1967-69, Social Security Administration, 1971-76, 1975-79; fellow of Midwest Council for Social Research on Aging, 1964-65.

WRITINGS: Occupation: Housewife, Oxford University Press, 1971; (contributor) *Aging and Modernization*, Appleton, 1972; (editor) *Marriage and Families*, Van Nostrand, 1973; *Widowhood in an American City*, Schenkman, 1973; *Polish Americans: Status Competition in an Ethnic Community*, Prentice-Hall, 1976; (editor) *Family Factbook*, Marquis Academic Media, 1978; *Women as Widows: Support Systems*, Elsevier-North Holland, 1979; (editor) *Research in the Interweave of Social Roles*, Volume I: *Women and Men*, Jai Press, 1980. Contributor to sociology journals. Review editor of *Sociological Quarterly*, 1969-72; associate editor of *Midwest Sociological Society Quarterly*, 1969-72; member of editorial board of *International Journal of Sociology and the Family*, 1970—.

BIOGRAPHICAL/CRITICAL SOURCES: Choice, October, 1976; *American Journal of Sociology*, July, 1977; *Contemporary Sociology*, July, 1979.*

*   *   *

LOPEZ, Claude-Anne   1920-

PERSONAL: Born October 17, 1920, in Brussels, Belgium; daughter of Sadi and Marguerite (Goldzieher) Kirschen; married Robert S. Lopez (a professor), August 27, 1946; children: Michael, Larry. *Education:* University of Brussels, M.A. (classics), 1940; University of Aix-Marseille, certificate, 1941; Columbia University, M.Phil., 1944. *Home:* 41 Richmond Ave., New Haven, Conn. 06515. *Office:* "Papers of Benjamin Franklin," Yale University, New Haven, Conn. 06520.

CAREER: Office of War Information, New York, N.Y., news editor, 1943-45; Yale University, New Haven, Conn., resident

assistant in classics for department of Near Eastern studies, 1950-53, assistant editor of "Papers of Benjamin Franklin," 1954—, Timothy Dwight College Fellow, 1968—, lecturer in history, 1972, research associate in history. *Member:* American Society for Eighteenth-Century Studies. *Awards, honors:* Rockefeller Serbelloni fellow, 1972; Guggenheim fellow, 1974; Luther Moss Award in Journalism, award from Colonial Dames of America, and book award from Boston Globe, all 1975, all for *The Private Franklin;* Knight of Royal Order of the Crown (Belgium), 1976.

WRITINGS: Mon Cher Papa: Franklin and the Ladies of Paris, Yale University Press, 1966; (with E. Herbert) *The Private Franklin: The Man and His Family*, Norton, 1975. Contributor to journals.

WORK IN PROGRESS: William Temple Franklin; Women in France.

*   *   *

Lo PINTO, Maria   1900(?)-1970

OBITUARY NOTICE: Born c. 1900 in New York, N.Y.; died June 12, 1970, in Kingston, N.Y. Attorney and author. Lo Pinto was the author of a number of cookbooks, for which she received the Amita Award in 1958. Her best-known book was *The Art of Italian Cooking*. Obituaries and other sources: *AB Bookman's Weekly*, July 20, 1970.

*   *   *

LORA, Josephine
See ALEXANDER, Josephine

*   *   *

LORCA, Federico Garcia
See GARCIA LORCA, Federico

*   *   *

LORD, Eda   1907-1976

OBITUARY NOTICE: Born in 1907 in Mexico; died October 23, 1976, in London, England. Author. Lord was raised in the United States but lived in Europe for most of her life. She was the author of several short stories and three novels, *Childsplay, A Matter of Choosing,* and *Extenuating Circumstances*. Obituaries and other sources: *New York Times*, October 26, 1976; *Publishers Weekly*, November 1, 1976.

*   *   *

LORD ALTRINCHAM
See GRIGG, John (Edward Poynder)

*   *   *

LORD DUNSANY
See DUNSANY, Edward John Moreton Drax Plunkett

*   *   *

LOUSLEY, J(ob) E(dward)   1907-1976

OBITUARY NOTICE: Born in 1907; died January 6, 1976, in England. Bank employee and author. Lousley wrote several books on botany, his lifelong hobby, including *Wild Flowers of Chalk and Limestone* and *Flora of the Isles of Scilly*. Obituaries and other sources: *AB Bookman's Weekly*, February 9, 1976.

* * *

LOVECRAFT, H(oward) P(hillips)   1890-1937
(Lawrence Appleton, Houdini, John J. Jones, Humphrey Littlewit, Gent., Henry Paget-Lowe, Ward Phillips, Richard Raleigh, Ames Dorrance Rowley, Edgar Softly, Edward Softly, Augustus Swift, Lewis Theobald, Jr., Frederick Willie, Zoilus)

BRIEF ENTRY: Born August 20, 1890, in Providence, R.I.; died of cancer and Bright's disease, March 15, 1937. American short story writer, novelist, poet, critic, and essayist. Noted for his work in the genre of supernatural fantasy, Lovecraft was considered a master of the Gothic tale of terror and a pioneer in science fiction. Written under various pseudonyms, Lovecraft's fiction was first published in pulp magazines and nonprofessional journals, such as *Weird Tales* and *Amazing Stories*. By the late 1920's his work was being reprinted in anthologies of horror stories, and two of his stories received honorable mentions in the O'Brien collections. It was not until the 1940's, however, that his work received major attention. His stories of Cthulhu Mythos, concerned with cosmic legend and the dislocation of space and time, have been the subject of renewed interest in the last decade since science fiction has come into vogue. A theorist as well as a fantasist, Lovecraft established a literary aesthetic for the genre of supernatural and fantasy literature in his critical survey *Supernatural Horror in Literature*. His writings include *The Shadow Over Innsmouth* (1936), *The Outsider and Others* (1939), *Beyond the Wall of Sleep* (1943), *Supernatural Horror in Literature* (1945), *Something About Cats and Other Pieces* (1949), and *The Horror in the Museum and Other Revisions* (1975). *Biographical/critical sources: Twentieth Century Authors: A Biographical Dictionary of Modern Literature*, H. W. Wilson, 1955; *Readers Encyclopedia of American Literature*, Crowell, 1962; Lin Carter, *Lovecraft: A Look Behind the "Cthulhu Mythos,"* Ballantine, 1972; L. Sprague de Camp, *Lovecraft: A Biography*, Doubleday, 1975; Barton Levi St. Armand, *The Roots of Horror in the Fiction of H. P. Lovecraft*, Dragon Press, 1977; *Twentieth-Century Literary Criticism*, Volume 4, Gale, 1981.

* * *

LOVELACE, Maud Hart   1892-1980

OBITUARY NOTICE—See index for *CA* sketch: Born April 25, 1892, in Mankato, Minn.; died March 11, 1980. Author. Known for her "Betsy-Tacy" series for children, Lovelace relied on her personal journals of her childhood to write the books. In 1961 Lovelace's hometown sponsored a Betsy-Tacy Day. Titles in the Betsy-Tacy series include *Betsy-Tacy, Betsy Was a Junior, Betsy and Joe,* and *Betsy's Wedding. Over the Big Hill* and *The Valentine Box* are among her other works of juvenile fiction, and *Black Angels* and *Gentlemen From England* are two of the adult novels Lovelace wrote with her husband. Obituaries and other sources: *Horn Book,* June, 1980.

* * *

LOVERING, Joseph Paul   1921-

PERSONAL: Born February 16, 1921, in Calais, Maine; son of Joseph J. and Gertrude (McVay) Lovering; married Eileen Quinn; children: Joseph, Eileen, Michael, David, Mary, Peter. *Education:* College of the Holy Cross, A.B., 1943; Boston

University, M.A., 1948; Ottawa University, Ph.D., 1956. *Home:* 254 Dexter Ter., Tonawanda, N.Y. 14150. *Office:* 2001 Main St., Buffalo, N.Y. 14208.

CAREER: St. Michael's College, Winooski, Vt., assistant professor of English, 1947-55; Canisius College, Buffalo, N.Y., associate professor, 1956-66, professor of English, 1967—. Violinist with Orchard Park, N.Y., Symphony Orchestra.

WRITINGS: Silas W. Mitchell, Twayne, 1971; *Gerald W. Brace*, G. K. Hall, 1981.

* * *

LOWE, David (Garrard)   1933-

PERSONAL: Born January 9, 1933, in Baltimore, Md.; son of Moses Vogel (an equestrian) and Grace (Garrard) Lowe. *Education:* Oberlin College, B.A., 1955; University of Michigan, M.A., 1958. *Politics:* Republican. *Religion:* Episcopalian. *Home:* 225 East 79th St., New York, N.Y. 10021. *Agent:* Carl Brandt, Brandt & Brandt Literary Agents, Inc., 1501 Broadway, New York, N.Y. 10036.

CAREER: Look, New York City, editor and writer, 1960-64; *American Heritage*, New York City, editor and writer, 1964-69; *McCall's*, New York City, editor and writer, 1969-71; Chanticleer Press, New York City, editor and writer, 1971-75; Dover Publications, New York City, staff writer, 1975—. Broadcaster for Canadian Broadcasting Corp., 1980—. Research associate at Newberry Library, 1975—. *Member:* Victorian Society of America (member of board of directors), Society of Architectural Historians, Writers Room (founding member of board of directors), Coffee House. *Awards, honors:* Avery Hopwood Award from University of Michigan; grant from Graham Foundation for Advanced Studies in the Fine Arts, 1974; awards from Cliff Dwellers Arts Foundation and Society of Midland Authors, both 1975, for *Lost Chicago.*

WRITINGS: (Editor) *New York, N.Y.: A Study of a City,* American Heritage Publishing, 1968; (editor with Douglas Cooper) *Braque: The Great Years,* Art Institute of Chicago, 1972; *Lost Chicago,* Houghton, 1975; *Postcard Views of Old Chicago,* Dover, 1976; *Postcard Views of Old Boston,* Dover, 1976; *Postcard Views of Old London,* Dover, 1977; *The Great Chicago Fire,* Dover, 1979; *Chicago Interiors: Views of a Splendid World,* Contemporary Books, 1979. Contributor of about twenty articles to magazines, including *Country Journal, Travel and Leisure, Horizon, Americana, Prairie Schooner,* and *Commonweal,* and newspapers.

WORK IN PROGRESS: A social history of Chicago.

SIDELIGHTS: Lowe wrote: "Beginning in 1959 I was an editor and writer for Cowles Communications in New York City. I specialized in the field of urban news and worked closely with stringers in London and Rome and with the Washington bureau of *Look* and *Christian Science Monitor.* Then I was with *American Heritage,* where I worked closely with such writers as Bruce Catton, James Flexner, and John Brooks. As senior editor with *McCall's,* in charge of architecture and conservation, I commissioned and edited pieces by Marcia Davenport, Josephine Johnson, and Kurt Vonnegut, as well as other leading writers.

"From 1972 to 1975 I was under contract to write *Lost Chicago,* on the vanished architecture of that city."

* * *

LOWE, Henry Paget
See LOVECRAFT, H(oward) P(hillips)

LOWE, Victoria Lincoln
See LINCOLN, Victoria

* * *

LOWELL, Amy 1874-1925

BRIEF ENTRY: Born February 9, 1874, in Brookline, Mass.; died of a cerebral hemorrhage, May 12, 1925. American poet, biographer, and essayist. Best known as the outspoken proponent of imagism, Lowell determinedly fought for the new style of poetry. In her flamboyant manner she provided young poets with a less restrictive environment in which to present their work. Lowell dedicated herself to imagism after meeting its founder Ezra Pound on a European journey. She espoused the school of poetry with such vigor that Pound caustically renamed the movement "Amygism." Although Lowell's "polyphonic prose" is considered less important than her advertisement and support of imagism, she won the Pulitzer Prize posthumously in 1926 for the volume *What's O'Clock.* The author also wrote a comprehensive biography of Keats entitled *John Keats* (1925). Lowell's biographers believe the strain of writing this two-volume book brought on her death. Her work comprises numerous volumes of poetry, including *A Dome of Many-Coloured Glass* (1912), *Sword Blades and Poppy Seed* (1914), *Men, Women, and Ghosts* (1916), *Can Grande's Castle* (1918), *Fir-Flower Tablets* (1921), and *Ballads for Sale* (1927). *Biographical/critical sources: Twentieth Century Writing: A Reader's Guide to Contemporary Literature,* Transatlantic, 1969; *Webster's New World Companion to English and American Literature,* World Publishing, 1973; *The Reader's Adviser: A Layman's Guide to Literature,* Volume I: *The Best in American and British Fiction, Poetry, Essays, Literary Biography, Bibliography, and Reference,* 12th edition, Bowker, 1974; *Twentieth-Century Literary Criticism,* Volume 1, Gale, 1978.

* * *

LUBALIN, Herb(ert Frederick) 1918-1981

OBITUARY NOTICE: Born March 17, 1918, in New York, N.Y.; died May 24, 1981, in New York, N.Y. Graphic designer, editor, and author best known for creating the formats for publications such as *Reader's Digest,* the *Saturday Evening Post, Eros,* and the *New Leader.* Lubalin had worked in advertising since 1940, and since 1964 he had been president of his own advertising agency. He was presented with a Cleo award for creating the best television commercial of 1963, and that year also received a citation from the U.S. Government for design of airmail postage stamps. Lubalin also designed book jackets, including Warner Books' edition of Richard Nixon's memoirs. He wrote for, edited, and designed *U&lc.* Obituaries and other sources: *Who's Who in Graphic Art,* Amstutz & Herdeg Graphis, 1962; *Who's Who in America,* 40th edition, 1978; *Publishers Weekly,* June 19, 1981.

* * *

LUCAS, Dione (Narnona Margaris Wilson) 1909-1971

OBITUARY NOTICE: Born October 10, 1909; died of pneumonia, December 18, 1971, in London, England. Restaurateur, cooking teacher, and author. Lucas studied the culinary arts at L'Ecole du Cordon Bleu in Paris, and in the early 1930's opened her own restaurant and cooking school in London. She came to the United States in 1940 and opened the Cordon Bleu restaurant and cooking school in New York two years later. In the mid-1940's Lucas had her own television show, on which she demonstrated culinary techniques with celebrity guests. In succeeding years she opened more restaurants and schools, and taught and wrote about cooking throughout the United States. She was the author of several cookbooks, including the best-selling *Cordon Bleu Cook Book.* Obituaries and other sources: *New York Times,* December 19, 1971; *Newsweek,* December 27, 1971; *AB Bookman's Weekly,* January 17, 1972.

* * *

LUCAS, Jim Griffing 1914-1970

OBITUARY NOTICE: Born June 22, 1914, in Checotah, Okla.; died of abdominal cancer in June, 1970, in Washington, D.C. Journalist and author. Lucas, a war correspondent for the Scripps-Howard newspaper chain, covered the Pacific theater during World War II, spent twenty-six months in the Korean war zone, was with French troops during the Indochina conflict, and reported from Vietnam in the 1960's. Lucas is best remembered for his 1954 interview with Douglas MacArthur, published in 1964 after MacArthur's death, in which the former general detailed plans he had proposed to President Truman to bring about an end to the Korean War by using nuclear weapons. Lucas wrote several books about his experiences, including *Dateline-Vietnam.* Obituaries and other sources: *Time,* August 3, 1970; *Who Was Who in America, With World Notables,* Volume V: *1969-1973,* Marquis, 1973.

* * *

LUCCHESI, Aldo
See von BLOCK, Bela W(illiam)

* * *

LUCE, Henry R(obinson) 1898-1967

PERSONAL: Born April 3, 1898, in Tengchow (now P'englai), Shantung Province, China; died February 28, 1967, in Phoenix, Arizona; son of Henry Winters (an American Presbyterian missionary) and Elizabeth Middleton (a missionary; maiden name, Root) Luce; married Lila Ross Hotz, December 22, 1923 (divorced October 4, 1935); married Clare Boothe Brokaw (a writer and congresswoman), November 23, 1935; children: (first marriage) Henry III, Peter Paul. *Education:* Yale University, B.A., 1920; attended Oxford University, 1920-21.

CAREER: Chicago Daily News, Chicago, Ill., cub reporter, 1921-22; *Baltimore News,* Baltimore, Md., reporter, 1922-23; co-founder and editor-in-chief of *Time* magazine, 1923-64; founder and editor-in-chief of *Fortune* magazine, 1930-64, *Life* magazine, 1936-64, and *Sports Illustrated* magazine, 1954-64; publisher of *Architectural Forum* magazine, 1932-64, and *House and Home* magazine, 1962-64; editorial chairman of *Time, Life, Fortune,* and *Sports Illustrated,* 1964-67; director of Time Inc. Organizer of United China Relief, 1940. Initiated committee on Freedom of the Press, 1944. Director of Union Theological Seminary; trustee of American Heritage Foundation, China Institute in America, Metropolitan Museum of Art (New York), and Roosevelt Hospital (New York). *Military service:* U. S. Army Field Artillery, 1918; became second lieutenant.

MEMBER: United Board of Christian Higher Education in Asia, New York Chamber of Commerce, Phi Beta Kappa, Omicron Delta Kappa, Alpha Delta Phi.

AWARDS, HONORS: Chevalier of French Legion of Honor, 1937; Order of Auspicious Star, China, 1947; Henry Johnson

Fisher Award from Magazine Publishers Association, 1965; Commander of Order of Orange-Nassau, the Netherlands; Commander of Order of Cedars of Lebanon; Commander of Royal Order of George I, Greece; Commander's Cross, Order of Danneborg, Denmark; Knight Commander's Cross, Order of Merit, Federal Republic of Germany. Honorary degrees: M.A. from Yale University, 1926; LL.D. from Rollins College, 1938, Grinnell College, 1942, Colgate University, 1948, Lafayette College, 1952, Occidental College, 1954, St. Louis University, 1955, Springfield College, 1961, Adelphi University, 1963, Williams College, 1965, Yale University, 1966, and Westminster College, 1967; Litt.D. from Boston University, 1941, Syracuse University, 1945, Rutgers University, 1949, and University of Arizona, 1961; L.H.D. from Hamilton College, 1942; H.H.D. from College of Idaho, 1951, and College of Wooster, 1962; Doctor of Journalism from Temple University, 1953.

WRITINGS: The American Century, Time Inc., 1941, 2nd edition, with comments by Dorothy Thompson, John Chamberlain, Quincy Howe, Robert G. Spivak, and Robert E. Sherwood, Farrar & Rinehart, 1941; *The Ideas of Henry Luce,* edited by John K. Jessup, Atheneum, 1969.

Addresses: *The Place of Art in American Life,* Time Inc., 1956; *Good Architecture Is Good Government,* Time Inc., 1957; *The Dangerous Age of Abundance,* Newcomen Society in North America, 1959; *The Rule of Law and the Administration of Justice,* American Judicature Society, 1961; *Sight and Insight,* University of Miami Press, 1961; *The Pursuit of Significance,* College of Wooster (Ohio), 1966.

SIDELIGHTS: Luce once described himself as "a Protestant, a Republican, and a free-enterpriser, which means I am biased in favor of God, Eisenhower, and the stockholders of Time Inc." Others have variously called him an empire builder and an imperialist, a publishing genius, and a totalitarian editor, but most would agree that, as Joseph Epstein in *Commentary* simply put it, Luce was "a genuine force in American life."

The son of American missionaries in China, Luce developed an unshakable Protestant ethic and belief in America's superiority. Nym Wales, in the *New Republic,* explained: "[Luce] was an Anglophile WASP—Ivy League and British-trained. . . . He received the British discipline intended to train empire-builders and administrators. . . . He had to be superhuman and a sophisticated Puritan. . . . He was an A Student at Hotchkiss in Connecticut and at Yale, with a postgraduate year at Oxford in England, essential for any American Cecil Rhodes tradition."

At Hotchkiss Luce met future publishing partner Briton Hadden. The two began their collaboration on the Hotchkiss school paper and then continued together on the Yale *Daily News.* Then in the early 1920's Luce and Hadden, believing that most Americans lacked the time to keep abreast of current events, conceived the idea of a weekly news magazine. They accumulated $86,000 from acquaintances and old school friends, and on March 3, 1923, the first issue of *Time* appeared. For four years the magazine ran at a loss, but by 1927 it was making a profit and, at the age of thirty, Luce was a self-made millionaire.

With the success of *Time* assured, the partners began work on a new magazine. They planned it, as stated in the prospectus, around the premise that "business is obviously the greatest single denominator of interest among the active leading citizens of the U.S.A. . . . the distinctive expression of the American genius." When Hadden died suddenly in 1929, Luce assumed sole control of *Time* and carried on with the new magazine, *Fortune,* which appeared for the first time in January, 1930.

Despite the stock market crash of 1929, *Fortune* was successful, and Time Inc.'s pattern of almost constant growth was established. "The March of Time," a radio broadcast presenting the news in dramatic form, came next; first aired on March 6, 1931, the program evolved into a newsreel series, first screened in February, 1935, and eventually seen thirteen times a year in over ten thousand movie theatres worldwide.

Venturing next into photojournalism, Luce brought out, on November 17, 1936, the first issue of *Life.* It has often been said that *Life* nearly died of success: advertising contracts were based on expected sales figures that were far below the number of copies actually sold. As a result, *Life* lost $3 million its first year. Once advertising rates were adjusted, *Life* recovered; its circulation at the time of Luce's death was seven and a half million. A fourth Luce magazine followed its successful predecessors; *Sports Illustrated* appeared on August 16, 1954, with an original circulation of over a half million, and it too grew steadily.

Luce experienced a few failures with magazines such as *Tide* and *Letters,* but they did not undermine his enormous business success. From the original investment of $86,000, he built a publishing empire with a market value at the time of his death of $690 million. (His own share was valued at $109,862,500.) In 1967, the combined circulation of his four major magazines exceeded fourteen million copies. Time Inc.'s expansion into other businesses, including book publishing and television and radio broadcasting, was consistently profitable.

In addition to his financial success, Luce was highly praised for his editorial acumen, his ability to personally control a huge journalistic staff, and his consistency of editorial style and content. He introduced a series of editorial innovations based on the idea that the news must entertain as well as inform. He himself once acknowledged: "I am all for titillating trivialities. I am all for the epic touch. I could almost say that everything in *Time* should be either titillating or epic or starkly, super-curtly factual." In fact, one of the fundamentals of *Time* editorial policy was to dramatize the news. A typical story began with a catchy lead, proceeded with an angle to a climax, and was brought to a neat conclusion. Epstein likened this approach to a B movie: "As a B-movie contorts human experience, snuffing out its complexity and tidying up its loose ends for an audience which has, after all, come primarily to be entertained, so does *Time* magazine: the B-movie of current events and personality."

While *Time*'s content emphasized personalities, its style fostered anonymity of authorship. This resulted from Luce's pioneering use of group journalism, a technique through which stories are produced by teams of researchers, correspondents, and editors. Nevertheless, by offering excellent salaries, Luce was able to attract and retain outstanding individual talent, including at various times such notables as James Agee, Stephen Vincent Benet, John Kenneth Galbraith, John O'Hara, Alfred Kazin, Archibald MacLeish, and Theodore H. White.

The criticism most often leveled at Luce has concerned the absence of objectivity in his publications. Yet objectivity seems never to have been among Luce's goals—even the original prospectus for *Time* included six points of "Editorial Bias." Herbert Mayes, in the *Saturday Review,* recalled a conversation that exemplified Luce's editorial influence: When asked what the magazines would do if his editors decided to support candidate A for President when he was for candidate B, Luce responded, "That's simple. They will support candidate B."

The interpretive slant at Time Inc. was all Luce's own. "Every substantive stand that *Time* ever took was, above all, the stand of Henry Luce," Epstein declared. "In a way that applies to few other recent publishers, Luce turned his magazines into his personal diaries." As reflected in his magazines, Luce's beliefs emphasized a foreign policy that would extend American economic resources and technology to all nations that would support American ideology. Specifically, this was manifested in a distrust of such men as Franklin Roosevelt and Adlai Stevenson and support for such men as Dwight Eisenhower and Richard Nixon, as well as in his promotion of free enterprise and condemnation of Communism. As Nym Wales explained: "When the Luce group-journalism got through mastering 10,000 reports, the result was not objective. It was slanted toward building up stone by stone the so-called American neoimperialism in all of its unconsciousness and contradictoriness." On the subject of China, Luce's subjective influence was most distinguishable. He believed that America should maintain a role of troublemaker toward Communist China, and he continually presented in his magazines a picture of a country in chaos. Epstein remarked: "It is safe to say, then, that Henry Luce's magazines have done more than their share to contribute to the mystification and general hysteria about Communist China."

Although Luce's editorial bias was undeniable, some defended his proprietary approach to journalism. Mayes, a personal friend and former president of the McCall Corporation, maintained: "If I think that Henry Luce tempered the news now and then, I do not believe that he tampered with the facts, ever." Others defined Luce's methods in the context of a broader purpose; when Luce died, Time published a letter from the staff which in part read: "H.R.L. was no press lord in the tradition of Britain's Lord Beaverbrook or America's William Randolph Hearst. Power was not his passion—what burned in him was the search for truth and the desire to communicate it."

BIOGRAPHICAL/CRITICAL SOURCES—Books: Profiles From the New Yorker, Knopf, 1938; Noel Busch, Briton Hadden: A Biography of the Co-Founder of Time, Straus & Cudahy, 1949; Kenneth Stewart and John Tebbel, Makers of Modern Journalism, Prentice-Hall, 1952; John Kubler, Luce, Doubleday, 1968; John K. Jessup, editor, The Ideas of Henry Luce, Atheneum, 1969; W. A. Swanberg, Luce and His Empire, Scribner, 1972; David Cort, The Sin of Henry Luce, L. Stuart, 1974.

Periodicals: Time, March 10, 1967, March 17, 1967; Life, March 10, 1967; Newsweek, March 13, 1967; U.S. News and World Report, March 13, 1967; Saturday Review, March 18, 1967, April 29, 1967; Nation, March 20, 1967; Fortune, April 1, 1967; New Republic, April 1, 1967; U.S. Camera, June, 1967; Esquire, September, 1967; Commentary, November, 1967.

OBITUARIES: New York Times, March 1, 1967; Publishers Weekly, March 13, 1967; New Yorker, March 18, 1967; National Review, March 21, 1967.*

—Sketch by Andrea Geffner

* * *

LUDDEN, Allen (Ellsworth)   1918(?)-1981

OBITUARY NOTICE: Born October 5, c. 1918, in Mineral Point, Wis.; died of cancer, June 9, 1981, in Los Angeles, Calif. Television and radio producer, game show host, and author. Ludden was best known as the host of the popular television shows "General Electric College Bowl" and "Password." His erudite, professorial manner won him the nickname "the happy highbrow." Ludden wrote several books of advice for young people, including Plain Talk for Men Under Twenty-one, Plain Talk for Women Under Twenty-one, and Plain Talk for Young Marrieds. Obituaries and other sources: Who's Who

in America, 40th edition, Marquis, 1978; New York Times, June 10, 1981; Newsweek, June 22, 1981; Time, June 22, 1981.

* * *

LUECKE, Janemarie   1924-

PERSONAL: Surname is pronounced Loo-kie; born April 24, 1924, in Okeene, Okla.; daughter of William (a farmer) and Gertrude (Boeckman) Luecke. Education: Attended Mount St. Scholastica College, 1941-43; Benedictine Heights College, B.A., 1948; Marquette University, M.A., 1956; University of Notre Dame, Ph.D., 1964. Politics: Democrat. Home: 1132 Northwest 32nd St., Oklahoma City, Okla. 73118. Office: Department of English, Oklahoma State University, Stillwater, Okla. 74078.

CAREER: Entered Order Sancti Benedicti (Order of St. Benedict; Benedictines; O.S.B.), 1943, became Roman Catholic nun, 1945; parochial high school teacher of English, journalism, Latin, and music in Tulsa, Oklahoma City, and McAlester, Okla., 1945-56; Benedictine Heights College, Tulsa, Okla., 1956-61, began as assistant professor, became associate professor of English and journalism, public relations director, and academic dean; St. Joseph's Convent, Tulsa, director of research project, 1964-66; Oklahoma State University, Stillwater, assistant professor, 1966-67, associate professor, 1967-73, professor of English, 1973—.

MEMBER: Modern Language Association of America (chairman of liaison advisory committee, 1977), Poetry Society of America, Poets and Writers, Modern Poetry Society, American Civil Liberties Union (member of state board of directors, 1969-77; state vice-president, 1976). Awards, honors: Named outstanding journalism adviser by Catholic School Press Association, 1953; outstanding teacher award from Redskin, Oklahoma State University, 1972; outstanding woman award from Association of Women Students, 1971; named one of "eighty women in the 80's" by Oklahoma Governor George Nigh, 1981.

WRITINGS: Measuring Old English Rhythm: An Application of the Principles of Gregorian Chant Rhythm to the Meter of Beowulf, University of Wisconsin Press, 1978; The Rape of the Sabine Women (poems), Wake-Brook, 1978. Contributor of about seventy articles and poems to professional journals and literary magazines, including Cimarron Review, Bitterroot, and Primavera.

WORK IN PROGRESS: The Prosody of Free Verse, publication expected in 1984.

SIDELIGHTS: Janemarie Luecke commented: "I am interested in giving lectures and poetry readings. I have done so extensively, and hope to make that, along with writing and publishing, a full-time career after retiring from teaching. I am also involved in movements concerned with peace, ecology, and energy conservation, all of them under the broad umbrella of the 'women's movement,' which I consider the kind of revolution that alone can save our planet for the next civilization. So understood, of course, the women's movement has to do with changing attitudes and judgmental views from male-oriented to fully human—that is, developing and esteeming the so-called 'female' traits in the human experience."

* * *

LUMMIS, Keith   1904-

PERSONAL: Born August 20, 1904, in Los Angeles, Calif.; son of Charles Fletcher (a writer) and Eve Frances (a translator;

maiden name, Douglas) Lummis; married Dorothy Fales, November 15, 1929 (died August 28, 1941); married Hazel Elinor McCausland. children: Charlotte Stuart, Charles Douglas, Suzanne Maria, James Bayard. *Education:* Attended University of Arizona. *Politics:* Republican. *Religion:* Episcopalian. *Home:* 5507 Anza St., San Francisco, Calif. 94121.

CAREER: U.S. Merchant Marine, New Orleans, La., seaman, 1920; U.S. Border Patrol, San Diego, Calif., inspector, 1927-29; special agent for U.S. Bureau of Prohibition and Alcohol Tax Unit, 1930-43; U.S. Secret Service, San Francisco, Calif., special agent, 1943-54; U.S. Department of State, Foreign Service, staff officer in Palermo, Italy, and Paris, France, 1954-57; manager of a ski lodge in Norden, Calif., 1957-65. *Member:* Westerners, California Historical Society, Southern California Historical Society, Southwest Museum, Delta Chi. *Awards, honors:* Western Heritage Wrangler Award, 1975-76; Border Regional Library Association Award, 1976.

WRITINGS: Charles F. Lummis: The Man and His West, University of Oklahoma Press, 1975. Contributor of historical articles to various magazines.

WORK IN PROGRESS: A television script based on the life of ''a great but forgotten Westerner''; a biography.

* * *

LUSTGARTEN, Edgar (Marcus) 1907-1979

OBITUARY NOTICE—See index for *CA* sketch: Born May 3, 1907, in Manchester, England; died December 15, 1979. Attorney, producer, journalist, broadcaster, and author. Lustgarten worked as a lawyer before becoming a producer, broadcaster, and journalist with the British Broadcasting Corp. (BBC). He stayed with the BBC, except for a stint at ATV Network, until his death. He was associated with several BBC programs, including ''In the News,'' ''Free Speech,'' ''Fair Play,'' ''Focus,'' and ''Famous Trials.'' Lustgarten wrote a number of books on the history of crime, such as *One More Unfortunate, Verdict in Dispute, The Woman in the Case,* and *A Century of Murderers.* Obituaries and other sources: *AB Bookman's Weekly,* February 12, 1979.

* * *

LYNCH, James
See ANDREYEV, Leonid (Nikolaevich)

* * *

LYNDON, Amy
See RADFORD, Richard F(rancis), Jr.

* * *

LYNN, Jonathan 1943-

PERSONAL: Born April 3, 1943, in Bath, England; son of Robin (a physician) and Ruth (a sculptor; maiden name, Eban) Lynn; married Rita Merkelis (a psychotherapist), August 1, 1967. *Education:* Pembroke College, Cambridge, M.A., 1964. *Home:* 29 Etheldene Ave., London N. 10, England. *Agent:* c/o Barry Burnett Organisation, Suite 409, Princess House, 190 Piccadilly, London W1 EN, England.

CAREER: Professional actor, 1964-76; Cambridge Theatre Company, Cambridge, England, director, 1976—. Actor on stage, on television, in repertory, and on tour. *Awards, honors:* Best musical awards from Society of West End Theatres and *Evening Standard,* both for directing ''Songbook''; Ivor Novello Award, 1979; ''Yes Minister'' named best television comedy by British Academy of Film and Television Arts and by Broadcasting Press Guild.

WRITINGS: A Proper Man (novel), Heinemann, 1976; *Yes Minister: The Diaries of the Right Honourable James Hackes,* Volume 1, BBC Publications, 1981. Also author of a film, ''The Internecine Project,'' and a play, ''Pig of the Month.''

Co-author of more than fifty television scripts for series, including ''My Brother's Keeper,'' on Granada Television, 1974-75; ''Doctor in Charge,'' ''Doctor at Sea,'' and ''My Name Is Harry Worth,'' all on London Weekend Television; and ''Yes Minister,'' on BBC-TV, 1980-81.

WORK IN PROGRESS: Second volume of *Yes Minister,* for BBC Publications.

SIDELIGHTS: Lynn has played drums in classical orchestras and worked as a jazz drummer. In the theatre he is a writer, director, and actor, though in recent years he has limited his acting appearances in favor of writing and directing. Much of his time is spent raising funds for theatrical productions, to replace, at least in part, funds that came from the British Government in better economic times.

* * *

LYRE, Pinchbeck
See SASSOON, Siegfried (Lorraine)

* * *

LYTE, Charles 1935-
(Charles Ewart)

PERSONAL: Born December 28, 1935, in Essex, England; son of Edwyn Trevor and Constance (Levinson) Lyte; married Sarah Jane Hale, May, 1960 (died June, 1963); married Sarah Mary Claire Carey-Foster, October 14, 1966; children: Caroline Martha, Sebastian John Charles, Benedict Edwyn Carey, Seamus Valentine. *Politics:* ''Moderate.'' *Religion:* Roman Catholic. *Home:* Carters Corner Place, Cowbeech, near Hailsham, East Sussex, England. *Agent:* Mark Hamilton, A. M. Heath & Co. Ltd., 40-42 William IV St., London WC2N 4DD, England.

CAREER: Worked at farms and nursery gardens in England, 1951-55; journalist with *East Grinstead Courier,* East Grinstead, England, *Bulawayo Chronicle,* Zimbabwe Rhodesia, *Evening Standard,* London England, *London Times,* London, and *Daily Express,* London; currently education correspondent for *Daily Mirror,* London. *Member:* Royal Geographical Society, Royal Horticultural Society.

WRITINGS: The Thames, Silver Burdett, 1980; *Sir Joseph Banks,* David & Charles, 1980.

Under pseudonym Charles Ewart: *The Healing Needles,* Elm Tree Books, 1973.

WORK IN PROGRESS: A political biography and a book about plant hunters.

M

MABON, John Scott 1910(?)-1980

OBITUARY NOTICE: Born c. 1910; died May 5, 1980, in Greenwich, Conn. Publishing executive and editor. Mabon worked for several publishers, including Alfred A. Knopf, Inc., and the University of Michigan Press, and was an associate editor of the Ladies' Home Journal. He was one of the first to recognize James Michener's talent, and helped Michener find a publisher for Tales of the South Pacific. Obituaries and other sources: Publishers Weekly, May 23, 1980.

*   *   *

MACAULAY, Rose 1881-1958

BRIEF ENTRY: Born August 1, 1881 (some sources say 1889), in Cambridge, England; died October 30, 1958, in London, England. British novelist, poet, and essayist. In her witty, satirical novels, Dame Rose Macaulay fought against ignorance, cruelty, and vulgarity by poking fun at British manners and political and religious organizations. The novel Potterism (1920), which was compared to Sinclair Lewis's Babbitt, presented a serious account of modern society and became one of her best-known works. Some critics felt her finest effort was They Were Defeated (1932), a historical novel set in the seventeenth century. She was an inveterate traveler in Europe and wrote several books on travel, including The Towers of Trebizond (1956), in which she revealed her fondness for the Mediterranean and its historical past. After World War II, Macaulay's writing appeared to contain more irony than satire and was marked by increased compassion for the people who were life's failures. Nevertheless, her reputation for satire had been so firmly established early in her career that many of her serious later works were labeled satires. Biographical/critical sources: Twentieth Century Authors: A Biographical Dictionary of Modern Literature, H. W. Wilson, 1942, 1st supplement, 1955; Papers on Language and Literature, summer, 1967; Kenyon Review, November, 1967.

*   *   *

MacGREGOR, Robert Mercer 1911-1974

OBITUARY NOTICE: Born August 5, 1911, in Pittsfield, Mass.; died of cancer, November 22, 1974, in New York, N.Y. Journalist, publisher, and editor. A foreign correspondent in Russia and China during the 1930's, MacGregor was best known as an editor and vice-president of New Directions Publishing,

where he worked with such authors as Henry Miller, Ezra Pound, and Tennessee Williams. He was also an editor and publisher of Theatre Arts Books, and he had been editor of Theatre Arts Monthly. Obituaries and other sources: The Biographical Encyclopaedia and Who's Who of the American Theatre, James Heineman, 1966; New York Times, November, 23, 1974; AB Bookman's Weekly, December 16, 1974; Publishers Weekly, January 6, 1975.

*   *   *

MACHADO (y RUIZ), Antonio 1875-1939

BRIEF ENTRY: Born July 26, 1875, in Seville, Spain; died February 22, 1939, in Collioure, France. Spanish educator and poet. Machado taught French and Spanish literature, acted, and became involved in the literary life of Madrid at the turn of the century, spending a few years in France as well. After his marriage Machado's work became more cheerful, though still tied closely to nature and the simple expression of human emotion, but after his wife's death in 1912 he returned to the melancholy that characterized his earlier work. When civil war broke out in Spain during the 1930's Machado experienced his most prolific period of writing. Allied with the cause of the common man, whose moral strength, honesty, and noble aspirations he admired, Machado accompanied exiled refugees of the collapsed republic on their walk across the Pyrenees in 1939; he died soon after in a small French village. His translated work includes Eighty Poems of Antonio Machado (1959), Juan de Mairena: Epigrams, Maxims, Memoranda, and Memoirs of an Apocryphal Professor (1963), and Castilian Ilexes: Versions From Antonio Machado (1963). Biographical/critical sources: Columbia Dictionary of Modern European Literature, Columbia University Press, 1947; The Concise Encyclopedia of Modern World Literature, Hutchinson, 1963; World Authors, 1950 1970, H. W. Wilson, 1975; Twentieth-Century Literary Criticism, Volume 3, Gale, 1980.

*   *   *

MacHARDY, Charles 1926-

PERSONAL: Born July 11, 1926, in Dundee, Scotland; son of Charles (an engineer) and Mary (Mabe) MacHardy; married Shirley Dawes (a model), November 7, 1966 (divorced). Education: Attended Naval Training Establishment, Shotley, 1941-46. Politics: "Leftish." Religion: "Tendency toward Buddhism." Home: 270 Perth Rd., Dundee, Scotland. Agent: John

Farquharson Ltd., Bell House, 8 Bell Yard, London WC2A 2JU, England.

CAREER: Associated with National Press, writing for the Sunday *Daily Express, Daily Herald,* and *Daily Sketch,* 1950-70; free-lance writer, 1970—. Worked for Television News Service (ITN). *Military service:* Royal Navy, petty officer, 1942-48.

WRITINGS: Send Down a Dove (novel), Collins, 1968, Coward, 1969; *The Ice Mirror* (novel), Collins, 1972; *Blowdown* (novel), Collins, 1978. Contributor to newspapers and magazines.

WORK IN PROGRESS: A long novel about mercenaries, publication by Collins expected in 1982; a radio play; a television series.

SIDELIGHTS: MacHardy wrote: "I wanted to be a writer since first reading Jack London as a kid, but I didn't start writing fiction till the late sixties. I am fascinated by man's struggle against nature, society, and himself, and my books tend to adopt this theme. I am by nature gregarious, but can be a bit of a recluse when writing.

"Writing requires enormous discipline, a fact I find difficult to equate with a life-style that, if not exactly hedonistic, is certainly geared to respond enthusiastically to the phone call suggesting a game of golf or a few days sailing on the magical west coast of England where I live. This is always the great problem and is only mitigated, in my own case, by a sense of duty that tells me that somewhere out there is an intelligent and imaginative public who, in spite of being nearly deafened by the screams from the marketplace to purchase a never-ending stream of consumer goods as a way to achieve happiness and self-fulfillment, have retained sufficient faith in literature to spare some of their hard-earned cash to buy books.

"Deeply conscious of this and my own shortcomings in both skill and industry, I feverishly scan the classified section of the national press in the hope that someday I will discover that someone has had the imagination—and temerity—to undertake the management of that unruly creature, the writer, for whom perhaps more than anyone else the need to bring forth the dark stirrings of the mind into the light of day and form of credibility is his only salvation. But we all have our dreams. Even writers."

AVOCATIONAL INTERESTS: Sailing, rock climbing, golf, playing jazz piano and classical guitar.

*   *   *

MACHEN, Arthur
See JONES, Arthur Llewellyn

*   *   *

MacKAY, Alfred F(arnum)   1938-

PERSONAL: Born October 1, 1938, in Ocala, Fla.; son of Kenneth Hood (an entrepreneur) and Julia (Farnum) MacKay; married Ann Wilson (an artist and architect), February 4, 1962; children: Douglas Kevin, Robert Wilson. *Education:* Davidson College, A.B., 1960; University of North Carolina, Ph.D., 1967. *Residence:* Oberlin, Ohio. *Office:* Department of Philosophy, Oberlin College, Oberlin, Ohio 44074.

CAREER: Oberlin College, Oberlin, Ohio, assistant professor, 1967-73, associate professor of philosophy, 1973—, chairman of department, 1978—. Visiting assistant professor at University of Illinois, 1970-71. *Military service:* U.S. Army Reserve, airborne counterintelligence, 1961-63; became first lieutenant.

Member: American Philosophical Association. *Awards, honors:* Woodrow Wilson fellowships, 1961, 1963, 1966; grant from Council for Philosophical Studies, Summer Institute in Philosophy of Language and Linguistics, 1966; fellowships from American Council of Learned Societies, 1973, and Rockefeller Foundation, 1981.

WRITINGS: (Editor with Robert H. Grimm) *Society: Revolution and Reform,* Press of Case Western Reserve University, 1971; (editor with Daniel D. Merrill) *Issues in the Philosophy of Language,* Yale University Press, 1976; *Arrow's Theorem: The Paradox of Social Choice,* Yale University Press, 1980. Contributor of articles and reviews to philosophy journals. Member of editorial board of *Oberlin Observer,* 1979—.

WORK IN PROGRESS: Research on the problem of interpersonal utility comparisons.

*   *   *

MACKAY, Shena   1944-

PERSONAL: Born in 1944 in Edinburgh, Scotland; married Robin Brown; children: three daughters. *Education:* Attended Tonbridge Girls Grammar School and Kidbrooke Comprehensive School. *Home:* 15 Fortis Green Ave., London N.2, England.

CAREER: Writer, 1959—.

WRITINGS—Novels: *Dust Falls on Eugene Schlumberger* [and] *Toddler on the Run,* Deutsch, 1964 (see below); *Music Upstairs,* J. Cape, 1965; *Dust Falls on Eugene Schlumberger,* Panther Books, 1966; *Toddler on the Run,* Simon & Schuster, 1966; *Old Crow,* J. Cape, 1967, McGraw, 1968; *An Advent Calendar,* J. Cape, 1971.

SIDELIGHTS: Mackay began writing when she was fifteen years old, and by the age of twenty-seven she had written five novels. According to a *Times Literary Supplement* reviewer, "extrapolating vividly-observed ordinariness into alarming and exuberant fantasy was her particular flair in all of them." *Listener* critic Brigid Brophy commented: "Her beautiful prose isolates homely objects into disconcertingness, and her macabre, overwhelmingly original imagination blooms into sheerly surrealist images caught in mid-metamorphosis." In *Old Crow,* for example, gloves sticking out of a man's coat pocket become "vestigial leather hands sprouting from his hips," and a woman in a black dress struggling with a jammed zipper becomes a "black bat flailing."

In addition to surrealistic and original imagery, Shena Mackay's work is noted for its black humor. Her "talent is to put the ruth back into ruthless rhymes," noted Brophy. "Her novels are visions of universal anguish composed in short, sharp reels." In the first chapter of *An Advent Calendar,* a butcher boy's finger is chopped into a pound of meat and eaten by an unknowing customer. *New Statesman* critic Clive Jordan suggested that the image of "the 'wild white drowned hair of the spaghetti' is not too fanciful when we already know that the meat sauce contains a human finger." In *Old Crow* an old man almost starves to death, having eaten nothing but toothpaste for four days, because he cannot make himself understood by a shopkeeper. Mackay's "odd charm is that she rushes her humour to the brink of bathos, then stops just short of the plunge," wrote a *Newsweek* reviewer. "But," the critic added, "her mockery is a measure of her sympathy."

BIOGRAPHICAL/CRITICAL SOURCES: New Statesman, June 12, 1964, July 2, 1971; *Newsweek,* January 17, 1966; *Observer Review,* June 11, 1967; *Listener,* June 15, 1967, July 8, 1971; *Times Literary Supplement,* June 15, 1967, July 2, 1971; *Il-*

lustrated London News, July, 1967; *Books and Bookmen*, September, 1967; *New York Times Book Review*, February 25, 1968; *Best Sellers*, March 1, 1968; *Saturday Review*, March 2, 1968; *Spectator*, July 10, 1971.*

* * *

MACKENZIE, W(illiam) J(ames) M(illar) 1909-

PERSONAL: Born April 8, 1909, in Edinburgh, Scotland; married Pamela Muriel Malyon, 1943; children: one son, four daughters. *Education:* Received M.A. from Balliol College, Oxford, and LL.B. from University of Edinburgh. *Home:* 5 Kirklee Circus, Glasgow G12 0TW, Scotland.

CAREER: Oxford University, Oxford, England, fellow of Magdalen College, 1933-48, fellow of Nuffield College and lecturer in politics, 1948; Victoria University of Manchester, Manchester, England, professor of government, 1949-66; University of Glasgow, Glasgow, Scotland, professor of government, 1966-74, professor emeritus, 1974—. Civil servant at Air Ministry, 1939-44; official war historian for Special Operations Executive, 1945-48. Special commissioner for constitutional development in Tanganyika, 1952; constitutional adviser in Kenya, 1959. Vice-chairman of Bridges Committee on Training in Public Administration for Overseas Countries, 1962; chairman of children's panel of advisory committee of the city of Glasgow, 1973-75; member of Manchester City Education Committee, 1953-64, British Wool Marketing Board, 1954-66, Royal Commission on Local Government in Greater London, 1957, Committee on Remuneration of Ministers and Members of Parliament, 1963-64, Maud Committee on Management in Local Government, 1964-66, Parry Committee on University Libraries, 1964-67, North-West Regional Economic Planning Council, 1965-66, and Social Science Research Council, 1965-69. *Member:* British Academy (fellow). *Awards, honors:* Commander of Order of the British Empire, 1963; LL.D. from University of Dundee, 1968, University of Lancaster, 1970, and Victoria University of Manchester, 1975; D.Litt. from University of Warwick, 1972.

WRITINGS: (With Jack William Grove) *Central Administration in Britain*, Longmans, Green, 1957, Greenwood Press, 1976; *Free Elections: An Elementary Textbook*, Rinehart, 1958; (editor with Kenneth Ernest Robinson) *Five Elections in Africa: A Group of Electoral Studies*, Clarendon Press, 1960; *Politics and Social Science*, Penguin, 1967; *Research in Political Science*, Heinemann, 1968; *The Study of Political Science Today*, Macmillan, 1971; *Explorations in Government: Collected Papers, 1951-1968*, Halsted, 1975; *Power, Violence, Decision*, Penguin, 1975; (editor with Douglas Chalmers Hague and Anthony P. Barker) *Public Policy and Private Interests: The Institutions of Compromise*, Macmillan, 1975; *Political Identity*, St. Martin's, 1978, revised edition, Manchester University Press, 1978; *Biological Ideas in Politics: An Essay on Political Adaptivity*, Manchester University Press, 1978, St. Martin's, 1979; *Power and Responsibility in Health Care: The National Health Service as a Political Institution*, Oxford University Press, 1979. Also co-author of *British Government Since 1918*, 1950, and *Social Work in Scotland*, 1969.

BIOGRAPHICAL/CRITICAL SOURCES: New Statesman, September 15, 1967; *Times Literary Supplement*, October 12, 1967; Brian Chapman and Allen Potter, editors, *W.J.M.M., Political Questions: Essays in Honour of W.J.M. Mackenzie*, Manchester University Press, 1974; *Economist*, June 2, 1979.*

MADDOCK, Kenneth   ?-1971

OBITUARY NOTICE: Died June 20, 1971, in Norwalk, Conn. Editor. Maddock edited a number of series of scientific and technical works for John Wiley & Sons, including the "Electrochemical Society" series, *Elderfield's Heterocyclic Compounds*, and *Environmental Science and Technology*. Obituaries and other sources: *Publishers Weekly*, July 26, 1971.

* * *

MAETERLINCK, Maurice   1862-1949

BRIEF ENTRY: Born August 29, 1862, in Ghent, Belgium; died May 6, 1949, in Nice, France. Belgian playwright and essayist. Maeterlinck's first writing was poetry, including *Serres chaudes* (1889), but his critical success was based on his symbolist plays such as "La Princesse Maleine" (1890). These highly allegorical, dreamy works earned him a Nobel Prize for literature in 1911. Maeterlinck was preoccupied with spiritualism, death, and a sense of fatality that often led his characters unquestioningly to their doom, as in "Pelleas and Melisanda" (1892), which was made into an opera by Claude Debussy. His later work included more philosophical writing, such as *The Treasure of the Humble* (1896), and the scientific work *The Life of the Bee* (1901). Eventually his writing indicated a shift from mystical convictions to a search for religious certainty, and finally to an acceptance of peaceful agnosticism, as in *Devant Dieu* (1937). Maeterlinck spent most of his time in Belgium and France, living as an exile in the United States during World War II and returning to the French Riviera for the last few years of his life. He was given the title of Count of the Kingdom of Belgium in 1932 and was elected to the French Academy in 1937. *Biographical/critical sources: Cyclopedia of World Authors*, Harper, 1958; W. D. Halls, *Maurice Maeterlinck: A Study of His Life and Thought*, Oxford University Press, 1961; *Encyclopedia of World Literature in the Twentieth Century*, updated edition, Ungar, 1967; *Twentieth-Century Literary Criticism*, Volume 3, Gale, 1980.

* * *

MAGUIRE, Michael   1945-

PERSONAL: Born November 19, 1945, in London, England; son of Leonard Francis (an engineer) and Irene Doris (an advertising agent; maiden name, Walker) Maguire. *Education:* Attended school in London, England. *Politics:* Social Democrat. *Religion:* Church of England. *Home:* 17 Sunbury Court Island, Sunbury-on-Thames, Middlesex TW16 5PP, England. *Office:* Studio Saratoga, 187 Manygate Lane, Shepperton, Middlesex TW17 9ER, England.

CAREER: Croydon Times, Croydon, England, press photographer, 1961-69; free-lance journalist, 1969-74; free-lance writer, 1974—. *Member:* Crime Writers Association.

WRITINGS: Shot Silk (novel), W. H. Allen, 1975; *Slaughter Horse* (novel), W. H. Allen, 1975; *Scratchproof* (novel), W. H. Allen, 1976; *Mylor, the Most Powerful Horse in the World* (juvenile novel), W. H. Allen, 1977; *Mylor: The Kidnap* (juvenile novel), W. H. Allen, 1978; *Superkids* (juvenile novel), W. H. Allen, 1980.

Scripts: "A Tale of Two Halves," first broadcast by Independent Television, A.T.V. Network, June, 1956. Writer for "Five Away," a prison escape series, and "The Vindicators," a suspense series for Universal Studios.

WORK IN PROGRESS: The Paranoid, a novel, with John Fredman; adapting his novels for a television series.

SIDELIGHTS: Maguire told *CA:* "I write about what I know best, research it well, pack it with thrills, and then stick at it. I wrote my first novel just to see if I could stay with the sixty-thousand-word course. I did it and then put the novel away for three months. When I took it out again and read it, it was so bad I burned it. This taught me a valuable lesson: I knew I had 'staying power,' but my writing needed a lot of polishing. I worked on it and eventually everything dovetailed. Vision is the most important factor in novel writing, plus a vivid imagination and a little bit of luck."

Maguire combined his fascination for horses and his desire to write thrilling detective stories in several works, including *Slaughter Horse,* later blamed for inciting a questionable practice at British racetracks. This novel concerns "blood doping," which involves removing a pint of blood from an athlete prior to competition, preserving the blood by refrigeration, and transfusing the blood back into its owner just prior to a race. Maguire learned of the practice from an Olympic athlete who avowed that the extra pint of blood and higher red blood count enables an athlete to run faster than his opponents. Wondering if blood doping would have the same effect on animals, particularly race horses, Maguire consulted a veterinarian, who verified that it would. Maguire then got the idea for *Slaughter Horse.*

Several months after *Slaughter Horse* was published, a London newspaper pointed to Maguire's novel as the reason that blood doping was being practiced at Britain's racetracks. The source noted that Maguire's novels were widely read by horse owners, jockeys, and trainers and claimed that *Slaughter Horse* helped to spread the practice. A lover of horses, Maguire did not intend for his fiction to become fact, but admitted: "It's nice to know that even the undesirables of the racing world buy my thrillers."

Each of Maguire's novels has been translated into seven languages, and the film rights of *Superkids* have been purchased by Walt Disney Productions.

*　　　*　　　*

MAHONEY, John Thomas　1905-1981
(Tom Mahoney)

OBITUARY NOTICE—See index for *CA* sketch: Born December 3, 1905, in Dallas, Tex.; died after a short illness, July 17, 1981, in Poughkeepsie, N.Y. Journalist, editor, executive, and author. Mahoney began his career working with the *El Paso Post, United Press,* and the *Buffalo Times.* He then became an editor with Fawcett Publications and later with *Look* and *Fortune* magazines. After leaving *Fortune,* Mahoney joined the public relations firm Publicity Associates. Remaining in the field of public realtions, he was an executive with Young & Rubicam, Inc., and Dudley-Anderson-Yutzy. Mahoney wrote several books, including *Public Relations for Retailers, The Merchants of Life: An Account of the American Pharmaceutical Industry, I'm a Lucky One,* and *Niagara.* Obituaries and other sources: *New York Times,* July 19, 1981.

*　　　*　　　*

MAHONEY, Tom
See MAHONEY, John Thomas

*　　　*　　　*

MAINE, Charles Eric
See McIlWAIN, David

MAITLAND, Margaret
See Du BREUIL, (Elizabeth) L(or)inda

*　　　*　　　*

MAKEBA, (Zensi) Miriam　1932-

PERSONAL: Born March 4, 1932, in Prospect, South Africa; came to United States, 1959; daughter of a teacher and a domestic worker; married Sonny Pillay (a singer; marriage ended); married Hugh Masekela (a musician; marriage ended); married Stokely Carmichael (a civil rights leader; marriage ended); children: Bongi (daughter). *Education:* Attended Kimerton Training Institute in Pretoria, South Africa. *Agent:* c/o Times Books, New York Times Co., 3 Park Ave., New York, N.Y. 10016.

CAREER: Domestic worker in Johannesburg, South Africa; Black Mountain Brothers, vocalist touring in South Africa, Rhodesia (now Zimbabwe), and the Belgian Congo, 1954-57; singer in concert halls and nightclubs in Africa, United States, England, France, Denmark, and Italy, 1957—. Recording artist of albums, including "The Voice of Africa," "Popular Songs and African Folk Songs," RCA, "Miriam Makeba Sings," RCA, "The World of Miriam Makeba," RCA, "Makeba Sings," RCA, "The Click Song," "Wimoweh," "Back of the Moon," Kapp, and "Miriam Makeba in Concert," Reprise. Actress, including appearances in opera "King Kong" and film "Come Back Africa," both 1959; guest on television and radio programs, including "Steve Allen Show," "Soul," and "Like It Is." Member of delegation from Guinea to United States, 1975. *Member:* American Society of Composers, Authors, and Publishers. *Awards, honors:* Grammy Award from National Academy of Recording Arts and Sciences, 1965, for best folk music for "An Evening with Belafonte/Makeba."

WRITINGS: The World of African Song, edited by Jonas Gwangwa and E. John Miller, Jr., Times Books, 1971. Author of musical compositions, including "Unhome," "Amampondo Dubala," "Pole Mze," "Boot Dance," and "Mangwene Mpulele."

SIDELIGHTS: Makeba gained international renown after starring in the anti-apartheid, semidocumentary film "Come Back Africa," in 1959. A black South African, Makeba was a well-known singer and actress in her native country before making the motion picture. When "Come Back Africa" was to be shown at the Venice Film Festival, she left her home for the first time and traveled to the city to attend. After the festival, Makeba journeyed to London where she met singer and performer Harry Belafonte. Extremely impressed with her renditions of unusual native African songs, Belafonte proclaimed her "easily the most revolutionary new talent to appear in any medium in the last decade." He became Makeba's promoter and introduced her to American audiences. In November, 1959, she was a guest on "The Steve Allen Show." Her nightclub debut at the Village Vanguard in New York City followed soon afterward. She quickly began performing in larger clubs and concert halls. Although most popular for singing African tunes in her Xhosan tribe dialect, Makeba also sings many other types of music. Her recordings include Hebrew and Yiddish songs, Portuguese fados and bossa novas, Haitian chants, and English ballads.

BIOGRAPHICAL/CRITICAL SOURCES: Newsweek, January 25, 1960; *Time,* February 1, 1960; *New York Times,* February 28, 1960; *Ebony,* April, 1963, July, 1968; Louise Crane, *Ms. Africa,* Lippincott, 1973; *Africa Report,* January, 1977.*

MAKSIMOV, Vladimir (Yemelyanovich)
See MAXIMOV, Vladimir (Yemelyanovich)

*   *   *

MALCOLM, Donald   1932(?)-1975

OBITUARY NOTICE: Born c. 1932; died August 15, 1975, in New York. Journalist, editor, and critic. A graduate of the University of Michigan, Malcolm worked as an assistant editor of the *Michigan Alumnus Magazine* and *Publishers Weekly* before moving to the *New Republic* as a staff writer and book critic in 1956. The following year he joined the staff of *New Yorker,* and in 1958 he became the magazine's first Off-Broadway drama critic, serving in that capacity throughout the 1959-60 season. He returned to book criticism, and shortly afterwards, at the age of thirty-two, he was overtaken by an illness from which he never recovered. Obituaries and other sources: *New York Times,* August 18, 1975; *Publishers Weekly,* September 1, 1975; *New Yorker,* September 8, 1975.

*   *   *

MALE, Roy R(aymond)   1919-

PERSONAL: Born March 15, 1919, in Brooklyn, N.Y.; son of Roy R. (a teacher) and Mary (a teacher; maiden name, Brooks) Male; married Carolyn Conlisk (in real estate sales), August 19, 1944; children: Marilyn Clare, Frank Wade. *Education:* Hamilton College, B.S., 1939; Columbia University, M.A., 1940; University of Texas, Ph.D., 1950. *Home:* 709 Chautauqua, Norman, Okla. 73069. *Office:* Department of English, University of Oklahoma, Norman, Okla. 73069.

CAREER: University of Texas, Austin, instructor in English, 1946-50; Texas Tech University, Lubbock, assistant professor of English, 1950-55; University of Oklahoma, Norman, assistant professor, 1955-59, associate professor, 1959-63, professor of English, 1963-66, Boyd Professor, 1966—. Visiting professor at University of Washington, Seattle, Bowling Green State University, and University of Texas at Arlington. *Military service:* U.S. Army, Infantry, 1940-46; became first lieutenant. *Member:* Modern Language Association of America, South Central Modern Language Association (president, 1967). *Awards, honors:* Ford Foundation fellow, 1954-55.

WRITINGS: (Editor with Martin Shockley and others) *Reading and Writings,* Rinehart, 1954; *Hawthorne's Tragic Vision,* University of Texas Press, 1957; (editor with Robert Anderson) *American Literary Masters,* Holt, 1965; *Enter Mysterious Stranger,* University of Oklahoma Press, 1979; (editor) *Money Talks,* University of Oklahoma Press, 1981. Contributor to journals.

WORK IN PROGRESS: The Threshold of American Romanticism, for University of Oklahoma Press.

SIDELIGHTS: Male commented: "I consider myself primarily a teacher who has enjoyed writing on the side. I do not have much use for writing that cannot be used somehow in the classroom. One of my favorite courses is called 'Sports and Literature.'" *Avocational interests:* Travel (France, Switzerland, Germany, the Philippines, Japan), tennis, Oklahoma football.

BIOGRAPHICAL/CRITICAL SOURCES: New York Times, June 13, 1981.

*   *   *

MALONY, H(enry) Newton   1931-

PERSONAL: Born May 17, 1931, in Birmingham, Ala.; son of Henry Newton and Amie (Milligan) Malony; married Suzanna Hayes Davis, November 23, 1953; children: Lawrence Edward, Allen Davis, Michael Newton. *Education:* Birmingham Southern College, A.B., 1952; Yale University, M.Div., 1955; George Peabody College, M.A., 1961, Ph.D., 1964. *Politics:* Democrat. *Home:* 1315 Medford Rd., Pasadena, Calif. 91107. *Office:* 177 North Madison Ave., Pasadena, Calif. 91101.

CAREER: Ordained Methodist minister, 1955; pastor of Methodist churches in Calera and Birmingham, Ala., 1950-52, New York, N.Y., 1955-56, and Sylacauga and Decatur, Ala., 1956-59; chaplain at Davidson County Psychiatric Hospital, 1959-61; Staff clinician at George Peabody College, Child Study Center, 1961-63; Topeka State Hospital, Topeka, Kan., intern in clinical psychology, 1963-64; Frankfort State Hospital, Frankfort, Ky., director of psychology, 1964-65; Tennessee Wesleyan College, Athens, 1965-69, began as associate professor, became professor of psychology, chairman of department of psychology and sociology, and director of counseling services; Fuller Theological Seminary, Pasadena, Calif., 1969—, began as associate professor, became professor of psychology and director of programs in the integration of psychology at Graduate School of Psychology. Diplomate of American Board of Professional Psychology and chairman of western region; private practice of clinical psychology, 1969—. Oral examiner for the psychology examining committee of California Board of Medical Examiners, 1973—. Member of board of directors of Robincroft Home for the Aged. *Military service:* Alabama and Tennessee National Guard, Chaplains Corps, 1958-64.

MEMBER: American Psychological Association, American Association of Pastoral Counselors, Society for the Scientific Study of Religion, Religious Research Association, Western Psychological Association, Western Association of Christians for Psychological Studies, California Psychological Association.

WRITINGS: (With Walter H. Clark) *Religious Experience: Its Nature and Function in the Human Psyche,* C. C Thomas, 1972; (with Richard L. Gorsuch) *The Nature of Man: A Social Psychological Perspective,* C. C Thomas, 1976; (editor) *Current Perspectives in the Psychology of Religion,* Eerdmans, 1977; *Understanding Your Faith,* Abingdon, 1978; (editor) *Psychology and Faith: The Christian Experience of Eighteen Psychologists,* University Press of America, 1978; *Living the Answers,* Abingdon, 1979; (editor) *A Christian Existential Psychology: The Contributions of John G. Finch,* University Press of America, 1980; (with G. Collins) *Psychology and Theology: Prospects for Integration,* Abingdon, 1981; (with A. Lovekin) *Glossolalia: Social and Psychological Perspectives,* Oxford University Press, 1982. Contributor of more than twenty articles to theology journals.

SIDELIGHTS: Malony told *CA:* "I am convinced of the value of religious faith for full development of the human personality. I am committed to relating faith in oneself and God to the task of psychotherapy." *Avocational interests:* Backpacking, swimming, square dancing.

*   *   *

MANDELSTAM, Osip (Emilievich)   1891(?)-1938(?)

BRIEF ENTRY: Born January 15, 1891 (some sources say 1892), in Warsaw, Poland; died December 27, 1938 (some sources say 1939, 1940, or 1942). Russian poet, novelist, essayist, and critic. A leading acmeist poet, Mandelstam was a member of the Guild of Poets, a radical faction of the acmeist movement. Reacting against the emotional excesses of the symbolists, Mandelstam wrote classical, impersonal poetry. In his verse, he expressed his pessimism with the chaotic state of revolutionary Russia and longed for the structure and orderliness of his classical ideal. Mandelstam also criticized the literary conformity demanded by the new communist government. In 1918 the poet narrowly escaped execution after destroying a stack of death warrants belonging to a government official. He was ultimately arrested in 1934 after reading an anti-Stalin poem to a group of friends. One of them informed the authorities, and Mandelstam spent the next three years in exile. With the help of Boris Pasternak, who personally petitioned Stalin, and other artists, the poet's release was obtained in 1937. A year later, however, Mandelstam was again arrested. Although the date and place of the poet's death remain uncertain, many biographers believe he died in 1938 near Vladivostok, Siberia, in a prison camp. During his imprisonments and despite ill health and occasional bouts of insanity, Mandelstam continued writing poetry. The work of his final years changed in style, becoming more emotional and metaphoric. Among his books are several volumes of poetry, including *Kamen* (1913; title means "Stone"), *Vtoraya kniga* (1923), and *Stikhotvoreniya* (1928), a collection of autobiographical essays entitled *Shum vremeni* (1925; title means "The Noise of Time"), and a novella, *Egipetskaya marka* (1928; title means "The Egyptian Stamp"). *Biographical/critical sources: Encyclopedia of World Literature in the Twentieth Century,* updated edition, Ungar, 1967; *The Penguin Companion to European Literature,* McGraw, 1969; *World Authors, 1950-1970,* H. W. Wilson, 1975; *Twentieth-Century Literary Criticism,* Volume 2, Gale, 1979.

* * *

MANDRAKE, Ethel Belle
See THURMAN, Wallace

* * *

MANIERE, J.-E.
See GIRAUDOUX, (Hippolyte) Jean

* * *

MANN, Thomas 1875-1955

BRIEF ENTRY: Born June 6, 1875, in Luebeck, Germany (now West Germany); came to United States in 1941, naturalized citizen, 1944; died of phlebitis, August 12, 1955, in Zurich, Switzerland. German novelist, short story writer, essayist, and critic. Considered one of the most important German novelists of the twentieth century, Mann was best known for the intellectual irony of his writings. He established himself as a writer with the publication of his second novel, *Buddenbrooks* (1901). One of Mann's prevalent themes was the relation of society's degeneration to the nihilism of art. This theme was most prominent in Mann's *Doctor Faustus* (1947), which explored the fall of a demonic musician and at the same time symbolized the decline of Nazi Germany. During the 1930's Mann openly opposed the national socialism in Germany and eventually was forced to leave the country. Even after renouncing his homeland, he continued to write in the classic German tradition and provided readers with a view of middle-class Germany and its problems. Mann received the Nobel Prize for literature in 1929 for *The Magic Mountain* (1924) and was awarded the Goethe Prize in 1949. His other writings include the novels *Gefallen* (1894) and *The Holy Sinner* (1951), a series of novels about the biblical character Joseph, and several books of short stories. *Biographical/critical sources:* Charles Neider, editor, *The Stature of Thomas Mann,* New Directions, 1948; *Cyclopedia of*

World Authors, Harper, 1958; Henry Hatfield, *Thomas Mann,* revised edition, New Directions, 1962; *Twentieth-Century Writing: A Reader's Guide to Contemporary Literature,* Transatlantic, 1969; Erich Heller, *Thomas Mann: The Ironic German,* revised edition, Regnery/Gateway, 1979.

* * *

MANSFIELD, Katherine
See BEAUCHAMP, Kathleen Mansfield

* * *

MAN WITHOUT A SPLEEN
See CHEKHOV, Anton (Pavlovich)

* * *

MARCUS, Fred H(arold) 1921-

PERSONAL: Born October 17, 1921, in Brooklyn, N.Y.; son of Jack (a rigger) and Anna (Brumberg) Marcus; married Edith Netreba (a high school dean), September 11, 1948; children: David, Joel. *Education:* Brooklyn College (now of the City University of New York), B.A., 1942; New York University, M.A., 1947, Ph.D., 1953. *Politics:* Liberal. *Religion:* Jewish. *Home:* 1470 Pegfair Estates Dr., Pasadena, Calif. 91103.

CAREER: New York University, New York, N.Y., instructor in education, 1948-52; State University of New York College at Oneonta, assistant professor of English, 1952-55; California State University, Los Angeles, assistant professor, 1955-58, associate professor, 1958-63, professor of English, 1963—. Visiting professor at University of Victoria, summer, 1960, summer, 1962, University of California, Los Angeles, summer, 1961, University of Southern California, summer, 1966, New York University, summer, 1967, and Hawaii Curriculum Center, summer, 1968. Director of National Defense Education Act Institute, summer, 1965. Literary supervisor of films, including "Young Goodman Brown," "The Legend of Sleepy Hollow," "The Legend of Paul Bunyan," "The Legend of John Henry," and "Plato's Cave." *Military service:* U.S. Army, Signal Corps, 1943-45. *Member:* National Council of Teachers of English.

WRITINGS: Perception and Pleasure, Heath, 1967; *Film and Literature: Contrasts in Media,* Chandler & Sharp, 1971; *Short Story/Short Film,* Prentice-Hall, 1977. Contributor to academic journals.

WORK IN PROGRESS: A textbook on children's film.

* * *

MARGARET, Karla
See ANDERSDATTER, Karla M(argaret)

* * *

MARK, Jon
See Du BREUIL, (Elizabeth) L(or)inda

* * *

MARKMAN, Sherwin J. 1929-

PERSONAL: Born January 19, 1929, in Des Moines, Iowa; son of Morris and Dorothy (Caspe) Markman; married Marilyn Louise Gates, August 26, 1951; children: Stephen Madison, Nicole Mari, Stacy Lynn. *Education:* Iowa State University, B.A., 1949; Yale University, LL.B., 1952. *Religion:* Jewish.

Home: 8100 Hamilton Spring Rd., Bethesda, Md. 20038. *Office:* Hogan & Hartson, 815 Connecticut Ave., Washington, D.C. 20006.

CAREER: Brody, Parker, Roberts & Thena, Des Moines, Iowa, partner, 1956-65; Agency for International Development, Washington, D.C., deputy director of Congressional liaison, 1965-66; assistant to president of the United States in Washington, D.C., 1966-68; Hogan & Hartson (law firm), Washington, D.C., partner, 1968—. State executive director of Iowa Citizens for Stevenson, 1956; state president of Iowa Young Democrats, 1967-68; delegate to Democratic National Convention, 1956, 1960, and 1964; state chairman of Iowa Citizens for Hughes, 1964. Chairman of Des Moines Planning and Zoning Commission, 1957-65. *Member:* American Bar Association, Iowa Bar Association, District of Columbia Bar Association.

WRITINGS: The Election (novel), Random House, 1970.

SIDELIGHTS: Markman's novel, *The Election,* is a thriller about a takeover of the United States Government. The coup d'etat occurs after a presidential election that results in a deadlock between the Democrats, Republicans, and a third-party candidate. The House of Representatives is engaged in numerous votes to break the tie, while a racial uprising and subsequent city takeover occurs in Oakland, Calif. The third-party candidate, who campaigned on a racist and anti-Semitic platform, takes advantage of the confusion and gains control of the federal government. Markman, a former aide of President Johnson, explained in a *Library Journal* interview one of his motives for writing *The Election.* "Upon leaving the White House, I began this book," he declared, "intending it as a distillation of my White House experience, a dramatic attack on a constitutional anachronism, the electoral college."

BIOGRAPHICAL/CRITICAL SOURCES: U.S. News and World Report, February 5, 1968; *Library Journal,* June 15, 1970; *Best Sellers,* October 1, 1970.*

*   *   *

MARKOV, Georgi   1929(?)-1978
(David St. George, a joint pseudonym)

OBITUARY NOTICE: Born c. 1929, in Bulgaria; died in 1978 in England. Playwright and author. A successful novelist and playwright in his homeland, Markov became critical of communism in his later works and moved to England in 1971. Shortly before his death, he collaborated with David Phillips, under the pseudonym David St. George, on a political novel, *The Right Honourable Chimpanzee.* Obituaries and other sources: *AB Bookman's Weekly,* October 23, 1978.

*   *   *

MARLIN, Henry
See GIGGAL, Kenneth

*   *   *

MARLOWE, Webb
See McCOMAS, J(esse) Francis

*   *   *

MARQUIS, Don(ald Robert Perry)   1878-1937

BRIEF ENTRY: Born July 29, 1878, in Walnut, Ill.; died of a stroke, December 29, 1937, in Forest Hills, N.Y. American poet and playwright. Marquis is remembered for his creation of *Archy and Mehitabel* (1927), the philosophical cockroach and adventurous alley cat who served as whimsical voices for his own views on contemporary life. Other popular characters include Clem Hawley, a reckless foe of Prohibition, featured in *The Old Soak* (1921) and *Hermione* (1916), through whom he satirized the pretentious "advanced thinkers" of Greenwich Village. Marquis's satire, sense of humor, and mastery of the folk style could not conceal the bitterness and cynicism that ran through his writing. The voice of protest emerged more stridently in *The Almost Perfect State* (1927). Penniless and crippled in his last years, Marquis worked on an autobiographical novel, *Sons of the Puritans* (1939). In it he put aside satire and recorded the events of his life in a sincere, realistic way that some critics considered his most valuable contribution to American letters. *Biographical/critical sources: Twentieth Century Authors: A Biographical Dictionary of Modern Literature,* H. W. Wilson, 1942, 1st supplement, 1955; *Webster's American Biographies,* Merriam, 1974.

*   *   *

MARSHALL, Margaret   1901(?)-1974

OBITUARY NOTICE: Born c. 1901, in Utah; died February 1, 1974, in Upland, Calif. Editor. Marshall was literary editor of the *Nation* for twenty-five years, working with such writers as James Agee, Diana Trilling, and Clement Greenberg. She was also a contributing editor and drama critic. Obituaries and other sources: *Publishers Weekly,* March 4, 1974.

*   *   *

MARSHALL, Robert L(ewis)   1939-

PERSONAL: Born October 12, 1939, in New York, N.Y.; son of Saul (an accountant) and Pearl (a secretary; maiden name, Shapiro) Marshall; married Traute Maass (a translator), September 9, 1966; children: Eric, Brenda. *Education:* Columbia University, A.B., 1960; Princeton University, M.F.A., 1962, Ph.D., 1968; attended University of Hamburg, 1962-65. *Home:* 5643 South Drexel Ave., Chicago, Ill. 60637. *Office:* Department of Music, University of Chicago, 5845 South Ellis, Chicago, Ill. 60637.

CAREER: University of Chicago, Chicago, Ill., instructor, 1966-68, assistant professor of music, 1968-71; Princeton University, Princeton, N.J., visiting associate professor of music, 1971-72; University of Chicago, associate professor, 1972-77, professor of music, 1977—, chairman of department, 1972-78. Member of music advisory board of Illinois Art Council, 1977-79. *Member:* American Musicological Society (member of board of directors, 1974-75), New Bach Society (chairman of American chapter, 1974-77), Phi Beta Kappa. *Awards, honors:* Otto Kinkeldey Prize from American Musicological Society, 1974, for *The Compositional Process of J. S. Bach.*

WRITINGS: The Compositional Process of J. S. Bach, two volumes, Princeton University Press, 1972; (editor) Johann Sebastian Bach, *New Complete Edition,* Series I, Volume XIX: *Cantatas for the Ninth and Tenth Sundays After Trinity,* Baerenreiter, in press. Editor of series, "Recent Researches in the Music of the Baroque Era," A-R Editions. Member of editorial board of *Journal of the American Musicological Society,* 1975-80.

WORK IN PROGRESS: Editing and translating *W. A. Mozart,* by Hermann Abert, two volumes, completion expected in 1984.

SIDELIGHTS: Marshall wrote: "Three individuals have been most significant in forming my approach to music: Gunther Schuller, with whom I studied the French horn during my student days from 1953 to 60; William J. Mitchell, who was instrumental in developing a deeper understanding of the workings of great music; and Arthur Mendel, who did the most to teach me how to think and write clearly about musical matters. My major areas of vocational interest are the music of Bach and Mozart and the Lutheran tradition."

AVOCATIONAL INTERESTS: Travel (Western Europe, especially Italy and Germany).

* * *

MARTIGNONI, Margaret E. 1908(?)-1974

OBITUARY NOTICE: Born c. 1908; died February 11, 1974, in New York, N.Y. Librarian, educator, and editor. Since 1970, Martignoni was executive secretary of the New York Library Association and editor of the *NYLA Journal*. Previously, she had worked in a number of public libraries, taught library science at Columbia University and Catholic University of America, and been a book editor. She edited *The Illustrated Treasury of Children's Literature*. Obituaries and other sources: *Publishers Weekly*, March 18, 1974; *Wilson Library Bulletin*, April, 1974.

* * *

MARTIN, Mary Steichen
See CALDERONE, Mary S(teichen)

* * *

MARTIN, William Keble 1877-1969

OBITUARY NOTICE: Born in 1877 in Radley, England; died November 26, 1969, in Woodbury, England. Clergyman, botanist, and author. Martin spent his entire life studying and drawing British plants. His *Concise British Flora in Colour* was a best-seller. Obituaries and other sources: *AB Bookman's Weekly*, January 19, 1970; *Brittanica Book of the Year*, 1970; *Country Life*, December 15, 1977; *Who Was Who Among English and European Authors, 1931-1949*, Gale, 1978.

* * *

MARTINEZ SIERRA, Gregorio 1881-1947

BRIEF ENTRY: Born May 6, 1881, in Madrid, Spain; died of cancer, October 1, 1947, in Madrid, Spain. Spanish playwright and theatrical producer. Martinez Sierra's best-known and most popular play is "The Cradle Song" (1910), a story of convent life written, as were most of his plays, with his wife, Maria de la O Lejarraga. Nearly all of Martinez Sierra's plays showed a delicate, almost sentimental emphasis on female characters, developed with a sympathy that approached feminism. Influenced by Benavente and later Maeterlinck, he wrote nearly fifty plays, described as uncomplicated, tender works in which piety always triumphs over human weakness, as in "Don Juan de Espana" (1921). Martinez Sierra has been hailed as a representative of Spain's theatre at its best. His first successful play was "The Housekeeper" (1910). "The Kingdom of God" (1915) was widely translated and was a success in English. Another significant contribution of Martinez Sierra to modern Spanish drama was his work as director and producer. He introduced new writers to Spanish audiences, translating nearly fifty plays himself, and revolutionized Spanish stage lighting and design techniques and production style by implementing ideas already in use outside Spain. *Biographical/critical sources:* *Cyclopedia of World Authors*, Harper, 1958; *Modern World Drama: An Encyclopedia*, Dutton, 1972; *McGraw-Hill Encyclopedia of World Drama*, McGraw, 1972.

MARVEL, Tom 1901-1970

OBITUARY NOTICE: Born in 1901; died April 13, 1970, in Fresno, Calif. Journalist and author. Marvel was an expert on wine and the co-author of several books on the subject. He was also the author of *The New Congo*. Obituaries and other sources: *AB Bookman's Weekly*, May 4, 1970.

* * *

MASLIN, Alice 1914(?)-1981
(Nancy Craig)

OBITUARY NOTICE: Born c. 1914 in St. Louis, Mo.; died of cancer, June 5, 1981, in New York, N.Y. Broadcaster and editor. Craig appeared on many radio programs, including "Women of Tomorrow." She also hosted a talk show for KMOX-Radio in St. Louis. From 1966 to 1978 she worked for *House Beautiful*. Obituaries and other sources: *New York Times*, June 7, 1981.

* * *

MASON, Nicholas 1938-

PERSONAL: Born December 30, 1938, in Harrow, England; son of Ronald (a lecturer and writer) and Margaret (a civil servant; maiden name, Coles) Mason; married Jane Nankivell (a health visitor), April 28, 1962; children: Peter Charles Christopher, Robert James, Anthony Alexander, Rosalind Jane. *Education:* Mansfield College, Oxford, B.A. (with honors), 1961. *Home:* 250 Stanstead Rd., Forest Hill, London S.E. 23, England. *Agent:* A. D. Peters & Co. Ltd., 10 Buckingham St., London WC2N 6BU, England. *Office:* London Sunday Times, 200 Gray's Inn Rd., London WC1X 8E2, England.

CAREER: Newcastle Evening Chronicle, Newcastle upon Tyne, England, reporter, 1961-65, reviewer, 1962-66, sub-editor, 1965-66; *London Sunday Times*, London, England, sub-editor, 1966-67, chief sub-editor, 1967-69, production editor, 1969-73, assistant editor, 1973-77, deputy sports editor, 1977—.

WRITINGS: (Editor) *The Olympics*, Times Newspapers, 1972; (editor with George Perry) *Rule Britannia: The Victorian World*, Times Books, 1974; *Football: The Story of All the World's Football Games*, Temple Smith, 1974; (editor with John Lovesey and Edwin Taylor) *The Sunday Times Sports Book*, World's Work, 1979.

* * *

MASSEY, Raymond 1896-

PERSONAL: Born August 30, 1896, in Toronto, Ontario, Canada; naturalized U.S. citizen in 1944; son of Chester Daniel (a manufacturer) and Anna (Vincent) Massey; married Margery Hilda Fremantle, 1921 (divorced, 1929); married Adrianne Allen (an actress), 1930 (divorced, 1939); married Dorothy Ludington Whitney (a lawyer), 1939; children: (first marriage) Geoffrey; (second marriage) Daniel, Anna. *Education:* Attended University of Toronto, 1914, and Balliol College, Oxford, 1919-21. *Home:* 913 Beverly Dr., Beverly Hills, Calif. 90210.

CAREER: Actor, director, and producer. Actor in stage productions, including "In the Zone," 1922, "At Mrs. Beams's," 1923, "The Rose and the Ring," 1924, "Saint Joan," 1925, "The Golden Calf," 1927, "An American Tragedy," 1927, "The Transit of Venus," 1927, "The Constant Nymph," 1928,

"The Second Man," 1928, "Topaze," 1930, "Hamlet," 1931, "Never Come Back," 1932, "The Ace," 1933, "The Shining Hour," 1934, "Ethan Frome," 1936, "Abe Lincoln in Illinois," 1938, "The Doctor's Dilemma," 1941, "Our Town," 1945, "Pygmalion," 1945, "The Father," 1950, "John Brown's Body," 1952, "Julius Caesar," 1957, "J.B.," 1960, "I Never Sang for My Father," 1970, and "The Night of the Iguana," 1975; actor in over seventy films, including "The Speckled Band," 1931, "The Scarlet Pimpernel," 1934, "Things to Come," 1935, "The Prisoner of Zenda," 1937, "Fire Over England," 1937, "Abe Lincoln in Illinois," 1940, "Santa Fe Trail," 1940, "Arsenic and Old Lace," 1944, "God Is My Co-pilot," 1945, "Stairway to Heaven," 1946, "Mourning Becomes Electra," 1947, "The Fountainhead," 1949, "David and Bathsheba," 1951, "Seven Angry Men," 1955, "Prince of Players," 1955, "East of Eden," 1955, "The Naked and the Dead," 1958, "The Great Imposter," 1960, "The Queen's Guards," 1961, "How the West Was Won," 1962, "Mackenna's Gold," 1969, and "All My Darling Daughters" (TV), 1972; appeared as Dr. Gillespie in television series "Dr. Kildare," 1961-65.

Director of over thirty-five stage productions, including "Tunnel Trench," 1925, "The White Chateau," 1927, "An American Tragedy," 1927, "The Sacred Flame," 1929, "The Man in Possession," 1930, "Grand Hotel," 1931, "Late Night Final," 1931, "Lean Harvest," 1931, "The Rats of Norway," 1933, "The Shining Hour," 1934, "Idiot's Delight," 1938, "The Winslow Boy," 1949, and "The Father," 1950. Producer of stage plays, including "Tunnel Trench," 1925, "An American Tragedy," 1927, "The Silver Tassie," 1929, "Lean Harvest," 1931, "The Shining Hour," 1934, "Idiot's Delight," 1938. Co-manager with Allen Wade and George Carr of Everyman Theatre (Hampstead, England), 1926-27. Narrator of radio programs, including "The Doctor's Fights" and "Harvest of Stars." *Military service:* Canadian Field Artillery, 1915-19, served in Siberian Expeditionary Force in France and in Siberia; became captain. Canadian Army, 1942-43; became major.

MEMBER: Actors' Equity Association (council member, 1946-55; first vice-president), American Federation of Television and Radio Artists, Screen Actors Guild, British Equity (council member, 1933-38), Century Association (New York City), Garrick Club (London). *Awards, honors:* D.Litt. from Layfayette University, 1939, and Hobart College, 1953; Delia Austria Medal from Drama League of New York, 1939, for performance in play "Abe Lincoln in Illinois"; Academy Award nomination for best actor from Academy of Motion Picture Arts and Sciences, 1940, for performance in film "Abe Lincoln in Illinois"; gold medal from Women's National Radio Committee, 1941, for participation in programs furthering democracy; LL.D. from Queen's University (Kingston, Ontario), 1949; D.F.A. from Northwestern University, 1959, and Ripon College, 1961; L.H.D. from American International College, 1960; D.H.L. from Wooster College, 1966.

WRITINGS: "The Hanging Judge" (three-act play; based on the novel by Bruce Hamilton), first produced on the West End at New Theatre, September 23, 1952; *When I Was Young* (autobiography), Little, Brown, 1976; *A Hundred Different Lives: An Autobiography,* foreword by Christopher Plummer, Little, Brown, 1979.

SIDELIGHTS: Best known for his stage and screen portrayals of Abraham Lincoln and as the character Dr. Gillespie from the "Dr. Kildare" television series, Raymond Massey has also appeared in hundreds of theatre, film, radio, and television productions, many of which he produced and directed himself.

Massey began his career in 1921 after leaving his Canadian home and the family farm implement business to take up acting—a vocation he pursued for the next fifty-five years.

Massey's autobiography, written after his retirement from the theatre in 1976, fills two volumes with eighty years of memories. The first volume, *When I Was Young,* covers the period from his birth to the early 1920's recounting his boyhood in turn-of-the-century Canada through his decision to become an actor. The second volume, *A Hundred Different Lives,* recollects his career using anecdotes of his encounters with the famous and the great: Charles Laughton, Dame Judith Anderson, Humphrey Bogart, Lord Lawrence Olivier, Dame Gladys Cooper, Gregory Peck, Richard Chamberlain, Ruth Gordon, Gertrude Lawrence, Robert Sherwood, Christopher Plummer, Gerald DuMaurier, John Ford, Tyrone Power, Katharine Cornell, Grace Kelly, and many others.

Massey's background seemed to preclude his choice of a theatrical career. "As a group the Massey's were industrious, responsible people who took the dimmest view of the theatre's flighty ways," observed Paul Showers in the *New York Times Book Review.* Descended from Puritan stock and boasting ancestors who fought in the American Revolution and for the North and the South in the Civil War, Massey's lineage includes the founder of the town of Watertown, New York, and the co-founder of the Chautauqua Institute, an important cultural influence during the post-Civil War period. His father, Chester, was president of the Massey-Harris Company, manufacturers of agricultural machinery in Toronto, and Massey's older brother, Vincent, was the first Canadian-born governor general of Canada. "The Masseys knew they were superior in a rather nice, unself-conscious way," opined *Times Literary Supplement* reviewer Phyllis Grosskurth, and the idea "that Raymond should go on the stage was undoubtedly an anomaly."

Massey's inclination toward the theatre began when he was seven years old and his mother promised to take him to the "'once-upon-a-time' place where people called actors and actresses tell stories." Within a few days of her promise, Massey's mother died from an appendectomy, but the impression she had made on her son was indelible. In *A Hundred Different Lives* Massey related: "Those moments when mother spoke of the theatre had been the last I spent with her before her sudden illness. It was as if she had left me a whole new world of enchantment and delight to explore. . . . I went to my own secret theatre as often as I could and dreamed stories just as mother told me, funny, sad, happy and scary." Overhearing his wife's talk with their son, Massey's father pledged to keep her promise. "Although he remained aloof from the theatre himself, he generously subsidized my attendance," Massey recalled. But, "this was not the dawn of a playwright, nor had I any thought of being one of those people called actors. I was just preparing to be an insatiable member of the audience."

According to Massey, the dream of becoming an actor had its real beginnings when he was eighteen years old and met a young woman who, after asking what he was going to be, announced that, as for herself, she was going to be "a professional actress on the stage—on Broadway." The woman was Katharine Cornell, and Massey credits her with awakening his desire to be an actor. "I knew all of a sudden that somehow I too would be a professional actor and act with Katharine Cornell—on Broadway," Massey wrote in his autobiography. "That was the moment . . . I had walked in my imagination through the pass-door from the front of the house onto the stage. I still had no idea whether or not I could act. But I now had that beacon which Kit [Cornell] had lighted and it stayed lighted."

World War I interrupted Massey's plans for a stage career. At nineteen he served as a lieutenant in the Canadian Field Artillery, and after being wounded in Belgium he became an artillery instructor for ROTC units at Princeton and Yale universities. Massey had his first real taste of show business while serving in Canada's Siberian Expeditionary Force in 1919. Impressed by a skit that Massey had put on at headquarter's mess, the force commander ordered him to prepare a full-length entertainment for the troops. "Road House Minstrels," a vaudeville-minstrel show, was prepared in two weeks and played fifteen performances to audiences that sometimes numbered in the thousands. The show was a huge success and bolstered Massey's determination to make his life in the theatre.

After the war and two years at Oxford University, Massey returned to Toronto and assumed his place in the family farm implement business. "Yet," Massey remembered in *A Hundred Different Lives,* "the theatre kept beckoning." Increasingly discontent with his job, he continued his involvement with the theatre, performing nights and weekends in amateur productions at a local playhouse. Then, after watching veteran actor John Drew perform in the Broadway production of "The Circle," Massey made what he has since called "my sudden but irrevocable decision." That evening he asked Drew "about the nuts and bolts of how to get a chance to work in the theatre." Warning him of the heartbreak awaiting young actors in New York City, Drew advised him to go to London. The next morning Massey quit his job with the family company; surprisingly, Chester Massey agreed to his son's decision, admonishing him only "to avoid self-conceit, to appear in good plays, and to abhor indecency in the theatre." Massey noted, "To the best of my powers, I have tried to do just that."

Within three weeks of his conversation with John Drew, Massey was in London playing the role of an American in Eugene O'Neil's "In the Zone." "He had no training and no experience to speak of, but he had unforgettable looks, unlimited nervous energy and an unmistakable way of speaking," commented *New York Times* reviewer John Russell. "London took to him and in no time at all . . . whether as actor or director he was almost every management's first choice."

In 1931 Massey made his Broadway debut in the title role of Norman Bel Geddes's "Hamlet." After the final matinee performance, playwright Robert Sherwood appeared in Massey's dressing room announcing that he would return for the evening show "If I can get a seat!" That evening Sherwood was backstage again, this time remarking on the similarities between Abraham Lincoln and Hamlet. He asked Massey, "Would you like to play a young Abe Lincoln?" Massey expressed genuine interest in the role, but six years passed before he received the script for "Abe Lincoln in Illinois."

Once it was written, Sherwood's play earned its author a Pulitzer Prize, and Massey's performance as Lincoln won the actor a New York Drama League medal for the most distinguished performance of the 1939 Broadway season. The movie version, filmed one year later, gained Massey an Academy Award nomination for best actor. "All actors who have played Mr. Lincoln have found it a glutinous role, liable to stick to a player offstage," assessed Massey. And, indeed, despite the numerous successes before and after his portrayal, Abe Lincoln remains one of the roles with which Massey is invariably identified.

Another Massey characterization that proved to be as "glutinous" as Abe Lincoln was the role of Dr. Gillespie on the "Dr. Kildare" television series. From 1961 to 1965 Massey starred with Richard Chamberlain in the hit series. "Many times the total number of people who had seen me in all the stage plays I had ever done would watch me in any single episode of a TV series," realized Massey. He thought "It was a pleasure to be greeted by a London bus conductor with 'and 'ow is Dr. Gillespie this rainy mornin'?'" Even so, Massey admitted that, after fifty months of production when the series finally ended, it was without any regret on the part of the principal actors.

For the next few years Massey did television guest spots and filmed several movies, but his activities were increasingly restricted by a degenerative arthritic condition. During the filming of "Mackenna's Gold" he had to be lifted onto the saddle of his horse. "Still," he confessed, "I longed to act just once more in the theatre." In 1968 he was offered the leading part in the London production of Robert Anderson's play "I Never Sang for My Father." He expressed concern to his wife Dorothy that the role would not have been offered to him had the producer known that he was lame. "Rubbish!," she replied. "The part they want you for is the father. He's supposed to be eighty. You'd have to learn to limp if you didn't know how to already." Recollecting his successful return to the English stage, although the play had only a seven-week run, Massey declared, "It was grand to walk or limp the London boards again."

Massey's physical condition continued to deteriorate, and when he made his last stage appearance in 1976 it was in the role of a very old man confined to a wheelchair in Tennessee Williams's "The Night of the Iguana." One evening during a preview performance of the play Massey went blank, momentarily forgetting some of the play's crucial lines. His doctor assured him that the isolated occurrence had probably been due to nervous strain, but Massey felt that "'nervous strain' is a euphemism for 'you've had it.'" At the end of the play's run, he declined an offer to repeat the role on the New York stage, choosing instead to retire and write his memoirs. Massey offered this explanation for his decision: "Oliver Wendell Holmes, Sr. once wrote: 'The riders in a race do not stop when they reach the goal. There is a little finishing canter before coming to a standstill. There is time to hear the kind voices of friends and say to one's self, "The work is done."' I had had my little finishing canter. I had the sense to know that my working years in theatre were over."

AVOCATIONAL INTERESTS: Golf, carpentry, reading play scripts.

CA INTERVIEW

CA interviewed Raymond Massey by phone on September 10, 1980, at his home in Beverly Hills, California.

CA: Theatre is your first professional love, and you wrote in A Hundred Different Lives *that "the actor who works on stage and screen must accept the sad truth that he is following two professional paths which do not converge." Was making movies generally frustrating for you?*

MASSEY: Yes, in a sense it was. The stage actor has the inestimable advantage of adequate preparation for public performance of the character which he is to interpret. In rehearsal he will be able to develop this character, experiment with identifying his own emotional reaction with that character—in short, obtain an objectivity detached from the actor's own personality; and he would reach the complete control of this interpretation of the author's creation. He or she is, so to speak, outside looking in, as far as this character is concerned.

The screenplayer, on the other hand, is allowed no such preparation. With rare exceptions, there will be virtually no rehearsal. He will not have the stage actor's privilege of knowing the character he is to portray as an entity. That character will be submitted to the screenplayer for performance in short, disjointed scenes, usually out of sequence, to be shot practically at sight.

In moviemaking, the character has no control of his voice. The sound mixer can blur the best diction. Inept editing can spoil the most skillful timing. And the very core of good acting, ensemble cooperation, team work, is denied the screenplayer, who is forced to be a soloist. There is always the possibility that his efforts will end up on the cutting-room floor. I once received a telegram from Darryl Zanuck congratulating me on two scenes I had played in the film "The Prince of Players" as Junius Brutus Booth. I had closed in the picture and was home in Connecticut. The telegram ended, "We will have a hard time living up to your performance in those two scenes." Zanuck's problem was quite easily solved by the elimination of those scenes from the film.

CA: You've written about the Method School of Acting in connection with James Dean in making the movie "East of Eden." Do you think the Method School has left behind anything of value?

MASSEY: I think the Method School has left behind nothing of value. There are some actors and actresses around who have discarded the theories of the Method, but their work is still clouded—even now—by the inherent, introspective selfishness, the disregard of diction and the resulting inaudibility. They still lack conscientious self-discipline—the obligation to learn their lines. There are not very many of them, but there are some.

CA: Do you think it's more difficult now to enter the acting profession than it was when you decided to become an actor?

MASSEY: I do not think it is any harder to get initial employment as an actor in the theatre today than it was nearly sixty years ago when I became a professional. In the movies, I think it is easier. Success in other vocations, such as professional sports, can sometimes lead to instant employment in the movies or television, sometimes with unfortunate results for the recruit and the public.

CA: Is it more difficult to get established?

MASSEY: The word *established* has no validity in the entertainment world, in my opinion. Its implication of security has no justification. Uncertainty will always remain a small cloud in the sky for the actor which can become a thunderhead when least expected.

CA: What changes have you seen in public opinion toward actors and the profession?

MASSEY: Actors can always expect their welcome nowadays from the public, commensurate with their professional popularity, should they wish to engage in activities other than those of the entertainment field. We of the profession know that the concept of actors as rogues and vagabonds is an almost forgotten prejudice.

CA: Would you have approached your excellent education any differently if you had known earlier you were going to become an actor?

MASSEY: No. A good liberal arts course at a university is of much advantage to an actor, although not a vocational course,

such as majoring in drama. The only way that an actor can learn his trade is by acting as a professional—for gain—in the professional theatre. I see no place for the academic training of actors except as amateur theatricals, but *not* to be included in the university course.

CA: When you told your father you were going to become an actor, he made you promise to abhor indecency in the theatre, which is something you still feel strongly about. Do you think the present license in movies and on stage will continue?

MASSEY: Well, as long as the present trend of permissiveness continues in all phases of human behavior, there will always be vulgarians anxious to ride the waves and make a fast profit. I think and I hope that the public will be bored sufficiently to defeat these exploitations of smut.

CA: Is there a single stage role you consider your finest, or a favorite role?

MASSEY: No. I do not think that superlatives or comparisons are applicable or appropriate to theatrical endeavor. Many characters I have acted on the stage and a few on the screen have become friends whom I would be loath to offend by invidious comparison. Some have been failures at the box office, but they are just as valued to me as those I have known during long runs. All of these friends have successfully survived the period of preparation, of rehearsal, and that is what counts, far more to the actor, I think, than the number of performances they were given.

CA: You are probably best known to many people from the television series "Dr. Kildare." Do you feel that television has a responsibility to the viewing public?

MASSEY: The networks certainly have a responsibility to the viewing public, a responsibility to provide leadership in programming, instead of committing the time-worn sin of producers of trying to anticipate public taste and pandering to it by providing nothing but endless copies of worn-out past successes. The theatre has long since learned the inefficacy of such unimaginative efforts.

CA: What do you think of current television programming?

MASSEY: I know the problems which the network producers of television face, and they are almost insurmountable, with the amount of time which they have to fill in. But I think they can make a better effort at creative programming.

CA: You refer more than once in your memoirs to reading Trollope. Is he still a favorite?

MASSEY: I'm very fond of Trollope, and I re-read him constantly. His novels allow me a refreshing escape from a world devoid of self-discipline and respect for tradition. Trollope offers a horse-drawn relief from the jet-paced speed at which we travel.

CA: You've also cited as influences Stephen Vincent Benet and, of course, Robert Sherwood, who wrote "Abe Lincoln in Illinois" for you. Are there others who have made a particular impact on your life and career?

MASSEY: Of course Stephen Benet, Bob Sherwood, Rudyard Kipling, Shaw, and a host of others I come back to, and they are all important to me. Not the least, I think, being James Herriot, the Yorkshire veterinarian. He's delightful. He supplies one of the most enchanting backgrounds and atmospheres that I've met in current writing.

CA: Did you originally plan to write your autobiography in two volumes?

MASSEY: No, but it soon looked like a seven-hundred page job, at least. So with the willing agreement of my publishers, I split it into two volumes.

CA: The reader is struck by the mass of memories and detail you recall. Did you have diaries or journals you had kept to draw on in writing the books?

MASSEY: Well, I had my numerous press books, but they really provided me only with a few quotes and cast lists and so forth. I never kept a diary or a journal in all my life, and I have retained very few letters. Both my books are filled almost entirely from memory and with details that I recalled.

CA: Looking back over the life you've recalled in When I Was Young *and* A Hundred Different Lives, *would you do anything differently if you could?*

MASSEY: Oh yes, of course. Many things, both professional and personal, I would handle differently. Two decisions I made I regret intensely. One was impetuous. Just before my final school at Oxford, I decided to leave the university without taking the examinations. I was piqued at the master of Balliol, my college, who admonished me that I was inadequately prepared for these examinations and advised me to stay another term. I have repented the rash decision of going down without a degree for nearly sixty years. The other mistake I regret was my continued neglect to exert my talent as a stage director when I worked in the United States; after "Abe Lincoln in Illinois," with one exception—I only directed one play, a revival. I had plenty of opportunities to do so, to carry on my directing. But I ignored them, and I deplore this lack of judgment.

CA: Unlike many writers, you found the work not lonely but very satisfying. Are you doing more writing now or would you like to do more?

MASSEY: The actor's life is filled with people, real and fictional, and to relive these associations has been a real joy to me. I was never lonely. I would like to write another book which would, among other things, answer adequately the questions which you have posed.

BIOGRAPHICAL/CRITICAL SOURCES: Raymond Massey, *When I Was Young,* Little, Brown, 1976; *Kirkus Review,* August 1, 1976, June 1, 1979; *Christian Science Monitor,* September 15, 1976; *Atlantic,* October, 1976, August, 1979; *New York Times Book Review,* October 3, 1976, September 16, 1979; *Canadian Forum,* November, 1976; *Times Literary Supplement,* June 3, 1977; Raymond Massey, *A Hundred Different Lives: An Autobiography,* Little, Brown, 1979; *Los Angeles Times Book Review,* June 22, 1979; *Washington Post Book World,* August 5, 1979; *Chicago Tribune Book World,* August 12, 1979; *New York Times,* August 20, 1979.

—Sketch by Lillian S. Sims

—Interview by Jean W. Ross

* * *

MASTERS, Edgar Lee   1869(?)-1950
(Lucius Atherton, Elmer Chubb, Webster Ford, Harley Prowler, Lute Puckett, Dexter Wallace)

BRIEF ENTRY: Born August 23, 1869 (some sources say 1868), in Garnett, Kan.; died March 5, 1950, in Melrose Park, Pa. American poet, novelist, essayist, dramatist, and biographer. Raised in rural Illinois, Edgar Lee Masters moved to Chicago as a young man and became a successful lawyer in partnership with the celebrated Clarence Darrow. Much of Masters's early poetry, which he wrote under a variety of pseudonyms, appeared in Chicago newspapers. His masterwork was a collection of verse entitled *Spoon River Anthology* (1915), in which he contrasted the epitaphs on the headstones in a small-town graveyard with those spoken by the dead men and women themselves. At a time when small-town America was still being depicted in literature as a bastion of traditional American values, Masters challenged that myth by demonstrating that a stifling small-town atmosphere could be conducive to the corruption and spiritual decay of its inhabitants. Throughout his life, Masters wrote prolifically, but none of his work matched the early success of the *Anthology.* His biography of Abraham Lincoln, *Lincoln, the Man* (1931), was significant only for its negative portrayal of the former president. He was also the author of an autobiography, *Across Spoon River* (1936). *Residence:* New York, N.Y. *Biographical/critical sources:* Cyclopedia of World Authors, Harper, 1958; *Encyclopedia of World Literature in the Twentieth Century,* updated edition, Ungar, 1967; *Twentieth-Century Writing: A Reader's Guide to Contemporary Literature,* Transatlantic, 1969; *Twentieth-Century Literary Criticism,* Volume 2, Gale, 1979.

* * *

MASTERSON, Whit
See McILWAIN, David

* * *

MATHEWS, Jackson   1907(?)-1978

OBITUARY NOTICE: Born c. 1907; died December 15, 1978, in Westminster, Maryland. Educator, poet, and translator. Mathews translated the works of a number of prominent French authors, including Gide, Baudelaire, and Paul Valery. His translation of Valery's *Monsieur Teste* won a National Book Award in 1974. Obituaries and other sources: *AB Bookman's Weekly,* February 12, 1979.

* * *

MATHIS, Cleopatra   1947-

PERSONAL: Born August 16, 1947, in Ruston, La.; daughter of James C. (a police officer) and Maxine (a waitress; maiden name, Theodos) Walton; married William J. Mathis (a state deputy assistant commissioner of education), June 20, 1973; children: Alexandra. *Education:* Attended Louisiana Technical University, 1965-67, and Tulane University, 1967-68; Southwest Texas State University, B.A., 1970; Columbia University, M.F.A., 1978. *Religion:* Greek Orthodox. *Home:* 5 Cadwalader Dr., Trenton, N.J. 08618.

CAREER: High school English teacher in Converse, Tex., 1970-72, at school for pregnant teenagers in Austin, Tex., 1972-73, in Lawrence, N.J., 1973-74, and at day school for emotionally disturbed and learning-disabled students in Trenton, N.J., 1974-75; artist in schools in New Jersey, 1978-81; Trenton State College, Trenton, instructor in English, 1981—. Director of workshops for teenagers and adults in New Jersey and Pennsylvania. *Member:* Poetry Society of America, Poets and Writers. *Awards, honors:* Dylan Thomas Award for Poetry from New School for Social Research, 1975, for "Two Memories"; scholarship from Bread Loaf writers Conference, 1976; fellowship from New Jersey State Council on the Arts, 1979-80; fellowship from Provincetown Fine Arts Work Center, 1981-82.

WRITINGS: Aerial View of Louisiana (poems), Sheep Meadow Press, 1980.

Work represented in anthologies, including *Leaving the Bough,* International Press, 1981; *Rising Tides,* edited by Joanna Cattonar, University of Arizona Press, 1982; *Poets Now: Eighty for the Eighties,* edited by E. V. Griffith, 1982. Contributor of dozens of poems to magazines, including *New Yorker, Nation, American Poetry Review, Ploughshares, The Southern Review,* and *Poetry Now.* Poetry and managing editor of *Columbia: Magazine of Poetry and Prose,* 1977-78.

WORK IN PROGRESS: A second volume of poetry, publication by Sheep Meadow Press expected in 1982.

*   *   *

MATISOFF, Susan 1940-

PERSONAL: Born August 30, 1940, in Detroit, Mich.; daughter of Edward H. (an advertising executive) and Hazel (Anderson) Kimball; married James A. Matisoff (a professor of linguistics), January 31, 1962; children: Nadja Rachel, Alexandra Lydia. *Education:* Radcliffe College, B.A., 1962; Columbia University, M.A., 1969, Ph.D., 1973. *Residence:* Berkeley, Calif. *Office:* Department of Asian Languages, Stanford University, Stanford, Calif. 94305.

CAREER: Stanford University, Stanford, Calif., assistant professor, 1973-79, associate professor of Asian languages, 1979—. *Member:* Association for Asian Studies (member of Northeast Asia Council, 1977-81), Japan Society, Association of Teachers of Japanese, American Literary Translation Association, American Society for Eastern Art. *Awards, honors:* Japan Foundation fellowship, 1976-77.

WRITINGS: The Legend of Semimaru, Blind Musician of Japan, Columbia University Press, 1978. Book review editor of *Journal of Asian Studies,* 1981—.

WORK IN PROGRESS: Research on medieval Japanese drama and literature.

SIDELIGHTS: Susan Matisoff observed: "The classical literature and drama of Japan provide a storehouse of delights still relatively unstudied in the West."

*   *   *

MATTLIN, Paula Plotnick 1934(?)-1981

OBITUARY NOTICE: Born c. 1934, in Cincinnati, Ohio; died June 10, 1981, in New York, N.Y. Editor. Mattlin worked as a free-lance book editor for several years before becoming editor of *Homelife* magazine. At the time of her death, she was a senior editor at Western Publishing Co. Obituaries and other sources: *Publishers Weekly,* July 3, 1981.

*   *   *

MAULE, Harry E(dward) 1886-1971

OBITUARY NOTICE: Born July 13, 1886, in Fairmount, Neb.; died April 8, 1971, in Glen Cove, Long Island, New York. Publishing executive, journalist, editor, and author. Maule was best known for editing the works of his friend Sinclair Lewis. Maule began his career in journalism and later worked in publishing for Doubleday's Country Life Press, where he began as an editor of *Short Story* magazine, later became an editor

in that firm's book publishing division, and eventually rose to vice-president and editor in chief. When Maule left Doubleday to join Random House as senior editor, he brought along many of Doubleday's top authors, including Sinclair Lewis. Maule co-edited *The Man From Main Street: A Sinclair Lewis Reader; Selected Essays and Other Writings, 1904-1950,* and was the author of *Boys' Book of New Inventions.* Obituaries and other sources: *New York Times,* April 9, 1971; *Publishers Weekly,* May 3, 1971; *AB Bookman's Weekly,* May 24, 1971; *Who Was Who Among North American Authors, 1921-1939,* Gale, 1976.

*   *   *

MAURER, David W(arren) 1906-1981

OBITUARY NOTICE—See index for *CA* sketch: Born April 12, 1906, in Wellston, Ohio; committed suicide, c. June 11, 1981, in Louisville, Ky. Educator, researcher, and author. Maurer worked briefly as a geologist before becoming a researcher at sea for General Seafoods Corp. He then taught at Ohio State University for five years. In 1935 Maurer joined the staff at the University of Louisville, where he stayed for thirty-seven years. An expert on the language of the underworld, Maurer wrote several books on crime, including *The Big Con: The American Confidence Man and the Confidence Game, Whiz-Mob: A Correlation of the Argot of Professional Pickpockets With Their Behavior Pattern,* and *The American Confidence Man.* Obituaries and other sources: *New York Times,* June 14, 1981.

*   *   *

MAUSKOPF, Seymour Harold 1938-

PERSONAL: Born November 11, 1938, in Cleveland, Ohio; son of Philip (in business) and Dora (Trompeter) Mauskopf; married Josephine Mary Album (a health economist), 1964; children: Deborah Carol, Philip Daniel, Alice Elizabeth. *Education:* Cornell University, B.A., 1960; Princeton University, M.A., 1962, Ph.D., 1966. *Residence:* Durham, N.C. *Office:* Department of History, Duke University, Durham, N.C. 27706.

CAREER: Duke University, Durham, N.C., instructor, 1964-66, assistant professor, 1966-72, associate professor, 1972-80, professor of history, 1980—, director of Program in Science, Society, and Human Values. *Member:* American Historical Association, History of Science Society (member of executive committee, 1980—).

WRITINGS: Crystals and Compounds, Transactions of the American Philosophical Society, 1976; (editor) *The Reception of Unconventional Science,* Westview, 1979; *The Elusive Science,* Johns Hopkins Press, 1980.

WORK IN PROGRESS: Research on science (chemistry) in Enlightenment Spain.

*   *   *

MAVOR, Osborne Henry 1888-1951
(James Bridie, Mary Henderson, Archibald P. Kellock)

BRIEF ENTRY: Born January 3, 1888, in Glasgow, Scotland; died of a vascular ailment, January 29, 1951, in Edinburgh, Scotland. Scottish physician, educator, and playwright. Mavor was a surgeon and a professor of medicine who, in middle age, turned to a new career as a dramatist. Known to the theatrical world as James Bridie, he wrote more than forty plays between 1928 and 1951, becoming the first modern playwright indigenous to Scotland. Although his plays often addressed such serious subjects as man's relationship to God and evil, Bridie shaped his works as sophisticated comedies with elements of farce and fantasy. Among those plays critics regard as his best are "The Anatomist" (1931), "Tobias and the Angel" (1932), "A Sleeping Clergyman" (1933), "Mr. Bolfry" (1943), and "The Baikie Charivari" (1952). A lifelong Scottish nationalist, Bridie refused to associate himself with the London stage, preferring instead to remain in Scotland and lead a revival of Scottish drama. He founded the Glasgow Citizens' Theatre in 1943. *Residence:* Glasgow, Scotland. *Biographical/critical sources: Encyclopedia of World Literature in the Twentieth Century,* updated edition, Ungar, 1967; *Twentieth Century Writing: A Reader's Guide to Contemporary Literature,* Transatlantic, 1969; *World Authors, 1950-1970,* H. W. Wilson, 1975; *Twentieth-Century Literary Criticism,* Volume 3, Gale, 1980.

* * *

MAXIMOV, Vladimir (Yemelyanovich) 1930-

PERSONAL: Birth-given name, Leon Samsonov; name legally changed; born December 9, 1930, in Moscow, Soviet Union; son of Emelian (a factory worker) and Tatiana (a bookkeeper; maiden name, Mikheev) Maximov; married Tatiana Poltoratskaia, September 15, 1973; children: Nathalie, Olga. *Education:* Educated in Moscow, Soviet Union. *Politics:* Christian Democrat. *Religion:* Christian Orthodox. *Home and office:* 11 bis rue Lauriston, 75116 Paris, France. *Agent:* B. Hofman, 77 boulevard St. Michel, 75006 Paris, France.

CAREER: Worked as reporter for Soviet radio stations, 1953-55; *Literaturnaya gazeta,* Moscow, Soviet Union, reporter, 1959-61; writer, 1961—. *Member:* International P.E.N. *Awards, honors:* Adenauer Literature Prize from Adenauer Foundation, 1975, for "continuing humanitarian traditions in European literature."

WRITINGS—Novels: *Jiv tchelovek,* translation by Anselm Hollo published as *A Man Survives,* Grove, 1963; *My objivaem zemliu,* translation by Albert Kaspin published as *We Tame the Land,* Ardis, 1973; *Sem dnei tvozenia,* translation published as *Seven Days of Creation,* Knopf, 1974; *Prochaniie is neotkouda,* translation by Michael Glenny published as *Farewell From Nowhere,* Doubleday, 1978; *Karantin,* translation by Glenny published as *Quarantine,* Doubleday, 1981. Also author of *Shaguik gozizontu* (title means "Steps to the Horizon") and *Kovcheg dlia nesvannyh* (title means "Arch for the Uninvited").

Scripts: "15 liet spoustia" (three-act play; title means "Fifteen Years Ago"), first produced in Moscow, Soviet Union, 1956; "Jiv tchelovek" (three-act play, based on own novel; title means "A Man Survives"), first produced in Moscow at Dramatic Theatre on Bronnaia, 1965; "Posyvhye tvoich paralleles" (title means "Signal Calls"), first broadcast by Central Television Network (Moscow), 1970; "Stahjza tchertou" (three-act play; title means "Across the Lines"), first produced in Georgia, Soviet Union, at Georgian Dramatic Theatre, 1971.

Chief editor of *Kontinent,* 1974—.

WORK IN PROGRESS: The second volume of *Farewell From Nowhere.*

SIDELIGHTS: In 1973 Maximov was exiled from the Soviet Union because of his outspoken opposition to the Soviet political system. Maximov told Anne Crutcher of the *Washington Post* that, as the son of an oppositionist who had twice been imprisoned for his support of Leon Trotsky, he "didn't become a dissident; he was born that way." Maximov was only eleven when he ran away from home, and he spent most of his rebellious adolescence in orphanages and reform schools.

On one occasion Maximov was arrested, beaten, and sent to a mental hospital for eight months because, in order to thwart the police and other authorities, Maximov had been using a false identity. In an interview with Herbert Lottman of *Publishers Weekly,* Maximov disclosed that much of the biographical data presently available about him is factually incorrect because it is based on the identity that he had assumed during that period. He told Lottman, for example, that he was born in Moscow (not Leningrad) in 1930 (not 1932) and that his name is really Leon Samsonov.

In response to an inquiry from *CA* regarding this discrepancy, Maximov commented: "My generation in Russia included sons and daughters of thousands, even millions, of people who suffered from Stalinist repressions during the late 1930's and World War II. Families were broken up and the children of 'enemies of the people' were scattered over the whole country. During the war they were thrown on the roads, and most of them landed in special asylums for children. In these homes half of the youngsters didn't know their own names, or their names were changed and new ones invented.

"My father was arrested, and I left home at the age of eleven. I spent several years in such "orphans homes," and in one of them my present name was given to me—Vladimir Maximov. Later this name was legalized and all my civil papers carried this name. My name at birth was Leon Samsonov, and I was born in 1930 in Moscow."

Although the circumstances of Maximov's life prevented him from receiving much formal schooling, Maximov educated himself by reading the works of William Shakespeare, Honore de Balzac, Mark Twain, Theodore Dreiser, Jack London, William Faulkner, Thomas Wolfe, and the great nineteenth-century Russian writers.

Maximov's writing career began when, as a nineteen-year-old farm laborer, he had his poems published in a Caucasus newspaper. A reporting job came next, and by 1959 he was writing for the prestigious literary journal *Literaturnaya gazeta.* Maximov's first novel, *A Man Survives,* was published three years later. The novel, about a man's estrangement from himself and his society, was enthusiastically received both within and outside the Soviet Union. *Saturday Review*'s Maurice Friedberg praised Maximov's novel for contributing to the survival of Russian literature "as a commentary on the human condition" and commended Maximov for "following in the footsteps of the great Russian novelists of the past." A *New York Herald Tribune* reviewer added, "Mr. Maximov is particularly reminiscent of Dostoevsky in his ability to imagine convincingly not only a man's total alienation from his own society . . . but also the redemptive power of human compassion."

The Soviets hailed Maximov as a boy wonder and granted him immediate entry into the Soviet Writers Union. The success of *A Man Survives* also prompted authorities to permit Maximov extraordinary freedom of speech in spite of the novel's many criticisms of what Friedberg called the "unseemly features of Soviet life." Maximov's increasingly outspoken dissent was tolerated until 1973. At that time he was expelled from the Writers Union and forced to leave the country because he violated a Soviet ban on publication of *Seven Days of Creation* when he arranged for a West German firm to publish the novel. Joshua Rubenstein of the *New York Times Book Review* observed that Maximov's "hatred for Soviet Communism suffuses the book, making it easy to understand why the authorities exiled him to Europe."

Critics responded ambivalently to *Seven Days of Creation,* praising Maximov's courage in writing the novel while disparaging its "hyperboles," "clumsy craftsmanship," and "melodramatic devices." *Time*'s Paul Gray, for example, said that the novel, a fictional account of Russian history since the turn of the century, "is another example of the human spirit speaking out when silence is prudent. Yet it is demeaning to praise something not because it is well done but because it was done at all." Susan Jacoby of *Saturday Review* concurred, maintaining that "it is extraordinarily difficult to criticize the writings of Russian dissenters who have paid so dearly for the right of free speech. But it is patronizing, and does no service to Russian literature, to hail every minor new work by a dissident as a successor to *The Brothers Karamazov* or *War and Peace.*"

Another reviewer, George Olkhovsky, insisted that *Seven Days of Creation* is a powerful book that is not adequately served by "existing English translations" that fail to "do justice to its profundity as poetry." Jacoby, meanwhile, conceded that Maximov's novel "has some political and literary interest" and "moments of poignant, subtle beauty."

Maximov's next book, an autobiographical novel entitled *Farewell From Nowhere,* was written during his exile in Paris and chronicles his life up to his departure from the Soviet Union. Herbert Lottman commented in *Publishers Weekly* that readers of *Farewell From Nowhere* will discover that Maximov is a writer "with some of the same life view found in mainstream American literature. Readers of Jack London, of the nineteenth-century American classics, and of Kerouac's Beats will recognize the world where one lives by one's wits, hopping freight cars, bumming food and a place to flop. A life in the American tradition, but with the added dimension of the 'prison-camp brotherhood.'" *Listener*'s Peter Kemp found the book "rambling" and complained that it "never really seems to know where it is going." Zahir Jamal of *New Statesman* agreed and added that "for all Maximov's abundant descriptive strength, his story-teller's imaginative composure remains desperately fragile."

Critics have often compared Maximov's work with that of another Soviet dissident, Aleksandr Solzhenitsyn. Both authors, said Friedberg, avoid "the sensational and the hysterical," and Anne Crutcher added that Maximov, like Solzhenitsyn, is very much a part of the pre-Soviet tradition in literature." Both authors have also continued during their exile to write books criticizing the Soviet political system.

BIOGRAPHICAL/CRITICAL SOURCES: New York Herald Tribune Books, August 4, 1963; *Saturday Review,* September 28, 1963, January 25, 1975; *Time,* February 3, 1975; *New York Times Book Review,* February 23, 1975; *Washington Star,* March 23, 1975; *Biography News,* March/April, 1975; *Observer,* November 12, 1978; *New Statesman,* November 17, 1978; *Listener,* November 30, 1978; *Publishers Weekly,* April 30, 1979.

—*Sketch by Susan M. Trosky*

*   *   *

MAY, Robert Lewis 1905-1976

OBITUARY NOTICE: Born in 1905; died of cancer, August 11, 1976, in Evanston, Ill. Advertising executive and author. May was the creator of Rudolph the Red-Nosed Reindeer, whose story he wrote in 1939 as a Christmas promotion for Montgomery Ward. He adapted the story into a poem, which later became a hit song performed by Gene Autry. Obituaries

and other sources: *Newsweek,* August 23, 1976; *Time,* August 23, 1976.

*   *   *

MAYAKOVSKI, Vladimir (Vladimirovich) 1893-1930

BRIEF ENTRY: Born July 19, 1893, in Bagdady (now Mayakovski), Georgia, Russia (now U.S.S.R.); committed suicide, April 14, 1930, in Moscow, U.S.S.R. Russian poet, playwright, and author. Considered the leading Soviet poet and the forerunner of futurist literature, Mayakovski was a sad and lonely figure whose poems and plays honoring Soviet life were characterized by the underlying despair of the author. His prerevolutionary poems *Oblako v shtanakh* (1915; title means "A Cloud in Trousers") and *Fleita pozvonochnik* (1916; title means "The Backbone Flute") deal with unrequited love in a chaotic world, while his subsequent verse presents an optimistic hope for a better world through Soviet societies. During the 1920's, Mayakovski served as a spokesman for the Communist party, painting signs with party slogans and writing propaganda for children. He wrote the lengthiest poem of his career, *Vladimir Ilyich Lenin* (1924), to mourn Lenin's passing and later wrote two satirical plays, *Klop* (1928; title means "The Bedbug") and *Banya* (1930; title means "The Bathhouse"). Mayakovski continually demonstrated a fervent need for love, particularly in his poems *Lyublyu* (1922; title means "I Love") and *Pro Eto* (1923; title means "About This"), and as a result was criticized by the Russian Association of Proletarian Writers (RAPP) for exhibiting individualism. This official criticism, followed by a broken love affair and the failure of his play "Banya," was thought to have led to Mayakovski's suicide in 1930. *Biographical/critical sources: The Reader's Encyclopedia of World Drama,* Crowell, 1969; *McGraw-Hill Encyclopedia of World Drama,* McGraw, 1972; *World Authors, 1950-1970,* H. W. Wilson, 1975; *Twentieth-Century Literary Criticism,* Volume 4, Gale, 1981.

*   *   *

McCAHILL, Thomas 1907(?)-1975

OBITUARY NOTICE: Born c. 1907; died of a heart attack in 1975 in Ormond Beach, Fla. Columnist and author. McCahill wrote a popular column on automobiles for *Mechanix Illustrated.* He was noted for his sarcastic comments on new model cars. Obituaries and other sources: *Time,* May 26, 1975.

*   *   *

McCAIG, Donald
(Steven Ashley)

PERSONAL—Office: c/o Rawson, Wade Publishers, Inc., 630 Third Ave., New York, N.Y. 10017.

CAREER: Novelist and poet.

WRITINGS—Novels: (Under pseudonym Steven Ashley) *Caleb, Who Is Hotter Than a Two-Dollar Pistol,* McKay, 1975; (under Ashley pseudonym) *Stalking Blind,* Dial, 1976; *The Butte Polka,* Rawson, Wade, 1980.

SIDELIGHTS: McCaig's three suspense novels are set in rural communities rather than in the urban centers usually associated with that type of novel. For example, the location for McCaig's *Caleb, Who Is Hotter Than a Two-Dollar Pistol* is a rustic commune in Virginia where Caleb, a fugitive from a terrorist organization, seeks shelter. The action in *Stalking Blind* takes place in the countryside of West Virginia, where a sheriff must track down a dangerous killer. Located in the small mining community of Butte, Montana, McCaig's *The Butte Polka* revolves around a miner's investigation into the mysterious disappearance of a fellow worker.

Critics applauded McCaig's ability to write convincingly about the cultural characteristics of rural communities. Douglas Bauer of *Washington Post,* for example, said that McCaig "clearly knows, and in many places marvelously conveys, the steps and ceremonies of a small, self-scrutinizing world." A *New York Times Book Review* critic added that McCaig "successfully manages to give the feeling of the rugged individualists who live a little apart from urban civilization."

BIOGRAPHICAL/CRITICAL SOURCES: New York Times Book Review, January 16, 1977; *Washington Post,* August 25, 1980.*

* * *

McCALLUM, James Dow 1893-1971

OBITUARY NOTICE: Born January 25, 1893, in Brooklyn, N.Y.; died December 30, 1971, in Hanover, N.H. Educator and author. A professor of English at Dartmouth College, McCallum was an authority on early Victorian literature. He edited a number of anthologies that have become standard college texts, including the six-volume series *English Literature.* He was also the author of *Eleazar Wheelock,* a biography of the founder of Dartmouth College. Obituaries and other sources: *AB Bookman's Weekly,* January 17, 1972; *National Cyclopaedia of American Biography,* Volume LVI, James T. White, 1975.

* * *

McCOMAS, J(esse) Francis 1911-1978
(Webb Marlowe)

OBITUARY NOTICE: Born in 1911; died April 19, 1978, in San Francisco, Calif. Editor and author. McComas was a founder and co-editor, with Anthony Boucher, of the *Magazine of Fantasy and Science Fiction.* With Boucher, he edited three anthologies of stories from the magazine. McComas also edited several other anthologies of science fiction and mystery stories, including *Special Wonder: The Anthony Boucher Memorial Anthology of Fantasy and Science Fiction,* and wrote stories under his own name and under the pseudonym Webb Marlowe. Obituaries and other sources: *Who's Who in Science Fiction,* Elm Tree Books, 1976; *Publishers Weekly,* June 5, 1978; *Science Fiction and Fantasy Literature,* Volume II: *Contemporary Science Fiction Authors II,* Gale, 1979; *The Encyclopedia of Science Fiction: An Illustrated A to Z,* Grenada, 1979.

* * *

McCONNELL, Frank D(eMay) 1942-

PERSONAL: Born May 20, 1942, in Louisville, Ky.; married, 1964; children: one. *Education:* University of Notre Dame, B.A., 1964; Yale University, M.A., 1965, Ph.D., 1968. *Office:* Department of English, Northwestern University, Evanston, Ill. 60201.

CAREER: Cornell University, Ithaca, N.Y., assistant professor of English, 1967-71; Northwestern University, Evanston, Ill., professor of English, 1971—.

WRITINGS: The Confessional Imagination: A Reading of Wordsworth's Prelude, Johns Hopkins Press, 1974; *The Spoken Seen: Film and the Romantic Imagination,* Johns Hopkins Press, 1975; *Four Postwar American Novelists: Bellow, Mailer, Barth,*

and Pynchon, University of Chicago Press, 1977; (editor) *Byron's Poetry: Authoritative Texts, Letters, Journals, Criticism, Images of Byron,* Norton, 1978; *Storytelling and Mythmaking: Images From Film and Literature,* Oxford University Press, 1979; *The Science Fiction of H. G. Wells,* Oxford University Press, 1981. Contributor to literature journals.

SIDELIGHTS: McConnell's volume of criticism, *Four Postwar American Novelists: Bellow, Mailer, Barth, and Pynchon,* received mixed reviews. Displeased with the book, Warren French of *American Literature* commented that "the aimless title of this book, its evasive conclusion . . . , and its lack of any bibliography of other speculations about much discussed authors puzzled me about the specific occasion for it." D. J. Leigh, however, praised the work in *Best Sellers.* He observed, "McConnell combines the formal analysis of old Yale 'new critical' mentors . . . with the sociophilosophical approaches of the new Yale gurus . . . to produce one of the finest critiques of contemporary fiction." The critic concluded that "few readers of these four novelists can afford to dismiss McConnell's excellent and provocative book."

BIOGRAPHICAL/CRITICAL SOURCES: Times Literary Supplement, August 13, 1976; *Journal of Aesthetics,* winter, 1976; *Encounter,* February, 1977; *Best Sellers,* October, 1977; *American Literature,* January, 1978; *Washington Post Book World,* March 22, 1981.

* * *

McCULLOCH, Alan McLeod 1907-

PERSONAL: Born August 5, 1907, in St. Hilda, Australia; son of Alexander (an engineer and writer) and Anne (McLeod) McCulloch; married Ellen Marion Bromley, September 1, 1947; children: Susan McLeod McCulloch. *Education:* Attended National Gallery of Victoria Art School, 1926-27. *Home address:* Tucks Rd., Shoreham, Victoria 3916, Australia. *Office:* Herald, Flinders St., Melbourne, Victoria 3000, Australia; and Mornington Peninsula Arts Centre, 4 Vancouver St., Mornington, Victoria 3931, Australia.

CAREER: Commonwealth Bank of Australia, Melbourne, bank officer, 1928-45; *Argus,* Melbourne, Australia, art critic, 1945-47; *Herald,* Melbourne, art critic, 1951—. Director of Mornington Peninsula Arts Centre, 1969—. *Member:* Australian Gallery Directors Council, Australian Society of Authors, Fellowship of Australian Writers, Regional Galleries Association of Victoria, Lawn Tennis Association of Victoria. *Awards, honors:* Officer of Order of Australia, 1975.

WRITINGS: Trial by Tandem (travel), Allen & Unwin, 1950; *Highway Forty* (travel), F. W. Cheshire, 1951; *Encyclopedia of Australian Art,* Hutchinson, 1968, revised edition, 1982; *The Golden Age of Australian Painting: Impressionism and the Heidelberg School,* Lansdowne, 1969; *Artists of the Australian Goldrush,* Landsdowne, 1975. Australian correspondent for *Art International,* 1969-73.

WORK IN PROGRESS: Encyclopedia of Australian Art.

SIDELIGHTS: McCulloch told *CA:* "The most important part of my early education came from family studies with my younger brother Wilfred (a painter killed in Singapore during World War II), from studies in the State Library of Victoria, and from lessons received in Melbourne as the self-elected protege of Will Dyson, the most celebrated Allied war cartoonist of World War I. Every artist/writer has to cross a desert if he/she is to amount to anything. Mine was the eighteen years spent in a bank, studying art at night. I came out of the bank like the Count of Monte Cristo came out of his dungeon. And I was lucky in my timing. I went into the *Argus* newspaper as an art critic, cartoonist, and editor of black-and-white contributions. My professional arrival on the art scene coincided with the advent of all those young Australian artists who later became famous as the antipodean school. Most of them were my co-llegues and friends. My part as a 'promoter' of my generation of artists is not for me to say. It's all recorded in four large volumes of newspaper clippings.

"My work in progress, the *Encyclopedia of Australian Art,* has been a kind of Frankenstein's monster that has kept me from my first love—drawing. But I can't see how I could have avoided writing it."

* * *

McDOUGALL, Anne 1926-

PERSONAL: Born June 16, 1926, in Montreal, Quebec, Canada; daughter of T.W.L. (a diplomat) and Elizabeth (Savage) MacDermot; married Robert McDougall (a professor), June 19, 1971; children: Richard, Ian, Christine. *Education:* McGill University, B.A., 1947; attended Middlebury College, 1950; Carleton University, M.A., 1981. *Home:* 24 Glen Ave., Ottawa, Ontario, Canada K1S 2Z7.

CAREER: Free-lance writer.

WRITINGS: Anne Savage: The Story of a Canadian Painter, Harvest House, 1977. Contributor to periodicals, including *Maclean's Magazine.*

WORK IN PROGRESS: Diamond Jenness: His Contribution to Eskimo Art History. .

* * *

McELWEE, William (Lloyd) 1907-1979

OBITUARY NOTICE—See index for *CA* sketch: Born September 13, 1907, in London, England; died c. April, 1979. Educator, historian, translator, editor, and author. McElwee taught history at the University of Liverpool, Stowe School, and the Royal Military Academy at Sandhurst. He was also a research scholar at the University of Vienna. With A.J.P. Taylor, McElwee translated and edited Heinrich Friedjung's *The Struggle for Supremacy in Germany.* He wrote several books on history, including *The Reign of Charles V, The Murder of Sir Thomas Overbury, The Story of England,* and *The Art of War: Waterloo to Mons.* McElwee also wrote a novel entitled *The House.* Obituaries and other sources: *AB Bookman's Weekly,* April 5, 1979.

* * *

McFADDEN, David 1940-

PERSONAL: Born October 11, 1940, in Hamilton, Ontario, Canada. *Residence:* Nelson, British Columbia, Canada. *Office:* David Thompson University Center, Nelson, British Columbia V1L 3C7, Canada.

CAREER: Hamilton Spectator, Hamilton, proofreader, 1962-70, reporter, 1970-76; Simon Fraser University, Burnaby, British Columbia, writer-in-residence, 1979; Kootenay School of Writing, David Thompson University Centre, Nelson, British Columbia, teacher of creative writing, 1979—. Gives poetry readings. Free-lance editor for Coach House Press and McClelland & Stewart. *Member:* Canadian Periodical Publishers' Association, League of Canadian Poets, Writers' Union of Canada. *Awards, honors:* Mickey Award, 1975, for *A Knight in Dried Plums;* Canada Council senior fellowship, 1976; Ne-

bula Award, 1977, for poem "I Don't Know"; winner of Canadian Broadcasting Corp. long poem competition, 1979, for *A New Romance;* National Magazine Award, 1981, for a series of six poems published in the *Capilano Review.*

WRITINGS—Poetry: *The Poem Poem,* Weed Flower Press, 1967; *Letters From the Earth to the Earth,* Coach House Press, 1968; *The Saladmaker,* Weed Flower Press, 1968, Cross Country, 1977; *Poems Worth Knowing,* Coach House Press, 1971, *Intense Pleasure,* McClelland & Stewart, 1972; *The Ova Yogas,* Weed Flower Press, 1972; *A Knight in Dried Plums,* McClelland & Stewart, 1975; *The Poet's Progress,* Coach House Press, 1977; *On the Road Again,* McClelland & Stewart, 1978; *I Don't Know,* Vehicle Press, 1978; *A New Romance,* Cross Country, 1979; *My Body Was Eaten by Dogs: Selected Poems,* introduction by George Bowering, Cross Country, 1981.

Fiction: *The Great Canadian Sonnet,* Coach House Press, 1970; *A Trip Around Lake Erie,* Coach House Press, 1981; *A Trip Around Lake Huron,* Coach House Press, 1981; *Animal Spirits* (short stories), illustrations by Greg Curnoe, Coach House Press, 1981.

Editor of *Mountain,* 1960-63; editor of *Writing.*

WORK IN PROGRESS: A novel.

SIDELIGHTS: David McFadden has lived in Hamilton, Ontario, for most of his life. "I believe in having strong roots," he told a writer for the *Quill & Quire.* "I write about the things that are closest to me." In both his poetry and his prose, McFadden draws from such ordinary elements of daily life as fast-food restaurants, mortgage payments, family pets, and camping trips. He calls attention to the many incongruities in the modern world, and he is known for his ability to depict the commonplace with insight and humor. "What is good about McFadden," noted Robert Gibbs in *Fiddlehead,* "is his honest happiness in the phenomena of living so often discarded by the high-minded."

AVOCATIONAL INTERESTS: Weight lifting, meditating, collecting mushrooms.

CA INTERVIEW

CA interviewed David McFadden by phone on August 28, 1980, and September 1, 1980.

CA: You're known mainly as a poet, although you have written novels and fiction. What is your approach to writing? What sort of routine do you go through? Do you write in the morning? Do you set aside time to write?

McFADDEN: That changes all the time. I've been writing for about twenty years, and I find that I go through phases. I went through a long period where my writing time was stolen from my sleeping time. I would wake up in the middle of the night and start writing, and I'd write till dawn. Or I wouldn't bother to go to bed at all; I'd just stay up all night and write. It was never planned. I think I'm more civilized in my approach, or perhaps more sensitive to the unconscious process.

CA: Do you use the typewriter when you're composing?

McFADDEN: I tend to use a typewriter more than I used to, but basically I still like to write the first draft by hand.

CA: Do you do many revisions?

McFADDEN: I do very rough drafts, and I make minimal changes in each revision, but I do several revisions. I find it's easier that way. I probably do more revising than most, but its actually less wear and tear, like putting on several thin coats rather than just one.

CA: The long poems that you've included in On the Road Again *and* A New Romance *seem to be a natural bent of yours. You've been toying with the long poem as a genre for a long time, haven't you?*

McFADDEN: My first book was one long poem. It was called *The Poem Poem.*

CA: Was that your first attempt at the long poem?

McFADDEN: No, I was working on long poems before that, but none of them ever made it into print. *A New Romance* was followed by two others in that series, *Night of Endless Radiance* and *Country of the Open Heart.* They're actually quite a bit longer. They're in the same series, a series which I call the *Kootenay Sonatas,* but I'm not very happy with the latter two—they're on the shelf right now. I don't know whether I'm going to go back to them or not. But now I'm writing mostly serial poetry. It may not fit the usual definition for serial poetry, but it's a long series of short poems with interconnecting content.

CA: Are you still drawing upon the same kinds of themes in your work? Poems and stories about the locale, common everyday people and events, the kind of writing you did about Hamilton, Ontario, your family, and the people there?

McFADDEN: That's still there, I think. But for the time being, some other priorities are taking over.

CA: What about Nelson, British Columbia? Are you able to draw on that like you did on Hamilton?

McFADDEN: Sure, but I'm not getting into things like I used to. There are things that are going on here that I don't find out about until people tell me. I think I should be doing that, not them. I should be writing about it. I guess I don't have that street sense like I used to.

CA: Speaking of "street sense," you used to work as a reporter for the Hamilton Spectator.

McFADDEN: Fourteen years, seven as a proofreader and the rest as a general assignment reporter and working on the police beat.

CA: Did it help your literary writing? Or was it a distraction? Did it cut into your time?

McFADDEN: I don't know, I was still writing a lot. How do you know whether it had a bad effect? One thing, I quickly lost my innocence. When I look back at some of the stuff that I wrote before that, I'm shocked at how innocent I was. It's downright embarrassing to read.

CA: You're teaching creative writing at Kootenay School of Writing now. How do you find that? Have you ever done it before?

McFADDEN: I've never done it on a full-time basis before. It certainly does have an effect on my writing. I think it slows my writing down a lot. I find it hard to go home and write when I'm talking about writing all day. But was I really surprised this summer. I seem to have made up for lost time—I've done an awful lot of writing this summer.

CA: How did you ever get into writing?

McFADDEN: Curiosity, I guess. I always wanted to write things down as a child. I come from a very strong diarist tradition. I started keeping a diary when I was about eight years old. I remember looking back on it after a few months and thinking: "This is terribly boring. My life is much more interesting than this." Then I started wondering why it was so boring, or why my accounts of certain days were so much more boring than my memories of those days. So I started working at that, and that's how I got to thinking about writing so early.

CA: Of all your books, The Great Canadian Sonnet *is perhaps the oddest in terms of format. It's in the Big Little style, isn't it? Was that your idea? Do you collect Big Little Books?*

McFADDEN: No, but Greg Curnoe [the illustrator of *The Great Canadian Sonnet*] did. So did Victor Coleman [a poet and former editor of Coach House Press in Toronto]. Coleman knew that Curnoe collected Big Little Books, so he gave him the idea of illustrating the book in that style. They're doing another one of my books—short stories—but in another children's book style, the Golden Books style. Apparently Curnoe hasn't finished all the pictures for the book yet, but there will be a full-page picture for each chapter or each story and a horizontal picture at the top of the title page for each story. This is a group of new stories that I call *Animal Spirits.* It was originally going to be called *Everyday Life in the Twentieth Century.* But one of the stories in the collection is called "Animal Spirits," and I decided to switch the titles around and call the story in the book "Everyday Life in the Twentieth Century," and call the book *Animal Spirits.* But some people at Coach House want me to change it back.

CA: Everday Life in the Twentieth Century *really sounds more like a McFadden book.*

McFADDEN: Yes, but maybe that's the problem.

CA: The thing about the Sonnet *book, however, is that the narrator kind of sums up your approach to writing. He says, "I guess I'm just a homey philosopher." Do you see yourself as a philosopher? In a sense, I see you doing the same kind of things in your poems, presenting situations and people, not with a moral, but in a casual, philosophizing manner.*

McFADDEN: I suppose so. I'm like everybody else, but I've never been into the professional or academic philosophers. I've never been able to read them all, but I think I take that view of looking at life.

CA: Margaret Atwood, a contemporary of yours, says if you want to make money and achieve fame or literary success, you've got to write fiction, because fiction is where it's at right now. What about you? You've turned to fiction, haven't you?

McFADDEN: Yes, I feel that way. I write a lot of fiction now. I've got two novels coming—the trips around the Great Lakes. They're books that explore Canadian-American relations. I'm having a lot of fun writing about the family, mom and dad and two kids. At the moment I'm still in the process of writing the others. I've done Lake Erie and Lake Huron. Lake Michigan is in rough, and Ontario and Superior, I haven't done yet. But I'm not just doing fiction. I'm still writing poetry. Cross Country Press in the United States is coming out with *My Body Was Eaten by Dogs.* George Bowering is doing the introduction.

CA: Is the process of writing a poem different from the process of writing a novel?

McFADDEN: Usually prose is more deliberate. Poetry, I feel, is almost already written—I just have to get it down. It has a quality of being dictated to you. But with prose, you have to think about it, work it all out, know exactly what you're doing. That's the difference with me, anyway. It's not necessarily the difference between prose and poetry, but the difference between fiction and poetry.

CA: Do you make a fairly complete outline? For example, did you write an outline for the Sonnet *novel?*

McFADDEN: No, but I had a pretty good idea of what I wanted to do in my mind. And in the Great Lakes books I had a very simple outline, a very simple structure, and I knew how it would go on.

CA: What about your affiliations? You're really not part of any movement of poetry or writers in this country, are you? You associate with the former Tish *[magazine] group, but you really aren't like them in the style of your work. You aren't at all like the Black Mountain poets, either.*

McFADDEN: No, I'm not. I can't read Robert Creeley, for one thing. I don't like his work. I don't know. I get along with the *Tish* people. They seem to like my work, and I like theirs, too, but my writing is different. In fact, it's different than anything else I've seen. I guess I'm alone in that. I don't think I belong to any movement in Candian poetry.

BIOGRAPHICAL/CRITICAL SOURCES: Canadian Forum May, 1968; *Fiddlehead,* summer, 1968; *Quill & Quire,* December, 1975; *Authors in the News,* Volume 2, Gale, 1976; *Windsor Star,* April 29, 1978.

—*Interview by C. H. Gervais*

* * *

McHUGH, Leroy 1891(?)-1975

OBITUARY NOTICE: Born c. 1891; died of heart disease in 1975 in Chicago, Ill. Journalist. A famous police reporter, McHugh covered over seven hundred murders. He was noted for his aggressive approach to reporting and used many tricks to get information, once posing as a coroner to get privileged information. His biggest scoop was a series of interviews with an escaped swindler in 1952. Obituaries and other sources: *Time,* May 26, 1975.

* * *

McILWAIN, David 1921-
(Charles Eric Maine, Bob Wade; Whit Masterson, a joint pseudonym)

PERSONAL: Born January 21, 1921, in Liverpool, England; son of David (an engineer) and Caroline (Jones) McIlwain; married Joan Lilian Hardy, 1947 (divorced, 1960); married Clare Mary Came, 1961; children: four daughters, two sons. *Agent:* c/o Ace Books, Charter Communications, Inc., 360 Park Ave. S., New York, N.Y. 10010.

CAREER: Journalist, 1948—. Free-lance writer and consultant. *Member:* Crime Writers Association, National Union of Journalists.

WRITINGS—Science fiction novels, except as noted; under pseudonym Charles Eric Maine: *Spaceways: A Story of the Very Near Future,* Hodder & Stoughton, 1953, published as *Spaceways Satellite,* Avalon, 1958; *Timeliner: A Story of Time and Space,* Rinehart, 1955; *Crisis 2000,* Hodder & Stoughton,

1955; *Escapement,* Hodder & Stoughton, 1956, published as *The Man Who Couldn't Sleep,* Lippincott, 1958; *High Vacuum,* Ballantine, 1957; *The Isotope Man,* Lippincott, 1957; *World Without Men,* Ace Books, 1958; *The Tide Went Out,* Hodder & Stoughton, 1958; *Fire Past the Future,* Ballantine, 1959 (published in England as *Count-Down,* Hodder & Stoughton, 1959); *Subterfuge,* Hodder & Stoughton, 1959; *He Owned the World,* Avalon, 1960 (published in England as *The Man Who Owned the World,* Hodder & Stoughton, 1961); *Calculated Risk,* Hodder & Stoughton, 1960; *The Mind of Mr. Soames,* Hodder & Stoughton, 1961; *The Darkest of Nights,* Hodder & Stoughton, 1962, published as *Survival Margin,* Fawcett, 1968; *Never Let Up,* Hodder & Stoughton, 1964; *B.E.A.S.T.: Biological Evolutionary Animal Simulation Test,* Hodder & Stoughton, 1966, Ballantine, 1967; *The World's Strangest Crimes* (nonfiction), Hart Publishing, 1967, reprinted as *The Bizarre and the Bloody: A Clutch of Weird Crimes, Each Shockingly True!,* 1972; *World-Famous Mistresses* (nonfiction), Odhams, 1970; *The Random Factor,* Hodder & Stoughton, 1971; *Alph,* Doubleday, 1972; *Thirst,* Ace Books, 1978.

Novels; under joint pseudonym Whit Masterson; published by Dodd: *Dead, She Was Beautiful,* 1955; *All Through the Night,* 1955; *Badge of Evil,* 1956; *A Shadow in the Wild,* 1957; *The Dark Fantastic,* 1959; *A Hammer in His Hand,* 1960; *Evil Come, Evil Go,* 1961; *Man on a Nylon String,* 1963; *711: Officer Needs Help,* 1965; *Play Like You're Dead,* 1967; *The Last One Kills,* 1969; *The Death of Me Yet,* 1970; *The Gravy Train,* 1971; *Why She Cries, I Do Not Know,* 1972; *The Undertaker Wind,* 1973; *The Man With Two Clocks,* 1974; *Hunter of the Blood: A Novel of Suspense,* 1977; *The Slow Gallows: A Novel of Suspense,* 1979.

Crime novels; under pseudonym Bob Wade: (With Bill Miller) *Pop Goes the Queen,* Farrar, Straus, 1947; *Knave of Eagles,* Random House, 1969. Also author of *Fatal Step,* 1948, *Uneasy Street,* 1948, *Devil on Two Sticks,* 1949, *Calamity Affair,* 1950, *Murder Charge,* 1951, *Shoot to Kill,* 1952, and *The Stroke of Seven,* Morrow.

Author of radio plays "Spaceways," first broadcast by British Broadcasting Corp. (BBC-Radio), 1952, and "The Einstein Highway." Contributor to periodicals, including *Amazing Stories.*

* * *

McINTOSH, E. 1894(?)-1970

OBITUARY NOTICE: Born c. 1894; died March 23, 1970, in Exmouth, England. Lexicographer and editor. McIntosh was best known as the chief editor of the *Concise Oxford Dictionary* and the *Pocket Oxford Dictionary* for over twenty-five years. Obituaries and other sources: *AB Bookman's Weekly,* May 4, 1970.

* * *

McINTOSH, James (Henry) 1934-

PERSONAL: Born February 4, 1934, in New York, N.Y.; son of Rustin (a pediatrician) and Millicent (a college president; maiden name, Carey) McIntosh; married Ingrid Hernandez (a librarian and musicologist), June 28, 1975. *Education:* Harvard University, A.B., 1955; Yale University, A.M., 1958, Ph.D., 1966; attended Free University of Berlin, 1959-60. *Residence:* Ann Arbor, Mich. *Office:* Department of English, University of Michigan, 2620 Haven Hall, Ann Arbor, Mich. 48109.

CAREER: Tufts University, Medford, Mass., assistant professor of English, 1966-67; Yale University, New Haven, Conn., assistant professor, 1967-73, associate professor of English, 1973-75, director of undergraduate studies, 1972-75; University of Michigan, Ann Arbor, assistant professor of English, 1975—. *Military service:* U.S. Navy, 1955-57. *Awards, honors:* Fulbright fellowship for West Germany, 1959-60; National Endowment for the Humanities fellowship, 1976.

WRITINGS: Thoreau as Romantic Naturalist, Cornell University Press, 1974; (editor) *The Norton Critical Edition of Selected Tales of Nathaniel Hawthorne,* Norton, in press. Contributor to *Yale Review, Forum,* and *Amerika Studien/American Studies.*

WORK IN PROGRESS: Research on the transformation of beliefs into fiction in nineteenth-century American literature; research on Melville, Schiller, and Goethe.

SIDELIGHTS: McIntosh wrote: "If I ever get done with nineteenth-century American literature, I'd like to write on Latin American literature. I'm drawn to poetry in foreign languages, to scriptures of origins, to originating eras in cultures, to the experience of the word unmolested by fashion and schedules."

*   *   *

McKAY, Claude   1890-1948
(Eli Edwards)

BRIEF ENTRY: Born September 15, 1890, in Sunny Ville, Jamaica; died May 22, 1948, in Chicago, Ill. American poet and novelist. McKay was a prominent figure in the Harlem literary renaissance of the 1920's. He came to the United States in 1912, and the racial prejudice he experienced caused him to drop his youthful conservatism in favor of a more militant stance. His experiences as a black immigrant were first portrayed in such early volumes of poetry as *Spring in New Hampshire* (1920). Much of his distinction as a poet lay in his theme of black vitality and in his role as a left-wing catalyst of social reform. He expressed his alienation and frustration at prejudice, halting his protest just short of the passionate hatred that would emerge in some later black literature. One of his most popular poems, "If We Must Die" (1919), is in this vein. *Home to Harlem* (1928) was his first novel and one of the first bestsellers by a black writer. He also wrote an autobiography, *A Long Way From Home* (1937). In these books, as in his poetry, McKay searched among ordinary black people for the common thread that could link them together in a black culture that would be distinctively their own. *Biographical/critical sources: Twentieth Century Authors: A Biographical Dictionary of Modern Literature,* H. W. Wilson, 1942, 1st supplement, 1955; Stephen H. Bronz, *Roots of Negro Racial Consciousness, the 1920's: Three Harlem Renaissance Writers,* Libra, 1964; *The McGraw-Hill Encyclopedia of World Biography,* McGraw, 1973.

*   *   *

McKNIGHT, Allan Douglas   1918-

PERSONAL: Born January 14, 1918, in Sydney, Australia; son of George (a clerk) and Alice Emma (Stephen) McKnight; married Marion Quigg, August 10, 1940; children: Patricia McKnight Triviere, Connor, Stephanie. *Education:* University of Sydney, LL.B. (with honors), 1938. *Politics:* Socialist. *Religion:* Agnostic. *Home:* Flat 4, Garden House, 13 Clifton Pl., Brighton BN1 3FN, England.

CAREER: Associated with Federal Attorney General's Department, 1938-52; Australian Cabinet, Canberra, Australia, deputy secretary, 1952-54; Australian Department of the Army, Melbourne, permanent secretary, 1955-58; International Atomic Energy Agency (IAEA), Vienna, Austria, Australian governor

in Sydney, 1958-64, chairman of board of governors, 1961, inspector general in Vienna, 1964-68; University of Sussex, Brighton, England, visiting fellow at Science Policy Research Unit, 1968-72; Civil Service College, London, England, lecturer in public administration, 1972—. Executive member of Australian Atomic Energy Commission, 1958-64; guest on television programs. *Military service:* Royal Australian Navy, 1940-45; became lieutenant. *Member:* United Nations Association (chairman of disarmament working group, 1970-80). *Awards, honors:* Commander of Order of the British Empire.

WRITINGS: Nuclear Nonproliferation: IAEA and Euratom, Carnegie Endowment for International Peace, 1970; *Atomic Safeguards: A Study in International Verification,* United Nations Institute for Training and Research, 1971; *Scientists Abroad: A Study of the International Movement of Persons in Science and Technology,* United Nations Educational, Scientific, and Cultural Organization (UNESCO), 1971; (editor) *Environmental Pollution Control,* Allen & Unwin, 1974; *World Disarmament,* United Kingdom United Nations Association, 1978. Contributor to journals.

WORK IN PROGRESS: Continuing research on disarmament.

SIDELIGHTS: McKnight wrote: "At fifty I found I had three children all over twenty-one. God, they had to rely on themselves. I had been a civil servant for nigh forty years. I was sick of expressing my thoughts with the ghoul of a national minister or another government looking over my shoulder. So I decided to get out of the rat race and think and write for myself. It was like removing a gag from one's throat or like the Czech dog saying in Poland, 'At least I can bark here.' I am now retired. After my interest in such subjects as the European Economic Community and science policy, I asked myself what matters for my grandchildren. The answer was simple—disarmament!"

BIOGRAPHICAL/CRITICAL SOURCES: Bulletin of Atomic Scientists, December, 1979.

*   *   *

McKOWN, Robert   1908-1973

OBITUARY NOTICE: Born in 1908 in London, England; died in 1973. Editor of British journals on industrial safety, including *Official Architecture and Planning.* McKown served as editorial officer of the industrial safety division of the Royal Society for the Prevention of Accidents. He was the author of *Comprehensive Guide to Factory Law.* Obituaries and other sources: *The Author's and Writer's Who's Who,* 6th edition, Burke's Peerage, 1971; *AB Bookman's Weekly,* October 15, 1973; *Who Was Who Among English and European Authors, 1931-1949,* Gale, 1978.

*   *   *

McPHERSON, Harry Cummings, Jr.   1929-

PERSONAL: Born August 22, 1929, in Tyler, Tex.; son of Harry Cummings and Nan (Hight) McPherson; married Clayton Read, August 30, 1952; children: Courtenay, Peter B. *Education:* University of the South, B.A., 1949; attended Columbia University, 1949-50; University of Texas, LL.B., 1956. *Politics:* Democrat. *Religion:* Episcopalian. *Home:* 30 West Irving St., Chevy Chase, Md. 20015. *Office:* 1660 L St. N.W., Washington, D.C. 20036.

CAREER: U.S. Senate, Washington, D.C., assistant general counsel to Democratic policy committee, 1956-59, associate counsel, 1959-61, general counsel, 1961-63; U.S. Department of the Army, Washington, D.C., deputy under-secretary of international affairs, 1963-64; U.S. Department of State, Washington, D.C., assistant secretary of state for educational and cultural affairs, 1964-65; special assistant to President Lyndon B. Johnson, 1965-66, special counsel, 1966-69; private practice of law in Washington, D.C., 1969—. Chairman of task force on domestic policy, of Democratic Advisory Council of Elected Officials, 1974-75. Vice-chairman of John F. Kennedy Center for Performing Arts, 1969-76, general counsel, 1977—; member of board of directors of Woodrow Wilson International Center for Scholars, 1969-74. *Military service:* U.S. Air Force, 1950-53; became second lieutenant. *Member:* District of Columbia Bar Association, Texas Bar Association, New York Council on Foreign Relations (member of board of directors, 1974-77). *Awards, honors:* Distinguished civilian service award from U.S. Department of the Army, 1964; Arthur S. Flemming Award, 1968.

WRITINGS: A Political Education, Little, Brown, 1972.

BIOGRAPHICAL/CRITICAL SOURCES: Charles Roberts, *L.B.J.'s Inner Circle*, Dial, 1965; Patrick Anderson, *The President's Men*, Doubleday, 1968.*

*   *   *

McQUEEN, Ian   1930-

PERSONAL: Born February 26, 1930, in Bournemouth, England; son of Peter Cowan (a civil engineer) and Phyllis (Palmer) McQueen; married Sheila Ford (a teacher and county councillor), August 17, 1957; children: Peter, Janet, Donald, Alexander. *Education:* University of Bristol, LL.B. (with first class honors), 1950. *Politics:* Conservative. *Religion:* Church of England. *Home:* 136 Norton Rd., Bournemouth BH9 2QB, England. *Office:* Andrews, McQueen & Co., Lansdowne, Bournemouth BH1 2NX, England.

CAREER: Andrews, McQueen & Co., Bournemouth, England, solicitor, 1954—. *Member:* English-Speaking Union (chairman, 1964-76; president, 1976—), Bournemouth and District Law Society (president, 1979-80), Mid-Wessex Samaritans (chairman, 1969-75), Bournemouth Philatelic Society (chairman, 1977-79).

WRITINGS: Bournemouth St. Peter's, Dorset Publishing, 1971; *Sherlock Holmes Detected,* Drake, 1974. Author of "Philately for Fun," a column in *Stamp Collecting.* Contributor to magazines.

WORK IN PROGRESS: Another book on Sherlock Holmes.

SIDELIGHTS: McQueen commented: "As a part-time writer who earns his bread as a lawyer, I enjoy the freedom to write what I like and when I like, insulated from any financial pressure. I enjoy the thrill of creation. To hold his newly published book may be, for a mere man, the nearest he will ever come to the thrill of a mother holding her newborn child. I write for fun, for my own amusement; if it gives pleasure to others, that is a bonus."

*   *   *

MEARNS, David Chambers   1899-1981
(Farragut Fraddle)

OBITUARY NOTICE—See index for *CA* sketch: Born December 31, 1899, in Washington, D.C.; died after a long illness, May 21, 1981. Administrator, librarian, lecturer, historian, and author. Associated with the Library of Congress for nearly fifty years, Mearns held a variety of positions ranging from reference assistant and director of the reference department to assistant librarian for the American collections, chief of the manuscript division, and holder of the chair of American history. He was a lecturer at colleges and universities and an Abraham Lincoln scholar. His works include *The Constitution of the U.S.: An Account of Its Travels, The Lincoln Papers, Three Presidents and Their Books,* and *Largely Lincoln.* Mearns received several awards for his research on Lincoln, including a medal of honor for the U.S. Abraham Lincoln Sesquicentennial Commission and the Lincoln diploma of honor from Lincoln Memorial University. Obituaries and other sources: *Library Journal*, September 1, 1981.

*   *   *

MEE, Fiona   1946(?)-1978

OBITUARY NOTICE: Born c. 1946; died of cancer, April 7, 1978, in Toronto, Ontario, Canada. Editor and publisher of *Quill & Quire.* During Mee's years with the magazine it was expanded from eight to forty-eight pages and came to be considered a comprehensive trade organ of Canadian publishing. Obituaries and other sources: *Publishers Weekly*, April 24, 1978.

*   *   *

MEIGS, Alexander James   1921-

PERSONAL: Born March 9, 1921, in Ancon, Panama Canal Zone; married, 1950; children: four. *Education:* Harvard University, A.B., 1948; University of Chicago, Ph.D., 1960. *Office:* Argus Research Corp., 140 Broadway, New York, N.Y. 10005.

CAREER: University of Arkansas, Fayetteville, assistant professor of economics and researcher, 1950-53; Federal Reserve Bank, St. Louis, Mo., business economist, 1953-61; New York Stock Exchange, New York City, economist, 1961-64; Argus Research Corp., New York City, vice-president and economist, 1964—. Lecturer at Washington University, St. Louis, Mo., 1954-56. *Military service:* U.S. Army Air Forces, 1943-46. *Member:* American Economic Association, American Statistical Association, American Association of Business Economists (fellow), American Finance Association.

WRITINGS: Free Reserves and the Money Supply, University of Chicago Press, 1962; *Money Matters: Economics, Markets, Politics,* Harper, 1972.*

*   *   *

MELONEY, William Brown   1905-1971

OBITUARY NOTICE: Born May 3, 1905, in New York City; died May 4, 1971, in Kent, Conn. Lawyer, educator, editor, and author best known for his stage plays and the radio series "Claudia." Meloney managed the 1932 New York gubernatorial campaign of William J. "Wild Bill" Donovan. Meloney was the author of *When Doctors Disagree.* Obituaries and other sources: *AB Bookman's Weekly*, June 7, 1971; *The Author's and Writer's Who's Who,* 6th edition, Burke's Peerage, 1971; *American Authors and Books, 1640 to the Present Day,* 3rd revised edition, Crown, 1972; *Who Was Who in America, With World Notables,* Volume V: *1969-1973,* Marquis, 1973.

*   *   *

MELSA, James L(ouis)   1938-

PERSONAL: Born July 6, 1938, in Omaha, Neb.; son of Louis F. and Ann (Pelnar) Melsa; married Katherine Smith,

June 25, 1960; children: Susan K., Elisabeth M., Peter J., Jon D., Jennifer A., Mark T. *Education:* Iowa State University, B.S.E.E., 1960; University of Arizona, M.S.E.E., 1962, Ph.D., 1965. *Home:* 53222 Martin Lane, South Bend, Ind. 46635. *Office:* Department of Electrical Engineering, University of Notre Dame, Notre Dame, Ind. 46556.

CAREER: Radio Corp. of America, Tucson, Ariz., associate member of technical staff, 1960-61; University of Arizona, Tucson, assistant professor of electrical engineering, 1965-67; Southern Methodist University, Dallas, Tex., associate professor, 1967-69, professor of information and control sciences, 1969-73; University of Notre Dame, Notre Dame, Ind., professor of electrical engineering and chairman of department, 1973—. Chairman of education committee of American Automatic Control Council, 1975-77; delegate to Popov Society Congress in Moscow, Soviet Union, 1975; member of board of directors of National Engineering Consortium, 1975-79; industrial publicity chairman of Joint Automatic Control Conference, 1976; co-chairman of National Engineering Consortium (NEC) international forum on multivariate control, 1977; chairman of technical program committee of MIDCON, 1981; consultant to Los Alamos Scientific Laboratory, Computer Sciences Corp., and Fuel Center Corp. of America.

MEMBER: Institute of Electrical and Electronic Engineers (fellow; chairman of professional groups on computers and automatic control, 1969-70; chairman of national membership committee, 1980-81), American Society for Engineering Education, Sigma Xi, Tau Beta Pi, Pi Mu Epsilon, Eta Kappa Nu, Phi Kappa Phi. *Awards, honors:* Western Electric Award from American Society for Engineering Education, 1973, for excellence in instruction of engineering students.

WRITINGS: (With D. G. Schultz) *State Functions and Linear Control Systems,* McGraw, 1967; (with Schultz) *Linear Control Systems,* McGraw, 1969; (with A. P. Sage) *Estimation Theory: With Applications to Control and Communications,* McGraw, 1971; (with Sage) *System Identification.* Academic Press, 1971; (with Sage) *Introduction to Probability and Random Process,* Prentice-Hall, 1973; (with J. D. Gibson) *Nonparametric Detection With Applications,* Academic Press, 1975; (with D. L. Cohn) *A Step by Step Introduction to 8080 Microprocessor Systems,* Dilithium, 1977; (with Cohn) *Decision and Estimation Theory,* McGraw, 1978; (editor with M. K. Sain and J. L. Peczkoswki) *Alternatives for Linear Multivariate Control,* National Engineering Consortium, 1978.

Contributor of nearly one hundred articles to technical journals. Associate editor of *Institute of Electrical and Electronic Engineers Transactions on Systems, Man, and Cybernetics,* 1972-79; member of editorial advisory board of *Journal of Computers and Electrical Engineering,* 1972—.

WORK IN PROGRESS: Microprocessor Systems and Applications, with D. L. Cohn, publication by Prentice-Hall expected in 1983.

*   *   *

MENOTTI, Gian Carlo   1911-

PERSONAL: Born July 7, 1911, in Cadegliano, Italy; came to the United States, 1928; son of Alfonso (a coffee importer) and Ines (Pellini) Menotti; children: Chip (adopted). *Education:* Attended Verdi Conservatory of Music, 1923-28; graduated from Curtis Institute of Music, 1933; *Home:* Yester House, East Lothian, Scotland; and 27 East 62nd St., New York, N.Y. 10021.

CAREER: Composer, librettist, and playwright. Curtis Institute of Music, Philadelphia, Pa., part-time teacher of composition,

1948-55; Metro-Goldwyn-Mayer (MGM), Hollywood, Calif., scriptwriter, c. 1948; director of film version of "The Medium," 1951; Festival of Two Worlds, Spoleto, Italy, cofounder, 1958, general manager and artistic director, 1958-68, president, 1968—. Director and producer of operas, including "Carmen," "Don Giovanni," and "La Boheme." *Member:* American Society of Composers, Authors, and Publishers, National Institute of Arts and Letters, Academy of St. Cecilia of Rome. *Awards, honors:* Carl R. Lauber Musical Award for "Variations on a Theme of Robert Schumann," 1931; B. M. from Curtis Institute of Music, 1945; Guggenheim fellowship, 1946 and 1947; Pulitzer Prize in music, 1950, for "The Consul," and 1955, for "The Saint of Bleecker Street"; New York Drama Critics' Circle Award, 1950, for "The Consul," and 1955, for "The Saint of Bleecker Street"; Cannes International Film Festival award for the film version of "The Medium."

*WRITINGS—*Operas: *Amelia Goes to the Ball* (one-act; first produced in Philadelphia at Academy of Music, April 1, 1937; produced on Broadway at Metropolitan Opera House, March 3, 1938), Ricordi, 1938; *The Old Maid and the Thief* (radio opera; first broadcast by NBC-Radio, April 22, 1939; first stage production in Philadelphia, February 11, 1941), Ricordi, 1942; *The Medium* (two-act; first produced in New York at Columbia University Brander Matthews Theatre, May 8, 1946; produced on Broadway at Ethel Barrymore Theatre, May 1, 1947), Schirmer, 1947; *The Telephone* (one-act; first produced in New York at Heckscher Playhouse, February 20, 1947; produced on Broadway at Ethel Barrymore Theatre, May 1, 1947), Schirmer, 1947.

The Consul (three-act; first produced in Philadelphia at the Shubert Theatre, February 22, 1950; produced on Broadway at Ethel Barrymore Theatre, March 15, 1950), Schirmer, 1950; *Amahl and the Night Visitors* (one-act television opera; first broadcast by NBC-TV, December 24, 1951), Schirmer, 1952; *The Saint of Bleecker Street* (three-act; first produced on Broadway at Broadway Theatre, December 27, 1954), Schirmer, 1955; *The Unicorn, the Gorgon, and the Manticore* (madrigal; first produced in Washington, D.C., at Library of Congress, October 21, 1956; produced on Broadway at New York City Center, January 15, 1957), Ricordi, 1956; *Maria Golovin* (three-act; first produced in Brussels at the American Pavilion, Brussels World's Fair, August 20, 1958; produced on Broadway at Martin Beck Theatre, November 5, 1958), Ricordi, 1958; *The Last Savage* (three-act; first produced as "Dernier Sauvage" in Paris at the Opera-Comique, October 22, 1963; produced on Broadway at Metropolitan Opera House, January 23, 1964), Colombo, 1964; (juvenile) *Help, Help, the Globolinks* (first produced in Santa Fe, N.M., August, 1969; produced on Broadway at New York City Center, December 22, 1969), published as *Gian Carlo Menotti's Help, Help, the Globolinks,* adapted by Leigh Dean, McGraw, 1970.

Unpublished operas: "The Island God," first produced on Broadway at Metropolitan Opera House, February 20, 1942; "Labyrinth" (television opera), first broadcast by NBC-TV, March 3, 1963; "Martin's Life," first produced in Bristol, England, at Bristol Cathedral, June 3, 1964; "The Most Important Man," first produced on Broadway at New York State Theatre, March 12, 1971; "Tamu-Tamu," first produced in Chicago, Ill., at Studebaker Theatre, September 5, 1973; "The Hero," first produced in Philadelphia by Philadelphia Opera Company, June 1, 1976; "The Egg," first produced in Washington, D.C., at the Cathedral, June 17, 1976; "The Trial of the Gypsy," first produced on Broadway at Lincoln Center, 1978. Also author of "The Last Superman" and "Arrival."

Plays: "A Copy of Madame Aupic," first produced in Paris, 1959; "The Leper," first produced in Tallahassee, Fla., at Florida State University, April 20, 1970.

Libretti: Samuel Barber, *Vanessa* (four-act; first produced on Broadway at Metropolitan Opera House, January 15, 1958), Schirmer, 1956, revised edition, 1964; Barber, "A Hand of Bridge," first produced in Spoleto, Italy, at Festival of Two Worlds, June 17, 1959; Lukas Foss, "Introductions and Goodbyes," first produced in 1959.

Musical compositions: *Poemetti* (juvenile), Ricordi, 1937; *Sebastian* (ballet), Ricordi, 1947; *Piano Concerto in F,* Ricordi, 1948; *Apocalypse,* Schirmer, c. 1951; *Ricercare and Toccata on a Theme From "The Old Maid and the Thief,"* Ricordi, 1953; *Violin Concerto in A Minor,* Schirmer, 1954; *The Death of the Bishop of Brindisi* (cantata), Schirmer, c. 1963. Also composer of "Variations on a Theme of Robert Schumann," c. 1931; "Pastorale," 1933; "Concerto in A Minor for Piano and Orchestra," 1945; "Errand Into the Maze" (ballet), 1947; "Concerto for Violin and Orchestra," 1955; "Canti della Lontananza" (song cycle), 1967; "Tripolo Concerto a Tre," 1970; "Suite for Two Celli and Piano," 1973; "The Halcyon" (symphony), 1976; "Landscapes and Remembrances" (cantata), 1976; "Trio for a House Warming Party."

SIDELIGHTS: The name Gian Carlo Menotti is associated with some of the most-performed, most widely recognized works in the field of contemporary opera. His name is affixed to the perennial Christmas favorite "Amahl and the Night Visitors," to the Pulitzer Prize-winning operas "The Consul" and "The Saint of Bleecker Street," and to the Broadway success "The Medium." It is no surprise, then, that the first American opera to be produced in Menotti's native Italy was one of his own works.

Menotti's name is also a familiar one in the town of Cadegliano, Italy, where the composer's family villa still stands. Menotti was the sixth of ten children born to a coffee importer and his wife. The family formed a chamber group, and Menotti was taught to play the violin, cello, and piano at an early age. He began composing music at six and wrote two operas, "The Death of Pierrot" and "The Little Mermaid," by the time he was thirteen. The Menottis had their own box at the famous opera house La Scala, and the young artist often went to hear opera classics directed by Arturo Toscanini.

Menotti was not a serious music student until 1928 when his mother brought him to the United States to study at Philadelphia's Curtis Institute. His professor of composition at Curtis was Rosario Scalero, who stressed the study and imitation of the masters. Menotti's teacher disliked opera, however, and so when Menotti wrote his first opera, he intended it to be his last. The opera, "Amelia Goes to the Ball," was originally written in Italian and later translated into English. It is an opera buffa, chronicling the escapades of a woman who is determined to go to a ball at all costs. After she puts her husband in the hospital and her lover in jail, she attends the ball, escorted by the detective investigating the case.

Nevertheless, with only one opera to his credit, Menotti was commissioned by NBC-Radio to write another, "The Old Maid and the Thief." This comic opera is about a spinster who takes in boarders and is so taken by one that she has him framed as a criminal to prevent him from moving on. After its original success on radio, the opera was brought to the stage. It was often performed by amateur groups for soldiers at hospitals and camps during World War II. Menotti's first undertaking in grand opera, "The Island God," was a critical flop. The composer felt that its poor staging contributed to its failure, so from that time on he insisted on directing his own operas.

Menotti's next major operatic effort, "The Medium," was distinct in that it had a successful Broadway run, a difficult feat for an original opera. Also presented with it on Broadway was his shorter opera, "The Telephone," which had been commissioned by the Ballet Society. "The Medium," the author feels, was the basis for all his other work. The world of the occult and the supernatural is explored through the life of a woman—a medium—caught between two worlds, one based on reality, the other on faith. This duality of character—cynical realism versus mysticism—is also dealt with in later works such as "The Saint of Bleecker Street."

Perhaps one of the most widely known of Menotti's operas is "Amahl and the Night Visitors," again commissioned by NBC. It is the story of a crippled boy who is cured of his handicap after giving his crutches to the three Wise Men as a gift for the new-born Jesus. First presented on television on Christmas Eve in 1951, the show ran annually on December 24th for thirteen years.

Menotti feels an opera written two decades later, "The Most Important Man," is one of his best, on a level with "The Saint of Bleecker Street." But William Bender, writing in *Time,* thought it hardly a step forward. "Menotti has turned out music that follows the pleasant, well-traveled road of early twentieth-century Italian opera. . . . None of the characters are very believable, even by opera's standards." Remarking on the composer's opinion that atonal music is pessimistic music, Bender added: "Menotti is correct about the joylessness of atonality. What he has failed to detect is the vast freedom that atonality has given certain contempoary composers who care about exploring the anxious mind and soul of modern man."

Menotti is also the co-founder, with Thomas Schippers, of the Festival of Two Worlds in Spoleto, Italy. The festival draws together artists, especially the young, from the Americas and Europe. Featured are presentations in the disciplines of music, dance, drama, and poetry. The concept has now jumped the Atlantic with the opening in Charleston, S.C., of Spoleto, U.S.A. Despite its success, Menotti has become slightly disillusioned with the amount of his time the festival requires. Some critics feel the effort expended in this project has led to a dissipation of his goals, accelerating his decline as a major composer of operas. Menotti, however, claims he would probably do it all over again if he had the chance.

While the plots of many operas exist only to string together a series of arias, Menotti's works have genuine dramatic substance. He uses simple language and presents experiences that are familiar to those uninitiated to opera. Although the author's approach has proven its general popularity, he has lost some credence with reviewers, who have criticized his operas for being too theatrical and over-simplified. Menotti commented on these judgments to his biographer, John Gruen, writing in the *New York Times:* "I have always felt that my musical home was New York. I have always felt that I had a very faithful audience in America. But this is no longer the case. I mean, when you live in a city like New York, and you know that any new opera of yours will be damned and panned by the chief music critic of the *New York Times* even *before* it's put on, then, naturally, you go somewhere else."

Ultimately, though, the veteran takes such unfavorable opinions in stride. To Gruen he elaborated: "I suppose, in a certain way, I can be accused of certain superficialities. . . . But the fact is that only my music, and a certain feeling that I owe something to the world, really mean anything to me. . . . A man only becomes wise when he begins to calculate the approximate depth of his ignorance." And to *Time*'s Bender he concluded, "I know I am alone in my road. I don't meet many critics or colleagues there—just people, which is very pleasant.''

In 1973 Menotti sold ''Capricorn,'' the home in Mount Kisco, N.Y., which he and his longtime friend and collaborator Samuel Barber had shared for over thirty years. He bought a house on the Scottish moors, where he enjoys the chilly, capricious weather. He regrets not being able to have his own opera house to run, which has been a lifelong dream. In the past, he has had several offers, but none has materialized.

BIOGRAPHICAL/CRITICAL SOURCES: New Yorker, May 4, 1963; *Holiday,* June, 1963; Samuel Chotzinoff, *A Little Nightmusic,* Harper, 1964; *Opera News,* February 8, 1964, May, 1977; David Ewen, editor, *Composers Since 1900,* Wilson, 1969; Melvin Berger, *Masters of Modern Music,* Lothrop, 1970; *Time,* March 22, 1971; Lyndal Grieb, *The Operas of Gian Carlo Menotti, 1937-1972,* Scarecrow, 1974; *New York Times,* April 14, 1974; John Gruen, *Menotti: A Biography,* Macmillan, 1978.*

—Sketch by Barbara A. Welch

* * *

MERRIMAN, John 1924-1974

OBITUARY NOTICE: Born in 1924; died in an airplane crash in 1974 in Charlotte, N.C. Journalist best known as news editor for ''The CBS Evening News With Walter Cronkite,'' from 1966 until his death. Merriman covered the Senate McCarthy hearings for CBS during the 1950's and was awarded an Emmy in 1972 for his coverage of the Apollo space flights. Obituaries and other sources: *Time,* September 23, 1974; Les Brown, *New York Times Encyclopedia of Television,* Times Books, 1977.

* * *

MESKILL, Robert 1918(?)-1970

OBITUARY NOTICE: Born c. 1918; died of a heart attack, January 6, 1970, in New York, N.Y. Editor for *Look* magazine and Cowles Book Co. Obituaries and other sources: *AB Bookman's Weekly,* January 19, 1970; *Publishers Weekly,* February 2, 1970.

* * *

MESSERER, Asaf Mikhailovich 1903-

PERSONAL: Born November 19, 1903; *Education:* Studied at Moscow School of Choreography. *Politics:* Communist. *Office:* State Academic Bolshoi Theatre, 1 Ploshchad Sverdlova, Moscow, Soviet Union.

CAREER: State Academic Bolshoi Theatre Moscow, Soviet Union, *premier danseur,* 1921-54, ballet instructor, 1946—. Lecturer at Moscow Choreographical Institute, 1923-60. *Awards, honors:* State prizes, 1941, 1957; named people's artist of Russian Socialist Federated Soviet Republic, 1951; honored worker of Arts of Lithuania, 1953.

WRITINGS: (With E. M. Golubkova) *Uroki klassicheskogo tantsa,* Istustvo, 1967, translation by Oleg Brainsky published as *Classes in Classical Ballet,* Doubleday, 1975.

BIOGRAPHICAL/CRITICAL SOURCES: Juri Slonimsky and others, *Soviet Ballet,* Philosophical Library, 1947.*

* * *

METZ, Jerred 1943-

PERSONAL: Born May 5, 1943, in Lakewood, N.J.; son of

Eli J. (a farmer) and Frances (a secretary; maiden name, Minnensohn) Metz; married Barbara Kapp, June 6, 1965 (divorced February, 1978); married Sarah Barker (a professor of movement for actors), May 14, 1978; children: Zachary, Ravenna Barker. *Education:* University of Rhode Island, B.A., 1965, M.A., 1967; University of Minnesota, Ph.D., 1972. *Home:* 2318 Albion Pl., St. Louis, Mo. 63104. *Agent:* Mary Yost Associates, Inc., 75 East 55th St., New York, N.Y. 10022. *Office:* Department of Welfare, 12 North Tucker Blvd., St. Louis, Mo. 63104.

CAREER: University of Minnesota, Minneapolis, instructor in literature, 1967-73; Webster College, St. Louis, Mo., assistant professor of literature, 1973-77; Department of Welfare, St. Louis, executive assistant to director, 1977—. Member of advisory board of St. Louis Area Agency on Aging and board of directors of local Anti-Defamation League.

WRITINGS: Speak Like Rain (poems), Singing Bone Press, 1975; *The Temperate Voluptuary* (poems), Capra, 1976; *Three Legs Up, Cold as Stone; Six Legs Down, Blood and Bone* (poems), Singing Bone Press, 1978; *Angels in the House* (poems), Heron Press, 1980; *Drinking the Dipper Dry: Nine Plain-Spoken Lives* (nonfiction) K. M. Gentile, 1980. Contributor to magazines, including *St. Louis.* Poetry editor of *Webster Review,* 1973—.

WORK IN PROGRESS: Circle of Hair Between the Eyebrows of the Buddha: Selected Poems, 1965-1980, for K. M. Gentile; *The Compleate Temperate Voluptuary,* for K. M. Gentile; *Tarzan of the Tetons: The Last Eleven Days of Earl Durand,* a novel; *The Angel of Mons,* a historical novel about the largest mass apparition in recorded history, completion expected in 1985; ''Broker's Tip,'' a play based on *Drinking the Dipper Dry,* for St. Louis Repertory Theater; a one-man play about John Philip Sousa.

SIDELIGHTS: Metz wrote: ''Exclusive of the poetry I wrote and published for fifteen years, my later work blends two distinct sources, oral and 'found' literature. First in *Drinking the Dipper Dry,* then in 'Broker's Tip,' the Durand saga, and the book on the World War I apparition, I used taped narratives from participants in the events described. I employ documentary sources that include affidavits, official reports, and newspaper and magazine coverage contemporaneous with the events.

''Among all the marvelous lessons the poets Yeats and Roethke taught me, the one manifested in my current writing, which consists of prose and plays, is the 'significance of the insignificant.' I am delighted and then compelled by those little oddities and curiosities which imply a life or a way of life behind them. Currently I tend to write 'documentaries' overlaid with themes and perspectives which create a novel out of history somewhat in the manner of Doctorow. For example, *Tarzan of the Tetons* (the name itself taken from a newspaper headline in the *Denver Post* at the time of the March, 1939, events) accurately renders the events of an actual eleven-day manhunt for Earl Durand, a mountain man who was arrested for poaching elk and went on from there to kill two law officers. As soon as a narrator, characters of considerable historic interest, and theories about the 'Wild Man' as seen in Greek and Biblical literature are inserted as 'overlays,' history becomes a novel.

''I find myself seeking to express the subtle interplay between simplicity, complexity and the downright inexplicable which strikes me as moving the action of individuals and cultures.''

BIOGRAPHICAL/CRITICAL SOURCES: St. Louis Post-Dispatch, September 18, 1980, September 28, 1980, November 5, 1980.

METZLER, Lloyd A(ppleton) 1913-

PERSONAL: Born April 3, 1913, in Lost Springs, Kan. *Education:* University of Kansas, B.S., 1935, M.B.A., 1938; Harvard University, M.A., 1941, Ph.D., 1942. *Office:* Department of Economics, University of Chicago, Chicago, Ill. 60637.

CAREER: University of Kansas, Lawrence, instructor in economics, 1935-37; Harvard University, Cambridge, Mass., instructor in economics, 1937-42; Office of Strategic Services, Washington, D.C., economist, 1943-44; member of board of governors of Federal Reserve System, 1944-46; Yale University, New Haven, Conn., assistant professor of economics, 1946-47; University of Chicago, Chicago, Ill., associate professor, 1947-49, professor of economics, 1949—. U.S. Information Service lecturer at University of Stockholm, University of Uppsala, University of Copenhagen, and University of Oslo, 1951-52; consultant to federal agencies, including U.S. Department of State. *Member:* American Economic Association, American Finance Association, Econometric Society (fellow), Royal Economic Society. *Awards, honors:* Guggenheim fellowship, 1942-43.

WRITINGS: (With Robert Triffin and Gottfried Haberler) *International Monetary Policies,* [Washington, D.C.], 1947, reprinted, Arno, 1978; (co-author) *Income, Employment, and Public Policy: Essays in Honor of Alvin H. Hansen,* Norton, 1948; *Collected Papers,* Harvard University Press, 1973.

BIOGRAPHICAL/CRITICAL SOURCES: George Horwitz and Paul A. Samuelson, editors, *Trade, Stability, and Macroeconomics: Essays in Honor of Lloyd A. Metzler,* Academic Press, 1974.*

* * *

MEURICE, Blanca
See von BLOCK, Bela W(illiam)

* * *

MEYNELL, Alice (Christina Gertrude Thompson) 1847-1922

BRIEF ENTRY: Born September 22, 1847, in Barnes, England; died November 27, 1922, in London, England. British poet and essayist. In her first book of poems, *Preludes* (1875), Alice Meynell adopted much of the simplicity and sincerity of seventeenth-century religious poets, and she was admired for the saintly image she evoked in her personal life. Her home was a center for such well-known contemporaries as Alfred Tennyson and George Meredith. She also played a large part in the discovery and rehabilitation of Francis Thompson, who wrote *Love in Dian's Lap* as a tribute to her. Meynell was a working journalist throughout her life. Her newspaper essays, collected in *The Rhythms of Life* (1893), show her as a feminist and as what she called a "Christian socialist." Meynell's philosophy was intensely religious (she converted to Roman Catholicism in 1872), but her writing showed an independence of spirit that appealed to her readers. Her output of verse was relatively small, and she was able to devote painstaking care to each poem, resulting in critical praise for her unusual mastery of the English language, her clarity, and her style. A complete edition of her poems was published in 1923. *Biographical/critical sources: Twentieth Century Authors: A Biographical Dictionary of Modern Literature,* H. W. Wilson, 1942; *Times Literary Supplement,* January 13, 1966.

MEYNERS, J. Robert 1922-

PERSONAL: Born August 31, 1922, in Palestine, Tex.; son of Conrad M. and Grace (House) Meyners; married Hazel Staats Westover, April 7, 1944 (divorced, 1971); married Claire Wooster (a writer), October, 1972; children: Dawn Meyners Thornburgh, Allan, Alexis. *Education:* Attended University of Southern California, 1941, University of Redlands, 1941-43, and University of Chicago, 1943-46; Chicago Theological Seminary, B.D., 1947; attended Cambridge University, 1949-50; Union Theological Seminary, New York, N.Y., Ph.D., 1956. *Agent:* Jane Rotrosen Agency, 318 East 51st St., New York, N.Y. 10022. *Office:* Masters & Johnson Institute, 4910 Forest Park Rd., St. Louis, Mo. 63108.

CAREER: Ordained minister of United Church of Christ, 1948; pastor of United Churches of Christ in San Francisco, Calif., and Hinsdale, Ill., 1947-52; Cornell College, Mount Vernon, Iowa, assistant professor of religion, 1954-56; Claremont Men's College, Claremont, Calif., associate professor of ethics, 1956-66; Chicago Theological Seminary, Chicago, Ill., professor of theology and urban culture, 1966-79; Masters & Johnson Institute, St. Louis, Mo., research and clinical associate, 1980—. Associate professor at Claremont Graduate School, 1956-66. *Member:* American Association of Sex Educators, Counselors, and Therapists, American Association of University Professors, American Academy of Religion. *Awards, honors:* Senior Fulbright grant for University of Hamburg, 1960-61.

WRITINGS: (With wife, Claire Wooster) *Solomon's Sword: Clarifying Values in the Church,* Abingdon, 1977; (with Wooster) *Sexual Style: Facing and Making Choices About Sex,* Harcourt, 1979.

WORK IN PROGRESS: Sexual Themes in Pastoral Counseling and *Dynamics of Intimacy,* completion of both expected in 1982.

SIDELIGHTS: Meyners told *CA:* "I am constantly asked how a theologian got involved in the subject of sex. Depending on the point of view of the speaker, this implies either 'What's a nice guy like you doing in a place like this?' or conversely, 'Can any good come out of Nazareth?' The answer is the same in either case: I have never seen a soul without a body, and until I do, I will believe that sex has religious meaning in human life."

* * *

MICHAEL, Ian (Lockie) 1915-

PERSONAL: Born November 30, 1915, in Scotland; son of Reginald Warburton and Margaret Campbell (Kerr) Michael; married Mary Harborne Bayley, 1942; children: Judith (Mrs. Ian Strachan) Jonathan. *Education:* University of London, B.A., 1938; University of Bristol, Ph.D., 1963. *Home:* 33 Tavistock Sq., London WC1H 9EZ England.

CAREER: Schoolmaster in Cambridge, England, 1935-40; teacher at junior school in Reading, England, 1941-45, headmaster, 1946-49; University of Bristol, Bristol, England, lecturer in education, 1950-63; University of Khartoum, Khartoum, Sudan, professor of education, 1963-64; University of Malawi, Zomba, vice-chancellor, 1964-73; University of London, Institute of Education, London, England, deputy director of institute, 1973—. Past chairman of Malawi Certificate in Education Examining Board. *Awards, honors:* Commander of Order of the British Empire, 1972; D.Litt. from University of Malawi, 1974.

WRITINGS: (Translator) Enrique Sordo, *Moorish Spain* (edited by Elizabeth Elek and Paul Elek), Elek, 1963; *English Grammatical Categories and the Tradition to 1800,* Cambridge University Press, 1970; *Treatment of Classical Material in the "Libro de Alexandre."* Manchester University press, 1970; *Alexander's Flying Machine: The History of a Legend,* University of Southampton, 1975; (editor) *Poem of the Cid* (translated from Spanish by Rita Hamilton and Janet Perry), Barnes & Noble, 1975; (editor and author of introduction and notes) *Poema de mio Cid* (title means "Poem of the Cid"), Castalia, 1976; *Gwyn Thomas,* University of Wales Press, 1977, Verry, 1978.*

*   *   *

MICHALCZYK, John Joseph   1941-

PERSONAL: Born June 26, 1941, in Dickson City, Pa.; son of John Anthony, Sr., and Sophie (Pezanowski) Michalczyk. *Education:* Attended University of Scranton, 1959-61, and St. Isaac Jogues Junior College, 1961-64; Boston College, B.A., 1966, M.A., 1967; Harvard University, Ph.D., 1972; Weston College, M.Div., 1974; postdoctoral study at Institut Catholique, Paris, France. *Politics:* Independent. *Office:* College of Arts and Sciences, Boston College, Chestnut Hill, Mass. 02167.

CAREER: Entered Society of Jesus (Jesuits), 1961, ordained Roman Catholic priest, 1974; teacher of French and film history and criticism at Roman Catholic high school in Towson, Md., 1967-69; Harvard University, Cambridge, Mass., teaching fellow in French, 1971-72; Boston College, Chestnut Hill, Mass., assistant professor, 1974-78, associate professor of fine arts, 1978—. Member of summer faculty at Rivier College, 1972, 1974, 1976.

MEMBER: Modern Language Association of America, American Association of Teachers of French, American Film Institute, Northeast Modern Language Association (chairman of film conference, 1980), Malraux Society, Bibliotheque Francaise de Boston. *Awards, honors:* Grants from Bryn Mawr Institute in Avignon, 1970, Polish Union of North America (for Poland), 1973, Fondation Camargo (for France), 1975-77, and Mellon, 1981.

WRITINGS: Andre Malraux's Film "Espoir": The Propaganda/Art Film and the Spanish Civil War, Romance Monographs, 1977; *Ingmar Bergman: La Passion d'etre homme aujourd'hui* (title means "Ingmar Bergman: Passion to Be Human Today"), Editions Beauchesne, 1977; *The French Literary Filmmakers,* Arts Alliance Press, 1980; (author of introduction) *Cinema and Society,* United Nations Educational, Scientific and Cultural Organization, 1981; *Costa-Gavras and the Political Fiction Film,* Arts Alliance Press, 1982. Contributor of about thirty articles and reviews to film, language, and French studies journals.

WORK IN PROGRESS: The Italian Political Film, publication by Arts Alliance Press expected in 1984.

SIDELIGHTS: Michalczyk commented: "Literature, film, and politics—three disciplines that at times may be considered independent of each other—are often significantly related. In my research as well as my teaching, my objective is to illustrate how they relate to each other, whether it is a cinematic adaptation from a novel or a propaganda work written or filmed during a war to motivate its intended audience."

*   *   *

MICHENER, Charles Thomson   1940-

PERSONAL: Born November 13, 1940, in Cleveland, Ohio;

son of Jesse Hamor and Virginia Marie (Callinan) Michener; married Fay Padelford, September 5, 1967 (divorced, 1971); married Diana Chatfield Davis (a photographer), September 13, 1975; children: (first marriage) Amanda Morgan. *Education:* Yale University, A.B., 1962; Columbia University, M.S., 1965. *Home:* 850 Park Ave., New York, N.Y. 10021. *Office: Newsweek,* 444 Madison Ave., New York, N.Y. 10022.

CAREER/WRITINGS: U.S. Peace Corps, Addis Ababa, Ethiopia, lecturer at Haile Selassie I University, 1962-64; *Seattle Magazine,* Seattle, Wash., staff writer, 1965-67, managing editor, 1967-70; *Newsweek,* New York, N.Y., associate editor, 1970-72, general editor, 1972-75, senior editor of cultural affairs, 1975—. Member of board of directors of Allied Arts of Seattle, 1967-70; lecturer at New School for Social Research, 1975; member of selection committee for New York Film Festival, 1975—. *Military service:* U.S. Army Reserve, 1965-70; became staff sergeant. *Member:* Yale Club, Zeta Psi. *Awards, honors:* Silver Gavel award from American Bar Association, 1971.

*   *   *

MIDDENDORF, John Harlan   1922-

PERSONAL: Born March 31, 1922, in New York, N.Y.; son of George Arlington and Margaret (Hofmann) Middendorf; married Beverly Bruner, July 14, 1943; children: Cathie Jean (Mrs. Robert B. Hamilton, Jr.), Peggy Ruth (Mrs. Lawrence J. Brindisi). *Education:* Dartmouth college, A.B., 1943; Columbia University, A.M., 1947, Ph.D., 1953. *Home:* 404 Riverside Dr., New York, N.Y. 10025. *Office:* Department of English, Columbia University, New York, N.Y. 10027.

CAREER: City College (now of City University of New York), New York City, lecturer in English, 1946; Hunter College (now of City University of New York), New York City, lecturer in English, 1946-49; Columbia University, New York City, began as instructor, became associate professor, 1947-65, professor of English, 1965—, director of graduate studies, 1971-74, chairman of Seminar on Eighteenth-Century Culture, 1973-75, vice-chairman of graduate studies, 1976—. *Military service:* U.S. Naval Reserve, active duty, 1943-46; became lieutenant junior grade.

MEMBER: Modern Language Association of America, American Society for Eighteenth Century Studies, American Association of University Professors, English Institute (member of supervising committee, 1963-66), Conference on British Studies, Economic History Society, Johnsonians (chairman, 1969, 1979), Oxford Bibliographical Society, Phi Beta Kappa, Grolier Club. *Awards, honors:* Fellow of Fund for the Advancement of Education, 1951-52; grants from Council for Research in the Humanities, 1958-59, American Philosophical Society and American Council of Learned Societies, both, 1962, and National Endowment for the Humanities, 1976-78.

WRITINGS: (With Ernest G. Griffin) *Manual of English Prose Composition,* Rinehart, 1956; (contributor) *Johnson, Boswell, and Their Circle,* Clarendon Press, 1965; (contributor) *Eighteenth-Century Studies in Honor of Donald F. Hyde,* Grolier, 1970; (editor and contributor) *English Writers of the Eighteenth Century,* Columbia University Press, 1971. Associate editor of "Works of Samuel Johnson," Yale University Press, 1962-66, general editor, 1966—. Contributor of articles and reviews to literature journals. Assistant editor of *Johnsonian Newsletter,* 1950-58, co-editor, 1958-78, editor, 1978—.*

MIDDLEMAN, Ruth J. Rosenbloom 1923-

PERONAL: Born November 11, 1923, in Pittsburgh, Pa.; daughter of Alfred A. and Corinne (Lorch) Rosenbloom; married Donald J. Middleman, January 30, 1949; children: Karl D., Philip H. *Education:* University of Pittsburgh, B.S, (with highest honors), 1944, M.S., 1946; further graduate study at University of Pennsylvania, 1960-61; Temple University, Ed.D., 1972. *Religion:* Jewish. *Office:* School of Social Administration, Temple University, Philadelphia, Pa. 19122.

CAREER: Jewish Center, Philadelphia, Pa., departmental supervisor, 1946-51, director of day camps, 1949-53; University of Pennsylvania, Philadelphia, affiliated with School of Social Work, 1950-68, affiliated with School of Occupational Therapy, 1960-61, 1966-69; Temple University, Philadelphia, professor of social administration, 1968—. Supervisor of students at Carnegie-Mellon University and University of Pennsylvania, 1946-53, 1966—, and Temple University, 1950-53. Director of activities at Philadelphia Neighborhood Center, 1951-53; social worker for Pennsylvania Association for Retarded Children, 1957-58; supervisor of Florence Crittenton Service, 1957-60, program director, 1965-66; group work supervisor for Children's Aid Society of Pennsylvania, 1965-68; active with New Jersey Division of Corrections. *Member:* American Orthopsychiatric Association, National Association of Social Workers, American Academy of Certified Social Workers, American Association of University Professor, Council on Social Work Education, Mortar Board, Alpha Epsilon Phi, Alpha Kappa Delta, Pi Lambda Theta.

WRITINGS: The Non-Verbal Method in Working With Groups, Association Press, 1968; (with Gale Goldberg) *Social Service Delivery: A Structural Approach to Social Work Practice,* Columbia University Press, 1974. Also author of *Social Group Work With Unmarried Mothers in a Maternity Home,* 1958. Co-author with Frank S. Seever and Erwin A. Carner of *A Game and Its Therapeutic Use,* 1968. Contributor to journals in the social sciences.*

*   *   *

MILHOUS, Katherine 1894-1977

OBITUARY NOTICE: Born November 27, 1894, in Philadelphia, Pa.; died December 5, 1977. Illustrator and author best known for illustrating *The Egg Tree,* for which she was awarded the Caldecott Medal in 1951. Milhous was the author of numerous books for children (all set in Pennsylvania), including her own favorite, *Through These Arches: The Story of Independence Hall.* Obituaries and other sources: *American Authors and Books, 1640 to the Present Day,* 3rd revised edition, Crown, 1972; *Publishers Weekly,* December 26, 1977; *Horn Book Magazine,* February, 1978.

*   *   *

MILKOMANE, George Alexis Milkomanovich 1903-
(George Alexis Bankoff, George Borodin, George Braddon, Peter Conway, Alec Redwood, George Sava)

PERSONAL: Born October 15, 1903, in Baku, Russia (now U.S.S.R.); came to England, 1932; naturalized British citizen, 1938; son of Ivan Alexandrovitch (a general) and Countess Maria Ignatiev Milkomane; married Jane Dorothy Hollingdale (a painter and sculptor), November 21, 1939; children: Alexandra, Peter, Lisa-Maria, Gregory. *Education:* Attended Russian Naval Academy, 1913, and University of Paris; studied medicine in Florence, Rome, Munich, Berlin, Bonn, Man-

chester, Glasgow, and Edinburgh. *Politics:* Conservative. *Religion:* Roman Catholic. *Home:* 101 Dukes Ave., New Malden, Surrey, England. *Agent:* Hilary Rubenstein, A.P. Watt Ltd., 26128 Bedford Row, London WC1R 4HL, England. *Office:* 6389 Florio St., Oakland, Calif. 94618.

CAREER: Private practice of plastic surgery; writer, 1938—. Lecturer in the United States, Italy, and Australia. *Military service:* Associated with Emergency Medical Service. *Member:* International College of Surgeons (fellow), Royal College of Surgeons (fellow). *Awards, honors:* Libero Docente Professorship of University of Rome, 1954; Commendatorre dell' Ordine al Merito Della Repubblica Italiana, 1961; Grand Chevalier of Crown of Bulgaria.

WRITINGS:—Under pseudonym George Sava; published by Faber, except as noted: *The Healing Knife: A Surgeon's Destiny,* Harcourt, 1938; *A Surgeon's Destiny,* 1939, reprinted, New Horizons Press, 1978; *Beauty From the Surgeon's Knife,* 1939; *Twice the Clock Round: One Day of a Surgeon's Life,* 1940; *A Ring at the Door: Personal Experiences,* 1940; *Donkey Serenade: Travels in Bulgaria,* 1940; *Valley of Forgotten People,* 1941; *They Stayed in London,* 1941; *Rasputin Speaks,* 1941; *A Tale of Ten Cities,* 1942; *The Chetniks,* 1942; *School for War,* 1942; *War Without Guns: The Psychological Front,* 1943; *Russia Triumphant: The Story of the Russian People,* 1943; *Surgeon's Symphony,* 1944; *Land Fit for Heroes,* 1945; *They Come by Appointment,* 1946; *Link of Two Hearts,* 1946; *Bride of Neptune,* Macdonald & Co., 1946; *Call It Life,* Macdonald & Co., 1947; *The Way of a Surgeon,* 1949; *Strange Cases,* 1950; *A Doctor's Odyssey,* 1951; *A Surgeon Remembers,* 1953; *Surgeon Under Capricorn,* 1954; *The Lure of Surgery,* 1955; *A Surgeon at Large,* 1956; *Surgery and Crime,* 1957; *All This and Surgery Too,* 1958; *The Emperor Story: A Historical Romance,* 1959.

Under Sava pseudonym; published by R. Hale, except as noted: *Punishment Deferred,* 1966; *Sex, Surgery, People,* Faber, 1967; *Man Without Label,* 1967; *The Gates of Heaven Are Narrow,* 1968; *Alias Doctor Holtzmann,* 1968; *Bitter-Sweet Surgery,* 1969; *City of Cain* 1969; *The Imperfect Surgeon,* 1969; *A Stranger in Harley Street,* 1970; *One Russian's Story* (biography of his father), 1970; *Of Guilt Possessed,* 1970; *Nothing Sacred,* 1970; *Beloved Nemesis* (historical novel), 1971; *A Skeleton for My Mate,* 1971; *Tell Your Grief Softly,* 1972; *The Sins of Andrea,* 1972; *On the Wings of Angels,* 1972; *Return From the Valley,* 1973; *Cocaine for Breakfast,* 1973; *Every Sweet Hath Its Sour,* 1974; *Sheilah of Buckleigh Manor,* 1974; *The Years of the Healing Knife: A Surgeon's Autobiography,* Kimber, 1976; *Pretty Polly,* 1976; *Of Men and Medicine,* 1976; *Mary Mary Quite Contrary,* 1977; *How to Write a Book That Sells,* New Horizons Press, 1977; *Mourning Becomes Argentina,* New Horizons Press, 1978; *Secret Surgeon,* Kimber, 1979.

Under Sava pseudonym, except as noted; "A Surgeon in . . ." Series; published by Faber: *A Surgeon in Rome; or, Passeggiata romana,* 1961; *. . . California,* 1962; (under pseudonym George Alexis Bankoff) *. . . New Zealand,* 1964; (under Bankoff pseudonym) *. . . Cyprus,* 1965; *. . . Australia,* 1966.

Under pseudonym George Alexis Bankoff: *Plastic Surgery,* Medical Publications, 1943; *The Practice of Local Anaesthesia,* Heinemann, 1943; *Appointments in Rome,* Faber, 1943; *The Boon of the Atom,* Faber, 1946; *Operative Surgery,* Medical Publications, 1946; *The Story of Surgery,* Arthur Barker, 1947; *The Story of Plastic Surgery,* Faber, 1952; *Plastic Repair of Genito-Urinary Defects,* Philosophical Library, 1956; *Surgery Holds the Door,* Faber, 1960; *Milestones in Medicine,* Pitman, 1961; *In Quest of Health,* Little Flower Co., 1968.

Under Bankoff pseudonym; "The Conquest of. . ." series; published by MacDonald & Co.: *The Conquest of Disease: The Story of Penicillin*, 1946; . . . *Pain: The Story of Anaesthesia*, 1946; . . . *Tuberculosis*, 1946; . . . *Brain Mysteries: The Story and Secrets of the Human Mind*, 1947; . . . *Cancer*, 1947; . . . *the Unknown: The Story of the Endocrine Glands*, 1947.

Under pseudonym George Borodin: *Street of a Thousand Misters*, Faber, 1939; *Those Borgias* (stories), Faber, 1940; *Bastard Angels* (novel), Hutchinson, 1942; *This Russian Land*, Hutchinson, 1943; *Peace in Nobody's Time*, Hutchinson, 1943; *Red Surgeon*, Museum Press, 1944; *Soviet and Tsarist Siberia*, Rich & Cowan, 1944; *This Thing Called Ballet*, Macdonald & Co., 1945; *The President Died at Noon* (novel), P. S. King & Staples, 1945; *Cradle of Splendour: The Song of Samarkand* (nonfiction), Staples Press, 1945; *Friendly Ocean*, Staples Press, 1946; *Pillar of Fire* (novel), Macdonald & Co., 1947, R. M. McBride, 1948; *One Horizon*, Laurie, 1948; *Invitation to Ballet*, Laurie, 1950; *The Charm of the Ballet*, Jenkins, 1955.

Under pseudonym George Braddon: *Judgment Deferred*, R. Trelawney, 1948; *Murdered Sleep*, P. Garnett, 1949; *Time Off for Death*, Roy, 1958.

Under pseudonym Peter Conway; published by Faber except as noted: *A Dark Side Also*, 1940; *The Unwanted Child*, 1941; *The Road Winds Back*, 1942; *Those That Have Eyes*, 1943; *Living Tapestry*, Staples Press, 1946.

WORK IN PROGRESS: The Beloved of God: The Life and Music of Mozart; Medical Malpractice; The Curse of Psoriasis; The Art of Acupuncture; The Killer Microbes, a novel, under pseudonym Alec Redwood; *Soviet Assignment*, a novel, under pseudonym Alec Redwood.

AVOCATIONAL INTERESTS: Tennis, golf, aviation, desert exploration, riding.

*   *   *

MILLAR, Gilbert John   1939-

PERSONAL: Surname is pronounced *Mill*-er; born April 7, 1939, in Kilwinning, Scotland; came to United States, 1952, naturalized citizen, 1960; son of Peter (a contractor) and Anne (a realtor; maiden name, Kennedy) Millar; married Mirilyn Mary Margaret Magdelyn Meibaum (a realtor), June 7, 1962; children: Lydia Ann, Peter Gilbert. *Education:* Southeastern Louisiana College, B.A., 1961; Louisiana State University, M.A., 1964, Ph.D., 1974. *Politics:* Independent. *Religion:* Presbyterian. *Home:* 13806 Nuttree Woods Ter., Midlothian, Va. 23113. *Office:* Department of History and Political Science, Longwood College, Farmville, Va. 23901.

CAREER: Arkansas State College (now Univeristy), State University, instructor in history, 1965-67; Longwood College, Farmville, Va., assistant professor, 1970-76, associate professor of history, 1976—. *Member:* American Association of University Professors, Society for Army Historical Research, American Military Institute, Conference on British Studies, Carolinas Symposium on British Studies.

WRITINGS: Tudor Mercenaries and Auxiliaries, 1485-1547, University Press of Virginia, 1980. Contributor to history and military journals.

SIDELIGHTS: Millar wrote: "To my thinking there is no higher calling than teaching, and there are few more challenging, rewarding, or instructive areas of study than history. I was drawn to the profession in general and to my discipline in particular by the example set by many of my own teachers,

stretching back to primary school. My parents, too, played their part; though not college-educated themselves, they have always had great respect for learning, and, I believe, from at least high school I knew someday I'd be a teacher. As a teacher, I see myself as a missionary, out to save not souls, but minds.

"The exciting thing about teaching is that it can be fun. To take oneself too seriously is an impediment, both to the learning process and to the enthusiasm for the subject, which every teacher should bring to the classroom. The rewards come, not in money or in the generously long and unpaid summer vacations, but in those occasional and chance moments when the instructor wins a convert to his discipline. Imitation, it is said, is the sincerest form of flattery: for me, then, the greatest professional thrill—after the renewal of my yearly contract—is the discovery of a new historian.

"As for writing, like teaching, if approached honestly it is immensely hard work, and my advice to those who would hope to succeed in either is to prepare thoroughly, have something meaningful to say, expect it to be rejected, and if it is, determine how to say it better. Neither a teacher nor a writer is made in a day. It is the work of a lifetime."

*   *   *

MILLAY, Edna St. Vincent   1892-1950
(Nancy Boyd)

BRIEF ENTRY: Born February 22, 1892, in Rockland, Me.; died October 19, 1950, in Austerlitz, N.Y. American poet, playwright, and author. Often called "the female Byron," Millay wrote modern sonnets of love and life, primarily based on her own experiences. She was most successful in the 1920's and 1930's when she was active in the artistic life of Greenwich Village. Among her most acclaimed work during that time was *Fatal Interview* (1931), a collection of fifty-two sonnets that were often compared with those of Shakespeare. Millay's popularity waned, however, during the 1940's when she turned from writing about affairs of the heart to focus on political and social problems. Millay's other collections of poetry include *A Few Figs From Thistles* (1921), *The Buck in the Snow, and Other Poems* (1928), and *Wine From These Grapes* (1934). She also wrote a collection of essays, under the pseudonym Nancy Boyd, entitled *Distressing Dialogues* (1924) and plays, including *The Lamp and the Bell* (1921). In 1923 Millay won the Pulitzer Prize for *Ballad of the Harp-Weaver* (1922). *Residence:* Austerlitz, N.Y. *Biographical/critical sources: Cyclopedia of World Authors*, Harper, 1958; *Reader's Encyclopedia of American Literature*, Crowell, 1962; *Twentieth Century Writing: A Reader's Guide to Contemporary Literature*, Transatlantic, 1969; *Twentieth-Century Literary Criticism*, Volume 4, Gale, 1981.

*   *   *

MILLEN, Clifford H.   1901(?)-1972

OBITUARY NOTICE: Born c. 1901; died May 23, 1972, in Des Moines, Iowa. Journalist. Millen was a political writer and editor for the *Des Moines Tribune*. Obituaries and other sources: *AB Bookman's Weekly*, December 4, 1972.

*   *   *

MILLER, Abraham H(irsh)   1940-

PERSONAL: Born May 20, 1940, in Chicago, Ill.; son of Irving (in sales) and Ida (a secretary) Miller; married Anne Radford (a management consultant), February 23, 1980; children: Ian C. *Education:* University of Illinois, B.A. (with honors), 1962;

University of Michigan, M.A., 1964, Ph.D., 1968. *Office:* Department of Political Science, University of Cincinnati, Cincinnati, Ohio 45221.

CAREER: University of Illinois, Urbana, assistant professor of political science, 1966-68; University of California, Davis, assistant professor of sociology, 1968-71; University of Cincinnati, Cincinnati, Ohio, associate professor, 1971-76, professor of political science, 1976—. Visiting fellow at National Institute of Justice and U.S. Department of Justice, 1976-77; consultant to National Institute of Justice. *Awards, honors:* Pi Sigma Alpha Award from Western Political Science Association, 1976, for article "The New Urban Blacks."

WRITINGS: (Editor with James McEvoy) *Black Power and Student Rebellion,* Wadsworth, 1969; *Terrorism and Hostage Negotiations,* Westview Press, 1980; (editor and contributor) *Terrorism, the Law, and the Media,* National Institute of Justice, 1981. Contributor to law and political science journals and popular magazines.

WORK IN PROGRESS: The Angels of Death, a political novel.

* * *

MILLER, Geoffrey Samuel 1945-

PERSONAL: Born August 9, 1945, in San Francisco, Calif.; son of Frederick Lloyd (a labor mediator) and Miriam (Levitsky) Miller. *Education:* University of California, Los Angeles, B.A., 1968, M.F.A. and M.L.I.S., both 1973. *Home:* 405 West Richmond Ave., Apt. 5, Richmond, Calif. 94801. *Agent:* Charlotte Sheedy Literary Agency, 145 West 86th St., New York, N.Y. 10024. *Office:* Richmond Public Library, Civic Center Plaza, Richmond, Calif. 94804.

CAREER: Richmond Public Library, Richmond, Calif., branch librarian, 1975—. *Member:* Alpha Mu Gamma.

WRITINGS: The Black Glove (novel), Viking, 1981. Also author of "Evan's Corner," a children's film, released by Stephen Bosustow Productions in 1970.

WORK IN PROGRESS: Something More Than Night, a novel; research for a novel set in Los Angeles in the 1930's.

SIDELIGHTS: Miller told *CA:* "I write urban stories, detective novels; my influences are Dashiell Hammett (in particular), Raymond Chandler, and Cornell Woolrich, as you would expect. Of equal importance are the Roman Polanski-Robert Towne film 'Chinatown' and that body of films made, roughly, from the close of World War II to the onset of the Korean conflict, usually referred to as 'film noir.' This genre is represented by such films as 'Out of the Past,' 'D.O.A.,' 'Criss Cross,' and 'Stranger on the Third Floor,' among others. Film noir is not exactly a genre like westerns or horror movies, but rather a body of films with a fatalistic attitude toward modern urban life. A line in a famous film noir called 'Detour' sums up what these films are about: 'Some day fate, or some mysterious force, can put the finger on you or me for no reason at all.'

"The truly great detective novels are not merely cleverly-constructed, fast-moving plots, but stories imbued with this 'noir' feeling—that there are forces at work as colorless and odorless as the air that make nothing seem as it is, that make an attitude of basic mistrust an inevitable result that is also vital for survival.

"If you've ever been involved in an accident of any kind, one of the first things you think afterward is: 'If only I'd done this or that a moment sooner or later.' In my writing I try to capture this 'noir' feeling, this feeling of 'if only.' Whether or not a person believes there is such a thing as fate, everyone knows that feeling of 'if only.' It is extremely powerful; the strongest characters in my stories, the ones for whom I have the most admiration, are those who know 'if only' does not really exist, and never ask themselves the question when a situation arises that would prompt it."

BIOGRAPHICAL/CRITICAL SOURCES: Los Angeles Times, May 13, 1981; *Houston Post/Sun,* May 24, 1981.

* * *

MILLER, Gerald 1928(?)-1970

OBITUARY NOTICE: Born c. 1928; died May 31, 1970, near Phnom-Penh, Cambodia. Journalist. Miller, a TV news reporter, was covering the U.S. incursion into Cambodia that was designed to eliminate sanctuaries of North Vietnamese forces when the jeep in which he was riding was hit by Viet Cong rocket fire, killing Miller, reporter George Syvertsen, and two others. Obituaries and other sources: *Newsweek,* June 22, 1970; *Time,* June 22, 1970.

* * *

MILLER, Leon Gordon 1917-

PERSONAL: Born August 3, 1917, in New York, N.Y.; son of Harry and Dora (Garod) Miller; married Pauline W. Gladish (a writer), April 21, 1948; children: Brandt Woodworth, Scott Gordon. *Education:* Attended Fawcett Art School, 1933-37, and Art Students League, 1941-42; Newark School of Fine and Industrial Arts, Certificate in Fine Arts, 1935; New Jersey State Teachers College, B.S, 1939; Newark College of Engineering, C.M.E., 1941. *Religion:* Jewish. *Home:* 16250 Aldersyde Rd., Shaker Heights, Ohio. *Office:* Leon Gordon Miller & Associates, Inc., 1220 Huron Rd., Cleveland, Ohio.

CAREER: Industrial designer. Teacher of art and design, 1939-40; U.S. War Department, Washington, D.C., chief designer, 1940-45; Cleveland Institute of Art, teacher, 1947-49; Leon Gordon Miller & Associates, Inc. (industrial design firm), Cleveland, Ohio, president, 1948—. Guest lecturer at Canadian Ministry of Commerce and Design Center of Yugoslavia; public speaker. Art work exhibited in galleries, museums, and solo shows and represented in private collections and Library of Congress; designer of stained glass windows, sculptures, and textiles; photographer. Founder of K.V. Design International, 1971, co-owner and chairman of board of directors, 1971-73; vice-president and member of board of trustees of Industrial Design Institute (founder and past president of Ohio Valley chapter); past member of board of trustees of Inter-Society Color Council; member of board of directors of fine arts advisory board of Rose Art Museum, 1972; chairman of board of directors of local Jewish Community Center. Delegate to international design congresses in Sweden, Italy, England, Mexico, Japan, and Yugoslavia; consultant to State of Israel; consultant for planning and design at Western Reserve University (now Case Western Reserve University). *Military service:* U.S. Army, engineer in technical intelligence, chief designer in Mobile Maintenance Division of Office of Army Ordnance, 1945-47; received two Bronze Stars.

MEMBER: World Craft Council, National Design Society (national president, 1960-62; chairman of board of directors, 1962), Industrial Design Society of America (fellow; president, 1960-62; chairman of board, 1962; member of board of directors), American Craftsmen's Council, Institute of Business Designers, Guild for Religious Art and Architecture (member of board of directors), Artists Equity Association, Stained Glass Association, Pierpont Morgan Library, Rotary International.

AWARDS, HONORS: Annual award for design in hardwoods, 1959; Institution's Interior Award, 1959; Design Derby Honor for space control, 1960; silver medal from Industrial Designers Institute, 1962; D.F.A. from Baldwin Wallace College, 1971, and Kean College of New Jersey, 1973; sculpture award from National Community Art Competition sponsored by U.S. Department of Housing and Urban Development, 1973.

WRITINGS: (With wife, Polly Miller) *Lost Heritage of Alaska: The Adventure and Art of the Alaska Coastal Indians,* World Publishing, 1967; *Light by Design,* General Electric Co., 1971; (author of preface) J. W. Bernstein, *Stained-Glass Craft,* Macmillan, 1973; *American First Editions: Their Prints and Prices,* Folcroft, 1973. Contributor to professional journals.

SIDELIGHTS: The Millers' *Lost Heritage of Alaska* describes the Northwest Indians as intelligent, artistic people who were cruelly exploited by the white trappers and explorers who came to the Alaskan wilderness. The book contains many photographs of artifacts that illustrate the artistic traditions of the Indians.

AVOCATIONAL INTERESTS: Collecting pre-Columbian and primitive art.

BIOGRAPHICAL/CRITICAL SOURCES: V. K. Ball and M. L. Shipley, *The Art of Interior Design,* Macmillan, 1960; Avram Kamph, *Contemporary Synagogue Art,* Union of American Hebrew Congregations, 1966.*

*   *   *

MILLETT, John D(avid)   1912-

PERSONAL: Born March 14, 1912, in Indianapolis, Ind.; son of Grover Allan (in business) and Helen Elizabeth (Welch) Millett; married Catherine Letsinger, September 2, 1934; children: Allan Reed, David Phillips, Stephen Malcolm. *Education:* DePauw University, A.B., 1933; Columbia University, A.M., 1935, Ph.D., 1938. *Religion:* Methodist. *Home:* 10444 Democracy Lane, Potomac, Md. 20854. *Office:* Academy for Educational Development, 1414 22nd St., Washington, D.C. 20037.

CAREER: Social Science Research Council, New York City, assistant secretary of committee on public administration, 1939-41; National Resources Planning Board, Washington, D.C., special assistant to director, 1941-42; Columbia University, New York City, associate professor, 1945-48, professor of public administration, 1948-53, director of Center of Administrative Studies, 1952-53; Miami University, Oxford, Ohio, president, 1953-64; Ohio Board of Regents, chancellor, 1964-72; Academy for Educational Development, Washington, D.C., vice-president, 1972—. Member of President's Commission on Administrative Management, 1936; executive director of Commission on Financing Higher Education, 1949-52; member of board of trustees of Educational Testing Service, 1959-63 and 1966-70, chairman, 1962-63 and 1969-70; member of board of trustees of College Entrance Examination Board, 1961-64, and DePauw University, 1977—; chairman of Ohio Commission for Education Beyond High School, 1962-63; member of National Board of Graduate Education and national commission for United Nations Educational, Scientific and Cultural Organization, 1965-70; commissioner of U.S. Department of Health, Education, and Welfare, 1964; delegate to international conferences; consultant to Ford Foundation. *Military service:* U.S. Army, Army Service Forces, 1942-45 and 1947; became colonel; Legion of Merit.

MEMBER: American Political Science Association (member of executive council, 1950), Academy of Political Science, American Society for Public Administration (president, 1960-61), National Association of State Universities, State Universities Association (president, 1961-63), National Academy of Public Administration (chairman, 1966-72), Institute of American Universities (member of board of trustees, 1963—), Phi Beta Kappa, Phi Delta Theta (president 1972-74), American Legion, Cosmos Club, Century Club. *Awards, honors:* Social Science Research Council fellow at University of London, 1938-39; LL.D. from DePauw University, 1950, Fenn College, 1954, Xavier University, 1959, Ohio State University, 1961, Denison University, 1963, Kent State University and University of Akron, 1964, Ohio Wesleyan University, 1966, University of Cincinnati, 1967, Central Michigan University and Central State University (Wilberforce, Ohio), 1968, Mount Union College and Chase College, 1969, and Urbana College, 1975; L.H.D. from Miami University (Oxford, Ohio), 1963, Findlay College, 1965, Waynesburg College, 1966, and Marion College, 1968; Litt.D. from University of Toledo, 1966; D.Ped. from Youngstown University, 1964, and University of Dayton, 1967; D.Public Service from Garfield College, 1973.

WRITINGS: The Works Progress Administration in New York City, Public Administration Service, 1938, reprinted, Arno, 1978; (with Arthur Whittier Macmahon) *Federal Administrators: A Biographical Approach to the Problem of Departmental Management,* Columbia University Press, 1939, reprinted, AMS Press, 1967; *British Unemployment Assistance Board: A Case Study in Administrative Anatomy,* McGraw, 1940 (published in England as *Unemployment Assistance Board: A Case Study in Administrative Anatomy,* G. Allen, 1940); (with Macmahon and Gladys Ogden) *The Administration of Federal Work Relief,* commission on Public Administration, 1941, reprinted, Da Capo, 1971; *The Process and Organization of Government Planning,* Columbia University Press, 1947, reprinted, Da Capo, 1972; (with Herman Struve Hensel) *Departmental Management in Federal Administration: A Report With Recommendations Prepared for the Commission on Organization of the Executive Branch of Government,* U.S. Government Printing Office, 1949.

Financing Higher Education in the United States: The Staff Report of the Commission on Financing Higher Education, Columbia University Press, 1952; (with others) *Natures and the Needs of Higher Education,* Columbia University Press, 1952; (editor) *An Atlas of Higher Education in the United States: The Geographical Distribution of Accredited Four-Year Colleges, Universities, and Technical Schools in 1950,* Columbia University Press, 1952; *Management in the Public Service: The Quest for Effective Performance,* McGraw, 1954; *The Organization and Role of the Army Service Forces,* Office of the Chief of Military History, U.S. Department of the Army, 1954; (editor with Macmahon) *Federalism Mature and Emergent,* Doubleday, 1955; *The Liberating Arts: Essays in General Education,* Howard Allen, 1957; *Government and Public Administration: The Quest for Responsible Performance,* McGraw, 1959; (with others) *What Is a College For?,* Public Affairs Press, 1961; *The Academic Community: An Essay on Organization,* McGraw, 1962; *Organization for the Public Service,* Van Nostrand, 1966; *Decision Making and Administration in Higher Education,* Kent State University Press, 1968.

Politics and Higher Education, University of Alabama Press, 1974; *Strengthening Community in Higher Education,* Academy for Educational Development, 1974; *Allocation Decisions in Higher Education,* Academy for Educational Development, 1975; *Mergers in Higher Education,* ACE, 1976; (editor) *Managing Turbulence and Change,* Jossey-Bass, 1977; *New Structures of Campus Power: Success and Failures of Emerging Forms of Institutional Governance,* Jossey-Bass, 1978; *Man-*

agement, Governance, and Leadership: A Guide for College and University Administrators, American Management Association, 1980. Contributor to scholarly journals.

BIOGRAPHICAL/CRITICAL SOURCES: New York Times, November 7, 1949; *Journal of Higher Education,* May-June, 1976.*

* * *

MILLS, David Harlow 1932-

PERSONAL: Born December 26, 1932, in Marshalltown, Iowa; son of Harlow Burgess (a biologist) and Esther Winifred (Brewer) Mills; married Janet Louise Anderson (a teacher), June 15, 1957; children: Ross Harlow, Anne Louise. *Education:* Iowa State University, B.S., 1955, M.S., 1957; Michigan State University, Ph.D., 1964. *Politics:* Democrat. *Religion:* Unitarian-Universalist. *Home:* 11919 Old Columbia Pike, Silver Spring, Md. 20904. *Office:* American Psychological Association, 1200 17th St. N.W., Washington, D.C. 20036.

CAREER: Iowa State University, Ames, assistant professor, 1965-68, associate professor of psychology, 1968-69, assistant director of Counseling Center, 1967-69; University of Maryland, College Park, associate professor, 1969-72, professor of psychology, 1972-81; American Psychological Association, Washington, D.C., administrative officer, 1981—. Research associate of National Register of Health Service Providers in Psychology; consultant to Veterans Administration and Iowa Women's Reformatory. *Military service:* U.S. Army, Medical Service Corps, 1957-61; became first lieutenant. *Member:* International Association of Counseling Services (vice-president, 1975-77; president, 1977-79), American Psychological Association (fellow), American Personnel and Guidance Association, Woodmoor-Pinecrest Citizens Association (president, 1973-74). *Awards, honors:* National Institute of Mental Health fellowship, 1964-65.

WRITINGS: (Contributor) L. Litwack, Getson, and Saltzman, editors, *Research in Counseling,* F. E. Peacock, 1968; *Licensing and Certification of Psychologists and Counselors,* Jossey-Bass, 1980. Also contributor to *Psychology and National Health Insurance: A Source Book,* edited by Kiesler, Cummings, and Vanden Bos. Contributor to psychology journals.

WORK IN PROGRESS: Ethics and Manpower Issues in Psychology, publication expected in 1982.

* * *

MILLUM, Trevor 1945-

PERSONAL: Born September 11, 1945, in Woking, England; son of George and Winifred Millum; married Christine Winn, 1968; children: Daniel, Joseph. *Education:* University of Birmingham, B.A. (with honors), 1967, Ph.D., 1970; University of Zambia, certificate in education, 1971. *Politics:* Labour. *Home:* Fern House, Barrow on Humber, South Humberside, England.

CAREER: English teacher at high school in Luapula, Zambia, 1971-74, and school in Cleethorpes, England, 1975-77. Baysgarth School, Barton on Humber, England, teacher of English and head of department, 1977-81; United World College of Southeast Asia, Singapore, head of faculty of English, 1981—.

WRITINGS: Images of Woman: Visual Communication in Advertising, Chatto & Windus, 1975; *Exercises in African History,* Longman, 1978. Contributor to academic journals.

WORK IN PROGRESS: A book of poems, *Warning: Too Much Schooling Can Damage Your Health.*

SIDELIGHTS: Millum told *CA:* "I used to write a lot. Now I am unsure why most of us write, or at least publish. Mostly, I suspect, it is for our *own* gratification. Is it really worth it? How many of us have something really original and worthwhile to say? I spend more time drawing and painting and running a small craft shop. Having spent four years in Africa, traveling widely, and visiting India, the world of publishing often seems rather remote from reality. However, I love to read. . . ."

* * *

MILNE, A(lan) A(lexander) 1882-1956

BRIEF ENTRY: Born January 18, 1882, in London, England; died January 31, 1956, in Hartfield, Sussex, England. English editor and author. Although primarily a writer of plays, essays, and novels for adults, Milne is best remembered for his whimsical "Winnie-the-Pooh" verses and stories. Inspired by his son, Christopher Robin, Milne wrote numerous books featuring Christopher and his personified, stuffed bear. Included in the beloved series are *When We Were Very Young* (1924), *Winnie-the-Pooh* (1926), *The House at Pooh Corner* (1928), and *The Christopher Robin Verses* (1932). Among his works for adults are *Mr. Pim* (1921) and a detective novel, *The Red House Murder* (1921). In addition, he wrote nearly thirty plays, most of them comedies. From 1906 until 1914 Milne was assistant editor of and a contributor to *Punch. Biographical/critical sources: Twentieth Century Authors: A Biographical Dictionary of Modern Literature,* H. W. Wilson, 1942; *Modern World Drama: An Encyclopedia,* Dutton, 1972; *McGraw-Hill Encyclopedia of World Drama,* McGraw, 1972; *Longman Companion to English Literature,* Longman, 1977.

* * *

MILNER, Ian Frank George 1911-

PERSONAL: Born June 6, 1911, in Oamaru, New Zealand; son of Frank (a headmaster) and Florence Violet (George) Milner; married Margaret L. Trafford, September 12, 1940 (divorced); married Jarmila Maranova, July 24, 1958; children: Linda Fruhaufova Servitova (stepdaughter). *Education:* Canterbury University College (now University of Canterbury), M.A. (with first class honors), 1933; Oxford University, B.A. (with first class honors), 1937; Charles University, Dr.Sc., 1971. *Home:* Lopatecka 11a, Prague 4, Czechoslovakia 147 00.

CAREER: Department of Education, Wellington, New Zealand, research officer, 1939; University of Melbourne, Parkville, Australia, lecturer in political science, 1940-44; Department of External Affairs, Canberra, Australia, temporary officer, 1945-46; United Nations, New York, N.Y., political affairs officer, 1947-51; Charles University, Prague, Czechoslovakia, lecturer, 1951-63, associate professor of English literature, 1964-76; writer, 1976—. Visiting professor at University of Otago, 1971. *Military service:* Australian Volunteer Defence Corps, lecturer with Army Education Service, 1942-44.

MEMBER: International Association of University Professors of English, Circle of Modern Philology, Friends of the Turnbull Library. *Awards, honors:* Rhodes scholar at Oxford University, 1934; Commonwealth Fund fellowship for University of California, Columbia University, and Institute of Pacific Relations, 1937-39; Bezruc Centennial Prize from North Moravian Council of Czechoslovakia, 1967, for translating Petr Bezruc's *Silesian Songs.*

WRITINGS: New Zealand's Interests and Policies in the Far East, Institute of Pacific Relations, 1940; *The Structure of Values in George Eliot*, Universita Karlova, 1968; (contributor) Ada Nisbet and Blake Nevius, editors, *Dickens Centennial Essays*, University of California Press, 1971.

Translator: (With Vilem Fried) Josef Macek, *The Hussite Movement in Bohemia* (edited by E. Lauer), Orbis, 1953, 3rd edition, 1965; (with wife, Jarmila Milner) Frantisek Kavka, *An Outline of Czechoslovak History*, Orbis, 1960, 2nd edition, 1963; Petr Bezruc, *Silesian Songs* (poems), Artia, 1966; (with George Theiner) Miroslav Holub, *Selected Poems*, Penguin, 1967; (with J. Milner) Holub, *Although* (poems), J. Cape, 1971; (with J. Milner; also author of introduction) Vladimir Holan, *Selected Poems*, Penguin, 1971; (with J. Milner) Holub, *Notes of a Clay Pigeon* (poems), Secker & Warburg, 1977; (with J. Milner) Alexej Pludek, *Carolus Quartus: Romanorum Imperator et Boemie Rex*, Orbis Press Agency, 1978; (with J. Milner; also author of introduction) Holan, *A Night With Hamlet* (poem), Oasis Books, 1980.

Contributor of articles and translations to scholarly journals and literary magazines, including *American Poetry Review, Transatlantic Review, New Statesman, Mosaic, London Magazine, Times Literary Supplement*, and *Encounter*. Co-editor of *Prague Studies in English*, 1973-76.

WORK IN PROGRESS: Translating, with wife, Jarmila Milner, *Anthology of Modern Czech Poetry*, covering the years 1920-70, completion expected in 1982; a biography of his father, a New Zealand high school headmaster, publication expected in 1983.

SIDELIGHTS: Milner told *CA:* "As a young New Zealander in the 1930's, I was mainly interested in English literature and current politics, especially in the Pacific and Far East. The latter took me for some years into the United Nations service, in the Secretariat. For the last thirty years I've been glad to return to my original field, teaching and research on English literature. I enjoy translating Czech poetry, with my Czech wife's assistance, partly because so much of it is concerned with the human essence and is rooted so deeply and imaginatively in the native earth and changing history of the Czech people.

"Apart from translation of Czech poetry, my writing has so far been mainly as literary critic of nineteenth-century English fiction, particularly George Eliot and Dickens. I'm old-fashioned enough to see literature as the imaginative creation and expression of social and historical reality. True, the house of Art has many mansions. But some things make me return, as reader and critic, to the great nineteenth-century fiction writers like Tolstoy, Dickens, Dostoevsky, George Eliot, and others: their Shakespeare-like, moving revelations of the ultimate worth of the human personality and its immense and varied potential for comedy, feeling, imagination, ambition, faith in human resources, love and passion, and stoic endurance; the way in which (each so different) they individualize and bring alive for the reader their chosen characters; the ways whereby they show us human character as 'history' rather than as 'destiny' so that we see the characters grow, adapt, and differ, for better or for worse, as inseparable units in a given historical and social milieu.

"I think it was the poet and critic Donald Davie who once remarked, 'For poetry to be great it must reek of the human.' Put that together with Matthew Arnold's view that poetry (and creative literature of any genre) is a criticism of life, and my credo is more or less said for me."

AVOCATIONAL INTERESTS: Reading (especially nineteenth-century English, French, and Russian fiction and contemporary poetry), music, walking, swimming.

* * *

MINEHAHA, Cornelius
See WEDEKIND, (Benjamin) Frank(lin)

* * *

MINK, Louis Otto, Jr.   1921-

PERSONAL: Born September 3, 1921, in Ada, Ohio; son of Louis Otto and Helen (Arndt) Mink; married Helen Louise Patterson, June 24, 1944; children: Louis Otto III, Sarah Patterson, Stephen Dorrance. *Education:* Hiram College, B.A., 1942; Yale University, M.A., 1948, Ph.D., 1952; Wesleyan University, M.A. (with honors), 1965. *Religion:* Congregationalist. *Home:* 73 Home Ave., Middletown, Conn. 06457. *Office:* Department of Philosophy, Wesleyan University, Middletown, Conn. 06457.

CAREER: Yale University, New Haven, Conn., instructor in philosophy, 1950-52; Wesleyan University, Middletown, Conn., 1952—, began as assistant professor, became professor of philosophy, 1965, Kenan Professor of Humanities, 1979—. Visiting professor at Carleton College, 1963; visiting lecturer at Yale University, 1977. *Military service:* U.S. Army, 1942-46; served in Pacific theater. *Member:* American Philosophical Association, American Association of University Professors, American Civil Liberties Union, Society for Values in Higher Education (Kent fellow; member of board of directors, 1953-56, 1973—; vice-president, 1974—), Metaphysical Society of America, American Society of Aesthetics.

WRITINGS: (Contributor) W. H. Dray, editor, *Philosophical Analysis and History*, Harper, 1966; *Mind, History, and Dialectic: The Philosophy of R. G. Collingwood*, Indiana University Press, 1969; (contributor) Ihab Hassan, editor, *Liberations: New Essays on the Humanities in Revolution*, Wesleyan University Press, 1971; (contributor) Michael Krausz, editor, *Critical Essays on the Philosophy of R. G. Collingwood*, Oxford University Press, 1972; *A Finnegan's Wake Gazetteer*, Indiana University Press, 1978; (contributor) Robert H. Canary and Henry Kozicki, editors, *The Writing of History*, University of Wisconsin Press, 1978. Contributor to scholarly journals. Managing editor of *Review of Metaphysics*, 1950-52, and associate editor of *History and Theory*, 1965—.*

* * *

MIREAUX, Emile   1885(?)-1969

OBITUARY NOTICE: Born c. 1885; died December 27, 1969, in Paris, France. Journalist and author of *Daily Life in the Time of Homer*. Obituaries and other sources: *AB Bookman's Weekly*, March 2, 1970.

* * *

MIRO (FERRER), Gabriel (Francisco Victor)   1879-1930

BRIEF ENTRY: Born in 1879 in Alicante, Spain; died in 1930 in Madrid, Spain. Spanish public administrator and novelist. Educated in a Jesuit school, Miro is best remembered for his novels that examine aspects of religion and religious figures while gently satirizing the clergy of Spain. *El humo dormido* (1919) and *Nuestro padre San Daniel* (1921) are typical of Miro's semi-autobiographical works in which he depicts the struggles and ironies of Jesuit life. Among his other works, which are noted for their richness of description and detail, are *Nomada* (1908), *Figuras de la pasion del Senor* (1916), and *El obispo leproso* (1926). Unable to earn his living by writing, Miro held a number of bureaucratic positions in Spain. *Biographical/critical sources: The Concise Encyclopedia of Modern World Literature*, Hutchinson, 1963; *The Penguin Companion to European Literature*, McGraw, 1969; *The Oxford Companion to Spanish Literature*, Clarendon, 1978.

*   *   *

MISRA, Bankey Bihari   1909-

PERSONAL: Born January 1, 1909, in Siwan, India. *Education:* Benares Hindu University, B.A., 1937; University of London, Ph.D., 1947. *Office:* Dayanand Ayurvedic Medical College, P.O. & Dist. Siwan, Bihar, India.

CAREER: Educator. Associated with Dayanand Ayurvedic Medical College, Siwan, India. *Member:* Bihar and Orisse Research Society. *Awards, honors:* D.Lit. from University of London, 1962.

WRITINGS: The Central Administration of the East India Company, 1773-1834, Manchester University Press, 1959; *The Indian Middle Classes: Their Growth in Modern Times*, Oxford University Press, 1961; *The Judicial Administration of the East India Company in Bengal, 1765-1782*, Motilal Banarsidass, 1961; (editor with Aditya Prasad Jha) *Select Documents on Mahatma Gandhi's Movement in Champaran, 1917-18*, Government of Bihar, 1963; *The Administrative History of India, 1834-1947: General Administration*, Oxford University Press, 1970; *The Indian Political Parties: An Historical Analysis of Political Behaviour up to 1947*, Oxford University Press, 1976; *The Bureaucracy in India: An Historical Analysis of Development up to 1947*, Oxford University Press, 1977. Contributor to administration journals.

BIOGRAPHICAL/CRITICAL SOURCES: Times Literary Supplement, December 23, 1977; *English Historical Review*, April, 1978; *Annals of the American Academy of Political and Social Science*, July, 1978.*

*   *   *

MISTRAL, Gabriela
See GODOY ALCAYAGA, Lucila

*   *   *

MITCHELL, Basil George   1917-

PERSONAL: Born April 9, 1917; son of George William and Mary (Loxston) Mitchell; married Margaret Eleanor Collin, 1950; children: one son, three daughters. *Education:* Graduated from Queen's College, Oxford (with first class honors), 1939. *Home:* Bridge House, Wootton, Woodstock, Oxford, England. *Office:* 26 Walton St., Oxford, England.

CAREER: Oxford University, Oxford, England, lecturer at Christ Church, 1946-47, tutor and fellow of Keble College, 1947-67, Nolloth Professor of Philosophy of the Christian Religion and fellow of Oriel College, 1968—, senior proctor, 1956-57, member of Hebdomadal Council, 1959-65. Stanton Lecturer in Philosophy of Religion at Cambridge University, 1959-62; visiting professor at Princeton University, 1963; Edward Cadbury Lecturer at University of Birmingham, 1966-67; Gifford Lecturer at University of Glasgow, 1974-76; visiting professor at Colgate University, 1976. *Military service:* Royal Navy,

1940-46; became lieutenant. *Awards, honors:* D.D. from University of Glasgow, 1977.

WRITINGS: (Editor) *Faith and Logic: Oxford Essays in Philosophical Theology*, Beacon Press, 1957; *Law, Morality, and Religion in a Secular Society*, Oxford University Press, 1967; *The Philosophy of Religion*, Oxford University Press, 1971; *The Justification of Religious Belief*, Macmillan, 1974; *Morality, Religious and Secular: The Dilemma of the Traditional Conscience*, Clarendon Press, 1980. Contributor to philosophy and theology journals.*

*   *   *

MITCHELL, James Leslie   1901-1935
(Lewis Grassic Gibbon)

BRIEF ENTRY: Born February 13, 1901, near Auchterless, Aberdeenshire, Scotland; died February, 1935, in Welwyn Garden City, Hertfordshire, England. Anglo-Scottish novelist, short story writer, science fiction writer, essayist, biographer, and journalist. James Leslie Mitchell, or Lewis Grassic Gibbon, as he is more commonly remembered, left the Scottish countryside of his boyhood to pursue a journalistic career in Glasgow. After a brief time in that field, he joined the armed services and spent several years stationed in such parts of the world as the Middle East and Central America. His studies in anthropology and archaeology, coupled with his dismay over the social injustices he had witnessed while in Glasgow, led him to embrace the diffusionist theory of civilization. The theory, to which Gibbon held throughout his short life, blamed the corruption of man's essential goodness on the "accidental" diffusion of civilization. Gibbon's loyalty to diffusionist principles was evident in his fiction, which presents characters constantly struggling to retain the purity and simplicity of a lifestyle threatened by industrialization. One such character was Christine Guthrie, the heroine of Gibbon's highly respected trilogy, *A Scots Quair* (1946). The novels were originally published separately under the titles *Sunset Song* (1932), *Cloud Howe* (1933), and *Grey Granite* (1934). What critics found particularly admirable about these works was Gibbon's unprecedented success at capturing the Scots idiom, not only in the dialogue, but also in the narrative. Under his own name he wrote *Spartacus* (1933) and several other historical novels, most of which were quickly forgotten. *Biographical/critical sources: Twentieth Century Authors: A Biographical Dictionary of Modern Literature*, H. W. Wilson, 1942; *The Concise Encyclopedia of Modern World Literature*, Hutchinson, 1963; *The Penguin Companion to English Literature*, McGraw, 1971; *Twentieth-Century Literary Criticism*, Volume 4, Gale, 1981.

*   *   *

MITCHELL, P(hilip) M(arshall)   1916-

PERSONAL: Born September 23, 1916; married, 1941; children: three. *Education:* Cornell University, B.A., 1938; University of Illinois, Ph.D., 1942. *Office:* Department of Germanic Languages, University of Illinois, Urbana, Ill. 61801.

CAREER: Harvard University, Cambridge, Mass., instructor in German, 1946-49; University of Kansas, Lawrence, assistant professor, 1950-54, associate professor of German, 1954-58; University of Illinois, Urbana, professor of German, 1958—. Managing editor of *Journal of English and German Philology*, 1959—.

WRITINGS: A Bibliographical Guide to Danish Literature, Munksgaard, 1951; *A History of Danish Literature*, Gyldendal, 1957, American-Scandinavian Foundation, 1958, 2nd edition,

Kraus-Thomson Organization, 1971; *A Bibliography of English Imprints of Denmark Through 1900,* Libraries, University of Kansas, 1960; *A Bibliography of Seventeenth-Century German Imprints in Denmark and the Duchies of Schleswig-Holstein,* three volumes, Libraries, University of Kansas, 1969-76; *Vilhelm Groenbech: En indfoering,* Gyldendal, 1970; *Halldor Hermannsson,* Cornell University Press, 1978; *Vilhelm Groenbech,* Twayne, 1978; *Henrik Pontoppidan,* Twayne, 1979.

Editor: (With Frederick Julius Billeskov-Jansen) *Anthology of Danish Literature* (bilingual), Southern Illinois University Press, 1964, reprinted in two volumes, Volume I: *Middle Ages to Romanticism,* Volume II: *Realism to the Present,* 1971; Johann Christopf Gottsched, *Ausgewaehlte Werke,* De Gruyter, Volume I: *Gedichte und Gedichtuebertragungen,* 1968, Volume II: *Saemtliche Dramen,* 1970, Volume III: *Saemtliche Dramenuebertragungen,* 1970, Volume VII: *Ausfuehrliche Redekunst,* Part 3: *Anhang und Variantverzeichnis,* 1975, Volume VI: *Versuch Einer Critischen Dichtkunst: Kommentar,* 1978; (with Kenneth H. Ober) *Bibliography of Modern Icelandic Literature in Translation, Including Works Written by Icelanders in Other Languages,* Cornell University Press, 1975.

Translator: (With W. D. Paden) Vilhelm Groenbech, *Religious Currents in the Nineteenth Century,* Southern Illinois University Press, 1973; (with K. H. Ober) *The Royal Guest and Other Classical Danish Narrative,* University of Chicago Press, 1977; (with Paden) Isak Dinesen, *Carnival: Entertainments and Posthumous Tales,* University of Chicago Press, 1977; (with Paden) Dinesen, *Daguerrotypes and Other Essays,* University of Chicago Press, 1979.

BIOGRAPHICAL/CRITICAL SOURCES: Times Literary Supplement, October 27, 1978.*

*   *   *

MITCHELSON, Marvin M. 1928-

PERSONAL: Born May 7, 1928, in Detroit, Mich.; son of Herbert and Sonia Mitchelson; married Marcella Ferri (an actress), 1961; children: Morgan. *Education:* University of California, Los Angeles, B.A., 1953; Southwestern University, J.D., 1956. *Residence:* Beverly Hills, Calif. *Office:* 1801 Century Park E., Suite 1900, Los Angeles, Calif. 90067.

CAREER: Marvin M. Mitchelson (law firm), Los Angeles, Calif., attorney, 1956—. Guest on television programs, including "60 Minutes," "Today," "Good Morning, America," "The Phil Donahue Show," and "Tomorrow"; speaker at law schools. *Member:* American Bar Association, American Trial Lawyers Association, Trial Lawyers of America, California Trial Lawyers, Century City Bar Association.

WRITINGS: Made in Heaven, Settled in Court, J. P. Tarcher, 1976; *Living Together,* Simon & Schuster, 1981.

SIDELIGHTS: "Marvin has the ability to baby fragile egos and still get the job done," said one of the attorney's friends when explaining why Marvin Mitchelson is one of the most popular lawyers for celebrities. He sees himself as "a friend, a part-time psychologist, a priest, sage, counselor, accountant, referee and detective" who is adept at handling personalities with kid gloves and at focusing on his clients' real lives. Though his practice has included such notable figures as Tony Curtis, Mel Torme, Stephen Stills, Sonny Bono, Carl Sagan, and Richard Harris, Mitchelson is known primarily as "a woman's lawyer." "I love women," the attorney told Pamela G. Hollie of the *New York Times.* "I am committed to their civil rights." In particular, Mitchelson is committed to the civil rights of the wives and unmarried partners of the rich and the famous. Fight-

ing against their husbands' and consorts' lawyers for their share of the couple's assets, Mitchelson secures what he terms "satisfactory" property and financial settlements for his clients. Pamela Mason, Rhonda Fleming, Eden Marx, Connie Stevens, Bianca Jagger, Soraya Khashoggi, Sara Dylan, and Michelle Triola Marvin are among his more prominent female clients.

As counsel for the plaintiff in the precedent-setting litigation *Marvin v. Marvin,* Mitchelson ended the doctrine of meretricious relationships and became famous in his own right. The California Supreme Court ruled that express or written contracts between unmarried couples who live together are binding and can be legally enforced. The court further established that in cases where no contract exists the individuals involved still must receive equitable remedies in order for their expectations to be protected.

In Michelle Triola Marvin's case, she claimed to have sacrificed a singing career to live with actor Lee Marvin, who the plaintiff said promised to support her for the rest of her life if she would carry out the duties of a wife without the benefit of a marriage license. After six years of the arrangement, Marvin married his high school sweetheart and stopped his financial support of Michelle Marvin. She contended that she was entitled to half of the couple's assets, one million dollars, because Marvin broke the verbal agreement they made in 1964. The court awarded Michelle Marvin $104,000 in "palimony" so that she could re-educate herself, and it recognized the rights of women to equitable shares of a couple's property. "I'm not trying to paint myself as a big crusader, but this was a case I believed in," Mitchelson revealed to a *People* interviewer. "I was waiting for one like it to come along. I believe that a woman who has lived exactly as a wife with everything but an $8 marriage license should have the same rights." He later told Steven Brill of *Esquire:* "I've always been fascinated by the question of why the existence or nonexistence of a marriage license should alter some people's rights. Any two idiots can get a marriage license."

A second notable case involving women's rights is Soraya Khashoggi's divorce from her Saudi-born husband Adnan, whom *People* called an "arms peddler and wheeler-dealer worth $4 billion." Asking for $2.54 billion for his client, supposedly the largest divorce settlement in history, Mitchelson "took the case because it is an extension of women's rights, the application of Western standards of law and fairness to Muslim women," he remarked in *People.*

At fifteen, Soraya Khashoggi, the former Sandra Jarvis-Daly, married a man ten years her senior and helped him make his fortune by acting as his full business partner for thirteen years. A possibly invalid Lebanese divorce in 1974 required that Khashoggi receive $400,000 and financial support for her four children and herself. The payments stopped shortly after she married an Englishman in 1979, and at one time *People* reported that Khashoggi had not seen her children in three months, which she considered "Adnan's revenge . . . for her divorce action." Mitchelson's petitions cite threats from Khashoggi's husband, warning that under Islamic law she could be killed for being a trouble-making wife. "But she had been a dutiful wife—Muslim, Christian or Jewish, any way you look at it," insisted Mitchelson. "And if women are equal, they're entitled to half." There is a technicality, however. Neither Khashoggi nor her husband are citizens of the United States, though she lives in California while he owns much of that state. Still, Khashoggi hopes that the case will "pave the way for other Muslim women to assert their rights."

Mitchelson was also involved in two other cases of special interest. The first was *People* v. *Douglas,* a case settled in the

United States Supreme Court in 1963. This case gave indigents the right to counsel and was adopted in all fifty states. The second case of considerable import was *People* v. *Raffalle Minichello.* In 1969 Minichello hijacked an airplane to Egypt which precipitated an international incident. Although he served a one-year sentence, had it not been for Mitchelson he could have been imprisoned for life.

The attorney's first book, *Made in Heaven, Settled in Court,* is the history of his career as a lawyer for public figures and dwells on his most memorable cases, such as the ones already mentioned. Critics have called the book "gossipy" and "entertaining," but they also note the respect and sympathy that the author has for his clients. And, like Charlotte Low of *BooksWest,* many found the book "quite insightful."

Living Together, his second book, is a guide for unmarried, married, and homosexual couples. In addition to discussing property and support payments, Mitchelson gives economic advice and suggests that partners "get it down in writing" and draw up contracts to make separating easier, shorter, and more efficient.

BIOGRAPHICAL/CRITICAL SOURCES: BooksWest, April, 1977; *People,* April 24, 1978, August 27, 1979, December 24, 1979; *Esquire,* May 9, 1978; *Time,* January 15, 1979; *New York Times,* January 6, 1980.

—Sketch by Charity Anne Dorgan

* * *

MITZMAN, Arthur Benjamin 1931-

PERSONAL: Born September 18, 1931, in Newark, N.J.; married, 1956; children: two. *Education:* Columbia University, B.S., 1956, M.A., 1959; Brandeis University, M.A., 1959, Ph.D., 1963. *Office:* Historisch Seminarium, University of Amsterdam, Herengracht 286, Amsterdam-C, Netherlands.

CAREER: Brooklyn College of the City University of New York, Brooklyn, N.Y., instructor in history, 1962-64; Goddard College, Plainfield, Vt., instructor in history, 1964-65; University of Rochester, Rochester, N.Y., assistant professor of history, 1965-69; Simon Fraser University, Burnaby, British Columbia, associate professor of social theory, 1969-71; University of Amsterdam, Amsterdam, Netherlands, professor of history, 1971—. *Member:* American Historical Association.

WRITINGS: The Iron Cage: An Historical Interpretation of Max Weber, Knopf, 1969; *Sociology and Estrangement: Three Sociologists of Imperial Germany,* Knopf, 1973. Contributor to *Encyclopaedia Britannica.* Contributor to history and sociology journals.*

* * *

MOGEL, Leonard Henry 1922-

PERSONAL: Born October 23, 1922, in Brooklyn, N.Y.; son of Isaac and Shirley (Goldman) Mogel; married Ann Vera Levy, October 23, 1949; children: Wendy Lynn, Jane Ellen. *Education:* City College (now of the City University of New York), B.B.A., 1947. *Religion:* Jewish. *Home:* 429 East 52nd St., New York, N.Y. 10022. *Office:* Leonard Mogel Associates, Inc., 635 Madison Ave., New York, N.Y. 10028.

CAREER: New York Printing Co., New York City, in sales, 1946-48; Pollak Printing Co., New York City, sales manager, 1948-52; Leonard Mogel Associates, Inc. (advertising representatives), New York City, president, 1952—. Vice-president of San Francisco Warriors (basketball team), 1962-63, prin-

cipal owner, 1963-64; president of Phoenix Press, Inc., 1952-67, and Twenty First Communications, Inc., 1967—; member of board of directors of Regents Publishing Co., 1960-67. Advertising director of Diners Club, Inc., 1952-56, publisher of *Signature,* 1956-67; publisher of *Bravo,* 1964-67, *Cheetah* and *Weight Watchers,* 1967—, *National Lampoon,* 1970—, *Liberty,* 1971—, *Ingenue,* 1973—, and *Heavy Metal,* 1977—. Adjunct professor at New York University, 1973—. Panelist at *Forum* Publishers Conference, 1975-76. Sponsor of Albert Einstein Medical College and Birch Wathen School. *Military service:* U.S. Army, 1942-46; served in China-Burma-India theater. *Member:* Society of Illustrators.

WRITINGS: The Magazine: Everything You Need to Know to Make It in the Magazine Business, Prentice-Hall, 1979.*

* * *

MOLODY, Konan Trofimovich
See LONSDALE, Gordon Arnold

* * *

MONTALE, Eugenio 1896-1981

OBITUARY NOTICE—See index for *CA* sketch: Born October 12, 1896, in Genoa, Italy; died of heart failure, September 12, 1981, in Milan, Italy. Poet, editor, translator, critic, journalist, and author. Montale was awarded the Nobel Prize for literature in 1975. Despite the fact that he published only five volumes of poetry in fifty years, the Swedish Academy pronounced Montale "one of the most important poets of the contemporary West." Presenting "an outlook on life with no illusions," Montale published his first collection of verse, *Ossi di seppia* (title means "Bone of the Cuttlefish"), in 1925. During his career, the poet worked in a variety of positions. He contributed articles and criticism to literary magazines such as *Primo Tempo* and held an editorial job with the publishing house Bemporad. While director of the Gabinetto Vieusseux Library in Florence in the late 1930's, Montale was forced to resign because he refused to join the Fascist party. He then supported himself by translating into Italian the works of Herman Melville, Eugene O'Neill, Shakespeare, T. S. Eliot, and Angus Wilson. In 1948 he joined the staff of the newspaper *Corriere della Sera.* Montale worked at the paper as a literary and sometime music critic until his death. His other volumes of poetry include *Le occasioni* (title means "The Occasions"), *La bufera e altro* (title means "The Storm and Other Things"), and *Satura.* Among his prose works are *La farfalla di Dinard* (title means "The Butterfly of Dinard") and *Nel nostro tempo.* Obituaries and other sources: *New York Times,* September 14, 1981; *London Times,* September 14, 1981; *Washington Post,* September 14, 1981; *Publishers Weekly,* September 25, 1981; *Time,* September 28, 1981; *Newsweek,* September 28, 1981; *AB Bookman's Weekly,* October 19, 1981.

* * *

MONTANARI, A(delio) J(oseph) 1917-

PERSONAL: Original name, Adelio Giuseppe Ambruano Pasquale Antonio Montanari, born May 25, 1917, in Winchendon Springs, Mass.; son of Antonio (a shipping clerk and truck driver) and Adelchisa (a weaver; maiden name, Guerra) Montanari; married Ann Belue (a teacher), 1943 (divorced, August, 1957); married Carol Straus, November 26, 1958; children: (first marriage) Antonio Garibaldi, Adele Ann; (second marriage) Karen, Herbert, Joyce (stepchildren). *Education:* Attended Antioch College, 1935-38; Western Carolina College (now University), B.S., 1955; received teaching certificate from University of Miami, Coral Gables, Fla. *Religion:* Jewish. *Home:* 19651 Northeast 19th Pl., North Miami Beach, Fla. 33162. *Office:* Montanari Clinical School, 291 East Second St., Hialeah, Fla. 33010.

CAREER: Worked at cotton mill in Winchenden, Mass., and at cooperative stores all over the United States; superintendent of vocational training at Brevard Junior College, Brevard, N.C.; teacher at public school in Little River, N.C.; teacher of educationally deprived children at school in Miami, Fla.; operated day school for hearing-impaired emotionally disturbed children in Hialeah, Fla., 1952-55; Montanari Clinical School (residential school for severely disturbed children), Hialeah, founder and teacher, 1955—. Lecturer at universities and public gatherings; guest on television programs, including "Today" and "The Mike Douglas Show." *Military service:* U.S. Army, Combat Engineers Battalion; served in European theater; became sergeant; received Purple Heart and Bronze Star. *Member:* Optimist Club, Kiwanis, Hialeah-Miami Springs Chamber of Commerce.

WRITINGS: (With Arthur Henley) *The Montanari Book: What the Other Child-Care Books Won't Tell You,* Stein & Day, 1972; (with Henley) *The Difficult Child,* Stein & Day, 1973.

BIOGRAPHICAL/CRITICAL SOURCES: Pageant, April, 1964; *Saturday Evening Post,* October 17, 1964; Arthur Henley, *Demon in My View,* Simon & Schuster, 1966.*

*   *   *

MONTGOMERY, (Robert) Bruce   1921-1978
(Edmund Crispin)

OBITUARY NOTICE: Born October 2, 1921, in Chesham Bois, Buckinghamshire, England; died September 15, 1978, in England. Musician and author best known for his series of detective novels featuring the Oxford sleuth, Gervase Fen. Montgomery was an accomplished pianist, organist, and writer by the age of fourteen. He was also a serious composer who wrote scores for British films, including "Carry On Nurse." Montgomery graduated from Oxford in 1943 and began to write the following year after outlining a story plot to his novelist friend Charles Williams. Williams was so impressed with Montgomery's plot synopsis that he encouraged its development into a novel. Between 1944 and 1953 Montgomery wrote nine crime novels and a collection of short stories under the pseudonym Edmund Crispin. In 1967 he became the mystery-fiction reviewer for the *London Sunday Times.* Montgomery's well-crafted plots and witty, highbrow humor earned him critical and popular acclaim as well as the respect of other mystery writers, including Ellery Queen and Julian Symons, who compared Montgomery's work to that of Agatha Christie. Obituaries and other sources: *Current Biography,* 1949, Wilson, 1950; *World Authors, 1950-1970,* H. W. Wilson, 1975; *Encyclopedia of Mystery and Detection,* McGraw, 1976; *London Times,* September 18, 1978.

*   *   *

MOORE, C(atherine) L(ucile)   1911-
(Lawrence O'Donnell, Lewis Padgett, joint pseudonyms)

PERSONAL: Born January 24, 1911, in Indianapolis, Ind.; daughter of Otto Newman and Maude Estelle (Jones) Moore; married Henry Kuttner (a writer), June 7, 1940 (died, 1958); married Thomas Reggie, June 13, 1963. *Education:* University of Southern California, B.A., 1956, M.A., 1964. *Residence:* Long Beach, Calif. *Agent:* Harold Matson Agency, 22 East 40th St., New York, N.Y. 10016.

CAREER: Writer. Fletcher Trust Co., Indianapolis, Ind., 1930-40, became president; University of Southern California, Los Angeles, instructor in writing and literature, 1958-61. Scriptwriter for Warner Bros., Inc. *Member:* Science Fiction Writers of America, Mystery Writers of America, Writers Guild, Phi Beta Kappa, Phi Kappa Phi.

WRITINGS:—Science fiction: *Judgment Night: A Collection of Science Fiction,* Gnome Press, 1952, reprinted, Dell, 1979; (with husband, Henry Kuttner, under joint pseudonym Lawrence O'Donnell) *Clash By Night* (story), American Science Fiction, 1952; *Shambleau and Others,* Gnome Press, 1953; *Northwest of Earth,* Gnome Press, 1954, revised edition, Consul, 1961; (with Robert E. Howard, Frank Belknap Long, H. P. Lovecraft, and A. Merritt) *The Challenge From Beyond,* privately printed, 1954, Necronomicon, 1978; *Jirel of Joiry,* Paperback Library, 1969, reprinted as *Black God's Shadow,* Donald M. Grant, 1977; *The Best of C. L. Moore,* Doubleday, 1975.

With Kuttner: *There Shall Be Darkness* (story), American Science Fiction, 1954; *No Boundaries,* Ballantine, 1955; *Doomsday Morning* (novel), Doubleday, 1957; *Earth's Last Citadel* (novel), Ace Books, 1964.

With Kuttner, under joint pseudonym Lewis Padgett: *A Gnome There Was and Other Tales of Science Fiction and Fantasy,* Simon & Schuster, 1950; *Tomorrow and Tomorrow* [and] *The Fairy Chessmen: Two Science Fiction Novels,* Gnome Press, 1951, reprinted as *Chessboard Planet,* Galaxy, 1956 (published in England as *The Far Reality,* Consul, 1963); *Robots Have No Tails,* Gnome Press, 1952; *Mutant* (novel), Gnome Press, 1953; *Well of the Worlds* (novel), Galaxy, 1953; *Line to Tomorrow,* Bantam, 1954.

With Padgett (pseudonym used solely by husband, H. Kuttner): *The Brass Ring,* Duell, Sloan & Pearce, 1946, published as *Murder in Brass,* Bantam, 1947; *The Day He Died,* Duell, Sloan & Pearce, 1947; *Beyond Earth's Gates* (novel), Ace Books, 1954.

Anonymous contributor to books by Kuttner: *Fury* (novel), Grosset & Dunlap, 1950, published as *Destination Infinity,* Avon, 1958; *Ahead of Time: Ten Stories of Science Fiction and Fantasy,* Ballantine, 1953; *Remember Tomorrow* (story), American Science Fiction, 1954; *Way of the Gods* (story), American Science Fiction, 1954; *Sword of Tomorrow* (story), American Science Fiction, 1955; *Bypass to Otherness,* Ballantine, 1961; *Return to Otherness,* Ballantine, 1962; *Valley of the Flame* (novel), Ace Books, 1964; *The Best of Kuttner,* Mayflower-Dell, Volume I, 1965, Volume II, 1966; *The Dark World* (novel), Ace Books, 1965; *The Time Axis* (novel), Ace Books, 1965; *The Mask of Circe* (novel), Ace Books, 1971.

Contributor of numerous short stories to periodicals, including *Weird Tales* and *Famous Fantastic Mysteries.*

SIDELIGHTS: Of the numerous works of science fiction that C. L. Moore has written, the short novel *Judgment Night* is considered one of her finest. Fletcher Pratt, for instance, deemed it "a classic." Published together with four short stories, the collection prompted a *New York Times* reviewer to comment: "The effect of the title story is marred a little by inclusion of some shorts that are by no means Miss Moore's best writing. But the startling and disturbing 'Judgment Night' is a perfect showcase for her romantic imagination at its absolute best."

CA INTERVIEW

C. L. Moore was interviewed by *CA* by phone on May 6, 1980, at her home in Long Beach, Calif.

CA: Your first story, "Shambleau," was published in Weird Tales *in 1933. At that time science fiction writers and fans were largely men. What drew you to the field?*

MOORE: I think probably, although this seems like a sort of off-beat answer, it was because I had a lot of illness in my childhood and didn't go to school until around fifth grade; I was taught at home. I spent a lot of time by myself, a lot of it in bed, and I couldn't do anything but read. I was furnished with the "Oz" books, the "Tarzan" books, and the "Mars" books, and I suppose those set me off in that direction.

CA: What were your favorites among the things you read?

MOORE: That would take a lot of hairsplitting to decide. I enjoyed them all tremendously. I suppose *Alice* perhaps would have been a favorite. It seems to me that was the thing I reread most often.

CA: When did you start reading actual science fiction?

MOORE: I wasn't really aware of such a thing at that period, because my parents quite naturally believed that those magazines with the screaming naked girls on the cover had to be unsuitable reading. At that time science fiction was the lowest of the low. It seemed so obviously impossible that anything like space travel, for instance, could ever happen that nobody but a nitwit would read about it. But at my first job I found myself without very much to do at times, and I had to look busy. I used to spend a lot of time reading science fiction in between the covers of bank reports and stuff like that. I did take it home, and mother gripped her fists and gritted her teeth and said it was all right if I wanted to read it. I think she probably looked it over first, and saw that it was really not indecent in spite of the naked girls.

My first discovery in the field of science fiction and fantasy was *Weird Tales* in July, 1933, and I was absolutely enchanted. I immediately began to write in this wonderful new field. The result was "Shambleau." And that's how it all began.

CA: You started writing, though, years before you submitted a story for publication. What held you back?

MOORE: There was no thought whatever of publishing. What happened was that I had a cousin with whom I was very close, and we used to make up romantic tales of mythical kingdoms. We would take long, long walks in the neighborhood under the trees—it was a lovely time in the world to be alive—and we each worked out our own fantasy kingdom with dashing young heroes and lots of swashbuckling adventure. Then we began separately to write it out. It was not anything that either of us considered offering for publication; it never occurred to us. I found some of it not too long ago, some writing from back in my early teens. The writing style has not changed very much except for one thing: I never said anything once when I could say it five times. It was intolerably dull to read. The writing is all right, but the repetition is hideous!

The first story I sold was "Shambleau," and I sent it off to *Weird Tales* just sort of wondering if anything would happen, or if they would throw it back at me or in the wastepaper basket. But I had a glowing letter of acceptance from the editor, and from then on they bought everything I submitted to them.

So, there was no problem in breaking in. It was a new field and there were not very many writers in it. The demand must have been greater than the supply. Anyhow, it was easy to break in at that time.

CA: One of the many good things about your writing is that the characters are well rounded, not stereotypes or the flat characters sometimes found in science fiction.

MOORE: Mine? I never thought of that. I can't think of any examples.

CA: All the heroes. The best known are Northwest Smith and Jirel of Joiry. That wasn't done through a conscious effort on your part?

MOORE: If that's true, maybe it's because it would have been terribly dull to write about characters with only one dimension. I think it might have come from a very heavy background of reading. I must have unconsciously learned the necessity of having a character with inner problems.

CA: The women characters were particularly unusual at the time you began writing science fiction; they are strong, liberated, independent. No deliberate effort involved in those characters either?

MOORE: Oh, no. Nothing I have ever written was given the slightest deliberation. It was there in the typewriter and it came out, a total bypassing of the brain. As I say, I think this background of reading was absorbed by my unconscious, and it knew what was what and took it from there. When I'm writing, I don't do a thing in the world except apply the fingers to the keys.

CA: Did you ever get any negative letters from men who felt women shouldn't be that kind of heroic character?

MOORE: No. You couldn't believe how much encouragement and support I got from all the men who wrote to me. They were delighted to have me around. And that was before we had even met personally. It was purely on the basis of the stories. Henry Kuttner was among them. In fact, he addressed his first letter to "Dear Mr. Moore." When he found out that I was not a mister, he was still just as pleasant, as encouraging, as anybody could have been, as they all were.

CA: You met Mr. Kuttner, then, through your writing?

MOORE: Yes. We corresponded for a while, and then I came out with a friend for my first visit to California and we met. He moved to New York shortly after that. Then he made several trips to Indianapolis, where I was living, and eventually he persuaded me that it would be a good idea to get married. He was perfectly right. We had a fine marriage.

CA: You did a lot of writing together?

MOORE: We had to. That was our only living. And the quickest way to get stories done is collaboration.

CA: Did your collaborative work follow a set pattern, or did it evolve in different ways for different books?

MOORE: Well, we would say, "The rent is coming due in about six days; what are we going to write this time?" And then we'd discuss ideas which we'd kick around until one of us could get a start on it. That one would sit down and write until he ran down, then look helpless and say, "What should happen next?" Usually—almost always, by then—whoever put it down baffled and let the other take it up would be refreshed by the new material and could carry it on from there.

CA: Did you work full time at the writing?

MOORE: Yes. We were paid a cent a word, and I think our rent was something like thirty-five dollars a month. It was fairly adequate pay for those days in New York—that was during the Depression and prices were low. So we wrote when the rent was due or when we needed grocery money or a new pair of shoes or whatever. It seemed—and it was true—the money was there for the taking, and the writing was there for the taking; we knew that one would produce the other, and we had no worries at all.

CA: Wasn't that unusual?

MOORE: Oh, I don't know. I imagine the other writers of the period worked more or less on that principle. I don't remember discussing this with other writers, although we knew a lot of them. When we got together, we didn't talk about money particularly. Mostly, as I recall it now, if we talked about writing we talked about editors and what problems *they* were. Never the stories themselves.

CA: You left college and went to work because of the Depression. You once commented that your first published story grew out of your extensive typing practice.

MOORE: It did, it did! Right halfway down the page, there it began.

CA: Would it have changed the course of your writing career much if you had stayed in college at that point?

MOORE: I doubt it. I think my cousin with whom I developed the mythical kingdom and I would have gone on in that vein if she hadn't had to move away and if I hadn't had the job. But it was there, and it would have to have come out one way or another.

CA: What prompted you to go back to college in the 1950's?

MOORE: Henry and I both went back to college. He ran into a slump in his writing, and he was the one who kept the rent paid. He was a fast writer and he never had to revise—if he revised, he made it worse. He couldn't revise, but heavens, he didn't need to. So he was the money-maker and I was the one who bought the frills. When the money-maker runs down, you're in trouble. He had been in the service, and we decided that it would be an interesting project for him to enroll for a semester in college. He would get a living allowance from the government, and from what we could write on the side, we could make out all right. So, he enrolled at the University of Southern California, and he liked it so much that he then enrolled full time and eventually I did too. That's how we got our college degrees at a fairly late stage in life. It took me a lot longer because I had to stop and earn enough money to go on; the government was paying for him.

CA: You were teaching writing and literature at the University of Southern California before you got your degrees. How did that come about?

MOORE: At one point we had made a contact at Warner Brothers and we were working on our first half-hour script there when Henry had a heart attack and died. He had just started to teach—I think he had met two classes. The university asked me to take it over, and I did. I continued to teach there and to write, and then they began to twist my arm to get at least my bachelor's degree. I took college courses while I was teaching and working at the studio. Then I went on eventually and got a master's degree for no particular reason except that it would be nice to have, and I needed to keep myself busy.

CA: How do you feel about the increasing acceptance of science fiction and fantasy as a genre?

MOORE: It's wonderful! How could I feel otherwise? It's as if I had started the whole thing—my own child that I'm very proud of! Well, I didn't start it, but I did contribute a lot of wordage in the early days when the genre was taking shape.

CA: You don't feel, as some science-fiction writers do, that with acceptance comes a loss of spontaneity or a sort of bastardization that changes the field?

MOORE: Of course one likes certain types of writing better than others; but we have a free press, and if anybody wants to buy what other people want to write, I have no objections to that.

CA: What do you consider the best work you've done?

MOORE: I liked *Judgment Night* best.

CA: What about the shorter work?

MOORE: The short story I liked best was called "Daemon." It was published in *Famous Fantastic Mysteries* in October, 1946. That was entirely my own work, and I still reread it now and then, enjoying it a lot.

CA: People have trouble, don't they, identifying which stories are yours and which are collaborations?

MOORE: Well, mine were probably a good deal more verbose, and I tended to have compound sentences. Henry wrote very tersely. That's about the only difference, except that I was greatly prone to adjectives and so forth, and he got his effect over without quite so much embellishment. There was a distinct difference, but in most cases I think not enough for the general reader to be aware of.

CA: Did you ever disagree over the individual styles?

MOORE: No. We had debates once in a while over plot actions, but we always ended up very quickly by, at worst, one of us saying, "I don't agree with you, but the rent is due, so go ahead and do it your way."

CA: Are you writing science fiction now?

MOORE: I'm not writing anything now, and I may never write again. I would like to, but somehow I don't. I think about it, and I do little dibs and dabs of it, but I'm living an entirely different life in a different world now. That part of it may be completely passed by.

I think sometimes that if Henry had lived and we had gone on writing together, we might have traveled a great deal and written more and different sorts of things. We were planning to take our first trip to Europe at the time of his death. We were swinging over into mystery novels at that time, and he was doing his master's thesis on a Victorian fantasy writer,

H. Rider Haggard. Science fiction at that time seemed to be taking a downswing, and some of the magazines were going out of print. So we went into mystery writing, and that led us rather directly into the television business.

We had joined Mystery Writers of America. Whenever they take on a new member, they force him to be the local vice-president since it's a job nobody wants. The only president is in the New York chapter, so the vice-president out here, or anywhere else, is responsible for the meetings and so forth. We had a mutual friend who knew a producer at Warner Brothers, and we got the producer to come and address our first meeting. We seated him between us at the table and plied him with questions, and the first thing you know he invited us to come out and look over the studio and talk to him about doing some scripts. So we did. It led to writing assignments, and I worked at Warner's for several years, up to the time of my second marriage.

CA: Have you done other work since you quit writing?

MOORE: No. I wish I had something of that sort, and I feel a lack of it. But somehow things go along. As you get further along into life, the days just go by like a flash, probably because they become a smaller and smaller percentage of your life. To a baby, a day is a year. When you get to be my age, a day is about fifteen minutes. I'd like very much to write, but just not quite enough to get down to do it. I make starts, think about it; then I go out and meet some friends and have coffee. That's the way it all ends.

BIOGRAPHICAL/CRITICAL SOURCES: New York Times, January 11, 1953; *New York Herald Tribune Book Review,* January 25, 1953; *Saturday Review,* June 6, 1953.

—*Interview by Jean W. Ross*

* * *

MOORE, Charles
See MOORE, Reg(inald Charles Arthur)

* * *

MOORE, Edward
See MUIR, Edwin

* * *

MOORE, George Augustus 1852-1933

BRIEF ENTRY: Born February 24, 1852, in Ballyglass, Ireland; died of bronchitis, January 21, 1933, in London, England. Irish novelist. Moore is best known for his autobiographical trilogy, *Hail and Farewell!* (1911-14), which chronicled his active involvement with Yeats and other prominent figures of the Irish literary renaissance. Though it was spiteful at times and not accepted as completely accurate, critics regarded it as one of his most important achievements. Moore's first success was the naturalist novel *The Mummer's Wife* (1885). His 1894 novel, *Esther Waters,* is considered a masterpiece of the realist movement. It is tinged with ideas gleaned from the impressionist artists he admired. Moore also wrote a symbolist work, *The Lake* (1905), which remained one of his own favorites. He constantly revised and refined his work, experimenting in all with a wide variety of form and genre. His other writings include *The Brook Kerith* (1916), an unusual elaboration of the crucifixion story of the Bible, and *Heloise and Abelard* (1921), a historical novel. *Biographical/critical sources: Twentieth Century Authors: A Biographical Dictionary of Modern Literature,* H. W. Wilson, 1942; *Cyclopedia of World Authors,* Harper, 1958; Graham Owens, editor, *George Moore's Mind and Art,* Barnes & Noble, 1970.

* * *

MOORE, Jerrold Northrup 1934-

PERSONAL: Born March 1, 1934, in Paterson, N.J. *Education:* Swarthmore College, B.A., 1955; Yale University, M.A., 1956, Ph.D., 1959. *Office:* History of Sound Recordings Program, Library, Yale University, New Haven, Conn. 06520.

CAREER: University of Rochester, Rochester, N.Y., instructor, 1958-61; Yale University, New Haven, Conn., curator of History of Sound Recordings program, 1961—. *Member:* Music Library Association.

WRITINGS: (Editor) *Elgar: A Life in Photographs,* Oxford University Press, 1972; *Elgar on Record: The Composer and the Gramophone,* Oxford University Press, 1974; *A Voice in Time: The Gramophone of Fred Gaisberg, 1873-1951,* Hamish Hamilton, 1976, published in the United States as *A Matter of Records: Fred Gaisberg and the Golden Era of the Gramophone,* Taplinger, 1977; (author of notes) *Music and Friends: Seven Decades of Letters to Adrian Boult From Elgar, Vaughan Williams, Holst, Bruno Walter, Yehudi Menuhin and Other Friends,* Hamish Hamilton, 1979.

BIOGRAPHICAL/CRITICAL SOURCES: Music Library Association Notes, December, 1975; *Times Literary Supplement,* September 10, 1976; *Choice,* March, 1980.*

* * *

MOORE, John Michael 1935-

PERSONAL: Born December 12, 1935, in Kent, England; son of Roy (a teacher) and Muriel (a teacher; maiden name, Shill) Moore; married Jill M. Maycock (a teacher), July 9, 1960; children: Nicholas Alan. *Education:* Clare College, Cambridge, B.A., 1957, Ph.D., 1960, M.A., 1962. *Home and office:* Radley College, 1 The Shrubbery, Abingdon OX14 2HU, England.

CAREER: Winchester College, Winchester, England, assistant master, 1960-64; Radley College, Abingdon, England, teacher of classics and head of department, 1964—, director of sixth form studies, 1974—. Junior fellow at Center for Hellenic Studies, Washington, D.C., 1970-71. *Member:* Joint Association of Classical Teachers, Society for the Promotion of Roman Studies.

WRITINGS: The Manuscript Tradition of Polybius, Cambridge University Press, 1965; (with P. A. Brunt) *Res Gestae Divi Augusti* (title means "Achievements of the Deified Augustus"), Oxford University Press, 1967; (with J. J. Evans) *Variorum,* Oxford University Press, 1969; *Timecharts,* Discourses, 1969; *Aristotle and Xenophon on Democracy and Oligarchy,* Chatto & Windus, 1974. Contributor of articles and reviews to journals.

WORK IN PROGRESS: A critical edition of Polybius, for Oxford University Press.

SIDELIGHTS: Moore told *CA:* "Life consists of a tug-of-war between the demands of teaching and the urge to get on with research—and yet, much of the best in writing arises from what you learn teaching and from what teaching shows you is lacking in existing publications. The contrast between long-term research projects and books produced to deal with individual needs is considerable, yet both sides contribute to what is needed in the classical world, and both must be informed by an understanding of what classical education is about. In education, the future of the classics depends on a flourishing market for classics in translation and suitable courses based on these translations. However, it is vital that the study of the languages and the works in the original should survive so that scholarly work may be based on real knowledge, not potentially misleading translations. Fascination and frustration. . . ."

AVOCATIONAL INTERESTS: Travel, art.

* * *

MOORE, Reg(inald Charles Arthur) 1930-
(Charles Moore)

PERSONAL: Born August 8, 1930, in Soham, Cambridgeshire, England; son of William Albert and Florence (Bobby) Moore; married Monique Cazelles, August 28, 1965; children: Isabelle. *Education:* Attended secondary school in Cambridge, England. *Politics:* Liberal. *Religion:* Church of England. *Home:* 1 Lowther Rd., Brighton, Sussex, England.

CAREER: Journalist with *Christchurch Press*, Christchurch, New Zealand, 1955-56, and *Crawley Courier*, Sussex, England, 1962; *Cambridge Daily News*, Cambridge, England, sports reporter, 1963-64; Berlitz School, Versailles, France, teacher of English, 1965; free-lance writer, 1968—. *Military service:* Royal Air Force, 1948-54.

WRITINGS: Sentiments (poems), Phoenix Publications, 1968.

Under name Charles Moore: *Free Spirits of the Pyrenees*, Gifford, 1971; *The Charm of Majorca*, Venton, 1973; *Where the Mountains Meet the Sea*, Venton, 1974; *The Scene From Amsterdam*, Venton, 1975; *Paris for All Seasons*, Venton, 1975; *Contrasting Spain*, Venton, 1977; *Vienna*, Venton, 1977.

WORK IN PROGRESS: Three books, *Music in Landscape, Creative Landscapes,* and *South Downland and Journalism.*

AVOCATIONAL INTERESTS: Travel (including France and Spain), sports, topography, health, music.

* * *

MOREAU, Reginald E(rnest) 1897-1970

OBITUARY NOTICE: Born in 1897; died May 30, 1970, in England. Ornithologist, editor, and author. Moreau was one of the founders of field ornithology and was also editor of *Ibis* from 1947 to 1960. He was the author of *Birds of Africa.* Obituaries and other sources: *AB Bookman's Weekly,* June 22, 1970.

* * *

MORELLA, Joseph (James) 1949-

PERSONAL: Born November 19, 1949, in Nutley, N.J.; son of Patrick Emil and Mary (Bonavita) Morella. *Home:* 63 Highfield Lane, Nutley, N.J. 07110.

CAREER: Variety, New York, N.Y., reporter and critic, 1970-73; free-lance writer, 1973—.

WRITINGS: (With Edward Z. Epstein) *Rebels: The Rebel Hero in Films,* Citadel, 1971; *Nutrition and the Athlete,* Van Nostrand, 1976; (with Epstein) *The It Girl,* Delacorte, 1976; (with Epstein) *The Ince Affair* (novel), New American Library, 1978; (with James Bliss) *The Left-Hander's Handbook,* A & W Publishers, 1980.

Plays: (Co-author) "Pennyman," first produced in Los Angeles, Calif., 1979; "The Rape of Maria Perez," first produced in Los Angeles, 1980.

WORK IN PROGRESS: Show Business Dictionary, with Bill Edwards; *Caves of America,* with James Bliss; "No Illusions," a play.

SIDELIGHTS: Morella commented: "Self-discipline is a hundred times harder than having a steady job. Friendships are all important. Travel (to Europe and South America) is necessary and welcome."

* * *

MORGAN, Dale L. 1914-1971

OBITUARY NOTICE: Born in 1914 in Salt Lake City, Utah; died March 30, 1971, in Accokeek, Md. Historian and author. Morgan, who lost his hearing after being afflicted with meningitis at the age of fourteen, developed an interest in reading during the long and psychologically difficult period of readjustment. He was graduated from the University of Utah in 1937 and secured employment as a historical editor on the Work Projects Administration's Historical Records Survey in Utah. It was during this period that Morgan first displayed his abilities in research and editing. From 1940 to 1942 Morgan was supervisor of the Utah Writers Project and also wrote the definitive *Utah, a Guide to the State.* During the remaining years of World War II he worked for the federal government's Office of Price Administration in Washington, D.C. Morgan resumed his historical studies of the American West when he joined the Utah Historical Society after the war ended. In 1954 he became an editor at the Bancroft Library at the University of California, where he remained until his retirement in 1970. Obituaries and other sources: *AB Bookman's Weekly,* May 24, 1971; *The Reader's Encyclopedia of the American West,* Crowell, 1977.

* * *

MORIARTY, Florence Jarman

PERSONAL: Born in Flushing, N.Y.; daughter of George W. L. and Sarah (Tuite) Jarman; married Robert Austin Schetty, January 22, 1938 (divorced); married Vincent Paul Moriarty, June 16, 1961. *Education:* New York University, A.B., 1936. *Home:* 69 West Ninth St., New York, N.Y. 10011. *Office:* Macfadden-Bartell Corp., 205 East 42nd St., New York, N.Y. 10017.

CAREER: Prentice-Hall, Inc., New York City, college textbook editor 1936-38; Iroquois Publishing Co., Syracuse, N.Y., school book editor, 1938-40; Dell Publishing Co., Inc., New York City, associate editor of *Modern Romances,* 1940-43; managing editor of *Personal Romances,* 1943-48, and editor of *Intimate Romances,* 1948-53, both for Ideal Publishing Corp.; founder and editor of *True Life Stories* for Pines Publications, 1953-54; Macfadden-Bartell Corp., New York City, editor-in-chief of *True Confessions,* 1954—. *Member:* Theta Upsilon, New York University Club (member of board of governors).

WRITINGS: (Editor) *True Confessions, 1919-1979: Sixty Years of Sin, Suffering, and Sorrow From the Pages of True Confessions, True Story, True Experience, True Romance, True Love, Secrets, Modern Romance,* Simon & Schuster, 1979.*

* * *

MORICE, Anne
See SHAW, Felicity

MOROWITZ, Harold Joseph 1927-

PERSONAL: Born December 4, 1927, in Poughkeepsie, N.Y.; son of Philip Frank and Anna (Levine) Morowitz; married Lucille Rita Stein, January 30, 1949; children: Joanna Lynn, Eli David, Joshua Alan, Zachary Adam, Noah Daniel. *Education:* Yale University, B.S., 1947, M.S., 1950, Ph.D., 1951. *Home address:* Ox Box Lane, Woodbridge, Conn. 06525. *Office:* 1937 Yale Station, Yale University, New Haven, Conn. 06520.

CAREER: Physicist with National Bureau of Standards, 1951-53; National Heart Institute, Bethesda, Md., physicist, 1953-55; Yale University, New Haven, Conn., assistant professor, 1955-60, associate professor, 1960-68, professor of molecular biophysics and biochemistry, 1968—. Lecturer at University of Maryland, 1952-53. Member of planetary biology committee of National Aeronautics and Space Administration, 1966-72; member of evaluation panel for physics and chemistry of National Bureau of Standards, 1969-74. *Member:* American Association for the Advancement of Science, American Institute of Biological Sciences (fellow), Biophysical Society (fellow; member of executive committee, 1965), New York Academy of Sciences (fellow), Sigma Xi.

WRITINGS: Life and the Physical Sciences: Introduction to Biophysics, Holt, 1963; (editor with Talbor Howe Waterman) *Theoretical and Mathematical Biology,* Blaisdell, 1965; *Energy Flow in Biology: Biological Organization as a Problem in Thermal Physics,* Academic Press, 1968; *Entropy for Biologists: An Introduction to Thermodynamics,* Academic Press, 1970; (with wife, Lucille S. Morowitz) *Life on the Planet Earth,* Norton, 1974; *Ego Niches: An Ecological View of Organizational Behavior,* Ox Bow, 1977; *Foundations of Bioenergetics,* Academic Press, 1978; *The Wine of Life and Other Essays on Societies, Energy, and Living Things,* St. Martin's, 1979. Author of a column in *Hospital Practice.* Contributor to scientific journals. Member of advisory board of *Journal of Theoretical Biology,* 1968—; associate editor of *Journal of Biomedical Computing,* 1969—.

BIOGRAPHICAL/CRITICAL SOURCES: Psychology Today, August, 1980.*

*   *   *

MORRA, Marion Eleanor

PERSONAL: Born in Hamden, Conn.; daughter of Italo and Eleanor (Tirone) Morra. *Education:* Attended University of New Haven; Fairfield University, M.A. *Office:* Yale Comprehensive Cancer Center, 333 Cedar St., P.O. Box 3333, New Haven, Conn. 06520.

CAREER: Advertising supervisor for Southern New England Telephone Co.; director of public information for New Haven Redevelopment Agency, New Haven, Conn.; director of communications for Greater Hartford Process, Inc.; Yale University, New Haven, communications director of Comprehensive Cancer Center, and clinical instructor at School of Medicine, 1975—. Chairman of the board of the American Cancer Society of Connecticut. *Awards, honors:* Achievement of Management Award from International Association of Business Communicators; national citation for cancer education from American Cancer Society; National Annual Report Award from Score; Corporate Publications Award from Greater Hartford Advertising Club.

WRITINGS: (Editor) *Cancer Chemotherapy Treatment and Care,* American Cancer Society and Yale Comprehensive Cancer

Center, 1979, revised edition, G. K. Hall, 1981; (with sister, Eve Potts) *Choices: Realistic Alternatives in Cancer Treatment,* Avon, 1980; (editor) *Cancer Therapy for the Eighties,* G. K. Hall, in press. Contributor of numerous articles to magazines, including *Good Housekeeping* and *Oncology Nursing Forum.*

WORK IN PROGRESS: Another book with Eve Potts.

SIDELIGHTS: Marion Morra and Eve Potts were inspired to write *Choices: Realistic Alternatives in Cancer Treatment* when one of their friends, a cancer patient, feared the cancer had spread to her throat, causing it to be sore and scratchy. As it turned out, the radiation treatment she'd been receiving, not the cancer, was causing the woman's discomfort, but she was afraid to talk to her physician. As a result of their friend's experience, Morra and Potts decided to write a handbook to alleviate some of the fears and answer many of the questions of cancer victims. "We felt that people needed information so they could ask intelligent questions of their doctors and nurses," Morra told Alberta Eiseman of the *New York Times.* "When the diagnosis is cancer, most of us are so full of fear we forget all the practical considerations."

Choices contains nearly eight hundred pages of information on cancer symptoms, tests, treatments (both conventional and controversial), hospitals, and doctors. Written in question-and-answer format, it is based on conversations the sisters had with cancer patients during a three-year period. *Choices* received favorable reviews from critics. In *Oncology Nursing Forum,* Joanna Pierce wrote: "The authors attempt to provide this incredible amount of information accurately, concisely, and understandably to the nonprofessional person. They succeed in large part, no small accomplishment for a subject as complex, confusing, and emotional as cancer." And Jory Graham, in her syndicated column "A Time For Living," called *Choices* "the best single source of a vast amount of information. It's far and away the best book of its kind."

Morra and Potts stress in their book that patients should talk frequently with their doctors, ask questions, and not take anything for granted. They also encourage family members to discuss the disease with the patient so that he won't feel alone in the battle. In short, the book contains information for anyone whose life is touched by cancer. Herb Hyde of the *Lincoln Evening Journal* remarked: "If you have cancer, you need this book. If you do not have cancer but one of your friends, family members, or other loved ones does, you need this book. If you merely want to know more about the dread disease, you need this book."

Morra told *CA:* "We wrote the book because we felt there was a need which was not being filled. But nobody prepared us for the feeling you get when someone tells you your book saved his or her life, which has happened to us several times. One of those experiences richly pays for the hours and hours of research and the getting up at 5 A.M. to write before going to work at your full-time job."

BIOGRAPHICAL/CRITICAL SOURCES: Oncology Nursing Forum 7, No. 3, 1980; *New York State Journal of Medicine,* April, 1980; *New York Times,* April 14, 1980, April 15, 1981; *Los Angeles Times Book Review,* May 4, 1980; *Lincoln Evening Journal,* May 18, 1980; *Vogue,* May, 1980; *New Haven Advocate,* September, 1980; *Rochester Post-Bulletin* (Rochester, Minn.), October 6, 1980; *Chicago Sun-Times,* November 10, 1980.

MORRIS, Phyllis Sutton   1931-

PERSONAL: Born January 25, 1931, in Quincy, Ill.; daughter of John Guice and Helen Elizabeth (Provis) Sutton; married John Martin Morris, February 4, 1950; children: William Robert, Katherine Jill. Education: University of California, Berkeley, A.B. (with honors), 1953; Colorado College, M.A., 1963; University of Michigan, Ph.D., 1969. Politics: Democrat. Religion: Unitarian-Universalist. Home: 4 Proctor Ave., Clinton, N.Y. 13323. Office: Department of Philosophy, Hamilton College, Clinton, N.Y. 13323.

CAREER: University of Colorado, Colorado Springs, lecturer in philosophy, 1963-64; Michigan State University, East Lansing, instructor in humanities, 1968-69; Kirkland College, Clinton, N.Y., instructor, 1969-70, assistant professor, became associate professor of philosophy, 1970-78, research professor, 1971; Hamilton College, Clinton, associate professor of philosophy, 1978—. Member: American Association of University Professors, American Philosophical Association, American Civil Liberties Union (member of local board of directors, 1962-64), Society for Phenomenology and Existentialism, Society of Women in Philosophy, League of Women Voters, Creighton Club. Awards, honors: Huber Foundation grant, 1974.

WRITINGS: Sartre's Concept of a Person: An Analytic Approach, University of Massachusetts Press, 1976. Contributor to scholarly journals. Editor of newsletter of League of Women Voters, 1956-57.*

*   *   *

MORSE, John D.   1906-

PERSONAL: Born September 26, 1906, in Gifford, Ill.; Education: University of Illinois, A.B., M.A.; also attended Wayne State University and New York University. Home: 1871 Prospect St., Sarasota, Fla. 33579.

CAREER: University of Illinois, Champaign-Urbana, lecturer in art history, 1934-35; Detroit Institute of Art, Detroit, Mich., instructor in art history, 1935-41; Metropolitan Museum of Art, New York City, associate in radio, 1941-42; editor of Magazine of Art, 1942-47; art editor of '47 Magazine of the Year, 1947-48; Art Students League, New York City, director of publications, 1948-50; associate editor of American Artist, 1951-53; executive secretary and instructor in art history at Kent School, 1954-56; associated with Detroit Institute of Art, 1959-62; Henri Francis du Pont Winterthur Museum, Winterthur, Del., editor of publications, 1962-70; editor of American Art Journal, 1972-77; writer and consultant, 1977—. Managing editor of Art Quarterly, 1938-40. Conducted European tours for American Artist, 1950-52. Film producer. Member: Century Association.

WRITINGS: Old Masters in America: A Comprehensive Guide—More Than Two Thousand Paintings in the United States and Canada by Forty Famous Artists, Rand McNally, 1955, reprinted, Abbeville Press, 1979; (editor) The Artist and the Museum, American Artists Group, 1951; (editor) Ben Shahn, Praeger, 1972; (editor) Country Cabinetwork and Simple City Furniture, University Press of Virginia, 1970; (editor) Prints in and of America to 1850, University Press of Virginia, 1970. Contributor to magazines, including Esquire, and newspapers. Associate editor of American Boy, 1928-29, 1930-31.*

*   *   *

MORSE-BOYCOTT, Desmond (Lionel)   1892-1979

OBITUARY NOTICE: Born December 10, 1892; died August 9, 1979. Clergyman, educator, musician, journalist, and author. Morse-Boycott served as assistant curate of St. Mary the Virgin in Somers Town, England, from 1919 to 1935. With his wife he founded the St. Mary-of-the-Angels Song School in 1932 and served as the director of the school until his death. He contributed articles to many British newspapers and was the author of numerous books on theology, including Great Crimes of the Bible. Obituaries and other sources: Who's Who in Music and Musicians' International Directory, 6th edition, Hafner, 1972; Who's Who, 126th edition, St. Martin's, 1974; The Writers Directory, 1976-78, St. Martin's, 1976; Who Was Who Among English and European Authors, 1931-1949, Gale, 1978. (Date of death provided by Roland Chad, administrator of the Morse-Boycott Bursary Fund.)

*   *   *

MORTENSEN, Ben(jamin) F.   1928-

PERSONAL: Born February 1, 1928, in Phoenix, Ariz.; son of Joseph A. and Josephine C. (Barraza) Mortensen; married Rene Joyce Rhead (an administrative assistant), December 27, 1950; children: Stephen, Michele, Mathew, Jeanette, Pamela, Cheryl. Education: Brigham Young University, B.A., 1951, M.A., 1956; University of Utah, Ph.D., 1960. Politics: Republican. Religion: Church of Jesus Christ of Latter-day Saints. Home: 2808 Arapahoe Lane, Provo, Utah 84601. Office: 1395 North 150 E., Provo, Utah 84601.

CAREER: Dean of students at Utah Technical College, Provo; clinical psychologist at Utah State Hospital, Provo; clinical psychologist at Sutter Memorial Hospital, Sacramento, Calif.; management consultant for Edward N. Hay & Associates, San Francisco, Calif.; currently in private practice of clinical psychology. Bishop of Church of Jesus Christ of Latter-day Saints (Mormons). Military service: U.S. Army, chaplain, 1952-55; served in Korea; became captain; received Silver Star and Korean Chung-Mu Medal. Member: American Psychological Association, American Vocational Association, American Education Association, National Military Chaplains Association, Utah Psychological Association, Utah Education Association, Phi Kappa Phi, Rotary.

WRITINGS: If You're Mad, Spit! and Other Aids to Coping, Brigham Young University Press, 1978. Contributor to religious and popular magazines, including Instructor and New Era.

WORK IN PROGRESS: Frontline Chaplain, memoirs of the Korean War; Healing, a psychotherapy manual; The Psychology of Educational Administration.

SIDELIGHTS: Mortensen commented: "I am a Mexican-American, adopted at age ten. I think it is important for people to know that orphans, and particularly Mexican-American orphans, can succeed in the United States of America with the proper education."

*   *   *

MOSES, Robert   1888-1981

OBITUARY NOTICE—See index for CA sketch: Born December 18, 1888, in New Haven, Conn.; died of heart failure, July 29, 1981, in West Islip, Long Island, N.Y. Administrator, city planner, and author. For nearly a half century, Moses headed most of the commissions and authorities responsible for constructing the public parks, buildings, and highways in the state of New York. New York Times writer Paul Goldberger credited him with having "played a larger role in shaping the physical environment of New York State than any other figure in the

20th century.'' As the chief administrator of such agencies as the State Council of Parks, Triborough Bridge Authority, Triborough Bridge and New York City Tunnel Authority, and the New York State Power Authority, Moses built more than six hundred fifty parks, an excess of four hundred miles of highways, and thirteen bridges. He saw to the construction of the Triborough Bridge, West Side Highway, Jones Beach State Park, Verrazano-Narrows Bridge, and the Long Island parkway network. He was also instrumental in bringing the United Nations to New York City. Controversial in his later years, Moses came under fire for his views on city planning. He favored the construction of large buildings and wide parkways, often dislocating hundreds of people. Critics accused him of ignoring the needs of city dwellers while stressing those of suburbanites. His ability "to get things done" gradually eroded, and by 1968 Moses had lost his posts. After that year he served as a consultant to the Metropolitan Transportation Authority and briefly continued to work as the director of the Lincoln Center of the Performing Arts, a position he held since 1960. His books include *The Civil Service of Great Britain, Working for the People,* and an autobiography, *Public Works: A Dangerous Trade.* Obituaries and other sources: Cleveland Rogers, *Robert Moses: Builder for Democracy,* Holt, 1952; Robert Caro, *The Power Broker: Robert Moses and the Fall of New York,* Knopf, 1974; *New York Times,* July 30, 1981.

* * *

MOST, Bernard 1937-

PERSONAL: Born September 2, 1937, in New York; son of Max (a painter) and Bertha (Moskowitz) Most; married Amy Beth Pollack, February 12, 1967; children: Glenn Evan, Eric David. *Education:* Pratt Institute, B.F.A. (with honors), 1959. *Politics:* Independent. *Home:* 3 Ridgecrest E., Scarsdale, N.Y. 10583. *Office:* MCA Advertising, 405 Lexington, New York, N.Y. 10017.

CAREER: McCann-Erickson, Inc. (advertising agency), New York City, art director, 1959-65; Benton & Bowles, Inc. (advertising agency) New York City, associate creative director, 1965-78; MCA Advertising, Inc., New York City, senior vice-president and creative director, 1978—. *Awards, honors:* Awards from Art Directors Club, Type Directors Club, and American Institute of Graphic Arts; Clio Award; Andy Award.

WRITINGS—Self-illustrated children's books: *If the Dinosaurs Came Back,* Harcourt, 1978; *There's an Ant in Anthony,* Morrow, 1980; *Turn Over,* Prentice-Hall, 1980; *My Very Own Octopus,* Harcourt, 1980; *Boo,* Prentice-Hall, 1980; *There's an Ape Behind the Drape,* Morrow, 1981.

Contributor of illustrations to national magazines.

SIDELIGHTS: Most commented: "My books are 'concept books' in that they get children to participate in the ideas of the books beyond the actual reading of them."

* * *

MOTTAHEDEH, Roy Parviz 1940-

PERSONAL: Born July 3, 1940, in New York, N.Y.; married, 1973. *Education:* Harvard University, B.A., 1960, Ph.D., 1970. *Office:* Department of Near Eastern Studies, Princeton University, 110 Jones Hall, Princeton, N.J. 08540.

CAREER: Princeton University, Princeton, N.J., assistant professor of Near Eastern history, 1970—, research associate, 1976—.

WRITINGS: Loyalty and Leadership in an Early Islamic Society, Princeton University Press, 1980.*

* * *

MOYSE-BARTLETT, Hubert 1902(?)-1973(?)

OBITUARY NOTICE: Author of books on the military, including *Louis Edward Nolan and His Influence on the British Cavalry.* Obituaries and other sources: *AB Bookman's Weekly,* October 15, 1973.

* * *

MUEHLEN, Norbert 1909-1981

OBITUARY NOTICE—See index for *CA* sketch: Born September 20, 1909, in Fuerth, Bavaria, Germany (now West Germany); died of leukemia, August 20, 1981, in Manhattan, N.Y. Journalist and author. Muehlen worked as a foreign correspondent for *Deutsche Zeitung* and *Deutsche Welle* in Switzerland, Saarbruecken, France, and the United States for nearly a half century. Staunchly anti-Nazi, he left Germany soon after the Nazis came to power in 1933. Muehlen wrote several books, including *The Return of Germany: A Tale of Two Countries, The Incredible Krupps: The Rise, Fall, and Comeback of Germany's Industrial Family, The Survivors: A Report on the Jews in Germany Today,* and *Hitler's Magician, Schacht: The Life and Loans of Dr. Djalmar Schacht.* Obituaries and other sources: *New York Times,* August 21, 1981; *London Times,* August 25, 1981.

* * *

MUHLEN, Norbert
See MUEHLEN, Norbert

* * *

MUIR, Edwin 1887-1959
(Edward Moore)

BRIEF ENTRY: Born May 15, 1887, in Deerness, Orkney Islands; died January 3, 1959, in Cambridge, England. Scottish poet, critic, translator, essayist, and novelist. The son of a tenant farmer, Edwin Muir spent his childhood in the idyllic setting of the Orkney Islands. When Muir was in his mid-teens his family was forced to leave their farm and move to Glasgow. Traumatized by that move, as well as by the ensuing deaths of his parents and two of his brothers, Muir underwent psychoanalysis. The contrast between the pastoral setting of his boyhood and the grim slums of Glasgow is reflected in much of his writing, most notably in his autobiography, *The Story and the Fable* (1940), which was later revised and published as *An Autobiography* (1954), and in his collection of poetry entitled *The Labyrinth* (1949). His poetry, filled as it is with mythical and biblical allusions, is highly traditional, especially in comparison to the innovative work of his contemporaries T. S. Eliot and Ezra Pound. A well-respected literary critic, Muir was the author of several volumes of criticism, including *Latitudes* (1924), *Scott and Scotland: The Predicament of the Scottish Writer* (1936), and, under the pseudonym Edward Moore, *We Moderns: Enigmas and Guesses* (1918). He was also co-translator, with his wife, Willa, of the works of Franz Kafka. *Biographical/critical sources: Twentieth-Century Writing: A Reader's Guide to Contemporary Literature,* Transatlantic, 1969; *The Penguin Companion to English Literature,* McGraw, 1971; *Webster's New World Companion to English and American Literature,* World Publishing, 1973; *Twentieth-Century Literary Criticism,* Volume 2, Gale, 1979.

MULLEN, Dore
See MULLEN, Dorothy

*   *   *

MULLEN, Dorothy 1933-
(Dore Mullen)

PERSONAL: Born December 15, 1933, in Boston, Mass.; daughter of Harry (a civil engineer) and Esther (Uman) Sattin; married Donald R. Mullen, February 22, 1963 (died May 27, 1980). *Education:* University of Connecticut, B.A. (with honors), 1955. *Home:* 2070 20th Lane, Brooklyn, N.Y. 11214. *Agent:* Jane Rotrosen Agency, 318 East 51st St., New York, N.Y. 10022.

CAREER: Worked as actress, 1956, advertising copywriter, 1957, airline reservationist, 1959-60, travel agent, 1960, and tour leader in Africa, 1972-75; writer, 1977—. *Awards, honors:* Porgi Bronze Medal from *West Coast Review of Books,* 1981, for *All We Know of Heaven.*

WRITINGS—Under name Dore Mullen: *The Far Side of Destiny* (novel), Dell, 1979; *All We Know of Heaven* (novel), Dell, 1980; *Shanghai Bridge* (novel), Dell, 1982.

SIDELIGHTS: "Although I have written three novels," Dorothy Mullen told *CA,* "I feel as though I am still on the threshold of my career. I dreamed for many years about the 'writing life,' and I find that the reality is like my first-time trips to Africa and China, two other dreams come true: infinitely more complicated, difficult, and wonderful than the fantasy.

"I have two enthusiasms beside writing. One is New York City, with all its exasperating, expensive, nerve-wracking problems, still the only place in the world where I would care to live. The other is travel, and in order to do it I worked for many years in airline offices and travel agencies. I have made three safaris to East and Central Africa, and two trips to the People's Republic of China. I am planning my first trip to India, Nepal, and Sri Lanka. My books have reflected this fascination with exotic settings; one is set in Siberia, one in Shanghai, and one in wartime France."

BIOGRAPHICAL/CRITICAL SOURCES: Writer, April, 1979.

*   *   *

MUNRO, Hector Hugh 1870-1916
(Saki)

BRIEF ENTRY: Born December 18, 1870, in Akyab, Burma; killed in action during World War I, November 14, 1916, in Beaumont Hamel, France. Scottish novelist, short story writer, and journalist. Using the pseudonym he chose from Omar Khayyam's *The Rubaiyat,* Saki wrote humorous essays and stories that are frequently described as flippant, witty, ironic, and cynical. His writing career began in 1896 when he contributed satirical political essays to London's *Westminster Gazette.* These were later collectively printed as *The Westminster Alice* (1902). Saki's fame, however, came with his short stories, the first collection of which was entitled *Reginald.* Reginald, the title character, was a recurring figure in Saki's stories about Britain's middle and upper classes. Several of Saki's tales were influenced by his childhood experiences; he was raised by two eccentric and strict aunts. "Sredni Vashtar," a short story, concerns the destruction of an aunt and the resultant glee of her nephew. Other of Saki's writings contain scenes of violence that are commonly attributed to the abuse

Saki suffered as a child. *The Unbearable Bassington* (1912), *Beasts and Super-Beasts* (1914), and *When William Came: A Story of London Under the Hohenzollerns* (1914) are among Saki's writings. *Biographical/critical sources: Cyclopedia of World Authors,* Harper, 1959; *Who's Who in Twentieth Century Literature,* Holt, 1976; *Twentieth-Century Literary Criticism,* Volume 3, Gale, 1980.

*   *   *

MURPHY, C. L.
See MURPHY, Lawrence A(gustus)

*   *   *

MURPHY, Lawrence A(gustus) 1924-
(Steven C. Lawrence; C. L. Murphy, a joint pseudonym)

PERSONAL: Born May 17, 1924, in Brockton, Mass.; son of John J. (a postal supervisor) and Rose M. (Clairmont) Murphy; married Charlotte A. Heuser (an artist and writer), January 14, 1950; children: Steven Lawrence. *Education:* Massachusetts Maritime Academy, B.S. (navigation and seamanship), 1944; Boston University, B.S. (journalism), 1950, M.A., 1951. *Religion:* Roman Catholic. *Home and office:* 30 Mercedes Rd., Brockton, Mass. 02401. *Agent:* Paul R. Reynolds, Inc., 12 East 41st St., New York, N.Y. 10017.

CAREER: Writer, 1950—; South Junior High School, Brockton, Mass., English teacher and department head, 1951-81. Instructor in creative writing at Stonehill College, North Easton, Mass., 1967. *Military service:* U.S. Naval Reserve, 1942-44. U.S. Maritime Service, chief officer and acting master of Liberty Ship, 1944-46; became lieutenant senior grade. U.S. Navy, 1946-47; served in the Atlantic and the Mediterranean.

MEMBER: Disabled American Veterans, National Trust for Historic Preservation, U.S.S. Constitution Museum Foundation, Tin Can Sailors, Destroyermen's League, Authors Guild, Western Writers of America, Masters, Mates, and Pilots, Navy League, National Education Association, Massachusetts Teachers Association, Brockton Teachers Association, Brockton Historical Society, University Club of Brockton, Boston University Alumni Association, Massachusetts Maritime Academy Alumni Association. *Awards, honors:* Scroll Award from Western Writers of America, 1967, for *Buffalo Grass;* certificate of merit from Knights of Columbus, 1980.

WRITINGS—Novels, under pseudonym Steven C. Lawrence: *The Naked Range,* Ace Books, 1956; *Saddle Justice,* Fawcett, 1957; *Brand of a Texan,* Fawcett, 1958; *The Iron Marshal,* Avon, 1960; *Night of the Gunmen,* Avon, 1961; *Gun Fury,* Avon, 1961; *Slattery,* Ace Books, 1961; *Bullet Welcome for Slattery,* Ace Books, 1961; *A Noose for Slattery,* Ace Books, 1962; *Walk a Narrow Trail,* Ace Books, 1962; *With Blood in Their Eyes,* Ace Books, 1962; *Slattery's Gun Says No,* Ace Books, 1962; *Longhorns North,* Ace Books, 1962; *A Texan Comes Riding,* Fawcett, 1966; *That Man From Texas,* Curtis Books, 1972; *Edge of the Land,* Ace Books, 1974; *Sixgun Junction,* Curtis Books, 1974; *North to Montana,* Leisure Books, 1975, revised edition, 1981; *Slattery Stands Alone,* Leisure Books, 1976; *Trial for Tennihan,* Ace Books, 1976; *A Northern Saga: The Account of the North Atlantic-Murmansk, Russia Convoys,* Playboy Press, 1976; *Gun Blast,* Belmont-Tower, 1977; *Day of the Comancheros,* Leisure Books, 1977.

With wife, Charlotte Murphy, under joint pseudonym C. L. Murphy: *Buffalo Grass* (juvenile), Dial, 1966.

WORK IN PROGRESS: In Which We Serve, a juvenile version of *A Northern Saga*, with C. Murphy; *Into the Beach*, a biographical novel about the D-Day invasion of Europe; *Staging Area—Tinian*, a novel about a planned invasion of Japan in World War II; a novel based on Murphy's thirty years as a public school teacher.

SIDELIGHTS: Murphy wrote: "*A Northern Saga*, first in a series of World War II sea novels, is the complete story of the convoys in the North Atlantic, to Murmansk, Russia. Critics have compared it to *The Cruel Sea* and *Two Years Before the Mast*. This series of wartime historical novels follows my own accounts of convoys, invasions, and surface-submarine battles, based on my own service aboard six merchant vessels and a destroyer escort doing hunter-killer patrols with aircraft carriers. Future works will cover U.S. history since 1946.

"*Buffalo Grass*, which has been optioned by a Los Angeles film producer, has been reviewed as the full picture of the days of the buffalo hunts. The 'Slattery' series of twelve novels draws the history of the frontier settlements from the end of the Civil War to the Custer massacre."

Murphy, who began writing while at sea during World War II, has written numerous historical novels about the American West, World War II, and present-day America because he feels that the present can be understood and faced through knowledge of the past. The author says that his series of war novels is intended "to give the factual material which is no longer included in most American public school history books." The first of that series is the highly acclaimed *A Northern Saga*, which aims to show the futility of war and the possibility of having a war that will end civilization. Murphy is writing a young reader's edition of *A Northern Saga* entitled *In Which We Serve*. Commenting on this volume Murphy said, "I would want it to be read by all young Americans and young Russians. Possibly, through writing, and a motion picture of serious depth and scope, my writing can help head us off the course we are now headed—toward a collision that can be the end for humanity."

He continued: "I believe there is a parallel to teaching and writing. Both the true educator and the author of depth live to work and inform, believing that factual knowledge can lead to progress in all ways known to man and that peace is a primary necessity—whether it be between two people, within a home, a city or state or a nation—and must be maintained among all the nations of the world."

BIOGRAPHICAL/CRITICAL SOURCES: Roundup, July, 1957, August, 1958, August, 1960, December, 1960, November, 1962, May, 1966, December, 1972, June, 1974, July, 1974, January, 1977; *New York Times Book Review*, September 7, 1958, May 10, 1960, September 6, 1966.

* * *

MURRAY, Eugene Bernard 1927-

PERSONAL: Born December 22, 1927, in Chicago, Ill.; married, 1963. *Education:* Kenyon College, A.B., 1952; Columbia University, M.A., 1957, Ph.D., 1965. *Office:* Department of English, University of Missouri, St. Louis, Mo. 63121.

CAREER: Rutgers University, New Brunswick, N.J., instructor in English, 1961-62; Indiana University, Fort Wayne, lecturer, 1962-65, assistant professor of English, 1965-66; University of Missouri, St. Louis, assistant professor, 1966-68, associate professor, 1968-77, professor of English, 1977—. *Military service:* U.S. Army, 1946-47. *Member:* Modern Language Association of America.

WRITINGS: Ann Radcliffe, Twayne, 1972. Contributor to literature journals.*

* * *

MUSE, Clarence 1889-1979

OBITUARY NOTICE: Born October 7, 1889, in Baltimore, Md.; died of a cerebral hemorrhage, c. October 6, 1979, in Perris, Calif. Actor, director, songwriter, and playwright. Muse gave up a legal career to become a singer. With his appearance in the film "Way Down South," Muse became the first black to star in a movie; he eventually made appearances in over two hundred films and wrote several screenplays, including "Heaven Can Wait." During the 1960's and 1970's Muse drew criticism from some segments of the black community for having portrayed what they felt to be demeaning representations of blacks early in his career. Muse's last role was in the 1979 film "The Black Stallion." Obituaries and other sources: *The Versatiles: A Study of Supporting Character Actors and Actresses in the American Motion Picture, 1930-1955*, A. S. Barnes, 1969; *Who's Who Among Black Americans*, 2nd edition, Who's Who Among Black Americans, 1977; *New York Times*, October 17, 1979, *Time*, October 29, 1979.

* * *

MUSTO, David Franklin 1936-

PERSONAL: Born January 8, 1936, in Tacoma, Wash.; son of Charles Hiram and Hilda Marie (Hanson) Mustoe; married Emma Jean Baudendistel, June 2, 1961; children: Jeanne Marie, David Kyle, John Baird, Christopher Edward. *Education:* University of Washington, Seattle, B.A., 1956, M.D., 1963; Yale University, M.A., 1961; studied at National Hospital for Nervous Diseases, London, England, 1961. *Office:* Child Study Center, Yale University, 333 Cedar St., New Haven, Conn. 06510.

CAREER: Pennsylvania Hospital, Philadelphia, intern, 1963-64; Yale University, Medical Center, New Haven, Conn., resident in psychiatry, 1964-67; National Institute of Mental Health, Bethesda, Md., special assistant to director, 1967-69; Yale University, assistant professor, 1969-73, associate professor of psychiatry and history, 1973-78, senior research scientist at Child Study Center and lecturer in history and American studies, 1978—. Visiting assistant professor at Johns Hopkins University, 1968-69. Research fellow of Drug Abuse Council, Washington, D.C., 1972-73; program director of National Humanities Institute, 1977-78; historian for President's Commission on Mental Health, 1977—; U.S. delegate to United Nations Narcotics Commission, 1978; consultant to White House Strategy Council and National Commission on Marijuana and Drug Abuse. *Military service:* U.S. Public Health Service, surgeon, 1967-69.

MEMBER: American Historical Association, American Psychiatric Association (fellow; chairman of history committee, 1973—), American Association for the History of Medicine, American Institute for the History of Pharmacy, Group for the Advancement of Psychiatry, Connecticut Medical Society, Connecticut Trust for Historic Preservation, New York C.S. Lewis Society. *Awards, honors:* William Osler Medal from American Association for the History of Medicine, 1960; Kremers Award from American Institute for the History of Pharmacy, 1974.

WRITINGS: The American Disease: Origins of Narcotic Control, Yale University Press, 1973; (contributor) Charles V. Willie and others, editors, *Racism and Mental Health*, University of Pittsburgh Press, 1973. Also author of *The Concept of Familial Continuity,* Smithsonian Institution Press. Advisory editor of "Papers of James Boswell," Yale University Press, 1975—. Contributor to *American Handbook of Psychiatry.* Contributor to academic journals.*

*   *   *

MY BROTHER'S BROTHER
  See CHEKHOV, Anton (Pavlovich)

*   *   *

MYERS, Alonzo F(ranklin)   1895-1970

OBITUARY NOTICE: Born April 6, 1895, in Grover Hill, Ohio; died after a long illness, May 24, 1970, in Venice, Fla. Educator and author. Myers was regarded as an authority on retirement planning and advocated a gradual withdrawal from working life. He wrote or co-wrote books on retirement planning and teacher training, including *A Teacher-Training Program for Ohio.* Obituaries and other sources: *New York Times,* May 26, 1970.

*   *   *

MYERS, (Eugene Victor) Debs   1911-1971

OBITUARY NOTICE: Born October 22, 1911, in Wichita, Kan.; died of hepatitis, February 2, 1971, in New Haven, Conn. Political adviser, public relations expert, and journalist. Myers was managing editor of *Newsweek* magazine after World War II and later entered political public relations work. Myers served under a variety of titles for former New York City Mayor Robert F. Wagner and advised Adlai E. Stevenson during his two unsuccessful presidential campaigns. He also advised Robert F. Kennedy in his 1964 bid for the United States Senate in New York. Obituaries and other sources: *New York Times,* February 3, 1971; *Time,* February 15, 1971.

*   *   *

MYERS, Desaix B. III   1945-

PERSONAL: Born in 1945; son of Desaix B. Myers, Jr. *Home:* 1712 Seaton St. N.W., Washington, D.C. 20009.

CAREER: U.S. Department of State, Agency for International Development, Washington, D.C., intern in Nairobi, Kenya, 1968, field operations officer and assistant program officer in Dacca, Bangladesh, 1970-71, officer in charge of Nepal-Ceylon desk, 1972; Investor Responsibility Research Center, Washington, D.C., deputy director, 1972—. Consultant to U.S. Senate Foreign Relations Committee, Rockefeller Foundation, and Carnegie Corp.

WRITINGS: Labor Practices of U.S. Corporations in South Africa, Investor Responsibility Research Center, 1976; *The Nuclear Power Debate: Moral, Economic, Technical, and Political Issues,* Praeger, 1977; *The Nuclear Power Alternative: Two Years Later,* Investor Responsibility Research Center, 1977; *U.S. Business and South Africa: The Withdrawal Issue,* Investor Responsibility Research Center, 1977; *Business and Labor in South Africa,* Investor Responsibility Research Center, 1979; (with Kenneth Propp) *The Motor Industry and South Africa,* Investor Responsibility Research Center, 1979; (with Propp, David Hauck, and David McLiff) *U.S. Business in South Africa: The Economic, Political, and Moral Issues,* Indiana University Press, 1980.

N

NADAN, Paul 1933(?)-1978

OBITUARY NOTICE: Born c. 1933; died March 23, 1978, in New York, N.Y. Editor. Nadan was a senior editor specializing in science books at Crown Publishing, where he worked with such authors as Max Lerner, Isaac Asimov, Lawrence Galton, and Ruth Winter. He was working with John Lear on a book about recombinant DNA at the time of his death. Obituaries and other sources: *New York Times,* March 25, 1978; *Publishers Weekly,* April 10, 1978.

*   *   *

NASH, Eno
See STEVENS, Austin N(eil)

*   *   *

NATSUME, Kinnosuke 1867-1916
(Soseki Natsume)

BRIEF ENTRY: Born in 1867 in Edo (now Tokyo), Japan; died of stomach ulcers, December 9, 1916, in Tokyo, Japan. The youngest of six children, Soseki Natsume was given up for adoption to a neighbor couple when he was two years old. When the couple divorced five years later, Soseki was returned to his birth parents, whom he had been told were his grandparents. His lifelong struggle against insanity has been attributed partially to that early trauma; the themes of madness and mental breakdown are predominant in his writing. During his lifetime Soseki witnessed the decline of ancient Japanese tradition and the subsequent westernization of his country. His work reflects the opposition of old and new, and he was highly regarded for his skill in creating a balance between Japanese lyricism and western analytical and psychological thought. His position as literary editor of *Asahi,* a national Japanese newspaper, provided Soseki with a showcase for his writing, and many of his novels first appeared there in serialized form. Included among his novels are *Botchan* (1906), *Gubijinso* (1907), *Sanshiro* (1908), *Mon* (1910) and *Michikusa* (1915). *Biographical/critical sources: Encyclopedia of World Literature in the Twentieth Century,* updated edition, Ungar, 1967; *World Authors, 1950-1970,* H. W. Wilson, 1975; *Twentieth-Century Literary Criticism,* Volume 2, Gale, 1979.

*   *   *

NATSUME, Soseki
See NATSUME, Kinnosuke

NELSON, Alan H(olm) 1938-

PERSONAL: Born November 4, 1938, in Boston, Mass.; married, 1961; children: two. *Education:* St. Olaf College, B.A., 1960; University of California, Berkeley, M.A., 1963, Ph.D., 1966. *Office:* Department of English, University of California, Berkeley, Calif. 94720.

CAREER: University of Chicago, Chicago, Ill., assistant professor of English and humanities, 1966-71; University of California, Berkeley, assistant professor, 1971-76, associate professor of English, 1976—. *Member:* Modern Language Association of America, Mediaeval Academy of America.

WRITINGS: (Editor with Jerome Taylor) *Medieval English Drama: Essays Critical and Contextual,* University of Chicago Press, 1972; *The Medieval English Stage: Corpus Christi Pageants and Plays,* University of Chicago Press, 1974; (editor) *The Plays of Henry Medwall,* Rowman & Littlefield, 1980. Contributor to drama journals.

BIOGRAPHICAL/CRITICAL SOURCES: Times Literary Supplement, January 17, 1975.*

*   *   *

NELSON, Carl Leroy 1910-

PERSONAL: Born June 25, 1910, in Minneapolis, Minn.; son of John and Amanda (Anderson) Nelson; married Charlotte Butler, June 1, 1936; children: Dowlan Richard, David Brian. *Education:* University of Minnesota, B.B.A., 1931, Ph.D., 1944. *Home:* 560 Riverside Dr., New York, N.Y. 10027. *Office:* Graduate School of Business, Columbia University, 603 Uris Hall, New York, N.Y. 10027.

CAREER: University of Kansas, Lawrence, instructor in accounting, 1934-35; Kansas State College (now University), Manhattan, assistant professor of accounting, 1935-40; University of Nebraska, Lincoln, 1940-47, began as assistant professor, became associate professor of accounting; University of Minnesota, Minneapolis, 1947-63, began as associate professor, became professor of accounting, chairman of department, 1961-63; Columbia University, New York, N.Y., George O. May Professor of Financial Accounting, 1963—. Instructor at University of California, summer, 1949, U.S. Navy Postgraduate School, summers, 1956-57, University of Idaho, summers, 1954, 1956, and 1959, University of Turku, 1959-60, and Norwegian School of Economics, 1964-65. Resident partner of Congdon, O'Hara & Becker, 1942-47. *Member:* American Institute of Certified Public Accountants, American Accounting Association, American Economic Association, National Accountants Association, Controllers Institute, Minnesota Institute of Certified Public Accountants.

WRITINGS: (With Roy G. Blakey and Gladys C. Blakey) *Sales Taxes,* League of Minnesota Municipalities, 1935; (with W. W. Heller and F. M. Boddy) *Savings in the Modern Economy,* University of Minnesota Press, 1952. Also editor and contributor of *Accountants' Handbook,* 1956.*

*   *   *

NERLOVE, Marc L(eon)   1933-

PERSONAL: Born October 12, 1933, in Chicago, Ill.; son of Samuel Henry and Evelyn (Andelman) Nerlove; married Mary Ellen Lieberman, February 5, 1956; children: Susan, Miriam. *Education:* University of Chicago, B.A., 1952; Johns Hopkins University, M.A., 1955, Ph.D., 1956. *Office:* Department of Economics, Northwestern University, Anderson Hall, 629 Noyes St., Evanston, Ill. 60201.

CAREER: U.S. Department of Agriculture, Washington, D.C., analytical statistician, 1956-57; U.S. Senate, Washington, D.C., economist for subcommittee on antitrust and monopoly, 1958; Johns Hopkins University, Baltimore, Md., lecturer in political economy, 1958-59; University of Minnesota, Minneapolis, associate professor of economics, 1959-60; Stanford University, Stanford, Calif., professor of economics, 1960-65; Yale University, New Haven, Conn., professor of economics, 1965-69; University of Chicago, Chicago, Ill., professor of economics, 1969-74; Northwestern University, Evanston, Ill., visiting Cook Professor, 1973-74, Cook Professor of Economics, 1974—. F. W. Taussig Research Professor of Economics at Harvard University, 1967-68; visiting professor at University of Mannheim, 1968, and University of British Columbia, 1971. Fulbright lecturer, 1963; Henry Schultz Memorial Lecturer of Economic Society, 1970. Member of advisory committee of U.S. Bureau of the Census, 1964-69, and advisory panel of National Science Foundation, 1968-70; consultant to RAND Corp., U.S. Department of Defense, and Office of International Security Affairs. *Military service:* U.S. Army, 1957-59; became first lieutenant.

MEMBER: American Statistical Association (fellow), American Association for the Advancement of Science (fellow), American Academy of Arts and Sciences (fellow), American Economic Association (member of executive committee, 1977-79), National Academy of Sciences, Population Society of America, Econometric Society (fellow; vice-president, 1980; president, 1981), Royal Economic Society, Phi Beta Kappa.

AWARDS, HONORS: Awards from American Farm Economic Association, 1956, 1958, 1961, and 1979; National Science Foundation grants, 1961-72, senior fellow, 1971-72; Fulbright fellow and Guggenheim fellow at Netherlands School of Economics, 1962-63; Ford Foundation fellow, 1963-64; M.A. from Yale University, 1965; John Bates Clark Medal from American Economic Association, 1969; Rockefeller Foundation grant, 1970-76; P.C. Mahalanobis Medal from Indian Economic Society, 1975.

WRITINGS: Distributed Lags and Demand Analysis for Agricultural and Other Commodities, U.S. Government Printing Office, 1958; *The Dynamics of Supply: Estimation of Farmers' Response to Price,* Johns Hopkins Press, 1958, reprinted, AMS Press, 1978.

Spectral Comparisons of Two Seasonal Adjustment Procedures, Institute for Mathematical Studies in the Social Sciences, Stanford University, 1964; *Two Models of the British Economy: A Fragment of a Critical Survey,* Institute for Mathematical Studies in the Social Sciences, Stanford University, 1964; (with Pietro Balestra) *Pooling Cross-Section and Time-Series Data,* Stanford University, 1964; *Estimation and Identification of Cobb-Douglas Production Functions,* Rand McNally, 1965; *Notes on Recent Empirical Studies of the CES and Related Production Functions,* Institute for Mathematical Studies in the Social Sciences, Stanford University, 1965; *A Tabular Survey of Macro-Econometric Models,* Institute for Mathematical Studies in the Social Sciences, Stanford University, 1965; (with D. Couts) *Forecasting Nonstationary Economic Time Series,* Stanford University, 1965; *Preliminary Results on Factors Affecting Differences Among Rates of Return on Investments in Individual Common Stocks,* Institute of Economic Research, Harvard University, 1968; (with D. M. Gerther) *Some Properties of "Optimal" Seasonal Adjustment,* Cowles Foundation for Research in Economics, Yale University, 1968; (with George Eads) *A Long-Run Cost Function,* Harvard University, 1968.

(Editor with John W. Hooper) *Selected Readings in Econometrics From Econometrica,* M.I.T. Press, 1970; (with T. Paul Schultz) *Love and Life Between the Censuses: A Model of Family Decision Making in Puerto Rico, 1950-1960,* RAND Corp., 1970; (with S. James Press) *Univariate and Multivariate Log-Linear and Logistic Models,* RAND Corp., 1973; (contributor) Press and Alvin J. Harman, *Methodology for Subjective Assessment of Technological Advancement,* RAND Corp., 1975; (with David M. Grether and Jose L. Carvalho) *Analysis of Economic Time Series: A Synthesis,* Academic Press, 1979. Contributor to economic journals.*

*   *   *

NESSI, Pio Baroja y
See BAROJA (y NESSI), Pio

*   *   *

NEUMAN, Abraham A(aron)   1890-1970

OBITUARY NOTICE: Born September 23, 1890, in Brezan, Austria; died November 20, 1970, in Philadelphia, Pa. Educator, scholar, clergyman, editor, and author. Neuman was regarded as a leading scholar and writer on Jewish history. He edited *The World History of the Jews* and wrote the book *Cyrus Adler.* Obituaries and other sources: *AB Bookman's Weekly,* January 4, 1971; *The National Cyclopaedia of American Biography,* Volume LV, James T. White, 1974; *Who Was Who Among English and European Authors, 1931-1949,* Gale, 1978.

*   *   *

NEVILLE, Robert   1905-1970

OBITUARY NOTICE: Born May 12, 1905, in Vinita, Okla.; died of heart disease, February, 1970, in Rome, Italy. Journalist and author. Neville was a foreign correspondent best known for being in the right place at the right time. Covering Europe in the days prior to World War II, Neville turned up in Spain just before the Spanish civil war broke out and happened to be in Warsaw on September 1, 1939, when Germany invaded Poland and officially began World War II. Later he served as *Time*'s bureau chief in New Delhi, Hong Kong, and Rome. Neville was the author of *The World of the Vatican.* Obituaries and other sources: *New York Times,* February 18, 1970; *Time,* March 2, 1970; *Who Was Who in America, With World Notables,* Volume V: *1969-1973,* Marquis, 1973.

NEWELL, Allen 1927-

PERSONAL: Born March 19, 1927, in San Francisco, Calif.; son of Robert R. and Jeannette (LeValley) Newell; married Noel Marie McKenna, December 20, 1947; children: Paul Allen. *Education:* Stanford University, B.A., 1949; graduate study at Princeton University, 1949-50; Carnegie Institute of Technology (now Carnegie-Mellon University), Ph.D., 1957. *Office:* Department of Computer Science, Carnegie-Mellon University, Schenley Park, Pittsburgh, Pa. 15213.

CAREER: Rand Corp., Santa Monica, Calif., research scientist, 1950-61; Carnegie-Mellon University, Pittsburgh, Pa., 1957—, served as lecturer, research scientist, and instructor, became professor of computer science and U. A. and Helen Whitaker Professor of Computer Science, 1976—. John Danz Lecturer at University of Washington, Seattle, 1972. Member of computer study section of National Institutes of Health, 1967-71; chairman of National Academy of Sciences computer panel, 1967-69; consultant to Xerox Corp. *Military service:* U.S. Naval Reserve, active duty, 1945-46.

MEMBER: American Association for the Advancement of Science (fellow), American Psychological Association, National Academy of Sciences, American Academy of Arts and Sciences, Association for Computing Machinery, Institute of Management Science, Institute of Electrical and Electronics Engineers. *Awards, honors:* Harry Goode Memorial Award from American Federation of Information Processing Societies, 1971; shared A. M. Turing Award from Association for Computing Machinery, 1975.

WRITINGS: (With Herbert Alexander Simon) *The Logic Theory Machine: A Complex Information Processing System*, RAND Corp., revised edition, 1956; (with Simon) *What Have Computers to Do With Management?*, RAND Corp., 1959; (editor) *Information Processing Language: V Manual*, RAND Corp., 1960, 2nd edition, Prentice-Hall, 1964; *Some Problems of Basic Organization in Problem-Solving Programs*, RAND Corp., 1962; *A Guide to the General Problem-Solver Program GPS-2-2*, RAND Corp., 1963; *IPL-V Programmers' Reference Manual*, RAND Corp., 1963; (with George W. Ernst) *GPS: A Case Study in Generality and Problem Solving*, Academic Press, 1969.

(With Jeffrey Barnett, James W. Forgie, and others) *Speech-Understanding Systems: Final Report of a Study Group*, Computer Science Department, Carnegie-Mellon University, 1971; (editor with C. Gordon Bell) *Computer Structures: Readings and Examples*, McGraw, 1971; (with D. A. Waterman) *Preliminary Results With a System for Automatic Protocol Analysis*, Departments of Psychology and Computer Science, Carnegie-Mellon University, 1972; *A Theoretical Exploration of Mechanisms for Coding the Stimulus*, Carnegie-Mellon University, 1972; (editor with Bell and J. Grason) *Designing Computers and Digital Systems*, Digital Press, 1972; (with H. A. Simon) *Human Problem Solving*, Prentice-Hall, 1972.*

*   *   *

NEWELL, Norman Dennis 1909-

PERSONAL: Born January 27, 1909, in Chicago, Ill.; son of Virgil Bingham and Nellie (Clark) Newell; married Valerie Zirkle, February 25, 1928 (deceased); married Gillian Wendy Wormall Schacht, April 28, 1973. *Education:* University of Kansas, B.S., 1929, A.M., 1931; Yale University, Ph.D., 1933. *Home:* 135 Knapp Ter., Leonia, N.J. 07605. *Office:*

Department of Geology, Columbia University, New York, N.Y. 10027.

CAREER: Kansas Geological Survey, assistant geologist, 1929-33; University of Kansas, Lawrence, geologist, 1934-35, assistant professor of geology, 1936-37; University of Wisconsin—Madison, associate professor of geology, 1937-45; Columbia University, New York, N.Y., professor of geology, 1945—. Chairman and curator of invertebrate paleontology at American Museum of Natural History, 1945-77, curator emeritus, 1977—; research affiliate in invertebrate paleontology at Yale University. Leader of Peruvian government geological expedition to Lake Titicaca, 1943-44, and expeditions in Texas, the Bahamas, and the South Pacific; participated in expeditions to Morocco, Tunisia, and the Marshall and Caroline Islands; member of Scripps Institute oceanographic expedition to Micronesia, 1967. Delegate to U.S. State Department to international geological congress in Moscow, U.S.S.R., 1937; adviser on petroleum geology to government of Peru, 1942-45; member of Smithsonian Council, 1961-69.

MEMBER: American Geological Institute (member of board of directors, 1950-51), Geological Society of America (fellow), American Association for the Advancement of Science, American Association of Petroleum Geologists, American Philosophical Society, Society for the Study of Evolution (president, 1949), Society of Systematic Zoology (president, 1972-73), Paleontological Society (fellow; vice-president, 1948-49; president, 1960-61), Society of Economic Paleontologists and Mineralogists, Sociedad Geologica del Peru, London Geological Society (honorary member), Sigma Xi.

AWARDS, HONORS: Sterling fellow at Yale University, 1933-34; Mary Clark Thompson Medal from National Academy of Sciences, 1960; distinguished service award from University of Kansas, 1960; medal from University of Hiroshima, 1964; Hayden Medal from Philadelphia Academy of Sciences, 1965; Verrill Medal from Yale University, 1966.

WRITINGS: (With John M. Jewett) *The Geology of Johnson and Miami Counties, Kansas, and the Geology of Wyandotte County, Kansas*, University of Kansas, 1935; *Late Paleozoic Pelecypods: Pectinacea and Mytilacca*, University of Kansas, 1937, reprinted, Arno, 1980; *Geology of the Lake Titicaca Region, Peru, and Bolivia*, Geological Society of America, 1949; (with others) *The Permian Reef Complex of the Guadalupe Mountains Region, Texas and New Mexico: A Study in Paleoecology*, W. H. Freeman, 1953, 2nd edition, 1970; (with John Chronic and Thomas G. Roberts) *Upper Paleozoic of Peru*, Geological Society of America, 1953; *Organism Communities and Bottom Facies, Great Bahama Bank*, American Museum of Natural History, 1959.

(Editor with John Imbrie) *Approaches to Paleoecology*, Wiley, 1964; (with Donald W. Boyd) *Hinge Grades in the Evolution of Crassatellacean Bivalves as Revealed by Permian Genera*, American Museum of Natural History, 1969; (with Bruce Runnegar) *Caspian-Like Relict Molluscan Fauna in the South American Permian*, American Museum of Natural History, 1971; (with Boyd) *Parallel Evolution in Early Trigoniacean Bivalves*, American Museum of Natural History, 1975. Also author of *The Nature of the Fossil Record*, 1959, *Origin of Oysters*, 1960, *Recent Terraces of Tropical Limestone Shores*, 1961, *Crises in the History of Life*, 1963, *Problems of Geochronology*, 1966, *Paraconformities*, 1967, *Revolutions in the History of Life, in Uniformity and Simplicity*, 1967, *Permian Bivalves of Japan*, with Keiji Nakazawa, 1967, *South American Permian*, 1971, *History of Tropical Organic Reefs*, 1971, *Special Creation and Organic Evolution*, 1973, *Paleozoic Era*,

1973, and *Tunisian Permian,* 1976. Contributor to scientific journals. Co-editor of *Journal of Paleontology,* 1939-42.*

* * *

NEWMAN, G(ordon) F.   1942-

PERSONAL: Born in 1942 in Westminster, England; married Angela Harding (divorced); married Janet Orga (divorced); children: one son, one daughter. *Home:* 12/58 Dean St., London W.1, England; and Cullinagh, Dunmanway, County Cork, Ireland. *Agent:* Giles Gordon.

CAREER: Film producer, screenwriter, playwright, and author. *Awards, honors:* Edgar Allan Poe Award from the Mystery Writers of America for *Sir, You Bastard. Member:* Writers Guild of Great Britain.

WRITINGS—Novels: *Sir, You Bastard,* Simon & Schuster, 1970, published as *Rogue Cop,* Lancer, 1973; *You Nice Bastard,* New English Library, 1972; *The Player and the Guest,* New English Library, 1972; *Billy: A Family Tragedy,* New English Library, 1972; *The Abduction,* New English Library, 1972; *The Split,* New English Library, 1973; *Three Professional Ladies,* New English Library, 1973; *The Price,* New English Library, 1974, published as *You Flash Bastard,* Sphere Books, 1978; *The Streetfighter,* Star Books, 1975; *A Prisoner's Tale,* Sphere Books, 1977; *The Guvnor,* Hart-Davis, 1977; *A Detective's Tale,* Sphere Books, 1977; *A Villain's Tale,* Sphere Books, 1978; *Trade-Off,* Dell, 1979; *The List,* Secker & Warburg, 1980; *The Obsession,* Granada, 1980.

Author of "Sun in the Hunter's Eye," a screenplay.

SIDELIGHTS: Newman is best known for the "Terry Sneed" detective series, including *Sir, You Bastard* and *You Nice Bastard. Avocational interests:* Flying, fencing, chess.*

* * *

NEWTON, Douglas   1920-

PERSONAL: Born September 22, 1920, in Malacca, Malaysia.

CAREER: Director and member of board of trustees of Museum of Primitive Art, New York City; chairman of department of primitive art of Metropolitan Museum of Art, New York City.

WRITINGS: Art Styles of the Papuan Gulf, Museum of Primitive Art, 1961; *Primitive Art of New Guinea,* Parrish Art Museum, 1963; (editor) *Bibliography of Sepik District Art Annotated for Illustrations,* Museum of Primitive Art, 1965; *New Guinea Art in the Collection of the Museum of Primitive Art,* Museum of Primitive Art, 1967.

Crocodile and Cassowary: Religious Art of the Upper Sepik River, New Guinea, Museum of Primitive Art, 1971; (with David Finn) *Oceanic Images,* Abrams, 1978; (with Lee Bolton) *The Nelson A. Rockefeller Collection: Masterpieces of Primitive Art,* foreword by Andre Malraux, introduction by Nelson A. Rockefeller, Knopf, 1978; (with Peter Gathercole and Adrienne L. Kaeppler) *The Art of the Pacific Islands,* National Gallery of Art, 1979. Contributor to journals, including *Man: A Monthly Record of Anthropological Science.*

BIOGRAPHICAL/CRITICAL SOURCES: Christian Science Monitor, December 4, 1978; *New York Times Book Review,* December 31, 1978.*

* * *

NEWTON, Norman Thomas   1898-

PERSONAL: Born April 21, 1898, in Corry, Pa.; son of John Peter and Jessie Bertha (King) Newton; married Lyyli E.E. Lamsa, July 30, 1966. *Education:* Cornell University, B.S., 1919, Master of Landscape Design, 1920. *Home:* 20 Prescott St., Cambridge, Mass. 02138.

CAREER: Bryant Fleming, Wyoming, N.Y., landscape architect, 1920-23; Ferruccio Vitale, New York City, landscape architect, 1926-31, associate, 1931; private practice of landscape architecture in New York City, 1931-42; Harvard University, Cambridge, Mass., assistant professor, 1939-47, associate professor, 1947-55, professor, 1955-66, Charles Eliot Professor of Landscape Architecture, 1963-66, professor emeritus, 1966—, chairman of department of architectural sciences, 1949-64. American Academy in Rome, fellow, 1923-26, resident landscape architect, 1967; associate landscape architect for U.S. National Park Service, 1933-39; senior monuments officer for British Army during World War II and director of subcommission for monuments, fine arts, and archives of Allied Commission in Italy. Member of board of directors of Hubbard Educational Trust. *Military service:* U.S. Marine Corps Reserve, aviation cadet, 1918. U.S. Army Air Forces, Air Service Group, 1942-46; became lieutenant colonel. U.S. Air Force Reserve, 1946-53.

MEMBER: American Society of Landscape Architects (member of board of trustees; national president, 1957-61), American Association of University Professors, New England Historic Genealogical Society, Alumni Association of American Academy in Rome, Theta Delta Chi, Gamma Delta Psi, Century Club, Savage Club, Cambridge Faculty Club. *Awards, honors:* Rome Prize in Landscape Architecture from American Academy in Rome, 1923; commander of Saints Maurice and Lazarus and grand officer of Crown of Italy, 1946; Order of Star of Solidarity (Italy), 1950; A.M. from Harvard University, 1957; Bradford Williams Medal from American Society of Landscape Architects, 1975.

WRITINGS: The Structure of Design: Preliminary Notes, Addison-Wesley, 1949; *An Approach to Design,* Addison-Wesley, 1951, revised edition, 1973; *Design on the Land: The Development of Landscape Architecture,* Belknap Press, 1971.

Editor: State Park Master Planning Manual, 1937; *War Damage to Monuments and Fine Arts of Italy,* 1946; *Uncle Johnny: A Soldier's Journal,* 1974.

Contributor to academic journals.*

* * *

NEWTON, Roy   1904(?)-1974

OBITUARY NOTICE: Born c. 1904; died July 27, 1974, in Big Rapids, Mich. Educator and author of a textbook on applied psychology. Newton collected and was regarded as an authority on dictionaries. He was professor of English and psychology at Ferris State College. Obituaries and other sources: *AB Bookman's Weekly,* October 7, 1974.

* * *

NICHOLS, David A(llen)   1939-

PERSONAL: Born February 4, 1939, in Lyons, Kan.; son of Arthur Alvin (a carpenter) and Merle (Allen) Nichols; married Esther Wells (a church musician), May 30, 1960; children: Preston, John, Yolanda. *Education:* Southwestern College, Winfield, Kan., B.Mus., 1960; Northwestern University, M.Mus., 1964; Roosevelt University, M.A., 1970; College of William and Mary, Ph.D., 1975. *Religion:* Lutheran. *Home:* 888 West Illinois S.W,, Huron, S.D. 57350. *Office:* Huron College, Huron, S.D. 57350.

CAREER: Director of orchestras at public schools in Huron, S.D., 1960-63; director of music at Methodist church in Des Plaines, Ill., 1963-65; director of orchestras at public schools in Glenview, Ill., 1964-67; Huron College, Huron, 1967—, began as assistant professor, became associate professor of history and humanities, director of community services, 1975—. Member of South Dakota Board of Cultural Preservation, 1973-74; member of Beadle County Democratic Committee. *Member:* South Dakota Historical Society.

WRITINGS: Lincoln and the Indians: Civil War Policy and Politics, University of Missouri Press, 1978. Contributor to history journals.

SIDELIGHTS: Nichols commented: "My interest is in integrating Indian history into the mainstream of American history. Therefore, I deal with the politics of Indian affairs and Indian subjects as they touch other major political issues of the era under study. I plan an integrative project concerning the reconstruction period following the Civil War."

* * *

NICHOLS, Peter 1927-

PERSONAL: Born July 31, 1927, in Bristol, England; son of Richard George and Violet Annie (Poole) Nichols; married Thelma Reed (a painter), December 26, 1959; children: Abigail (deceased), Louise, Daniel, Catherine. *Education:* Attended Bristol Old Vic Theatre School, 1921-23, and Trent Park Teachers College, 1928-30. *Politics:* "Utopian socialist." *Religion:* None. *Agent:* Margaret Ramsay Ltd., 14a Goodwin's Court, St. Martin's Lane, London WC2N 4LL, England.

CAREER: Professional actor, 1950-55; playwright, 1959—. Visiting playwright at Guthrie Theatre, Minneapolis, Minn.; member of Arts Council drama panel, 1973-76; member of board of governors of Greenwich Theatre, 1971-75. *Awards, honors:* Best play award from *Evening Standard,* 1967, for "A Day in the Death of Joe Egg," 1969, for "The National Health," and best comedy award, 1978, for "Privates on Parade"; best comedy award from Society of West End Theatres, 1978, for "Privates on Parade."

WRITINGS—Plays: The Hooded Terror (two-act; first produced in 1964), [England], 1965; *A Day in the Death of Joe Egg* (two-act; first produced in Glasgow, Scotland, at Citizens Theatre, 1967), Samuel French, 1967 (also see below); *The National Health* (two-act; first produced in London, England, at Old Vic National Theatre, 1969), Samuel French, 1970 (also see below); *Forget-Me-Not Lane* (two-act; first produced in London at Greenwich Theatre, 1973), Samuel French, 1971; *Chez Nous* (two-act; first produced in London at Globe Theatre, 1974), Faber, 1974; *The Freeway* (two-act; first produced in London at Old Vic National Theatre, 1974), Faber, 1975; (also director) *Born in the Garden* (two-act; first produced in Bristol, England, at Bristol Old Vic Theatre Royal, 1979; produced in London at Globe Theatre, 1980), Faber, 1979; *Passion Play* (two-act; first produced in London at Aldwych Theatre, 1981), Methuen, 1981.

Unpublished plays: "Hardin's Luck" (two-act; adapted from a work by E. Nesbit), first produced in London at Greenwich Theatre, 1977; "Privates on Parade" (two-act), first produced in London at Aldwych Theatre, 1977.

Screenplays: "Georgy Girl" (adapted from the novel by Margaret Forster), Columbia, 1966; "Joe Egg" (adapted from his play "A Day in the Death of Joe Egg"), Columbia, 1972; "National Health" (adapted from his play "The National Health"), Columbia, 1974.

Also author of fifteen television plays and two adaptations of short stories for television.

WORK IN PROGRESS: "Poppy," a musical play for the Royal Shakespeare Company; another musical; a television series.

SIDELIGHTS: "A Day in the Death of Joe Egg," Peter Nichols's first stage success, concerns two young parents coping with their mute, mongoloid child. It is also a comedy, noted *Time's* T. E. Kalem, which places Nichols in the circle of contemporary British playwrights who treat serious subjects with a caustic, mordant sense of humor. In Kalem's view, "No one in contemporary theater orchestrates mordant laughter with a surer hand than . . . Nichols." Although many reviewers focused on the comic strengths of the play, *Encounter* critic John Spurling praised the seriousness of its subject: "*Joe Egg* . . . [gave] a hearty music-hall humour to a gloomy subject, but the basis of its considerable appeal for audiences was that it dealt in straightforward naturalistic terms with a topical problem—what is it like to have a spastic child?"

In his next play, "The National Health," Nichols sets the action in a London hospital ward for the dying. Brendan Gill wrote in the *New Yorker:* "'The National Health' . . . is a play about the physical and spiritual indignities of sickness, old age, and approaching death. . . . The dreadfulness of suffering and the still greater dreadfulness of the certain end to suffering hang in the antiseptic air. . . . Hard as it may be to believe, Mr. Nichols' play is an unbroken series of successful jokes: gallows humor of a kind that makes us simultaneously gasp and laugh. . . . Mr. Nichols' close, compassionate scrutiny of life and death heightened my sense of well-being instead of diminishing it."

The black comedy of "Joe Egg" and "The National Health" exemplified British theatre in the late 1960's, according to Kalem, and reflected a national mood about conditions of life in England. For nearly two decades the London stage had been dominated by the angry, antiestablishment plays of writers like John Osborne ("Look Back in Anger"), but the change in dramatic tone, from hostility to a grim, mocking humor, corresponded to the decline of the welfare state. "Underlying that mockery is a sour nagging resentment of the present sorry state of England," Kalem contended. "Thus it is no unintended irony that *The National Health* is set in a hospital ward," where terminally ill patients meet their suffering without a loss of humor, however grisly. "Laughter," Kalem explained, "is a wonder drug by which man anesthetizes his consciousness" of dismal circumstances.

One criticism made against Nichols, that he does not fully exploit the dramatic potential of his plays, came from Stanley Kauffmann, whose review of "The National Health" appeared in the *New Republic:* "In all his work so far Nichols has shown irreverence for sentimentality and theatrical taboos but, fundamentally, not much more. He seems to bite bullets—in *Joe Egg* the anguish of having a brain-damaged child, in this play the implacability of the hospital beds waiting for every one of us—but he just mouths them for a while before he spits them out, he never really crunches. We keep waiting for the author's gravity as distinct from the subject's."

Ronald Bryden raised similar concerns in his review of "Chez Nous," arguing that the conflict between gravity and farce, reality and fantasy, is central to the kind of plays Nichols writes. "Unfortunately," he remarked, "it becomes clear in *Chez Nous* that this recurring opposition expresses an equivalent tug-of-war within Nichols' talent." This time Nichols constructs a domestic comedy around two English couples, Liz and Dick, Diana and Phil, one visiting the other. In the middle of the quartet, though never seen onstage, is Liz and Dick's thirteen-year-old daughter, Jane, who turns out to be the mother of Phil's baby. This revelation comes early in the play and serves as the departure point for an examination of marriage, sexual relationships, and such contemporary subjects as pubescent liberation.

Bryden began his discussion of "Chez Nous" by observing that Nichols partly uses "plays as play: as fantasies exploring the alternatives to real life. The other half is . . . the realist who . . . [reminds us] that you can have real emotions only about reality." In his estimation the central incident, Jane and Phil's parenthood, "is an improbability, a deliberate alternative to real life, engineered as a play-experiment to see what emotions one should have about it. Because it's unreal . . . most of the emotions it generates are unreal too. . . . I haven't said anything, I hope, which suggests that he's capable of writing a really bad play. But he spends far too much of his evening exploring all the unreal emotions. . . . His indulgence of fantasy has made things too artificial for . . . much conviction."

Some of the particular strengths of the play and Nichols's talent were described by Benedict Nightingale in his review for the *New Statesman:* "This is a very intelligent, careful play, which regards its protagonists with humour, horror, exasperation and compassion, though not always in equal proportion. . . . Diana and Phil prove rather more sympathetic—she for all her fastidiousness and melodramatics, he, with his ostentatious crudity, his pathetic yen for youth and craving for paternity. Their reconciliation, in which she unfurls the hysterectomy-scarred body she's always kept hidden, is unexpectedly moving, a declaration that affection can survive a mangling. As Nichols sees it, men are in thrall to their sexual drives, women doomed to humour them, but both sexes more tenaciously committed to marriage than they sometimes realise."

In "The Freeway," Nichols again joins fantasy and reality to launch an attack against rampant capitalism and acquisitiveness. Here he projects an England of the future in which all but the poorest own an automobile. Further, he envisions an eighty-mile long traffic jam that lasts for three days on Britain's Fl, a colossal freeway running the length of the nation. Members of the aristocracy and working class are forced to contend with each other as well as with the lack of food, water, and sanitation. Kenneth Hurren of the *Spectator* stated, "Fl and the trouble that develops on it are a tortured metaphor for British democracy, class-ridden and acquisitive, careering along a freeway to disaster."

"The Freeway" fared less well with critics than Nichols's previous works. Hurren commented: "[Nichols] is a dramatist who has hitherto seemed possessed of as vivaciously original a comic talent as anyone presently operating in the theatre, and it is as surprising as it is dismaying to find that talent . . . foundering bleakly in contemplation of the menace of the motor car. . . . It would plainly be possible to develop the situation pretty humorously, but Nichols on this occasion seems to be altogether too embittered (he must have had some really terrible times in the Peugeot), and it is a measure, I suppose, of his desperation—and of the extraordinary fall in his standards of comedy—that he is reduced to the desolate business of trying to get a laugh or two out of people going to the lavatory in rather primitive circumstances."

In his review of the play Nightingale talked about some of the ideas Nichols raises: "We learn that individual self-indulgence can produce social misery; that labour tends to equate happiness with possessions, and that capital is only too glad to keep its power with the odd handout; that freedom, in short, may be slavery. But anyone who has read a little 19th-century history

. . . will want to see more slippery questions tackled. . . . I found *The Freeway* not unenjoyable, a deliberately negative recommendation. As a play of ideas, it could be more provocative; as a comedy about people in a jam, more trenchant and amusing."

BIOGRAPHICAL/CRITICAL SOURCES: J. R. Taylor, *The Second Wave,* Methuen, 1971; *New Statesman,* February 15, 1974, October 11, 1974; *Plays and Players,* March, 1974; *Spectator,* October 12, 1974; *New Yorker,* October 21, 1974; *Time,* October 21, 1974; *New Republic,* November 2, 1974; *Encounter,* January, 1975; *Contemporary Literary Criticism,* Volume 5, Gale, 1976; Oleg Kerensky, *The New British Drama,* Hamish Hamilton, 1977.

—*Sketch by B. Hal May*

*　　*　　*

NICOLSON, Victoria Mary
See SACKVILLE-WEST, V(ictoria Mary)

*　　*　　*

NIELSEN, Sven Sigurd   1901-1976

OBITUARY NOTICE: Born November 13, 1901, in Olgod, Denmark; died December 31, 1976, in Paris, France. Publisher. Nielsen started a book exporting firm after moving to France in 1924. Following World War II Nielsen expanded his business by publishing American and English authors for a French book market. Obituaries and other sources: *Publishers Weekly,* January 17, 1977; *AB Bookman's Weekly,* February 14, 1977.

*　　*　　*

NIXSON, Frederick Ian   1943-

PERSONAL: Born June 15, 1943, in London, England; son of Frederick A. (a personnel manager) and Emily Mary (Shaw) Nixson; married Susan Mary Taylor (a lecturer), July 22, 1972; children: Matthew James, Jonathan Charles, Andrew Thomas. *Education:* University of Leeds, B.A., 1964, Ph.D., 1970. *Religion:* None. *Home:* 42 Buxton Old Rd., Disley, Cheshire SK12 2BW, England. *Office:* Department of Economics, Victoria University of Manchester, Manchester M13 9PL, England.

CAREER: Makerere University, Kampala, Uganda, lecturer in economics, 1968-71; Victoria University of Manchester, Manchester, England, lecturer, 1971-79, senior lecturer in economics, 1979—. *Member:* Royal Economic Society.

WRITINGS: Economic Integration and Industrial Location: An East African Case Study, Longman, 1973; (with David Colman) *Economics of Change in Less Developed Countries,* Halsted, 1978; (editor with C. H. Kirkpatrick, and contributor) *The Industrialisation of Less Developed Countries,* Manchester University Press, 1982. Contributor to economic and international studies journals.

WORK IN PROGRESS: A textbook on industrial economics, tentatively titled *Industrial Structure and Policy in Less Developed Countries,* with C. H. Kirkpatrick and N. Lee, publication by Allen & Unwin expected in 1983.

AVOCATIONAL INTERESTS: Travel (including East Africa).

*　　*　　*

NOBLE, Dudley (Henry)   1893(?)-1970

OBITUARY NOTICE: Born c. 1893; died July 18, 1970, in

London, England. Journalist and author best known for his autobiography, *Milestones in a Motoring Life*. Obituaries and other sources: *AB Bookman's Weekly*, September 21, 1970.

* * *

NOBLE, J(ames) Kendrick 1896(?)-1978

OBITUARY NOTICE: Born c. 1896; died November 15, 1978, in Austin, Tex. Aviator and publisher. Noble's love of flying began during World War I when he served as a pilot with the Northern Bombardment Group in France. Noble raced airplanes during the 1920's and maintained an interest in aviation throughout his life. As president of his own publishing firm, Noble & Noble, he was best known for developing a series of remedial readers for adults. Obituaries and other sources: *New York Times*, November 17, 1978; *Publishers Weekly*, November 27, 1978; *AB Bookman's Weekly*, April 5, 1979.

* * *

NOBLE, Stanley R(odman) 1904(?)-1977

OBITUARY NOTICE: Born c. 1904; died August 24, 1977, on Fire Island, N.Y. Publisher. As executive vice-president of Noble & Noble Publishers, he helped develop a remedial reading series for junior and senior high school students. Obituaries and other sources: *New York Times*, August 25, 1977; *AB Bookman's Weekly*, October 17, 1977.

* * *

NOKES, Gerald Dacre 1899-1971

OBITUARY NOTICE: Born in 1899 in London, England; died November 15, 1971, in Worthing, England. Educator and author. Nokes taught law at King's College, London, and revised legal texts, including *Cockle's Evidence* and *Halsbury's Laws of England*. Obituaries and other sources: *The Author's and Writer's Who's Who*, 6th edition, Burke's Peerage, 1971; *AB Bookman's Weekly*, December 13, 1971.

* * *

NOLEN, Barbara 1902-

PERSONAL: Born December 19, 1902, in Ardmore, Pa.; daughter of John and Barbara (Schatte) Nolen; married David Fales Strong, June 14, 1927; children: Stephen Lewis, Deborah Louisa. *Education:* Smith College, A.B. (cum laude), 1924; Stanford University, M.A., 1925. *Home address:* Trotta Lane, Morris, Conn. 06763.

CAREER: Macmillan Publishing Co., Inc., New York, N.Y., assistant to children's book editor, 1926-27; Century Co., editor of children's books, 1931-32; *Story Parde*, editor, 1936-54; *Washington Star*, Washington, D.C., children's book reviewer, 1954-63; *Children's Digest*, children's book reviewer, 1963-70. George Washington University, director of workshops, 1953-61, lecturer, 1954-56; lecturer at American University, 1959-61. Chairman of action committee of District of Columbia School Libraries, 1960-62; member of board of directors of Morris Public Library, 1969—; consultant to International Cooperation Administration. *Member:* Children's Book Guild of Washington (charter member), Morris Historical Society. *Awards, honors:* Community service awards from District of Columbia Education Association and American Association of School Librarians, both 1962.

WRITINGS: (Editor) *Children of America* (juvenile stories), foreword by Lucy Sprague Mitchell, John C. Winston Co.,

1939; (editor) *Fun and Frolic*, illustrations by Emma Brock, Heath, 1942; (editor) *Luck and Pluck*, illustrations by Decie Merwin, Heath, 1942; (editor) *Merry Hearts and Bold* (juvenile stories), illustrations by Fritz Kredel, Heath, 1942; (editor) *The Brave and Free*, illustrations by Harve Stein, Heath, 1942.

(Editor) *Do and Dare*, Heath, 1951; (editor with Eleanor M. Johnson) *What Next?: Adventure and Surprise* (juvenile stories), American Education Publications, 1957; (with Delia Goetz) *Writers' Handbook for the Development of Educational Materials*, Office of Education, U.S. Department of Health, Education and Welfare, 1959; (editor of abridgement) Anna Sewell, *Black Beauty: The Autobiography of a Horse* (juvenile), illustrations by Tom Gill, Golden Press, 1963; (editor) *Spies, Spies, Spies*, (stories), F. Watts, 1965; (editor) *Africa Is People: Firsthand Accounts From Contemporary Africa*, introduction by Mercer Cook, Dutton, 1967.

Ethiopia (juvenile), F. Watts, 1971; (editor) *Africa Is Thunder and Wonder: Contemporary Voices from African Literature*, introduction by Abioseh Nicol, Scribner, 1972; (editor) *Mexico Is People: Land of Three Cultures*, introduction by Concha Romero James, Scribner, 1973; (editor) *Voices of Africa*, Fontana, 1974; (editor) *More Voices of Africa: Contemporary Voices From African Literature*, Fontana, 1975. Also editor of *The Morris Academy: Pioneer in Coeducation, 1790-1888*, 1976.*

* * *

NOONE, Richard 1918(?)-1973

OBITUARY NOTICE: Consultant and author. Noone advised the Southeast Asia Treaty Organization (SEATO) and wrote a book about his experiences with tribesmen in northern Malay. Obituaries and other sources: *AB Bookman's Weekly*, October 15, 1973.

* * *

NORA, James Jackson 1928-

PERSONAL: Born June 26, 1928, in Chicago, Ill.; son of Joseph James (a physician) and Mae (a nurse; maiden name, Jackson) Nora; married Audrey Hart (a physician), April 9, 1966; children: Wendy, Penelope, Marianne, James, Jr., Elizabeth. *Education:* Harvard University, A.B., 1950; Yale University, M.D., 1954; University of California, Berkeley, M.P.H., 1978. *Politics:* Democrat. *Religion:* Presbyterian. *Home:* 6135 East Sixth Ave., Denver, Colo. 80220. *Office:* Department of Pediatrics, Medical Center, University of Colorado, Denver, Colo, 80262.

CAREER: Detroit Receiving Hospital, Detroit, Mich., rotating intern, 1954-55; private practice, Cambridge, Wis., 1955-59; University of Wisconsin—Madison, pediatric resident, 1959-61, chief resident, 1961; private practice in pediatrics, Beloit, Wis., 1961-62; University of Wisconsin—Madison, instructor, 1962-64, assistant professor of pediatrics, 1965; Baylor College of Medicine, Houston, Tex., assistant professor, 1965-69, associate professor of pediatrics, 1969-71, head of section of human genetics and director of Birth Defects Center, 1967-71; University of Colorado School of Medicine, Denver, Color., associate professor, 1971-74, professor of pediatrics, 1974—, professor of preventative medicine, 1979—, professor of biochemistry, biophysics, and genetics, 1979—, director of Pediatric Cardiovascular-Pulmonary Training Center, 1972-78, director of Preventative Cardiology, 1978—.

Research fellow in cardiology at University of Wisconsin—Madison, 1962-64; special N.I.H. fellow in genetics at McGill University and at Montreal Children's Hospital, Montreal,

Quebec, Canada. Associate director of cardiology, 1965-71, and chief of genetics service, 1967-71, at Texas Children's Hospital, Houston, Tex.; director of pediatric cardiology at Colorado General Hospital, 1971-77, and of division of genetics at Rose Medical Center. Served on task force of National Heart, Blood Vessel, Lung, and Blood Program, 1973, in U.S.-U.S.S.R. Exchange Program on Congenital Heart Disease, 1975, and on Human Research Committee of Children's Hospital of Denver. Diplomate of National Board of Medical Examiners, of American Board of Pediatrics, and of American Sub-Board of Pediatric Cardiology. Served on institutional committees at University of Colorado, including faculty council, human research committee, computer committee, faculty risk committee, fourth year pediatric curriculum committee, 1972-74. Associated with National Foundation-March of Dimes, American Heart Association, Colorado Heart Association, American College of Cardiology. *Military service:* U.S. Army Air Corps, 13th Air Force, 1945-47; became second lieutenant; stationed in Philippine Islands.

MEMBER: Transplantation Society, Genetics Society of America, Teratology Society, American Pediatric Society, American Society of Human Genetics, American Federation for Clinical Research, American Institute of Biological Sciences, American Heart Associations and Councils, American College of Cardiology (member of ad hoc committee on pediatric cardiology), American Academy of Pediatrics (fellow), American College of Cardiology, Society for Pediatric Research, Society for Experimental Biology and Medicine, Southern Society for Pediatric Research, Western Society for Pediatric Research. *Awards, honors:* Received grants from National Foundation-March of Dimes, 1966-71, from National Heart and Lung Institute, 1972-78, from National Institute of Child Health and Human Development, 1974-77, from Johnson Foundation, 1978—, from American Heart Association, from Junior League of Denver, and from local heart associations; Virginia Apgar Memorial Award.

WRITINGS: Introduction to Immunology, Kimtec, 1970; (editor; with D. Bergma and others) *Birth Defects Atlas and Compendium*, Williams & Wilkins, 1973, 2nd edition, 1979; (with F. C. Fraser) *Medical Genetics: Principles and Practice*, Lea & Febiger, 1974, 2nd edition, 1981; (with Fraser) *Genetics of Man*, Lea & Febiger, 1975; *Genetics and Cardiology*, ACCEL, 1976; (with wife, Audrey Hart Nora) *Genetics Counseling in Cardiovascular Diseases*, C. C Thomas, 1978; *The Whole Heart Book*, Holt, 1980.

Contributor: Hamish Watson, editor, *Pediatric Cardiology*, Lloyd-Luke, 1968; Oscar Jaffe, editor, *Cardiac Development With Special Reference to Congenital Heart Disease: Proceedings of the 1968 International Symposium*, University of Dayton Press, 1970; C. Henry Kempe, H.K. Silver, and D. O'Brien, editors, *Current Pediatric Diagnosis and Treatment*, Lange Medical Publications, 2nd edition, 1972, 3rd edition, 1974, 4th edition, 1976; *Birth Defects Compendium*, National Foundation, 1973, 2nd edition, Alan R. Liss, 1979; W. F. Friedman, M. Lisch, and E. H. Sonnenblick, editors, *Neonatal Heart Disease*, Grune, 1973; B. S. Langford Kidd and Richard D. Rowe, editors, *The Child With Congenital Heart Disease After Surgery*, Futura Publishing, 1976; A. J. Moss, F. Adams, and G. C. Ammanouilides, editors, *Heart Disease in Infants, Children and Adolescents*, Williams & Wilkins, 2nd edition, 1977; H. A. Kaminetzky and L. Iffy, editors, *New Techniques and Concepts in Maternal and Fetal Medicine*, Van Nostrand, 1979; R. Neil Schmike and Laird G. Jackson, editors, *Clinical Genetics: A Source Book for Physicians*, Wiley, 1979; Richard Van Praagh and Atsuyoshi Takao, editors, *Etiology and Morphogenesis of Congenital Heart Disease*, Futura

Publishing, 1980. Contributor of over one hundred papers and articles to journals.

Member of editorial board of *Circulation* and of *Blakiston's New Gould Medical Dictionary*, 4th edition.

WORK IN PROGRESS: Preventative Cardiology, with H. L. Brammell, publication by Lea & Febiger; two novels, one titled *The Last Vikings;* a nonfiction book.

SIDELIGHTS: Nora's major research fields include the etiology of cardiovascular diseases, congenital heart disease, atherosclerosis, hypertentsion, and rheumatic fever. He is also interested in general topics in the areas of cardiology, genetics, teratology, human development, maternal and child health, epidemiology, and preventative medicine.

* * *

NORDELL, (Hans) Roderick 1925-

PERSONAL: Born June 26, 1925, in Alexandria, Minn.; son of Wilbur Eric (a salesman) and Amelia (a teacher; maiden name, Jasperson) Nordell; married Joan Projansky (a university administrator), April 30, 1955; children: Eric Peter, John Roderick, Elizabeth Sabin. *Education:* Harvard University, A. B. (magna cum laude), 1948; University of Dublin, B.Litt., 1951. *Religion:* Christian Scientist. *Home:* 25 Meadow Way, Cambridge, Mass. 02138. *Office: Christian Science Monitor*, Boston, Mass. 02115.

CAREER: Christian Science Monitor, Boston, Mass., reporter, 1948-50, movie and theatre reviewer, 1951-55, book editor, 1955-63, assistant chief editorial writer, 1964-66, 1973—, assistant feature editor, 1966-68, arts editor, 1968-73. Part-time teacher of adult education courses. Member of board of directors of Community Music Center of Boston, 1970—, and Young Audiences, 1970—; trustee of Berklee College of Music; member of advisory committee of Berlin Jazz Festival; member of Committee for the Harvard Theatre Collection. *Military service:* U.S. Marine Corps, 1943-46; became staff sergeant; received commendation ribbon. *Member:* Phi Beta Kappa. *Awards, honors:* Rotary Foundation fellowship, 1950-51.

WRITINGS: (Editor with Erwin D. Canham) *Man's Great Future* (condensation of *Christian Science Monitor's* Fiftieth Anniversary Issue), Longmans, Green, 1959. Contributor of articles to magazines.

WORK IN PROGRESS: A novel.

* * *

NORDEN, Denis 1922-

PERSONAL: Born February 6, 1922; son of George and Jenny (Lubell) Norden; married Avril Rosen, 1943; children: one son, one daughter. *Education:* Attended schools in London, England. *Home:* 16 Neal's Yard, Monmouth St., London W.C.2, England.

CAREER: Broadcaster and scriptwriter. Theatre manager, 1939-42; Variety Agency, staff writer, 1945-47; writer and broadcaster, 1947—. Chairman of "Looks Familiar," a program on Thames Television, 1973—, and "It'll Be Alright on the Night," on LWT, 1977. Guest on television and radio game programs; affiliated with television programs "My Word!" and "My Music"; consultant to British Broadcasting Corp. *Military service:* Royal Air Force, 1942-45. *Member:* Saturday Morning Odeon Club, Queen's Club. *Awards, honors:* Shared award from Screenwriters Guild, 1961, for best contribution to light entertainment; best radio personality award from Variety Club of Great Britain, 1978.

WRITINGS—With Frank Muir: *You Can't Have Your Kayak and Heat It: Stories From "My Word,"* introduction by Jack Longland, Eyre Methuen, 1973; *Upon My Word!: More Stories from "My Word!,"* Eyre Methuen, 1974; *The "My Word!" Stories,* contains "You Can't Have Your Kayak and Heat It" and "Upon My Word!," Eyre Methuen, 1976, Stein & Day, 1977; *Take My Word for It: Still More Stories from "My Word!,"* Eyre Methuen, 1978; *The Glums,* Robson, 1979; *Oh, "My Word!,"* Eyre Methuen, 1980.

Films: (With Alec Coppel) "The Bliss of Mrs. Blossom," Paramount, 1968; (with Melvin Frank and Sheldon Keller) "Buona Sera, Mrs. Campbell," United Artists, 1969; "The Best House in London," MGM, 1969; "The Statue," Cinerama, 1971. Also scriptwriter of "Every Home Should Have One" and "Twelve Plus One."

Writer (and sometimes producer) with Muir of television and radio programs, including "Take It From Here," 1947-58, "Bedtime With Braden," 1950-54, "And So to Bentley," 1956, "Whack-O!," 1958-60, and "The Seven Faces of Jim," 1961. Author of television commercials and revues.*

* * *

NORDLAND, Gerald John 1927-

PERSONAL: Born July 10, 1927, in Los Angeles, Calif. *Education:* Received A.B. and J.D. from University of Southern California. *Office:* Milwaukee Art Center, 750 North Lincoln Memorial Dr., Milwaukee, Wis. 53202.

CAREER: California Institute of the Arts, Valencia, dean of Chouinard Art School, 1960-64; Washington Gallery of Modern Art, Washington, D.C., director, 1964-66; San Francisco Museum of Art, San Francisco, Calif., director, 1966-72; University of California, Los Angeles, director of Frederick S. Wight Galleries, 1973-78; Milwaukee Art Center, Milwaukee, Wis., director, 1978—. Arranged collections at Whitney Museum of American Art and Los Angeles County Art Museum; member of National Endowment for the Arts museum advisory panel, 1970-73. *Member:* Association of Art Museum Directors.

WRITINGS: Paul Jenkins Retrospective, Houston Museum of Fine Arts, 1971; *Gaston Lachaise: The Man and His Work,* Braziller, 1974; *Recent Work by Master of Fine Art Graduates of University of California, Santa Barbara,* Santa Barbara Museum of Art, 1974; *Franklin D. Murphy Sculpture Garden: An Annotated Catalog of the Collection, 1976,* University of California, Los Angeles, 1976; *Alberto Burri: A Retrospective View, 1948-77,* Frederick S. Wight Art Gallery, University of California, Los Angeles, 1977. Author of museum and exhibition catalogs.*

* * *

NORTH, Helen Florence 1921-

PERSONAL: Born January 31, 1921, in Utica, N.Y.; daughter of James H. and Catherine (Debbold) North. *Education:* Cornell University, A.B., 1942, M.A., 1943, Ph.D., 1945. *Home:* 604 Ogden Ave., Swarthmore, Pa. 19081. *Office:* Department of Classics, Swarthmore College, Swarthmore, Pa. 19081.

CAREER: Rosary College, River Forest, Ill., instructor in classical languages, 1946-48; Swarthmore College, Swarthmore, Pa., assistant professor, 1948-53, associate professor, 1953-62, professor of classics, 1962—, Centennial Professor of Classics, 1966-73, William J. Kenan Professor, 1973—, chairman of department, 1959—. Visiting assistant professor at Cornell

University, 1952—; visiting associate professor at Barnard College, Columbia University, 1954-55; visiting professor at LaSalle College, 1965, and American School of Classical Studies, Athens, Greece, 1975; Martin Classical Lecturer at Oberlin College, 1972—; Blegen Distinguished Visiting Research Professor at Vassar College, 1979. Member of advisory council of American School of Classical Studies, Athens, 1960-62 and 1964; member of board of directors of King's College, Wilkes-Barre, Pa., 1969-71 and 1973—, LaSalle College, 1973—, and American Council of Learned Societies, 1977—; member of board of trustees of American Academy in Rome, 1972-75 and 1977-79. Chairman of Catholic Commission on Intellectual and Cultural Affairs, 1968-69.

MEMBER: American Philological Association (member of board of directors, 1968—; first vice-president, 1975; president, 1976—), American Academy of Arts and Sciences, American Association for the Advancement of Science, Society for Religion in Higher Education, Classical Association of the Atlantic States, Classical Society of the American Academy in Rome (president, 1960-61), Phi Beta Kappa, Phi Kappa Phi.

AWARDS, HONORS: Scholarship from American Academy in Rome, 1942-43; grants from American Council of Learned Societies, 1943-45 and 1973, fellowship, 1971-72; Mary Isabel Sibley fellowship from Phi Beta Kappa Foundation, 1945-46; fellowship from Ford Fund for the Advancement of Education, 1953-54; Fulbright fellowship, 1953-54; Guggenheim fellowships, 1958-59 and 1975-76; grant from Danforth Foundation, 1962; American Association of University Women fellowship, 1963-64; grant from Lindbach Foundation, 1966; senior fellow of National Endowment for the Humanities, 1967-68; Harbison Prize from Danforth Foundation, 1969, for distinguished teaching; Charles J. Goodwin Award of Merit from American Philological Association, 1969, for *Sophrosyne.*

WRITINGS: Sophrosyne: Self-Knowledge and Self-Restraint in Greek Literature, Cornell University Press, 1966; (contributor) Don M. Wolfe, editor, *The Complete Prose Works of John Milton,* Volume IV, Yale University Press, 1966; (editor with Anne King) Harry Caplan, *Of Eloquence: Studies in Ancient and Medieval Rhetoric,* Cornell University Press, 1970; *From Myth to Icon: Reflections of Greek Ethical Doctrine in Literature and Art,* Cornell University Press, 1979; (editor) *Interpretations of Plato: A Swarthmore Symposium,* Humanities, 1979. Contributor to classical journals. Editor of *Journal of the History of Ideas;* member of editorial board of *Catalogues Translationum et Commentariorum,* 1979—.*

* * *

NORTH, John 1894-1973

OBITUARY NOTICE: Born in 1894 in Cambridge, England; died February 15, 1973. Author of military works, including *Gallipoli: The Fading Vision* and *Men Fighting: Battle Stories.* Obituaries and other sources: *The Author's and Writer's Who's Who,* 6th edition, Burke's Peerage, 1971; *AB Bookman's Weekly,* March 19, 1973.

* * *

NORTH, Morgan 1915(?)-1978

OBITUARY NOTICE: Born c. 1915; died March 21, 1978, in Berkeley, Calif. Mining engineer and publisher. North co-founded Howell-North Books, publishers of books on mining and railroading. He was also a successful miner of quicksilver. Obituaries and other sources: *Publishers Weekly,* May 1, 1978.

NORTHEDGE, Frederick Samuel 1918-

PERSONAL: Born October 16, 1918, in Derby, England; son of William (a molder) and Alice (Bryan) Northedge; married Betty Cynthia Earnshaw, May 25, 1939; children: Christopher Phillip, Alastair, Theresa Felicity. *Education:* Attended Merton College, Oxford, 1937-39, and University of Nottingham, 1945-46; London School of Economics and Political Science, London, B.Sc., 1949, Ph.D., 1953, D.Sc., 1976. *Politics:* Labour. *Religion:* Church of England. *Home:* 21 Marlborough Rd., Chiswick, London W.4, England. *Office:* London School of Economics and Political Science, University of London, Houghton St., Aldwych, London WC2A 2AE, England.

CAREER: University of London, London School of Economics and Political Science, London, England, assistant lecturer, 1949-52, lecturer, 1952-60, reader, 1960-68, professor of international relations, 1968—, convener of department, 1969—. *Member:* Royal Institute of International Affairs, Association of University Teachers. *Awards, honors:* Carnegie Prize for Research in International Organisation from Carnegie Endowment for International Peace, 1955.

WRITINGS: British Foreign Policy: The Process of Readjustment, 1945-1961, Praeger, 1962; *The Troubled Giant: Britain Among the Great Powers, 1916-1939,* G. Bell, 1966, Praeger, 1967; (editor) *The Foreign Policies of the Powers,* Faber, 1968, 2nd edition, 1974, Praeger, 1969, 2nd edition, Free Press, 1975; *Order and the System of International Politics,* Nigerian Institute of International Affairs, 1971; (with M. J. Grieve) *A Hundred Years of International Relations,* Praeger, 1971; (with Michael D. Donelan) *International Disputes: The Political Aspects,* St. Martin's, 1971; (editor) *The Use of Force in International Relations,* Free Press, 1974; *Descent From Power: British Foreign Policy, 1945-1973,* Allen & Unwin, 1974; *East-West Relations: Detente and After,* University of Ife Press, 1975; *The International Political System,* Faber, 1976; (with A. Wells) *Britain and Soviet Communism,* Macmillan, 1981.

WORK IN PROGRESS: A book tentatively titled *The Cold War,* publication by Athlone Press expected in 1983; a book tentatively titled *The League of Nations,* publication by Leicester University Press expected in 1983.

SIDELIGHTS: Northedge told *CA:* "I was drawn to the study of international politics by my lifelong concern with the problem of war, in my opinion the greatest evil afflicting human society. The fact that I was born at the end of the First World War, grew to manhood with the Second World War, and have spent all my writing and teaching career in the shadow (or glare) of a third, no doubt largely accounts for my feelings. My interest in international organizations created for the prevention of war is one natural expression of this interest, and my choice of British foreign policy as my principal subject of research is another.

"Britain has had her share of great wars, especially in the twentieth century, and this fact has, I think, had much to do with the country's recent troubles and its long decline from world power during my lifetime. This subject has brought me to the study of our relations with Russia and with Soviet Communism, not that I have any ideological sympathy with either, but because I believe that our prejudices on these subjects have prevented the cooperation between the two countries needed to reduce the incidence of war, and because the dangers of a violent clash between my own country and its allies, on one side, and Russia, on the other, are at the present time so great."

NOTZ, Rebecca Love 1888-1974

OBITUARY NOTICE: Born December 8, 1888, in Richardsville, Va.; died November 16, 1974, in Concord, Mass. Librarian, educator, and author. Notz was a legal analyst in the Legislative Reference Division of the Library of Congress and professor emeritus at American University's Washington College of Law in Washington, D.C. She was the author of several books, including *Legal Bibliography and Legal Research.* Obituaries and other sources: *Who's Who of American Women,* 3rd edition, Marquis, 1964; *AB Bookman's Weekly,* January 27, 1975.

*   *   *

NOYES, Alfred 1880-1958

BRIEF ENTRY: Born September 26, 1880, in Wolverhampton, England; died June 28, 1958. English author. Noyes was among the most popular and prolific British poets of the early twentieth century. Though his verse offended some critics as the antithesis of the intellectual style popularized by T. S. Eliot, many readers enjoyed his ballads and romantic narrative poems. Among the best known of his early works is *Drake: An English Epic* (1906-08), which was serialized in *Blackwood's Magazine. Drake* concerned life at sea, and was followed by more collections containing similar themes, including *The Golden Hunde* (1908) and *The Enchanted Island* (1909). Because of his success, Noyes was able to devote his time solely to writing, an unheard of situation for poets of his generation. He continued in his career with poems of scientific discovery, many of which revealed his knowledge of astronomy, and added criticism and novels to his voluminous canon. Noyes's conversion to Roman Catholicism in 1925 profoundly altered the course of his work, for his subsequent writings are explicit in their adherence to Catholic doctrine. In 1938, Noyes's biography *Voltaire* sparked a conflict with his Catholic superiors in Rome, who found the book "worthy of condemnation." He contested the criticism and was eventually exonerated. Throughout his career Noyes resisted the influence of Eliot and fellow modernist Ezra Pound. He claimed Tennyson as his mentor and continued writing traditional verse into the 1940's. Noyes wrote his autobiography, *Two Worlds for Memory,* in 1953. *Biographical/critical sources: Everyman's Dictionary of Literary Biography, English and American,* revised edition, Dutton, 1960; *The Reader's Encyclopedia,* 2nd edition, Crowell, 1965; *Longman Companion to Twentieth Century Literature,* Longman, 1970.

*   *   *

NOYES, David 1898(?)-1981

OBITUARY NOTICE: Born c. 1898; died of a heart attack in 1981 in Los Angeles, Calif. Journalist. Noyes went to Washington, D.C., during World War II to help the Roosevelt administration organize the War Production Board and later became a presidential assistant and adviser to Harry Truman. Noyes advised Truman on many historic decisions, including approval to develop the atomic bomb, the implementation of the Marshall Plan, the establishment of the Central Intelligence Agency, and the firing of General Douglas MacArthur. Obituaries and other sources: *New York Times,* August 10, 1981; *Time,* August 24, 1981.

*   *   *

NUSSBAUM, Aaron 1910-1981

OBITUARY NOTICE—See index for *CA* sketch: Born July 9, 1910, in New York, N.Y.; died June 6, 1981, in New York,

N.Y. Attorney and author. Nussbaum founded and served as the national director of the Amnesty League of America, an organization which proposed that first felony offenders be given amnesty and that their records be made secret after they served their sentences. Nussbaum worked as an assistant district attorney for the Criminal Appeals Bureau of Kings County, N.Y., for twenty-seven years. His works include *Second Chance: Amnesty for the First Offender*. Obituaries and other sources: *New York Times*, June 10, 1981.

*　　*　　*

NUTTALL-SMITH, Margaret Emily Noel   1919- (Peggy Fortnum)

PERSONAL: Born December 23 (some sources cite December 22), 1919, in Harrow-on-the-Hill, Middlesex, England; married Ralph Nuttall-Smith (a painter, sculptor, and teacher), 1958; children: two stepsons. *Education:* Attended Royal Tunbridge Wells School of Arts and Crafts and Central School of Arts and Crafts, London, England. *Home:* Swinview, West Mersea, Essex, England.

CAREER: Author and illustrator of books for young people. Has worked as an art teacher and textile designer. *Wartime service:* British Auxiliary Territorial Service, signals operator during World War II.

WRITINGS—All under name Peggy Fortnum; self-illustrated: *Running Wild* (autobiography), Chatto & Windus, 1975.

Illustrator; "Paddington Bear" series; written by Michael Bond; original editions published by Collins: *A Bear Called Paddington*, 1958, Houghton, 1960; *More About Paddington*, 1959; *Paddington Helps Out*, 1960; *Paddington Abroad*, 1961,

Houghton, 1972; *Paddington at Large*, 1962, Houghton, 1963; *Paddington Marches On!*, 1964, Houghton, 1967; *The Adventures of Paddington* (contains *A Bear Called Paddington* and *More About Paddington*), 1965; *Paddington at Work*, 1966, Houghton, 1967; *Paddington Goes to Town*, Houghton, 1968; *Paddington Takes the Air*, 1970, Houghton, 1971; *Paddington on Top*, 1974, Houghton, 1975; Bond and Alfred Bradley, *Paddington on Stage* (plays), 1974, Houghton, 1977.

Other illustrated works: Beverley Nichols, *The Mountain of Magic*, J. Cape, 1950, revised edition, Collins, 1975; Patricia Lynch, *Brogeen Follows the Magic Tune*, Burke, 1952; Lynch, *Brogeen and the Green Shoes*, Burke, 1953; Helen Clare, *Bel the Giant, and Other Stories*, Bodley Head, 1956; Lynch, *The Bookshop on the Quay*, Dent, 1956; Eleanor Farjeon, *The Children's Bells: A Selection of Poems*, Oxford University Press, 1957, Walck, 1960; Lynch, *Fiona Leaps the Bonfire*, Dent, 1957, published as *Shane Comes to Dublin*, Criterion, 1958; Lynch, *The Old Black Sea Chest: A History of Bantry Bay*, Dent, 1958; Kenneth Grahame, *The Reluctant Dragon*, Bodley Head, 1959, Dufour, 1965; Lynch, *Jinny the Changeling*, Dent, 1959; Ursula Williams, *Adventures of the Little Wooden Horse*, Penguin, 1959.

Anna Rutgers van de Loeff, *Children of the Oregon Trail*, University of London Press, 1961; Margaret Mackprang MacKay, *Dolphin Boy: A Story of Hawaii*, Harrap, 1963; Ivy Eastwick, *A Camel for Saida*, Roy, 1964; Oscar Wilde, *The Happy Prince and Other Stories*, Dutton, 1968; Noel Streatfeild, *Thursday's Child* (Junior Literary Guild selection), Collins, 1970, Random House, 1971; Jane Gardam, *A Few Fair Days*, Hamilton, 1971, Macmillan, 1972.

BIOGRAPHICAL/CRITICAL SOURCES: Peggy Fortnum, *Running Wild*, Chatto & Windus, 1975.*

O

OAK, Liston M. 1895-1970

OBITUARY NOTICE: Born in 1895; died February 6, 1970, in Tel Aviv, Israel. Journalist and editor best known for his association with the *New Leader*. Oak was a political activist of the American left wing who became disenchanted with Soviet communism after his participation in the Spanish civil war in the 1930's. Obituaries and other sources: *New York Times*, February 9, 1970; *AB Bookman's Weekly*, March 2, 1970.

* * *

OAKLEY, Barry K(ingham) 1931-

PERSONAL: Born February 24, 1931, in Melbourne, Australia; married Carmel Hart; children: four sons, two daughters. *Education:* University of Melbourne, received B.A. *Home:* 12 Francis St., Richmond 3121, Victoria, Australia.

CAREER: High school teacher, 1955-62; Royal Melbourne Technical Institute, Melbourne, Australia, lecturer in humanities, 1963; worked as copywriter for advertising agencies, 1964-65; Australian Department of Trade and Industry, writer, 1966—. *Member:* Australian Society of Authors. *Awards, honors:* Captain Cook Bicentenary Award, 1970.

WRITINGS—Novels, except as noted: *A Wild Ass of a Man*, F. W. Cheshire, 1967; *A Salute to the Great McCarthy*, Heinemann, 1970; *Let's Hear It for Prendergast*, Heinemann, 1970; *How They Caught Kevin Farrelly*, illustrations by Barbara Day, Cassell, 1973; *Walking Through Tigerland* (stories), University of Queensland Press, 1978.

Plays: *A Lesson in English* (first produced in Melbourne, Australia, 1967), Eyre Methuen, 1976; "Witzenhausen, Where Are You?," first produced in Melbourne, 1967; "It's a Chocolate World," first produced in Melbourne, 1968; *The Feet of Daniel Mannix* (musical; first produced in Melbourne, 1970), Angus & Robertson, 1975; "Beware of Imitations," first produced in Melbourne, 1972; *Bedfellows* (first produced in Melbourne, 1975), Currency, 1975; *The Great God Mogadon and Other Plays*, University of Queensland Press, 1980.

Contributor to periodicals, including *Meanjin Quarterly*, *Quadrant*, *Australian Letters*, *Southerly*, *Vital Decade*.

SIDELIGHTS: Oakley is an Australian novelist and playwright whose writing deals mainly with life in his native land. Gary Davenport of *Hudson Review* noted that "the characters in Barry Oakley's stories are sometimes neurotically conscious of their nationality. . . . But admittedly many of these stories could take place anywhere, and almost never are they doctrinaire about national or any other matters." He added that the stories in *Walking Through Tigerland* "are most noteworthy for their style and their comedy."

BIOGRAPHICAL/CRITICAL SOURCES: Times Literary Supplement, April 23, 1971; *Hudson Review*, spring, 1979.*

* * *

OBELE, Norma Taylor 1933-

PERSONAL: Surname is pronounced *Oh*-bell-ee; born July 27, 1933, in Sugar City, Colo.; daughter of Evan Nolen and Bessie Leona (Bunker) Taylor; married Daniel Joseph Obele (in chemical sales), February 14, 1953; children: Debra Kathleen Obele MacMurdo, Mark Edward, Matthew Nolen. *Education:* Attended Colorado College, 1951-53. *Home and office:* 5302 East Flower, Phoenix, Ariz. 85018.

CAREER: Neonatology Associates Ltd., Phoenix, Ariz., business manager, 1967—.

WRITINGS: (With Harold E. McNeely) *Psychotherapy: The Private and Very Personal Viewpoints of Doctor and Patient*, Nelson-Hall, 1973.

SIDELIGHTS: Norma Obele wrote: "I have worked in medical fields for the past twenty-five years, first with general practitioners, ten years with psychologists, psychoanalysts, and psychiatrists, and the past thirteen years with men and women in the field of neonatology (care of premature and sick newborns)." *Avocational interests:* Interior design, antiques (primarily eighteenth-century furniture and Oriental porcelains, ivories, and temple pieces).

* * *

O'DONNELL, Lawrence
See MOORE, C(atherine) L(ucile)

* * *

O'DONNELL, Mark 1954-

PERSONAL: Born July 19, 1954, in Cleveland, Ohio; son of Hubert John (a welder) and Frances (Novak) O'Donnell. *Education:* Attended American Academy of Dramatic Art, 1971; Harvard University, B.A. (magna cum laude), 1976. *Home and office:* 202 Riverside Dr., New York, N.Y. 10025. *Agent:* Gil Parker, William Morris Agency, 1350 Avenue of the Americas, New York, N.Y. 10019.

CAREER: Esquire, New York, N.Y., member of research staff, 1977-78; writer, 1978—. *Awards, honors:* First place in *Dramatics*'s National Student Playwrights' Competition, 1972, for "Bricks"; Varsity Show Award from Broadcast Music, Inc., 1975, for "Keep Your Pantheon"; prize from Academy of American Poets, 1976, for eight poems; Rotary International fellowship for Ireland, 1976; Lecomte du Nouy Prize, 1980, for "Fables for Friends."

WRITINGS: (With Kurt Andersen and Roger Parloff) *Tools of Power: An Elitist Guide to the Ruthless Exploitation of Everything and Everybody,* Viking, 1980; (contributor) Charles Rubin and Jonathan Etya, editors, *Junk Food,* Dell, 1980; (contributor) Jeffrey Lant and Cynthia Cook, editors, *Our Harvard,* Taplinger, 1982.

Plays: "Do It Yourself" (two-act comedy), first produced in Cambridge, Mass., at Harvard Premiere Society, November, 1976; "Summer Work" (two-act), first produced in Cambridge at Harvard Premiere Society, November, 1977; "Caught in the Act" (two-act comedy), first produced in Charleston, S.C., at Spoleto Festival, June, 1978; "Fables for Friends" (two-act comedy), first produced in New York, N.Y., at Playwrights Horizons, June, 1980.

Contributor of poems and articles to periodicals, including *Canto, Ploughshares, Esquire, Saturday Review, Quest,* and *Oui.* Past editor of *Harvard Lampoon.*

WORK IN PROGRESS: Nature Made Natural, a book of essays expected in 1983; "People From Heaven," a play.

SIDELIGHTS: O'Donnell wrote: "I cherish Santayana's observation that life is simultaneously comic and tragic, an interplay that creates the lyrical."

*   *   *

OGDEN, Schubert Miles   1928-

PERSONAL: Born March 2, 1928, in Cincinnati, Ohio; son of Edgar Carson and Neva Louetta (Glancy) Ogden; married Joyce Ellen Schwettman, August 26, 1950; children: Alan Scott, Andrew Merrick. *Education:* Ohio Wesleyan University, A.B., 1950; attended Johns Hopkins University, 1950-51; University of Chicago, B.D., 1954, Ph.D., 1958. *Home:* 7232 Hillwood Lane, Dallas, Tex. 75240. *Office:* Graduate Program in Religious Studies, Perkins School of Theology, Southern Methodist University, Dallas, Tex. 75275.

CAREER: Ordained United Methodist minister, 1958; Southern Methodist University, Dallas, Tex., instructor, 1956-58, assistant professor, 1958-61, associate professor, 1961-64, professor of theology, 1964-69; University of Chicago, Chicago, Ill., professor of theology, 1969-72; Southern Methodist University, professor of theology, 1972—, director of graduate program in religious studies, 1974—. Fulbright professor at University of Marburg, 1962-63; Merrick Lecturer at Ohio Wesleyan University, 1965; visiting fellow of Council of Humanities at Princeton University, 1977-78.

MEMBER: American Academy of Religion (president, 1976-77), American Philosophical Association, American Theological Society, Society for Values in Higher Education, Phi Beta Kappa, Omicron Delta Kappa, Phi Mu Alpha. *Awards, honors:* Susan Colver Rosenberger Award from University of Chicago, 1959; Guggenheim fellow, 1962-63; Litt.D. from Ohio Wesleyan University, 1965.

WRITINGS: (Editor, translator and author of introduction) *Existence and Faith: Shorter Writings of Rudolf Bultmann,* Meridian, 1960; *Christ Without Myth: A Study Based on the Theology of Rudolf Bultmann,* Harper, 1961; *The Reality of God and Other Essays,* Harper, 1966; *Theology in Crisis: A Colloquium on the Credibility of God,* Muskingum College, 1967; *Faith and Freedom: Toward a Theology of Liberation,* Abingdon, 1979.

Contributor: *The Future of Empirical Theology,* University of Chicago Press, 1969; *The Future of Philosophical Theology,* Westminster, 1971; *Language, Truth, and Meaning,* Gill & Macmillan, 1972; *God, Secularization, and History,* University of South Carolina Press, 1974; *Our Common History as Christians,* Oxford University Press, 1975. Also contributor to theology journals.

Member of editorial board of *Journal of Theology and the Church,* 1963—, *Journal of Religion,* 1972—, *Review of Books and Religion,* 1976—, and *Journal of the American Academy of Religion,* 1977—.

BIOGRAPHICAL/CRITICAL SOURCES: Time, May 25, 1962; *Encounter,* spring, 1967; *Times Literary Supplement,* May 11, 1967; *Christian Century,* May 16, 1979.*

*   *   *

O'GRADA, Sean
See O'GRADY, John (Patrick)

*   *   *

O'GRADY, John (Patrick)   1907-
(Nino Culotta, Sean O'Grada)

PERSONAL: Born October 9, 1907, in Sydney, Australia; son of John Edward and Margaret (Gleeson) O'Grady; married Lorna Schreiber, October 9, 1929; children: John Patrick, Denis James, Francis Joseph. *Education:* University of Sydney, Ph.C., 1928. *Home:* 68 Algernon St., Oatley, New South Wales 2223, Australia.

CAREER: Worked in pharmaceutical field as chemist, representative, owner of a pharmaceutical business, and Samoan Government pharmacist; construction worker, 1954-56; writer, 1959—. *Military service:* Australian Army, Medical Corps, 1942-50; became captain. *Member:* International P.E.N., Society of Authors (member of council), Sydney Journalists Club.

WRITINGS—Published by Ure Smith: *The Things They Do to You* (nonfiction), 1966; (with Douglass Baglin) *Ladies and Gentlemen,* 1966; *Gone Troppo,* 1968; *O'Grady Sez,* 1969; *So Sue Me!,* 1970; *No Kava for Johnny,* 1971; *Aussie Etiket; or, Doing Things the Aussie Way* (nonfiction), 1971; *It's Your Shout, Mate!: Aussie Pubs and Aussie Beers,* 1972; *Smoky Joe, the Fish Eater* (nonfiction), 1972; *Survival in the Doghouse,* 1973; *Autobiography,* 1977; *There Was a Kid* (nonfiction), 1977.

Under pseudonym Nino Culotta: *They're a Weird Mob* (novel), Ure Smith, 1957, Simon & Schuster, 1961; *Cop This Lot* (novel), Ure Smith, 1960; *Gone Fishin',* Ure Smith, 1962; *Aussie English: An Explanation of the Australian Idiom,* Tri-Ocean Books, 1965; *Gone Gougin': The Weird Mob in the Opal Fields,* Ure Smith, 1975.

Under name Sean O'Grada: *Are You Irish or Normal?* (nonfiction), Kaye & Ward, 1970.

BIOGRAPHICAL/CRITICAL SOURCES: John Hetherington, *Forty-Two Faces,* F. W. Cheshire, 1962.*

O'GRADY, Standish James   1846-1928

BRIEF ENTRY: Born September 18, 1846, in Castletown Berehaven, Ireland; died May 18, 1928, in Shanklin, Isle of Wight. Irish historian. By using Irish legends as a basis for his own literature, O'Grady broke ground for writers of the Celtic revival. He also encouraged young writers through his weekly periodical, *All-Ireland Review.* His two-volume *History of Ireland* (1878-80) retold the country's ancient heroic legends, presenting them as real historical events. Though some critics objected to the Victorian moral overtones he added to tales of antiquity that were essentially amoral, O'Grady's history was praised as a fine expression of the scholarly imagination. O'Grady was not fluent in the Irish language, yet his aim was to revive public interest in old Irish literature and Ireland's heroic past. To attract the general reader he turned to the form of the historical novel, or adventure story, writing about such epic characters as Cu Cuchulainn. Since O'Grady was more adept at journalism than fiction writing, critics felt the value of his novels lay almost exclusively in their historical background; but O'Grady's later fiction, including *The Flight of the Eagle* (1897), drew a more positive critical response. *Biographical/critical sources: Twentieth Century Authors: A Biographical Dictionary of Modern Literature,* H. W. Wilson, 1st supplement, 1955.

* * *

OHLIN, Lloyd E(dgar)   1918-

PERSONAL: Born August 27, 1918, in Belmont, Mass.; son of Emil (a bakery owner) and Elise (Nelson) Ohlin; married Helen Barbara Hunter, January 27, 1946; children: Janet, George, Robert, Nancy. *Education:* Brown University, A.B., 1940; Indiana University, M.A., 1942; University of Chicago, Ph.D., 1954. *Politics:* Democrat. *Home:* 9 Red Coat Lane, Lexington, Mass. 02173. *Office:* School of Law, Harvard University, Cambridge, Mass. 02138.

CAREER: Indiana University, Bloomington, instructor in sociology, 1941-42; Illinois Parole and Pardon Board, sociologist and actuary in Joliet, 1947-50, supervising research sociologist in Chicago, 1950-53; University of Chicago, Chicago, Ill., director of Center for Education and Research in Corrections, 1953-56; Columbia University, New York, N.Y., professor of sociology, 1956-67, director of Research Center, 1962-66; Harvard University, Cambridge, Mass., Roscoe Pound Professor of Criminology, 1967—. Investigator of Korean prisoner-of-war camps for Human Resources Research Office, at George Washington University, 1953; special assistant to secretary for juvenile delinquency, Office of the Secretary of U.S. Department of Health, Education, and Welfare, 1961-62; member of research council of Division of Youth of the State of New York, 1963-65; associate director of President's Commission on Law Enforcement and Administration of Justice, 1966-67; chairman of advisory board of Massachusetts Department of Youth Services, 1970-72, and National Institute of Law Enforcement and Criminal Justice, 1978—. Chairman of Social Science Research Council committee on sociocultural contexts of delinquency, 1959-60; consultant to Ford Foundation, National Institute of Mental Health, and American Bar Foundation. *Military service:* U.S. Army, Counterintelligence Corps, 1942-45; served in Europe; became technical sergeant. *Member:* American Sociological Association (chairman of criminology section, 1962-63), Council on Social Work Administration, National Council on Crime and Delinquency (member of council, 1959—), Phi Beta Kappa.

WRITINGS: Selection for Parole: A Manual of Parole Prediction, Russell Sage, 1951; *Sociology and the Field of Corrections,* Russell Sage, 1956; (with Richard A. Cloward) *Delinquency and Opportunity: A Theory of Delinquent Gangs,* Free Press, 1960; (editor) *Combating Crime,* American Academy of Political and Social Science, 1967.

(Editor) *Prisoners in America: Perspectives on Our Correctional System,* Prentice-Hall, 1973; (with Alden D. Miller and Robert B. Coates) *Juvenile Correctional Reform in Massachusetts: A Preliminary Report of the Center for Criminal Justice of the Harvard Law School,* U.S. Government Printing Office, 1977; (with Miller) *A Theory of Social Reform,* Ballinger, 1977; (with Coates) *Diversity in a Youth Correctional System,* Ballinger, 1978; (with Coates) *Reforming Youth Corrections: The Massachusetts Experience in the Nineteenth and Twentieth Centuries,* Ballinger, 1980. Contributor to newspapers.

BIOGRAPHICAL/CRITICAL SOURCES: New York Post, June 9, 1961; *New York Times,* August 16, 1962.*

* * *

OLIVEIRA, Antonio Ramos
See RAMOS-OLIVEIRA, Antonio

* * *

OLSCAMP, Paul James   1937-

PERSONAL: Born August 29, 1937, in Montreal, Quebec, Canada; son of James J. and Luella M. (Brush) Olscamp; married, 1958 (marriage ended); married Ruth I. Pratt, December 2, 1978; children: (first marriage) Rebecca Ann, Adam James. *Education:* University of Western Ontario, B.A., 1958, M.A., 1960; University of Rochester, Ph.D., 1962. *Office:* Western Washington University, 516 High St., Bellingham, Wash. 98225.

CAREER: Ohio State University, Columbus, instructor, 1962, assistant professor, 1963-66, associate professor of humanities, 1966-69; Roosevelt University, Chicago, Ill., professor of philosophy and dean of faculty, 1970-71, vice-president for academic affairs, 1971-72; Syracuse University, Syracuse, N.Y., professor of philosophy, 1972-75, executive assistant to chancellor, 1972, vice-chancellor of student programs, 1972-75; Western Washington University, Bellingham, president, 1975—. Member of board of directors of Adult Education Council of Greater Chicago, 1971-72. *Member:* American Philosophical Association. *Awards, honors:* Danforth associate, 1966—; Alfred J. Wright Award from Ohio State University, 1970.

WRITINGS: (Translator) Rene Descartes, *Discourse on Method, Optics, Geometry, and Meteorology,* Bobbs-Merrill, 1965; *The Moral Philosophy of George Berkeley,* Nijhoff, 1970; *An Introduction to Philosophy,* Ronald, 1971; (editor with Thomas M. Lennon) *The Search After Truth and Elucidations of the Search After Truth,* Ohio State University Press, 1980. Contributor to philosophy and aesthetics journals.*

* * *

OLSCHKI, G. Cesare   1890-1971

OBITUARY NOTICE: Born February 24, 1890, in Verona, Italy; died December 23, 1971, in Pisa, Italy. Book dealer, scholar, and publisher best known for discovering and publishing the critical edition of the diary of Machiavelli's father in 1954. Along with his brother, Aldo, Olschki directed his father's firm, Libreria Leo S. Olschki, during the 1920's and

1930's, and rebuilt the firm in the wake of World War II. Obituaries and other sources: *AB Bookman's Weekly*, October 6, 1980.

*   *   *

O'NEILL, Michael J.

PERSONAL: Born in England. *Education:* Attended Cambridge University. *Agent:* Clive Goodwin, 79 Cromwell Rd., London S.W.7, England.

CAREER: Teacher and writer.

WRITINGS: Lennox Robinson, Twayne, 1964; (editor with Robert Hogan) *Joseph Holloway's Abbey Theatre: A Selection From His Unpublished Journal, "Impressions of a Dublin Playgoer,"* Southern Illinois University Press, 1967; (editor) Holloway, *Joseph Holloway's Irish Theatre,* Proscenium Press, 1968; *The Ever Birds of Space,* Excello & Bollard, 1977.

Co-author of stage plays: "Life Price," first produced in London, England, 1969; "Morality," first produced in London, 1971; "Millenium," first produced in London, 1973; "Our Sort of People," first produced in London, 1974; "Sex and Kinship in a Savage Society," first produced in London, 1975.

Radio and television plays: "A Clear Cut Case," first broadcast in 1973; "Soap Opera in Stockwell," first broadcast in 1973; "The Bosom of the Family," first broadcast in 1975; "Children of the Sun," first broadcast in 1975; "Beyond the Call of Duty," first broadcast in 1976. Also author of "A State of Welfare."*

*   *   *

ORAM, Malcolm   1944(?)-1976

OBITUARY NOTICE: Born c. 1944; died June 29, 1976, in Buckinghamshire, England. Journalist and editor best known for his work as London correspondent for *Publishers Weekly*. Obituaries and other sources: *Publishers Weekly,* July 12, 1976.

*   *   *

O'RAND, Angela M(etropulos)   1945-

PERSONAL: Born August 6, 1945, in Chicago, Ill.; daughter of William Chris and Mary (Demos) Metropulos; married Michael Gene O'Rand (a professor of anatomy), June 18, 1967; children: Christopher J. M. *Education:* University of the Pacific, B.A. (with honors), 1967; University of Oregon, M.A. (with honors), 1969; Temple University, Ph.D., 1974. *Home:* 621 Caswell Rd., Chapel Hill, N.C. 27514. *Office:* Department of Sociology, Duke University, Durham, N.C. 27706.

CAREER: Temple University, Philadelphia, Pa., instructor in sociology, 1969-70; Institute for Survey Research, Philadelphia, coding supervisor, 1970; Florida Atlantic University, Boca Raton, assistant professor of sociology and social psychology, 1974-76; University of Florida, Gainesville, assistant research professor of sociology and graduate program coordinator at Center for Gerontological Studies, 1976-79; Duke University, Durham, N.C., assistant professor of sociology, 1979—.

MEMBER: American Sociological Association, Gerontological Society, Southern Sociological Society, Phi Kappa Phi, Mortar Board. *Awards, honors:* Award from Alpha Lambda Delta; grants from National Institutes of Health, 1977, 1979-80, Administration on Aging, 1977-78, State of Florida Program Office on Aging and Adult Services, 1976-79, and Social Security Administration, 1978-79.

WRITINGS: (With C. C. Osterbind) *Older People in Florida: A Statistical Abstract, 1978,* University Presses of Florida, 1979; (contributor) D. J. Mangen and W. A. Peterson, editors, *Research Instruments in Social Gerontology,* University of Minnesota Press, 1980; (contributor) C. L. Fry, editor, *Anthropological Dimensions of Aging,* Bergin Publishers, 1980. Contributor of articles and reviews to journals in the social sciences. Associate editor of *Journal of Marriage and the Family,* 1978—.

WORK IN PROGRESS: The Retirement Patterns of Older Women; Comparative Scientific Systems.

*   *   *

ORCZY, Emma Magdalena Rosalia Maria Josefa
   Barbara   1865-1947
   (Emmuska Orczy)

BRIEF ENTRY: Born September 23, 1865, in Tarna-Ors, Hungary; died November 12, 1947, in London, England. British artist and author. The Baroness Orczy wrote dozens of romantic novels, plays, and short stories, but the best-remembered is undoubtedly *The Scarlet Pimpernel* (1905), which was a huge success on stage in 1903 and was eventually made into a feature film. The adventures of Sir Percy Blakeny during the French Revolution have continued to entertain readers ever since *The Scarlet Pimpernel* and its sequels were published. Orczy also wrote detective stories during the time that public attention was focused on that genre through Sherlock Holmes. Orczy created "the old man in the corner," one of the first "armchair" detectives, in stories collected in *The Case of Miss Elliott* (1905). In another short story collection, *Lady Molly of Scotland Yard* (1910), Orczy experimented with the character of a woman detective. Her work forms an important background to the modern detective story. *Biographical/critical sources: Twentieth Century Authors: A Biographical Dictionary of Modern Literature,* H. W. Wilson, 1942.

*   *   *

ORCZY, Emmuska
   See ORCZY, Emma Magdalena Rosalia Maria
   Josefa Barbara

*   *   *

ORENGO, Charles   1913(?)-1974

OBITUARY NOTICE: Born c. 1913; died after a long illness, December 12, 1974. Editor and publisher. The internationally known French publisher was the founder of the publishing firm Editions du Rocher in Monaco and later became chief editor at Librarie Plon. After a period at Hachette publishers, Orengo reorganized Editions Fayard and turned it into one of the most respected international publishing firms. Obituaries and other sources: *Publishers Weekly,* January 13, 1975.

*   *   *

ORNIS
   See WINCHESTER, Clarence

*   *   *

ORPEN, Eve   1926(?)-1978

OBITUARY NOTICE: Born c. 1926 in Vienna, Austria; died November 13, 1978. Co-founder of the publishing firm Lester and Orpen. Orpen also worked for General Publishing Co. and

Collier Macmillan. Obituaries and other sources: *Publishers Weekly*, December 4, 1978.

*   *   *

ORTHWINE, Rudolf   1900(?)-1970

OBITUARY NOTICE: Born c. 1900; died July 13, 1970, in New York, N.Y. Printer, publisher, and author. Orthwine was the publisher of *Dance* magazine and the author of his memoirs, *Wild Grass*. Obituaries and other sources: *The Biographical Encyclopaedia and Who's Who of the American Theatre*, James Heineman, 1966; *New York Times*, July 15, 1970; *AB Bookman's Weekly*, September 21, 1970.

*   *   *

ORWELL, George
See BLAIR, Eric Hugh

*   *   *

OSBORN, Albert D.   1896(?)-1972

OBITUARY NOTICE: Born c. 1986; died October 27, 1972. Graphologist and author best known as the key handwriting expert to testify in the Lindbergh kidnapping case. Osborn was the co-author of *Questioned Document Problems*. Obituaries and other sources: *AB Bookman's Weekly*, November 13, 1972.

*   *   *

OSBORN, Percy George   1899(?)-1972

OBITUARY NOTICE: Born c. 1899; died February 28, 1972 in England. Legal historian and author best known for the authoritative *Concise Law Dictionary*. Obituaries and other sources: *AB Bookman's Weekly*, May 15, 1972.

*   *   *

OSWALD, J(oseph) Gregory   1922-

PERSONAL: Born March 18, 1922, in Chicago, Ill.; son of Gregory Thomas (a railroad engineer) and Mary Magdalen (Toman) Oswald; married Audrey Marie Prolo, September, 1949 (divorced, 1960); married Norma Manol Flores (an art teacher), April 27, 1975; children: (first marriage) Melanie Marie, Gregory John, Marc Wayne. *Education:* Attended University of Illinois, 1941-43; University of California, Berkeley, B.A., 1948; Loyola University, Chicago, Ill., M.A., 1950; Stanford University, Ph.D., 1958. *Politics:* Democrat. *Religion:* Roman Catholic. *Home:* 1121 West Camino Desierto, Tucson, Ariz. 85704. *Office:* Department of History, University of Arizona, Tucson, Ariz. 85721.

CAREER: Stanford University, Stanford, Calif., instructor in history, 1955-58; University of Arizona, Tucson, assistant professor, 1958-63, associate professor, 1963-67, professor of history, 1967—. Visiting professor at University of Oklahoma, 1967-68, and Institute for the Study of the U.S.S.R., Munich, West Germany, 1968; consultant to Hispanic Foundation, Library of Congress. *Military service:* U.S. Army, Military Intelligence, Russian interpreter for General Patton and at Dachau concentration camp trial, 1943-47, commander of interrogation team, 1950-52; served in Germany and Korea; became first lieutenant; received battle star.

MEMBER: American Historical Association, American Association for the Advancement of Slavic Studies, Latin American Studies Association, Conference on Slavic and East Eu-
ropean History, Western Slavic Association, Tucson Civitan Club (president, 1980-81), Knights of Columbus, Society of St. Vincent de Paul. *Awards, honors:* Mershon fellow at Ohio State University, 1962-63; Ford Foundation grant, 1964-66.

WRITINGS: (Editor and translator) *The Soviet Image of Contemporary Latin America: A Documentary History, 1960-1968*, University of Texas Press, 1970; (editor with Anthony Stover) *The Soviet Union and Latin America*, Praeger, 1970; (contributor) *The Communist Tide in Latin America*, University of Texas Press, 1972. Contributor to *Foreign Relations of the Soviet Union*, edited by Thomas Hammond, and to history and international studies journals.

WORK IN PROGRESS: Understanding the History of World War II Thirty-Five Years Later.

SIDELIGHTS: Oswald wrote: "My World War II experiences convinced me to become a historian of twentieth-century affairs. My love of university students and the campus spirit motivate me constantly. I consider the U.S.S.R. as a political continuum of the past thousand years which shall become even more humanized in the twenty-first century, and I appreciate it as a nation whose people I love as I do my own Slovak ancestors."

AVOCATIONAL INTERESTS: International travel.

*   *   *

OWEN, Guy (Jr.)   1925-1981

OBITUARY NOTICE—See index for *CA* sketch: Born February 24, 1925, in Clarkton, N.C.; died of liver cancer, c. July 23, 1981, in Raleigh, N.C. Educator, editor, poet, novelist, and author. Owen taught at several schools, including Davidson College, Elon College, and Stetson University before moving to North Carolina State University at Raleigh, where he taught for nearly twenty years. Owen was best known for his novel *The Ballad of the Flim-Flam Man*, the story of an enterprising con artist. The author of collections of verse such as *Cape Fear Country and Other Poems* and *The White Stallion and Other Poems*, Owen was the founder and editor of the *Southern Poetry Review* (formerly entitled *Impetus*). He also edited the anthologies *Essays in Modern American Literature, New Southern Poets*, and *Contemporary Poetry of North Carolina*. Obituaries and other sources: *New York Times*, July 25, 1981; *Washington Post*, July 25, 1981; *AB Bookman's Weekly*, October 19, 1981.

*   *   *

OWEN, Oliver S.   1920-

PERSONAL: Born June 14, 1920, in Watertown, Wis.; son of Ernest S. (a pharmacist) and Hattie (a music teacher; maiden name, Fels) Owen; married Carol Elizabeth Lundberg (a social worker), June 13, 1964; children: Tom, Timothy, Stephanie. *Education:* University of Wisconsin, Madison, B.A., 1946, M.A., 1948; Cornell University, Ph.D., 1950. *Politics:* Democrat. *Religion:* Lutheran. *Home:* 3718 Rimridge Rd., Eau Claire, Wis. 54701. *Office:* Department of Biology, University of Wisconsin—Eau Claire, Eau Claire, Wis. 54701.

CAREER: University of Notre Dame, Notre Dame, Ind., instructor in ornithology, 1956-58; Mankato State College, Mankato, Minn., instructor in zoology, 1958-63; University of Minnesota, Minneapolis, instructor in conservation, 1963-67; University of Wisconsin—Eau Claire, instructor in conservation and ornithology, 1967—. *Military service:* U.S. Army, 1943-45; became technical sergeant; received Bronze Battle

Star. *Member:* Wilson Ornithological Society, Wisconsin Society for Ornithology.

WRITINGS: Natural Resource Conservation: An Ecological Approach, Macmillan, 1971, 3rd edition, 1980.

SIDELIGHTS: Owen commented: "My deep concern about the environmental degradation that is occurring not only in the United States but in the world as a whole, was the one overriding factor which prompted me to write *Natural Resource Conservation.* Currently I derive great satisfaction from teaching conservation and ornithology."

AVOCATIONAL INTERESTS: Hiking, fishing, attending concerts, lectures, plays, and athletic events.

*　　*　　*

OWEN, Wilfred   1893-1918

BRIEF ENTRY: Born March 18, 1893, in Oswestry, Shropshire, England; killed in World War I action, November 4, 1918, at Sambre Canal, France. English poet. After attending school in Liverpool, Owen worked as a tutor in France from 1913 to 1915, when he joined the British Army. He served in a rifle company for seven months until he was invalided to a war hospital in Scotland. There he was encouraged to write by his fellow-patient, poet Siegfried Sassoon. Unable to secure a post in England following his convalescence, Owen returned to France as a company commander during World War I and was later awarded the Military Cross for gallantry under fire. His poems, including "Strange Meeting" and "Anthem for Doomed Youth," portray the horrors of war with angered pity. Owen was killed by enemy gunfire while leading his troops across the Sambre Canal only a week before the Armistice. *Poems,* collected and published by Sassoon in 1920, had a great influence on such English poets as W. H. Auden and Stephen Spender. *Biographical/critical sources: Twentieth Century Authors: A Biographical Dictionary of Modern Literature,* H. W. Wilson, 1942; *The Concise Encyclopedia of Modern World Literature,* Hutchinson, 1963; *Twentieth Century Writing: A Reader's Guide to Contemporary Literature,* Transatlantic, 1969; *Longman Companion to Twentieth Century Literature,* Longman, 1970; *Who's Who in Twentieth Century Literature,* Holt, 1976.

P

PADGETT, Desmond
See von BLOCK, Bela W(illiam)

*   *   *

PADGETT, Lewis
See MOORE, C(atherine) L(ucile)

*   *   *

PAFFORD, John Henry Pyle   1900-

PERSONAL: Born March 6, 1900, in Bradford-on-Avon, England; son of John and Bessie (Pyle) Pafford; married Elizabeth R. Ford, May 29, 1941; children: Katharine Pafford Ford. *Education:* Attended University College, London. *Home:* Hillside, Allington Park, Bridgport, Dorsetshire DT6 5DD, England.

CAREER: Writer. University College, London, England, library assistant, 1923-25; Selly Oak Colleges, Birmingham, England, librarian and tutor, 1925-31; National Central Library, London, sub-librarian, 1931-45; University of London, London, lecturer at School of Librarianship, 1937-61, Goldsmiths' Librarian, 1945-67; *Somerset and Dorset Notes and Queries,* England, Dorset editor, 1971—. Library advisor to Inter-University Council for Higher Education Overseas, 1960-68. Fellow of University College, London. *Wartime service:* Served in War Office in Book and Libraries for Army Education, 1944-45.

WRITINGS: Library Cooperation in Europe, Library Association (London), 1935; (editor) *Accounts of the Parliamentary Garrisons of Great Chalfield and Malmesbury, 1845-1946,* [England], 1940, Devizes, 1966; *American and Canadian Libraries: Some Notes on a Visit in the Summer of 1947,* Library Association (London), 1949; *W. P. Ker, 1855-1923: A Bibliography,* University of London Press, 1950; (editor) Anthony Munday, *Chrusothriambos: The Triumphs of Gold,* [London], 1962; (editor) William Shakespeare, *The Winter's Tale,* Harvard University Press, 1963; (editor) Isaac Watts, *Divine Songs Attempted in Easy Language for the Use of Children,* Oxford University Press, 1971; (editor and author of introduction) *Literary Works of Lodowick Bryskett: A Discourse of "Civill Life," "The Mourning Muse of Thestylis," [and] "A Pastorall Aeglogue Upon the Death of Sir Phillip Sydney Knight"; With John Milton's "Lycidas,"* Farnborough, Gregg, 1972; (with wife, Elizabeth R. Pafford) *Employer and Employed: Ford*

Ayrton & Co. Ltd., Silk Spinners With Worker Participation, Leeds and Low Bentham, 1870-1970, Pasold Research Fund, 1974.

BIOGRAPHICAL/CRITICAL SOURCES: A. T. Milne, *Librarianship and Literature: Essays in Honour of Jack Pafford,* Athlone Press, 1970.

*   *   *

PAGET, Violet   1856-1935
   (Vernon Lee)

BRIEF ENTRY: Born October 14, 1856, in Boulogne-sur-Mer, France; died February 13, 1935, in San Gervasio, Italy. British novelist and essayist. Writing as Vernon Lee, Violet Paget presented her English-speaking readers with one of the first comprehensive views of Italy and Italian culture. Her first book, *Studies in the Eighteenth Century in Italy* (1880), was admired in Italy as well as England for its intelligent and imaginative treatment of its topic. Also popular were her essays, including *Euphorion* (1884), and the writings based on her extensive European travels, such as *Genius Loci* (1899). Later Paget wrote fiction and drama, and she expressed her belief in pacifism in the allegorical play "Satan the Waster" (1920). The unpopularity of her pacifism, coupled with the arrogance she sometimes expressed, caused her readership to decline. Her other writings include *Ariadne in Mantua* (1903), *Gospels of Anarchy* (1908), and *Vital Lies* (1912). *Biographical/critical sources: Twentieth Century Authors: A Biographical Dictionary of Modern Literature,* H. W. Wilson, 1942; Vineta Colby, *The Singular Anomaly: Women Novelists of the Nineteenth Century,* New York University Press, 1970; *Quarterly Journal of Speech,* October, 1970.

*   *   *

PAGET-LOWE, Henry
See LOVECRAFT, H(oward) P(hillips)

*   *   *

PALYI, Melchior   1892(?)-1970

OBITUARY NOTICE: Born c. 1892; died July 29, 1970, in Chicago, Ill. Economist, columnist, and author of works in his field, including *Managed Money at the Crossroads: The European Experience* and *The Chicago Credit Market.* Obituaries and other sources: *AB Bookman's Weekly,* September 21, 1970.

*   *   *

PANAMA, Norman   1920-

PERSONAL: Born April 21, 1920, in Chicago, Ill.; son of Herman H. and Tessie (Nevins) Panama; married Marcia Engel (divorced, 1970); married Gloria Dobson (divorced, 1981); children: Steven, Kathleen Panama Brown. *Education:* University of Chicago, Ph.B., 1938. *Home and office:* 1721 Stone Canyon Rd., Los Angeles, Calif. 90024. *Agent:* Mitchell Kaplan, Kaplan-Stahler Agency, 119 South Beverly Dr., Beverly Hills, Calif. 90211.

CAREER: Writer, 1940—. Co-owner of Parkwood Productions; film producer and director; producer of Broadway version of "Li'l Abner," 1956. *Military service:* U.S. Army, writer for overseas radio program "Command Performance," 1942-45. *Member:* Dramatists Guild, Writers Guild of America (West), Directors Guild of America. *Awards, honors:* Nominations for Oscars from Academy of Motion Picture Arts and Sciences, 1946, for "Road to Utopia," 1948, for "Mr. Blandings Builds His Dream House," 1953, for "Above and Beyond," 1954, for "Knock on Wood," and 1960, for "The Facts of Life"; nominations for awards from Writers Guild of America, 1953, for "Above and Beyond," 1954, for "Knock on Wood," and 1960, for "Facts of Life."

WRITINGS: (With Larry Gelbart) *Not With My Wife You Don't!* (novelization of own screenplay), Warner Books, 1967; (with Albert E. Lewin) *I Will, I Will . . . for Now* (novelization of own screenplay), Warner Books, 1975; (with Lewin) *The Glass Bed* (novel), Morrow, 1980.

Feature films: (With Melvin Frank) "Knock on Wood," Paramount, 1954; (with Frank) "White Christmas," Paramount, 1955; (with Frank) "Court Jester," Paramount, 1956; "Li'l Abner" (based on own musical play), Paramount, 1958; "The Road to Hong Kong," United Artists, 1963; "Not With My Wife You Don't!," Warner Bros., 1966; "I Will, I Will . . . for Now," Twentieth-Century Fox, 1975.

Plays: (With Frank) "A Free Hand," 1954; "Li'l Abner," first produced on Broadway at Ethel Barrymore Theatre, October 1, 1981.

WORK IN PROGRESS: "The Bats of Portobello," a play with Jerome Chodorov; "The Glass Bed," a screenplay with Albert Lewin based on their novel; "The Divine Comedy," an original screenplay with Lary Levinson; "Hellfire!," an original screenplay with Victor Bullick.

SIDELIGHTS: Panama told *CA:* "Through a long and varied career as a writer for radio, the stage, then motion pictures, and then adding producing and directing to the above, I know that the *writing,* the root idea, the blank piece of paper, the writing and rewriting, and polishing and repolishing is the most important facet of creativity. Producing (at least in motion pictures and television) is just to hold the creative process together and stop too many cooks from spoiling the souffle. Directing is the most exacting and most fun, but all hard-nosed professionals know that first there has to be the word . . . and *another* word and *another* word.

"A word of caution: No matter what your friends, producers, directors, or other well-meaning fools mean by help and suggestions, *remember* the root idea . . . why you set out to write the piece in the first place. Don't ruin with improvements!"

PANDIT, Vijaya Lakshmi   1900-

PERSONAL: Born August 18, 1900, in Allahabad, India; daughter of Motilal (a lawyer) and Sarup (Rani) Nehru; married Ranjit Sitaram Pandit (a lawyer, classicist, and historian), May 10, 1921 (died, 1944); children: Chandralekha Mehta, Nayantara Sahgal, Rita Dar. *Education:* Educated privately. *Politics:* Indian National Congress. *Religion:* Hindu. *Home and office:* 181-B Rajpur Rd., Dehra Dun, Uttar Pradesh, India.

CAREER: Allahabad Municipal Board, Allahabad, India, member of board and chairman of education committee, 1934-36; minister in charge of portfolios of local self-government and public health, Uttar Pradesh Congress Cabinet, 1936-39, 1946-47; ambassador to the Soviet Union, 1947-49, ambassador to the United States and Mexico, 1949-52; member of Parliament of Independent India, 1953-54; high commissioner to Court of St. James in England and ambassador to Ireland and Spain, 1954-61; governor of Maharashtra, India, 1962-64; member of parliament, 1964-68; leader of Indian delegation to Human Rights Commission, 1978-79. Delegate to Pacific Relations Conference, 1944; leader of Indian delegation to the United Nations, 1946-51, 1963; member of Lok Sabha, 1952-54, 1964-68; president of General Assembly of United Nations, 1953-54; lecturer in the United States.

MEMBER: International Women's League for Peace and Freedom, All India Women's Conference. *Awards, honors:* Honorary doctorates from University of Allahabad, 1947, Wellesley College, New York University, Howard University, West Virginia State College, St. Louis University, and Lafayette University, all 1950, Oklahoma City University, 1951, University of Hawaii and Nagpur University, both 1954, University of London, 1955, University of Wales and University of Leeds, both 1956, McMaster University, 1957, and University of Edinburgh, 1960; D.C.L. from Oxford University, 1964; award from Beta Mu Lambda chapter of Alpha Phi Alpha, 1950; Robert S. Abbot Memorial Award, 1950; award from Bethune-Cookna College, 1951; One World Award, 1952; named Key Woman of the Year, 1954; woman of achievement award from American Federation of Soroptimist Clubs, 1956; appreciation award from city of Dayton, Ohio, 1957; Dorothes Schlozer Gold Medal from University of Goettingen, 1958; Padna Vibushan, 1962.

WRITINGS: So I Became a Minister, Kitabistan, 1939; *Prison Diary,* Signet Press, 1945; *The Evolution of India,* Oxford University Press, 1958; *The Scope of Happiness: A Personal Memoir,* Crown, 1979.

SIDELIGHTS: Vijaya Lakshmi Pandit was born of a wealthy family whose members were active loyalists of India; they devoted their lives to fighting for India's independence from British rule. Pandit's father, Motilal Nehru, was a political associate of Mahatma Gandhi and penned the Nehru report, detailing plans for dominion status for India. Her brother, Jawaharal Nehru, was India's first prime minister, serving from 1950 to 1966.

Like her brother, father, and husband, Pandit was imprisoned several times for participating in nationalist activities. But neither she nor her family ever resisted arrest; they were peaceful prisoners willing to sacrifice their lives of comfort and pleasure if the result would be India's release from British rule. They followed the rules of Gandhi, who said: "When you go, there must be no trace of anger or resentment. Remember it is a privilege to go. You cannot fight for truth with hatred in your hearts, your thoughts, or your actions." As a result of their stoic protests, the Nehru and Pandit families were greatly respected and revered by their many nationalist comrades.

In 1936 Vijaya Pandit became the first woman to be elected to India's legislative assembly and was appointed minister of local self-government and public health. As an official she set many precedents. While minister of public health, she personally toured epidemic-plagued villages, trying to help where needed and encouraging the local medics and the families of victims. Previously, one of the minister's subordinates went to observe disaster areas, but Pandit wanted to see firsthand the problems that needed to be resolved.

In her role as minister of local self-government, Pandit piloted the bill that gave villages the power of local administration. Though they had once been locally governed, self-government had been abolished after the British took control. Pandit, however, found the villagers to be happier and more cooperative under local leadership and thus restored self-rule.

Pandit was reelected to the legislature in 1946, and in 1947 she began a career as a diplomatic ambassador. Between 1947 and 1961, she was the Indian envoy to the United Nations, Soviet Union, United States, Mexico, England, Ireland, and Spain. She was the first female president of the General Assembly of the United Nations, serving from 1953 to 1954. Returning to India after her diplomatic journeys, Pandit was elected governor of Maharashtra before serving for four years in India's parliament.

During her many excursions to other nations, Pandit was lauded with several honorary degrees. While serving as the High Commissioner to England's Court of St. James, she received an honorary Doctor of Laws degree from the University of Edinburgh. In *Madame Ambassador* by Anne Guthrie, L. M. Walsh of Edinburgh's *Scotsman* is quoted: "Mrs. Pandit will go down in history as one of the greatest statesmen of our time. She has taken politics out of the market place into the hearts and conscience of men and women and she has done it without abating a jot of her patience, serenity, humour, and tolerance for the modern world. With the years her great personal beauty has seemed to deepen, as though her experiences of the worst and the best of human behaviour have served only to strengthen the inner flame."

Often called the "Lamp of India," Pandit illuminates her life in *The Scope of Happiness: A Personal Memoir.* This autobiography details Pandit's life in an affluent family and tells of their sacrifices of wealth and tranquility made in order to fully involve themselves in the nationalist movement. Critics have warmly accepted Pandit's story. Emily Hahn of the *New York Times Book Review* called it a "wise and fascinating book." An *Economist* reviewer wrote: "Mrs. Pandit's [book] . . . is an engrossing self-portrait of a magnanimous, even— if it may be said without misunderstanding—imperial figure."

BIOGRAPHICAL/CRITICAL SOURCES: Anne Guthrie, *Madame Ambassador: The Life of Vijaya Lakshmi Pandit,* Harcourt, 1962; Robert Hardy Andrews, *A Lamp for India: The Story of Madame Pandit,* Prentice-Hall, 1967; *New York Times Book Review,* August 19, 1979; *Economist,* September 29, 1979.

*   *   *

PARDIS, Marjorie B.   1886(?)-1970

OBITUARY NOTICE: Born c. 1886; died July 2, 1970, in New York, N.Y. Playwright and author. Pardis wrote the novel *This Side of Heaven.* Obituaries and other sources: *AB Bookman's Weekly,* September 7, 1970.

PARKER, Gail Thain   1943-

PERSONAL: Born February 8, 1943, in Chicago, Ill; daughter of Richard Jenness (a university administrator) and Jane (Noyes) Thain; married Thomas David Parker (a university administrator), June 9, 1964 (divorced, 1978); married Paul Wickes (an attorney); children: (first marriage) Julia Thain. *Education:* Radcliffe College, A.B., 1964; Harvard University, Ph.D., 1969. *Residence:* Burlington, Vt. *Office:* c/o Simon & Schuster, 1230 Avenue of the Americas, New York, N.Y. 10020.

CAREER: Harvard University, Cambridge, Mass., assistant professor of history and literature, 1969-72; Bennington College, Bennington, Vt., president, 1972-76; free-lance writer, beginning, 1976; director of Vermont Association for the Retarded. Trustee of Amherst College. *Member:* Phi Beta Kappa. *Awards, honors:* Woodrow Wilson fellow 1964-65; Charles Warren Center fellow, Rockefeller Foundation fellow, and Radcliffe Institute fellow, all 1972-73.

*WRITINGS—*Nonfiction: (Editor) *The Oven Birds: American Women on Womanhood, 1820-1920,* Doubleday, 1972; *Mind Cure in New England: From the Civil War to World War I,* University Press of New England, 1973; (with Gene R. Hawes) *College on Your Own: How You Can Get a College Education at Home,* Bantam, 1978; *The Writing on the Wall: Inside Higher Education in America,* Simon & Schuster, 1979.

SIDELIGHTS: Parker became the youngest college president in the nation in 1972 when prestigious Bennington College selected her as its chief administrative officer. Parker's appointment was reported in newspapers and periodicals across the country. According to Nora Ephron of *Esquire,* this publicity was largely due to Parker's youth, her sex, and her husband's willingness to work for her as vice-president. Three years later Parker received even more publicity when her involvement in a bitter row with the Bennington faculty ended with her forced resignation.

Although Parker began her administration amicably, she soon became impatient with tedious, nonproductive faculty meetings. Faculty members, in turn, grew irritated with what Parker called her "tough managerial style." Resentment erupted into hostility in 1975 when Parker presented a set of proposals for improving Bennington's financial status and educational program to the school's board of trustees. The faculty was outraged by Parker's proposals to increase tuition fees, to require students to pursue advanced study in at least two disciplines, and to eliminate the school's presumptive tenure system under which a faculty member is presumed to have attained permanent employment status merely by remaining on the teaching staff for five years. Angry faculty members unanimously agreed that they would no longer work with Parker. The board of trustees at first supported Parker but ultimately requested her resignation when it became clear that without faculty cooperation she would be unable to function effectively as Bennington's president. Parker told a *Time* reporter that she agreed to quit because "it wasn't worth it. I'm not willing to be abused unless I'm damned sure there will be some real gain."

Parker later insisted that her proposals had been "reasonable" and had contained nothing "inflammatory." A *Newsweek* reporter suggested that the Bennington faculty may have become incensed by Parker's proposed reforms out of concern that the proposals would affect their job security.

In *The Writing on the Wall* Parker indicates that her own concern is for the entire collegiate system, which she concludes is in a chaotic state brought about by unfavorable economic factors, inadequate curriculums, and the declining marketability of the liberal arts degree. In addition, she also accuses inflexible professors of contributing to the chaos in higher education by preventing administrators from establishing new programs to deal with these problems.

The Writing on the Wall contains a number of suggestions for alleviating the collegiate crisis that are similar to the proposals Parker presented to the Bennington trustees; most notable are those to eliminate B.A. degrees and faculty tenure systems.

Several reviewers criticized Parker's "vituperative style" and her "jibes at the faculty," yet they praised her proposals for improving the condition of higher education. Megan Marshall of *New Republic,* for example, commended Parker's proposed elimination of the tenure system which would, said Marshall, result in more competition for faculty posts thereby assuring "more lively professors." *New York Times Book Review* critic Joseph Featherstone was impressed with Parker's suggestion that colleges and universities abolish their degree programs and focus instead on adult education as a means to "real intellectual development."

Parker acknowledged that some people believe her to be a "fundamentally hostile person," but she contended that she is, in reality, a disappointed idealist who feels an "obligation to bring disciplined habits of mind to the consideration of all questions."

BIOGRAPHICAL/CRITICAL SOURCES: New York Times, June 17, 1972; *Saturday Review,* August 12, 1972; *New England Quarterly,* December, 1973; *Time,* December 15, 1975, February 23, 1976, August 30, 1976; *Newsweek,* December 15, 1975, May 26, 1980; *Esquire,* September, 1976; *Atlantic,* September, 1976, January, 1980; *Washington Post Book World,* January 6, 1980; *New Republic,* February 2, 1980; *New York Times Book Review,* February 3, 1980; *Los Angeles Times,* March 11, 1980.*

* * *

PARKER, H(enry) M(ichael) D(enne)   1896(?)-1971

OBITUARY NOTICE: Born c. 1896; died December 2, 1971, in London, England. Educator, historian, and author best known for his writings on ancient Rome, including *The Roman Legions.* Parker was a professor of ancient history at Oxford University and was active in academic and civil politics. Obituaries and other sources: *AB Bookman's Weekly,* January 17, 1972.

* * *

PARKES, James William   1896-1981
(John Hadham)

OBITUARY NOTICE: Born December 22, 1896, in Guernsey, Channel Islands; died August 6, 1981. Theologian, scholar, and author best known for his attempts to reconcile Christianity and Judaism as mutually complimentary religions. Parkes became an outspoken opponent of anti-Semitism while working with the International Student Service in Geneva, Switzerland, during the 1930's. Parkes's efforts to aid Jewish students led to an attempt on his life by Fascists. After World War II Parkes devoted his time to scholarly study and writing such books as *The Foundations of Judaism and Christianity.* Parkes also wrote several books under the pseudonym John Hadham, including *Good God,* which achieved popular success while provoking critical comment from the theological community. Obituaries and other sources: *The Author's and Writer's Who's Who,* 6th edition, Burke's Peerage, 1971; *Who's Who,* 126th edition, St. Martin's, 1974; *London Times,* August 8, 1981.

PARKES, Terence   1927-
(Larry)

PERSONAL: Born in 1927 in Birmingham, England; married Jean Pauline Woodward; children: one son, one daughter. *Education:* Attended College of Arts and Crafts, Birmingham, England.

Home: 204 Marshall Lake Rd., Shirley, Solihull, Warwickshire, England.

CAREER: Teacher at secondary school, 1950-54; free-lance cartoonist, 1957—. *Member:* Cartoonists Club.

WRITINGS—Cartoon books; under pseudonym Larry: *Man in Apron and Others,* Museum Press, 1959; *More Man in Apron,* Museum Press, 1960; *Man in Office,* Museum Press, 1961; *Man at Large,* Stephen Greene, 1964; *Man and Wife,* Stephen Greene, 1965; *Man in Garden,* Museum Press, 1966; *Man's Best Friend,* Stephen Greene, 1966; *Large Economy Man,* Stephen Greene, 1967; *More Man in Garden; and, Man in Factory,* Museum Press, 1967; *The Larry Omnibus,* Museum Press, 1967; *Man in Motor Car,* Museum Press, 1968; *Man in Motion,* Stephen Greene, 1971; *Man in School,* Pitman, 1972; *Bumper Book of Boobs,* Deutsch, 1973; *Man on Holiday,* Pitman, 1974; *One Hundred Best Jokes of Larry,* Deutsch, 1974; *The Way the Money Goes: A Consumer's Handbook,* BBC Publications, 1978; *Larry's Art Collection,* A. P. Rushton, 1978.

Illustrator: Jerome Beatty, editor, *Double Take,* Stephen Greene, 1971; James Herriot, *Let Sleeping Vets Lie,* M. Joseph, 1973; Leonard Sutherland Powell, *Lecturing,* Pitman, 1973; *Sandy Molloy, The Dog's Guide to London,* Garnstone Press, 1973; Gerald Haigh, *The School and the Parent,* Pitman, 1975; Donald Kilbourn, *Pots and Pants: Man's Answer to Women's Lib, a Cookbook for Men,* Mitchell Beazley, 1975; Haigh, *Pastoral Care,* Pitman, 1975; Hamish Donaldson, *Computer by the Tail: A User's Guide to Computer Management,* Allen & Unwin, 1976; Herriot, *Vets Might Fly,* M. Joseph, 1976; Michael Hardwick, *The Jolly Toper,* I. Henry, 2nd edition, 1978; Eve Harlow, *One Hundred and One Instant Games,* Macdonald & Co., 1978.

Contributor to magazines, including *Punch, Spectator,* and *Holiday,* and newspapers.*

* * *

PARKIN, Molly   1932-

PERSONAL: Born in 1932 in England.

CAREER: Worked as fashion editor for *Nova, Harper's Bazaar,* and *Sunday Times* in London, England; currently free-lance writer.

WRITINGS—Novels: *Love—All,* Blond & Briggs, 1974, Nash Publishing, 1975; *Up Tight,* Blond & Briggs, 1975; *Full Up,* St. Martin's, 1976; *Write Up,* M. Joseph, 1977; *Good Golly Ms. Molly* (edited by Richard Barber), W. H. Allen, 1978; *Fast and Loose,* W. H. Allen, 1979; *Switchback,* Star Books, 1979; *Molly Parkin's Purple Passages,* Star Books, 1980.*

* * *

PARRISH, Stephen Maxfield   1921-

PERSONAL: Born June 11, 1921, in Minneapolis, Minn.; son of Wayland Maxfield and Blanche Greeta (Leigh) Parrish; married Jean Jacob, February 26, 1945 (divorced, September, 1969); married Priscilla Alden Kiefer Baker-Carr, December, 1969; children: (first marriage) Madeleine, Anne Leigh. *Education:* University of Illinois, A.B., 1942; Harvard University, M.A., 1947, Ph.D., 1954. *Politics:* Democrat. *Religion:* Society of Friends (Quakers). *Home:* 116 The Parkway, Ithaca, N.Y. 14850. *Office:* Department of English, Cornell University, Ithaca, N.Y. 14853.

CAREER: Cornell University, Ithaca, N.Y., 1954—, began as instructor, became assistant professor, then associate professor, professor of English, 1966—, associate dean of College of Arts and Sciences. Visiting professor at U.S. Military Academy, 1964. Regional chairman of Woodrow Wilson Fellowship Foundation, 1962-70. *Military service:* U.S. Naval Reserve, active duty, 1942-46, 1950-52; became captain. *Member:* Modern Language Association of America, Phi Beta Kappa. *Awards, honors:* Guggenheim fellow, 1959.

WRITINGS: (Editor with Hyder Edward Rollins) *Keats and the Bostonians: Amy Lowell, Louise Imogen Guiney, Louis Arthur Holman, and Fred Holland Day—Letters and Papers, 1889-1931,* Harvard University Press, 1951, reprinted, Russell, 1972; *A Concordance to the Poems of Matthew Arnold,* Cornell University Press, 1959; (with James A. Painter) *A Concordance to the Poems of W. B. Yeats,* Cornell University Press, 1963.

(Editor) Jane Austen, *Emma: An Authoritative Text, Backgrounds, Reviews, and Criticism,* Norton, 1972; *The Art of the Lyrical Ballads,* Harvard University Press, 1973; (editor with J. Allen Tyler) *A Concordance to the Fables and Tales of Jean De la Fontaine,* Cornell University Press, 1974; (editor with Demetrius J. Koubourlis) *A Concordance to the Poems of Osip Mandelstam,* Cornell University Press, 1974; (editor) William Wordsworth, *The Prelude, 1798-1799,* Cornell University Press, 1977. Also author of *Freud,* (with S. A. Guttman and Randall Jones,) 1980. General editor of "The Cornell Concordances" and "The Cornell Wordsworth," both Cornell University Press.

SIDELIGHTS: Parrish made a sound recording, "Sense and Sensibility," on the work by Jane Austen, released by Everett/Edwards in 1976.

BIOGRAPHICAL/CRITICAL SOURCES: Antiques, June, 1979.*

*   *   *

PARSONS, Jack 1920-

PERSONAL: Born December 6, 1920, in Greasely, England; son of Joseph (a coal miner) and Frances Dora (Bagguley) Parsons; married Barbara Jean Barker (an artist), April 4, 1960; children: Miranda, Gerard. *Education:* Attended University of Nottingham, 1950-51; University of Keele, B.A., 1955. *Politics:* "A sort of hard-headed ecological socialist." *Religion:* "Humanist." *Home:* Treferig Cottage Farm, Llantrisant, Pontyclun, Mid-Glamorganshire CF7 8LQ, Wales. *Office:* David Owen Centre for Population Growth Studies, University College, University of Wales, P.O. Box 78, Cardiff CF1 1XL, Wales.

CAREER: Worker and apprentice at mechanical engineering factories in and around Nottingham, England, 1934-41; Fairey Aviation Co., Hayes, England, trainee aero draftsman and designer, 1946; Caffin & Co. (civil engineers), London, England, laborer, foreman, trainee engineer, and site engineer and manager, 1946-48; J. B. Edwards (civil engineering contractors), London, England, site engineer in Wilton, 1948-49; farm worker, 1950; National Coal Board, London, England, sociological researcher, 1955-59; Brunel University, Uxbridge, England,

Nuffield Research Associate in department of management and production technology, 1959-61, lecturer in social institutions, 1961-74, founder of Environment Group, 1971; University of Wales, University College, Cardiff, senior lecturer in population studies and deputy director of David Owen Centre for Population Growth Studies, 1975—. Member of Liberal party's environment and economics panel, 1971-74; member of Independent Commission on Transport, 1973-74. Public speaker to educational, political, medical, and conservation groups, humanists, and women's organizations; broadcaster on radio and television, including "Woman's Hour," "Science Now," and "Newsbeat." *Military service:* Royal Air Force Volunteer Reserve, pilot, 1941-46; served in Rhodesia, Europe, and India; became warrant officer, first class. *Member:* British Society for Population Studies, Fertility Studies Group, Conservation Society (founding member; first honorary education officer; member of council and chairman of South Buckinghamshire branch, 1971-75), British Humanist Association, Fabian Society.

WRITINGS: Population Versus Liberty, Pemberton Books, 1971, Prometheus, 1973; (editor with Bishop Hugh Montefiore, and contributor) *Changing Directions,* Coronet Books, 1974; *The Economic Transition* (monograph), Conservation Trust, 1975; *Population Fallacies,* Elek, 1977.

Contributor: D. J. Stewart, editor, *Planners Versus People,* Pemberton Books, 1970; L. R. Taylor, editor, *The Optimum Population for Britain,* Academic Press, 1970; M. B. Hamilton and K. G. Robertson, editors, *Britain's Crisis in Sociological Perspective,* University of Reading Press, 1976; Nicholas Holmes, editor, *Environment and the Industrial Society,* Hodder & Stoughton, 1976; M. A. Elder and D. F. Hawkins, *Human Fertility Control: Theory and Practice,* Butterworth, 1979. Also contributor to *The Pollution of Our Environment,* John Burton, editor, 1971.

Author and director of "The Blackhill Campaign," a documentary film, released by British Film Institute, 1964. Contributor of articles, stories, and reviews to scholarly journals, popular magazines, and newspapers, including *New Statesman* and *Nation.*

WORK IN PROGRESS: A book on migration control, publication expected in 1983; research on competitive breeding, population control, and migration control, with emphasis on individual liberty, population optimization, application of the principle of "difference-control" in population theory, critical appraisal of the alleged rationality of high-fertility norms in conditions of abject poverty, and evolutionary survival strategies in the field of human sexuality and reproductive behavior.

SIDELIGHTS: Parsons told *CA:* "In my liberal studies days in the early 1960's, I developed a strong interest in the population/resources problem and began to feed some of the material into my teaching. I also became active as a publicist. Although my background is unorthodox and my approach distinctly idiosyncratic, I think I now have quite a good standing in this field and find it deeply satisfying to have the comradeship of scholars of the stature of Paul Ehrlich and Garrett Hardin.

"What I have increasingly struggled for is a deeper, more rational, and more humane appreciation of the place of human beings in society and society's place in the environment. My feeling is that the odds are heavily in favor of the extinction of our species, not because we are particularly unecological, let alone stupid or wicked, but because we are simply in the natural order of things. If we are to survive and evolve to a reasonably high and sustainable quality of life, then we have to really understand the dynamics of psychological, social, ethical, and ecological systems and use this knowledge in a sane fashion in order to 'invent' our own failure, and then reinvent and maintain it as long as the galaxy can sustain us.

"Paradoxically it seems possible that if we were to abandon all thought of controlling ourselves and the environment, we might stand a better chance of evolving into a survival-worthy state. But that would, of course, entail a vigorous rejection of health care, crime and pollution control, and many other unthinkables, and we might go on to wreck the environment anyway, and insure extinction by that means.

"My first solid attack on this series of interlocking problems was an attempt to legitimize the principle of population control in the eyes of intelligent, liberal-minded people; my second was to demolish the myth of continuous economic growth; my third, to foster a rational analysis of the population/resources balance-of-nature problem; my next is on the practice, rationales, and ethics of migration and migration control. All these, particularly the ongoing work, have led me even deeper into the complex and difficult area of the mechanisms, morality, and functionality of resource allocation and survival strategies.

"What I really would like to achieve is not a utopia (I don't believe in them), but a recognizable contribution toward a sane, more realistic, more peaceful, humane, permanent, and satisfying future. Perhaps even that is a utopian idea, but it seems a worthwhile goal to struggle for. If we don't struggle, the self-fulfilling prophecy mechanism takes over in the negative direction, and things tend to get worse instead of better.

"In pursuit of the mechanisms, morality, and functionality of resource allocation and survival strategies, I recently found myself espousing the pursuit of individual, group, and national self-interest. I have always valued altruism very highly and felt the necessity for a stronger moral code than we have in the West now that other-worldly religion has lost much of its binding force, and utopian socialism is another 'God that failed.' I still feel passionately against anti-social behavior and my problem is reconciling these seemingly irreconcilable positions. I want to see individuals and groups pursuing their self-interests with zest and clear conscience, but I also want most of us, most of the time, to accept and behave in accordance with what I have called a 'socio-centric' ethic.

"Dimly I see the beginnings of a reconciliation in distinguishing self-interested behavior from purely selfish behavior, the latter being behavior which has no regard for the self-interests of others. What I am advocating is energetic, intelligent, informed long-term self-interest that has due regard for others on a basis of reciprocity.

"Only now am I beginning to think of myself as an 'author,' despite the fact that I have always wanted to be a writer and have in fact published quite a varied lot of stuff in one way or another.

"I really would like to be able to feel, at least, as those shutters finally come fluttering down on me that, somewhere, some few men and women of sensibility, intelligence, and good will, would be moved to think, or better to say out loud, 'Well, maybe he was a queer fish and not too easy to get on with, but somehow the genes and the memes came together in him in such a way that he managed to create and transmit something inspiring, something worth carrying over for at least the vanguard of our posterity.' In my more Walter Mitty-like moments I have even dreamed up the epitaph I would like to have earned: 'He was a good chap; he tried hard.'''

AVOCATIONAL INTERESTS: Handcrafts, gardening, theatre, cinema, swimming.

PATMORE, John Allan 1931-

PERSONAL: Born in 1931 in Leeds, England; married Barbara Fraser; children: one son, two daughters. *Education:* Pembroke College, Oxford, B.Litt., M.A. *Home:* 22 Brancote Rd., Birkenhead, Cheshire, England. *Office:* Department of Geography, University of Liverpool, Liverpool, England.

CAREER: University of Liverpool, Liverpool, England, lecturer, 1954-70, senior lecturer in geography, 1970—. Visiting professor at Southern Illinois University, 1962-63. *Awards, honors:* Fellow of British Academy, 1967-69.

WRITINGS: An Atlas of Harrogate, Harrogate Public Library, 1963; (contributor) David St. John Thomas, editor, *A Regional History of the Railways of Great Britain,* David & Charles, 1964; (with John Clarke) *Railway History in Pictures: North-West England,* Augustus Kelley, 1968; *Land and Leisure in England and Wales,* David & Charles, 1970, Fairleigh Dickinson University Press, 1971; (editor with Alan Goeffrey Hodgkiss) *Merseyside in Maps,* Longmans, Green, 1970. Contributor to geography and transportation journals.*

* * *

PATRICK, James (Arthur) 1933-

PERSONAL: Born December 24, 1933, in Paris, Tenn.; son of James Arthur (in real estate) and Neva Lois (Harris) Patrick; married Mary Wellford Pringle Smith (an architectural draftsman), December 19, 1955; children: Michael Harris Heaton. *Education:* Auburn University, B.Arch., 1956; University of the South, B.D., 1962, S.T.M., 1963; University of Toronto, Th.D., 1968; University of Wisconsin—Milwaukee, M.A., 1972. *Religion:* Roman Catholic. *Home:* 8417 Bluebonnet Rd., Dallas, Tex. 75209. *Office:* Department of Theology, University of Dallas, Irving, Tex. 75061.

CAREER: Trinity College, Toronto, Ontario, lecturer in religious knowledge, 1965-66; All Saints' Church, Morristown, Tenn., rector, 1966-69; University of Tennessee, Knoxville, assistant professor, 1968-69; Nashotah House, Nashotah, Wis., associate professor of ethics, 1969-71; Christ Church, Delevan, Wis., rector, 1970-71; University of Tennessee, professor of architecture, 1971-75, acting dean, 1972-73; University of Dallas, Irving, Tex., associate professor of theology, 1975—, chairman and director of graduate programs of theology department, 1975-78, academic dean, 1977-79, dean for university affairs, 1979-80. Partner of Knight Associates (architecture and planning firm). *Military service:* U.S. Army, Field Artillery, 1956-58; became first lieutenant. *Member:* American Society of Christian Ethics, American Catholic Philosophical Association, Society for Biblical Literature, Society of Architectural Historians.

WRITINGS: Architecture in Tennessee, 1768-1897, University of Tennessee Press, 1981. Contributor to history journals.

WORK IN PROGRESS: Immortal Self, O Brave New World!: The Christian Idea in the Crucible of Technological Totalitarianism, publication expected in 1982; *The Eighteenth-Century Architecture of the Upper Counties,* publication expected in 1983; *The Charles Coffin Journals, 1800-1822: Learning About Piety in Early Eighteenth-Century East Tennessee,* publication by East Tennessee Historical Society expected in 1983; *Art, Catholicism, and Reform: Imagination, Progress, and Technique From Pugin to Eric Gill,* publication expected in 1984; *C. S. Lewis and the Metaphysical Tradition,* publication expected in 1984.

SIDELIGHTS: Patrick commented: "I am interested chiefly in the Western theological and metaphysical tradition as it shaped our civilization, and in the art and architecture which image the relation of the intellectual tradition to time and place. I enjoy exploring the implications of these relationships in their particularity in the American regional civilization I know best, the South, as well as in the larger, more abstract matrix of Western civilization generally. The problem which concerns me most is the maintenance of the humane image and of the possibility of moral significance in a world in which the forms of nature have been broken by technique."

*   *   *

PATRICK, Vincent 1935-

PERSONAL: Born in 1935 in Bronx, N.Y.; married, 1954. *Education:* Received B.S. from New York University.

CAREER: Worked as Bible salesman, as garment worker, as design engineer, as vice-president of engineer consulting firm, for waterbed manufacturer, as restaurant manager, as bartender, and as instructor at community college.

WRITINGS: The Pope of Greenwich Village, Seaview, 1979.

SIDELIGHTS: The Pope of Greenwich Village, Patrick's best-selling first novel, is the story of a trio of small-time hustlers whose dreams of escaping the obscurity of their lives in lower Manhattan prompt them to burglarize a trucking company. Their scheme backfires when a policeman is killed during the theft and the stolen money turns out to be underworld cash intended for police payoffs.

Critics praised Patrick's novel for its tight story line and descriptive language. *Washington Post Book World* reviewer Joseph McLellan wrote: "Patrick handles his abundant plot with neat complications and occasional surprises. . . . More important ingredients are the dialogue . . . and the picture of an alien world, an almost totally corrupt society, in which the people are still recognizably members of our own species."

Chicago Tribune Book World critic Merryl Maleska found the book to contain more than just a charming story. "What becomes apparent," Maleska wrote, "is a complex inquiry into issues of loyalty, trust, and altruism. . . . The message is grim and important. But, almost magically, the book keeps us laughing."

BIOGRAPHICAL/CRITICAL SOURCES: Library Journal, June 15, 1979; *Village Voice,* October 15, 1979; *New York Times Book Review,* October 21, 1979; *Washington Post Book World,* November 16, 1979; *Chicago Tribune Book World,* December 9, 1979; *Newsweek,* January 7, 1980; *New York Times,* February 20, 1980; *National Review,* May 16, 1980.*

*   *   *

PATTERSON, Lawrence Thomas II 1937-

PERSONAL: Born August 8, 1937, in Cincinnati, Ohio; son of Lawrence Thomas and Helen Adelaide (Wintering) Patterson; children: Page Patrick, Lawrence Thomas III, Blake Shannon. *Education:* Miami University, Oxford, Ohio, B.S. (cum laude), 1957; University of Michigan, M.B.A., 1959; graduate study at University of Pennsylvania, 1958. *Home:* 6785 East Beechlands Dr., Cincinnati, Ohio 45237. *Office address:* Box 37432, Cincinnati, Ohio 45237; and P.O. Box 1059, Basel, Switzerland.

CAREER: Secretary-treasurer of P-G Products, Inc., 1959-60; associated with Arrington Van Pelt Management Consultants,

1960-61; Patterson International Corp., Cincinnati, Ohio, founder and president, 1964-75; American Youth Marketing Corp., Cincinnati, founder and president, 1969-77; L. T. Patterson Strategy, Cincinnati, owner and president, 1974—; retirement and financial planning consultant. Publisher of *L. T. Patterson Strategy Letter* (PSL), *Index of the Independent Press,* 1975, and *The Conspiracy Theory Catalogue,* 1975. Chairman of Center for Financial Freedom. *Military service:* U.S. Air Force, 1961-62, stationed in Berlin. *Member:* International Association of Financial Planners (life member), American Numismatic Association (life member), Commission for Monetary Research and Education, Phi Beta Kappa, Phi Eta Sigma.

WRITINGS: Swiss Real Estate and How to Retire in Switzerland.

*   *   *

PATTERSON, Peter
See TERSON, Peter

*   *   *

PAUCK, Wilhelm 1901-1981

OBITUARY NOTICE—See index for *CA* sketch: Born January 31, 1901, in Laasphe, Westphalia, Germany (now West Germany); died after a long illness, c. September 3, 1981, in Palo Alto, Calif. Educator, theologian, editor, translator, and author. An authority on church history and the Reformation, Pauck taught at such schools as the Chicago Theological Seminary, University of Chicago, Union Theological Seminary, Vanderbilt University, and Stanford University. He wrote several books in his field, including *Karl Barth: Prophet of a New Christianity?, Harnack and Froeltsch: Two Historical Theologians,* and the two-volume biography *Paul Tillich.* Pauck also translated and edited *Luther: Lecturers on Romans.* Obituaries and other sources: *New York Times,* September 5, 1981, September 6, 1981; *AB Bookman's Weekly,* October 19, 1981.

*   *   *

PAVESE, Cesare 1908-1950

BRIEF ENTRY: Born September 9, 1908, in Santo Stefano Belbo, Italy; committed suicide, August 27, 1950, in Turin, Italy. Italian novelist, poet, short story writer, and translator. In 1935 Pavese was imprisoned by Italy's Fascist government for surreptitious political activity. His ten months of captivity greatly influenced the writings that followed: confinement, solitude, and death were recurring themes in his works, and his characters continually sought means by which they could detach themselves from life. *Paesi tuoi* (1939; title means "Your Country"), *La casa in collina* (1949; title means "The House on the Hill"), and *La luna e i falo* (1950; title means "The Moon and the Bonfires") are among Pavese's escapist novels. Artistically and emotionally stifled by fascism, Pavese managed to bring uninhibited and uncensored literature to his countrymen by translating the works of English and American authors under the guise of literary criticism. He translated into Italian his favorite book, Melville's *Moby Dick,* as well as works by Steinbeck, Joyce, and Gertrude Stein. In 1950, the same year in which he took his life, Pavese won the Strega Prize, Italy's most distinguished literary award. Pavese's other writings include *Lavorare stanca* (1936; title means "Hard Labor"), *Il carcere* (1949; title means "The Political Prisoner"), and *Il mestiere di vivere: Diario 1935-1950* (1952; title means "The Burning Brand: Diaries 1935-1950"). *Residence:* Turin, Italy. *Biographical/critical sources: Twentieth*

Century Authors: A Biographical Dictionary of Modern Literature, 1st supplement, H. W. Wilson, 1955; *Encyclopedia of World Literature in the Twentieth Century,* updated edition, Ungar, 1967; *The Penguin Companion to European Literature,* McGraw, 1969; *Twentieth-Century Literary Criticism,* Volume 3, Gale, 1980.

*   *   *

PEARCE, Charles A.   1906-1970

OBITUARY NOTICE: Born July 21, 1906, in Chicago, Ill.; died February 1, 1970, in Tarrytown, N.Y. Editor and co-founder of Duell, Sloan & Pearce. Obituaries and other sources: *New York Times,* February 2, 1970; *AB Bookman's Weekly,* February 16, 1970; *Publishers Weekly,* February 16, 1970; *Who Was Who in America, With World Notables,* Volume V: *1969-1973,* Marquis, 1973.

*   *   *

PEARSON, James Larkin   1879-1981

OBITUARY NOTICE: Born September 13, 1879, in Moravian Falls, N.C.; died of natural causes, August 27, 1981, in Wilkes County, N.C. Journalist, poet, and author. Pearson covered Theodore Roosevelt's administration for the national political journal *Yellow Jacket;* he later edited and published the *Fool-Killer,* a humorous monthly magazine. In 1953 Pearson was named poet laureate of North Carolina. He was the author of six books of poetry, including *Early Harvest.* Obituaries and other sources: Bernadette Hoyle, *Tar Heel Writers I Know,* Blair, 1956; *American Authors and Books, 1640 to the Present Day,* 3rd revised edition, Crown, 1972; *Who Was Who in America, With World Notables,* Volume VI: *1974-1976,* Marquis, 1976; *Chicago Tribune,* August 29, 1981.

*   *   *

PECK, John B.   1918(?)-1973

OBITUARY NOTICE: Born c. 1918; died after a brief illness, September 27, 1973, in New York. Editor. Peck served as an editor with the publishing company Farrar, Straus, & Giroux from its founding in 1946. At his death he was senior editor. Recognized for his editorial skills, Peck edited a number of books by authors such as Harry T. Moore, Edmund Wilson, M. Halsey Thomas, and Milton Lomask. Obituaries and other sources: *Publishers Weekly,* October 8, 1973.

*   *   *

PECK, Paula   1927(?)-1972

OBITUARY NOTICE: Born c. 1927; died April 26, 1972, in New York, N.Y. Cooking expert, educator, and author. Peck was the author of two cookbooks, *The Art of Good Cooking* and *The Art of Fine Baking.* Both were highly acclaimed by gourmets such as Craig Claiborne and James Beard. Obituaries and other sources: *New York Times,* April 27, 1972; *AB Bookman's Weekly,* May 15, 1972.

*   *   *

PECKENPAUGH, Angela J(ohnson)   1942-

PERSONAL: Born March 21, 1942, in Richmond, Va.; daughter of Clarence Hazelton and Mary (Chamberlayne) Johnson; married C. W. Peckenpaugh (an artist; divorced). *Education:* Denison University, B.A., 1965; Ohio University, M.A., 1966; University of Massachusetts, M.F.A., 1978. *Home:* 2513 East Webster Pl., Milwaukee, Wis. 53211. *Office:* Division of Urban Outreach, University of Wisconsin—Milwaukee, Garland Hall, Milwaukee, Wis. 53201.

CAREER: Ohio University, Chillicothe, lecturer in English, 1966-67; University of Wisconsin—Milwaukee, instructor in English, 1968-74, coordinator of freshman seminar program, 1974-75; Milwaukee Institute of Art and Design, Milwaukee, director of development, 1977-78; University of Wisconsin—Milwaukee, director of writing program for adults, 1978—. Performer with ArtReach Milwaukee; guest lecturer at Universities; workshop leader. Member of board of directors of Historic Third World Development, 1976-77; volunteer worker for Planned Parenthood, 1968-70. *Member:* Zero Population Growth (local coordinator, 1970-72), Adult Education Association of the United States of America, Committee of Small Press Editors, Feminist Writers Guild, Wisconsin Regional Writers, Wisconsin Council for Writers.

WRITINGS: Letters From Lee's Army (poems), Morgan Press, 1979; *Discovering the Mandala* (poems), Lakes and Prairies Press, 1981. Also co-author with Lois Beebe Hayna of *A Book of Charms* (poems), Barnwood Press.

Work represented in anthologies, including *I, That Am Ever Stranger,* Westminster; *Moving to Antarctica,* Dustbooks, 1976; *Poetry Out of Wisconsin.* Contributor of poems, translations, and reviews to magazines, including *Margins, Spectrum, Southern Poetry Review, Moving Out, Northwest Review,* and *Exile.* Editor of *Sackbut Review.*

SIDELIGHTS: Angela Peckenpaugh commented: "My becoming a writer had a lot to do with being a teacher of literature during the period, around 1970-74, when so many women were writing about topics of pertinence to the 'women's movement.' I found the writing of women interesting, and felt my own experiences would be of interest to other women. Perhaps the writing of Anne Sexton and Adrienne Rich meant the most to me in the beginning. I learned style from them and in some way found them appropriate role models. I have since rejected them as such: Sexton because she chose suicide, and Rich because she became a separatist. I guess the work of May Sarton, Theodore Roethke, and Robert Bly sustains me now, although I find many writers of poetry today adept and stimulating.

"The writings of Carl Jung and Abraham Maslow were important to my early work. I found Jung's theory of individuation a good handle for the development of my personality, and his research on mandala symbolism relevant to symbols in my writing. In both I found discussions of peak states and mystical experiences that supplied me with a substitute for my abandoned Episcopalian religion. Writing, then, provided me a means of expression for my personality, a lasting literary identity when teaching jobs were in question, a link to the women's movement, and a basis for a religion. About 1978 I became interested in the charm as a literary form and that led me to an exploration of the pagan religion. I now consider myself a pagan, although I live in an urban setting and do not meet or participate in rituals with other pagans. By calling myself that, I mean that I find nature an adequate symbol of the godhead and feel that its models of cycles provide an adequate meaning for my everyday existence. I see the order of things as basically cyclical. I try to represent this intuitive stance in my poetry. The use of charms as a form of 'prayer' or healing device is appealing to me. I hope my charms will be taken as more than mere literary works.

"My vocation as a director of a writing program for adults seems appropriate to my background and education. Being thirty-five when I returned to graduate school for a third degree made me particularly aware of the motivations and conflicts of the adult student. I see people daily who are highly motivated to write but have a hard time fitting it into their busy schedules. They are also greatly in need of a careful reader and supportive leader, or role model. I am pleased to have the opportunity to set up writers' conferences, making local writers whose work is professional and sustaining available to students who derive valuable advice from them on writing technique and marketing strategy. I enjoy figuring out what type of writing might be usefully highlighted in a short course, such as travel writing, or writing about food preparation. Recently I entered into the field of instruction about book publishing. It turned out to be a subject that held great interest for the local adult population, and it was exciting to see the course catch hold as it did.

"For the last three years I have been in touch with writers all over the United States via the little magazine I edit. I have been intensely involved with this project, fundraising, editing, choosing graphics, and seeing to the printing and distribution. This has made me much more conscious of the workings of editorial policy, and has made me less in awe of other editors and of grant-providing bodies. It has also made me more familiar with the long hours editors put in, and the incredible variety of personalities they must interact with. The Reagan budget cuts may cause me to abandon the magazine, but I will continue to operate a 'small press' in some capacity."

* * *

PEDERSEN, Knut   1859-1952
(Knut Hamsun)

BRIEF ENTRY: Born August 4, 1859, in Lom, Norway; died February 19, 1952, in Grimstad, Norway. Norwegian author. Hamsun is considered one of Scandinavia's finest twentieth-century writers. His initial work, *Cultural Life of Northern America* (1889), drew from his experiences as a farm worker and horse-car conductor. Hamsun followed the essay with his first novel, *Hunger* (1890), which ranks with his finest work. The novel concerns a starving artist whose self-confidence and disdain for society is unaffected by his impoverished condition. The novel proved immensely successful for Hamsun, and he was afterwards able to devote his energy to writing without worrying about an income. For the next twenty-five years Hamsun wrote several novels, including *Mysteries* (1892) and *Pan* (1894). These works revealed the considerable influence of Strindberg, Schopenhauer, and Dostoevsky in their realistic depictions of irrational behavior. Hamsun's pressimism was overshadowed by his simplistic celebrations of nature in later novels such as *The Growth of the Soil* (1917), for which he received the Nobel Prize for literature in 1920, and *The Woman at the Pump* (1920). When his pro-German sentiments during World War II drew the ire of his countrymen, Hamsun refrained from writing and seeking publicity. After the liberation of Norway in 1945, Hamsun was arrested and charged with collaborating with German forces. The charges were later dropped, however, and Hamsun was allowed to remain in Norway. Hamsun resumed writing with the semi-autobiographical *Pa gjengrodde stier* (1949), which most critics consider a partial apology for his conduct during the war. Throughout his life Hamsun also wrote for the stage. *Biographical/critical sources: Cyclopedia of World Authors*, Harper, 1958; *Who's Who in Twentieth Century Literature*, Holt, 1976; *Twentieth-Century Literary Criticism*, Volume 2, Gale, 1979.

PEMAN, Jose Maria   1897-1981

OBITUARY NOTICE: Born in 1897 in Cadiz, Spain; died in 1981 in Cadiz, Spain. Linguist, poet, playwright, and author. A devout Roman Catholic, Peman wrote numerous novels, poems, and plays. Included among his works are *El divino impaciente* ("The Anxious Saint"), *Callados como muertos* ("Silent as the Dead"), *La santa virreina* ("The Holy Vicereine") and *La divini pelea* ("The Heavenly Quarrel"). His adaptation of *Edipo* is considered his masterpiece. Peman was a loyal monarchist who gained fame in Spain with his political television appearances and newspaper articles. He served as president of the Royal Spanish Academy. Obituaries and other sources: *Crowell's Handbook of Contemporary Drama*, Crowell, 1971; *Modern World Drama: An Encyclopedia*, Dutton, 1972; *International Who's Who in Poetry*, 5th edition, Melrose, 1977; *London Times*, July 24, 1981.

* * *

PENNINGTON, Chester Arthur   1916-

PERSONAL: Born September 16, 1916, in Delanco, N.J.; son of Chester Arthur and Emily Bolton (Lush) Pennington; married Marjorie Elizabeth Bruschweiler, September 13, 1941; children: Celeste Ann, Lawrence Arthur. *Education:* Temple University, A.B., 1937; Drew Theological Seminary, B.D., 1940; Drew University, Ph.D., 1948; postdoctoral study at Oxford University, 1949. *Home:* 7515 Clinton St., Los Angeles, Calif. 90036.

CAREER: Ordained Methodist minister, 1940; pastor of Methodist church in Spring Lake, N.J., 1941-43, assistant pastor in East Orange, N.J., 1945-47, pastor in Hackettstown, N.J., 1947-51, and New York, N.Y., 1951-55, senior minister in Minneapolis, Minn., 1955-72; Iliff School of Theology, Denver, Colo., professor of preaching and worship, 1972-79. Professor at Centenary College, Hackettstown, 1947-51. Director of Ministers Life and Casualty Union. *Military service:* U.S. Naval Reserve, active duty as chaplain, 1943-45. *Awards, honors:* L.H.D. from Ohio Northern University, 1961; D.D. from McKendree College, 1968.

WRITINGS: Even So, Believe, Abingdon, 1966; *With Good Reason*, Abingdon, 1967; *A More Excellent Way*, Abingdon, 1969; *Half-Truths or Whole Gospels?*, Abingdon, 1972; *Liberated Love*, United Church Press, 1972; (with wife, Marjorie J. Pennington) *After the Children Leave Home*, Graded Press, 1972; *Christian Counter Culture*, Abingdon, 1973; *The Word Among Us*, United Church Press, 1973; *The Thunder and the Still Voice*, Graded Press, 1974; *A New Birth of Freedom*, Discipleship Resources, 1976; *God Has a Communication Problem*, Hawthorn, 1976; (with Jack D. Kingsbury) *Lent*, Fortress, 1980.*

* * *

PENNY, Prudence
See GOLDBERG, Hyman

* * *

PEREIRA, W(ilfred) D(ennis)   1921-

PERSONAL: Born November 16, 1921, in London, England; son of Ernani Horace (an export agent) and Helen Elizabeth (Gonsalves) Pereira; married Irene Elizabeth Crawford, June 12, 1948; children: Helen Elizabeth. *Education:* College of Aeronautical Engineering, London, England, Diploma (with honors), 1948. *Home:* Woodfold Cottage, Down Hatherley, Gloucestershire, England.

CAREER: Technical writer for De Havilland Aircraft Co., 1948-50; Rotol, Bristol, England, technical writer, 1950-58; press officer for Dowty Group, 1958-61; publicity manager for Daniels/Unochrome International, 1961-73; owner and director of advertising agency in Cheltenham, England, 1973—.

WRITINGS: Time of Departure, R. Hale, 1956; *The Wheat From the Chaff,* Dent, 1967; *Serene Retreat,* R. Hale, 1957; *Johnson's Journey,* R. Hale, 1958; *The Lion and the Lambs,* R. Hale, 1959; *North Flight,* R. Hale, 1959.

Lark Ascending, R. Hale, 1960; *The Cauldrons of the Storm,* R. Hale, 1961; *Arrow in the Air,* Jarrolds, 1963; *An Uncertainty of Marriages,* Dent, 1969.

Aftermath Fifteen (science fiction novel), R. Hale, 1973; *The Charon Tapes,* R. Hale, 1975; *Contact,* R. Hale, 1977; *King of Hell,* R. Hale, 1978; *Celeste,* R. Hale, 1979. Also author of *Another Eden,* 1976. Contributor of articles and stories to magazines.*

*   *   *

PERKINS, Wilma Lord   1897-1976

OBITUARY NOTICE: Born in 1897; died November 29, 1976, in Rochester, N.Y. Editor and author. Wilma Lord Perkins edited *The Fannie Farmer Cook Book* for forty-five years and wrote *The Fannie Farmer Junior Cook Book.* In 1929 she became the editor of *The Boston Cooking School Cook Book,* which was written in 1896 by her husband's aunt, Fannie Merritt Farmer. Obituaries and other sources: *New York Times,* December 1, 1976; *AB Bookman's Weekly,* January 10, 1977.

*   *   *

PERRY, Barbara Fisher
See FISHER, Barbara

*   *   *

PERRY, Brighton
See SHERWOOD, Robert E(mmet)

*   *   *

PERRY, Elizabeth Jean   1948-

PERSONAL: Born September 9, 1948, in Shanghai, China; American citizen born abroad; daughter of Charles E. (a missionary and a professor) and Carey (a missionary and a professor; maiden name, Coles) Perry. *Education:* William Smith College, B.A. (summa cum laude), 1969; University of Washington, Seattle, M.A., 1971; University of Michigan, Ph.D., 1978. *Home:* 4048 Northeast 55th, Seattle, Wash. 98105. *Office:* School of International Studies, University of Washington, Seattle, Wash. 98195.

CAREER: University of Arizona, Tucson, assistant professor of political science, 1977-78; University of Washington, Seattle, assistant professor of international studies and political science, 1978—. Member of Seattle China Council and National Committee on U.S.-China Relations. *Member:* Phi Beta Kappa, Pi Gamma Mu, Alpha Lambda Delta. *Awards, honors:* Social Science Research Council fellowship for East Asia, 1974-76; grant from U.S.-China National Educational Exchange Program, 1979-80.

WRITINGS: Rebels and Revolutionaries in North China, 1845-1945, Stanford University Press, 1980; *Chinese Persectives on the Nien Rebellion,* M.E. Sharpe, 1981. Contributor of articles

and reviews to Asian studies and political science journals. Member of editorial board of *Modern China.*

SIDELIGHTS: Elizabeth Perry has lived and studied in China, Japan, Taiwan, and Korea.

She wrote: "I am presently engaged in two long-term projects. The first focuses on several cases of peasant rebellion in nineteenth- and twentieth-century China. The aim is to explain varying patterns of rural protest in terms of differences in social ecology. I spent the 1979-80 academic year in China conducting field and documentary research on this topic. The second project is a study of the local politics of water control in contemporary China. I was also able to undertake some field work on this topic when I was in China, but most of the research lies ahead."

*   *   *

PERRY, John Curtis   1930-

PERSONAL: Born July 18, 1930, in Orange, N.J.; son of Gerald Eugene (in business) and Dorothy Lyman (Burt) Perry; married Sarah Hollis French (a photographic researcher), September 14, 1957; children: five. *Education:* Yale University, B.A., 1952, M.A., 1953; Harvard University, Ph.D., 1962. *Office:* Fletcher School of Law and Diplomacy, Tufts University, Medford, Mass. 02155.

CAREER: Connecticut College, New London, instructor, 1962-64, assistant professor of history, 1964-66; Carleton College, Northfield, Minn., assistant professor, 1966-68, associate professor, 1968-74, professor of history, 1974—, chairman of department, 1971-74, director of Asian studies program, 1966-73; Tufts University, Fletcher School of Law and Diplomacy, Medford, Mass., Henry Willard Denison Professor of Diplomatic History, 1981—. Visiting research associate at Fairbank East Asia Research Center, Harvard University, 1976-77 and Japan Institute, 1977-80. *Member:* American Historical Association, Association for Asian Studies, Japan Society.

WRITINGS: Beneath the Eagle's Wings: Americans in Occupied Japan, Dodd, 1981; (with James C. Thomson and Peter W. Stanley) *Sentimental Imperialists: The American Experience in East Asia,* Harper, 1981.

WORK IN PROGRESS: A study of American-Japanese cultural relations since 1952; a novel.

SIDELIGHTS: Sentimental Imperialists traces American relations with eastern Asia since the late eighteenth century. Perry, an expert in United States-Japan relations, worked with James C. Thompson, Jr., and Peter W. Stanley, experts in American-Chinese and American-Philippino relations respectively, in fashioning a comprehensive account of events that included five wars. The authors attribute much of the conflict between the U.S. and eastern Asia to America's attitude of superiority towards Orientals. This racist stance, which the authors trace to the failure of American missionaries in China in the 1780's, is analyzed with respect to its implications in the Spanish-American War, World War II, the Korean War, and the war in Vietnam. In *Sentimental Imperialists,* the authors blame much of the hostility between the two nationalities on America's attempts "to put East Asia into our image of world history."

Sentimental Imperialists was called "a description and deflation of a series of illusions" by Gaddis Smith. In *New York Times Book Review,* Smith praised the writers as "confident scholars" and called the book "fine." *Newsweek's* Elizabeth Peer agreed. In an analysis of the book's account of the Spanish-American War, she declared, "For its diligence in tracing this bitter precedent alone, 'Sentimental Imperialists' deserves a thoughtful audience.'" Peer added, "Equally impressive is the book's analysis of the singular fickleness of U.S. affections toward China and Japan." She called *Sentimental Imperialists* an "original, tough-minded study."

BIOGRAPHICAL/CRITICAL SOURCES: *Washington Post Book World,* August 23, 1981; *New York Times,* August 27, 1981; *New York Times Book Review,* September 13, 1981; *Newsweek,* September 14, 1981.

* * *

PETERS, Arthur King 1919-

PERSONAL: Born October 17, 1919, in Charleston, W.Va.; son of Arthur Cushing and Jessie (King) Peters; married Sarah Jebb Whitaker, October 21, 1943; children: Robert Bruce, Margaret Allen, Michael Whitaker. *Education:* Cornell University, A.B., 1940; Columbia University, M.A., 1954, Ph.D., 1969. *Religion:* Reformed Church. *Home:* 14 Village Lane, Bronxville, N.Y. 10708. *Office:* A. K. Peters Co., 230 Park Ave., New York, N.Y. 10017; and French-American Foundation, 680 Park Ave., New York, N.Y.

CAREER: Associated with W. R. Grace & Co., 1940-50; A. K. Peters Co. (import-export company), New York, N.Y., owner and president, 1950—. President of French-American Foundation, 1977—, chairman, 1978—; president of National Council of American Importers, 1965, senior counselor, 1966—. Assistant professor at Hunter College of the City University of New York, 1971-74; speaker at international trade conferences; guest on television and radio programs. Member of U.S. trade mission to Peru and Argentina, 1957. Member of board of directors of Bronxville Community Fund, 1962-65. *Military service:* U.S. Army, 1941-46; became major. *Member:* U.S. Chamber of Commerce, Modern Language Association of America, American Association of Teachers of French, American Arbitration Association, Phi Delta Theta, American Alpine Club, Coffee House Club, University Club, Bronxville Field Club.

WRITINGS: *Jean Cocteau and Andre Gide: An Abrasive Friendship,* Rutgers University Press, 1973. Contributor of articles and reviews to scholarly journals.*

* * *

PETERS, Frederick George 1935-

PERSONAL: Born May 9, 1935, in Philadelphia, Pa.; married, 1965; children: one. *Education:* University of Pennsylvania, B.A., 1957; Columbia University, M.A., 1959, M.A., 1962; Oxford University, B.Litt., 1965; Cambridge University, Ph.D., 1970. *Office:* Department of German, Milbank Hall, Barnard College, Columbia University, 120th St. and Broadway, New York, N.Y. 10027.

CAREER: Cambridge University, Cambridge, England, tutor in German at Christ's College and Jesus College, 1968-69; Columbia University, New York, N.Y., assistant professor of German, 1970—. Member of faculty at New School for Social Research, 1974—; adjunct assistant professor at New York University, 1975—; Harvard-Mellon fellow at Harvard University, 1978-79. *Member:* Modern Language Association of America, Germanics Institute.

WRITINGS: (Contributor) *Oxford German Studies,* Volume I, Oxford University Press, 1966; *Robert Musil, Master of the Hovering Life: A Study of the Major Fiction,* Columbia University Press, 1978; (translator with Diana L. S. Peters) Hein-

rich Von Kleist, *Prince Friedrich of Homburg,* New Directions, 1978.*

* * *

PETERS, Ruth Marie 1913(?)-1978

OBITUARY NOTICE: Born c. 1913; died December 16, 1978, in Englewood, N.J. Editor and author. In addition to her editorial work for the *New York Times,* Peters wrote several books on horticulture, including *Bulb Magic in Your Window* and *Your Garden in Town.* Obituaries and other sources: *New York Times,* December 18, 1978; *AB Bookman's Weekly,* February 12, 1979.

* * *

PETERS, S. H.
See PORTER, William Sydney

* * *

PETERSON, James Alfred 1913-

PERSONAL: Born May 11, 1913, in Glendive, Mont.; son of John Martin and Hilda (Moline) Peterson; married Audrey Mount Crawford, June 2, 1936; children: Jon Chrispin, Mary Louise (Mrs. Peter Hamlet), Nancy Lea. *Education:* Ripon College, A.B., 1934; Chicago Theological Seminary, B.D., 1938; University of Southern California, Ph.D., 1950. *Home:* 2428 North Highland St., Altadena, Calif. 91001. *Office:* Peterson-Guedel Family Center, 8530 Wilshire Blvd., Beverly Hills, Calif. 90211.

CAREER: Ordained Congregationalist minister, 1936; pastor of community church in Manhattan Beach, Calif., 1939-50; University of Southern California, Los Angeles, professor of sociology, 1950-58; Peterson-Guedel Family Center, Beverly Hills, Calif., director, 1960—. Lecturer at University of Oregon, 1975; chairman of department of sociology at University of Southern California, 1962-65, 1970, acting director of School of Gerontology and founding director of Rossmoor Cortese Institute for the Study of Retirement and Aging, 1963-65. President of El Dorado Corp. for Mining and Recreation; executive vice-president of Christian Services, Inc. *Member:* American Association of Marriage and Family Counselors (president, 1967-68), American Sociological Association, National Council on Family Relations, Southern California Association of Marriage and Family Counselors (president, 1962), Southern California Conference on the Family (president, 1961).

WRITINGS: *Education for Marriage,* Scribner, 1956, 2nd edition, 1964; (with Eleanor Metheny) *The Trouble With Women,* Vantage, 1957; *Toward a Successful Marriage,* Scribner, 1960; *Married Love in the Middle Years,* Association Press, 1968; (editor) *Marriage and Family Counseling: Perspective and Prospect,* Association Press, 1968.

Counseling and Values: A Philosophical Examination, International Textbook Co., 1970; *Finding and Preparing Precious and Semiprecious Stones,* Association Press, 1974; (with Barbara Payne) *Love in the Later Years: The Emotional, Physical, Sexual, and Social Potential of the Elderly,* Association Press, 1975; (editor) *Journey's End: A Discussion Guide,* University of Southern California Press, 1976; (with Michael P. Briley) *Widows and Widowhood: A Creative Approach to Being Alone,* Association Press, 1977; (with Arthur N. Schwartz) *Introduction to Gerontology,* Holt, 1979.*

PETRES, Robert E(van) 1939-

PERSONAL: Born February 11, 1939, in Fairmont, W.Va.; son of Paul (a supervisor) and Frances (Worley) Petres; married Betty Confehr, December 1, 1963 (divorced June, 1981). *Education:* West Virginia University, B.S., 1961, M.D., 1965. *Home address:* Route 14, Box 333 F, Richmond, Va. 23231. *Office:* Medical College of Virginia, Station Box 34, Richmond, Va. 23298.

CARREER: Good Samaritan Hospital, Dayton, Ohio, intern, 1965-66; Medical College of Virginia, Richmond, resident, 1968-71, instructor, 1971-72, assistant professor, 1972-75, associate professor of obstetrics and gynecology, 1975—; private practice of obstetrics and gynecology, 1971—. *Military service:* U.S. Army, 1966-68; became medical officer. *Member:* American College of Obstetrics and Gynecology, American Institute of Ultrasound in Medicine, Planned Parenthood.

WRITINGS: (With Robert Bluford) *Unwanted Pregnancy*, Harper, 1973.

WORK IN PROGRESS: Research on high-risk pregnancy and ultrasound.

SIDELIGHTS: Petres's interests include humanism in medicine and public education in medicine and health.

* * *

PETTINGILL, Amos
See HARRIS, William Bliss

* * *

PFINGSTON, Roger 1940-

PERSONAL: Born April 6, 1940, in Evansville, Ind.; son of Walter Carl (in business) and Esther (Sandage) Pfingston; married Nancy Weber (an elementary school teacher), December 15, 1962; children: Brett, Jenna. *Education:* Indiana University, B.A., 1962, M.S., 1967. *Residence:* Bloomington, Ind. *Office:* Department of English, Bloomington High School North, Bloomington, Ind. 47401.

CAREER: Junior high school English teacher in Virginia Beach, Va., 1964-65; high school English teacher at university school in Bloomington, Ind., 1967-72; Bloomington High School North, Bloomington, teacher of English and photography, 1972—. Member of Indiana Arts Commission literature advisory panel, 1979-80. Photographer, with work exhibited in group and solo shows, including Midwest Photo 80. *Military service:* U.S. Navy, 1962-64. *Member:* Poetry Society of America, National Education Association, Indiana State Teachers Association. *Awards, honors:* Robert W. Mitchner poetry scholar at Indiana University writer's conference, 1976; grant from National Endowment for the Arts, 1978; resident at MacDowell Colony, 1978.

WRITINGS—Poetry chapbooks: *A Poem for Tom Sandage*, Raintree, 1976; *Stoutes Creek Road*, Raintree, 1976; *Nesting*, Sparrow, 1978; *Poems From a Snow Journal*, Raintree, 1978; *The Presence of Trees*, Raintree, 1979; *Hazards of Photography*, Writers' Center Press, 1980; *Poems and Photographs*, Years Press, 1981.

Work represented in anthologies, including *Traveling America With Today's Poets*, Macmillan, 1977; *The Indiana Experience*, Indiana University Press, 1977; *Bear Crossings*, New South Co., 1978. Contributor of poems and photographs to more than one hundred fifty magazines and newspapers, including *Modern Photography, Nation, Prairie Schooner, West*

Coast Review, Malahat Review, and *Yankee.* Associate editor of *Stoney Lonesome.*

WORK IN PROGRESS: Breaking Ground (tentative title), poems.

SIDELIGHTS: Pfingston wrote: "For many years now I have given equal attention to poetry and photography, sometimes letting the two merge to produce a cross-pollination of sorts. When this happens, it's usually a poem derived from the photographic image(s).

"I started making photographs while still in high school; the poems began a few years later. About a dozen years ago it occurred to me that I might write poems based on photographs (other photographers' work as well as my own), or some aspect of photography. I like the idea of 'walking around' inside the framed image, describing what was there or wasn't there—dealing with what was missing and making it whatever I imagined. I write other types of poems, too, but the photography poems are fun to do, and they can be valuable as a loosening up device. It seems to me a healthy activity—letting one art 'trigger' another. Think of all the poems *after* paintings, or for that matter, poems *after* poems. Why not poems *after* photographs?"

BIOGRAPHICAL/CRITICAL SOURCES: Indiana Alumni, April, 1978; *Indianapolis Star,* September 28, 1980; *Evansville Press,* March 5, 1981.

* * *

PHARR, Emory Charles 1896(?)-1981

OBITUARY NOTICE: Born c. 1896; died of a heart attack, July 18, 1981, in Arlington, Va. Poet and journalist. Pharr worked for the Weather Bureau (now the National Weather Service) for thirty-six years, retiring in 1965 to work part-time as an editor and reporter for the *Northern Virginia Sun.* He wrote two volumes of poetry, *Wild Geese Fly High* and *Calling Winds.* His poems also appeared in the *New York Times, Minneapolis Star, Good Housekeeping,* and *Woman's Home Companion.* Obituaries and other sources: *Washington Post,* July 25, 1981.

* * *

PHELPS, Phelps 1897-1981

OBITUARY NOTICE: Born May 4, 1897, in Bonn, Germany (now West Germany); died June 10, 1981, in Wildwood, N.J. Lawyer, politician, and author. Phelps was a Republican assemblyman in Greenwich Village, N.Y., from 1924 to 1928 before pledging himself to the Democratic Party in 1932. He served as a Democratic assemblyman from 1937 to 1938 and as a New York state senator from 1939 until 1942. Phelps was also the first civilian governor of American Samoa and was an ambassador to the Dominican Republic. Widely known for his letters to newspapers in which he expressed his opinions on various political and domestic issues, Phelps wrote two books: *Our Defenses Within and Without* and *America On Trial.* Obituaries and other sources: *Who's Who in America,* 39th edition, Marquis, 1976; *New York Times,* June 12, 1981.

* * *

PHILBROOK, Clem(ent E.) 1917-

PERSONAL: Born October 30, 1917, in Old Town, Me.; son of Earle W. (a business executive) and Harriet (Crocker) Philbrook; married Leone Fissette (a teacher), June 23, 1941 (died, 1976). *Education:* Attended Bryant & Stratton Commercial School. *Address:* Box 158, Pittsburg, N.H. 03592.

CAREER: New England Power Co., Worcester, Mass., field accountant, 1941-56; Harrison Publishing House, Sugar Hill, N.H., office manager, 1956-71; real estate salesman, 1971—. Writer.

WRITINGS—All for children: *Hickory Wings,* Macmillan, 1951; *Key Log,* Macmillan, 1953; *The Magic Bat,* illustrated by Clifford N. Geary, Macmillan, 1954; *Skimeister,* Macmillan, 1955; *Captured by the Abnakis,* illustrated by Joshua Tolford, Hastings House, 1966; *Live Wire,* illustrated by Tolford, Hastings House, 1966; *Slope Dope,* illustrated by Frank Kramer, Hastings House, 1966.

"Ollie" series; all published by Hastings House; all illustrated by Francis Chauncy: *Ollie's Team and the Baseball Computer,* 1967; *. . . and the Football Computer,* 1968; *. . . and the Basketball Computer,* 1969; *. . . Plays Biddy Baseball,* 1970; *Ollie, the Backward Forward,* 1970; *Ollie's Team and the Alley Cats,* 1971; *. . . and the 200 pound Problem,* 1972; *. . . and the Million Dollar Mistake,* 1973.

WORK IN PROGRESS: Another book in the "Ollie" series, publication expected in 1982.

SIDELIGHTS: Clem Philbrook offers much variety for young sports enthusiasts in his "Ollie" series and other publications. His adventure tales revolve around a number of sports, including baseball, basketball, football, and skiing. In each of Philbrook's books the main character is a young boy. With a playing field as a backdrop, Philbrook explores the development of such things as camaraderie and sportsmanship in a boy's character.

Philbrook told *CA:* "My wife died in 1976, after a long and painful illness, and only now am I 'getting it back together' again. As a superb school teacher and the most inspirational human being I have ever known, my wife was a constant source of motivation in my writing career. As I begin another passage in my life, she continues to motivate me. She was the inspiration for Miss Carmody, the lovable teacher in my popular 'Ollie' series. As I revise the ninth 'Ollie' book, I find that Miss Carmody lives on."

*   *   *

PHILLIPS, Ward
See LOVECRAFT, H(oward) P(hillips)

*   *   *

PICKERING, Samuel Francis, Jr.   1941-

PERSONAL: Born September 30, 1941, in Nashville, Tenn. *Education:* University of the South, B.A., 1963; Cambridge University, B.A., 1965, M.A., 1970; Princeton University, Ph.D., 1970. *Office:* Department of English, Dartmouth College, Hanover, N.H. 03755.

CAREER: Dartmouth College, Hanover, N.H., assistant professor of English, 1970—. Fulbright lecturer at University of Jordan, 1975-76. *Awards, honors:* National Endowment for the Humanities fellowship, 1974; American Council of Learned Societies grant, 1976.

WRITINGS: The Moral Tradition in English Fiction, 1785-1850, University Press of New England, 1976; *Be Merry and Wise: John Locke and Eighteenth-Century English Children's Books,* University of Tennessee Press, 1980. Contributor to scholarly journals.

BIOGRAPHICAL/CRITICAL SOURCES: Times Literary Supplement, June 24, 1977.*

PICON, Molly   1898-

PERSONAL: Surname is pronounced Pee-*kahn;* born June 1, 1898, in New York, N.Y.; daughter of Lewis (a shirtmaker) and Clara (a wardrobe mistress; maiden name, Ostrow) Picon; married Jacob Kalich (a producer, actor, and author), June 29, 1919 (died March 16, 1975). *Education:* Attended William Penn High School, Philadelphia, Pa., 1911-14. *Religion:* Jewish. *Home:* 1 Lincoln Plaza, New York, N.Y. 10023. *Agent:* William Morris Office, 1350 Sixth Ave., New York, N.Y. 10019.

CAREER: Actress, 1904—. Appeared in vaudeville acts in nickelodeon theatres in Philadelphia, Pa., and in Camden and Red Bank, N.J., 1904 and 1912-15; appeared in Yiddish repertory productions in Philadelphia, 1904-1912, including "Gabriel," "The Silver King," "Uncle Tom's Cabin," "Sapphro," "Shulamith," "Girl of the West," "God of Revenge," "Medea," "King Lear," and "The Kreutzer Sonata"; appeared in plays at Chester Street Theatre in Philadelphia, 1915, including "Broadway Jones" and "Bunty Pulls the Strings"; toured with vaudeville show "Four Seasons," 1918-19; appeared in Boston and toured Europe with Jacob Kalich's Yiddish repetory company, 1919-20.

Appeared in theatrical productions, including "Yonkele," 1923 and 1932, "Tzipke," 1924, "Schmendrik," 1924-25, "Gypsy Girl," 1925-26, "Rabbi's Melody," 1926, "Little Devil," 1926-27, "Little Czar," 1926, "Kid Mother," 1927, "Some Girl," 1927, "Raizele," 1927-28, "Mazel Brocke," 1928, "Circus Girl" 1928, "Hello Molly," 1928-29 and 1979, "The Radio Girl," 1929, "The Jolly Orphan," 1929, "The Little Clown," 1930, "Comedienne," 1930, "Girl of Yesterday," 1931, "Love Thief," 1931, "Mamale," 1932, "One in a Million," 1934, "Motel Peissi, the Cantor's Kid," 1934, "What Girls Do," 1935, "My Malkele," 1937, "Bablitchki," 1938, "Vaudeville Marches On," 1938, "Morning Star," 1940, "Oy Is Dus a Leben," 1942, "For Heaven's Sake, Mother!," 1948, "Sadie Is a Ladie," 1949, "Abi Gezunt," 1949 and 1980, "Mazel Tov, Molly," 1950, "Take It Easy," 1950, "Make Momma Happy," 1953, "Farblonjet Honeymoon," 1956, "The World of Sholem Aleichem," 1957, "The Kosher Widow," 1959, "A Majority of One," 1960-61, 1965, 1966, and 1974, "Milk and Honey," 1961-64, 1966, and 1968, "Madame Mousse," 1965, "Dear Me, the Sky Is Falling," 1966, "The Rubiyat of Sophie Klein," 1967, "Funny Girl," 1967, "How to Be a Jewish Mother," 1967, "The Milliken Show," 1968 and 1971, "The Solid Gold Cadillac," 1969, "The Front Page," 1969, "Paris Is Out!," 1970 and 1971, "Hello Dolly!," 1971 and 1972, "Come Blow Your Horn," 1973, "How Do You Live With Love?," 1975, "The Second Time Around," 1977, "Those Are the Days," 1979.

Appeared in vaudeville shows at Palace Theatre in New York and throughout the United States, 1931, in Paris, France, and Johannesburg, South Africa, 1932, at London Palladium and throughout England, 1937, throughout United States and Canada, 1942, and at Alhambra Theatre, Paris, 1953.

Appeared in films, including "Yiddle and His Fiddle," produced in Warsaw, Poland, 1936, "Mamale," produced in Warsaw, 1938, "Come Blow Your Horn," Paramount, 1963, "Fiddler on the Roof," United Artists, 1970, "For Pete's Sake," Columbia, 1973.

Performer on radio and television programs, including "Car 54, Where Are You?," 1961, "The Ed Sullivan Show," 1961, "The Jack Paar Show," 1961, "The Mike Wallace Show,"

1961, "Dr. Kildare," 1961, "The Johnny Carson Show," 1961, "The Merv Griffin Show," 1965, 1966, and 1969, "The Mike Douglas Show," 1967 and 1971, "Gomer Pyle," 1968, "My Friend Tony," 1968, "The Jack O'Brien Show," 1968, "The David Frost Show," 1969.

Appeared in concerts, including tour of Israel, Poland, and Russia, 1933, tour of United States, Canada, and Israel, 1939, world tour, 1941, tour of United States military camps and displaced person camps in Europe, 1944-45, tour of United States and Africa, 1946-47, U.S.O. tour of Korea and Japan, 1951, tour of United States and Canada with Israel Bond Tour, 1952, concert at Carnegie Hall, New York City, for Ladies' Garment Workers Union, 1970, and tours of United States, Canada, and Israel, 1975—. Also appeared in revue, 1975.

MEMBER: American Federation of Radio Artists, American Guild of Variety Artists, American Actors Association, Actors Equity, Jewish Theatrical Guild, Hebrew Actor's Union, Jewish Theatrical Alliance, Yiddish Composers Guild, Leeds Jewish Institute (first honorary woman member). *Awards, honors:* First actress from the Yiddish theatre elected to Theatre Hall of Fame, 1981; received Abram Leon Sachar Award with Helen Hayes from Brandeis University.

WRITINGS: (With Eth Clifford Rosenberg) *So Laugh a Little,* Messner, 1962; (with Jean Bergantini Grillo) *Molly!: An Autobiography,* Simon & Schuster, 1980. Also author of character sketches.

Lyricist of songs for plays, including "The Radio Girl," 1929, "The Jolly Orphan," 1929, "Oy Is Dus a Leben," 1942, "Abi Gezunt," 1949, "Sadie Is a Lady," 1950, "Mazel Tov, Molly," 1950, and "The Kosher Widow," 1959.

Composer of about one hundred songs, including "East Side Symphony," "Song of the Tenement," "The Story of Grandma's Shawl," "Working Goil," "Hands," and "That's How You Go With Me."

SIDELIGHTS: Once known as "the sweetheart of Second Avenue," Molly Picon is a leading figure in the Yiddish theatre. She began her career at the age of five when she won a five-dollar gold piece in a children's amateur night performance at the Bijou Theatre in Philadelphia. After that, Picon appeared in other amateur shows until she began steady professional work with Michael Tomashefsky's Yiddish stock company. Picon was six years old and received fifteen cents for each performance. Years later, when she was alone in Boston after the stock company with which she was touring dissolved, Picon appealed to Jacob Kalich, the manager of the Grand Opera House, for employment. Within a year, Kalich made Picon his wife; within three years, he made her a star.

Kalich wrote or adapted most of Picon's material. Beginning in 1921 with a tour of Europe to perfect his wife's Yiddish, Kalich wrote "dopey boy roles" for her, notably "Schmendrik" and "Yonkele." The latter he named after himself, and the persona of his nickname became Picon's first major success. In its European tour, the production revolutionized the Yiddish theatre, changing its mode from heavy dramas to humorous musicals. By 1979, Picon had starred in three thousand performances of her "Peter Pan of the Yiddish Theatre."

Not exclusively the property of the Yiddish theatre, Picon moved from the Second Avenue Theatre to the Palace Theatre for a salary of $3,500 a week in 1931. With the move, she became "one of the most successful of the Yiddish actors who left downtown Second Avenue for uptown Broadway," reported Fred Ferretti. "Once the idol of Second Avenue," Picon became "the darling of the world," noted Brooks Atkinson.

Throughout her career, Picon traveled extensively, averaging between five thousand and fifty thousand miles per year. She performed all over the world and for all types of audiences, including a tribe of Zulus whom she entertained with an imitation of Charlie Chaplin, complete with the chief's derby hat. She has even provided impromptu performances while vacationing in out of the way places like Spitsbergen, the Norwegian archipelago where Picon sang in a bar for an audience of three. And in 1946 the entertainer toured postwar Europe, performing in hospitals, orphanages, and displaced person camps as well as raising money for relief institutions. One of the first entertainers to perform for concentration camp survivors, Picon brought cosmetics, jewelry, candy, and laughter back to the refugees. She remembered: "A woman came up with a child and said: 'My child is two years old and she has never heard the sound of laughter,' Yonkele told me: 'Molly, that's our job. Make them laugh.'"

Still touring at eighty-three, Picon is able to do deep-knee bends and dance the can-can. "Age is a problem to many," she revealed to Nan Robertson in the *New York Times*. "It isn't for me. I've no time to bother with it. I think it's just a matter of genes and luck." The last of the Yiddish theatre, the entertainer still appears in the productions that made her famous. In 1980, she once again presented "Abi Gezunt," a production which Richard Shepard of the *New York Times* hailed as "a pleasant journey to another time." And at her eightieth birthday show, held during the Eighth Annual Sholem Aleichem Festival of the Jewish Arts at Queens College, the same critic found Picon to be "the whole show, singing, dancing, telling jokes, making the same faces with those ganayvishe oygen, which you might translate as mischievous eyes, that were her trademark more than a half century ago." Her vivacity makes an audience forget her age, Shepard said, "two minutes into the show."

Reflecting on Picon's long career, which is chronicled in her autobiography *Molly!*, Ethel Goldberg commented: "It would be difficult to estimate how many plays she starred in, but it's easy to remember that no matter what roles she played, she was ever the lovable darling of the Yiddish Stage." As an entertainer, Picon has done everything: the theatre, motion pictures, radio programs, television, and concerts all over the world. Whatever the endeavor, Goldberg put forth, "it was a shot in the arm," as enjoyable at the third viewing of a performance as at the first.

To write *Molly!*, Picon relied on the diaries and the journals that she has kept for fifty years. "She tells her life story," observed a critic in the *New York Times Book Review*, "in a homey, unaffected pastiche of Yiddishisms, unashamed cliches, colloquialisms, enthusiastic outbursts of love, faith and devotion to her beloved husband and mother, and unabashed affection for almost everyone she has ever known or met." According to the reviewer, Picon "is indomitable." To Goldberg, as to many others, the entertainer "will always be a bright, shining star that will never lose its luster."

Picon told *CA* a story to explain her attitude about being an author: "On the Jewish Passover in Poland, children always get new clothes and run around boasting. One little boy says: 'See, I have a new hat.'; another: 'I have a new coat'; a third: 'I have new shoes.' But one poor kid, having nothing new, boasts, 'So what! I have a belly button, too.' (It's funnier in Yiddish—'Ich hob oich a pippik.') So when I have to face real authors, all I can say is: 'Ich hob oich a pippik.'"

AVOCATIONAL INTERESTS: Gardening, walking.

BIOGRAPHICAL/CRITICAL SOURCES: New York Times, February 27, 1927, March 6, 1927, December 24, 1927, October 21, 1928, June 24, 1929, July 1, 1929, July 8, 1929, September 9, 1929, October 19, 1929, December 23, 1929, March 15, 1930, September 27, 1930, January 19, 1931, September 20, 1934, November 4, 1934, November 17, 1934, November 29, 1934, January 14, 1935, September 20, 1937, January 17, 1938, December 30, 1938, April 17, 1940, October 13, 1942, October 2, 1946, November 17, 1948, October 10, 1949, November 13, 1949, January 28, 1950, October 2, 1950, December 25, 1950, September 27, 1955, November 2, 1959, March 10, 1960, October 11, 1961, January 28, 1962, November 21, 1962, December 29, 1967, February 3, 1970, February 22, 1970, April 10, 1977, April 15, 1977, March 30, 1979, April 2, 1979, May 12, 1979, April 11, 1980, July 11, 1980, August 10, 1980, August 13, 1980, August 15, 1980, March 3, 1981; *New York Post*, April 6, 1940; *New York Herald Tribune*, April 7, 1940, October 11, 1942, November 14, 1948; *Cue*, April 20, 1940.

New York World Telegram, October 13, 1942, November 6, 1950; Louis Nizer, *Between You and Me*, Beechhurst Press, 1948; *Variety*, October 19, 1949; *Washington Post*, May 16, 1950; Molly Picon and Eth Clifford Rosenberg, *So Laugh a Little*, Messner, 1962; *New York Times Book Review*, March 2, 1980; Picon and Jean Bergantini Grillo, *Molly!: An Autobiography*, Simon & Schuster, 1980; *Broward Jewish Journal*, September 3, 1981.

—Sketch by Charity Anne Dorgan

*   *   *

PIERCE, Robert N(ash)   1931-

PERSONAL: Born December 5, 1931, in Greenville, Miss.; son of Fred Paul (a bookkeeper) and Virginia (a teacher; maiden name, Henry) Pierce; married Ann Courter, December 28, 1953 (divorced, 1978); children: Douglas, Diana. *Education:* Attended University of Missouri, 1950; Arkansas State University, B.A., 1951; University of Texas, M.J., 1955; University of Minnesota, Ph.D., 1968. *Politics:* Democrat. *Religion:* Presbyterian. *Home address:* Route 1, Box 840, Micanopy, Fla. 32667. *Office:* College of Journalism and Communications, University of Florida, Gainesville, Fla. 32611.

CAREER: Arkansas Democrat, Little Rock, reporter, 1953-55, assistant state editor, 1954-55, acting state editor, 1955; *San Angelo Standard-Times*, San Angelo, Tex., reporter and real estate editor, 1955-56; *Sarasota News*, Sarasota, Fla., news editor, 1956-60, associate editor, 1958-60; Florida Presbyterian College, St. Petersburg, public relations director, adviser to student publications, and chairman of Board of Student Publications, 1960-62; *St. Petersburg Evening Independent*, St. Petersburg, assistant city editor, 1962-63; University of Minnesota, Minneapolis, instructor in journalism, 1964-65; Louisiana State University, Baton Rouge, assistant professor of journalism and member of executive committee of Latin American Studies Institute, 1965-70; University of Florida, Gainesville, associate professor, 1970-76, professor of journalism, 1976—, graduate studies director of College of Journalism and Communications, 1978—. Reporter for Associated Press, winter, 1953; state legislative correspondent for *Shreveport Journal*, summer, 1970; copy editor of *Miami Herald*, summer, 1972. Guest lecturer at Panamanian Syndicate of Journalists, Colombian-American Cultural Institute, Seminar for Rectors and Deans of Colombian Universities, Mendoza Association of Argentine-American Cultural Exchange, and Instituto Wells, 1973; visiting lecturer at Catholic University of Minas Gerais, 1973; Fulbright-Hays lecturer at Universidad Argentina de la Empresa, 1973. Member of U.S. State Department Latin American Scholar-Diplomat Seminar, 1972; judge of writing competitions. *Member:* Association for Education in Journalism, Sigma Delta Chi (past chairman of freedom of information committee), Kappa Tau Alpha. *Awards, honors:* Fulbright-Hays grant for Latin America, 1976; grant from U.S. Office of Education, 1976; grant from Foreign Affairs Ministry of Sweden, 1978.

WRITINGS: (Contributor) James W. Markham, editor, *International Communication as a Field of Study*, Department of Publications, University of Iowa, 1970; *Lord Northcliffe and Trans-Atlantic Journalistic Influences*, Journalism Monographs, 1975; (contributor) Richard R. Cole, editor, *Mass Communication in Mexico*, Association for Education in Journalism, 1975; *Keeping the Flame: Media and Government in Latin America*, Hastings House, 1979. Contributor to journalism magazines. Contributing northern Latin American editor of *World Encyclopedia of the Press*.

WORK IN PROGRESS: An anthology, with commentary on journalism as literature.

SIDELIGHTS: Pierce commented: "Too often the United States Government, in seeking political and economic advantage abroad, has taken a shortsighted view that we must support certain political factions and oppose others. We overlook the fact that our greatest appeal for the minds of people around the world is the way we traditionally have forged our national destiny through free and open discussion, letting the most popular opinions rise to the top and become policy but still allowing the 'despised minority' to work toward the day when it can take control. Thus to win support abroad we must stand by what is truest to our nature. Woodrow Wilson realized this, and so did Franklin Roosevelt and John Kennedy, but our diplomacy often thwarts this approach. So we are puzzled when foreigners say, 'We like Americans, but we do not like American policy.' We accordingly end up on the side of regimes that are hated by the great majority of the people. Inevitably, the dictators will be overthrown, and then our interests will suffer.

"We do not have to overthrow governments to demonstrate our intention; rather, that is resented as meddling. But if we will show our sympathy for dissident journalists and other spokesmen, whether of the left or the right, we should find our natural claim to hemispheric leadership once again respected. Actually, this is the easiest path to follow, because in nearly every country of the world there are many courageous journalists willing to risk everything for their causes. All they need is a spark of international attention to give them the will to act. And experience shows that one persistent editor can often embarrass a government into changing its policies."

*   *   *

PIETSCH, Paul Andrew   1929-

PERSONAL: Born August 8, 1929, in New York, N.Y.; son of Elwood Paul and Bridget (McDonnell) Pietsch; married Myrtle Evelyn Miller (a nurse aide and laboratory technician), 1950; children: Samuel Hart, Benjamin Elwood, Mary Theresa Pietsch Randall, Abigail Lisa. *Education:* Syracuse University, A.B., 1954; University of Pennsylvania, Ph.D., 1960. *Politics:* Democrat. *Home:* 2600 East Fifth St., Bloomington, Ind. 47401. *Agent:* Harriet Wasserman, Russell & Volkening, Inc., 551 Fifth Ave., New York, N.Y. 10017. *Office:* School of Optometry, Indiana University, Bloomington, Ind. 47401.

CAREER: University of Pennsylvania, Philadelphia, instructor in physiology, 1958; Bowman Gray School of Medicine, Winston-Salem, N.C., instructor in anatomy, 1960-61; State

University of New York at Buffalo, assistant professor of anatomy, 1961-64; Dow Chemical Co., Midland, Mich., senior research molecular biologist in biochemistry, 1964-70; Indiana University, Bloomington, associate professor, 1970-78, professor of anatomy at School of Optometry, 1978—, chairman of department of basic health sciences, 1977—. *Military service:* U.S. Army, 1946-49, 1951.

MEMBER: American Association of Anatomists, Society for Developmental Biology, American Federation of Teachers (president, 1974-75), Pan-American Association of Anatomists, British Society for the Philosophy of Science. *Awards, honors:* Medical journalism award from American Medical Association, 1972, for article "Shuffle Brain."

WRITINGS: Shufflebrain, Houghton, 1981. Contributor of more than one hundred fifty articles to technical journals and popular magazines, including *Harper's* and *Quest.*

WORK IN PROGRESS: A book on the relationship between memory and regeneration; a novel dealing with the relationship of philosophy and art to science; laboratory investigations of memory and regeneration.

SIDELIGHTS: Pietsch wrote: "My scientific research is into the logic of recurring biological events; that is, memory and regeneration. I teach human neuroanatomy, microanatomy (histology), and ocular biology. I began writing for the general reader initially with the desire to export scientific knowledge beyond the cloister of the laboratory, but soon found that the common language opened up a view of nature I had not seen before. Science and philosophy need art to complete their destiny. I backed into writing as a free-lance journalist."

*   *   *

PILINSZKY, Janos   1921-1981

OBITUARY NOTICE: Born November 25, 1921, in Budapest, Hungary; died May 27, 1981, in Budapest, Hungary. Poet. Largely inspired by the atrocities he witnessed as a soldier at the close of World War II, Pilinszky wrote poems that attempted to capture the feelings of humiliation and terror experienced by the victims of the holocaust. Among his books of poetry that have been translated into English are *Trapeze and Parallel Bar, On the Third Day, Splinters, Denouement,* and *Crater.* Obituaries and other sources: *Who's Who in the Socialist Countries,* K. G. Saur, 1978; *Who's Who in the World,* 4th edition, Marquis, 1978; *London Times,* June 2, 1981.

*   *   *

PIRANDELLO, Luigi   1867-1936

BRIEF ENTRY: Born June 28, 1867, in Girgenti, Sicily; died in his sleep, December 10, 1936, in Rome, Italy; cremated. Italian playwright, novelist, short story writer, essayist, and poet. Pirandello is considered by some critics to be the greatest short story writer of the twentieth century, and others have listed him with Brecht, Synge, and O'Neill among the greatest modern playwrights. He is credited with inventing "grottesco," the expressionistic theatre of the grotesque that explores the drama of disillusionment or the psychological realities that lie beneath social appearances. Pirandello also innovated the play-within-a-play, play-outside-the-play, and scripted improvisation techniques. A pessimistic philosopher and a grim humorist, Pirandello believed that truth is nonexistent and that personalities are continually evolving. His plots are more psychological and symbolic than philosophical in that they center on trauma and schizophrenia. Through his explorations of the conflict between reality and illusion, Pirandello revealed his main themes: that man creates his life, that reality is relative, and that art is reality. Pirandello, who was patronized by Mussolini, joined the Fascist party in 1924 and was named a High Commander of St. Maurice. In 1934 he was awarded the Nobel Prize in literature. The writer was also named Commander of the Crown by the Italian Government and a member of the Legion of Honor by the French Government. His works include *L'Esclusa* (1893; title means "The Outcast"), *Il fu Mattia Pascal* (1904; title means "The Late Mattia Pascal"), and *Sei personaggi in cerca d'autore* (1921; title means "Six Characters in Search of an Author"). *Residence:* Rome, Italy. *Biographical/critical sources: The Reader's Encyclopedia of World Drama,* Crowell, 1969; *Reader's Companion to World Literature,* second edition, New American Library, 1973; *Twentieth-Century Literary Criticism,* Volume 4, Gale, 1981.

*   *   *

PIRIE-GORDON, (Charles) Harry (Clinton)   1883(?)-1969

OBITUARY NOTICE: Born c. 1883; died December 8, 1969, in London, England. Genealogist and author. Pirie-Gordon collaborated with Frederick Rolfe, writing *Hubert's Arthur, Being Certain Curious Documents Found Among the Literary Remains of Mr. N.C., Here Produced by Prospero and Caliban* and *The Weird of the Wanderer, Being the Papyrus Records of Some Incidents in One of the Previous Lives of Mr. Nicholas Crabbe, Here Produced by Prospero and Caliban.* Obituaries and other sources: *AB Bookman's Weekly,* January 19, 1970; *Science Fiction and Fantasy Literature,* Volume II: *Contemporary Science Fiction Authors II,* Gale, 1979.

*   *   *

PITCHFORD, Kenneth S(amuel)   1931-

PERSONAL: Born January 24, 1931, in Moorhead, Minn.; married Robin Morgan (a poet), 1962; children: one. *Education:* University of Minnesota, B.A. (summa cum laude), 1952; attended University of Washington, Seattle, and Magdalen College, Oxford, 1956-57; New York University, M.A., 1959. *Home:* 109 Third Ave., New York, N.Y. 10003.

CAREER: New York University, New York, N.Y., 1958-62; free-lance writer and editor. Member of faculty at New School for Social Research, 1964; writer-in-residence at Yaddo Colony, summer, 1958. *Military service:* U.S. Army, Infantry, 1953-55; became sergeant. *Awards, honors:* Fulbright fellowship, 1956-57; award from *Isis* short story contest, 1956, for "Templates for a Family Group"; Eugene Lee-Hamilton Award for Poetry, 1957; Borestone Mountain Award, 1964.

WRITINGS: The Blizzard Ape (poems), Scribner, 1958; *A Suite of Angels and Other Poems,* University of North Carolina Press, 1967; *Color Photos of the Atrocities* (poems), Little, Brown, 1973. Also author of *The Contraband Poems.*

Work represented in anthologies, including *Poets of Today,* Volume V, Scribner, 1958; *New World Writing Twenty-One,* 1963; *A Controversy of Poets,* 1965. Contributor to magazines and newspapers, including *Chicago Review, Listener, New Statesman, New Yorker, Transatlantic Review,* and *Kenyon Review.* Associate editor of *New International Yearbook,* 1960-66.

BIOGRAPHICAL/CRITICAL SOURCES: Poetry, July, 1968.*

PLIMMER, Charlotte 1916-
(Charlotte Denis, a joint pseudonym)

PERSONAL: Born in 1916 in Cleveland, Ohio; daughter of Saul and Mary (Gootkin) Fingerhut; married Clifford Straus, 1937 (divorced, 1949); married Denis Plimmer (a writer), 1950. *Education:* Attended Oberlin College, 1934-35; Ohio State University, B.A., 1938. *Home:* 41 Randolph Ave., London W.9, England.

CAREER: Writer. Radio producer for Office of War Information, 1941-42; contract scriptwriter for Mutual Broadcasting Co., 1941-44; career and education editor for *Seventeen*, 1945-47; correspondent in Israel and Europe for Women's National News Service, 1949-50; managing editor of *Photoplay*, 1952-54. *Member:* Phi Beta Kappa.

WRITINGS—All with husband, Denis Plimmer: *Slave Master*, Popular Library, 1971 (published in England as *The Damn'd Master: An Authentic Account of an Eighteenth-Century Slaver*, New English Library, 1971); *Slavery: The Anglo-American Involvement*, Barnes & Noble, 1973; (under joint pseudonym Charlotte Denis) *King's Wench*, Star Books, 1975, Pocket Books, 1976; (under joint pseudonym Charlotte Denis) *King's Bastard*, Star Books, 1976; *London: A Visitor's Companion*, Norton, 1977; *A Matter of Expediency: The Jettison of Admiral Sir Dudley North*, Quartet Books, 1978; (with Celia Hunter) *Positive Beauty*, Hutchinson, 1979; *A Pictorial History of Marks and Spencer*, Sundial Books, in press.

Television plays: "Insurrection's Child," first broadcast by Rediffusion, 1968; "The Diary and the Devil's Advocate," first broadcast by Rediffusion, 1968; "The Ordeal of Sister Paul," first broadcast by Rediffusion, 1968; "The Chequers Manoeuvre," first broadcast by British Broadcasting Corp. (BBC-TV), 1968; "Cause of Death," first broadcast by BBC-TV, 1968; "Where Have They Gone, All the Little Children?," first broadcast by BBC-TV, 1969; "And Was Invited to Form a Government," first boradcast by BBC-TV, 1969; "Formula for Treason," first broadcast by BBC-TV, 1969; "The Wrong Side of the Hill," first broadcast by Rediffusion, 1969; "You've Got to Keep Them Talking," first broadcast by BBC-TV, 1969; "Paradise Destruct," first broadcast by London Weekend TV, 1970; "The Ambassador's Chauffeur," BBC-TV, 1975.

Radio plays, except as noted; first broadcast on BBC-Radio: "Slavery, the Bloody Commerce," 1972; "The Penkovsky Riddle," 1973; "Where There's a Will," 1973; "Napoleon Aboard *Bellerephon*," 1975; "Autobiography of Mark Twain" (abridgement), 1976; "Somebody's Telling the Truth" (adaptation of work by Patricia McGerr), 1975; "The Mountain of Light," 1977; "Antigua Penny Puce" (abridgement of work by Robert Graves), 1978; "Women of Words" (documentary about Dorothy Parker and Elinor Glyn), 1980. Also author of "Tallulah" and dramatizations of fourteen short stories by Ernest Hemingway.

Contributor to periodicals, including *Saturday Evening Post, Reader's Digest, Saturday Review, Life, McCall's, Redbook, Good Housekeeping, Holiday, Esquire, Look, Chatelaine, Punch, Observer, Sunday Times Magazine, Telegraph, New York Times Magazine,* and *Herald Tribune Magazine.*

WORK IN PROGRESS: The Power Seekers; two novels.

SIDELIGHTS: Charlotte Plimmer told *CA:* "It is a constant source of amazement to friends and editors that any marriage could have survived over three decades of creative collaboration. As far as Denis and I are concerned, the living together has been enhanced by the writing—and vice versa. We can,

however, have knock-down, drag-out battles over the choice of a punctuation mark. We are frequently asked how we divide the work. We don't. The approach, even the technique, varies from project to project, but they are always shared. We have, for interviews, evolved a stock answer: 'Charlotte supplies the verbs, Denis the adjectives, and we split the infinitives between us.'"

*   *   *

PLIMMER, Denis 1914-
(Charlotte Denis, a joint pseudonym)

PERSONAL: Born September 27, 1914, in Melbourne, Australia; son of Harry (an actor) and Ena (an actress; maiden name, Shanahan) Plimmer; married Charlotte Fingerhut Straus (a writer), July 1, 1950. *Education:* Columbia University, B.A., 1937. *Home:* 41 Randolph Ave., London W.9, England.

CAREER: Office of War Information, radio writer and producer, 1942-43; *Time* (magazine), foreign news editor, 1943-46, editor-in-chief of radio program "Time Views the News," 1944-45; *New York Post*, New York City, foreign correspondent, 1946; Overseas News Agency, New York City, bureau chief in London and Paris, 1946-50; Foote, Cone & Belding, Switzerland, director of public relations, 1950; writer, 1950—. Commentator at WQXR-Radio, New York, 1944-46.

WRITINGS—All with wife, Charlotte Plimmer: *Slave Master*, Popular Library, 1971 (published in England as *The Damn'd Master: An Authentic Account of an Eighteenth-Century Slaver*, New English Library, 1971); *Slavery: The Anglo-American Involvement*, Barnes & Noble, 1973; (under joint pseudonym Charlotte Denis) *King's Wench*, Star Books, 1975, Pocket Books, 1976; (under joint pseudonym Charlotte Denis) *King's Bastard*, Star Books, 1976; *London: A Visitor's Companion*, Norton, 1977; *A Matter of Expediency: The Jettison of Admiral Sir Dudley North*, Quartet Books, 1978; (with Celia Hunter) *Positive Beauty*, Hutchinson, 1979; *A Pictorial History of Marks and Spencer*, Sundial Books, in press.

Television plays: "Insurrection's Child," first broadcast by Rediffusion, 1968; "The Diary and the Devil's Advocate," first broadcast by Rediffusion, 1968; "The Ordeal of Sister Paul," first broadcast by Rediffusion, 1968; "The Chequers Manoeuvre," first broadcast by British Broadcasting Corp. (BBC-TV), 1968; "Cause of Death," first broadcast by BBC-TV, 1968; "Where Have They Gone, All the Little Children?," first broadcast by BBC-TV, 1969; "And Was Invited to Form a Government," first broadcast by BBC-TV, 1969; "Formula for Treason," first broadcast by BBC-TV, 1969; "The Wrong Side of the Hill," first broadcast by Rediffusion, 1969; "You've Got to Keep Them Talking," first broadcast by BBC-TV, 1969; "Paradise Destruct," first broadcast by London Weekend TV, 1970; "The Ambassador's Chauffeur," BBC-TV, 1975.

Radio plays, except as noted; first broadcast on BBC-Radio: "Slavery, the Bloody Commerce," 1972; "The Penkovsky Riddle," 1973; "Where There's a Will," 1973; "Napoleon Aboard *Bellerephon*," 1975; "Autobiography of Mark Twain" (abridgement), 1976; "Somebody's Telling the Truth" (adaptation of work by Patricia McGerr), 1975; "The Mountain of Light," 1977; "Antigua Penny Puce" (abridgement of work by Robert Graves), 1978; "Women of Words" (documentary about Dorothy Parker and Elinor Glyn), 1980. Also author of "Tallulah" and dramatizations of fourteen short stories by Ernest Hemingway.

Contributor to periodicals, including *Saturday Evening Post, Reader's Digest, Saturday Review, Life, McCall's, Redbook,*

Good Housekeeping, Holiday, Esquire, Look, Chatelaine, Punch, Observer, Sunday Times Magazine, Telegraph, New York Times Magazine, and *Herald Tribune Magazine.*

WORK IN PROGRESS: *The Power Seekers;* two novels.

SIDELIGHTS: Denis Plimmer told *CA:* "The great Dr. Johnson said that only a fool would write for anything except money. And the only way to achieve professionalism is to write so effectively that someone will pay you for it. Of course the mighty lexicographer was being slightly duplicitous; one does indeed write for money, but one also does so out of a deep, unanalyzable need to write. Otherwise why embark on the world's least lucrative profession (except for acting)? Why not be a crooked politician and have your memoirs ghost-written; or a fee-splitting doctor; or a pop singer with the requisite nasal whine? I do not aim these questions at my fellow writers. We know the answer: *Quem Jupitor vult perdere, dementat prius.*

"My first writing, a short story, was sold to the *Minneapolis Journal* for five dollars; I was then fifteen. I wrote easily in those days; now with difficulty. The more you know about your craft, the more there is to learn.

"Writers in English have one great advantage over all others; our language is the finest, most beautiful, most flexible, least formal, and most expressive of all the languages in history. We should thank God for it. Shakespeare, said Ben Jonson, had small Latin and less Greek. He should worry!"

*   *   *

PLOGHOFT, Milton E(rnest) 1923-

PERSONAL: Surname is pronounced *Ploe*-hoft; born May 15, 1923, in Atlantic, Iowa; son of Grover Cleveland (a farmer) and Jennie Ora (Freeman) Ploghoft; married Zella I. Mitchell (a realtor), May 22, 1945; children: Milton Eugene, Philip, Shelley, Tara. *Education:* Northwest Missouri State University, B.S.Ed., 1949; Drake University, M.S., 1951; attended University of Missouri, 1953-54, and University of Minnesota, 1955; University of Nebraska, Ed.D., 1957. *Politics:* Democrat. *Religion:* Unitarian Universalist. *Home:* 133 Longview Heights, Athens, Ohio 45701. *Office:* Department of Curriculum/Instruction, Ohio University, 206 McCracken Hall, Athens, Ohio 45701.

CAREER: Teacher of social studies at junior high schools in Quitman, Mo., 1943-44, and Coin, Iowa, 1944-45; elementary school principal in Audubon, Iowa, 1946-50; elementary supervisor at schools in Kearney, Neb., 1950-52, and McCook, Neb., 1952-56; Ohio University, Athens, principal of university school, 1957-58; University of Nebraska, Lincoln, associate professor of elementary education, 1958-62; U.S. Agency for International Development, Washington, D.C., project director in Kano, Nigeria, 1963-65; Ohio University, professor of curriculum and instruction, 1965—, director of Social Science Center, 1966—, and Office of Graduate Studies, 1971-74. Visiting lecturer at University of Saigon, 1971. Chairman of Nebraska Civil Service System, 1958-60. Member of Ohio Division of Corrections Educational Planning Commission, 1971-72; director of First National Conference on Television and Children, 1979. Program development director for U.S. Agency for International Development team in Botswana, 1980. *Military service:* U.S. Army, 1942-43.

MEMBER: National Education Association, Association for Supervision and Curriculum Development, National Association of Elementary School Principals, National Council for the Social Studies, Kiwanis International. *Awards, honors:* Grants from George Gund Foundation, 1979 and 1981; Three Best

Papers Award from International Communication Association, 1980, for "Receivership Skills: The Television Experience"; grant from Charles Stewart Mott Foundation, 1980.

WRITINGS: *The Emerging Elementary School Curriculum,* C. E. Merrill, 1963, 3rd edition, 1975; *Social Science Education in the Elementary School,* C. E. Merrill, 1971, 2nd edition, 1976; *Television and You: Textbook for Children,* Ohio University, 1975; (with James A. Anderson) *Education for the Television Age,* C. C Thomas, 1981; (with Anderson) *Teaching Critical TV Viewing Skills, an Integrated Approach,* C. C Thomas, 1981. Contributor to education journals.

SIDELIGHTS: Ploghoft told *CA:* "All of my efforts have been directed to a single purpose: that of assessing man's contemporary condition in order to identify the adequacy of traditional education and the need for innovations to fill the gaps that may be found."

*   *   *

POBO, Kenneth 1954-

PERSONAL: Born August 24, 1954, in Elmhurst, Ill.; son of Louis G. (a chemist) and Myrtle (Swanson) Pobo. *Education:* Wheaton College, Wheaton, Ill., B.A., 1976; University of Wisconsin—Milwaukee, M.A., 1978. *Politics:* "Extremely liberal Democrat." *Religion:* "Mystical agnostic." *Home:* 2319 East Park Pl., Milwaukee, Wis. 53211. *Office:* Department of English, University of Wisconsin—Milwaukee, Milwaukee, Wis. 53201.

CAREER: University of Wisconsin—Milwaukee, teaching assistant in English, 1977—.

WRITINGS: *Musings From the Porchlit Sea* (poems), Branden Press, 1979; *Postcards From America* (poems), Hidden People, 1980; *Billions of Lit Cigarettes* (poems), Raw Dog, 1980. Contributor to magazines, including *Gay Sunshine, Poem, Tendril,* and *Another Chicago.* Poetry editor of *Cream City Review,* 1980-81.

WORK IN PROGRESS: *A Vision Tested in the Flower: The Aaron Stern Poems; The Burning Boats,* a poetry chapbook.

SIDELIGHTS: Pobo commented: "I consider myself a poet in the tradition of the modernist writers Eliot, Pound, Stevens, and Auden. Like my heroine Bette Davis, I believe (as she says), 'In the arts, you *must* contribute.' Like her, I would like someone to write on my tombstone, 'She did it the hard way.' My poetry combines juke-box music, conversational dialogue, and much character development. I hope to see an end to the boring 'I' poems of contemporary writing. I distrust the vast majority of literary academic critics. I also still believe Baudelaire's ideas on modernity are applicable to modern poets. I am extremely interested in how the arts intermingle and connect.

"I believe the poet must read avidly but also must understand how to boogie in a disco if necessary. I am fervently committed to the gay rights movement and would hope my own work reflects this perspective without seeming pedagogical. I am also a feminist and would like to see the Reagan patriarchy go plop-plop in the sea.

"I was raised in Villa Park, Illinois, that dead town, village of the vast ennui. I enjoy my family and friends. I expect to continue writing until they pry my cold dead hand from the typewriter. Is there any hope for the human race? No. Is there any hope for individuals? Yes."

POLAK, Jacques Jacobus   1914-

PERSONAL: Born April 25, 1914, in Rotterdam, Netherlands; son of James and Elisabeth Flora Polak; married Josephine Weening, December 21, 1937; children: Herman-Joost, Willem Louis. *Education:* University of Amsterdam, M.A., 1936, Ph.D., 1937. *Home:* 3420 Porter St. N.W., Washington, D.C. 20016. *Office:* International Monetary Fund, 700 19th St. N.W., Washington, D.C. 20431.

CAREER: League of Nations, economist in Geneva, Switzerland, and Princeton, N.J., 1937-43; Netherlands Embassy, Washington, D.C., economist, 1943-44; United Nations Relief and Rehabilitation Administration, Washington, D.C., 1944-46, began as assistant financial adviser, became economic adviser; International Monetary Fund, Washington, D.C., chief of Statistics Division, 1947-48, assistant director of research and statistics department, 1948-52, deputy director, 1952-58, director of department, 1958—, economic counselor, 1966—. Professorial lecturer at Johns Hopkins University, 1949-50, and George Washington University, 1950-55. *Member:* Econometric Society (fellow), American Economic Association, Cosmos Club, International Club. *Awards, honors:* D.H.C. from Erasmus University, 1972.

WRITINGS: (Editor and translator) Jan Tinbergen, *The Dynamics of Business Cycles: A Study in Economic Fluctuations,* University of Chicago Press, 1950; *An International Economic System,* University of Chicago Press, 1953; *The National Income of the Netherlands Indies, 1921-1939,* University of Indonesia, c. 1966; (editor with Robert A. Mundell) *The New International Monetary System,* Columbia University Press, 1977. Also author of *Economic Recovery of the Countries Assisted by the United Nations Relief and Rehabilitation Administration,* 1946.

In Dutch: *Publieke werken als vorm van conjunctuurpolitiek,* (title means "Public Works as a Form of Business Cycle Policy"), Nijhoff, 1938; (with S. Posthuma and I. H. Vos) *Internationale coordinatie der economische politiek,* Nijhoff, 1960.

Contributor to professional journals.*

*   *   *

POLEVOI, Boris
    See KAMPOV, Boris Nikolayevich

*   *   *

POLIAKOV, Leon   1910-

PERSONAL: Born November 25, 1910, in St. Petersburg, Russia (now Leningrad, U.S.S.R.); came to France in 1924; son of Wladimir and Fanny (Friedman) Poliakov; married Germaine Rousso (a choir director), January 8, 1952; children: Jean-Michael. *Education:* Received Dr. d'Etat es Lettres from University of Paris. *Home:* 35 Avenue du President Kennedy, 91300 Massy, France. *Agent:* A. D. Peters & Co. Ltd., 10 Buckingham St., London WC2N 6BU, England.

CAREER: Writer. Centre de Documentation Juive Contemporaine, Paris, France, head of research department, 1945-54; associated with Ecole Pratique des Hautes Etudes, Paris, 1954—. Director of research at Centre National de Recherche Scientifique, Paris. *Military service:* French Army, 1939-45. *Awards, honors:* Anisfield-Wolf Award, 1975, for *The Aryan Myth.*

In English translation: (Editor with Jacques Sabille) *La Condition des juifs en France sous l'occupation italienne,* [Paris], 1946, translation published as *Jews Under the Italian Occupation,* Editions du Centre, 1955; *Breviaire de la haine: Le*

IIIe Reich et les juifs, [Paris], 1951, translation published as *Harvest of Hate: The Nazi Program for the Destruction of the Jews of Europe,* Syracuse University Press, 1954, revised and expanded edition, Holocaust Library, 1979; *Histoire de l'antisemitisme,* four volumes, Calmann-Levy, 1955, translation by Richard Howard published as *The History of Anti-Semitism,* Vanguard Press, 1965-81; *Les Banquiers juifs et le Saint-Siege du XIIIe au XVIIe siecle,* S.E.V.P.E.N., 1965, abridged edition, Calmann-Levy, 1967, translation by Miriam Kochan published as *Jewish Bankers and the Holy See From the Thirteenth to the Seventeenth Century,* Routledge & Kegan Paul, 1977; *Le Mythe aryen: Essai sur les sources du racisme et des nationalismes,* Calmann-Levy, 1971, translation by Edmund Howard published as *The Aryan Myth: A History of Racist and Nationalist Ideas in Europe,* Basic Books, 1974.

In French: *L'Etoile jaune,* Editions du Centre, 1949; (contributor) Itzhak Ben-Zvi, *Les Tribus dispersees,* Editions de Minuit, 1949; *Petite histoire de l'antisemitisme,* Comptoir du livre du Keren Hasefer, 1956; *De Mahomet aux marranes, suivi de les juifs au Saint-Siege, les Morisques d'Espagne et leur expulsion,* Calmann-Levy, 1961; (editor) *Les Proces de Jerusalem,* Calmann-Levy, 1963; (editor) *Auschwitz,* Julliard, 1964; *De Voltaire a Wagner,* Calmann-Levy, 1968; *Le Developpement de l'antisemitisme en Europe aux temps modernes, 1700-1850,* Floch, 1968; *De l'antisionisme a l'antisemitisme,* Calmann-Levy, 1969; *Le Proces de Nuremberg,* Julliard, 1971; *Les Idees anthropologiques des philosophes du Siecle des Lumieres,* P. Geuthner, 1971; *Les Juifs et notre historie* (addresses, essays, and lectures), Flammarion, 1973; (author of preface) *Hommes et betes: Entretiens sur le racisme,* Mouton, 1975; (with Christiar Delacampagne and Patrick Girard) *Le Racisme,* Seghers, 1976; *La Causalite diabolique,* Calmann-Levy, 1980.

Other; in German, except as noted: *Di gele late* (Hebrew), [Paris], 1952; (editor with Josef Wulf) *Das Dritte Reich und die Juden,* Arani, 1955; (with Wulf) *Das Dritte Reich und Diener,* Arani, 1956; (editor with Wulf) *Das Dritte Reich und seine Denker,* Arani, 1959.

*   *   *

POLIER, Justine Wise   1903-

PERSONAL: Born April 12, 1903, in Portland, Ore.; daughter of Stephen S. (a rabbi) and Louise (Waterman) Wise; married Leon Arthur Tulin, June 14, 1927 (died December 12, 1932); married Shad Polier, March 26, 1937; children: (first marriage) Stephen Wise; (second marriage) Trudy H. Polier Festinger, Jonathan W., Michael W. (deceased). *Education:* Attended Bryn Mawr College, 1920-22, and Radcliffe College, 1922-23; Barnard College, A.B., 1924; studied at International Labor Office, Geneva, Switzerland, 1925; Yale University, LL.B., 1928. *Religion:* Jewish. *Home:* 175 East 64th St., New York, N.Y. 10021. *Office:* 100 East 85th St., New York, N.Y. 10028.

CAREER: New York State Department of Labor, referee in Workmen's Compensation Division, 1929-34; City of New York, New York City, assistant corporate counsel, 1934-35, counsel to mayor's committee on unemployment relief, 1934-35, and Emergency Relief Bureau, 1935, justice of Domestic Relations Court, 1935-62; New York State Family Court, judge, 1962-73; Children's Defense Fund, Washington Research Project, director of program for juvenile justice, 1973-76. President of Louise Wise Services, 1941-78; president, 1960-66, and member of board of directors of Wiltwyck School for Boys. Member of Joint Commission of Institute of Juvenile Administration and American Bar Association; member of advisory review board of Human Resources Administration; vice-president of Field Foundation; delegate to White House Planning Conference on Civil Rights, 1965.

Chairperson of Eleanor Roosevelt Institute, 1980—; president of Kenontis-Swift Foundation. Member of New York State Department of Education advisory council for children with handicapping conditions, New York State Task Force on Mental Health Services for Children and Youth, and New York State Task Force on Juvenile Violence; member of New York Citizens for Foster Care of Children. Vice-president of New York City Citizens Committee for Children, 1945-61; member of board of trustees of New York School for Nursery Years and Church Peace Union; member of board of visitors of School of Law at Antioch College. Honorary president of Women's Division of American Jewish Congress, 1948-56, chairman of National executive committee, 1956-60. Consultant to Office of Civilian Defense.

MEMBER: American Orthopsychiatric Association (fellow), National Council on Crime and Delinquency (member of advisory council of judges), Association of the Bar of the City of New York. *Awards, honors:* Named woman of the month by American Women's Association, 1948; Isaac Ray Award from American Psychiatric Association, 1964, for outstanding contributions to law and psychiatry; Naomi Lehman Award from Federation of Jewish Philanthropies, 1965, for distinguished service; distinguished service award from City of New York, 1973; Human Services Award from New York and Bronx Mental Health Association and New York Association of University Women, both 1973; Hannah G. Solomon Award from National Council of Jewish Women, 1975, for distinguished efforts to achieve justice for children; Eleanor Roosevelt Humanitarian Award from board of directors of Wiltwyck School for Boys, 1975; LL.D. from Princeton University, 1976, Kenyon College, 1977, City University of New York, 1978, and Yale University, 1979; Gertrude F. Zimand Memorial Award from National Child Labor Committee, 1976; Marion E. Kenworthy Award from School of Social Work at Columbia University, 1979; Fowler Harper fellow at Yale University; Ittleson Award from American Orthopsychiatric Association, 1980.

WRITINGS: Everyone's Children, Nobody's Child: A Judge Looks at Underprivileged Children in the United States, Scribner, 1941, reprinted, Arno, 1974; (editor with James Waterman Wise) *The Personal Letters of Stephen Wise,* Beacon Press, 1956; *A View From the Bench: The Juvenile Court,* National Council on Crime and Delinquency, 1964; *The Rule of Law and the Role of Psychiatry,* Johns Hopkins Press, 1968; (author of foreword) *Juvenile Justice Confounded: The Pretensions and Realities of Treatment Services,* National Council on Crime and Delinquency, 1972. Contributor to learned journals.

BIOGRAPHICAL/CRITICAL SOURCES: New York Times, February 17, 1973.

* * *

POLINGER, Elliot Hirsch 1898-1970

OBITUARY NOTICE: Born in 1898; died March 2, 1970, in New York, N.Y. Educator and author. A professor emeritus of romance languages at City College (now of the City University of New York), Polinger wrote *Pierre Charles Roy: Playwright and Satirist (1688-1764),* a biography. Polinger also wrote a volume on Diderot and several French textbooks. Obituaries and other sources: *New York Times,* March 4, 1970; *AB Bookman's Weekly,* March 16, 1970.

POLONSKY, Abraham (Lincoln) 1910-
(Emmett Hogarth, a joint pseudonym)

PERSONAL: Born December 5, 1910, in New York, N.Y.; son of Henry and Rebecca (Rosoff) Polonsky; married Sylvia Marrow, 1937; children: Susan, Henry Victor. *Education:* City College of New York (now of the City University of New York), B.A., 1932; Columbia University, LLB., 1935. *Religion:* Jewish. *Residence:* Beverly Hills, Calif.

CAREER: City College of New York (now City College of the City University of New York), New York City, instructor in English, 1932-42; called to the bar, 1935. Screenwriter; director of motion pictures, including "Force of Evil," 1949, "Romance of a Horse Thief," 1971. *Military service:* U.S. Office of Strategic Services, 1943-45, served in European theater.

WRITINGS—Novels: (With Mitchell A. Wilson under joint pseudonym Emmett Hogarth) *The Goose Is Cooked,* Simon & Schuster, 1940; *The Enemy Sea,* Little, Brown, 1943; *The World Above,* Little, Brown, 1951; *A Season of Fear,* Cameron Associates, 1956; *Zenia's Way,* Lippincott, 1980.

Screenplays: (With Frank Butler and Helen Deutch) "Golden Earrings" (adapted from the novel by Yolanda Foldes), Paramount, 1946; "Body and Soul," United Artists, 1947; (with Ira Wolfert; and director) "Force of Evil," (adapted from the novel by Wolfert, *Tucker's People*), Metro-Goldwyn-Mayer, 1949; "I Can Get It for You Wholesale" (adapted from the novel by Jerome Weidman), Twentieth Century-Fox, 1951; (with Howard Rodman) "Madigan" (adapted from the novel by Robert Dougherty, *The Commissioner*), Universal, 1968; (and director) "Tell Them Willie Boy Is Here," (adapted from the book by Harry Lawton, *Willie Boy*.), Universal, 1969; "Avalanche Express," Twentieth Century-Fox, 1979.

Author of essays, short stories, and scripts for radio and television.

WORK IN PROGRESS: "Monsignore," a screenplay for Twentieth Century-Fox; "Assassination On Embassy Row," a television screenplay adapted from the book by John Dinges and Saul Landau; "Mario and the Magician," a screenplay adapted from the novella by Thomas Mann; *Children of Eden,* a novel.

SIDELIGHTS: In 1947, after writing the original screenplay of "Body and Soul," Polonsky was hired by John Garfield and Robert Roberts to write and direct "Force of Evil." Ostensibly a film about the numbers racket, "Force of Evil" is an experiment in words and images, portraying its characters and social scene in great depth. In England, reviewers Lindsay Anderson and others hailed Polonsky as an important filmmaker, and U.S. critics later echoed that praise. In 1968 Andrew Sarris called "Force of Evil" "one of the great films of the modern American cinema."

During the McCarthy period, Polonsky's career suffered. He appeared as a hostile witness before the House Un-American Activities Committee in 1951 and was blacklisted until 1967. During that time he wrote using "fronts"—other writers submitting Polonsky's work as their own.

His novels include *The Enemy Sea,* a love-triangle drama set on an oil tanker during World War II; *The World Above,* a character study of a psychiatrist working with war veterans and the effects of McCarthyism on scientific experiment; *A Season of Fear,* a drama of loyalties under political fear; and *Zenia's Way,* a drama of a young man and his beloved aunt involved in important political and moral decisions in 1922, and then in the 1970's, after fifty years of separation.

CA INTERVIEW

CA interviewed Abraham Polonsky on April 14, 1980.

CA: What was Hollywood like when you first arrived there?

POLONSKY: I first came to Hollywood with Gertrude Berg, who was a client in the law office in which I worked. Hollywood was lively and passionate over the Spanish civil war. We heard Hemingway and Malraux, went to parties to raise money for ambulances for the Republicans, and so on. I met some young people in the movies. I was a writer, always had been, but I had no ambition to work in films.

CA: What were you writing?

POLONSKY: Short stories. A novel. I was still close to the student excitement and hopes of a little literary society at City College. In this group were Leonard Boudin, Milton Millhauser, Paul Goodman, William Barrett, myself, and one or two others. I went to the movies, Russian, for one set of reasons, American, for another.

CA: Were the Russian movies a learning experience?

POLONSKY: They were classics of aesthetics and the current drama of political hope. I went to see our movies because we adored them and they were fun. I was also intrigued by the German expressionist films. It took some time to realize how deep and advanced were the aesthetics of American films, how hidden in my familiarity with them, and my long life as a Saturday moviegoer. My closest friend was Bernard Herrmann, whose musical career was beginning and through whom an intense musical exploration sort of drifted within and around me. He was also a movie fan and a great finder of the unusual in literature. I was also deeply concerned with radical politics. I became friends with Mitchel Wilson, a physicist. He was trying to be a writer. We wrote a mystery story together, *The Goose Is Cooked.* I then wrote a serial for *American* magazine, *The Enemy Sea,* This led to a contract to write movies for Paramount, which I signed, although I was on my way to England for the OSS (Office of Strategic Services).

After the war I arrived at Paramount. The town was lively with the victory in the war, the problems of politics, radical and otherwise, the ominous presence of the bomb, and the crazy excitement of trying to write movies. But all the while I considered myself a novelist. John McNulty warned me to leave. He was himself always getting ready to leave. He showed me my first set, with Alan Ladd standing on a box for a close two-shot kiss with his leading lady. Everything McNulty considered awful I thought magical, and magical it has remained through bad times and bad pictures as well as good.

You can't understand those times unless you realize that radical politics, the beginnings of the cold war, the bomb, and for me the new world of making movies, were in a boiling mix. I think my films reflect this in one way or another.

I got to write "Body and Soul" for Enterprise because my friend Arnold Manoff gave up on a Barney Ross prizefight picture. It had too many censorship problems. He came to Paramount and sent me over to meet with Garfield and Bob Roberts to see what I could do. I did a new story. "Body and Soul" was a success and led to my becoming a director of "Force of Evil." In that film my early New York life and my thrashing about in Hollywood came together in a personal and political way. Although technique in any medium is basic, being an artist, a mathematician, a good whistler, or a film director is something in your mind. We are prisoners and liberators of the symbolism of consciousness.

Our family went to France then. I wrote *The World Above,* returned and wrote "I Can Get It for You Wholesale," went back to Europe to try out "Mario," started a new novel, *A Season of Fear,* and came home again to be blacklisted.

CA: Were you expecting it?

POLONSKY: Yes.

CA: You refused to hide?

POLONSKY: It wasn't that at all. I thought I had to be home then. Others thought it best to go abroad to work if they could.

CA: You now think you were wrong?

POLONSKY: There's no morality in either position. It's a question of personality and temperament. Or just chance and the moment. The idea of exile, of a world of exiles, is part of the picture of our times. Always has been, I suppose. You become an exile when you have to. You fight to come back and come back when you can. Anyway, I returned and was blacklisted; that is, I was exiled within my own country. I think the Russians call it "internal exile."

CA: Did they then think you were even more dangerous because you were a radical in a top security organization?

POLONSKY: They pretended to. But, in fact, I was taken into the OSS because of my radical knowledge and experience, because of the work that had to be done with the radical base of the resistance movements (not that I ever did.) I was blacklisted because everyone like me was, not because of anything special. What was special was the Cold War. But, you see, it's not so special after all. I lived through the Depression, which generated hope again, and a passionate war that was fatal to lose. I've spent the rest of my life in the cold war which still poisons the world with an endless political smog.

CA: Then what did you do?

POLONSKY: My family moved to New York, and there Arnold Manoff, Walter Bernstein, and myself organized a guerilla movement against the television industry in order to work on some systematic basis not at the whim of the blacklist. Through Walter's friend Charles Russell, a brilliant, young, and brave producer, indifferent to the crazy, fearful politics of the time, we were able first to write on "Danger" and later to help organize under his leadership a program called "You Are There." All the forbidden subjects of the day became through history the drama on television. Free speech, democracy, human rights, the courage to confront oppression, whatever is still good and worth living for became our subjects. The show was a success, and we earned a living.

CA: Did you write under different names?

POLONSKY: At first we used pseudonyms, but as the blacklist became more intense and a business in which lists and magazines were published with names added each week, as the country seemed to tremble under a new inquisition, we finally were forced to use real people instead of imaginary ones. Real people were called fronts, and Walter Bernstein later wrote a film, "The Front," which reflected some of our blacklist experiences. Director Martin Ritt, after each credit, mentioned those who had been blacklisted.

CA: Were there any limitations?

POLONSKY: We couldn't use our own names on anything. I couldn't even get a novel published under my own name.

CA: You couldn't know for certain that your writing would be published?

POLONSKY: It was certain enough. My novel *Season of Fear* was several times accepted and then returned because the accepting editors found it was a little too difficult. In the end, Angus Cameron, who had been editor in chief at Little, Brown, and my publisher formed a company with Carl Marzani and published many blacklisted books, mine among them. But of course the press, itself victimized by the blacklist into firing named reporters, didn't review any of these books, in the main. Certainly not mine.

During this unceasing smog I wrote *Season of Fear,* helped Tyrone Guthrie make *Oedipus Rex* in Canada as a film, did a series in Canada called "Seaway," and with Harry Belafonte sketched out a series of films on the black struggle in our country. The only film Belafonte could get done was one directed by Robert Wise. I later got Universal to buy another, but after much preparation it was buried unborn. Martin Ritt tried to break the blacklist for me, after he had become acceptable through the passage of time, but Paramount wouldn't accept my name. That was the "The Spy Who Came in From the Cold." It seemed I was still out in the cold.

Finally Frank Rosenberg, with the powerful help of Jennings Lang, broke the blacklist, and I was able to work on "Madigan." Then Phillip Waxman, once again under the supervision and with the help of Jennings Lang, helped me become a director again, and "Tell Them Willie Boy" was made. The only other film I directed was "Romance of a Horse Thief." Since then I've worked steadily as a writer, although, like Ring Lardner, few if any of my pictures get made. Right now, because of Frank Yablans it seems my name may once more appear on something besides late-night television. Of course I just had a book published (*Zenia's Way*), which was a great satisfaction to me since I've been trying to write it for twenty years.

CA: Are there things you still can't do?

POLONSKY: Things that age and time have made impossible. The blacklist struck down many of us so that we couldn't work when we were youngest and perhaps most productive. The purpose of the blacklist was to destroy people and in this way frighten those who were not blacklisted. In this it was successful. Some died. Some changed professions. Some became informers and destroyed what is most human in ourselves, our integrity as persons. But most of us survived, and as with survivors in wars, revolutions, nightmares of social change and personal difficulty, those who survived were changed. In the main, they became what they now know more deeply as themselves. This I consider a personal victory of the spirit and the mind.

BIOGRAPHICAL/CRITICAL SOURCES: New York Times, September 15, 1940, June 13, 1943, April 22, 1951, December 19, 1969; *New York Herald-Tribune Book Review,* June 3, 1951; *Sight and Sound,* summer, 1957, spring, 1971; *Film Comment,* fall, 1965; Andrew Sarris, *The American Cinema,* Dutton, 1968; *Film Quarterly,* winter, 1969-70; *Cue,* December 27, 1969; *Film Culture,* fall/winter, 1970; *Washington Post,* October 24, 1979; *Los Angeles Times Book Review,* June 1, 1980; *Chicago Tribune Book World,* August 10, 1980.

—*Interview by Judith Spiegelman*

POOL, Tamar de Sola 1891(?)-1981

OBITUARY NOTICE: Born c. 1891 in Jerusalem, Israel; died June 1, 1981, in New York, N.Y. Educator and author. Tamar de Sola Pool was active in Hadassah, the Zionist women's organization, serving as president of the New York chapter from 1929 until 1935, and of the national chapter from 1938 to 1943. With her husband, Rabbi David de Sola Pool, she wrote several books, including *An Old Faith in the New World: Portrait of Shearith Israel, 1654-1954,* and *The Passover Haggadah: Is There an Answer? An Inquiry Into Some Dilemmas.* She also wrote a play, "Israel and the United Nations: In the Spirit of '76," and a novel, *Triple Cord.* Obituaries and other sources: *Who's Who in World Jewry: A Biographical Dictionary of Outstanding Jews,* Pitman, 1972; *Who's Who in America,* 40th edition, Marquis, 1978; *New York Times,* June 2, 1981.

* * *

PORTER, Mark
See COX, James Anthony

* * *

PORTER, William Sydney 1862-1910
(O. Henry, Oliver Henry, S. H. Peters)

BRIEF ENTRY: Born September 11, 1862, in Greensboro, N.C.; died from the effects of alcoholism, June 5, 1910, in New York. American short story writer, poet, journalist, and editor. One of the most dramatic events of Porter's life occurred while he was a bank teller in Austin, Texas. Accused of embezzlement, he fled to Central America. Turning himself over to the authorities when his wife died, Porter was convicted, though neither his guilt nor his innocence had been adequately proved, and served over three years of a five-year term. Many believe that Porter knew who the criminal was, but would not divulge his identity. After his early release for good behavior, Porter continued writing under the pseudonym O. Henry, a diversion had begun while in prison. One of America's greatest short story writers, Porter received much of his inspiration from his experiences in prison. Although Porter also wrote of the southwest and Latin America, he was considered the prose laureate of Manhattan, and his "Bagdad-on-the-subway" series was a kind of Arabian Nights of New York. Porter possessed a good sense of the romantic and the mysterious as well as great narrative skill. He used the expanded anecdote formula, a method conducive to showing the workings of fate. Most of his stories have a surprise ending, a technique that he was the first to perfect. Porter is known for his inventiveness of plot and character, his compassion for unfortunates, and his understatement of character. Like Dickens, he concentrated on ordinary people, and his favorite topic was habit. "The Gift of the Magi" and "The Ransom of Red Chief" are his most famous stories. His works include *Cabbages and Kings* (1904), *The Four Million* (1906), and *Strictly Business* (1910). *Biographical/critical sources: The Reader's Encyclopedia of American Literature,* Crowell, 1962; *Twentieth-Century Literary Criticism,* Volume 1, Gale, 1978.

* * *

POSTHUMUS, Cyril 1918-

PERSONAL: Born in 1918 in Sunbury-on-Thames, England;

married Betty Margaret Mason; children: one son. *Home:* 35 Stane Way, Ewell, Surrey, England.

CAREER: Free-lance writer. Worked as associate editor of *Autosport,* 1950-57; editor of *Motoring News,* 1957-58, 1960-62; staff writer for *Motor,* 1962-66; editor of *Motor Racing,* 1966-68; European editor of *Road and Track,* 1968. Editor of *Autoworld,* 1967-70. *Member:* Veteran Car Club of Great Britain, Guild of Motoring Writers, Vintage Sports Car Club, Institute of Journalists.

WRITINGS: Miniature Car Construction, Percival Marshall, 1949; (with Cecil Clutton and Denis Jenkinson) *The Racing Car: Development and Design,* Batsford, 1956, revised edition, 1962; *The British Competition Car,* Batsford, 1959.

Sir Henry Seagrave, Batsford, 1961; *World Sports Car Championship,* MacGibbon & Kee, 1961; *The German Grand Prix,* George Newnes, 1966; *Land Speed Record: A Complete History of the Record-Breaking Cars From Thirty-Nine to Six Hundred-Plus Miles per Hour,* Osprey, 1971; (with Gianni Rogliatti) *Period Cars,* Hamlyn, 1973; *Vintage Cars: Motoring in the 1920's,* Hamlyn, 1973; (with Jenkinson) *Vanwall: The Story of Tony Vandervell and His Racing Cars,* Stephens, 1975; *Classic Racing Cars,* Rand McNally, 1977; *The Story of Veteran and Vintage Cars,* Hamlyn, 1977; *The Motorcycle Story,* Phoebus, 1979; *Graham Hill Remembered,* Aztex, 1979.

The Roaring Twenties, Blandford, 1980; *Classic Sports Cars,* Hamlyn, 1980. Also author of *How to Build a Scale-Model Monoposto Alfa Romeo.* Contributor to *Encyclopedia of the Automobile.* Contributor to magazines, including *On Four Wheels* and *Steering Wheel.*

BIOGRAPHICAL/CRITICAL SOURCES: Booklist, September 1, 1978.*

* * *

POSTON, Theodore Roosevelt Augustus Major 1906-1974

OBITUARY NOTICE: Born July 4, 1906, in Hopkinsville, Ky.; died after a long illness, January 11, 1974, in Brooklyn, N.Y. Journalist and author. Poston was a waiter and free-lance writer before taking a full-time job as a journalist with New York's *Amsterdam News* in 1929. He became city editor of that paper in 1934, later leaving for the *New York Post* where he was the first black to work full time for a New York daily paper. His by-line appeared in the *Post* for more than thirty-three years. Among Poston's early stories were exclusive interviews with Huey Long and Wendell Wilkie and special coverage of civil rights confrontations in the South. Poston also served as chief of the Negro news desk in the news bureau of the Office of War Information. In addition to his journalistic work, Poston wrote several short stories and contributed to numerous anthologies and periodicals. Obituaries and other sources: *Newsweek,* April 11, 1949; *New York Times,* January 12, 1974; *Time,* January 24, 1974.

* * *

POTTER, Kathleen Jill 1932-
(Kathleen Kinder)

PERSONAL: Born October 10, 1932, in Sussex, England; daughter of Claude Stanley (an artist) and Marie Priscilla (Blake) Kinder; married John Gilbert Lidster, January 9, 1951 (divorced, 1955); married David John Potter (a professional tennis coach), February 5, 1957; children: (second marriage) Carol Elizabeth, Simon David. *Education:* Attended private school

in Sussex, England. *Residence:* Surrey, England. *Agent:* c/o William Collins Sons & Co. Ltd., 14 St. James Pl., London SW1A 1PS, England.

CAREER: Worked as teacher, hairdresser, and cook. Writer, 1972—.

WRITINGS: (Under name Kathleen Kinder) *The Raven and the Dove* (novel), Collins, 1980.

WORK IN PROGRESS Another novel.

SIDELIGHTS: Kathleen Kinder Potter wrote: "I learned to read when I was three—before I went to school, fortunately—and have read avidly ever since. Although I went to many schools, both day and boarding, beginning with a convent in Sussex before World War II, mathematics has remained a mystery to me. During the war years I attended several small private schools in Oxford (two of them are described, without exaggeration, in my novel) and at eleven I went to a grammar school where I stayed until the war ended. My education was finally completed in July, 1946, at yet another little private school three months before my fourteenth birthday. Writing about *The Clergyman's Daughter,* George Orwell mentioned the fact that his publishers were skeptical about the description of the private school in his book and considered it to be farfetched; it was not in the least, as I can verify! Some of the schools I attended were much worse and they were in existence at a later date than the one Orwell wrote about. However, in retrospect, I would not have missed the experience because it gave me an insight into Victorian schooling methods I might otherwise find difficult to believe.

"I have had no other education apart from that which I glean involuntarily. In Oxford I had the tremendous advantage of living among beautiful and historic buildings with access not only to museums and the Bodleian Library, but also to a unique open space called Port Meadow which dates back before Domesday. It has never been plowed up and is therefore rich in flora. Here I learned something about plants and wildlife, and I learned to ride. Oxford freemen had, and I believe have still, their grazing rights on the meadow, and at eleven years old, already smitten with horse-fever, I set out to catch a horse. I caught a great many over the next few years and fortunately no one caught me! I gained much firsthand knowledge, too, from my interest in boats; in a hazardous cockleshell made out of a motorcycle sidecar, which I pitched and tarred myself, I explored the waterways of Oxford. There are many canals and rivers, and their negotiation involved much manual opening and closing of enormous lock gates; this must have been a great nuisance to the lock keepers who so often discovered no one other than me when summoned to the waterside. In common with many solitary children, I constantly made up stories in my head and at the same time wrote my first book and sent it, bright with ambition, to a publisher whose name I had taken from my Bible. I imagined this must indicate he was the best!

"When I left school I worked as a riding instructor for several years, but the position was poorly paid and I could not afford to continue in it. I then took a temporary post as an infant teacher in a Jewish school, where my additional duties included supervising the senior girls at their preparation work. As I was barely a year older than they, discipline was not achieved without something of a struggle, and I was extremely relieved when, after an absence of two terms, the permanent teacher returned. I then trained to be a hairdresser and as such I worked until the birth of my first child, although I disliked the work intensely. I didn't start writing until I was forty when, due to a financial disaster, I was again in need of a job. Without any qualifications and after more than twenty years as a housewife

I was well aware that I had little to offer. However, I took a job as a restaurant cook and stayed there for the next five years. It was during this period that I wrote my first novel, and completed the first draft of my second. Only at this ridiculously late stage did I realize that writing was what I wanted to do, that it was in fact what I had been doing, albeit merely in thought, all my life.''

* * *

POWELL, James V(irgil) 1938-

PERSONAL: Born December 17, 1938, in Minneapolis, Minn.; son of James C. (a merchant and poet) and Helen (Campbell) Powell; married Janice Johnson (divorced); married Vickie Dee Jensen (a photographer and writer); children: Nels Jensen, Jensa. *Education:* Wheaton College, Wheaton, Ill., B.A., 1959; University of Denver, M.A.L.S., 1965; University of Hawaii, Ph.D., 1972. *Office:* Department of Anthropology, University of British Columbia, Vancouver, British Columbia, Canada V6T 1W5.

CAREER: Archaeological fieldworker in the Near East, 1958-65; American Bible Society, New York, N.Y., research librarian, 1965-68; linguistic fieldworker among Indians of the Northwest Coast, 1968-72; University of British Columbia, Vancouver, assistant professor, 1972-81, associate professor of anthropology, 1981—. Linguistic fieldworker among Northwest Coast Indians, 1972—. *Military service:* U.S. Army, Security Agency, translator, 1960-62; served in West Germany. *Member:* American Anthropological Association (fellow), Linguistic Society of America, Royal Anthropological Society, Canadian Sociology and Anthropology Association.

WRITINGS: (With wife, Vickie Jensen) *Quileute,* University of Washington Press, 1975; *Quileute Dictionary,* Northwest Anthropological Research Notes (Idaho State University, Moscow), 1975. Compiler of Indian alphabets and calendars. Author of language materials on Northwest Coast Indians. Contributor of articles and reviews to scholarly journals.

SIDELIGHTS: Powell wrote: "In 1970 I realized that North Americans were losing an irretrievable aspect of our identity: the native languages of our continent were going extinct as the Indian communities became English-speakers. Language programs to revitalize the use of these languages among Indians were largely unsuccessful. One of the reasons appeared to be that the Indian languages were usually taught out of handfuls of mimeographed handouts, rather than having professional-quality language books to use in native language classes. Vickie Jensen and I set out to make books for Indian kids that would inspire the kind of respect in the students that their cultural heritage deserves. Working with languages called Shuswap, Quileute, Kwakwala (Kwakiutl), Gitksan, Halkomelem, and Chinook Jargon, among others, my wife and I turned out more than forty books of language lessons in eight years. We have become a family of fieldworkers, living five months a year on Indian reservations and traveling in a van complete with typewriters equipped to write such sounds as a glottalized lateral fricative, a sound common to the complex tongues of the North Pacific Coast Indian tribes.

"*Quileute* derives from the Quileute community, who asked me to write a book that would answer all of the questions that visitors to the reservation ask. We wrote an introduction to the tribe that answered every question that had been asked about the Quileutes in the seven years we had been working with them. Eventually I became more of a community member than a linguist, and am called 'Kwashkwash' by the Quileute, 'Gwinxsiwiliksxw' (a mythic character) by the Wolf Clan of the Gitksan, and 'Gwasdi' (raven) by some Kwakiutl.

"The demand for language materials by Indian communities is so intense that we usually plan fieldwork commitments three years in advance. At a time when anthropologists are finding it increasingly difficult to be welcome in their research on Amerindian groups, my wife and I sometimes have to turn down as many as a dozen requests from tribes each year, simply because there isn't time to research and write materials in more than three languages a year. No shift in professional direction is in sight as long as our native languages are dying out and there are Indian communities that would like to welcome a linguist and his family among themselves for part of a summer in return for language textbooks."

* * *

POWELL, Lawrence N(elson) 1943-

PERSONAL: Born January 10, 1943, in Santa Monica, Calif.; son of Stewart N. (in the military) and Elizabeth D. Powell; married Diana Skirven (a teacher), June 10, 1967; children: Justin S. *Education:* University of Maryland, B.A., 1967; Yale University, M.Phil., 1970, Ph.D., 1976. *Home:* 2310 Metairie Court, Metairie, La. 70118. *Office:* Department of History, Tulane University, New Orleans, La. 70118.

CAREER: Yale University, New Haven, Conn., assistant editor of "Frederick Douglass Papers," 1973-76, associate editor, 1977-78; Tulane University, New Orleans, La., assistant professor, 1978-79, associate professor of history, 1980—. *Military service:* U.S. Army, 1960-63. *Member:* American Historical Association, Organization of American Historians, Southern Historical Association, Louisiana Historical Association.

WRITINGS: (Editor with John W. Blassingame) *Papers of Frederick Douglass,* Volume I, Yale University Press, 1979; *New Masters: Northern Planters During the Civil War and Reconstruction,* Yale University Press, 1980.

WORK IN PROGRESS: The Politics of Southern Reconstruction.

* * *

POWER, Catherine
See Du BREUIL, (Elizabeth) L(or)inda

* * *

PRESSBURGER, Emeric 1902-
(Richard Imrie)

PERSONAL: Born December 5, 1902, in Miskolc, Hungary; married; children: one daughter. *Education:* Attended University of Prague and University of Stuttgart.

CAREER: Writer. Associated with Universum-Film Aktien-Gesellschaft, Berlin, Germany; co-owner of Archers Film Producing Co., England, 1941-56; co-owner of Vega Productions Ltd. Producer of more than fifteen films, including "The Small Back Room" (alternate title "Hour of Glory"), Snader Productions, 1948, and "Behold a Pale Horse" (adapted from his novel *Killing a Mouse on Sunday*), Columbia, 1964.

WRITINGS: (With Michael Powell) *Story of the Film: "One of Our Aircraft Is Missing,"* H.M.S.O., 1942; *Killing a Mouse on Sunday* (novel), Harcourt, 1961 (reprinted in England as *Behold a Pale Horse,* Collins, 1964); *The Glass Pearls* (novel), Heinemann, 1966; (with Powell) *The Red Shoes,* Avon, 1978.

Screenplays: "The Spy in Black" (alternate title "U-Boat Twenty-Nine"), Columbia, 1939; (author of screen story)

"Contraband" (original title "Blackout"), Anglo American, 1940; (with Gordon Welesley and Edward Dryhurst) "Sons of the Sea" (alternate title "Atlantic Ferry"), Warner Bros., 1941; "The Invaders" (alternate title "The Forty-Ninth Parallel), Columbia, 1942; "Colonel Blimp" (alternate title "The Life and Death of Colonel Blimp"), Archers-General, 1943; (with Powell) "Black Narcissus," Universal, 1947; (under pseudonym Richard Imrie; with Derry Quinn and Ray Rigby; also director) "Operation Crossbow" (alternate title "The Great Spy Mission"), MGM, 1965; (and director) "Twice Upon a Time," 1952; "Miracle in Soho," 1957; "They're a Weird Mob," 1966; "The Boy Who Turned Yellow," 1972.

Screenplays written and directed with Powell: "One of Our Aircraft Is Missing," United Artists, 1942; "I know Where I'm Going," Universal, 1945; "Stairway to Heaven" (original title "A Matter of Life and Death"), Universal, 1946; "The Red Shoes," Eagle Lion, 1948; "The Wild Heart" (original title "Gone to Earth"), RKO, 1950; "The Tales of Hoffmann," Lopert, 1951; "Pursuit of the Graf Spee" (original title "Battle of the River Plate"), J. Arthur Rank, 1956; "Night Ambush," J. Arthur Rank, 1957; "Oh, Rosalinda!," 1955.

BIOGRAPHICAL/CRITICAL SOURCES: Ian Christie, editor, *Powell, Pressburger, and Others,* British Film Institute, 1978.*

* * *

PRICE, Byron 1891-1981

OBITUARY NOTICE: Born in 1891; died of a heart attack, August 6, 1981, in Hendersonville, N.C. Newsman and diplomat. Price served as director of the U.S. Board of Censorship and was the chief censor during World War II. In addition he acted as assistant secretary-general of the United Nations, vice-president of the Motion Picture Association of America, and executive editor of the Associated Press. Price received numerous awards during his career. King George VI named him an honorary Knight Commander of the Order of the British Empire, and President Truman presented him the Medal of Merit. In 1944 Price won a Pulitzer Prize for his development of media censorship codes. Obituaries and other sources: *Newsweek,* October 2, 1961; *New York Times,* August 8, 1981; *Detroit Free Press,* August 10, 1981.

* * *

PRICE, Emerson 1902(?)-1977

OBITUARY NOTICE: Born c. 1902; died August 31, 1977, in Cuyahoga Falls, Ohio. Journalist and author. Price was a feature writer and reporter for the *Akron Times-Press, Cincinnati Post,* and *Cleveland Press* and served as a senior news editor for the Office of War Information during World War II. He was also the author of a novel, *Inn of That Journey,* a story about boyhood in a small Ohio town. Obituaries and other sources: *Publishers Weekly,* September 9, 1977.

* * *

PRICE, Frank James 1917-

PERSONAL: Born March 1, 1917, in Logansport, La.; son of William Hall and Mary Elizabeth (Loving) Price; married Lucile Kendrick, November 16, 1940; children: Virginia, James Patrick. *Education:* Louisiana Polytechnic Institute, B.A. (cum laude), 1938; Louisiana State University, M.A., 1940; Iowa State University, Ph.D., 1956. *Religion:* Presbyterian. *Home:* 545 Centenary Dr., Baton Rouge, La. 70808. *Office:* School of Journalism, Louisiana State University, Baton Rouge, La. 70803.

CAREER: Interstate Progress, Logansport, La., reporter, summers, 1937-38; University of Georgia, Athens, instructor in journalism, spring, 1940; Louisiana State University, Baton Rouge, 1942—, began as instructor, became assistant professor, then associate professor, professor of journalism, 1956—, director of School of Journalism, 1956-69. Reporter and alternate telegraph editor of *Baton Rouge Morning Advocate,* summer, 1941, editorial writer, 1941-42; reporter for *Baton Rouge State-Times,* summers, 1942-43, editorial writer, 1943-44, 1946-53; legislative reporter for Associated Press in Baton Rouge, 1948; copy editor of *Florida Times Union,* summer, 1962. President of Southwestern Journalism Congress, 1950. *Military service:* U.S. Army, 1945-46; became second lieutenant.

MEMBER: International Association of Business Communicators, Association for Education in Journalism, American Association of University Professors, Society of Professional Journalists, Louisiana Scholastic Press Association (executive director, 1956-70), Louisiana Press Association, Quill and Scroll, Sigma Delta Chi (president, 1963-64), Kappa Tau Alpha, Phi Kappa Phi. *Awards, honors:* Member of Hall of Fame at School of Journalism, Louisiana State University.

WRITINGS: Troy H. Middleton: A Biography, Louisiana State University Press, 1974. Also author of *Story of the Baton Rouge Refinery* and *Two Minutes of Basketball.* Contributor to magazines, including *Quill, Progressive Farmer, Ford Times,* and *Forests and People.**

* * *

PRITIKIN, Robert C(harles) 1929-

PERSONAL: Born May 6, 1929, in Chicago, Ill.; son of Arnold and Adelaide (Hoffing) Pritikin; married Louise Brown, 1960 (divorced); children; Tracy, Scott. *Education:* University of California, Los Angeles, B.A., 1951. *Home and office:* 2835 Clay St., San Francisco, Calif. 94113.

CAREER: Young & Rubicam Advertising Agency, New York, N.Y., copywriter, 1956-59; Dailey & Associates, San Francisco, Calif., creative director, 1959-72, senior vice-president, 1968-71; Pritikin & Gibbons Communications, San Francisco, president and creative director, 1971—. Partner of Pritikin/Eglin Productions, 1980—; creator and owner of San Francisco's historic Mansion Hotel. Instructor at San Francisco State College, 1965—. Guest on television and radio programs. *Military service:* U.S. Coast Guard Reserve, journalist, 1952-56. *Member:* Zeta Beta Tau (president), World Trade Club. *Awards, honors:* Recipient of hundreds of advertising awards from American Advertising Federation, 1962-79, and from IBA, 1962-80.

WRITINGS: Christ Was an Ad Man: The Amazing New Testament in Advertising, Harbor/Putnam, 1980. Author of several thousand commercial advertisements for television. Contributor to magazines.

WORK IN PROGRESS: A feature film.

SIDELIGHTS: Pritikin told *CA:* "The painful truth is that advertising rarely works. Maybe General Motors or General Foods or General Dynamics can waste a few million dollars on nonsense sloganeering—but the average struggling merchant or even the burgeoning entrepreneur can ill-afford to waste even a nickel. If these conglomnivorous spendthrifts would study the dogmas, dictums, and directives in my book, they might recoup billions in advertising waste, then perhaps pass on that savings in reduced costs for their services and goods. When the small advertiser discovers a few simple truths he will quadruple the value of his advertising budget.

"What happens under the covers of the advertising business is revealed between the covers of my book. In my 'Amazing New Testament' on advertising, I attempt to show how hype, weaseling, and subterfuge can sometimes lead to advertising successes. But the miraculous advertising campaigns are born from deep convictions, inspiration, and simple honesty.

"My collection of true case histories will enrage some pros and expose some cons. And I hope it will become the advertising bible for those visionaries who aspire to brilliant campaigns and miracle results. For the rest, the unbaptized, my irreverent but very relevant book might be something else: a hoot!''

Pritikin added: "In addition to my writing, I am billed as America's foremost concert saw player. I have released a record album, 'There's a Song in Your Saw,' released by P&G Records in 1976.''

BIOGRAPHICAL/CRITICAL SOURCES: *San Francisco Examiner,* March 2, 1961; *Ad Age,* April 9, 1962, September 12, 1966; *Playboy,* June, 1973; *Atlantic,* July, 1973; *San Francisco Chronicle,* December 8, 1974, June 16, 1977, March 19, 1979, August 13, 1979; *New West,* November 5, 1979.

*   *   *

PROHIAS, Antonio 1921-

PERSONAL: Born January 17, 1921, in Cuba; son of Dario and Maria Luisa Prohias; married twice; children: Marta Rosa, Antonio, Susana. *Education:* Attended University of Havana, 1940. *Politics:* "International democrat." *Religion:* Roman Catholic. *Home:* 4250 Southwest 94th Ave., Miami, Fla. 33165. *Office: Mad,* 485 Madison Ave., New York, N.Y. 10022.

CAREER: Free-lance cartoonist; *Mad,* New York, N.Y., creator of monthly cartoon feature "Spy Versus Spy." *Awards, honors:* Juan Gualberto Gomez Award, 1946, 1953, 1955, 1957, 1958; Mergenthaler Prize from Interamerican Press Association, 1960.

WRITINGS—Books of cartoons; all published by Warner Books, except as noted: *Mad's Spy Vs. Spy: Follow-up File,* edited by Albert B. Feldstein, foreword by Jerry De Fuccio, New American Library, 1968; *The Third Mad Dossier of Spy Vs. Spy,* 1972; *The All New Mad Secret File on Spy Vs. Spy,* 1973; *Spy Vs. Spy Follow-up File,* 1975; *Fifth Mad Report on Spy Vs. Spy,* 1978; *Mad's Big Book of Spy Vs. Spy Capers and Other Surprises,* 1978.

WORK IN PROGRESS: "Spy Versus Spy," to be included in *Galaxy Seven.*

SIDELIGHTS: Prohias's books have been published in fourteen countries, including Germany, Brazil, Spain, and Switzerland. In his cartoons, he expresses his views without words.

*   *   *

PROPPER, Dan 1937-

PERSONAL: Born April 15, 1937, in Brooklyn, N.Y. *Education:* Attended Queens College (now of the City University of New York), 1955-57, and New School for Social Research, 1957-58. *Politics:* "Anarchosocialist." *Religion:* "Judeotaoist." *Home:* 61-26 213th St., New York, N.Y. 11364.

CAREER: Poet. Worked as truckdriver, merchant seaman, copywriter, and ranch hand. Star of television programs, "Po-

etry/Jazz," for Columbia Broadcasting System (CBS), and "Focus."

WRITINGS: *The Fable of the Final Hour and Other Poems,* Energy, 1958; *The Tale of the Amazing Tramp and Other Poems,* Cherry Valley, 1977; (translator) *Pablo Neruda: Twenty-Three Poems,* Wilderness Press, 1979; *For Kerouac in Heaven,* Energy, 1980. Author of "Books," a column in *Nugget,* 1961-64.

WORK IN PROGRESS: Editing *Works,* contemporary American poetry; translating poems by Pablo Neruda.

SIDELIGHTS: Propper wrote: "I associate with other artists, but avoid factions. I don't apply for grants, but find an honorable method of making a living, such as farming or selling ice cream, or driving a truck. I always try to be entertaining."

*   *   *

PROUST, Marcel 1871-1922

BRIEF ENTRY: Born July 10, 1871, in Auteuil, France; died of bronchitis and pneumonia, November 18, 1922, in Paris, France. French novelist. Most of Proust's career was dedicated to the creation of his massive autobiographical novel, *Remembrance of Things Past* (1913-27), which marked him as one of the twentieth century's premier writers. In earlier writing, like *Jean Santeuil* (written in the 1890's; published in 1952), he experimented with theme and character, exploring the effects of nature, memory, imagination, and events on truth. After his mother's death in 1905, Proust began to write his seven-volume masterpiece, beginning with *Swann's Way* (1913), which was ignored by the critics of his day but later considered by many to be the best volume of the series. His prose style was unique; his plots detailed and complex, but unconfused. He presented a vast panorama of French life and a painstaking self-analysis. Proust clarified his view that reality, and therefore truth, is no more than each man's individual perception of it, influenced by events, memories, and personality. He emphasized the importance of everyday events as catalysts in the formation of reality, and of man's selective memory as the key to inner truth. Proust was one of the first writers to record in fiction such a theory of subjective human consciousness. *Biographical/critical sources: Cyclopedia of World Authors,* Harper, 1958; *The McGraw-Hill Encyclopedia of World Biography,* McGraw, 1973; *Modern Language Quarterly,* June, 1980; *Contemporary Literature,* autumn, 1980.

*   *   *

PROWLER, Harley
See MASTERS, Edgar Lee

*   *   *

PRYS-JONES, Arthur Glyn 1888-

PERSONAL: Surname is pronounced Preece-Jones; born March 7, 1888, in Denbigh, Wales; son of Robert (a lecturer) and Annie (a headmistress) Prys-Jones; married Elizabeth Jane Gibbon (a bank assistant; died, 1976); children: D.R.V., Barbara Prys-Jones Vaughan. *Education:* Jesus College, Oxford, B.A. (with honors) and M.A., both 1912. *Politics:* "None taken seriously." *Religion:* Church of Wales. *Home:* 50 Coombe Lane W., Kingston-upon-Thames, Surrey KT2 7BY, England.

CAREER: Teacher at grammar schools in Macclesfield, England, and Walsall, England; assistant master at private boys' school in London, England, 1916-19; staff inspector of schools in Wales, 1919-46; staff inspector of secondary education in

Wales, 1946-49; secretary of Welsh committee of Festival of Britain, 1950-52; writer, 1952—. Broadcaster of talks, poems, and stories for British Broadcasting Corp., Wales. Co-founder and past chairperson of Cardiff Little Theatre; past member of governing board of National Museum of Wales. *Member:* Welsh Academy (president of English section), Cardiff Literary Society (past chairperson), Cardiff Writers Circle (vice-president), Honourable Society of Cynmradarian (vice-president). *Awards, honors:* Officer of Order of the British Empire, 1949.

WRITINGS: (Editor) *Welsh Poets: A Representative English Selection From Contemporary Writers,* Erskine Macdonald, 1917; *Poems of Wales,* Basil Blackwell, 1923; *Green Places: Poems of Wales,* Gwasg Aberystwyth, 1948; (editor) *The Fountain of Life: Prose and Verse From the Authorized Version of the Bible,* Pan Books, 1949, Beacon Press, 1950; *A Little Nonsense* (poems), Eastgate Press, 1954; *Gerald of Wales: His "Itinerary" Through Wales and His "Description" of the Country and Its People,* Harrap, 1955; *The Story of Carmarthenshire,* Christopher Davies, Volume I, 1959, Volume II, 1972; *High Heritage: Poems of Wales,* Christopher Davies, 1969; *Valedictory Verses,* Gomer Press, 1978.

Contributor to magazines and newspapers, including *British Weekly.* Literary editor of *The National Songs of Wales,* Boosey & Hawkes, 1959.

WORK IN PROGRESS: Another *Little Book of Nonsense.*

SIDELIGHTS: Prys-Jones wrote: "As a bilingual Welshman, speaking both Welsh and English from early childhood, I am naturally interested in the survival of my native tongue. I also take great interest in Welsh social and political history, and find pleasure in the study of comparative religion, psychic research, and the whole field of humor in English verse and prose.

"Avant-garde modern poetry leaves me unmoved, as does much so-called modern 'art.' Both impress me as being insincere, fraudulent, and trivial."

*   *   *

PUCKETT, Lute
See MASTERS, Edgar Lee

*   *   *

PURSER, Philip John   1925-

PERSONAL: Born August 28, 1925, in Letchworth, England; son of John W. G. (a representative) and Phyllis (an artist; maiden name, Palmer) Purser; married Ann Elizabeth Goodman (a writer), May 18, 1957; children: Harriet, Emily, Matthew. *Education:* Attended King's College, Cambridge, 1943;

University of St. Andrews, M.A., 1950. *Home:* c/o Lois Weedon, Towcester, Northamptonshire NN12 8PL, England. *Agent:* David Higham Associates Ltd., 5/8 Lower John St., Golden Sq., London W1R 4HA, England. *Office: Sunday Telegraph,* 135 Fleet St., London EC4P 4BL, England.

CAREER: Bon Accord, Aberdeen, Scotland, editorial assistant, 1950-51; *Scottish Daily Mail,* Edinburgh, Scotland, reporter, 1951-55; *Daily Mail,* London, England, television reporter, 1955-56; *News Chronicle,* London, television critic, 1957-60; *Sunday Telegraph,* London, television critic, 1961—. Chairman of National Film Archive television selection committee, 1960-70. *Military service:* British Army, Royal Engineers, 1943-47; became sergeant. *Member:* Writers Guild of Great Britain, Critics Circle. *Awards, honors:* Named critic of the year by International Publishing Corp., 1965.

WRITINGS: Peregrination Twenty-Two (novel), J. Cape, 1962; *Four Days to the Fireworks* (novel), Hodder & Stoughton, 1964; *The Twenty Men* (novel), Hodder & Stoughton, 1967; *Night of Glass* (novel), Hodder & Stoughton, 1968; "Dr. Glas" (two-act play; adapted from novel by Hjalmer Soderberg), first produced in Derby, England, at Derby Playhouse, December 10, 1970; *The Holy Father's Navy* (novel), Hodder & Stoughton, 1971; *The Last Great Tram Race* (short stories), Hodder & Stoughton, 1974; *Where Is He Now?* (biographical profile), Quartet, 1978; (with Jenny Wilkes) *The One and Only Phyllis Dixey* (biography), Future, 1978; *A Small Explosion* (novel), Secker & Warburg, 1979; (contributor) George Brandt, editor, *The Television Dramatist,* Cambridge University Press, 1981.

Television and radio plays: "Anatomy of the Hero," first broadcast by ABC-TV, October 14, 1962; "Calf Love" (adapted from novel by Vernon Bartlett), first broadcast by BBC-TV, January 26, 1966; "Hawks and Doves," first broadcast by Rediffusion Television, July 13, 1967; "Hazard," first broadcast by Granada-TV, January 21, 1971; "Night of Glass" (adapted from own novel), first broadcast by BBC-Radio 4, May 8, 1971; "Heydays Hotel," first broadcast by Granada-TV, November 10, 1976; "The One and Only Phyllis Dixey," first broadcast by Thames Television, November 1, 1978.

Contributor of articles and stories to magazines, including *Telegraph, Encounter,* and *Radio Times,* and to newspapers.

WORK IN PROGRESS: A novel, publication by Secker & Warburg expected in 1982; a television A–Z guide, with Leslie Halliwell, publication by Granada Publishing expected in 1982; a collection of television reviews, publication by Telegraph Publications expected in 1982.

SIDELIGHTS: Purser commented: "My most personal predilection as a writer is for fiction purporting to be fact (and occasionally vice versa), as in *The Last Great Tram Race,* short stories for *Encounter,* 'The Longest Quietest War of All,' in *Telegraph* on April Fools' Day, 1979, and 'Wot a Karajan.'"

Q-R

QUIGLEY, Aileen 1930-
(Ruth Fabian, Erica Lindley)

BRIEF ENTRY: Born in 1930, in Luton, England. British author. Aileen Quigley has written for British Broadcasting Corp. programs "Morning Story" and "Woman's Hour," and for such magazines as *My Weekly* and *Woman's Day.* Her books include *A Scent of Violets* (1973), *The Brackenroyd Inheritance* (1975), *Empress to the Eagle* (R. Hale, 1975), *Devil in Crystal* (New American Library, 1977), *Belladonna* (New American Library, 1978), and *Harvest of Destiny* (New American Library, 1979). *Address:* 14 Newquay Rd., Park Hall, Walsall, Staffordshire, England.

* * *

QUINN, Seabury (Grandin) 1889-1969

OBITUARY NOTICE: Born January 1, 1889; died December 24, 1969, in Washington, D.C. Lawyer and author. Quinn was a prolific writer of stories of the supernatural, contributing ninety-three works to the publication *Weird Tales.* Recurring characters in Quinn's stories are Jules de Grandin, an occult detective, and his aide, Dr. Trowbridge. Among Quinn's works are *The Phantom-Fighter, Is the Devil a Gentleman?,* and *The Horror Chambers of Jules de Grandin.* Quinn also edited an undertaker's trade journal, *Casket and Sunnyside.* Obituaries and other sources: *New York Times,* December 26, 1969; *AB Bookman's Weekly,* February 2, 1970; *The Encyclopedia of Science Fiction: An Illustrated A to Z,* Granada, 1979.

* * *

RABINOVITCH, Sholem 1859-1916
(Solomon Rabinowitz; Sholom Aleichem, pseudonym)

BRIEF ENTRY: Born March 2, 1859, in Pereyaslev, Ukraine (now Pereyaslav-Khmelnitski, U.S.S.R.); died May 13, 1916, in New York, N.Y. Yiddish novelist, playwright, and short story writer. Writing under the name Sholom Aleichem, a traditional Hebrew greeting which means "Peace be unto you," Rabinovitch became the most widely read Yiddish author of all time. One of the founders of modern Yiddish literature, Sholom Aleichem was best known for his tales of Tevye the dairyman, which were adapted into the highly successful Broadway musical "Fiddler on the Roof." Noted for its humor and for capturing the lifestyle and traditions of the Yiddish-speaking Jews of Eastern Europe, Aleichem's work earned him the reputation as "the Jewish Mark Twain." Aleichem began writing in his mid-twenties, and after publishing his first story in 1883 he devoted himself to the dissemination of Jewish culture. In 1892 the first episode of the epistolary series *Menahem Mendl* appeared, followed in 1894 by the first story of *Tevye der Milkhiker.* These two characters, which he returned to often throughout the years, are the ones most readily associated with his name. Almost all of Aleichem's works have been translated into English as well as most major European languages. English translations of his principal works include the following: *The Old Country* (1946), *Tevye's Daughters* (1949), *Adventures of Mottel, The Cantor's Son* (1953); *The Tevye Stories, and Others* (1959), and *The Adventures of Menahem-Mendl* (1969). *Residence:* New York, N.Y. *Biographical/critical sources: Encyclopedia of World Literature in the Twentieth Century,* updated edition, Ungar, 1967; *Twentieth-Century Literary Criticism,* Volume 1, Gale, 1978.

* * *

RABINOWITZ, Peter MacGarr 1956-

PERSONAL: Born January 21, 1956, in New York, N.Y.; son of Alan (a professor of urban planning) and Andrea (a psychiatric social worker; maiden name, Wolf) Rabinowitz. *Education:* Amherst College, B.A., 1978; University of Washington, Seattle, M.D., 1982. *Residence:* Seattle, Wash. *Agent:* Carol Mann Literary Agency, 168 Pacific St., Brooklyn, N.Y. 11201. *Office:* School of Medicine, University of Washington, Seattle, Wash. 98195.

CAREER: Writer. *Member:* American Medical Association Student Association (coordinator of regional occupational health task force, 1979-80), Physicians for Social Responsibility.

WRITINGS: Talking Medicine (nonfiction), Norton, 1981. Member of editorial board of *New Physician.*

WORK IN PROGRESS: A book of interviews "with people in the United States and overseas who are intimately associated with nuclear armament, from soldiers who make their daily patrols and test runs of weapons to military strategists and politicians who juggle such immensely destructive entities."

SIDELIGHTS: Rabinowitz told *CA:* "Medicine and writing both demand mastery of the skills of observation, attention to detail, and an attempt to discover underlying causes and truths. Both disciplines also require large commitments of time and emotional energy. I wrote a book about what American doctors feel it is like to be a physician. Now I am discovering how hard it is to put my ideas (based on the conclusions I arrived at in *Talking Medicine*) into daily practice as a medical student. The balance of writing and doing continues: precarious and, to me, essential."

BIOGRAPHICAL/CRITICAL SOURCES: Los Angeles Times, February 5, 1981.

*   *   *

RABINOWITZ, Solomon
See RABINOVITCH, Sholem

*   *   *

RAD, Gerhard von
See von RAD, Gerhard

*   *   *

RADFORD, Edwin Isaac   1891-

PERSONAL: Born in 1891 in West Bromwich, England; married Mona Augusta Mangan (a writer). *Education:* Received M.A. from Cambridge University. *Home:* Manor Dea, Apt. 119, Boundary Rd., Worthing, Sussex, England.

CAREER: Associated with *Wisbech Advertiser,* 1912; subeditor of *Daily News,* 1918; subeditor of *Star and Daily Mirror,* 1919-35; caption editor, 1936, art editor, 1937, and columnist for *Daily Mirror;* acting editor of *Evening Argus,* Bradford, England; production editor of *Mail,* Leicester, England; chief subeditor and deputy editor of *Evening News,* Nottingham, England; drama and music critic for *Daily Express,* Nottingham. *Member:* Authors Club, Savage Club.

WRITINGS—Folklore: *Unusual Words and How They Come About,* Philosophical Library, 1946 (published in England as *Crowther's Encyclopaedia of Phrases and Origins,* J. Crowther, 1947), revised edition published as *To Coin a Phrase: A Dictionary of Origins,* Arrow Books, 1973; (with wife, Mona Augusta Radford) *Encyclopaedia of Superstitions,* Rider & Co., 1948, Philosophical Library, 1949, revised edition (edited by Christina Hole), Hutchinson, 1961, Dufour, 1969, reprinted by Arrow Books as three-volume set, 1978, Volume I: *Superstitions of Death and the Supernatural,* Volume II: *Superstitions of Love and Marriage,* Volume III: *Superstitions of the Countryside.* Also author of *Dictionary of Allusions,* with M. A. Radford, and of *Superstitions, Manners, and Customs of Peoples.*

Detective novels; published by Melrose, except as noted: *Murder Isn't Cricket,* 1946; *Who Killed Dick Whittington?,* 1947; *It's Murder to Live,* 1947; *John Kyleing Died,* 1949; *Death Has Two Faces,* R. Hale, 1972, Thorpe, 1975.

With M. A. Radford; published by R. Hale, except as noted: *Heel of Achilles,* Melrose, 1950; *Look in at Murder,* John Long, 1956; *Death on Broads,* Melrose, 1957; *The Six Men,* 1958; *Married to Murder,* 1959; *Death of a Frightened Editor,* 1959; *Murder on My Conscience,* 1960; *Death at the Chateau Noir,* 1960; *Death and the Professor,* 1961; *Death's Inheritance,* 1961; *Death Takes the Wheel,* 1962; *From Information Received,* 1962; *Murder of Three Ghosts,* 1963; *A Cosy Little Murder,* 1963; *The Hungry Killer,* 1964; *Jones's Little Murder,* 1967; *The Middleford Murders,* 1967; *The Safety First Murders,* 1968; *Death of an Ancient Saxon,* 1969; *Death of a Peculiar Rabbit,* 1969; *Two Ways to Murder,* 1969; *Murder Speaks,* 1970; *Murder is Ruby Red,* 1970.

"Dr. Manson" detective novels; first published by R. Hale: *Mask of Murder,* 1965; *Murder Magnified,* 1965; *Death of a "Gentleman,"* 1966, Ulverscroft Large Print Books, 1976; *No Reason for Murder,* 1967; *Trunk Call to Murder,* 1968; *Dead Water,* 1971; *The Greedy Killers,* 1971, Ulverscroft Large Print Books, 1976.

"Inspector Manson" novels; published by Melrose: *Inspector Manson's Success,* 1944; *Murder Jigsaw,* 1944; *Crime Pays No Dividends,* 1945.

BIOGRAPHICAL/CRITICAL SOURCES: Books and Bookmen, July, 1973, March, 1975.*

*   *   *

RADFORD, Richard F(rancis), Jr.   1939-
(Lynne Critchley, Amy Lyndon)

PERSONAL: Born February 15, 1939, in Boston, Mass.; son of Richard F. (a banker) and Lorraine (Lally) Radford; married Lynne S. Critchley (an executive secretary), August 20, 1966; children: Amy, Richard F. III. *Education:* Attended University of Massachusetts and Boston University; Boston State College, B.A. (with honors), 1979. *Politics:* Independent Democrat. *Religion:* Roman Catholic. *Home:* 31 Harvard St., Brookline, Mass. 02146; Camp Serenity, Thompson Point, Naples, Me.

CAREER: Sales representative in New York and New Jersey, 1958-64; bartender in Boston, Mass., 1964-69; surveyor, 1969-70; worked as a golf starter and caddy master in Brookline, Mass., 1970—. Operates a summer trading post in the Maine woods. Member of Human Relations Youth Resources Commission, 1974-77; president of 631 Committee (mental health organization); alcoholism consultant. *Military service:* U.S. Army, Operations and Intelligence, 1959-62; served in Europe; became acting sergeant.

WRITINGS—Novels; under pseudonym Amy Lyndon, except as noted: *Opal Moon,* MacFadden, 1979; *One White Rose,* MacFadden, 1980; *Tournament of Love,* MacFadden, 1980; (under pseudonym Lynne Critchley) *Brief Summer,* Avon, 1982.

Work represented in anthologies, including *Pegasus: The Best of 1977; Having Been There,* edited by Alan Luks, Scribner, 1979; *Dreams,* 1980. Contributor of poems and stories to magazines, including *American Man, New Earth Review, Word,* and *New England Sampler.*

WORK IN PROGRESS: A trilogy dealing with "the reality of evil in the world today and modern man's refusal to recognize it," completion expected in 1983.

SIDELIGHTS: Radford told *CA:* "My poetry I believe to be inspired by a gracious God as a reward for 'hanging in there.' My prose, on the other hand (despite the unflappable exterior I maintain for my young children), is a boil on a canker in my gut that keeps erupting in new stories and revised novels—regardless of failure and rejection. I'm really only an apprentice at the craft, but I aspire to be a Master. Roughly paraphrased: Johnson said, 'None but a boob writes for anything but money.' I'm beginning to agree."

AVOCATIONAL INTERESTS: Etymology, golf, travel.

BIOGRAPHICAL/CRITICAL SOURCES: Publishers Review, May, 1979; *Tab,* October 31, 1979.

*   *   *

RAE, Evonne   1928-1974

OBITUARY NOTICE: Born June 17, 1928, in Detroit, Mich.;

died in an automobile accident, June 3, 1974, in East Hampton, N.Y. Editor. Associated with various publishing houses for more than twenty years, Rae was editor in chief of Dell Purse Books at the time of her death. Obituaries and other sources: *Publishers Weekly,* July 15, 1974.

*   *   *

RAFFERTY, S.S.
    See HURLEY, John J(erome)

*   *   *

RAINER, George
    See GREENBURGER, Ingrid Elisabeth

*   *   *

RALEIGH, Richard
    See LOVECRAFT, H(oward) P(hillips)

*   *   *

RAMOS-OLIVEIRA, Antonio   1907-1973

OBITUARY NOTICE: Born in 1907; died in 1973 in Mexico City, Mexico. Historian, journalist, and author. Ramos-Oliveira wrote books on analytical history, including *Catholics and the Civil War in Spain, Historia de Espana,* and *Politics, Economics, and Men of Modern Spain, 1808-1946.* Obituaries and other sources: *AB Bookman's Weekly,* October 15, 1973.

*   *   *

RANDOLPH, Gordon
    See von BLOCK, Bela W(illiam)

*   *   *

RANGEL, Carlos   1929-

PERSONAL: Born September 17, 1929, in Caracas, Venezuela; son of Jose Antonio and Magdalena (Guevara) Rangel; married Sofia Imber (a journalist, editor, critic, and museum director), 1968. *Education:* Bard College, B.A., 1951; University of Paris, certificat d'etudes de civilisation francaise, 1950; New York University, M.A., 1959. *Politics:* "Whig liberal." *Religion:* Agnostic. *Home:* 24 Calle El Mirador, San Rafael, La Florida, Caracas 1050, Venezuela.

CAREER: New York University, New York, N.Y., instructor, 1958-59; Venezuelan Foreign Service, Brussels, Belgium, first rank secretary, 1959-60; Channel Four Television, Caracas, producer and moderator of daily public affairs program, "Buenos Dias," 1961—. Assistant professor at University of Caracas, 1961-63; vice-president of Caracas City Council, 1964-68. Member of board of trustees of Caracas Museum of Contemporary Art. *Member:* Venezuelan Association of Journalists, Television Workers Union, Society for the Prevention of Cruelty to Animals. *Awards, honors:* Banda de honor of Orden Andres Bello; Venezuelan Orden Francisco de Miranda, first class; commendator of Order of Merit of the Italian Republic.

WRITINGS: Del Buen Salvaje al Buen Revolucionario, Monte Avila, 1976, translation by Ivan Kats published as *The Latin Americans,* Harcourt, 1977. Contributor to periodicals, including *Vuelta, Commentary,* and *O Estado de Sao Paulo.* Managing editor of *Memento* (weekly magazine), 1961-69; contributing editor of *Newsweek International;* associate editor of *World Paper;* member of editorial board of *Commentaire.*

WORK IN PROGRESS: A book, tentatively entitled *Le Tiermondisme,* publication by R. Laffont expected in 1981 or 1982.

SIDELIGHTS: Rangel told *CA:* "In my writing I try to dispel the myth that the difference in the wealth and development of nations is due entirely or mainly to the exploitation of poor by rich nations. This pernicious notion has obscured economic and political discourse much more than the former ethnocentric conviction of the West that its expansion and domination was an unmixed blessing for mankind."

On their morning television show "Buenos Dias," Rangel and wife Sofia Imber voice their opinions on current events and interview people in the news. Their guests have included Margaret Mead, Willy Brandt, William Fulbright, George Reedy, Max Lerner, Mario Soares, Jean-Francois Revel, Arthur Schlesinger, Jr., Jules Feiffer, Roy Lichtenstein, Manuel Fraga Iribarne, Sarah Caldwell, Naum Goldmann, and Herman Kahn.

*   *   *

RANKIN, Paula C(lark)   1945-

PERSONAL: Born January 3, 1945, in Newport News, Va.; daughter of Paul (an engineer) and Ruth (a teacher; maiden name, Jackson) Clark; married Terry W. Rankin (an engineer), December 1, 1962; children: Jennifer, Walter. *Education:* Christopher Newport College, B.A., 1974; William and Mary College, M.A., 1975; doctoral study at Vanderbilt University, 1978—. *Home:* 135 Medearis Dr., Old Hickory, Tenn. 37138. *Office:* Department of English, Vanderbilt University, Nashville, Tenn. 37215.

CAREER: Old Dominion University, Norfolk, Va., instructor in English, 1975-77; Volunteer State Community College, Gallatin, Tenn., adjunct instructor in English, 1978—. *Member:* Associated Writing Programs.

WRITINGS—Poems: *By the Wreckmaster's Cottage,* Carnegie-Mellon University Press, 1977; *Augers,* Carnegie-Mellon University Press, 1981.

Contributor to magazines, including *Nation, North American Review, Poetry Northwest, Ploughshares, Poetry Now,* and *Missouri Review.*

WORK IN PROGRESS: Research on John Clare's poetry, "particularly his practice of 'search and retrieval' for values which can be salvaged from the 'scrap heap' of waste, change, and loss."

SIDELIGHTS: Paula Rankin commented: "I live the most ordinary and quiet life, married to the same man for seventeen years and the mother of two children. Poetry is my way of appreciating, understanding, fracturing, and defeating that ordinariness, and I am always a beginner.

"It is not an exaggeration to say that I'd never have written poetry, nor even have been aware of contemporary poetry's being written if Dave Smith had not come to Newport News (my hometown) in 1970. He was stationed at Langley Field in the Air Force and was offering a poetry-writing course at the local college. It was the first course of its kind that the college ever offered. I read about the course in the newspaper and enrolled. As unbelieveable as this may seem to many people, I had absolutely *no* idea that people were still writing, much less publishing, poems. I really thought the last poet was Robert Frost. The revelation had all the elements of a religious conversion, and even now I shudder at how unbearable my life might have remained had David not brought poetry to Newport News.

"I began writing, naturally, during the course, and *Westigan Review* published my first poem in the summer of 1970. In 1976 Gerald Costanzo, an editor at Carnegie-Mellon Press, called me and asked to publish my first book—he'd not even seen a manuscript, only poems in periodicals. He also published my second book, *Augurs*.

"The past year has been the most difficult period I've had with my writing; and though I want to blame doctoral exams and guilt over not beginning my dissertation, the truth is that I've allowed everydayness to gain the upper hand—children growing up, parents aging, so many things seem to be working to defeat the *curiosity* which is indispensible. Thus I see my new poems as trying to survive and to *triumph* over Keats's 'sense of real things'—and as the struggle is more intense, I suspect the voice in these poems is fiercer, less patient, and, I hope, more determined and persistent.''

*   *   *

RAPHAEL, Dan   1952-

PERSONAL: Born June 7, 1952, in Fargo, N.D.; son of Raphael John (a reporter) and Cecelia (Dlugonski) Raphael. *Education:* Cornell University, B.A., 1973; Bowling Green State University, M.F.A., 1975. *Politics:* Humanist. *Religion:* "Pseudo-taoist." *Home:* 3281 Northeast Fremont, Portland, Ore. 97212. *Office address:* NRG P.O. Box 14072, Portland, Ore. 97214.

CAREER: KSOR-FM Radio, Ashland, Ore., disc jockey, 1976-77; Sam's Bull Feeder, Durango, Colo., meat carver, 1977; Oregon Department of Transportation, Medford, weighmaster, 1977-78; U.S. Postal Service, Portland, Ore., mail carrier, 1978—. Volunteer worker for Metropolitan Crisis Service, 1979—; reading organizer for Northwest Artists Workshop, 1980—. *Member:* Coordinating Council of Literary Magazines, Committee of Small Magazine Editors and Publishers.

WRITINGS—Poems: *Truck,* Pisspoor Press, 1973; *Energumen,* Cherry Valley, 1976; *Polymerge,* Skydog Press, 1979; *Dawn Patrol,* Contraband Press, 1979; *Zone du Jour,* Poets and Poets Press, 1981.

Editor of *NRG,* 1975—.

WORK IN PROGRESS: The Hot and the Sideways, poems; compilation of journal material; a book length essay on the redefinition of craft in contemporary parasyntactic literature.

SIDELIGHTS: Raphael told *CA:* "All my comments are post-factum. I do not make money with my writing nor do I expect to, but language hence thought, knowledge, and perception must be explored and not de-liberated. My poems work best in performance, and it is my hope to tour nationally, as well as to work more with cassette-books and eventually video-tapes.''

Raphael later commented *CA:* "dont read much contemporary poetry, fail to reach to understand to have the patience and/or desire to probe the nuances. feel too outside this world of 'professional writers,' even the level of state grants & medium press prizes, what does this have to do with writing. seems like writers always say they write coz they have to, i guess many are lucky that what they have to do is vendable, accessible, in fashion.

"seems all th art forms made acceptable transition into non-representational a while back but poetry continues th most anachronistic, precious, hung up in expectations & traditions like a private club clinging dearly to its tiny outmoded magic.

"where does language come from? it is not a pure medium like music or painting, words are both heard and seen and more importantly processed, or how much of language is learned and what is there in a deeper, universal, cosmic, etc sense? language is this energy that taps into me—is the base of my work, a flow i do not understand & highly respect.

"its damned frustrating to build a body of polished work, work that can speak to many people in different voices, and have no way of getting it out, have no channels that will accept it for distribution or even for itself. yet this is th way i am committed to, and must accept others for what theyre doing & believe they have as much integrity as i do, & vision, & skill—we are just walking different paths.

"to talk more makes no difference. the more ideas i formulate th more they may block th free unassuming flow of language, which tho dependent on my circumstances, exposures etc., my instrumentality, must be given open rein (craft, in relation to my work, is a fine tuning, just whacking th words & going for th right tone; newness is important; not repeating nor taking an easy path, tho i begin to realize th potential of recognizable structures & linkages within th work, how repetition w/variation can be highly dimensional.)

"th channel that works best for me in presenting my work is reading, as ive some dramatic training & experience, & th aural (i seem to have a natural tho eccentric ear for rhythm & interrelation of sound) underpinnings of my poetry, couple with the works lack of syntax, of recognizable clues to how to read—people dont know what to do with it when seen On th page, but reactions in public are always strong, in all parts of th country ive read, & th couple times ive read to older & non-poetry audience. since books are becoming a thing of th past, it may be time for poetry to become multi-media, & i hope to eventually tour more as a reader, to make tapes to accompany written texts (for i feel th poems work well as written, and w/angles that cant be perceived thru hearing, that poetry can fill both aural & visual spaces & unite these in th mind and deeper) as well as eventual appearances in radio & video.''

*   *   *

RAPHAEL, Sandra (Joan)   1939-

PERSONAL: Born July 18, 1939, in London, England; daughter of Jack and Lily (Woolf) Raphael. *Education:* Victoria University of Wellington, B.A., 1959; University of London, Diploma in Librarianship, 1962. *Home:* 18 Argyle St., Oxford OX4 1SS, England. *Agent:* Curtis Brown Ltd., 1 Craven Hill, London W2 3EP, England. *Office:* Dictionary Department, Oxford University Press, 37A St. Giles', Oxford OX1 3LD, England.

CAREER: Linnean Society, London, England, librarian and archivist, 1963-69; Oxford University Press, Oxford, England, senior editor of natural history and library research in dictionary department, 1969—. *Member:* Society for the Bibliography of Natural History, Garden History Society, Society of Indexers, Oxford Bibliographical Society.

WRITINGS: Folio 21: A Bibliography of the Folio Society, 1947-1967, Folio Press, 1968; (with Wilfred Blunt) *The Illustrated Herbal,* Thames & Hudson, 1979; (contributor) *Of Oxfordshire Gardens,* Oxford Polytechnic Press, 1982.

WORK IN PROGRESS: Research on botanical and horticultural history.

RASCHKE, Carl A(llan) 1944-

PERSONAL: Born September 11, 1944, in New York, N.Y.; son of Charles Frederick (a chemist) and Grace (a librarian; maiden name, Van Nostrand) Raschke; married Lorita Elaine Lagiglia, March 2, 1968 (divorced May 5, 1981); children: Erik Nathan. *Education:* Pomona College, B.A., 1966; Graduate Theological Union, Berkeley, Calif., M.A., 1969; Harvard University, Ph.D., 1973. *Residence:* Denver, Colo. *Office:* Department of Religious Studies, University of Denver, Denver, Colo. 80208.

CAREER: Livermore Herald and News, Livermore, Calif., reporter, 1967-68; University of Denver, Denver, Colo., assistant professor, 1972-77, associate professor of philosophy and religion, 1977—. President of Omega Foundation, 1981—. *Member:* American Academy of Religion (regional president, 1978-79; leader of philosophy of religion section, 1980—), American Philosophical Association, American Society for Christian Ethics, Phi Beta Kappa. *Awards, honors:* Deutsche Akademische Austauschdienst, 1974; National Endowment for the Humanities fellowship, 1978-79.

WRITINGS: Moral Action, God, and History, Scholars Press (Chico, Calif.), 1975; (with Mark Taylor and James Kirk) *Religion and the Human Image,* Prentice-Hall, 1977; *The Bursting of New Wineskins,* Pickwick, 1978; *The Alchemy of the Word,* Scholars Press, 1979; *The Interruption of Eternity,* Nelson-Hall, 1980; (editor) *New Dimensions in Philosophical Theology,* Scholars Press, 1981; (editor with Thomas J. J. Altizer) *Deconstruction and Theology,* Cross Roads, 1982. Editor of "Academy Series," American Academy of Religion.

WORK IN PROGRESS: The Omega Moment, on contemporary apocalypse themes; research on "parasciences and religion."

SIDELIGHTS: Raschke told *CA:* "I am currently working within what might be described as a 'unified field theory' of the sciences and humanities. Inspired by the recent breakthroughs in the so-called 'new physics,' I am endeavoring to show that in writing and teaching there is currently underway a silent revolution which challenges our conventional picture of the cosmos, dominant since the seventeenth century, as a machine-like march of matter in motion. The popular image of science, which predominated among the counterculture of the sixties, as a hard-fisted discipline with narrow research concerns that sought to banish all mystery and a sense of the wondrous totality from the domain of human awareness, is no longer tenable. Instead we have a new spirit in some key quarters of the academic community, which aims to reconcile science and religion, to integrate empirical research into the study of consciousness, culture, and symbolism.

"The Omega Foundation is chartered for the public dissemination and utilization in a day-to-day context of this new knowledge. It will endeavor to bring within the ken of informed public discussion various issues and subject areas that are situated at the new frontiers of the sciences, humanities, and culture. For example, our public lectures and seminars will treat such controversial topics as UFOs, psychic archaeology, and other 'dimensions of reality.' However, unlike so-called 'new age' groups and purveyors of mass media sensationalism, we enlist the expertise of bona fide professional lecturers and researchers. And we have no specific 'doctrine' to promote, other than showing how, as one of Shakespeare's characters puts it 'there are more things in heaven and earth, Horatio, than are imagined in your philosophy.'"

RASKIN, A(braham) H(enry) 1911-

PERSONAL: Born April 26, 1911, in Edmonton, Alberta, Canada; came to the United States in 1913, naturalized citizen, 1920; son of Henry (a fur trader) and Mary (Slatkin) Raskin; married Rose Samrock (an artist), September 27, 1933; children: Jane, Donald. *Education:* City College (now of the City University of New York), B.A., 1931. *Politics:* Liberal party. *Religion:* Jewish. *Home:* 136 East 64th St., New York, N.Y. 10021. *Office:* National News Council, 1 Lincoln Plaza, New York, N.Y. 10023.

CAREER: New York Times, New York City, local college correspondent, 1931-34, labor reporter, 1934-42, chief labor correspondent, 1948-61, member of editorial board, 1961-64, assistant editor of editorial page, 1964-76, author of labor column, 1976-77; National News Council, New York City, associate director, 1978—. Lecturer at New York School of Social Work, 1947-52; adjunct professor at Columbia University, 1976. Member of board of directors of Jewish Family Service of New York, 1950-62, and Legal Aid Society, New York City, 1967-74; member of board of trustees of Lowell Mellett Fund for a Free and Responsible Press, 1968—, and James Gordon Bennett Foundation, 1971—. Member of President's Committee on Universal Training, 1947. *Military service:* U.S. Army, chief of labor branch of Industrial Services Division, 1942-46; became lieutenant colonel; received Distinguished Service Medal.

MEMBER: International Press Institute, Industrial Relations Research Association (member of national executive board), American Academy of Political and Social Science, New York Newspaper Guild (vice-chairman, 1948-62), Phi Beta Kappa, Society of Silurians. *Awards, honors:* Sidney Hillman Memorial Award, 1961 and 1964, the latter for report on New York City's newspaper strike; George Polk Memorial Award from Long Island University, 1953 and 1964, the latter for report on newspaper strike; Page One Award from New York Newspaper Guild, 1961 and 1964, the latter for report on newspaper strike; Heywood Broun Memorial Citation, 1964, for report on newspaper strike; award from Society of Silurians, 1964, for report on newspaper strike, and 1970; journalism award from Columbia University, 1976, and distinguished service award from university's Institute of Collective Bargaining and Group Relations, 1978.

WRITINGS: (Editor) *A Selection From the Winning Entries in the 1958 Science Teacher Achievement Recognition Program,* National Science Teachers Association, 1958; (with David Dubinsky) *David Dubinsky: A Life With Labor,* Simon & Schuster, 1977; (with Herbert C. Morton and Julius Duscha) *Views on Employment Statistics From the Press, Business, Labor, and Congress: Reports,* National Commission on Employment and Unemployment Statistics, 1979.

Work represented in anthologies, including *Labor in a Changing America,* Basic Books, 1966; *American Labor Since the New Deal,* Quadrangle, 1971. Contributor to magazines, including *Commentary, Saturday Review, Atlantic,* and *Reporter.* Editor of *Journal of International Labor Affairs,* 1978.

SIDELIGHTS: During his long career in journalism, Raskin was highly respected among his colleagues. One of his major achievements was his detailed report on the printers' strike that paralyzed newspapers in New York City for more than nine months in the early 1960's.

Raskin retired from journalism when he reached the *New York Times*'s mandatory retirement age and became associated with the National News Council, a nonprofit body that works to protect the Constitutional rights of the press and investigates abuses of those rights by the media.

BIOGRAPHICAL/CRITICAL SOURCES: Newsweek, January 13, 1958; Gay Talese, The Kingdom and the Power, World Publishing, 1969; New York Times, December 1, 1977, October 28, 1979; New Yorker, January 29, 1979; Monthly Labor Review, February, 1979; New Leader, June 4, 1979; Change, July, 1979; Fortune, August 27, 1979, December 31, 1979.*

*   *   *

RATHMELL, Neil 1947-

PERSONAL: Born May 15, 1947, in Leeds, England; son of Rowland (a printer) and Dorothy (Escritt) Rathmell; married Lynne Anderson, July 29, 1972; children: Katherine, Rebecca. Education: Jesus College, Cambridge, B.A. (with honors), 1968. Home: 3 Bridge Lane, Hanwood, Shrewsbury, Shropshire, England. Agent: David Higham Associates Ltd., 5-8 Lower John St., Golden Sq., London W1R 4HA, England. Office: Upper School, Stirchley, Telford, Shropshire, England.

CAREER: Teacher at boys' grammar school in Wirral, England, 1968-71; teacher of English and drama at secondary school in Durham, England, 1971-75; Upper School, Telford, England, teacher of drama and head of faculty of movement studies, 1975—.

WRITINGS: The Old School (novel), Faber, 1976.

Author of "Glorious Technicolor" (two-act musical play for young people), first produced in Telford, Shropshire, England, at Stirchley Studios, March, 1981.

Work represented in anthologies, including Introduction Four, Faber, 1970.

WORK IN PROGRESS: Festival, a novel.

AVOCATIONAL INTERESTS: Gardening (especially garden design).

*   *   *

RAWLINGS, Marjorie Kinnan 1896-1953

BRIEF ENTRY: Born August 8, 1896, in Washington, D.C.; died of a cerebral hemorrhage, December 14, 1953, in St. Augustine, Fla.; buried in Antioch Cemetery, Cross Creek, Hawthorne, Fla. American novelist, short story writer, journalist, and poet. Rawlings is considered by some critics to be one of the best regional American writers. In 1928 Cross Creek, Florida, became her home and the subject of her writings. The Yearling (1938), a novel about a young boy and his pet fawn, has been called her most significant contribution to regional fiction. The novel earned Rawlings a Pulitzer Prize in 1938 and was adapted into a motion picture starring Gregory Peck and Jane Wyman. The Yearling, South Moon Under (1933), and Cross Creek (1942) were all Book-of-the-Month Club selections. Two of Rawlings's short stories, "Gal Young Un" and "Black Secret," received O. Henry Memorial Awards, and "Gal Young Un" was also adapted into a motion picture in 1980. Among her other writings are Golden Apples (1935), When the Whipporwill (1940), and The Sojourner (1953). Residence: Cross Creek, Hawthorne, Fla. Biographical/critical sources: Twentieth Century Authors: A Biographical Dictionary of Modern Literature, H. W. Wilson, 1942; Notable American Women, 1607-1950: A Biographical Dictionary, Belknap Press, 1971; Twentieth-Century Literary Criticism, Volume 4, Gale, 1981.

RAY, Paul C(harles) 1926-

PERSONAL: Born May 15, 1926, in Antwerp, Belgium; married, 1955. Education: Columbia University, B.S., 1950, M.A., 1951, Ph.D., 1962. Office: Department of English, York College, 150-14 Jamaica Ave., Jamaica, N.Y. 11432.

CAREER: Hofstra University, Hempstead, N.Y., instructor in English, 1959-62; Queens College of the City University of New York, Flushing, N.Y., instructor in English, 1964-67; York College, Jamaica, N.Y., assistant professor, 1967-71, associate professor of English, 1971—. Member: Modern Language Association of America, American Association of University Professors.

WRITINGS: The Surrealist Movement in England, Cornell University Press, 1971. Contributor to literature journals.*

*   *   *

RAYMOND, Harold 1887-1975

OBITUARY NOTICE: Born in 1887 in Rose Lawn, Worcestershire, England; died in 1975 in England. Publisher. The first chairman of the publishing firm Chatto & Windus, Raymond was the creator of book tokens, gift certificates that can be redeemed for a book of the token's value at any bookstore. This concept, begun in 1932, is an integral part of England's book trade. A speech that Raymond delivered in 1938 was published as Publishing and Bookselling: A Survey of Post-War Developments and Present-Day Developments and Present-Day Problems. Obituaries and other sources: Who's Who, 126th edition, St. Martin's, 1974; AB Bookman's Weekly, December 8, 1975.

*   *   *

RAYMOND, Margaret E(lmendorf) 1912-

PERSONAL: Born December 14, 1912, in New York, N.Y.; daughter of John Baldwin (a surgeon) and Mai E. (Hackstaff) Walker; married Richard Candage Raymond (an administrator and poet), May 15, 1942 (divorced, December, 1977); children: Jonathan, Margaret, Rosanne Raymond Wilczynski. Education: Vassar College, A.B., 1935; Columbia University, M.S.W., 1937; exchange student at the Kosciuszko Foundation (Poland). Politics: Liberal. Religion: Unitarian Universalist. Home: 20 Mary Dyer Lane, North Easton, Mass. 02356.

CAREER: Cambridge-Somerville Youth Study, Cambridge, Mass., caseworker, 1938-42; Norwich State Hospital, Norwich, Conn., psychiatric social worker, 1941-42; American Red Cross, Washington, D.C., 1942-44, psychiatric social worker at Walter Reed Hospital, and psychiatric social worker, becoming supervisor, at St. Elizabeth's Hospital; Veteran's Administration, New York City, psychiatric social worker at mental health clinic, 1946-47; State Charities Aid Association, New York City, caseworker, 1947; National Council of Jewish Women, Department of Service to the Foreign Born, Brooklyn, N.Y., 1947-50, caseworker, became supervisor; Family Service Association, Mt. Vernon, N.Y., executive director and part-time caseworker, 1951-53; Childrens Village, Dobbs Ferry, N.Y., part-time psychiatric social worker, 1958-60; Pelham Family Service, Pelham, N.Y., part-time caseworker, 1961-63; Griffin Hospital, Alice Ross Cochran Psychiatric Clinic, Derby, Conn., part-time social worker, 1964-68; Orange Street Clinic, New Haven, Conn., social worker, 1968-69; Connecticut Mental Health Center, New Haven, social worker and supervisor, 1969—; private practice of psychiatric social work in the Clinton Mental Health Center, 1969—. Chairman of Scarsdale Fair Housing Committee and New Haven Women's

Counseling Center project; member of board of directors of Homemaker's Service; consultant for New Haven Half-Way House; clinical instructor in social work in psychiatry for the Yale University School of Medicine. Worked on community resources directory for Connecticut Mental Health Center.

MEMBER: Amnesty International, National Association of Social Workers, American Civil Liberties Union, National Association for the Advancement of Colored People, American Committee on Africa, Academy of Certified Social Workers, Wilderness Society, Southern Poverty Law Center. *Awards, honors: The Healing Alliance* was named mental health book of the year by American Nursing Association, 1975.

WRITINGS: (With Andrew Slaby and Julian Lieb) *The Healing Alliance,* Norton, 1975. Contributor to *Social Casework.*

WORK IN PROGRESS: Research on the search for an intentional community, with publication expected to result.

SIDELIGHTS: Margaret Raymond told *CA:* "I have always been eagerly interested in other people and their ways of meeting everyday, tragic, or happy situations. I believe people should appreciate differences. I am optimistic, but grounded in reality. I believe every person should take responsibility for his own life and limit dependence, although we do need each other. Basically, my approach to life is religious, from the Quaker and Unitarian point of view.

"I am now working on the search for an intentional community. At my age this is an extraordinary search, for people reaching out to live in a community harmoniously and healthily, freed up to work. Multi-generational extended families should live in communities."

AVOCATIONAL INTERESTS: Photography, Japanese flower arrangements, Sumi brush-stroke painting, the arts, music, theatre, travel (Greece, Scandinavia, Poland, England, the Caribbean).

*   *   *

REASON, James T(ootle)   1938-

PERSONAL: Born in 1938, in Watford, England; married Rea Jaari; children: two daughters. *Education:* Attended University of London, Victoria University of Manchester, and University of Leicester. *Agent:* International Authors Agency, Wadhurst, Sussex, England.

CAREER: Royal Air Force, Institute of Aviation Medicine, psychologist, 1962-64; University of Leicester, Leicester, England, lecturer in psychology, 1964—. Research psychologist at U.S. Naval Aerospace Medical Institute, 1968-70. *Member:* British Psychological Society, Aerospace Medical Association.

WRITINGS: Introducing Psychology: An Experimental Approach, Penguin, 1970; (with M. Herbert) *Introducing Psychology,* Kahn & Averill, 1970; *Man in Motion: The Psychology of Travel,* Walker & Co., 1974; (with J. J. Brand) *Motion Sickness,* Academic Press, 1976. Contributor to scientific and medical journals and popular magazines, including *First Features, New Scientist,* and *New Society.*

BIOGRAPHICAL/CRITICAL SOURCES: Times Literary Supplement, May 24, 1974.*

*   *   *

REDPATH, (Robert) Theodore (Holmes)   1913-

PERSONAL: Born in 1913, in London, England; married Sarah Campbell Taylor; children: one son, one daughter. *Education:*

Attended St. Catharine's College, Cambridge, and St. John's College, Cambridge. *Home:* 49 Madingley Rd., Cambridge, England.

CAREER: Called to the Bar at Middle Temple, 1948; reader in chambers, 1948-49; Cambridge University, Cambridge, England, fellow, 1950—, and tutor, 1960—, of Trinity College, lecturer in English, 1954—. *Military service:* British Army, 1940-46. *Member:* Aristotelian Society, University Pitt Club.

WRITINGS: (Editor and author of introduction) John Donne, *Songs and Sonets,* Methuen, 1956, Barnes & Noble, 1957; *Tolstoy,* Hillary House, 1960, 2nd edition, 1969; (editor with W. G. Ingram) William Shakespeare, *Shakespeare's Sonnets,* University of London Press, 1964, Barnes & Noble, 1965, published as *Sixty-Five Sonnets of Shakespeare,* University of London Press, 1967; (editor with Margaret Patricia Hodgart) *Romantic Perspectives: The Work of Crabbe, Blake, Wordsworth, and Coleridge as Seen by Their Contemporaries and by Themselves,* Barnes & Noble, 1964; *The Young Romantics and Critical Opinion, 1807-1824: Poetry of Byron, Shelley, and Keats as Seen by Their Contemporary Critics,* St. Martin's, 1973.*

*   *   *

REDWOOD, Alec
See MILKOMANE, George Alexis Milkomanovich

*   *   *

REECK, Darrell (Lauren)   1939-

PERSONAL: Born January 25, 1939, in Tacoma, Wash.; son of Clarence (an educator) and Orleen (Colburn) Reeck; married Lucille Ruth Wonderly, June 23, 1963; children: David L.A., Christina Ruth. *Education:* Seattle Pacific University, B.A., 1960; Garrett-Evangelical Theological Seminary, B.D., 1965; Boston University, Ph.D., 1970. *Office:* Department of Religion, University of Puget Sound, Tacoma, Wash. 98416.

CAREER: Ordained minister in United Methodist Church; ordained in Evangelical United Brethren Church, 1965, pastor of church in Portland, Ore., 1965-66; University of Sierra Leone, Freetown, visiting research fellow at African Studies Institute, 1968-69; University of Puget Sound, Tacoma, Wash., assistant professor, 1969-74, associate professor, 1974-81, professor of religion, 1981—, chairman of department, 1977—. Visiting research scholar at University of Ghana, 1978; workshop leader. Member of board of directors of Tacoma Community House, 1970-76, 1978—, vice-president, 1972-73, president, 1974-76, chairman of program and planning committee, 1978—; member of Standing General Commission on Archives and History, United Methodist Church, 1972-76. Member of coordinating council of Washington Two Thousand, 1972-74; founding member of board of directors of Northwest Institute for Ethics and Life Sciences, 1975-77; member of human research review board of Washington State Department of Social and Health Services, 1979—; social ethics consultant at Christian Counselling Service, 1981—.

MEMBER: Society for Values in Higher Education, Society for Christian Ethics, American Academy of Religion, Phi Kappa Phi, Alpha Kappa Sigma. *Awards, honors:* Grants from African Studies Association, 1970, American Council of Learned Societies (for Ethiopia), 1973, and National Endowment for the Humanities, 1975.

WRITINGS: Deep Mende: Religious Interactions in a Changing African Rural Society, E. J. Brill, 1976; *Ethics for the Professions: A Christian Perspective,* Augsburg, 1982. Contributor of about twenty-five articles and reviews to magazines, including *Bioethics Quarterly, Africa Today,* and *Christian Century,* and newspapers.

SIDELIGHTS: Darrell Reeck wrote: "It is very difficult to both teach well in an excellent undergraduate institution that stresses excellence in teaching and to write. Either pursuit alone is more than a full-time occupation. If I have done either well, it is because I write what I teach and teach what I write. Leroy Ostransky, author of *Anatomy of Jazz* and my former colleague, taught me that if I were going to write and also teach undergraduates, the two pursuits would have to feed each other. *Ethics for the Professions,* my 1982 book, illustrates perfectly Ostransky's lesson. The main organizing concepts of the book and much of the research grew directly out of my teaching of a course with the same title."

* * *

REED, Henry 1914-

PERSONAL: Born February 22, 1914, in Birmingham, Warwickshire, England; son of Henry and Mary Ann (Bell) Reed. *Education:* University of Birmingham, M.A., 1937. *Address:* c/o Johnathan Cape, Ltd., 30 Bedford Square, London WC1B 3EL, England.

CAREER: Teacher and free-lance journalist, 1937-41; British Foreign Office, London, England, staff member, 1942-45; writer, critic, translator, broadcaster, 1945—. *Military service:* British Army, 1941-42. *Member:* Savile Club.

WRITINGS: A Map of Verona: Poems, Cape, 1946, Reynal, 1947; (translator) Paride Rombi, *Perdu and His Father,* Hart-Davis, 1954; (translator) Dino Buzzati, *Larger Than Life,* Secker & Warburg, 1962; (translator) Honore de Balzac, *Eugenie Grandet,* New American Library, 1964; *Lessons of the War* (poems), Chilmark Press, 1970.

Plays; translator and adaptor: Ugo Betti, "The Burnt Flower Bed," first produced in London, 1955 (published in *Three Plays;* see below); Betti, *The Queen and the Rebels* (two-act; first broadcast, 1954; first produced in London, 1955), Samuel French, 1957; Betti, *Summertime* (three-act; first produced in London, 1955), Samuel French, 1957; Betti, "Island of Goats" (three-act), first produced in New York, 1955, published as *Crime on Goat Island,* Samuel French, 1960; Betti, "Corruption in the Palace of Justice," first produced in New York, 1963; Natalia Ginzburg, *The Advertisement* (first produced on the West End at Old Vic Theatre, September 24, 1968; produced in New York, 1974), Faber, 1969.

Radio plays: "Noises On," 1947; "Noises: Nasty and Nice," 1947; *Moby Dick: A Play for Radio From Herman Melville's Novel* (first broadcast, 1947), Cape, 1947; "Pytheas," 1947; "Leopardi: The Unblest, The Monument," 1949; "A By-Election of the Nineties," 1951; "The Dynasts," 1951; "Malatesta," 1952; "The Streets of Pompeii," 1952; "The Great Desire I Had," 1952; "Return to Naples," 1953; "All for the Best," 1953; "A Very Great Man Indeed," 1953; "The Private Life of Hilda Tablet," first broadcast on British Broadcasting Corp. BBC-Radio, 1953; "Hamlet; or, The Consequences of Filial Piety," 1954; "The Battle of the Masks," 1954; "The Queen and the Rebels," 1954; "Emily Butler," 1954; "The Burnt Flower-Bed," 1955; "Vincenzo," 1955; "Crime on Goat Island," 1956; "A Hedge, Backwards," 1956; "Don Juan in Love," 1956; "Alarica," 1956; "Irene," 1957; "Corruption in the Palace of Justice," 1958; "The Primal Scene, As It Were . . . ," 1958; "The Auction Sale," 1958; "The Island Where the King Is a Child," 1959; "One Flesh,"

1959; "Not a Drum Was Heard," 1959; (with Donald Swann) "Musique Discrete," 1959; "The House on the Water," 1961; "A Hospital Case," 1961; "The America Prize," 1964; "Zone 36," 1965; "Summertime," 1969; "The Two Mrs. Morlis," 1971.

Omnibus volumes: (Translator and adaptor) Betti, *Three European Plays* (contains "The Queen and the Rebels," "The Burnt Flower-Bed," and "Summertime"), Gollancz, 1956; *The Streets of Pompeii and Other Plays for Radio* (contains "Leopardi: The Unblest, The Monument," "The Great Desire I Had," "Return to Naples," and "Vincenzo"), BBC Publications, 1971; *Hilda Tablet and Others: Four Pieces for Radio* (contains "A Very Great Man Indeed," "The Private Life of Hilda Tablet," "A Hedge, Backwards," "The Primal Scene, As It Were . . ."), BBC Publications, 1971.

Contributor of poetry and criticism to periodicals, including *Poetry, New Yorker, Theatre Arts, Nation, Newsweek,* and *Time.*

SIDELIGHTS: Reed began writing as a student at Birmingham University where his circle of friends included writers W. H. Auden, Walter Allen, and Louis MacNiece. Like that of his contemporaries, Reed's early poetry was concerned with the political events of the period just prior to and including World War II. His most admired pieces include the poems "Naming of the Parts" and "Judging Distances," which are based on his experiences in cadet training.

The range of Reed's talents is represented in his first volume of poetry, *A Map of Verona.* In this book he demonstrates his abilities as a writer not only of stately, formal verse, but of humorous poetry as well. "Chard Whitlow," a parody of T. S. Eliot, won Reed recognition as a masterful satiric writer.

The "Hilda Tablet" series is probably the best known of Reed's satiric work. Produced by BBC-Radio in the 1960's, these programs lampooned British society as it was in the 1930's. Reed is also famous for his radio adaptations of *Moby Dick* and of the works of Italian playwright Ugo Betti.

In 1972 Reed's poem "Naming of the Parts" was adapted as a motion picture and released by Contemporary Films.

BIOGRAPHICAL/CRITICAL SOURCES: Times Literary Supplement, May 11, 1946, November 1, 1947; December 6, 1947; *New York Times,* December 28, 1947; *Commonweal,* January 16, 1948; John Russell Taylor, *Anger and After,* Hill & Wang, 1962.*

* * *

REED, Willis 1942-

PERSONAL: Born June 25, 1942, in Hico, La.; son of Willis, Sr. (a warehouse foreman) and Inell Reed; married Geraldine Oliver (divorced); children: Carl Vance, Veronica. *Education:* Attended Grambling College. *Residence:* Bernice, La. *Office:* New York Knickerbockers, 4 Pennsylvania Plaza, New York, N.Y. 10010.

CAREER: New York Knickerbockers (professional basketball team), New York City, forward, 1964-68, center, 1968-74, coach, 1977—. Owner of businesses in New York City. *Awards, honors:* Member of National Basketball Association (NBA) all-star team, 1965-71 and 1973, and World Championship basketball team, 1970 and 1973; named rookie of the year by basketball writers and broadcasters, 1965; Podoloff Cup from NBA players, 1970, for most valuable player of regular season; named most valuable player of NBA playoff, 1970 and 1973, and all-star game, 1970.

WRITINGS: (With Phil Pepe) *View From the Rim: Willis Reed on Basketball,* Lippincott, 1971; *A Will to Win: The Comeback Year,* photographs by George Kalinsky, Prentice-Hall, 1974.

SIDELIGHTS: Although Reed had led his college basketball team to three conference championships, he was passed over during the first round of the NBA's annual draft in 1964. The Knicks chose Reed on the next round and he went on to become the team's captain and its most valuable player. "Few rookies broke into the pro basketball scene more explosively than did Reed," said a *New York Times* reporter. "He scored 1,560 points for the season and was named rookie of the year." What is more, the reporter noted, Reed "had gained the respect of teammates, opposing players, coaches and fans." After eleven seasons with the Knicks, Reed was forced to retire when a knee injury failed to respond to therapy. According to the *New York Times*'s Sam Goldaper, during his pro career Reed "played in 650 regular-season games, scored 12,183 points (an 18.7 average) and grabbed 8,414 rebounds."

BIOGRAPHICAL/CRITICAL SOURCES: Look, January 24, 1967; *Newsweek,* February 24, 1969; Larry Fox, *Willis Reed: Take-Charge Man of the Knicks,* Grosset, 1970; Phil Pepe, *Greatest Stars of the NBA* (juvenile), Prentice-Hall, 1971; *Sports Illustrated,* May 21, 1973; *New York Times,* June 21, 1974, March 10, 1977.*

*   *   *

REES, David Morgan   1904-

PERSONAL: Born March 29, 1904; son of Rees Rees (a justice of the peace); married Marjorie Griffith, 1935; children: one son, one daughter. *Education:* Received certificate in English and qualified as mining engineer, University of Birmingham. *Home:* Tynewydd, Abergolech, Dyfed, Wales.

CAREER: Mining engineer in Wales, 1930-36; B. A. Colliery, agent, 1936-46; National Coal Board, area general manager of East Midlands Division, 1947-52, chairman of South Western Division, 1952-61; Justice of the peace in Newcastle, Ogmore, and Bridgend, Wales; member of Council for Wales and Monmouthshire, 1953-56. *Member:* Cardiff and County Club, Royal Porthcawl Golf Club. *Awards, honors:* Commander of Order of the British Empire, 1956; commander of Order of St. John.

WRITINGS: Mines, Mills, and Furnaces: An Introduction to Industrial Archaeology in Wales, H.M.S.O., 1969, published as *The Industrial Archaeology of Wales,* David & Charles, 1975; *Rhys Davies,* Verry, 1975; *Wales,* Moorland Publishing, 1979.

In Welsh: *Agweddau ar archaeoleg diwydiannol: Erthyglau a gyhoeddwyd yn wreiddiol yn Y Gwyddondydd,* Angueddfa Genedlaethol Cymru, 1974.*

*   *   *

REES, (George) Leslie (Clarence)   1905-

PERSONAL: Born December 28, 1905, in Perth, Western Australia; married Coralie Clarke (a writer), 1931 (died, 1972); children: Megan, Dymphna. *Education:* University of Western Australia, B.A., 1929; graduate study at University College, London, 1930. *Home:* 4/5 The Esplanade, Balmoral Beach 2088, New South Wales, Australia.

CAREER: Writer, editor, and drama critic. *Era,* London, England, senior drama critic, 1931-35; Playwrights Advisory Board, Sydney, Australia, co-founder, 1937, continuing honorary chairman; Australian Broadcasting Commission, chief drama editor, 1937-57, assistant director of drama, 1957-66; Mt. Law-

ley College of Advanced Education, Perth, Australia, writer-in-residence, 1975. *Member:* International P.E.N. (president of Sydney Centre, 1968-76). *Awards, honors:* Australian Children's Book-of-the-Year Award, 1946, for *The Story of Karrawingi, the Emu;* award from Townsville Literary Foundation, 1978, for *A History of Australian Drama;* member of the Order of Australia, 1981.

WRITINGS—With wife, Coralie Rees: *Spinifex Walkabout: Hitch-Hiking in Remote North Australia,* Harrap, 1953; *Westward From Cocos: Indian Ocean Travels,* Harrap, 1956; *The Coasts of Cape York: Travels Around Australia's Pearl-Tipped Peninsula,* Angus & Robertson, 1960; *People of the Big Sky Country,* Ure Smith, 1970.

Juvenile; published by John Sands, except as noted: *Digit Dick on the Barrier Reef,* 1942; *Gecko: The Lizard Who Lost His Tail,* 1944 (see below); *The Story of Shy, the Platypus,* illustrations by Walter Cunningham, 1945 (see below); *Digit Dick and the Tasmanian Devil,* 1946; *The Story of Karrawingi, the Emu,* illustrations by Cunningham, 1946; *The Story of Sarli, the Barrier Reef Turtle,* 1947 (see below); *Bluecap and Bimbi,* Trinity House, 1948 (see below); *Mates of the Kurlalong,* illustrations by Alfred Wood, 1948; *The Story of Kurri Kurri, the Kookaburra,* illustrations by Margaret Senior, 1950; *Quokka Island,* illustrations by Arthur Horowicz, Collins, 1951; *Danger Patrol: A Young Patrol Officer's Adventures in New Guinea,* Collins, 1954; *Two Thumbs: The Story of a Koala,* illustrations by Senior, Ryerson Press, 1954; *The Story of Koonaworra, the Black Swan,* illustrations by Senior, 1957; *The Story of Aroora, the Red Kangaroo,* illustrations by John Singleton, 1958 (see below); *Australian Nature Tales* (contains *The Story of Aroora, the Red Kangaroo, The Story of Shy, the Platypus,* and *The Story of Sarli, the Barrier Reef Turtle*), 1958.

The Story of Wy-lah, the Cockatoo, illustrations by Cunningham, 1960; *The Story of Russ, the Australian Tree Kangaroo,* illustrations by Cunningham, 1964; *Boy Lost on Tropic Coast: Adventure With Dexter Hardy,* Ure Smith, 1968; *Digit Dick on the Great Barrier Reef,* illustrations by F. Hutchings, Hamlyn, 1969; *Digit Dick in Black Swan Land,* Hamlyn, 1972; *Mokee, the White Possum,* illustrations by Tony Oliver, Hamlyn, 1973 (see below); *Panic in the Cattle Country,* Rigby, 1974; *Bluecap and Bimbi, Gecko, and Mokee* (contains *Mokee, the White Possum, Gecko, the Lizard Who Lost His Tail,* and *Bluecap and Bimbi*), illustrations by Oliver, Hamlyn, 1975. Also author of *The Story of Shadow, the Rock Wallaby* and *Here's to Shane: The Story of a Boy Born Deaf.*

Other: (Editor) *Australian Radio Plays,* Angus & Robertson, 1946; (editor) *Modern Short Plays,* Angus & Robertson, 1951; *Towards an Australian Drama,* Angus & Robertson, 1953, revised edition published as *The Making of Australian Drama: A Historical and Critical Survey From the 1830's to the 1970's,* 1973 (see below); (editor) *Mask and Microphone* (plays), Angus & Robertson, 1963; *Australian Drama in the 1970's: A Historical and Critical Survey,* Angus & Robertson, 1978 (see below); *A History of Australian Drama* (contains a revised version of *The Making of Australian Drama: A Historical and Critical Survey From the 1830's to the 1970's* and *Australian Drama in the 1970's: A Historical and Critical Survey*), Angus & Robertson, 1978.

WORK IN PROGRESS: Hold Fast to Dreams, memoirs.

SIDELIGHTS: Some of Rees's popular children's books are based on his childhood experiences near Perth, Australia. Rees spent many holidays exploring about the countryside and often camped along the Swan River or on coastal islands. *Digit Dick in Black Swan Land, Quokka Island,* and *Kurri Kurri, the*

Kookaburra recapture the scenes of these adventures. His love and knowledge of Australian wildlife is also reflected in his many other books, but especially in *The Story of Shy, the Platypus, The Story of Karrawingi, the Emu,* and *The Story of Koonaworra, the Black Swan.*

*   *   *

REES, William 1887-1978(?)

OBITUARY NOTICE—See index for *CA* sketch: Born December 14, 1887, in Brecon, Wales; died c. 1978 in Penarth; England. Educator, historian, editor, cartographer, and author. Rees taught history at the University College of South Wales and at Monmouthshire of the University of Wales for more than thirty years. He wrote several historical works, including *The Making of Europe, South Wales and the March, The Great Forest of Brecknock,* and *Industry Before the Industrial Revolution.* Rees also edited *A Bibliography of the History of Wales.* As a cartographer, he published *Historical Map of South Wales and the Border in the Fourteenth Century* and *An Historical Atlas of Wales From Early to Modern Times.* Obituaries and other sources: *AB Bookman's Weekly,* January 29, 1979.

*   *   *

REGAN, Thomas Howard 1938-
(Tom Regan)

PERSONAL: Born November 28, 1938, in Pittsburgh, Pa.; married, 1962; children: two. *Education:* Thiel College, A.B., 1960; University of Virginia, M.A., 1962, Ph.D., 1966. *Office:* Department of Philosophy, North Carolina State University, Raleigh, N.C. 27607.

CAREER: Sweet Briar College, Sweet Briar, Va., assistant professor of philosophy, 1965-67; North Carolina State University, Raleigh, assistant professor, 1967-72, associate professor of philosophy, 1972—. *Member:* American Association of University Professors.

WRITINGS—Under name Tom Regan: *Understanding Philosophy,* Dickenson, 1974; (editor with Peter Singer) *Animal Rights and Human Obligations,* Prentice-Hall, 1976; *Matters of Life and Death,* Random House, 1980. Contributor to philosophy journals.*

*   *   *

REGAN, Tom
See REGAN, Thomas Howard

*   *   *

REGUEIRO, Helen 1943-

PERSONAL: Born September 18, 1943, in Montevideo, Uruguay. *Education:* Brandeis University, B.A., 1964; Brown University, Ph.D., 1969. *Office:* Department of English, State University of New York at Albany, Albany, N.Y. 12222.

CAREER: Columbia University, New York, N.Y., assistant professor of English and comparative literature, 1969-75; Yale University, New Haven, Conn., assistant professor of English, 1975-77; State University of New York at Albany, associate professor of English, 1977—. *Member:* Modern Language Association of America, American Association of University Professors. *Awards, honors:* Junior fellow of Society for Humanities of Cornell University, 1973-74.

WRITINGS: The Limits of Imagination: Wordsworth, Yeats, and Stevens, Cornell University Press, 1976.*

*   *   *

REICHMANN, Felix 1899-

PERSONAL: Born September 14, 1899, in Vienna, Austria; came to the United States in 1939, naturalized citizen, 1944; son of Alois and Emma (Loewy) Reichmann; married Lilly Doerfler (a teacher), March 5, 1933; children: Ingrid Reichmann Matheson. *Education:* University of Vienna, Ph.D., 1923; University of Chicago, M.A., 1942. *Home:* 217 Willard Way, Ithaca, N.Y. 14850. *Office:* Libraries, Cornell University, Ithaca, N.Y. 14853.

CAREER: Bookdealer in Vienna, Austria, 1925-38; Carl Schurz Foundation, Philadelphia, Pa., librarian, 1939-43; associated with Office of Strategic Services, Washington, D.C., 1943-45; U.S. Military Government, Stuttgart, Germany (now West Germany), head of Publications Control Division, 1943-45; worked at Library of Congress, Washington, D.C., 1945-47; Cornell University Libraries, Ithaca, N.Y., assistant director for technical services, 1947-66; Cornell University, Ithaca, professor of bibliography, 1967-72, professor emeritus, 1973—. *Member:* Mediaeval Academy of America. *Awards, honors:* Fulbright fellow, 1955; Guggenheim fellow, 1955.

WRITINGS: Gotische wandmalerei in Niederoesterreich (title means "Gothic Mural Paintings in Lower Austria"), Amalthea-Verlag, 1925; (with Eugene E. Doll) *Ephrata as Seen by Contemporaries,* Pennsylvania German Folklore Society, 1953; *Sugar, Gold, and Coffee: Essays on the History of Brazil, Based on Francis Hull's Books,* Library, Cornell University, 1959; (with Josephine Tharpe) *Bibliographic Control of Microforms,* Greenwood Press, 1972; *The Sources of Western Literacy: The Middle Eastern Civilization,* Greenwood Press, 1980. Contributor to history journals.

WORK IN PROGRESS: A History of Booktrade in Medieval Europe, publication expected in 1983.

SIDELIGHTS: Felix Reichmann commented: "My main interest is the development of literacy and of commercial booktrade, with main emphasis on Western Europe. The literature on this topic, treating classical antiquity, is extensive. My own contribution, 'The Booktrade at the Time of the Roman Empire,' appeared in *Library Quarterly* in 1938. My recent book, *The Sources of Western Literacy,* summarizes most of the facts we know about the Middle East. Comparatively little has been published about literacy and the booktrade during the Middle Ages. However, I hope to prove widespread literacy among laymen, including women, and extensive book publishing activities not connected with monastic scriptoria before the invention of printing."

*   *   *

REILLY, John M(arsden) 1933-

PERSONAL: Born February 18, 1933, in Pittsburgh, Pa.; son of John Francis (in business) and Virginia (Marsden) Reilly; married Joyce Whisler (an office worker), 1952; children: John David, Bridget Anne, Michael Timothy. *Education:* West Virginia University, B.A. (with high honors), 1954; Washington University, St. Louis, Mo., M.A., 1963, Ph.D., 1967. *Home:* 293 Washington Ave., Albany, N.Y. 12206. *Office:* Department of English, State University of New York at Albany, Humanities Building, 1400 Washington Ave., Albany, N.Y. 12206.

CAREER: Washington University, St. Louis, Mo., instructor in English, 1960-61; University of Puerto Rico, San Juan, assistant professor of English, 1961-63; State University of New York at Albany, assistant professor, 1963-70, associate professor of English, 1970—. Visiting assistant professor at University of Oregon, 1970. Member of board of directors of Albany County New Liberal Coalition, 1980—.

MEMBER: United University Professions (president of Albany chapter, 1979—), American Studies Association, Modern Language Association of America, Mystery Writers of America, College Language Association, Popular Culture Association, Society for the Study of the Multi-Ethnic Literature of the United States (program chairman, 1980-81), Society for the Study of Southern Literature, Northeastern Modern Language Association, Phi Beta Kappa. *Awards, honors:* Woodrow Wilson fellow, 1954-55; National Endowment for the Humanities Younger humanist fellow, 1960-61; Edgar Allan Poe Award from Mystery Writers of America, 1981, for *Twentieth-Century Crime and Mystery Writers; Twentieth-Century Crime and Mystery Writers* was named outstanding reference book by Reference and Adult Services Division of American Library Association, 1981.

WRITINGS: (Editor) *Twentieth-Century Interpretations of Invisible Man*, Prentice-Hall, 1970; (editor) *Richard Wright: The Critical Reception*, B. Franklin, 1978; (editor) *Twentieth-Century Crime and Mystery Writers*, St. Martin's, 1980; (editor with Robert B. Stepto) *Afro-American Literature: The Reconstruction of a Literary History*, Modern Language Association of America, 1982.

Contributor: (Author of afterword) Richard Wright, *Native Son*, Harper, 1966; (author of afterword) Wright, *Black Boy*, Harper, 1966; Nagayo Honma and Shunsuke Kamei, editors, *Amerika no Taisha Bunka* (title means "American Popular Culture"), Kenkyusha, 1974; Louis Filler, editor, *Seasoned Authors for a New Season*, Bowling Green University, 1980; James Woodress, editor, *American Literary Scholarship*, Duke University Press, 1979 edition, 1981, 1980 edition, 1982, 1981 edition, in press; Earl Bargainnier, editor, *Ten Women of Mystery*, Bowling Green University, 1981; Yoshinobu Hakutani, editor, *Critical Essays on Richard Wright*, G. K. Hall, 1981; Kimberly Benston, editor, *Essays on Ralph Ellison*, Center for Southern Studies, 1982.

Contributor of about thirty articles and reviews to literature journals and popular magazines, including *Armchair Detective, Georgia Review, Alternative Futures, Minority Voices,* and *Clues: Journal of Detection.* Contributing editor of *Obsidian/ Black Literature in Review;* member of advisory board, St. James Editorial Ltd., 1972—; member of editorial advisory board of *Melus*, 1977-79; member of board of continuing critics and reviewers of *Callaloo: Journal of the Black South.*

WORK IN PROGRESS: Research on the uses of history in Afro-American literature and on genres of popular story and narrative.

SIDELIGHTS: Reilly told *CA:* "A good deal of my writing represents an attempt to apply the training I have received as an academic to the principles I have found in popular political practice; thus, the choice of Afro-American writing as subject matter for my first publication originally derived from experience in the civil rights movement. As a participant in the St. Louis chapter of CORE during the 1950's I thought it necessary to unite what I was learning about the brave efforts of blacks to live the construction of a democratic society with the techniques of the profession I wanted to enter. Later, the fight against racism evolved into a movement for social reconstruc-

tion, and the thrill of that development stimulated me to seek additional subjects that would integrate action and investigation. So, I read social reform literature only to discover that the institution I work in (the university) is itself in need of reform as much as any other. In 1970, therefore, I did what many others at that time did—joined the strike. The consequence for my professional work was an interest in revising the subjects of literary study—particularly the canon of 'acceptable' works—and participating as I could in humanizing the relationships within the university and between the university and broader society.

"All this sounds neatly linear, and a mite too simple, for there is also a motive of pleasure to account for. My work on popular literature may have something to do with smashing the pantheon of greats, but it also has a lot to do with delight in storytelling—the means for establishing consciousness of our communities—and with reading that, appearing to have no utility, testifies on another level to the wonderful ability of people to make the world for themselves."

BIOGRAPHICAL/CRITICAL SOURCES: Edward Margolies and David Bakish, *Afro-American Fiction, 1853-1976: A Guide to Information Sources*, Gale, 1979; J. Albert Robbins, editor, *American Literary Scholarship, 1978*, Duke University Press, 1980; *Poisoned Pen*, July-August, 1980; *Mystery Fancier*, September-October, 1980, January-February, 1981; *New Republic*, October 11, 1980; *Ellery Queen's Mystery Magazine*, December 1, 1980; *New York Times Book Review*, December 28, 1980; *Reference Quarterly*, December, 1980; *Wilson Library Bulletin*, January, 1981; *Enigmatika*, February, 1981; *Armchair Detective*, winter, 1981; *Times Literary Supplement*, June 5, 1981.

*   *   *

REINHART, Charles (Franklin) 1946-

PERSONAL: Born March 9, 1946, in Lancaster, Pa.; son of Charles F., Sr. (an electrician) and Thelma Jane (Zink) Reinhart; married Erna Weigel (a credit clerk), May 27, 1967; children: Jeffrey Neil, Gregory Steven. *Education:* Millersville State College, B.S., 1968, M.A., 1971. *Home:* 1616 Robert Rd., Lancaster, Pa. 17601.

CAREER: High school science teacher in Quarryville, Pa., 1968-70; Columbia High School, Columbia, Pa., science teacher, 1970—. Announcer for WGAL-AM/FM Radio, 1970-77, and WQXA-FM Radio, 1977—. East Lampeter Recreation Association, baseball coach, 1978—, vice-president, 1980-81.

WRITINGS: Beatle Novelty Discography, privately printed, 1976; *You Can't Do That* (nonfiction), Pierian, 1981; *Beatle People* (nonfiction), Pierian, 1982. Contributor to magazines, including *Goldmine* and *Beatlefan.*

WORK IN PROGRESS: The Solo Beatles Trivia Book; Paul McCartney and Wings, a history for teenagers.

SIDELIGHTS: "My writing is a direct result of my hobby of record collecting," Reinhart told *CA.* "Since 1964 I have amassed nearly twenty thousand 45 rpm records and five thousand albums. My first love has been the Beatles and I have followed their careers both as a group and as solo artists. My interest in collecting Beatles novelty records and bootlegs led me to write *You Can't Do That* as a guide for collecting these two types of records.

"My radio work has also given me a chance to use my writing ability. At WGAL I wrote and announced my own news for nearly two years, wrote and produced specials on subjects ranging from nuclear energy to education, and wrote and produced my own nightly hour-long 'oldies' show. Just recently I wrote, announced, and produced a two-hour tribute to the late John Lennon for WQXA.

"I have also written and performed two break-in records, 'Beatles/Best Ex-Beatle' and 'History of the Beatles, Part I: Early Days/Hamburg Days.' Break-in records are those in which questions are asked by the artist and bits of records are used as the answers. This is the type of record that Dickie Goodman has made so popular over the years."

BIOGRAPHICAL/CRITICAL SOURCES: Stereo Review, July, 1981; *Columbia News,* July 11, 1981.

* * *

REISMAN, George Gerald 1937-

PERSONAL: Born January 13, 1937, in New York, N.Y. *Education:* Columbia University, A.B., 1957; New York University, M.B.A., 1959, Ph.D., 1963. *Home:* 420 East 72nd St., New York, N.Y. 10021. *Office:* Department of Economics, College of Business Administration, St. John's University, Jamaica, N.Y. 11439.

CAREER: U.S. Trust Co., New York, financial analyst, 1963-64; Adelphi University, Garden City, N.Y., assistant professor of economics, 1964; St. John's University, Jamaica, N.Y., assistant professor, 1964-66, associate professor of economics, 1966—. *Member:* American Economic Association, American Academy of Political and Social Science.

WRITINGS: (Translator) Ludwig von Mises, *Epistemological Problems of Economics,* Van Nostrand, 1960; *The Government Against the Economy: The Story of the U.S. Government's On-Going Destruction of the American Economic System Through Price Controls,* foreword by William E. Simon, Caroline House, 1979. Contributor to political and social science journals.

WORK IN PROGRESS: Capitalism: The Cure for Racism.

BIOGRAPHICAL/CRITICAL SOURCES: National Review, December 7, 1979.*

* * *

REITLINGER, Gerald R. 1900(?)-1978

OBITUARY NOTICE: Born c. 1900; died in March, 1978, in England. Artist and author. Among Reitlinger's writings is *Economics of Good Taste,* a three-volume history of the art market from the 1700's through the 1960's. Obituaries and other sources: *AB Bookman's Weekly,* July 10, 1978.

* * *

RENDEL, John 1906(?)-1978

OBITUARY NOTICE: Born c. 1906; died April 16, 1978, in Bradenton, Fla. Journalist and author. Rendel was a sports columnist for the *New York Times* for forty-five years, specializing in the coverage of yacht races and dog and horse shows. The author of *The Dog Book* and *The Horse Book,* Rendel formerly served as president of the Dog Writers of America. He was named Writer of the Year four times by that organization. Obituaries and other sources: *New York Times,* April 18, 1978; *AB Bookman's Weekly,* July 10, 1978.

* * *

REYMONT, Wladyslaw (Stanislaw) 1868(?)-1925

BRIEF ENTRY: Born c. May, 1868, in Kobiele Wielkie, Po-

land; died December 5, 1925, in Warsaw, Poland. Polish novelist and short story writer. Reymont's international reputation rests on his novel *The Peasants* (1902-09), for which he received a Nobel Prize in literature in 1924. This epic of village life illustrated Reymont's firsthand knowledge of rural society and his fluency in the peasant idiom. Reymont held various positions, including that of a journalist, before he began writing full time. His talent for reporting and mass description is apparent in his early books *A Pilgrimage to Jasna Gora* (1895) and *The Comedienne* (1896). He had entered the literary arena during the sway of the Polish positivists. Their influence was waning, partly because the industrialization of Poland, in which they had placed their faith, had failed to free the people from foreign domination and dire poverty. Reymont introduced a new view in *The Promised Land* (1899), a grim novel of industrial expansion in Lodz, emphasizing its dehumanization of the people and their enslavement to factory life. Reymont continued to write short stories and novels on such diverse subjects as spiritualism and war, but none received the acclaim of *The Peasants. Biographical/critical sources: Twentieth Century Authors: A Biographical Dictionary of Modern Literature,* H. W. Wilson, 1942; *Columbia Dictionary of Modern European Literature,* Columbia University Press, 1947.

* * *

REYNOLDS, (Alfred) Christopher 1911-

PERSONAL: Born in 1911, in Brinscall, England; married Doreen Betty Kearsley; children: two sons. *Education:* Received A.R.C.A. from Royal College of Art.

CAREER: High school art teacher, 1947-64; biology teacher at grammar schools, 1965—. *Military service:* British Army, Royal Armoured Corps, 1942-46. *Member:* Zoological Society.

WRITINGS: Small Creatures in My Back Garden (juvenile), self-illustrated, Deutsch, 1965, published in the United States as *Small Creatures in My Garden,* Ariel Books, 1966; *The Pond on My Window-Sill* (juvenile), self-illustrated, foreword and appendix by John C. Pallister, Pantheon, 1969; *Creatures of the Bay* (juvenile), Deutsch, 1974.

Work represented in anthologies, including *Miscellany Four* and *Christmas Anthology.* Contributor to *Encyclopedia of Gardening.* Contributor to magazines, including *Animals.*

AVOCATIONAL INTERESTS: Drawing and painting, nature photography, collecting natural history books, walking in the country, gardening.*

* * *

RHOADS, Jonathan E(vans) 1907-

PERSONAL: Born May 9, 1907, in Philadelphia, Pa.; son of Edward G. and Margaret Ely (Paxson) Rhoads; married Teresa Folin; children: Margaret Rhoads Kendon, Jonathan Evans, Jr., George Grant, Edward Otto Folin, Philip Garrett, Charles James. *Education:* Haverford College, B.A., 1928; Johns Hopkins University, M.D., 1932; University of Pennsylvania, D.Sc.Med., 1940. *Politics:* Republican. *Religion:* Society of Friends (Quakers). *Residence:* Philadelphia, Pa. *Office:* Department of Surgery, Hospital of the University of Pennsylvania, Philadelphia, Pa. 19104.

CAREER: University of Pennsylvania, Philadelphia, intern at hospital, 1932-34, assistant chief resident physician, 1934, fellow in general surgery, 1934-39, research associate in surgery, 1939-47, assistant surgeon, 1940-46, acting chief of Surgical

Service B, 1942-46, acting director of Harrison Department of Surgical Research, 1944-45 (assistant director, 1946-59, director, 1959-72), chief of Surgical Division II, 1946-56, assistant chief of department of surgery, 1956-59, chairman of department of surgery, 1959-72; assistant instructor at university, 1934-35, instructor, 1935-39, assistant professor, 1945-47, associate professor, 1947-49, professor of surgery, 1949—, J. William White Professor of Surgical Research, 1949-51, John Rhea Barton Professor of Surgery, 1959-72, provost of university, 1956-59, provost emeritus, 1977—. Assistant surgeon at Pennsylvania Hospital, 1939-46, director of department of surgery, 1972-74, consulting surgeon, 1974—; assistant surgeon at Children's Hospital of Philadelphia, 1942-47, senior visiting surgeon, 1948-72; surgeon-in-chief pro tempore at Rhode Island Hospital, 1957; consulting surgeon at Monmouth Medical Center, 1959—, and Bryn Mawr Hospital, 1960—.

Visiting professor at University of Manitoba, 1958, Hartford Hospital, 1960, University of Illinois, Allegheny General Hospital, Vanderbilt University, and State University of New York Downstate Medical Center, 1973, University of Mississippi, Norfolk General Hospital, Eastern Virginia Medical School, and State University of New York at Stony Brook, 1974, University of Texas, Houston, 1975, Hospital for Joint Diseases and Medical Center, New York, N.Y., and Medical Center of Western Massachusetts, 1976, Yeshiva University, 1977, Duke University, 1979, and Ohio State University, 1980; visiting lecturer at Roswell Park Memorial Institute, 1973, Washington Hospital Center, Rutgers University's Medical School, Piscataway, N.J., Maui Memorial Hospital, and Bryn Mawr Hospital, 1974, California Institute of Technology, 1975, Massachusetts General Hospital, 1978, and Cancer Institute, Melbourne, Australia, 1979.

Curator of Osler Library, McGill University, 1952-54; committee member of National Research Council; chairman of U.S. Food and Drug Administration surgical drugs advisory committee, 1971-74; member of national advisory general medical sciences council of National Institutes of Health, 1963-67; member of U.S. Senate panel of consultants on the conquest of cancer, 1970; chairman of National Cancer Advisory Board of U.S. Public Health Service, 1972-79. Member of National Foundation for Ileitis and Colitis, Digestive Disease Foundation, Philadelphia Medico-Legal Institute, Worcester Foundation for Experimental Biology, Adult Education Council of Philadelphia, Crime Commission of Philadelphia, Franklin Institute, and Philadelphia Medical Political Action Committee; member of advisory council of Life Insurance Medical Research Fund, 1961-65, scientific advisory committee of Papanicolaou Cancer Research Institute, 1971-76, and advisory board of Widows and Single Women's Society of Philadelphia, 1973—; member of board of trustees of Institute for Medical Research, 1957— (vice-president for scientific affairs, 1964-76), Bryn Mawr College, 1960-79, Associated Universities, Inc., 1961-63, and General Motors Cancer Research Foundation, 1978—; member of board of directors of Provident Mutual Life Insurance Co., 1956-77, Pennwalt Corp., 1966-77, Bryn Mawr College, 1969-79, Benjamin and Mary Siddons Measey Foundation, 1971— (chairman, 1978—), InTerAx, 1973-75, Philadelphia Health Management Corp., 1973—, Philadelphia Professional Standards Review Organization, 1974— (member of executive committee and president, 1974—), Fox Chase Cancer Center, 1975—, J. E. Rhoads & Sons, 1976—, and Quadrangle, 1981—. Member of board of managers of Haverford College, 1947— (president of corporation, 1963-77; chairman of board, 1963-72), and Friends Hospital, 1952—.

MEMBER: Collegium Internationale Chirurgiae Digestivae, International Federation of Surgical Colleges (member of executive council, 1969—; vice-president, 1972-78; president, 1978—), International Society of Blood Transfusion, International Surgical Group (president, 1958-59), Societe Internationale de Chirurgie, World Medical Association, Pan-American Medical Association, Pan-Pacific Surgical Association (vice-president, 1974-77), American Academy of Arts and Sciences (member of council, 1977-81), American Association for the Advancement of Science, American Association for Cancer Research, American Association for the Surgery of Trauma, American Association of University Professors, American Board of Surgery (senior member), American Geriatric Society, American Heart Association, American Institute of Biological Sciences, American Institute of Nutrition, American Medical Association, American Medical Writers Association, American Philosophical Society (president, 1976—), American Physiological Society, American Public Health Association, American Society for Parenteral and Enteral Nutrition (member of board of advisers), American Surgical Association (president, 1972-73; member of council, 1972-76), American College of Surgeons (member of board of governors, 1954-61; member of board of regents, 1961-70; chairman of board of regents, 1967-69; president, 1971-72), American Trauma Society (founding member; member of board of directors; member of executive committee), American Council for the United Nations University, American Cancer Society (honorary life member; member of executive committee, 1967-71; chairman of medical and scientific committee, 1967-68; vice-president, 1968-69; president, 1969-70; member of local board of directors, 1951—; local president, 1955-56).

Association for Academic Surgery (member of executive council, 1971), Association for the Advancement of Medical Instrumentation, Association of American Medical Colleges (distinguished service member; member of executive council, 1967-72; chairman of council of academic societies, 1968-69; member of administrative board, 1969-72), Association of Community Cancer Centers, Association of Governing Boards of Colleges and Universities, Council of Medical Specialty Societies (chairman, 1968-69), Federation of American Societies for Experimental Biology, Fellows in American Studies, Gerontological Society, Hawthorne Surgical Society, Medical Society for the Study of Education, John Morgan Society, Ravdin-Rhoads Surgical Society, Society for Academic Achievement, Society for Health and Human Values, Society of Clinical Surgery (president, 1958-60), James Ewing Society (honorary member), Philomathean Society, H. William Scott, Junior Society (honorary member), Sphinx Senior Society (honorary member), Society of Surgical Chairmen (president, 1966-68), Society of University Surgeons, Surgical Infection Society (founding member; chairman of education committee), Allen O. Whipple Surgical Society, Wistar Association (member of executive committee, 1971-73), Council of Biology Editors, Society for Surgery of the Alimentary Tract (president, 1967-68; member of board of trustees, 1968-70).

Association of Surgeons of India (honorary fellow), Deutsches Gesellschaft fuer Chirurgie (corresponding member), Hollandsche Maatchappij der Wetenschappen (foreign fellow), Kollege van Geneeskunde van Suid-Afrika (honorary fellow), Polish Association of Surgeons (fellow), Royal College of Physicians and Surgeons of Canada (fellow), Royal College of Surgeons of Edinburgh (fellow), Royal College of Surgeons (England; fellow), Royal Society of Arts (fellow), Royal Society for the Promotion of Health, Royal Society of Medicine, Southeastern Surgical Congress (fellow), Southern Surgical Association, Pennsylvania Association of Blood Banks, Pennsylvania Medical Society, Pennsylvania Public Health Association, Pennsylvania Society for Advancing Medical Research, Pennsylvania Citizens Association, Pennsylvania Society, New York Academy of Sciences (life member), Buffalo Surgical Society (fellow), Chicago Surgical Society (fellow), College of Physicians of Philadelphia (chairman of library committee, 1952-54; president, 1958-60).

Medical Club of Philadelphia, Philadelphia Academy of Surgery (chairman of committee on scientific business, 1955-59; president, 1964-66), Philadelphia County Medical Society (president, 1970), Physiological Society of Philadelphia, Philadelphia Athenaeum, Philadelphia Orchestra Association, Philadelphia Society for the Preservation of Landmarks, Science and Art Club of Germantown, Independence Hall Association (member of board of directors, 1980), Society of Graduate Surgeons of Los Angeles County Hospital (honorary), Johns Hopkins Medical and Surgical Association, Johns Hopkins University Philadelphia Alumni Association, Phi Beta Kappa, Phi Beta Kappa Associates, Sigma Xi, Alpha Omega Alpha, Surgeons Travel Club (president, 1975-76), Sunday Breakfast Club, Cosmos Club, Faculty Club of University of Pennsylvania, Haverford Club of Philadelphia, Peale Club, Penn Club, Philadelphia Art Alliance, Rittenhouse Club, Union League of Philadelphia.

AWARDS, HONORS: LL.D. from University of Pennsylvania, 1960, M.A., 1971; D.Sc. from Haverford College, 1962, Swarthmore College, 1969, Medical College of Pennsylvania, 1974, Hahnemann Medical College, 1978, Duke University, 1979, and Georgetown University, 1981; D.Litt. from Jefferson University, 1979; distinguished service award from American Cancer Society, 1957, national award, 1973; humanitarian award from Kain Moses Group for Cancer Research, 1963; Strittmatter Award from Philadelphia County Medical Society, 1968; shared Joseph Goldberger Award in Clinical Nutrition from American Medical Association, 1970; citation from Association for Academic Surgery, 1971; Mount Scopus citation of honor from American Friends of Hebrew University, 1972; Dr. Roswell Park Medal from Buffalo Surgical Society, 1973; distinguished achievement award from *Modern Medicine,* 1974; lecturer award from James Ewing Society, 1974; distinguished service award from Pennsylvania Medical Society, 1975; Papanicolaou Award from Papanicolaou Cancer Research Institute, 1977; Philadelphia Award, 1977; distinguished service award from American Surgical Association and American Trauma Society, both 1979; prize from Societe Internationale de Chirurgie, 1979; Dr. Rodman E. and Thomas G. Sheen Award for Scientific Accomplishment from American Medical Association, 1980.

WRITINGS: (Editor with J. G. Allen, H. N. Harkins, and C. A. Moyer, and contributor) *Surgery: Principles and Practice,* Lippincott, 1957, 4th edition, 1970; (with J. M. Howard) *The Chemistry of Trauma,* C. C Thomas, 1963; (editor with J. G. Fortner, and contributor) *Accomplishments in Cancer Research, 1980,* Lippincott, 1980.

Contributor: H. L. Bockus, editor, *Gastroenterology,* Saunders, 1945, 3rd edition, 1976; Frederick Christopher, editor, *Christopher Textbook of Surgery,* 4th edition (Rhoads was not included in earlier editions), Saunders, 1945, 11th edition, edited by David C. Sabiston, Jr., 1977; J. M. Howard and G. L. Jordan, editors, *Surgical Diseases of the Pancreas,* Lippincott, 1960; C. P. Artz and James D. Hardy, editors, *Complications of Surgery and Their Management,* Saunders, 1960; Clarence Morris, editor, *Trends in Modern American Society,* University of Pennsylvania Press, 1962; T. F. Nealon, Jr., editor, *Management of the Patient With Cancer,* Saunders,

1965, 2nd edition, 1976; *The Management of Soft Tissue Injuries and Fractures,* Saunders, 1965; (author of introduction) Philip Syng Physick, *Medical Affairs,* University of Pennsylvania Press, 1965; Gerhard Berg, editor, *Advances in Parenteral Nutrition,* Georg Thieme Verlag, 1970; C. L. Fox, Jr. and G. G. Nahas, editors, *Body Fluid Replacement in the Surgical Patient,* Columbia University Press, 1970; H. G. Barker, editor, *The Continuing Education of the Surgeon,* C. C Thomas, 1971; Hardy, editor, *Critical Surgical Illness,* Saunders, 1971; Konrad Lang, Werner Fekl, and Berg, editors, *Balanced Nutrition and Therapy,* Georg Thieme Verlag, 1971; G. F. Cowan, Jr. and W. L. Scheetz, editors, *Intravenous Hyperalimentation,* Lea & Febiger, 1972; R. W. Raven, editor, *Modern Trends in Oncology-1, Part 2: Clinical Progress,* Butterworth, 1973; Hardy, editor, *Rhoads Textbook of Surgery: Principles and Practice* (5th edition of *Surgery: Principles and Practice*), Lippincott, 1977; H. E. Nieburgs, editor, *Prevention and Detection of Cancer,* Part I, Volume I, Dekker, 1977; J. L. Mullen and others, editors, *Surgical Nutrition and Metabolism,* Saunders, 1981.

Contributor to *Encyclopedia Americana* and *Year Book of Cancer.* Contributor of more than three hundred articles to medical journals. Editor of *Cancer: Journal of the American Cancer Society,* 1972—; founding member of editorial board of *Journal of Surgical Research,* 1960-71; member of editorial board of *Annals of Surgery,* 1947— (chairman of board, 1971-73), and *Oncology Times,* 1979—; member of editorial committee of *Transactions and Studies of the College of Physicians of Philadelphia,* 1979—; senior member of editorial advisory board of *Journal of Clinical Surgery,* 1981—.

WORK IN PROGRESS: Prefaces for *Parenteral and Enteral Nutrition for the Hospitalized Patient,* by Howard Silberman and Daniel Eisenberg, for Appleton-Century-Crofts, and *The Management of Intestinal Fistulas,* by John Alexander-Williams and Miles Irving, for John Wright; forward for *Enteral Hyperalimentation: Tube Feeding,* edited by John L. Rombeau and Michael D. Caldwell, for Saunders.

* * *

RICE, Charles D(uane)   1910-1971

OBITUARY NOTICE: Born in 1910; died of cancer, January 30, 1971, in New York. Editor, journalist, and author. Rice was associated with *This Week* magazine for more than thirty years and was the creator of the column "Charlie Rice's Punchbowl." He also wrote children's books, including *Minty's Magic Garden,* and *The Little Boy Who Wore Earmuffs.* He wrote *Fields for President* with W. C. Fields and served on the usage panel of the *American Heritage Dictionary.* Obituaries and other sources: *New York Times,* February 1, 1971; *Publishers Weekly,* February 15, 1971.

* * *

RICHARDS, Kent David   1938-

PERSONAL: Born August 7, 1938, in Kenosha, Wis.; married, 1960; children: two. *Education:* Knox College, B.A., 1960; University of Wisconsin (now University of Wisconsin—Madison), M.S., 1961, Ph.D., 1966. *Office:* Department of History, Central Washington State College, Ellensburg, Wash. 98926.

CAREER: Central Washington State College, Ellensburg, 1966—, began as assistant professor, became associate professor of history. *Member:* American Historical Association, Organization of American Historians, Western History Association.

WRITINGS: Isaac I. Stevens: Young Man in a Hurry, Brigham Young University Press, 1979. Contributor to history journals.*

* * *

RICHARDSON, Dorothy Miller 1873-1957

BRIEF ENTRY: Born May 17, 1873, in Abington, Berkshire, England; died June 17, 1957, in Beckenham, Kent, England. English educator, novelist, and journalist. A pioneer in psychological fiction, Richardson was one of the first to conceive and to develop the stream of consciousness technique and the use of interior monologues. Though she initiated these experimental techniques, which are used to reveal personal reactions to experiences, other writers such as Joyce, Woolf, and Proust practiced them more successfully. Richardson, influenced by Bergson's philosophy, illuminated the feminine consciousness and enlarged the scope of the novel. Her most notable work is *Pilgrimage,* a thirteen-volume novel presented through the consciousness of the author's alter ego, Miriam Henderson. An "adventure of personality," the sequence novel traces Henderson's search for self-realization. *Pilgrimage* is considered one of the most significant novels of the twentieth century. Richardson's other writings include *The Quakers Past and Present* (1914) and *John Austen and the Inseparables* (1930). *Biographical/critical sources: Cyclopedia of World Authors,* Harper, 1958; C. R. Blake, *Dorothy Richardson,* University of Michigan Press, 1960; *Encyclopedia of World Literature in the Twentieth Century,* updated edition, Ungar, 1967; *Twentieth-Century Literary Criticism,* Volume 3, Gale, 1980.

* * *

RICHARDSON, Frank Howard 1882-1970

OBITUARY NOTICE: Born July 1, 1882, in Brooklyn, N.Y.; died May 26, 1970, in Asheville, N.C. Physician and author. Richardson wrote numerous books on the care and development of children, including *For Boys Only, For Girls Only, The Nursing Mother, A Christian Doctor Talks with Young Parents,* and *Grandparents and Their Families: A Guide for Three Generations.* Obituaries and other sources: *Publishers Weekly,* October 5, 1970; *Authors and Illustrators of Children's Books for Young People,* 2nd edition supplement, Scarecrow, 1971; *American Authors and Books, 1640 to the Present Day,* 3rd revised edition, Crown, 1972; *Who Was Who in America, With World Notables,* Volume VI: *1974-1976,* Marquis, 1976.

* * *

RICHARDSON, Leopold John Dixon 1893-1979(?)

OBITUARY NOTICE: Born August 3, 1893; died c. 1979 in Cardiff, England. Educator and author. Richardson was a professor of Greek and classical literature at universities in England and Ireland. He issued numerous articles on Mycenean dialect and inscription and contributed to many English and Irish journals. Among his writings is *Ta Indika.* Obituaries and other sources: *Who's Who,* 126th edition, St. Martin's, 1974; *AB Bookman's Weekly,* April 16, 1979.

* * *

RIDDELL, Alan 1927-

PERSONAL: Born April 16, 1927, in Townsville, Queensland, Australia. *Education:* Received M.A. from University of Edinburgh.

CAREER: Lines Review, Edinburgh, Scotland, founding editor, 1952-55 and 1962-67; *Daily Telegraph,* London, England, sub-

editor, 1963—. Has had group and solo shows of concrete and visual poetry in Scotland, England, Australia, Argentina, Yugoslavia, the Netherlands, and Belgium. *Awards, honors:* Heinemann Award, 1956; prize from Scottish Arts Council, 1968.

WRITINGS: Beneath the Summer (poems), William Macdonald, 1953; *Majorcan Interlude* (poems), William Macdonald, 1960; (editor with others) *Young Commonwealth Poets '65,* Heinemann, 1965; *The Stopped Landscape and Other Poems,* Hutchinson, 1968; *Eclipse* (poems), Calder & Boyars, 1972; (editor) *Typewriter Art,* London Magazine Editions, 1975. Editor of education supplement of *Sydney Morning Herald,* 1969-70.*

* * *

RIDGE, Antonia (Florence) ?-1981

OBITUARY NOTICE—See index for *CA* sketch: Born in Amsterdam, Holland; died c. June 24, 1981. Translator, editor, playwright, songwriter, broadcaster, and author. Ridge is best known for her talks and narrations on the British Broadcasting Corp. (BBC) program "Woman's Hour." She also wrote for children, publishing such books as *The Handy Elephant and Other Stories, Jan and His Clogs, The Little Red Pony,* and *The Royal Pawn.* Her works for young people include the play "How Jan Klaassen Cured the King," the collection *Puppet Plays for Children,* and the song "The Happy Wanderer." Ridge regularly supplied material to the Obernkirken Children's Choir. She also translated and edited *Mission Underground* by Norbert Casteret. Among her other writings are *For Love of a Rose* and *Melodia: A Story From Holland.* Obituaries and other sources: *London Times,* June 24, 1981.

* * *

RIDLEY, B(rian) K(idd) 1931-

PERSONAL: Born March 2, 1931, in Newcastle-upon-Tyne, England; married; children: two. *Education:* University of Durham, B.Sc., 1953, Ph.D., 1957. *Office:* Department of Physics, University of Essex, Colchester, England.

CAREER: Philips Research Laboratories, Redhill, England, research physicist, 1956-64; University of Essex, Colchester, England, lecturer, 1964-71, reader in physics, 1971—. Visiting professor; consultant. *Member:* Institute of Physics (fellow).

WRITINGS: Time, Space, and Things, Penguin, 1976; *The Physical Environment,* Ellis Horwood, 1979; *Quantum Processes in Semiconductors,* Oxford University Press, 1981.

WORK IN PROGRESS: Research on semiconductor physics and the physical basis of life.

SIDELIGHTS: Ridley commented: "The physical universe, for me, is a magical place. Along with electrons and Einstein there is music (particularly Mozart), French wine, pretty women, and tennis. The difficulty is fitting in some writing. . . ."

* * *

RIKER, Tom L. 1936-

PERSONAL: Born April 17, 1936, in Syracuse, N.Y.; son of Irwin A. and Agnes L. Riker. *Agent:* Collier Associates, 280 Madison Ave., New York, N.Y. 10016.

CAREER: Horticultural consultant, archivist, graphic designer, painter, art teacher, and songwriter. *Military service:* U.S. Army, served during late 1950's.

WRITINGS: (With Harvey Rottenberg) *The Gardener's Catalogue,* Morrow, 1974; (with Rottenberg) *Food Gardens,* Morrow, 1975; *The Guide to Buying Plants*, Morrow, 1976; *Sex in the Garden*, Morrow, 1976; *City and Suburban Gardens*, Prentice-Hall, 1977; (with Erik Darling) *The Hip Pocket Chord Book*, McAfee Music Co., 1978; *The Healthy Garden Book*, Stein & Day, 1978; (with Darling) *The Illustrated American Five-String Banjo*, McAfee Music Co., 1979; *The Directory of Natural and Health Foods*, Putnam, 1979; (with Darling) *Chords for the Guitar*, E. C. Schirmer, 1980.

WORK IN PROGRESS: A book of poems, a novel, another garden book, two plays, and a screenplay.

*   *   *

RILEY, Miles O'Brien   1937-

PERSONAL: Born August 31, 1937, in South Bend, Ind.; son of William T. (in business) and Frances (O'Brien) Riley. *Education:* St. Patrick's College, B.A., 1960; Gregorian University, S.T.B., 1962, S.T.L., 1964; attended Graduate Theological Union, 1975-81; University of California, Berkeley, Ph.D., 1981. *Politics:* Republican. *Home:* 3321 16th St., San Francisco, Calif. 94114. *Office:* Archdiocese of San Francisco, 445 Church St., San Francisco, Calif. 94114.

CAREER: Ordained Roman Catholic priest, 1963; associate pastor of Roman Catholic churches in San Rafael, Calif., 1964-68, and San Francisco, Calif., 1968-70; Archdiocese of San Francisco, San Francisco, director of Communications Center, 1970-78, and Office of Information, 1978—. Director of board of advisers of San Francisco Junior League; chairman of children's advisory committee of Field Communications. *Member:* National Academy of Television Arts and Sciences (member of board of governors and national board of trustees), National Association of Religious Public Relations. *Awards, honors:* Emmy Award from San Francisco chapter of Academy of Television Arts and Sciences, 1971, for "A Part of Me Is Still Crying"; Gabriel Awards from UNDA-USA, 1971, for best local television program and best television spots, and 1972-78, for best local radio programs and best local radio spots.

WRITINGS: With a Song in My Ark (fiction), Mitchell, 1970; *Fish Book* (fiction), Wichlander, 1972; *To Whom It May Concern* (essays), Practical Press, 1976; *Set Your House in Order* (nonfiction), Doubleday, 1980.

Films; produced by Communications Center: "Respect Life," 1971; "Priest," 1974; "Go in Peace," 1975; "Sister," 1975; "Birthday," 1976; "Excuse Me, America," 1977; "Everyone Everywhere," 1978.

Plays; Two-act musicals, first produced in San Francisco: "Bye, Bye Beatles," 1965; "Teenagent," 1966; "Pleasant Place," 1967; "The Impossible Mission," 1968; "Ark," 1969.

Author of about three hundred television and two thousand radio scripts, including "In the Beginning," "For Heaven's Sake," "For God's Sake," and "I Believe." Author of syndicated newspaper columns, including "The Life of Riley," "Father Knows Best," and "To Whom It May Concern."

WORK IN PROGRESS: Training church communicators in television news interviews.

AVOCATIONAL INTERESTS: International travel.

*   *   *

RILEY, Sandra   1938-

PERSONAL: Born November 12, 1938, in Detroit, Mich.; daughter of Joseph and Florence (a buyer; maiden name, Alexander) Riley. *Education:* Barry College, B.A., 1960; University of Michigan, M.A., 1963. *Agent:* Liz Basile, 8650 Northwest 17th Court, Pembroke Pines, Fla. 33024.

CAREER: Drama director at high school in Hialeah, Fla., 1960-67; Barn Theatre, Miami Lakes, Fla., producer and director, 1965-68; Yarmouth Playhouse, Yarmouth, Mass., producer and director, 1968; drama director at high school in Miami Springs, Fla., 1969-72; Zama American Workshop Theatre, Camp Zama, Japan, director, 1972-73; Columbus Landings Co., San Salvador, Bahamas, historical researcher, 1973-74; Coral Gables High School, Coral Gables, Fla., instructor in drama, 1975—, director of drama, 1980—. Director of Players Theatre, Coconut Grove, Fla., 1968-69; acting instructor at Players State Theatre Conservatory, 1978-79. Historical researcher for Provident Ltd., Providentiales, British West Indies, 1979. Member of National Archives Associate. *Member:* International Women's Writing Guild, Bahamas Historical Society, Florida Historical Society, Historical Association of Southern Florida.

WRITINGS: Bloody Bay (historical novel), Tower, 1980. Contributor to history journals.

WORK IN PROGRESS: History of Abaco, from Loyalist days to the present, completion expected in 1983; four sequels to *Bloody Bay*, one on Anne Bonny and the Maroon Uprisings in Jamaica in the middle 1700's, one on Deborah Sampson and American Revolutionary soldiers in the late 1700's, one on an American Loyalist in the out-islands of the Bahamas in the early 1800's, and the last about a wrecker in Key West in the middle 1800's.

SIDELIGHTS: Sandra Riley commented: "My experiences doing historical research in the Bahamas include flying in a small plane wedged between truck tires and batteries with my feet propped on boxes of groceries, chopping my way through the dense bush with the thorns of the haulback vine snatching at my clothes on the way to an out-island plantation ruin, straining my eyes on faded illegible documents in the stifling Nassau library, and sitting on a porch of a native hut talking to the island people, and, above all, watching the color of the sea. A stroke of chance brought me into this work, and nothing could induce me to give it up."

*   *   *

RILKE, Rainer Maria   1875-1926

BRIEF ENTRY: Born December 4, 1875, in Prague, Austria (now Czechoslovakia); died of blood poisoning, December 29, 1926, in Montreux, Switzerland. European author. A lifelong traveler of Europe, Rilke shunned companionship in favor of observation and contemplation. His early verse, including *Das Studenbuch* (1905), reveals the influence of the German folk tradition and offers reverent, if frequently melancholic, celebrations of nature. Upon publication of his initial works, Rilke accepted a position in Paris as secretary to the sculptor August Rodin. Organizing the sculptor's voluminous correspondence proved too demanding, however, and in 1906 Rilke and Rodin parted. Rilke followed the break with the publication of *Neue Gedichte* (1907), a collection of poems most critics consider his first important work. More mystical than their predecessors, the poems of *Neue Gedichte* are Rilke's attempts to lend profundity to everyday experiences and the behavior of children and animals. Rilke's health fluctuated during this period, and his travels to Spain and Italy were disrupted by frequent bedrest. When World War I began in 1914, Rilke enlisted in the Austrian infantry only to be dismissed because of his health. For the duration of the war, Rilke avoided writing poetry in favor of reading Tolstoy and Freud. In 1919 he settled in

Switzerland and lived in a medieval tower. In the next few years he wrote his two greatest works. *Duineser Elegien* (1922) marks Rilke's acceptance of death as the key to life's mystery and pleasures. The collection of ten poems is often considered his finest work, for in them he successfully fused his love of nature with his mystical belief in suffering. In his other masterpiece, *Die Sonette an Orpheus* (1923), Rilke evoked a highly symbolic world in which man's holiness is measured by the depth of his acceptance of death. He died after a rose thorn pierced his finger and caused an infection. *Biographical/critical sources: The Reader's Companion to World Literature,* 2nd edition, New American Library, 1973; *Twentieth-Century Literary Criticism,* Volume 1, Gale, 1978.

*   *   *

RINALDI, Nicholas   1934-

PERSONAL: Born April 2, 1934, in Brooklyn, N.Y.; son of Frank A. (in business) and Rose (Lopena) Rinaldi; married Jacqueline Tellier (a university teacher), August 29, 1959; children: Christina, Paul, Stephen, David. *Education:* Shrub Oak College, A.B., 1957; Fordham University, M.A., 1960, Ph.D., 1963. *Residence:* Fairfield, Conn. *Office:* Department of English, Fairfield University, North Benson Rd., Fairfield, Conn. 06430.

CAREER: Fordham University, Bronx, N.Y., lecturer in English, 1960-61; St. John's University, Jamaica, N.Y., instructor, 1960-63, assistant professor of English, 1963-66; Fairfield University, Fairfield, Conn., assistant professor, 1966-67, associate professor, 1967-71, professor of English, 1971—, chairman of department, 1974-76, director of writing program, 1981—. Lecturer at City University of New York, spring, 1966; associate professor at Columbia University, summer, 1969; professor at University of Connecticut, summer, 1972. Gives readings at universities, museums, libraries, and on radio programs.

MEMBER: Modern Language Association of America, American Association of University Professors, Poetry Society of America, American Association for Higher Education, Associated Writing Programs. *Awards, honors:* Scholar of Harcourt, Brace & World at Colorado University Writers Conference, 1969; fellow at Indiana University Writers Conference, summer, 1969; Joseph P. Slomovich Memorial Award for Poetry from *Cedar Rock,* 1979, for poem "The Window"; All Nations Award in Poetry, 1981, for poem "The Bird."

WRITINGS: The Resurrection of the Snails (poems), Blair, 1977; *We Have Lost Our Fathers* (poems), University Presses of Florida, 1981.

Work represented in anthologies, including *Anthology of Magazine Verse and Yearbook of American Poetry,* edited by Alan F. Pater, Monitor, 1980. Contributor of poems, stories, and articles to magazines and newspapers, including *Prairie Schooner, New England Review, Descant, Epoch, Early American Life,* and *Southwest Review.*

WORK IN PROGRESS: Hitler in Chains, poems; *Medieval Miracles,* poems; a novel.

SIDELIGHTS: Rinaldi told *CA:* "For me, poetry operates at the far edges of consciousness, groping for insight, awareness, fresh angles of perception. My poems rely heavily on dream imagery and fantasy situations, techniques that were popularized by the surrealists, yet I consider myself basically a realist, working with the problems and preoccupations of the current mood. I write about waiting rooms, hospitals, movies, bombers, museums, postage stamps, money, the strangeness of

growing up in Brooklyn during World War II. If I use surreal devices when I write of these things, it's because they help me locate the human factors—the ironies and the pathos, the confusion, terror, uncertainty, the comedy. Occasionally I use historical subjects as a way of focusing a contemporary attitude (as when I write about George Washington and Benjamin Franklin), and there are times, too, when I go beyond history into fairytales and lies.

"I like a poetry that is lucid and accessible, and a poetry that knows how to deal with serious themes through humor. I regard humor as a vital instrument for probing the paradoxes and exasperations of daily living. Too often, I feel, the comic capability is undervalued in contemporary poetry, which continues to be strongly influenced by romantic and existential tendencies. Much of my own work derives from those tendencies, yet I also have deep affinities with the complex traditions of wit and humor that were set long before private anguish and dark vision became the fashion.

"*The Resurrection of the Snails and Other Poems* opens with the transformation of skyscrapers into cabbages and ends with an army of snails invading Manhattan. In these poems, and in many of the pieces which they frame, the focus is on the interaction between nature and modern technological society, an interaction that may be subtle or obvious, harsh or surprisingly gentle, but always ongoing and compelling. It is not my purpose, in all of this, to predict the triumph of nature over technology, though there are times when such a triumph may seem to be inevitable; rather, my aim is to trace the contours of the interaction, and to explore the transformations in feeling, tone, attitude, and personality that accrue when these two forces, these two massive systems of imagery, engage each other dialectically."

BIOGRAPHICAL/CRITICAL SOURCES: Choice, June, 1978.

*   *   *

RINEHART, Frederick Roberts   1903(?)-1981

OBITUARY NOTICE: Born c. 1903 in Allegheny, Pa.; died June 15, 1981, in New York, N.Y. Publisher. Rinehart, the son of mystery writer Mary Roberts Rinehart, founded the publishing company of Farrar & Rinehart with John Farrar. The firm became Rinehart & Co. when Farrar left to form Farrar & Straus. Among the notable authors published by Rinehart were Norman Mailer, Vincent Benet, and Erich Fromm. In 1960 Rinehart merged with Henry Holt and John C. Winston to become Holt, Rinehart & Winston. After retiring in 1963, Rinehart was president of the Mary Roberts Rinehart Foundation, organized to aid aspiring writers financially and through editorial advice. Obituaries and other sources: *New York Times,* June 17, 1981; *Publishers Weekly,* July 3, 1981; *AB Bookman's Weekly,* July 27, 1981.

*   *   *

RIPS, Rae Elizabeth   1914-1970

OBITUARY NOTICE: Born June 4, 1914, in Omaha, Neb.; died November 4, 1970, in Detroit, Mich. Librarian. Associated with the Detroit Public Library for nearly thirty years, Rips was chief of the library's history and travel department at her death. In 1950 she edited the *U.S. Government Publications,* third edition. Obituaries and other sources: *Wilson Library Bulletin,* December, 1970; *AB Bookman's Weekly,* January 4, 1971; *Who's Who of American Women,* 7th edition, Marquis, 1972.

RIZZOLI, Angelo 1889-1970

OBITUARY NOTICE: Born in 1889; died of complications from gall bladder disease, September 24, 1970, in Milan, Italy. Publisher, film producer, and businessman. Rizzoli started his own printing company at the age of twenty. Nine years later, the company grossed twenty million dollars in one year. Eventually, his organization published a dozen weekly magazines for an audience of twenty million readers. Rizzoli also produced movies, including "La Dolce Vita," "Red Desert," and "8½," and owned a chain of bookstores in numerous countries. Obituaries and other sources: Newsweek, January 4, 1965, October 5, 1970; New York Times, September 26, 1970; Time, October 5, 1970; Publishers Weekly, October 12, 1970.

* * *

ROADARMEL, Gordon 1932-1972

OBITUARY NOTICE: Educator and author. Roadarmel wrote numerous books on Asian culture, including Cues and Clues for the American in India, The Theme of Alienation in the Modern Hindi Novel, and A Death in Delhi. Obituaries and other sources: Journal of Asian Studies, August, 1972.

* * *

ROBERTS, Susan F. 1919-

PERSONAL: Born in 1919, in New Orleans, La.; daughter of Frank and Margaret (Jackson) Bryson; children: Susan M., Laura S. Education: Graduate of Tulane University. Home: 170 Carroll St., Brooklyn, N.Y. 11231. Office: Family Service Association of America, 44 East 23rd St., New York, N.Y.

CAREER: Reporter, 1943-53; Louisiana State University, New Orleans, La., public relations director at medical center, 1953-63; Family Service Association of America, New York, N.Y., staff consultant, 1963—. Member: Public Relations Society of America, Overseas Press Club of America.

WRITINGS: (With Yogi Vithaldas) Yogi Cookbook, Crown, 1968; Witch America, Dell, 1970; Witches U.S.A., Phoenix House, 1974; The Magician of the Golden Dawn: The Story of Aleister Crowley, Contemporary Books, 1974.

BIOGRAPHICAL/CRITICAL SOURCES: Best Sellers, November, 1978.*

* * *

ROBERTSON, Alec
See ROBERTSON, Alexander Thomas Parke Anthony Cecil

* * *

ROBERTSON, Alexander Thomas Parke Anthony Cecil 1892-
(Alec Robertson)

PERSONAL: Born June 3, 1892; son of J.R.S. (a physician) and Elizabeth (Macrory) Robertson. Education: Studied at Collegio Beda, 1930; Royal Academy of Music, A.R.A.M., F.R.A.M., 1945. Religion: Roman Catholic. Home: The Platt, Apsley Farm, Pulborough, West Sussex M20 2LJ, England.

CAREER: Organist at parish churches in Frensham, England and Farnham, England, 1914; Gramophone Co., England, lecturer in education department, 1920-25, became head of department, 1925; British Broadcasting Corp., England, gramophone department, 1940-41, music department, 1941-44, talks department, 1944, senior talks producer (music), 1944-53; writer, lecturer, and broadcaster, 1953—. Military service: British Army, Hampshire Regiment, 1914-17; served in India and Palestine (now Israel); became lieutenant. Awards, honors: Member of Order of the British Empire, 1972.

WRITINGS—Under name Alec Robertson: (Editor) The Golden Treasury of Recorded Music (Other Than Opera) on "His Master's Voice," Gramophone Co., 1928; The Interpretation of Plainchant: A Preliminary Study, Oxford University Press, 1937, reprinted, Greenwood Press, 1970; Introductions and Analytical Notes to Accompany Gramophone Records of Mozart's Pianoforte and Violin Sonatas, Volume I: Sonatas for Pianoforte and Violin, Mozart Chamber Music Society, 1937; Christian Music, Scholarly Press, 1941; Dvorak, Dutton, 1945, revised edition, Dent, 1964; Contrasts: The Arts and Religion—Keats, Milton, Blake, Housman, Hopkins, S.C.M. Press, 1947, reprinted, Folcroft, 1973; How to Listen to Music, Feature Books, 1948.

Sacred Music, Chanticleer Press, 1950; Music, Penguin, 1952; Music and Musicians: Reader's Guide, Cambridge University Press, 1956; (editor) Chamber Music, Penguin, 1957; (editor with Denis Stevens) The Pelican History of Music, Penguin, Volume I: Ancient Forms to Polyphany, 1960, Volume II: Renaissance and Baroque, 1963, Volume III: Classical and Romantic, 1968, reprinted as A History of Music, Cassell, 1962.

Music of the Catholic Church, Burns & Oates, 1961; More Than Music (autobiography), Collins, 1961; Requiem: Music of Mourning and Consolation, Cassell, 1967, Greenwood Press, 1977; Church Cantatas of J. S. Bach, Praeger, 1972; Bach: A Biography, With a Survey of Books, Editions, and Recordings, Shoe String, 1977. Also suthor of Schubert's Song: In Symposium, 1946.

Contributor to Chambers's Encyclopedia and Grove's Dictionary of Music and Musicians. Contributor to music journals. Music editor of Gramophone.

WORK IN PROGRESS: Revising Contrasts: The Arts and Religion.

SIDELIGHTS: Robertson commented: "I have traveled to South India, Mesopotamia, and Italy. I believe my greatest achievement was becoming known to everyone in the great medieval city of Hyderabad. I had never been abroad before, and I left India with sorrow. A maharajah told a London priest it was inspiring because I went with love in my heart for the people of India."

BIOGRAPHICAL/CRITICAL SOURCES: Alec Robertson, More Than Music, Collins, 1961; Dear Alec: A Tribute for His Eightieth Birthday From Friends, Known and Unknown, Abbey, 1972.

* * *

ROBERTSON, Charles Martin 1911-
(Martin Robertson)

PERSONAL: Born September 11, 1911; son of Donald Struan (a professor) and Petica Coursolles (Jones) Robertson; married Theodosia Cecil Spring Rice, 1942; children: four sons, two daughters. Education: Trinity College, Cambridge, B.A., 1934, M.A., 1947; attended British School of Archaeology, Athens, Greece, 1934-36. Home: 7a Parker St., Cambridge CB1 1JL, England.

CAREER: British Museum, London, England, assistant keeper in department of Greek and Roman antiquities, 1936-40 and

1946-48; University of London, University College, London, Yates Professor of Classical Art and Archaeology, 1948-61; Oxford University, Oxford, England, Lincoln Professor of Classical Art and Archaeology, 1961-78, fellow of Lincoln College, 1978—. Chairman of managing committee of British School of Archaeology, Athens, Greece, 1958-68; member of Institute for Advanced Study, Princeton, N.J., 1968-69. *Military service:* Served in World War II. *Member:* British Academy (fellow), German Archaeological Institute (corresponding member). *Awards, honors:* D.Lit. from Queen's University, Belfast, 1978.

WRITINGS: (Under name Martin Robertson) *Greek Painting,* Skira, 1959, Rizzoli International, 1979; (contributor) Hugh Lloyd-Jones, editor, *The Greeks,* C. A. Watts, 1962, World Publishing, 1963; (under name Martin Robertson) *Crooked Connections* (poems), Outposts, 1970; (editor and contributor) John Beazley, *Paralipomena,* 2nd edition, Clarendon Press, 1971; (under name Martin Robertson) *The Parthenon Frieze,* photographs by Alison Frantz, Oxford University Press (New York), 1975; (under name Martin Robertson) *A History of Greek Art,* two volumes, Cambridge University Press, 1975; (under name Martin Robertson) *A Hot Bath at Bedtime: Poems, 1933-1977,* Dugdale, 1977; (under name Martin Robertson; editor with John Boardman) *Corpus vasorum antiquorum, Castle Ashby,* Oxford University Press (London), 1979.

Also author of *For Rachel* (poems) and *The Sleeping Beauty's Prince* (a poem). Contributor of articles and reviews to journals in England and abroad.*

*   *   *

ROBERTSON, Martin
See ROBERTSON, Charles Martin

*   *   *

ROBIN, Arthur de Quetteville   1929-

PERSONAL: Born March 3, 1929, in Melbourne, Australia; son of Laurence Hugh (a bank manager) and Mary (McLaughlin) Robin; married Mavis Elizabeth Boreham, May 7, 1955; children: Elizabeth Anne de Quetteville (Griffiths). *Education:* University of Melbourne, B.A., 1957; Cambridge University, B.A., 1961, M.A., 1965; University of Western Australia, Ph.D., 1971. *Politics:* "Non-aligned." *Home and office:* 1 Pakington St., New Victoria 3101, Australia.

CAREER: Ordained priest of Church of England, 1955; vicar of Church of England in Kallista, Australia, 1956-59, and Croydon, Australia, 1961-64; St. George's College, University of Western Australia, Nedlands, Australia, sub-warden, 1964-68; vicar of St. Paul's Church of England in Geelong, Australia, 1969-78, rural dean, 1971-78; Holy Trinity Church, Kew, Australia, vicar, 1978—. Visiting tutor at University of Western Australia, 1964-68; visiting lecturer at University of Melbourne, 1962-63. Member of council of Yarra Valley Church of England School, 1963-64, Hermitage Church of England Girls' Grammar School, 1971-77, and Trinity Grammar School, Kew, 1978—. *Member:* Fellowship of Australian Writers, Royal Victorian Historical Society.

WRITINGS: Charles Perry, Bishop of Melbourne: The Challenges of a Colonial Episcopate, 1847-1876, University of Western Australia Press, 1967; *Mathew Blagden Hale: The Life of an Australian Pioneer Bishop,* Hawthorn, 1976; *Making Many Rich: A Memoir of Joseph John Booth,* Diocese of Melbourne, 1978; (editor) Richard C. Perry, *Contributions to an Amateur Magazine,* Queensberry Hill Press, 1981. Contributor

to history and theology journals and to *Australian Dictionary of Biography.*

SIDELIGHTS: Robin told *CA:* "I began serious writing at Cambridge, where I rediscovered my interest in history, and have concentrated on biography because I believe that people make history. After my success with *Charles Perry* I turned to research on Mathew Hale, partly as a means of discovering more about Western Australia, but also as an excuse to discover the history of my church in three other Australian colonies. At Geelong I wrote the Booth memoir because I was in the parish which he had served, because I admired him very much, and because I felt the need to get out of the nineteenth century for a time.

"Writing is very much a happy (if somewhat compulsive) occupation. My vocation as a clergyman absorbs most of my time and also commands much of my writing energy. I still write my sermons in full to keep them short. Words are a precious gift and should not be wasted; otherwise the reader or listener switches off."

AVOCATIONAL INTERESTS: Birdwatching, reading, travel (Israel, Greece, Europe, England), cricket, the Australian countryside.

*   *   *

ROBINSON, E(dwin) A(rlington)   1869-1935

BRIEF ENTRY: Born December 22, 1869, in Head Tide, Me.; died of cancer, April 6, 1935, in New York, N.Y.; ashes buried in Gardiner, Me. American poet whose style is regarded as the bridge between nineteenth- and twentieth-century poetry. A string of personal and family disasters clouded young Robinson's life, which he termed "a tragedy from the beginning." This depression and sense of failure runs through much of Robinson's early work, considered by most critics to be his best. His poetry first appeared in the privately published *The Torrent and the Night Before* (1896), which, with some revision, was published the following year as *The Children of the Night.* Robinson was hounded by poverty and alcoholism after moving to New York City in 1898. *Captain Craig* (1902) caught the attention of President Theodore Roosevelt, who secured a government job for Robinson. He continued doing character portraits of small-town America in *The Town Down the River* (1910), which contained elements of his hometown, Gardiner, Me. After *The Man Against the Sky* (1916) Robinson gained national literary attention and began to write longer, more involved narratives, such as his Arthurian trilogy, *Merlin* (1917), *Lancelot* (1920), and *Tristram* (1927). Robinson finally gained popular and financial success during the 1920's. He won three Pulitzer Prizes. *Biographical/critical sources: The Reader's Encyclopedia of American Literature,* Crowell, 1962; *The Concise Encyclopedia of Modern World Literature,* Hutchinson, 1963; *Encyclopedia of World Literature in the Twentieth Century,* updated edition, Ungar, 1967; *The Penguin Companion to American Literature,* McGraw, 1971; *Cassell's Encyclopaedia of World Literature,* revised edition, Morrow, 1973.

*   *   *

ROCHE, Alphonse Victor   1895-

PERSONAL: Born May 7, 1895, in Caderousse, France; married in 1927; children: one. *Education:* Washington State College (now University), A.B., 1928; University of Illinois, A.M., 1931, Ph.D., 1935. *Home:* 421 North Sawtelle Ave., Tucson, Ariz. 85716.

CAREER: Washington State College (now University), Pullman, instructor, 1924-29; University of Illinois, Champaign-

Urbana, instructor, 1935-36; Northwestern University, Evanston, Ill., 1937-63, began as assistant professor, became professor of Romance languages, professor emeritus, 1963—; University of Arizona, Tucson, professor of Romance languages, 1963-77; writer, 1977—. Visiting professor at University of Wisconsin, spring, 1967, University of Illinois, spring, 1968, University of Minnesota, spring, 1969, Illinois State University, spring, 1970, University of Missouri, spring, 1971, and University of Dallas, autumn, 1973. *Member:* Modern Language Association of America, American Association of Teachers of French, Society of Professors of French in America.

WRITINGS: (Editor with Lila Nalder Roche) *Au pays du soleil: Twenty-Three Stories From Provence,* Heath, 1950; *Provencal Regionalism: A Study of the Movement in the Revue Felibreenne, Le Feu, and Other Reviews of Southern France,* Northwestern University Press, 1954, reprinted, AMS Press, 1970; *Alphonse Daudet,* Twayne, 1976.

BIOGRAPHICAL/CRITICAL SOURCES: Choice, July-August, 1976; *Modern Language Journal,* April, 1977.*

* * *

RODENBERG, Julius 1884-1970

OBITUARY NOTICE: Born in 1884; died January 23, 1970, in Berlin, Germany. Author. Among Rodenberg's major works is *Groesse und Grenze der Typographie.* Obituaries and other sources: *AB Bookman's Weekly,* May 25, 1970.

* * *

ROEDER, Ralph Leclerq 1890-1969

OBITUARY NOTICE: Born in 1890 in New York, N.Y.; committed suicide, October 22, 1969, in Mexico City, Mexico. Author. Roeder wrote a highly acclaimed biography of Mexican statesman Benito Pablo Juarez, entitled *Juarez and His Mexico.* Other works include *The Man of the Renaissance,* and *Catherine de Medici and the Lost Revolution.* Obituaries and other sources: *New York Times,* February 21, 1970; *AB Bookman's Weekly,* March 16, 1970; *Publishers Weekly,* March 16, 1970.

* * *

ROGALY, (Henry) Joseph 1935-

PERSONAL: Surname is pronounced Ro-*gay*-lee; born October 23, 1935, in Johannesburg, South Africa; son of Nelson Julius and Isobel Rose (Lyons) Rogaly; married Susan Baring (a teacher), June 18, 1962; children: Benjamin, Sarah, Rachel, Jessica. *Education:* University of the Witwatersrand, B.A., 1957. *Agent:* Deborah Rogers Ltd., 5-11 Mortimer St., London W1N 7RH, England.

CAREER: Worked at *Rand Daily Mail,* Johannesburg, South Africa, until 1959; worked at *Economist,* London, England, 1960-65; *Financial Times,* London, author of column, 1965-78; *World Business Weekly,* London, editor and publisher in London and New York, N.Y., 1978-80; *Financial Times,* assistant editor, 1980—.

WRITINGS: Parliament for the People, Temple Smith, 1976; *Grunwick,* Penguin, 1977.

SIDELIGHTS: Rogaly wrote: "My first book was about proportional representation—a fair voting method, the second about a labor strike. The strikers lost. Both were in the European mold: one writer, one book. On many contemporary issues,

American writers work only in flocks. They produce compendiums. Can't any U.S. social and economic writers write books themselves any more?"

* * *

ROGERS, William R(aymond) 1932-

PERSONAL: Born June 20, 1932, in Oswego, N.Y.; son of W. Raymond (a minister) and A. Elizabeth (a teacher; maiden name, Hollis) Rogers; married Beverley C. Partington (a teacher), August 14, 1954; children: John, Susan, Nancy. *Education:* Kalamazoo College, A.B., 1954; University of Chicago, B.D., 1958, Ph.D., 1965. *Religion:* Society of Friends (Quakers). *Home:* 1107 Nathan Hunt Rd., Greensboro, N.C. 27410. *Office:* Guilford College, Friendly Ave., Greensboro, N.C. 27410.

CAREER: University of Chicago, Chicago, Ill., member of counseling staff, 1959-62; Earlham College, Richmond, Ind., assistant professor, 1962-65, associate professor of psychology and religion, 1965-70, director of student counseling, 1962-68; Harvard University, Cambridge, Mass., professor of psychology and religion, 1970-80, Parkman Professor, 1977-80; Guilford College, Greensboro, N.C., president, 1980—. Private practice of psychology. Member of Boston Symphony Chorus, 1976-80, and Greensboro Symphony Society, 1981—.

MEMBER: American Association of University Professors, American Psychological Association, American Association of Higher Education, American Council on Education, American Academy of Religion, Society for the Scientific Study of Religion, Society for Values in Higher Education. *Awards, honors:* A.M. from Harvard University, 1970.

WRITINGS: The Alienated Student, Methodist Press, 1962; *Project Listening,* Beacon Press, 1974; *Nourishing the Humanistic in Medicine,* University of Pittsburgh Press, 1980.

WORK IN PROGRESS: Phenomenology of Helplessness and *Dynamics of Psychology and Religion,* publication of both expected in 1984.

SIDELIGHTS: Rogers told *CA:* "I have a strong interest in the relations of religion and psychology and in values in higher education." *Avocational interests:* Sailing, sculpting, restoring antique automobiles.

* * *

ROLLINS, Charlemae Hill 1897-1979

OBITUARY NOTICE—See index for *CA* sketch: Born June 20, 1897, in Yazoo City, Miss.; died February 3, 1979. Educator, librarian, editor, and author. For more than thirty years, Rollins worked as the children's librarian at the George C. Hall Branch of the Chicago Public Library. She also taught concurrently at Roosevelt University. Her books include *We Build Together, Black Troubadour: Langston Hughes, The Magic World of Books,* and *Famous Negro Entertainers of Stage, Screen, and TV.* In addition, Rollins edited *Call of Adventure* and *Christmas Gif': An Anthology of Christmas Poems, Songs, and Stories, Written by and About Negroes.* Obituaries and other sources: *Library Journal,* May 1, 1979.

* * *

ROMANOFF, Harry 1892(?)-1970

OBITUARY NOTICE: Born c. 1892; died in 1970 in Chicago, Ill. Journalist. A reporter in Chicago, Romanoff was known for his wily methods of scooping a story more quickly than his journalistic competitors. Obituaries and other sources: *Time,*

July 29, 1966, December 28, 1970; *Newsweek,* August 18, 1969, December 28, 1970.

*   *   *

ROODENBURG, Nancy McKee   1909-1972

OBITUARY NOTICE: Born July 23, 1909, in Pittsburgh, Pa.; died from injuries suffered in a fall, September 28, 1972, in New York, N.Y. Psychologist and editor. Formerly an editorial assistant to Dr. Erich Fromm, Roodenburg was a consulting psychologist from 1945 until 1960. She later acted as an administrative assistant and contract supervisor at Doubleday & Co. At the time of her death Roodenburg was an editor with Prentice-Hall. Obituaries and other sources: *Publishers Weekly,* October 7, 1972; *Who's Who of American Women,* 8th edition, Marquis, 1974.

*   *   *

ROOK, Earnest Robert   1917-

PERSONAL: Born July 27, 1917, in Portland, Ore.; son of Michael and Theresa (Ernst) Rook. *Education:* Attended Pasadena City College, 1936-39, and University of California, Berkeley, 1939-41. *Home:* 866 33rd Ave., San Francisco, Calif. 94121. *Office:* California Academy of Sciences, Golden Gate Park, San Francisco, Calif. 94118.

CAREER: Worked as designer at World Publishing Co., Cleveland, Ohio, and at Alfred A. Knopf, Inc., New York, N.Y.; worked as manager at Amthor & Co., San Francisco, Calif.; California Academy of Sciences, San Francisco, associate producer of television series "Science in Action," 1955-63; University of California, San Francisco, special audio-visual lecturer at medical center, 1964-66; California Academy of Sciences, curator of exhibits, 1966—. Member of board of directors of Science Fair of the San Francisco Bay Area, 1966—. *Military service:* U.S. Army, Transport Service, 1943. *Member:* Artists' Embassy, Astronomical Society of the Pacific, Northern California Academy of Television Arts and Sciences (member of board of governors, 1961-63). *Awards, honors:* Grants from National Endowment for the Arts, 1972, 1976, 1977.

WRITINGS: Once Upon a Time They Lived Happily Ever After, Celestial Arts, 1973.*

*   *   *

ROSE, Norman Anthony   1934-

PERSONAL: Born December 29, 1934, in London, England; son of Simon and Minnie Rose; married Tslilla Kuper (a television producer), February 21, 1959; children: Inbal. *Education:* London School of Economics and Political Science, London, B.Sc. (with honors), 1965, Ph.D., 1968. *Office:* Department of International Relations, Hebrew University of Jerusalem, Jerusalem, Israel.

CAREER: Weizmann Letters, Rechovot, Israel, senior research editor, 1968-70; Hebrew University of Jerusalem, Jerusalem, Israel, senior lecturer, 1974-78, professor of international relations, 1978—. *Member:* Institute of Historical Research (England).

WRITINGS: The Gentile Zionists: A Study in Anglo-Zionist Diplomacy, 1929-1939, Frank Cass, 1973; *Baffy: The Diaries of Blanche Dugdale, 1936-1947,* Valentine, Mitchell, 1973; *Vansittart: Study of a Diplomat,* Heinemann, 1978; *The Letters of Chaim Weizmann, 1939-40,* Israel Universities Press, 1979; *Lewis Namier and Zionism,* Oxford University Press, 1980.

WORK IN PROGRESS: A study of British foreign and imperial policy in the twentieth century, publication by Oxford University Press expected in 1984.

SIDELIGHTS: Rose commented: "My vocational interests are nineteenth- and twentieth-century European diplomatic history, and a special interest in British foreign policy and Anglo-Zionist relations. *Avocational interests:* Travel, architectural history, English literature.

*   *   *

ROSEDALE, Valerie
See HARRON, Don(ald)

*   *   *

ROSENBERG, Jerome Roy   1926-

PERSONAL: Born October 5, 1926, in New York, N.Y.; son of Louis and May (Schack) Rosenberg; married Julia Daniels, April 21, 1968; children: Louise I., Daniel M. *Education:* New York University, B.S., 1949, J.D., 1953, LL.M., 1972; graduate study, Oxford University, 1949. *Home:* 50 Park Ave., New York, N.Y. 10016.

CAREER: Admitted to the Bar of New York State, 1956; Apfel & Englander (certified public accountants), New York City, staff accountant, 1950-52; Abraham J. Briloff (certified public accountant), New York City, staff accountant, 1952-54; Samuel Aronowitz & Co. (certified public accountants), New York City, staff accountant, 1955-57; David Berdon & Co. (certified public accountants), New York City, tax accountant, 1957-64; private practice of law, 1965—. Lecturer at New York University, 1971. *Military service:* U.S. Army Air Forces, 1943-45. *Member:* American Bar Association, New York State Society of Certified Public Accountants.

WRITINGS: Managing Your Own Money, edited by Bernard Hassan, Newsweek, 1979. Senior technical editor of *Income Tax Workbook,* Macmillan, 1970-74. Assistant technical editor of *Journal of Taxation,* 1965; member of editorial board of *Practical Accountant,* 1968—.

*   *   *

ROSENSTONE, Steven J(ay)   1952-

PERSONAL: Born January 20, 1952, in Chicago, Ill. *Education:* Washington University, St. Louis, Mo., A.B., 1973; University of California, Berkeley, M.A., 1974, Ph.D., 1979. *Office:* Department of Political Science, Yale University, New Haven, Conn. 06520.

CAREER: Yale University, New Haven, Conn., assistant professor of political science, 1979—. Polling consultant for WNBC, New York, N.Y., 1980. *Member:* American Political Science Association.

WRITINGS: (With Raymond E. Wolfinger) *Who Votes?,* Yale University Press, 1980; *Third Parties in Presidential Politics,* Yale University Press, 1982. Contributor to political science journals.

WORK IN PROGRESS: Forecasting Presidential Elections, publication by Yale University Press expected in 1983; research on American politics, public opinion, elections, political parties, and public policy.

SIDELIGHTS: Who Votes? presents the results of a statistical analysis of voter activity to isolate and identify the determinates of voter participation. Based on interviews with eighty-eight thousand voters gathered by the U.S. Bureau of the Census following the 1972 and 1974 general elections, the authors concluded that education was the single most influential factor in identifying potential voters.

BIOGRAPHICAL/CRITICAL SOURCES: New York Times Book Review, April 13, 1980; *Los Angeles Times,* July 6, 1980.

*   *   *

ROSENTHAL, Mitchell S(tephen)   1935-

PERSONAL: Born June 12, 1935, in Brooklyn, N.Y.; son of Abner H. and Adele (Fiering) Rosenthal; married Ellen May Slosberg, April 2, 1967; children: Claudia, Alexis, David. *Education:* Lafayette College, B.A., 1956; State University of New York Downstate Medical Center, M.D., 1960. *Home:* 1174 Park Ave., New York, N.Y. 10028. *Office:* 164 West 74th St., New York, N.Y. 10023.

CAREER: Jersey City Medical Center, Jersey City, N.J., intern, 1960-61; Kings County Psychiatric Hospital, Kings County, N.Y., resident in adult and general psychiatry, 1961-65; Phoenix House, New York City, program director and president of Phoenix House Foundation, Inc., 1967—. Resident in child and community psychiatry at Staten Island Mental Health Society, 1963-65; assistant attending psychiatrist at St. Vincent's Medical Center, Staten Island; associate attending psychiatrist at Roosevelt Hospital and Morris Bernstein Institute. Director of South Shore Mental Health Clinic, Staten Island, 1964-65. Assistant clinical professor at Tufts University; lecturer at University of California, Los Angeles, and Langley-Porter Neuropsychiatric Institute. Deputy commissioner for rehabilitation of New York City's Addiction Services Agency, 1967-70. *Military service:* U.S. Naval Reserve, active duty, 1965-67; became lieutenant commander. *Member:* American Medical Association, American Psychiatric Association, American Society of Psychoanalytic Physicians, New York Academy of Sciences, East Bay Psychiatric Society, Alameda-Contra Costa County Medical Association.

WRITINGS: (With Ira Mothner) *Drugs, Parents, and Children: The Three-Way Connection,* Houghton, 1972. Also editor (with George De Leon) of *The Therapeutic Community, a Generation Later: A Conference at the National Drug Abuse Conference* and contributor to medical journals.*

*   *   *

ROSS, Angus
See GIGGAL, Kenneth

*   *   *

ROSS, Diana
See DENNEY, Diana

*   *   *

ROSSI, Lino   1923-

PERSONAL: Born December 31, 1923, in Milan, Italy; son of Emilio and Anna Visco (Gilardi) Rossi; married Graziella Belluschi, June 25, 1955. *Education:* University of Milan, M.D., 1947; University of Turin, Lib.Doc.Pathol., 1956, specialist in cardiology, 1959, specialist in endocrinology, 1961. *Home:* 23 Via Annunciata, Milan, Italy.

CAREER: University of Bristol, Bristol, England, member of research staff in department of pharmacology, 1951; University of Hamburg, Hamburg, West Germany, member of research

staff in department of anatomy, 1953; University of Milan, Milan, Italy, instructor in pathology, 1956—. Head of pathology and laboratory at Civic Hospital, Gallarate, Italy, 1964—. *Military service:* 1939-45; served in Mediterranean theater; received award from Supreme Allied Command. *Member:* Italian Society of Pathology and Cardiology, Instituto de Studi Romani, American Heart Association (fellow of Council of Clinical Cardiology), Society for Roman Studies (England). *Awards, honors:* Distinguished service medal from Fatebenefratelli Hospital, 1963.

WRITINGS: Histopathologic Features of Cardiac Arrhythmias, Casa Editrice Ambrosiana, 1969; *Trajan's Column and the Dacian Wars,* Cornell University Press, 1971; *Histopathology of Cardiac Arrhythmias,* Lea & Febiger, 1979.

In Italian: *Sistema di conduzione e nervi nel cuore dell'uomo,* Casa Editrice Ambrosiana, 1954; (with Giorgio Tusini) *Neoformazioni Epitelio-linfatiche della tiroide: Tumore de Heurthle, adenolinfoma tiroideo, struma di Hashimoto,* Casa Editrice Ambrosiana, 1956. Also author (with C. Cavallero) of *Iperparatiroidismo renale.*

Contributor to medical and archaeology journals.

WORK IN PROGRESS: Arrhythmologic Pathology of Sudden Cardiac Death; Guerra e Pace Romana in rotocalchi di marmo.

SIDELIGHTS: Rossi described his interests as "morphological investigation and interpretation of biological, as well as archaeological material, with specific interests in the basic histopathology of the heart's rhythm disorders and, respectively, iconographic-historical questions of Imperial Rome and the Army."

*   *   *

ROSTAND, Edmond (Eugene Alexis)   1868-1918

BRIEF ENTRY: Born April 1, 1868, in Marseilles, France; died December 2, 1918, in Paris, France. French poet and playwright. A neo-romantic who revived the dramatic traditions of Hugo and Musset, Rostand created colorful, lyrical, sentimental plays at a time when realism and naturalism reigned on the stage. His first popular success was an 1894 romantic satire entitled *Les Romanesques* (translated as *The Romancers,* 1899, *The Fantasticks,* 1900). The play won its author the Toirac Prize in 1894. Rostand gained a worldwide reputation with his 1897 drama *Cyrano de Bergerac,* a romantic tragedy presenting the hero Cyrano in a conflict of love and friendship. Audiences and critics praised the verse drama for its lyric eloquence, dramatic intensity, and subtle wit. The graceful sentimentality of Rostand's plays presented three roles created for the legendary actress Sarah Bernhardt; she portrayed the title roles in *La Princesse Lointaine* (1895; translated as *The Princess Far-away,* 1899), *La Samaritaine* (1897; translated as *The Woman of Samaria,* 1921), and *L'Aiglon* (1900; translated as *The Eaglet,* 1921). In 1900 Rostand was made Officer in the French Legion of Honor and a year later became the youngest writer to be named to the Academie Francaise. Ill health forced Rostand to retire to the south of France, where he spent a decade producing his next play, *Chantecler* (1910; translated as *Chanticleer,* 1921), a satirical animal allegory about a rooster's disillusionment with life and his fellow animals. Although not as popular as his previous plays, *Chantecler* received favorable critical comments. At his death in 1918 Rostand left unfinished what some critics consider to be his best work, *La Dernier Nuit de Don Juan* (1921; translated as *The Last Night of Don Juan,* 1922). His plays have enjoyed lasting popular appeal; more than fifty years after its first production *The Fantasticks* was successfully revived in New York. *Biographical/critical sources:* Cyclopedia of World Authors, Harper, 1958; *Encyclopedia of World Literature in the Twentieth Century,* updated edition, Ungar, 1967; *The Reader's Encyclopedia of World Drama,* Crowell, 1969; *McGraw-Hill Encyclopedia of World Drama,* McGraw, 1972; *Modern World Drama: An Encyclopedia,* Dutton, 1972.

* * *

ROTH, David M. 1874(?)-1971

OBITUARY NOTICE: Born c. 1874; died June 10, 1971, in Los Angeles, Calif. Mnemonist and author. A specialist in the field of memory, Roth wrote self-help books designed to improve mind power. His writings include *Roth Memory Course: A Simple and Scientific Method of Improving the Memory and Increasing Mental Power* and *Roth Course in Mental Power: Clear Thinking, Memory, Quick Decision, and Good Judgment in Business and Everyday Life.* Obituaries and other sources: *New York Times,* June 11, 1971; *AB Bookman's Weekly,* July 19, 1971.

* * *

ROTH, Peggy (Meehan) ?-1973

OBITUARY NOTICE: Died of complications following viral pneumonia, August 8, 1973, in New York, N.Y. Editor and author. Roth was editor in chief for Dell Books. Prior to her years at Dell she worked at various publishing houses and as a writer and editor in Hollywood for Metro-Goldwyn-Mayer (MGM) and Columbia Pictures. She was the author of one novel, *Moon Set.* Obituaries and other sources: *New York Times,* August 11, 1973; *Publishers Weekly,* August 27, 1973.

* * *

ROTSTEIN, Abraham 1929-

PERSONAL: Born April 10, 1929, in Montreal, Quebec, Canada; son of Hyman and Fanny (Mosenson) Rotstein; married Diane Louise Whitman, February 18, 1966; children: Daniel, Eve. *Education:* McGill University, B.A., 1949; graduate study at University of Chicago, 1949-50, and Columbia University, 1950-51; University of Toronto, Ph.D., 1967. *Religion:* Jewish. *Home:* 102 Admiral Rd., Toronto, Ontario, Canada M5R 2L6. *Office:* University of Toronto, 100 St. George St., Toronto, Ontario, Canada M8V 2S4.

CAREER: Worked as industrial economist, 1951-59; University of Toronto, Toronto, Ontario, began as associate professor of economics, became senior fellow of Massey College. Managing editor of *Canadian Forum,* 1968-73. Founding member of University League for Social Reform, 1962, and Committee for an Independent Canada, 1970; member of federal task force on foreign ownership and structure of Canadian industry, 1967-68.

WRITINGS: (Editor) *The Prospect of Change: Proposals for Canada's Future,* McGraw, 1965; (with Karl Polanyi) *Dahomey and the Slave Trade,* University of Washington Press, 1967; (editor) *Power Corrupted: The October Crisis and the Repression of Quebec,* New Press, 1971; (author of introduction) Philip Mathias, *Forced Growth: Five Studies of Government Involvement in the Development of Canada,* Lorimer, 1971; (editor with Robert Fulford and Dave Godfrey) *Read Canadian: A Book About Canadian Books,* Lorimer, 1972; (editor with Gary Lax) *Independence: The Canadian Challenge,* Committee for an Independent Canada, 1972; (editor) *An Industrial Strategy for Canada,* New Press, 1972; *The Pre-*

carious Homestead: Essays on Economics, Technology, and Nationalism, New Press, 1973; (with Viv Nelles) *Nationalism or Local Control,* New Press, 1973; (editor with Lax) *Getting It Back: A Program for Canadian Independence,* Clarke, Irwin, 1974; (editor) *Beyond Industrial Growth,* University of Toronto Press, 1976; (with Leon Dion and William A. Dimma) *Goals for Canada 1977-78,* Free Paper, 1978. Also author of foreword to *Reclaiming the Canadian Economy,* by Gunnar Adler-Karlson, and editor of *A Citizen's Guide to the Herb Gray Report.*

BIOGRAPHICAL/CRITICAL SOURCES: Canadian Forum, July, 1967; *Maclean's,* August 4, 1980.*

* * *

ROTTER, Marion 1940(?)-1973

OBITUARY NOTICE: Born c. 1940; died in 1973. Editor and author. Rotter was the fashion editor of *Woman and Home.* She wrote *Dressmaking: The Easy Way* as well as other volumes on dressmaking. Obituaries and other sources: *AB Bookman's Weekly,* October 15, 1973.

* * *

ROULAC, Stephen E. 1945-

PERSONAL: Surname is pronounced *Rue*-lack; born August 15, 1945, in San Francisco, Calif.; son of Phil Williams (a real estate developer) and Elizabeth (an interior decorator; maiden name, Young) Roulac; married Nancy Silver (divorced); married Holly Anne Gibson (a writer), November 18, 1978; children: (first marriage) Arthur Young. *Education:* Pomona College, B.A., 1967; Harvard University, M.B.A. (with distinction), 1970; University of California, Berkeley, J.D., 1976; Stanford University, Ph.D., 1978. *Residence:* San Francisco, Calif. *Office:* Questor Associates, 115 Sansome St., San Francisco, Calif. 94104.

CAREER: Roulac Construction Co., Pasadena, Calif., 1963-66, worked in apartment leasing, management, and general administration, became foreman of labor crew and assistant construction superintendent; Economics Research Associates, Los Angeles, Calif., research assistant, 1966-67; Urbanomics Research Associates, Claremont, Calif., associate economist, 1967; Litton Industries, Inc., Beverly Hills, Calif., acquisition auditor, 1967-68; Coopers & Lybrand, Los Angeles, real estate tax consultant, 1968; Owens-Corning Fiberglas Corp., Toledo, Ohio, consultant, 1969-70; California State University, Hayward, lecturer in business and economics, 1970-71; Questor Associates, San Francisco, Calif., founder and president, editor-in-chief and publisher of *Real Estate Securities Letter,* 1972—. Certified public accountant, 1978. Lecturer at Northeastern University, 1969-70, Stanford University, 1971-79, and University of California, Berkeley, 1972-77; adjunct professor at Hastings College of Law, 1977-78; instructor at Pacific Coast Banking School, 1978. Member of real estate advisory committee of California Commissioner of Corporations, 1973, member of blue ribbon committee on projections and track records, 1973-74; expert witness for U.S. Securities and Exchange Commission.

MEMBER: American Real Estate and Urban Economics Association, American Economics Association, American Finance Association, Harvard Club of New York City, Harvard Business School Association of Northern California, Commonwealth Club of California, Adventurers Club (Los Angeles). *Awards, honors:* W. T. Grant Fellowship, 1969-70; Harvard Business School Student Association award, 1970;

George F. Baker Trust scholarship, 1970; elected to Pomona College Athletic Hall of Fame, 1981.

WRITINGS: Real Estate Syndication Digest, 1972: Principles and Applications, Real Estate Syndication Digest, 1972; *Case Studies in Property Development*, Property Press, 1973; *Syndication Landmarks*, two volumes, Practising Law Institute, 1974; (contributor) Robert N. Anthony and James S. Reece, editors, *Management Accounting: Text and Cases*, Irwin, 5th edition (Roulac was not included in earlier editions), 1975; *Tax Shelter Sale-Leaseback Financing: The Economic Realities*, Ballinger, 1976; (with Sherman Maisel) *Real Estate Investment and Finance*, McGraw, 1976; *Modern Real Estate Investment: An Institutional Approach*, Property Press, 1976; (contributor) Peter L. Bernstein, editor, *Portfolio Management and Efficient Markets*, Institutional Investor Books, 1977.

Editor: *Notable Syndications Sourcebook*, two volumes, Practising Law Institute, 1972; *Real Estate Securities and Syndication: A Workbook*, National Association of Real Estate Boards, 1973; *Due Diligence in Real Estate Transactions*, two volumes, Practising Law Institute, 1974; *Real Estate Venture Analysis*, 1974, two volumes, 3rd edition (Roulac was also associated with two earlier editions), Practising Law Institute, 1974; *Real Estate Securities Regulation Sourcebook*, two volumes, Practising Law Institute, 1975.

Contributor of more than eighty articles and reviews to investment, real estate, tax, and construction industry journals. Editor of *Real Estate Syndication Digest*, 1971-72; contributing editor of *Real Estate Review*, 1973-75, and *Real Estate Law Journal*, 1973-78; special editor of *California Management Review*, spring, 1976; member of editorial advisory board of *Financial Education Journal*, 1976-80, *American Real Estate and Urban Economics Association Journal*, 1977-81 and *Housing Development Reporter*, 1978-80; member of editorial advisory committee of *Real Estate Securities Journal*, 1980—.

WORK IN PROGRESS: Revising *Modern Real Estate Investment*.

SIDELIGHTS: Roulac is a nationally recognized expert on investment management, housing economics, real estate valuation, and finance and investment analysis. His experience includes real estate strategy studies, housing policy, and real estate performance measurement. As a member of California's blue ribbon committee on track records and projections, he played a key role in developing the financial feasibility disclosure model which has become the standard for reporting real estate investment securities.

Questor Associates is a financial consulting firm that provides information, analysis, and representation for significant real estate decisions. The company's services include feasibility studies for tax-exempt revenue bond financing, assistance in converting under-utilized property to competitive financial investments, negotiation and structuring of real estate transactions, legal economic analysis, and expert witness testimony.

Roulac told *CA:* "Approximately ten years ago my ideas crystalized regarding the need for a new financial services organization to provide a caliber of service to the discriminating real estate participant, similar to that provided by attorneys and accountants, and I subsequently founded Questor Associates. Questor Associates is organized to provide a high standard of professional real estate services by applying modern management methods and contemporary economics to a significant sector of the economy which has often lacked the quality of services traditionally available to other businesses. By means of our Information Services division—through newsletters, journals, books, conferences, and performance measurement data bases—Questor is closing the gap between the information available to the real estate decision maker and that for the stock market participant.

"*Modern Real Estate Investment: An Institutional Approach* has received national acclaim, and is my statement of how I believe real estate investment decisions should be made. In it are various discussions of more contemporary investment analysis and valuation methods.

"Many of our publications are in the forefront of the field, in that we are providing innovative suggestions and insights in a rapidly changing sector of the business world. I am editor-in-chief of the *Real Estate Securities Letter*, which covers the broad institutional real estate market, with the distinctive focus of integrating superior journalistic reporting with a contemporary analytic orientation.

"By membership in various regulatory commissions and in numerous presentations, I have participated in raising standards in the real estate business. As the president and chief executive officer, I encourage the members of Questor Associates to practice the highest standards of excellence."

BIOGRAPHICAL/CRITICAL SOURCES: Appraisal Briefs, October 4, 1972; *Real Estate Review*, autumn, 1972, spring, 1973, summer, 1973, winter, 1974, summer, 1975, autumn, 1977, winter, 1977, spring, 1978; *Texas Bar Journal*, March, 1973, September, 1976; *Real Estate Law Journal*, summer, 1973, autumn, 1975, spring, 1976; *Appraisal Journal*, July, 1973, October, 1975, April, 1977; *Scope*, April, 1974; *Mortgage Banker*, April, 1975, January, 1976, February, 1977; *Mortgage and Real Estate Executives Report*, December 1, 1975; *Real Estate Disclosure Digest*, March 4, 1977; *RESSI Review*, June, 1977; *U.S. News and World Report*, December 29, 1980/January 5, 1981.

*   *   *

ROULSTON, Marjorie Hillis   1890-1971

OBITUARY NOTICE: Born May 25, 1890, in Peoria, Ill.; died of a stroke, November 8, 1971, in Manhattan, N.Y. Editor and author. Roulston served on the editorial staff of *Vogue* magazine from 1918 until 1936, acting as executive editor from 1932 to 1936. Her first book, *Live Alone and Like It*, was written as a self-help book for unmarried women. Subsequent books include *Orchids on Your Budget, Corn Beef and Caviar, You Can Start All Over*, and *Keep Going and Liking It*. Roulston was the wife of Thomas Roulston, the owner of a chain of grocery stores in New York. Obituaries and other sources: *New York Times*, November 10, 1971; *Newsweek*, November 22, 1971; *Time*, November 22, 1971; *Who's Who of American Women*, Marquis, 8th edition, 1974.

*   *   *

ROWE, Clarence J(ohn), Jr.   1916-

PERSONAL: Born May 24, 1916, in St. Paul, Minn.; son of Clarence John and Sayde (Mabin) Rowe; married Patricia McNulty (a psychiatric society's executive secretary), January 15, 1945; children: Padraic, Rory, Kelly Michael. *Education:* College of St. Thomas, St. Paul, Minn., B.A., 1938; University of Minnesota, M.B., 1942, M.D., 1943, postdoctoral study, 1946-49. *Religion:* Roman Catholic. *Home:* 1770 Colvin Ave., St. Paul, Minn. 55116. *Office:* 551 South Snelling Ave., St. Paul, Minn. 55116.

CAREER: St. Joseph's Hospital, St. Paul, Minn., rotating intern, 1942-43; University of Minnesota, Minneapolis, instructor, 1949-52, assistant professor, 1952-54, clinical assistant professor, 1954-57, clinical associate professor, 1957-64, clinical professor of psychiatry, 1964—. Diplomate of American Board of Psychiatry and Neurology; private practice of psychiatry in St. Paul, 1957—. Director of Hamm Memorial Psychiatric Clinic, 1954-57; president of Mental Health Consultants Ltd., 1970—; medical director of Adult Psychiatric Services of United Hospitals, 1979—. Lecturer at College of St. Catherine, 1957-72; member of adjunct faculty at Antioch College, 1974—.

Member of governor's advisory council on employment of the handicapped and chairman of its committee on the mentally restored and mentally retarded, 1954-65; chairman of Minnesota Mental Health Planning Council, 1963-69; member of Social Security Administration's advisory bureau for hearing and appeals, 1965; member of St. Paul mayor's committee on drug use and abuse, 1969-71; member of Minnesota Supreme Court Commission on Rights of the Mentally Disabled, 1971-81. Member of board of directors of St. John's University Institute for Mental Health, Collegeville, Minn., 1954-78, chairman of board, 1965-70, board of trustees of St. Thomas Academy, 1970-76, and board of advisers of Institute for Religion and Human Development, Collegeville, 1977—; consultant to Constance Bultman Wilson Center, St. Paul Family Service, and Minnesota Mining & Manufacturing Co. *Military service:* U.S. Army, Medical Corps, 1943-46; became captain.

MEMBER: American Psychiatric Association (fellow), American Medical Association (chairman of committee on mental health in industry, 1968-70), American Society of Adolescent Psychiatry, American Medical Writers Association, Academy of Psychiatry and the Law, Group for the Advancement of Psychiatry (chairman of committee on psychiatry in industry, 1969-74), Minnesota Psychiatric Society (president, 1973-75), Minnesota Society of Adolescent Psychiatry (president, 1977-78), St. Paul Society of Psychiatry and Neurology (president, 1970-71, 1978-79).

WRITINGS: An Outline of Psychiatry, W. C. Brown, 1954, 7th edition, 1980; (with A. A. McLean, John MacInver, Richard Proctor, and others) *The Mentally Ill Employee: His Treatment and Rehabilitation,* Harper, 1965; (contributor) Dana Farnsworth and Francis Braceland, editors, *Psychiatry, the Clergy, and Pastoral Counseling,* Liturgical Press, 1969. Contributor of about a dozen articles to medical journals.

WORK IN PROGRESS: Co-editing a revision of *Psychiatry, the Clergy, and Pastoral,* with Richard Sipe, for St. John's University Press.

* * *

ROWLEY, Ames Dorrance
   See LOVECRAFT, H(oward) P(hillips)

* * *

ROYAL, D.
   See Du BREUIL, (Elizabeth) L(or)inda

* * *

RUDWICK, Elliot M.   1927-

PERSONAL: Born July 19, 1927, in Philadelphia, Pa.; divorced. *Education:* Temple University, B.S., 1949; University of Pennsylvania, M.A., 1950, Ph.D., 1956. *Office:* Department of Sociology, Kent State University, Kent, Ohio 44242.

CAREER: Beaver College, Glenside, Pa., instructor in sociology, 1950-51; Bates College, Lewiston, Me., instructor in

sociology, 1951-53; Elizabethtown College, Elizabethtown, Pa., 1954-56, began as instructor, became assistant professor of sociology; University of Tampa, Tampa, Fla., assistant professor of sociology, 1956-58; Florida State University, Tallahassee, assistant professor of social work, 1958-60; Southern Illinois University, Carbondale, 1960-68, began as associate professor, became professor of sociology; Kent State University, Kent, Ohio, professor of sociology, 1968—, and history, 1971—, senior research fellow at Center of Urban Regionalism, 1968—. Fellow of Center for Advanced Studies in the Behavioral Sciences, Palo Alto, Calif., 1976-77; consultant to U.S. Civil Rights Commission, President's Commission on Civil Disorders, and President's Commission on Causes and Prevention of Violence. *Member:* American Sociological Association, American Historical Association. *Awards, honors:* Guggenheim fellowship, 1971-72; National Endowment for the Humanities fellowship, 1975-76.

WRITINGS: W.E.B. Du Bois: A Study in Minority Group Leadership, University of Pennsylvania Press, 1960, 2nd edition published as *W.E.B. Du Bois: Propagandist of the Negro Protest,* 1968; *Race Riot at St. Louis, July 2, 1917,* Southern Illinois University Press, 1964; (with August Meier) *From Plantation to Ghetto,* Hill & Wang, 1966, 3rd edition, 1976; (editor with Meier) *The Making of Black America,* Volume I: *The Origins of Black Americans,* Volume II: *The Black Community in Modern America,* Atheneum, 1969.

(Editor with A. Meier) *Black Protest in the Sixties,* Quadrangle, 1970; (editor with John H. Bracey) *Black Nationalism in America,* Bobbs-Merrill, 1970; (editor with Bracey) *American Slavery: The Question of Resistance,* Wadsworth, 1971; (editor with Bracey) *Black Matriarchy: Myth or Reality?,* Wadsworth, 1971; (editor with Bracey) *The Black Sociologist: The First Half Century,* Wadsworth, 1971; (editor with Bracey) *Black Workers and Organized Labor,* Wadsworth, 1971; (editor with Bracey) *Blacks in the Abolitionist Movement,* Wadsworth, 1971; (editor with Bracey) *Conflict and Competition: Studies in the Recent Black Protest Movement,* Wadsworth, 1971; (editor with Bracey) *Free Blacks in America, 1800-1860,* Wadsworth, 1971; (editor with Bracey) *The Rise of the Ghetto,* Wadsworth, 1971; (editor with Meier) *Black Protest Thought in the Twentieth Century,* 2nd edition (Rudwick was not associated with first edition), Bobbs-Merrill, 1971; (editor with Bracey) *The Afro-Americans,* Allyn & Bacon, 1972; (with Meier) *CORE: A Study in the Civil Rights Movement, 1942-1968,* Oxford University Press, 1973; (with Meier) *Along the Color Line: Explorations in the Black Experience,* University of Illinois Press, 1976; (with Meier) *Black Detroit and the Rise of the U.A.W.,* Oxford University Press, 1979.

BIOGRAPHICAL/CRITICAL SOURCES: Yale Review, autumn, 1967; *New Republic,* October 27, 1979; *Nation,* December 1, 1979.*

* * *

RUFFIAN, M.
   See HASEK, Jaroslav (Matej Frantisek)

* * *

RUSH, Philip   1908-

PERSONAL: Born February 24, 1908, in Palmers Green, London, England; married Geraldine Gould, 1931; children: two daughters, one son. *Education:* Attended London School of Economics and Political Science, London. *Home:* 45 Castle St., Canterbury, Kent CT1 2PY, England. *Agent:* John

Johnson, 51-54 Goschen Buildings, 12-13 Henrietta St., London WC2E 8LF, England.

CAREER: Borough of East Ham, London, England, local government officer, 1930-63; chief inspector of weights and measures, 1963-65; Borough of Bexley, London, chief inspector of weights and measures, 1965-68. Historical novelist, biographer, and author of books for children.

WRITINGS: Rogue's Lute, Andrew Dakers, 1944; Mary Read, Buccaneer, T. V. Boardman, 1945; Freedom Is the Man, Andrew Dakers, 1946; Crispin's Apprentice, Andrew Dakers, 1948.

For children: He Sailed With Dampier, T. V. Boardman, 1947; A Cage of Falcons, Collins, 1954; Queen's Treason, Collins, 1954; The Minstrel Knight, Collins, 1955, revised edition, Bobbs-Merrill, 1956; Great Men of Sussex, Bodley Head, 1956, Richard West, 1973; King of the Castle, Collins, 1956; He Went With Dampier, Harrap, 1957, Roy Publishers, 1958; My Brother Lambert: A Story of the Simnel Rebellion, Roy Publishers, 1957; Red Man's Country, Collins, 1957; Strange People: The Later Hanoverians, Hutchinson, 1957; More Strange People: The Early Hanoverians, Hutchinson, 1958; London's Wonderful Bridge, Harrap, 1959; Strange Stuarts, 1603-1714, Hutchinson, 1959.

Apprentice at Arms, Collins, 1960; He Went With Franklin, Harrap, 1960; How Roads Have Grown, Routledge & Kegan Paul, 1960; The Young Shelley, Parrish, 1961, Roy Publishers, 1962; Weights and Measures, Methuen, 1962, Roy Publishers, 1964; The Castle and the Harp, Collins, 1963, McGraw-Hill, 1964; The Book of Duels, Harrap, 1964; Frost Fair, Collins, 1965, Roy Publishers, 1967; That Fool of a Priest, and Other Tales of Early Canterbury, Pergamon, 1970; A Face of Stone, Brockhampton Press, 1973; Guns for the Armada, Hodder & Stoughton, 1975; Death to the Strangers!, Hodder & Stoughton, 1977.

SIDELIGHTS: Philip Rush's writings focus on events and characters from history. He presents his settings realistically, including the hardships and violence endured by his characters.

One of Rush's earlier publications, The Minstrel Knight, was based on a documentary found in the British Museum. Rush retold the story of Fulk Fitz-Warin, which had been recorded by a minstrel between 1256 and 1264. Rush set the tale in England during the reign of King John, writing of battles and chivalry in Robin Hood style.

BIOGRAPHICAL/CRITICAL SOURCES: Chicago Sunday Tribune, March 24, 1957, September 2, 1962.*

*   *   *

RUSH, Theressa Gunnels   1945-

PERSONAL: Born September 2, 1945, in Morrilton, Ark.; daughter of Fred J. (a farmer) and Florence (Pledger) Gunnels; married J. D. Rush, January 9, 1966 (divorced, 1970); married John W. Wesley (a service station dealer), June 18, 1976; children: (first marriage) Dwayne; (second marriage) Rashida, Kameelah, Jameel. Education: Philander Smith College, B.A., 1967; Kent State University, M.M., 1972. Home and office: 14508 Sara Dr., Little Rock, Ark. 72206.

CAREER: High school English teacher in Springfield, Mo., 1967-69, and North Little Rock, Ark., 1969-70; University of Wisconsin, Eau Claire, instructor in English, 1972-74; reading specialist at public schools in Minneapolis, Minn., 1974-75; Philander Smith College, Little Rock, Ark., career development director, 1975-78. Awards, honors: Black American Writers

was selected as an outstanding reference book by select group of librarians, 1975.

WRITINGS: (With Carol Myers and Ester Arata) Black American Writers Past and Present: A Biographical and Bibliographical Directory, Scarecrow, 1975.

WORK IN PROGRESS: A philosophical autobiography; a supplement to Black American Writers Past and Present.

SIDELIGHTS: Theressa Rush wrote: "I began a factual autobiography because I felt that my experiences could offer inspiration and hope to young people, but as I allowed my mind and creativity to expand and unfold, I began incorporating a philosophical dimension, which accomplishes my purpose much better."

*   *   *

RUSSELL, George William   1867-1935
(A.E.)

BRIEF ENTRY: Born April 10, 1867, in Lurgan, County Armagh, Ireland; died of cancer, July 17, 1935, in Bournemouth, England. Irish painter, economist, poet, and critic. Rather than being remembered for his poetry or his paintings, Russell is best known as a main figure in the Irish intellectual movement, particularly important in the Irish literary revival. Russell was a mystic and his writings often combined Irish nationalism with mystical imagination. Among his works are a book of critical essays that he published with William Butler Yeats, pamphlets on the Irish economy, and poetry dealing with magic, visions, and Eastern religions. Other interests explored in his writings were Buddhism, theosophy, and the Irish National Theatre. Active in Irish agrarian and political affairs, especially in the Home Rule movement, Russell organized the Irish Agricultural Co-Operative movement and was associated with the Irish Agricultural Organization Society, for which he edited the Irish Homestead and later the Irish Statesman. He co-founded the Dublin League of the Theosophical Society as well as the famous Abbey Theatre. Russell never wrote under his own name. His intended pseudonym was AEon, but a compositor found only the first two letters legible so the accidental pen name of A.E. evolved. His works include Homeward: Songs by the Way (1894), The Mask of Apollo (1904), The National Being, Thoughts on Irish Policy (1916), Collected Poems (1926), Song and Its Fountains (1932), and The Avatars (1933). Residence: London, England. Biographical/critical sources: D. Figgis, George W. Russell: A Study of a Man and of a Nation, Maunsel, 1916; Twentieth Century Authors: A Biographical Dictionary of Modern Literature, H. W. Wilson, 1942; Twentieth-Century Literary Criticism, Volume 3, Gale, 1980.

*   *   *

RYAN, William (Howard)   1914-

PERSONAL: Born March 8, 1914, in Rochester, N.Y.; son of Willis James (an engineer) and Amelia Mary (Ginter) Ryan; married Mary Elizabeth Black, August 9, 1941. Education: New York State Normal School (now State University of New York College at Geneseo), diploma and license, 1936; Boston University, B.S., 1955. Home address: Todd Pond Rd., Lincoln, Mass. 01773. Office: Polyphor Corp., 4 New York Ave., Framingham, Mass. 01701.

CAREER: Automatic Electric Co., Chicago, Ill., equipment engineer, 1937-39; Polaroid Corp., Cambridge, Mass., research scientist, 1939-65, research consultant, 1965-71; Polyphor Corp., Framingham, Mass., president, 1970—. Member:

American Chemical Society, Society of Architectural Historians, Society of Motion Picture and Television Engineers (delegate to Inter-Society Color Council, 1946-71), Society of Photographic Scientists and Engineers, Royal Photographic Society, Society of Architectural Historians (England).

WRITINGS: (Contributor) Martin Quigley, Jr., editor, *New Screen Techniques,* Quigley, 1953; (with Desmond Guinness) *Irish Houses and Castles,* Viking, 1971, revised edition, Crescent Books, 1981; (with Guinness) *The White House: An Architectural History,* McGraw, 1980.

WORK IN PROGRESS: Research on American architectural views published before 1800.

* * *

RYSKAMP, Charles (Andrew) 1928-

PERSONAL: Born October 21, 1928, in East Grand Rapids, Mich.; son of Henry Jacob and Flora (DeGraaf) Ryskamp. *Education:* Calvin College, A.B., 1950; Yale University, M.A., 1951, Ph.D., 1956; graduate study at Pembroke College, Cambridge, 1953-54. *Home:* 12 Cleveland Lane, Princeton, N.J. 08540. *Office:* Pierpont Morgan Library, 29 East 36th St., New York, N.Y. 10016.

CAREER: Princeton University, Princeton, N.J., instructor, 1955-59, assistant professor, 1959-63, associate professor, 1963-69, professor of English, 1969—, John E. Annan Preceptor, 1961-64, curator of English and American literature at library, 1967-69. Director of Pierpont Morgan Library, 1969—. Member of advisory committee of "Horace Walpole Correspondence" and "Private Papers of James Boswell" of Yale University; member of board of trustees of Museum of Broadcasting (also member of executive committee), Andrew W. Mellon Foundation, Gerard B. Lambert Foundation (also vice-president), and Corning Museum of Glass; member of board of advisers of Gunston Hall; member of board of managers of Lewis Walpole Library of Yale University.

MEMBER: Association Internationale de Bibliophilie (member of committee of honor), Modern Language Association of America, Keats-Shelley Association of America (vice-president), Master Drawings Association (secretary-treasurer), Drawing Society, Academy of American Poets, Association of Art Museum Directors (vice-president), Cowper Society, Museums Council of New York City (past vice-president), Friends of Princeton University Library (member of council), Metropolitan Opera Association, Johnsonians, Pilgrims, William Blake Trust, Lotos Club, Grolier Club, Coffee House Club, Century Association, Round Table Club, Elizabethan Club, Turf Club, Roxburghe Club. *Awards, honors:* Fellowship from Procter & Gamble Co., 1958-59; junior fellowship from Council of Humanities at Yale University, 1960-61; Bollingen Foundation fellowship, 1965-67; Guggenheim fellowship, 1966-67; Litt.D. from Trinity College, Hartford, Conn., 1975; L.H.D. from Union College, Schenectady, N.Y., 1977; Order of St. John of Jerusalem; commander of the Order of Orange Nassau (The Netherlands) and officer of the Order of Leopold II (Belgium), both 1980.

WRITINGS: William Cowper of the Inner Temple, Esq.: A Study of His Life and Works to the Year 1768, Cambridge University Press, 1959; *William Blake, Engraver: A Descriptive Catalogue of an Exhibition,* Princeton University Library, 1969; (author of preface and general editor) *William and Mary and Their House,* Pierpont Morgan Library, 1979; (with Herbert Cahoon and Thomas V. Lange) *American Literary Autographs: From Washington Irving to Henry James,* Dover, 1977; (with Cahoon and Verlyn Klinkenborg) *British Literary Manuscripts: From 800 to 1914,* two volumes, Dover, 1881.

Editor: (With Frederick A. Pottle) *Boswell: The Ominous Years, 1774-1776,* McGraw, 1963; *The Cast-Away,* Princeton University Library, 1963; *Wilde and the Nineties: An Essay and an Exhibition by Richard Ellmann, E.D.H. Johnson, and Alfred L. Bush,* Princton University Library, 1966; *William Blake: The Pickering Manuscript,* Pierpont Morgan Library, 1972; *Introduction to the Pierpont Morgan Library,* Pierpont Morgan Library, 1974; (with James King) *The Letters and Prose Writings of William Cowper,* Oxford University Press, Volume I: *1750-1781,* 1979, Volume II: *Letters, 1782-1786,* 1981; (with Richard Wendorf) *The Works of William Collins,* Oxford University Press, 1979; (with John D. Baird) *The Poems of William Cowper,* Volume I: *1748-1782,* Oxford University Press 1980. Editor of *Report to the Fellows of The Pierpont Morgan Library,* 1969—.

WORK IN PROGRESS: Completing volumes of William Cowper's correspondence and poems.

S

SACKVILLE-WEST, V(ictoria Mary) 1892-1962

PERSONAL: Born March 9, 1892, at Knole Castle, Sevenoaks, Kent, England; died June 2, 1962, at Sissinghurst Castle, Cranbrook, Kent, England; daughter of Lionel Edward and Victoria Sackville-West; married Harold Nicolson (a journalist and diplomat), October 1, 1913; children: Benedict, Nigel. *Education:* Studied privately with tutors.

CAREER: Novelist and poet. Gardening correspondent for *Observer;* member of National Trust's Garden Committee. *Wartime service:* Organizer of Kent's Women's Land Army during World War II. *Member:* Royal Society (fellow). *Awards, honors:* Hawthornden Prize, 1927, for *The Land;* Heinemann Prize, 1946, for *The Garden;* Companion of Honor, 1948.

WRITINGS—Poetry: Chatterton, privately printed, 1909; *Constantinople,* privately printed, 1915; *Poems West and East,* John Lane, 1918; *The Land,* Heinemann, 1927; *King's Daughter,* Doubleday, 1930; *Invitation to Cast Out Care,* illustrated by Graham Sutherland, Faber, 1931; *Sissinghurst,* Hogarth, 1931, reprinted, National Trust, 1972; *Collected Poems: Volume I,* Hogarth, 1933, Doubleday, 1934; *Some Flowers,* Cobden-Sanderson, 1937; *Solitude,* Hogarth, 1938, Doubleday, 1939; *Selected Poems,* Hogarth, 1941; *The Garden,* Doubleday, 1946. Also author of *Orchards and Vineyards,* 1921.

Novels: *Heritage,* George H. Doran, 1919; *The Dragon in Shallow Waters,* Putnam, 1922; *Challenge,* George H. Doran, 1923, Collins, 1974; *Grey Wethers: A Romantic Novel,* George H. Doran, 1923; *The Edwardians,* Doubleday, Doran, 1930, reprinted, Hogarth, 1966; *All Passion Spent,* Doubleday, Doran, 1931, reprinted, Hogarth, 1965; *Family History,* Doubleday, Doran, 1932; *The Dark Island,* Doubleday, Doran, 1934; *Grand Canyon,* Doubleday, Doran, 1942; *The Devil at Westease* (detective story), Doubleday, 1947; *The Easter Party,* Doubleday, 1953, reprinted, Greenwood Press, 1972; *No Sign-Posts in the Sea,* Doubleday, 1961.

Short stories: *The Heir* (contains "The Heir," "The Christmas Party," "Patience," "Her Son," and "The Parrot"), George H. Doran, 1922, reprinted, Cedric Chivers, 1973; *Seducers in Ecuador,* George H. Doran, 1925; *Thirty Clocks Strike the Hour and Other Stories,* Doubleday, Doran, 1932. Also author of *Death of Noble Godavary and Gottfried Kuenstler,* 1932.

Biographies: *The Diary of Lady Anne Clifford,* 1923, reprinted, Norwood Editions, 1979; *Aphra Ben, the Incomparable Astrea,* G. Howe, 1927, Viking, 1928, reprinted, Russell, 1970; *Andrew Marvell,* Faber, 1929, reprinted, Folcroft, 1969; *St. Joan of Arc,* Doubleday, 1936, reprinted, M. Joseph, 1969; *Pepita,* Doubleday, 1937, reprinted, Hogarth, 1970; *The Eagle and the Dove: A Study in Contrasts* (biographies of St. Theresa of Avila and St. Theresa of Lisieux), M. Joseph, 1943, Doubleday, 1944, reprinted, M. Joseph, 1969; *Daughter of France: The Life of Anne Marie Louise d'Orleans,* Doubleday, 1959.

Books on gardening: *Country Notes,* M. Joseph, 1939, Harper, 1940, reprinted, Books for Libraries, 1971; *Country Notes in Wartime,* Hogarth, 1940, Doubleday, 1941, reprinted, Books for Libraries, 1970; *In Your Garden,* M. Joseph, 1951, published as *V. Sackville-West's Garden Book,* edited by Philippa Nicolson, Atheneum, 1968, published in England as *V. Sackville-West's Garden Book: A Collection Taken From In Your Garden,* M. Joseph, 1968; *In Your Garden Again,* M. Joseph, 1953; *More for Your Garden,* M. Joseph, 1955; *A Joy of Gardening: A Selection for Americans,* Harper, 1958; *Even More for Your Garden,* M. Joseph, 1958.

Other: *Knole and the Sackvilles,* Heinemann, 1923, Benn, 1950; *Twelve Days: An Account of a Journey Across the Bakhtiari Mountains in Southwestern Persia,* Doubleday, 1928; *English Country Houses,* Collins, 1941; *Passenger to Teheran,* Penguin, 1943; *The Women's Land Army,* M. Joseph, 1944; *Nursery Rhymes* (a study of the history of nursery rhymes), Dropmore, 1947; *Faces: Profiles of Dogs,* Harvill, 1961, Doubleday, 1962; (with husband, Harold Nicolson) *Another World Than This* (anthology), M. Joseph, 1945; (author of introduction) Alice Christiana Meynell, *Prose and Poetry,* J. Cape, 1947; *Berkeley Castle: The Historic Glouchestershire Seat of the Berkeley Family Since the Eleventh Century,* English Life Publications, 1972; *Dearest Andrew: Letters From V. Sackville-West to Andrew Reiber, 1951-1952,* edited by Nancy MacKnight, Scribner, 1979. Contributor of critical essays to Royal Society of Literature of the United Kingdon, c.1927-45.

SIDELIGHTS: Victoria Sackville-West, who was called Vita and published under the name V. Sackville-West, was a member of one of Britain's most socially prominent families. She was born in Knole Castle, which her son Nigel Nicolson described in *Portrait of a Marriage* as "the largest house in England still in private hands." Her social milieu included people of noble birth and wealth, namely, Rudyard Kipling, Auguste Rodin, Pierpont Morgan, William Waldorf Astor, and Henry Ford. She was courted by nobility, including Lord Lascelles and Lord Granby.

A solitary person, Sackville-West for many years enjoyed Knole as her only companion. "Through Knole and her preferred solitude," Nicolson revealed, "she discovered the joy of writing." Her first works, written at the age of eleven, were ballads in the Horatius manner, and the first money she ever earned was one pound for a poem published in the *Onlooker* in 1907. Commenting on her early style, her son noted: "She taught herself the techniques of narrative and dialogue by careful observation of what she read, since she had no literary mentor and was yet to go to school." A prolific young writer, she wrote eight full-length novels (one in French) and five plays between 1906 and 1910. For her plots, Sackville-West turned to the stories of Knole and the Sackvilles. "The Sackvilles, who were on the whole a modest family given to lengthy bouts of melancholia," related Nicolson, "were transformed by Vita into troubadors who played the most dramatic roles at the most dramatic moments of English history, and behaved in every situation with the utmost gallantry."

Some of the drama in the author's life was not made public until after her death when her son discovered an autobiography that his mother wrote in 1920. Incorporated into *Portrait of a Marriage*, the autobiography described Sackville-West's relationships with two women, Rosamund Grosvenor, a relative of the Duke of Westminster, and Violet Keppel. Sackville-West's affair with Grosvenor coincided with her engagement to Harold Nicolson, and by nearly eloping with Keppel the novelist came close to destroying her marriage.

Apart from disclosing the homosexuality within Britain's upper classes, Sackville-West's autobiography is the remarkable story of the author's relationship with her husband, Harold Nicolson. Their son called his parents' marriage "the strangest and most successful union that two gifted people have ever enjoyed." Theirs "is the story of two people who married for love and whose love deepened with every passing year, although each was constantly and by mutual consent unfaithful to the other. Both loved people of their own sex, but not exclusively. Their marriage not only survived infidelity, sexual incompatibility and long absences, but it became stronger and finer as a result. . . . Marriage succeeded because each found permanent and undiluted happiness only in the company of the other," observed Nicholson.

A large part of Sackville-West's renown stems from her association with the Bloomsbury group, a clique of literary elites, and from her relationship with a member of that group, Virginia Woolf, with whom she shared a deep, lasting, and briefly sexual friendship. Some believe that Sackville-West is the central figure of *Orlando*, Woolf's experimental novel that traces a character through several centuries as well as identities. Based on the novelists' friendship, the novel took on genuine importance in Sackville-West's life. Nicolson explained: "Virginia by her genius has provided Vita with a unique consolation for having been born a girl, for her exclusion from her inheritance, for her father's death earlier that year. The book, for her, was not simply a brilliant masque or pageant. It was a memorial mass."

Woolf often commented on Sackville-West's writings. In a letter dated January 26, 1926, Sackville-West summarized Woolf's reaction to *The Land*. She said: "She was disappointed, but very sweet about it. She says it is a contribution to English literature, and is a solid fact against which one can lean up without fear of its giving way. She also says it is one of the few *interesting* poems—I mean the information part." Woolf, however, did like *Seducers in Ecuador*, as she told Sackville-West in a letter written September 15, 1924. "I like its texture," Woolf wrote, "the sense of all the fine things

you have dropped in to it, so that it is full of beauty in itself when nothing is happening—nevertheless such interesting things do happen, so suddenly—barely, too; and I like its obscurity so that we can play about with it—interpret it different ways, and the beauty and the fantasticallity of the details."

Other critics also praised Sackville-West's endeavors. In *Bookman*, for example, Hugh Walpole stated: "I find among all the writers in England no one else who has achieved such distinction in so many directions. The novelists who are also poets, the poets who are also novelists, are very rare always." L.A.G. Strong made a similar observation in *Spectator:* "Every novel written by a poet is in one sense an allegory. If it moves him as a poet—and he has no business with it otherwise—its characters and scenes will bear more than their literal meaning. Like a poem, it will contain more than the poet is consciously aware of as he writes. Miss Sackville-West's work has always had this double validity. Even where she is least conscious of her intentions, the truth of her work rings on more than one level."

Among her literary works, Sackville-West's long poem *The Land*, her novel *The Edwardians*, and the biography of her grandmother *Pepita* received the most critical attention. As a writer she brought consciousness to bear on her choice of genres, and in her poetry, fiction, and biographies she stayed within traditional forms. In his critical biography, Michael Stevens put forth: "The quality most immediately apparent in VS-W's work is the beauty of her prose, an observation which applies equally to her fiction, her biographies, and her travel books. It is, however, a style that she had to discipline herself to achieve; restraint was not a trait that came naturally to her passionate nature. The tranquility and balance which are such noticeable features of *No Sign-Posts in the Sea*, her last novel, are by no means equally obvious in *Heritage*, her first."

Later in life, Sackville-West became greatly admired for her formal gardens. Her enthusiasm for this country art, about which she wrote several books, seemed at first in sharp contrast with the nonconformity of her youth. But Walpole discerned the inconsistency in Sackville-West's nature. He claimed: "She has done everything in her life, I imagine, simply because it would be a delightful thing to do. . . . I would say that she has never definitely chosen anything or anybody all her life long, but that when a place or a person or a book has appeared close to her and has seemed the sort of place or person or book natural to her, she has attached it to herself without consciously thinking about it." This makes her romantic, the reviewer continued, "because the essence of romantic living is to find pleasure in the things around one, and she has found intense pleasure in them. This intensity of approach is at the basis of all her work."

BIOGRAPHICAL/CRITICAL SOURCES: Nigel Nicolson, editor, *The Diaries and Letters of Harold Nicolson*, three volumes, Atheneum, 1966-68; Norah Smaridge, *Famous British Women Novelists*, Dodd, 1967; Sarah Ruth Watson, *V. Sackville-West*, Twayne, 1972; Quentin Bell, *Virginia Woolf: A Biography*, Harcourt, 1972; Nicolson, *Portrait of a Marriage*, Atheneum, 1973; Michael Stevens, *V. Sackville-West: A Critical Biography*, Scribner's, 1974; Jane Rule, *Lesbian Images*, Doubleday, 1975; Jullian Philippe and John Phillips, *The Other Woman: A Life of Violet Trefusis*, Houghton, 1976.

Periodicals: *Bookman*, September, 1930; *Spectator*, June 2, 1953; *PMLA*, March, 1955, March, 1956; *Vogue*, September 1, 1956, October 15, 1961, November, 1973; *Newsweek*, April 24, 1961, November 5, 1973; *New York Times*, June 3, 1962; *Time*, June 8, 1962, November 12, 1973; *Publishers Weekly*, June 25, 1962; *Wilson Library Bulletin*, September, 1962; *New*

York Public Library Bulletin, May, 1967; *New York Times Book Review,* October 28, 1973, July 28, 1974; *Horticulture,* July, 1977.*

—Sketch by Charity Anne Dorgan and Andrea Geffner

*   *   *

(el-)SADAT, Anwar   1918-1981

OBITUARY NOTICE—See index for *CA* sketch: Born December 25, 1918, in Mit Abu el Kom, Egypt; assassinated, October 6, 1981, in Cairo, Egypt. Politician, statesman, military officer, editor, and author. Committed to peace in the Middle East, Sadat was the first Arab leader to initiate and sign a peace treaty with Israel. Arriving in Jerusalem in 1977 bearing the traditional olive branch of peace, Sadat ended the thirty-year state of war existing between Egypt and Israel. The effort won him the Nobel Peace Prize in 1978. Sadat surprised his colleagues with his "creative diplomacy." After the death of Egypt's President Abdel Nasser in 1970, Sadat came into power with a reputation as "Nasser's poodle." Because of his strong loyalty to Nasser and an apparent lack of ambition, Sadat was viewed as an interim ruler only. He quickly took command, however, and crushed a Communist plot to overthrow him. In 1973 he ejected all Soviet military personnel from Egypt and firmly allied himself with the West. Yet, on October 6th of the same year, Egyptian armies crossed the Suez Canal and unexpectedly attacked Israel. Sadat claimed he warred on his Jewish neighbor in an effort to regain the self-respect Egypt had lost in the Arab-Israeli conflict of 1967. Although Egypt eventually lost the war, Sadat accomplished his aim and was thereafter known as the "Hero of the Crossing." With Egypt's newly acquired image, Sadat turned to his self-imposed mission to restore peace in the Middle East, which ultimately resulted in the agreement with Israel. Sadat began his career in 1938 as a soldier dedicated to ridding Egypt of its British inhabitants. During the fight, Sadat spent several years in prison. After helping to unseat British-supported King Farouk in 1952, Sadat became a member of the new government and was vice-president when Nasser died. In addition to editing the newspaper *al-Gomhouriya,* Sadat wrote two books, *Revolt on the Nile* and *In Search of Identity: An Autobiography.* Obituaries and other sources: *New York Times,* October 7, 1981; *London Times,* October 7, 1981; *Time,* October 19, 1981; *Newsweek,* October 19, 1981.

*   *   *

ST. GEORGE, David
See MARKOV, Georgi

*   *   *

SAKI
See MUNRO, Hector Hugh

*   *   *

SALK, Lee   1926-

PERSONAL: Born December 27, 1926, in New York, N.Y.; son of Daniel Bonn and Dora (Press) Salk; divorced; children: Eric, Pia. *Education:* Attended Rutgers University, 1944, and University of Louisville, 1946; University of Michigan, A.B., 1949, M.A., 1950, Ph.D., 1954. *Office:* 941 Park Ave., New York, N.Y. 10028.

CAREER: University of Michigan, Ann Arbor, Mich., assistant in psychology department, 1948-50, research assistant in Re-

search Center Group Dynamics, 1949, instructor in psychology of adjustment in Extension Service, 1951-54, clinical psychologist at psychology clinic of Institute of Human Adjustment, 1952-53; Michigan Department of Mental Health, Lansing, Mich., research assistant, 1949, research program director, 1951-52, research consultant, 1953-54; Pontiac Child Clinic, Pontiac, Mich., chief clinical psychologist, 1952; Detroit Veterans Mental Hygiene Clinic, Detroit, Mich., intern in clinical psychology, 1952-53; Dearborn Veterans Administration Hospital, Dearborn, Mich., intern in clinical psychology, 1953-54; McGill University, Montreal, Quebec, Canada, research associate in department of psychiatry of Allen Memorial Institute of Psychiatry, 1954-57, instructor at Industrial Relations Center, 1954-55, instructor at McGill Extension Service, 1955, visiting lecturer in human relations, 1957-59; University Settlement House, New York City, chief psychologist of psychiatric consulting service, 1957-58; City Hospital, Elmhurst, N.Y., instructor of scientific methods in resident training program of department of psychiatry, 1958-63, clinical director of deprol research program, 1960; Lenox Hill Hospital, N.Y., chief psychologist for pediatric psychiatry service, 1962-66, consulting psychologist in department of pediatrics, 1976—; New York Hospital-Cornell University Medical Center, New York City, chief psychologist for child psychiatry service, 1966-67, attending psychologist in pediatrics, 1966—, director of division of pediatric psychology, 1968-76; attending psychologist at Payne Whitney Psychiatric Clinic, 1976—.

Researcher at Lab Group Research, 1950; research associate at Wayne State University, Detroit, 1950-51; and associate research scientist at New York College of Dentistry, New York City, 1971-72. Private practice as diagnostic consultant, 1952-54, in diagnosis and psychotherapy, 1954-57, and in intensive psychotherapy diagnosis, 1957-66. Adjunct professor of child development at Child Study Center of Brown University, Providence, R.I., 1979—; professor of psychology in psychiatry and pediatrics at Cornell University Medical College. Macklin Memorial Lecturer, U.S. Naval Medical Hospital, Portsmouth, Va., 1971, and Jonas E. Berg Memorial Lecturer, 1973.

Syndicated on NBC-Radio News and Information Service, 1975-77; NBC-TV News Doctor's Office, New York City and Chicago, Ill., 1976. Task force member of American Psychiatric Association, Head Start Child Abuse and Neglect Prevention. Member of Boys' Club of America citizens' committee on population and the American future, 1973-75.

Member of the advisory board of The Floating Hospital, 1972—, International Childbirth Education Association, 1972—, Postgraduate Center for Mental Health of Guanabara, Brazil, 1973, League for Parent Education, Inc., 1974-77, Foundation for Education in Human Relations, 1976—, Public Action Coalition for Toys (PACT), 1976—, Boys' Club of America's National Health Project, 1977, and National Organization for Non-Parents, 1978—. Special adviser on family law to American Bar Association. Trustee of Youth Consultation Service, 1976—, and Learning-for-Living Institute.

Consultant to American Red Cross, 1973—, American Foundation for Maternal and Child Health, Girl Scouts of the U.S.A., Dalton School (New York City), and National Broadcasting Co. (NBC). Member of board of directors of Council for the Advancement of the Psychological Professions and Sciences, Interdisciplinary Association for the Study and Prevention of Filicide (FILIUM), 1973-76, New York State Citizens' Council for Children, Youth, and Their Families, 1973—, and Bide-A-Wee, 1979—; member of executive board of American Association for Child Care in Hospitals, 1970-74; honorary board member of Artists Family Theatre Project, Inc., 1977—. *Mil-*

itary service: U.S. Army, Armor Corps, served in World War II; became staff sergeant.

MEMBER: World Federation for Mental Health, International Society for Political Psychology, American Psychological Association (president of clinical child psychology section, 1976-77; president of child and youth services, 1979-80), American Academy of Psychotherapists, Society for the Psychological Study of Social Issues, Society of Research in Child Development, Society of Pediatric Psychology (president, 1970-72), Royal Society of Medicine, Harvey Society, New York Academy of Sciences.

AWARDS, HONORS: Key to the City of Chattanooga, Tenn., and named Ambassador of Good Will by city of Chattanooga, both 1973, for "distinguished contributions to the field of pediatric psychiatry and warm understanding of the needs of the human family"; Pearl Merrill Award, 1974; American Red Cross special citation, 1974, for "service in parent education"; Key to the City of Indianapolis, Ind., 1974; National Media Award from American Psychological Foundation, 1977; Hannah G. Solomon Award from National Council of Jewish Women, 1977, for "outstanding work with children"; Distinguished Contributions Award from Society of Pediatric Psychology, 1977, for "outstanding efforts on behalf of the Society, in the field of pediatric psychology and for service to the public"; Distinguished Professional Contributions in Clinical Child Psychology Award from American Psychological Association, 1978; Commission of Honor Award from State University of New York Agricultural and Technical College, 1979.

WRITINGS: (With Rita Kramer) *How to Raise a Human Being,* Random House, 1969; *What Every Child Would Like His Parents to Know,* Warner Books, 1973; *Preparing for Parenthood: Understanding Your Feelings About Pregnancy, Childbirth, and Your Baby,* Bantam, 1975; *What Every Child Would Like His Parents to Know About Divorce,* Harper, 1978; *Dear Dr. Salk: Answers to Your Questions About Your Family,* Harper, 1979; *Ask Dr. Salk,* Bobbs-Merrill, 1981; *Fathers and Sons, An Intimate Relationship,* Putnam, 1982. Columnist for *Pediatrics Annals,* 1972-74, *McCall's,* and other magazines; author of syndicated newspaper column "Talk to Dr. Salk," 1973-75; contributor of numerous articles to professional publications. Author of audio cassette programs.

WORK IN PROGRESS: Encyclopedia of Child Behavior, publication expected in fall, 1983.

SIDELIGHTS: "I kept getting the recurring thought," said Lee Salk, "that I wish I could have gotten to the parents of the [emotionally disturbed] person." A prominent psychologist and the brother of Jonas Salk, the inventor of the polio vaccine, Salk is concerned with communicating to his readers the crucial role that parents play in the art of total child care. Margo Huston of the *Milwaukee Journal* reported that Salk, in *Preparing for Parenthood,* "talks about how important it is for an infant and young child to spend time during the day with one parent or the other."

As Salk points out in *How to Raise a Human Being,* babies are able to learn from their environments even during the first twenty-four hours of their lives, so early care like holding and cuddling an infant is a major factor in preventing the development of emotional problems. Expressing the doctor's theory, a *Harper's* reviewer explained that, without motherly love, a "baby not only fails to develop the capacity for any kind of emotional attachment, it is also severely stunted in its ability to learn—an ability on which its very survival is predicated."

But, the psychologist purported, "the father is every bit as important as the mother." Fathers as well as mothers should make their children feel that they are very important and that they come first above all other things in their parents' life. For instance, Salk, a divorced father with custody of his two children, arranges his business trips so that his children are able to accompany him or juggles his schedule so that he can attend his son's school plays. "Even busy fathers," he remarked in the *Milwaukee Journal* interview, "can do these kinds of things for their children."

BIOGRAPHICAL/CRITICAL SOURCES: Harper's, October, 1969; *Milwaukee Journal,* February 20, 1975; *Authors in the News,* Volume 1, Gale, 1979.

* * *

SAMSONOV, Leon
    See MAXIMOV, Vladimir (Yemelyanovich)

* * *

SANCHEZ, Ramiro Guerra y
    See GUERRA y SANCHEZ, Ramiro

* * *

SANSOM, Clive   1910-

PERSONAL: Born June 21, 1910, in London, England. *Education:* Attended London Polytechnic, Speech Institute, and University of London. *Agent:* David Higham Associates Ltd., 5-8 Lower John St., Golden Sq., London W1R 4HA, England.

CAREER: Examiner in speech and drama at London Academy of Music and Dramatic Art and at University of London; supervisor of speech education in Tasmania, 1950-65; writer, 1935—. Lecturer. *Member:* Society of Authors. *Awards, honors:* Poetry award from Festival of Britain for "The Witness"; award from Arts Council of Great Britain.

WRITINGS: (With Rodney Bennett) *Adventures in Words: Speech Training for Canadian Schools,* University of London Press, 1935; (with Marjorie Gullan) *The Poet Speaks,* Methuen, 1940, 4th edition, 1951; *Speech Training as a Career,* Vawser & Wiles, 1947; *Speech in the Primary School,* A. & C. Black, 1965, reprinted as *Speech and Communication in the Primary School,* 1966, 2nd edition, 1979.

Poetry; published by Methuen, except as noted: *In the Midst of Death,* privately printed, 1940; *The Unfailing Spirit,* Faril Press, 1943; *The Witness and Other Poems,* 1956; *The Cathedral,* 1958; *Dorset Village,* 1962; *Return to Magic,* Leslie Frewin, 1969; *The Witnesses,* 1971.

Juveniles; published by A. & C. Black, except as noted: *The Green Dragon and Other Plays* (edited by Cyril Swinson; contains "The Green Dragon," "In the Street," "At the Zoo," and "Three Bags Full"), 1941; *Speech Rhythms: Introductory Book* (poetry), 1942, reprinted, 1966; *Acting Rhymes,* 1948, 2nd edition, 1975; *Chorus Plays,* 1952; *The Golden Unicorn* (poetry), Methuen, 1965; *Microphone Plays,* Macmillan, 1966; *More Microphone Plays,* Macmillan, 1971; *Counting Rhymes,* 1974; *An English Year,* Chatto & Windus, 1975.

Other writings: *The World Turned Upside Down: A Modern Morality Play* (verse play), Muller, 1948; *Passion Play* (novel), Methuen, 1951. Also author of *Blackbird Pie and Other Plays.*

Editor: *The English Heart: An Anthology of English Lyric Poetry,* Falcon Press, 1946; *Plays in Verse, With Spoken Choruses* (juvenile), A. & C. Black, 1947; *Speech of Our Time,* Hinrichsen, 1948; *By Word of Mouth: An Anthology of Prose for Reading Aloud,* Methuen, 1950; *Briar Rose, and Other Plays With Choruses* (juvenile), A. & C. Black, 1950; *The World of Poetry: Poets and Critics on the Art and Functions of Poetry,* Phoenix House, 1959; (and author of introduction) Helen Power, *A Lute With Three Strings* (poetry), R. Hale, 1964.

Work represented in anthologies, including *The World of Poetry,* 1959. Contributor to magazines and newspapers, including *Observer, Punch, Poetry Review,* and *Countryman.*

SIDELIGHTS: An English Year contains poetry about the countryside and its animal and human citizens. In a *Books and Bookmen* review of Sansom's work, Derek Sanford remarked that the poet captures life in the country for the child who delights in it. Sansom, he said, is able "to enrich life through verbal definition."

BIOGRAPHICAL/CRITICAL SOURCES: Books and Bookmen, December, 1975.*

*   *   *

SAPINSLEY, Alvin   1921-

PERSONAL: Surname is pronounced Sapp-INZ-lee; born November 23, 1921, in Providence, R.I.; son of Alvin Theodore (an attorney) and Charlotte (Lewine) Sapinsley; married Elizabeth York, September 4, 1951 (deceased); children: Gregory, Ann. *Education:* Bard College, B.A., 1942. *Home:* 15029 Greenleaf St., Sherman Oaks, Calif. 91403. *Agent:* Adams Ray Rosenberg, 9200 Sunset Blvd., Los Angeles, Calif. 90069.

CAREER: Writer, 1947—; Granville Productions, Inc., Hollywood, Calif., president, 1978—. *Member:* American Civil Liberties Union, Dramatists Guild, Writers Guild, Phi Beta Kappa. *Awards, honors:* Award from Mystery Writers of America, 1955, for "Sting of Death"; TV-Writers' Annual Award, 1966-67, for "Code Name Heraclitus."

WRITINGS—Television programs; broadcast by Columbia Broadcasting System (CBS-TV): "Teias, the King," February 3, 1950; "Mr. Mummery's Suspicion," February 17, 1950; "Sanctuary in Paris," April 14, 1950; "The Good Companions," June 23, 1950; "Sredni Vashtar," October 3, 1950; "Over Twenty-One," December 19, 1950; "Ruggles of Red Gap," February 27, 1951; "Don Quixote," January 14, 1952; "The Angel Was a Yankee," February 3, 1952; "Adventures of Tom Sawyer," February 10, 1952; "The Rose and the Ring," February 24, 1952; "A Connecticut Yankee in King Arthur's Court," May 19, 1952; "The Astonishing Mr. Glencannon," November 10, 1952.

Broadcast by National Broadcasting Co. (NBC-TV), except as noted: "Phantom Lady," April 24, 1950; "A Star Is Born," February 26, 1951; "Stairway to Heaven," April 29, 1951; "Cashel Byron's Profession," January 14, 1952; "Mr. Loveday's Little Outing," April 20, 1953; "Fred Allen's Sketchbook," first broadcast by American Broadcasting Co. (ABC-TV), May 24, 1953; "Cakes and Ale," October 26, 1953; "Our Hearts Were Young and Gay," February 15, 1954; "Ten Minute Alibi," September 13, 1954; "Notre Dame de Paris," November 8-15, 1954; "Fred Allen's Sketchbook Number Two," first broadcast by ABC-TV, November 9, 1954; "A Matter of Dignity," March 7, 1955; "The Great Gatsby," May 9, 1955; (original story) "Even the Weariest River," April 15, 1956; "Key Largo," October 14, 1956; "Lee at Gettysburg," first produced by ABC-TV, January 20, 1957; "The Trials of Captain Kidd," first broadcast by ABC-TV, March 10, 1957.

Author of scripts for television series, including "Front Page," "Danger," "Crime Photographer," "Crime Syndicated," "Suspense," "Philip Morris Playhouse," "CBS Workshop," "Eyewitness," "Justice," "The Web," "Tales of Tomorrow," "Studio One," "Robert Montgomery Presents," "Elgin Hour," "Prudential Family Playhouse," "Motorola," "Omnibus," "Alcola/Goodyear Hour," "Spencer's Pilots," "Chrysler Theatre," "Night Gallery," "Judd for the Defense," "Young Lawyers," "The Virginian," "Hawaii Five-O," "Bonanza," "Ironside," "Kojak," "The Great Adventure," "Our Man Higgins," "Yancey Derringer," "Espionage," "Name of the Game," "The Man From U.N.C.L.E.," "Adventures in Paradise," "Robert Taylor's Detectives," and "Shirley Temple's Storybook."

Other: "Famous Jury Trials" (radio program), 1947; "Code Name Heraclitus" (teleplay), first broadcast by NBC-TV, December 28, 1966; "Sherlock Holmes in New York" (movie), first broadcast by NBC-TV, October 18, 1976; "The Scarlet Letter" (movie), first broadcast by WGBH-TV, 1979; "Moon of the Wolf" (movie), produced by Filmways, 1972; "Once Upon a Family" (movie), first broadcast by CBS-TV, January 23, 1980.

SIDELIGHTS: Public television's production of "The Scarlet Letter" very nearly never came to be. In 1977, Allan Knee completed a series of six scripts which were submitted to the National Endowment for the Humanities for funding. The director, Rick Hauser of WGBH, the public television station in Boston planning to produce the classic, thought that the scripts were "dynamite," but, according to Joan Kufrin of *New York,* "though the Endowment admired the work that had been done, it believed 'the proposal and scripts should be seriously reexamined before a production request can be recommended.'"

To save "The Scarlet Letter," Hauser hired Sapinsley to rewrite the scripts. "In less than six months," wrote Kufrin, "Sapinsley pared the six scripts down to four, and inserted, where possible, Hawthorne's own dialogue." When two of Sapinsley's scripts were submitted to the Endowment, WGBH received its production grant.

Critical reactions to "The Scarlet Letter" were varied. In the opinion of Michael J. Arlen of the *New Yorker,* "public television's version of 'The Scarlet Letter' was not terrible," but it was not "much good," either. The reviewer felt that the production did not follow Hawthorne's book as closely as it should have. Because the production had to appeal to so many sensibilities, Arlen maintained, it ceased to be Hawthorne's version of *The Scarlet Letter.* He called the movie's creators "serious and dutiful fellows—bound not merely by a responsibility to 'art' but also . . . by a responsibility to trustees and educators and government committees and so forth."

On the other hand, *Newsweek*'s David Gelman and Cynthia H. Wilson claimed that the movie was a "striking production that might well set the mark for a TV masterpiece series of America's own." Though they cited the teleplay's "slow start" and its "off-center casting" as problems, the critics concluded that "both the acting and the ambience seem to work in the end." Apparently, Chloe Aaron agreed since she told *Smithsonian*'s Peter Neill, "We should have a 52 weeks a year of drama like *The Scarlet Letter,* Sunday nights, nine o'clock, and I don't care where it comes from."

Besides "The Scarlet Letter," Sapinsley's other works have achieved critical acclaim. In 1976 his television movie "Sherlock Holmes in New York" proved most popular. A *Los Angeles Times* writer, Kevin Thomas, called the script "witty, painstaking, and imaginative." "What's more," he added,

"Sapinsley's dialogue is as good as his plotting." Earlier, in 1972, Sapinsley penned what *Variety* labeled "the most ambitious venture in the history of 'Hawaii Five-O.'" Written in three episodes, "V for Vashon" was "tv's version of 'The Godfather.'" "The Sapinsley teleplays," the *Variety* reviewer purported, "are expertly woven together."

Among Sapinsley's greatest critical successes are television productions written in blank verse. One, "Lee at Gettysburg," was a historical drama written, according to *Time*, in "lucid, often eloquent blank verse." The other, a western, was hailed by Jack Gould of the *New York Times* as "one of the season's fine achievements." "'Even the Weariest River,'" he lauded, "had much the quality of a Sandburg work brought to life."

BIOGRAPHICAL/CRITICAL SOURCES: *New York Times*, April 16, 1956; *Time*, January 28, 1957; *Variety*, November 30, 1972; *Los Angeles Times*, October 18, 1976; *Smithsonian*, March, 1979; *Newsweek*, April 2, 1979; *New York*, April 9, 1979; *New Yorker*, April 23, 1979.

*   *   *

SARMIENTO, Felix Ruben Garcia   1867-1916
(Ruben Dario)

BRIEF ENTRY: Born January 18, 1867, in Metapa, Nicaragua; died February 6, 1916, in Leon, Nicaragua. Nicaraguan poet, novelist, short story writer, journalist, critic, and essayist, under the pseudonym Ruben Dario. Although ranked among the greatest writers in world literature, Ruben Dario has remained relatively unknown in the United States. He was a highly cosmopolitan man, aristocratic and aloof by nature, who lived most of his life in foreign lands, either as a world-traveling correspondent for Central and South American newspapers, or as a diplomatic representative of the Nicaraguan Government. Dario is recognized as the founder and foremost exponent of Spanish modernism, and his literary reputation rests chiefly on three volumes of poems and collected short stories, beginning with *Azul* (1888) and followed by *Prosas profanos, y otros poemas* (1896; translated as *Prosas Profanos and Other Poems*, 1922) and *Cantos de vida y esperanza* (1905). The first of these works marked a revolution in Spanish literature, introducing not only the aesthetics of modernism but also a profound break from the Romantic tradition that had left Spanish literature stifled in rhetoric and convention. Evident in these poems and short stories are new metres and lengths of line, the influence of the French Parnassian poets, and Dario's adherence to the principle of "art for art's sake." *Prosas profanos*, which many critics consider Dario's best work, shows the poet at his highest point of formal development. Dario was especially interested in these poems to exploit the new poetic possibilities of French Symbolism. *Cantos de vida y esperanza*, although artistically equal or superior to *Prosas profanos*, reveals a growing melancholy in a poet changed by age and world events. His earlier, exclusive concern with art is displaced by historical and political subjects, a deepening disillusionment, and a call to a distinctly Hispanic humanism. *Biographical/critical sources: Encyclopedia of World Literature in the Twentieth Century*, updated edition, Ungar, 1967; *Twentieth Century Writing: A Reader's Guide to Contemporary Literature*, Transatlantic, 1969; *Who's Who in Twentieth Century Literature*, Holt, 1976; *Twentieth-Century Literary Criticism*, Volume 4, Gale, 1981.

*   *   *

SASSOON, Siegfried (Lorraine)   1886-1967
(Saul Kain, Pinchbeck Lyre)

PERSONAL: Born September 8, 1886, in Brenchley, Kent,

England; died September 1, 1967, in Wiltshire, England; buried in Mells, Somerset, England; son of Alfred and Theresa (Thornycroft) Sassoon; married Hester Gatty, December 18, 1933; children: George Thornycroft. *Education:* Attended Clare College, Cambridge. *Politics:* Labour. *Religion:* Catholic. *Home:* Heytesbury House, Wiltshire, England.

CAREER: Poet and author. Literary editor of the *Daily Herald*, 1919. *Military service:* British Army, 1914-18; became captain; received Military Cross. *Member:* Reform Club (London). *Awards, honors:* Hawthornden Prize and James Tait Black Memorial Prize, both 1928, both for *Memoirs of a Fox-Hunting Man;* D. Litt. from University of Liverpool, 1932, and Oxford University, 1965; Commander of the Order of the British Empire, 1951; Queen's Medal for Poetry, 1957.

WRITINGS—Poems; published anonymously: *Poems*, privately printed, 1906; *Orpheus in Diloeryum*, J. E. Francis, 1908; *Sonnets*, privately printed, 1909; *An Ode for Music*, privately printed, 1912; *Hyacinth*, 1912; *Melodies*, [London], 1912; *Apollo in Diloeryum*, 1913; *Discoveries*, privately printed, 1915; *Morning Glory*, [London], 1916; *Recreations*, privately printed, 1923; *Lingual Exercises for Advanced Vocabularians*, privately printed, 1925. Also author of *Twelve Sonnets*, 1911, and another volume entitled *Poems*.

Other poems: (Under pseudonym Saul Kain) *The Daffodil Murderer, Being the Chantrey Prize Poem*, John Richmond, 1913; *The Redeemer*, W. Heffer, 1916; *The Old Huntsman and Other Poems*, Heinemann, 1917, Dutton, 1918; *Counter-Attack and Other Poems*, introduction by Robert Nichols, Dutton, 1918; *Four Poems*, R. I. Severs, 1918; *The War Poems of Siegfried Sassoon*, Heinemann, 1919; *Picture Show*, privately printed, 1919, Dutton, 1920.

Selected Poems, Heinemann, 1925; *Satirical Poems*, Heinemann, 1926, enlarged edition, 1933; *Siegfried Sassoon*, Benn, 1926; *Nativity*, designs by Paul Nash, Faber & Gwyer, 1927; *The Heart's Journey*, C. Gaige, 1927; *To My Mother*, illustrations by Stephen Tennant, Faber & Gwyer, 1928; *On Chatterton: A Sonnet*, privately printed, 1930; *In Sicily*, illustrations by Tennant, Faber, 1930; (under pseudonym Pinchbeck Lyre) *Poems*, Duckworth, 1931; *To the Red Rose*, illustrations by Tennant, Faber, 1931; *Prehistoric Burials*, illustrations by Witold Gordon, Knopf, 1932; *The Road to Ruin*, Faber, 1933; *Vigils*, Heinemann, 1935, Viking, 1936; *Rhymed Ruminations*, Faber, 1940; *Poems Newly Selected, 1916-1935*, Faber, 1940.

Early Morning Long Ago, Chiswick Press, 1941; *Selected Poems*, Eyre & Spottiswoode, 1943; *Collected Poems*, Faber, 1947, Viking, 1949; *Common Chords*, Mill House Press, 1950; *Emblems of Experience*, Rampant Lions Press, 1951; *The Tasking*, privately printed, 1954; *An Adjustment*, foreword by Philip Gosse, Golden Head Press, 1955; *Sequences*, Faber, 1956, Viking, 1957; *Poems*, selected by Dennis Silk, Marlborough College Press, 1958; *Lenten Illuminations and Sight Sufficient*, privately printed, 1958, Downside Review, 1959; *The Path to Peace*, Stanbrook Abbey Press, 1960; *Collected Poems, 1908-1956*, Faber, 1961; *Something About Myself*, illustrations by Margaret Adams, Stanbrook Abbey Press, 1966; *An Octave: 8 September 1966*, London Arts Council of Great Britain, 1966; *Selected Poems*, Faber, 1968; *A Poet's Pilgrimage*, edited by Felicitas Corrigan, Gollancz, 1973. Also author of *Arbor Vitae and Unfoldment*, Stanbrook Abbey Press, and *A Prayer at Pentecost (1960)*, Stanbrook Abbey Press.

Prose: *Memoirs of a Fox-Hunting Man* (novel), Faber & Gwyer, 1928, Coward, 1929, new edition, Faber, 1954; special children's edition with illustrations by Arnrid Johnston, Coward, 1931; *Memoirs of an Infantry Officer* (novel), Coward-Mc-

Cann, 1930, reprinted with illustrations by Barnett Freedman, Faber, 1966, Collier, 1969; *Sherston's Progress* (novel), Doubleday, Doran, 1936; *The Memoirs of George Sherston* (contains *Memoirs of a Fox-Hunting Man, Memoirs of an Infantry Officer,* and *Sherston's Progress*), Doubleday, Doran, 1937, reprinted, Stackpole Books, 1967 (published in England as *The Complete Memoirs of George Sherston,* Faber, 1937, reprinted, 1964); *The Old Century and Seven More Years* (autobiography), Faber, 1938, Viking, 1939, reprinted with introduction by Michael Thorpe, Faber, 1968; *On Poetry,* University of Bristol, 1939; *The Flower Show Match and Other Pieces,* Faber, 1941; *The Weald of Youth* (autobiography), Viking, 1942; *Siegfried's Journey, 1916-1920* (autobiography), Faber, 1945, Viking, 1946, reprinted, White Lion, 1973; *Meredith: A Biography,* Viking, 1948; (author of introduction) Isaac Rosenberg, *The Collected Poems,* Chatto & Windus, 1962; *Letters to a Critic,* introduction and notes by Michael Thorpe, Kent Editions, 1976.

SIDELIGHTS: Sassoon was born into a wealthy family and lived the leisurely life of a cultivated country gentleman, pursuing his two major interests, poetry and fox hunting. His early work, which was printed in several slim volumes between 1906 and 1916, is considered minor and imitative, heavily influenced by John Masefield (of whose work *The Daffodil Murderer* is a parody).

His angry and compassionate poems of World War I were the first to bring him public and critical acclaim. Avoiding the sentimentality and jingoism of many war poets, Sassoon wrote of the horror and brutality of trench warfare and contemptuously satirized generals, politicians, and churchmen for their incompetence and their blind support of the war. After being wounded and decorated for heroism, Sassoon wrote an open letter of protest, refusing to fight any more. He expected to be court-martialed, but instead he was hospitalized and treated for shell-shock. Though his opinions did not change, he was persuaded by his friends to rejoin his unit at the front, where he was again wounded.

After the war, Sassoon became involved in Labour party politics, lectured on pacifism, and continued to write. His most successful works of this period were his trilogy of autobiographical novels, *The Memoirs of George Sherston.* In these he gave a thinly fictionalized account, with little changed except names, of his wartime experiences, contrasting them with his nostalgic memories of country life before the war and recounting the growth of his pacifist feelings. He later complemented the novels with three explicitly autobiographical books.

Sassoon's critical biography of Victorian novelist and poet George Meredith was well received. Sassoon recounted numerous anecdotes about Meredith portraying him vividly as a person as well as an author: "The reader lays the book down with the feeling that a great author has become one of his close neighbors," wrote G. F. Whicher in the *New York Herald Tribune Weekly Book Review.* The critical portions of the book were also praised, though some found the writing careless. But the *New Yorker* noted Sassoon's "fresh and lively literary criticism," and the *Times Literary Supplement* declared that "Mr. Sassoon gives us a poet's estimate, considered with intensity of insight, skilfully shaped as biography, and written with certainty of style."

In 1957 Sassoon became a convert to Catholicism. For some time before, his spiritual concerns had been the predominant subject of his writing. Though his later poems are usually considered markedly inferior to those written between 1917 and 1920, *Sequences* (published shortly before his conversion) has been praised by some critics. Derek Stanford, in *Books*

and Bookmen, wrote, "the poems in *Sequences* constitute some of the most impressive religious poetry of this century."

Critics differ widely in their evaluation of Sassoon's works, though it is generally acknowledged that his reputation rests mainly on the war poems and the autobiographical novels. "The dynamic quality of his war poems," according to the *Times Literary Supplement,* "was due to the intensity of feeling which underlay their cynicism." Many critics have felt that the later poems, lacking that intensity, lapsed into a facile romanticism and stilted, artificial diction. The more elaborate vocabulary and syntax contrast sharply with the blunt, economic, and colloquial language that gives the war poems much of their power. Though Sassoon's craftsmanship continued to be recognized, Stanley Kunitz called a 1935 book, *Vigils,* "sincere, pathetic, grey, monotonous and deadening," and others handed down similar judgments of that and other of Sassoon's works from the late 1920's on.

Some have maintained that Sassoon's best work is his prose, particularly the first two Sherston novels. *Memoirs of a Fox-Hunting Man* was described by the *Springfield Republican* as "a novel of wholly fresh and delightful content," and Robert Littrell of *Bookman* called it "a singular and a strangely beautiful book." While many were attracted by its portrayals of country life and the sport of fox hunting, the *Spectator* noted: "We have met no book which analyses better than this one the spirit in which the war was fought; which exposes more pitilessly the wickedness of warfare. Bitterness and irony tinge the narrative, but the poet's outlook remains."

That book's sequel was also well received. The *New Statesman* called *Memoirs of an Infantry Officer* "a document of intense and sensitive humanity." In a review in the *Times Literary Supplement,* after Sassoon's death, one critic wrote: "His one real masterpiece, *Memoirs of an Infantry Officer.* . . . is consistently fresh. His self scrutiny is candid, critical, and humourous. . . . If Sassoon had written as well as this consistently, he would have been a figure of real stature. As it is, English literature has one great work from him—almost by accident."

After Sassoon's death, Felicitas Corrigan assembled *A Poet's Pilgrimage,* consisting of selections of Sassoon's prose and poetry and emphasizing the growth of his religious feelings.

BIOGRAPHICAL/CRITICAL SOURCES: New York Times, January 27, 1918, February 3, 1929, October 12, 1930, January 2, 1949; *Times Literary Supplement,* July 11, 1918, June 3, 1926, November 1, 1947, September 18, 1948; January 4, 1957, December 7, 1973; *Saturday Review of Literature,* February 23, 1929, January 29, 1949; *Bookman,* March, 1929; *Springfield Republican,* March 3, 1929; *New Statesman,* September 20, 1930; *Poetry,* August, 1936; Siegfried Sassoon, *The Memoirs of George Sherston,* Doubleday, Doran, 1937; Sassoon, *The Old Century and Seven More Years,* Viking, 1939; Sassoon, *The Weald of Youth,* Viking, 1942; Sassoon, *Siegfried's Journey, 1916-1920,* Viking, 1946; *New Yorker,* October 9, 1948; *New York Herald Tribune Weekly Book Review,* October 24, 1948; Michael Thorpe, *Siegfried Sassoon: A Critical Study,* Oxford University Press, 1966; Sassoon, *A Poet's Pilgrimage,* edited by Felicitas Corrigan, Gollancz, 1973; *Books and Bookmen,* November, 1973.

OBITUARIES: New York Times, September 3, 1967; *London Times,* September 4, 1967; *Time,* September 15, 1967; *Newsweek,* September 18, 1967; *Publishers Weekly,* September 18, 1967; *Brittanica Book of the Year,* 1968.*

—*Sketch by Tim Connor*

SAUVAIN, Philip Arthur 1933-

PERSONAL: Born March 28, 1933, in Burton on Trent, Staffordshire, England; son of Alan (an education officer) and Norah (a teacher; maiden name, Humphreys) Sauvain; married June Maureen Spenceley (a teacher), July 27, 1963; children: Richard Philip, Rachel Anne. *Education:* Emmanuel College, Cambridge, M.A. (with honors), 1956; Institute of Education, London, postgraduate certificate in education, 1957. *Home and office:* 70 Finborough Rd., Stowmarket, Suffolk 1P14 1 PU, England.

CAREER: Steyning Grammar School, Sussex, England, head of geography department, 1957-61; Penistone Grammar School, Sheffield, England, head of geography department, 1961-63; James Graham College, Leeds, England, senior lecturer in geography, 1963-68; Charlotte Mason College of Education, Ambleside, England, head of environmental studies department, 1968-74; writer, 1974—. Member of committee of Educational Writers' Group, 1978. *Member:* Incorporated Society of Authors, Playwrights, and Composers. *Awards, honors:* Honorary senior scholar of Emmanuel College, Cambridge, 1956; *Looking Around in Town and Country* named runner-up, 1975, for Times Educational Supplement Information Book Award.

WRITINGS—All juvenile; published by Hulton Educational Publications, except as noted: *A Map Reading Companion,* 1961; *Lively History,* Volume I: *Lord and Peasant: Old Stone Age to 1485 A.D.,* 1970, Volume II: *Town and Country: 1485-1789,* 1971, Volume III: *Empire, City, and Industry: 1789-1901,* 1973, Volume IV: *Conflict, Science, and Society: The Twentieth Century,* 1973; *Practical Geography,* Volume I: *Pictures and Plans,* 1970, Volume II: *Facts, Maps, and Places,* 1970, Volume III: *Man and Environment,* 1971, Volume IV: *Advanced Techniques and Statistics,* 1972.

The First Men on the Moon, 1972; *The Great Wall of China,* 1972; *Looking Around in Town and Country,* F. Watts, 1975; *Looking Back,* F. Watts, 1975; *Junior Guide to Arundel Castle,* F. Watts, 1978; *Certificate Mapwork,* 1979; *Macmillan Local Studies Kit,* Macmillan, 1979; *First Elements of Geography: The British Isles,* 1980; (with Michael Carrier) *Topics for Discussion and Language Practice: Books I and II,* 1980; *The World About Us: Science Discussion Pictures,* Macmillan, 1981.

"Environmental Studies" series; published by Hulton Educational Publications: *Exploring at Home,* 1966; *Exploring Britain,* 1966; *Exploring the World,* 1967.

"Discovery" series; published by Macmillan: *Where You Live,* 1970; *Where You Go to School,* 1970; *About the Weather,* 1970; *In a Garden,* 1970; *Along a Road,* 1970; *Near Your Home,* 1970.

"Breakaway" series; published by Hulton Educational Publications: *Finding a Job and Settling Down,* 1973; *People With Problems,* 1973; *Keeping the Peace,* 1974; *Living in Towns,* 1974; *Vanishing World,* 1974; *World of Adventure,* 1974; *Enjoying Ourselves,* 1976; *Where the Money Goes,* 1976.

"Exploring the World of Man" series; published by Hulton Educational Publications: *Man the Builder,* 1973; *Man the Farmer,* 1973; *Man the Traveller,* 1973; *Man the Manufacturer,* 1974; *Man the Pleasure Lover,* 1974; *Man the Warrior,* 1974; *Man the Discoverer,* 1975; *Man the Citizen,* 1976; *Man the Artist,* 1977; *Man the Thinker,* 1977.

"First Look" series; published by F. Watts: *Maps and How to Read Them,* 1973; *Winds,* 1975, *Dinosaurs,* 1976; *Discoveries and Inventions Before the Age of Steam,* 1977; *Rain,* 1978; *Snow and Ice,* 1978.

"Environment Book" series; published by Macmillan: *By Land, Sea, and Air,* 1974; *On a Farm,* 1974; *On a Holiday,* 1974; *Under Your Feet,* 1974; *Back in the Past,* 1978; *Dial 999,* 1978; *In Town,* 1978; *Made in Britain,* 1978.

"Imagining the Past" series; published by Macmillan: *Prehistoric Britain,* 1976; *Roman Britain,* 1976; *A Castle,* 1976; *An Abbey,* 1976; *A Medieval Town,* 1976; *A Tudor Mansion,* 1976; *Stuart Britain,* 1980; *An Eighteenth-Century Village,* 1980; *A Georgian Town,* 1980; *A Regency Coaching Inn,* 1980; *A Victorian Factory Town,* 1980; *The Victorian Seaside,* 1980.

"Looking Around" cards series; published by F. Watts: *Houses and Towns,* 1978; *Villages and Farms,* 1978; *Hills and Coasts,* 1979; *Valleys and Routeways,* 1979.

"Story of Britain" series; published by Macmillan: *Early Britain,* 1980; *Britain in the Middle Ages,* 1980; *Tudors, Stuarts, and Georgians,* 1980; *From Nelson to the Present,* 1980.

"Junior History of Britain" series, four books, Macmillan, in press.

Contributor of articles to periodicals, including *Times Educational Supplement, Teachers World, Child Education, Pictorial Education,* and *British Heritage.*

WORK IN PROGRESS: "Junior Geography" series, four books, publication by Macmillan expected in 1983; "Secondary School Geography" series; a book on Britain's heritage.

SIDELIGHTS: Sauvain's book *Looking Around in Town and Country* is a treasure chest of information for young readers. The author explores towns, coasts, railways, and other locations. He describes buildings along the way and explains the purposes of objects encountered. Designed as a pictorial guide to the environment of the British Isles, the book offers several indexes that are useful to young readers of varied levels of understanding. Sauvain drew on his experience as a teacher of environmental studies when preparing the work, and in 1975 the book was runner-up for the *Times Educational Supplement* Information Book Award.

Sauvain followed *Looking Around in Town and Country* with *Looking Back,* a pictorial encyclopedia to British history that highlights the key events, personalities, and facets of everyday life in the past. The author used his own color transparencies to show children the many buildings, relics, and monuments still seen today in all parts of Britain.

Sauvain told *CA:* "I always find it helpful to envisage the final layout of words and pictures at the time of writing the text. For some time now I have been photographing many of the characteristic features that illustrate the history and geography of the British Isles. My color transparencies and monochrome prints illustrate most of the books I have written. Indeed, some of my recent work, notably a set of science-discussion pictures for five to seven year olds, has been largely photographic.

"I first started to write in response to a challenge from an old acquaintance who said, 'Why not write a book for schools?' It was also something of a family tradition. My father and my maternal grandfather (G. A. Humphreys) had both written school textbooks in the 1930's, and my great-grandfather Aime Sauvain wrote a French textbook, *Presque mot a mot,* in 1887. I shall always remember the day my first book appeared in November, 1961, because I drove into the back of a vehicle half an hour after receiving my complimentary copies through the post!

"Writing and preparing materials for use by children in schools is one of the essential, but least glamorous, branches of authorship. It imposes certain constraints that many general writers might find particularly irksome, such as restricted vocabulary and writing within strict word limits to the page."

BIOGRAPHICAL/CRITICAL SOURCES: Teachers World, June 3, 1966, January 6, 1967, June 18, 1976; *Geographical Journal,* March, 1965; *Times Educational Supplement,* July 24, 1970, June 8, 1973; *Educational Development Centre Review,* January, 1972; *Teacher,* June 8, 1973, August 23, 1974, October 25, 1974; *Learning for Living,* May, 1974; *Growing Point,* September, 1975, November, 1977, September, 1978, February, 1979; *Secondary Teacher,* summer, 1977.

*   *   *

SAVA, George
See MILKOMANE, George Alexis Milkomanovich

*   *   *

SAVAGE, D(erek) S(tanley)   1917-

PERSONAL: Born March 6, 1917, in Harlow, England; son of Thomas William (a soldier) and Jessie (Wilmott) Savage; married Constance Kiernan, December 11, 1937; children: Richard, Mark, Romer, Chris, Edward, Perry. *Education:* Attended private boys' school in Edmonton, England. *Politics:* "Pacifist." *Religion:* Christian. *Residence:* Cornwall, England. *Agent:* John Farquharson Ltd., Bell House, 8 Bell Yard, London WC2A 2JU, England.

CAREER: Writer. Addenbrooke's Hospital, Cambridge, England, orderly (as conscientious objector to military service), 1941-43; land worker in Bromsash, England (as conscientious objector), 1944-48. *Member:* Amnesty International, Anglican Pacifist Fellowship (general secretary, 1960-62), Fellowship of Reconciliation.

WRITINGS: The Autumn World (poetry), Fortune Press, 1939; *Don Quixote and Other Poems,* Right Review, 1939; *A Time to Mourn* (poems), Routledge & Kegan Paul, 1943; *The Personal Principle* (criticism), Routledge & Kegan Paul, 1944; *The Withered Branch* (criticism), Eyre & Spottiswoode, 1950; *Hamlet and the Pirates* (criticism), Eyre & Spottiswoode, 1950; *The Cottager's Companion* (handbook), P. Davies, 1975, published as *Self-Sufficient Country Living,* St. Martin's, 1978.

Radio plays: "And Also Much Cattle," first broadcast by British Broadcasting Corp., November 4, 1956; "The Bow and the Beads," first broadcast by British Broadcasting Corp., January 2, 1959. Contributor to magazines and newspapers.

WORK IN PROGRESS: The Mystery of Meaulnes, a study of *Le Grand Meaulnes* by Alain-Fournier, publication expected in 1983; *England Made Them,* studies of English novelists of the 1930's.

SIDELIGHTS: Savage commented: "My major interests as a writer are literature, philosophy, and psychology. As a man and citizen I care about religious and social reform, world peace and total disarmament, abolition of the death penalty and preservation of human rights (including the right of objection to enforced military service), conservation of the natural environment, encouragement of small-scale husbandry and small industries, diminution of the powers of nation-states and multinational business enterprise, and the abolition of excessive wealth and excessive poverty."

SAVERY, Ranald   1903(?)-1974

OBITUARY NOTICE: Born c. 1903; killed by intruders who broke into his home, October 4, 1974, in Plainfield, N.J. Editor and journalist. Savery was an editor at United Press International, copy chief with Blanchard Press, editor of *Bookbinding Magazine,* and was associated with *Inland Printer.* In 1948 Savery became an associate editor of *Printing News,* where he later served as executive editor. He was also on the board of governors of the New York Club of Printing House Craftsmen. Obituaries and other sources: *Publishers Weekly,* November 4, 1974.

*   *   *

SAYERS, Dorothy L(eigh)   1893-1957
(Johanna Leigh)

BRIEF ENTRY: Born June 13, 1893, in Oxford, England; died of a thrombosis, December 17, 1957, in Witham, England. English novelist, essayist, playwright, poet, and theologian. Although best known and remembered for her detective stories, Sayers considered herself primarily a Christian apologist. After becoming one of the first women to earn a degree from Oxford, she turned to writing mysteries as a source of income. Among her detective novels are *Lord Peter Views the Body* (1928), *Strong Poison* (1930), and *Busman's Honeymoon: A Love Story With Detective Interruptions* (1937). From 1937 until her death, Sayers wrote religious essays and dramas and translated Dante's *Divine Comedy.* Her radio play *The Man Born to Be King: A Play-Cycle on the Life of Our Lord and Savior Jesus Christ, Written for Broadcasting* (1943) ran on British Broadcasting Corporation (BBC) radio for numerous years as a Christmas and Easter classic. *Biographical/critical sources: Twentieth Century Writing: A Reader's Guide to Contemporary Literature,* Transatlantic, 1969; *The Penguin Companion to English Literature,* McGraw, 1971; *Twentieth-Century Literary Criticism,* Volume 2, Gale, 1979.

*   *   *

SCADUTO, Anthony
(Tony Scaduto)

PERSONAL—Agent: Stephanie Bennett, Stephanie Bennett Agency, 148 East 53rd St., New York, N.Y. 10022.

CAREER: Feature writer for *New York Post,* New York, N.Y.; free-lance writer and journalist.

WRITINGS: The Beatles, New American Library, 1968; *Bob Dylan,* Grosset, 1972, revised edition, New American Library, 1979; (under name Tony Scaduto) *Mick Jagger: Everybody's Lucifer,* McKay, 1974; (under name Tony Scaduto) *Frank Sinatra,* M. Joseph, 1976; *Who Killed Marilyn?,* Manor, 1976; *Scapegoat: The Lonesome Death of Bruno Richard Hauptmann,* Putnam, 1976; *A Terrible Time to Die,* Putnam, 1978.

SIDELIGHTS: Though his later books have focused on crime, Scaduto is best known for his biographies of popular musicians, especially Bob Dylan and Mick Jagger. An earlier, brief biography of the Beatles attracted little attention, but *Bob Dylan* was a popular success.

Bob Dylan was carefully researched: Scaduto interviewed dozens of people who had known Dylan during his boyhood in Minnesota and his early years in New York, and finally interviewed Dylan himself. He uncovered many facts about Dylan's life that Dylan had concealed, and exposed much of the biographical information Dylan had given reporters over the years as fiction. J. D. O'Hara, in the *New Republic*, praised the biography for its effectiveness in doing away "with many of the old stories about Dylan's childhood—the cruel parents; the rebellious kid who ran away eight times and was brought back seven; the wanderer . . . Dylan wasn't that kind of kid: he was too busy studying."

Peter Marin of the *New York Times Book Review* conceded that "in a few of its moments the book deeply reveals life," but "its usual tone is one of plodding and corrosive scholarship." The rock press, however, generally approved of Scaduto's biography, and Dylan himself said, upon reading an early version of the manuscript, "some of it is pretty straight, some of it is *very* straight, some of it is *exactly* the way it happened."

In *Mick Jagger: Everybody's Lucifer*, Scaduto tells the story of the Rolling Stones, portraying lead singer Jagger as a superstar whose carefully cultivated stage persona came to dominate his private life so strongly that one of his entourage suggested he had become a parody of himself. Discussing this book's style in the *Washington Post Book World*, J. D. O'Hara called it "florid" and "godawful," though he noted that Scaduto's description of the infamous Altamont concert, where a spectator was stabbed to death by Hell's Angels who had been hired to guard the stage, was "nicely done."

In *Scapegoat*, Scaduto, who was a police reporter for several years, turned from pop music to the subject of crime, examining the trial of Bruno Richard Hauptmann. Scaduto concludes that Hauptmann, who was executed in 1936 for the kidnapping and murder of the infant son of Charles Lindbergh, was framed. In an interview quoted in *Newsweek* Scaduto said: "Every piece of physical evidence introduced at the trial was fabricated, distorted or tampered with. Each of the key witnesses lied." The book details the flaws in the prosecution's case, points out the failure of Hauptmann's lawyer to make use of exculpatory evidence, and asserts that the judge, the police, the prosecutor, and the witnesses, believing Hauptmann to be guilty, and under the pressure of violent public opinion, were willing to twist the truth to prevent his acquittal.

Reviewers found Scaduto's arguments persuasive. Hugh Brogan, critic for the *Times Literary Supplement*, wrote: "By page 200 I was convinced that Richard Hauptmann, the alleged kidnapper and murderer of Charles Lindbergh's son, was indeed the victim of a gross miscarriage of justice. . . . Mr. Scaduto has done much in proving, by patient honest argument, that Clarence Darrow was right when he said that no man should be executed on such flimsy evidence; and that a fair trial would have set Hauptmann free without a stain on his character." And "even the most skeptical reader of this fascinating inquiry," observed John L. Hess of the *New York Times Book Review*, "must conclude that Hauptmann's life was taken without due process of law."

In 1978 Scaduto published *A Terrible Time to Die*, a novel about a New York reporter investigating organized crime and political corruption.

BIOGRAPHICAL/CRITICAL SOURCES: Commentary, April, 1969; Anthony Scaduto, *Bob Dylan*, Grosset, 1972; *New York Times Book Review*, February 20, 1972, January 16, 1977; *New Republic*, May 20, 1972; *Washington Post Book World*, July 21, 1974; *Newsweek*, December 6, 1976; *Spectator*, April 2, 1977; *Times Literary Supplement*, April 22, 1977.*

* * *

SCADUTO, Tony
    See SCADUTO, Anthony

SCHAEFER, Nicola Caroline 1939-

PERSONAL: Born January 11, 1939, in Oxford, England; daughter of Hubert Frederick (an inventor) and Cordelia Mary Vashti (an artist; maiden name, Saleeby) Sewell; married Ted Schaefer (a university professor), December 12, 1960; children: Catherine, Dominic, Benjamin. *Education:* Attended Catholic girls' school and Radcliffe Infirmary. *Politics:* "Vague." *Religion:* "Vague, but with a strong bent, in my middle age, back to Catholicism." *Home:* 210 Oak St., Winnipeg, Manitoba, Canada R3M 3R4.

CAREER: Writer.

WRITINGS: Does She Know She's There?, Doubleday, 1978. Also author of numerous articles on mental and physical disabilities and of radio shows.

SIDELIGHTS: According to Laird Rankin of *Trib Magazine*, Nicola Schaefer writes in order to spread her philosophy "that even the multiple handicapped are people who . . . deserve a home or a place in the community instead of isolated lives in institutions." *Does She Know She's There?*, the author's first book, promotes this belief by recounting Schaefer's life with her daughter Catherine. Catherine was born with brain damage so extreme that it impaired her mental and physical development and left her vulnerable to other ailments such as circulatory and respiratory problems. "I decided to accept and enjoy Catherine for what she was—which never would be much—and resigned myself to the fact that I would have a much more definite role towards her than Ted [Schaefer's husband] would, and a more immediate responsibility for her, because I would be with her most of the time," Schaefer told Rankin.

From her life with Catherine, the author produced a book that, said Rankin, "will break you up and break your heart." Whether in the book or in articles, Schaefer stresses "the inherent dignity of all people, however disabled, and their right to live as normally as possible in the community." Recognizing that there is not enough material of this sort, Schaefer abandoned "an inconsequential, funny, dirty novel about amateur musicians" to continue fighting for society's understanding of the handicapped.

She told *CA:* "I wrote *Does She Know She's There?*, the biography of my daughter, Catherine, who was born with severe and widespread brain damage, to show that even someone who is very retarded, speechless, screwed up in a wheelchair, etc., is as important as anyone else and can, *IF* good community support programs are available, lead a happy, dignified life—rather than end up a twisted, tube-fed wreck in an institution. My main interest these days is helping to create community programs for people of all ages with severe multiple handicaps."

AVOCATIONAL INTERESTS: Classical music.

BIOGRAPHICAL/CRITICAL SOURCES: Trib Magazine, May 17, 1980.

* * *

SCHARLATT, Hal 1936(?)-1974

OBITUARY NOTICE: Born c. 1936; died of a heart attack, February 19, 1974, in West End, N.J. Editor. Scharlatt was vice-president and editor in chief of the publishing firm E. P. Dutton & Co., having joined the firm in 1969. At his death he was editing a biography by Richard Holmes entitled *Shelley:*

The Pursuit. Obituaries and other sources: *New York Times*, February 21, 1974; *Publishers Weekly*, March 4, 1974.

*   *   *

SCHERER, Raymond Lewis 1919-

PERSONAL: Born June 7, 1919, in Fort Wayne, Ind.; son of Arnold F. and Eleanor M. (Vonderau) Scherer; married Barbara Hetzner, December 28, 1950; children: Nancy, David. *Education:* Valparaiso University, A.B., 1942; University of Chicago, M.A., 1947. *Home:* 3550 Springland Lane, Washington, D.C. 20008. *Office:* RCA Corp., 1800 K St., Northwest Suite 810, Washington, D.C. 20006.

CAREER/WRITINGS: Fort Wayne Journal-Gazette, Fort Wayne, Ind., in business department, 1940-41, general assignment reporter and feature writer, 1942 and 1947; National Broadcasting Co. (NBC), New York, N.Y., news editor, 1947-49, broadcaster from Pentagon, 1949-52, White House correspondent, 1952-69, London correspondent, 1969-73, Washington, D.C., correspondent, 1973-75; RCA Corp., Washington, D.C., vice-president, 1975—. *Military service:* U.S. Naval Reserve, 1942-46; became lieutenant. *Member:* Sigma Delta Chi, National Press Club, Cosmos Club, Federal City Club, F Street Club, Carlton Club, International Club, George Town Club, Garrick Club.

*   *   *

SCHMITZ, Ettore 1861-1928
(Italo Svevo)

BRIEF ENTRY: Born December 19, 1861, in Trieste, Austria (now part of Italy); died in an automobile accident, September 13, 1928, in Motta di Livenza, Italy. Italian novelist. Schmitz was born of Italian-German parents, and he grew up speaking both languages. He became a successful businessman before trying his hand at writing under the pseudonym Italo Svevo. His first two novels, *A Life* (1892) and *As a Man Grows Older* (1898), were ignored by Italian critics. After this initial failure, Svevo gave up writing for many years, but his work came to the attention of James Joyce, who encouraged him and helped publicize Svevo's next book, *The Confessions of Zeno* (1923). Though French critics were enthusiastic, some Italian critics found Svevo's style unpolished and even ungrammatical. His novels have little in common with either the aristocratic romances or the realistic novels of peasant life that dominated Italian literature during his lifetime: Svevo wrote of the middle class and focused on the individual consciousness, using the principles of psychoanalysis. He remains the only major Italian psychological novelist, and some regard him as the greatest Italian author since Giovanni Verga. In addition to his novels, Svevo wrote several short stories, which were collected after his death in *The Nice Old Man and the Pretty Girl and Other Stories* (1930) and *Short Sentimental Journey and Other Stories* (1967). *Residence:* Trieste, Italy. *Biographical/critical sources: Times Literary Supplement,* March 30, 1962; P. N. Furbank, *Italo Svevo: The Man and the Writer,* University of California Press, 1966; *Encyclopedia of World Literature in the Twentieth Century,* updated edition, Ungar, 1967; *New York Times Book Review,* January 21, 1968; *Penguin Companion to European Literature,* McGraw, 1969; *Twentieth-Century Literary Criticism,* Volume 2, Gale, 1979.

*   *   *

SCHNEIDER, Lambert 1900-1970

OBITUARY NOTICE: Born in 1900; died May 26, 1970, in Heidelberg, West Germany. Publisher. Schneider founded a publishing firm, Verlag Lambert Schneider, in Germany in 1925. Among the books his company published were *The Diary of Anne Frank* and a Bible translated by Martin Buber. Schneider also served as manager of the publishing house Schocken Verlag from 1932 until its close in 1938. One of the first German publishers to be licensed by the American military government, Schneider was executive secretary of the German book trade association German Boersenverein for twelve years. Obituaries and other sources: *Publishers Weekly,* June 29, 1970.

*   *   *

SCHNITZLER, Arthur 1862-1931
(Anatol)

BRIEF ENTRY: Born May 15, 1862, in Vienna, Austria; died October 21, 1931, in Vienna, Austria. Austrian physician, short story writer, dramatist, and novelist. Schnitzler's works reflected the end of Vienna's bourgeois society, which occurred at the turn of the century. His plays and novels have psychological and sociological interests in that they explore marriage, feminism, anti-Semitism, and, mostly, the subconscious aspects of sex. A practitioner of the stream of consciousness technique, Schnitzler experimented with interior monologues and produced *Leutnant Gustle* (1901), a novel some have called the first European masterpiece to utilize the technique. A friend of Sigmund Freud, the author was interested in human psychology; his writings show a deep concern for the individual as well as his personal fear of old age and death. With Hermann Bahr, Richard Beer-Hofmann, Hugo von Hofmannsthal, and Felix Salten, Schnitzler formed the "Jungwien," or the Young Vienna Group, an association opposed to German naturalism and the pseudo-classicism of Grillparzen. The Jungwien movement remained in vogue until World War I. With the coming of the war and the destruction of the Hapsburg Empire, Schnitzler grew despondent and pessimistic, feelings which are apparent in his later writings. His work, banned by the Nazis during World War II, never regained the popularity it had achieved prior to World War I. Some of his writings include *Anatol* (1893), *Liebelie* (1896; title means "Light O' Love"), *Reigen* (1897; title means "Hand Around"), *Der gruen Kakadu* (1899; title means "The Green Cockatoo"), *Der Weg ins Freie* (1908; title means "The Road to the Open"), and *Professor Bernhardi* (1912). *Residence:* Vienna, Austria. *Biographical/critical sources: McGraw-Hill Encyclopedia of World Drama,* McGraw, 1972; *Modern World Drama: An Encyclopedia,* Dutton, 1972; *Twentieth-Century Literary Criticism,* Volume 4, Gale, 1981.

*   *   *

SCHOCKEN, Theodore 1914-1975

OBITUARY NOTICE: Born October 8, 1914, in Zwickau, Germany (now East Germany); died after a long illness, March 20, 1975, in White Plains, N.Y. Schocken became manager of his family's German publishing company, Schocken Verlag, at the age of nineteen when the rest of his family emigrated to Palestine. Schocken Verlag, formed in 1931, held exclusive rights to the works of Franz Kafka. After Kafka's works were banned by the Nazis, Schocken, a Jew, fled to the United States. He fought with the United States against Germany and took part in the invasion of Italy during World War II. Returning from military duty, Schocken established Schocken Books, Inc. in White Plains. Obituaries and other sources: *Who's Who in World Jewry: A Biographical Dictionary of Outstanding Jews,* Pitman, 1972; *New York Times,* March 21,

1975; *Publishers Weekly,* March 31, 1975; *Time,* March 31, 1975.

* * *

SCHOENBAUM, Thomas John 1939-

PERSONAL: Born August 15, 1939, in Washington, D.C.; son of Matthew H. (a professor) and Cecilia M. (Konzal) Schoenbaum; married Sarajane Love (a professor), August 16, 1978; children: Lucius, Elizabeth, Geoffrey. *Education:* St. Joseph's College, Renesselaer, Ind., B.A. (summa cum laude), 1961; attended Catholic University of Louvain, 1961-62; Univeristy of Michigan, J.D. (with distinction), 1965; postdoctoral study at University of Munich, 1965-66. *Religion:* Episcopalian. *Home:* 6031 Annunciation St., New Orleans, La. 70118. *Office:* School of Law, Tulane University, New Orleans, La. 70118.

CAREER: Jenner & Block, Chicago, Ill., attorney, 1966-68; University of North Carolina, Chapel Hill, assistant professor, 1968-71, associate professor, 1971-75, professor of law, 1975-79; Tulane University, New Orleans, La., professor of law, 1980—, and director of graduate program in law and maritime law graduate program. Visiting professor at Duke University, 1973, 1978, and Hokkaigakuen University, autumn, 1980; senior Fulbright lecturer at University of Cologne, 1972-73, and University of Liege, 1978. Counsel with Smith, Patterson, Follin, Curtis, James & Harkavy, 1971-79. Member of International Council of Environmental Law; U.S. State Department law scholar in Moscow, Soviet Union, summer, 1975; member of U.S.S. *Monitor* Commission, 1979. Counsel to North Carolina governor's Commission on Economics and Environment, 1970-71; chairman of committee to formulate a coastal zone management act for North Carolina, 1972; member of North Carolina Marine Science Commission, 1975-79; member of board of directors of State of North Carolina Botanical Garden, 1978-79; member of International Commission for Environmental Law. *Member:* Maritime Law Association of the United States. *Awards, honors:* W.D. Weatherford Award from Berea College, 1979, for *The New River Controversy.*

WRITINGS: Ocean and Coastal Law Teaching Materials, two volumes, University of North Carolina Sea Grant, 1977; *The New River Controversy: The Story of a Conflict Between Energy Development and Environmental Quality* (foreword by Sam Ervin, Jr.), Blair, 1979; *Islands, Capes, and Sounds: The North Carolina Seacoast,* Blair, 1981; *Environmental Policy Law: Cases and Text,* Foundation Press, 1982. Also contributor to *La Protection du Littoral* (title means "The Protection of the Shore"), M. L. Prieur and A. C. Kiss, editors, 1977. Contributor to law journals.

SIDELIGHTS: Schoenbaum told *CA:* "In my writings thus far I have tried to demonstrate the human side of environmentalism. Preservation of natural resources is more than protecting birds, rocks and trees; it is preserving our cultural heritage, our way of life, and even our identity as a nation. That is why it is short-sighted to measure everything on the basis of cost-benefit analysis and economic and technological feasibility. We must not lose sight of the broader concerns when making decisions about our natural resources."

BIOGRAPHICAL/CRITICAL SOURCES: Raleigh News and Observer, October 24, 1976.

* * *

SCHOENBERNER, Franz 1892-1970

OBITUARY NOTICE: Born in 1892; died April 11, 1970, in Teaneck, N.J. Editor and author. Schoenberner was the last pre-Nazi editor of the anti-Nazi *Simplicissimus,* a German satirical magazine. He fled Munich for France in 1933 and in 1941 came to the United States, where he worked for the Office of War Information. Schoenberner wrote his autobiography in three volumes: *Confessions of a European Intellectual, The Inside Story of an Outsider,* and *You Still Have Your Head: Excursions From Mobility.* In addition, he contributed articles to numerous American periodicals. Obituaries and other sources: *New York Times,* April 14, 1970; *Publishers Weekly,* May 4, 1970; *AB Bookman's Weekly,* May 4, 1970.

* * *

SCHOLDERER, Victor 1880-1971

OBITUARY NOTICE: Born in 1880 in Putney, England; died September 11, 1971, in Aberystwyth, Cardiganshire, Wales. Librarian, editor, and author. Scholderer was affiliated with the British Museum for his entire career, retiring as deputy keeper of illuminated books. His publications include *Greek Printing Types, 1465-1927.* Scholderer also edited the *Catalogue of Books Printed in the XV Century.* Obituaries and other sources: *AB Bookman's Weekly,* September 27, 1971; *Medical Library Association Bulletin,* January 3, 1972; *Who Was Who Among English and European Authors, 1931-1949,* Gale, 1978.

* * *

SCHOLT, Grayce 1925-

PERSONAL: Born August 2, 1925, in Oak Harbor, Ohio; daughter of Otto L. (a carpenter) and Clara (Bebow) Scholt. *Education:* Bowling Green State University, B.S., 1948, M.A., 1949; also attended University of Vienna, 1953-54, University of Wisconsin—Madison, 1954-55, University of Michigan, 1957-62, and Oakland University, 1971-74. *Home:* 805 Kensington Ave., Flint, Mich. 48503. *Office:* Department of Language, Literature, and Philosophy, Mott Community College, 1401 East Court, Flint, Mich. 48503.

CAREER: Bowling Green State University, Bowling Green, Ohio, instructor in English, 1949-53; Mott Community College, Flint, Mich., instructor in English, 1955—. Member of board of directors of WFBE-Radio. *Member:* International Wildlife Association, National Education Association, American Association of University Professors, Children's Literature Association, Flint Institute of Music, Flint Institute of Art, Friends of the Detroit Public Library, Friends of the Flint Public Library, Friends of the Sloan Museum. *Awards, honors:* First place award from Michigan Community Theater, 1962, for play, "A Shrine for Galatea."

WRITINGS: (With Jane Bingham) *Fifteen Centuries of Children's Literature,* Greenwood Press, 1980. Also author of one-act play "A Shrine for Galatea." Contributor to magazines, including *Christian Century, Red Cedar Review, Blue Heron, Poet and Critic, Language Arts,* and *Choice.* Editor of *Three R's: A Magazine of the Arts for Children.*

WORK IN PROGRESS: The Space Behind the Wheel, poems; continuing research on history of children's literature.

SIDELIGHTS: Grayce Scholt commented: "Having long been aware of the influence that teachers had over me as a child and young adult, I should not be surprised to find that I have just completed my thirtieth year of teaching. Yet I *am* surprised, since writing has always been what I feel I really 'do.' Has the teaching interfered? Of course. There is simply no way to remain fresh to do one's own work when one spends the greater part of each working day wading through students' all-too-often murky language and thought. And yet that very act of having to deal so concretely with language has taught me more than anyone who hasn't done it could possibly understand. Most importantly, it has kept me in touch with my underpinnings; in effect, it has given my life structure. And the older I get the more I understand that lack of structure, at least for me, is devastating. In my poems, I have tried to capture the structure as well as the feel of the experience, the time, the place, the persons I write about. In my research, I have tried to shape the form as well as the feel of the data. Perhaps that, after all, is what all writing is at base, selecting, connecting, emphasizing, and all to build the structure, the architecture of a thought.''

* * *

SCHOSSBERGER, Emily Maria 1905-1979

OBITUARY NOTICE: Born September 26, 1905, in Budapest, Hungary; died of cancer, May 15, 1979. Editor. Schossberger immigrated to the United States from Vienna, Austria, in 1940. In 1941 she became the first full-time director of the University of Nebraska Press, a position she held for seventeen years. Subsequently, Schossberger served as senior foreign language editor for the University of Chicago Press and assistant director of Fordham University Press. From 1960 until her retirement in 1972, Schossberger was director of the University of Notre Dame Press. Among the honors she received during her career were the Cross of Merit from the Republic of Austria and the distinguished service medal from the Association of American University Presses. Obituaries and other sources: *Who's Who of American Women,* 2nd edition, Marquis, 1961.

* * *

SCHRAMM, Percy Ernst 1894-1970

OBITUARY NOTICE: Born in 1894; died November 13, 1970, in Goettingen, West Germany. Historian and author. Among Schramm's many writings are *Geschichte des Zweiten Weltkrieges; Hamburg, Deutschland und die Welt; Kaufleute zu Haus und ueber See;* and *Der Koenig von Frankreich.* Schramm also edited a seven-volume World War II diary of the German High Command. Obituaries and other sources: *New York Times,* November 14, 1970; *AB Bookman's Weekly,* January 4, 1971.

* * *

SCHULTZ, Philip 1945-

PERSONAL: Born January 6, 1945, in Rochester, N.Y.; son of Samuel B. and Lillian (a clerk; maiden name, Bernstein) Schultz. *Education:* Attended University of Louisville, 1963-65; San Francisco State University, B.A., 1967; University of Iowa, M.F.A., 1971. *Politics:* Democrat. *Religion:* Jewish. *Home:* 78 Charles St., No. 2R, New York, N.Y. 10014. *Office:* Department of English, New York University, 19 University Pl., Room 200, New York, N.Y. 10003.

CAREER: San Francisco Department of Social Service, San Francisco, Calif., clerk-typist, 1969-70; Kalamazoo College, Kalamazoo, Mich., writer-in-residence, 1971-72; University of Massachusetts, Boston, lecturer in creative writing, 1973-75; New York University, New York, N.Y., lecturer in creative writing, 1978—. *Member:* International P.E.N., Poetry Society of America, Writers Guild of America. *Awards, honors:* Poetry award from *Kansas City Star,* 1971; Creative Arts Public Service fellow of New York Council on the Arts, 1976, 1980; National Book Award nomination, 1979; literature award from American Academy and Institute of Arts and Letters, 1979.

WRITINGS: Like Wings (poems), Viking, 1978.

WORK IN PROGRESS: A novel; *Deep Within the Ravine,* poems; a play, for educational television.

SIDELIGHTS: Schultz commented: ''I tend to write about my personal experience and how it affects and is affected by my times. My past, in particular, has proven to be a rich source of material. My father was born in Russia, and the street I grew up on—now a lost world—was filled with immigrants from several eastern European countries. This culture offered a mysterious, if not bewildering, contrast to the American life I now lead. I write about those things which most obsess me, things I feel passionately about.''

BIOGRAPHICAL/CRITICAL SOURCES: Coda, November-December, 1979.

* * *

SCHWARTZ, George 1908-1974

OBITUARY NOTICE: Born in 1908; died September 15, 1974. Biologist, educator, and author. A fellow of the New York Academy of Sciences, Schwartz wrote biology textbooks, biology programs for the Encyclopaedia Britannica Educational Corporation, and numerous books, including *Life in a Drop of Water, Life in a Log,* and *Food Chains and Ecosystems.* Obituaries and other sources: *American Medical Association Journal,* January 28, 1950; *New York Times,* September 17, 1974; *Publishers Weekly,* September 30, 1974.

* * *

SCHWARTZ, K(arlene) V. 1936-

PERSONAL: Born February 18, 1936; married Lowell M. Schwartz. *Education:* University of Wisconsin (now University of Wisconsin—Madison), B.S., 1958, M.S., 1963; attended University of Illinois, 1963-64, and Harvard University, 1964-65. *Office:* Department of Biology, University of Massachusetts, Boston, Mass. 02125.

CAREER: University of Massachusetts, Boston, biologist, 1972—. Free-lance photographer.

WRITINGS: (With Lynn Margulis) *The Kinds of Life on Earth: An Illustrated Guide to the Five Kingdoms,* W. H. Freeman, 1981. Contributor to scientific journals.

WORK IN PROGRESS: Bibliography of Edible Wild Plants of the United States and Canada (tentative title).

* * *

SCITOVSKY, Tibor 1910-

PERSONAL: Born November 3, 1910, in Budapest, Hungary; came to the United States in 1939, naturalized citizen, 1944; son of Tibor and Hanna (Hodosi) Scitovsky; married Anne M. Aickelin, 1942 (divorced, 1966); married Elisabeth Vida (a librarian), June 21, 1968; children: Catherine M. *Education:* University of Budapest, D.J., 1932; London School of Economics and Politics, London, M.Sc., 1938. *Home:* 1175 North Lemon Ave., Menlo Park, Calif. 94025.

CAREER: Worked as bank clerk in Budapest, Hungary, 1933-34; researcher for London & Cambridge Economic Service, 1938-39; associated with Department of Commerce, 1938-46; Stanford University, Stanford, Calif., professor of economics, 1946-58; University of California, Berkeley, professor of economics, 1958-66; Yale University, New Haven, Conn., Heinz Professor of Economics, 1968-70; Stanford University, Eberle

Professor of Development Economics, 1970-76; University of London, London School of Economics and Political Science, London, England, professor of economics, 1976-78; University of California, Santa Cruz, professor of economics, 1978—. Fellow at Development Centre of Organization for Economic Cooperation and Development, Paris, France, 1966-68. *Military service:* Hungarian military, 1932-33; U.S. Army, 1943-45; became second lieutenant; received Bronze Star. *Member:* American Academy of Arts and Sciences, American Economic Association (fellow; vice-president, 1969-70).

WRITINGS: Welfare and Competition, Irwin, 1951; *Economic Theory and Western European Integration,* Stanford University Press, 1958; *Papers on Welfare and Growth,* Stanford University Press, 1964; (with I.M.D. Little and M. F. Scott) *Industry and Trade in Some Developing Countries,* Oxford University Press, 1970; *Money and the Balance of Payments,* Rand McNally, 1970; *The Joyless Economy,* Oxford University Press, 1976.

WORK IN PROGRESS: The Common Sense of Macroeconomics, for Oxford University Press; research on the causes and process of inflation.

* * *

SCOBIE, James R(alston) 1929-1981

OBITUARY NOTICE—See index for *CA* sketch: Born June 16, 1929, in Valparaiso, Chile; died June 4, 1981, in Del Mar, Calif. Educator, editor, and author. An expert in Latin American history, Scobie taught at the University of California at Berkeley and Indiana University before joining the University of California at San Diego in 1977 as a professor of history. He wrote several books in his field, including *Argentina: A City and a Nation, Revolution on the Pampas: A Social History of Argentina Wheat, 1860-1910,* and *La lucha por la consolidacion de la nacionalidad argentina, 1852-1862.* Scobie also edited *Correspondencia Mitre-Elizalde* and *Three Years in California: William Perkins' Journal of Life at Sonora, 1849-52.* Obituaries and other sources: *New York Times,* June 11, 1981.

* * *

SCOTT, Cecil Alexander 1902(?)-1981

OBITUARY NOTICE: Born c.1902 in Stone Haven, Scotland; died after a brief illness, July 10, 1981, in Mount Kisco, N.Y. Editor. Scott was best known for editing the Pulitzer Prize-winning books *Tales of the South Pacific* by James Michener, *The Crooked Corridor* by Elizabeth Stevenson, and *The Guns of August* by Barbara Tuchman. He also worked on Harriet Arnow's *The Dollmaker.* Obituaries and other sources: *Chicago Tribune,* July 17, 1981; *Publishers Weekly,* August 7, 1981.

* * *

SCOTT, Duncan Campbell 1862-1947

BRIEF ENTRY: Born August 2, 1862, in Ottawa, Ontario, Canada; died December 19, 1947, in Ottawa, Ontario, Canada. Canadian public official, poet, and short story writer. Considered one of Canada's best early twentieth-century poets, Scott was a regionalist whose works usually studied the Indians inhabiting the northern wilderness of Canada. Scott's position as deputy superintendent of the department of Indian affairs enabled him to accurately portray the lives of North American Indians as well as those of the other inhabitants of French Canada. His poetry is marked by its descriptive and rhythmic qualities in addition to its verbal color and poetic jest. The

most common theme found in his poetry is man's conflict with nature. At one time Scott collaborated with Archibald Lampan, a man who greatly influenced him, and with Wilfred Campbell to produce "At the Mermaid Inn," a weekly series that appeared in the *Toronto Globe.* He also edited a series of biographies, *The Makers of Canada,* with Pelham Edgar. In 1934, King George V named the poet a Companion of the Order of St. Michael and St. George, and in 1899 he was made a fellow of the Royal Society of Canada. Scott was a fellow of the Royal Society of Literature of Great Britain, and he received honorary degrees from the University of Toronto and from Queen's University in Kingston. His writings include *In the Village of Viger* (1896), *The Witching of Elspie* (1923), and *Green Cloister* (1935). *Residence:* Ottawa, Ontario, Canada. *Biographical/critical sources: Twentieth Century Authors: A Biographical Dictionary of Modern Literature,* H. W. Wilson, 1942, first supplement, 1955; *The Oxford Companion to Canadian History and Literature,* Oxford University Press, 1967.

* * *

SCOTT, Evelyn 1893-
(Ernest Souza)

PERSONAL: Given name, Elsie Dunn; born January 17, 1893, in Clarksville, Tenn.; married Frederick Creighton Wellman (a painter and writer under pseudonym Cyril Kay Scott), December 20, 1913 (marriage ended); married John Metcalfe (a writer), February 20, 1928; children: (first marriage) Creighton. *Education:* Attended Tulane University. *Home:* Jove Cottage, Walberswick, Suffolk, England.

CAREER: Writer. *Member:* Authors League of America (vice-president). *Awards, honors:* Guggenheim fellowship, 1932.

WRITINGS—Novels: *The Narrow House,* Boni & Liveright, 1921 (published in England as *Bewilderment,* Duckworth, 1922), reprinted, Arno, 1977; *Narcissus,* Harcourt, 1922, reprinted, Arno, 1977; *The Golden Door,* F. Seltzer, 1925; *Migrations: An Arabesque in Histories,* A. & C. Boni, 1927; *The Wave,* J. Cape & H. Smith, 1929; (under pseudonym Ernest Souza) *Blue Rum,* J. Cape & H. Smith, 1930; *A Calendar of Sin: American Melodramas,* two volumes, J. Cape & H. Smith, 1931; *Eva Gay: A Romantic Novel,* H. Smith & R. Haas, 1933; *Breathe Upon These Slain,* H. Smith & R. Haas, 1934; *Bread and a Sword,* Scribner, 1937; *The Shadow of the Hawk,* Scribner, 1941.

Other: *Precipitations* (poems), N.L. Brown, 1920; *Escapade* (autobiography), T. Seltzer, 1923, reprinted, Scholarly Press, 1971; (with husband, Cyril Kay Scott) *In the Endless Sands: A Christmas Book for Boys and Girls* (juvenile), Holt, 1925; *Ideals: A Book of Farce and Comedy* (short stories), A. & C. Boni, 1927; *Witch Perkins: A Story of the Kentucky Hills* (juvenile), Holt, 1929; *The Winter Alone* (poems), J. Cape & H. Smith, 1930; *Billy, the Maverick* (juvenile), Holt, 1934; *Background in Tennessee* (autobiography), R. M. McBride, 1937; *The Fourteen Bears, Summer and Winter* (juvenile), Golden Press, 1973.

Contributor to periodicals, including *Mercury, American Spectator, American Poetry Journal, Dial, Everyman, Nation, New Republic, Outlook, Poetry, Saturday Review of Literature, Scribner's,* and *Yale Review.*

SIDELIGHTS: Evelyn Scott began publishing short stories at the age of fourteen. She was also the youngest student to be admitted to the H. Sophie Newcomb Memorial College of Tulane University. At the age of twenty, she ran away to Brazil with Frederick Wellman, a writer under the pseudonym Cyril Kay Scott. The couple lived in the South American country for three years, enduring poverty and isolation. Out of her experiences in Brazil came her first autobiography, *Escapade*. In the book she describes her psychological states as they shift with her misfortunes. Although many critics acknowledged the book's lasting literary worth, they also noted Scott's tendency to dwell on her often depressing turn of mind. A *Boston Transcript* reviewer complained: "Her autobiography is precisely what we should expect from a reading of her novels. She is clearly more interested in the sickness than in the health of her mind. She delights in exposing both sicknesses." R. M. Lovett of *New Republic* concurred, stating that "Scott is too constantly preoccupied with her art, naturalistic or psychic, and relief from this insistence is even more needed than from the intense brooding bitterness with which she sees her world."

Scott's first novel, *The Narrow House*, received mixed reviews. A *Nation* critic praised the author, asserting that "the acuteness of her perceptions, both sensory and psychical, is so high that she has achieved the purpose she entertained with consummate skill and completeness." Agreeing, Sinclair Lewis raved: "Salute to Evelyn Scott! She belongs, she understands, she is definitely an artist. 'The narow house' is an event; it is one of those recognitions of life by which life itself becomes the greater." R. D. Townsend of *Outlook* thought otherwise, finding the book "so unhappy and so revolting in its realism that neither the reader nor anybody in the book has a happy moment from beginning to end."

A later novel, *Eva Gay*, received generally favorable reviews. Mary Ross, writing for *Books*, claimed that "here in even more striking degree than in her earlier books is the almost savage sincerity that is the quality of Evelyn Scott's writing, a will to realize the emotions that surge beneath protective idealizations we have built for them." Dorothy Van Doren of *Nation* wrote, "Scott has always been and still is a highly serious and a far more than commonly powerful novelist; and her novels are important works of art."

Breathe Upon These Slain, Scott's next novel, met with an enthusiastic reception. Van Doren applauded the author, commenting that "Scott has done in prose what T. S. Eliot did in poetry." Lewis Gannett of the *New York Herald Tribune* likewise added that "it is the passionate will to freedom, to honesty, the unflinching integrity, which gives its dignity and its agony to all Evelyn Scott's work. . . . When the tumult and the shouting over more 'popular novels' die, I think Evelyn Scott's work will still be read and remembered."

Scott's following novel, *Bread and a Sword*, took fourteen years to complete. The work impressed some critics, including Van Doren, who wrote: "Nobody describes family bickering brought on by poverty more relentlessly than Mrs. Scott does. Nobody delineates stupidity and vulgarity more devastatingly." *Saturday Review*'s Paula Snelling was also impressed with the work. "It is doubtful if anyone now using the novel form has brought to the task so clear, so informed, so unillusioned a mind as has Evelyn Scott." Some other critics, however, called the story boring and crude, and a *Time* reviewer found Scott's style to be entirely lacking in humor and discipline.

Scott's poetry has not fared well with critics. *Precipitations*, the author's first book of poems, provoked a *Springfield Republican* reviewer to observe that Scott's "poems are sometimes poignant, sometimes so lacking in detail as to be meaningless." A *Dial* critic contended that the book "loses when taken as a whole; it seems to borrow its colour from the bad poems rather than from the good." Scott's next volume of

verse did not appear until ten years later. Of *The Winter Alone*, the *New York Evening Post*'s Emanuel Eisenberg wrote, "when everything has been said, Evelyn Scott is not a poet and 'The Winter Alone' is less a book of poems than a series of expositions of the way this woman lives." Babette Deutsch found the book "disappointing, mainly because Mrs. Scott does not sustain her own highest standards of excellence."

BIOGRAPHICAL/CRITICAL SOURCES: New York Times, March 13, 1921, July 2, 1922, April 10, 1927, October 18, 1931, May 27, 1934, April 18, 1937, April 27, 1941; *Literary Review of the New York Evening Post*, April 2, 1921, July 15, 1922; *Nation*, April 20, 1921, November 11, 1931, April 12, 1933, June 13, 1934, April 24, 1937; *Dial*, May, 1921; *Springfield Republican*, May 8, 1921; *Outlook*, June 8, 1921; *Boston Transcript*, April 15, 1923; *New Republic*, August 22, 1923, May 19, 1937; *Greensboro Daily News*, September 16, 1923; *New York Sun*, April 14, 1925; *New York Herald Tribune Books*, January 24, 1926, October 23, 1927, October 6, 1929, April 27, 1930, October 11, 1931, April 9, 1933, May 20, 1934, April 25, 1937, October 17, 1937; *New York Evening Post*, October 29, 1927, March 29, 1930; *Saturday Review of Literature*, October 31, 1931, April 15, 1933, May 26, 1934; *Bookman*, November, 1931; *New York Herald Tribune*, May 21, 1934; *Time*, April 19, 1937.*

*   *   *

SCOTT, Justin
(J. S. Blazer)

PERSONAL: Son of Leslie (a writer) and Lily K. (a writer) Scott. *Residence:* New York, N.Y. *Office:* c/o Dial Press, 1 Dag Hammarskjold Plaza, 245 East 47th St., New York, N.Y. 10017.

CAREER: Writer. *Awards, honors:* Nomination for best first novel of the year from Mystery Writers of America for *Many Happy Returns*.

WRITINGS: Many Happy Returns, McKay, 1973; (under pseudonym J.S. Blazer) *Deal Me Out*, Bobbs-Merrill, 1973; *Treasure for Treasure*, McKay, 1974; (under Blazer pseudonym) *Lend a Hand*, Bobbs-Merrill, 1975; *The Turning*, Dell, 1978; *The Shipkiller* (alternate selection of Book-of-the-Month Club, Playboy Book Club, Dolphin Book Club, and Nautical Book Club), Dial, 1978; *Normandie Triangle*, Atheneum, 1981.

SIDELIGHTS: Scott was born into a family of writers—his mother was a novelist, and his father wrote the "Walt Slade" western series. Scott told a *Publishers Weekly* reporter that although his childhood ambition was to follow his parents' career, he "somehow . . . just didn't" until boredom with his job on an industrial magazine eventually led him to try his hand as a writer.

Scott's first book, a humorous crime novel titled *Many Happy Returns*, fared well with critics and received a nomination from the Mystery Writers of America for the best first novel of the year. Although Scott's subsequent comic novels were similarly well received, he observed a decline in the market for humorous fiction and began writing thrillers instead. His first, *The Turning*, was a psychological chiller about a fanatical religious cult that takes over a small town in the Adirondacks.

This book was followed by Scott's best-selling novel, *The Shipkiller*. It is the story of a modern-day Captain Ahab who sets out to destroy an immense oil tanker that had capsized his sailboat, killing his wife and leaving him for dead. After arming his thirty-eight-foot sloop with an antitank missile, Scott's protagonist relentlessly pursues the monster ship through the Atlantic Ocean and the Persian Gulf seeking to avenge his wife's death. Like his other books, *The Shipkiller* has proved popular with critics, who noted that Scott's careful research and skillfull writing resulted in an authentically detailed and exciting suspense novel.

BIOGRAPHICAL/CRITICAL SOURCES: New York Times Book Review, May 6, 1973, October 7, 1973, July 21, 1974, October 19, 1975; *Best Sellers,* July 1, 1974; *Publishers Weekly,* September 12, 1977; *Time,* November 10, 1978.*

*   *   *

SCOTT-TAGGART, John   1897-1979

OBITUARY NOTICE: Born May 27, 1897, in Bolton-le-Moors, England; died July 30, 1979. Attorney, specialist in radio engineering, and author of books on electronics, including *Wireless Valves Simply Explained* and *Book of Practical Radio.* Obituaries and other sources: *Who's Who,* 126th edition, St. Martin's, 1974; *The Writers Directory, 1980-82,* St. Martin's, 1979. (Date of death provided by wife, Elizabeth Scott-Taggart.)

*   *   *

SEELY, Rebecca Z(ahm)   1935-

PERSONAL: Born April 2, 1935, in Johnstown, Pa.; daughter of Daniel Z. (a newspaper reporter) and Anne Hindman (Zahm) Seely; married Early Edwin Seely (in computer field), June 22, 1957; children: Laura, Daniel, Elizabeth. *Education:* Pennsylvania State University, B.A., 1957; George Washington University, B.B.A., 1979, graduate study, 1979—. *Religion:* Presbyterian. *Home:* 6609 Tina Lane, McLean, Va. 22101. *Office: Washington Post,* 1150 15th St., Washington, D.C. 20071.

CAREER: Associated with Smith Kline Corp., 1957-58; *Washington Post,* Washington, D.C., 1970—, manager of corporate advertising, beginning 1978.

WRITINGS: Tidewater Dynasty, Harcourt, 1981.

*   *   *

SEGAL, David I.   1928(?)-1970

OBITUARY NOTICE: Born c. 1928; died of a heart attack, December 27, 1970, in New York, N.Y. Editor. Obituaries and other sources: *Publishers Weekly,* January 11, 1971; *AB Bookman's Weekly,* January 18, 1971.

*   *   *

SEGRE, Dan V(ittorio)   1922-
(R. Bauduc)

PERSONAL: Born April 12, 1922, in Turin, Italy; son of Arthur Yedidia and Henriette Segre; married Rosetta Bauducco, December 8, 1948; children: Michael, Immanuel. *Education:* University of Turin, J.D., 1950; attended Ecole Sciences Politiques, 1952-55. *Religion:* Jewish. *Home:* 1 Ben Yehuda St., Jerusalem, Israel. *Agent:* Eric Linder, Manzoni, 41, Milan, Italy; and Peter Halban, P.O. Box 7474, 91-073, Jerusalem, Israel. *Office:* Department of Political Science, University of Haifa, Haifa, Israel.

CAREER: State of Israel, Ministry of Foreign Affairs, worked as diplomatic counselor, attache in Rome, first secretary in Paris, charge d'affairs in Tananarive, and deputy director of African affairs, 1949-67; Bar-Ilan University, Ramat-Gan, Is-

rael, lecturer in modern African history, 1964, senior lecturer, 1965, head of department of political science, 1966; Massachusetts Institute of Technology, Cambridge, visiting professor of comparative history, 1968; fellow at St. Antony's College, Oxford, 1967-68; Haifa University, Haifa, Israel, visiting professor, 1969-70, associate professor, 1970-80, professor of international relations, 1980—. Seminar director for Aspen Institute for Humanistic Studies. Director of Israel Overseas Broadcasting Service, 1958-60. *Military service:* British Army, 1941-46; served in Palestine; became warrant officer. Israeli Army, intelligence officer, 1948-49. *Member:* Israeli Institute for the Study of International Affairs, Societe Europeenne de Culture (member of council, 1976), Ettore Majorana Center for Scientific Culture (corresponding member), Leonard Davis Institute of International Affairs (fellow), Cosmos Club. *Awards, honors:* Officer of National Order of the Ivory Coast, 1962. Commander of Order of Merit of the Republic of Italy, 1979.

WRITINGS: Israel: A Society in Transition, Oxford University Press, 1971, revised edition published as *Israele: Societa in Transizione,* Rizzoli, 1973; *The High Road and the Low: A Study in Authority, Legitimacy, and Technical Aid,* Allen Lane, 1974; *Jerusalem Executive Seminar Readings,* Aspen Institute for Humanistic Studies, 1977; *A Crisis of Identity,* Oxford University Press, 1980. Editor with P. Mendes Flohr of *Monotheism, Tradition, and Modernisation.*

Other writings: *Israele e i suoi problemi* (title means "Israel and Its Problems"), Comunita, 1962; *Hayabeshet Hashehora* (title means "The Black Continent"), Am Hasefer, 1967.

Editor of *Jerusalem Journal of International Relations,* 1974-78. Contributor to periodicals under pseudonym R. Bauduc, including *Le Figaro* and *Il Giornale Nuovo.*

WORK IN PROGRESS: History of a Happy Jew: The Historical Record of the Segre-Ovazza Banking and Industrialist Family From 1880 to 1980.

SIDELIGHTS: Segre wrote: "What does it mean to create a national state at the end of the twentieth century? How can modernization fit into tribalism? How can tribalism—social, religious, or ideological—accomodate itself to a world standardized by technology? What does it mean to be a Jew, and in particular a nationalist Jew, in a pluralistic society? These are my main interests."

*   *   *

SELIG, Elaine Booth   1935-

PERSONAL: Born August 28, 1935, in Brooklyn, N.Y.; daughter of Harry and Ellen (Humbert) Booth; married Werner Selig, December 31, 1959 (deceased); children: Paul Booth, Joshua Simon. *Education:* Attended Pratt Institute, 1956-57, New School for Social Research, 1958-60, and School of Visual Arts, 1967. *Politics:* Liberal. *Religion:* "Humanitarian." *Home:* 252 East Seventh St., New York, N.Y. 10009. *Agent:* Alfonso Tafoya, 655 Sixth Ave., No. 212, New York, N.Y. 10010. *Office:* American Electric Power Co., 2 Broadway, New York, N.Y. 10004.

CAREER: American Electric Power Co., New York City, chartist and cartographer, 1957-61; free-lance technical illustrator, chartist, and cartographer, 1961-67; American Broadcasting Co. (ABC), New York City, designer, 1967-69; Children's Television Workshop, New York City, graphic artist for "Sesame Street," 1969-73; free-lance writer and illustrator, 1973-79; Falmouth Nursing Facility, Falmouth, Mass., community relations coordinator, publicist, and graphic artist, 1979-80; American Electric Power Co., technical illustrator, 1980—.

Artist, with one-man and group shows in New York City; consultant to "Plaza Sesamo," the Spanish-language version of "Sesame Street." *Member:* CODA, Seventh Street Cooperative Association.

WRITINGS—Novels: *Scorpion Summer,* Pocket Books, 1977; *Mariner's End,* Pocket Books, 1977; *Demon Summer,* Pocket Books, 1979. Contributor to periodicals, including *Ms.* and *Nightbeat.*

WORK IN PROGRESS: Studying the lives of older gay women.

SIDELIGHTS: Elaine Selig wrote: "My literary endeavors have been temporarily suspended since moving to New York City from Cape Cod in 1980. I am working as a technical illustrator in a detestable corporation that allows little room for individuality.

"Writing did not provide me with a living wage, and I had difficulty writing popular, salable books. In a real way, I was ahead of my time, having written a novel about widowhood in 1967 and several partial books with homosexual/transsexual themes before this topic was acceptable or salable. At present I am somewhat disenchanted with the publishing world since it, like the corporation I work for, is strictly 'big business.'

"I feel as though my life is temporarily in abeyance now that I am not writing. To console myself (or perhaps gain information for a later book) I am deeply involved with people—knowing them, observing them. Since I am gay (this transition in the last five years), I am deeply interested in women's lives, their transitions, and strengths.

"I do not intend to work at a full-time job forever. My creativity and independence are constantly assailed and beaten down. There is a terrible loss of dignity when one works for a paternalistic corporation. I intend to go back to free-lancing so as to have time to write and travel, which I have always done in the past. Traveling is *the* greatest turn-on for me, and my three published books have come out of my traveling experiences. Right now my major preoccupation is renovating an apartment I have recently purchased in 'Junkie Heaven' on the Lower East Side of New York City. The low, low maintenance will soon buy my freedom from nine-to-five drudgery.

"Freedom to *be* is essential to artists, and I am now devoting a great deal of time and energy to figuring out the angles that will allow for maximum flexibility in my life. Staying free has always been my major goal in life, and except for the past year I have lived my life the way I wanted to."

*   *   *

SELLER, Maxine Schwartz   1935-

PERSONAL: Born May 23, 1935, in Wilmington, N.C.; daughter of Benjamin David (a retail merchant) and Sylvia (Wolk) Schwartz; married Robert H. Seller (a physician), June 3, 1956; children: Michael Scott, Douglas Adam, Stuart Laurence. *Education:* Bryn Mawr College, B.A., 1956; University of Pennsylvania, M.A., 1957, Ph.D., 1965. *Politics:* "Democrat/Liberal/Feminist." *Religion:* Jewish. *Home:* 125 Crestwood Lane, Williamsville, N.Y. 14221. *Office:* Department of Social Foundations of Education, State University of New York at Buffalo, 428 Baldy Hall, Buffalo, N.Y. 14260.

CAREER: Temple University, Philadelphia, Pa., instructor, 1964, assistant professor of history, 1965-66; Bucks County Community College, Newtown, Pa., associate professor, 1966-70, professor of history, 1970-74; State University of New York at Buffalo, assistant professor, 1974-77, associate professor of social foundations of education, 1977—. Member of

editorial board of State University of New York Press, 1981-84. *Member:* American Historical Association, Organization of American Historians, American Educational Studies Association (member of executive board), Immigration History Society (member of executive board), American Educational Research Association, History of Education Society.

WRITINGS: To Seek America: A History of Ethnic Life in the United States, Jerome S. Ozer, 1977; *Ethnic Communities and Education in Buffalo, New York: Politics, Power, and Group Identity, 1838-1979* (monograph), Buffalo Community Studies Group, 1979; (editor) *Immigrant Women,* Temple University Press, 1981; *Ethnic Theater in the United States,* Greenwood Press, 1982. Contributor to education, history, ethnic studies, and women's studies journals. Member of editorial advisory board of *History Teacher,* 1976—; book review editor of *Journal of American Ethnic History,* 1981—.

WORK IN PROGRESS: The Education of Women in the United States: A Social History, publication by Temple University Press expected in 1984; earch on American Jewish women.

SIDELIGHTS: Maxine Seller commented: "Growing up in a second-generation East European Jewish family in a small town in the South during World War II (and the Holocaust) undoubtedly stimulated my interest in ethnic identity and the costs, benefits, and mechanisms for preserving it. A respect for differences—a pluralist position—runs through my scholarship on ethnicity. My feminism comes from my own experiences as wife, mother, daughter, professor, and writer—and from my observation of the lives of my grandmothers, my mother, and my women colleagues and friends.

"I write not only because academics must, but also because I enjoy it and it gives me a sense of contributing. Books, like children, have a life of their own and survive when one is gone."

AVOCATIONAL INTERESTS: Traveling, skiing, riding.

*   *   *

SETH-SMITH, Leslie James   1923-
(James Brabazon)

PERSONAL: Born January 12, 1923, in Kampala, Uganda; son of Leslie Moffat (a surveyor) and Ursula Seth-Smith; married Elizabeth Marka Webb, June 23, 1950 (divorced); married Margaret L. Lord (a researcher and script editor), June 22, 1974; children: Elizabeth Naomi, Nigel James, Penelope Marka, Helena Margaret. *Education:* Attended Sidney Sussex College, Cambridge; London University, B.A. (with honors), 1944. *Politics:* "Liberal to Left." *Religion:* "Non-dogmatic Christian." *Home:* 36 Kingswood Rd., Chiswick, London W4 5ET, England.

CAREER: British Admiralty, London, statistician, 1940-45; professional actor, under name James Brabazon, 1946-54; British Broadcasting Corp. (BBC-TV), London, dramatist, 1958—, story editor, 1963-68, director, 1968-69; Granada Television, Manchester, England, producer, 1970-81. *Member:* Royal Society of Literature (fellow), Writers Guild of Great Britain, Association of Directors and Producers, Association of Cinematograph and Television Technicians, Association of Independent Producers, British Association of Film and Television Arts.

WRITINGS—All under pseudonym James Brabazon: *Albert Schweitzer,* Putnam, 1975; *Dorothy L. Sayers: The Life of a Courageous Woman,* Scribner, 1981.

Plays: "People of Nowhere" (three-act), first produced in London at St. Thomas's Church, November 3, 1959; "Jack Adams" (three-act), first produced in Scunthorpe, England, at Civic Theatre, May 16, 1960; "The Last Alley" (three-act), first produced in London at Lyric Theatre, April 3, 1962; "Don't Talk to Me About Love" (three-act), first produced in London at Wyndham Theatre, September 29, 1963.

Television scripts: "Notes for a Love-Song," first broadcast by Associated Rediffusion Television, March 20, 1959; "Fifty-Five Columns," first broadcast by British Broadcasting Corp. (BBC-TV), August 18, 1967; "I Measured the Skies," first broadcast by BBC-TV, November 4, 1970.

SIDELIGHTS: Brabazon commented: "I've been very lucky in being able to divide my life between the lonely business of writing and the gregarious business of drama production—both of them connected with the basic business of telling stories, which I believe is still the most effective method man has devised for exploring and understanding himself.

"Theories about life—economic, political, or religious—always seem to end up by diminishing humanity. The meaning of a good story is as many-sided and ambiguous as life itself. It comes from the writer's instincts and emotions as well as his intellect, and it speaks to the instinct, emotion, and intellect of the reader, the viewer, the audience. It operates below surface level, it goes straight into the bloodstream.

"This carries a heavy responsibility. Stories that are distorted by propagandist or commercial pressures damage the mind more surely and dangerously than bad diet damages the body. Our confused age badly needs storytellers with insight, honesty, and the skill to communicate. Even to attempt the task is to be part of an honorable tradition."

BIOGRAPHICAL/CRITICAL SOURCES: London Times, May 7, 1981; *Chicago Tribune Book World*, June 21, 1981.

* * *

SHAFFER, Samuel 1910-

PERSONAL: Surname rhymes with "wafer"; born July 10, 1910, in Washington, D.C.; son of Morris (a tailor) and Fannie (Siegel) Shaffer; married Helen Buchalter (a journalist), July 9, 1933 (died July 18, 1978); children: Joan, Susan Shaffer Vaillant, Karen Shaffer Baskin. *Education:* George Washington University, A.B. (cum laude), 1931; graduate study at University of Michigan, 1931, and University of Chicago, 1932-33. *Politics:* Independent. *Home:* 3750 Kanawha St. N.W., Washington, D.C. 20015. *Office: Newsweek*, 1750 Pennsylvania Ave. N.W., Washington, D.C. 20006.

CAREER: Washington Herald (became *Washington Times-Herald*), Washington, D.C., reporter, 1936-42; *Newsweek*, New York, N.Y., White House correspondent, 1945-46, chief Congressional correspondent, 1947-75, consultant, 1975-76. *Military service:* U.S. Marine Corps, combat correspondent, 1942-45; served in Pacific theater; received Purple Heart, two battle stars, and Presidential Unit Citation. *Member:* National Press Club, White House Correspondents Association, Periodical Galleries Association (president, 1975-76), George Washington Faculty and Alumni Club.

WRITINGS: (With Jim Lucas, Pete Zurlinden, and Earl Wilson) *Betio Beachhead*, Putnam, 1945; *On and Off the Floor: Thirty Years as a Correspondent on Capitol Hill*, Newsweek, 1979.

SIDELIGHTS: Shaffer covered four Presidential election campaigns, traveling with Dwight D. Eisenhower, Adlai Steven-

son, Richard M. Nixon, and John F. Kennedy, and fourteen nominating conventions.

* * *

SHAINMARK, Eliezer L. 1900-1976
(Lou Shainmark)

OBITUARY NOTICE: Born September 13, 1900, in Warsaw, Poland; died after a long illness, January 5, 1976, in Bronx, N.Y.; buried in Beth David Cemetery, Elmont, N.Y. Executive, journalist, and editor of newspapers and magazines, including *Richmond Times Dispatch, New York Graphic, New York Evening Journal, Chicago Herald American, Esquire*, and *Coronet*. Shainmark became well known during the investigation into the kidnapping of Charles Lindbergh's son. Shainmark's advice that authorities compare the handwriting in the ransom notes with that of suspect Bruno Richard Hauptmann led to Hauptmann's later conviction. Shainmark also covered the Sacco and Vanzetti murder case in the 1920's, and he was the first journalist to expose Nazi atrocities in American newspapers. Obituaries and other sources: *Who's Who in World Jewry: A Biographical Dictionary of Outstanding Jews*, Pitman, 1972; *Who Was Who in America, With World Notables*, Volume VI: *1974-76*, Marquis, 1976; *New York Times*, January 6, 1976; *Time*, January 19, 1976.

* * *

SHAINMARK, Lou
See SHAINMARK, Eliezer L.

* * *

SHARMAT, Mitchell 1927-

PERSONAL: Born April 18, 1927, in Brookline, Mass.; son of H. Leon (a lawyer and investor) and Lucille (Brenner) Sharmat; married Marjorie Weinman (a writer), February 24, 1957; children: Craig, Andrew. *Education:* Harvard University, A.B., 1949. *Residence:* Tucson, Ariz. *Office:* c/o Doubleday & Co., Inc., 501 Franklin Ave., Garden City, N.Y. 11530.

CAREER: William Filene's, Boston, Mass., coordinator of branch store, 1949-53; Gimbel Brothers, New York City, research analyst, 1953-55; B. Altman, New York City, consultant, 1956; investor, New York City, 1957-75, and Tucson, Ariz., 1975—. *Military service:* U.S. Navy, 1945-46; became seaman first class. *Awards, honors:* Children's Choices Award from International Reading Association, 1980, for *I Am Not a Pest*.

WRITINGS—Children's books: *Reddy Rattler and Easy Eagle*, Doubleday, 1979; (with wife, Marjorie Weinman Sharmat) *I Am Not a Pest*, Dutton, 1979; *Gregory, the Terrible Eater*, Four Winds, 1980; *Come Home, Wilma*, Albert Whitman, 1980; (with M. W. Sharmat) *The Day I Was Born*, Dutton, 1980; *Spring Talk*, Houghton, 1981; *The Seven Sloppy Days of Phineas Pig*, Harcourt, 1982.

SIDELIGHTS: Sharmat wrote: "When I was in the second grade, my father encouraged me to write. He insisted that I write a composition a day. He would pay me a nickel a composition. Each was to be at least one hundred words and was to be finished by the time he got home for supper so we could discuss it before I went to bed. When I asked him what I could write about every day, he replied, 'Anything you want. Your life experiences.' So I wrote about going to school, the policeman at the corner, the gang I belonged to that terrorized the lunch recess, the dog who walked to school with me every day. About the third week, new ideas became pretty hard to come by. I got discouraged. My father got mad. I quit writing. And except for classroom assignments, I never tried writing again until a few years ago.

"My wife is a well-known children's writer. Through the years she has consulted with me when she has had problems with her own writing. As a result I've picked up by osmosis a pretty good idea of how to write stories for children. Couple that knowledge with some of the frustrations of my childhood plus a personal quirky way of looking at the world, and the result has been seven books.

"Recently I was asked what I thought was the appeal of my books to children. I replied, 'Humor, of course.' Then I reflected, and discovered that in each of my books I had also touched on some feeling that children have. As long as children have feelings, and as long as I can touch upon them in some original and entertaining way, I'll be writing new books that I hope the young public will have a chance to read."

BIOGRAPHICAL/CRITICAL SOURCES: Arizona Daily Star, January 10, 1980.

* * *

SHARP, Zerna A.   1889-1981

OBITUARY NOTICE: Born August 12, 1889, in Hillisburg, Ind.; died June 17, 1981, in Frankfort, Ind. Educator and originator of the "Dick and Jane" reading series that was used for many years in American schools. Sharp did not write the "Dick and Jane" texts, but she worked with illustrator Eleanor Campbell and several others to produce the books. In recent years feminist groups have criticized the series for portraying Jane as subordinate to Dick. Obituaries and other sources: *New York Times,* June 19, 1981; *Washington Post,* June 20, 1981; *Time,* June 29, 1981; *AB Bookman's Weekly,* July 27, 1981.

* * *

SHARPTON, Robert E(arl)   1936-

PERSONAL: Born November 23, 1936, in Tampa, Fla.; son of George and Alma (Beamon) Sharpton. *Education:* Central State University, Wilberforce, Ohio, B.S., 1958; Michigan State University, M.A., 1967, Ph.D., 1977. *Home:* 11069 Southwest 70 Ter., Miami, Fla. 33173. *Office:* Department of Mathematics, Miami-Dade Community College, Miami, Fla. 33176.

CAREER: High school mathematics teacher in West Palm Beach, Fla., 1958-61, and Elizabethtown, N.C., 1961-63; Fulbright Commission, Tehran, Iran, science and mathematics adviser to Iranian Ministry of Education, 1963-66; Fulbright Commission, Ankara, Turkey, master teacher of mathematics at Ankara College, 1966-67; high school science and mathematics teacher at school of the American community in Beirut, Lebanon, 1967-69; Miami-Dade Community College, Miami, Fla., assistant professor, 1969-71, associate senior professor of mathematics, 1971—, head of career college department, 1969-71. Lecturer at University of Maryland, summer, 1969, and University of Miami, Coral Gables, Fla., summer, 1973. Professional model and television actor; guest on television programs; consultant on mathematics and fashion. *Member:* American Association of University Professors, Association of Educational Communications and Technology, Council for Exceptional Children, Screen Actors Guild, Florida Association of Community Colleges.

WRITINGS: Designing in Strings, Cunningham, 1973; *Designing Pictures in String,* Emerson, 1974; *String Art: Step by Step,* Chilton, 1975. Contributor of articles and covers to magazines, including *Design* and *Creative Craft.*

WORK IN PROGRESS: Fashion Design; a mathematics textbook.

* * *

SHAW, Evelyn S.   1927-

PERSONAL: Born January 19, 1927, in Jersey City, N.J.; married Fred Wertheim. *Education:* New York University, B.A., 1947, M.S., 1948, Ph.D., 1952. *Home:* 3421 Jackson St., San Francisco, Calif. 94118. *Office:* Department of Biological Sciences, Stanford University, Stanford, Calif. 94305.

CAREER: Rutgers University, New Brunswick, N.J., assistant professor of biology, 1951-54; American Museum of Natural History, New York City, United States Public Health Service fellow, 1955-57, research associate, 1957-63, director of undergraduate research program, 1959-71, associate curator and curator, 1963-71; Stanford University, Stanford, Calif., senior research associate, 1972-75, adjutant professor of biological sciences, 1975—. Lecturer at Rutger's University, 1956; adjutant assistant professor at Columbia University, 1960, and adjutant professor at City University of New York, New York City, 1969-71. *Member:* American Academy of Arts and Sciences, American Society of Zoology, American Society of Ichthyologists and Herpetologists, Animal Behavior Society. *Awards, honors:* Guggenheim fellowship, 1963-64; research career development award from United States Public Health Service, 1963-71; research science award from National Institute of Mental Health, 1972—.

WRITINGS—All for children; all published by Harper: *Fish Out of School,* illustrated by Ralph Carpentier, 1970; *Octopus,* illustrated by Carpentier, 1971; *Alligator,* illustrated by Frances Zweifel, 1972; *A Nest of Wood Ducks,* illustrated by Cherryl Pape, 1976; *Elephant Seal Island,* illustrated by Pape, 1978; *Sea Otters,* 1980.

Other: (Editor with Ethel Tobach and Lester R. Aronson) *The Biopsychology of Development,* Academic Press, 1971; (contributor) Charles M. Schulz, *The Snoopy Doghouse Cook Book,* illustrated by Schulz, Determined Productions, 1979. Also author of scientific monographs and contributor of articles to periodicals, including *Natural History.*

SIDELIGHTS: Evelyn Shaw has conducted much research in the area of marine biology. She has extensively studied the physiology and habits of fish, including their mating and schooling habits. From her scientific studies, Shaw has written several informational books for children. Written for beginning readers, her volumes, such as *A Nest of Wood Ducks* and *Elephant Seal Island,* chronologically detail the life of a particular animal. Shaw presents information on how the animal eats, escapes predators, and trains its young, and she also describes the animal's home.

BIOGRAPHICAL/CRITICAL SOURCES: Fred Brewer, *Challengers of the Unknown,* Four Winds Press, 1965.

* * *

SHAW, Felicity   1918-
(Anne Morice)

PERSONAL: Born in 1918 in Kent, England; daughter of Harry (a general practitioner) and M. R. (Morice) Wolthington; married Alexander Shaw (a film director), 1939; children: three. *Education:* Attended secondary school in London, England. *Politics:* "Varies." *Religion:* Church of England. *Home:* 41

Hambleden Village, Henley-on-Thames, Oxfordshire, England.

CAREER: Writer.

WRITINGS—Novels: *The Happy Exiles*, Harper, 1956; *Sun Trap*, Anthony Blond, 1958.

Novels; under pseudonym Anne Morice: *Death in the Grand Manor*, Macmillan, 1970; *Murder in Married Life*, Macmillan, 1971; *Death of a Dutiful Daughter*, St. Martin's, 1974; *Death of a Heavenly Twin*, St. Martin's, 1974; *Killing With Kindness*, St. Martin's, 1975; *Nursery Tea and Poison*, St. Martin's, 1975; *Death of a Wedding Guest*, St. Martin's, 1976; *Murder in Mimicry*, St. Martin's, 1977; *Scared to Death*, Macmillan, 1977, St. Martin's, 1978; *Murder by Proxy*, St. Martin's, 1978; *Murder in Outline*, St. Martin's, 1979; *The Men in Her Death*, Macmillan, 1981. Also author of *Death in the Round*, St. Martin's, *Death of a Dog*, 1972, and *Murder on French Leave*, 1973.

Author of "Dummy Run" (two-act play), first produced in Henley-on-Thames, England, at Kenton Theatre, 1977.

WORK IN PROGRESS: A crime novel.

SIDELIGHTS: Felicity Shaw wrote: "I have never engaged in any research, beyond making a telephone call to one of numerous friends connected with the theater, films, and television.

"Perhaps the single slightly unusual thing about my life has been the number and variety of foreign countries I have lived in (Egypt, Kenya, Cyprus, Sudan, Tunisia, Uganda, India, France, Taiwan, and the United States), and from this the vast collection of friends I have been lucky enough to acquire in different parts of the world."

Some of her travels have been on behalf of her husband's work with UNESCO and the World Bank.

BIOGRAPHICAL/CRITICAL SOURCES: Murder Ink, September, 1977; *Murderess Ink*, October, 1979.

*   *   *

SHAW, Fred   ?-1972

OBITUARY NOTICE: Died of a heart attack, January 2, 1972, in Eatonton, Ga. Educator and columnist for the *Miami Sunday Herald*. Obituaries and other sources: *Publishers Weekly*, February 7, 1972.

*   *   *

SHAW, George Bernard   1856-1950
(Corno di Bassetto)

BRIEF ENTRY: Born July 26, 1856, in Dublin, Ireland; died November 2, 1950, in Ayot St. Lawrence, Hertfordshire, England. Anglo-Irish playwright, critic, and novelist. Considered the best-known English dramatist since Shakespeare, Shaw is known not only for his writings but for the eccentric personality he adopted. Prior to devoting himself to playwriting, the author worked as a book reviewer as well as an art and music critic. In 1882 Shaw became a socialist; by 1885 he was a prominent member of the Fabian Society. In addition, he helped to found the *New Statesman* in 1913. Shaw espoused the philosophy of creative evolution, believing that a life force is central to the evolution of man and that creative will brings intellectual evolution. Shaw was influenced by Shakespeare, Mozart, and Wagner, and, like Shelley and Dickens, he sought to reform the world. In his method of writing he was a poetic dramatist,

dealing with social and political issues plus religious and philosophical ideas. Two of his plays, "Heartbreak House" (1919) and "St. Joan" (1924), are held to be masterpieces of the twentieth century. "Mrs. Warren's Profession" (1893), an early play, was banned because it concerned a controversial subject, prostitution. In 1925, Shaw accepted the Nobel Prize, using the money to establish the Anglo-Swedish Literary Foundation. Nevertheless, he declined an Order of Merit and a peerage from the first Labour Government. His works include the plays "Man and Superman" (1903) and "Pygmalion" (1914), and *The Intelligent Woman's Guide to Socialism and Capitalism* (1928). *Residence:* Shaw's Corner, Ayot St. Lawrence, Hertfordshire, England. *Biographical/critical sources: Webster's New World Companion to English and American Literature*, World Publishing, 1973; *Twentieth-Century Literary Criticism*, Volume 3, Gale, 1980.

*   *   *

SHELLEY, Noreen   1920-

PERSONAL: Born June 21, 1920, in Lithgow, New South Wales, Australia; daughter of Frederick Thomas (a Methodist clergyman) and Mary Melvina Annie (a music teacher; maiden name, King) Walker; married Ralph Shelley (a commercial artist and sculptor); children: Jan Elisabeth, Roger James. *Education:* Attended Methodist Ladies College, 1932-38, Sydney Teachers College, 1939-40, and Sydney Art School, 1939-42. *Home:* 20 Bromborough Rd., Roseville, New South Wales 2069, Australia.

CAREER: Writer. Teacher at elementary school in Sydney, Australia, 1940-42; Sydney Teachers' Training College, Sydney, lecturer in art, beginning 1941; Abbotsleigh College, Wahroonga, New South Wales, art instructor, 1943-46; Australian Broadcasting Commission, Sydney, writer for "Children's Session" and "Kindergarten of the Air" radio shows, 1943-45; *School Magazine*, Sydney, assistant editor, 1949-60, editor, 1960-69; writer, 1969—. *Awards, honors:* Book of the year award from Australian Book Council, 1973, for *Family at the Lookout*.

WRITINGS—Juveniles: *Animals of the World*, Robertson & Mullens, 1952; *King of Spain and Other Plays* (includes "Silly Billy," "The Toys That Came Alive," "The Five Little Rabbits," and "A Different Santa Claus"), Robertson & Mullens, 1953; *The Runaway Scooter*, Robertson & Mullens, 1953; *Snowboy*, John Sands, 1958; *The Baker*, Volume I: *The Baker*, Volume II: *The Dentist*, Volume III: *The Life Savers*, Volume IV: *The Postman*, Longman, 1963; *Roundabout I* (reader), Horwitz, 1967; *Family at the Lookout*, Oxford University Press, 1972; *Faces in a Looking-Glass*, Oxford University Press, 1974; *Cat on Hot Bricks*, Oxford University Press, 1975; *Legends of the Gods: Strange and Fascinating Tales From Around the World*, Crane, Russak, 1976; *The Other Side of the World*, Angus & Robertson, 1977; (contributor) Michael Dugan, editor, *The Early Dreaming*, Jacaranda, 1980.

"Piggy Grunter" series; published by Johnson, except as noted: *Piggy Grunter's Red Umbrella*, 1944; *Piggy Grunter's Nursery Rhymes*, 1944; *Piggy Grunter at the Fire*, 1944; *Piggy Grunter at the Circus*, 1944; *Piggy Grunter Stories*, Angus & Robertson, 1954; *Three Cheers for Piggy Grunter!*, Angus & Robertson, 1960.

Contributor to periodicals, including *School Paper* and *Reading Times*.

WORK IN PROGRESS: The Jenkins Affair; It Takes All Sorts.

SIDELIGHTS: Shelley told *CA:* "I began to write stories and 'poems' when I was very young, and had filled a fat black exercise book with them before I was eight. In elementary school I wrote plays, which my friends and I put on with great gusto on the school playground. When I was ten, a special friend and I began to produce a monthly magazine (hand written) which we called *The Young Australian*—though its only readers were the members of our own immediate families. The magazine persisted for three and a half years, until my friend moved to a suburb too far away for us to continue our frequent and essential editorial conferences. I always designed the covers and wrote the serials, which began on a note of high drama and suspense, but usually petered out after a few months because I couldn't think of a satisfactory ending. My teachers told me I would be a writer when I grew up—but I had already decided this long before. In my opinion there could never be enough stories in the world, and I intended to add to their number.

"I choose to write for children and young people rather than for adults, because they are the most receptive and demanding of readers. You can't blind them with knowledge or trick them with a display of verbal fireworks—they see through that. They demand sincerity and understanding. Writing for children is a serious business, requiring complete dedication. But it is also a lot of fun, and I intend to go on writing books for them as long as I keep my wits about me!

"As a writer my chief interest is in human relationships. I like to explore the actions, reactions and interactions of a group of people. Of my own novels, my favorite is *Cat on Hot Bricks*, which I wrote following a chance meeting with an old Spanish woman on a train while traveling from Spain to France. I knew I *had* to write about her. The problem was, *how?* In the end I had to invent dozens of characters and incidents in order to bring her into a story—it was like erecting a large building to contain one room! Actually, the old woman appears in only a few pages somewhere in the middle of the book, but I wrote the whole story because I had to write about her. A challenging and a fascinating exercise."

*   *   *

SHER, Zelig   1888-1971

OBITUARY NOTICE: Born in 1888; died November 11, 1971, in Silver Springs, Md. Newspaper editor and author of Hebrew stories and novels, including *Azoy is bashert* and *Oyf alter un nayer erd*. Obituaries and other sources: *New York Times*, November 13, 1971; *AB Bookman's Weekly*, December 13, 1971.

*   *   *

SHERIDAN, Martin   1914-

PERSONAL: Born August 1, 1914, in Providence, R.I.; son of S. H. and Edna Sheridan; married Margaret Ann Cooke, June 10, 1944 (died June 20, 1981); children: Margaret (Mrs. R. A. Schmidt), Jean Randall. *Education:* Attended College of William and Mary, 1932-33, and Rhode Island State College, 1933. *Home:* 2545 Greeley Ave., Evanston, Ill. 60201. *Office:* National Electronic Distributors Association, 1480 Renaissance Dr., Park Ridge, Ill. 60068.

CAREER: Free-lance writer and photographer, 1933-43; *Boston Globe*, Boston, Mass., war correspondent, 1943-46; worked for Carl Byoir and Associates in New York, N.Y., 1946-51; Admiral Corp., Chicago, Ill., vice-president, 1951-71; free-lance writer. National Electronic Distributors Association, Park Ridge, Ill., editor of *NEDA Journal*, 1977—. Public relations consultant. *Member:* Overseas Press Club of America, Adventurers Club of Chicago, Sigma Delta Chi.

WRITINGS: Comics and Their Creators, Hale, Cushman & Flint, 1942, 3rd edition, 1974; *Overdue and Presumed Lost* (nonfiction), Marshall Jones, 1947. Contributor to more than two hundred fifty periodicals in the United States and Canada. Editor of *NARDA News* (of National Appliance and Radio-TV Dealers Association), 1971-74.

SIDELIGHTS: Sheridan commented: "In 1936 I was assistant to Russ Westover, cartoonist of 'Tillie the Toiler' comic strip, which led to the writing of the first book ever done about comic strips. I was the only war correspondent permitted to go on a submarine war patrol, which led to the second book, the biography of the last ship lost in World War II."

*   *   *

SHERWOOD, Robert E(mmet)   1896-1955
(Brighton Perry)

BRIEF ENTRY: Born April 4, 1896, in New Rochelle, N.Y.; died November 14, 1955, in New York, N.Y. American playwright, editor, and author. Sherwood was wounded in France during World War I and returned from that experience cynical and disillusioned with society. His plays captured the changing American attitudes toward the country and war during the 1920's and 1930's. Sherwood expressed his pacifism and disdain for traditional values in his early plays, and by the mid-1930's he showed an increasing concern for social problems, developing this attitude in such plays as *The Petrified Forest* (1935) and *Idiot's Delight* (1936), which earned him the first of four Pulitzer Prizes. In 1938 the specter of fascism in Europe convinced him that military action was a responsible act in defense of liberty. This motif runs through two other Pulitzer Prize-winning works, *Abe Lincoln in Illinois* (1939) and *There Shall Be No Night* (1940). Serving as a speechwriter and adviser to President Franklin Roosevelt during World War II provided Sherwood with much of the material for the book *Roosevelt and Hopkins: An Intimate History* (1948), for which he won his fourth Pulitzer. He also won an Academy Award for his scenario for the film "The Best Years of Our Lives." *Biographical/critical sources: New York Times Book Review*, October 24, 1948; *Saturday Review of Literature*, August 6, 1949; *Theatre Arts Monthly*, February, 1956; Jean Gould, *Modern American Playwrights*, Dodd, 1966; *Twentieth-Century Literary Criticism*, Volume 3, Gale, 1980.

*   *   *

SHINKLE, James D.   1897(?)-1973
(Tex Shinkle)

OBITUARY NOTICE: Born c. 1897; died January 3, 1973. Educator and author of books on frontier history, including *Fort Sumner and the Bosque Redondo Indian Reservation*, *Robert Casey and the Ranch on the Rio Hondo*, and *Fifty Years of Roswell History, 1867-1917*. Obituaries and other sources: *AB Bookman's Weekly*, February 5, 1973.

*   *   *

SHINKLE, Tex
See SHINKLE, James D.

*   *   *

SHOBIN, David   1945-

PERSONAL: Born May 2, 1945, in Baltimore, Md.; son of Jack (a dentist) and Gertrude (Goldberg) Shobin; married Sharyn Sokoloff, January 16, 1975; children: Rick, Jon. *Education:*

University of Pennsylvania, B.A., 1965; University of Maryland, M.D., 1969. *Religion:* Jewish. *Agent:* Henry Morrison, Inc., 58 West Tenth St., New York, N.Y. 10011. *Office:* 363 Route 111, Smithtown, N.Y. 11787.

CAREER: Montefiore Hospital and Medical Center, Bronx, N.Y., intern, 1969-70; New York Medical College/Flower Fifth Avenue Hospital, New York, N.Y., resident in obstetrics and gynecology, 1971-75; private practice of obstetrics and gynecology in Smithtown, N.Y., 1975—. Diplomate of American Board of Obstetrics and Gynecology; assistant clinical professor at State University of New York at Stony Brook. *Military service:* U.S. Army Reserve, Medical Corps, 1970-80; became captain. *Member:* American College of Obstetrics and Gynecology (fellow), Writers Guild of America, Alpha Omega Alpha.

WRITINGS: The Unborn (suspense thriller), Linden Press, 1981.

WORK IN PROGRESS: Two novels for Linden Press.

SIDELIGHTS: Shobin commented: "My genre as a novelist is medical melodrama."

*   *   *

SHOMRONI, Reuven
See von BLOCK, Bela W(illiam)

*   *   *

SHORES, Louis   1904-1981

OBITUARY NOTICE—See index for *CA* sketch: Born September 14, 1904, in Buffalo, N.Y.; died after a long illness, June 19, 1981. Educator, librarian, editor, and author. After working briefly with the New York Public Library, Shores was a librarian and professor at Fisk University and George Peabody College. In 1946 he joined Florida State University, where he was a professor and dean of the library school for more than twenty years. Shores served as the editor in chief of *Colliers Encyclopedia* in addition to writing several works in his field. His books include *How to Use Your Library: A Series of Articles on Libraries for High School and College Students, Library-College USA: Essays on a Prototype for an American Higher Education,* and *Looking Forward to 1999.* Obituaries and other sources: *School Library Journal,* September, 1981; *Library Journal,* September 14, 1981.

*   *   *

SHU-JEN, Chou   1881-1936
(Chou Ch'o, Lu Hsun)

BRIEF ENTRY: Born September 25, 1881, in Shaohsing, Chekiang, China; died of tuberculosis, October 19, 1936, in Shanghai, China. Chinese educator, short story writer, essayist, and translator. Considered one of China's greatest modern writers, Lu Hsun, the name under which the author established his reputation, is regarded as one of the leaders of the Chinese cultural revolution of the early twentieth century. In his numerous essays and short stories, Lu Hsun bitterly attacked feudalism and imperialism, both of which stalled China's move towards modernization. Beginning his career in the navy, he soon became interested in medicine. After briefly studying in that field, however, Lu Hsun decided to teach and write. In these professions he felt more able to influence people and institute change. Lu Hsun taught at several schools, including Peking University, National Teachers College, Peking Women's Normal College, and Sun Yat-sen University. In 1930 he helped found the China League of Left Wing Writers, an im-

portant achievement in the cultural revolution. The author also successfully fought for the use of vernacular Chinese in literature rather than the classical form of the language that had been favored for centuries. In addition, Lu Hsun translated the works of Western authors into Chinese, thereby exposing his countrymen to the social ideas evolving in the West. The author's work includes *Na han* (1923), *Chung-kuo hsiao shuo shih lueen* (1924; title means "A Brief History of Chinese Fiction"), *Ku shih hsin pien* (1936; title means "Old Tales Retold"), and *Yeh ts'ao* (1953; title means "Wild Grass"). *Residence:* Shanghai, China. *Biographical/critical sources: The Concise Encyclopedia of Modern World Literature,* Hutchinson, 1963; *Cassell's Encyclopaedia of World Literature,* revised edition, Morrow, 1973; *Twentieth-Century Literary Criticism,* Volume 3, Gale, 1980.

*   *   *

SHULTZ, George P(ratt)   1920-

PERSONAL: Born December 13, 1920, in New York, N.Y.; son of Birl E. (founder and director of New York Stock Exchange Institute) and Margaret Lennox (Pratt) Shultz; married Helena Maria O'Brien (a military nurse), February 16, 1946; children: Margaret Ann, Kathleen Pratt Shultz Jorgensen, Peter Milton, Barbara Lennox, Alexander George. *Education:* Princeton University, B.A. (cum laude), 1942; Massachusetts Institute of Technology, Ph.D., 1949. *Religion:* Episcopalian. *Home:* 776 Dolores St., Stanford, Calif. 94305. *Office:* Bechtel Corp., 50 Beale St., San Francisco, Calif. 94105.

CAREER: Massachusetts Institute of Technology, Cambridge, instructor, 1948-49, assistant professor, 1949-55, associate professor of industrial relations, 1955-57; University of Chicago, Chicago, Ill., professor of industrial relations, 1957-68, dean of Graduate Business School, 1962-68; Executive Office of the President, Washington, D.C., U.S. secretary of labor, 1969-70, director of Office of Management and the Budget, 1970-72, U.S. secretary of the treasury and assistant to the president, 1972-74; Bechtel Corp., San Francisco, Calif., executive vice-president, 1974-75, president and member of board of directors, 1975—. Professor at Stanford University, 1974—; Sperry & Hutchinson Lecturer at Tulane University; fellow of Center for Advanced Study in the Behavioral Sciences, Palo Alto, Calif., 1968; member of board of visitors at U.S. Naval Academy.

Senior staff economist of President's Council of Economic Advisers, 1955-56; member of steering committee of Study of Collective Bargaining in the Basic Steel Industry, 1960; director of Public Interest in National Labor Policy, 1961; co-chairman of Automation Fund Committee, 1962-68; member of research advisory board of Committee for Economic Development, 1965-67; chairman of U.S. Department of Labor Task Force on U.S. Employment Service, 1965-68; member of National Manpower Policy Task Force, 1966-68; member of President Nixon's Cost of Living Council and National Commission on Productivity; chairman of Council on Economic Policy, 1972-74, and East-West Trade Policy Committee, 1973-74; member of U.S. board of governors of International Monetary Fund, International Bank for Reconstruction and Development, Inter-American Development Bank, and Asian Development Bank, 1972-74; member of Foreign Intelligence Advisory Board, 1974—, and Treasury Advisory Committee on Reform of the International Monetary System, 1975—; U.S. representative to General Agreement on Trade and Tariffs (GATT), 1973; member of arbitration panels.

Member of Illinois governor's committee on unemployment, 1961-62, and committee on job vacancies, 1963-64. Member of board of directors of National Opinion Research Center, 1962-69, Borg-Warner Corp., 1964-69, J. I. Case Corp., 1964-68, General American Transportation Corp., 1966-69, Stein, Roe & Farnham Stock Fund and Balanced Fund, 1966-69, Morgan Guaranty Trust Co., Sears, Roebuck & Co., and Alfred P. Sloan Foundation. Guest on television programs, including "Issues and Answers." *Military service:* U.S. Marine Corps Reserve, active duty, 1942-45; served in Pacific theater; became captain.

MEMBER: American Economic Association, Industrial Relations Research Association (member of executive board, 1963-66; president, 1968), National Academy of Arbitrators, American Association of University Professors. *Awards, honors:* LL.D. from University of Notre Dame, 1969, Loyola University, 1972, and University of Pennsylvania, 1973; Sc.D. from University of Rochester and Princeton University, both 1973, and Carnegie-Mellon University, 1975.

WRITINGS: Pressures on Wage Decisions: A Case Study in the Shoe Industry, Wiley, 1951; (with Charles Andrew Myers) *The Dynamics of a Labor Market: A Study of the Impact of Employment Changes on Labor Mobility, Job Satisfactions, and Company and Union Policies,* Prentice-Hall, 1951, reprinted, Greenwood Press, 1976; (editor with John R. Coleman) *Labor Problems: Cases and Readings,* McGraw, 1953, 2nd edition, 1959; (editor with Thomas L. Whisler) *Management Organization and the Computer,* Free Press, 1960; (editor and author of introduction, with Robert Z. Aliber) *Guidelines, Informal Controls, and the Market Place: Policy Choices in a Full Employment Economy,* University of Chicago Press, 1966; (with Arnold R. Weber) *Strategies for the Displaced Worker: Confronting Economic Change,* Harper, 1966; (with Albert Rees) *Workers and Wages in an Urban Labor Market,* University of Chicago Press, 1970; *Leaders and Followers in an Age of Ambiguity,* New York University Press, 1975; (with Kenneth W. Dam) *Economic Policy Beyond the Headlines,* Stanford Alumni Association, 1977.

SIDELIGHTS: Before his appointment to the Nixon Cabinet in 1969, George Shultz distinguished himself in the fields of industrial economics, job displacement and unemployment, and labor-management relations. When he was named as the incoming president's secretary of labor, the announcement was hailed by labor and business leaders who welcomed Shultz's moderate political views and his philosophy of government nonintervention in the marketplace. During his tenure as labor secretary he worked out a successful conclusion to the 1970 postal strike, pushed for integration of federal construction projects, and prepared the way for the peaceful desegregation of Southern schools.

In 1972, after serving as the first director of the Office of Management and Budget, Shultz was appointed secretary of the treasury in place of the departing John Connally. Although the country faced a yearly inflation rate of 10 percent, Shultz earnestly campaigned against wage-price controls, believing still that government should not intervene in the marketplace. Instead, his plan called for tighter fiscal and monetary policies that would slow the rate of economic growth. The Nixon administration favored a wage-price freeze, however, and Shultz helped implement a program of phased controls. According to *Newsweek,* "Shultz's basic abhorrence of controls, coupled with his occasional willingness to go along with them as a political necessity, helped to produce the erratic lurches from Phase to freeze that marked Nixonian economic policy."

In 1973 the Watergate scandal and a distracted president hampered the development of an effective economic policy, and Shultz decided to leave government service. Following an appeal from the president, Shultz agreed to stay on long enough to oversee the phaseout of economic controls. He resigned in March, 1974. A *Newsweek* reporter commented: "As Treasury Secretary and the President's chief adviser on domestic and economic affairs, Shultz exercised more clout at the White House than anyone save Secretary of State Henry Kissinger. . . . His resignation deprives the President of one of his two most trusted advisers and of a man whose integrity has never been questioned. It was Shultz who kept alive a flicker of faith in the early Nixon goals amid the mounting scandals involving leading Administration figures."

Shultz made a casette recording, "A New International Monetary System," released by *Encyclopedia Americana* and Columbia Broadcasting System Resource Library in 1972.

BIOGRAPHICAL/CRITICAL SOURCES: Earl Mazo and Stephan Hess, *Nixon: A Political Portrait,* 1969; Robert I, Vexler, *Vice-Presidents and Cabinet Members,* Oceana, 1975; *New York Times,* December 12, 1968, March 1, 1969, August 23, 1970, May 17, 1972, May 13, 1973; *Washington Post,* December 12, 1968; *Christian Science Monitor,* December 13, 1968; *Business Week,* December 14, 1968, December 21, 1968, May 28, 1979, May 5, 1980; *Newsweek,* December 23, 1968, August 18, 1969, June 22, 1970, November 15, 1971, May 29, 1972, December 11, 1972, March 25, 1974; *U.S. News and World Report,* December 23, 1968, January 27, 1969, April 6, 1970, March 29, 1971, February 11, 1974, March 10, 1980; *Time,* January 24, 1969, November 7, 1969, June 22, 1970, August 10, 1970, May 29, 1972, February 26, 1973, June 11, 1973, March 25, 1974; *Nation's Decisions,* March, 1971; *Reader's Digest,* March, 1971; *Banking,* June, 1972; *Dun's,* October, 1972; *National Review,* April 12, 1974; *Forbes,* February 20, 1978, April 16, 1979; *Chronicle of Higher Education,* February 27, 1978; *Library Journal,* March 15, 1978; *Best Sellers,* April, 1978.*

*   *   *

SIBERELL, Anne

PERSONAL: Born in Los Angeles, Calif.; daughter of Estill Brown (in business) and Bernice (a writer and musician; maiden name, Cornell) Hicks; married G. Peter Siberell; children: Peter, Brian, Justin. *Education:* Attended University of California, Los Angeles, 1949-51; Chouinard Art Institute, B.F.A., 1954; attended Silvermine College of Art, 1960-62, and College of San Mateo, 1968-71. *Home and office:* 1041 La Cuesta Rd., Hillsborough, Calif. 94010.

CAREER: Walt Disney Productions, Burbank, Calif., assistant art editor of publications, 1955-59; art director for advertising agency, 1960-64; free-lance artist, 1964—. Member of faculty at Silvermine College of Art, 1966-68, Martin Luther King, Jr. Center, San Mateo, 1969-70; guest lecturer at California State College, Bakersfield, and San Jose State University, 1977; adult education teacher, 1969-72. Work exhibited at solo shows in California and Chicago, Ill., group shows in the United States, Mexico, England, and Norway, and represented in international collections. *Member:* Pacific Center for the Book Arts, California Society of Printmakers, Los Angeles Printmaking Society. *Awards, honors: Our Friend the Atom* was a selection of American Institute of Graphic Arts, 1955-57; award from Los Angeles Rounce and Coffin Club, 1972, for *Lamb, Said the Lion, I Am Here.*

WRITINGS—Self-illustrated children's books: (With Ivy Eastwick) *Rainbow Over All,* McKay, 1967; (with Mark Taylor) *Lamb, Said the Lion, I Am Here,* Golden Gate Junior Books, 1971; (with Johanna Johnston) *Who Found America?,* Childrens Press, 1973; (with June Behrens) *Feast of Thanksgiving,* Childrens Press, 1974; (with Behrens) *Martin Luther King, Jr.: The Story of a Dream,* Childrens Press, 1979; *Houses: Shelters from Prehistoric Times to Today,* Holt, 1979.

Illustrator: Walt Disney and Hans Haber, *Our Friend the Atom,* Simon & Schuster, 1956; John Beatty and Patricia Beatty, *A Donkey for the King,* Macmillan, 1966; Jean Montgomery, *The Wrath of the Coyote,* Morrow, 1968; Montgomery, *Passage to Drake's Bay,* Morrow, 1972; Marjorie Thayer and Elizabeth Emanuel, *Climbing Sun: The Story of a Hopi Indian Boy,* Dodd, 1980; *Whale in the Sky,* Unicorn Books, 1982.

SIDELIGHTS: Anne Siberell is best known for the woodcuts that illustrate her books, but she uses other media as well, including pen and ink. Her studio contains a woodcut press and she prefers to make her own paper by hand, a durable paper that will stand the test of time.

Siberell told *CA:* "In grade school I began to write, illustrate, and make books. My very short stories were typed, then, along with pictures, were pasted onto newsprint pages. Later I started using wallpaper sample books for jackets and end pages. Some of these books were class assignments.

"Later on in school my orientation was more towards graphic design. After graduating from Chouinard Art Institute I worked on publications at the Disney studios and learned much about the processes involved in the making of books.

"The shift to fine arts, painting, printmaking, especially woodcut, broadened my understanding—and when I started illustrating for publication I took extensive notes during research. I found that I was indeed writing again. *Houses* was to be the first book published that I wrote as well as illustrated. Now I am working in the woodcut medium. I also make books which I show in 'artist's books' exhibitions throughout the country. I am pleased that this involvement has been many-faceted— and that the work that I produce for young readers is a reflection of the activities of my childhood."

BIOGRAPHICAL/CRITICAL SOURCES: San Mateo Times, December 15, 1980.

* * *

SIDNEY, Neilma
   See GANTNER, Neilma

* * *

SIEGEL, Max   1904-1972

OBITUARY NOTICE: Born in 1904; died April 25, 1972. Bookseller, agent, and author of *Boy's Club.* Obituaries and other sources: *Publishers Weekly,* May 22, 1972.

* * *

SIEMANOWSKI, Richard F.   1922(?)-1981

OBITUARY NOTICE: Born c. 1922; died September 25, 1981, in Jersey City, N.J. Producer and author of television documentaries, including "Lamp Unto My Feet" and "Look Up and Live." He specialized in producing documentaries focused on the arts and civil rights. Obituaries and other sources: *New York Times,* September 26, 1981.

* * *

SIENKIEWICZ, Henryk (Adam Aleksander Pius) 1846-1916
   (Litwos)

BRIEF ENTRY: Born May 5, 1846, in Wola Okrzejska, Poland;

died November 15, 1916, in Vevey, Switzerland. Polish journalist and author. Although much of Sienkiewicz's work is unknown outside his native Poland, he achieved international status with the historical novel *Quo Vadis: A Narrative of the Time of Nero* (1896), which was made into several motion pictures. Critics blame his relative obscurity on the poor quality of English translations. His principal works include *Na marne* (1872; translated as *In Vain,* 1899), *Potop* (1886; translated as *The Deluge,* 1891), *Bex dogmatu* (1891; translated as *Without Dogma,* 1893), and the multi-volumed *Drzyzacy* (1897-1900; translated as *Knights of the Cross,* 1897-1900). Sienkiewicz was an ardent nationalist who fought for social reform and Polish independence from Russia. He was in Switzerland organizing Polish relief efforts at the time of his death. Sienkiewicz was awarded the Nobel Prize for literature in 1905. *Biographical/critical sources: Cyclopedia of World Authors,* Harper, 1958; Waclaw Lednicki, *Henryk Sienkiewicz: A Retrospective Synthesis,* Mouton, 1960; *The Penguin Companion to European Literature,* McGraw, 1969; *Twentieth-Century Literary Criticism,* Volume 3, Gale, 1980.

* * *

SIERRA, Gregorio Martinez
   See MARTINEZ SIERRA, Gregorio

* * *

SILBER, Joan   1945-

PERSONAL: Born June 14, 1945, in Millburn, N.J.; daughter of Samuel S. (a dentist) and Dorothy (a teacher; maiden name, Arlein) Silber. *Education:* Sarah Lawrence College, B.A., 1967; New York University, M.A., 1979. *Home:* 43 Bond St., New York, N.Y. 10012. *Agent:* Jane Rotrosen, 318 East 51st St., New York, N.Y. 10022.

CAREER: Holt, Rinehart, and Winston, New York City, copy editor, 1967-68; *New York Free Press,* New York City, reporter, 1968; waitress, 1968-71; assistant teacher in day-care centers in New York City, 1972; salesclerk, 1971-72; Ideal Publishing, New York City, editor of fan magazines *Movie Stars* and *Movie Life,* 1975; Kirkus Service, New York City, reviewer, 1976; Warner & Gillers, New York City, lawyer's assistant, 1977-78; Women's Action Alliance, New York City, legal proofreader, 1981. *Member:* P.E.N., Authors Guild. *Awards, honors:* New writer's award honorable mention from Great Lakes Colleges Association, 1980, and Ernest Hemingway Foundation Award for best first novel from P.E.N., 1981, both for *Household Words.*

WRITINGS: Household Words (novel), Viking, 1980. Contributor of short stories to *Redbook* and book reviews to *Ms.* and *Newsday.*

WORK IN PROGRESS: A second novel.

SIDELIGHTS: Silber's first novel, *Household Words,* depicts the life of Rhoda Taber, a middle-class housewife living in New Jersey in the 1940's and 1950's. After her pharmacist husband dies, Rhoda determinedly cares for her family and "goes on" for "where else is there to go?" Her "life is relatively unremarkable," explained Susan Isaacs in the *New York Times Book Review.* "There are no thunderous confrontations here. . . . Rhoda's consciousness never rises, her horizons never soar. Instead she stays in New Jersey, raises her two daughters, visits with friends, works, vacations, suffers." Isaacs continued: "The heroine exhibits strength and integrity under the most mundane circumstances—comforting a wailing baby, presiding over a lonely Thanksgiving dinner." Marilyn

Murray Wilson of the *Los Angeles Times* maintained, though, that the lack of drive on the part of the main character is the novel's weakness. "What Rhoda does not have—and I can't help but perceive it as a flaw in the book—is a goal of some sort. . . . She . . . floats from day to day, year to year, with no plan, no dream, no real reason for living. . . . Her life has no urgency." Isaacs disagreed. *Household Words* "is about ordinary life," she observed. "There is no zippy dialogue, no literary razzle-dazzle. People live, die, raise children, put on girdles and teach school. But the details add up to a novel full of dignity and humanity." Linda B. Osborne concurred in the *Washington Post Book World*. "Silber's writing is strong and richly detailed, spotlighting the drama inherent in ordinary lives without sentiment or pretension."

BIOGRAPHICAL/CRITICAL SOURCES: Washington Post Book World, January 31, 1980; *New York Times Book Review*, February 3, 1980; *Los Angeles Times*, March 6, 1980.

* * *

SILURIENSIS, Leolinus
   See JONES, Arthur Llewellyn

* * *

SILVERMAN, Joseph H(erman) 1924-

PERSONAL: Born October 15, 1924, in New York, N.Y.; son of Samuel and Edna (Leviloff) Silverman; married June A. Chavez, June 16, 1951; children: Suzanne, Sheryl, Laura. *Education:* City College (now of the City University of New York), B.S.S., 1946; University of Southern California, M.A., 1950, Ph.D., 1955. *Politics:* Democrat. *Religion:* Jewish. *Home:* 614 Trevethan Ave., Santa Cruz, Calif. 95065. *Office:* Stevenson College, University of California, Santa Cruz, Calif. 95064.

CAREER: University of Southern California, Los Angeles, instructor in Spanish literature, 1952-54; University of California, Los Angeles, instructor, 1954-55, assistant professor, 1955-60, associate professor, 1961-66, professor of Spanish literature, 1967-68; University of California, Santa Cruz, professor of Spanish literature, 1968—, provost of Stevenson College, 1974-81. *Member:* Phi Beta Kappa. *Awards, honors:* National Endowment for the Humanities fellow, 1971-72; first prize in folklore from University of Chicago, 1973, for *Judeo-Spanish Ballad Chapbooks of Yacob Abraham Yona;* Guggenheim fellow, 1977-78.

WRITINGS: Siglo veinte (title means "Twentieth Century"), Holt, 1968; *Judeo-Spanish Ballads From Bosnia*, University of Pennsylvania Press, 1971; *Judeo-Spanish Ballad Chapbooks of Yacob Abraham Yona*, University of California Press, 1971; *Romances judeo-espanoles de Tanger* (title means "Judeo-Spanish Ballads From Tangins"), Castalia, 1977. Member of editorial board of *Romance Philology*, 1952-62, *Studia humanitatis*, 1975—, and *Journal of Hispanic Philology*, 1979—.

WORK IN PROGRESS: A book on Jews and New Christians in Old Christian Spain, publication expected in 1984; a multivolume edition of Judeo-Spanish ballads, publication by University of California Press expected in 1983; research on Cervantes, the picaresque novel, and the theater of Lope de Vega.

* * *

SILVIUS, G(eorge) Harold 1908-1981

OBITUARY NOTICE—See index for *CA* sketch: Born April 4, 1908, in Virdi, Minn.; died August 13, 1981, in Detroit, Mich. Educator, editor, and author. Silvius was a teacher of industrial arts and the supervisor of vocational education in the Detroit public school system before joining Wayne State University. Associated with the university for more than thirty years, he taught industrial education and vocational and applied arts. During this time, Silvius developed a well-known plan for industrial teacher education. In addition to serving as editor in chief of *Guild News*, he wrote several books in his field, including *Safe Work Practice in Sheet Metal Work, Teaching Successfully in Industrial Education*, and *Organizing Course Materials for Industrial Education*. Obituaries and other sources: *Detroit News*, August 18, 1981.

* * *

SIMMONDS, James D(udley) 1933-

PERSONAL: Born December 15, 1933, in Mt. Magnet, Australia; came to the United States in 1965, naturalized citizen, 1975; son of James and Jessie (Fabre) Simmonds; married Barbara M. Clegg (a medical technician), September 27, 1980; children: (from a previous marriage) Peta Michele Anson. *Education:* University of Western Australia, B.A. (with first class honors), 1954; University of Melbourne, M.A., 1958; Louisiana State University, Ph.D., 1961. *Politics:* Independent. *Office:* Department of English, University of Pittsburgh, Pittsburgh, Pa. 15260.

CAREER: University of Kentucky, Lexington, instructor in English, 1960-61; University of Sydney, Sydney, Australia, lecturer in English, 1961-63; Preston Technical College and Royal Melbourne Institute of Technology, Melbourne, Australia, lecturer in English, 1963-65; University of Pittsburgh, Pittsburgh, Pa., assistant professor, 1965-66, associate professor, 1966-74, professor of English, 1974—. Member of executive board of Pittsburgh Laboratory Theatre, 1975-78. Member of professional advisory board and speakers' consortium of Holocaust Center of Greater Pittsburgh, 1981—. *Member:* Modern Language Association of America, Milton Society of America (past member of executive committee), Pennsylvania College English Association (past president). *Awards, honors:* Melbourne University Research Fellow, 1952-58; University of Pittsburgh Humanities Research Fellow, 1963, and Charles E. Merrill Research Fellow, 1967.

WRITINGS: (With E. L. Marilla) *Henry Vaughan: A Bibliographical Supplement, 1946-1960*, University of Alabama Press, 1963; *Masques of God: Form and Theme in the Poetry of Henry Vaughan*, University of Pittsburgh Press, 1972.

Plays: "And What Were They Going to Do With the Holy Grail When They Found It, Mr. Rossetti?" (one-act comedy), first produced in Pittsburgh, Pa., at Pittsburgh Laboratory Theatre, March 31, 1976; "The Albatross" (one-act); "Wedlock" (one-act); "The Enemy" (one-act); "The Aquarium" (full length).

Contributor to scholarly journals. Editor of *Milton Studies*.

WORK IN PROGRESS: Three plays, tentatively titled "Fugitives," "Ceremonies of the Horsemen," and "Wednesday in Vienna; or, Did Beethoven Ever Find a Piano That Made Him Truly Happy?"; monographs on the English sonnet and on the treatment of death in literature.

SIDELIGHTS: Simmonds told *CA:* "When friends ask what something I'm writing is about, I say, 'Madness and death, madness and death—what else is there to write about?'

"I was twelve years old when this century's second 'war to end all wars' left over seventy million dead and Europe in ruins. Though far away and (after the Battle of the Coral Sea) safe in the southwest corner of Australia, I was deeply affected by constant news of the war and by the disillusioning discovery, when it was over, that it had not made the world a better place, as expected, but a worse one. Raised in a colonial outpost on the edge of a desert wasteland, I thought of England and Europe as home, looked to them for a sense of identity with something more habitable and durable than the ramshackle houses, scratchy farms, and dirt tracks that I lived among.

"But the war destroyed the Europe I had read about, and I could never be at home in England's class-ridden, xenophobic society. In the limbo of the Australian bush, having lost my family in infancy, I identified with the homeless refugees from Europe who settled in Australia after the war, as they encountered the casual bigotry that, like the White Australia Policy and the banning of books, expresses the country's barbaric innocence. My sense of kinship with Anne Frank, two years older than me when she died in Auschwitz, was so strong that I could not read her diary until twenty-five years later. The unprecedented cruelty of both sides in the war (most vivid to me in the death camps, the firebombings of German cities, and the nuclear bombings of Hiroshima and Nagasaki), together with the ignorant brutality of the people around me, filled me with horror and disgust. I decided that either human beings were not images of God, as I had been taught, or, if they were, then God was like Hitler, Himmler, and 'The Bitch of Buchenwald,' Ilse Koch. In either case, religion was a lie, and the world as cursed and godforsaken as the Australian desert.

"I discovered the magical powers of language when I read Shakespeare's 'Hark, hark, the lark / At heaven's gate sings' at about the age of ten or eleven, and when, about the same time, I found that I could defend myself from my elders and peers with verbal tirades whose eloquence awed even me. These were the beginnings of my fascination with the mixed powers of language—to heal, charm, humor, humanize, liberate, and make whole, and to terrify, control, stereotype, polarize, distort, and destroy. Since the protean, paradoxical nature of language, verbal and nonverbal, expresses the protean, paradoxical nature of human beings and the realities they inhabit and make, my writing brings diverse modes of language, perception, and being into sharp (usually unresolved) conflict, existing somewhere along the spectrum of tragicomedy or irony.

"Writing poetry as an undergraduate, I admired Eliot, Yeats, and Walt Whitman, but was besotted by the lushness of Shakespeare, Milton, the Romantics, Tennyson, and Swinburne. A desire to write for the theatre was awakened in me in 1964 by a performance of Albee's *Who's Afraid of Virginia Woolf?* The solitary meditations of poetry suddenly seemed pallid and effete compared to the startling clash and communal ritual of the theatre. And Albee's language excited in me the hope of escaping from my neo-Romantic impasse (I had long ago abandoned poetry in despair), by fashioning a style that (like his, and, in their different ways, the styles of Eliot, Yeats, Whitman, Joyce, Arthur Miller, and Tennessee Williams) would be built out of the language of everyday life and yet be capable of eloquence, power, and grace. Beckett, Pinter, Arrabal, and Ionesco have also been major influences, both on my sense of theatre and on my use of language and symbols.

"The decisive events in my growth as a writer were my immigration to the United States in 1965 and my experience of psychoanalysis in the early seventies. I came to the United States in the middle of the most turbulent period in its history since the Civil War and the Indian Wars, and my first play grew out of my feelings about the assassination of President Kennedy. It seems to me that the New World is doomed (has always been doomed) to experience anew all the ancient trag-

edies of the Old. That is the 'complex fate' of being an American, and, in the broadest terms, is what I write about."

BIOGRAPHICAL/CRITICAL SOURCES: *University Times* (of University of Pittsburgh), March 18, 1976; *Pittsburgh Post-Gazette*, April 8, 1976, September 17, 1977; *Pittsburgh Press*, July 5, 1978.

* * *

SIMMONS, Geoffrey 1943-

PERSONAL: Born July 28, 1943, in Camp Gordon, Ga. *Agent:* Gary Cosay, Cosay, Werner & Associates, Inc., 9744 Wilshire Blvd., Suite 310, Beverly Hills, Calif. 90212.

CAREER: Physician, specializing in internal medicine, in Eugene, Ore.

WRITINGS: *The Z Papers* (novel), Arbor House, 1976; *The Adam Experiment* (novel), Arbor House, 1978; *Pandemic* (novel), Arbor House, 1980.

SIDELIGHTS: Simmons told *CA:* "I've been writing for about ten years and often type late in the night because I have a full-time practice and a family that take priority. My interests, naturally, lie in medicine, but not the soap opera stuff or scandals or diets, but more so on potential problems now and in the future. To express any of my ideas in a nonfiction manner would be boring, to me and any readers, I'm sure, but in a thriller pace the perspective changes considerably. In *The Z Papers*, I explore what happens if a national figure is poisoned with a toxin we can't diagnose or treat; in *The Adam Experiment* what happens when the first child is born on a space lab; and in *Pandemic* what happens if one of the more worrisome bacteria becomes resistant to our antibiotics such as is happening with other organisms on a daily basis in the hospitals."

* * *

SIMON, Solomon 1895-1970

OBITUARY NOTICE: Born July 4, 1895, in Kolikovichi, Russia (now U.S.S.R); died November 8, 1970, in Miami, Fla. Dentist and author of Yiddish stories and books, including *In the Thicket, More Wise Men of Helm and Their Merry Tales,* and *The Wandering Beggar.* Obituaries and other sources: *New York Times*, November 10, 1970; *AB Bookman's Weekly*, January 4, 1971; *Who's Who in World Jewry: A Biographical Dictionary of Outstanding Jews*, Pitman, 1972.

* * *

SIMONIN, Albert (Charles) 1905-1980

OBITUARY NOTICE: Born April 18, 1905, in Paris, France; died February 15, 1980, in Paris, France. Author of police thrillers, including *Voila taxi, Touchez pas au grisbi,* and *Grisbi or not grisbi.* Obituaries and other sources: *AB Bookman's Weekly*, May 5, 1980.

* * *

SIMONS, Beverley 1938-

PERSONAL: Born March 31, 1938, in Flin Flon, Manitoba, Canada; daughter of Jack (a lumber dealer) and Zita (in business; maiden name, Schacter) Rosen; married Sidney B. Simons (a lawyer); children: Paris, Darren, Keir. *Education:* Attended McGill University; University of British Columbia, B.A. (with honors), 1959. *Home:* 5202 Marine Dr., West Vancouver, British Columbia, Canada V7W 2P3. *Agent:* Peter Hay, 1521 Kemper St., Los Angeles, Calif. 90065.

CAREER: Writer, 1968—. *Awards, honors:* Scholarship from Banff School of Fine Arts; national short story award from Canadian Broadcasting Corp.; received grant and senior artist award from Canada Council.

WRITINGS—Published plays: *Crabdance* (three-act; first produced in Seattle, Wash., at Contemporary Theatre, 1969), In Press, 1969; *Green Lawn Rest Home* (one-act; first produced in Vancouver, British Columbia, at Simon Fraser University, 1969), Playwrights Co-Operative, 1973; *Preparing: A Collection of Short Plays*, Talonbooks, 1975.

Author of "Leela Means to Play" (two-act; first produced in Waterford, Conn., at Eugene O'Neill Theatre Center, 1978), published in *Canadian Theatre Review*, winter, 1976.

Unpublished plays: "The Elephant and the Jewish Question" (three-act), first produced in Vancouver, British Columbia, 1968; "Preparing" (one-act monologue), first produced in Vancouver, at Simon Fraser University, 1973; "Preparing, Triangle, Crusader," first produced in Toronto, Ontario, at York University, 1976.

WORK IN PROGRESS: Encounter, a collection of stories written between 1962 and 1978; *The Boy With a Piece of Dark,* a children's book; *Tabernacles,* a novel; "Judith," a three-act play.

SIDELIGHTS: Beverley Simons's agent, Peter Hay, told *CA:* "Beverley Simons could have been a concert pianist; her love of music, ranging from classical to jazz to modern, informs the rhythms of her writing. Her dialogue is written like music. She has wide-ranging intellectual interests in philosophy, mythology, and great literature. She has traveled widely in Europe and Asia; many of her plays show a fascination with Oriental thought, art, and theatre. She gives birth to each work after long gestation and with great labor (including the pains); she has great love of nature and lives amidst a forest over the ocean, almost a recluse, but caring passionately for family and friends."

BIOGRAPHICAL/CRITICAL SOURCES: Capilano Review, summer, 1976; *Canadian Theatre Review,* winter, 1976.

*   *   *

SIMOS, Miriam 1951-
(Starhawk)

PERSONAL: Surname is pronounced *Sigh*-mose; born June 17, 1951, in St. Paul, Minn.; daughter of Jack (a social worker) and Bertha (a clinical social worker and writer; maiden name, Goldfarb) Simos; married Edwin W. Rahsman (a plumber), January 22, 1977. *Education:* University of California, Los Angeles, B.A. (cum laude), 1972, graduate study, 1973; graduate study at Antioch West University, 1980-82. *Politics:* "Feminist." *Religion:* Wicca. *Residence:* San Francisco, Calif. *Agent:* Ken Sherman & Associates, 9507 Santa Monica Blvd., Beverly Hills, Calif. 90210. *Office:* Reclaiming: A Center for Feminist Spirituality and Counseling, c/o Covenant of the Goddess, P.O. Box 14404, San Francisco, Calif. 94704.

CAREER: Producer of educational videotapes and slide series for Environmental Communications, 1971-72; coordinator of Westside Women's Center, 1972, gave workshops for women in photography, writing, poetry, and feminist thought, 1973-74; adult education teacher at Bay Area Center for Alternative Education, 1975-77; free-lance film writer, 1978-80; Reclaiming: A Center for Feminist Spirituality and Counseling, Berkeley, Calif., director, teacher, and counselor, 1980—. Minister and elder of Covenant of the Goddess, West Coast publicity

chairperson and national president, 1976-77. Organizer of "community rituals"; speaker at colleges and universities, including Union Theological Seminary, New York, N.Y., University of California, San Francisco, American River College, and California State University in San Franciso, San Jose, and Chico. *Member:* Media Alliance, Information Film Producers Association, American Academy of Religion.

WRITINGS—Under pseudonym Starhawk: *The Spiral Dance: A Rebirth of the Ancient Religion of the Great Goddess,* Harper, 1979; *Dreaming in the Dark: Magic, Sex, and Politics,* Beacon Press, 1982.

Contributor: Carol Christ and Judith Plaskow, editors, *Womanspirit Rising,* Harper, 1979; Naomi Goldenberg, editor, *The Changing of the Gods,* Beacon Press, 1979; Ann Forfreedom, editor, *The Book of the Goddess,* Feminist Spirituality Center Press, 1980; Charlene Spretnak, editor, *The Politics of Women's Spirituality: Essays on the Rise of Spiritual Power Within the Women's Movement,* Doubleday, 1981.

Plays: "The Loss Ritual" (five-act), first produced in San Francisco, Calif., at Project One, May, 1976; "Winter Solstice" (one-act), first broadcast by KPFA-Radio, December 22, 1977; "The Spiral Dance Ritual: In Celebration of the True Halloween" (one-act), first produced in San Francisco, at Fort Mason, October, 1979.

Author of scripts, including "Learning," "Managing for Competence," "Ground in Motion: Earthquake Engineer," "Thinking About the Future: Technology Assessment," "The Information Era," "Hemophilia," "Mary," and "The Origins of Consciousness in the Breakdown of the Bicameral Mind" (based on book by Julian Jaynes). Contributor to magazines, including *Anima, Lady-Unique,* and *Inclination-of-the-Night.*

WORK IN PROGRESS: To the Wild Places, "a novel about the spiritual, emotional, sexual, and political aspects of the sixties, seventies, and eighties."

SIDELIGHTS: Miriam Simos described her first book as "an overview of the growth, suppression, and modern-day reemergence of the Old Religion of the Goddess, the pre-Christian tradition know as paganism, Wicca, or witchcraft. The book presents the history, philosophy, theology, and practice of this serious and much misunderstood religion, and explores its growing influence on the feminist and ecology movements. It is currently being used as a text in religious studies and women's studies courses. *Dreaming in the Dark* is a further exploration of the Goddess as a catalyzing symbol of the immanent consciousness that challenges the present social order."

She added: "My motivation in most of my work has been the integration of a strong feminist vision and commitment to social justice with a strong spiritual search. I was born and raised Jewish, with a strong Hebrew education. Presently, I am a leader of the religion of the Great Goddess, the life force manifest in nature, human beings, and the world. To me the Goddess is a symbol that evokes women's strength and men's nurturing capabilities, and restores deep value to nature, sexuality, and the ecological balance.

"I am a co-director of Reclaiming, a center that offers classes, workshops, public rituals, and private counseling in the tradition of Goddess religion. I am also a graduate student, working toward a master's degree in the feminist therapy program at Antioch West that combines women's studies and psychology.

"Up until now, and sporadically even now, I have been a free-lance writer for educational and industrial films, ninety per cent of which have yet to be produced. I've tended to specialize in technical subjects, purely by accident and in spite of absolutely no technical background or inclination.''

AVOCATIONAL INTERESTS: ''I was an art major in college, but am not doing much along those lines any more except appreciating. I enjoy wilderness, backpacking, hiking, and watching things like tidepools, and am glad we live close to the ocean. I have traveled extensively in this country and Europe, including bicycling trips in Oregon, Ireland, and Wales. My husband and I have two dogs, three cats, and a boa constrictor and are the obnoxious sort of people that treat their pets like children.''

BIOGRAPHICAL/CRITICAL SOURCES: Vortex: A Journal of New Vision, spring, 1981.

*   *   *

SINCLAIR, Julian
    See SINCLAIR, Mary Amelia St. Clair

*   *   *

SINCLAIR, Mary Amelia St. Clair   1865(?)-1946
    (Julian Sinclair, May Sinclair)

BRIEF ENTRY: Born c. 1865 in Rock Ferry, Cheshire, England; died November 14, 1946, in Aylesbury, Buckinghamshire, England. English feminist and author. Strongly influenced by the psychological theories of Freud, Sinclair was a pioneer in the stream of consciousness technique and was the first to apply that term to a literary style. Her writing was largely ignored in her native England until the American success of *The Divine Fire* (1904). Sinclair redefined what was considered to be ''appropriate'' subject matter for women writers and, through her novels, opposed constricting Victorian mores. She employed psychoanalytic theories of the subconscious in *Mary Olivier* (1919), considered her best work, and in *The Three Sisters* (1914). Much of the material she used in *The Tree of Heaven* (1917) and *The Romantic* (1920) was culled from her experiences with an ambulance unit on the Belgian front during World War I. Well-versed in many areas, Sinclair was considered by her contemporaries to be one of the important writers and thinkers of her time. *Biographical/critical sources: New York Times Book Review,* September 7, 1919; *Nation and Athenaeum,* August 5, 1922; Walter L. Myers, *The Later Realism: A Study of Characterization in the British Novel,* University of Chicago Press, 1927; Frank Swinnerton, *The Georgian Literary Scene: 1910-1935,* Hutchinson, 1969; *Twentieth-Century Literary Criticism,* Volume 3, Gale, 1980.

*   *   *

SINCLAIR, May
    See SINCLAIR, Mary Amelia St. Clair

*   *   *

SINGER, Jack W(olfe)   1942-

PERSONAL: Born November 9, 1942, in New York, N.Y.; son of Leon E. (a dentist) and Sarah (a poet; maiden name, White) Singer; married Thalia Syracopoulos (a legal assistant), December 26, 1965; children: Constantine, Jeremiah. *Education:* Columbia University, B.A., 1964; State University of New York Downstate Medical Center, Brooklyn, M.D., 1968. *Home:* 2766 Westlake N., Seattle, Wash. 98109. *Office:* Seattle Veterans Administration Medical Center, 4435 Beacon Ave. S., Seattle, Wash. 98108.

CAREER: Internship and residency in internal medicine at University of Chicago Hospitals; University of Washington Hospitals, Seattle, fellowship in hematology and oncology, assistant professor, 1975-79, associate professor of medicine and oncology, 1979—. Assistant member of Hutchinson Cancer Center, 1975—. *Military service:* U.S. Public Health Service, 1970-72; became lieutenant commander. *Member:* International Society for Experimental Hematology, American Society of Clinical Oncology, American Society of Hematology, Western Society for Clinical Research.

WRITINGS: (With Harold Glucksberg) *Cancer Care: A Personal Guide,* Johns Hopkins Press, 1980. Contributor to medical journals.

WORK IN PROGRESS: A screenplay about fishing in Alaska.

SIDELIGHTS: Singer told *CA:* ''We wrote *Cancer Care* to help provide cancer victims with enough information about their illness to assure them that they would be intelligent health care consumers. We felt that the quality of care available varied widely and that only the consumer could be sure he or she was getting the best care available. We also felt that there was so much widely-disseminated misinformation that an accurate, complete source of lay information was needed. We enjoyed the opportunity to attempt a non-scholarly work in which we could state our opinions, biases, and feelings.''

*   *   *

SINGER, Rochelle   1939-

PERSONAL: Born February 6, 1939, in Minneapolis, Minn.; daughter of Ralph (a grocer) and Dorothy (Lewis) Singer. *Education:* University of Minnesota, B.A., 1961. *Home and office:* 5117 Lawton Ave., Oakland, Calif. 94618. *Agent:* Elizabeth Lay, 4321 Gilbert St., Oakland, Calif. 94611.

CAREER: Worked as a journalist, editor, production artist, antique restorer, welfare worker, and advertising copywriter; owner of boutique, Chicago, Ill., 1968-70; employed as landscaper, gardener, and carpenter, 1979—. President of Tamalpais Canyon Community Association, 1976.

WRITINGS: The Demeter Flower (novel), St. Martin's, 1980.

WORK IN PROGRESS: Another ''Demeter'' book; a suspense novel.

SIDELIGHTS: Rochelle Singer commented: ''I want to tell a good story and to communicate my ideas to as many people as possible.

''I grew up in a ma-and-pa grocery store. Perhaps I would not have become a writer had my childhood been more sheltered. Perhaps I would have been better off—bored, but better off.''

*   *   *

SINJOHN, John
    See GALSWORTHY, John

*   *   *

SINNEN, Jeanne   1926-1976

OBITUARY NOTICE: Born July 25, 1926, in St. Paul, Minn.; died after a long illness, July 19, 1976. Editor of the University of Minnesota Press. Obituaries and other sources: *Foremost Women in Communications,* Bowker, 1970; *Who's Who in America,* 39th edition, Marquis, 1976; *Publishers Weekly,* August 9, 1976.

SIONS, Harry   1906-1974

OBITUARY NOTICE: Born February 20, 1906, in Philadelphia, Pa.; died March 26, 1974, in Philadelphia, Pa. Editor. In 1965 a dispute over editorial policy caused Sions to resign his eighteen-year post as editorial director of *Holiday* magazine. He became senior editor of Little, Brown & Co., where he worked with many well-known authors, including Stephen Birmingham, Langston Hughes, William Manchester, V.S. Pritchett, Irwin Shaw, and John Steinbeck. Obituaries and other sources: *New York Times,* March 28, 1974; *Publishers Weekly,* April 15, 1974; *Who Was Who in America, With World Notables,* Volume VI: *1974-76,* Marquis, 1976.

*   *   *

SIROF, Harriet   1930-

PERSONAL: Born October 18, 1930, in New York, N.Y.; daughter of Herman (a dress manufacturer) and Lillian (Miller) Hockman; married Sidney Sirof (a psychologist), June 18, 1949; children: Laurie, David, Amy Sirof Bordiuk. *Education:* New School for Social Research, B.A., 1962. *Home and office:* 792 East 21st St., Brooklyn, N.Y. 11210.

CAREER: Remedial reading teacher at elementary schools in Brooklyn, N.Y., 1962-76; St. John's University, Jamaica, N.Y., instructor in creative writing, 1978—. Instructor at South Shore Adult Center, 1977—, Long Island University, 1978-79, and Brooklyn College of the City University of New York, 1980-81. *Member:* International Women's Writing Guild, Authors Guild, Authors League of America, League of Women Voters (past president of Brooklyn branch), Bank Street College Writers Laboratory.

WRITINGS—Juveniles: *A New-Fashioned Love Story* (novel), Xerox Education Publications, 1977; *The IF Machine* (novel), Scholastic Book Services, 1978; *The Junior Encyclopedia of Israel,* Jonathan David, 1980; *Save the Dam!* (novel), Crestwood, 1981.

Work represented in anthologies, including *Voices of Brooklyn,* edited by Sol Yorick, American Library Association, 1973; *Remember Me and Other Stories,* edited by Mary Verdick, Xerox Education Publications, 1976; *Triple Action Play Book* (contains "Itchy Feet," a one-act play for children), edited by Jeri Schapiro, Scholastic Book Services, 1979.

Author of "Your Child," a column in *Flatbush News,* in *Kings Courier,* in *Bay News,* and in *Canarsie Digest,* all 1962-65. Contributor of stories and articles to magazines for adults and young people, including *North American Review, Descant, Highlights for Children, Rainbow,* and *Maine Review.*

WORK IN PROGRESS: A juvenile historical novel.

SIDELIGHTS: "I came to writing late," Harriet Sirof commented. "After many years devoted to being a mother and teacher, I began to write short stories for adults. Sales to the literary quarterlies and the interest of an agent persuaded me to attempt an adult novel. It took me nearly two years and two thousand discarded pages to discover that it was not for me.

"Deeply discouraged, I was considering giving up writing when I received a letter from Scholastic (for whom I had previously written some educational materials) looking for novels for children with reading problems. I tried one and found to my surprise that I loved writing it. I have since published three novels and one nonfiction book for young adults and am now working on a historical novel for nine- to twelve-year-olds.

"My life is representative of many women of my generation. At the age of ten, sure that I would be a famous writer when I grew up, I dictated stories to my friend Boopsie who planned to be a secretary. When I entered college at seventeen I still held onto the dream of writing someday, but was persuaded to train for something practical like teaching English. I married at eighteen, left school to plunge wholeheartedly into domesticity, and soon had three small children. Although writing had been relegated to the status of an abandoned adolescent fantasy, I began to feel that something was missing in my life. I returned to school, earned a scholarship, wrote term papers while the children watched 'Romper Room' on television, and graduated first in my class. Teaching was the next obvious step for a woman whose own children were entering school, so I taught reading.

"I don't know what eventually reactivated the old dream of being a writer—probably a combination of the ideas of the women's movement and my own personal growth. In any case, I hauled out the old term-paper typewriter and began. At first it seemed necessary to reject the years of child rearing and child teaching and to assume a new identity by writing adult literature. Only gradually did it dawn on me that those years had not been wasted, that I had spent so much time with children because I liked them, and that I really wanted to write for children. I have been doing so ever since.

"Today I look at my daughter, who is now in her early twenties. She earned her M.A. in English literature before she married, then decided to postpone children for the future and took an editorial job on a magazine. Recently she arranged to work part-time while she writes her first novel. I contrast the direct path she is taking with my round-about one. She was born into a different generation with different options. I wonder whether my unborn granddaughter will want to be a writer and, if so, how she will go about it. Maybe I'll write a book for girls on the subject.

"I am now working on a historical novel based on the second century Bar-Kokba revolt in Judea. While researching *The Junior Encyclopedia of Israel,* I became interested in the recent archaeological discovery of letters written by Simon Bar-Kokba to his captains during the revolt. The idea for the novel grew out of the contrast between the very human leader revealed in the letters and the larger-than-life hero of the legends. Perhaps I chose to write the novel for nine- to twelve-year-olds because those are the years when reality supplants early childhood fantasies."

*   *   *

SISLER, Rebecca   1932-

PERSONAL: Born October 16, 1932, in Mount Forest, Ontario, Canada; daughter of Byron Cooper (a bank manager) and Mildred (a registered nurse; maiden name, Ramsden) Sisler; marriage annulled; children: Adam. *Education:* Attended Ontario College of Art, 1951-52, and Royal Danish Academy of Fine Arts, 1953-55. *Politics:* Liberal. *Religion:* Christian. *Home address:* P.O. Box 950, Durham, Ontario, Canada N0G 1R0. *Office:* Royal Canadian Academy of Arts, 11 Yorkville Ave., No. 601, Toronto, Ontario, Canada M4V 1L3.

CAREER: Educational director of McMichael Canadian Collection, 1969-70; Royal Canadian Academy of Arts, Toronto, Ontario, executive director, 1978—. Sculptor, with commissioned works. *Member:* Ontario Society of Arts. *Awards, honors:* Sculpture award from Art Gallery of Toronto, 1959; Canadian National Exhibition, Toronto, 1968.

WRITINGS: The Girls: A Biography of Frances Loring and Florence Wyle, Clarke, Irwin, 1972; *Passionate Spirits: A His-*

tory of the Royal Canadian Academy of Arts, 1880-1980, Clarke, Irwin, 1980; *Tom Forrestall: His Painting*, Merritt Publishing, 1982.

WORK IN PROGRESS: A History of Canadian Sculpture; Wild Apples, a novel about art and artists.

SIDELIGHTS: Rebecca Sisler told *CA:* "All my writing to date has been connected to the visual arts, which is not surprising. I consider myself something of an evangelist in my attempts to interpret the visual arts to the public through the written word. My hobby, if it can be termed that, has been to travel to sites of ancient civilizations noted for their artistic achievements (such as Egypt, Mexico, and Peru), and it is my secret ambition to extend my travels and write a book that would bring these sites and their significance to life for the general reader."

*   *   *

SKELTON, Red   1913-

PERSONAL: Given name, Richard Bernard Skelton; born July 18, 1913, in Vincennes, Ind.; son of Joseph (a circus clown) and Ida Mae Skelton; married Edna Marie Stillwell, June, 1932 (divorced, 1940); married Georgia Maureen Davis, March, 1945 (divorced, 1973); married Lothian Toland, March, 1973; children: (second marriage) Valentina Maris Alonso, Richard Freeman (deceased). *Education:* Attended Northwestern University. *Office:* Van Bernard Productions, 37-715 Thompson Rd., Rancho Mirage, Calif. 92270.

CAREER: Worked as comedian and singer with tent and minstrel shows and on a showboat; clown with Hagenbeck & Wallace Circus; entertainer in burlesque shows in the Midwest; worked as master of ceremonies in walkathons; Loew's Montreal Theatre, Montreal, Quebec, comedian in vaudeville shows, 1936; made Broadway debut, 1937; made radio debut on "The Rudy Valee Show," 1937; regular guest on radio show "Avalon Time," 1939; actor and comedian in more than forty-five motion pictures, including "Having a Wonderful Time," 1938, "Lady Be Good," 1941, "Whistling in the Dark," 1941, "The People vs. Dr. Kildare," 1941, "Ship Ahoy," 1942, "Whistling in Dixie," 1942, "Panama Hatti," 1942, "DuBarry Was a Lady," 1943, "I Dood It," 1943, "Whistling in Brooklyn," 1943, "Thousands Cheer," 1943, "Bathing Beauty," 1944, "Ziegfeld Follies," 1946, "The Show-Off," 1946, "Merton of the Movies," 1947, "Neptune's Daughter," 1949, "Three Little Words," 1950, "Texas Carnival," 1951, "The Clown," 1953, "The Great Diamond Robbery," 1954, "Public Pigeon Number One," 1957, and "Those Magnificent Men in Their Flying Machines," 1965; host of "Red Skelton Scrapbook of Satire" radio show, 1941-53; television star of "The Red Skelton Show," Columbia Broadcasting System (CBS-TV), 1951-69, National Broadcasting Co. (NBC-TV), 1969-70; businessman, painter, and occasional entertainer, 1970—. Founder and member of board of directors of Red Skelton's Needy Children's Fund. *Military service:* U.S. Army Field Artillery, 1944-45; entertained servicemen.

MEMBER: American Federation of Television and Radio Artists, American Society of Composers, Authors, and Publishers, Masons. *Awards, honors:* Emmy Awards from National Academy of Television Arts and Sciences; Silver Helmet Americanism Award from American Veterans of World War II, Korea, and Vietnam, 1968; Freedom Foundation Award, 1970; National Commanders award from American Legion, 1970; Golden Globe Award, 1978.

WRITINGS: (Editor) *A Red Skeleton in Your Closet: Ghost Stories Gay and Grim*, Grosset, 1965; *Red Skelton's Gertrude*

and Heathcliffe, Desert Publications, 1971, reprinted as *Gertrude and Heathcliffe* (self-illustrated), Scribner, 1974.

WORK IN PROGRESS: An autobiography.

SIDELIGHTS: Red Skelton has been in the entertainment business since the age of ten. His father, a clown with the Hagenbeck & Wallace Circus, died two months before Skelton was born. The elder's death left the family in financial straits, so young Skelton worked as soon as he was able. At seven, he hawked newspapers and racked balls in a local pool hall. At ten, he broke wooden crates for J.C. Penney's. While thus employed, Skelton auditioned for a job as a "mammy singer" with "Doc" R. E. Lewis's traveling medicine show. During the tryout, he accidentally tumbled from the stage, shattering dozens of medicine bottles. "When I got up, the audience laughed," Skelton later explained. "I decided to fall again to see if I could get another laugh. But that time I jumped up real quick to let them know I wasn't hurt, and the laugh was louder." The budding entertainer was hired at fifteen dollars a week, and his clumsy falls became one of his most reliable comic devices.

Quitting school in the seventh grade, Skelton ran away from home with his older brother's birth certificate and a wig his mother had given him. He took up show business on a full-time basis, touring with a variety of companies, including the John Lawrence Stock Company's tent show, Clarence Stout's Minstrels, and Captain Happy's company on the showboat *Cotton Blossom*, which plied the Ohio and Missouri rivers. Skelton then followed his father's footsteps by joining the Hagenbeck & Wallace Circus as a clown.

By the age of fifteen, the comedian was covering the burlesque circuit, playing in such cities as St. Louis, Kansas City, Buffalo, and Indianapolis. It was while performing at a burlesque engagement in Kansas City that the entertainer met his wife Edna. They were married shortly before Skelton's eighteenth birthday and began working at "walkathons" all over the country. Skelton entertained, and Edna collected the entrance fees. The couple then moved into vaudeville, with Edna filling such positions as scriptwriter and agent for her husband. Unable to achieve recognition in the United States, they eventually sought work in Canada at Loew's Montreal Theatre.

On August 12, 1937, Skelton got his big break with a radio spot on "The Rudy Vallee Show." His appearance was a hit, and the comic made several return visits. He regularly starred on the radio show "Avalon Time" in 1939 and obtained his own show, "Red Skelton's Scrapbook of Satire," in 1941. Supported by the writing abilities of Edna and the musical talents of Ozzie and Harriet Nelson, Skelton's show became a national favorite. Although suspended briefly while the comedian served his stint in the armed forces during World War II, the program returned to the air waves with a vigor which lasted until 1953. Through the radio show, Americans became familiar with such Skelton creations as Clem Kadiddlehopper, Deadeye, Freddie Freeloader, Junior, Bolivar Shagnasty, and Willie Lump-Lump.

With his radio successes came motion picture offers. In numerous films, Skelton displayed his comic facial expressions and pantomimic talents beside such well-known movie stars as Fred Astaire, Lucille Ball, Gene Kelly, Esther Williams, and Ginger Rogers.

It was through television, however, that Skelton established himself as an entertainment legend. "The Red Skelton Show" ran nearly twenty years on television, a record surpassed by no other comedian except Jack Benny. Skelton, who once asserted that "humor is truth . . . [and that] wit is an exaggeration on that truth," has performed before seven presidents.

After the television show was cancelled in 1970, Skelton went into business selling his own oil paintings of sad-faced clowns. He runs a mail-order operation which offers his original paintings, reproductions on canvas, and lithographs to consumers.

AVOCATIONAL INTERESTS: Gardening, writing music.

BIOGRAPHICAL/CRITICAL SOURCES: Life, October 22, 1951; *Newsweek,* March 17, 1952, December 28, 1959; *Look,* April 2, 1957, October 13, 1959; *Time,* October 3, 1960; *Life,* April 21, 1961; *Saturday Evening Post,* June 2, 1962, June 17, 1967; *McCalls,* October, 1966; *National Review,* July 27, 1971; *New York Times,* March 9, 1977; Leonard Maltin, *Great Movie Comedians,* Crown, 1978.*

*　　*　　*

SKIRA, Albert   1904-1973

OBITUARY NOTICE: Born August 10, 1904, in Geneva, Switzerland; died September 14, 1973, in Dully, Switzerland. Publisher of books on art. Known throughout the world for the fine quality of the art books he published, Skira worked meticulously on their composition, often spending several years on a single edition. His publishing career began in 1928 when he convinced Pablo Picasso to illustrate a limited edition of Ovid's *Metamorphoses.* Although the volume later became a collector's item, selling for $12,500 in 1966, the book sold slowly at its original price of $400. Skira, however, continued to publish literary classics, including *Florilege des amours de Ronsard,* with etchings by Henri Matisse, and *Les Chants de Maldoror,* with illustrations by Salvador Dali. He also published art journals and works on the history of art, including "The Great Centuries of Painting" series. Obituaries and other sources: *Current Biography,* Wilson, 1967; *New York Times,* September 15, 1973; *Publishers Weekly,* October 1, 1973; *Who's Who,* 126th edition, St. Martin's, 1974.

*　　*　　*

SKOUSEN, Mark

PERSONAL—Education: George Washington University, Ph.D. *Home:* 600 Beulah Rd., Vienna, Va. 22180. *Office:* Suite 1200 N, 7315 Wisconsin Ave., Washington, D.C. 20014.

CAREER: Economist. Worked as economic analyst for Central Intelligence Agency, Washington, D.C.; writer and editor. *Member:* National Press Club.

WRITINGS: The 100 Percent Gold Standard: Economics of a Pure Money Commodity, University Press of America, 1977; *Playing the Price Controls Game: How Some People Will Profit From the Coming Controls,* Arlington House, 1977; *The Insider's Banking and Credit Almanac,* Kephart Communications, 1977, 4th edition, 1979; *Mark Skousen's Complete Guide to Financial Privacy,* foreword by Robert Kinsman, Alexandria House, 1979, revised edition, 1980. Also author of *New Profits From Your Insurance Policy.* Contributor of articles to business and financial publications. Special consultant to *Ruff Times;* associate editor of *Tax Angles* and *Personal Finance;* editor of *Forecast and Strategies.*

SIDELIGHTS: Skousen's books on economics are directed toward the individual who is concerned about investment protection and personal finance. His book *Playing the Price Controls Game,* for example, includes Skousen's suggestions for worthwhile investments in a business climate where the government has instituted price controls in an attempt to curb inflation. He says his newsletter *Forecasts and Strategies* provides subscribers with "a continuing source of information and advice on government interference with private investors and with the whole economy." Skousen has conducted economics seminars and has been a guest speaker for various financial organizations.

*　　*　　*

SKOYLES, John   1949-

PERSONAL: Born December 11, 1949, in New York, N.Y.; son of Gerard (in sales) and Olga (Bertolotti) Skoyles. *Education:* Fairfield University, A.B., 1971; University of Iowa, M.A., 1972, M.F.A., 1974. *Home:* 37-15 81st St., Apt. 5D, Jackson Heights, N.Y. 11372. *Office:* Fine Arts Work Center, Provincetown, Mass. 02657.

CAREER: Southern Methodist University, Dallas, Tex., assistant professor of English, 1976-77, 1978-79; Fine Arts Work Center, Provincetown, Mass., chairman of writing committee, 1979-81; Sarah Lawrence College, Bronxville, N.Y., assistant professor, 1981—. *Awards, honors:* Fellow of National Endowment for the Arts, 1976; resident fellow at Yaddo Colony, 1977, 1981.

WRITINGS: The Sadness of Music (poetry chapbook), Borogove Press, 1974; *A Little Faith* (poems), Carnegie-Mellon University Press, 1981.

Work represented in anthologies, including *Aspen Anthology; The Ardis Anthology of New American Poetry.* Contributor to literary journals, including *American Poetry Review, Chicago Review, Margins, New Letters, Rolling Stone,* and *Poetry Northwest.*

WORK IN PROGRESS: Another book of poems, for publication by Carnegie-Mellon University Press.

*　　*　　*

SLACK, Adrian (Charles)

PERSONAL: Born in Bosbury, Herefordshire, England; son of Austin and Joan (Hicking) Slack. *Education:* Attended Heatherleys (art school) and Cannington College of Horticulture. *Politics:* "Independent, anti-left." *Religion:* "My own, based largely on Christianity." *Home:* Gregory's Orchard, Barton St. David, Somerton, Somerset, England. *Agent:* James Service, 6 Maiden Lane, London WC2E 7NN, England. *Office:* Marston Exotics, Frome, Somerset, England.

CAREER: Worked as landscape designer for several landscape contracting firms in England, 1958-64; in private practice as landscape architect, 1964-76; Marston Exotics (carnivorous plants) Spring Gardens, Frome, England, partner, 1976—. Guest on British radio and television programs. *Member:* Royal Horticultural Society (fellow), Carnivorous Plant Society (founding member), Alpine Garden Society, English Civil War Society (colonel), Sons of King Ina (co-founder).

WRITINGS: Carnivorous Plants, M.I.T. Press, 1980. Contributor to horticulture journals.

WORK IN PROGRESS: Research on *Drosera binata.*

SIDELIGHTS: Slack commented: "I don't think I'm particularly interested in my *own* being, but am intensely interested in things of nature, be they protozoans or primitive algae under the microscope, or some newly discovered Sundew from Western Australia. I do not think I'm the eccentric some have made me out to be.

"I attended more schools than I can remember, and was sacked or taken away from all but, I think, one. I never worked at school, which explains the frequent removals, though I could read very well at the age of five. I saw no point in work, only learning my lesson when confronted with the obvious *need* to pursue a matter, so I am largely self-taught, even in botany.

"I came from an environment in which little thought was given to such things, for neither my father nor my uncles had careers! They preserved their own game and were all excellent shots, which fitted in nicely with the world of that time. Even had that world continued, however, I could not have joined it, for at five I read the 'Peter Rabbit' books and wanted to live in a rabbit burrow. What I saw on my first shoot (and last) made me the vegetarian I remain, though I am actually in favor of one field sport as providing the best and kindest means of limiting the fox population.

"My main interests are the plants and the countryside, especially carnivorous plants. I have been a keen amateur gardener and plantsman for as long as I can remember. In my youth the first fly-eater I cultivated was the common Round-headed Sundew (you get this over much of the U.S.A. too). This kindled my interest in the study of carnivorous plants, and led to the formation of what ultimately became one of the largest collections of these plants in the world. Six years ago it had become so large that I was forced to light pyres of excess material for which I could find no room. A depressing task, so I was glad when a friend suggested it would be a good plan to form a partnership which could grow this material for sale. Marston Exotics is now a thriving business.

"From early days it had occurred to me that no book existed in English which dealt adequately with all known genera of carnivorous plants, their natural history, biology, and cultivation, in language which was intelligible to layman as well as scientist. To fill this gap I wrote *Carnivorous Plants.*

"I like to write at a south window in the freshness of early morning, when ideas and words come most easily to me. Writing later in the day can be difficult to impossible, so it is then that I study live material and research information from other authorities, or prepare the diagrams and drawings with which I illustrate many of my points.

"I am presently conducting research on the *Drosera binata* complex. These are the giant Forked Sundews of eastern Australia and New Zealand, and have been inadequately studied in the past. I suspect that more than one distinct species may hide under this name.

"Another interest is attending amusing dinner parties, in particular those of the Sons of King Ina. I am a retired colonel of the English Civil War Society, for which I like to organize battle reenactments at old castles with *massive* use of explosives, owners permitting!"

AVOCATIONAL INTERESTS: Looking at paintings, listening to music (especially Bach, Handel, and Beethoven).

BIOGRAPHICAL/CRITICAL SOURCES: Julian Pettifer and Robin Brown, *Naturewatch,* M. Joseph, 1981.

* * *

SLAVENS, Thomas Paul 1928-

PERSONAL: Born November 12, 1928, in Cincinnati, Iowa; son of William Blaine and Rhoda (Bowen) Slavens; married Cora Hart (a school library media specialist), July 9, 1950; children: Mark Thomas. *Education:* Phillips University, B.A., 1951; Union Theological Seminary, New York, N.Y., M.Div.,

1954; University of Minnesota, M.A., 1962; University of Michigan, Ph.D., 1965. *Office:* School of Library Science, University of Michigan, Ann Arbor, Mich. 48109.

CAREER: Ordained minister of Christian Church (Disciples of Christ), 1953; pastor of Christian churches in Sac City, Iowa, 1953-56, and Sioux Falls, S.D., 1956-60; Divinity School of Drake University, Des Moines, Iowa, librarian, 1960-64; University of Michigan, Ann Arbor, teaching fellow, 1964-65, instructor, 1965-66, assistant professor, 1966-69, associate professor, 1969-77, professor, 1977—, faculty associate of Center for Research on Learning and Teaching. Visiting professor at College of Librarianship of Wales, summers, 1978, 1980; member of advisory board of publisher Marcel Dekker, Inc., 1980—; consultant to Agency for International Development. *Military service:* U.S. Army, 1946-48; became staff sergeant.

MEMBER: Association of American Library Schools (president, 1972), American Association of University Professors, American Library Association (chairman of media research committee, 1965-71; member of executive board of Reference and Adult Services Division, 1968-72, and Library Education Division, 1971-72; chairman of Dartmouth Medal committee, 1976-77), Beta Phi Mu. *Awards, honors:* Warner G. Rice Award from University of Michigan, 1977, for *Sources of Information in the Humanities.*

WRITINGS: The Bethany Bible Teacher, Christian Board of Publication, 1965; *The Development and Testing of Materials for Computer-Assisted Instruction in the Education of Reference Librarians,* U.S. Department of Health, Education & Welfare, 1970; *Informational Interviews and Questions,* Scarecrow, 1978; *Computer-Assisted Instruction in the Education of Reference Librarians,* Science Associates/International, 1979; (editor) *Sources of Information in the Humanities,* six volumes, American Library Association, 1982; (editor) *Library Problems in the Humanities,* K. G. Saur, 1981; *The Retrieval of Information in the Humanities and the Social Sciences,* Dekker, 1981.

WORK IN PROGRESS: A systems approach to the teachings of Jesus prayers for public and private worship.

AVOCATIONAL INTERESTS: Travel (Europe, Asia, the Caribbean).

* * *

SLAVICK, William H(enry) 1927-

PERSONAL: Born July 7, 1927, in Memphis, Tenn.; son of Henry William (a radio and television executive) and Lenore (O'Hara) Slavick; married Ursula Lukas (a high school teacher of foreign languages), May 24, 1955; children: Susanne, Elisabeth, Sarah, Stephen, John Henry (deceased), Madeleine, Ellen. *Education:* University of Notre Dame, B.A., 1949, M.A., 1951, Ph.D., 1971; attended University of Munich, 1957-58. *Politics:* Democrat. *Religion:* Roman Catholic. *Home:* 242 Ludlow St., Portland, Maine 04102. *Office:* Department of English, University of Southern Maine, College Ave., Gorham, Maine 04038.

CAREER: Notre Dame College, Wilcox, Saskatchewan, instructor in English, 1951-52, teaching fellow, 1955-57; associated with St. Bernard Abbey, 1952-53; Louisiana State University, Baton Rouge, instructor in English, 1958-60; St. Mary's College, South Bend, Ind., assistant professor of English, 1961-63; State University of New York College at Geneseo, assistant professor of English, 1963-67; Marquette University, Milwaukee, Wis., assistant professor of English, 1967-68; Mount St.

Paul College, Waukesha, Wis., associate professor of English and chairman of Division of Humanities, 1968-70; University of Southern Maine, Gorham, associate professor of English, 1970—, chairman of department, 1974-76. Senior Fulbright Lecturer at Gesamthochschule Kassel, Kassel, West Germany, 1977. Director of Downeast Southern Renascence Conference, 1978, Seeing New Englandly Conference, 1980, State, Religion, and Education Conference, 1980, and Elizabeth Madox Roberts Centenary, 1981; member of national board of directors of Citizens for Educational Freedom, 1961-68. *Military service:* U.S. Army, 1953-55.

MEMBER: Modern Language Association of America, Society for the Study of Southern Literature, National Collegiate Honors Council, American Association of University Professors (chapter president, 1973-75; chairman of state conference, 1974-76). *Awards, honors:* Fulbright grant, 1957-58; Southern Fellowship, 1960-61, Fulbright Senior Lectureship, 1977 and 1981-82; National Endowment for the Humanities grant, summer, 1979.

WRITINGS: DuBose Heyward, Twayne, 1981. Contributor to journals, including *Cross Currents, Commonweal, Studies in the Literary Imagination, Southern Literary Journal,* and *America.*

WORK IN PROGRESS: Editing papers of Downeast Southern Renascence Conference, papers of Seeing New Englandly Conference, and papers of Elizabeth Madox Roberts; editing Roberts's unpublished poems; editing writings by students of Frank O'Malley.

AVOCATIONAL INTERESTS: Travel (Western Europe).

* * *

SMILEY, Jane (Graves) 1949-

PERSONAL: Born September 26, 1949, in Los Angeles, Calif.; daughter of James Laverne (in U.S. Army) and Frances Graves (a writer; maiden name, Nuelle) Smiley; married John Whiston, September 4, 1970 (divorced November, 1975); married William Silag (an editor), May 1, 1978; children: (second marriage) Phoebe Graves. *Education:* Vassar College, B.A., 1971; University of Iowa, M.A., 1975, M.F.A., 1976, Ph.D., 1978. *Politics:* "Skeptical." *Religion:* "Vehement agnostic." *Agent:* Elaine Markson Literary Agency, Inc., 44 Greenwich Ave., New York, N.Y. 10011. *Office:* Department of English, Iowa State University, Ames, Iowa 50011.

CAREER: Iowa State University, Ames, assistant professor of English, 1981—. Visiting assistant professor at University of Iowa, spring, 1981. *Member:* Authors Guild. *Awards, honors:* Fulbright fellowship, 1976-77; grant from National Endowment for the Arts, 1978.

WRITINGS: Born Blind (novel), Harper, 1980; *At Paradise Gate* (novel), Simon & Schuster, 1981.

Work represented in anthologies, including *Pushcart Anthology.* Contributor of stories to magazines, including *Redbook, Mademoiselle, Fiction, TriQuarterly,* and *Playgirl.*

WORK IN PROGRESS: Duplicate Keys, a novel set in New York City, publication by Simon & Schuster expected in 1983.

* * *

SMITH, Gretchen L. ?-1972

OBITUARY NOTICE: Died August 19, 1972. Editor of books, including *Van Nostrand's Scientific Encyclopedia, Modern*

Steamship, and *Sourcebook on Atomic Energy.* Obituaries and other sources: *Publishers Weekly,* September 25, 1972.

* * *

SMITH, Leslie James Seth
   See SETH-SMITH, Leslie James

* * *

SMITH, Margaret Emily Noel Nuttall
   See NUTTALL-SMITH, Margaret Emily Noel

* * *

SMITH, Mortimer B(rewster) 1906-1981

OBITUARY NOTICE: Born February 17, 1906, in Mt. Vernon, N.Y.; died April 26, 1981, in Scottsdale, Ariz. Executive and author of books on education. Smith was an advocate of academic excellence in public schools, particularly in the area of basic skills. His books on education include *And Madly Teach, A Citizen's Manual for Public Schools,* and *A Consumer's Guide to Educational Innovations.* Obituaries and other sources: *Leaders in Education,* 5th edition, Bowker, 1974; *Who's Who in America,* 40th edition, Marquis, 1978; *New York Times,* April 30, 1981.

* * *

SMITH, Paul Jordan
   See JORDAN-SMITH, Paul

* * *

SMITH, Wendell 1914-1972

OBITUARY NOTICE: Born June 27, 1914, in Detroit, Mich.; died of cancer, November 26, 1972, in Chicago, Ill.; buried in Burr Oak Cemetery. Sportswriter, broadcaster, and author. One of the first black members of the Baseball Writers Association, Smith became known for his role in integrating professional baseball. While sports editor for the *Pittsburgh Courier* in the 1930's, Smith polled players and managers and found that most favored integrating the teams, thus refuting the argument of club owners who claimed that white players would refuse to play with blacks. Later he arranged to have Jackie Robinson scouted by the Brooklyn Dodgers. The Dodgers offered Robinson a contract in 1946, and he became the first black athlete to play on a major league baseball team in more than sixty years. Smith and Robinson wrote *Jackie Robinson: My Own Story* in 1948. Obituaries and other sources: *New York Times,* November 27, 1972; *Time,* December 11, 1972; *Who Was Who in America, With World Notables,* Volume V: *1969-1973,* Marquis, 1973; *Chicago Sun-Times,* May 29, 1974; *Biography News,* July, 1974.

* * *

SMITHIES, Arthur 1907-1981

OBITUARY NOTICE: Born December 12, 1907, in Hobart, Tasmania, Australia; died of a heart attack, September 9, 1981, in Cambridge, Mass.; buried in Belmont Cemetery. Economist, educator, and author. Smith, an expert on the fiscal affairs of both industrially advanced and developing nations, held positions with the Bureau of the Budget, the Economic Cooperation Administration, and Harvard University. His book *The Federal Budget and Fiscal Policy* became a standard reference work. Obituaries and other sources: *Who's Who in America,*

40th edition, Marquis, 1978; *New York Times,* September 11, 1981.

* * *

SMOTHERS, Frank A(lbert) 1901-1981

OBITUARY NOTICE: Born in 1901; died after a brief illness, June 14, 1981. Journalist and author. During his long career, Smothers covered gangland violence in the United States, the Spanish civil war, the European and Pacific theaters during World War II, and the Greek civil war, which he wrote about in his book, *Report on the Greek.* Obituaries and other sources: *New York Times,* June 15, 1981.

* * *

SNODGRASS, Thomas Jefferson
See CLEMENS, Samuel Langhorne

* * *

SNOW, Frances Compton
See ADAMS, Henry (Brooks)

* * *

SNYDER, William 1951-

PERSONAL: Born October 7, 1951, in Sellersville, Pa.; son of Bruce (a plumber) and Pauline (an antique dealer; maiden name, DeCicco) Snyder. *Education:* Attended Temple University, 1969-72. *Residence:* San Francisco, Calif. *Agent:* Michael Larsen/Elizabeth Pomada, 1029 Jones St., San Francisco, Calif. 94109.

CAREER: Gourmet Foods, Philadelphia, Pa., in retail management, 1972-78; writer, 1978—.

WRITINGS: Tory's (novel), Avon, 1981.

WORK IN PROGRESS: Another novel.

SIDELIGHTS: Snyder's first novel, *Tory's,* traces the life of Tory, a young man torn by the death of David, his lover. When financially depressed, Tory is attracted to the glittery world of high-priced prostitution, later running a brothel and nightclub, and falling in love with George, who wants to abandon the call-boy life and settle down. After three years in the mob-controlled business, Tory and George make a clean break and commit themselves to each other.

Snyder wrote: "My original motivation for writing was that it appeared to be a painless way to make a living. I could sleep late, work in a bathrobe, and meet friends for long lunches. After a best-seller, I could also move to a seaside villa and hire help to keep the ashtrays empty. Jacqueline Susann made it look so easy to write mindless fiction. Apparently she knew something I don't, but I shall continue to search."

* * *

SOFTLY, Edgar
See LOVECRAFT, H(oward) P(hillips)

* * *

SOFTLY, Edward
See LOVECRAFT, H(oward) P(hillips)

SOLOGUB, Fyodor
See TETERNIKOV, Fyodor Kuzmich

* * *

SOMERSET FRY, (Peter George Robin) Plantagenet 1931-

PERSONAL: Born January 3, 1931, in Kent, England; son of P. K. Llewellin (a naval engineer) and Ruth (a concert pianist; maiden name, Marriott) Fry; married Audrey Russell (marriage ended, 1957); married Daphne Yorke (an actress; died, 1961); married Leri Butler (divorced, 1973); married Pamela Fiona Ileene Whitcombe (a writer), March, 1974. *Education:* Attended St. Thomas's Hospital Medical School, 1948-49, London University, 1949-52, and St. Catherine's College, Oxford, 1954-57. *Politics:* Social democrat. *Home:* Wood Cottage, Wattisfield, Bury St. Edmunds, Suffolk, England.

CAREER: Worked as history master at preparatory school, 1952-54 and 1958-60, as public relations executive, 1960-63, and as director of public relations agency, 1963-64; Incorporated Association of Architects and Surveyors, London, England, information officer, 1965-67; worked as information officer at Ministry of Public Buildings and Works, 1967-70, as head of information services for Council for Small Industries in Rural Areas, 1970-74, and as first book editor of Her Majesty's Stationery Office, 1975-80; writer, 1955—. Visiting scholar at Wolfson College, Cambridge, 1980—. Guest on numerous television programs. *Member:* National Union of Journalists, Royal Society of Literature, Royal Archaeological Institute, Cambridge Antiquarian Society, East Anglian Writers Association.

WRITINGS: Mysteries of History, Muller, 1957; *The Cankered Rose, Elizabeth Tudor: A Sketch of Her Life and Times,* Muller, 1959; *The World of Antiques,* Hamlyn, 1970; *Antique Furniture,* Hamlyn, 1971; *Collecting Inexpensive Antiques,* Hamlyn, 1973; *British Medieval Castles,* David & Charles, 1974; *Two Thousand Years of British Life: A Social History of England, Wales, Scotland, and Ireland,* Collins, 1976; *Chequers: The Country Home of Britain's Prime Ministers,* H.M.S.O., 1977; *Plantagenet Somerset Fry's Three Thousand Questions and Answers Book,* Collins, 1977; *The David & Charles Book of Castles,* David & Charles, 1980; *Great Commanders,* Weidenfeld & Nicholson, 1982; *British History From the Air,* Cambridge University Press, 1983. Also author of *Fountains Abbey,* an official souvenir guide, 1981.

Children's books: *Rulers of Britain,* Hamlyn, 1967; *They Made History: Great Men and Women From Britain's Past,* Hamlyn, 1970; *Constantinople,* Purnell, 1970; *The Wonderful Story of the Jews,* Purnell, 1970; *The Hamlyn Children's History of the World,* Hamlyn, 1972, 8th edition, 1980; *The Answer Book of History,* Hamlyn, 1972; *The Zebra Book of Famous Men,* Evans Brothers, 1972; *The Zebra Book of Famous Women,* Evans Brothers, 1972; *The Zebra Book of Castles,* Evans Brothers, 1974; *Great Caesar,* Collins, 1974; *One Thousand Great Lives,* Hamlyn, 1975; *Questions and Answers to Who, What, When, How, Why, and Where,* Collins, 1976; *Boudicca,* W. H. Allen, 1978. General editor of "Macmillan History in Pictures Series for Children," Macmillan, 1978—.

WORK IN PROGRESS: David and Charles Book of Roman Britain, completion expected in 1983.

SIDELIGHTS: Somerset Fry wrote: "I am very much interested in communicating knowledge, and my career has been devoted to that end since the early 1950's. I have been teacher, writer, broadcaster, and information specialist. I am inspired by history and have a desire to communicate that enthusiasm to others. I was fortunate to have good teachers when young. I also believe that academic history is essential *but,* and it's a big *but,* the results of academic historical research and study must be communicated to the general public in terms they can readily and swiftly appreciate. My work is academically based and researched in depth, but I attempt to present it in easily readable form. I believe this to be crucial.''

* * *

SONENBLICK, Jerry 1931-

PERSONAL: Born July 22, 1931, in Chicago, Ill.; son of Benjamin (in real estate) and Fae (Jacobson) Sonenblick; married Phyllis Rowley, November 5, 1961; children: Beth, Chip, Andy. *Education:* University of Arizona, D.S., 1953, LL.B., 1957. *Politics:* Democrat. *Religion:* Jewish. *Home:* 1542 North Estate, Tuscon, Ariz. 85712. *Agent:* Diane Cleaver, 825 Third Ave., New York, N.Y. 10022. *Office:* 5656 East Grant Rd., Suite 100, Tuscon, Ariz. 85712.

CAREER: Private practice as attorney, Tuscon, Ariz., 1957—; real estate developer, Tuscon, Ariz., 1961—. Chairman of board of Empire West Companies, Inc. Chairman of public relations committees of State Bar of Arizona and of Pima County Bar Association; chairman of a political action committee; former chairman of Pima County Democratic Party Central Committee. Former moderator of legal information television program. Alternate delegate to 1980 Democratic Party National Convention. *Member:* State Bar of Arizona, State Bar of California, Pima County Bar Association.

WRITINGS: (With Martha Sowerwine) *The Legality of Love,* Jove, 1981.

SIDELIGHTS: In *The Legality of Love,* Jerry Sonenblick, an attorney and an expert in contracts, discusses what Jack Russell of the *San Mateo Times* called ''the hottest topic in legal circles these days'': the legal rights of lovers living together. Inspired by the *Marvin* v. *Marvin* case, which the lawyer says posed rather than answered questions, Sonenblick produced a paperback guide explaining the legal ramifications of ''living together.'' In the landmark case, Michelle Triola Marvin sued actor Lee Marvin, with whom she cohabitated for six years, for a percentage of his earnings accrued while they lived together. The California Supreme Court awarded Michelle Marvin $104,000 in ''palimony'' and ended, according to Sonenblick, ''no-strings attached'' relationships. ''If you believe in a no-strings free union,'' the attorney advised, ''get it in writing.''

Since courts are beginning to consider ''homemates,'' the author's name for those who live together, equal to married couples, Sonenblick suggests that couples balance romance with pragmatism and adopt an ''I love you, but you are not going to take all my assets and leave me in debt'' attitude. A contract provides such insurance. As Sonenblick told Jayne Clark of the *Phoenix Gazette,* a contract is ''a hedge against illness, accident or death. The whole purpose of having one is to look into the crystal ball and think about the future from a legal standpoint. Or, as a business associate once said, 'The faintest of ink is better than the keenest of memories.'''

Each homemate should retain an attorney; then together with their counselors the homemates should draw up an agreement specifying their wishes about living expenses, housework, property rights, inheritance, palimony, custody of children and pets, and the like. Without a contract, as is exemplified by a scenario from *The Legality of Love,* the couple's wishes may

be ignored. ''Take for instance Roger and Ellen who have been living together for 10 years,'' wrote Sonenblick. ''Roger wants Ellen to have everything if he passes away. He gets hit by a car and dies. But since there are no provisions in inheritance laws for homemates, a distant relative, Aunt Nellie, say, inherits everything. At best, Ellen could go to court and try to establish that they had an oral agreement.''

But insurance is not the only reason for a contract, and an agreement, as Bob Womack of the *Arizona Daily Star* put it, does not ''throw cold water on a hot romance.'' In fact, Womack reported, ''far from destroying the rapture of romance, . . . couples who draw up contracts actually deepen the bond between them.'' A contract enhances a romance by opening lines of communication and by deepening the relationship. ''Everyone should have a contract,'' Sonenblick disclosed to Russell. ''It is the best way to maintain a loving atmosphere.'' Even married couples should draw up contracts, just as the author and his wife did.

In writing *The Legality of Love,* Sonenblick discovered inconsistencies between state laws as well as inequalities in laws when men and women are concerned. Looking back on the book, he revealed that he ''never realized when I started this thing what I was getting into.'' Yet, in Womack's opinion, the author produced ''a clearly written book loaded with colorful anecdotes as well as a wealth of practical information about the law as it relates to love in every state.''

Sonenblick told *CA:* ''My investment of lost weekends, midnight rewriting sessions, and extensive research, despite its intensity, proved to be a worthwhile investment to experience an 'essence' of life—the writing of a book. How very satisfying to crystallize ideas, impart useful information, and buck the odds against publication.''

BIOGRAPHICAL/CRITICAL SOURCES: Arizona Daily Star, March 5, 1981; *San Mateo Times,* March 12, 1981; *Phoenix Gazette,* April 28, 1981.

* * *

SOUZA, Ernest
See SCOTT, Evelyn

* * *

SPAETH, Eloise O'Mara 1904-

PERSONAL: Born June 19, 1904, in Decatur, Ill.; daughter of James and Alice Margaret (Moroney) O'Mara; married Otto Lucien Spaeth, October 4, 1925; children: Marna (Mrs. G. H. Doherty), Deborah (Mrs. Frank Shakespeare), Otto Lucien, Mary Louise. *Education:* Attended Millikin University. *Home:* 65 East 76th St., New York, N.Y. 10021.

CAREER: Art Institute, Dayton, Ohio, member of board of trustees and director of Contemporary Gallery, 1938-44; chairman of extension service, 1949-59, and of East Division of Architecture, 1959—, for American Federation of the Arts. Chairman of art committee and member of board of trustees of studio school at Guild Hall, Easthampton, N.Y., 1952—; member of UNESCO national commission; member of fine art committee of Smithsonian Institution; member of commission of National Collection of Fine Arts; member of board of trustees of Dayton's Art Institute and Archives of American Art; vice-president of Friends of Whitney Museum. *Member:* American Federation of Arts (member of board of trustees), College Art Association of America, National Council of Women of the United States, Museum Association, Art Collectors Club, Cosmopolitan Club, Maidstone Club.

WRITINGS: American Art Museums and Galleries: An Introduction to Looking, Harper, 1960, 3rd edition, 1975. Contributor to art journals and religious magazines.*

*   *   *

SPALDING, Frances 1950-

PERSONAL: Born July 16, 1950, in Surrey, England; daughter of Hedley Stinston (an aeronautical engineer) and Margaret (Holiday) Crabtree; married Julian Spalding (an art gallery director), April 20, 1974. *Education:* University of Nottingham, B.A. (with first class honors), 1972, Ph.D., 1978. *Home and office:* 74 Ashland Rd., Sheffield S7 1RJ, England.

CAREER: Sheffield City Polytechnic, Sheffield, England, part-time lecturer in art history, 1978—. Guest lecturer at University of San Francisco, summer, 1977. *Member:* Society of Authors.

WRITINGS: Magnificent Dreams: Burne-Jones and the Late Victorians, Phaidon, 1978; *Whistler,* Phaidon, 1979; *Roger Fry: Art and Life,* University of California Press, 1980. Contributor to art journals and to periodicals, including *Times Literary Supplement.*

WORK IN PROGRESS: Vanessa Bell: A Biography, publication expected by Weidenfeld & Nicolson.

SIDELIGHTS: Frances Spalding wrote: "Like most biographers, I realized as a child that there was more going on in books than in the world around me. I admired the achievement of Michael Holroyd and was given a boost of self-confidence by an invitation to lecture on Robert Fry at the University of San Francisco. This visit to California and my reading of the first volume of Virginia Woolf's diary made me determined to become a writer. My touchstone (or Bible, or whatever) is Rainer Maria Rilke's small pamphlet, 'Letters to a Young Poet.'

"The cumbersome business of writing another person's life makes inroads on the author's own life. It is only justified if the writer is able to give back life to his or her subject. Often, however, there is the surprising discovery that what seemed lost in one's own life has in fact been redeemed."

BIOGRAPHICAL/CRITICAL SOURCES: Times Literary Supplement, March 21, 1980; *Burlington,* July, 1980; *New York Times Book Review,* October 5, 1980; *Los Angeles Times,* November 13, 1980; *American Scholar,* winter, 1980-81.

*   *   *

SPALDING, Lucile
See SPALDING, Ruth

*   *   *

SPALDING, Ruth
(Marion Jay, Lucile Spalding)

PERSONAL—Education: Received M.A. from Somerville College, Oxford. *Home:* 34 Reynards Rd., Welwyn, Hertfordshire AL6 9TP, England.

CAREER: Worked as artistic director and general manager of Rock Theatre Company Ltd., and as national adviser and lecturer of National Union of Townswomen Guilds, London, England; Association of Head Mistresses, London, general secretary, 1960-75; writer, 1975—. *Member:* Royal Historical Society (fellow), Royal Society of Arts (fellow). *Awards, honors:* Whitbread Literary Award, 1975, for *The Improbable Puritan.*

WRITINGS: The Improbable Puritan: A Life of Bulstrode Whitelocke, 1605-1675, Faber, 1975.

Under pseudonym Marion Jay: *Pleasure or Pain in Education* (documentary play), University of London Press, 1958; *Mistress Bottom's Dream,* (one-act play), Evans Brothers, 1958; (with Alison Graham Campbell) *Why Not Write a Documentary Play?,* University of London Press, 1960.

Plays: (Co-author) "With This Sword: A Modern Masque," first produced in London, England, at Royal Festival Hall, 1954; "The Word," first broadcast by BBC-TV, 1957.

Also author of *Craft Standards,* 1956, and *Craft-Judging,* both under pseudonym Lucile Spalding.

WORK IN PROGRESS: Editing diary of Bulstrode Whitelocke, completion expected in March, 1982, for publication by British Academy.

SIDELIGHTS: Ruth Spalding commented: "Two, among many, influences on my work have been (1) the advice given to me many years ago by the late Charles Williams: 'Always remember the rules of melodrama—something must happen on every page,' and (2) acting in the plays of Bernard Shaw, whose words are balanced to a hair. I love words and the sandwich of excitement, boredom, and excitement in historical research."

AVOCATIONAL INTERESTS: Family and friends, organic gardening, whole foods, travel (including walking tours).

*   *   *

SPALEK, John M. 1928-

PERSONAL: Born July 28, 1928, in Warsaw, Poland; son of Bronislaw and Augusta (Gomse) Spalek; married Dortha Ann Tillman, June 16, 1957; children: Anne Margaret, Frederick Carter. *Education:* Whitworth College, B.A., 1954; Stanford University, M.A., 1957, Ph.D., 1961. *Home:* 23 Pheasant Lane, Delmar, N.Y. 12054. *Office:* Department of Germanic Languages and Literatures, HU 209, State University of New York at Albany, Albany, N.Y. 12222.

CAREER: University of Southern California, Los Angeles, 1960-70, began as assistant professor, became professor of German; State University of New York at Albany, professor of German, 1970—, chairman of department of Germanic languages and literatures, 1970-76. *Member:* International Arthur Schnitzler Society (chairman of research seminar on German literature in exile), Modern Language Association of America, American Association of Teachers of German, Brecht Society. *Awards, honors:* Fulbright grant for Germany, 1958-59; Andrew Mellon fellowship from University of Pittsburgh, 1967-68; National Endowment for the Humanities grant, 1972-73 and 1974-78.

WRITINGS: Ernst Toller and His Critics: A Bibliography, Bibliographical Society, University of Virginia, 1968, 2nd edition, 1973; (editor) *Medieval Epic to the "Epic Theater" of Brecht,* University of Southern California Press, 1968; (editor) *Lion Feuchtwanger: The Man, His Ideas, His Work, a Collection of Critical Essays,* Hennessey & Ingalls, 1972; (with others) *German Expressionism in the Fine Arts: A Bibliography,* Hennessey & Ingalls, 1977; (with Adrienne Ash and Sandra H. Hawrylchak) *Guide to the Archival Materials of the German-Speaking Emigration to the United States After 1933: Verzeichnic der Quellen und Materialien der deutschsprachigen Emigration in den U.S.A. seit 1933,* University Press of Virginia, 1978.

In German: (Editor with Joseph Strelka) *Deutsche Exhilliteratur seit 1933,* Volume I, Part 2, Francke, 1976; (with Wolfgang Fruehwald) *Der Fall Toller: Kommentar und Materialien,* Hanser, 1979. Also editor of *Gesammelte Werke,* five volumes, by Ernest Toller.

BIOGRAPHICAL/CRITICAL SOURCES: Choice, July-August, 1977.*

* * *

SPEARS, Richard A(lan)   1939-

PERSONAL: Born October 28, 1938, in Kansas City, Mo.; son of Richard Frank (in sales) and Marguerite A. (a singer; maiden name, Sowell) Spears; married Nancy Hopper (a medical technologist), June 30, 1961; children: Elaine, Joel, Rachel, Andrew. *Education:* Texas Christian University, B.A., 1961; Indiana University, Ph.D., 1965. *Office:* Department of Linguistics, Northwestern University, Evanston, Ill. 60201.

CAREER: Operated pipe organ tuning and service company, 1958-65; Northwestern University, Evanston, Ill., assistant professor, 1965-71, associate professor of linguistics, 1971—. Member of board of trustees of Glenview Public Library, 1979-85; consultant to Brand Group, Inc.

WRITINGS: Basic Course in Mende, U.S. Office of Education, 1967; *Short Course in Mende,* U.S. Office of Education, 1967; *Basic Course in Maninka-kan,* U.S. Office of Education, 1973; *Slang and Euphemism: A Dictionary of Oaths, Curses, Insults, Sexual Slang and Metaphor, Racial Slurs, Drug Talk, Homosexual Lingo, and Related Matters,* Jonathan David, 1981.

WORK IN PROGRESS: The Slang and Jargon of Drugs and Drink; collecting material for other historical slang dictionaries.

SIDELIGHTS: Spears told *CA:* "It may sound strange, but the need to write dictionaries has been part of me for as long as I can remember. Every term paper I ever wrote in school was just an elaboration of a small dictionary. My doctoral dissertation and subsequent African language textbooks all contain dictionaries which are vital to the rest of the work. In fact, before I began *Slang and Euphemism,* I only knew that I had to write a *whole* dictionary; the choice of topic came along later. I chose the topic 'euphemism and taboo' because (1) it is of universal interest, (2) very few lexicographers have approached the subject seriously, and (3) it points to a historical framework for explaining the vastness of our vocabulary of euphemisms and the persistence of our prohibitions against slang.

"The hazards of writing about low-life vocabulary have been the same for at least two centuries. The most reliable dictionaries are those written on 'historical principles,' i.e., dates and definitions based on citations of usage by respectable authors. Since respectable authors tend not to know or use low-life vocabulary, it is impossible to write a historical dictionary of slang, etc., that is as reliable as *The Oxford English Dictionary,* for instance.

"Even more of a problem is that when one includes the 'taboo words,' some people focus on them exclusively. News of my research interests often becomes 'silly season' filler in the local newspapers. In August, 1980, during a lengthy interview about *Slang and Euphemism,* I mentioned some minor point about the big bad word that starts with F. Before things settled down I had done seventy-six radio, television, and print interviews, had a lively correspondence with some extraordinary people, and received a small helping of hate mail. It is very sobering to learn that there is a handful of souls somewhere praying for my early demise in the name of truth and beauty. Unfortu-

nately, the book was not due out for a year when this hit the fan.

"All of this has not dulled my lexicographical zeal. I am currently working on a drug slang dictionary. Somewhere, off in the future, I will probably write *The Anatomy of Hate Mail.*"

* * *

SPEED, Frank Warren

PERSONAL: Born in Ballarat, Australia; son of Frank and Jean Hastie (Good) Speed; married Joyce Irene Ackroyd (a university professor), May 12, 1962; children: Roderic Euen Warren, Jennifer Dorothy Callaghan. *Education:* Attended Middle East Staff College, 1940. *Home and office:* 50 Vanwall Rd., Moggill, Queensland 4070, Australia.

CAREER: Australian Citizen Military Forces, served in Victorian Scottish Regiment, 1929-39, leaving service as captain; Australian Imperial Force, served in infantry battalion, 1939-46, leaving service as lieutenant colonel; Australian Regular Army, senior instructor at Australian Staff College, 1947-54, commander of Australian Army Force of Far East Landforces, 1954-59, director of quartering and personnel administration and inspector of administration, 1959-66, retiring as brigadier. President of United Service Institute of Queensland, 1969-74. *Member:* Regular Defence Forces Welfare Association (president of Queensland branch, 1969—), Most Excellent Order of the British Empire (president of Queensland Association, 1977-80).

WRITINGS: The South East Asian Peninsula Today, Angus & Robertson, 1970; *Indonesia Today,* Angus & Robertson, 1971; *Malaysia and Singapore,* Angus & Robertson, 1973; *Your Journey Into the South East Asian Peninsula,* Angus & Robertson, 1973; *Your Journey Into Indonesia,* Angus & Robertson, 1974; (contributor) I. F. Nicolson and Colin A. Hughes, editors, *Pacific Polities,* Pitman, 1974; *The Leadership of Monash: A Military, Industrial, and Commercial Case Study,* about General Sir John Monash, in press.

SIDELIGHTS: Speed told *CA:* "Each sentence in a piece of nonfiction should be so clear that it needs to be read only once in order to take in its meaning. A reader may wish, subconsciously, to reread a sentence—to savour the thought it expresses, to understand the implication of a technical word it contains, or even to enjoy the quality of its style. But it is an affront to the reader's intelligence if a sentence is so constructed that it must be read more than once before its meaning becomes clear."

* * *

SPEER, Albert   1905-1981

OBITUARY NOTICE—See index for *CA* sketch: Born March 19, 1905, in Mannheim, Germany (now West Germany); died of a cerebral hemorrhage, September 1, 1981, in London, England. Nazi official, administrator, architect, educator, and author. Speer served as the minister for armaments and ammunition of Nazi Germany from 1942 to 1945. In this position he was responsible for supplying Nazi armies with guns, aircraft, tanks, bullets, and fuel. Despite repeated Allied bombings of German industrial complexes, Speer succeeded and more than doubled pre-1942 armament output. He also developed and supervised the production of synthetic fuel, which eventually filled more than half of Germany's energy requirements. To accomplish this, Speer used slave labor. After Nazi Germany's surrender, he was arrested on May 23, 1945, and tried for his war crimes at Nuremburg. Although the only Nazi to confess his guilt, he denied knowledge of the death camps. Speer once wrote, "My mortal failure is not a matter of this item or that; it resides in my active association with the whole course of events." Charged primarily with using conscripted workers, he was sentenced to twenty years in Spandau prison. His books on Nazi Germany are entitled *Inside the Third Reich: Memoirs, Spandau: The Secret Diaries,* and *The Slave State.* Prior to his Nazi involvement, Speer was an asssistant professor of architecture at the Technical University of Berlin. He also worked as an architect for Hitler before becoming the minister of armaments. Speer engineered the famous "cathedrals of light" of Nazi rallies in addition to constructing various monuments praising the Fascist regime. Obituaries and other sources: *London Times,* September 3, 1981; *Time,* September 14, 1981; *Newsweek,* September 14, 1981.

* * *

SPENGLER, Edwin H(arold)   1906-1981

OBITUARY NOTICE: Born April 4, 1906, in Brooklyn, N.Y.; died June 8, 1981, in Rockville Centre, N.Y. Economist, educator, and author of textbooks on economics and business. Spengler became known as a leader in continuing education when, as dean of Brooklyn College (now of the City University of New York), he introduced evening classes for working adults in 1950. Among Spengler's books are *Land Values in New York in Relation to Transit Facilities* and *Urban Taxation.* Obituaries and other sources: *Who's Who in America,* 39th edition, Marquis, 1978; *New York Times,* June 11, 1981.

* * *

SPIEGEL, Richard Alan   1947-

PERSONAL: Born January 24, 1947, in New York, N.Y.; son of Morris (a real estate broker) and Sylvia (in newspaper advertising; maiden name, Iskowitz) Spiegel. *Education:* Syracuse University, B.A., 1967; New York University, M.A., 1981. *Home and office:* 799 Greenwich St., New York, N.Y. 10014.

CAREER: Teacher at community center in New York City, 1967-68; U.S. Peace Corps, Washington, D.C., volunteer teacher in Liberia, 1968-69; teacher at international school in Vilstern, Netherlands, 1970-71; teacher at public schools in Charlotte Amalie, Virgin Islands, 1971-72; Scribblers, New York City, director and editor of *Scribblers Sheet,* 1972-75; Bantam Books, Inc., New York City, in sales department, 1974-77; Bard Press, New York City, publisher and editor, 1974-80; Ten Penny Players, New York City, co-director, 1979—. Producer of poetry and folk music programs on cable television, 1972-75; play reader for playwright development program of Public Theater, 1975-76; director of New York Poetry Festival, 1976-78; co-director of Waterways Project, 1979-80. *Awards, honors:* National Endowment for the Arts fellow, 1978.

WRITINGS—Poems: *Icarus,* Bard Press, 1975; *Lust's Last,* Bard Press, 1976; *Harbor,* Bard Press, 1979.

Work represented in anthologies, including *From Hudson to the World,* Hudson River Sloop Clearwater, 1978; *More Than a Gathering of Dreamers,* Coordinating Council of Literary Magazines, 1980. Contributor of poems to magazines, including *Jewish Currents, Dodeka, Home Planet News, AIM, Public Press,* and *Poet.* Member of editorial board of *American Review,* 1974-77; co-editor of *Waterways,* 1979-81.

WORK IN PROGRESS: Syg's Saga, an epic, with own illustrations.

SIDELIGHTS: Ten Penny Players produces and publishes books and theatrical materials by and for children. The Waterways Project is a series of small press book fairs, poetry readings, and workshops. It also operates a children's awareness project and deals primarily, but not exclusively, with children who have special needs.

Spiegel told *CA:* "I'm a visual artist as well as an author. In 1979 I founded the school of Romantic Abstract Sensualism."

* * *

SPILSBURY, Richard   1919-

PERSONAL: Born in 1919 in Great Britain.

CAREER: University of Wales, University College of Wales, Aberystwyth, Wales, lecturer in philosophy, 1947-57. University of Toronto, Toronto, Ontario, visiting professor of philosophy, 1960-61.

WRITINGS: Providence Lost: A Critique of Darwinism, Oxford University Press, 1975.*

* * *

SPINDLER, Arthur   1918-

PERSONAL: Born December 13, 1918, in New York, N.Y.; son of Morris and Fannie (Mintzer) Spindler; married Pearl Goldstein, August 24, 1941; children: Nancy Spindler Callahan, Kenneth, Janet. *Education:* Brooklyn College (now of the City University of New York), B.A., 1940; American University, M.A., 1946; Strayer College of Accounting, B.C.S., 1953. *Home and office:* 9210 Ewing Dr., Bethesda, Md. 20034.

CAREER: District of Columbia General Hospital, Washington, D.C., comptroller, 1959-60; District of Columbia Public Health Department, Washington, D.C., public health program adviser, 1960-63; District of Columbia Public Welfare Department, Washington, D.C., chief of planning and research, 1963-67; U.S. Department of Health, Education and Welfare, Washington, D.C., program analysis officer for Welfare Administration, 1967-68, director of Program Planning Division of Social Rehabilitation Service, 1968—. Visiting professor at colleges and universities; consultant on social and health systems. *Member:* American Public Health Association, American Public Welfare Association, Operations Research Society of America (chairman of social sciences applications section), District of Columbia Public Health Association.

WRITINGS: Federal Administration: A Management Plan, [Bethesda, Md.], 1958; *Public Welfare,* Human Sciences, 1978.*

* * *

SPIRO, Herzl Robert   1935-

PERSONAL: Born April 22, 1935, in Burlington, Vt.; married, 1955; children: three. *Education:* University of Vermont, B.A., 1955, M.D., 1960; attended Harvard University, 1955-56, Washington Psychoanalytic Institute, 1966-71, Washington School of Psychiatry, 1968, Tavistock Institute of Human Relations, 1970, and National Institute of Applied Behavioral Science, 1970-71; Rutgers University, Ph.D., 1975. *Office:* Medical College of Wisconsin, 9191 Watertown Plank Rd., Milwaukee, Wis. 53226.

CAREER: Cornell University, Ithaca, N.Y., intern in internal medicine, 1960-61; Johns Hopkins University, Baltimore, Md., resident in psychiatry, 1961-64, instructor, 1964-66, assistant professor, 1966-69, associate professor of psychiatry, 1969-

71, research fellow, 1961-64, associate physician in charge of psychiatric liaison service at Johns Hopkins Hospital and administrator of Psychosomatic Clinic, 1964-66, psychiatrist in charge of Henry Phipps Outpatient Service, 1966-70, director of outpatient and community mental health programs and Division of Group Process, 1969-71; Rutgers University, Medical School, Piscataway, N.J., professor of psychiatry and social psychology and director of Mental Health Center, 1971-76; Medical College of Wisconsin, Milwaukee, professor of psychiatry and chairman of department, 1976—. Member of National Task Force for Psychiatric Research, 1972-73; director of psychiatry and mental health for Milwaukee County, 1975—; president of medical staff at Milwaukee Psychiatric Hospital, 1975—; consultant to Social Security Administration and National Institute of Mental Health.

MEMBER: American Association for the Advancement of Science, American Psychiatric Association (fellow), American College of Psychiatrists (fellow), American Public Health Association (fellow), American Psychosomatic Society, American Group Psychotherapy Association, American Association of Social Psychiatry, American Psychopathological Association, American Association of University Professors, American Association of Chairmen of Departments of Psychiatry, National Council of Community Mental Health Centers, Group for the Advancement of Psychotherapy.

WRITINGS: (Contributor) *Science and Psychoanalysis*, Grune, 1971; (co-author) *Reform Is a Verb*, Union of American Hebrew Congregations, 1972; (with Guido M. Crocetti and Iradj Siassi) *Contemporary Attitudes Toward Mental Illness*, University of Pittsburgh Press, 1974. Contributor to journals in the behavioral sciences.

SIDELIGHTS: Spiro made a sound recording, "The Construct of Mental Illness," released by the Health Sciences Centre at University of British Columbia in 1974.*

*   *   *

SPIVACK, Robert (Gerald)   1915-1970

OBITUARY NOTICE: Born April 28, 1915, in Dayton, Ohio; died of a heart attack, June 25, 1970, in Riverside, Conn. Journalist and editor of a political affairs newsletter. Obituaries and other sources: *New York Times*, June 26, 1970; *AB Bookman's Weekly*, September 21, 1970; *Who's Who in World Jewry: A Biographical Dictionary of Outstanding Jews*, Pitman, 1972; *Who Was Who in America, With World Notables*, Volume V: *1969-1973*, Marquis, 1973.

*   *   *

SPONG, John Shelby   1931-

PERSONAL: Born June 16, 1931, in Charlotte, N.C.; son of John Shelby (in sales) and Doolie Boyce (Griffith) Spong; married Joan Lydia Ketner, September 5, 1952; children: Ellen Elizabeth, Mary Katharine, Jaquelin Ketner. *Education:* University of North Carolina, A.B., 1952; Virginia Theological Seminary, M.Div., 1955. *Home:* 43 Ogden, Morristown, N.J. 07960. *Office:* 24 Rector St., Newark, N.J. 07102.

CAREER: Ordained Episcopal minister, 1955; rector of Episcopal churches in Durham, N.C., 1955-57, Tarboro, N.C., 1957-65, Lynchburg, Va., 1965-69, and Richmond, Va., 1969-76; Northern New Jersey Episcopal Church, Diocese of Newark, Newark, bishop, 1976—. Chaplain at Duke University, 1955-57, Randolph-Macon Woman's College, 1965-69, and Medical College of Virginia, 1969-76; member of executive council of National Episcopal Church. Chairman of board of

directors of Christ Hospital, Jersey City, N.J.; chairman of Youth Consultative Service. *Member:* Phi Beta Kappa. *Awards, honors:* Brotherhood Award from National Conference of Christians and Jews, 1974.

WRITINGS: Honest Prayer, Seabury, 1973; *This Hebrew Lord*, Seabury, 1974; *Dialogue: In Search of Jewish-Christian Understanding*, Seabury, 1975; *Christpower*, Thomas Hale Co., 1975; *The Living Commandments*, Seabury, 1977; *The Easter Moment*, Seabury, 1980; *The Changing Shape of the Church*, Seabury, 1982. Contributor to theology journals and religious magazines, including *Christian Century*, *Living Church*, and *Witness*.

SIDELIGHTS: Spong commented: "I write as a believing skeptic inside the structures of the church for those who have drifted outside these structures. I try to keep one foot in tradition and one in the radical secularity of the twentieth century. I seek the inner meaning of the Christian symbol beyond the literal words of scripture and creed."

*   *   *

SPOTTISWOODE, Raymond J.   1913-1970

OBITUARY NOTICE: Born in 1913; died in an automobile accident, August 18, 1970, in England. Filmmaker and author of *A Grammar of the Film, Film and Its Techniques*, and *The Focal Encyclopedia of Film and Television*. Obituaries and other sources: *Publishers Weekly*, September 7, 1970; *The Oxford Companion to Film*, Oxford University Press, 1976.

*   *   *

SPRADLING, Mary Elizabeth Mace   1911-

PERSONAL: Born December 31, 1911, in Winchester, Ky.; daughter of Minor Jeremiah (a minister) and Ella Nora (a teacher; maiden name, Trivers) Mace; married Louis Lee Spradling (a teacher and elementary school principal), August 8, 1936 (died, 1964). *Education:* Kentucky State College, A.B., 1933; Atlanta University, B.L.S., 1949; Rutgers University, Certificate, 1959. *Religion:* Christian Church (Disciples of Christ). *Home and office:* 307 South Dartmouth, Kalamazoo, Mich. 49007.

CAREER: Lynch High School, Lynch, Ky., teacher of French, 1933-37; Mather Academy, Camden, S.C., teacher, 1937-38; Eminence Junior High, Eminence, Ky., teacher, 1942-43; Douglass High School, Lexington, Ky., teacher, 1943-44; Shelbyville Junior High, Shelbyville, Ky., 1944-47; Louisville Public Library, Louisville, Ky., branch librarian, 1948-57; Kalamazoo Public Library, Kalamazoo, Mich., young adult librarian, 1957-61, head of young adult department, 1961-76, organizing librarian of Alma Harrod Powell branch library, 1969-70; compiler, 1976—. Guest lecturer at Western Michigan University; guest instructor at Rutgers University. Member of Louisville Family Service Organization Community Council; member of Kalamazoo Council on Human Relations, County Community Services Council, Youth Committee, Council of Churches, County Library Board, and Mayor's Advisory Committee on Problems of Law Enforcement; Secretary and member of board of directors of King Memorial Fund; member of board of trustees of Nazareth College; public speaker.

MEMBER: American Library Association (member of board of directors of Young Adult Services Division; member of council), Association of Young People's Librarians, National Association for the Advancement of Colored People (Kalamazoo Branch; vice-president; secretary of executive committee), Michigan Library Association, Kentucky Library Association, Kentucky Negro Education Association (chairman of librarians' section), Delta Kappa Gamma (Epsilon chapter), Delta Sigma Theta.

AWARDS, HONORS: Citations from Midwest region of Delta Sigma Theta, 1968, for campus chapter advisory service; Kalamazoo alumnae of Delta Sigma Theta citation, 1976, for *In Black and White: Afro-Americans in Print;* award from Adero Sisterhood, 1977, for devotion to young people and their learning; citation from Black Educators of Kalamazoo, 1977, for contributions to all young people of Kalamazoo.

WRITINGS: (Editor) *In Black and White: Afro-Americans in Print,* Kalamazoo Public Library, 1971, 3rd edition, Gale, 1980. Contributor to magazines.

WORK IN PROGRESS: Compiling and editing a bibliography of books written by and about black American women, publication expected in 1982; a supplement to *In Black and White.*

SIDELIGHTS: "I grew up in a separate society," Mary Mace Spradling told *CA,* "in a small Kentucky town, with one parent, one grandparent, one sister, one uncle, one great-uncle, whose talents and competencies furnished me with all the 'tools' necessary for a black American child to survive. When my father died in Kansas, my mother brought us back to her home town to live and keep house for her father and brother. My sister and I came to know the small neighborhood called Kohlassville. All black neighborhoods in different areas of the city had distinctive names. We grew up among other children, other elders whose combined contributions to our lives were significant. I do not remember much 'preaching' about what to do and what not to do. There were admonitions, delivered with firmness. Elders in Kohlassville and at home were our mentors, models, friends.

"School was clear across town—grades one through twelve, with girls' and boys' basketball the only sport except football and track. Our all-black teaching staff, which stood tall in the community, viewed education as being serious and set and kept the standards for excellence. It was customary for teachers to return to college during the summers, to acquire the necessary credentials to validate their teaching certificates, or to attain another degree. Not all teachers were Kentucky born and educated, so students shared life vicariously outside home, city, state.

"'Programs'—church, school, community—attracted prominent black Americans from outside, thus supplying the black community with opportunities to expand horizons, as well as become accustomed to performing and singing before audiences. Much was made of music. Those gifted musically were inspirations to the whole community. Among the places to display musical talent was the annual teachers' conference of the Kentucky Negro Education Association in Kentucky's largest city, Louisville.

"There were always newspapers at our house—the *Chicago Defender* arrived on Fridays, the *Cincinnati Enquirer* every day. The high point of my day came when I spread out the two newspapers and read them from cover to cover. The *Chicago Defender* was my weekly course in black American history.

"'Educational and cultural opportunities' are my words to describe the motivating forces which eventually led (although I was not aware of this) to my becoming a librarian, or working in a place where *In Black and White* could be conceived and/or published. The major factor in my motivation for education was my mother, who could not imagine any child or young person dropping out of school. College graduation led to a profession which claims many young black Americans—teaching. After fifteen years of teaching in South Carolina and Kentucky came library school and a job away from the South in Michigan. My awareness, after coming to Kalamazoo, of the lengths patrons had to go to in area libraries to locate material about black Americans led to the pursuit of trying to make such information readily available.

"'Biography—collective and individual—just has to be the most exciting section of Dewey's Decimal Classification System! Here are the evidences of the greatness of the human spirit. Here are the examples of the achievements black Americans made over often insurmountable obstacles. Nowhere in all of literature can there be found more dramatic examples of courage, endurance, and survival than in the sagas of black people wherever they live.

"*In Black and White* does not attempt to assess the contributions of the individuals who are listed. It is almost enough that their names found the way into print. This fact, in itself, unleashes the whole issue of the absence of the names and the absence of sufficient information concerning contributions of black people in books, newspapers, magazines, radio, and television. I wanted also to remember (and to rescue) literary giants, black men and women, whose works are 'out of sight and out of mind.'"

* * *

SPRAGUE, W.D.
See von BLOCK, Bela W(illiam)

* * *

SPRAY, Sherrad L(ee)   1935-

PERSONAL: Born October 7, 1935, in Union, Ore.; married, 1961; children: two. *Education:* University of Oregon, B.S., 1958, Ph.D., 1962. *Office:* Department of Sociology and Anthropology, Kent State University, Kent, Ohio 44242.

CAREER: Louisiana State University, Baton Rouge, assistant professor of sociology, 1962-64; University of Chicago, Chicago, Ill., assistant professor of sociology and research associate of Committee on Human Development, 1964-69; York University, Downsview, Ontario, associate professor of sociology, 1969-72, director of graduate program, 1970-72; Kent State University, Kent, Ohio, professor of sociology and anthropology, 1972—. Member of National Institute of Mental Health interdisciplinary conference on training in the community mental health field, 1972—; consultant to Social Planning Council of Metropolitan Toronto. *Member:* American Sociological Association, Canadian Mental Health Association, Canadian Sociological Association, Society for Applied Anthropology, Society for the Study of Social Problems.

WRITINGS: (With William Earl Henry and John H. Sims) *The Fifth Profession: Becoming a Psychotherapist,* Jossey-Bass, 1971; (with Henry) *Public and Private Lives of Psychotherapists,* Jossey-Bass, 1973; (editor) *Organizational Effectiveness: Theory, Research, Utilization,* Comparative Administration Research Institute, Kent State University, 1976. Contributor to *Research in Psychotherapy,* Volume III, 1968. Contributor to journals in psychiatry and the behavioral sciences.*

* * *

SPURLING, Hilary   1940-

PERSONAL: Born December 25, 1940, in Stockport, England; daughter of G. A. (a judge) and E. M. (a teacher; maiden name, Armstrong) Forrest; married John Spurling (a playwright), April 4, 1961; children: Amy, Nathaniel, Gilbert. *Education:* Somerville College, Oxford, B.A., 1962. *Residence:* London, England. *Agent:* Curtis Brown Ltd., 1 Craven Hill, London W2 3EP, England.

CAREER: Spectator, London, England, arts editor and theatre critic, 1964-70, literary editor, 1967-70; free-lance writer, 1970—. *Awards, honors:* Rose Mary Crawshay Prize from British Academy, 1976, for *Ivy When Young.*

WRITINGS: Ivy When Young: The Early Life of Ivy Compton Burnett, Gollancz, 1974; (editor) *Mervyn Peake: Drawings,* Davis Poynter, 1974; *Handbook to Anthony Powell's Music of Time,* Heinemann, 1977. Contributor to magazines, including *Observer* and *New Statesman.*

WORK IN PROGRESS: A second volume of biography of Ivy Compton Burnett, publication expected in 1983.

*   *   *

STADTER, Philip A(ustin) 1936-

PERSONAL: Born November 29, 1936, in Cleveland, Ohio; son of John Martin (a purchasing agent) and Mary Louise (Jones) Stadter; married Lucia A. Ciapponi (a professor), July 6, 1963; children: Paul, Maria Francesca, Mark. *Education:* Princeton University, A.B., 1958; Harvard University, M.A., 1959, Ph.D., 1963. *Religion:* Roman Catholic. *Residence:* Chapel Hill, N.C. *Office:* Department of Classics, University of North Carolina, 030A Murphey Hall, Chapel Hill, N.C. 27514.

CAREER: University of North Carolina, Chapel Hill, instructor, 1962-64, assistant professor, 1964-67, associate professor, 1967-72, professor of classics, 1972—, chairman of department, 1976—. *Member:* American Philological Association (member of board of directors, 1977-80), Association of Ancient Historians, Classical Association of the Middle West and South, North Carolina Classical Association (president, 1968-69). *Awards, honors:* Fulbright fellowship, 1960-61; Guggenheim fellowship, 1967-68; National Endowment for the Humanities senior fellowship, 1974-75.

WRITINGS: Plutarch's Historical Methods, Harvard University Press, 1965; (with B. L. Ullman) *The Public Library of Renaissance Florence,* Antenore, 1972; (editor) *The Speeches in Thucydides,* University of North Carolina Press, 1973; *Arrian of Nicomedia,* University of North Carolina Press, 1980.

WORK IN PROGRESS: Preparing an edition of Plutarch's *Life of Pericles* for American Philological Association textbook series.

*   *   *

STAENDER, Gilbert F(rank) 1930-

PERSONAL: Born February 25, 1930, in Chicago, Ill.; son of Frank X. (a machinist) and Frieda (Ballmaier) Staender; married Vivian Tiller (a writer), July 30, 1955. *Education:* Portland State University, B.A., 1964. *Home and office:* Indian Ford Rd., Sisters, Ore. 97759.

CAREER: In automobile sales in Portland, Ore., 1955-60; teacher at elementary schools in Portland, 1963-69, and Sisters, Ore., 1973-77; Wildhaven, Sisters, photographer and operator of wildlife sanctuary, 1977—. Worked at Oregon Museum of Science and Industry. *Military service:* U.S. Army, Signal Corps, 1951-53. *Member:* National Audubon Society, National Wildlife Federation, Wilderness Society, Nature Conservancy,

Sierra Club, Mazamas, Defenders of Wildlife, Friends of the Earth.

WRITINGS: (With wife, Vivian Staender) *Adventures With Arctic Wildlife,* Caxton, 1970; (with V. Staender) *Our Arctic Year,* Alaska Northwest Publishing, 1981. Contributor of photographs to magazines, including *National Wildlife, Ranger Rick, Birds of Alaska, Earth,* and *Great Weather.*

SIDELIGHTS: Staender wrote: "I am very interested in conservation, wildlife, and nature photography. I spent four summers and one year in the Brooks Range of Alaska observing nature. We have a 160-acre wildlife sanctuary near Sisters, Oregon. Our hand-built stone house, Nature House, is host to many nature-oriented groups. I feel that we must learn to live in harmony with our environment, or we are lost."

BIOGRAPHICAL/CRITICAL SOURCES: Living Wilderness, autumn, 1971; *Portland Oregonian,* November 5, 1967, July 20, 1970, October 14, 1979; *Madras Pioneer,* August 28, 1980.

*   *   *

STAFFORD, David Alexander Tetlow 1942-

PERSONAL: Born March 10, 1942, in Newcastle upon Tyne, England. *Education:* Cambridge University, B.A., 1963; University of London, Ph.D., 1968. *Office:* Department of History, University of Victoria, Victoria, British Columbia, Canada V8W 2Y2.

CAREER: British Diplomatic Service, London, England, third secretary at Foreign Office, 1967-68, second secretary, 1968; University of London, London School of Economics and Political Science, London, research associate at Centre of International Studies, 1968-70; University of Victoria, Victoria, British Columbia, assistant professor, 1970-76, associate professor of history, 1976—. Senior associate member of St. Antony's College, Oxford, 1976-77.

WRITINGS: From Anarchism to Reformism: A Study of the Political Activities of Paul Brousse Within the First International and the French Socialist Movement, 1870-90, University of Toronto Press, 1971; *Britain and European Resistance, 1940-1945: A Survey of the Special Operations Executive, with Documents,* University of Toronto Press, 1980. Contributor to history and political science journals.

BIOGRAPHICAL/CRITICAL SOURCES: Times Literary Supplement, March 28, 1980; *Quill and Quire,* April, 1980.*

*   *   *

STAHL, Nancy 1937-

PERSONAL: Born in 1937 in Chicago, Ill.; married; children: Laurie, Eric. *Education:* Attended DePauw University and University of Massachusetts. *Office: Calgary Herald,* 206 Seventh Ave., Calgary, Alberta, Canada.

CAREER: Iowa Farm Science, Ames, editorial assistant, 1959-60; *Calgary Herald,* Calgary, Alberta, author of syndicated column, "Jelly Side Down," 1969—. Guest lecturer.

WRITINGS: If It's Raining This Must Be the Weekend, Andrews & McMeel, 1979.

Illustrator: Ellen Liman, *The Spacemaker Book,* Viking, 1977 (published in England as *Everything in Its Place: A Practical Guide to Room Improvement,* David & Charles, 1977).*

STAHR, John W. 1904-1981

OBITUARY NOTICE: Born in 1904; died of cancer, June 17, 1981, in Larchmont, N.Y. Sportswriter, public relations executive, and author. An authority on the rules of tennis, Stahr became one of the game's leading officials. He wrote a handbook for tennis officials entitled *A Friend at Court* and a public relations manual, *Write to the Point.* Obituaries and other sources: *Who's Who in Public Relations (International),* 4th edition, PR Publishing, 1972; *New York Times,* June 20, 1981.

* * *

STALLIBRASS, (Helen) Alison 1916-

PERSONAL: Born September 18, 1916, In London, England; daughter of Gilbert James (an engineer) and Helen M. (Low) Scott; married Geoffrey Ward Stallibrass, May 12, 1940; children: Chloe, James, Julia, William, Lucy. *Education:* Studied at Pioneer Health Centre, 1936-39. *Home:* Turkey Island Corner, Eart Harting, Petersfield, Hampshire, England.

CAREER: Operated pre-school play group in Croydon, Surrey, England, 1952-72; writer, 1972—.

WRITINGS: Self-Respecting Child, Thames & Hudson, 1974.

WORK IN PROGRESS: A book on the Pioneer Health Centre (the Peckham experiment); a book on child development.

SIDELIGHTS: Stallibrass told *CA:* "The Pioneer Health Centre was a social and scientific experiment designed and directed by George Scott Williamson and his wife, I. H. Pearse. Also known as the Peckham experiment, it operated in Peckham, South London, from 1935 to 1950, although interrupted by World War II from 1939 to 1946. It was a club for families, membership to which gave families living in its vicinity the opportunity to be healthy in the fullest sense of the word. Most importantly, it enabled them to create—and be part of—a community of families. They retained the privacy of their homes but each member of the family could seek occupations and friends of his or her own choice within a territory common to the whole family. Within the club building neither parents nor children were obliged to breathe down each others' necks, yet each knew that the others were available if desired. Children could use the club on their own, since it was within walking distance of their homes.

"Scott Williamson said that the proper place for children was at the edge of the shadow cast by the parent tree, where they are free to nourish themselves on the sun and air and dew, but also to rely on shelter from a familiar and stable source. His concept of health includes a situation in which every individual member of a community is able to be himself and to choose what to nourish his unique personality and powers upon, and, moreover, to practice responsibility for the course of his own life and for the health of the environment on which he depends for his own health and happiness. Such a definition of environment, of course, includes his neighbors. The 'Centre,' as it was called, gave the family a chance to fulfill its purpose as a social institution—a chance to be healthy.

"For three years I was a part of the Peckham experiment at Pioneer Health Centre and used the methods I studied there in the play group I operated in my home. At present I am interested in the progress of the theory of development of the faculties, general ability, and individuality of the human being from birth onward, and on the nature of the environment and opportunities for activity that are necessary for full development, self-esteem, and joy in life. My view of the nature of human nature and its environmental needs is based on that of

Williamson and J. C. Smuts, on Piaget's little known theory of the process of mental growth in children, and on R. W. White's theory of motivation."

* * *

STANBURY, David 1933-

PERSONAL: Born in 1933 in Leeds, England. *Education:* Imperial College of Science and Technology, London, B.Sc.

CAREER: Senior biologist and deputy headmaster at comprehensive school in London, England, 1955-70. *Member:* Royal College of Science (fellow), Zoological Society (fellow), Field Studies Council, St. Kilda Club.

WRITINGS: (Translator and editor of adaptation) Marcel Orieux and M. Everaere, *The Living World* (edited by Joseph Elder), two volumes, Macmillan, 1970. Contributor to magazines, including *Nature.**

* * *

STAPLETON, Constance 1930-

PERSONAL: Born June 16, 1930, in Norwood, Mass.; daughter of James Joseph (an editor) and Teresa (an editor; maiden name, Welch) Hurney; married Walter Stapleton, January 31, 1953 (divorced, 1975); children: Jill, John, Brooke, Michael, Christopher. *Education:* Attended Museum of Fine Arts School, Boston, Mass., 1943-44, extension courses at Harvard University and Massachusetts Institutute of Technology, 1946-52, American University, 1961-62, Museum of Fine Arts, Houston, Tex., 1963-64, and George Mason University, 1977-78. *Home and office:* Marameade, 2439A Old National Pike, Middletown, Md. 21769. *Agent:* Gail Hochman, Paul R. Reynolds, Inc., 12 East 41st St., New York, N.Y. 10017.

CAREER: Worked at S. D. Warren Co. in Boston, Mass., 1949-53; portrait painter, 1960-68; *Baltimore Catholic Review,* Baltimore, Md., correspondent and historiographer, 1968-73; Frederick County, Md., director of tourism, 1974; Constance Stapleton (public relations firm), president, 1974-77; EBON Research Systems, Washington, D.C., chief psychology writer, 1978-80. Instructor at St. Joseph College, Emmitsburg, Md., 1969-70. Member of advisory board of Folk Art Center, Asheville, N.C., 1977-78; consultant to American Craft Enterprises. *Member:* Authors Guild. *Awards, honors:* Community service award from Maryland-Delaware-District of Columbia Press Association, 1968; Bread Loaf scholarship, 1975.

WRITINGS: (With Nelson Way) *Antiques Don't Lie,* Doubleday, 1975; (with Phyllis Richman) *Barter: How to Get Almost Anything Without Money,* Scribner, 1978. U.S. correspondent for *Architectural Digest,* 1976-80. Contributor to magazines and newspapers, including *Reader's Digest, Woman's Day, Quest, Ladies' Home Journal, Writer,* and *Parade.* Contributing editor of *Washingtonian,* 1975—, and *Baltimore,* 1977—.

WORK IN PROGRESS: How to Do Everything Well, humorous essays; *One Hundred Best-Designed Products Under One Dollar,* to teach design through ordinary objects; "Turnabout," a film for television.

SIDELIGHTS: Stapleton told *CA:* "I was born to two newspapers in Norwood, Massachusetts. My father edited the daily and my mother published a shoppers weekly. Although I started writing for newspapers in high school, I was determined to become a portrait painter (perhaps because no one else in my family had). When faced with the need to support my children, I returned to what I knew best: writing. From the first word, it was like coming home, and I haven't had time to paint since.

My forte is translating complicated data into easy-to-understand language, I want to know more about a subject than any reader. Consequently, I learn from everything I write. After I've researched a subject, I enter a typing marathon with myself, often rewriting the first paragraph twenty times (and frequently throwing it away). When an article or book is finished and not one more word can be changed or deleted, I feel like a tube of toothpaste that's been squeezed empty. But it's a good feeling; the effort is always worth it.''

*   *   *

STARHAWK
See SIMOS, Miriam

*   *   *

STAUBACH, Roger (Thomas)   1942-

PERSONAL: Born February 5, 1942, in Cincinnati, Ohio; son of Robert Joseph and Elizabeth (Smyth) Staubach; married Marianne Jeanne Hoobler, September 4, 1965; children: Jennifer Anne, Michelle Elizabeth, Stephanie Marie, Jeffrey Roger, Amy Lynn. *Education:* U.S. Naval Academy, B.S., 1965. *Religion:* Roman Catholic. *Office:* Holloway-Staubach Co., Realtors, 6750 LBJ Freeway, Suite 1100, Dallas, Tex. 75240.

CAREER: Dallas Cowboys Football Club, Dallas, Tex., quarterback, 1969-79; Holloway-Staubach Co. (realtors), Dallas, owner, 1977—. Assistant vice-president and saleman for Henry S. Miller Realty, 1970-77; sports spokesman for Fuqua Industries; advisor to president of Aurora Toys and Games; recruiter for sports program at U.S. Naval Academy. Member of board of directors of Reunion Bank, Paul Anderson Youth Home, and Jesuit High School; member of Salvation Army Advisory Board. Easter Seals, national chairman and Texas state chairman. *Military service:* U.S. Navy, 1965-69; became lieutenant.

MEMBER: American Diabetes Association, Fellowship of Christian Athletes. *Awards, honors:* Thompson Trophy Cup from U.S. Naval Academy, 1962, 1963, 1964; Heisman Trophy for college football's most valuable player, 1963; Walter Camp Memorial Trophy from Touchdown Club, Washington, D.C., 1963; Maxwell Award, 1964, and Bert Bell Award, 1971, both from Maxwell Club; Naval Academy Athletic Association Sword, 1965; voted most valuable player by players of National Football League, 1971; *Sporting News* National Football Player of the Year, 1971; most valuable player of Super Bowl VI, 1971; National Football Conference Pro Bowl selection, 1972, 1977, 1978, 1979, 1980; Byron "Whizzer" White Humanitarian Award, 1972; Texas Pro Athlete of the Year, 1975; Vince Lombardi Sportsman of the Year, 1975; Field Scovill Award from All-Sports Association of Dallas for athletic achievement and community service, 1975; Golden Plate Award for outstanding citizenship from the American Academy of Achievement, 1976; National Football Conference Player of the Year from Touchdown Club, Columbus, Ohio, 1976, 1978; National Football League Players' Association Offensive Player of the Year, 1978; National Football Conference Offensive Player of the Year from 100 Club, 1978; National Football League leading passer, 1978, 1979; National Football League Players' Assocation passing champion, 1979; Brian Piccolo Award, 1979; Distinguished Service Award from the Sports Association of Dallas, 1980; Ohio Governor's Award, 1980.

WRITINGS: (With Sam Blair and Bob St. John) *First Down, Lifetime to Go,* Word, Inc., 1974; (with Frank Luksa) *Time Enough to Win,* Word, Inc., 1980.

SIDELIGHTS: During his ten years as quarterback for the Dallas Cowboys, Stauback was "one of the most calmly efficient quarterbacks in N.F.L. [National Football League] history," said *Time* reporter Peter Ainslie. "Stauback's greatest asset [was] his fierce competitiveness, fierce even by the standards of a league filled with men who brood for days after a defeat."

Staubach is a family man with a strong religious inclination and an interest in learning. He told Ainslie: "I'm really learning new things all the time. I'm constantly growing." As a player, Staubach enjoyed analyzing defensive strategies of other teams. "My real asset [was] reading defenses and throwing to the right receiver," he observed.

Staubach's first book, *First Down, Lifetime to Go,* is an autobiographical account of his personal life and his sports career.

BIOGRAPHICAL/CRITICAL SOURCES. Time, January 22, 1979.

*   *   *

STAVENHAGEN, Lee   1933-

PERSONAL: Born March 12, 1933, in Galveston, Tex.; son of Ernest (a ship supplier) and Henrietta (Kressmann) Stavenhagen; married Jill Mattingly (a potter), January 12, 1957; children: Lotte, Lucien, Julia. *Education:* University of Texas, B.A., 1958, M.A., 1960; attended Free University of Berlin, 1959-60; University of California, Berkeley, Ph.D., 1964. *Politics:* "Liberal cynic." *Religion:* "Great Spirit (homebrew)." *Home address:* Route 2, Caldwell, Tex. 77836.

CAREER: Rice University, Houston, Tex., assistant professor of German, 1964-71; Brandeis University, Waltham, Mass., assistant professor of Germanic and Slavic languages and lecturer in philosophy and history of ideas, 1972-76, director of literary studies colloquium, 1972-73, chairman of coordinating committee of medieval studies program, 1973-75; Texas A & M University, College Station, associate professor of modern languages, 1976—. Farmer; technical translator and editorial consultant, 1964—. *Military service:* U.S. Army, 1953-55. *Member:* Mediaeval Academy of America, Society for the History of Alchemy and Chemistry.

WRITINGS: (Editor and translator from Latin) Morienus, *A Testament of Alchemy: Being the Revelation of Morienus, Ancient Adept and Hermit of Jerusalem to Khalid ibn Yazid ibn Mu'awiyya, King of the Arabs,* University Press of New England, 1974. Contributor to academic journals.

WORK IN PROGRESS: Editing and translating *Lord and Lady, Monk and Merchant, Devil, Saint, and Thief,* late medieval popular stories, publication expected in 1982.

SIDELIGHTS: Stavenhagen wrote: "I have driven a bookmobile, gone to sea, worked as a carpenter and electrician, and now dabble in subsistence farming. I don't yet know 'what I'm going to be when I grow up.'

"With my cluttered mind, I'm always on the fringes (as in my book on science, religion, and literature). I deplore the gulf between academic and other writing and find myself adrift therein."

*   *   *

STEDMAN, Ray C.   1917-

PERSONAL: Born October 5, 1917, in Temvik, N.D.; married Elaine L. Smith (a writer and speaker), October 22, 1945; children: Sheila (Mrs. Steven Kappe), Susan (Mrs. Richard Christensen), Linda (Mrs. Rod Buchstaber), Laurie. *Educa-*

tion; Attended Witworth College; Dallas Theological Seminary, received degree in 1950. *Residence;* Palo Alto, Calif. *Office:* Peninsula Bible Church, 3505 Middlefield Rd., Palo Alto, Calif. 94306.

CAREER: Ordained minister. Worked as assistant office manager at Libby Pineapple Plantations, Honolulu, Hawaii; Peninsula Bible Church, Palo Alto, Calif., pastor, 1950—. Member of board of directors of Christian National's Evangelism Commission, Bible Study Fellowship, and Youth for Christ International. *Military service:* Served in U.S. Navy. *Awards, honors:* D.D. from Talbot Thelogical Seminary, 1971.

WRITINGS: What on Earth's Going to Happen?, Regal Books, 1970; *Body Life,* revised edition, Regal Books, 1972; *Folk Psalms of Faith,* Regal Books, 1973; *What More Can God Say?: A Fresh Look at Hebrews,* Regal Books, 1974; *Birth of the Body* (foreword by Hal Lindsey), Vision House, 1974; *Authentic Christianity,* Word, Inc., 1975, study guide, 1977; *Jesus Teaches on Prayer* Word, Inc., 1975; *Secrets of the Spirit,* Revell, 1975; *Understanding Man,* Word, Inc., 1975; *Riches in Christ,* Word, Inc., 1976; *Growth of the Body,* Vision House, 1976; *Death of a Nation,* Word, Inc., 1976; *Behind History,* Word, Inc., 1976; *The Servant Who Rules,* Word, Inc., 1976; *The Ruler Who Serves,* Word, Inc., 1976; *The Queen and I,* Word, Inc., 1977; *The Beginnings,* Word, Inc., 1978; *From Guilt to Glory,* Word, Inc., Part I, 1978; *Highlights of the Bible,* Regal Books, 1979; *Triumphs of the Body,* Vision House, 1980. Also author of *Spiritual Life Trilogy* (contains *Body Life, Authentic Christianity,* and *Spiritual Warfare*).

SIDELIGHTS: Stedman conducted a tour of the Holy Land in 1967 and later traveled around the world to visit ministers, missionaries, and congregations in Mexico, Guatemala, Brazil, Italy, Greece, Singapore, Indonesia, Vietnam, the Philippines, Hong Kong, and Taiwan. He has also traveled widely in Latin America, Europe, and the Far East.

*   *   *

STEELE, Colin Robert   1944-

PERSONAL: Born March 2, 1944, in Hartlepool, England; son of Robert Warnock (a personnel manager) and Mary (Carter) Steele; married Anna Elizabeth Creer (a teacher); children: Christopher, Jonathan. *Education:* University of Liverpool, B.A., 1965, M.A., 1971; University of London, Diploma in Librarianship, 1967. *Home:* 11 Elsey St., Hawker, Canberra, Australian Capital Territory 2614, Australia. *Office:* Library, Australian National University, P.O. Box 4, Acton, Canberra, Australian National Territory 2600, Australia.

CAREER: University of Liverpool, Liverpool, England, trainee of Standing Conference of National University Libraries, 1965-66; Oxford University, Bodleian Library, Oxford, England, assistant librarian, 1967-76; Australian National University, Canberra, deputy librarian, 1976-80, university librarian, 1980—. *Member:* Library Association of Australia, Australian Institute of Tertiary Educational Administrators, Bibliographical Society of Australia and New Zealand, Higher Education Research and Development Society of Australia, Library Association (England), Hakluyt Society, British Society for Eighteenth-Century Studies, Colophon Society, Oxford Bibliographical Society, Commonwealth Club. *Awards, honors:* Visiting fellow of British Academy in the United States, 1974.

WRITINGS: (Editor) Bartolome de las Casas, *The Tears of the Indians,* Oriole, 1972; (with M. P. Costeloe) *Independent Mexico,* Mansell, 1973; (contributor) D. B. Quinn, editor, *The Hakluyt Handbook,* Hakluyt Society, 1974; (with Bernard Nay-

lor and Laurence Hallewell) *Directory of Libraries and Special Collections on Latin America and the West Indies,* Athlone Press, 1975; *English Interpreters of the Iberian New World From Purchas to Stevens: A Bibliographical Survey, 1603-1726,* Dolphin, 1975; (with G.P.M. Walker) *European Acquisitions and Their Bibliographical Control,* Lancaster University Library, 1975; *Major Libraries of the World: A Selective Guide,* Bowker, 1976, 2nd edition, 1982; (editor) *Steady State/Zero Growth Libraries,* Bingley, 1978; Contributor to *Academic American Encyclopedia.* Contributor to library and Latin American studies journals.

SIDELIGHTS: Steele told *CA;* "I am particularly interested in the understanding of Latin America in Western civilization, and my books have attempted to assess this relationship through the printed word. This was, historically, perhaps the most important factor in disseminating information and views of Latin America.

"As a repository of information, libraries, within their particular geographical setting, are also vital. My book *Major Libraries of the World* attempted to establish this commonality of information provision in a number of countries. Access to information is one of the key factors for development and understanding in the latter part of the twentieth century and control of information sources must not be left in the hands of a previleged few."

*   *   *

STEEVES, Harrison R(oss)   1881-1981

OBITUARY NOTICE: Born April 8, 1881, in New York, N.Y.; died August 1, 1981, in Kingston, R.I. Educator and author. Steeves served on the faculty of Columbia College (now University) for more than forty years. His books include a volume of literary criticism, *Before Jane Austen,* and a mystery novel, *Good Night, Sheriff.* Obituaries and other sources: *American Authors and Books, 1640 to the Present Day,* 3rd revised edition, Crown, 1972; *Who's Who in America,* 40th edition, Marquis, 1978; *New York Times,* August 4, 1981; *AB Bookman's Weekly,* September 7, 1981.

*   *   *

STEIN, Gertrude   1874-1946

BRIEF ENTRY: Born February 3, 1874, in Allegheny, Pa.; died of cancer, July 27, 1946, in Paris, France. American poet, novelist, and critic. While a student at Radcliffe College, Gertrude Stein studied under psychologist and philosopher William James. She later attended Johns Hopkins Medical School where she specialized in the anatomy of the brain. Admittedly bored by the requirements of academic life, Stein abandoned her studies and moved to Europe, settling in France in 1903. The Paris apartment that she shared with her secretary and lifelong companion, Alice B. Toklas, became a cultural center for avant-garde writers and painters. Independently wealthy, Stein served as patron to such painters as Pablo Picasso, Georges Braque, and Henri Matisse, and she encouraged the literary efforts of such writers as Ernest Hemingway, Sherwood Anderson, and F. Scott Fitzgerald. Her own artistic endeavors were highly controversial, angering many for their blatant disregard for literary convention. Although capable of lucid writing, as evidenced by the celebrated *Autobiography of Alice B. Toklas* (1933) and *Wars I Have Seen* (1945), Stein seldom chose to demonstrate that ability. She concentrated instead on a unique, abstract style of writing that was characterized by repetition of words and phrases. The famed quote, "A rose is a rose is a rose," from *Geography and Plays* (1922), exemplifies Stein's technique. Her other works include *Three Lives* (1909), *The Making of Americans* (1925), and *Everybody's Autobiography* (1937). *Residence:* Paris, France. *Biographical/critical sources: Reader's Encyclopedia of American Literature*, Crowell, 1962; *The Oxford Companion to American Literature*, 4th edition, Oxford University Press, 1965; *Who's Who in Twentieth Century Literature*, Holt, 1976; *Twentieth-Century Literary Criticism*, Volume 1, Gale, 1978.

* * *

STEIN, William B. 1915-

PERSONAL: Born May 25, 1915, in Congo, Ohio; son of Peter (a coal miner) and Mary (Seeman) Stein; married Gertrude M. Scholz, June 8, 1946. *Education:* Rutgers University, B.A., 1948; University of Florida, M.A., 1949, Ph.D., 1950. *Religion:* Buddhist. *Home:* 605 Old Lane Rd., Binghamton, N.Y. 13903. *Office:* Department of English, State University of New York at Binghamton, Binghamton, N.Y. 13901.

CAREER: Princeton University, Princeton, N.J., instructor in English, 1950-51; Washington and Jefferson College, Washington, Pa., assistant professor, 1951-55, associate professor, 1955-61, professor of English, 1961-66; State University of New York at Binghamton, professor of English, 1966—. Exchange professor at various institutions. Bollingen fellowship and research grant on Melville's poetry, 1953-55. *Member:* Phi Beta Kappa. *Awards, honors:* Fulbright lecturer at University of Mainz, West Germany, 1959-60.

WRITINGS: Hawthorne's Faust, University of Florida Press, 1953; (editor and author of introduction) *Two Brahman Sources of Thoreau and Emerson*, Scholars' Facsimiles and Reprints, 1967; (editor and author of introduction) *The Hitopadesa*, Scholars' Facsimiles and Reprints, 1968; *The Poetry of Melville's Late Years: Time, History, Myth, and Religion*, State University of New York Press, 1970; (editor and author of introduction) *The Four Chinese Books*, Scholars' Facsimiles and Reprints, 1970.

Contributor: Bo Harkness, editor, *Conrad's Heart of Darkness and the Critics*, Wadsworth, 1960; E. Stone, editor, *Henry James: Seven Stories and Studies*, Heath, 1961; William T. Stafford, editor, *Perspectives on James's Portrait of a Lady*, New York University Press, 1966; J. B. Vickery, editor, *Myth and Literature*, University of Nebraska Press, 1966; M. Hassan, editor, *Stephen Crane: Twentieth-Century Views*, Prentice-Hall, 1967; *Twentieth-Century Interpretations of Walden*, Prentice-Hall, 1968; C. A. Patrides, editor, *Aspects of Time*, University of Toronto Press, 1976; Thomas A. Gullason, editor, *Maggie: A Girl of the Streets (Eighteen Ninety-Three)*, Stephen Crane, 1979. Contributor of nearly one hundred articles to literature journals.

SIDELIGHTS: Stein told *CA:* "After thirty years of literary criticism, I have come to the conclusion that it's a game of intellectual nonsense. Since every generation interprets literature in its own framework, one must conclude that the extracted meaning involves nothing except language interpreting itself in a constant round of Humpty-Dumptyism."

* * *

STEINBERG, Jeffrey 1947(?)-1981

OBITUARY NOTICE: Born c. 1947 in New York, N.Y.; died of injuries sustained in an automobile accident, June 3, 1981, in Hempstead, N.Y. Owner and publisher of Stonehill Communications. Steinberg founded *Rolling Stone*'s Straight Arrow Press with Alan Rinzler. He is best known for publishing Philip

Agee's expose of the Central Intelligence Agency, *Inside the Company*. Other books published by Steinberg include Aldous Huxley's *Moksha*, Anthony Burgess's *Moses*, and Christina Rossetti's *Goblin Market*. Obituaries and other sources: *New York Times*, June 3, 1981; *Publishers Weekly*, June 19, 1981; *AB Bookman's Weekly*, July 27, 1981.

* * *

STEINHARDT, Anne Elizabeth 1941-

PERSONAL: Born February 21, 1941, in Brooklyn, N.Y.; daughter of Alfred Tennyson and Henrietta (Nachman) Vogel; married Richard Antony Steinhardt (a professor of biology; divorced); children: Alicia Anne. *Education:* Columbia University, B.A., 1962, doctoral study; Cornell University, M.A., 1963. *Religion:* Humanist. *Home:* 4760 Glen Haven Rd., Soquel, Calif. 95073.

CAREER: University of California, Santa Cruz, acting assistant professor, 1967-70; writer, 1971—. Musician.

WRITINGS: The Healthy Season, Grove, 1971; *Thunder la Boom*, Viking, 1974; *How to Get Balled in Berkeley*, Viking, 1976. Contributor to *California Today*.

WORK IN PROGRESS: Philologist Uncovers Billion Buck Bamboozle, a novel, with father, Alfred Vogel.

SIDELIGHTS: Anne Steinhardt commented: "In between writing stints I am a professional swing fiddler, and am currently supporting myself by playing in a cowboy bar."

* * *

STEINITZ, Paul 1909-

PERSONAL: Born August 25, 1909, in Chichester, England; son of Charles Edward (a clerk in Holy Orders) and Sarah Jessie (Prior) Steinitz; married wife, Margaret Anne (an organizing secretary), October 30, 1976. *Education:* Royal Academy of Music, F.R.C.O., L.R.A.M.; University of London, B.Mus., 1934, D.Mus., 1940. *Religion:* Society of Friends (Quakers). *Home:* 73 High St., Old Oxted, Surrey RH8 9CN, England.

CAREER: Royal Academy of Music, London, England, professor of music, 1945—. Principal lecturer at University of London, 1971-78; founder and conductor of London Bach Society and Steinitz Bach Players. *Member:* Incorporated Society of Musicians, Royal Academy of Music (fellow), Royal Academy of Music Club, Athenaeum Club.

WRITINGS: (Editor) *Harmony and Counterpoint With the Masters*, Novello, 1963; *Commonsense Harmony: A Study of Composers' Music*, Belwin-Mills Music, 1967; (with Stella Sterman) *Harmony in Context: A New Approach to Understanding Harmony Without Conventional Exercises*, Belwin-Mills Music, 1974, workbook, 1976; *Bach's Passions*, Scribner, 1978; *Performing Bach's Vocal Music*, Addington Press, 1980. Contributor to *A New Oxford History of Music*. Record reviewer for *Records and Recording*.

* * *

STELTZER, Ulli 1923-

PERSONAL: Born October 2, 1923, in Frankfurt, Germany; daughter of Oswald H. (an art historian) and Lili (an art historian; maiden name, Guenthes) Goetz; married Werner Steltzer, April 27, 1947 (divorced, 1952); children: Michael, Christian. *Education:* Attended high school in Frankfurt, West Germany;

studied music privately. *Politics:* Social democrat. *Religion:* Lutheran. *Home and office:* 3666 West 14th Ave., Vancouver, British Columbia, Canada V6R 2W5.

CAREER: Windsor Mountain School, Lenox, Mass., music teacher, 1953; photographer in New York, N.Y., 1954-57, Princeton, N.J., 1957-72, and Vancouver, British Columbia, 1972—. *Awards, honors:* Eaton's sixth annual British Columbia Book Award, 1980, for *Coast of Many Faces.*

WRITINGS—All illustrated with own photographs: *Indian Artists at Work,* University of Washington Press, 1976; (with Catherine Kerr) *Coast of Many Faces,* University of Washington Press, 1979; *Building an Igloo* (juvenile), Douglas & McIntyre, 1981; *Inuit of Canada's Arctic,* Douglas & McIntyre, 1982; (with Elisabeth Behrhorst and Carroll Behrhorst) *Chimaltenango,* University of Washington Press, 1982.

SIDELIGHTS: Ulli Steltzer commented: "Over the years my interest in people and their environment has surpassed my interest in photography for photography's sake. Hence my regional and thematic books. I don't consider myself a writer. Introductions are a terrible headache. The text for most all my books is based on interviews with their subjects."

* * *

STENTON, Doris Mary (Parsons)   1894-1971

OBITUARY NOTICE: Born in 1894; died December 29, 1971, in Reading, England. Historian and author of books on medieval England, including *King John and the Courts of Justice, English Society in the Middle Ages,* and *The English Woman in History.* Obituaries and other sources: *Longman Companion to Twentieth Century Literature,* Longman, 1970; *AB Bookman's Weekly,* February 7, 1972; *American Historical Review,* February, 1974.

* * *

STEPHENS, James   1882(?)-1950
(James Esse)

BRIEF ENTRY: Born February 2, 1882 (some sources say February 9, 1880) in Dublin, Ireland; died December 26, 1950, in London, England. Irish poet, playwright, and author. Stephens, one of the more popular and engaging personalities of the Irish literary revival, was a passionate nationalist who incorporated Irish folklore into his tales of fantasy. He began to attract attention soon after his short stories and poems began to appear in Arthur Griffith's newspaper, *Sinn Fein,* in 1905. In 1907 he met A.E. (George Russell), who brought Stephens into contact with other Irish writers and introduced him to the concepts of theosophy. In 1909 *Insurrections,* a book of poetry, was published, followed by the novels *The Charwoman's Daughter* (1912), *The Crock of Gold* (1912), and *The Demi-Gods* (1914). Stephens planned a five-volume epic based on the mythological tales that comprise the "Tain Bo Cualinge" saga, but abandoned the physically and mentally exhaustive project after completing the first two books, *Deirdre* (1923) and *In the Land of Youth* (1924). Stephens became good friends with James Joyce during the 1920's, and Joyce insisted that if he should die before completing *Finnegan's Wake* Stephens would be the only person capable of finishing the book. Stephens's creativity and literary importance peaked early in his career, and by the 1930's his output was reduced to occasional reflective poems. Stephens moved to London in 1925 and during the 1930's conducted yearly lecture tours of the United States. From 1937 until his death, Stephens was featured on BBC-Radio as a lecturer on poets and poetry. *Biographical/*

critical sources: The Poetry Review, January, 1914; *The Forum,* January, 1915; *The Atlantic Monthly,* April, 1958; Patricia McFate, *The Writings of James Stephens: Variations on a Theme of Love,* Macmillan, 1979; *Twentieth-Century Literary Criticism,* Volume 4, Gale, 1981.

* * *

STERN, J(ulius) David   1886-1971

OBITUARY NOTICE: Born April 1, 1886, in Philadelphia, Pa.; died of a heart ailment, October 10, 1971, in Palm Beach, Fla. Publisher and author. Stern, a liberal who supported Franklin D. Roosevelt and the New Deal, was owner and publisher of the *Philadelphia Record,* the *New York Post,* the *Camden Evening Courier,* and the *Camden Morning Post.* Concerned about the economic welfare of his editorial employees, Stern became the first American newspaper publisher to sign a labor contract with the American Newspaper Guild. When fellow publishers refused to follow suit, Stern resigned from the American Newspaper Publishers Association in protest. Several years later a bitter dispute with Guild members over wages caused Stern to regret his earlier support of the union. Announcing that his recognition of the Guild had been "a grave mistake," Stern sold his newspapers and retired from publishing. His autobiography, *Memoirs of a Maverick Publisher,* was published in 1962. He also wrote a science fiction novel entitled *Eidolon.* Obituaries and other sources: *New York Times,* October 11, 1971; *Time,* October 25, 1971; *Who's Who in World Jewry: A Biographical Dictionary of Outstanding Jews,* Pitman, 1972.

* * *

STERN, Philip M(aurice)   1926-

PERSONAL: Born May 24, 1926, in New York, N.Y.; son of Edgar Bloom and Edith Stern; married Helen Phillips Burroughs Sedgwick, August 30, 1957 (marriage ended); married Nellie L. Gifford, June 14, 1975; children: (first marriage) Henry D., Michael P., Helen P., David M., Eve. *Education:* Harvard University, A.B. (magna cum laude), 1947; graduate study at Georgetown University, 1975-76. *Home:* 27 West 67th St., New York, N.Y. 10023.

CAREER: New Orleans Item, New Orleans, La., reporter and editorial writer, 1948; legislative assistant to U.S. Representative Henry M. Jackson, 1949-50, and U.S. Senator Paul Douglas, 1951-52; personal assistant to Wilson W. Wyatt (campaign manager to Adlai E. Stevenson), 1952; director of research and senior editor of *Democratic Digest* for Democratic National Committee, 1953-56; *Northern Virginia Sun,* Arlington, editor, 1957-60, publisher, 1960; deputy assistant secretary of state for public affairs, 1961-62; *Washington Post,* special assignment reporter for national staff, 1974-75; writer, 1962—. Director of Council Foundations and Fair Campaign Practices Committee; President of the Center for Public Financing of Campaigns, 1975-76. Member of Health and Welfare Council of the Greater Washington Area, 1960. Chairman of Virginia United Givers Fund, 1960. *Member:* Phi Beta Kappa, Federal City Club. *Awards, honors:* Rockefeller fellow, 1948-49.

WRITINGS: The Great Treasury Raid, New American Library, 1964; (with wife, Helen B. Stern) *O, Say Can You See?,* Colortone Press, 1965; (with George de Vincent) *The Shame of a Nation,* Astor-Honor, 1965; (with Harold P. Green) *The Oppenheimer Case: Security on Trial,* Harper, 1969; *The Rape of the Taxpayer,* Random House, 1973; *Lawyers on Trial: A*

Book for People Who Are Fed Up With Lawyers, Times Books, 1980.

SIDELIGHTS: Public servant and investigative journalist Philip Stern has concentrated on writing books that describe the ways in which governmental systems can abuse the individual. He is best known for his highly acclaimed book *The Oppenheimer Case: Security on Trial*, which details the 1954 hearings of the Atomic Energy Commission's loyalty board and its subsequent decision to revoke the security clearance of J. Robert Oppenheimer, who had been director of the Los Alamos atomic bomb project during World War II.

The board had accused Oppenheimer of disloyalty because he opposed U.S. military plans for a crash program to develop the hydrogen bomb and because he had friends of leftist political persuasion: a fact known to the government when it hired Oppenheimer in 1943. Although Oppenheimer was declared "loyal" by the board, he was found guilty of "defects of character" and of other secret charges never revealed even to Oppenheimer.

"By transcribing the sorry record of Oppenheimer's hearing," *Nation* critic Allen Weinstein wrote, "Philip Stern exposes the grave abuse of individual rights perpetrated by the government's loyalty-security program upon thousands of similarly honorable public servants since the program's inception in 1947." Alfred Friendly of the *Washington Post* declared that Stern "has taken an episode of hideous complexity, with a cast of characters approaching that of 'War and Peace' and organized it into a flow of such lucidity as to thrill any historical craftsman." *New York Review of Books* critic H. Stuart Huges voiced similar praise for the book. "Stern's book on the case itself is altogether admirable," Hughes wrote. "Thoroughly documented, carefully organized and reasoned, it is that rare and always welcome phenomenon, the work of a non-historian which amply meets professional requirements."

BIOGRAPHICAL/CRITICAL SOURCES: Atlantic, November, 1969; *New York Times*, November 3, 1969, April 20, 1973; *Washington Post*, November 7, 1969, April 5, 1970, April 10, 1970, April 17, 1970; *Newsweek*, November 10, 1969; *New Republic*, November 22, 1969, May 12, 1973; *Saturday Review*, December 27, 1969; *New York Times Book Review*, January 4, 1970, June 7, 1970, April 8, 1973, October 5, 1980; *Nation*, April 27, 1970, September 27, 1980; *New York Review of Books*, July 2, 1970, April 19, 1973; *Virginia Quarterly Review*, autumn, 1970; *New Statesman*, June 11, 1971; *The Observer*, June 13, 1971; *Times Literary Supplement*, June 25, 1971; *Washington Post Book World*, March 18, 1973, February 10, 1974; *Time*, March 26, 1973; *National Review*, November 9, 1973; *U.S. News and World Report*, October 6, 1980.*

*   *   *

STERNBERG, Vernon (Arthur)   1915-1979

OBITUARY NOTICE: Born August 12, 1915, in Wausau, Wis.; died of a heart attack, February 27, 1979, in Carbondale, Ill. Editor and founding director of Southern Illinois University Press. Sternberg was responsible for publishing several notable book series, including "Lost American Fiction," "Crosscurrents," and "The London Stage in the Eighteenth Century." Obituaries and other sources: *Who's Who in America*, 40th edition, Marquis, 1978; *Publishers Weekly*, March 12, 1979; *AB Bookman's Weekly*, May 7, 1979.

STERNBERGER, Dolf   1907-

PERSONAL: Born July 28, 1907, in Wiesbaden, Germany (now West Germany); son of Georg and Luise (Schauss) Sternberger; married Ilse Rothschild, 1931. *Education*: Attended University of Heidelberg, University of Freiburg, and University of Frankfurt. *Home*: 6 Frankfurt/M., Grueneburgweg 153, West Germany.

CAREER: Worked as professor of political science at University of Heidelberg, Heidelberg, West Germany; director of Institut fuer Politische Wissenschaft; writer. Member of German commission for United Nations Educational, Scientific and Cultural Organization. *Member*: International P.E.N. (president of German club), German Association of Political Science (past chairman), German Academy of Language and Literature (vice-president). *Awards, honors*: Grosses Bundesverdienstkreuz der Bundesrepublik Deutschland, 1974.

WRITINGS—In English: *Panorama: Oder, Ansichtem vom Neunzehnte Jahrhundert*, H. Govert, 1938, reprinted, Suhrkamp, 1974, translation by Joachim Neugroschel published as *Panorama of the Nineteenth Century*, Urizen Books, 1977; *The Social Sciences in Western Germany: A Post-War Survey*, European Affairs Division, Library of Congress, 1950.

In German: *Der verstandege Tod: Eine Untersuchung zu Martin Heideggers Existenzial-Ontologie, mit einer monographischen Bibliographie Martin Heidegger*, S. Hirzel, 1934, reprinted, Garland Publishing, 1979; *Dreizehn Politische Radioreden*, [Germany], 1947; *Nur die Freiheit macht stark*, (bound with *Die rechtliche Verantwortung des Journalisten*, by Otto Kuester), L. Schneider, 1949.

Figuren der Fabel, [Germany], 1950; *Der Stand der sozialwissenschaftlichen Forschung und Lehre in der Bundesrepublik Deutschland, Abgeschlossen im Maerz, 1950*, European Affairs Division, Library of Congress, 1950; *Lebende Verfassung: Studien ueber Koalition und Opposition*, A. Hain, 1956; *Ueber den Jugendstil und andere Essays*, Claassen, 1956; *Indische Miniaturen: Aus einem Reisetagebuch*, Societaets-Verlag, 1957; (with Gerhard Storz and Wilhelm Emmanuel Sueskind) *Aus dem Woerterbuch des Unmenschen*, Claassen, 1957, new edition, 1968; *Gefuehl der Fremde*, Insel Verlag, 1958.

Wahlen und Waehler in Westdeutschland, Ring-Verlag, 1960; *Grund und Abgrund der Macht: Kritik und Rechtmaessigkeit heutiger Regierungen*, Insel-Verlag, 1962; *Die grosse Wahlreform: Zeugnisse einer Bemuehung*, Westdeutschen Verlag, 1964; *Ekel an der Freiheit?: Und Fuenfzig andere Leitartikel*, R. Piper, 1964; *Kriterien: Ein Lesebuch*, Insel-Verlag, 1965; *Ich wuenschte ein Buerger zu sein*, Suhrkamp, 1967; (editor with Bernard Vogel) *Die Wahl der Parlamente und anderer Staatsorgane: Ein Handbuch*, three volumes, De Gruyter, 1969.

Nicht alle Staatsgewalt geht vom Volke sus: Studien ueber Repraesentation, W. Kohlhammer, 1971; *Heinrich Heine und die Abschaffung der Suende*, Claassen, 1972; (editor with Bernd Hueppauf) *Ueber Literatur und Geschichte: Festschrift fuer Gerhard Storz*, Athenaeum-Verlag, 1973; *Peter Menzel's Darmstaedter Bilderbogen*, Justus von Liebig Verlag, 1974; *Machiavellis "Principe" und der Begriff des Politischen*, Steiner, 1974; *Gerechtigkeit fuer das neunzehnte Jahrhundert: Zehn historisch Studien*, Suhrkamp, 1975; (co-author) *Recht und Macht in Politik und Wirtschaft*, Schulthess Polygraphischer Verlag, 1976; *Schriften*, Insel-Verlag, 1977; *Res Publica*, W. Fink, 1977. Contributor to language and literature journals. Editor of *Die Wandlung*, 1945—.*

STERTZ, Eda   1921-

PERSONAL: Born September 14, 1921, in Fernandina Beach, Fla.; daughter of John Jacob (a seafood dealer) and Ira (Satterwhite) Klarer; married James Gail Stertz (a minister), May 20, 1946; children: Joseph, Kathryn Stertz Driver, James Gail, Jr., John, Luke. *Education:* Tift College, A.B., 1944; attended Woman's Missionary Union Training School (now Southern Baptist Theological Seminary), 1946. *Politics:* Democrat. *Religion:* Southern Baptist. *Home and office:* 3725 Meyer Pl., Sarasota, Fla. 33579.

CAREER: School teacher in Louisville, Ky., 1946-47; substitute school teacher in Greenville, S.C., 1969-72; writer, 1937—.

WRITINGS: Young Man, Young Man (novel), Zondervan, 1972; *Katie's Treasure* (juvenile), Zondervan, 1980. Author of church school curriculum material, church magazine articles, and devotionals. Contributor of poetry to newspapers.

WORK IN PROGRESS: A children's book set in early 1900's in Florida; research for adult novel in same time period and setting.

SIDELIGHTS: Eda Stertz wrote: "As a minister's wife I have lived and worked in eight states and one foreign country, Germany. Christian ministry and the rearing of five children has taken up most of my adult life—my writing, for the most part, relegated to stolen or left over hours. Fiction I write for the sheer love of spinning yarns. My religious material is written out of a sense of responsibility to use whatever gifts I have in practical service to others.

"My most recent activities outside my home and church have been related to resettlement of Vietnamese and Laotian refugees, and social ministries such as teaching literacy classes and finding practical help for people needing housing, jobs, and medical care."

*   *   *

STEVENS, Austin N(eil)   1930-
(Stephen Austin, Eno Nash)

PERSONAL: Born May 10, 1930, in New York, N.Y.; son of Neil C. (a general practitioner of medicine) and Evelyn (Noble) Stevens; married Cynthia Fisher, July 23, 1952; children: Sara, Alexander. *Education:* Tufts University, B.A., 1956; School of the Museum of Fine Arts, Boston, Mass., Certificate, 1952. *Politics:* Republican. *Religion:* Unitarian-Universalist. *Home address:* Watkins Hill, Walpole, N.H., 03608. *Office:* Blackbird Studio, Walpole, N.H. 03608.

CAREER: Endicott Junior College, Beverly, Mass., assistant professor of art, 1958-62; *Boston* (magazine), Boston, Mass., executive publisher, 1962-65; free-lance copywriter and illustrator, 1965-68; Endicott Junior College, associate professor of art, 1965-68; Yankee, Inc., Dublin, N.H., art director and managing editor of *Yankee* (magazine), director of book division, and executive director of *New Englander* (now *New England Business*), 1968-78; Blackbird Studio, Walpole, N.H., owner, writer, and illustrator, 1978—. Advertising and public relations representative for Harvard University, Massachusetts Port Authority, Boston Redevelopment Authority, Boston Chamber of Commerce, National Grange Mutual Insurance Co., and Tufts University. *Military service:* U.S. Army.

WRITINGS: (Editor) *Yankees Under Steam: An Anthology of the Best Stories on the World of Steam Published in Yankee Magazine Since 1935,* Yankee, Inc., 1970; (editor) *Mysterious New England,* Yankee, Inc., 1971; (contributor under pseudonym Stephen Austin, and illustrator) Clarissa M. Silitch, ed-

itor, *A Little Book of Yankee Humor,* Yankee, Inc., 1977. Also author of *Walpole '76* and, under pseudonym Eno Nash, *The Best of Tintinnabulations,* both self-illustrated. Illustrator of *Life on the Mississippi, Beowulf, How Now You,* and *The Secret Life of Walter Mitty.* Contributor of illustrations to newspapers and magazines, including *New York Times, Time, Life, Business Week, U.S. News & World Report,* and *New York Times Magazine.* Contributing editor to *Yankee.*

SIDELIGHTS: Austin Stevens wrote: "Many professional writers and artists are surprised to learn that I both write *and* illustrate for a living. But for the writer who claims he 'can't draw a straight line,' let me say the thought and work experience is much the same. A good writer is graphic, and a good illustrator is literary. It's all one thing. After all, the language evolved from pictures. I'll allow the responsibilities are subtly different. If I illustrate another man's fiction, my responsibility is to create (an image) sympathetically with the writer's mood. And if he's a great writer, then you have to try to be a great illustrator. That's tough. It's hard enough just trying to be a *good* illustrator. As for my responsibility as a writer, I go along with the school of thought that says one should never let the truth interefere with a good story. I think I've done *that,* anyway."

*   *   *

STEVENS, Gwendolyn   1944-

PERSONAL: Born February 29, 1944, in Los Angeles, Calif.; daughter of Oscar and Alice (Whalen) Stevens; married David Nicholos, February 24, 1962 (divorced, 1972); married Sheldon Gardner (a psychologist), October 27, 1972; children: Loren Ann Gardner, Stephen Forest. *Education:* California State University, Los Angeles, B.A., 1973, M.A., 1974; University of California, Riverside, Ph.D., 1978. *Politics:* Libertarian. *Home:* 2006 Bend Rd., Cape Girardeau, Mo. 63701. *Office:* Department of Psychology, Southeast Missouri State University, Cape Girardeau, Mo. 63701.

CAREER: Hyperkinesis Clinic, Pasadena, Calif., administrative director, 1973; Rancho Los Amigos Hospital, Downey, Calif., research assistant, 1974-76; California State Department of Rehabilitation, Downey, research director of clinical assistance program, 1976-78; Southeast Missouri State University, Cape Girardeau, assistant professor of psychology, 1978—. *Member:* International Council of Psychologists, American Psychological Association, American Educational Research Association, National Women's Studies Association, Cherion.

WRITINGS: (With husband, Sheldon Gardner) *Care and Cultivation of Parents,* Simon & Schuster, 1979; (with Gardner) *Women of Psychology: Pioneers and Innovators,* Schenkman, 1981; (with Gardner) *Women of Psychology: Expansion and Refinement,* Schenkman, 1981. Contributor to scientific journals.

WORK IN PROGRESS: Decisions, a novel, publication expected in 1983; *Psychology of Women,* a textbook, with husband, Sheldon Gardner, 1983.

SIDELIGHTS: Gwendolyn Stevens commented: "An 'unhappy housewife,' I returned to school to complete my education. I had wanted to be a psychologist since I was thirteen, but became sidetracked as a sixteen-year-old undergraduate. Being an academician allows a wide audience for my feminist views.

"My writing and research centers primarily on women's issues. Not necessarily polemic in nature, my work more often details contributions made by women and general public opinion concerning women's issues.

"I believe that adequate role models are necessary for the encouragement of young women. I use my position as a professor, a returning woman, a mother to provide what I believe is a very good role model for college-age women. They need to know that competence doesn't mean being homely and alone.

"Most of the work produced so far is in collaboration with my husband. The senior authorship is decided by who originates the idea. We work well together; petty arguments do not develop because we keep in mind the goal, the final project.

"The main reason for writing the first book, *Care and Cultivation of Parents,* was a response to all those other books telling children that they had rights and to demand them. That's not the way the world is! We thought that by telling adolescents how parents develop psychologically, we could provide alternative coping mechanisms for these children, helping both them and their parents to mature.

"The motive for the latest work, *Women of Psychology,* was to set the official history of psychology straight. Nowhere else is there adequate documentation of the contributions that women made to psychology."

*   *   *

STEVENS, Wallace   1879-1955

BRIEF ENTRY: Born October 2, 1879, in Reading, Pa.; died August 2, 1955, in Hartford, Conn. American poet. Regarded by critics as one of the most important American poets of the twentieth century, Stevens was vice-president of an insurance company and wrote in his spare time. His first book of poetry, *Harmonium* (1923), was not published until Stevens was in his forties. Stevens, an agnostic, sought philosophical reassurance in what he termed "Supreme Fiction," an explanation of a universe in constant change. This concept has brought the frequent criticism that Stevens's poetry is too abstract, a condition necessitated by Stevens's view that the only access to reality is through the creative use of imagination. His ability to create an illogical verse structure out of logical thought combined well with his philosophical approach as outlined in both *Ideas of Order* (1935) and *Notes Toward a Supreme Fiction* (1942). Stevens won the National Book Award in 1950 and the Pulitzer Prize in 1955. Two books were published after his death, *Opus Posthumous* (1957) and *Letters* (1966). *Residence:* Hartford, Conn. *Biographical/critical sources:* Robert Buttel, *Wallace Stevens: The Making of "Harmonium,"* Princeton University Press, 1967; *The Yale Review,* spring, 1967; *Contemporary Literature,* autumn, 1975; *Southern Review,* October, 1979; *Twentieth-Century Literary Criticism,* Volume 3, Gale, 1980.

*   *   *

STEWART, Desmond (Stirling)   1924-1981

OBITUARY NOTICE—See index for *CA* sketch: Born April 20, 1924, in Leavesden, England; died June 12, 1981, in London, England. Educator, poet, translator, and author. Stewart taught English at the University of Baghdad and served as an inspector of English in Islamic schools in Beirut before becoming a full-time writer. He wrote many books, including *Leopard in the Grass, The Sequence of Roles, New Babylon: A Portrait of Iraq,* and *T.E. Lawrence.* Stewart also translated such works as Plato's *Socrates and the Soul of Man* and *The Man Who Lost His Shadow* by Fathi Ghanem. Obituaries and other sources: *London Times,* June 22, 1981.

STEWART, Dorothy Mary   1917-1965
(Mary Elgin)

OBITUARY NOTICE: Born October 7, 1917, on Isle of Man; died in March, 1965. Secretary and author of *A Man From the Mist* and *Highland Masquerade.* (Date of death provided by husband, Walter Stewart.)

*   *   *

STEWART, Frank   1946-

PERSONAL: Born May 3, 1946, in Grand Island, Neb.; son of Emmett and Frances (Swann) Stewart; married in 1968 (divorced 1974); children: Chloe. *Education:* Attended University of New Mexico, 1964-65, and American University, 1965-66; University of Hawaii, B.A., 1968, M.A., 1972; attended Harvard University, summer, 1972. *Office:* Department of English, University of Hawaii, Honolulu, Hawaii 96822.

CAREER: Barre Publishers and Imprint Society, Barre, Mass., production manager and editor, 1972-73; free-lance technical editor and compositor in Honolulu, Hawaii, 1973-74; University of Hawaii, Honolulu, instructor, 1974-80, assistant professor of English, 1980—. Director of Petronium Press, 1975-81; acting managing editor of *Hawaii Observer,* 1978. Member of various committees of Hawaii State Foundation on Culture and the Arts; writing awards judge for Honolulu City and County Council on the Arts; writer and consultant for the Kamehameha Schools, Bernice Pauahi Bishop estate. *Member:* Hawaii Literary Arts Council (founding president, 1974; member of board of directors, 1975—), Hawaii Printmakers (member of board of directors, 1980—), Arts Council of Hawaii (member of board of directors, 1979—), InterArts Hawaii (member of executive board, 1979-80). *Awards, honors:* All-Nations Poetry Award from Triton College, 1978.

WRITINGS: (Editor with Eric Chock, Darrell Lum, Gail Miyasaki, Dave Robb, and Kathy Uchida) *Talk Story: An Anthology of Hawaii's Local Writers,* Petronium Press, 1978; (editor with John Unterecker,) *Poetry Hawaii: A Contemporary Anthology,* University Press of Hawaii, 1979; (editor with Linda Spalding) *InterChange: A Symposium on Regionalism, Internationalism, and Ethnicity in Literature,* InterArts Hawaii, 1980; *The Open Water* (poetry), Floating Island Publications, 1981.

Work represented in anthologies, including *Anthology of Magazine Verse and Yearbook of American Poetry,* edited by Alan F. Pater, Monitor Books, 1981; *Peace Is Our Profession: Poems and Passages of War Protest,* East River Anthology, 1981. Contributor of poems, translations, articles, and reviews to journals, magazines, and newspapers, including *Epoch, Ironwood, Poetry Now, The Little Magazine, Brick,* and *Modern Poetry Studies.* Art critic for *Honolulu Star-Bulletin,* 1977-80.

WORK IN PROGRESS: A collection of poems and stories about Hawaii; a videotape-script about Hawaiian children.

SIDELIGHTS: Stewart told *CA:* "My poetry and other art from the beginning has been personal, lyrical, concerned principally with the separation, loss, and betrayal characterizing human relationships—and our attempts to salvage love and even grace from them by whatever means.

"Much of my other work—essays, criticism, editing—flows from a commitment to the people and art of Hawaii and the Pacific; few regions continue to be so abused and misunderstood by the rest of the nation and therefore bear such deep, complex scars. The artists and writers of Hawaii today are crucial to the renaissance of ethnic values and to the emergence of historical truth that began here after statehood. No writer in contemporary Hawaii—myself included—can be unaffected.''

* * *

STICKGOLD, Bob 1945-

PERSONAL: Born October 24, 1945, in Chicago, Ill.; son of Morris and Annabelle (Sorokin) Stickgold; married wife, Becky Sarah, July 21, 1968 (marriage ended, 1978); married Sarah Carleton (a carpenter), June 21, 1980; children: Jessie, Sarah. *Education:* Harvard University, B.A., 1966; University of Wisconsin, Madison, M.S., Ph.D., 1972. *Politics:* "Socialist-feminist.'' *Religion:* None. *Home:* 9 Leonard Ave., Cambridge, Mass. 02139. *Agent:* Blassingame, McCauley & Wood, 60 East 42nd St., New York, N.Y. 10017. *Office:* Department of Physiology, Medical School, University of Massachusetts, Worcester, Mass. 01605.

CAREER: Stanford University, Stanford, Calif., postdoctoral fellow in biochemistry, 1972-75; Harvard University, Cambridge, Mass., postdoctoral fellow in neurobiology, 1975-79; University of Massachusetts, Medical School, Worcester, assistant professor of physiology, 1979—. *Member:* Nine Leonard Avenue Collective.

WRITINGS: Margo Makes a Mess, New Seed Press, 1972; (with Mark Noble) *Gloryhits,* Ballantine, 1977; *California Coven Project,* Ballantine, 1981. Contributor to professional journals and *Worlds of If.*

WORK IN PROGRESS: The Rape of Just About Everyone, a novel about the role of the advertising industry in presidential elections; research on the mechanical properties of the uterus during childbirth.

SIDELIGHTS: Stickgold commented: "My science fiction deals with the political and social interface between science and society. My writings deal with the abuse of scientific knowledge by political and economic groups within the United States. The analysis is made from a socialist-feminist perspective.''

* * *

STOCKWELL, John R(obert) 1937-

PERSONAL: Born August 27, 1937, in Angleton, Tex.; son of William Foster (an engineer) and Wilora (Baker) Stockwell; married Betty McCallum, September 25, 1959 (divorced July, 1974); married Thach Xu Lit (a secretary), January 26, 1979; children: (first marriage) Mary Kathleen, Arthur McCallum, Mel Foster; (second marriage) Thuy Xa, Jonathan Lit. *Education:* Received degree from University of Texas, 1959. *Politics:* Liberal. *Religion:* Humanist. *Home and office:* 5504 Jim Hogg, Austin, Tex. 78756. *Agent:* Wendy Lipkind Agency, 225 East 57th St., New York, N.Y. 10022.

CAREER: Central Intelligence Agency (CIA), Washington, D.C., field case officer, 1964-77; free-lance writer and television journalist, 1978—. *Military service:* U.S. Marine Corps Reserve, 1955-77; active duty, 1959-62; became major.

WRITINGS: In Search of Enemies: A CIA Story (nonfiction), Norton, 1978.

WORK IN PROGRESS: Sondafi: The Burundi Gambit Declined, a novel, for Morrow.

SIDELIGHTS: Stockwell was the chief of the CIA's task force in Angola during 1975 and 1976. He headed a secret paramilitary operation in support of UNITA and FNLA, two pro-

Western guerilla groups, against the pro-Moscow MPLA. He became disillusioned by what he saw as the incompetence, irrationality, and amorality of many of his colleagues, and after the operation ended in failure, he quit the agency to write *In Search of Enemies.* The book was published without the CIA's approval, and in 1980 the agency filed suit against Stockwell, charging him with violating the secrecy agreement he signed when he was hired. The CIA sought all Stockwell's profits from the book, but in a June, 1980, agreement, Stockwell consented to pay the Federal Government any future profits from the book.

In Search of Enemies tells of the growth of the Angola operation from an attempt to insure free elections into a war to guarantee victory for UNITA and FNLA. In the process, the CIA's role grew far beyond that authorized by Congress or the White House. At first American support was just financial, but soon the CIA was sending the guerillas arms. The guerillas were unable to use the weapons effectively, so advisers were sent to train them. The agency recruited foreign mercenaries to reinforce the UNITA and FNLA forces, and sometimes advanced money to "recruiters'' who simply pocketed it. Though it was claimed that the operation was a response to Soviet intervention in Africa, Stockwell reveals that American aid to FNLA began some two months before the first Soviet arms shipments. In addition, Stockwell writes, the agency and its chief, William Colby, lied to Congress, the State Department, and the White House advisory committee on covert operations about the nature and extent of CIA activity in Angola. "There were several levels of untruth functioning simultaneously,'' Stockwell writes, "different stories for different aspects of our activities, one for the working group, another for unwitting State Department personnel, yet another for the U.S. Congress.''

Colby, whom Stockwell called "a disciplined, amoral bureaucrat,'' denied lying to Congress and also denied that CIA officers were engaged in combat or training in Angola. Colby also remarked about Stockwell's disillusionment: "If he says that suddenly it didn't turn out to be the Boy Scouts, I think he was asking a little much.'' *Time* called Stockwell's account "overdrawn in important respects,'' pointing out that some "maintain it was not U.S. activity that provoked the heavy Soviet-Cuban response but South Africa's early move to send troops.''

John Kenneth Galbraith, in the *New York Review of Books,* called *In Search of Enemies* "impressive and convincing.'' He cited the Angola misadventure as an example of the irrationality of "strategic thought,'' which is obsessed with spheres of influence and gives rise to covert operations to defend or expand them. "All who are alarmed by such strategic thinking,'' Galbraith wrote, "should strongly welcome Mr. Stockwell's book.'' And Norman Cousins, editor of *Saturday Review,* wrote: "The constitutional design does not give the government the right to deceive its people. . . . What John Stockwell has done is to document what is in effect an undeclared war by the CIA against American institutions.''

BIOGRAPHICAL/CRITICAL SOURCES: John Stockwell, *In Search of Enemies: A CIA Story,* Norton, 1978; *Newsweek,* May 15, 1978; *Time,* May 22, 1978; *Saturday Review,* July 8, 1978; *New York Times Book Review,* July 16, 1978; *New York Review of Books,* October 12, 1978; *Washington Post,* March 4, 1980; *New York Times,* June 26, 1980.

* * *

STONE, Gerald (Charles) 1932-

PERSONAL: Born August 8, 1932, in Surbiton, England; son

of Albert (a secretary) and Grace (Varndell) Stone; married Vera Konnova (a teacher of languages), April 10, 1974; children: Lydia Grace. *Education:* University of London, B.A. (with honors), 1964, Ph.D., 1968. *Home:* 6 Barns Hay, Old Marston, Oxford, England. *Office:* Hertford College, Oxford University, Oxford OX1 3BW, England.

CAREER: University of Nottingham, Nottingham, England, lecturer, 1966-71; Cambridge University, Cambridge, England, assistant director of research, 1971-72; Oxford University, Oxford, England, lecturer in Slavonic languages and fellow of Hertford College, 1972—. *Military service:* British Army, 1951-53; became sergeant. *Member:* Philological Society.

WRITINGS: The Smallest Slavonic Nation: The Sorbs of Lusatia, Athlone Press, 1972; (with B. Comrie) *The Russian Language Since the Revolution,* Oxford University Press, 1978; *An Introduction to Polish,* Oxford University Press, 1980. Contributor to Slavic studies journals.

WORK IN PROGRESS: Research on the history of the Polish language and on sociolinguistics.

*   *   *

STORNI, Alfonsina 1892-1938

BRIEF ENTRY: Born May 29, 1892, in Ticino, Switzerland; committed suicide, May 11, 1938, in Buenos Aires, Argentina. Argentinian poet. Though her poetry concerns such timeless subjects as love and desolation, Storni's emotional tone and her form are modernist. Her first collection, *La inquietud del rosal* (1916), gave traditional love poems an intelligent, new, and refreshing voice. Storni's best work is considered to be embodied in *Ocre* (1925). She has been admired for the candor with which she discussed her own sexuality and related problems. Storni spent her early career working in a theatrical troupe and with theatre for young people. In her mid-forties she learned she had cancer and took her own life by drowning. *Biographical/critical sources:* Rachel Phillips, *Alfonsina Storni: From Poetess to Poet,* Tamesis, 1975; Sonia Jones, *Alfonsina Storni,* Twayne, 1979.

*   *   *

STOTT, Mary 1907-

PERSONAL: Born July 18, 1907, in Leicester, England; daughter of Robert Guy (a journalist) and Amalie (a journalist; maiden name, Bates) Waddington; married Kenneth Stott (a journalist), February 18, 1937 (died, 1967); children: Catherine Lindsey Stott Lewis. *Education:* Attended girls' secondary school in Leicester, England. *Home:* Flat 4, 11 Morden Rd., Blackheath, London SE3 0AA, England.

CAREER: Worked as journalist for *Manchester Evening News,* Manchester, England, *Co-Operative Press,* Manchester, *Bolton Evening News,* Bolton, England, and *Leicester Evening Mail,* Leicester, England; *Guardian,* London, England, editor of "Woman's Page," 1957-72. *Member:* National Union of Journalists (life member), Women in Media, Fawcett Society (chairman, 1978—), Press Club of London (life member), University Women's Club. *Awards, honors:* Fellow of Manchester Polytechnic; officer of Order of the British Empire, 1975.

WRITINGS: Forgetting's No Excuse, Faber, 1973; *Is This Your Life: Images of Women in the Media,* Virago/Quartet, 1977; *Organization Woman: The Story of the National Union of Townswomen's Guilds,* Heinemann, 1978; *Ageing for Beginners,* Basil Blackwell, 1981. Contributor to women's magazines and newspapers.

SIDELIGHTS: Mary Stott commented: "Because most of my work has been in women's pages I have become very much caught up in the women's movement, especially since I moved from Manchester to London in 1970 after the death of my husband, but I am also interested in music and other cultural matters."

AVOCATIONAL INTERESTS: Singing in a choir, painting.

BIOGRAPHICAL/CRITICAL SOURCES: London Times, July 4, 1981; *Times Literary Supplement,* July 24, 1981.

*   *   *

STOTT, Mike 1944-

PERSONAL: Born January 2, 1944, in Rochdale, England. *Education:* Attended Victoria University of Manchester. *Agent:* Michael Imison, Jan Van Loewen Ltd., 81-83 Shaftesbury Ave., London W1V 8BX, England.

CAREER: Writer. Worked as stage manager at Scarborough Library Theatre; play reader at Royal Shakespeare Theatre, England; BBC-Radio, London, England, script editor, 1970-72; Hampstead Theatre Club, Hampstead, England, Thames Television resident writer, 1975.

WRITINGS: Funny Peculiar (farce; first produced in Bochum, West Germany, 1973; produced in London, England, 1976), I. Henry, 1977; *Soldiers Talking, Cleanly,* Eyre Methuen, 1979.

Unpublished plays: "Mata Hari," first produced in Scarborough, England, 1965; "Erogenous Zones" (sketches), first produced in London, England, 1969; "Lenz" (adaptation of story by Georg Buechner), first produced in London, 1974; "Plays for People Who Don't Move Much," first produced in London, 1974; "Midnight," first produced in London, 1974; "Other People," first produced in London, 1974; "Men's Talk" (contains "Hard Slog," "The Force," and "Fixtures"), first produced in Edinburgh, Scotland, 1974, produced in London, 1974; "Ghosts" (adaptation of play by Wolfgang Bauer), first produced in London, 1975; "Lorenzaccio" (adaptation of play by Alfred de Musset), first produced in Exeter, England, 1976.

Radio plays: "Lucky," first broadcast in 1970; "When Dreams Collide," first broadcast in 1970; "Early Morning Glory," first broadcast in 1972; "Lincoln," first broadcast in 1973; "Richard Serge," first broadcast in 1973; "The Bringer of Bad News," first broadcast in 1973; "The Doubting Thomases," first broadcast in 1973.

Television plays: "The Flaxton Boys," first broadcast in 1969; "Susan," first broadcast in 1973; "Thwum," first broadcast in 1975.*

*   *   *

STRADLING, Leslie Edward 1908-

PERSONAL: Born February 11, 1908, in Reading, England; son of Walter Herbert (a minister) and Mary (Collier) Stradling. *Education:* Queen's College, Oxford, B.A., 1930, M.A., 1934; also studied at Westcott House, Cambridge. *Home:* 197 Main Rd., Kalk Bay, Cape 7975, South Africa.

CAREER: Ordained Anglican minister, 1934; curate of Anglican church in London, England, 1933-38; vicar of Anglican churches in London, 1938-45; bishop of Anglican churches in Tasmania, 1945-53, and Tanganyika, 1952-61; bishop of Anglican church in Johannesburg, South Africa, 1961-74; writer, 1974—. *Member:* United Oxford and Cambridge Universities Club, City and Civil Service Club. *Awards, honors:* D.C.L. from Bishop's University, Lennoxville, Quebec, 1968.

WRITINGS: A Bishop at Prayer, S.P.C.K., 1971; *Prayers of Love,* ELD, 1973; *Prayers of Faith,* ELD, 1974; *Praying Now,* ELD, 1976; *Praying the Psalms,* Fortress Press, 1977.

WORK IN PROGRESS: Markan Meditations, commentary on the New Testament gospel of Mark.

SIDELIGHTS: Stradling commented: "I have traveled widely in the continent of Africa; I am fluent in Swahili (preach sermons in it) and have a smattering of other African languages.

"There is a part of me which writes because I want to see myself in print and hear myself referred to as a successful author; but what I like to think of as my better self writes because I believe I have something to say which can help others. Though it is nice to be paid for writing, I do not depend on this money and do not need to write when I have nothing to say.

"My books are comparable to sermons though they are not produced in sermon style, which rarely looks well in print. I deal with such subjects as the possibility of communicating with God, bringing the Bible to life, and being a Christian in this technological age. I draw extensively from my experience in the primitive—and now not so primitive—culture of Africa."

* * *

STRAKOSCH, Avery
   See DENHAM, Avery Strakosch

* * *

STRAUSS, Harold   1907-1975

OBITUARY NOTICE: Born June 18, 1907, in New York, N.Y.; died of a heart attack, November 27, 1975, in New York, N.Y. Editor. Contemporary American readers were introduced to modern Japanese literature when Strauss persuaded his employer, Alfred A. Knopf, to publish Jiro Osaragi's novel *Homecoming.* During his many years with Knopf, Strauss also edited works by other Japanese authors, including Kobo Abe, Junichiro Tanizaki, Yukio Mishima, and Nobel Prize-winner Yasunari Kawabata. Western writers whose works were edited by Strauss include John Hersey, Edwin Reischauer, and Christopher Lash. Obituaries and other sources: *American Authors and Books, 1640 to the Present Day,* 3rd revised edition, Crown, 1972; *New York Times,* November 30, 1975; *Publishers Weekly,* December 8, 1975; *AB Bookman's Weekly,* January 5, 1976; *Who Was Who in America, With World Notables,* Volume IV: *1974-1976,* Marquis, 1976.

* * *

STRETTON, Hugh   1924-

PERSONAL: Born in 1924, in Melbourne, Australia; son of Leonard (a lawyer) and Norah (Crawford) Stretton; married Jennifer Gamble (a painter), 1951 (marriage ended, 1962); married Pat Gibson (a historian), 1963; children: Simon, Fabian, Timothy, Sally. *Education:* Attended University of Melbourne, 1942, 1946; Oxford University, M.A., 1948; attended Princeton University, 1948-49. *Office:* Department of History, University of Adelaide, Adelaide, South Australia 5000.

CAREER: Oxford University, Oxford, England, fellow of Balliol College, 1948-54; University of Adelaide, Adelaide, Australia, professor, 1954-68, reader in history, 1969—. Visiting lecturer or researcher at Smith College, 1960-61, Australian National University, 1966, Centre for Environmental Studies,

London, England, 1973, University of London, 1977, and York University, 1981. Member of Australian Cities Commission, 1974-75; member of board of directors of Australian Housing Corp., 1975-76; deputy chairman of South Australian Housing Trust, 1972—. *Member:* Australian Academy of the Humanities (fellow), Australian Academy of the Social Sciences (fellow).

WRITINGS: The Political Sciences: General Principles of Selection in Social Science and History, Basic Books, 1969; *Ideas for Australian Cities,* Georgian House, 1971, 2nd revised edition, 1975; *Housing and Government,* Australian Broadcasting Commission, 1974; *Capitalism, Socialism, and the Environment,* Cambridge University Press, 1976; *Urban Planning in Rich and Poor Countries,* Oxford University Press, 1978.

SIDELIGHTS: Stretton commented: "I am currently writing on institutional economics, chiefly against the current lurch to the right in English-speaking countries."

* * *

STRINDBERG, (Johan) August   1849-1912

BRIEF ENTRY: Born January 22, 1849, in Stockholm, Sweden; died of stomach cancer, May 14, 1912, in Stockholm, Sweden. Swedish playwright, poet, novelist, and critic. Strindberg is variously hailed as the originator of modern drama, the father of expressionism in the theatre, and one of Sweden's greatest authors. Stressing the cruelty and harshness of life, he produced more than sixty-five plays in addition to several novels and autobiographical works. Strindberg had an unhappy childhood and school career, and his young adulthood was marked with bouts of alcoholism. He unsuccessfully embarked on a number of occupations, including private tutor, actor, journalist, insurance agent, translator, and librarian. Although he began writing while a student, Strindberg did not obtain recognition until 1879 when his novel *Roeda Rummet* (title means "The Red Room") was published. Considered Sweden's first realistic novel, the book was controversial in its criticism of Swedish society. The author followed this book with other bitterly satirical works. One of them, *Giftas* (title means "Married"), resulted in Strindberg being tried for blaspheming the holy sacrament. Although he was acquitted, the incident affected his already unstable mental state. He became a misogynist and felt persecuted by feminists. After the break-up of his first marriage, he slipped into insanity. Returning to mental health, Strindberg began a period of renewed creative activity writing expressionistic plays. Regarded as his finest, these plays often ignore plot and realistic stage settings in order to express what Strindberg thought was man's hell on earth. His other works include *Froken Julie* (1888; translated as *Miss Julie,* 1913), *Till Damascus* (1898-1904; translated as *To Damascus,* 1933-35), *Doedsdansen* (1901; translated as *The Dance of Death,* 1912), and *Spoeksonaten* (1907; translated as *The Spook Sonata,* 1916). *Biographical/critical sources: Cyclopedia of World Authors,* Harper, 1958; *McGraw-Hill Encyclopedia of World Drama,* McGraw, 1972; *The McGraw-Hill Encyclopedia of World Biography,* McGraw, 1973; *Twentieth-Century Literary Criticism,* Volume 1, Gale, 1978.

* * *

STROMAN, Duane F(rederick)   1934-

PERSONAL: Born March 8, 1934, in Fostoria, Ohio; son of F. Harry (in business) and M. Cena (a bookkeeper; maiden name, Yeasting) Stroman; married June Charles (a teacher), March 24, 1958; children: Steven, Susan, Karen, David. *Education:* Ohio Wesleyan University, B.A., 1956; Boston University, S.T.B., 1959, Ph.D., 1966; postdoctoral study at Pennsylvania State University. *Home:* 2200 Cassady Ave., Huntingdon, Pa. 16652. *Office:* Department of Sociology, Juniata College, Huntingdon, Pa. 16652.

CAREER: Juniata College, Huntingdon, Pa., instructor, 1963-65, assistant professor, 1965-67, associate professor, 1967-76, professor of sociology, 1976—, chairman of department of sociology and anthropology, 1965-73, assistant dean, 1972-74, director of continuing education, 1975—. Conducts marketing surveys. Member of Keystone Health Systems Agency task force on specialized care, 1977, and advisory committee of Pennsylvania Department of Education's Pennsylvania Educational Information Centers Project; member of board of directors of Tri-County Community Action Agency, 1968-74 and 1976-77. Vice-president of Skills of Central Pennsylvania, 1969-74; chairman of Huntingdon County Redevelopment Authority, 1970-74, and Comprehensive Health Planning Council of the Southern Alleghenies, 1973-74; consultant to Federal Trade Commission, Pennsylvania Electric Co., and Stephen V. Heine Engineering Co. *Member:* American Sociological Association, Rotary International. *Awards, honors:* Honorary fellow at Harvard University, 1974-75.

WRITINGS: The Medical Establishment and Social Responsibility, Kennikat, 1976; *The Quick Knife: Unnecessary Surgery in the U.S.A.,* Kennikat, 1979. Contributor to *Social Science Quarterly.*

WORK IN PROGRESS: Two books on minorities, one on the handicapped and one on behavioral minorities, publication by Kennikat expected in 1982; *Placebos: Ethical and Medical Aspects,* 1983.

SIDELIGHTS: Stroman wrote: "*The Quick Knife* reviews the evidence for an expensive problem in the United States: unnecessary surgery." *Avocational interests:* Playing and coaching golf.

*   *   *

STRONG, Kenneth William Dobson   1900-

PERSONAL: Born September 9, 1900; son of John (a professor) Strong. *Education:* Attended Royal Military College, Sandhurst, England. *Home:* 25 Kepplestone, Eastbourne, East Sussex, England.

CAREER: British Army, career officer, 1920-47, served as battalion commander of Royal Scots Fusiliers, member of Saar force, 1935, defense security officer in Malta, and Gibraltar, head of German section at War Office, military attache in Berlin, Germany, Italy, France, and Spain, head of Intelligence Home Forces, 1942, head of General Eisenhower's intelligence staff, 1943-45 (serving in Africa, Sicily, Italy, France, and Germany), member of delegations for conducting armistice negotiations with Italy in Lisbon, Portugal and in Sicily, 1943, and armistice negotiations with Germany in Rheims and Berlin, 1945, director general of political intelligence department of Foreign Office, 1945-47, retiring as major general; Ministry of Defence, England, first director of Joint Intelligence Bureau, 1948-64, first director-general of intelligence, 1964-66; director of Philip Hill Investment Trust and Eagle Star Insurance Co., 1966-77.

MEMBER: Army and Navy Club. *Awards, honors*—Military: mentioned in British dispatches, U.S. distinguished service medal; U.S. Legion of Merit; chevalier and officer of French Legion of Honor; French Croix de Guerre, with palms; Russian Order of the Red Banner. Other: Officer of Order of the British

Empire, 1942, knight commander, 1966; Companion of Order of the Bath, 1945; knighted, 1952.

WRITINGS: Intelligence at the Top: The Recollections of an Intelligence Officer, Cassell, 1968, Doubleday, 1969; *Men of Intelligence: A Study of the Roles and Decisions of Chiefs of Intelligence From World War I to the Present Day,* Cassell, 1970, St. Martin's, 1972. Contributor to newspapers.*

*   *   *

STRUEVER, Stuart McKee   1931-

PERSONAL: Born August 4, 1931, in Peru, Ill.; son of Carl Chester and Martha McKee (Scobee) Struever; married Alice Russell Melcher, August 21, 1956; children: Nathan Chester, Hanna Russell. *Education:* Dartmouth College, A.B., 1953; Northwestern University, M.A. 1960; University of Chicago, Ph.D., 1968. *Home:* 2000 Sheridan Rd., Evanston, Ill. 60201. *Office:* Department of Anthropology, Northwestern University, Evanston, Ill. 60201.

CAREER: University of Chicago, Chicago, Ill., instructor in anthropology, 1964-65; Northwestern University, Evanston, Ill., instructor, 1965-68, assistant professor, 1968-69, associate professor, 1969-72, professor of anthropology, 1972—, chairman of department, 1975-78, director of archaeology program, president of Center for American Archaeology, 1980—. Lecturer at University of Chicago, 1969—. Director of Foundation for Illinois Archaeology, 1956-58, chairman of board of directors, 1958—; member of Illinois Historic Sites Advisory Council, 1969—; director of Illinois Archaeological Survey; member of National Science Foundation anthropology advisory panel and board of archaeological consultants of Tennessee Valley Authority, 1976—; member of north central accreditation committee of Commission on Institutions of Higher Education.

MEMBER: Society for American Archaeology (member of executive committee, 1970-72; president, 1975-76), Society of Professional Archaeologists (member of executive board, 1976-77), American Anthropological Association, Adventurers Club. *Awards, honors:* Grants from National Science Foundation, 1968-70, National Geographical Society National Endowment for the Humanities, National Park Service, American Philosophical Society, Wenner-Gren Foundation for Anthropological Research, 1968-69, and Illinois Department of Conservation.

WRITINGS: (Contributor) *New Perspectives in Archaeology,* Aldine, 1968; (editor) *Prehistoric Agriculture,* Natural History Press, 1971; (with Felicia Antonelli Holton) *Koster: Americans in Search of Their Prehistoric Past,* Doubleday, 1979. General editor of "Studies in Archaeology," a series, Academic Press. Contributor to scholarly journals. Editor of *Memoirs* (of Society for American Archaeology), 1969—.

BIOGRAPHICAL/CRITICAL SOURCES: Science Digest, May, 1979.*

*   *   *

STUART, Colin   1910-

PERSONAL: Born December 17, 1910; married, September 16, 1941; children: two sons, two daughters. *Education:* Received B.A., 1934, M.A., 1940, and Ph.D., 1954. *Agent:* Sidney Porcelain, Box J, Rocky Hill, N.Y. 08553.

CAREER: Merchant seaman, laborer, and commercial salmon fisherman, 1926-38; history teacher and college administrator,

1947-74. *Military service:* U.S. Army, Infantry, 1940-46; became major; received Purple Heart.

WRITINGS: Shoot an Arrow to Stop the Wind (novel), Dial, 1971; *Walks Far Woman* (novel), Dial, 1976.

SIDELIGHTS: Stuart commented briefly: "I have had lunch with Chief Two Guns White Calf of the Blackfeet, Admiral Byrd, Eleanor Roosevelt, and Raquel Welch."

* * *

STUERMER, Nina Roberta 1933-

PERSONAL: Born August 12, 1933, in Oklahoma City, Okla.; daughter of Robert Treat (a roofer) and Mary Lucille (Beal) Payne; married Gordon Gene Stuermer (a naval architect and writer), April 10, 1955; children: Ernest Gordon. *Education:* Attended high school in Long Beach, Calif. *Home:* Yacht "Starbound," P.O. Box 26, Annapolis, Md. 21404.

CAREER: Writer.

WRITINGS: (With husband, Gordon Stuermer) *Starbound*, McKay, 1977; (with G. Stuermer) *Deep Water Cruising*, McKay, 1980.

* * *

STURTEVANT, Catherine ?-1970

OBITUARY NOTICE: Born in Sterling, Colo.; died April 2, 1970, in Charlottesville, Va. Editorial director of the University Press of Virginia. Sturtevant edited *Man and Wife and Other Plays* by Augustin Daly. Obituaries and other sources: *Publishers Weekly*, May 4, 1970; *Who's Who of American Women*, 7th edition, Marquis, 1972.

* * *

STURTEVANT, David Reeves 1926-

PERSONAL: Born September 20, 1926, in Zanesville, Ohio; married, 1947; children: three. *Education:* Muskingum College, B.A., 1950; Stanford University, M.A., 1951, Ph.D., 1958. *Office:* Department of History, Muskingum College, New Concord, Ohio 43762.

CAREER: Muskingum College, New Concord, Ohio, began as assistant professor, 1955, became professor of history, 1967—. Conducted seminars at Ateneo de Manila University and University of the Philippines; visiting professor at University of Hawaii, 1976-77. *Member:* Association for Asian Studies. *Awards, honors:* Fulbright grant for the Philippines, 1965-66; American Council of Learned Societies-Social Science Research Council grant for Asia, 1970.

WRITINGS: Popular Uprisings in the Philippines, 1840-1940, Cornell University Press, 1976. Contributor to history journals.*

* * *

SUDBERY, Rodie 1943-

PERSONAL: Born April 22, 1943, in Chalmsford, Essex, England; daughter of William (a designer) and Barbara (a writer; maiden name, Jones) Tutton; married Anthony Sudbery (a lecturer in mathematics), July 4, 1964; children: Lucy, Clare. *Education:* Girton College, Cambridge, B.A., 1964. *Home:* 5 Helsington Croft, Fulford, York YO1 4NB, England.

CAREER: Writer.

WRITINGS:—All juvenile; all published by Deutsch, except as noted: *The House in the Wood*, 1968, published as *A Sound of Crying*, McCall Publishing, 1970; *Cowls*, 1969; *Rich and Famous and Bad*, 1970; *The Pigsleg*, 1971; *Warts and All*, 1972; *A Curious Place*, 1973; *Inside the Walls*, 1973; *Ducks and Drakes*, 1975; *Lighting Cliff*, 1975; *The Silk and the Skin*, 1976; *Long Way Round*, 1977; *Somewhere Else*, 1978; *A Tunnel With Problems*, 1979; *The Village Secret*, 1980.

SIDELIGHTS: Sudbery told *CA:* "I like to write about conflicts and often see my books in terms of power shifts from one character, or group of characters, to another (though readers need not and usually don't). This is particularly true of *Somewhere Else*, in which a boy and girl move in and out of an imaginary world; their relationship in the real world is echoed by that of their counterparts in the other. The girl begins by dominating the boy and ends up at his mercy, and the situation is resolved in the real world when he realizes his power over her and chooses not to use it."

In *Pigsleg*, Sudbery examines a problem involving four families. The children of these families begin daring members of their gang to perform various feats. One girl is dared to remain silent for a year's time, and her attempt to live up to the dare creates much irritation at home. The adults become aware of the gang's activities and finally subdue Cressida, the bossy leader of the gang.

Sudbery's *A Tunnel With Problems* involves the children of two families in York engaged in typical childhood amusements. A tunnel near the children's homes becomes blocked, and they embark on a search for a buried treasure. The fun comes to a quick halt when one boy gets trapped in the tunnel.

Sudbery has published five books as part of her "Polly Devenish" series. The books follow Polly and the events in her life from age twelve in *The House in the Wood* to her first experiences at York University at age eighteen in *Ducks and Drakes*.

* * *

SULLIVAN, Martin Gloster 1910-1980

OBITUARY NOTICE: Born March 30, 1910, in Auckland, New Zealand; died September 5, 1980, in Auckland, New Zealand. Clergyman and author. After his ordination in 1934, Sullivan was associated with churches in New Zealand, was a chaplain in Asia and Europe, and was a clerical staff member of several institutions in London. Prior to serving as dean of St. Paul's Cathedral in London, a position he held from 1967 to 1977, Sullivan served as the rector of St. Mary in Bryonston Square, as the archdeacon of London, and as the canon residentiary of St. Paul's. Though a "traditionalist with regard to texts," Sullivan incorporated innovations into his worship services so that young people would be attracted to them. For instance, the clergyman invited the cast of the rock musical "Hair" to a celebration of the Eucharist. And in 1968 he sponsored a Festival of Youth at St. Paul's Cathedral, complete with rock musicians and a simulated parachute jump. A powerful speaker, Sullivan was a leading figure at Winston Churchill's funeral in 1965 and at Queen Elizabeth's Silver Jubilee Thanksgiving service in 1977. His most popular works include *On Calvary's Tree, Watch How You Go*, and his autobiography *A Funny Thing Happened to Me on My Way to St. Paul's*. Obituaries and other sources: *Who's Who in the World*, 3rd edition, Marquis, 1976; *The Writers Directory, 1980-82*, St. Martin's, 1979; *Obituaries Annual 1980*, St. Martin's, 1980.

SULLIVAN, Richard 1908-1981

OBITUARY NOTICE—See index for *CA* sketch; Born November, 29, 1908, in Kenosha, Wis.; died September 13, 1981, in South Bend, Ind. Educator and author. Prior to embarking on his teaching career, Sullivan worked as a free-lance writer for five years, beginning in 1931. A professor of English, he was associated with the University of Notre Dame for forty-five years. Sullivan wrote radio and television plays and contributed stories and reviews to magazines and to newspapers; he often reviewed books for the *Chicago Tribune* and the *New York Times*. He wrote a play entitled "Our Lady's Tumbler" and several novels, including *Summer After Summer, The World of Idella May,* and *Three Kings.* His most famous work is the nonfiction book *Notre Dame: The Story of a Great University.* Obituaries and other sources: *Chicago Tribune,* September 16, 1981.

* * *

SUMICHRAST, Michael M. 1921-

PERSONAL: Born March 31, 1921, in Trencin, Czechoslovakia; came to the United States in 1955, naturalized citizen; son of Michal and Vilma (Medzihradska) Sumichrast; married Marika Elisabeth Spacek, June 1, 1949; children: Michael, Marek, Martin. *Education:* University of Bratislava, B.S., 1948; University of Melbourne, degree, 1953; Ohio State University, M.B.A., 1957, Ph.D., 1962. *Home:* 11527 Le Havre Dr., Potomac, Md. 20854.

CAREER: Worked as editor of *Obrana Ludu,* Bratislava, Czechoslovakia; co-editor of *Nove Prudy,* Bratislava; J. J. Clift Co. Ltd., Melbourne, Australia, building manager, 1950-55; Carlyle Construction Co., New York, N.Y., construction engineer and supervisor, 1955-57; Nationwide Insurance Co., Columbus, Ohio, consulting engineer, 1957-58; Ernest G. Fritsche & Co., Columbus, production manager and director of market research, 1958-62; National Association of Home Builders of the United States, Washington, D.C., assistant economist, 1963-64, associate economist, 1964-66, chief economist and vice-president, 1966—. Lecturer at American University, 1966-67, associate professor, 1967—. Consulting engineer for Tectum Corp., 1957-58; chairman of economic committee of National Housing Council, 1964-66; co-chairman of statistics committee of Construction Industry Joint Conference, 1964-68; member of Homer Hoyt Institute; consultant to National Academy of Sciences. *Member:* American Marketing Association, American Economic Association, National Association of Business Economists, American Statistical Association, American Political Science Association.

WRITINGS: (Editor) Uriel L. Manheim, *How to Do Housing Market Research: A Handbook for Local Home Builders Associations,* National Association of Home Builders, 1963; (editor) *Components of Future Housing Demand,* National Housing Center, 1966; (with Norman Farquhar) *Demolition and Other Factors in Housing Replacement Demand,* Homebuilding Press, 1967. Also author of *Net Removal Rate From Housing Inventory,* 1967, and co-author of *Urban Development Planning,* 1969.

(With Sara A. Frankel) *Profile of the Builder and His Industry,* National Association of Home Builders, 1970; (with Maury Seldin) *The Uniform Building Permit Reporting System: A Demonstration in the Washington, D.C. SMSA,* U.S. Department of Housing & Urban Development, 1970; (with Charles P. McMahon) *Opportunities in Building Construction,* Universal Publishing & Distributing Corp., 1971, revised edition, Vocational Guidance Manuals, 1976; (with Robert Enzel)

Housing Component Costs, National Association of Home Builders, 1974; (with Seldin) *Housing Markets: The Complete Guide to Analysis and Strategy for Builders, Lenders, and Other Investors,* Dow Jones-Irwin, 1977; (with Robert J. Sheehan and Gopal Ahluwalia) *Condominium Management and Operation,* National Association of Home Builders, 1979; (with Sheehan and Ahluwalia) *Kitchen Appliances and Other Equipment in New Homes,* National Association of Home Builders, 1979; (with Sheehan and Ahluwalia) *Profile of a Condominium Buyer,* National Association of Home Builders, 1979; (with Sheehan and Ahluwalia) *Profile of the Builder,* National Association of Home Builders, 1979.

(With Ronald G. Shafer) *The Complete Book of Home Buying,* Dow Jones 1979, revised edition published as *The Complete Book of Home Buying: A Consumer's Guide to Housing in the Eighties,* 1980. Contributor to professional journals.*

* * *

SUMMER, Brian
See Du BREUIL, (Elizabeth) L(or)inda

* * *

SUTNAR, Ladislav 1897-1976

OBITUARY NOTICE: Born November 9, 1897, in Pilsen, Czechoslovakia; died after a brief illness, November 13, 1976, in New York, N.Y. Graphic designer and author. Sutnar came to the United States in 1939 to design the Czech pavilion for the World's Fair, and he remained in America because of the Nazi domination of his homeland. He received design commissions from a variety of employers, including McGraw-Hill, International Business Machines (IBM), and the United Nations. He also worked for Sweet's Catalog Service for almost twenty years. Sutnar held many one-man exhibitions, and his work is on permanent display in the Museum of Modern Art in New York. His books include *Controlled Visual Flow: Shape, Line and Color, Package Design: The Force of Visual Selling,* and *Visual Design in Action: Principles, Purposes.* Obituaries and other sources: *Who's Who in Graphic Art,* Amstutz & Herdeg Graphis, 1962; *Publishers Weekly,* December 27, 1976.

* * *

SVAREFF, Count Vladimir
See CROWLEY, Edward Alexander

* * *

SVEVO, Italo
See SCHMITZ, Ettore

* * *

SWIFT, Augustus
See LOVECRAFT, H(oward) P(hillips)

* * *

SYNGE, (Edmund) J(ohn) M(illington) 1871-1909

BRIEF ENTRY: Born April 16, 1871, in Newton Little, Ireland; died of tuberculosis, March 24, 1909, in Dublin, Ireland. Irish poet and playwright. Synge wrote only five plays before his death at age thirty-seven. His poetic drama was inspired by the inhabitants of the Aran Islands, whom poet and fellow Irishman W. B. Yeats advised him to study in 1898. In the early 1900's, Synge turned to playwrighting under the continued encouragement of Yeats, who was coordinating a revival in Irish drama. Synge's first play, *In the Shadow of the Glen* (1903), caused a scandal with its depiction of an adulterous Irish wife. He followed it with *Riders to the Sea* (1904), a one-act tragedy of man's resignation to the unsympathetic nature of fate. Synge continued with three comedies, *The Well of the Saints* (1905), *The Playboy of the Western World* (1907), and *The Tinker's Wedding* (1908). The comedies were initially condemned for their unromantic portrayals of the Irish—especially *The Playboy of the Western World,* in which a murderer receives friendship and shelter from an Irish peasant. Since Synge's death, however, *The Playboy of the Western World* has risen in stature with *Riders to the Sea* to rate among the finest twentieth-century plays. Synge also wrote a collection of stories and sketches entitled *The Aran Islands* (1907). His poems were published posthumously. *Biographical/critical sources: Cyclopedia of World Authors,* Harper, 1958; *Longman Companion to Twentieth Century Literature,* Longman, 1970; *Modern World Drama: An Encyclopedia,* Dutton, 1972; *Cassell's Encyclopaedia of World Literature,* revised edition, Morrow, 1973.

*   *   *

SZYDLOW, Jarl
   See SZYDLOWSKI, Mary Vigliante

*   *   *

SZYDLOWSKI, Mary Vigliante   1946-
   (Mary Vigliante; Jarl Szydlow, a pseudonym)

PERSONAL: Born September 8, 1946, in Albany, N.Y.; daughter of Frank A. (a chef) and Nataly (Nicita) Vigliante; married Frank Joseph Szydlowski (an insurance account executive), April 17, 1971; children: Carrie Ann. *Education:* State University of New York at Albany, B.A. (cum laude), 1971; also studied at American Academy of Dramatic Arts and Circle in the Square. *Home and office:* 92B Columbia Turnpike, Rensselaer, N.Y. 12144.

CAREER: New York State Department of Mental Hygiene, Albany, administrator, 1974-78; writer, 1978—. *Member:* Authors Guild, Authors League of America, National Organization for Women.

WRITINGS: Silent Song (novel), Everest House, 1980.

Novels, under name Mary Vigliante: *The Colony* (fantasy), Manor, 1979; *The Land* (fantasy), Manor, 1979; *Source of Evil* (science fiction), Manor, 1980; *Worship the Night* (horror), Leisure/Tower Books, 1981.

Under pseudonym Jarl Szydlow: *The Ark* (science fiction novel), Manor, 1978. Contributor to newspapers.

WORK IN PROGRESS: Act of Vengeance, a feminist suspense novel, under name Mary Vigliante Szydlowski; *Messiana,* a fantasy novel, under name Mary Vigliante Szydlowski.

SIDELIGHTS: Mary Szydlowski commented: "All my books have decidedly feminist themes and are about women who struggle to control their lives and destinies. My first novel, *The Colony,* concerns the adjustment of a feminist who is forced to live in a post-holocaust society dominated by males. Most of my succeeding books have built on that theme: the endless battle females must fight to gain equality. No matter what genre I'm working in, be it science fiction (*The Ark* and *Source of Evil*), fantasy (*The Colony, The Land* and *Messiana*), horror (*Worship the Night*), or contemporary (*Silent Song* and *Act of Vengeance*), I write about the type of situations I see affecting women today. My characters are strong willed and intelligent and always triumph over their antagonists in the end. I guess that I write the kinds of books that I enjoy reading: those in which women are portrayed not as objects, powerless and vulnerable, at the mercy of outside forces, but instead as capable, thinking, feeling individuals who take responsibilities for their lives, and through diligent effort manage to overcome their problems, emerging battered but victorious. I am a longtime advocate of women's rights and think that it is one of the most important issues facing contemporary society. Writing is my way of conveying that message."

BIOGRAPHICAL/CRITICAL SOURCES: Troy Sunday Record, March 25, 1979; *Greenbush Area News,* February 6, 1979, August 25, 1980; *Albany Times Union,* November 13, 1980.

T

TACK, Alfred 1906-

PERSONAL: Born in 1906, in London, England; married Vera Davies; children: one daughter. Education: Attended private boys' school in Hammersmith, England. Home: 1 Chelsea House, 24 Lowndes St., London S.W.1, England.

CAREER: Writer. Managing director of Tack Organisation.

WRITINGS—Nonfiction: Sell Your Way to Success, Jenkins, 1950, 6th edition, Business Books, 1978; (editor) Professional Salesmanship, World's Work, 1953; One Thousand Ways to Increase Your Sales, World's Work, 1954, Prentice-Hall, 1961; How to Overcome Nervous Tension and Speak Well in Public, World's Work, 1954, reprinted as How to Speak Well in Public, Baker Book, 1973; (editor) Successful Sales Management, World's Work, 1955; How to Double Your Income in Selling, World's Work, 1957; Sell Better—Live Better, World's Work, 1958; (with George Tack) How to Sell Successfully Overseas, World's Work, 1963; How to Train Yourself to Succeed in Selling, World's Work, 1964; Marketing: The Sales Manager's Role, World's Work, 1968, revised edition, 1973; Profitable Letter Writing, World's Work, 1972; How to Increase Sales by Telephone, World's Work, 1971; How to Increase Your Sales to Industry, World's Work, 1975.

Novels: Selling's Murder!, Jenkins, 1946; Interviewing's Killing, Jenkins, 1947; The Prospect's Dead, Jenkins, 1948; The Test Match Murder, Jenkins, 1948; Killing Business, Jenkins, 1949; A Murder Is Staged, Jenkins, 1949; Death Takes a Dive, Jenkins, 1950, Roy, 1957; Death Kicks a Pebble, Jenkins, 1951; P.A. to Murder, John Long, 1966; Murder Takes Over, John Long, 1966; Forecast: Murder, John Long, 1967; The Top Steal, Doubleday, 1968; The Spy Who Wasn't Exchanged, John Long, 1968, Doubleday, 1969; The Big Kidnap, John Long, 1969; The Great Hi-Jack, Doubleday, 1970; Return of the Assassin, Putnam, 1974.

* * *

TAGGART, John Scott
See SCOTT-TAGGART, John

* * *

TAGLIAVIA, Sheila 1936-

PERSONAL: Surname is pronounced Tal-ya-vee-a; born November 17, 1936, in Toronto, Ontario, Canada; daughter of Edmond Cecil (an office manager) and Nan (Faickney) Bourke; married Angelo Tagliavia (a management consultant), July 18, 1959; children: Irene, Jamie, Gian Paolo. Education: Attended University of Toronto, 1955-57. Politics: "In Italy this is too complicated to go into." Religion: Presbyterian. Home: Via XX Settembre 150, Perugia, Italy 06100. Agent: Elizabeth Trupin, JET Literary Associates, Inc., 124 East 84th St., Suite 4A, New York, N.Y. 10028.

CAREER: Writer.

WRITINGS: The Heritage, Harper, 1977; An Arrangement for Life, Harper, 1980.

WORK IN PROGRESS: A biography of Julia Beccaria, mother of Italian writer Alessandro Manzoni.

SIDELIGHTS: Sheila Tagliavia wrote: "Having lived in Italy for twenty years, my reality, the raw material from which I draw my stories, is here. On the other hand, writing for publication in America, I must draw on those elements which will be meaningful for readers there. This involves a constant sifting process, to bring to light enough common ground to illuminate situations and problems that go beyond mere local color, touching chords of wider, and I hope deeper, interest."

* * *

TAGORE, Rabindranath
See THAKURA, Ravindranatha

* * *

TAHARA, Mildred Machiko 1941-

PERSONAL: Born May 15, 1941, in Hilo, Hawaii. Education: University of Hawaii, B.A., 1963, M.A., 1965; Columbia University, Ph.D., 1969. Office: Department of East Asian Literature, University of Hawaii, Honolulu, Hawaii 96822.

CAREER: University of Hawaii, Honolulu, assistant professor, 1969-76, associate professor of Japanese literature, 1976—. Member: Association for Asian Studies, Association of Teachers of Japanese, Japan Society.

WRITINGS: (Translator) Sanuko Ariyoshi, The River Ki, Kodansha, 1980; (translator) Yamato Monogatari, Tales of Yamato: A Tenth-Century Poem-Tale, University Press of Hawaii, 1980. Contributor of articles and stories to scholarly journals, including Japan Quarterly.*

TALBOT, Nathan B(ill) 1909-

PERSONAL: Born November 25, 1909, in Boston, Mass.; son of Fritz B. and Beatrice B. Talbot; married Anne Perry, 1934; children: N. Dennison, Frederick B. *Education:* Harvard University, A.B., 1932, M.D., 1936. *Home:* 176 Warren St., Brookline, Mass. 02146.

CAREER: Worked as intern at children's hospital, 1936-38; Harvard University, Cambridge, Mass., 1939-1962, began as assistant professor, became associate professor, Charles Wilder Professor of Pediatrics and head of department, 1962—; Massachusetts General Hospital, Boston, consultant, 1942-62, chief of children's services, 1962—. *Member:* American Academy of Arts and Sciences, American Pediatric Society, Society for Pediatric Research, Endocrine Society, Century Association. *Awards, honors:* Mead Johnson Award; Borden Award from American Academy of Pediatrics.

WRITINGS: (Editor with Jerome Kagan and Leon Eisenberg) *Behavioral Science in Pediatric Medicine,* Saunders, 1971; (editor) *Raising Children in Modern America,* Volume I: *What Parents and Society Should Be Doing for Their Children,* Volume II: *Problems and Prospective Solutions,* Little, Brown, 1976. Also author of *Functional Endocrinology,* Harvard University Press, and *Metabolic Homeostasis,* Harvard University Press.

Contributor of more than a hundred articles to medical journals.

SIDELIGHTS: Talbot commented: "I was trained basically in the natural sciences. In the course of time I became convinced of the need to apply behavioral sciences to diagnosis and care of children by physicians and teachers." *Avocational interests:* Art, cruising.

*   *   *

TANDY, Clifford Ronald Vivien 1919(?)-1981

OBITUARY NOTICE: Born c. 1919; died July 3, 1981. Landscape architect and author of *Landscape of Industry.* He worked on many reclamation projects, including the restoration of the Aberfan disaster site and the creation of parks and recreation areas at Stoke-on-Trent, England. Obituaries and other sources: *London Times,* July 7, 1981.

*   *   *

TANNER-RUTHERFORD, C.
See WINCHESTER, Clarence

*   *   *

TARG, Russell 1934-

PERSONAL: Born April 11, 1934, in Chicago, Ill.; son of William (an editor and publisher) and Anne (in publicity; maiden name, Jesselson) Targ; married Joan Fischer (a teacher), 1958; children: Elisabeth, Alexander, Nicholas. *Education:* Queens College (now of the City University of New York), B.S., 1954; graduate study at Columbia University, 1954-56. *Politics:* Independent. *Residence:* Palo Alto, Calif. *Agent:* Roslyn Targ Literary Agency, Inc., 250 West 57th St., Suite 1932, New York, N.Y. 10019. *Office:* Stanford Research Institute International, Menlo Park, Calif. 94025.

CAREER: Conducted research on lasers and microwave physics, 1956-62; General Telephone and Electronics Corp.—Sylvania, Mountain View, Calif., engineering specialist in lasers,

1962-72; Stanford Research Institute International, Menlo Park, Calif., engaged in parapsychological research, 1972—. Founder of Parapsychology Research Group, president, 1963—. *Member:* American Association for the Advancement of Science, Institute of Electrical and Electronics Engineers, American Society for Psychical Research, Parapsychological Association.

WRITINGS: Mind Reach: Scientists Look at Psychic Ability, Delacorte, 1977; (editor) *Mind at Large: Institute of Electrical and Electronics Engineers Symposia on the Nature of Extrasensory Perception,* Praeger, 1979. Contributor of more than forty articles to scientific and parapsychological research journals.

*   *   *

TATELBAUM, Judith Ann 1938-
(Judy Tatelbaum)

PERSONAL: Born September 22, 1938, in Rochester, N.Y.; daughter of Abraham Joseph (a physician) and Esther (Beckler) Tatelbaum; married David Allan Gross, 1965 (divorced, 1966). *Education:* Syracuse University, B.S. (cum laude), 1959; Simmons College, M.S.W., 1961. *Religion:* Jewish. *Home and office:* 60 Middle Canyon Rd., Carmel Valley, Calif. 93924. *Agent:* Jed Mattes, International Creative Management, 40 West 57th St., New York, N.Y. 10019.

CAREER: Massachusetts Mental Health Center, Boston, psychiatric social worker, 1961-63; Payne Whitney Psychiatric Clinic, New York City, caseworker at adult outpatient clinic, 1963-71; private practice of psychotherapy in New York City, 1968-71, and Carmel Valley, Calif., 1972—. Instructor at University of California, Berkeley and Santa Cruz, California Polytechnic State University, and Monterey Peninsula College, 1974—; public speaker on grief, psychology, and women's issues. *Member:* American Academy of Psychotherapists, National Association of Social Workers, American Group Psychotherapy Association, Association for Humanistic Psychology, Association for Transpersonal Psychology, National Organization for Women, Mensa.

WRITINGS: (Under name Judy Tatelbaum) *The Courage to Grieve,* Crowell, 1980. Author of "On the Road to Enlightenment," a column in *Health and Happiness.*

SIDELIGHTS: Tatelbaum's *The Courage to Grieve* is a guidebook for those experiencing the death of a loved one. Intended to illustrate that grief is a natural, human experience, the book deals with many aspects of grief, such as resentment, loneliness, and loss of the will to live.

Tatelbaum told *CA:* "Writing *The Courage to Grieve* was the most satisfying experience of my life. Everyday I set aside first two, then four, then eight hours to write about my experiences with grief. It was as if I turned on a faucet that flowed. Since then writing is as it always was: something I enjoy and not something I do with ease. Clearly that book was meant to be for me personally, to complete my grief with my brother, and to be my memorial to him. And I believe it was meant to be given to the world, as the response from readers is that it got them through their most difficult life experiences. All I ever wanted to do was to contribute to people's lives, and through this book I've done that on a larger scale than I had as a psychotherapist."

AVOCATIONAL INTERESTS: Metaphysics, foreign travel.

TATELBAUM, Judy
See TATELBAUM, Judith Ann

* * *

TATUM, Jack
See TATUM, John David

* * *

TATUM, John David 1948-
(Jack Tatum)

PERSONAL: Born November 18, 1948, in Cherryville, N.C. *Education:* Attended Ohio State University. *Agent:* c/o Catherine Hartman, Everest House Publishing, 1133 Avenue of the Americas, New York, N.Y. 10036. *Office:* c/o The Houston Oilers, 6910 Fannin, Houston, Tex. 77025.

CAREER: Oakland Raiders (professional football team), Oakland, Calif., defensive back, 1971-80; Houston Oilers (professional football team), Houston, Tex., defensive back, 1980—. *Awards, honors:* Named New Jersey All-State high school fullback, 1966; selected for Sporting News College All-America Team, 1969-70; selected for All-Rookie National Football League (NFL) team, 1971; named to Pro-Bowl team, 1973-74 and 1977; selected for American Football Conference (AFC) All-Star team, 1975-77.

WRITINGS: (Under name Jack Tatum; with Bill Kushner) *They Call Me Assassin*, Everest House, 1979.

SIDELIGHTS: They Call Me Assassin provides an inside look at the more brutal aspects of professional football from the viewpoint of one of the game's most aggressive players, Jack Tatum. In recounting his early career, Tatum emphasized having learned from high school and college coaches that his success in football would be judged by how hard he could hit opponents on the field. Tatum discovered that this criterion for success also applied in the professional ranks when he joined the Oakland Raiders in 1971.

Shortly after Tatum's arrival in Oakland, fellow teammate George Atkinson instructed him in the use of the now illegal "hook," a headlock-like tackle designed, in Tatum's words, "to strip the receiver of the ball, his helmet, his head and his courage." The hook proved to be so effective at disabling opponents that Tatum and Atkinson held a clandestine contest: two points were awarded for each opponent rendered unconscious; one point for those who could eventually leave the field under their own power. "Actually," Tatum wrote in *They Call Me Assassin*, "it was all part of our job, but we made a game out of it. Guess who won?"

Tatum insisted that his aggressive behavior on the field was not only essential to the game but was also encouraged by team officials. Before the 1978 season, for example, the Oakland Raiders management accused Tatum of not hitting as hard as he had earlier in his career and in effect reminded him that his "job was that of a paid assassin," said Tatum. He responded to the criticism by knocking two players unconscious during that year's exhibition season opener. During a game the following week, on August 12, 1978, Tatum was, he wrote, "involved in a terrible accident with Darryl Stingley," a wide receiver for the New England Patriots: Tatum's hook tackle left Stingley paralyzed from the neck down. In his book, Tatum expressed regret over Stingley's injury: "To think that my tackle broke another man's neck and killed his future . . . well, I know it hurts Darryl, but it hurts me too." Because Tatum was acting within the rules when he tackled Stingley, no disciplinary action was taken against him by league officials.

At the time Stingley was injured, *They Call Me Assassin* was being written. "To be honest," co-author Bill Kushner confessed, "at first I felt the book would sell only medium-well. Then came the Stingley incident and we decided to add the section about the need to change the rules to eliminate some of the high risks." The book sold well, but many professional football players and sports observers were critical of Tatum's attempts to hold football's rules responsible for no-field brutality. *New York Times* writer Dave Anderson commented, "To put Jack Tatum's book in perspective, it's almost as if John Wilkes Booth's autobiography glorified his murder of Abraham Lincoln while suggesting that thereafter a president be prohibited from attending the theatre." But the book's publisher, Lewis W. Gillenson, insisted that *They Call Me Assassin* is "the most misunderstood book that has ever come down the pike. Jock-minded people say Tatum's destroying the image of football, but in fact Tatum is saying this is football—these are the rules, and that's how I'll play the game, and if you don't want people hurt, then change these rules."

BIOGRAPHICAL/CRITICAL SOURCES: Jack Tatum and Bill Kushner, *They Call Me Assassin*, Everest House, 1979; *New York Times*, January 13, 1980; *Washington Post*, January 19, 1980, January 20, 1980; *Time*, January 28, 1980; *Chicago Tribune*, February 17, 1980; *New York Times Book Review*, April 6, 1980; *Sport*, August, 1980.*

* * *

TAUBES, Frederic 1900-1981

*OBITUARY NOTICE—See index for *CA* sketch:* Born April 15, 1900, in Lwow, Poland; died after a long illness, June 20, 1981, in Nyack, N.Y. Artist, educator, editor, and author. Taubes exhibited his paintings and drawings all over the world. His work is represented in the collections of the Metropolitan Museum of Art, San Diego Fine Arts Gallery, San Francisco Museum, and High Museum of Atlanta. He taught as a visiting professor at several schools, including the University of Illinois, Mills College, University of Hawaii, University of Wisconsin, and University of Alberta. Taubes also edited the magazines *Artist* and *American Artist*. His numerous books include *Oil Painting for the Beginner*, *New Essays on Art*, *The Guide to the Great Art of Europe*, and *A Judgment of Art, Fact and Fiction*. Obituaries and other sources: *New York Times*, June 21, 1981; *AB Bookman's Weekly*, July 27, 1981.

* * *

TAUBES, Susan
See FELDMANN, Susan Judith

* * *

TAVE, Stuart M(alcolm) 1923-

PERSONAL: Born April 10, 1923, in Brooklyn, N.Y.; son of Max and Gertrude (Goldinger) Tave; married Edel Petersen, December 28, 1948; children: Douglas, Niels, Karen, Janice. *Education:* Columbia University, B.A., 1943; Harvard University, M.A., 1947; Oxford University, D.Phil., 1950. *Home:* 1461 East 55th Pl., Chicago, Ill. 60637. *Office:* Department of English, University of Chicago, Chicago, Ill. 60637.

CAREER: Columbia University, New York, N.Y., lecturer in English, 1950-51; University of Chicago, Chicago, Ill., 1951-64, began as instructor, became assistant professor, then associate professor, professor of English, 1964—, William Rainey Professor of Humanities, 1971—, chairman of department of English, 1972-78, associate dean of college, 1966-70. Visiting associate professor at University of Wisconsin, Madison, 1962, and Stanford University, 1963; visiting professor at University of Washington, Seattle, 1966. *Military service:* U.S. Naval Reserve, active duty, 1943-46. *Member:* Modern Language Association of America. *Awards, honors:* Guggenheim fellowship, 1959-60; American Council of Learned Societies fellowship, 1970-71; Laing Prize from University of Chicago Press, 1974, for *Some Words of Jane Austen;* National Endowment for the Humanities fellowship, 1978-79.

WRITINGS: The Amiable Humorist: A Study in the Comic Theory and Criticism of the Eighteenth and Early Nineteenth Centuries, University of Chicago Press, 1960; (editor) Thomas De Quincey, *New Essays by De Quincey: His Contributions to the Edinburgh Saturday Post and the Edinburgh Evening Post, 1827-1828,* Princeton University Press, 1966; *Some Words of Jane Austen,* University of Chicago Press, 1973.

SIDELIGHTS: Tave made a sound recording, "Persuasion," on the work by Jane Austen, released by Everett-Edwards in 1976.*

* * *

TAYLOR, Joshua Charles 1917-1981

PERSONAL: Born August 22, 1917, in Hillsboro, Ore.; died April 26, 1981, in Washington, D.C.; son of James Edmond and Anna L. M. (Scott) Taylor. *Education:* Attended Museum Art School, Portland, Ore., 1935-39; Reed College, B.A., 1939, M.A., 1946; Princeton University, M.F.A., 1949, Ph.D., 1956. *Home:* 1250 31st St. N.W., Washington, D.C. 20007. *Office:* National Collection of Fine Arts, Smithsonian Institution, 8th and G Sts. N.W., Washington, D.C. 20560.

CAREER: San Francisco Opera Ballet, San Francisco, Calif., designer, 1936-37; designer for theater, 1937-39; Reed College, Portland, Oregon, instructor in theater, 1939-41; Princeton University, Princeton, N.J., instructor in art history, 1948-49; University of Chicago, Chicago, Ill., professor of art and William Rainey Harper Professor of Humanities, 1963-74; Smithsonian Institution, Washington, D.C., director of National Collection of Fine Arts, beginning 1970. Lecturer and guest on television programs; lecturer at Instituto Interuniversitario, Argentina, 1962. Member of council of Archives of American Art; member of board of directors of American Federation of Arts (also vice-president), Museum of Contemporary Art, Chicago, and National Humanities Faculty; member of advisory committee on twentieth-century art, Art Institute of Chicago; member of faculty advisory committee of *Encyclopaedia Britannica;* member of advisory board of Lillie P. Bliss International Study Center at Museum of Modern Art. *Military service:* U.S. Army, Infantry, 1941-46; served in European theater; became major; received Bronze Star. *Member:* International Instutute for the Conservation of Historic and Artistic Works, College Art Association of America (member of board of directors; vice-president), Association of Art Museum Directors, American Association of Museums, Royal Society of Arts (Benjamin Franklin fellow), Phi Beta Kappa.

WRITINGS: Learning to Look: A Handbook for the Visual Arts, University of Chicago Press, 1957; *William Page: The American Titan,* University of Chicago Press, 1957; *Futurism,* Museum of Modern Art, 1961; *The Graphic Work of Umberto Boccioni,* Museum of Modern Art, 1961; (translator) Justino Fernandez, *A Guide to Mexican Art From Its Beginning to the Present,* University of Chicago Press, 1969; (with Jane Dillenberger) *The Hand and the Spirit: Religious Art in America, 1700-1900,* University Art Museum, University of California, Berkeley, 1972; (with Lois Marie Fink) *Academy: The Aca-*

demic Tradition in American Art, Smithsonian Institution Press, 1975; *To See Is to Think: Looking at American Art,* Smithsonian Institution Press, 1975; *America as Art,* Smithsonian Institution Press, 1976; *The Fine Arts in America,* University of Chicago Press, 1979; (co-authors) *Perceptions and Evocations: The Art of Elihu Vedder,* Smithsonian Institution Press, 1979. Contributor of articles and reviews to art history journals. Also author of *Giacomo Manzu: Recent Sculpture,* 1957. Contributor to *Theories of Modern Art,* edited by Herschel Browning Chipp.

BIOGRAPHICAL/CRITICAL SOURCES: American Historical Review, June, 1977; *Commonweal,* August 5, 1977; *Best Sellers,* October, 1979; *Smithsonian,* October, 1979; *Art News,* October, 1979.

OBITUARIES: New York Times, April 27, 1981; *Washington Post,* April 28, 1981.*

* * *

TAYLOR, Lois Dwight Cole
See COLE, Lois Dwight

* * *

TCHEKHOV, Anton
See CHEKHOV, Anton (Pavlovich)

* * *

TEASDALE, Sara 1884-1933

BRIEF ENTRY: Born August 8, 1884, in St. Louis, Mo.; committed suicide, January 29, 1933, in New York, N.Y. American poet. Sara Teasdale's delicate and sensitive lyrics made her one of the most popular poets of the early twentieth century, though her work had little in common with contemporary poetic trends such as imagism. Her themes were love, beauty, and, in later years, death; she wrote of them in spare, usually rhymed quatrains that expressed simple but intense emotions. Some critics dismissed her work as shallow, sentimental, and conventional, but others praised the musical qualities of her verse and its purity of feeling, finding her antecedents in Sappho, Christina Rossetti, and Emily Dickinson. Louis Untermeyer described her poetic gift as "authenticity, rather than originality . . . her muse was frankly communicative." Teasdale won a Pulitzer Prize in 1918, as well as a Poetry Society award, for *Love Songs* (1917). Torn between her passion for life and a neurotic craving for solitude, she became increasingly withdrawn and unhappy in the late 1920's. Failing health and the death of her close friend, the poet Vachel Lindsay, intensified her depression. She died of an overdose of sleeping medicine in 1933. Her works include *Sonnets to Duse and Other Poems* (1907), *Rivers to the Sea* (1915), *Dark of the Moon* (1926), and *The Collected Poems of Sara Teasdale* (1937). *Residence:* New York, N.Y. *Biographical/critical sources: Saturday Review of Literature,* February 11, 1933; *Twentieth Century Authors: A Biographical Dictionary of Modern Literature,* H. W. Wilson, 1942; *The Reader's Encyclopedia of American Literature,* Crowell, 1962; Margaret Haley Carpenter, *Sara Teasdale: A Biography,* Pentelic, 1977; *Twentieth-Century Literary Criticism,* Volume 4, Gale, 1981.

* * *

TELEMAQUE, Eleanor Wong 1934-

PERSONAL: Born January 1, 1934, in Albert Lea, Minn.; daughter of Sang and Mei-Lee (See) Wong; married Jean-Raoul

Middleton, 1953 (divorced); married Maurice Telemaque (in business), April 11, 1960; children: (second marriage) Adrienne Love. *Education:* Attended University of Chicago, 1947-49; University of Minnesota, B.A., 1952. *Home:* 230 East 88th St., New York, N.Y. 10028. *Agent:* Frances Schwartz Literary Agency, 60 East 42nd St., Suite 413, New York, N.Y. 10017. *Office:* U.S. Commission on Civil Rights, 26 Federal Plaza, Suite 1639, New York, N.Y. 10278.

CAREER: CARE, Inc., New York City, researcher, 1956-59, member of UNESCO relations staff in Washington, D.C., 1952-54; New York City Commission on Human Rights, New York City, in public relations, 1963-70; U.S. Department of Justice, Community Relations Service, Northeast Regional Office, New York City, communications specialist, 1970-73; Equal Employment Opportunity Commission, Newark, N.J., conciliator, 1973-74; U.S. Commission on Civil Rights, New York City, field representative in Massachusetts, 1974-79, New Hampshire, 1974-79, and New York City, 1974—. Once active in civil rights and anti-war movements; gives readings.

WRITINGS: It's Crazy to Stay Chinese in Minnesota (novel), Thomas Nelson, 1978; *Haiti Through Its Holidays* (juvenile), Edward Blyden, 1981; *Tai-Wang* (novel), Richard Marek, 1982. Also author of *Ru-Wen Goes to the Golden Mountain* (juvenile), Council on Urban Education (New York City).

Co-author of "Picture Bride for Peter," a film released by Revue Studios. Contributor to *New York.*

SIDELIGHTS: Eleanor Telemaque wrote: "It has been difficult being a minority writer reviewed by Caucasians from their point of view. You become schizo; most writers are that way anyway, because they have to get inside another person's skin. It's hard when a manuscript wins a semi-finalist award for fiction but is reviewed as having 'nasty characters.' Why? Because all Chinese women are supposed to be passive and nice—they don't fit the stereotype. Then that is followed by a lawsuit for a million dollars for 'libel.'

"Why do I write? It is a source of creativity. I can get angry and have my characters shoot someone; I can fall in love and have my heroine get the man of her dreams. I can get angry at the apathy and cruelty of the world, but I am not a person who writes tirades or tracts. I hope to create characters who feel pain and can shout their fury to the gods. Some persons who knew me as a child in Minnesota and who read *It's Crazy to Stay Chinese in Minnesota* claimed I was 'bitter.' I guess the book missed its mark with them. *It's Crazy* is not an autobiography—it is the story of discovery by a teenager, the discovery of sex, the discovery that sex knows no race, and the discovery that growing up is painful for everyone, especially Chinese girls who are not passive and who hate being Chinese.

"What are important subjects? The relationships of human beings. Being mostly Chinese, I am fascinated by family—at one end of the spectrum the Asian concept of family and loyalty and subjugation of rights to the good of the members—at the other end, the Western ideology of individualism which becomes material. I learned from Edward McClure (E. Daniel McClure), who wrote a marvelous book called *Freckles* about how we are all interrelated—one family—black, white, yellow—we all are 'others.'"

*   *   *

TEMPLE, Philip (Robert)   1939-

PERSONAL: Born March 20, 1939, in England; son of George (an aviation engineer) and Mary (Wilson) Lamb; married Daphne Evelyn Keen (a secretary), June 12, 1965; children: Fiona Jane, Roger Philip. *Education:* Attended secondary school in London, England. *Politics:* "Environmentalist." *Religion:* "Nature mystic." *Home:* Little Akaloa, Banks Peninsula, New Zealand. *Agent:* Curtis Brown Ltd., 2 Craven Hill, London W2 3EP, England.

CAREER: Mountain climber, 1959—. Collector of animals and ectoparasites in New Guinea and the Solomon Islands for Bishop Museum, Honolulu, Hawaii, 1963-64; entomologist, scribe, and climber for South Indian Ocean expedition to Heard Island, 1964-65; instructor in Cobham, New Zealand, 1965-68; free-lance photographer, 1972—, with exhibitions in England, Scotland, and New Zealand. *Member:* Amnesty International, International P.E.N. (awards judge), New Zealand Alpine Club, New Zealand Council of Recreation and Sport. *Awards, honors:* Wattie Award, 1970, for *The World at Their Feet;* grants from New Zealand Literary Fund, 1972, 1976; Katherine Mansfield Memorial fellowship, 1979; Robert Burns fellowship from University of Otago, 1980.

WRITINGS: Nawok!, Dent, 1962; *The Sea and the Snow,* Cassell, 1966; *The World at Their Feet,* Whitcoulls, 1969; *Castles in the Air,* McIndoe, 1973; *The Explorer* (novel), Hodder & Stoughton, 1975; *Stations* (novel), Collins, 1979; *Beak of the Moon* (novel) Collins, 1981.

Photographic books: *Mantle of the Skies,* Whitcoulls, 1971; *Christchurch,* Whitcoulls, 1973; *Patterns of Water,* Whitcoulls, 1974; *Philip Temple's South Island,* Whitcoulls, 1975; *Ways to the Wilderness,* Whitcoulls, 1977. Also photographer for *Shell Guide to New Zealand,* and *Images of Wellington,* 1976.

Author of column in *New Zealand Listener,* 1973, 1976. Contributor to magazines, including *Reader's Digest.* Features editor of *New Zealand Listener,* 1968-72; editor of *New Zealand Alpine Journal,* 1968, 1969, 1970, 1973; associate editor of *Landfall,* 1972-75.

WORK IN PROGRESS: The Disappearance of Stephen Lowrie, a psychological novel; *The Explorers,* on New Zealand explorers and their journeys, with accompanying television series; *Tikimana,* a mystic saga of South Pacific prehistory, completion expected in 1989.

SIDELIGHTS: Temple wrote: "In a world edging closer to self-destruction, a modern novelist's most important role lies in helping to fashion the kind of moral framework that might yet give us a choice of futures. Today, writers cannot afford to be side-tracked by current 'issues,' 'isms' of 'where it's at.' The world is where it's at, and the fashioning of basement philosophies that will allow the survival of civilized societies. Writers, in fact, have no need to be consciously 'relevant,' to deal with *now* and *it.* Remember the Jorge Luis Borges truism that no matter *what* you write—science fiction, belles lettres, poetry, or whatever—you automatically reflect yourself and your times.

"My chief moral concern is humankind's increasing estrangement from and purposeful destruction of the natural world, and thus our loss of knowledge of our real selves. The arrogance of humanism (of any kind—Western, Soviet, Chinese, Japanese) has led to an increasing misapprehension of our place on the planet.

"Additionally, in my own part of the world, New Zealand, I am concerned at the paucity of indigenous mythology for a post-colonial society that causes white settlers and their descendants to still look elsewhere for social and cultural reassurance; and often to treat one of the most ancient and magnificent natural environments in the world with indifference, rejection, or downright hostility.

"Through imaginative writing I am trying to encourage a new moral ambience, a new climate of feeling that sees values less in material growth and the gratification of ego and more in care for and understanding of the world fabric of which we are a part and not the whole. That way we will surely care for and finally understand ourselves."

* * *

TENDRYAKOV, Vladimir Fyodorovich   1923-

PERSONAL: Born December 5, 1923, in Makorovskaya, U.S.S.R.; son of Feodor Vasilyevich and Tatyana Petrovna (Zukova) Tendryakov; married Natalya Grigoryevna Asmolova, June, 1961; children: Tatyana, Mariya. *Education:* Attended Gorky Literary Institute, 1946-51. *Politics:* Communist.

CAREER: Correspondent to *Ogonyok,* 1951-54; free-lance writer, 1954—. *Military service:* Soviet Army, 1941-43. *Member:* Union of Writers of the Union of Soviet Socialist Republics. *Awards, honors:* Order of Red Banner of Labor.

WRITINGS—In English translation: *Three, Seven, Ace, and Other Stories* (contains "Three, Seven, Ace," "Justice," and "Creature of a Day"; translated by David Alger, Olive Stevens, and Paul Fella), Harper, 1973. Also author of *Son-in-Law,* Foreign Languages Publishing House.

Other writings: *Sredi lesov: Povesti i ocherki,* Sovetski Pisatel,' 1954; *Padenie Ivana Chuprova: Ne ko dvoru* (title means "The Fall of Ivan Chuprov"), Gos. Izd-vo khudozh. lit-ry, 1956; *Ukhavy: Povesti i rasskazy* (novel; title means "Road Holes" Molodaia Gvardia, 1957; *Tugoi uzel,* Kirovskoe Knizh, 1958; *Chudotvornaia,* Molodaia Gvardia, 1958.

Za begushchim dnem (novel), Molodaia Gvardia, 1960; *Sud* (novella; title means "The Trial"), Sovetski Pisatel,' 1961; *Povesti,* Moskovski rabochi, 1961; *Chrezvychalnoe,* Sovetskaia Rossia, 1962; *Rasskazi i skazki russkikh pisatelei* (juvenile stories), Gos. Izd-vo khudozh. lit-ry, 1962; *Korotkoe zamykanie,* Sovetskaia Rossia, 1962; *Mednyi krestik,* Gos. Izd-vo detskoi lit-ry, 1963; *Izbrannye proizvedeniia,* two volumes, Gos. Izd-vo khudozh. lit-ry 1963; *Ne ko dvoru, Chudotvornaia, Sud, Chrezv'ichainoye, Korotkoe zam'ikanie,* Volgo-Vyatskoe knizhnoe Izd-vo, 1964; *Kostry na snegu,* Sovetskaia Rossia, 1964; *Puteshestvie dlinoi v vek: Nauchno-Fantasticheskaia povesti,* Severo-Zapadnoe knizhnoe Izd-vo, 1965; *Svidanie s Nefertiti* (novel; title means "Meeting With Nefertiti"), Molodaia Gvardia, 1965; *Nakhodka,* Sovetskaia Rossia, 1966; *Podenka: Vek Korotkii,* Sovetski Pisatel,' 1967; *Three Novellas* (in Russian; contains "Road Holes," "Three, Seven, Ace," and "The Trial"; edited by J.G. Garrard), Pergamon, 1967; *Podenka: Vek korotkii, Chudotvornaia, Chrezv'ichainoe, Korotkoe zam'ikanie, Onega,* Molodaia Gvardia, 1969.

Svidanie s Nefertiti: Roman—Nakhodka, Povest—Kostr'i na snegu, Rasskaz'i—Ill, Sovetski Pisatel,' 1970; *Padenie Ivana Chuprova, Ne ko dvoru, Podenka—Vek korotkii,* Kn. Izd-vo, 1971; *Izbrannoe* (contains "Svidanie s Nefertiti," "Nakhodka," "Tugoi uzel," and "Novi chas drebnevo Samarkanda"), Izd-vo Izvestia, 1973; *Perebert'yshi: Povestii* (contains "Tri meshka sornoi pshenits'i," "Lonchina," "Podenka— Vek korotkii," "Sud," "Troika, semerka, tuz," and "Vecennie perevert'ishi"), Sovremennik, 1974; *Grazhdane Goroda Solntsa,* Molodaia Gvardia, 1977; *Sobranie sochinenii,* Khydozh. lit., 1978.

Work represented in anthologies, including *Modern Russian Short Stories,* 1968.

Scripts; titles in translation: "Alien In-Laws," 1955; "Miracle Worker," 1960; "Short Circuit," 1961; "The Trial," 1962; "Spring Changes," 1975.

BIOGRAPHICAL/CRITICAL SOURCES: Soviet Literature, July, 1954; *Problems of Communism,* September-October, 1962; *Slavic and East European Journal,* spring, 1965; *Books Abroad,* winter, 1965, summer, 1966; Mihajlo Mihajlov, *Russian Themes,* Farrar, Straus, 1968.*

* * *

TENISON, Marika Hanbury
See HANBURY-TENISON, Marika

* * *

TERRY, Michael   1899-1981

PERSONAL: Born May 3, 1899, in Gateshead, England; died September 21, 1981; son of Arthur Michael (a major in the military) and Catherine Beaufoy (Neagle) Terry; married Ursula Livingstone-Learmonth, 1940 (marriage ended, 1945). *Education:* University of Durham, B.Sc. *Religion:* Church of England. *Home address:* War Veterans Home, Unit 105E, Narrabeen, New South Wales 2101, Australia.

CAREER: Explorer and writer. Farmer in New South Wales, Australia, 1946-60. *Military service:* Served in Russia. *Member:* Royal Geographical Society of Australia (life fellow), Australian Society of Authors (life member), Royal Geographical Society (life fellow), Royal Empire Society (fellow), National Geographical Society (United States), Path Finders Association of New South Wales (life associate). *Awards, honors:* Cuthbert-Peek expedition grant, 1925; award for *War of the Warramullas.*

WRITINGS: Across Unknown Australia, Jenkins, 1925; *Through a Land of Promise: With Gun, Car, and Camera in the Heart of Northern Australia,* Jenkins, 1927; *Hidden Wealth and Hiding People,* Putnam, 1931; *Untold Miles: Three Gold-Hunting Expeditions Amongst the Picturesque Borderland Ranges of Central Australia,* Selwyn & Blount, 1933; *Sand and Sun: Two Gold-Hunting Expeditions With Camels in the Dry Lands of Central Australia,* M. Joseph, 1937; *Bulldozer: The War Role of the Department of Main Roads, New South Wales, Through the Courtesy of the Commissioner,* D. Craig, Esquire, F. Johnson, 1945; *War of the Warramullas,* Rigby, 1974. Also author of *And Now This* and *Thanks, Kind Fate* (autobiography), 1979. Contributor to magazines, including *Modern Motor, Little Folks, Sphere, Walkabout,* and *National Geographic,* and newspapers.

SIDELIGHTS: After his discharge from military service, Terry went to Australia as an explorer. On his second expedition, from Darwin to Broome, he gave names to Mount Rosamund and the Drummer Range. He made gold and potassium nitrate discoveries on his third expedition. In the late 1920's and early 1930's he traveled by camel, collecting data for Australia's Department of Lands and Waite Research Institute, and discovered Hidden Basin. He was received by the Prince of Wales in 1926 and presented to King George in 1940.*

* * *

TERSON, Peter   1932-
(Peter Patterson)

PERSONAL: Birth-given name Peter Patterson; known professionally as Peter Terson; born February 24, 1932, in Tyne, England; son of Peter (a joiner) and Jane (a playwright) Patterson; married Sheila Bailey, May 25, 1955; children: Bruce, Neil, Janie. *Education:* Attended Newcastle-upon-Tyne Technical College and Redland Training College, Bristol, 1952-54. *Home:* 87 Middlebridge St., Romsey, Hampshire, England. *Agent:* Harvey Unna & Stephen Durbridge, 14 Beaumont Mews, Marylebone High St., London, England.

CAREER: Worked as draftsman; schoolteacher of physical education, 1953-65; playwright, 1965—. Resident playwright, Victoria Theatre, Stoke-on-Trent, England, 1966-67; writer for National Youth Theatre, 1966. *Military service:* Royal Air Force, 1950-52. *Awards, honors:* Arts Council bursary, 1966; m20John Whitney Award, 1967; Writers Guild of Great Britain award, 1971; Radio Scriptwriter award, 1972; promising playwright's award from Lord Goodman.

WRITINGS—All under name Peter Terson; all plays: "A Night to Make the Angels Weep" (first produced in Stoke-on-trent, England, at Victoria Theatre, 1964; produced in London, 1971), published in *New English Dramatists Eleven*, Penguin, 1967; "The Mighty Reservoy" (first produced in Stoke-on-Trent at Victoria Theatre, 1964; produced in London, 1967), published in *New English Dramatists Fourteen*, Penguin, 1970; "The Rat Run," first produced in Stoke-on-Trent, 1965; "All Honour Mr. Todd," first produced in Stoke-on-Trent at Victoria Theatre, 1966; "I'm in Charge of These Ruins," first produced in Stoke-on-Trent at Victoria Theatre, 1966; (with others) "Sing an Arful Story," (first produced in Stoke-on-Trent, 1966; "Jock-on-the-Go" (adaptation of story, "Jock-at-a-Venture," by Arnold Bennett), first produced in Stoke-on-Trent, 1966; "Holder Dying," first produced in part in Stoke-on-Trent, 1966.

Zigger Zagger (first produced in London, 1967), published in *Zigger Zagger and Mooney and His Caravans*, Penguin, 1970 (also see below); (with Joyce Cheeseman) "Clayhanger" (adaptation of the novel by Bennett), first produced in Stoke-on-Trent, 1967; "The Ballad of the Artificial Mash," first produced in Stoke-on-Trent at Victoria Theatre, 1967; *The Apprentices* (first produced in London, 1968), Penguin, 1970; *The Adventures of Gervase Beckett; or, The Man Who Changed Places* (first produced in Stoke-on-Trent, 1969), Eyre Methuen, 1973; "Fuzz," first produced in London, 1969.

"Inside-Outside," first produced in Nottingham, England, 1970; "The Affair at Bennett's Hill, Worcestershire," first produced in Stoke-on-Trent, 1970; "Spring-Heeled Jack" (first produced in London, 1970), published in *Plays and Players*, November, 1970; "The 1861 Whitby Lifeboat Disaster," first produced in Stoke-on-Trent, 1970, produced in London, 1971; (with Mike Butler) "The Samaritan," (first produced in Stoke-on-Trent, 1971, produced in London, 1971), published in *Plays and Players*, July, 1971; "Cadium Firty," first produced in London, 1971; "Good Lads at Heart," first produced in London, 1971, produced in New York at Brooklyn Academy of Music Opera House, 1979; "Slip Road Wedding," first produced in Newcastle-upon-Tyne, England, 1971, produced in London, 1971; "Prisoners of the War," first produced in Newcastle-upon-Tyne, 1971.

"But Fred, Freud Is Dead" (first produced in Stoke-on-Trent, 1972), published in *Plays and Players*, March, 1972; "Moby Dick," first produced in Stoke-on-Trent, 1972; "The Most Cheerful Man," first produced in Stoke-on-Trent, 1973; "Georgie's March," first produced in London, 1973; "The Trip to Florence," first produced in London, 1974; "Lost Yer Tongue?," first produced in Newcastle-upon-Tyne, 1974; "Vince Lays the Carpet, and Fred Erects the Tent," first produced in Stoke-on-Trent, 1975; "The Ballad of Ben Bagot,"

published in *Prompt Two*, edited by Alan Durband, Hutchinson, 1976; (with Paul Joyce) "Love Us and Leave Us," first produced in London, 1976; "The Bread and Butter Trade," first produced in London, 1976.

Also author of "Family Ties," "The Cul de Sac," "V.E. Night," "Dobson's Drie Bobs," "The Launching of the Esso Northumbria," and "I Would Prefer Not To" (adaptation of the novella *Bartleby* by Herman Melville); co-author of "The Knotty," a musical.

Television plays: *Mooney and His Caravans* (first broadcast in 1966; produced on stage in London, 1968), published in *Zigger Zagger and Mooney and His Caravans* (also see above); "The Heroism of Thomas Chadwick," first broadcast in 1967; "The Last Train Through the Harecastle Tunnel," first broadcast in 1969; "The Gregorian Chant," first broadcast in 1972; "The Dividing Fence," first broadcast in 1972; "Shakespeare—or Bust," first broadcast in 1973; "Three for the Fancy," first broadcast in 1973; "Dancing in the Dark," first broadcast in 1974; "The Rough and the Smooth," first broadcast in 1975; (with Joyce) "The Jolly Swagman," first broadcast in 1976.

Radio plays: "The Fishing Party," first broadcast in 1971.

WORK IN PROGRESS: "The Romsey Gibbet," a radio play.

SIDELIGHTS: Terson had already launched a career as a physical education teacher when the birth of his first child revived an interest in writing that had been dormant for years. In order to fill time while caring for his infant son Terson began work on a novel; he eventually abandoned the project in favor of writing plays, a decision based on his interest in writing dialogue. His first two plays were optioned by the BBC but never produced because they were judged to need too much work to adapt them for broadcast. Terson was encouraged by the sale, however, and continued to write in his spare time for the next seven years.

During much of this period Terson lived in the Vale of Evesham, a rural, fruit-growing area in central England. His early plays are set in Evesham and contain a sinister undercurrent: progress and civilization threaten nature and alienate humankind. Terson sent samples of his work to Peter Cheeseman, director of the Victoria Theatre in Stoke-on-Trent, an in-the-round theatre committed to regionalism. Cheeseman was impressed with Terson's work and "A Night to Make the Angels Weep" was performed at the Victoria in 1964. Other Terson plays set in the Vale of Evesham and sharing the theme of rural tradition opposing the forces of change include "The Mighty Reservoy," "Mooney and His Caravans," "All Honour Mr. Todd," and "I'm in Charge of These Ruins." As a collection the plays constitute a cycle, emphasizing themes in a quiet, dialogue-centered fashion.

Typical of Terson's writing during this period is "Mooney and His Caravans." The story centers on a married couple, Charley and Mave, who are so determined to escape city life that they are willing to submit themselves to repeated degradation in a rural trailerpark community run like a concentration camp by the evil, cunning Mooney. Humiliated and stripped of all pretense, with Mave carrying Mooney's baby, the couple rediscovers their love for each other and returns to the city. Although deciding that the play was not one of Terson's best, *Observer Review* critic Ronald Bryden wrote: "I wish all disciples of Artaud who preach the death of language in drama could compare that blurred vision with Peter Terson's comedy."

Terson was named resident playwright of the Victoria Theatre in 1966, and was also invited to write a play for the National Youth Theatre by its director, Michael Croft. Terson's acceptance of the offer required a major change in his writing style; whereas the productions at the Victoria Theatre were small in scale and represented regional, rural interests, the London-based National Youth Theatre presented large, showy productions, staged by schoolchildren and young adults, and dealt with themes that appealed to urban youth. Terson responded to the challenge with ''Zigger Zagger,'' a look at almost fanatical adoration of and identification with professional soccer teams as seen through the eyes of Harry Philton, a school dropout seeking his niche in a society in decline. Harry bounces from job to job, falling into unhappy relationships and a dead-end career.

''The perception of [soccer] as a substitute religion,'' wrote *New Statesman* critic Brian Glanville, ''of the fan as aimless victim of an industrialised society, is hardly original, but Mr. Terson tricks it out with fine vigour and invention.'' The play was considered by some critics to be too simplistic, but Philip French, in a later *New Statesman* review, wrote that he felt the play possessed ''a coherence and consistency in its over-simplification, and important questions are asked in a way too rarely done in the theatre.'' Bryden, again writing in *Observer Review,* praised Terson as being ''that rare thing, a poet of the theatre.''

Terson gave up his post as resident playwright at the Victoria Theatre in 1967 and began to devote more time to working with the National Youth Theatre, evolving the themes he had developed in ''Zigger Zagger.'' ''The Apprentices'' is an elaboration on those themes in a more naturalistic fashion; the hopes and dreams of a working class youth are stripped away one by one until he finds himself trapped in a colorless, meaningless world with no future. *Listener* critic D.A.N. Jones wrote: ''Terson presents aspects of that huge body of individuals known as the working class, from his own angle, in a strong and serious way. I wish he had rivals, with different angles.''

Terson's ability to tailor a play to fit a particular cast and director has led some observers to classify him as a ''primitive'' to describe his unsophisticated natural talents and observations of human nature. However, the versatility required to be able to write for both the small, in-the-round Victoria Theatre and the National Youth Theatre with its large company of amateur players is considerable. In order to fully utilize the potential of the National Youth Theatre Terson would start with a basic outline and, working with cast and director Croft, work out staging details and dialogue.

An example of the success of this technique was observed by *New York Times* critic Richard Eder when ''Good Lads at Heart'' played in New York City in 1979. The play, which examines the life and relationships of eighteen boys in reform school, presented the difficult task of adequately developing each of the characters. After seeing the play Eder wrote: ''The play, written by Peter Terson for the group, is descriptive and instructive. Mr. Terson has not created a notable play but he has created a very useful one; and one that beautifully fits the nature and abilities of the performers.''

BIOGRAPHICAL/CRITICAL SOURCES: Spectator, September 2, 1967, September 6, 1969; *The Observer Review,* September 3, 1967, May 19, 1968, August 25, 1968; *New Statesman,* September 29, 1967, March 22, 1968, August 28, 1968, May 15, 1970; *Drama,* winter, 1968; *Punch,* March 20, 1968, September 2, 1970; *London Magazine,* June, 1968; *The Listener,* August 29, 1968; *Times Literary Supplement,* April 23, 1970; *Stage,* August 27, 1970, September 17, 1970, December 3, 1970, August 5, 1971, September 30, 1971; *Plays and Players,* September, 1970, October, 1970, November, 1970,

March, 1972; *Variety,* October 6, 1971; *New York Times,* March 28, 1979.

—*Sketch by Michael L. LaBlanc*

*   *   *

TETERNIKOV, Fyodor Kuzmich   1863-1927
(Fyodor Sologub)

BRIEF ENTRY: Born March 1, 1863, in St. Petersburg (now Leningrad), Russia (now U.S.S.R.); died December 5, 1927, in Leningrad, U.S.S.R. Russian poet, playwright, and novelist. In the style of the symbolists, Teternikov introduced to Russian literature the European decadent theories of art, beauty, life and death, reality and dream. His most successful work was the novel *The Petty Demon* (1916). In this and other novels he created a vision of the real world as one of repulsive pettiness and grotesque evil, from which the only escapes were the comfort of death or a beautiful world of dreams. Teternikov's poems, *Collected Works* (1913-14), reflected in hypnotic cadence his brilliant, perverse imagination, his hatred of life and love of death, and his search for beauty that for him existed only in dream and fantasy. In such plays as ''The Triumph of Death'' (1907) his heroes consistently met their dooms in the futile quest to cover natural chaos with a layer of beauty. Despite Teternikov's vulgar subject matter and morbid themes, he was recognized for his simple style and musical language. His contemporaries compared him favorably to Dostoyevsky. Some of his stories were published in *The Old House and Other Tales* (1915) and *Little Tales* (1917). *Biographical/critical sources: The Concise Encyclopedia of Modern World Literature,* Hutchinson, 1963; *Encyclopedia of World Literature in the Twentieth Century,* updated edition, Ungar, 1967; *Modern Fiction Studies,* summer, 1980.

*   *   *

THAKURA, Ravindranatha   1861-1941
(Rabindranath Tagore)

BRIEF ENTRY: Born May 7, 1861, in Calcutta, India; died August 7, 1941, in Calcutta, India; cremated. Indian poet, playwright, novelist, short story writer, essayist, and philosopher. In addition to writing more than one thousand poems, Tagore pioneered the use of conversational idioms in Indian prose. He sought political independence for India and the cooperation of the East and the West. William Butler Yeats introduced Tagore to the English-speaking world after reading *Gitanjali* (1910), for which Tagore was awarded the Nobel Prize for literature in 1913. Although sometimes tragic in tone, Tagore's work always carries a message of respect for human dignity. Among his principal works are *Sandhya sangit* (1882; translated as *Evening Songs*), *Raja* (1910; translated as *The King of the Dark Chamber,* 1914), *Dakghar* (1912; translated as *The Post Office,* 1914), and *Sesher Kavita* (1929; translated as *Farewell, My Friend,* 1949). *Residence:* Calcutta, India. *Biographical/critical sources: Saturday Review of Literature,* August 16, 1941; *The Dalhousie Review,* April, 1945; *Encyclopedia of World Literature in the Twentieth Century,* updated edition, Ungar, 1967; *Twentieth-Century Literary Criticism,* Volume 3, Gale, 1980.

*   *   *

THEOBALD, Lewis, Jr.
See LOVECRAFT, H(oward) P(hillips)

THOMAS, Dylan (Marlais)   1914-1953

BRIEF ENTRY: Born October 27, 1914, in Swansea, Wales; died November 9, 1953, in New York, N.Y.; buried in Laugharne, Wales. Welsh poet. Thomas is as famous for his life as for his poetry. The sudden success of his early work made him a public figure when he was in his mid-twenties; the accompanying stress intensified the bohemian lifestyle and heavy drinking that finally broke his health. Unashamedly romantic, Thomas intended his poems to be experienced rather than interpreted. They are intensely emotional and sensual, relying on striking, often private images and on the sounds of the words to produce their effects; their themes are nature, birth, sex, and death. Some critics have dismissed Thomas as clumsy, sentimental, and needlessly obscure, but others regard him as the greatest lyric poet of his generation; he was certainly among the most influential poets of his time. Thomas also wrote several prose works, the best known of which is the radio play *Under Milk Wood* (1954). Other works include *18 Poems* (1934), *Twenty-five Poems* (1936), *Portrait of the Artist as a Young Dog* (1940), *Deaths and Entrances* (1946), and *Collected Poems 1934-1952* (1952). *Residence:* Laugharne, Wales. *Biographical/critical sources:* Elder Olson, *The Poetry of Dylan Thomas*, University of Chicago Press, 1954; Caitlin Macnamara Thomas, *Leftover Life to Kill*, Little, Brown, 1957; *Cyclopedia of World Authors*, Harper, 1958; John Malcolm Brinnin, *A Casebook on Dylan Thomas*, Crowell, 1960; Paul Ferris, *Dylan Thomas*, Dial, 1977; *Twentieth-Century Literary Criticism*, Volume 1, Gale, 1978.

*   *   *

THOMAS, Edward Llewellyn
See LLEWELLYN-THOMAS, Edward

*   *   *

THOMAS, Harold Becken   1888-1971

OBITUARY NOTICE: Born in 1888; died August 12, 1971, in Bexhill-on-Sea, England. Authority on East African history and author of *The Story of Uganda*. Obituaries and other sources: *AB Bookman's Weekly*, October 4, 1971.

*   *   *

THOMAS, Lionel H(ugh) C(hristopher)   1922(?)-1978

OBITUARY NOTICE: Born c. 1922; died in February, 1978, in England. Translator and author of *Willibald Alexis: A German Writer of the Nineteenth Century* and *Comic Spirit in Nineteenth-Century German Literature*. Obituaries and other sources: *AB Bookman's Weekly*, July 10, 1978.

*   *   *

THOMAS, Lowell (Jackson)   1892-1981

OBITUARY NOTICE—See index for *CA* sketch: Born April 6, 1892, in Woodington, Ohio; died of a heart attack, August 29, 1981, in Pawling, N.Y. Journalist, explorer, broadcaster, producer, educator, lecturer, editor, and author. A familiar figure to millions of Americans, Thomas broadcast news on the radio for nearly a half century. Greeting his listeners with the unchanging line "Good evening, everybody," he presented the day's events in an eloquent, homespun manner and invariably signed off with "So long until tomorrow." Thomas traveled around the world many times in quest of stories. He broadcast his programs from such locations as Cairo, India, Iwo Jima, and Chongquing, and he was the first person to speak to a radio audience from a ship, an airplane, and a helicopter. Thomas began his career as an editor and reporter with the *Rocky Mountain News* and the *Chicago Journal*, but gained prominence as a public speaker while showing his travel films of Alaska. Drawing the attention of the Department of the Interior, the journalist was asked by the government to film and report on World War I. While covering the conflict, Thomas went to the Middle East where he met T. E. Lawrence. He filmed and interviewed the British archaelogist-turned-solider during Lawrence's campaign with the Arabs against the Turks. On his return to the United States, Thomas established his reputation with a successful film about Lawrence called "The Last Crusade." His first book was *With Lawrence in Arabia;* other books include *Raiders of the Deep*, *The Untold Story of Exploration*, and *Burma Jack*. Thomas began reading the news on the radio in 1930 and in 1939 broadcast the first news program on television. He hosted several television programs, but he considered radio his specialty and broadcast in that medium until 1976. Obituaries and other sources: Lowell Thomas, *Good Evening Everybody: From Cripple Creek to Samarkand*, Morrow, 1976; *New York Times*, August 30, 1981; *Washington Post*, August 30, 1981; *Newsweek*, September 7, 1981; *Time*, September 7, 1981.

*   *   *

THOMASMA, David Charles   1939-

PERSONAL: Born October 31, 1939, in Chicago, Ill.; son of Charles W. (a company president) and Rosemary (Olma) Thomasma; married Evalyn R. Ryan, December 20, 1969; children: Pieter Jon, Elizabeth Rose. *Education:* Aquinas College, B.S., 1961; Aquinas Institute of Philosophy and Theology, B.A., 1964, Ph.L. and M.A., both 1965; College of the Immaculate Conception, S.T.B., 1967, S.T.L., 1969; Catholic University of America, Ph.D., 1972. *Politics:* Democrat. *Religion:* Roman Catholic. *Home:* 424 Butterfield Rd., Elmhurst, Ill. 60126. *Office:* Medical Humanities Program, Stritch School of Medicine, Medical Center, Loyola University, 2160 South First Ave., Maywood, Ill. 60153.

CAREER: Ordained Roman Catholic priest, 1968; Catholic University of America, Washington, D.C., instructor in philosophy, 1967-69; Christian Brothers College, Memphis, Tenn., assistant professor of philosophy, religious studies, and humanities, 1969-73, chairman of department of humanities, 1973; University of Tennessee, Memphis, associate professor, 1973-79, professor of human values and ethics, 1979-81, director of human values and ethics, 1973-81; Loyola University, Stritch School of Medicine, Maywood, Ill., professor of medical humanities and director of medical humanities program, 1981—. Writer and host of television series, "The State of Health," on WKNO-TV, and "Americans and Death," WKNO-TV. President of Tennessee Center for Human Values and Health Sciences, 1976-79; member of Tennessee Committee for Humanities, 1974-81; member of board of directors of Hospice of Memphis, 1979-81; consultant to Institute for Human Values and Medicine.

MEMBER: American Philosophical Association, American Catholic Philosophical Association, American Academy of Religion, Society for Health and Human Values (member of council, 1981-84), Institute for Social Ethics and Life Science. *Awards, honors:* Named patron of the humanities by Tennessee Committee for the Humanities, 1978, and public citizen of the year (for Memphis) by National Association of Social Workers, 1980, for television program, "Americans and Death."

WRITINGS: (With Edmund D. Pelligrino) *A Philosophical Basis of Medical Practice: Toward a Philosophy and Ethic of the Healing Profession*, Oxford University Press, 1981; *Health Care: Its Psychosocial Dimensions*, Duquesne University Press, 1981. Contributor to scholarly journals.

WORK IN PROGRESS: Person and Disease, completion expected in 1984; *Theory and Practice in Medical Ethics*, 1984; *Theological Basis of Medical Practice*, 1985.

SIDELIGHTS: Thomasma commented: "I advise students to consider a career in medical ethics and philosophy of medicine. These subsets of moral problems facing humanity in a technological society are vital and exciting.

"Medical ethics has grown as a discipline since World War II. Now it is almost impossible to read all the literature on a single issue within the field. Where is it going in the future? I think in two directions. First it will move into the arena of public policy. Creative minds are definitely needed for this task, because there is so little consensus in American moral life today. Second it will move in the direction of case resolution. More and more physicians and other health professionals are taking serious interest in medical ethics. In the main their interests have to do with improving patient care, underlining the human and value aspects of the doctor-patient relationship, and establishing the rights and limits of professional responsibilities.

"I am also convinced that the field of medical ethics will not prosper unless more work is done on a new field of philosophy of medicine. Further, medical ethics must also come to depend upon the insights developed in clinical psychology and medical sociology. These latter disciplines contribute a great deal of descriptive data for critical issues in medical ethics. For example, many medical ethicists believe that more and more autonomy should be given to patients. Physicians, while agreeing with this general model of interpersonal relations, also think that undue emphasis on autonomy might lead to an abridgement of their own responsibilities in the relation. Finally, clinical psychology would contribute studies on the impact of disease on personal autonomy, so that the medical ethicist's assumptions about autonomy could be checked against the facts.

"This scenario is a good example of the importance of joining together the insights of many disciplines in the development of any new field of inquiry. It also enhances the prospects for significant insights and influence on other features of life in the twentieth century."

*   *   *

THOMPSON, Francis Joseph 1859-1907

BRIEF ENTRY: Born December 18, 1859 in Preston, Lancashire, England; died of tuberculosis, November 13, 1907, in London, England. English poet, critic, and biographer. Educated in the Catholic faith at Ushaw College, Thompson studied medicine for six years before deciding that he was emotionally and physically unsuited for that profession. In 1885 he moved to London, where he became addicted to opium and supported himself by selling matches and delivering messages. Thompson's poetry first appeared in Wilfried Meynell's literary magazine, *Merry England*. Meynell and his wife befriended the destitute Thompson, taking him into their home for the remainder of his life. Thompson's best-known poem, "The Hound of Heaven," appeared in his first collection, *Poems* (1893). Thompson's other two books of poetry, *Sister Songs* (1895) and *New Poems* (1897), deal with religious themes and have been compared to the poetry of the seventeenth-century meta-

physical poet Richard Crashaw. Thompson's poetry established him as one of the most important figures of the Catholic Revival. After the publication of *New Poems*, Thompson wrote essays, literary criticism, and two biographies, *Saint Ignatius Loyola* (1910) and *The Life and Labours of Saint John Baptist de la Salle* (1911). *Residence:* London, England. *Biographical/ critical sources: The Fortnightly Review*, January, 1894; *The Yale Review*, October 1, 1914; *British Authors of the Nineteenth Century*, H. W. Wilson, 1936; Brigid Brophy, Michael Levey, and Charles Osborne, *Fifty Works of English and American Literature We Could Do Without*, Stein & Day, 1967; *Twentieth-Century Literary Criticism*, Volume 4, Gale, 1981.

*   *   *

THOMPSON, (Eu)Gene (Allen) 1924-

PERSONAL: Born June 28, 1924, in San Francisco, Calif.; son of Andrew A. and Rose (Greenblat) Thompson; married Sylvia Vaughn Sheekman (a writer), June 15, 1955; children: David Oxley, Benjamin Stuart, Dinah Vaughn, Amanda Greenleaf. *Education:* University of California, Berkeley, B.A., 1949; attended Oxford University, 1959; studied music in Heidelberg, West Germany. *Politics:* Democrat. *Religion:* Jewish. *Home:* 3567 Serra Rd., Malibu, Calif. 90265. *Agent:* Robert Lescher, 155 East 71st St., New York, N.Y. 10021. *Office:* AVO Productions, P.O. Box 156, Malibu, Calif. 90265.

CAREER: Free-lance writer; writer for AVO Productions, Malibu, Calif. *Member:* Writers Guild of America (West).

WRITINGS: Lupe, Random House, 1977; *Murder Mystery*, Random House, 1980.

WORK IN PROGRESS: A sequel to *Murder Mystery*.

SIDELIGHTS: Thompson told *CA:* "My writing has been greatly influenced by the fact that most of my work was written for radio and television and performed before an audience. I began this work when I was sixteen, under the tutelage of Groucho Marx, who brought me to Hollywood as one of his writers. I left when I was twenty-one and went to the university and then to Europe. I returned to Hollywood afterward and wrote both comedy and drama for such people as Lucille Ball and 'Baretta,' before leaving television to devote myself exclusively to fiction."

BIOGRAPHICAL/CRITICAL SOURCES: Los Angeles Times, November 21, 1980.

*   *   *

THOMPSON, George Clifford 1920-

PERSONAL: Born May 3, 1920, in New York, N.Y.; son of W. Stuart and M. Gladys (Slade) Thompson; married Barbara F. Churchill, 1962; children: Elizabeth, Stuart, Anne. *Education:* Columbia University, B.A., 1942, M.S., 1943, J.D., 1949. *Home:* 164 Shore Rd., Old Greenwich, Conn. 06830. *Office:* Columbia University, New York, N.Y. 10027.

CAREER: Associate of Arthur Andersen (certified public accountant), 1943-47; Columbia University, New York, N.Y., assistant professor, 1949-54, associate professor, 1954-58, professor, 1958—, James L. Dohr Professor of Accounting and Business Law, 1960—. Member of board of directors of corporations and foundations; chairman of board of directors of Yale Express System, Inc. Member of financial survey of Western Europe, 1946-47. *Member:* New York State Bar Association, Phi Beta Kappa, Beta Gamma Sigma, Phi Delta Phi, Alpha Kappa Psi, Rocky Point Club, Indian Harbor Yacht Club, Columbia University Club.

WRITINGS: (With Gerald P. Brady) *Shortened CPA Law Review*, Wadsworth, 1959, 4th edition, 1977; (with Brady) *Law in a Business Environment*, Wadsworth, 1963; (with Brady) *Negotiable Instruments and Sales*, Wadsworth, 1964; (with Brady) *Antitrust Fundamentals*, Wadsworth, 1964, 2nd edition published as *Text, Cases, and Materials on Antitrust Fundamentals*, West Publishing, 1974, 3rd edition, 1979; (with Brady) *Essentials of Business Law*, Wadsworth, 1968; (with James Louis Dohr) *Accounting and the Law: Cases and Materials*, 4th edition (Thompson was not associated with earlier editions), Foundation Press, 1978, supplement published as *Problem Material*, 1978. Also author of *Law in an Economic Environment*, two volumes. Contributor to professional journals.*

*   *   *

THOMSON, Robert William   1934-

PERSONAL: Born March 24, 1934, in Cheam, England; came to the United States in 1963; son of David William and Lilian (Cramphorn) Thomson; married Judith Ailsa Cawdry, April 20, 1963; children: Jasper Rupert, Crispin Simon. *Education:* Cambridge University, B.A., 1955, M.A., 1958, Ph.D., 1962; University of Louvain, Licence, 1962. *Home:* 77 Kensington Park, Arlington, Mass. 02174. *Office:* Department of Near Eastern Languages, Harvard University, 6 Divinity Ave., Cambridge, Mass. 02138.

CAREER: Dumbarton Oaks, Washington, D.C., junior fellow, 1960-61; Harvard University, Cambridge, Mass., instructor, 1963-65, 1965-69, began as assistant professor, became associate professor, professor of Armenian studies, 1969—, chairman of department of Near Eastern languages, 1973-78. Member of British School of Archaeology in Ankara and British Institute for Persian Studies in Teheran. *Member:* American Oriental Society, Mediaeval Academy of America. *Awards, honors:* M.A. from Harvard University, 1969.

WRITINGS: (Editor with J. Neville Birdsall) *Biblical and Patristic Studies in Memory of Robert Pierce Case*, Herder, 1963; (editor and translator) *Athanasiana Syriaca*, Secretariat du CorpusSCO, Part I: *De incarnatione*, Volume I: *Syriac Texts*, Volume II: *English Translations*, 1965, Part II: *Epistula ad Epictetum*, Volume I: *Syriac Texts*, Volume II: *English Translations*, 1967, Part III: Volume I: *Syriac Texts*, Volume II: *English Translations*, 1972, Part IV: Volume I: *Syriac Texts*, Volume II: *English Translations*, 1977.

(Translator and author of notes) Agatangeghos, *The Teaching of Saint Gregory: An Early Armenian Catechism*, Harvard University Press, 1970; *Athanasius: Contra Gentes and De Incarnation*, Oxford University Press, 1970; *An Introduction to Classical Armenian*, Caravan Books, 1975; (translator and author of notes) Agatangeghos, *History of the Armenians*, State University of New York Press, 1976; (with Kevork B. Bardakjian) *A Textbook of Modern Western Armenian*, Caravan Books, 1977; (translator and author of notes) Moses Khorenatsi, *History of the Armenians*, Harvard University Press, 1978; (editor of reprint) Patmowtiwn Hayots, *Hayots' Patmowtiwn*, Caravan Books, 1980. Editor of *Recent Studies in Modern Armenian History*, 1972.

*   *   *

THORER, Konrad
    See GREVE, Felix Paul (Berthold Friedrich)

*   *   *

THORNE, Edouard
    See GREVE, Felix Paul (Berthold Friedrich)

THORP, Margaret Farrand   1891-1970

OBITUARY NOTICE: Born in 1891; died October 3, 1970, in Princeton, N.J. Journalist and author of *America at the Movies*. Obituaries and other sources: *AB Bookman's Weekly*, October 26, 1970.

*   *   *

THURMAN, Wallace   1902-1934
    (Patrick Casey, Ethel Belle Mandrake)

BRIEF ENTRY: Born August 16, 1902, in Salt Lake City, Utah; died of tuberculosis, December 22, 1934. American editor, novelist, playwright, and screenwriter. An integral part of the Harlem Renaissance, Thurman is known for his representations of Harlem "low life." In his writings Thurman mocked the prejudices of his fellow blacks and attacked certain aspects of the New Negro movement, arguing that the movement had produced no major literary talents. Though Thurman showed great talent as a satirist during his short life, he was sometimes criticized for his sensationalism. In addition to being a member of *The Messenger*'s editorial staff and an employee of Macauley Publishing Co., the writer founded two magazines, *Fire* and *Harlem*. H. L. Mencken and Carl Van Vechten were his major influences. Thurman's writings include the play "Harlem" (1929) and novels such as *The Blacker the Berry* (1929), *Infants of the Spring* (1932), and *The Interne* (1932). *Biographical/critical sources: The Reader's Encyclopedia of American Literature*, Crowell, 1962; *American Authors and Books, 1640 to the Present Day*, 3rd edition, Crown, 1972.

*   *   *

TICHI, Cecelia   1942-

PERSONAL: Born April 10, 1942, in Pittsburgh, Pa.; daughter of James (a manager) and Mary Louise (a clerk; maiden name, Doherty) Halbert; married William Tichi (a psychologist and administrator), September 8, 1967; children: Claire, Julia. *Education:* Pennsylvania State University, B.A., 1964; Johns Hopkins University, M.A., 1965; University of California, Davis, Ph.D., 1968. *Home:* 29 Crowninshield Rd., Brookline, Mass. 02146. *Office:* Department of English, Boston University, 236 Bay State Rd., Boston, Mass. 02215.

CAREER: Boston University, Boston, Mass., assistant professor, 1968-74, associate professor, 1975-79, professor of English, 1980—. *Member:* Modern Language Association of America, American Studies Association (member of council, 1981-84).

WRITINGS: New World, New Earth: Environmental Reform in American Literature From the Puritans Through Whitman, Yale University Press, 1979. Contributor to magazines and newspapers, including *William and Mary Quarterly*, *Genre*, *Prospects*, and *Christian Science Monitor*.

WORK IN PROGRESS: A book on American literature in the "age of efficiency," 1890-1920.

*   *   *

TIEMPO, Edith (Lopez)   1919-

PERSONAL: Born April 22, 1919, in Bayombong, Philippines; married E. K. Tiempo; children: two. *Education:* Silliman University, B.S.E., 1947; University of Iowa, M.A., 1949; University of Denver, Ph.D., 1958. *Office:* Department of English, Silliman University, Dumaguete City, Philippines.

CAREER: Silliman University, Dumaguete City, Philippines, professor of English, 1961—, chairman of department. Visiting professor at Western Michigan University, 1963-64 and 1965-66, and Wartburg College, 1964-65. *Awards, honors:* Rockefeller Foundation grants, 1949 and 1971; Palanca National Literary Award, 1951, 1955, and 1956, for poem, and 1969, for story; Free Press Literary Award, 1955 and 1959; Asia Foundation grant, 1971; special citation in poetry from Focus Philippines, 1975.

WRITINGS: Abide, Joshua, and Other Stories, Cellar Book Shop, 1964; *The Tracks of Babylon, and Other Poems,* Alan Swallow, 1966; *A Blade of Fern* (novel), Heinemann, 1978; *His Native Coast* (novel), Cellar Book Shop, 1979. Also author of *College Writing and Reading,* with husband E. K. Tiempo, 1964, *Introduction to Literature,* with E. K. Tiempo and F. A. Bernard, 1976, and *Poetry Through Image and Statement,* 1976. Contributor to poetry magazines, including Chicago's *Poetry.**

*   *   *

TILLION, Germaine Marie Rosine   1907-

PERSONAL: Born May 30, 1907, in Allegre, France; daughter of Jacques and Emilie (Cussac) Tillion. *Education:* Received M.A. from University of Paris and diplomas from Practical School of Advanced Studies, National School of Living Oriental Languages, and School of the Louvre. *Home:* 3 avenue Daumesnil, 94 Saint-Mande, France.

CAREER: Writer. Conductor of ethnographic missions in the Aures, 1934-40; investigator of German war crimes and Soviet concentration camps, 1945-54, investigator in Algeria, 1954-62; educational director at Professional School of Advanced Studies, 1957—. Participated in National Science Research Center missions among the Tauregs and Moors, 1964-65 and 1966. *Wartime service:* Head of resistance network in France, 1940-42; prisoner of war in Germany, 1942-45. *Awards, honors:* Commander of Legion of Honor; Croix de Guerre; Rosette of Resistance.

*WRITINGS—*In English translation: *Ravensbrueck: Temoignages,* Editions de la Baconniere, 1946, translation by Gerald Satterwhite published as *Ravensbrueck,* Anchor Press, 1946; *L'Algerie en 1957,* Editions de Minuit, 1957, translation by Ronald Matthews published as *Algeria: The Realities,* Knopf, 1958; *Les Ennemis-complementaires,* Editions de Minuit, 1960, translation by Richard Howard published as *France and Algeria: Complementary Enemies,* Knopf, 1961.

In French: *L'Afrique bascule vers l'avenir: L'Algerie en 1957 et autres textes,* Editions de Minuit, 1960; *Le Harem et les cousins,* Editions du Seuil, 1966.

Contributor to journals.

BIOGRAPHICAL/CRITICAL SOURCES: Best Sellers, October, 1975.*

*   *   *

TIMMERMANS, Claire   1938-

PERSONAL: Born August 5, 1938, in Netherlands; daughter of Peter Hendricus (a small-goods manufacturer) and Siebrigje (Mulder) van Wees; married Tim Timmermans (a partner in a child development center), October 11, 1958; children: Andrea, Mark, Chad. *Education:* Larnook Domestic Science Teacher's College, Secondary Teacher's Certificate, 1960; also studied at Institute for the Achievement of Human Potential, Philadelphia, Pa. *Home and office:* 10 Koornalla Cres., Mount Eliza, Victoria 3930, Australia.

CAREER: Teacher at primary school in Geelong, Australia, 1955; swimming teacher at school in Melbourne, Australia, 1957-77; Timmermans Child Development Centre, Australia, teacher of child development to parents, 1980—. Certified swimming teacher and coach; Royal Lifesaving Diploma. *Member:* Victoria Amateur Swimming Association. *Awards, honors:* Medalba de Ouro de Honra ao Merita from Centro de Reabilitacao, Nossa Senhora da Gloria, Rio de Janeiro, Brazil, 1973.

WRITINGS: How to Teach Your Baby to Swim, Stein & Day, 1975.

WORK IN PROGRESS: How to Teach Your Baby Anything.

SIDELIGHTS: In a brochure for Timmermans Child Development Centre, Claire Timmermans wrote: "How often have we parents and those of us who are planning to be parents wished that there could be some training available for parenthood. After all, if you want to be a plumber, carpenter, doctor, dentist, lawyer, or whatever trade, craft, or profession you wish to name, somewhere in our community there is a group of people or organization that will teach you step by step how to become capable in your chosen career through study, experience, and guidance.

"Parenthood is by far the most interesting, the most challenging, the most demanding and, if well done, the most rewarding experience in our lives and you also do not get any second chances. Up till now parents have turned to grandparents, friends, neighbors, and professionals for advice. However, these people often give such conflicting advice that the parents are left none the wiser. It is, therefore, in many families, not until the parents have their second or third child that they feel confident through experience in handling these children.

"Because most babies born these days were conceived by choice, we find that our community goes more towards quality than quantity. Because parents are having fewer children, they want to ensure that each of them gets the best quality of parenting right from conception. Through our course parents and parents-to-be learn each step in this development. Thus they know how to recognize what happens *and* why."

The subjects covered in Timmermans's course include how to have a healthy baby, how to teach a baby reading, mathematics, swimming, general physical development, foreign languages, music, and how to develop a baby's intelligence.

*   *   *

TIMMIS, John Henry III   1934-

PERSONAL: Born January 1, 1934, in Warren, Pa.; son of John Henry Timmis, Jr.; married, 1970; children: three. *Education:* Pennsylvania State University, B.A., 1959, M.A., 1962, Ph.D., 1966; attended University of Munich, 1960 and 1966. *Office:* College of Communication, Ohio University, Athens, Ohio 45701.

CAREER: Pennsylvania State University, University Park, instructor in communications, 1960-66; Ohio University, Athens, 1966—, began as assistant professor, became associate professor of communications. Research engineer for HRB-Singer, Inc., 1962-67; consultant to Naval Command and Control Systems, U.S. Department of State Arms Control and Disarmament Agency, and Office of Naval Intelligence. *Military service:* U.S. Marine Corps, 1953-56; became sergeant. *Member:* Speech Communication Association of America, American Historical Association, Operations Research Association of America, Historical Society (England), Speech Association of the Eastern States.

WRITINGS: *Thine Is the Kingdom: The Trial for Treason of Thomas Wentworth, Earl of Strafford, First Minister to King Charles I and Last Hope of the English Crown*, University of Alabama Press, 1974. Contributor to history journals.*

* * *

TIMMONS, Bascom N(olly) 1890-

PERSONAL: Born March 31, 1890, in Collin County, Tex.; son of Commodore Amplias and Martha Ann (Crenshaw) Timmons; married Ethel Boardman, August 8, 1925 (died October, 1970). *Education:* Attended military academy. *Religion:* Methodist. *Home:* 1316 30th St. N.W., Washington, D.C. 20007.

CAREER: *Fort Worth Record*, Fort Worth, Tex., reporter, 1906; *Dallas Times Herald*, Dallas, Tex., reporter, 1907; *Amarillo News*, Amarillo, Tex., managing editor, 1910; journalist with *Milwaukee Sentinel*, Milwaukee, Wis., 1911, and *Washington Post*, Washington, D.C., 1912-13; *Daily Panhandle*, Amarillo, owner and editor, 1914-16; *Houston Chronicle*, Houston, Tex., Washington correspondent, 1917-73. Writer. *Member:* National Press Club (president, 1932), Philosophical Society of Texas, Gridiron Club, Elks. *Awards, honors:* Biography award from Texas Heritage Foundation, 1958.

WRITINGS: *Garner of Texas*, Harper, 1948; *Portrait of an American: Charles G. Dawes*, Holt, 1953; *Jesse H. Jones: The Man and the Statesman*, Holt, 1956.*

* * *

TINDALL, William York 1903-1981
(A. P. Yorick)

OBITUARY NOTICE—See index for *CA* sketch: Born March 7, 1903, in Williamstown, Vt.; died September 8, 1981, in Salisbury, Md. Educator, editor, and author. A well-known authority on James Joyce, Tindall was a professor of English at Columbia University for forty years. He had previously taught at New York University, where in 1928 he had his students read Joyce's still prohibited book, *Ulysses*. Tindall was the president of the James Joyce Society for several years. His books, dealing primarily with British authors, include *D. H. Lawrence and Susan His Cow*, *James Joyce: His Way of Interpreting the Modern World*, and *John Bunyan, Mechanick Preacher*. Tindall also edited *Later D. H. Lawrence* and Joyce's *Chamber Music*. Obituaries and other sources: *New York Times*, September 9, 1981.

* * *

TINKLE, (Julien) Lon 1906-

PERSONAL: Born March 20, 1906, in Dallas, Tex.; son of James Ward and Mary (Gardenhire) Tinkle; married Maria Ofelia Garza, December 27, 1939; children: Jon Richard, James Alan, Anthony Robert. *Education:* Southern Methodist University, A.B., 1927, A.M., 1932; Sorbonne, University of Paris, diplome de phonetique, 1933. *Politics:* Democrat. *Religion:* Christian. *Home:* 3615 Amherst St., Dallas, Tex. 75225.

CAREER: Southern Methodist University, Dallas, Tex., 1932-74, began as instructor, became professor of French and comparative literature. Writer. Guest professor at Columbia University, summer, 1947. Vice-president of Margo Jones Theater-in-the-Round, 1945-47; member of board of directors of Dallas Museum of Fine Arts, Dallas Civic Music Association, and Dallas Friends of the Library.

MEMBER: Philosophical Society of Texas, Texas Institute of Letters (president, 1949-52), Dallas Chamber of Commerce.

Awards, honors: Prize from Texas Institute of Letters, 1959; book award from Sons of the Republic of Texas, 1959; Palmes Academiques of France; LL.D. from St. Mary's University, 1963.

WRITINGS: *Thirteen Days to Glory: The Siege of the Alamo*, McGraw, 1958, reprinted as *The Alamo*, New American Library, 1960; (editor with Allen Maxwell) *The Cowboy Reader*, Longmans, Green, 1959; *The Story of Oklahoma* (juvenile), Random House, 1962; (editor with Wynn Rickey) *Treson Nobel: An Anthology of French Nobel Prize-Winners*, Heath, 1963; *The Valiant Few: Crisis at the Alamo* (juvenile), Macmillan, 1964; *Miracle in Mexico: The Story of Juan Diego* (juvenile), Hawthorn, 1965; *The Key to Dallas* (juvenile), Lippincott, 1965; (author of preface) William Harvey Vann, *The Texas Institute of Letters, 1936-1966*, Encino Press, 1967; *J. Frank Dobie: The Makings of an Ample Mind*, Encino Press, 1968; *Mr. De: A Biography of Everette Lee DeGolyer* (foreword by Norman Cousins), Little, Brown, 1970; (author of introduction) Norman Kotker, editor, *Texas: A Picture Tour*, Scribner, 1976; *An American Original: The Life of J. Frank Dobie*, Little, Brown, 1978. Also author of *Les Deux Idoles*, with C. F. Zeek.

BIOGRAPHICAL/CRITICAL SOURCES: *Journal of American History*, September, 1979.*

* * *

TIPPIT, Sammy 1947-

PERSONAL: Born July 27, 1947, in Baton Rouge, La.; son of David Thomas (a factory worker) and Lavada (in sales; maiden name, Morgan) Tippit; married Debara Sirman, June 8, 1968; children: Paul David, Rachel Renee. *Education:* Attended Louisiana College, 1966-68. *Office address:* P.O. Box 563, Gresham, Ore. 97030.

CAREER: Ordained Southern Baptist minister, 1968; God's Love in Action, San Antonio, Tex., president and director, 1968-78; pastor of Baptist church in Lautzenhausen, West Germany, 1978-81; Mount Hood Baptist Church, Gresham, Ore., pastor, 1981—. President of East Baton Rouge Parish Youth Council, 1964-65; chairman of evangelism committee of European Baptist Convention, 1979-80, chairman of Interlaken committee, 1980-81.

WRITINGS: (With Jerry Jenkins) *Sammy Tippit: God's Love in Action, as Told to Jerry Jenkins*, Broadman, 1973; (with Jenkins) *Three Behind the Curtain*, Whitaker House, 1975; (with Jenkins) *You, Me, He: Sex Really Isn't a Dirty Word!* (juvenile), Victor Books, 1978; (with Jenkins) *Reproduced by Permission of the Author: You Can Be Like Jesus* (juvenile), Victor Books, 1979. Contributor to *Moody Monthly*.

SIDELIGHTS: Tippit commented: "Upon speaking in West Berlin I felt a tremendous desire to share my faith with the thousands of young people in the Eastern bloc countries. I have had the opportunity to preach in East Germany, the Soviet Union, Czechoslovakia, and Romania. Many of the books I have written refer to these experiences. I have discovered a deep hunger for spiritual things among Christians in Communist bloc countries. It is my desire to see that kind of thirst for God here in America."

BIOGRAPHICAL/CRITICAL SOURCES: *The Jesus Revolution*, Broadman, 1972.

TODD, Barbara Euphan 1890-1976
(Barbara Bower; Euphan, a pseudonym)

PERSONAL: Born January 9, c. 1890, in Arksey, Doncaster, England; died February 2, 1976, in Newbury, England; daughter of Thomas (a priest) and Alice Maud Mary (Bentham) Todd; married John Graham Bower (a naval officer and a writer under the pseudonym Klaxon), 1932 (died, 1940). *Education:* Attended school in Guildford, Surrey, England. *Politics:* Conservative. *Religion:* Church of England. *Home:* Cleeve Cottage, Blewbury, Berkshire, England. *Agent:* A. M. Heath & Co., 40-42 William IV St., London WC2N 4DD, England.

CAREER: Writer. *Wartime service:* Voluntary Aid Detachment, 1914-18.

WRITINGS: (Under name Barbara Bower) *Miss Ranskill Comes Home* (novel), Putnam, 1946.

For children: (With Marjory Royce and Moira Meighn) *The 'Normous Saturday Fairy Book,* Paul, 1924; (with Royce and Meighn) *The 'Normous Sunday Story Book,* Paul, 1925; (with Royce) *The Very Good Walkers,* illustrations by H. R. Miller, Methuen, 1925; *Hither and Thither* (poems), Harrap, 1927; *Mr. Blossom's Shop,* Nelson, 1929, reprinted, illustrations by E. S. Duffin, 1954.

(With Royce) *Happy Cottage,* Collins, 1930; (under pseudonym Euphan) *The Seventh Daughter* (poems), Burns & Oates, 1935; (under pseudonym Euphan; with husband, John Graham Bower under pseudonym Klaxon) *South Country Secrets,* Burns & Oates, 1936; (under pseudonym Euphan; with Klaxon) *The Touchstone,* Burns & Oates, 1935; *Worzel Gummidge; or, The Scarecrow of Scatterbrook,* illustrations by Elizabeth Alldridge, Burns & Oates, 1936, reprinted, illustrations by Jill Crockford, Evans, 1964; (under pseudonym Euphan; with Klaxon) *Stories of the Coronations,* Burns & Oates, 1937; *Worzel Gummidge Again,* illustrations by Alldridge, Burns & Oates, 1937, Evans, 1959; *The Mystery Train,* University of London Press, 1937; *The Splendid Picnic,* University of London Press, 1937; *More About Worzel Gummidge,* Burns & Oates, 1938; *Mr. Dock's Garden,* illustrations by Ruth Westcott, E.J. Arnold, 1939; *Gertrude the Greedy Goose,* illustrations by Benjamin Rabier, Muller, 1939.

(With Ester Boumphry) *The House That Ran Behind,* Muller, 1943; *Worzel Gummidge and Saucy Nancy,* illustrations by John Harwood, Harmandsworth, 1947; *Worzel Gummidge Takes a Holiday,* illustrations by Will Nickless, Hollis & Carter, 1949; (with Klaxon) *Aloysius Let Loose,* illustrations by A. E. Batchelor, Collins, 1950; *Earthy Mangold and Worzel Gummidge,* illustrations by Crockford, Hollis & Carter, 1954; *Worzel Gummidge and the Railway Scarecrows,* illustrations by Crockford, Evans, 1955; (with Mabel Constanduros) *The Frog Prince* (play), Samuel French, 1956; (with Constanduros) *The Sleeping Beauty* (play), Samuel French, 1956; *Worzel Gummidge at the Circus,* illustrations by Crockford, Evans, 1956; *The Boy With the Green Thumb,* illustrations by Charlotte Hough, Hamish Hamilton, 1956; *The Wizard and the Unicorn,* illustrations by Prudence Seward, Hamish Hamilton, 1957; *Worzel Gummidge and the Treasure Ship,* illustrations by Crockford, Evans, 1958; *The Shop Around the Corner,* illustrations by Olive Coughlan, Hamish Hamilton, 1959.

Detective Worzel Gummidge, illustrations by Crockford, Evans, 1963; *The Shop by the Sea,* illustrations by Sarah Garland, Hamish Hamilton, 1966; *The Clock Shop,* illustrations by Crockford, World's Work, 1967; *The Shop on Wheels,* illustrations by Crockford, World's Work, 1968; *The Box in the Attic,* illustrations by Lynnette Hemmant, World's Work, 1970;

The Wand From France, illustrations by Hemmant, World's Work, 1972.

Contributor of poems and stories to *Punch* and *Cornhill Magazine.* Author of radio and television scripts for British Broadcasting Corp. (BBC).

SIDELIGHTS: Barbara Euphan Todd lived in the rural English village of Blewbury, where in the 1930's she created her most famous character, the scarecrow Worzel Gummidge. The adventures of Worzel gradually became popular with British children, leading Todd to write a Worzel Gummidge series. Following World War II Todd worked in cooperation with BBC writers Mabel Constanduros and Denis Constanduros to produce a series of radio plays introducing the Worzel Gummidge cast. These popular performances were later adapted for television.

[Sketch verified by stepdaughter, Mrs. U.V.G. Betts]

*   *   *

TOLSTOY, Leo (Nikolaevich) 1828-1910

BRIEF ENTRY: Born September 9, 1828, in Yasnaya Polyana, Russia (now U.S.S.R.); died of pneumonia, November 20, 1910, in Astapovo, Russia (now U.S.S.R.); buried in Yasnaya Polyana, U.S.S.R. Russian author and moral philosopher. Tolstoy is ranked among the world's greatest novelists on the strength of his two most important works, *War and Peace* and *Anna Karenina.* His first published works, a trilogy of autobiographical novels entitled *Childhood* (1852), *Boyhood* (1854), and *Youth* (1857), were written during his brief military career and were praised for their psychological insight and evocative descriptive passages. When Tolstoy left the army in 1856, he traveled in Europe, writing several stories critical of Western European society, then returned to his estate to start a progressive school for peasant children. He was married in 1862 and during the next two decades devoted himself to family life and to the writing of his major novels. *War and Peace* (1869), a chronicle of two aristocratic families during the Napoleonic wars, was immediately recognized as a masterpiece; some critics have called it the greatest novel ever written. *Anna Karenina* (1877) is the story of a woman who is destroyed by her own passions and by society's hypocrisy. Its moralistic themes prefigure the moral obsessions that came to dominate Tolstoy's life and work. About 1880, he experienced a religious conversion and dedicated himself to propagating his own religious and political creed, a radical Christian anarchism. He repudiated his earlier work, asserting that art could be valuable only when it inspired religious and moral feelings. His later work is usually considered inferior to that of the early phase, but such works as *The Death of Ivan Ilyitch* (1886), *The Kreutzer Sonata* (1890), and *Resurrection* (1899), are recognized as powerful works of literature, though marred by his obsession with nonviolence and sexual abstinence. *Residence:* Yasnaya Polyana, Russia (now U.S.S.R.). *Biographical/critical sources:* Aylmer Maude, *The Life of Tolstoy,* revised edition, Oxford University Press, 1930; *The Reader's Encyclopedia,* 2nd edition, Crowell, 1965; Harry J. Mooney, *Tolstoy's Epic Vision: A Study of War and Peace and Anna Karenina,* University of Tulsa, 1968; R. F. Christian, *Tolstoy: A Critical Introduction,* Cambridge University Press, 1969; *Twentieth-Century Literary Criticism,* Volume 4, Gale, 1981.

*   *   *

TOMLINSON, Reginald R(obert) 1885-1979(?)

OBITUARY NOTICE: Born October 10, 1885, in Overton,

Hampshire, England; died c. 1979. Painter and author of books about art, including *Lettering for Arts and Crafts, Children as Artists,* and *Crafts for Children.* His paintings have been exhibited at the Royal Academy and the English Art Club. Obituaries and other sources: *The Author's and Writer's Who's Who,* 6th edition, Burke's Peerage, 1971; *Who's Who,* 126th edition, St. Martin's, 1974; *Who Was Who Among English and European Authors, 1931-1949,* Gale, 1978; *AB Bookman's Weekly,* January 29, 1979.

* * *

TOOLE, John Kennedy   1937-1969

PERSONAL: Born in 1937 in New Orleans, La.; committed suicide, March 26, 1969, in Biloxi, Miss.; son of John (a car salesman) and Thelma (a teacher; maiden name, Ducoing) Toole. *Education:* Received degree from Tulane University, 1958; Columbia University, M.A., 1959; graduate studies at Tulane University, mid-1960's.

CAREER: Teacher at colleges in New York and Louisiana, including University of Southwestern Louisiana, Lafayette, and St. Mary's Dominican College, New Orleans, La., 1959-68. *Military service:* U.S. Army, 1962-63. *Awards, honors:* Pulitzer Prize in fiction and Faulkner Award nomination from P.E.N., both 1981, both for *A Confederacy of Dunces.*

WRITINGS: A Confederacy of Dunces (novel), foreword by Walker Percy, Louisiana State University Press, 1980. Also author of an unpublished novel, "Neon Bible."

SIDELIGHTS: Toole wrote *A Confederacy of Dunces* in the early 1960's, when he was a soldier stationed in Puerto Rico. It was rejected by Simon & Schuster in 1966 and remained unpublished when Toole committed suicide in 1969. During the next seven years, his mother submitted the novel to eight more publishers, all of whom rejected it. In 1976 she took the manuscript to novelist Walker Percy, who agreed, reluctantly, to read it. He perused the opening pages of the smudged carbon copy, "first with the sinking feeling that it was not bad enough to quit, then with a prickle of interest, then a growing excitment, and finally an incredulity: surely it was not possible it was so good."

Percy recommended *A Confederacy of Dunces* to Louisiana State University Press, a scholarly publisher that had accepted only a few novels in the past. The book was published in the spring of 1980, and by summer Toole was, posthumously, a successful author, critically and commercially. *Confederacy* went through five printings, a total of 45,000 hardcover copies—an amazing number for an academic press. The novel was selected by the Book-of-the-Month Club, Grove Press bought the paperback rights, and Twentieth Century-Fox bought the movie rights. The hardcover edition made local best-seller lists in several cities, and the Grove edition was number one on the *New York Times* trade paperback best-seller list for over a month.

The critics' response was also enthusiastic. Jean Strouse of *Newsweek* called *A Confederacy of Dunces* "an astonishingly good novel, radiant with intelligence and artful high comedy." Richard Brown of the *Times Literary Supplement* praised "the clarity of its episodic architecture, its ability to rely effectively on dialogue for the evocation of scene and character, and . . . some splendid close observation, which arises mainly from a determination to work with the peculiarities of a New Orleans setting and language." The book was commended for being highly accessible and entertaining as well as a serious literary work, "a great rumbling farce of Falstaffian dimensions," as Percy called it.

A Confederacy of Dunces is the story of Ignatius J. Reilly, who is "a misfit, an iconoclast, a liar, a virgin, a raconteur, and, above all, a grossly overweight mamma's boy," in the words of *Detroit News* reviewer Charles J. Larson. Ignatius is devoted to medieval philosophy and spends much of his time in bed, writing indictments of the modern world and its trespasses against "theology and geometry." His outrage is directed at diverse targets, including Greyhound Scenicruisers, Doris Day, fashion, ambition, and sex. His mother thinks he should get a job, his girlfriend thinks he needs sex, and several people think he should be locked up in a jail or an asylum. Ignatius, however, considers himself a genius and aspires to be a reformer; when he has to take a job in a pants factory he organizes the black workers in a "Crusade for Moorish Dignity." When the crusade and the job end in chaos, he becomes a hot dog vendor in the French Quarter, selling few hot dogs but sowing a good deal of confusion when he tries to organize homosexuals as "sodomites for peace." Finally he is caught up in the exposure of a pornography ring that operates out of the Night of Joy nightclub, and he has to flee to New York to escape his mother's plan to commit him to a mental hospital. "The form of the novel represents a triumph all its own," wrote Phelps Gay in the *New Republic.* "Characters run into each other with an excess of coincidence rather like a Hardy novel, but every thread of the tale is followed and resolved with clarity and comedy."

Called "one of the funniest books ever written" by Gay and "a masterwork of comedy" by *New York Times Book Review* critic Alan Friedman, *A Confederacy of Dunces* has been compared favorably with such comic novels as John Irving's *The World According to Garp,* Joseph Heller's *Catch-22,* and Miguel Cervantes's *Don Quixote.* Much of the humor arises from the bizarre characters who populate the book: Ignatius's vapid, alcoholic mother; Patrolman Mancuso, who dons grotesque disguises to entice suspicious characters and is repeatedly arrested; Miss Trixie, the senile secretary of Levy Pants, who occasionally becomes lucid enough to look about her and ask, "am I retired?"; and Burma Jones, the black janitor at the Night of Joy, "a superb comic character of immense wit and resourcefulness," who plots sabotage in his perpetual cloud of cigarette smoke. "Caricature . . . is an art that Toole handles at his best with a nearly Dickensian skill." Friedman pointed out.

A Confederacy of Dunces also won praise from several critics, including Andrew Sinclair of the *Times Literary Supplement,* for its vivid depiction of "the gingerbread squalor and raffish charm of the delta city" of New Orleans. Gay wrote that Toole is "uncannily accurate in portraying the sights and sounds of New Orleans." Several reviewers applauded the authenticity of Toole's rendering of New Orleans speech, particularly in the character of Jones, "whose comedy," Brown noted, "comes from his language as much as from his situation: 'Hey! I'm working in modren slavery. If I quit, I get report for bein vagran. If I stay, I'm gainfully employ on a salary ain ever startin to be a minimal wage.'"

Some critics found the novel less satisfying, arguing that the plot is disorganized, many of the characters implausible, and the work as a whole insubstantial. Paul Gray of *Time* acknowledged the book's funniness, but added, "Pratfalls can pass beyond slapstick only if they echo, and most of the ones in this novel do not." The *Chicago Tribune's* Shirley Ann Grau wrote: "*A Confederacy of Dunces* isn't a very good novel. . . . It seems to move in many directions at once. . . . The background is so lightly sketched in that many references will make no sense to a reader who does not know the city of New Orleans. The parade of grotesques . . . is often confusing and pointless. The humor . . . is curiously restrained and old-fashioned with its parodies of fluttering fairies, Jewish pants manufacturers, tricky blacks, dumb Italian cops.'' But Grau noted that the book ''is the work of a promising writer,'' remarking on its ''passages of beauty and sensitivity.''

Even the book's defenders acknowledged its imperfections. Friedman conceded that it is ''flawed in places by its very virtues. Characters are overdone; caricatures are done to death; there are swatches of repetition. . . . Toward the end especially, there are doldrums and crudities.'' But Friedman, like others, found the flaws minor: ''No attack can seriously damage a text as energetic, resourceful and supple as this one. It resists the corrosion of our criticism. . . . The novel astonishes with its inventiveness, it lives in the play of its voices. *A Confederacy of Dunces* is nothing less than a grand comic fugue.''

BIOGRAPHICAL/CRITICAL SOURCES: John Kennedy Toole, *A Confederacy of Dunces*, forword by Walker Percy, Louisiana State University Press, 1980; *Newsweek*, May 26, 1980; *Time*, June 2, 1980; *Detroit News*, June 17, 1980; *New York Times Book Review*, June 22, 1980; *Chicago Tribune Book World*, June 29, 1980; *Times Literary Supplement*, July 18, 1980, June 12, 1981; *New Republic*, July 19, 1980; *Horizon*, September, 1980; *People*, September 22, 1980; *Contemporary Literary Criticism*, Volume 19, Gale, 1981; *Publishers Weekly*, June 12, 1981.

[Sketch verified by mother, Thelma D. Toole]

—*Sketch by Tim Connor*

* * *

TOVEY, Doreen Evelyn 1918-

PERSONAL: Born in 1918 in Bristol, England; married Rene C.D. Tovey. *Home:* White Cottage, Rowberrow, near Winscombe, Somerset, England.

CAREER: Writer.

WRITINGS—Illustrations by Maurice Wilson, except as noted: *Cats in the Belfry*, Elek, 1957, Doubleday, 1958; *Cats in May*, Elek, 1959, published as *Cats in Cahoots*, Doubleday, 1960; *Donkey Work*, Elek, 1962, Doubleday, 1963; *Life With Grandma*, illustrations by Ffolkes, Elek, 1964; *Raining Cats and Donkeys*, M. Joseph, 1967, Norton, 1968; *The New Boy*, Norton, 1970; *Double Trouble*, Norton, 1972; *Making the Horse Laugh*, Norton, 1974; *The Coming of Saska*, St. Martin's, 1977; *A Comfort of Cats*, M. Joseph, 1979, St. Martin's, 1980.*

* * *

TOYNBEE, (Theodore) Philip 1916-1981

OBITUARY NOTICE—See index for *CA* sketch: Born June 25, 1916, in Oxford, England; died June 15, 1981. Journalist, editor, reviewer, and author. Toynbee was an editor with the *Birmingham Town Crier* and a literary adviser for Constant Publications before joining the *Observer* in 1950. He began with the publication as a foreign correspondent and later became a book reviewer. Toynbee wrote several novels, including *The Savage Days, School in Private*, and *Friends Apart*. He also edited such books as *Underdogs*. Obituaries and other sources: *London Times*, June 17, 1981.

* * *

TRAIN, Arthur K(issam) 1902(?)-1981

OBITUARY NOTICE: Born c. 1902; died of heart failure, July 18, 1981, in Emerson, N.J. Translator and author of *Spoken Like a Frenchman*. Obituaries and other sources: *New York Times*, July 21, 1981.

* * *

TRAKAS, Pedro N(icholas) 1923-

PERSONAL: Born May 19, 1923, in Spartanburg, S.C.; son of Nicholas Saranto (a merchant) and Joanna (Harakas) Trakas; married Anna Patterson (an executive director), December 25, 1946; children: Nyko, Deno, Joanne Trakas Baizan, Irene, Chris. *Education:* Wofford College, A.B., 1944; Universidad Nacional de Mexico, M.A., 1945; University of North Carolina, Ph.D., 1954. *Politics:* Democrat. *Religion:* Greek Orthodox. *Home:* 5048 43rd St. S., St. Petersburg, Fla. 33711. *Office:* Department of Spanish Language and Literature, Eckerd College, P.O. Box 12560, St. Petersburg, Fla. 33733.

CAREER: Davidson College, Davidson, N.C., assistant professor, 1946-48, 1951-54, associate professor of Spanish language and literature, 1954-60; Eckerd College, St. Petersburg, Fla., professor of Spanish language and literature, 1960—. Member of summer adjunct faculty at University of Miami, Coral Gables, Fla. Church choir director, 1961-79. *Member:* Modern Language Association of America, American Association of University Professors, American Association of Teachers of Spanish and Portuguese (state president in North Carolina and Florida), South Atlantic Modern Language Association (member of executive committee), Phi Beta Kappa, Sigma Delta Pi, Delta Phi Alpha. *Awards, honors:* Grant from U.S. Department of State for Cuba, 1949; Litt.D. from Wofford College, 1972.

WRITINGS: (Editor) Antonio Buero-Vallejo, *El concierto de San Ovidio* (title means ''The Concert of St. Ovid''), Scribner, 1965; (with D. K. Barton and R. W. Tyler) *Beginning Course in Spanish*, Heath, 1976. Contributor to *Kentucky Quarterly* and *Bohemia*. Editor of *Wofford Journal*, 1944.

WORK IN PROGRESS: Research on Spanish novelist Dolores Medio, with a book or monograph expected to result.

SIDELIGHTS: Trakas told *CA:* ''The book that has had the greatest effect on me is Cervante's *Don Quixote de la Mancha*. My basic philosophy is summed up in two proverbs: 'Where there's a will there's a way' and 'Make hay while the sun shines.'

''The six months I spent in Cuba in 1949 doing research for my doctoral dissertation ('The Life and Works of Alfonso Hernandez-Cata') were the highest point of my academic pursuit. I not only received a wealth of invaluable information from the family of the deceased Hernandez-Cata, but I was also privileged to meet the top writers of Cuba who also knew him and acclaimed him as a great writer of short stories.''

AVOCATIONAL INTERESTS: Travel (Mexico, Cuba, Spain, France, Germany, Italy, Switzerland, Greece), singing, dancing, painting, playing guitar and piano.

* * *

TRAKL, Georg 1887-1914

BRIEF ENTRY: Born February 3, 1887, in Salzburg, Austria; died from an overdose of cocaine, November 3, 1914, in Krakow, Poland. Austrian poet. Encouraged by Austrian philosopher Ludwig Wittgenstein, Trakl wrote his best works, *Gedichte* (1913) and *Sebastian Dreaming* (1914). His career was remarkably brief. Neurotic to the point of madness, alternating between violence and childlike simplicity, Trakl took his own life, perhaps accidentally, at age twenty-seven. Nevertheless in just two years he had managed to produce the poems that place him among the most important and original poets of the German language. Trakl's work was sometimes called a precursor to expressionism. He saw the world collapsing around him and taking him with it. He described his poetry as "imperfect penance" for "unabsolved guilt." Trakl's language was simple and clear, even in translation, resembling the work of Hoelderlin. His strong and precise imagery, darkly brooding sensitivity, and feeling for color bolstered his reputation. He wrote about death, decay, and doom, hiding himself in lyrical metaphor and the ambiguity of his images, but some critics saw a positive side to his work: a compassionate view of life, based on a pantheism acquired from Hoelderlin. The bulk of critical acclaim for Trakl's work came after World War II with the publication of *Gesammelte Werke* (1948-53) and *Dichtungen und Briefe* (1970). *Biographical/critical sources: The Concise Encyclopedia of Modern World Literature*, Hutchinson, 1963; *Listener*, October 24, 1968; Herbert Lindenberger, *Georg Trakl*, Twayne, 1971; Maire Jaanus Kurrik, *Georg Trakl*, Columbia University Press, 1974.

*   *   *

TREE, Gregory
See BARDIN, John Franklin

*   *   *

TROEN, Selwyn K.   1940-

PERSONAL: Born September 15, 1940, in Boston, Mass.; married, 1964; children: four. *Education:* Brandeis University, B.A., 1963; Hebrew Teachers College, B.J.Ed., 1962; University of Chicago, M.A., 1965, Ph.D., 1970.

CAREER: University of Missouri, Columbia, assistant professor of American history, beginning in 1969. Visiting fellow at Princeton University, 1972-73. *Member:* Organization of American Historians, History of Education Society, Southern Historical Association.

WRITINGS: A Guide to Resources on the History of St. Louis, Washington University (St. Louis, Mo.), 1971; (contributor) R. A. Mohl and J. F. Richardson, editors, *The Urban Experience: Themes in American History*, Wadsworth, 1973; (contributor) *Education and Society*, Princeton University Press, 1974; *The Public and the Schools: Shaping the St. Louis System, 1838-1920*, University of Missouri Press, 1975; (editor with Glen E. Holt) *St. Louis*, New Viewpoints, 1977. Contributor to education journals.

BIOGRAPHICAL/CRITICAL SOURCES: Journal of American History, March, 1976; *American Historical Review*, April, 1976.*

*   *   *

TRUDEL, Marcel   1917-

PERSONAL: Born May 29, 1917, in Saint-Narcisse-de-Champlain, Quebec, Canada; son of Hermyle (a carpenter) and Antoinette (Cossette) Trudel; married Anne Chretien, July 11, 1942 (marriage ended); married Micheline d'Allaire, August 27, 1970; children: Jeanne, Madeleine, Marc. *Education:* Laval University, B.A., 1938, Lic. es Lettres, 1941, Dr. es Lettres (summa cum laude), 1945. *Office:* Department of History, University of Ottawa, Ottawa, Ontario, Canada J9H 1G1.

CAREER: Bourget College, Rigaud, Quebec, professor of Greek and Latin, 1941-45; Harvard University, Cambridge, Mass.,

postdoctoral research fellow, 1945-47; Laval University, Quebec, Quebec, professor of Canadian history, 1947-65, director of Institute of History and Geography, 1954-55, and Institute of History, 1955-64; Carleton University, Ottawa, Ontario, professor of Canadian history and director of Institute of Canadian Studies, 1965-66; University of Ottawa, Ottawa, research professor of history, 1966—, director of department, 1966-68. Speaker at French Canadian Institute, Sorbonne, University of Paris, and University of Poitiers; Gray Lecturer at University of Toronto, 1966. Member of Commission des Monuments et Lieux Historiques du Canada.

MEMBER: Royal Society of Canada (fellow), Academie Canadienne/Francaise, Canadian Historial Association (president), Academie Berrichonne, Institute for French-American History, Conseil des Arts de Quebec (president). *Awards, honors:* Prix David from Government of Quebec, 1945, for *L'Influence de Voltaire*, and 1951, for *Louis XVI: Le Congres americain et le Canada, 1774-1789;* Leo-Pariseau Medal from Association Canadienne-Francaise pour l'Avancement des Sciences, 1960, for contribution to history; Prix Casgrain from Laval University, 1961, for *L'Esclavage au Canada francais;* Prix Concours Litteraire du Quebec from government of Quebec, 1963, for *Histoire de la Nouvelle-France*, Volume I, and 1966, for Volume II of the same work; Tyrrell Medal from Canadian History Association, 1964, for contribution to history; Prix Duvernay from Societe Saint-Jean-Baptiste, 1966, for contribution to history; prize from governor-general of Canada, 1967, for *Histoire de la Nouvelle-France*, Volume II; member of Order of Canada, 1971; Molson Award from Molson Company, 1980, for contribution to history.

WRITINGS: Atlas historique du Canada francais des origines a 1867, Presses de l'Universite Laval, 1961, bilingual edition published as *Atlas de la Nouvelle-France: An Atlas of New France*, 1968, 2nd edition, 1973; *Histoire de la Nouvelle-France*, Fides, Volume I: *Les Vaines tentatives, 1524-1603* (title means "Futile Attempts"), 1963, Volume II: *Le Comptoir, 1604-1627* (title means "The Trade Post"), 1966, Volume III: *La Seigneurie des cent-associes* (title means "The Domain of the Hundred Associates"), part 1: *Les Evenements* (means "The Events"), 1980, part 2: *La Societe* (means "Society"), 1982; translation of first two volumes by Patricia Caxton published as *The Beginnings of New France, 1524-1663*, McClelland & Stewart, 1973; (editor with George W. Brown and Frances Halpenny) *Dictionary of Canadian Biography*, Volume I: *1000-1700*, University of Toronto Press, 1966; (with Paul Cornell and others) *Canada: Unity in Diversity*, Holt, 1967; *Initiation a la Nouvelle-France: Histoire et institutions*, Holt, 1968, translation published as *Introduction to New France*, Holt, 1968; (with Genevieve Jain) *L'Histoire du Canada: Enquete sur les manuels*, Imprimeur de la Reine, 1969, translation published as *Canadian History Textbooks: A Comparative Study*, Queen's Printer for Canada, 1970.

In French: *L'Influence de Voltaire au Canada* (title means "Voltaire's Influence in Canada"), Volume I: *De 1700 a 1850*, Volume II: *De 1850 a 1900*, Fides, 1945; *Vezine* (novel), 1946, revised edition, Fides, 1963; *Louis XVI: Le Congres americain et le Canada, 1774-1789* (title means "Louis XVI: The American Congress and Canada, 1774-1789"), Editions du Quartier Latin, 1949, reprinted as *La Revolution americaine: Pourquoi la France refuse le Canada, 1775-1783* (title means "The American Revolution: Why France Does Not Wish to Have Canada Back"), Editions du Boreal Express, 1976.

Le Regime militaire dans le gouvernement des Trois-Rivieres, 1760-1764 (title means "The Military Rule in the Government of Trois-Rivieres"), Editions du Bien Public, 1952; (editor with Michel Brunet and Guy Fregault) *Histoire du Canada par les textes* (title means "A Study of History Through the Primary Sources"), 1952, Volume I: *1534-1854*, Volume II: *1855-1960*, revised edition (with Brunet only), Fides, 1963; *Chiniquy* (biography), Editions du Bien Public, 1955; (editor and author of notes) *Champlain* (biography), Fides, 1956, revised edition, 1968; *L'Eglise canadienne sous le regime militaire, 1759-1764* (title means "The Church of Canada Under the Military Rule"), Presses Universitaires Laval, Volume I: *Les Problemes*, 1956, Volume II: *Les Institutions*, 1957.

L'Esclavage au Canada francais: Histoire et conditions de l'esclavage (title means "Slavery in French Canada: Its History and Nature"), Presses Universitaires Laval, 1960, abridged edition published as *L'Esclavage au Canada francais*, Horizon, 1963; (editor) *Jacques Cartier* (biography), Fides, 1968; *La Population du Canada en 1663*, Fides, 1973; *Le Terrier du Saint-Laurent en 1663* (title means "A Catalogue of Lands in Canada in 1663"), Editions de l'Universite d'Ottawa, 1973; *Les Debuts du regime seigneurial au Canada* (title means "The Beginnings of the Seigneurial Regime in Canada"), Fides, 1974; *Montreal: La Formation d'une societe, 1642-1663* (title means "Montreal: The Birth of a Society"), Fides, 1976; *Melanges d'histoire du Canada francais offerts au professeur Marcel Trudel* (title means "A Miscellany of Historical Writings Dedicated to Professor Marcel Trudel"), Editions de l'Universite d'Ottawa, 1978. Also author of *L'Affaire Jumonville* (title means "The Jumonville Skirmish"), 1953.

* * *

TSURUTANI, Taketsugu 1935-

PERSONAL: Born December 15, 1935, in Iki, Japan; came to the United States in 1954; son of Taketshi (in business) and Chizu (Yamauchi) Tsuruya; married Cassandra Schilberg (a librarian); children: Gabriella. *Education:* Lawrence College (now University), B.A., 1958; attended University of Strasbourg, 1958-59; University of Wisconsin (now University of Wisconsin—Madison), M.A., 1964, Ph.D., 1966. *Home:* Northwest 1558 Turner Dr., Pullman, Wash. 99163. *Office:* Department of Political Science, Washington State University, Pullman, Wash. 99164.

CAREER: University of Nevada, Las Vegas, assistant professor of political science, 1966-67; University of Maine, Orono, assistant professor of political science, 1967-69; Washington State University, Pullman, assistant professor, 1969-71, associate professor, 1971-75, professor of political science, 1975—. *Member:* American Political Science Association.

WRITINGS: The Politics of National Development: Political Leadership in Transitional Societies, Chandler, 1973; *Political Change in Japan: Response to Postindustrial Challenge*, McKay, 1977; *Japanese Policy and East Asian Security*, Praeger, 1981; (with Alex Dragnich and John Dorsey) *Politics and Government: A Brief Introduction*, Chatham Bookseller, 1982.

WORK IN PROGRESS: Academics in Politics: Their Role and Influence in Contemporary Japan.

SIDELIGHTS: Tsurutani told *CA:* "As a Japanese scholar working in the United States, I feel it is part of my role to describe, analyze, and explain Japanese politics and society to the American public. It is for this reason that in recent years I have been engaged in research on Japan.

"As one of the post-industrial societies, Japan is undergoing a range of significant and largely unanticipated changes caused by her all-too-successful drive toward international economic superstardom. Trials and tribulations precipitated by these changes render her future uncertain and unpredictable. But studying Japan's situation is important not only because Japan is unique in that she is the only non-Western post-industrial society, but also because hers are the kinds of problems that all advanced industrial societies of the West share with varying degrees of explicitness and significance. In short, studying Japan will help us understand other post-industrial societies.

"The only advanced industrial and stable democratic state in Asia, Japan is destined to play an increasingly significant role in the maintenance of peace and stability in the region and beyond. In performing this role, Japan will be working in close cooperation and coordination with the United States because of their mutual security arrangement. The pattern of Japanese-American relations that would be most appropriate to this end remains to be clearly defined, however, because of a certain ambivalence with which the two nations still view each other. To the extent that Japanese-American relations are the foundation of peace and stability in Asia, the future of Asia will be determined in large measure by the way in which Japanese-American relations are defined during the current decade."

* * *

TSVETAEVA (EFRON), Marina Ivanovna 1892-1941

BRIEF ENTRY: Born in 1892 in Moscow, Russia (now U.S.S.R.); committed suicide in 1941 in Yelabuga, U.S.S.R. Russian poet. Marina Tsvetaeva's modernist poetry is characterized by a concise style and versatility of inflection and rhythm. Her first book, *Vechernii al'bom* (1910), secretly published when she was eighteen, won immediate critical acclaim. She wrote about her homeland and the Russian people, and much of her work was anti-Bolshevik, including *Lebediny stan* (1957). Tsvetaeva so abhorred the 1917 revolution that she lived in western Europe from 1922 to 1939; her literary independence was so fierce that during her voluntary exile she was outcast from the Russian emigre community. She also suffered at the hands of publishers who edited much of the strength from her unusual work and critics who interpreted the brevity of her style as carelessness. Still, she continued to write lyrics that were extremely compressed, in rhythms that sometimes approached the chant. She created miniature fairy tales and recreated myths, with inflection reminiscent of the folk song, as in *Tsar'-devitsa* (1922). Her work was enlivened by outbursts of passion and occasional, unexpected use of colloquial speech. The poems in *Posle rossii* (1928), which were written and published abroad, were later considered to be Tsvetaeva's most outstanding work, but since all her writing was banned in the Soviet Union for some thirty years, it did not reach the Russian people until long after her death. *Biographical/critical sources: The Penguin Companion to European Literature*, McGraw, 1969; *Slavic Review*, December, 1979.

* * *

TUCKER, Anthony 1924-

PERSONAL: Born June 1, 1924, in Urmston, England; son of Harold Leslie (in business) and Lucy (Steggles) Tucker; married Eileen Lloyd, 1950; children: Lesley Tucker Christensen, John Dixon, Helen Beatrix. *Education:* Attended Queen's University, Belfast, 1941-42; received D.A., A.T.D., and N.D.D. from Regional College of Art, Manchester, England. *Office: Guardian*, 119 Farringdon Rd., London EC1R 3ER, England.

CAREER: Guardian, London, England, art critic, 1953-64, northern features editor, 1960-64, science correspondent, 1964—, futures editor, 1979—. Broadcaster for British Broadcasting Corp. (BBC). *Military service:* Royal Air Force, fighter pilot, 1942-47, served in Italy; became flying officer. *Member:* British Ecological Society, American Association for the Advancement of Science, Institute of Contemporary Arts, New York Academy of Sciences. *Awards, honors:* British National Science Writers award, 1966 and 1980.

WRITINGS: Climate for Living, Queen Anne Press, 1967; *The Toxic Metals,* Ballantine, 1972; (with J. A. Lauwerys and Keith Reid) *Man, Nature, and Ecology,* Aldus, 1974. Contributor to magazines, including *Brassey's, Tropical Science,* and *New Scientist.*

WORK IN PROGRESS: Research for monographs on the escalation and disarmament of nuclear weapons and on the effects of low-level radiation.

SIDELIGHTS: Tucker wrote: "My motivation is curiosity and the search for a new ethic that will allow a transition into the post-industrial (post-materialistic) world, as well as an awareness of (perhaps even reverence for) the intricate beauty of living structures." *Avocational interests:* People, dogs ("not necessarily in that order"), walking, talking, looking, "finding time to browse."

*   *   *

TUMELTY, James J.   1921(?)-1979(?)

OBITUARY NOTICE: Educator and author of *Britain Today.* Obituaries and other sources: *AB Bookman's Weekly,* January 29, 1979.

*   *   *

TUNNICLIFFE, C(harles) F(rederick)   1901-

PERSONAL: Born December 1, 1901, in Langley, England; son of William and Margaret Tunnicliffe; married Winifred Wonnacott (an artist), 1929 (died, 1969). *Education:* Attended Macclesfield School of Art and Manchester School of Art; Royal College of Art, diploma in painting, 1923, and A.R.C.A. *Address:* c/o CBS Educational and Professional Publishing, 383 Madison Ave., New York, N.Y. 10017.

CAREER: Painter, engraver, and illustrator. *Member:* Royal Academy (associate). *Awards, honors:* Named royal artist, 1954; gold medal from Royal Society for the Protection of Birds, 1975; officer of Order of the British Empire, 1978.

WRITINGS—Self-illustrated: My Country Book, Studio, 1942; *Bird Portraiture,* Studio, 1945; *How to Draw Farm Animals,* Studio, 1947; *Mereside Chronicle, With a Short Interlude of Lochs and Lochans,* Scribner, 1948; *Shorelands Summer Diary,* Collins, 1952; *Birds of the Estuary,* Penguin, 1955; *A Sketchbook of Birds,* Holt, 1979.

Illustrator: Derek Henry Chapman, *The Seasons and the Woodman* (juvenile), Cambridge University Press, 1941; H. Williamson, *Tarka, the Otter* (juvenile), Putnam, 1949; Anthony Julian Huxley, *Wild Flowers of the Countryside,* Blandford, 1962; Richard Jefferies, *Wild Life in a Southern County* (reprint of 1879 edition), Moonraker Press, 1978; Linda Bennett, *The Royal Society for the Protection of Birds Book of Garden Birds,* Hamlyn, 1978. Also illustrator of *Orielton* by Ronald Lockley, 1977.*

*   *   *

TUOHY, William Klaus   1926-

PERSONAL: Born October 1, 1926, in Chicago, Ill.; son of John Marshall and Lolita (Klaus) Tuohy; married Johanna Iselin, November 24, 1964; children: Cyril Iselin. *Education:* Northwestern University, B.S., 1951. *Office:* c/o Foreign Editor, *Los Angeles Times,* Los Angeles, Calif. 90053.

CAREER: San Francisco Chronicle, San Francisco, Calif., 1952-59, began as copy boy, became night city editor; *Newsweek,* 1959-66, began as associate editor, became foreign correspondent, 1966; *Los Angeles Times,* Los Angeles, Calif., Vietnam correspondent, 1966-68, Middle East correspondent in Beirut, Lebanon, 1969-71, bureau chief in Rome, Italy, 1971-77, bureau chief in London, England, 1977—. *Military service:* U.S. Naval Reserve, active duty, 1944-46. *Awards, honors:* National Headliner Award, 1965, for Vietnam coverage; Pulitzer Prize for international reporting, 1969, for Vietnam coverage; award from Overseas Press Club of America, 1970, for Middle East coverage.

WRITINGS: Sicily, Berlitz, 1979; *The Italian Adriatic,* Berlitz, 1981.

*   *   *

TURNBULL, Stephen (Richard)   1948-

PERSONAL: Born Feburary 6, 1948, in London, England. *Education:* Downing College, Cambridge, M.A., 1969. *Home:* 9 Victoria Dr., Horsforth, Leeds LS18 4PN, England.

CAREER: Writer. Deputy headmaster of Whitehill School, Stockport, England, 1974; lecturer on Japanese culture. *Member:* To-Ken Society of Great Britain, British Association of Japanese Studies, Japan Society of London.

WRITINGS: The Samurai: A Military History, Macmillan, 1977; *Samurai Armies,* Osprey, 1979; *Warlords of Japan,* Sampson Low, 1979; *The Mongols,* Osprey, 1980.

WORK IN PROGRESS: Samurai: A Social History (tentative title).

AVOCATIONAL INTERESTS: All aspects of Japanese culture, collecting Japanese arms and armor, photography, wargaming, including designing model soldiers and wargames.

*   *   *

TURNER, George William   1921-

PERSONAL: Born October 26, 1921, in Dannevirke, New Zealand; son of Albert George (a farmer) and Elinor Jessie (a dressmaker; maiden name, Anderson) Turner; married Beryl Horrobin (an academic), April 18, 1949; children: Anton Eric, Neil Thurstan. *Education:* University of New Zealand, M.A., 1948; University of London, Diploma in English Linguistic Studies, 1964. *Home:* 3 Marola Ave., Rostrevor, South Australia 5073. *Office:* Department of English, University of Adelaide, Adelaide, South Australia 5001.

CAREER: Teacher of science and agriculture at a high school in Dannevirke, New Zealand, 1944, and Auckland Teachers' College in Auckland, New Zealand, 1945; teacher of languages at Wellington College, Wellington, New Zealand, 1946; University of Canterbury, Canterbury, New Zealand, University Library, head of orders department, 1949-52; Canterbury Public Library, Canterbury, New Zealand, head of reference department, 1953-54; University of Canterbury, lecturer, 1955-64, senior lecturer in English, 1964; University of Adelaide, Adelaide, Australia, reader in English, 1965—, chairman of department, 1975-77. Lecturer in Germany, Sweden, England, France, Yugoslavia, and Canada. *Military service:* Served in New Zealand Army, 1942. *Member:* Australia and New Zealand Association for Medieval and Renaissance Studies, Linguistic Society of Australia, Australian Universities Language and Literature Association, Academy of the Humanities (fellow).

WRITINGS: (Author of introduction) Joseph Furphy, *Rigby's Romance*, Rigby, 1972; *German for Librarians*, Massey University, 1972; *The English Language in Australia and New Zealand*, Longmans, Green, 1966, 2nd edition, 1972; *Stylistics*, Penguin, 1973; (editor) *Good Australian English*, A. H. & A. W. Reed, 1973.

WORK IN PROGRESS: Revising *Australian Pocket Oxford Dictionary;* with Frances Devlin Glass and P. R. Eaden, an annotated edition of *Such Is Life*, by Joseph Furphy.

SIDELIGHTS: Turner wrote: "In my early years I worked in a cheese factory, as a builder's laborer and shop assistant, in a radio factory, and as a meter reader. I became interested in books and language early.

"My writing has owed much—really everything—to academic colleagues. My main books have been commissioned for series; unprompted, I, a New Zealand country boy, would not have had the temerity to write them.

"I have two opposite ambitions in writing. In one mood I would simply like to establish a fact, however minute, that was not known before. This ambition comes nearest to fulfillment in the work I do as a consultant for the *Oxford English Dictionary* (second supplement) checking entries for Australian and New Zealand words, in which it is sometimes possible to fill in the earlier history of a word with quotations of earlier date than those collected by previous informants. The opposite ambition is symoptic, a desire to break down barriers between academic subjects. Articles I have written link linguistics with science or logic, or journalism or history. Especially important in this connection is an ambition to heal the old feud between linguistic and literary study.

"My habit when writing a book is to plan the outline in about eight or ten chapters, setting aside a folder for each chapter and putting all quotations, ideas, and facts into the appropriate folder as they come to hand. The book then organizes itself around the material. Quotations and illustrative examples often seem to come in very aptly this way, because in fact they precede the connecting text they illustrate."

* * *

TURNER, Kermit 1936-

PERSONAL: Born December 29, 1936, in Lincolnton, N.C.; son of William Martin and Clara (McRee) Turner; married Carol Thompson (a grants coordinator), December 26, 1965; children: Jason William. *Education:* Lenoir-Rhyne College, B.A., 1960; University of Arkansas, M.A., 1967; University of North Carolina, Greensboro, M.F.A., 1973. *Home:* 1282 12th Street Dr., Hickory, N.C. 28601. *Agent:* Richard Huttner Agency, Inc., 330 East 33rd St., New York, N.Y. 10016. *Office:* Department of English, Lenoir-Rhyne College, Box 518, Hickory, N.C. 28601.

CAREER: Lenoir-Rhyne College, Hickory, N.C., instructor, 1967-73, assistant professor, 1973-79, associate professor of English, 1979—. Gives readings. *Member:* Associated Writing Programs, South Atlantic Modern Language Association. *Awards, honors:* Resident at Yaddo, 1980.

WRITINGS: *Rebel Powers* (novel), Warne, 1979. Contributor to literary journals, including *Phylon, Greensboro Review*, and *Roanoke Review*. Editor of *Graffiti*, 1973-79.

WORK IN PROGRESS: Trials of a Teenage Redneck, a novel; *Tenure*, a novel.

SIDELIGHTS: Turner wrote: "In my fiction I try to depict life in the late twentieth-century South as I have experienced and witnessed it. I try to be authentic and original and to avoid traditional modes or schools of southern literature, since I believe that the South as traditionally presented in fiction is rapidly disppearing."

* * *

TURNER, Merfyn (Lloyd) 1915-

PERSONAL: Born in 1915 in Wales; married wife, Shirley (a magistrate); children: Geraint, Glyn, Catrin, Lowri, and Nerys (triplets). *Education:* Received B.A. from University of Wales and diploma in education from University of London. *Home:* 24 Harberton Rd., London N.19, England.

CAREER: Social worker, 1946—. Worked as school teacher; writer. Guest on television and radio programs.

WRITINGS: (Translator from Welsh) Rhys John Davies, *The Christian and War*, Gee's Press, c. 1940; *Y meini hyn* (one-act play), Aberystwyth, 1950; *Nid hon yw y ddinas* (one-act play), Aberystwyth, 1950; *Ship Without Sails: An Account of the Barge Boys' Club*, University of London Press, 1953; *Norman House: The First Five Years*, Norman House, 1961; *Safe Lodging: The Road to Norman House*, Hutchinson, 1961; *A Pretty Sort of Prison*, Pall Mall, 1965; *O Ryfedd Rym: Hynt a helynt troseddwyr yng ngharchar ac allan o garchar*, Gomer Press, 1970; (with Stuart Whiteley and Briggs) *Dealing With Deviants*, Schocken, 1971; *Who Cares?*, British Broadcasting Corp., 1972. Contributor to journals.

WORK IN PROGRESS: Two books of commentary, based on Turner's thirty-five years of experience in the penal field.

SIDELIGHTS: Turner told *CA:* "My main interest in living is my involvement with society's rejects, misfits, and failures, particularly when they are socially isolated and in prison or mental hospitals. I think I live, sleep, dream, and talk prison and prisoners. I have traveled to prisons of all the various European countries, and am currently involved with English-speaking drug offenders in Turkish prisons. In England I visit prisons and security hospitals. I have been an official visitor at Pentonville Prison since 1947, where I spend much time with prisoners awaiting deportation."

Turner himself was imprisoned in 1941 as a pacifist and conscientious objector.

* * *

TURSUN-ZADE, Mirzo 1911-1977

OBITUARY NOTICE: Born in 1911 in Tadzhik, Russian Turkistan (Now Tadzhik Soviet Socialist Republic); died in September, 1977, in Moscow, U.S.S.R. Poet, playwright, and essayist. A recipient of four Orders of Lenin, the Stalin Prize, and the Lenin Prize, Tursun-Zade was secretary of the Soviet Writer's Union from 1959 until his death. His writings include *Banner of Victory*, a collection essays and verse; "Spring and Autumn," a poem; "Verdict," a play; and "The Vose Rebellion," an opera libretto. Obituaries and other sources: *AB Bookman's Weekly*, February 6, 1978.

* * *

TURYN, Alexander 1900-1981

OBITUARY NOTICE: Born December 26, 1900, in Warsaw,

Poland; died after a long illness, August 26, 1981, in Urbana, Ill. Philologist, educator, and author. Turyn was best known for his textual transmissions of the works of Greek tragedians. His research in the study of manuscripts and ancient handwriting earned him several philology awards, including the Golden Cross of the Order of the Phoenix from the Greek Government in 1934 and the Goodwin Award of Merit in 1960. He was named professor extraordinary of classical philology by the University of Warsaw in 1935 and professor emeritus of the University of Illinois in 1969. Turyn was also a research collaborator with the Vatican and a 1959 Guggenheim fellow. His writings include *Studies in the Manuscript Tradition of Aeschylus, Studies in the Manuscript Tradition of the Tragedies of Sophocles,* and *The Byzantine Manuscript Tradition of the Tragedies of Euripides.* Obituaries and other sources: *International Who's Who,* Europa, 1978; *New York Times,* August 31, 1981.

* * *

TWAIN, Mark
  See CLEMENS, Samuel Langhorne

* * *

TWELVEPONIES, Mary
  See CLEVELAND, Mary

* * *

TYNAN, Katharine   1861-1931
  (Katharine Tynan Hinkson)

BRIEF ENTRY: Born January 23, 1861, in Clondalkin, County Dublin, Ireland; died April 2, 1931; buried in London, England. Irish poet, novelist, and journalist. Tynan's first poem was published when she was seventeen; she went on to write several volumes of poetry and more than one hundred popular romantic novels. Her verse is usually considered minor but distinctive, influenced by Christina Rossetti. Much of her poetry is devotional, reflecting her pious Catholicism. She also wrote of nature, motherhood, and Irish patriotism, but unlike other Celtic revival poets, she rarely drew on Irish pagan mythology in her work. Considered less significant than her poems, her novels are sentimental and sensational, and she made no secret of her commercial motives. Nevertheless, critics have recognized Tynan's gift for storytelling. Tynan is remembered primarily as an early member of the Celtic revival and as a friend of W. B. Yeats, A.E. (George Russell), Alice Meynell, and other Irish writers. Her works include *Louise de la Valliere, and Other Poems* (1885), *Ballads and Lyrics* (1890), *The Way of a Maid* (1895), *A Lover's Breast Knot* (1896), *The Holy War* (1916), and *Collected Poems* (1930). *Residence:* London, England. *Biographical/critical sources:* Katharine Tynan, *Twenty-Five Years: Reminiscences,* Smith, Elder, 1913; *Catholic World,* May, 1913; *Catholic Authors: Contemporary*

Biographical Sketches, 1930-1947, St. Mary's Abbey, 1948; W. B. Yeats, *Letters to Katharine Tynan,* Clonmore & Reynolds, 1953; Marilyn Gaddis Rose, *Katharine Tynan,* Bucknell University Press, 1974; *Twentieth-Century Literary Criticism,* Volume 3, Gale, 1980.

* * *

TYRE, Nedra

PERSONAL: Given name is pronounced *Nee*-dra; born in Offerman, Ga.; daughter of Henry and Frances C. (Hull) Tyre. *Education:* Georgia School of Technology (now Georgia State University), B.A.; Emory University, M.A.; also attended Richmond School of Social Work. *Home:* 1118 Grove Ave., Apt. 34, Richmond, Va. 23220. *Agent:* Scott Meredith Literary Agency, Inc., 845 Third Ave., New York, N.Y. 10022.

CAREER: Worked at various jobs, including teacher of sociology at Richmond Professional Institute, Richmond, Va., and book reviewer for *Richmond News Leader,* Richmond, and *Atlanta Journal,* Atlanta, Ga.; currently free-lance writer. Social worker at American Red Cross field station, 1943-44.

WRITINGS: Red Wine First (stories), Simon & Schuster, 1974; *Mouse in Eternity* (novel), Knopf, 1952, reprinted as *Death Is a Lover,* Spivak, 1953; *Death of an Intruder* (novel), Knopf, 1953; *Journey to Nowhere* (novel), Knopf, 1954; *Hall of Death* (novel), Simon & Schuster, 1960, reprinted as *Reformatory Girls,* Ace Books, 1962; *Everyone Suspect* (novel), Macmillan, 1964; *Twice So Far* (novel), Random House, 1971.

Work represented in anthologies, including *Ellery Queen's Searches and Seizures,* Davis Publications (New York), 1977; *Alfred Hitchcock's Tales to Scare You Stiff,* edited by Eleanor Sullivan, Davis Publications (New York), 1978; *Ellery Queen's Napoleons of Mystery,* Davis Publications (New York), 1978. Contributor of more than thirty stories to magazines, including *Ellery Queen's Mystery Magazine, Alfred Hitchcock's Mystery Magazine, Mystery Monthly, Signature,* and *Sleuth.*

SIDELIGHTS: Nedra Tyre wrote: "I've worked in offices, been a social worker, library assistant, clerk in a book department, done copy in an advertising agency, and taught sociology. I've done everything and it seems to me I've never made even minimum wage. Life is real and life is earnest, but most of all, it's ridiculous. Now I am a staff writer in an agency that gives financial assistance to desperately poor children in twenty-five countries.

"For the last four years I have been totally deaf. It's amazingly interesting to be deaf, though it's awkward socially. Politically I am what would be called a liberal and religiously I am a protestant with a small *p.* Almost everything defeats me and everything amazes me."

AVOCATIONAL INTERESTS: Painting (as a spectator), tours, reading.

U

UEHLING, Theodore Edward, Jr. 1935-

PERSONAL: Born July 31, 1935, in Scranton, Pa.; son of Theodore Edward (a business executive) and Ella Cuthbertson (Macmurrey) Uehling; married Anne Stewart Bevis (a writer), August 10, 1957; children: Theodore III, Thomas A., Trent S., Robert A. *Education:* Ohio State University, B.A., 1959; Ph.D., 1965. *Office:* Department of Philosophy, University of Minnesota, 207 Camden Hall, Morris, Minn. 56267.

CAREER: University of Minnesota, Morris, instructor, 1963-65, assistant professor, 1965-68, associate professor, 1968-72, professor of philosophy, 1972—. *Member:* American Philosophical Association, Australasian Association of Philosophy, Minnesota Philosophical Society.

WRITINGS: The Notion of Form in Kant's Critique of Aesthetic Judgment, Mouton, 1971; (editor with Peter A. French and Howard K. Wettstein) *Midwest Studies in Philosophy,* University of Minnesota Press, Volume I: *Studies in the History of Philosophy,* 1976, Volume II: *Studies in the Philosophy of Language,* 1977, Volume III: *Studies in Ethical Theory,* 1978, Volume IV: *Contemporary Perspectives in the Philosophy of Language,* 1979, Volume V: *Studies in Metaphysics,* 1979, Volume VI: *Studies in Epistemology,* 1980, Volume VII: *The Foundations of Analytic Philosophy,* 1981, Volume VIII: *Social and Political Philosophy,* 1982, Volume IX: *Contemporary Perspectives on the History of Philosophy,* in press.

Also author of *A Commentary to Kant's Prolegomena,* 1982, and *Kant: The Forgotten Principles,* in press.

*   *   *

ULLMAN, Leslie 1947-

PERSONAL: Born April 28, 1947, in Chicago, Ill.; daughter of Fredrick Ernest (a technical engineer) and Ann (Riegelman) Ullman; married Rush M. Rankin, June 21, 1975 (divorced, March, 1979). *Education:* Skidmore College, B.A., 1969; University of Iowa, M.F.A., 1974. *Home:* 4141 Westcity Court, No. 112, El Paso, Tex. 79902. *Agent:* Bill Thompson, Lordly & Dome, 51 Church St., Boston, Mass. 02116. *Office:* Creative Writing Program, University of Texas, El Paso, Tex. 79968.

CAREER: Mademoiselle, New York, N.Y., assistant to managing editor, 1969-70, guest editor, 1969; Bennington College, Bennington, Vt., managing editor of publications, 1970-72;

University of Missouri, Columbia, instructor in composition, 1974-75; William Jewell College, Liberty, Mo., lecturer in composition, 1975; Park College, Parkville, Mo., lecturer in creative writing, 1976-77; Ottawa University, Ottawa, Kan., lecturer in creative writing, 1978; University of Missouri, Kansas City, lecturer in creative writing, 1978-79; Baker University, Baldwin City, Kan., lecturer in creative writing, 1978-79; University of Texas, El Paso, poet-in-residence, 1979-80, associate professor of English, 1980—. Instructor at University of Iowa, summer, 1974; member of faculty at Goddard College, 1981—; member of summer workshop faculty at Bennington College, 1981—. Gives readings at colleges; guest on radio and television programs.

MEMBER: Associated Writing Programs. *Awards, honors:* Shared prize from *Mademoiselle* college poetry competition, 1969, for "Journey"; National Endowment for the Arts fellowship, 1976; award from "Series of Younger Poets," Yale University Press, 1978, for "Natural Histories"; new writers award from Great Lakes College Association, 1979, for "Natural Histories."

WRITINGS: Natural Histories (poems), Yale University Press, 1979.

Work represented in anthologies, including *Intro Number Six.* Contributor of poems, articles, and reviews to magazines and newspapers, including *New Yorker, Nation, Shenandoah, Epoch, Poetry Northwest* and *American Poetry Review.*

WORK IN PROGRESS: Another book of poems.

SIDELIGHTS: Leslie Ullman wrote: "I travel a lot to give readings. I like the communication between a real me and real people, and I like to talk about the difficulty and rewards of the *process* of writing—to de-mythologize it and make it more accessible."

BIOGRAPHICAL/CRITICAL SOURCES: American Poetry Review, January-February, 1981.

*   *   *

ULRICH, Carolyn F. 1881(?)-1970

OBITUARY NOTICE: Born c. 1881; died November 23, 1970, in Winter Park, Fla. Librarian and editor. Emeritus chief of the New York Public Library periodicals division, Ulrich was best known as originator and editor of *Ulrich's Periodical*

Directory. Obituaries and other sources: *AB Bookman's Weekly*, January 19, 1970.

*   *   *

UNAMUNO (y JUGO), Miguel de   1864-1936

BRIEF ENTRY: Born September 29, 1864, in Bilbao, Spain; died December 31, 1936, in Salamanca, Spain. Spanish educator, poet, novelist, and playwright. One of the greatest influences on Spanish letters, Unamuno was a man of many contradictions. As part of the generation that witnessed Spain's demise as a world power, the writer wondered about the nation's tragedy in addition to the tragedies of men. Unamuno's early writings were patterned in the Hegelian thesis-antithesis-synthesis tradition until, after experiencing a personal and religious crisis in 1897, the author changed his writing style from a deterministic bent to a pre-existential vision. Unamuno grew suspicious of reason, took an anguished view of man, and decided that virtue was attained by accepting God in spite of reason. Opposed to dogmatism, the writer was exiled for six years by the dictator Primo de Rivera and subsequently began to doubt whether he was primarily a writer or a politician. Condemned by the Church, he nevertheless accepted Spanish Catholicism to gain immortality, which he saw as the fundamental problem of men. Possessing the philosophical attitude of "creative doubt," Unamuno held a transcendental interpretation of life. His works, though tranquil, provoked thought. They generally dealt with doubt and religious faith or with man's personal immortality, which was the theme of Unamuno's principal poem, "El Cristo de Velazquez" (title means "The Velasquez Christ"). He ignored the norms of fiction and theatrical productions, but he loved and portrayed Castillian virtues and landscapes. His works include *Paz en la guerra* (1897; title means "Peace in War"), *Vida de Don Quijote y Sancho* (1905; title means "The Life of Don Quixote and Sancho"), and *La agonia del cristianismo* (1928; title means "The Agony of Christianity"). *Biographical/critical sources: Twentieth Century Writing: A Reader's Guide to Contemporary Literature*, Transatlantic, 1969; *Twentieth-Century Literary Criticism*, Volume 2, Gale, 1979.

*   *   *

UNDERWOOD, Peter   1923-

PERSONAL: Born May 16, 1923, in Letchworth, England; married wife, Joyce Elizabeth (an antique dealer), July 15, 1944; children: Christopher Paul, Pamela Anne. *Education:* Educated privately. *Home address:* c/o Savage Club, Berkeley Sq., London W.1, England. *Agent:* Andrew Hewson, John Johnson, Clerkenwell House, 45-47 Clerkenwell Green, London EC1R 0HT, England.

CAREER: J.M. Dent & Sons (book publishers), London, England, c. 1945-1971, production manager, 1966-71; writer, 1971—. Consultant to British Broadcasting Corp. *Military services:* British Army, Suffolk Regiment, 1942. *Member:* Society for Psychical Research, Ghost Club (president, 1960—), Unitarian Society for Psychical Studies (vice-president, 1969—), Savage Club (honorary librarian, 1974-79), Sesame Club, Constitutional Club (honorary librarian, 1968-74).

WRITINGS: A Gazetteer of British Ghosts, Souvenir Press, 1971; *Into the Occult*, Harrap, 1972; *Karloff*, Drake, 1972 (published in England as *Horror Man: The Life of Boris Karloff*, Frewin, 1972); *A Gazetteer of Scottish and Irish Ghosts*, Souvenir, Press, 1973, reprinted as *A Gazetter of Scottish Ghosts*, 1974; *Haunted London*, Photographs by Chris Underwood, Harrap, 1973; (with Paul Tabori) *The Ghosts of Borley: Annals*

of the Haunted Rectory, David & Charles, 1973; *A Host of Hauntings: A Shuddersome Book of Ghosts and Ghostly Adventures*, Frewin, 1973; *Life's a Drag: A Life of Danny La Rue*, Frewin, 1974; *Deeper Into the Occult*, Harrap, 1975; *The Vampire's Bedside Companion*, Frewin, 1975; (with Leonard Wilder) *Lives to Remember: A Casebook on Reincarnation*, R. Hale, 1975; *Hauntings*, Dent, 1977; (editor) *Thirteen Famous Ghost Stories*, Dent, 1977; *Ghosts of North West England*, Collins, 1978; *Dictionary of the Supernatural*, Harrap, 1978; *Ghosts of Wales*, Christopher Davies, 1978; *A Ghost Hunter's Handbook*, Hutchinson, 1980; *Complete Book of Dowsing and Divining*, Hutchinson, 1980; *Ghosts of Hampshire and the Isle of Wight*, St. Michael's Press, 1981.

WORK IN PROGRESS: Research for *International Who's Who of Ghosts; Haunted National Trust Properties*.

SIDELIGHTS: Underwood wrote: "A lifelong interest in ghosts and haunted houses, dating from school days when my grandparents lived in a haunted house, culminated in publication of the gazetteers, the first two comprehensive collections of Britain's hauntings ever compiled. I was literary executor to the Harry Price estate, 1974-77. I have made many television and radio broadcasts, several hundred over many years, including a four-hour television marathon in Madrid. I have lectured in most English universities and to fellow members of the Society for Psychical Research."

BIOGRAPHICAL/CRITICAL SOURCES: Bunte Deutsche, March 7, 1959; Paul Tabori and Phyllis Raphael, *Beyond the Senses*, Souvenir, 1971; *Merian*, November 11, 1977; Daniel Farson, *The Hamlyn Book of Ghosts*, Hamlyn, 1989; *TV Times*, March 4-10, 1978.

*   *   *

UNDSET, Sigrid   1882-1949

BRIEF ENTRY: Born May 20, 1882, in Kalundborg, Denmark; died after a stroke, June 10, 1949, in Lillehammer, Norway. Norwegian novelist. One of the most prominent Scandinavian novelists, Undset achieved widespread popularity with her third novel, *Jenny* (1911). In it she told of a sensitive, artistic young woman, her affair with an older man, and its tragic aftermath. While some critics found parts of the plot melodramatic and improbable, Undset's ability to render setting and character by the use of small but significant details drew praise. Undset's trilogy of historical novels, *Kristin Lavransdatter* (including *The Bridal Wreath*, 1920, *The Mistress of Husaby*, 1922, and *The Cross*, 1922) is considered her greatest work. It was praised for its vivid portrayal of medieval life and for its integration of convincing characters with its moralistic theme. "Undset knows how to project her ideals through living characters," Hanna Astrup Larsen noted. "They are never the puppets of her theories." In 1924 Undset converted to Catholicism, and her subsequent work is permeated by orthodox Catholic dogma. Critics found her use of religious themes effective and natural in the medieval settings of her historical novels such as the tetralogy *The Master of Hestviken* (1925-27). But in the contemporary settings of her later writings, many found the Catholic emphasis artificial and obtrusive and characters and settings less strikingly drawn. Undset's other works include *Gunnar's Daughter* (1909), *The Wild Orchid* (1929), and *The Faithful Wife* (1936). *Residence:* Lillehammer, Norway. *Biographical/critical sources: American-Scandinavian Review*, June, 1929, July, 1929; Sigrid Undset, *Return to the Future* (autobiography), Knopf, 1942; A. H. Winsnes, *Sigrid Undset: A Study in Christian Realism*, Sheed & Ward, 1953; Carl F. Bayerschmidt, *Sigrid Undset*, Twayne, 1970; *Twentieth-Century Literary Criticism*, Volume 3, Gale, 1980.

UPITS, Andrejs 1877-1970

OBITUARY NOTICE: Born December 5, 1887, in Skriveri, Latvia; died November 18, 1970, in Riga, Latvian Soviet Socialist Republic. Translator, literary critic, historian, and author. Upits's "Robezniek trilogy," which includes *Jauni avoti, Zida tikla,* and *Ziemela vejs,* is one of the best-known works in Latvian literature. The author of an eleven-volume history of Latvian and world literature as well as several historical novels, Upits was awarded a Soviet State prize for *Zala zeme* (title means "The Green Land"), an account of nineteenth-century Latvian village life. Among his other works are *Plaisa makonos* (title means "Break in the Clouds") and *Outside Paradise and Other Stories.* Obituaries and other sources: *AB Bookman's Weekly,* January 4, 1971; *Cassell's Encyclopaedia of World Literature,* revised edition, Morrow, 1973.

* * *

URRUTIA LLEO, Manuel 1901-1981

OBITUARY NOTICE: Born December 8, 1901, in Yaguajay, Las Villas Province, Cuba; died July 5, 1981, in Queens, N.Y. Lawyer, judge, educator, political leader, and author. A former judge, Urrutia became provisional president of Cuba on January 2, 1959, at the request of Fidel Castro, the leader of the rebel forces against President Fulgencio Batista's government. Inaugurated after a civil war that lasted two years, Urrutia was expected to govern for eighteen months to two years at which time free elections were to be held. In July, 1959, however, Castro publicly accused the president of treasonous actions and the latter was forced to resign. Urrutia maintained that his ouster was Castro's means of preventing the "neutralization of his own march toward Communism," and in order to set matters straight, the former president wrote the book *Fidel Castro and Company, Inc.: Communist Tyranny in Cuba.* Although he realized that many of Castro's supporters were Communists, Urrutia insisted that he had thought Castro himself was not. Eventually, he said, he came to believe that the leader of the Cuban uprising had been a Communist from the beginning and that he had used deception to accomplish his ends. After arriving in the United States in 1963, Urrutia became a university professor, teaching at several institutions. Obituaries and other sources: *Current Biography,* Wilson, 1959; *New York Times,* July 6, 1981.

* * *

USBORNE, Richard Alexander 1910-

PERSONAL: Born May 16, 1910, in India (now Pakistan); son of Charles Frederick (a civil servant) and Janet (Lefroy) Usborne; married Monica MacArthur, April 19, 1938; children: David Stuart MacArthur, Karen Elizabeth. *Education:* Received B.A. (with honors) from Balliol College, Oxford. *Politics:* Socialist. *Religion:* Church of England. *Home:* Fenton House, Windmill Hill, London N.W.3, England. *Agent:* A. D. Peters & Co. Ltd., 10 Buckingham St., London WC2N 6BU, England.

CAREER: Worked for advertising agencies, 1933-1936; *London Week,* London, England, co-owner and editor, 1936-37; London Press Exchange, 1937-39; British Broadcasting Corp. Monitoring Service, 1939-41; *Strand,* assistant editor, 1947-50; Graham & Gillies Advertising Agency, London director, 1962-70. Book critic for British Broadcasting Corp., 1950—. Custodian of National Trust. *Military service:* British Army, 1941-45; became major.

WRITINGS: Clubland Heroes: A Nostalgic Study of Some Recurrent Characters in the Romantic Fiction of Donford Yates, John Buchan and Sapper, Costable, 1953, revised edition, Barrie & Jenkins, 1974; *Wodehouse at Work,* Barrie & Jenkins, 1961, revised edition published as *Wodehouse at Work to the End,* 1977; (editor) *A Century of Summer Fields,* Eyre Methuen, 1964; (editor) *Vintage Wodehouse,* Barrie & Jenkins, 1973; (editor) P. G. Wodehouse, *Sunset at Blandings* (novel), Chatto & Windus, 1977; *A Wodehouse Companion,* 1981. Adapted Wodehouse's novels for series, "What Ho, Jeeves!," on BBC-Radio. Contributor to newspapers.

AVOCATIONAL INTERESTS: Reading and writing verse.

V

VACCARO, Joseph P(ascal) 1935-

PERSONAL: Born February 7, 1935, in Cambridge, Mass.; son of Orazio E. (a social worker) and Margaret (Grosso) Vaccaro; married Patricia A. Murphy, June 29, 1963; children: Paul J., Anne M., Theresa M., Rose P. *Education:* Boston College, B.S.B.A., 1957; Suffolk University, M.B.A., 1969, J.D., 1976. *Home:* 36 Oakwood Rd., Auburndale, Mass. 02166. *Office:* Department of Marketing, School of Management, Suffolk University, Boston, Mass. 02114.

CAREER: J. M. Fields, Natick, Mass., member of executive training program, 1957; Prince Leaning Tower of Pizza, Somerville, Mass., and West Yarmouth, Mass., manager, 1959-60; Vaccaro's Iron Rail Restaurant, Waltham, Mass., owner and manager, 1961-66; Burdett College, Boston, Mass., instructor in marketing and management, 1966-71; Suffolk University, Boston, Mass., assistant professor of marketing, 1971—. Marketing researcher and analyst for businesses, colleges, and industry. *Military service:* U.S. Army, 1957-59.

MEMBER: American Academy of Marketing, American Marketing Association, American Advertising Federation, Delta Sigma Pi, Auburndale Community Association, Corpus Christi Holy Name Society (past president), Newton Junior Chamber of Commerce (past president), Newton High School Alumni Association, Boston College Alumni Association, Suffolk University Alumni Association. *Awards, honors:* Certificates of recognition from American Marketing Association, 1971-80, for "advancing the discipline of marketing," and Massachusetts Press Association, 1975.

WRITINGS: Decision-Making With Cases in Marketing, Prentice-Hall, 1971; *Consumer Behavior Cases: A Marketing Management Approach,* Interface Press, 1977; *Marketing Management Cases,* Alfred Publishing, 1982.

WORK IN PROGRESS: Sales Management, publication expected in 1983.

SIDELIGHTS: Vaccaro told *CA:* "I write textbooks for one main reason: to become a better teacher to my students. Nothing is more gratifying to a teacher than successfully arousing in the alert minds of students the curiosity of searching for the truth. An indication of their interest and desire to face and solve problems is shown by their questions during class discussions and after class. Teaching is much like marketing; we have a product to sell—knowledge and its use. I therefore write with the pragmatic approach in mind leading students in case work, reading in their field, as well as textual material to ultimately reach my goal."

*   *   *

VAILLANCOURT, Pauline M(ariette)

PERSONAL: Born in Fall River, Mass.; daughter of Leo E. and Rhea (Godbout) Vaillancourt. *Education:* St. John's University, Jamaica, N.Y., B.S.; Columbia University, M.S.L.S., 1953, D.L.S., 1968. *Religion:* Roman Catholic. *Residence:* Albany, N.Y. *Office:* School of Library and Information Science, State University of New York at Albany, Albany, N.Y. 12222.

CAREER: Mary Immaculate Hospital, Jamaica, N.Y., nursing librarian, 1952-58; Kings Park State Hospital, Kings Park, N.Y., chief librarian, 1958-60; library directory of Memorial Sloan-Kettering Cancer Center, 1960-68; consultant, 1968-70; State University of New York at Albany, associate professor of library science, 1970—. Visiting associate professor of library science at Washington University, summer, 1975, and McGill University, summer, 1978; consultant and visiting professor at National University of Mexico, 1976. Member of Albany Area Health Library Affiliates, 1974—; member of board of directors of National Commission on Libraries and Information Sciences, 1974-75; member of advisory committee of Hudson Valley Community College, 1973-76, 1977-80, chairman of committee, 1975-76.

MEMBER: American Library Association, Special Libraries Association (chairman of biological sciences group, 1951-52; chairman of education committee, 1974-77), Medical Library Association (chairman of education interest group, 1974-75), Association of American Library Schools (chairman of continuing education committee, 1977-79), American Association for the Advancement of Science, American Chemical Society, New York Academy of Sciences (member of advisory committee of section on computer and information science, 1970-74), New York Library Club (member of council, 1964-68).

WRITINGS: Bibliographic Control of the Literature of Oncology, 1800-1960, Scarecrow, 1969; *Institute for Health Care Libraries: Training of Personnel,* ERIC Clearinghouse, 1975; *International Dictionary of Acronyms in Library, Information, and Computer Science,* Bowker, 1980. Contributor of about thirty-five articles and reviews to library and information science journals. Editor of *Scientific Information Notes,* 1969-70.

WORK IN PROGRESS: Various studies in Latin American library education for publication as journal articles.

SIDELIGHTS: Vaillancourt told *CA:* "My first trip abroad was a gift on completion of my master's degree and lasted seven weeks, including attendance at my first international conference in London, a Papal audience in Rome, a lucky trip to Monoco where I won the money for my first gold charm at roulette, and an excellent assortment of photographs which made recall of the trip relatively easy, especially since it was accompanied by the most detailed diary that I have ever kept of travels.

"My second trip was during the course of completing my doctoral dissertation and was both a pleasure trip and a working trip and included visits to several cancer libraries, where the chiefs were most friendly, cordial, and helpful. Many of them also served as hosts inviting me to their homes. This trip covered seven countries, and my diaries were coupled with cassette recordings to supplement details that I would later need.

"A conference in California afforded the opportunity to visit American cancer centers in Houston and other cities for the dissertation on *Bibliographic Control of the Literature of Oncology, 1800-1960,* which was subsequently published. I had the good fortune of having the famous Ralph Shaw, founder of library schools at Rutgers and University of Hawaii, as my editor. It was interesting to receive copy from him marked with cigarette burns and suggesting changes which I had originally had in the earlier drafts of my dissertation but which had been changed by the authorities on my committee! This resulted in my first book, the revision of my doctoral dissertation, bibliographic research which took eight years during which time I was employed in a very demanding administrative position.

"My professional writing began early in my professional career. My first substantial article, at the invitation of Estelle Broadman, then editor of the *Bulletin of the Medical Library Association* was also in a referred journal. This was on the subject of nursing libraries in which I was employed at the time.

"Later writings dealt with integrating libraries, internship as a means of library education, continuing education for librarians, and Latin American library education, especially in regard to medical librarianship. Some of these articles were previously read at international conferences, one in the Philippines at the International Association for Agricultural Librarians and Documentalists (March, 1980; later published in the *UNESCO Journal for Librarians and Information Scientists and Documentalists*), another two papers at the International Medical Library Congress in Yugoslavia in August, 1980.

"Travel by ship is a particular joy of mine, especially on the lovely luxury cruise ships. Other forms that I have enjoyed include returning from Seattle by way of western Canada by train; driving to the South in winter vacations; short bus trips; flying for long distances; perhaps, some day, a freighter trip (especially on one of the larger ones). Perhaps that might provide the time and relaxation to consider a different kind of writing: a novel!!''

*   *   *

VALERY, Paul (Ambroise Toussaint Jules) 1871-1945

BRIEF ENTRY: Born October 30, 1871, in Cette (now Sete), France; died of heart disease, July 20, 1945, in Paris, France. French poet, critic, and essayist. A man of diverse interests, Valery first became known as a poet of the symbolist school associated with Stephane Mallarme, Andre Gide, and Pierre Louys. In 1892, after an emotional and intellectual crisis, Valery gave up poetry and dedicated himself to mathematics, science, and philosophy, focusing on inquiry into the nature of mental processes. In 1912, at Gide's request, Valery agreed to revise his early poems for collection; in the process he began a new poem, "La Jeune Parque," which was not finished until 1917. It is considered one of the great masterpieces of French verse and immediately made Valery a major literary figure. Like all his poems, it is noted for its classical form, sensuous imagery, and brilliant metrical effects; it has also been called "the most obscure poem in French." After writing the volume of poetry *Charmes* (1922), Valery again abandoned poetry for essays, writing on a wide variety of topics, including architecture, the arts, history, and politics. He developed a theory of poetry that excluded inspiration, insisting that technique alone was sufficient for the process of creation. His ideas have been controversial, but their importance has been acknowledged even by Valery's detractors. Valery was elected to the French Academy in 1925. His works include *An Evening with Mr. Teste* (1919), *Variete I-V* (1924-44), *Reflections on the World Today* (1931), and *L'Idee fixe* (1932). *Residence:* Paris, France. *Biographical/critical sources:* C. M. Bowra, *The Heritage of Symbolism,* Macmillan, 1943; *New York Times Book Review,* May 7, 1950; Elizabeth Sewell, *Paul Valery: The Mind in the Mirror,* Yale University Press, 1952; *Twentieth Century Authors: A Biographical Dictionary of Modern Literature,* 1st supplement, H. W. Wilson, 1955; *Hudson Review,* autumn, 1969; *Twentieth-Century Literary Criticism,* Volume 4, Gale, 1981.

*   *   *

VAN CASPEL, Venita 1922-

PERSONAL: Born October 3, 1922, in Sweetwater, Okla.; daughter of Leonard (in sales) and Ella Belle (Jarnagin) Walker; married Charles Nehring (deceased). *Education:* Attended Duke University, 1944-46; University of Colorado, B.A., 1948, graduate study, 1949-51; further graduate study at New York Institute of Finance, 1962. *Politics:* Republican. *Religion:* Presbyterian. *Home:* 165 Sage Rd., Houston, Tex. 77056. *Office:* Van Caspel & Co., Inc., 1540 Post Oak Tower, Houston, Tex. 77056.

CAREER: Kirby Petroleum/Carter Oil & Gas, Houston, Tex., executive assistant, 1951-58; Rauscher Pierce, Houston, stockbroker, 1962-65; A. G. Edwards, Houston, stockbroker, 1965-68; Van Caspel & Co., Inc. (stockbrokers, financial planners, and insurance agents), Houston, president, 1968—. Member of Pacific Stock Exchange. Member of board of directors of West Loop National Bank and Greater Houston Convention Council; member of Billy Graham Crusade Committee. *Member:* International Association of Financial Planners (member of board of directors), Institute of Certified Financial Planners, Phi Beta Kappa, University Club, Houstonian Club. *Awards, honors:* Outstanding woman award from Young Women's Christian Association, 1981; Matrix Award.

WRITINGS: Money Dynamics, Reston, 1975; *The New Money Dynamics,* Reston, 1978; *Money Dynamics for the 1980's,* Reston, 1980. Contributor to magazines, including *Money Maker, Working Woman, Success Unlimited, National Tax Shelter Digest,* and tax and financial planning journals.

WORK IN PROGRESS: Articles for *Next Magazine, Financial Planner Magazine, Working Woman,* and *National Tax Shelter Digest.*

SIDELIGHTS: Van Caspel told *CA:* "My desire is to help everyone that attends my seminars or reads my books to become financially independent. We are raising a nation of financial illiterates. We are spending millions to teach our youth how to earn dollars but nothing to teach them what to do with money, and they are making some terrible mistakes. Consequently, of every one hundred of our citizens who reach sixty-five, only two are financially independent, twenty-three must continue to work, and seventy-five are dependent on friends, charity, or relatives. This is a tragedy I'm striving to prevent by writing books on financial planning in lay language. My books are designed to educate, inspire, and motivate.''

AVOCATIONAL INTERESTS: Listening to tapes, nutrition, physical fitness, psychology.

BIOGRAPHICAL/CRITICAL SOURCES: New York Times, March 10, 1981.

* * *

Van der ZEE, James (Augustus Joseph) 1886-

PERSONAL: Born June 29, 1886, in Lenox, Mass.; son of John (a butler) and Elizabeth (a maid) Van der Zee; married Kate Brown, 1906 (deceased); married Gaynella Greenlee, 1920 (deceased); married Donna Mussenden, June 15, 1978; children: (first marriage) Rachael (deceased), Emil (deceased). *Education:* Attended Carlton Conservatory, 1906. *Home:* 220 West 93rd St., New York, N.Y. 10025.

CAREER: Gertz Department Store, Newark, N.J., darkroom developer, 1907; first violinist with John Wanamaker Orchestra; Guarantee Photo Studio, New York City, owner, 1918-32; GGG Photo Studio, New York City, owner, 1932-71; photographer and writer, 1971—. Photographs exhibited in museums and private collections, including Metropolitan Museum of Art. *Awards, honors:* Pierre Toussaint Award, 1978; Living Legacy Award from president of the United States, 1979; award from American Society of Magazine Photographers.

WRITINGS—With own photographs: *The World of James Van der Zee,* Grove, 1969; *James Van der Zee* (edited by Liliane De Cock and Reginald McGhee), Morgan & Morgan, 1973; (with Owen Dodson and Camille Billops) *The Harlem Book of the Dead,* Morgan & Morgan, 1978. Also author of *Harlem on My Mind,* 1969, revised edition, 1979, and *James Van der Zee: The Picture Takin' Man,* 1979.

BIOGRAPHICAL/CRITICAL SOURCES: New York Times, October 17, 1971.*

* * *

Van DRUTEN, John (William) 1901-1957

BRIEF ENTRY: Born June 1, 1901; died in 1957. British-born American director and playwright. Van Druten wrote several successful Broadway plays that were later produced as motion pictures, including *Leave Her to Heaven* (1940), *The Voice of the Turtle* (1944), *I Remember Mama* (1945), and *I Am a Camera* (1952), an adaptation of Christopher Isherwood's *Berlin Stories. I Am a Camera,* winner of the Drama Critics Circle Award in 1952, was later produced as the popular stage musical and motion picture ''Cabaret.'' Van Druten is also remembered as the director of the Rodgers and Hammerstein musical *The King and I. Residence:* Thermal, Calif. *Biographical/critical sources: Current Biography,* Wilson, 1944; *New York Times Book Review,* January 25, 1953; John Van Druten, *Playwright at Work,* Harper, 1953; Van Druten, *The Widening Circle,* Scribner, 1957; *Twentieth Century Writing: A Reader's Guide to Contemporary Literature,* Transatlantic, 1969; *Twentieth-Century Literary Criticism,* Volume 2, Gale, 1979.

Van SERTIMA, Ivan 1935-

PERSONAL: Born January 26, 1935, in Kitty Village, Guyana; came to the United States in 1970; son of Frank Obermuller (an administrator and trade union leader) and Clara (Smith) Van Sertima; married Maria Nagy, October 24, 1964; children: Lawrence Josef. *Education:* London School of Oriental and African Studies, London, B.A. (with honors), 1969; Rutgers University, M.A., 1977. *Home:* 59 South Adelaide Ave., Highland Park, N.J. 08904. *Office:* Department of Africana Studies, Douglass College, Rutgers University, New Brunswick, N.J. 08904.

CAREER: Government Information Services (Guyana Civil Service), Georgetown, Guyana, press and broadcasting officer, 1956-59; Central Office of Information, London, England, broadcaster, 1960-70; Rutgers University, Douglass College, New Brunswick, N.J., instructor, 1970-72, assistant professor, 1972-79, associate professor of African studies, 1978—. Nominator for Nobel Prize in Literature, 1976-80. President of *Journal of African Civilizations* Ltd. Inc. *Member:* African Heritage Association, American Association of University Professors. *Awards, honors:* Clarence L. Holte Prize from Twenty-First Century Foundation, 1981, for *They Came Before Columbus.*

WRITINGS: River and the Wall, Miniature Poets, 1958; *Caribbean Writers,* New Beacon Books, 1968; *Swahili Dictionary of Legal Terms,* Tanzania, 1968; *They Came Before Columbus: The African Presence in Ancient America* (Book-of-the-Month Club selection), Random House, 1977.

Contributor: Rhoda Goldstein, editor, *Black Life and Culture in the United States,* Crowell, 1971; Anna Rutherford, editor, *Enigma of Values,* Dangaroo Press, 1975; Tom Trebasso, editor, *Seminar in Black English,* Lawrence Erlbaum Associates, 1976. Contributor to journals.

Editor of *Journal of African Civilizations.*

WORK IN PROGRESS: Research on the African presence in the art of the Americas.

SIDELIGHTS: Van Sertima's languages include Hungarian and Swahili. He wrote: ''The single greatest influence on my thought and life are the works of the novelist Wilson Harris. I consider his novels the most important now emerging from the English-speaking world.''

BIOGRAPHICAL/CRITICAL SOURCES: Washington Post, May 1, 1977; *New York Times,* May 8, 1977.

* * *

VAN SLYKE, Donald Dexter 1883-1971

OBITUARY NOTICE: Born March 29, 1883, in Pike, N.Y.; died of cancer, May 4, 1971, in Garden City, Long Island, N.Y. Biological chemist and author. Van Slyke was best known for his studies on acidosis, which revolutionized the treatment of diabetes, and for his studies of kidney diseases. At the time of his death, Van Slyke was senior scientist emeritus at the Brookhaven National Laboratory and professor emeritus of the Rockefeller University. The author or co-author of six books and nearly five hundred scientific papers, Van Slyke was internationally recognized for his discoveries in chemistry, physiology, and medicine. He received fourteen international scientific awards, including the Willard Gibbs Medal of the American Chemical Society, the Kober Medal of the Association of American Physicians, the First Scientific Achievement

Award of the American Medical Association, and the National Medal of Science of the United States. In addition, he held honorary memberships in thirteen foreign and six domestic scientific societies and academies, and he was awarded five foreign decorations. From 1914 to 1924 Van Slyke was managing editor of the *Journal of Biological Chemistry*. A textbook he co-authored, *Quantitative Clinical Chemistry*, is used extensively by medical students and biochemical investigators throughout the world. Obituaries and other sources: *Current Biography*, Wilson, 1943; *New York Times*, May 6, 1971; *Time*, May 17, 1971; *Publishers Weekly*, May 24, 1971.

*   *   *

VARDAMAN, James M(oney)   1921-

PERSONAL: Born June 1, 1921, in Memphis, Tenn.; son of James Money and Martha (Middleton) Vardaman; married Virginia Bradley; children: James M., Jr., John Bradley, Virginia Kimble, Stewart Wynne, Emily Money, David Middleton, Sally Wolfe. *Education:* Attended University of Virginia, 1938-40; University of Michigan, B.S., 1942. *Home:* 5346 Farnsworth, Jackson, Miss. 39211. *Office address:* P.O. Drawer 22766, Jackson, Miss. 39205.

CAREER: Forester near Memphis, Tenn., 1946-47; Hobac Veneer and Lumber Co., Caruthersville, Mo., forester, 1947-48; Masonite Corp., Laurel, Miss., district forester, 1948-51; James M. Vardaman & Co. (consulting foresters), Laurel, founder and owner, 1951-61; James M. Vardaman & Co., Jackson, Miss., owner, 1961-67, partner, 1967-69, president, 1970—. Member of board of directors of Mississippi Bank, Jackson, 1973. Licensed forester and real estate broker. *Military service:* U.S. Army, Armored Division, 1942-46; served in European theater; became captain; received Silver Star, Purple Heart, and five battle stars. *Member:* Society of American Foresters, American Forestry Association, Forest Farmers Association, Mississippi Forestry Association (president, 1970).

WRITINGS: Tree Farm Business Management, Ronald, 1965, revised edition, 1978; *How to Make Money Growing Trees*, privately printed, 1967; *Call Collect, Ask for Birdman* (nonfiction), St. Martin's, 1980. Contributor to trade magazines and newspapers.

SIDELIGHTS: Vardaman told *CA:* "My forestry work is concentrated on management of small tracts (less than four thousand acres), owned by private individuals, in the eastern United States. We have full-time, professional staffs at thirty-five branch offices in eleven states from Texas to Virginia, and our firm is the largest of its kind in the United States. We have the highest respect for the collective wisdom of these private landowners; in our opinion, they know much more about how to handle the timberlands of our country than does any conceivable array of government and business entities.

"Birding has been my hobby since I joined the Boy Scouts in 1933, and the bird book is the story of 1979, a year spent doing what I had always wanted to do. Birding got me in the right business for the wrong reason. I entered forestry as a teenager because I thought it was mostly birding, whereas, as an adult, I have always been fascinated by the economic aspects of forestry."

*   *   *

VAUGHN, Toni
See Du BREUIL, (Elizabeth) L(or)inda

VEDER, Bob   1940-

PERSONAL: Surname is pronounced *Vee*-der; born May 6, 1940; son of Morris (a concert violinst) and Mary (a teacher; maiden name, Hyman) Veder; married Tina Cristiani (a restorer of carousel carvings), September 28, 1979; children: Sean, Ryan, Rivka. *Education:* Hunter College of the City University of New York, A.B., 1965. *Religion:* "Messianic Jew/Born-Again Christian." *Home:* 70 Gateway Rd., Yonkers, N.Y. 10703. *Agent:* Nat Sobel, 128 East 56th St., New York, N.Y. 10022. *Office:* Grey Advertising, 777 Third Ave., New York, N.Y. 10017.

CAREER: Grey Advertising, New York, N.Y., vice-president and creative supervisor, 1970—. *Military service:* U.S. Navy, 1957-61.

WRITINGS: Play With Fire, Simon & Schuster, 1980. Contributor of stories to magazines, including *Northwest Review, Descant, Chelsea Review, Forum, Colorado Quarterly*, and *Prairie Schooner*.

WORK IN PROGRESS: A novel, tentatively titled *Ordnueng*, set in Germany in 1938.

SIDELIGHTS: Veder told *CA:* "All writing should teach. Unfortunately, too many writers use books to make the reader love or hate or enjoy the writer, instead of the characters. The writer should be subordinate to the characters.

"*Ordnueng* is about Jews and Nazis in Hitler's first experimental death camp, set just after the 'Crystal Night' of November, 1938."

BIOGRAPHICAL/CRITICAL SOURCES: Washington Post Book World, January 4, 1981.

*   *   *

VERGA, Giovanni   1840-1922

BRIEF ENTRY: Born September 2, 1840, in Catania, Sicily; died January 27, 1922, in Catania, Sicily. Italian novelist, short story writer, and playwright. Verga is known as "the father of the modern realist novel" and is considered one of the greatest Italian novelists. His early books were melodramatic historical novels of adultery and duels among the aristocracy; they were popular, but of slight literary value. His first use of the subject matter and style for which he is remembered was in "Nedda" (1874), a short story about a Sicilian peasant girl. But it was not until 1881 that he published *The House by the Medlar-Tree*, his first realistic novel. In it he told the story of the destruction of a peasant family, using simple language close to peasant dialect. Verga attempted to eliminate the authorial presence, letting his characters tell the story and the subject matter dictate its form. He planned a series of novels entitled *The Defeated*, which would realistically portray all levels of Italian society; only two of the five books were completed. Verga also applied his realistic, or "veristic," method to the theatre, writing several successful plays. His works include *Eva* (1873), *Il marito di Elena* (1882), *Little Novels of Sicily* (1883), *Cavalleria Rusticana* (1884), and *Master Don Gesualdo* (1889). *Residence:* Catania, Sicily. *Biographical/critical sources:* D. H. Lawrence, *Phoenix: The Posthumous Papers of D. H. Lawrence*, Viking, 1936; *New Republic*, January 11, 1954; *Cyclopedia of World Authors*, Harper, 1958; *Encyclopedia of World Literature in the Twentieth Century*, Ungar, 1967; Alfred Alexander, *Giovanni Verga: A Great Writer and His Work*, Grant & Cutler, 1972; *Twentieth-Century Literary Criticism*, Volume 3, Gale, 1981.

VERNEY, Stephen Edmund 1919-

PERSONAL: Born April 17, 1919, in Claydon, England; son of Harry Calvert and Rachel (Bruce) Verney; married Priscilla Schwerdt, December 13, 1947 (deceased); children: Robin, Rachel, Helen, Katharine. *Education:* Balliol College, Oxford, M.A., 1948; attended Westcott House Theological College, 1948-50. *Home:* Repton House, Lea, Matlock, Derbyshire, England.

CAREER: Ordained minister of Church of England, 1950; curate of Church of England in Nottingham, England, 1950-52; priest in charge and first vicar of Church of England in Clifton, England, 1952-58; vicar of Church of England in Leamington Hastings, England, 1958-64; canon of Coventry Cathedral, Conventry, England, 1964-70, and St. George's, Windsor, England, 1970-77; bishop of Repton, England, 1977—. *Military service:* Friends Ambulance Unit, 1939-43. British Army, Intelligence Corps, 1943-46; served in Greece; became captain; member of Order of the British Empire.

WRITINGS: Fire in Coventry, Hodder & Stoughton, 1964; (with others) *People and Cities,* Revell, 1969; *Into the New Age,* Fontana, 1976.

WORK IN PROGRESS: St. John's Gospel, publication by Collins expected in 1983.

SIDELIGHTS: Verney wrote: "There is a need to rediscover the Judaeo-Christian tradition in the context of today, to rediscover, above all, the key word of that tradition—repentance. It means a change of mind—new consciousness—coming to see, feel, desire, choose differently. It means to know God. It is a gift, which man can only ask for and wait for."

*   *   *

VERNON, Lee M.
See von BLOCK, Bela W(illiam)

*   *   *

VESEY-FitzGERALD, Brian Seymour 1900-

PERSONAL: Born July 5, 1900, in Wrexham, Wales; son of Percy Seymour and Mary Brigid (Jones) Vesey-FitzGerald; married Amy Catherine Nash, September 12, 1930 (died, 1960); married Mary Julius Hunt, October 7, 1961. *Education:* Attended Keble College, Oxford. *Home:* Long Croft, Wrecclesham, Surrey, England. *Agent:* Laurence Pollinger Ltd., 18 Maddox St., London W1R OEU, England.

CAREER: Worked as journalist for Reuters News Agency; *Field,* 1938-46, began as naturalist editor, became editor-in-chief; County Books, editor, beginning 1946; naturalist and writer. Broadcast radio programs "Field Fare," 1940-45, and "There and Back," 1947-49. *Member:* British Ornithologists Union, Royal Entomological Society (fellow), Linnean Society (fellow), Royal Society of Arts (fellow), Gypsy Lore Society, Institute for the Study of Animal Behaviour, Association of School Natural History Societies (chairman, 1947-48), British Fairground Society (president, 1953-63), Gamekeepers Association (vice-president), Honourable Society of Cymmprodorion.

WRITINGS: A Book of British Waders, Collins, 1939; *Hampshire Scene,* Methuen, 1940; (editor) *Programme for Agriculture,* M. Joseph, 1941; *A Country Chronicle,* Chapman & Hall, 1942; *Hedgerow and Field,* Chapman & Hall, 1943, 2nd edition, 1949; *Gypsies of Britain: An Introduction to Their History,* Chapman & Hall, 1944, revised edition, David & Charles, 1973; *The British Countryside in Pictures,* Odhams,

1946; (editor) *The Book of the Horse,* Nicholson & Watson, 1946, Borden Publishing, 1947; *British Game,* Collins, 1946; *A Child's Biology,* Cassell, 1947; *It's My Delight,* Eyre & Spottiswoode, 1947; *Background to Birds,* Cassell, 1948; *Bird Biology for Beginners,* Cassell, 1948; (editor) *The Book of the Dog,* Nicholson & Watson, 1948; *British Bats,* Methuen, 1948; *Hampshire and the Isle of Wight,* R. Hale, 1949; *Rivermouth,* Eyre & Spottiswoode, 1949; (editor with Francesca Raimonde Lamonte) *Game Fish of the World,* Harper, 1949.

The Hampshire Avon, Cassell, 1950; (author of introduction) *English Villages in Pictures,* Odhams, 1951, Norton, 1960; *British Birds and Their Nests,* Wills & Hepworth, 1953; *Gypsy Borrow,* Dobson, 1953; *Winchester,* Phoenix House, 1953; *A Second Book of British Birds and Their Nests,* Wills & Hepworth, 1954; *The Nature Lover's Recognition Book,* Odhams, 1956; *A Third Book of British Birds and Their Nests,* Wills & Hepworth, 1956; *The Ladybird Book of British Wild Flowers,* Wills & Hepworth, 1957; *The Domestic Dog: An Introduction to Its History,* Routledge & Kegan Paul, 1957; *Cats,* Penguin, 1957; (author of introduction) *Historic Towns of England in Pictures,* Odhams, 1957, Norton, 1960; *Mammals* (juvenile) Museum Press, 1958.

The Ladybird Book of Garden Flowers, Wills & Hepworth, 1960; *Odhams Wonder-World of Knowledge in Colour,* Odhams, 1961; *The Ladybird Book of Trees,* Wills & Hepworth, 1963; *About Dogs,* Faber, 1963; *The Cat Owner's Encyclopaedia,* Pelham Books, 1963, House & Maxwell, 1964; (editor and author of introduction) *Best Animal Stories,* Faber, 1965; (editor) *Animal Anthology,* George Newnes, 1965; *Town Fox, Country Fox,* Deutsch, 1965; *Portrait of the New Forest,* R. Hale, 1966, 2nd edition, 1977; *Garden Alive,* Studio Vista, 1967; *Enquire Within About Animals,* Pelham Books, 1967; *The World of Fishes,* Pelham Books, 1968; *The World of Reptiles,* Pelham Books, 1968; *The Domestic Cat,* Pelham Books, 1969; *The Vanishing Wild Life of Britain,* MacGibbon & Kee, 1969; *The World of Ants, Bees, and Wasps,* Pelham Books, 1969.

Also author of *Amateur Boxing,* 1936, *Professional Boxing,* 1936, *Badgers Funeral,* 1937, *The Noctule,* 1941, *Farming in Britain,* 1942, *Field Fare,* 1942, *The River Avon,* 1951, *Borrow in Britain,* 1953, *Nature Recognition,* 1955, *Instructions to Young Naturalists,* 1959, *Foxes in Britain,* 1964, *The Dog Owner's Encyclopaedia,* 1965. General editor of "Regional Books Series," R. Hale, and "Faber Sporting Handbooks," Faber. Contributor to scientific journals.

BIOGRAPHICAL/CRITICAL SOURCES: Spectator, June 21, 1969.*

*   *   *

VETERE, Richard 1952-

PERSONAL: Born January 15, 1952, in New York, N.Y.; son of Albert (a clerk) and Angelina (Guiliano) Vetere. *Education:* St. John's University, Jamaica, N.Y., B.A., 1973; Columbia University, M.A., 1974. *Home:* 53-40 62nd St., Maspeth, N.Y. 11378. *Agent:* Fifi Oscard & Associates, Inc., 19 West 44th St., New York, N.Y. 10036. *Office:* Writing Co., 155-17 Sanford Ave., Flushing, N.Y. 11355.

CAREER: Queens Council on the Arts, New York City, literary chairman, 1975-78; Cultural Council Foundation/Comprehensive Employment Training Act (CETA), New York City, writer, 1978-80; free-lance writer, 1980—. Playwright-in-residence at Actors Studio. *Member:* Poetry Society of America, Dramatists Guild, Poets and Writers. *Awards, honors:* grants from

Mary Roberts Rinehart Foundation, 1977, Writing Center, 1978, and Coordinating Council of Literary Magazines, 1976-77, 1978-79.

WRITINGS: Memories of Human Hands (poems), Manyland Books, 1976; *The Last Detective* (novella), Seagull, 1978.

Plays: "Nero" (two-act), first produced in New York City at Nighthouse Theatre, 1974; "Hadrian's Hill" (two-act), first produced in New York City at Provincetown Playhouse, 1975; "Night Over the Tiber" (two-act), first produced in New York City at Provincetown Playhouse, 1976; "Rockaway Boulevard" (two-act), first produced in New York City at Actors Studio, 1978; "Johnny on the Pony" (two-act), first produced in New York City at Actors Studio, 1979; "The New Living Newspaper, Volume I, Number 2" (two-act), first produced in New York City, 1979; "Brooklyn Voices" (one-act), first produced in New York City at New York Technical College, 1980. Also author of "Paradise" (two-act) and "Joey 'No Talk'" (two-act).

Films: "Nuts and Bolts," Legend Films/CBS Records, 1979; "A Night to Dismember," American/East End Films, 1981; "Downtown," East End Films, to be released; "Vigilante," Magnum Motion Pictures, to be released.

Librettos for operas: "The First Born," first produced in New York City at Cami Theater; "A Letter," first produced in New York City at Cami Theater; "The Forgotten," first produced in New York City at Cami Theater, 1977.

Work represented in anthologies, including *East Coast Writers Anthology*, East Coast Writers, 1976; *Words to Go Anthology*, Cultural Council Foundation, 1980. Also author of *Maniac*, a novelization of a feature film. Contributor to literary journals. Editor-in-chief of *Source*, 1976-79, contributing editor, 1979-80.

WORK IN PROGRESS: The Capitalists, a novel; *Dead Body*, poems; *Poetry and American Capitalism*, nonfiction; "The Arrogance of a Fat Man," a play.

SIDELIGHTS: Vetere wrote: "I am currently doing films, plays, fiction, and poetry. I earn a nice living from it and I am still in my twenties. I want my career to show that a serious writer can make a living in this country and still be able to contribute to literature.

"For several years I have been committed to the realities of the working class, since I see in their lives real drama and conflict. I also seem to be most successful in this area commercially and critically. My poetry, however, has somewhat different aims and is not limited to urban and/or the New York City area. Ideas and emotions generate the force behind my work, sometimes coming from literature, painting, and life, but generally and always from my own heart and mind."

BIOGRAPHICAL/CRITICAL SOURCES: Village Voice, December 22, 1975, September 11, 1978; *New York Daily News*, August 8, 1978; *Show Business*, January 4, 1979; *New York Times*, January 17, 1980; *Backstage*, February 15, 1980.

*   *   *

VIGLIANTE, Mary
    See SZYDLOWSKI, Mary Vigliante

*   *   *

VILMORIN, Louise Leveque de   1902-1969

OBITUARY NOTICE: Born in 1902; died of a heart attack,

December 26, 1969, in a suburb of Paris, France. Poet, painter, and author best known for her novels. Her books include *Julietta, Erica's Return*, and *Madame De*. Obituaries and other sources: *Publishers Weekly*, January 12, 1970.

*   *   *

VINCIGUERRA, Mario   1887-1973

OBITUARY NOTICE: Born in 1887; died in 1973 in Rome, Italy. Journalist and author best known for his studies in English literature. His works include *I partiti italiani dal 1848 al 1955, Romanticismo, Romanticismo: Discussioni attuali*, and *Stampa in democrazia*. Obituaries and other sources: *AB Bookman's Weekly*, February 5, 1973.

*   *   *

VINEBERG, Arthur   1903-

PERSONAL: Born May 24, 1903, in Montreal, Quebec, Canada; son of Abraham M. and Anna (Berman) Vineberg; married Ann Porter, December, 1942. *Education:* McGill University, B.Sc., 1924, M.Sc. and M.D., both 1928, Ph.D., 1933. *Religion:* Jewish. *Office:* 1390 Sherbrooke St. W., Montreal, Quebec, Canada.

CAREER: Bellevue Hospital, Presbyterian Division, staff surgeon, 1928-39; private practice of surgery, beginning 1939; surgeon in charge of cardiac surgery, Royal Victoria Hospital. Consultant surgeon at Jewish General Hospital (developed cardio-thoracic service), Queen Mary Veterans Hospital, and Montreal Institute of Cardiology (developed cardiac surgery). *Military service:* Canadian Army Reserve, Medical Corps, 1939-42, active duty, 1942-45.

MEMBER: Physiological Society of Canada, Entomological Society, American College of Surgeons (fellow), American Association of Thoracic Surgery, American Board of Thoracic Surgery (founding member), Canadian Physiological Society of Montreal, McGill Faculty Club. *Awards, honors:* Rockefeller Foundation fellow, 1929-30; Casgrain-Charbonneay Prize from McGill University, 1942.

WRITINGS: How to Live With Your Heart: The Family Guide to Heart Health, Quadrangle, 1975; *Myocardial Revascularization by Arterial Ventricular Implants*, PSG Publishing, 1980. Contributor to *Textbook of Surgery*, 1952, 2nd edition, 1955, and to medical journals.*

*   *   *

VINER, Jacob   1892-1970

OBITUARY NOTICE: Born in 1892; died September 12, 1970, in Princeton, N.J. Educator and economist. A professor emeritus of economics and international finance, Viner was best known as the author of books on international trade. Among his works are *The Customs Union Issue, The Intellectual History of Laissez-Faire*, and *International Trade and Economic Development*. Obituaries and other sources: *New York Times*, September 13, 1970; *AB Bookman's Weekly*, October 5, 1970.

*   *   *

VOGEL, Alfred T(ennyson)   1906-

PERSONAL: Born August 4, 1906, in Brooklyn, N.Y.; son of Abraham (a lawyer) and Elizabeth (a teacher; maiden name, Brodsky) Vogel; married Henrietta Nachman (divorced); married Signe Sandstrom (a musician), July 16, 1950; children: Jane Austen, Lynn Ward, Anne E. Steinhardt. *Education:* City

College (now of the City University of New York), B.A., 1923; graduate study at Columbia University, 1924-26; New York University, M.A., 1936. *Religion:* Jewish. *Home:* 11 Riverside Dr., New York, N.Y. 10023.

CAREER: English teacher, 1927-49, and chairman of English department, 1959-71, at high schools in New York, N.Y. Assistant examiner for New York City Board of Education. Associate of Fashion Institute of Technology, 1956-70; president of Civil Service Merit Council, 1978-81. *Member:* City College Alumni Association (member of board of directors), Phi Beta Kappa.

WRITINGS: The Owl Critics (on education), University of Alabama Press, 1980. Contributor to language journals, including *English Journal* and *English Record*.

WORK IN PROGRESS: A book on "the intellectual fallacies that are undermining our culture, such as astrology and parapsychology," publication expected in 1982.

SIDELIGHTS: Vogel wrote: "The purpose of *The Owl Critics* was to define the direction in which education must go in the next decade, namely, toward a restoration of a sound curriculum and a focus on teaching method. In my book I hoped to achieve this purpose by exploring the irrationality of some of the current trends in our schools."

* * *

VOLGYES, Ivan 1936-

PERSONAL: Born August 25, 1936, in Budapest, Hungary; came to the United States in 1957, naturalized citizen, 1962; son of Miklos (an economist) and Klara (a clerk; maiden name, Heller) Volgyes; married second wife, Nancy A. (a writer), October 29, 1974; children: Gabriella, Elizabeth. *Education:* American University, A.B., 1960, M.A., 1961, Ph.D., 1968. *Religion:* Jewish. *Home:* 2724 Bradfield, Lincoln, Neb. 68502. *Office:* Department of Political Science, University of Nebraska, Lincoln, Neb. 68583.

CAREER: University of Maryland, Overseas Division, Heidelberg, West Germany, lecturer in political science, 1961-65; Denison University, Granville, Ohio, instructor in history, 1965-66; University of Nebraska, Lincoln, assistant professor, 1966-70, associate professor, 1970-76, professor of political science, 1976—, coordinator of Slavic and East European area study program, 1966-76, director of East European exchange program, 1976—, and Slavic and East European studies, 1979—. Visiting associate professor at University of Arizona, summer, 1970; director of U.S. State Department seminar on modernization in Poland, 1973.

MEMBER: American Association for the Advancement of Slavic Studies, American Political Science Association. *Awards, honors:* U.S. Office of Education grants, 1973-78, 1975, 1976-78; International Research and Exchanges Board fellowship, 1974-75, grant, 1978-79; U.S. Department of Agriculture grants, 1977-78, 1979-80; Fulbright-Hays grant, 1978-79; American Council of Learned Societies grant, 1978-79; National Endowment for the Humanities grant, 1980-81.

WRITINGS: The Hungarian Soviet Republic, Hoover Institution, 1970; (with wife, Mary Volgyes) *Czechoslovakia, Hungary, Poland: The Breadbasket and the Battleground,* Thomas Nelson, 1970; (with Peter A. Toma) *The Politics of the Communist Party States in Eastern Europe: Hungary,* W. H. Freeman, 1976; (with wife, Nancy Volgyes) *The Liberated Female: Life, Work, and Sex in Socialist Hungary,* Westview, 1977; *The Government and Politics of Eastern Europe,* Cliff's Notes, 1979; (with Joseph Held, Bela Keraly, and others) *The Mod-*

ernization of Hungarian Agriculture, Columbia University Press, 1980; *Modern Hungary,* Westview, 1980; *From Tradition to Modernity: The Modernization of the Rural Countryside in Hungary,* Columbia University Press, 1981.

Editor: (Also contributor) *Revolution in Hungary, 1918-1919,* University of Nebraska Press, 1971; (with Roger Kanet) *On the Road to Communism: Fifty Years of Soviet Domestic and Foreign Policy,* University of Kansas Press, 1972; (also contributor) *Comparative Political Socialization: Eastern Europe,* Praeger, 1975; *Environmental Deterioration in the U.S.S.R. and in Eastern Europe,* Praeger, 1975; *Eastern Europe: An Interdisciplinary Multi-Media Approach,* ten volumes, with audio cassettes and filmstrips, Cliff's Notes, 1979; (also contributor) *Social Deviance in Eastern Europe,* Westview, 1979; (with Dale Herspring; also contributor) *Civil-Military Relations in Communist States,* Westview, 1979; *The Eastern European Peasantry,* two volumes, Pergamon, 1979; (with Hans Brisch) *Czechoslovakia: The Heritage of Ages Past,* Columbia University Press, 1979; (with William P. Avery and Richard Lonsdale) *The Process of Rural Transformation,* Pergamon, 1980; (with Avery and Lonsdale; also contributor) *Rural Change and Public Policy,* Pergamon, 1980.

Contributor: Jaroslaw Piekalkiewicz and Edward Czerwinski, editors, *The Soviet Occupation of Czechoslovakia, 1968,* Praeger, 1972; Ronald A. Francisco, Betty A. Laird, and Roy Laird, editors, *The Political Economy of Collectivized Agriculture: A Comparative Study of Communist and Non-Communist Systems,* Pergamon, 1979; Charles Gati and Jon F. Triska, editors, *The Working Class in Eastern Europe,* Allen & Unwin, 1981; Gregory Varhall and Kenneth Curry, editors, *The Soviet Union in the 1980's,* U.S. Government Printing Office, 1981; Morris Janowitz, editor, *New Aspects on Civil-Military Relations,* Sage Publications, 1981; Vernon V. Aspaturian, editor, *Authoritarianism and Development in Communist Systems,* Pennsylvania State University Press, 1981; Charles Gati and Jon F. Triska, editors, *Blue-Collar Workers in Eastern Europe,* Allen & Unwin, 1981.

Co-author of "Eastern Europe: A Multi-Media Kit for High Schools," with films and records, Educational Activities, 1972. Contributor of more than twenty-five articles to political science journals, *Choice,* and *Prairie Schooner.*

WORK IN PROGRESS: Murder by Cancer, an espionage novel.

SIDELIGHTS: Ivan Volgyes wrote: "Having traveled extensively in all the states of Eastern Europe and having learned the various cultures of the people of the area, I have tried to relate the goals and aspirations, ideals and ideas, hopes and dreams of the people of this region to both my scholarly research and to the 'creative' writing I have chosen to undertake. In a sense, this is by way of appreciation, expressed in writing, for the many found moments that I have had the pleasure of sharing with friends and colleagues from an area many thousands of miles and eons of life-styles away."

* * *

VOLTZ, Jeanne Appleton 1920-

PERSONAL: Born November 12, 1920, in Collinsville, Ala.; daughter of James Lamar and Marie (Sewell) Appleton; married Luther Manship Voltz, July 31, 1943; children: Luther Manship, Jr., Jeanne Marie. *Education:* University of Montevallo, A.B., 1942; attended Academie Cordon Bleu, 1960, and University of California, Los Angeles, 1970. *Religion:* Methodist. *Home:* 170 West End Ave., Apt. 9-P, New York, N.Y. 10023; and 3695 Bay Homes Dr., Miami, Fla. 33133. *Office: Woman's Day,* 1515 Broadway, New York, N.Y. 10036.

CAREER: Birmingham News, Birmingham, Ala., correspondent, 1940-42; *Mobile Press-Register,* Mobile, Ala., reporter, 1942-45; *Miami Herald,* Miami, Fla., reporter, 1947-51, food editor, 1951-60; *Los Angeles Times,* Los Angeles, Calif., food editor, 1960-73; *Woman's Day,* New York, N.Y., food editor, 1973—. Member of trade advisory committee of Los Angeles Trade Technical College, 1960-73, agricultural advisory council of University of California, 1971-73, and agricultural advisory committee of California Polytechnic University, 1972. Also member of National Nutrition Exchange, and Citizens' Commission on the Science of Law and Food Supply.

MEMBER: Institute of Food Technologists, Society for Nutrition Education, American Home Economics Association, Food Industry Gourmet Society (president, 1966-68), Home Economists in Business, Les Dames d'Escoffier (New York City; founding member), Porcelain Enamel Institute (member of advisory council), Electrical Women's Round Table, Knights of the Vine, La Confrerie St. Etienne, Confrerie de la Chaine de Rotisseurs (dame), Theta Sigma Phi (vice-president, 1970-72), Phi Tau Sigma, Nut Club (Chicago). *Awards, honors:* Awards from Florida Women's Press Club, 1955, 1956, and 1957, all for articles in the *Miami Herald;* Vesta Awards from American Meat Institute, 1963, for articles in *Los Angeles Times,* and 1965, 1966, 1967, and 1968 for editing food section of *Los Angeles Times Home* magazine section; honorary service award from California Home Economics Association, 1972, for service to the home economics profession; alumnus of the year award from University of Montevallo, 1981.

WRITINGS: Famous Florida Recipes, Miami Herald, 1954; *The California Cookbook,* Bobbs-Merrill, 1970; (with Burks Hamner) *The L.A. Gourmet: Favorite Recipes From Famous Los Angeles Restaurants,* Doubleday, 1971; *The Los Angeles Times Natural Food Cookbook,* illustrations by Ellen Friedman, Putnam, 1973; *The Flavor of the South: Delicacies and Staples of Southern Cuisine,* illustrations by Mel Klapholz, Doubleday, 1977; (with Elayne J. Kleeman) *How to Turn a Passion for Food Into Profit,* Rawson, Wade, 1979.

SIDELIGHTS: Voltz told *CA:* "Only romantic love is more sensuous than the pleasures of gastronomy. For me the pleasure in food extends to the very feeling, smells, tastes, and creative pleasure of preparing foods. Consequently, as a writer, my interests ultimately came to writing about foods, how man and woman treat it and enjoy it, and the pleasures of gastronomy. I am handicapped by a note pad and pen every time I go into the kitchen to create my culinary miracles. But the rewards of sharing an honest pleasure with thousands is reward-in-full for stopping to note my successes. Every writer is a show-off in print. Seeing the children of our typewriters in print is as stimulating as a glass of the best champagne. I chose food to write about, or it chose me, when an editor said, 'We've lost our food writer; will you take over temporarily?' That was more than thirty years ago and I've revelled in every word, every bite, and every change for the better in readers' tastes."

*   *   *

von ABELE, Rudolph (Radama)   1922-

PERSONAL: Born October 15, 1922, in Englewood, N.J.; son of Tassilo Radama (a banker) and Amalie Helene Jenny (Krug) von Abele; children: Annette, Stephen Erich, Susan, Rudolph, Jr. *Education:* Columbia University, B.A., 1943, Ph.D., 1946. *Home:* 3040 Idaho Ave. N.W., No. 115, Washington, D.C. 20016. *Office:* Department of Literature, American University, 209 Gray Hall, Washington, D.C. 20016.

CAREER: American University, Washington, D.C., assistant professor, 1947-50, associate professor, 1950-54, professor of English, 1954-68, professor of literature, 1969—.

WRITINGS: Alexander H. Stephens: A Biography, Knopf, 1946; *The Death of the Artist,* Nijhoff, 1955; *The Vigil of Emmeline Gore,* Houghton, 1962; *The Party,* Houghton, 1963; *A Cage for Loulou,* Louisiana State University Press, 1978.

WORK IN PROGRESS: Continuing research on Samuel Beckett and James Joyce; an autobiographical book.

SIDELIGHTS: Von Abele wrote: "I have always been interested in science, especially physics, and in philosophy, particularly of the twentieth century. I do not like to travel, but am in love with Ireland. When I die I shall go to Dublin. I believe that poetry, as an object of interest, is finished. I don't know about the novel: there may be some hope. The arts in general are in poor condition in this century. Long live Beethoven!

"My own writing has always been focused on the problem of the interface between individualism and society, how the individual can and does comprehend himself as part of a larger entity. I guess it is, in the end, the classical problem of philosophy, that of the Same and the Different. I think my partisanship for the IRA, even though I am absolutely terrified by guns ,and cannot imagine being present at a scene of real violence, stems from this preoccupation. One flees to physics and astronomy and the material universe mainly to get away from the tensions these other problems feed."

*   *   *

von BLOCK, Bela W(illiam)   1922-
(Jonathan Black, Mercedes Endfield, Creighton La Barr, Aldo Lucchesi, Blanca Meurice, Desmond Padgett, Reuven Shomroni, Lee M. Vernon; Ilya Chambertin, Caroline Hennessey, Gordon Randolph, W. D. Sprague, joint pseudonyms)

PERSONAL: Born April 2, 1922, in Cleveland, Ohio; son of Bela C. W. and Cornelia (Makranczy) von Block; married Sylvia Guttenplan (a writer), December 31, 1952. *Education:* Attended high school in Los Angeles, Calif. *Politics:* "Not interested in politics as generally understood." *Residence:* Europe. *Agent:* Roslyn Targ Literary Agency, Inc., 250 West 57th St., Suite 1932, New York, N.Y. 10019.

CAREER: Worked as reporter, 1939; publicity representative, 1939-40; self employed, 1946-48; newspaper editor, 1949-50; free-lance writer, 1953—. *Military service:* U.S. Army, Infantry, 1940-45, 1951-53; became master sergeant.

WRITINGS—With wife, Sylvia von Block: *The Worldrapers,* Lancer, 1968, Bantam, 1977; *Super-Detective: The Many Lives of Tom Ponzi, Europe's Master Investigator,* Playboy Press, 1972; *The Best Pieces,* Dell, 1976.

Under pseudonym Jonathan Black: *Oil,* Morrow, 1974; *Ride the Golden Tiger,* Morrow, 1976; *The House on the Hill,* Berkley Publishing, 1977; *Megacorp,* New American Library, 1981; *The Expatriates,* New American Library, 1982.

Under pseudonym Mercedes Endfield: "Ms. Squad" series, New American Library, 1973.

Under pseudonym Creighton La Barr: *The New Astrology,* Midwood Tower, 1968.

Under pseudonym Reuven Shomroni: *Astrological Secrets of the Jews Revealed,* Lancer, 1969.

With S. von Block, under joint pseudonym Ilya Chambertin: *Astro-Analysis*, Lancer Books, 1970; *How to Get What You Want Out of Life Through Astrology*, Lancer Books, 1970; *How to Keep Your Man Through Astrology*, Lancer Books, 1971; *Personal Psychology: Your Star Guide to Love and Romance*, Lancer Books, 1971; *Encyclopedia of Astrology*, Lancer Books, 1972; *How to Astroanalyze Yourself*, Lancer, 1972. Also author of several other books under this joint pseudonym.

With S. von Block, under joint pseudonym Caroline Hennessey: *I, Bitch*, Lancer Books, 1970; *Strategy of Sexual Struggle*, Lancer Books, 1971.

With S. von Block, under joint pseudonym Gordon Randolph: *Beyond Yoga*, Lancer Books, 1973. Also author of several other books under this joint pseudonym.

With S. von Block, under joint pseudonym W.D. Sprague: *Sexual Behavior of American Nurses*, Lancer Books, 1963; *Sex Behavior of the American Secretary*, reprinted as *Sex and the Secretary*, Lancer Books, 1964; *Patterns of Adultery*, Lancer Books, 1964; *Case Histories From the Communes*, Lancer Books, 1972. Also author of numerous other books under this joint pseudonym.

Author of more than thirty novels under pseudonyms Aldo Lucchesi, Blanca Meurice, Desmond Padgett, and Lee M. Vernon.

SIDELIGHTS: Von Block told *CA:* "Before I started doing books I was a magazine writer—with credits including *Male, Men, Stag, Cavalier,* and most of the old men's mags, *Confidential* and most of the old expose mags, several confession mags, a very large number of the old detective (true detective-police) mags, and so on. Later, I got into a more legitimate magazine market, with credits in *True, American Weekly, Look, This Week, Better Homes and Gardens* (believe it or not), and quite a few others.

"From 1957 until 1976 I collaborated with J. Paul Getty on a total of seventy-two magazine articles and six Gettybooks. I didn't work for Getty—the publishers, mag and book, paid (for the use of his name as a grabby lute, natch), and I got the money, while Getty got the free publicity and the image. It was, incidentally, a great and friendly relationship. Contrary to what you may have heard, J. Paul G. was a great guy."

*   *   *

VONDRA, Josef Gert 1941-

PERSONAL: Born June 11, 1941, in Vienna, Austria; son of Josef (an architect) and Theresa (an actress; maiden name, Knoll) Vondra; married wife, Ena Rosemary Monica. *Education:* Attended De La Salle College. *Home and office:* P.O. Box 5, South Yarra, Victoria 3141, Australia.

CAREER: Sun, Melbourne, Australia, journalist, 1960-63; Austrian Airlines, Vienna, Austria, press officer, 1964; Australian Broadcasting Commission, sub-editor for Radio Australia, 1966-68; free-lance writer, 1968—. Foundation and editorial director of Cavalier Press. *Member:* Australian Journalists Association, Fellowship of Australian Writers. *Awards, honors:* Senior fellowship from Australian Literature Board, 1974.

WRITINGS: Timor Journey, Lansdowne Press, 1968; *The Other China,* Lansdowne Press, 1969; *Hong Kong: City Without a Country,* Lansdowne Press, 1969; *A Guide to Australian Cheese,* Thomas Nelson, 1970; *Paul Zwilling,* Wren Publishing, 1974; *Hellas Australia,* Widescope Publishing, 1979; *Germania Australia,* Cavalier Press, 1981. Contributor to *Aspect.*

WORK IN PROGRESS: A novel about a father-son relationship, in terms of sexuality and psychology.

SIDELIGHTS: Vondra wrote: "I am essentially interested in the sociological aspect of migration and the influence of migration on aspects of Australian life. Much of my writing concerns themes of this expression. *Germania Australia* is a study of the history and contribution of the German-speaking groups to the Australian way of life."

*   *   *

von HEIDENSTAM, (Carl Gustaf) Verner
See HEIDENSTAM, (Carl Gustaf) Verner von

*   *   *

von HEYSE, Paul (Johann Ludwig)
See HEYSE, Paul (Johann Ludwig von)

*   *   *

von RAD, Gerhard 1901-1971

OBITUARY NOTICE: Born in 1901; died October 31, 1971, in Heidelberg, West Germany. Biblical scholar and author best known for his works on the theology of the Old Testament. Among von Rad's writings are *Moses, Deuteronomy: A Commentary, Old Testament Theology,* and *Genesis: A Commentary.* Obituaries and other sources: *AB Bookman's Weekly,* December 13, 1971.

*   *   *

VOORHIES, Barbara 1939-

PERSONAL: Born March 10, 1939, in New York, N.Y. *Education:* Tufts University, B.S., 1961; Yale University, Ph.D., 1969. *Office:* Department of Anthropology, University of California, Santa Barbara, Calif. 93107.

CAREER: San Diego State College (now San Diego State University), San Diego, Calif., assistant professor of anthropology, 1969-70; University of California, Santa Barbara, visiting assistant professor, 1970-71, assistant professor of anthropology, 1971—. *Member:* American Anthropological Association, Society for American Archaeology. *Awards, honors:* National Science Foundation fellowship, 1972-73.

WRITINGS: (With M. Kay Martin) *Female of the Species,* Columbia University Press, 1975; (editor with Barbara L. Stark) *Prehistoric Coastal Adaptations: The Economy and Ecology of Maritime Middle America,* Academic Press, 1978.*

*   *   *

VOSKOVEC, George 1905-1981

OBITUARY NOTICE: Born June 19, 1905, in Sazava, Czechoslovakia; died July 1, 1981, in Pearlblossom, Calif. Actor, director, and playwright best known for his character roles on the New York stage. Voskovec was forced to leave Czechoslovakia in 1939 because of his anti-Fascist comedy reviews and plays. Earlier, he had formed a theatre company with his partner Jan Werich, and together they created one of the most popular and influential theatres in Prague. Voskovec composed more than three hundred songs and wrote and co-authored twenty-six plays while with the company, including "Heavy Barbara," "The Ass and the Shadow," and "Fist in the Eye." In 1945 he made his first New York stage appearance, and during the next twenty-five years he acted in scores of Broadway and Off Broadway productions. His credits included the roles of Einstein in "The Physicists," Mr. Alper in "The Tenth Man," Herr Schultz in "Cabaret," and the Player King in the John Gielgud-Richard Burton version of "Hamlet." In 1956 he won an Obie for his performance in the title role of "Uncle Vanya." While returning from Europe in 1950, Voskovec was detained at Ellis Island for ten months while the government investigated charges that he had ties with the Communist party in Czechoslovakia. Voskovec played himself in a television drama based on the experience. In 1965 he published a book of essays and verse entitled *A Hat in the Bush*. Obituaries and other sources: *Notable Names in the American Theatre*, James T. White, 1976; *Who's Who in the Theatre: A Biographical Record of the Contemporary Stage*, 16th edition, Pitman, 1977; *New York Times*, July 3, 1981; *Newsweek*, July 13, 1981; *Time*, July 13, 1981.

* * *

VOYNICH, Ethel Lillian (Boole)   1864-1960

OBITUARY NOTICE: Born in 1864 in Cambridge, England; died July 27, 1960. Composer and author. In 1955, when Voyich was ninety years old, she learned from a group of Soviet journalists touring the United States that in the Soviet Union her fame as a novelist ranked with that of writers Mark Twain, Theodore Dreiser, and Charles Dickens. Voynich's novel *The Gadfly* sold 2.5 million copies in the Soviet Union, and the book was made into a Soviet motion picture. In 1957 an opera based on the plot of *The Gadfly* was performed in the Urals. Beginning in 1956 Voynich received royalty checks from the Soviet Union for the sale of her books. Among her other novels are *The Interrupted Friendship* and *Put Off My Shoes*. Voynich also wrote original musical compositions, primarily cantatas and oratorios. Obituaries and other sources: *Look*, July 8, 1958; *New York Times*, July 29, 1960; *Publishers Weekly*, August 8, 1960; *Time*, August 8, 1960; *Who Was Who Among English and European Authors, 1931-1949*, Gale, 1978.

WAAGE, Frederick 1943-

PERSONAL: Surname is pronounced *Wah*-gee; born December 1, 1943, in Ithaca, N.Y.; son of Frederick Oswin (a college teacher) and Dorothy (Boylan) Waage; married Virginia Rose Renner (an editor and teacher), June 18, 1977; children: Melissa Rose. *Education:* Princeton University, A.B., 1965, Ph.D., 1971. *Politics:* Liberal Democrat. *Home:* 2127 Sinking Creek Rd., Johnson City, Tenn. 37601. *Office:* Department of English, East Tennessee State University, Johnson City, Tenn. 37614.

CAREER: Northwestern University, Evanston, Ill., instructor in English, 1968-71; California State University, Los Angeles, lecturer in English and comparative literature, 1971-73; Friends of the Earth, San Francisco, Calif., business manager of organization's magazine, 1974; Rutgers University, Douglass College, New Brunswick, N.J., assistant professor of English, 1974-77; College Misericordia, Dallas, Pa., assistant professor of language and literature, 1977-78; East Tennessee State University, Johnson City, assistant professor of English, 1978—, assistant chairperson of department of English, 1980—. Junior research associate at Huntington Library, 1971-73. Co-founder of Joyce Kilmer Poetry Center, 1977; member of community advisory board of WETS-FM Radio, 1979—.

MEMBER: Modern Language Association of America (delegate to assembly, 1977-80), Committee of Small Magazine Editors and Publishers, Popular Culture Association, American Society for Environmental History, Sierra Club, Friends of the Earth (state chairperson, 1974-75), Phi Beta Kappa. *Awards, honors:* Fellow of Huntington Library, 1975, 1979; fellow of Southeast Institute of Renaissance and Medieval Studies, 1975; first prize for fiction from Virginia Highlands Creative Writing Contest, 1979, for novel, *Bohemians;* Danforth Associate with wife, Virginia Renner, 1981-86.

WRITINGS: (Editor) *Uncollected Writings of Samuel Rowlands,* Scholars' Facsimiles and Reprints, 1971; *The End of the World: California Stories,* Gallimaufry, 1977; *Thomas Dekker's Pamphlets and Jacobean Popular Literature,* Salzburg Studies in English, 1977; (editor) *Teaching Environmental Literature,* MLA Publications Bureau, 1982. Contributor of articles, poems, and stories to scholarly journals and literary magazines, including *Journal of Popular Culture, Tales, Antigonish Review, Shakespeare Studies, Contemporary Poetry,* and *Southern Poetry Review.* Editorial assistant for *Journal of Cryosurgery,* 1971; assistant editor of *Research Opportunities in Renaissance Drama,* 1970-71; book review editor of *Wetlands,* 1974-76; editor of *Second Growth: Appalachian Nature and Culture.*

WORK IN PROGRESS: Webster's Major Tragedies; editing *Jacobean Popular Literature; Mint Springs Stories,* short stories; *Bohemians,* a novel; research on agrarianism in contemporary Southern literature.

SIDELIGHTS: Waage commented: "My major areas of interest and competence (academically) include Renaissance and twentieth-century literature and its cultural context. I am fluent in French and deeply interested in French art and culture. My other most compelling concern is environmental action and reflection; I am committed to the need for survival and preservation of nature and human life, and the consciousness that this survival is jeopardized.

"I am involved with publishing and the small press movement. I have been hoping to be a creator of imaginative literature as well as a student of literature and society, and to be a communicator of both committed values and tangible, sensory natures of things. At this point in my career I am aware of the truth of Tillie Olsen's *Silences;* I have found my face turning inward for the short term. I share many of the value orientations of the Nashville agrarians, without the conservatism associated with some of their ideology."

*   *   *

WADE, Bob
See McILWAIN, David

*   *   *

WAKEMAN, Robert Parker 1914(?)-1981

OBITUARY NOTICE: Born c. 1914; died September 14, 1981, in Newark, N.J. Engineer and author best known as an authority on contract bridge. A photographic systems engineer associated with Fairchild Camera and Instrument Corp. for more than thirty years, Wakeman also wrote a weekly bridge column for the *Newark Evening News* for fifteen years. He was a member of the New Jersey squad that won the National Men's Team Championships in 1960; in the same year he earned the New England Mixed Team title, and in 1971 he won the Pacific Northwest Regional Open Pair Championship. His writings include *Instant Play Methods for Beginners, Modern Bidding Techniques,* and *Elements of Declarer Play and*

Defense. Obituaries and other sources: *New York Times*, September 17, 1981.

* * *

WALDINGER, Ernst   1896-1970

OBITUARY NOTICE: Born October 16, 1896, in Vienna, Austria; died February 1, 1970, in New York, N.Y. Educator and poet. A retired professor of German literature at Skidmore College, Waldinger wrote several books of lyric poetry, including *Die Kuppel, Zwischen Hudson und Donau,* and *Gesang vor dem Abgrund*. Obituaries and other sources: *AB Bookman's Weekly,* February 16, 1970; *Cassell's Encyclopaedia of World Literature,* revised edition, Morrow, 1973.

* * *

WALKER, David   1950-

PERSONAL: Born November 11, 1950, in Aberdeen, Scotland; son of John (a steelworker) and Irene (a teacher; maiden name, Connor) Walker; married Karen Irving (a social worker). *Education:* University of Sussex, M.A., 1972; St. Catharine's College, Cambridge, M.A., 1975. *Home:* 11 Waterlow Rd., London N.19, England. *Agent:* Michael Sissons, A.D. Peters & Co. Ltd., 10 Buckingham St., London WC2N 6BU, England.

CAREER: Times Newspapers Ltd., London, England, journalist, 1973-77; *Economist,* London, journalist, 1979-81; *London Times,* London, journalist, 1981—. *Awards, honors:* Harkness fellowship from Harkness Foundation's Commonwealth Fund, 1977-79.

WRITINGS: (With Jeremy Tunstall) *Media Made in California,* Oxford University Press, 1981; (contributor) *Yearbook of Social Policy,* Routledge & Kegan Paul, 1981. Contributor to magazines and newspapers, including *New Society* and *Chronicle of Higher Education.*

SIDELIGHTS: Walker told *CA:* "A problem for a journalist writing a book is expanding the usual short deadlines over a long period and writing at length instead of at breadth. But once the new rhythm is learned, books take on a weightiness which journalism lacks. Book-writing, the immortality offered by library shelves, beckons!"

* * *

WALKER, Mary Alexander   1927-

PERSONAL: Born September 24, 1927, in Beaumont, Tex.; daughter of James Cosper (a mechanic and pilot) and Mary Helen (a painter; maiden name, Johnson) Alexander; married Tom Ross Walker (a physician), December 23, 1952; children: Timothy Ross, Mark Thomas, Miles Stephen. *Education:* Lamar Technological College, A.A., 1947; Texas Woman's University, B.A., 1950; San Francisco State University, M.A., 1981; further graduate study at Academy of Art College, San Francisco. *Home:* 22 Corte Lodato, Greenbrae, Calif. 94904.

CAREER: Teacher at public schools in Texas, Washington, Ohio, Arkansas, and Iowa, 1947-57; Marin Country Day School, Corte Madera, Calif., teacher, 1967-68; A Joy Forever (design business), San Rafael, Calif., owner, 1973-76; Dominican College, San Rafael, part-time instructor in writing, 1972-80, director of writer's conference, 1978-80. Instructor of class on writing children's literature at Lone Mountain College, San Francisco, Calif., spring, 1976, and Indian Valley College, Novato, Calif., fall, 1978. *Member:* American Association of University Women, Society of Children's Book Writers, Mystery Writers of America.

AWARDS, HONORS: First prize from Pacific Northwest Writers Conference, 1971, for "Les Ailes du Papillon," 1973, for *Catching a Zombie,* and 1979, for story "Brimstone"; *Weekly Reader* fellowship for Bread Loaf Writers Conference, 1972; nomination for Dorothy Canfield Fisher Award from Vermont State PTA and State Department of Libraries, 1972, for *The Year of the Cafeteria;* award from Santa Rosa Actors' Theatre, 1977, for adaptation of "Ozma and the Nome King's Palace."

WRITINGS—Children's books: *The Year of the Cafeteria,* Bobbs-Merrill, 1971, reprinted as *Bread and Roses,* Grosset, 1972; *To Catch a Zombi,* Atheneum, 1979; *Maggot,* Atheneum, 1980.

Other: (With Peggy Ford) "Ozma and the Nome King's Palace" (musical play for children; adaptation), first produced in San Leandro, Calif., at Lilliput Theatre, 1982. Work represented in anthologies, including *Awards,* edited by William K. Durr, Rita M. Beau, and others, Houghton, 1981. Author of "College Column," in *Beaumont Journal,* 1943-47, and "Children and Books," a column in *Pacific Sun,* 1965. Contributor of stories, articles, and reviews to magazines and newspapers, including *American Girl, In,* and *Extension.*

WORK IN PROGRESS: Screenplays based on her books; research on Celtic legends and designs, early medicine in America, and the history of law in the United States.

SIDELIGHTS: Walker told *CA:* "Coming from a background in more than one of the arts, I do not strive to write naturalistically, but rather to present an art form, composing and selecting. I work with ideas about which I feel passionately or with craft problems that challenge me greatly, or sometimes both. My novel *Maggot* is about a young dancer, developed from a line I read in the autobiography of Martha Graham: 'The body does not lie.' The greatest challenge to me in craft is using a verbal art to grasp the essence of a non-verbal art."

* * *

WALL, Patrick (Henry Bligh)   1916-

PERSONAL: Born October 14, 1916, in Bidston, Cheshire, England; son of Henry Benedict (a mining engineer) and Gladys (Finney) Wall; married Sheila Elizabeth Putnam, November 19, 1953; children: Rosemary Elizabeth Beverley Wall Normand. *Education:* Attended Royal Naval Staff College and Joint Services Staff College. *Religion:* Roman Catholic. *Home:* Westminster Gardens, Marsham St., London S.W.1, England. *Office:* House of Commons, London S.W.1, England.

CAREER: Royal Marines, served as commanding officer, naval gunnery officer, and parachutist, 1935-50, leaving service as major; House of Commons, London, England, parliamentary private secretary to Minister of Agriculture, Fisheries, and Food, 1950-57, and to chancellor-of-the-exchequer, 1958-59, Conservative member for Haltemprice Division of Hull, 1954-55, Conservative member for Haltemprice Division of East Riding of Yorkshire, 1955—, member of British delegation to the United Nations, 1962; chairman of Conservative parliamentary fisheries subcommittee, vice-chairman of Conservative Parliamentary Defence Committee, 1965-77. Member of Westminster City Council, 1953-63. Chairman of Military Committee of North Atlantic Assembly, 1977—. *Member:* Institute of Directors, Royal Naval Yachting Association, Royal Yacht Squadron. *Awards, honors*—Military: Military Cross; U.S. Legion of Merit. Other: Knight of Sovereign Military Order of Malta.

WRITINGS: Royal Marine Pocket Book, Gale & Polden, 1944; *Student Power*, Monday Club, 1968; *Defence Policy*, Monday Club, 1969; *Overseas Aid*, Monday Club, 1969; *The Soviet Maritime Threat*, Monday Club, 1973; *The Indian Ocean and the Threat to the West*, Stacey International, 1975; *Prelude to Detente*, Stacey International, 1975; *Southern Oceans and the Security of the Free World*, Stacey International, 1977.

WORK IN PROGRESS: A comparison of British and U.S. parliamentary systems, publication expected in 1982.

SIDELIGHTS: Wall wrote: "I am a specialist in defense and foreign affairs, particularly in Africa and the Middle East. I am a frequent traveler due to my parliamentary and North Atlantic Assembly duties. I visit south and central Africa every second year, and the Far East and the United States three or four times a year.

"The British and American parliamentary systems were founded on an entirely different basis and yet there are signs that they are now moving some way to adopt some of each other's procedures. For example, the House of Commons has recently introduced select committees to monitor the work of each government department, somewhat on the lines of the congressional committees.

"So far as security is concerned, the danger of war increases as the Soviet Union faces new leadership and economic decline. War can be avoided in Europe only by the strength of the North Atlantic Treaty Organization (NATO). The danger is that NATO may be bypassed by Soviet attempts to secure, either directly or indirectly, the oil of the Middle East and the minerals of southern Africa. As yet the West has not coordinated their plans for checking this form of indirect aggression."

*   *   *

WALLACE, Dexter
See MASTERS, Edgar Lee

*   *   *

WALLS, Ian G(ascoigne)   1922-

PERSONAL: Born April 28, 1922, in Yoker, Scotland; son of William and Mary Louisa (Jackson) Walls; married Eleanor McCaig, August 11, 1947; children: Moira Lindsay, Eleanor Mary. *Education:* West of Scotland Agricultural College, Diploma in Horticulture, 1949. *Home and office:* 17 Dougalston Ave., Milngavie, Glasgow G62 6AP, Scotland. *Agent:* Rupert Crew Ltd., King's Mews, London WC1N 2JA, England.

CAREER: Dobbie & Co. Ltd. (seed company), 1936-39; Asmer Seeds, Leicester, England, 1949-50; West of Scotland Agricultural College, Glasgow, horticultural adviser, 1950—. Horticultural consultant to companies including D. T. Brown & Co. Ltd., Clovis Lande Associates Ltd., Frederick Muller Ltd., and R. D. Ltd., and to numerous bowling clubs. *Military service:* British Army, 1941-46. *Member:* National Farmers Union, Scottish Technical Education Committee, Milngavie Horticultural Society (president), Victoria Park Club, Glasgow Wheelers Cycling Club.

WRITINGS: Tomato Cultivation for the Amateur, West of Scotland Agricultural College, 1952; *Gardening Month by Month*, Collins, 1962; *Creating Your Garden*, Collins, 1967; *The Lady Gardener*, Collins, 1968; *Greenhouse Gardening*, Ward, Lock, 1970; *Tomato Growing Today*, David & Charles, 1972, 2nd edition, 1978; *The Complete Book of the Greenhouse*, Ward, Lock, 1974, published in the United States as *The Complete Book of Greenhouse Gardening*, preface by E. W. Curtis,

Quadrangle, 1975; (with A. S. Horsburgh) *Making Your Garden Pay: Profit From Garden and Nursery*, David & Charles, 1974; (editor of revised edition for temperate zones, with A.M.M. Berrie) Dudley Harris, *Hydroponics: Growing Without Soil, Easy-to-Follow Instructions for the Flatdweller, Modern Gardener, and Commercial Grower*, David & Charles, 1975; *Simple Tomato Growing*, Ward, Lock, 1975; *Making the Most of Your Greenhouse*, Ward, Lock, 1975; *The Care and Maintenance of Bowling Greens*, Scottish Bowling Association, 1979; *Collins A-Z of Garden Pests and Problems*, Collins, 1979. *Commercial Vegetable Growing Under Protection*, Fred Miller, 1981; *Commercial Flower Growing Under Protection*, Fred Miller, 1981. Contributor to magazines and newspapers. Consulting editor for Fred Miller Ltd.

SIDELIGHTS: Walls told *CA:* "I now act as a consultant to a number of different companies. I also have a small 'self-pick' fruit farm near my home—growing strawberries and raspberries. I am becoming much more specialized in all my consulting work—as so many nonprofessional people are cashing in on the gardening scene in the U.K. I feel this is essential for writers and consultants."

*   *   *

WALPOLE, Hugh (Seymour)   1884-1941

BRIEF ENTRY: Born March 13, 1884, in Auckland, New Zealand; died of heart failure, June 1, 1941, in Keswick, Cumberland, England. English novelist. A prolific and highly popular writer, Walpole wrote short stories, criticism, and essays, but he is best known for his romantic and mystical novels. An early, realistic work, *Mr. Perrin and Mr. Traill* (1911), was inspired by his experiences as a schoolteacher and is considered by some critics to be his best book, though it was not especially successful when first published. It was his next novel, *Fortitude* (1913), that brought him public and critical recognition. Walpole's books vary widely in style and subject as well as in quality: he wrote psychological novels of the English upper and middle classes, macabre thrillers like *Portrait of a Man With Red Hair* (1925), and swashbuckling historical romances like his tetralogy *The Herries Chronicle* (1930-33). Though his ability is generally acknowledged, much of his later work is considered mediocre and superficial. Walpole won the James Tait Black Memorial Prize in 1919, and again in 1920 for *The Secret City*. He was knighted in 1937. *Residence:* Keswick, Cumberland, England. *Biographical/critical sources: Twentieth Century Authors: A Biographical Dictionary of Modern Literature*, H. W. Wilson, 1942; Rupert Hart-Davis, *Hugh Walpole*, Macmillan, 1952; Elizabeth Steele, *Hugh Walpole*, Twayne, 1972.

*   *   *

WALSH, Ellen Stoll   1942-

PERSONAL: Born September 2, 1942, in Baltimore, Md.; daughter of Joseph Adolphus and Nell (Orum) Stoll; married David Albert Walsh (a professor), August 25, 1964; children: Benjamin Martin. *Education:* Maryland Institute of Art, B.F.A., 1964; also attended University of Minnesota, 1966-69. *Home:* 29 West St., Fairport, N.Y. 14450.

CAREER: Writer. *Awards, honors:* Merit award from Art Directors Club exhibition and award of excellence from American Institute of Graphic Arts, both 1980, for *Brunus and the New Bear*.

WRITINGS—Self-illustrated children's books: *Brunus and the New Bear*, Doubleday, 1979; *Theodore All Grown Up*, Doubleday, 1981.

SIDELIGHTS: Ellen Walsh told *CA:* "I first became interested in writing and illustrating books for children while reading to my son, Benjamin, and it was not long before I realized just how difficult book-making is. Since I had never had any practical experience in illustrating, I explored many media before deciding upon pen and colored inks for *Brunus and the New Bear*. The story itself underwent many transformations before it was finished.

"During 1968 and 1969 my husband and I spent nine months traveling in Europe, primarily in the Mediterranean. Since 1973 we have been involved in the archaeology of a medieval Cistercian abbey in England where we spend several weeks every summer. For the past few years I have been occupied with the drawing and cataloging of the stained glass fragments which we have uncovered there."

*   *   *

WALSH, James Edward   1891-1981

OBITUARY NOTICE: Born April 30, 1891, in Cumberland, Md.; died of a heart ailment, July 29, 1981, in Ossining, N.Y. Clergyman, missionary, and author. A Roman Catholic bishop and a former superior general of the Maryknoll Mission Society, Walsh spent more than forty years in China as a missionary. He was known to the Chinese Catholics as Wha Lee Sou, or Pillar of Truth. As the second superior general of the Maryknoll Fathers, he also supervised from 1936 to 1946 the order's first mission efforts in Africa and Latin America. Charged with spying and subversion by the Peoples Republic of China in 1958, Walsh spent the next twelve years in a Shanghai prison. He denied the charges, but he was eventually forced to sign a confession. His 1970 release was seen as an important step toward improved relations between Peking and the United States. His writings include *The Man on Joss Stick Alley, Tales of Xavier, Maryknoll Spiritual Directory,* and *The Young Ones.* Obituaries and other sources: *Who's Who in America,* 40th edition Marquis, 1978; *New York Times,* July 30, 1981; *Newsweek,* August 10, 1981; *Time,* August 10, 1981.

*   *   *

WALSHE, R(obert) D(aniel)   1923-

PERSONAL: Born December 28, 1923, in Sydney, Australia; son of Eric Dalrymple (a process worker) and Helen (Moore) Walshe; married Patricia Mary McEvoy. *Education:* University of Sydney, B.A. (with honors), 1950; Sydney Teachers College, Diploma in Education, 1951. *Home:* 74 Linden St., Unit 5, Sutherland, New South Wales 2232, Australia.

CAREER: High school teacher of English and history in Sydney, Australia, 1952-63; Martindale Press, Sydney, publisher and managing director, 1963-70; A. H. & A. W. Reed (publisher), Sydney, editorial director, 1970-75; free-lance writer, 1975—. Member of faculty at Sutherland Shire Evening College, 1969-78. Honorary publications editor for Primary English Teaching Association, 1972—. *Military service:* Australian Army, 1942-44. *Member:* Australian Society of Authors.

WRITINGS: (With P. M. Wheeler) *Mastering Words,* Longman Cheshire, 1962; *Student's Guide to World History Since 1789,* Longman Cheshire, 1963; (with Peter O'Meara and Don Shirley) *How to Study Better,* Longman Cheshire, 1963; (with Wheeler) *Mastering English,* Longman Cheshire, 1969.

(Editor with N. A. Little) *Ways We Teach History,* History Teachers Association (Sydney), 1971; (editor) *My Machine Makes Rainbows,* Longman Cheshire, 1972; (editor) *Exploring the New English,* Primary English Teaching Association, 1973;

(with J. J. Cosgrove and E. B. McKillop) *Power and Persuasion: Twenty Modern Biographies of Great Men,* Longman Cheshire, 1974; (editor) *The New English in Action,* Primary English Teaching Association, 1974; (editor) *New English, New Ways,* Primary English Teaching Association, 1975; (editor) *Speaking of Writing,* Longman Cheshire, 1975; (editor) *The New English: How To,* Primary English Teaching Association, 1976; (editor) *Better Reading/Writing—Now!,* Primary English Teaching Association, 1977; (with Norman McCulla) *Balance in the Classroom: K-Seven,* Primary English Teaching Association, 1979; *Better Writing, Clearer Thinking,* Longman Cheshire, 1979; (editor) *One-Hundred-One Questions Primary Teachers Ask,* Primary English Teaching Association, 1980; (editor) *Donald Graves in Australia: "Children Want to Write . . . ,"* Primary English Teaching Association, 1981. Contributor to history and English journals.

WORK IN PROGRESS: A text on the teaching of writing in primary schools, publication by Primary English Teaching Association expected in 1981.

SIDELIGHTS: Walshe told *CA:* "I write to make things clearer for teachers and schoolchildren in the midst of a knowledge explosion. I would like to write in other fields, but education always seems more significant than anything else and I see no prospect of release."

*   *   *

WARD, Robert   1943-

PERSONAL—Address: c/o Rawson Associates Publishers, Inc., 630 Third Ave., New York, N.Y. 10017.

CAREER: Writer. Worked as welfare worker, playground director, teacher, and musician.

WRITINGS—Novels: *Shedding Skin,* Harper, 1971; *Cattle Annie and Little Britches,* Morrow, 1978; *The Sandman,* Rawson Associates, 1978. Contributor of articles to magazines.

SIDELIGHTS: Ward's first book, *Shedding Skin,* is an autobiographical novel about growing up in the 1950's and 1960's. The main character, Bob Ward, takes to the highway in search of himself, eventually winding up in the Haight-Ashbury district of San Francisco in the late 1960's. *New York Times Book Review* critic Sheldon Frank wrote that *Shedding Skin* is "a novel in overdrive—vulgar, outrageous, totally hyperbolic, exceptionally funny, and written with an uncommon attention to the wonders of language."

Cattle Annie and Little Britches, Ward's second novel, is a western about two girls who join the Doolin-Dalton Gang during the 1890's. Frank found the book "considerably better" than most westerns, but thought it to be a disappointment after Ward's promising first novel. Based on a true story, *Cattle Annie and Little Britches* offers a typical fare of shootouts, robberies, and romance.

Cattle Annie and Little Britches was followed by *The Sandman,* a suspense thriller about an insane anesthesiologist in a New York City hospital who takes up the practice of mercy-killing. In order to cover his tracks he begins killing staff members who suspect him. Several reviewers praised Ward for his detailed knowledge of pathology and surgical procedures, which provided a "convincing background" for the tale.

BIOGRAPHICAL/CRITICAL SOURCES: *New York Times,* January 29, 1972; *New York Times Book Review,* April 16, 1972, February 5, 1978; *Crawdaddy,* May, 1978; *West Coast Review of Books,* March, 1979; *New Statesman,* June 27, 1979.*

WARNER, Alan   1912-

PERSONAL: Born December 4, 1912, in Shipston-on-Stour, England; son of Alfred Nicholas (a minister) and Elizabeth (Young) Warner; married Phyllis Mercer, July 23, 1937 (died December 20, 1965); married Hazel Izon, July 30, 1968; children: (first marriage) Alison Mary Warner Poole, John Nicholas. *Education:* St. Catharine's College, Cambridge, B.A., 1935, M.A., 1938. *Home:* 33 Lodge Rd., Coleraine, County Londonderry BT52 1NA, Northern Ireland.

CAREER: Rhodes University College (now Rhodes University), Grahamstown, South Africa, lecturer in English literature, 1939-46; University of the Witwatersrand, Johannesburg, South Africa, lecturer in English literature, 1946-50; Makerere University College (now Makerere University), Kampala, Uganda, professor of English, 1951-60; Magee University College, Londonderry, Northern Ireland, professor of English 1961-68; New University of Ulster, Coleraine, Northern Ireland, professor of English, 1968-78; writer, 1978—. *Member:* International Association for the Study of Anglo-Irish Literature.

WRITINGS: *A Short Guide to English Style,* Oxford University Press, 1961; *Clay Is the Word: Patrick Kavanagh, 1904-1967,* Dolmen, 1973; *William Allingham,* Bucknell University Press, 1975; *A Guide to Anglo-Irish Literature,* Gill & Macmillan, 1981; (editor) *The Selected John Hewitt* (poems), Blackstaff, 1981; *On Foot in Ulster,* Blackstaff, in press.

SIDELIGHTS: Warner told *CA:* "Always interested in Anglo-Irish literature, I have become increasingly absorbed by it since I moved to Ireland. But academic pursuits have never monopolized my time and energy. I have climbed many mountains, including Kilimanjaro and Ruwenzori, and walked many miles in different parts of the world. I celebrated my retirement by making the first circuit of the Ulster Way, a five hundred-mile footpath route around Ulster."

*   *   *

WARREN, Louise   1909(?)-1981

OBITUARY NOTICE: Born c. 1909; died June 18, 1981. Author of more than one hundred short stories and screenplays. Warren wrote "Party Line" and "Snips and Snarls," which were combined and made into the motion picture "Her Twelve Men," starring Greer Garson. Also a civic leader, Warren was a member of the National Advisory Council on Vocational Rehabilitation, a delegate to the White House Conference on Childhood and Youth, and a trustee of Pomona College. Obituaries and other sources: *Chicago Tribune,* June 26, 1981.

*   *   *

WARREN, Mary Douglas
See GREIG, Maysie

*   *   *

WASHBURN, Charles   1890(?)-1972

OBITUARY NOTICE: Born c. 1890, in Chicago, Ill.; died January 9, 1972, in Jersey City, N.J. Press agent, playwright, and author. Best known as a theatrical press agent, Washburn included George M. Cohan, Al Jolson, Billy Rose, Mike Todd, and John Barrymore among his clients. Co-author of the 1936 Broadway production "All Editions," Washburn also wrote *Press Agentry* and *Come Into My Parlor,* an unconventional view of Chicago nightlife. Obituaries and other sources: *New York Times,* January 10, 1972; *AB Bookman's Weekly,* January 24, 1972.

*   *   *

WASHBURNE, Heluiz Chandler   1892-1970

OBITUARY NOTICE—See index for *CA* sketch: Born January 25, 1892, in Cincinnati, Ohio; died September 23, 1970, in Falls Church, Va. Journalist and author. Washburne worked as a home fashion adviser for the Carson, Pirie, Scott & Co. department store and as a travel columnist with the *Chicago Daily News* before becoming a full-time writer. She wrote several books for children, including *Letters to Channy: A Trip Around the World, Little Elephant Catches Cold,* and *Thomas Goes Trading.* Obituaries and other sources: *AB Bookman's Weekly,* October 5, 1970.

*   *   *

WASSERMANN, (Karl) Jakob   1873-1934

BRIEF ENTRY: Born March 10, 1873, in Fuerth, Germany (now West Germany); died January 1, 1934, in Alt-Aussee, Austria. German novelist and short story writer. Wassermann's family opposed his literary aspirations and tried to discourage him, but after two aborted attempts at a business career, a year in the army, and a period of destitute wandering, he succeeded in establishing himself as an author with his second novel, *Dark Pilgrimage* (1897). His subsequent books were more popular; by the late 1920's he was among the world's most prominent authors, widely read in many countries in addition to his homeland. In such books as *Caspar Hauser* (1908), *The Goose Man* (1915), and *The World's Illusion* (1919), Wassermann examined all levels of German society, attacking injustice as he probed his characters' psychological problems. His work is considered uneven in quality, possessing considerable psychological insight and, at its best, a Dostoyevskian intensity, but sometimes flawed by Wassermann's tendency toward abstract philosophical discussion. Though Wassermann always considered himself German, he spent most of his adult life in Austria to avoid the anti-Semitism he encountered in Germany. In his autobiography *My Life as a German and a Jew* (1921) he wrote of the problems of his dual cultural identity. Shortly before his death, his books were banned by the Nazis and he was expelled from the Prussian Academy of Letters. *Residence:* Alt-Aussee, Austria. *Biographical/critical sources: Twentieth Century Authors: A Biographical Dictionary of Modern Literature,* H. W. Wilson, 1942, 1st Supplement, 1955; John C. Blankenagel, *The Writings of Jakob Wassermann,* Christopher, 1942; *Cyclopedia of World Authors,* Harper, 1958.

*   *   *

WATKINS, Alan (Rhun)   1933-

PERSONAL: Born April 3, 1933, in Swansea, Wales. *Education:* Queen's College, Cambridge, M.A., LL.B. *Home:* 12 Battishill St., London N1 1TE, England *Agent:* Felicity Bryan, Curtis Brown, Ltd., 1 Craven Hill, London W2 3EP, England. *Office: Observer,* 8 St. Andrews Hill, London EC4V 5JA, England.

CAREER: Called to the Bar at Lincoln's Inn, 1957; *Sunday Express,* London, England, member of editorial staff, 1959-64; *Spectator,* London, political correspondent and author of column, 1964-67; *New Statesman,* London, political correspondent and author of column, 1967-76; *Observer,* London, author of political column, 1976—. *Awards, honors:* "What the Papers Say" Award from Granada Television; named political columnist of the year, 1973.

WRITINGS: The Liberal Dilemma, MacGibbon & Kee, 1966; (contributor) Gerald Kaufman, editor, *The Left,* Blond Educational, 1966; (with Andrew Alexander) *The Making of the Prime Minister 1970,* MacDonald & Co., 1970. Author of columns in *Sunday Mirror,* 1968-69, and *Evening Standard,* 1974-75.

* * *

WATKINS, Evan Paul 1946-

PERSONAL: Born October 25, 1946, in Wichita, Kan.; married, 1968; children: one. *Education:* University of Kansas, B.A., 1968; University of Iowa, Ph.D., 1972. *Office:* Department of English, Morrill Hall, Michigan State University, East Lansing, Mich. 48824.

CAREER: Michigan State University, East Lansing, assistant professor, 1972-77, associate professor of English, 1977—. *Member:* Modern Language Association of America. *Awards, honors:* Fulbright-Hays fellow in Italy, 1978-79.

WRITINGS: The Critical Art: Criticism and Community, Yale University Press, 1978. Contributor to journals, including *Boundary Two.*

BIOGRAPHICAL/CRITICAL SOURCES: Journal of Aesthetics, autumn, 1979.*

* * *

WATKINS, Mary M. 1950-

PERSONAL: Born December 15, 1950, in Houston, Tex.; daughter of Henry C. (a financial executive) and Pauline (Orgill) Watkins; married Robert Alan Rosenthal (a psychologist), March 1, 1980. *Education:* Attended Rice University, 1968-70; Princeton University, A.B. (cum laude), 1972; attended Jung Institute, Zurich, Switzerland, 1973-74; Duquesne University, M.A., 1975; further graduate study at Clark University, 1976—. *Home:* 81 Oliver Rd., Belmont, Mass. 02178.

CAREER: Cambridge City Hospital, Cambridge, Mass., mental health worker, 1972-73; Psychotherapy Associates, Cambridge, psychotherapist, 1975-77; Judge Baker Guidance Center, Boston, Mass., psychology intern, 1978-79.

WRITINGS: Waking Dreams, Gordon & Breach, 1976. Contributor to psychology journals.

WORK IN PROGRESS: Research on imaginal dialogues in childhood and adulthood.

* * *

WATSON, Graham (Angus) 1913-

PERSONAL: Born June 8, 1913, in Newcastle-on-Tyne, England; son of Angus and Ethel (Reid) Watson; married Dorothy Vasey, March 6, 1946; children: Julia Dorothy, Hester Sophie. *Education:* Cambridge University, B.A. (with honors), 1934. *Home:* Lamb House, Rye, Sussex, England. *Office:* John Cushman Associates, Inc., 25 West 43rd St., New York, N.Y. 10036.

CAREER: Editorial director for Nicholson & Watson (publisher), 1934-40; *Spectator,* London, England, journalist, 1946-47; Curtis Brown Ltd. (literary agents), London, director, 1947-67, managing director, 1967—. Chairman of literary agency, John Cushman Associates, Inc., New York, N.Y., 1967—. *Military service:* British Army, served during World War II in Europe and North Africa; mentioned in dispatches. *Member:* Brooks's Club.

WRITINGS: A Guide to the Fishing Inns of Scotland, revised edition, Constable, 1977; *Book Society* (memoirs), Deutsch, 1979, Atheneum, 1980.

BIOGRAPHICAL/CRITICAL SOURCES: Graham Watson, *Book Society,* Atheneum, 1980; *New York Times,* February 29, 1980; *Times Literary Supplement,* April 25, 1980; *New York Times Book Review,* May 25, 1980.*

* * *

WATSON, Jack Brierley 1927-

PERSONAL: Born June 20, 1927, in Rochdale, England; son of Robert (a builder) and Alice (a draper; maiden name, Hallowell) Watson; married Margaret Cowin Sim (a lecturer), March, 1951; children: Roger, Lorelei. *Education:* University of London, B.A., 1948, M.A., 1959. *Home:* 436 Queen's Promenade, Blackpool FY5 1QT, England. *Office:* Preston Polytechnic, Preston, England.

CAREER: Teacher at secondary schools in Rochdale, England, 1951-53; head of history and general studies at grammar school in Stockton-on-Tees, England, 1953-56; teacher of history and general studies and department head at grammar school in Eccles, England, 1956-63; Queen Mary School, Lytham, England, teacher of history and government and head of department, 1963-68; Preston Polytechnic, Preston, England, senior lecturer in history, 1968—. Member of Commonwealth Institute colleges of education panel.

WRITINGS: The Public Services of the Lancashire Gentry, 1529-1558, Lancashire and Cheshire Antiquarian Society, 1960; *The Member for Eccles,* Eccles and District History Society, 1963; *Empire to Commonwealth, 1919-1970,* Dent, 1971; (with I. F. Burton, R. J. Moore, and L.C.B. Seaman) *Multiple Choice Testing in History Examinations: A Teacher's Guide,* Chatto Educational, 1973; (with Burton, Moore, and Seaman) *Multiple Choice Practice Items in History,* Chatto Educational, 1973; *Success in Twentieth-Century World Affairs Since 1919,* J. Murray, 1974; (with E. G. Rayner and R. F. Stapley) *New Objective Tests in Twentieth-Century History,* Hodder & Stoughton, 1974.

(With Rayner and Stapley) *New Objective Tests in British and European History, 1760-1848,* Hodder & Stoughton, 1977; (with Rayner and Stapley) *Practice Questions in West Indian History,* J. Murray, 1979; *The West Indian Heritage,* J. Murray, 1979; *European History, 1815-1941,* J. Murray, 1981; *Twentieth-Century British History,* J. Murray 1981. Co-author of "Evidence in Question," a series, Oxford University Press, 1980. Co-editor of *Panelview,* 1970-73, editor, 1973-74.

WORK IN PROGRESS: Western Europe Since 1945, for Harrap; *World History Since 1945,* for J. Murray.

SIDELIGHTS: Watson wrote: "My teaching and research interests are the Commonwealth, the Caribbean and race relations, especially the building of multicultural societies in a world where racism remains all too prevalent." *Avocational interests:* Music, philately, politics.

* * *

WATSON, Philip S(aville) 1909-

PERSONAL: Born October 15, 1909; married Joyce Margaret Saville, June 30, 1942; children: one son, one daughter. *Education:* University of Durham, B.A., 1931, M.A., 1934; Cambridge University, B.A., 1934, M.A., 1939, B.D., 1950, D.D., 1960; studied at University of Tuebingen and University of Lund, 1934-36. *Home:* Timbers, 60 Court Ave., Old Coulsdon, Surrey CR3 1HE, England.

CAREER: Ordained Methodist minister; Wesley College, Leeds, England, assistant tutor, 1936-39; pastor of Methodist churches in Barrhead, Scotland, 1939-44, and Bristol, England, 1944-46; Handsworth College, Birmingham, England, tutor in systematic theology and philosophy of religion, 1946-55; Wesley House, Cambridge, England, tutor in systematic and pastoral theology, 1955-59; Garrett Theological Seminary, Evanston, Ill., professor of systematic theology, 1959-73; writer, 1973—. Ferneley-Hartley Lecturer, 1947; Merrick Lecturer, 1962; Brashares Visiting Professor, 1968-69. *Awards, honors:* D.D. from University of Glasgow, 1959, and Ohio Wesleyan University, 1962.

WRITINGS: (Translator) Anders Nygren, *Agape and Eros: A History of the Christian Idea of Love,* two volumes, Macmillan, 1938-39, revised edition, 1953, reprinted, Harper, 1970; *The State as a Servant of God: A Study of Its Nature and Tasks,* S.P.C.K., 1946; *Let God Be God: An Interpretation of the Theology of Luther,* Epworth, 1947, reprinted, Fortress, 1970; (editor and translator) Martin Luther, *A Commentary on the Epistle to the Galatians,* Revell, 1953; *The Concept of Grace,* Epworth, 1959; *The Message of the Wesleys,* Macmillan, 1964; (editor with E. G. Rupp) *Luther and Erasmus: Free Will and Salvation,* S.C.M. Press, 1969; (editor and translator) *The Bondage of the Will,* Concordia, 1972; (translator) *Meaning and Method,* Fortress, 1972. Also translator of *Essence of Christianity,* 1960.

Contributor to books, including *The Catholicity of Protestantism,* 1950, *Lutherforschung Heute,* 1958, *World Lutherism of Today,* 1960, *The Christian Replies,* 1960, and *The Doctrine of the Church,* 1964. Contributor to *A Dictionary of Christian Theology.* Contributor of about twenty-five articles to scholarly journals, including *Dialog, Cresset, Ecumenical Review, Expository Times,* and *London Quarterly.*

*   *   *

WATTENMAKER, Richard J.   1941-

PERSONAL: Born February 22, 1941, in Philadelphia, Pa.; son of Nathan and Frances (Rynes) Wattenmaker; married Eva Augusta Oscarsson, June 25, 1968; children: Adrian Ezra, Barnaby Leo. *Education:* Studied at Barnes Foundation, 1959-66; University of Pennsylvania, B.A., 1963; New York University, M.A., 1965, Ph.D., 1972. *Home:* 37 Lonsdale Rd., Toronto, Ontario, Canada M4V 1W4. *Office:* Art Gallery of Ontario, 317 Dundas St. W., Toronto, Ontario, Canada M5T 1G4.

CAREER: Rutgers University, New Brunswick, N.J., director of art gallery, 1966-69; Art Gallery of Ontario, Toronto, chief curator, 1972—. *Member:* College Art Association of America.

WRITINGS: The Art of Charles Prendergast, Art Gallery, Rutgers University, 1968; *The Art of Jean Hugo,* Art Gallery of Ontario, 1973; (author of introduction) *Handbook* (translated by Louis Le Gall), Art Gallery of Ontario, 1974; *Puvis de Chavannes and the Modern Tradition,* Art Gallery of Ontario, 1975, revised edition, 1976; (author of introduction) *The Dutch Cityscape in the Seventeenth Century and Its Sources,* Historical Museum (Amsterdam, Netherlands), 1977.*

*   *   *

WAUGH, Alec
See WAUGH, Alexander Raban

WAUGH, Alexander Raban   1898-1981
(Alec Waugh)

OBITUARY NOTICE—See index for *CA* sketch: Born July 8, 1898, in Hampstead, London, England; died after suffering a stroke, September 3, 1981, in Tampa, Fla. Poet, biographer, and author best known for his novel *Island in the Sun.* Waugh's story of an interracial love affair on an imaginary tropical island garnered for its author a popularity that had eluded him for most of his career. In the year after its publication, Waugh observed, "I made more in one month with 'Islands in the Sun' than I did in 40 years of writing with about 38 books and countless stories." The novel's success allowed him to lead the nomadic life for which he was famous. The older brother of writer Evelyn Waugh, Waugh explained that he and his sibling had parceled the world between them. "He [Evelyn] was a devout Catholic so he took the Catholic countries," remarked Waugh. "I am a devout cricketer so I took the cricket-playing countries." Spending much of his time in warm climates, the author wrote several travel books on the places he lived and visited. Such works include *Hot Countries, The Sugar Islands,* and *Most Women.* Waugh's first novel, *The Loom of Youth,* caused a minor scandal in Britain. Written in 1917, *The Loom of Youth* was the first book to deal with homosexuality in English public schools. Its publication resulted in the deletion of Waugh's and his father Arthur's names from the alumni records of the public school they had both attended. The author's other novels include *The Lonely Unicorn, Playing With Fire,* and *A Spy in the Family.* He also wrote a book of poetry entitled *Resentment* and *The Lipton Story,* a biography. Obituaries and other sources: Alec Waugh, *The Early Years of Alec Waugh,* Cassell, 1962; *New York Times,* September 4, 1981; *Washington Post,* September 5, 1981; *Time,* September 14, 1981; *Newsweek,* September 14, 1981; *Publishers Weekly,* September 18, 1981; *AB Bookman's Weekly,* October 19, 1981.

*   *   *

WAYMAN, Alex   1921-

PERSONAL: Born January 11, 1921, in Chicago, Ill.; son of Phillip and Katie (Grostern) Wayman; married Hideko Shimomaki, August 25, 1956. *Education:* University of California, Los Angeles, B.A., 1948, M.A., 1949; University of California, Berkeley, Ph.D., 1959. *Home:* 560 Riverside Dr., New York, N.Y. 10027. *Office:* Columbia University, New York, N.Y. 10027.

CAREER: University of Wisconsin (now University of Wisconsin—Madison), assistant professor, 1961-65, associate professor of Indian studies, 1965-67; Columbia University, New York, N.Y., professor of Sanskrit, 1967—. Visiting lecturer at University of Michigan, autumn, 1960, spring, 1961; visiting associate professor at Columbia University, autumn, 1966. *Military service:* U.S. Army Air Forces, 1942-46; became staff sergeant. *Member:* American Oriental Society, Association for Asian Studies. *Awards, honors:* Fellow of Bollingen Foundation, 1958-60, and American Institute of Indian Studies (in India), 1963-64; grants from American Council of Learned Societies, summer, 1966, and American Philosophical Society (for India), spring, 1970.

WRITINGS: (Contributor) *Indo-Iranian Monographs,* Mouton, 1968; (contributor) *Historia Religionum,* Volume II, E. J. Brill, 1971; *The Buddhist Tantras: Light on Indo-Tibetan Esotericism,* Samuel Weiser, 1973; (translator) Srimalasutra, *The Lion's*

Roar of Queen Srimala: A Buddhist Scripture on the Tatha-gatagarbha Theory, Columbia University Press, 1974; *Yoga of the Guhyasamajatantra: The Arcane Lore of Forty Verses; A Buddhist Tantra Commentary*, Motilal Banarsidass, 1977; (translator) Tson-kha-pa Blo-bzan-grags-pa, *Calming the Mind and Discerning the Real: Buddhist Meditation and the Middle View, From the Lam rim chenmo Tson-kha-pa*, Columbia University Press, 1978; (with F. D. Lessing) *Introduction to the Buddhist Tantric System*, Motilal Banarsidass, 1978. Contributor to philosophy, theology, and Oriental studies journals.*

* * *

WEAVER, Frank Parks 1904-

PERSONAL: Born March 17, 1904, in Greensburg, Pa.; son of Amos P. (a blacksmith and farrier) and Oma (Parks) Weaver; married Margaret E. Hay, July 7, 1933 (died November, 1963); married Katherine Crockett Allard (a teacher of English), July 31, 1966; children: (first marriage) Samuel Alan, Frank Parks, Marion Hay (deceased), Sarah. *Education:* University of Michigan, A.B., 1926; University of Washington, Seattle, LL.B., 1928. *Politics:* Republican. *Religion:* Episcopalian. *Home:* 1404 Boulevard Park Dr., Lacey, Wash. 98503.

CAREER: Gonzaga University, Spokane, Wash., professor of real property, 1928-49, secretary of Law School, 1939-45, dean, 1945-48; Supreme Court of Washington, Olympia, justice, 1951-70, chief justice, 1959-61; writer, 1970—. Lawyer in Spokane, 1928-51. Member of Washington Judiciary Council; delegate to Republican National Convention, 1944. *Member:* Washington State Bar Association, Spokane County Bar Association (president, 1946), Phi Beta Kappa, Coif, Beta Theta Pi, Spokane Sailing Club, Olympia Yacht Club, Washington Athletic Club. *Awards, honors:* LL.D. from Gonzaga University, 1949, and Whitman College, 1959.

WRITINGS: (With Charles Sheldon) *Politicians, Judges, and the People*, Greenwood Press, 1980.

SIDELIGHTS: Weaver wrote: "Three years after I retired in 1970, I was called back in service to organize, direct, work as chief justice, and finally to write the opinion of the first all pro tempore court of its kind in the state's history."

* * *

WEBB, Harri 1920-

PERSONAL: Born September 7, 1920, in Swansea, Glamorgan, Wales. *Education:* Attended Magdalen College, Oxford. *Politics:* Welsh Nationalist (Plaid Cymru). *Home:* 2 Roserow, Cumbach, Aberdare, Wales.

CAREER: Journalist, politician, balladist, and poet. Chief librarian at Mountain Ash Library, Glamorgan, Wales. *Awards, honors:* Prize from Welsh Arts Council, 1970.

WRITINGS: (With Peter Gruffydd and Meic Stephens) *Triad: Thirty-Three Poems*, Triskel Press, 1963; *Our National Anthem: Some Observations on "Hen wlad fy nhadau,"* Triskel Press, 1964; *The Green Desert* (poems), Gomer, 1969; *A Crown for Branwen* (poems), Gomer, 1974. Also author of *Rampage and Revel* (poems), 1977.*

* * *

WEBB, Jon (Edgar) 1905(?)-1971

OBITUARY NOTICE: Born c. 1905; died June 9, 1971, in Nashville, Tenn. Typographer, editor, and author. Webb was best known as the editor and typographer of *The Outsider*, an avant-garde magazine that he edited with his wife, the artist and novelist Gypsy Lou Webb. He was also responsible for producing several hand-press limited editions, including Henry Miller's *Order and Chaos Chez Hans Reichel*. Obituaries and other sources: *AB Bookman's Weekly*, August 2, 1971.

* * *

WEBB, Phyllis 1927-

PERSONAL: Born April 8, 1927, in Victoria, British Columbia, Canada. *Education:* University of British Columbia, B.A., 1949; received degree from McGill University, 1953. *Address:* P.O. Box 11, Fulford, British Columbia, Canada.

CAREER: Secretary in Montreal, Quebec, 1956; University of British Columbia, Vancouver, member of staff, 1961-64; Canadian Broadcasting Corporation (CBC), Toronto, Ontario, program organizer, 1964-67, executive producer, 1967-69; freelance writer and broadcaster. *Awards, honors:* Overseas Award from Government of Canada, 1957; Canada Council grant, 1963, senior fellowship, 1969.

*WRITINGS—*Poems: (With Gael Turnbull and Eli Mandel) *Trio*, Contact Press, 1954; *Even Your Right Eye*, McClelland & Steward, 1956; *The Sea Is Also a Garden: Poems*, Ryerson Press, 1962; *Naked Poems*, Periwinkle Press, 1965; *Selected Poems, 1954-1965*, edited and introduced by John Hulcoop, Talonbooks, 1971.

WORK IN PROGRESS: The Kropotkin Papers, a sequence of poems on the theme of imprisonment.

SIDELIGHTS: Phyllis Webb's "intensely, painfully personal" poems have earned her a reputation as one of Canada's important contemporary poets though her output has been small. Her poetry is intellectually and emotionally complex, and, as Robert Weaver of *Saturday Night* notes, "that nakedness of feeling shouldn't obscure the fact that she is a patient and professional craftsman." She takes as her themes "love, history, time, public life," writes Peter Stevens in *Canadian Literature*, "and they are expressed in images of bones, the sea, open landscapes and nakedness."

BIOGRAPHICAL/CRITICAL SOURCES: Canadian Literature, summer, 1961, spring, 1967, spring, 1972; Phyllis Webb, *Selected Poems*, Talonbooks, 1971; *Saturday Night*, November, 1971; *Contemporary Literary Criticism*, Gale, Volume 18, 1981.*

* * *

WEBB, Stephen S(aunders) 1937-

PERSONAL: Born May 25, 1937, in Syracuse, N.Y.; married, 1959; children: two. *Education:* Williams College, B.A., 1959; University of Wisconsin (now University of Wisconsin—Madison), M.S., 1961, Ph.D., 1965. *Office:* Department of History, Syracuse University, Maxwell Hall, Syracuse, N.Y. 13210.

CAREER: St. Lawrence University, Canton, N.Y., assistant professor of history, 1964-65; College of William and Mary, Williamsburg, Va., assistant professor of history, 1965-68; Syracuse University, Syracuse, N.Y., associate professor of history, 1968—. Fellow of Institute of Early American History and Culture, 1965-68, associate, 1977—; associate of Columbia University seminar on early American history and culture, 1968—, chairman, 1976-77; fellow of Charles Warren Center, Harvard University, 1971-72, 1974-75. *Awards, honors:* National Endowment for the Humanities fellow, 1971-72.

WRITINGS: Government in Britain and America, Harper, 1978; *The Governors-General: The English Army and the Definition* *of the Empire, 1569-1681*, University of North Carolina Press, 1979. Contributor to history journals.*

* * *

WEBSTER, Grant T. 1933-

PERSONAL: Born March 15, 1933, in Fargo, N.D.; son of Grant C. (a manager) and Mabel E. (a teacher; maiden name, Thompson); married Mary L. Rose (a framer), December, 1963; children: William, Charles. *Education:* Carleton College, A.B., 1954; Columbia University, A.M., 1958; Ohio State University, Ph.D., 1963. *Home:* 11 Edgewood Rd., Binghamton, N.Y. 13903. *Office:* Department of English, State University of New York at Binghamton, Binghamton, N.Y. 13901.

CAREER: University of Southern California, Los Angeles, assistant professor of English, 1963-67; State University of New York at Binghamton, assistant professor, 1967-72, associate professor of English, 1972—. *Military service:* U.S. Army, 1954-56. *Member:* Modern Language Association of America. *Awards, honors:* Fellowship from American Council of Learned Societies, 1980-81.

WRITINGS: The Republic of Letters: A History of Postwar American Literary Opinion, Johns Hopkins Press, 1979. Contributor to journals, including *Criticism* and *Denver Quarterly*.

WORK IN PROGRESS: Volume II of the history of postwar American literary criticism.

SIDELIGHTS: Webster told *CA:* "Like most English professors of my generation, I began to study English literature because I was an Anglophile, or came to love England through the study of English literature. London in the fifties seemed the center of the English-speaking world, as it is still the pleasantest and safest city for a night at the theatre. I have visited England several times, and lived there twice for some months, and have found these periods to be the most rewarding of my life so far. One of the interesting critical problems of the present is to find a new central tradition for the study of literature now that the England and the WASP elements in American culture have declined so sharply in influence because of the rise in interest in other ethnic literatures, woman's literature, and the like.

"The problems in literary criticism that interest me most are the social and historical values implicit in various critical approaches: What does it mean to see literature in Formalist, Marxist, Structuralist, mythic, or scholarly terms, and what is the relation of such interpretative strategies to broader cultural currents? In seeking answers to such questions, I have found a model for the history of criticism in the history of science of Thomas S. Kuhn, for the thought of the New York Intellectuals in the historian of the avant-garde Renato Poggioli, for a new theory of myth as oral literature in the anthropologist Jack Goody and the classicist Eric A. Havelock. Such thinkers, and others like the historian of printing Elizabeth Eisenstein, and the historian of education Laurence Veysey, seem to me now to be doing work both more exciting and more sensible than the Structuralism of Levi-Strauss and Barthes, and the post-modernism of Derrida and Heidegger now fashionable in advanced literary and critical circles. In the second volume of my history of modern criticism I try to deal with the current state of English studies and criticism in terms suggested by some of these thinkers.

"Personally I live a quiet family- and university-centered life in a pleasant and safe, but hardly dynamic, small American city. I have been meeting classes since 1956, play tennis, take care of the garden, and watch the children, a sort of regular existence that is essential for the scholarly life."

BIOGRAPHICAL/CRITICAL SOURCES: Nation, January 26, 1980.

* * *

WEBSTER, James 1925-1981

OBITUARY NOTICE—See index for *CA* sketch: Born March 8, 1925, in New Barhet, Hertfordshire, England; killed in a glider crash, June 15, 1981, in Stratford-upon-Avon, England. Educator and author. An authority on literacy and dyslexia, Webster was a professor of education at such schools as the Newton Park College of Education, Redland College of Education, and University of Bristol. In 1964 he founded England's first institution to aid dyslexic children. While participating in a Gloucester Gliding Club competition, Webster was killed when his glider crashed into a housing project. Among his works are *Practical Reading: Some New Remedial Techniques* and *Reading Failure, With Particular Reference to Rescue Reading*. Webster also wrote books for children, including *The Red Robber of Larado, The Ladybird Book of Tricks and Games and Others,* and *Ladybird Readers*. Obituaries and other sources: *Chicago Tribune*, June 17, 1981.

* * *

WEBSTER, Norman William 1920-

PERSONAL: Born August 21, 1920, in Barrow-in-Furness, England; son of John William and Sarah (Hayward) Webster; married Phyllis Joan Layley, February 17, 1945; children: Gwendolen Webster Freundel, Stella Webster Birchall. *Education:* University of London, B.Sc., 1954. *Politics:* "European Democrat." *Religion:* Church of England. *Home:* Wetherlam, Ecchinswell, Newbury RG15 8UB, England.

CAREER: Associated with Ministry of Defence, Scientific Civil Service, 1938-80; writer, 1980—. Part-time lecturer at Reading College of Technology. Member of local parish council. *Military service:* Royal Air Force, Fighter Command, 1941-46. *Member:* Institute of Physics, Jane Austen Society, European Society.

WRITINGS: Joseph Locke, Railway Revolutionary, Allen & Unwin, 1970; *Britain's First Trunk Line: The Grand Junction Railway*, Adams & Dart, 1972; *The Great North Road*, Adams & Dart, 1974. Contributor of more than two hundred articles to scientific journals and popular magazines, including *Antiquarian Book Review, Book Collector, Cornhill, Cumbria,* and *Hertfordshire Countryside*.

WORK IN PROGRESS: The Outskirts of Success, a collection of his previously published articles on such women as Cecile Chaminade, Jean Ingelow, Anne Hathaway, Felicia Hemans, Vernon Lee, Daisy Ashford, and Alice Liddell; *John Webster*, a biographical study of the Jacobean dramatist.

SIDELIGHTS: Webster wrote: "I have a strong topographical sense which forms my preference for places rather than people, except that I have a keen interest in those I feel are now unjustly neglected. For example, I think my study of French composer Chaminade has not been matched. I have a keen interest in Europe (and thus such writers as Henry James), and my wife and I travel as often as possible to France, Italy, and Germany. The United States is also fine for a holiday break, when we can afford it."

BIOGRAPHICAL/CRITICAL SOURCES: Berkshire Mercury, October 19, 1972.

WEDDE, Ian 1946-

PERSONAL: Born October 17, 1946, in Blenheim, New Zealand; son of Frederic Albert and Linda (Ogilvie) Wedde; married Rosemary Beauchamp (a puppeteer), 1967; children: Carlos Beauchamp, Thomas Conrad. *Education:* University of Auckland, M.A. (with honors), 1968. *Home:* 118A Maidavale Rd., Roseneath, Wellington, New Zealand.

CAREER: Teacher with British Council in Jordan, 1969-70; *London*, London, England, poetry reviewer, 1970-71; Broadcasting editor for New Zealand Broadcasting Corp., 1972. Also worked as forester, factory worker, gardener, and mail carrier. Member of State Literary Fund, 1971-79. *Member:* International P.E.N., New Zealand Scriptwriters Guild. *Awards, honors:* Robert Burns fellowship from University of Otago, 1972; Arts Council grant, 1974; National Book Award for fiction, 1976, and for poetry, 1977.

WRITINGS: Homage to Matisse (poems), Amphedesma, 1971; (translator with Fawwas Tuqan) Mahmud Darwish, *Selected Poems,* Carcanet Press, 1973, Dufour, 1974; *Made Over* (poems), Stephen Chan, 1974; *Pathway to the Sea* (poem), Hawk Press, 1975; *Earthly: Sonnets for Carlos,* Amphedesma, 1974; *Dick Seddon's Great Dive* (novel), Islands, 1976; *Spells for Coming Out* (poems), Oxford University Press, 1977; *Castaly* (poems), Oxford University Press, 1980; *The Shirt Factory* (stories), Price Milburn, 1981. Also author of two radio plays, "Stations" (musical), 1969, and "Pukeko" (musical), 1972.

WORK IN PROGRESS: A novel; "The Gringos," a film, for TV-New Zealand.

* * *

WEDEKIND, (Benjamin) Frank(lin) 1864-1918 (Cornelius Minehaha)

BRIEF ENTRY: Born July 24, 1864, in Hanover, Germany (now West Germany); died March 9, 1918, in Munich, Germany (now West Germany). German playwright. Wedekind scandalized German audiences with plays that expressed, with missionary zeal, his belief that men and women are merely animals, healthiest when acting purely out of natural instinct regardless of education and attempts at civilization. His first success, "The Awakening of Spring" (1891), reflected a remarkable knowledge of adolescents. It was a protest against the sexual secrecy that he felt doomed youth to a future of hypocritical immorality. Wedekind's best-known play was "Earth Spirit" (1893). In its heroine, Lulu, Wedekind personified his vision of woman as sex incarnate, ageless and unchanging despite the havoc she wreaked. In "The Marquis of Keith" (1900), he accented his belief that the shady characters of the underworld, by indulging their natural animal instincts, were vital agents of the will of God. Wedekind drew some of his subject matter from the naturalists and some of his style from the romantics, but his distortion of reality pointed toward expressionism and, later, surrealism. He relied on the language patterns of his characters to create a background and on the bizarre dramatic action and essential absurdity to shock his audiences into awareness and moral reform. *Biographical/ critical sources: Columbia Dictionary of Modern European Literature,* Columbia University Press, 1947; *German Quarterly,* March, 1966; *Modern World Drama: An Encyclopedia,* Dutton, 1972; *McGraw-Hill Encyclopedia of World Drama,* McGraw, 1972.

WEDELL, Eberhard (Arthur Otto) George 1927-

PERSONAL: Surname is accented on last syllable; born April 4, 1927; son of John (a minister) and Gertrude (Bonhoeffer) Wedell; married Rosemarie Winckler (a professor of religion); children: Martin, Crispin, Philip, Rebecca. *Education:* London School of Economics and Political Science, London, B.Sc., 1947. *Politics:* Liberal. *Religion:* Anglican. *Home:* 335 avenue Louise, 1050 Brussels, Belgium. *Office:* European Economic Community Commission, 200 rue de la Loi, 1049 Brussels, Belgium; and School of Business, Victoria University of Manchester, Manchester 15, England.

CAREER: Associated with Ministry of Education, London, England, 1950-60; Independent Television Authority, London, secretary, 1960-64; Victoria University of Manchester, Manchester, England, professor of adult education, 1964-75, honorary professor of employment policy, 1975—. Head of Division of Employment and Vocational Training of European Economic Community Commission, 1973—. *Awards, honors:* Book of the year award from National Association of Educational Broadcasters of the United States of America, 1978, for *Broadcasting in the Third World.*

WRITINGS: The Use of Television in Education, Association of Technical Institutions, 1963; *Broadcasting and Public Policy,* M. Joseph, 1968; (with H. D. Perraton) *Teaching at a Distance,* National Institute of Adult Education, 1968; (editor and contributor) *Structures of Broadcasting,* Manchester University Press, 1970; (with Ron Glatter) *Study by Correspondence,* Longman, 1971; *Teachers and Educational Development in Cyprus,* United Nations Educational, Scientific and Cultural Organization, 1971; (editor and contributor) *Education and the Development of Malawi,* Centre for Overseas Educational Development, Victoria University of Manchester, 1973; (with Elihu Katz) *Broadcasting in the Third World,* Harvard University Press, 1978. Also author of *Correspondence Education in Europe,* 1971.

WORK IN PROGRESS: A series of radio talks, "The Corridors of Power"; a symposium, "Broadcasting in Africa."

SIDELIGHTS: Wedell commented: "I am a student of human motivation and how to change it; hence my interest (both academic and in terms of policy making) in mass media."

* * *

WEIGER, John George 1933-

PERSONAL: Born February 6, 1933, in Dresden, Germany (now East Germany); came to the United States in 1938, naturalized citizen, 1945; son of Willy and Elisabeth (Prinz) Weiger; married Leslie Lawrence Carpenter, December 28, 1955; children: Robert Boyden, Mark Owen, Heidi Elaine. *Education:* Middlebury College, B.A., 1955; University of Colorado, M.A., 1957; Indiana University, Ph.D., 1966. *Home address:* Woodbine Rd., Shelburne, Vt. 05482. *Office:* Department of Romance Languages, University of Vermont, 521 Waterman Building, Burlington, Vt. 05403.

CAREER: University of Colorado, Boulder, instructor in Spanish, 1955-57; Lawrence College (now University), Appleton, Wis., instructor in Spanish, 1957-58; University of Vermont, Burlington, instructor, 1958-62, assistant professor, 1964-67, associate professor, 1967-73, professor of Romance languages, 1973—, dean of College of Arts and Sciences, 1971-76. Visiting lecturer at University of Bologna, 1978.

MEMBER: International Association of Hispanists, Modern Language Association of America (chairman of comedia section, 1970-71), Renaissance Society of America, American Association of Teachers of Spanish and Portuguese, American Council of Academic Deans, American Association for Higher Education, Joint Operations Committee of New England Deans, Council of Colleges of Arts and Sciences, Association for General and Liberal Studies, Comediantes, Phi Sigma Iota. *Awards, honors:* American Council of Learned Societies grant, 1978.

WRITINGS: The Valencian Dramatists of Spain's Golden Age, Twayne, 1976; *Cristobal de Virues,* Twayne, 1978; *The Individuated Self: Cervantes and the Emergence of the Individual,* Ohio University Press, 1979. Also wrote *Introduction to the Youthful Deeds of the Cid,* 1969, and *Hacia la Comedia: De los Valencianos a Lope,* 1978.

Contributor: Steven M. Cahn, editor, *Scholars Who Teach: The Art of College Teaching,* Nelson-Hall, 1978. Also contributor to *Studies in Honor of Gerald F. Wade,* 1978, and to academic journals.

Member of editorial board of *Bulletin of Comediantes,* 1978—.*

* * *

WEINBERG, Daniela 1936-

PERSONAL: Born April 4, 1936, in Prague, Czechoslovakia; came to the United States in 1939, naturalized citizen, 1945; daughter of Boris (a physician) and Dala (a physician's assistant; maiden name, Perper) Libon; married Gerald M. Weinberg (a writer), 1961. *Education:* Columbia University, A.B., 1956, A.M., 1959; University of Michigan, A.M., 1965, Ph.D., 1970. *Office:* Department of Anthropology, University of Nebraska, Lincoln, Neb. 68588.

CAREER: Hunter College of the City University of New York, New York, N.Y., instructor in anthropology, 1965-67; State University of New York at Binghamton, assistant professor of anthropology and director of summer field school in Europe, 1970-74; University of Nebraska, Lincoln, associate professor of anthropology, 1973-80, professor of anthropology, 1980—. *Member:* American Anthropological Association, Central States Anthropological Society, Swiss Ethnological Society. *Awards, honors:* Grants from Ford Foundation, 1968-69, State University of New York, 1971-72, Commune of Bagnes, Switzerland, 1971, and University of Nebraska, Lincoln, 1973-74.

WRITINGS: Experimental Use of a Computer in the Field: Kinship Information, Social Science Information, 1972; *Bruson: Etude socio-ethnologique sur les relations humaines dans un village de montagne* (title means "Ethnological Study of Human Relations in a Mountain Village"), Annales Valaisannes, 1975; *Peasant Wisdom: Cultural Adaptation in a Swiss Village,* University of California Press, 1975; (with husband, Gerald M. Weinberg) *On the Design of Stable Systems,* Wiley, 1979.

WORK IN PROGRESS: Models of Mental Health in American Culture; Thinking, Shminking—What's the Difference?, with husband, G. M. Weinberg.

SIDELIGHTS: Weinberg told *CA:* "I do not consider myself primarily a writer but a teacher. For me, writing is a way of working out ideas, testing them for clarity, wholeness, and honesty. I try to teach my students to do the same in their writing, rather than to imitate the mostly dreadful models of social-science writing they find in the professional journals and monographs. As a non-native speaker of English and a student of culture, I find language fascinating and powerful. This sensitivity to language has made me a very demanding writer and reader."

WEINBERG, Nathan Gerald 1945-

PERSONAL: Born June 15, 1945, in Los Angeles, Calif.; son of David (a tailor) and Ruth (a secretary; maiden name, Bercovitz) Weinberg; married Virginia Mia Alexander (a librarian), August 29, 1969; children: Zachary. *Education:* University of California, Riverside, B.A., 1966; University of California, Davis, M.A., 1968, Ph.D., 1974. *Home:* 22858 Calabash, Woodland Hills, Calif. 91364. *Office:* Department of Sociology, California State University, 18111 Nordhoff St., Northridge, Calif. 91330.

CAREER: University of California, Davis, lecturer in sociology, 1971 and 1972; California State University, Northridge, assistant professor, 1972-77, associate professor of sociology, 1977—. *Awards, honors:* California State graduate fellowship, 1969-71; grant from M. M. Lewis Memorial Foundation, 1971-72, for doctoral research.

WRITINGS: (Contributor) *Sociology Today,* CRM Books, 1971; *Preservation in American Towns and Cities,* Westview Press, 1979.

WORK IN PROGRESS: A study of the development of town and city planning.

SIDELIGHTS: Weinberg's concept of preservation as a social movement includes research on neglect, speculation, architecture, revolving funds, tourist development, community involvement, demonstration projects, and conflicts between preservation and development. He addresses these issues in his book *Preservation in American Towns and Cities. AIA Journal's* Richard Wagner noted that the book "has provided a good introductory examination of the current practice of historic preservation in the U.S."

BIOGRAPHICAL CRITICAL SOURCES: AIA Journal, mid-May, 1980.

* * *

WEINSTEIN, Nathan Wallenstein 1903(?)-1940 (Nathanael West)

BRIEF ENTRY: Born October 17, c. 1903, in New York, N.Y.; died in an automobile accident, December 22, 1940, in El Centro, Calif. American screenwriter, editor, and author of *The Dream Life of Balso Snell* (1931), *Miss Lonely Hearts* (1933), *A Cool Million* (1934), and *The Day of the Locust* (1939). West's novels were largely ignored until 1957 when the posthumous publication of *The Complete Works of Nathanael West* brought them critical recognition. West's books are now regarded by many critics as masterpieces of black humor. While writing his novels, West was employed as a hotel manager and later as a Hollywood screenwriter. He also worked as associate editor of *Contact* with William Carlos Williams and as an associate of *Americana* with George Grosz. *Biographical/critical sources: New York Times,* December 23, 1940; James F. Light, *Nathanael West: An Interpretive Study,* Northwestern University Press, 1961; Victor Comerchero, *Nathanael West: The Ironic Prophet,* Syracuse University Press, 1964; Randall Reid, *The Fiction of Nathanael West,* University of Chicago Press, 1968; *Encyclopedia of World Literature in the Twentieth Century,* updated edition, Ungar, 1971; *Twentieth-Century Literary Criticism,* Volume 1, Gale, 1978.

* * *

WEISBUCH, Robert 1946-

PERSONAL: Born November 22, 1946, in Rochester, N.Y.;

children: one. *Education:* Wesleyan University, Middletown, Conn., B.A., 1968; Yale University, M.Phil., 1970, Ph.D., 1972. *Office:* 1619 Haven Hall, University of Michigan, Ann Arbor, Mich. 48104.

CAREER: University of Michigan, Ann Arbor, assistant professor, 1972-75, associate professor of English, 1976—, director of undergraduate studies, 1977—. *Member:* Modern Language Association of America. *Awards, honors:* American Council of Learned Societies fellowship, 1976-77.

WRITINGS: Emily Dickinson's Poetry, University of Chicago Press, 1975.

BIOGRAPHICAL/CRITICAL SOURCES: Times Literary Supplement, May 7, 1976.*

* * *

WEISENFELD, Murray 1923-

PERSONAL: Born June 20, 1923, in New York, N.Y.; son of Harry (a tailor) and Toby (Wilk) Weisenfeld; married Shirley Segerman (assistant in husband's practice); children: Harry, Janet, Irv, Lori. *Education:* Attended New York University, 1946-48; New York College of Podiatry, D.P.M., 1952. *Religion:* Jewish. *Residence:* Brooklyn, N.Y. *Agent:* Sue Zechendorf, 57th St., New York, N.Y. *Office:* 47 West 34th St., New York, N.Y. 10001.

CAREER: Podiatrist.

WRITINGS: (With Barbara Burr) *The Runner's Repair Manual,* St. Martin's, 1980; (with Burr) *The Foot Book,* St. Martin's, 1980.

* * *

WEISS, Abraham 1895-1971

OBITUARY NOTICE: Born March 23, 1895, in Podhajce, Galicia; died October 4, 1971, in Jerusalem, Israel. Educator and author. A professor of Talmud at Bar-Ilan University, Weiss wrote ten major works on the Talmud, including *On the History of the Development of the Babylonian Talmud, The Development of the Talmud as a Literary Unit, The Talmud in Its Development,* and *Studies in the Law of the Talmud on Damages. The Abraham Weiss Jubilee Volume,* an eight hundred-page Festschrift, was published in his honor in 1964. Obituaries and other sources: *AB Bookman's Weekly,* January 4, 1971; *Who's Who in World Jewry,* Pitman, 1972.

* * *

WEISS, Lillian ?-1972

OBITUARY NOTICE: Born in New York, N.Y.; died February 22, 1972, in New York, N.Y. Editor, columnist, and author. Weiss's book, *The Concise Dictionary of Interior Decorating,* was completed just before her death and was published posthumously. Obituaries and other sources: *Who's Who of American Women,* 4th edition, Marquis, 1966; *New York Times,* February 24, 1972; *AB Bookman's Weekly,* May 15, 1972.

* * *

WELBER, Robert

PERSONAL—Education: Bank Street College of Education, M.S.

CAREER: Nursery and kindergarten teacher in New York City; founder and teacher at The Studio on Eleventh Street (alternative school), New York City.

WRITINGS—All for children; all published by Pantheon: *The Winter Picnic,* 1970; *Frog, Frog, Frog,* 1971; *The Train,* 1972; *Song of the Seasons,* 1973; *Goodbye, Hello* (Junior Literary Guild selection), 1974; *The Winter Wedding,* 1975.*

* * *

WELCH, D'Alte Aldridge 1907-1970

OBITUARY NOTICE: Born in 1907; died of gunshot wounds, January 4, 1970, in Cleveland, Ohio. Educator and bibliographer. Welch was a professor of biology at John Carroll University and an authority on early children's books. *His Bibliography of American Children's Books Printed Prior to 1821* appeared serially in the *Proceedings of the American Antiquarian Society* beginning in 1963 and was published in book form posthumously in 1972. Welch was shot in a hold-up on December 10, 1969, and subsequently died of his wounds. Obituaries and other sources: *AB Bookman's Weekly,* February 16, 1970; *Childhood in Poetry,* 2nd supplement, volume 1, Gale, 1976.

* * *

WELCH, Don 1932-

PERSONAL: Born June 3, 1932, in Hastings, Neb.; son of Howard L. (an automobile dealer) and Genevieve B. (Greenslit) Welch; married Marcia Lee Zorn, June 14, 1953; children: Shannon, Timaree, Erin, Kael, Chad, Keir. *Education:* Kearney State College, B.A., 1954; University of Northern Colorado, M.A., 1957; University of Nebraska, Ph.D., 1965. *Home:* 611 West 27th, Kearney, Neb. 68847. *Office:* Department of English, Kearney State College, Kearney, Neb. 68847.

CAREER: High school teacher of English and speech in Fort Morgan, Colo., 1957-58; high school teacher of English and French in Gothenburg, Neb., 1958-59; Kearney State College, Kearney, Neb., professor of English, 1959-80, Martin Professor of English, 1980—. Publicity director for American Homing Pigeon Union, 1972. *Military service:* U.S. Army, Counter-Intelligence Corps, 1954-56. *Member:* Poets and Writers Association. *Awards, honors:* Pablo Neruda Prize for Poetry from *Nimrod,* 1980, for "The Rarer Game."

WRITINGS—Poetry: *Dead Horse Table,* Wildflower, 1975; *Handwork,* Kearney State College Press, 1978; *The Rarer Game,* Kearney State College Press, 1980.

Work appeared in anthologies, including *Traveling America With Today's Poets,* Macmillan, 1977; *A Geography of Poets,* Bentam, 1979; *The Wildflower Home Almanac of Poetry,* Wildflower Press, 1980.

Contributor to *Pebble, Prairie Schooner,* and *Nimrod.*

WORK IN PROGRESS: Beasts of a Stranger Field, a tentative title, poems about imaginary birds and animals, with some reworkings of legendary creatures; a series of four poetic broadsides, publication by Waterleaf Press expected in 1982.

SIDELIGHTS: Welch wrote: "My works are strongly rooted in the feelings I have for nature. This can be seen in the epigraph of my most recent book, *The Rarer Game,* in which I said, 'The world of animals and birds is innocent, visceral, predatory, and beautiful.' In an age of literary disbelief and chaos, there is a blood pulse in nature which is both redemptive and, in its own way, orderly. I have consistently drawn on it, as well as the gut-toughness of the Midlanders who survived the Great Depression of the 1930's."

WELCH, Mary-Scott (Stewart)   1914-

PERSONAL: Born in December, 1914, in Chicago, Ill.; daughter of William Scott (an attorney) and Myrtle (Ferrin) Stewart; married Barrett Farley Welch (in business), March 23, 1943; children: Farley, Laura, Margaret, Mary Barrett. *Education:* University of Illinois, A.B., 1940. *Politics:* "Feminist/Democrat." *Religion:* None. *Home:* 55 Park Ave., New York, N.Y. 10016. *Agent:* Alexandria Hatcher Agency, 150 West 55th St., New York, N.Y. 10019. *Office:* 333 East 33rd St., New York, N.Y. 10016.

CAREER: Free-lance writer. Held several positions on magazines, including editor of *Homemaker's Digest,* food editor of *Glamour,* entertainment editor of *Look,* and associate editor of *Pageant;* also columnist for *Vogue,* 1972—, *McCall's,* 1974—, *Executive Female,* and *Seventeen.* Member of advisory board of Working Women and Cornell University's Institute on Women and Work; past member of faculty at Womanschool and Ethical Culture Society; founding member of Friends of NOW. Lecturer; conducts workshops; guest on radio and television programs. *Military service:* U.S. Navy, Women Accepted for Volunteer Emergency Service (WAVES), 1942-43.

MEMBER: American Society of Journalists and Authors, American Civil Liberties Union, Feminist Writers Guild, Authors Guild, National Women's Political Caucus, National Press Club, Women in Communications, National Organization for Women (member of advisory board; coordinator of rape prevention committee), Wilderness Society, Sierra Club, New York Civil Liberties Union, Phi Beta Kappa, Kappa Kappa Gamma.

WRITINGS: Your First Hundred Meals, Scribner, 1948; (co-editor) *Esquire Handbook for Hosts,* Grosset, 1949, enlarged edition, 1953; (co-editor) *Esquire Etiquette: A Guide to Business, Sports, and Social Conduct,* Lippincott, 1953; (co-editor) *The Esquire Cook Book,* introduction by Arnold Gingrich, illustrated by Charmatz, McGraw, 1955; (co-editor) *The Art of Keeping Fit; or, How the Successful Male Can Avoid Going to Seed,* Harper, 1959; (co-editor) *What Every Young Man Should Know,* Geis, 1962; (co-editor with Ronnie Welch) *The Esquire Party Book,* illustrated and designed by Seymour Chwast, [New York], 1965; *The Seventeen Guide to Travel: How, When, Where,* Macmillan, 1970; *The Family Wilderness Handbook,* Ballantine, 1974; *Networking: The Great New Way for Women to Get Ahead,* Harcourt, 1980.

Contributor to popular magazines, including *Redbook, Ladies' Home Journal,* and *Working Woman.* West Coast editor of *Esquire* and *Coronet.*

WORK IN PROGRESS: A book on sex discrimination in employment, with Carolyn Bird and Catherine East.

SIDELIGHTS: Mary-Scott Welch wrote: "*Networking* has thrust me into a new life as lecturer and conductor of workshops, as well as (it seems) a constant interviewee on how this system really works." *Avocational interests:* Bicycling in Manhattan, swimming.

*   *   *

WELLESLEY, Gerald   1885-1972

OBITUARY NOTICE: Born in 1885; died January 4, 1972, in England. Diplomat, soldier, architect, publisher, editor, and author. The seventh Duke of Wellington, Wellesley edited and published several books on his ancestry, including *The Iconography of the First Duke of Wellington.* Wellesley gave the Duke's Hyde Park Corner residence and its contents to the nation as the Wellington Museum. He was married to the poet Dorothy Violet Ashton from 1914 until her death in 1956. Obituaries and other sources: *AB Bookman's Weekly,* February 7, 1972.

*   *   *

WELLS, Bella Fromm   1901(?)-1972

OBITUARY NOTICE: Born c. 1901; died February 9, 1972, in New York, N.Y. Journalist. Wells was a diplomatic correspondent in Berlin for *Ullstein* and *The Times* prior to World War II. While in Germany she kept a secret diary on Nazi activities, *Blood and Banquets: A Berlin Social Diary.* Her papers were given to the Boston University Library. Obituaries and other sources: *AB Bookman's Weekly,* February 28, 1972.

*   *   *

WELLS, John Campbell   1936-

PERSONAL: Born November 17, 1936, in Ashford, England; son of Eric George (a minister) and Dorothy Amy (Thompson) Wells. *Education:* St. Edmund Hall, Oxford, M.A., 1961. *Home and office:* 1-A Scarsdale Villas, London W8 6PT, England. *Agent:* A. D. Peters & Co. Ltd., 10 Buckingham St., London WC2N 6BU, England.

CAREER: Eton College, Windsor, England, teacher of modern languages, 1961-63; co-editor of *Private Eye,* 1964-66; author of column "Afterthought" in *Spectator,* 1966-70; full-time free-lance writer, 1970—. Visiting lecturer at Central School of Art and Design. *Military service:* British Army, Royal Sussex Regiment, 1957-58; served in Korea; became lieutenant. *Awards, honors:* Ondas Prize from Spanish radio, 1975, for radio musical "Alice in Wonderland."

WRITINGS: (With Richard Ingrams) *Mrs. Wilson's Diary* (play; first produced on West End at Stratford and at Criterion Theatres, 1967), Anthony Blond, 1967; *The Exploding Present* (essays), Sidgwick & Jackson, 1971; *A Melon for Ecstasy* (novel), Weidenfeld & Nicolson, 1971; (with Ingrams) *Dear Bill* (collection of columns), Deutsch, 1980; "Anyone for Denis," first produced in London, May 7, 1981; (translator and author of prefaces) Beaumarchais, *The Figaro Plays: "The Barber of Seville"; "The Marriage of Figaro"; "A Mother's Guilt,"* J. Calder, 1981; *Where We Went Wrong: A Secret History of the Twentieth Century,* Routledge & Kegan Paul, 1982.

Unpublished plays: "Alice in Wonderland" (adapted from the story by Lewis Carroll), first broadcast by BBC-Radio, 1975; (translator) Georg Buechner, "Danton's Death" (two-act), first produced in London at National Theatre, 1970; (translator) "The Marriage of Figaro," first produced in London, at National Theatre, 1973. Contributor to *Private Eye.*

SIDELIGHTS: Wells commented: "The thing I enjoy doing most is teaching; at the moment I am teaching theatre design. Second to that—writing and performing jokes, ideally with old friends, some almost as old as the jokes.

"I have a very profound insight about the twentieth century and would argue if pressed that the proof of the pudding is in the eating rather than in its scientific analysis or the philosophical outpourings of the code."

*   *   *

WELLS, Samuel F(ogle, Jr.)   1935-

PERSONAL: Born September 13, 1935, in Mullins, S.C.; son

of Samuel Fogle (a teacher) and Mildred (a teacher; maiden name, Meeks) Wells; married Sherrill Brown (a historian and editor), June 7, 1969; children: Lauren, Anthony, Jeffrey. *Education:* University of North Carolina, A.B., 1957; Harvard University, A.M., 1961, Ph.D., 1967. *Home:* 1509 Woodacre Dr., McLean, Va. 22101. *Office:* Wilson Center, Smithsonian Institution Building, Washington, D.C. 20560.

CAREER: Wellesley College, Wellesley, Mass., instructor in history, 1963-65; University of North Carolina, Chapel Hill, assistant professor, 1965-70, associate professor of history, 1970-78; Wilson Center, Washington, D.C., secretary of International Security Studies Program, 1977—. Member of board of trustees of Z. Smith Reynolds Foundation; consultant to U.S. Department of Defense and National Broadcasting Co. (NBC) News. *Military service:* U.S. Marine Corps, 1957-60; became captain.

MEMBER: International Institute for Strategic Studies, International Studies Association, Association for Public Policy Analysis and Management, Society for Historians of American Foreign Relations, American Historical Association, Organization of American Historians, Phi Beta Kappa. *Awards, honors:* Woodrow Wilson fellow, 1960-61; Danforth fellow, 1960-65; fellow of Hoover Institution on War, Revolution, and Peace, 1972-73, Woodrow Wilson International Center for Scholars, 1976-77, and Ford Foundation, 1976-79.

WRITINGS: (With Robert H. Ferrell and David F. Trask) *The Ordeal of World Power: American Diplomacy Since 1900,* Little, Brown, 1975; (with Paul Gordon Lauren and others) *Diplomacy: New Approaches in History, Theory, and Policy,* Free Press, 1979; *Economics and American Diplomacy: An Assessment,* Columbia University Press, 1982; *The Tenuous Entente: Anglo-American Strategy and Diplomacy, 1904-1914,* Oxford University Press, 1982. Contributor to political science and international studies journals.

WORK IN PROGRESS: Escalation of the Cold War: The Impact of Korea, 1950-1954.

SIDELIGHTS: Wells told *CA:* "More than the citizens of most nations, Americans should strive to learn about their past interactions in world affairs in order to understand the complexity of contemporary international politics and to better manage the future."

*   *   *

WELMERS, William Evert   1916-

PERSONAL: Born April 4, 1916, in Orange City, Iowa; son of Thomas E. and Jane (Waalkes) Welmers; married Beatrice Faye Fairbanks, June 21, 1940; children: R. Bruce, Margaret Jean, Richard C. *Education:* Hope College, B.A., 1936; Westminster Theological Seminary, Th.B. and Th. M., both 1939; University of Pennsylvania, Ph.D., 1943. *Home:* 2272 Overland Ave., Los Angeles, Calif. 90064. *Office:* University of California, Los Angeles, Calif. 90024.

CAREER: Ordained Orthodox Presbyterian minister, 1943; University of Pennsylvania, Philadelphia, instructor, 1943-44, 1945-46; Lutheran Mission in Liberia, missionary, 1946-48; Cornell University, Ithaca, N.Y., visiting assistant professor, 1950-51, acting associate professor of linguistics, 1951-54; Lutheran Mission in Liberia, missionary, 1954-55; Hartford Seminary Foundation, Hartford, Conn., associate professor of linguistics and African languages at Kennedy School of Missions, 1955-60; University of California, Los Angeles, professor of linguistics and African languages, 1960—. Pastor of Orthodox Presbyterian church in Philadelphia, 1943-46.

MEMBER: International African Institute, Linguistic Society of America, Society for Ethnomusicology, African Music Society, African Studies Association, West African Linguistic Society, Linguistic Society of Liberia. *Awards, honors:* Fellow of American Council of Learned Societies in Africa, 1948-50; Litt.D. from Hope College, 1967.

WRITINGS: A Descriptive Grammar of Fanti, Linguistic Society of America, 1946, reprinted, Kraus Reprint, 1966; *Jukun Language: Analysis of Two Dialects Known as Jukun; Notes on the Structure of Kutep,* H. A. Gleason, 1956; (with Ruth C. Sloan) *A Preliminary Survey of Existing Resources for Training in African Languages and Linguistics,* Georgetown University Press, 1957.

(Contributor) G. Reginald Bishop, Jr., editor, *Culture in Language and Learning,* Northeast Conference on the Teaching of Foreign Languages, 1960; (with John Massie Stewart) *The Typology of the Twi Tone System,* Institute of African Studies, University of Ghana, 1965; *Jukun of Wukari and Jukun of Takum,* International Publications Service, 1968; *Efik,* Institute of African Studies, University of Ibadan, 1968; (with wife, Beatrice F. Welmers) *Igbo: A Learner's Dictionary,* African Studies Center, University of California, Los Angeles, 1968; (contributor) John Gay, editor, *Mathematics and Logic in the Kpelle Language,* Institute of African Studies, University of Ibadan, 1971; *African Language Structures,* University of California Press, 1973; *A Grammar of Vai,* University of California Press, 1976; (co-author) *Structural Notes and Corpus,* Spoken Language Services, 1980. Contributor to language and linguistic journals.

BIOGRAPHICAL/CRITICAL SOURCES: American Anthropologist, June, 1975.*

*   *   *

WELSH, Paul   1911-

PERSONAL: Born September 29, 1911, in Philadelphia, Pa.; son of Harry and Anne (Dolan) Welsh; married Ethel Butcher Van Order, November 24, 1942; children: one. *Education:* Bowdoin College, B.S., 1937; Cornell University, Ph.D., 1947. *Office:* Department of Philosophy, Duke University, 6846 College Station, Durham, N.C. 27708.

CAREER: Cornell University, Ithaca, N.Y., instructor in English, 1940-47; Duke University, Durham, N.C., assistant professor, 1948-57, associate professor, 1957-62, professor of philosophy, 1962—, chairman of department, 1968-76. Visiting professor at University of Iowa, 1955-56. *Member:* American Philosophical Association, Linguistic Society of America, Phi Beta Kappa.

WRITINGS: (Co-author) *Introduction to Logic,* Van Nostrand, 1962; (editor and contributor) *Fact, Value, and Perception: Essays in Honor of Charles A. Baylis,* Duke University Press, 1975.*

*   *   *

WENDT, Viola (Sophia)   1907-

PERSONAL: Born March 31, 1907, in Boise, Idaho; daughter of C. William (a brick manufacturer) and Ella L. (Koelsch) Wendt. *Education:* University of Wisconsin (now University of Wisconsin—Madison), B.A., 1928, M.A., 1936, Ph.D., 1947; graduate study at Radcliffe College, 1928-29. *Home:* 119 West Newhall Ave., Waukesha, Wis. 53186.

CAREER: Platteville State Teachers College (now University of Wisconsin—Platteville), Platteville, Wis., interim instructor, 1942; Carroll College, Waukesha, Wis., instructor, 1942-47, assistant professor, 1947-51, associate professor, 1951-71, professor of English literature and writing, 1971-75, professor emeritus, 1975—; Carroll College Press, Waukesha, editor, 1976-79; writer and teacher of continuing education course in writing, 1979—.

MEMBER: Modern Language Association of America, Academy of American Poets, Wisconsin Fellowship of Poets, Wisconsin Regional Writers Association, Phi Beta Kappa. Awards, honors: Borestone Mountain Poetry Award from Stanford University Press, 1955, for "On Reading Marianne Moore"; Uhrig Foundation Award for excellent teaching from Carroll College, 1962; second place award from Council for Wisconsin Writers, 1976, for You Keep Waiting for Geese; D.H.L. from Carroll College, 1977; woman of achievement award from Altrusa Club, 1979.

WRITINGS: You Keep Waiting for Geese: Selected Poems, Carroll College Press, 1975; (editor) Alfred Lunt and Lynn Fontanne: A Bibliography, Carroll College Press, 1978; The Wind Is Rising: New Poems, Carroll College Press, 1979; (editor) Carroll College: The First Century, 1846-1946, Carroll College Press, 1980.

WORK IN PROGRESS: A book of poems tentatively titled The Voice of the Turtle for publication by Bittern Press.

SIDELIGHTS: Wendt told CA: "My first poem shaped itself in a dream when I was nine. It was complete when I woke—though it had a syntactical and rhythmical problem that I was even then frustrated by, and that has not yet been resolved.

"The source of poetry as I have experienced it would appear to be the subconscious mind, with its ever-accreting contents. It sends up, dislodged by association or by its own mysterious intention, the material of a poem. The principle of order inherent in the subconscious supplies a certain structure; often the conscious mind has to set to and supplement that order by deliberate manipulation of concept, of rhythm, of sound. For a poem is many things: a constructed intellectual statement, the distillation of an attitude or a mood, and a crafted sensuous object, a work of art.

"All experience, personal and vicarious, goes into the storage place of the subconscious. Lodged in my hold are flora and fauna from Idaho and Wisconsin: roses, sagebrush, little flying insects, spiders, coyotes, frogs. 'Kinsmen' I call them in one section of a book. My reading in English, German, Latin, Greek, and French literature also imbues the hoard from which I draw.

"I have done a series of poems based on 'touchstones,' as Matthew Arnold uses the term, from my reading, and a series dealing with the nature of poetry. There is a section on love of many kinds. There are poems in many moods on the tragicomedy of the coming, and the inexorable settling-in, of age; there are a number on music and on the human condition, with special concern for the human comedy. The cause of women is presented with kindly—but edged—humor.

"Some of the critical comments applied to my work that I have particularly liked are: 'soberly, at times acidly, honest—and puckishly witty'; 'a subtle, almost shy classicism'; 'irony, wit, tough gaiety, warmth, and offbeat but profound spirituality.'

"I suggest these caveats for readers of poetry: (a) no life-time body of writing ever expresses the total person; (b) some poems say what may reasonably and competently be said about a given matter; others say what the writer considers truths, at least for him; let the reader be cautious in distinguishing the two sorts; (c) the persona of a poem may or may not be the poet."

*   *   *

WENGENROTH, Edith Flack Ackley   1887-1970

OBITUARY NOTICE: Born in 1887; died November 28, 1970, in Greenport, Long Island, N.Y. Puppeteer and author of books on dolls and marionettes. Wengenroth was best known for her book A Doll Shop of Your Own. Obituaries and other sources: New York Times, November 30, 1970; AB Bookman's Weekly, January 4, 1971.

*   *   *

WENGENROTH, Stow   1906-1978

OBITUARY NOTICE: Born July 25, 1906, in New York, N.Y.; died of emphysema, January 22, 1978, in Gloucester, Mass. Lithographer and author. Best known for his drawings of New England scenes, Wengenroth was called "the greatest black-and-white artist in America" by artist Andrew Wyeth. Elected to the National Institute of Arts and Letters in 1942, Wengenroth was also the recipient of many awards, such as the Medal of Honor of the Audubon Artists, the Samuel F.B. Morse Medal from the National Academy of Art, and the Pennell Memorial Medal of the Philadelphia Watercolor Club. Wengenroth illustrated several books, including The Susquehanna and The Hudson, and was the author of Making a Lithograph. Obituaries and other sources: Who's Who in America, 40th edition, Marquis, 1978; New York Times, January 23, 1978; AB Bookman's Weekly, May 8, 1978.

*   *   *

WERFEL, Franz (V.)   1890-1945

BRIEF ENTRY: Born September 10, 1890, in Prague, Bohemia (now Czechoslovakia); died of a heart attack, August 26, 1945, in Beverly Hills, Calif. Austrian novelist, playwright, and poet. One of the founders of the expressionist movement in German literature, Werfel began writing poetry when he was a boy and published his first play when he was twenty. His first book of verse, Der weltfreund (1911), was published the following year. In the 1920's Werfel won a reputation as an important dramatist; his plays "Goat Song" (1922) and "Juarez and Maximilian" (1925) were successfully produced in Europe and in New York. With the novel Verdi (1924), based on the life of the composer, Werfel turned to prose fiction and a more conventional, realistic style. His novels, like his earlier poems and plays, express a mystical and idealistic sensibility and stress the values of brotherhood and peace. Though Werfel was Jewish he was drawn to Roman Catholicism, and both religions figure prominently in his work. In 1940 Werfel fled Nazi-occupied Europe for the United States, where he spent the rest of his life and where he wrote The Song of Bernadette (1941), one of his most popular books. His last novel, The Star of the Unborn (1946), which expresses his utopian hopes for humanity's future, was finished only a few days before his death. Biographical/critical sources: Twentieth Century Authors: A Biographical Dictionary of World Literature, H. W. Wilson, 1942, 1st supplement, 1955; New Republic, February 18, 1946; Cyclopedia of World Authors, Harper, 1958; McGraw-Hill Encyclopedia of World Drama, McGraw, 1972.

*   *   *

WERNER, M(orris) R(obert)   1897-1981

OBITUARY NOTICE: Born March 6, 1897, in New York,

511

N.Y.; died August 5, 1981, in New York. Editor, historian, biographer, and author. Best known for his biographies, Werner worked as an editor of the *New York Tribune* and as a writer for the *New Yorker* magazine. The first of his sixteen books, *Orderly,* recounts his World War I experiences in military hospitals in France. After the war the author became obituary editor of the *Tribune* and the New York correspondent of the *Yorkshire Post* and the *Paris Herald Tribune.* Werner worked for the Office of War Information during the Second World War, following which he spent twenty years as associate editor of *Sports Illustrated.* His books include *Barnum; Brigham Young; Tammany Hall; Bryan;* and *Julius Rosenwald.* Obituaries and other sources: *Who Was Who Among English and European Authors, 1931-1949,* Gale, 1978; *New York Times,* August 16, 1981.

* * *

WESS, Martin 1906(?)-1975

OBITUARY NOTICE: Born c. 1906; died after a long illness, September 18, 1975, in Neuilly, France. Army officer, literary agent, and editor. Wess served as a major on General Dwight D. Eisenhower's staff during World War II. Following the liberation of France he worked as a relocator of refugees in Paris and was decorated by Charles de Gaulle for his services to France. An American expatriate, Wess stayed in Paris after the war and became a French literary agent representing authors such as Robert Courtine and Henry Charriere. He also represented American publishing houses in France, including Lyle Stuart and Julian Press, and was editor in chief of the *Encyclopedie de la femme.* Obituaries and other sources: *Publishers Weekly,* October 13, 1975.

* * *

WEST, (Mary) Jane 1939(?)-1981

OBITUARY NOTICE: Born c. 1939 in Evanston, Ill.; died September 9, 1981, at Memorial Sloan-Kettering Cancer Center, in New York, N.Y. Editor and publisher. Noted for the literary, artistic, and commercial quality of her books, West became vice-president and publisher of Clarkson N. Potter, an affiliate of Crown Publishers, in 1978. She began her publishing career at Ivan Obolensky and then worked at Frederick Praeger before joining the Potter company in 1967. West took over as publisher in 1976, and under her leadership editorial policies were redirected and the publishing list became more successful. West continued and enlarged the Potter "Annotated Classics" series, which includes works of Shakespeare, Swift, Thoreau, and Twain. She was also credited with the ability to spot a trend and was responsible for the publication of books such as *High Tech* and *American Country.* Two Potter best-sellers are *How to Make Love to a Man* and *101 Uses for a Dead Cat.* Among the authors and artists whose works were published by West are Sir John Gielgud, Isaac Asimov, Louise Nevelson, John Simon, and A.L. Rowse. Obituaries and other sources: *New York Times,* September 12, 1981; *Publishers Weekly,* September 25, 1981.

* * *

WEST, Nathanael
See WEINSTEIN, Nathan Wallenstein

* * *

WEST, V(ictoria Mary) Sackville
See SACKVILLE-WEST, V(ictoria Mary)

WESTON, Rubin Francis 1921-

PERSONAL: Born July 7, 1921, in Columbia, S.C.; divorced; children: six. *Education:* North Carolina Central University, B.A., 1951, M.A., 1955; Syracuse University, Ph.D., 1964. *Home:* 1265 Joyce Dr., Xenia, Ohio 45385. *Office:* Department of History, Central State University, Wilberforce, Ohio 45384.

CAREER: North Carolina Central University, Durham, instructor in history, 1951-53; high school history teacher in Atkins, N.C., 1953-54; North Carolina Central University, instructor in history, 1954-65; South Carolina State College, Orangeburg, professor of history and chairman of department, 1964-68; Central State University, Wilberforce, Ohio, professor of history, 1968—, chairman of department, 1969—. *Member:* American Historical Association, Organization of American Historians, Association for Studies of Afro-American Life and History.

WRITINGS: Racism in U.S. Imperialism: The Influence of Racial Assumptions on American Foreign Policy, 1893-1946, University of South Carolina Press, 1972.*

* * *

WETCHEEK, J. L.
See FEUCHTWANGER, Lion

* * *

WHARTON, Edith (Newbold Jones) 1862-1937

BRIEF ENTRY: Born January 24, 1862, in New York, N.Y.; died August 11, 1937, in St. Brice-sous-Foret, France; buried in Versailles, France. American novelist, poet, and short story writer. Wharton, a close friend and literary disciple of novelist Henry James, is best known for her novels about the decline of fashionable society, including *The House of Mirth* (1905), *The Custom of the Country* (1913), and *The Age of Innocence* (1920), winner of the Pulitzer Prize in 1921. Wharton spent much of her life in France, where she was awarded a Cross of the Legion of Honor for her work on behalf of Belgian orphans during World War I. In 1923 Wharton became the first female recipient of the honorary degree of Doctor of Letters from Yale University and was the first woman to be awarded the Gold Medal of the National Institute of Arts and Letters. She was elected to the Institute's membership in 1930 and was elected a member of the American Academy of Arts and Letters in 1934. Other well-known books by Edith Wharton include *Ethan Frome* (1911), *The Reef* (1913), and *The Children* (1928). *Residence:* Paris, France. *Biographical/critical sources:* Edith Wharton, *A Backward Glance,* Scribner, 1934; Percy Lubbock, *Portrait of Edith Wharton,* Appleton-Century, 1947; *The Reader's Encyclopedia of American Literature,* Crowell, 1962; *Encyclopedia of World Literature in the Twentieth Century,* Volume 3, Ungar, 1971; *Webster's American Biographies,* Merriam, 1974; *Twentieth-Century Literary Criticism,* Volume 3, Gale, 1980.

* * *

WHEATON, Bruce R. 1944-

PERSONAL: Born July 7, 1944, in Evanston, Ill.; son of Ralph W. (in business) and Julia E. (a teacher; maiden name, Sheedy) Wheaton; married Lois Segal (an educational resource specialist), 1966; children: Ariana M., Geoffrey S. *Education:*

Stanford University, B.S., 1966; University of California, Berkeley, M.A., 1971; Princeton University, M.A., 1974, Ph.D., 1978. *Office:* Office for History of Science and Technology, University of California, 470 Stephens Hall, Berkeley, Calif. 94720.

CAREER: University of California, Berkeley, assistant director of Office for History of Science and Technology, 1976—. Consultant to Exploratorium. *Member:* History of Science Society.

WRITINGS: (With J. L. Heilbron) *Literature on the History of Physics in the First Half of the Twentieth Century,* Berkeley Papers in History of Science, 1981; *The Tiger and the Shark: Empirical Roots of Wave-Particle Dualism,* Arno, 1981. Contributor to scholarly journals. Book review editor of *Historical Studies in the Physical Sciences.*

WORK IN PROGRESS: Research on the history of radiation theory and modern technology.

SIDELIGHTS: Wheaton told *CA:* "We live in a world increasingly dependent on science-based technology. Yet understanding of science as a cultural contribution is scarcely greater today than when C. P. Snow clearly pointed out the growing schism between the scientifically literate and those to whom modern science is virtual magic. Study of the evolution of scientific ideas and their application in technology frequently grants insights lost even to the modern practitioner of science. I believe that writing the history of science can contribute to widerspread appreciation of both the contribution and the limits of the scientific enterprise."

* * *

WHEATON, Philip D(amon) 1916-

PERSONAL: Born Feburary 1, 1916, in Putnam, Conn.; son of William E. (a lumber dealer) and Helen I. (Brigham) Wheaton; married Amy Bowles (a state commissioner of children's youth services), October 19, 1971; children: Sam, Bess, David. *Education:* Clark University, A.B., 1938, M.Ed., 1946; University of Connecticut, M.A., 1946; University of Maryland, Ph.D., 1952. *Politics:* Independent. *Religion:* Protestant. *Home and office:* 5000 Durham Rd., Guilford, Conn. 06437. *Agent:* Elaine Markson Literary Agency, Inc., 44 Greenwich Ave., New York, N.Y. 10011.

CAREER: High school teacher of science and English in Putnam, Conn., 1938-42; Sanborn Seminary, Kingston, N.H., teacher of physics, English, drama, and debate, 1942-45; University of New Hampshire, Durham, instructor in debating, speech, and stagecraft, 1946-50; University of Maryland, College Park, lecturer in diplomacy, international relations, and history, and administrator of armed services program overseas, 1955-65; Middlesex Community College, Middletown, Conn., president, 1966-76; writer, 1976—.

WRITINGS: Razzmatazz (novel), Everest House, 1980.

WORK IN PROGRESS: A novel about a college; a comedy play about a college.

SIDELIGHTS: Wheaton told *CA:* "A major experience of my life was working for the University of Maryland in Asia, Africa, and Europe. Another was the opportunity to develop a college from scratch.

"My work has provided much opportunity for non-fictional writing, none of it giving me the satisfaction that comes with writing fiction. In fiction, one can create and create endlessly. One makes his own world in which he or she must live while

in the process of writing, and if he persists, he can make his imprint on the real world for better or worse—hopefully for the former. As an artist paints himself into any painting he does with every brush stroke he makes on a canvas, so a writer does the same with every word he puts on paper. Writing is a marvelous form of escape; you can escape almost everything but yourself when you do it. The more you attempt to hide yourself in your writing; the more self-revealing you become. Why do I write: because I can't stop myself from doing."

BIOGRAPHICAL/CRITICAL SOURCES: Washington Post, November 4, 1980.

* * *

WHEELER, Thomas C. 1927-

PERSONAL: Born March 26, 1927, in Stamford, Conn.; son of Walter Heber (a businessman) and Florence (a civic worker; maiden name, Chilton) Wheeler; married Carol Einhorn, June 15, 1963 (separated June, 1979); children: Nicholas Einhorn. *Education:* Studied in France, 1947-48; Harvard University, A.B., 1950, M.A., 1952. *Politics:* Democrat. *Religion:* Episcopalian. *Home:* 156 West 77th St., New York, N.Y. 10024. *Agent:* Barbara Rhodes Literary Agency, 140 West End Ave., New York, N.Y. 10023. *Office:* Department of English, York College of the City University of New York, Jamaica, N.Y. 11451.

CAREER: Encyclopaedia Britannica, New York City, assistant to the publisher, 1952-54; *Life* (magazine), New York City, reporter and assistant editor, 1954-62; Holt, Rinehart, and Winston, New York City, editor, 1962-63; Brooklyn College, Brooklyn, N.Y., lecturer, 1966-70; York College of the City University of New York, Jamaica, N.Y., assistant professor, 1970—. *Military service:* U.S. Navy, 1945-46. *Member:* Harvard Club (New York City).

WRITINGS: (Editor) *A Vanishing America: The Life and Times of the Small Town,* Holt, 1964; (editor and author of introduction) Jack Agueros and others, *The Immigrant Experience: The Anguish of Becoming American,* Dial, 1971; *The Great American Writing Block: Causes and Cures of the New Illiteracy,* Viking, 1979.

SIDELIGHTS: In *The Great American Writing Block,* Wheeler draws upon his experience as a teacher of remedial English at York College to examine the problem of the diminishing language skills of college students and to offer suggestions for a solution. He places much of the blame for the decline of American literacy at the feet of educators, who in their push for objective standardization of tests have all but eliminated the essay test from public schools and college entrance exams. Wheeler's prescription for his students' language deficiency is a heavy dose of reading and writing, with an emphasis on writing as a form of self-expression.

Nation critic Leonard Kriegel agreed with Wheeler's diagnosis of the problem, but feared his solution may be too simplistic. "His 'cure,'" Kriegel wrote, "seems to amount to little more than having students write more papers in high school." Jeffrey Burke of *Harper's,* on the other hand, applauded Wheeler's approach, noting that his "methods are abundantly, effectively obvious, and he gives evidence of their effectiveness with numerous examples of his students' writing."

BIOGRAPHICAL/CRITICAL SOURCES: New York Times Book Review, August 29, 1971, December 5, 1971, September 2, 1979; *Nation,* October 6, 1979; *Chronicle of Higher Education,* October 29, 1979; *Harper's,* March, 1980.

WHITAKER, Malachi Taylor 1895-1976

OBITUARY NOTICE: Born September 23, 1895, in Bradford, Yorkshire, England; died January 7, 1976, in Skipton, England. Author of short stories. Whitaker began writing at the age of thirty-three and published her first short stories a year later. From 1929 to 1934, four volumes of her collected short stories were published by J. Cape: *Frost in April, No Luggage, Five for Silver,* and *Honeymoon.* In 1939 she published her journal, *And So Did I.* Two additional short story collections followed. Obituaries and other sources: *The Writers Directory, 1976-78,* St. Martin's, 1976; *AB Bookman's Weekly,* March 1, 1976.

* * *

WHITE, Antonia 1899-1980

PERSONAL: Born March 31, 1899, in London, England; died April 10, 1980; daughter of Cecil George (a classics professor) and Christine Julia (White) Botting; married in 1921 (annulled, 1924); married in 1924 (annulled, 1929); married H. Tom Hopkinson (a journalist), 1930 (divorced, 1938); children: Susan Chitty, Lyndall Passerini. *Education:* Attended Royal Academy of Dramatic Art, 1919-20. *Religion:* Roman Catholic. *Home:* 42D Courtfield Gardens, London S.W.5, England. *Agent:* Carmen Callil, 40 Bradmore Park Rd., London W6 0DT, England.

CAREER: Writer and translator. Actress, 1920-21; W. S. Crawford Ltd., London, England, copywriter, 1924-31; *Life and Letters,* London, assistant editor, 1928-29; free-lance journalist, 1931-34; *Time and Tide,* London, theatre critic, 1934; J. Walter Thompson (advertising), London, copywriter, 1934-35; London Theatre Studio, London, teacher and writer, 1935-36; *Daily Mirror,* London, fashion editor, 1935-37; *Sunday Pictorial,* London, fashion editor, 1937-39; British Broadcasting Corp. (BBC), London, writer, 1940-43; associated with Political Intelligence Department, French section of Foreign Office, London, 1943-45. Visiting lecturer in English at St. Mary's College, Notre Dame, Ind., 1959. *Member:* Royal Society of Literature (fellow). *Awards, honors:* Denyse Clairouin Prize, 1950, for translation of Maupassant's *Une Vie;* Arts Council grant, 1967, 1969; awarded Civic List Pension by Queen Elizabeth, for services to literature.

WRITINGS: Frost in May (novel), D. Harmsworth, 1933, Viking, 1934, second edition, Eyre & Spottiswoode, 1948, reprinted, Virago, 1978, Dial, 1980; *Three in a Room* (three-act comedy), Samuel French, 1947; *The Lost Traveller* (novel; first volume of trilogy), Viking, 1950, reprinted, Virago, 1979, Dial, 1980; *The Sugar House* (novel; second volume of trilogy), Eyre & Spottiswoode, 1952, reprinted, Virago, 1979, Dial, 1981; *Beyond the Glass* (novel; third volume of trilogy), Eyre & Spottiswoode, 1954, Regnery, 1955, reprinted, Virago, 1979, Dial, 1981; *Strangers* (short stories and poems), Harvill, 1954, reprinted, Virago 1981; *Minka and Curdy* (juvenile; illustrated by Janet Johnstone and Anne Johnstone), Harvill, 1957; *The Hound and the Falcon: The Story of a Reconversion to the Catholic Faith,* Longmans, 1965; *Living with Minka and Curdy: A Marmalade Cat and His Siamese Wife* (juvenile), Harvill, 1970.

Translator from the French: Guy de Maupassant, *A Woman's Life,* Pantheon, 1949; Henry Bordeaux, *A Pathway to Heaven,* Gollancz, 1952, Pelligrini & Cudahy, 1953; Alexis Carrel, *Reflections on Life,* Hamish Hamilton, 1952, Hawthorn, 1953; Colette, *Gigi* [*and*] *The Cat* (the former translated by Roger Senhouse; the latter translated by Antonia White), Secker & Warburg, 1953; Marguerite Duras, *A Sea of Troubles,* Meth-

uen, 1953; Serge Groussard, *A German Officer,* Putnam, 1955; Paul Andre Lesort, *The Wind Bloweth Where It Listeth,* Collins, 1955; Colette, *Claudine at School,* Secker & Warburg, 1956, Farrar, Straus, 1957; Christine Arnothy, *I Am Fifteen and I Do Not Want to Die,* Dutton, 1956; Arnothy, *God Is Late,* Dutton, 1957 (published in England as *Those Who Wait,* Collins, 1957); Lesort, *The Branding Iron,* Collins, 1958; Colette, *Claudine in Paris,* Farrar, Straus, 1958; Arnothy, *It Is Not so Easy to Live* (autobiography), Collins, 1958; *The Stories of Colette,* Secker & Warburg, 1958, published as *The Tender Shoot,* Farrar, Straus, 1959, reprinted as *The Stories,* Heinemann, 1962, and as *The Rainy Moon, and Other Stories,* Penguin, 1975; Fanny Rouget, *The Swing,* Bodley Head, 1958; Jean Marc Langlois-Berthelot, *Thou Shalt Love,* Methuen, 1958; Arnothy, *The Charlatan,* Dutton, 1959; Claire France, *Children in Love,* Eyre & Spottiswoode, 1959; Eveline Mahyere, *I Will Not Serve,* Muller, 1959, Dutton, 1960; Loys Masson, *The Tortoises,* Chatto & Windus, 1959.

Colette, *Claudine Married,* Farrar, Straus, 1960; Julie Storm, *Till the Shadow Passes,* Collins, 1960; Arnothy, *The Serpent's Bite,* Collins, 1961; Colette, *Claudine and Annie,* Secker & Warburg, 1962; Alfred Fabre-Luce, *The Trial of Charles de Gaulle,* Praeger, 1963; Masson, *Advocate of the Isle,* Knopf, 1963 (published in England as *The Whale's Tooth,* Chatto & Windus, 1963); Arnothy, *The Captive Cardinal,* Doubleday, 1964; Pierre Leulliette, *St. Michel and the Dragon,* Heinemann, 1964; Colette, *The Shackle,* Secker & Warburg, 1964; Therese de Sainte Phalle, *The Candle,* Harrap, 1968; Colette, *The Innocent Libertine,* Secker & Warburg, 1968; Frederick Gaillardet, *Memoirs of the Chevalier d'Eon,* Blond, 1970; Georges Simenon, *The Glass Cage,* Harcourt Brace, 1973; Paul-Gabriel Bouce, *The Novels of Smollett,* Longman, 1975; Colette, *The Complete Claudine,* Farrar, Straus, 1976; Voltaire, *The History of Charles XII, King of Sweden,* Folio Society, 1976.

Contributor to periodicals.

SIDELIGHTS: The conversion of White's parents to Catholicism when she was seven years old, and her subsequent education at a Catholic boarding school, precipitated events that deeply affected the author's life and affected her career as a novelist. In order to satisfy her father, whom she adored, White agreed at age nine to continue her education at a convent school. She did so despite the fact that she considered herself an outsider, "a middle-class convert among aristocratic 'born Catholics,'" noted Samuel Hynes of the *Times Literary Supplement.* When she was fifteen, she decided to surprise her father by writing a novel that exemplified his religious beliefs. The characters, wallowing in sin, were to experience a revelation and repent. "I made everybody as wicked as possible," White told an *Observer* interviewer. "As I couldn't think of anything bad enough for them to do, I said they were indulged in 'nameless vices.'"

With only five chapters written, and before she could develop the characters, the manuscript was confiscated by the nuns, and White was expelled from the convent. Her father's rage at the incident precluded any explanations. White believed that "she had offended both her father and his church and had been angrily rejected by both," opined Hynes. As a result, she did not resume writing novels until after her father's death, and she often commented that she was never again able to write original work without feelings of guilt and anxiety. Twenty years passed, including two failed marriages ending in annulment, and a mental breakdown resulting in institutionalization, before White attempted novel-writing again.

In 1933 White's third husband expressed interest in a novel that she had begun while still at the convent but had since set aside. At his insistence, she finished the story. The book, published soon afterwards as *Frost in May*, recounts White's experiences at the convent school, including the details of her expulsion. Written during a period when White considered herself a lapsed Catholic, the novel has two central themes according to *Commonweal* critic Philip Burnham: "Why are people Catholics? And in what manner should one break one's will completely . . . in order to offer to God the will and personality?" A reviewer for *Catholic World* criticized White's slanted depiction of Catholic life, remarking: "Granted that all the events of the story could happen, or have happened, this is not yet a full and true account. . . . The author discloses symptoms of that malady which often develops from the life-long nursing of a grievance. The poison has corroded her soul." On the other hand, Jean Holzhauer, reviewing for *Commonweal*, called *Frost in May* a "minor classic" and its author "one of the best Catholic women writers of the generation."

Because of her husband's encouragement, White began work on a second novel, believing that the jinx she associated with the writing of novels had finally been lifted. However, a short time later her marriage ended, and consequently fifteen years passed between the first and last chapters of her second novel, *The Lost Traveller*. "It must have seemed to my unconscious mind that writing drove away affection," White wrote in *The Book of Catholic Authors*, "and all the old sense of guilt returned."

After a second nervous breakdown and four years of psychoanalytical treatment, White reconverted to Catholicism and, in a five year period, managed to write the three novels that form the Clara Batchelor trilogy. The trilogy is largely autobiographical, and despite the change of name of the heroine, from Wanda Grey in *Frost in May* to Clara Batchelor in this trilogy, the three novels are a sequel to *Frost in May*. The first novel, *The Lost Traveller*, re-explores the traumas of White's Catholic upbringing; the second novel, *Sugar House*, examines the failure of her marriage; and the final novel, *Beyond the Glass*, recreates the author's bouts with mental illness and institutionalization.

White's four novels "came out of urgent psychic needs rather than out of a strict creative impulse," theorized Samuel Hynes. "The central impulse behind her novels was the will-to-testify, and by testifying to throw off the past." It seems that White never completely succeeded in throwing off the past, because novel-writing remained a problem for her throughout her life. She once reflected, "'Creative joy' is something I haven't felt since I was fourteen and don't expect to feel again."

BIOGRAPHICAL/CRITICAL SOURCES: Christian Century, February 21, 1934; *Commonweal*, March 16, 1934, November 11, 1955; *Catholic World*, April, 1934; *New Statesman and Nation*, April 15, 1950; *New York Herald Tribune*, April 16, 1950; *New York Times*, April 16, 1950; *New Republic*, May 20, 1950; *Saturday Review of Literature*, July 15, 1950; Walter Romig, editor, *The Book of Catholic Authors*, Fifth Series, Walter Romig, 1957; *Times Literary Supplement*, July 13, 1969; *Observer*, June 4, 1978.

OBITUARIES: London Times, April 12, 1980; *Daily Telegraph*, April 12, 1980; *Guardian*, April 12, 1980.

[Sketch verified by White's agent and literary executor, Carmen Callil.]

WHITE, Katherine Sergeant   1892-1977

OBITUARY NOTICE: Born September 17, 1892, in Winchester, Mass.; died July 20, 1977, at Blue Hill Memorial Hospital, in Maine. Journalist and editor. White joined the *New Yorker* in 1925, and she is credited with having shaped the magazine from a satirical weekly into a literary showcase. One of the first editors hired by publisher Harold Ross, "she was Ross's intellectual conscience," according to Brendan Gill, one of White's proteges. White introduced the fiction of John O'Hara and Vladimir Nabokov and encouraged the work of authors such as Mary McCarthy, John Cheever, Irwin Shaw, Ogden Nash, Shirley Hazzard and John Updike. With her husband, author E.B. White, she edited *A Subtreasury of American Humor*, which was published in 1941. White retired in 1959 but continued writing occasional columns for the *New Yorker* for many years. Obituaries and other sources: *Who's Who Among American Women*, 1st edition, 1958; *New York Times*, July 22, 1977; *Publishers Weekly*, August 1, 1977.

*   *   *

WHITE, Reginald James   1905-1971

OBITUARY NOTICE: Born in 1905 in Norwich, England; died November 13, 1971, in Cambridge, England. Educator and author best known for his writings on Cambridge life. Among his books are *The Road to the City, Young Leslie, Admiral Blades, The Breton*, and *Dinner at Night*. Obituaries and other sources: *AB Bookman's Weekly*, December 13, 1971; *Who Was Who Among English and European Authors, 1931-1949*, Gale, 1978.

*   *   *

WHITEHEAD, Evelyn Annette Eaton   1938-

PERSONAL: Born August 22, 1938, in New Orleans, La.; daughter of Homer Delbert and Evelyn Lewis (Farrell); married James D. Whitehead, January 24, 1970. *Education:* St. Louis University, B.A., 1962, M.A., 1964; University of Chicago, Ph.D., 1973. *Home:* 19120 Oakmont South Dr., South Bend, Ind. 46637.

CAREER: Loyola University, Chicago, Ill., lecturer in philosophy, 1966-67; Federation of Communities in Service, Knoxville, Tenn., director of evaluation and training for Appalachian Arts Project, 1970-71; Loyola University, Chicago, lecturer in pastoral studies and research director at Institute of Pastoral Studies, 1971-73; University of Notre Dame, Notre Dame, Ind., assistant professor of theology, 1973-78; Whitehead Associates, South Bend, Ind., consultant in education and ministry, 1978—. Educational director of Appalachian Study Center, Marquette University, 1966-68; co-director of Office of Field Education in Ministry, 1973-78; member of associate faculty at Loyola University, Chicago, 1978—.

MEMBER: International Council of Psychologists, American Psychological Association, Authors Guild, Gerontological Society, Society for the Scientific Study of Religion, Association of Theological Field Education (vice-chairman of steering committee, 1975-77), Association of Theological Schools. *Awards, honors:* Woodrow Wilson fellowship, 1962-63; St. Louis University fellowship, 1967-68; National Institute of Child Health and Human Development fellowship, 1968-70; National Endowment for the Humanities, research associate, 1975-77; grant from Lilly Endowment, 1976-78.

WRITINGS: (Editor) *The Parish in Community and Ministry*, Paulist/Newman, 1978; (contributor) Stuart F. Spiker and other editors, *Aging and the Elderly: Humanistic Perspectives in*

Gerontology, Humanities, 1978; (contributor) Maureen Gallagher, editor, *Paths of Life: Parenting,* Paulist/Newman, 1979; (with husband, James D. Whitehead) *Christian Life Patterns: The Psychological Challenges and Religious Invitations of Adult Life* (Catholic Book Club selection), Doubleday, 1979; (with J.D. Whitehead) *Method in Ministry: Theological Reflection and Christian Ministry,* Seabury, 1980; (with J. D. Whitehead) *Marrying Well: Possibilities in Christian Marriage Today,* Doubleday, 1981; (contributor) William Clements, editor, *Ministry With the Aging,* Harper, 1981; (with J. D. Whitehead) *Christians Gather in Community,* Seabury, 1982; (with J. D. Whitehead) *Community of Faith,* Seabury, 1982.

Co-author of audio tape series for N.C.R. Cassettes: "Sexuality and Christian Intimacy"; "Adulthood: The Context of Religious Development"; "Forming a Community of Faith"; "The Emerging Parish: An Adult Community of Faith." Contributor to theology journals and religious magazines, including *Living Light, Listening: Journal of Religion and Culture,* and *Sign.*

WORK IN PROGRESS: A book with husband, James D. Whitehead, tentatively titled *Personal Power: Psychological Maturity and Religious Experience.*

* * *

WHITMAN, Martin J. 1924-

PERSONAL: Born September 30, 1924, in New York, N.Y.; son of Irving and Dora (Cukier) Whitman; married Lois M. Quick (an attorney), March 10, 1956; children: James Q., Barbara E., Thomas I. *Education:* Syracuse University, B.S. (magna cum laude), 1949; attended Princeton University, 1950; New School for Social Research, M.A., 1956. *Religion:* Jewish. *Home:* 285 Central Park W., New York, N.Y. 10024. *Office:* M. J. Whitman & Co., Inc., 115 Broadway, New York, N.Y. 10006.

CAREER: Shearson Hammill & Co., New York City, research analyst, 1950-56; William Rosenwald, New York City, research analyst, 1956-58; Ladenburg, Thalmann & Co., New York City, head of research, 1958-59; Gerstley, Sunstein & Co., Philadelphia, Pa., general partner, 1960-67; Blair & Co., Inc., New York City, vice-president and member of board of directors, 1967-69; M. J. Whitman & Co., Inc. (securities dealer), New York City, president, 1969—. Adjunct professor at Yale University, 1972—. Chairman of board of directors of Alpha Group, Inc., 1969-80; member of board of directors of Mathematica, Inc. and Genimar, Inc.; financial consultant to corporations and government agencies. *Military service:* U.S. Naval Reserve, active duty, 1942-46; became pharmacist's mate first class. *Member:* Institute of Chartered Financial Analysts, New York Society of Security Analysts.

WRITINGS: (With Martin Shubik) *The Agressive Conservative Investor,* Random House, 1979. Contributor to professional journals.

WORK IN PROGRESS: A book on investment banking, publication by Random House expected in 1983.

* * *

WHITNEY, Thomas P(orter) 1917-

PERSONAL: Born January 26, 1917, in Toledo, Ohio; son of Herbert Porter and Louise (Metzger) Whitney; married Tryphena Gray, July 19, 1936 (divorced, 1949); married Julia Zapolskaya, August 3, 1953 (died August, 1965); married Judith Forrestel, October 14, 1966 (divorced June, 1973); married

Marguerite Carusone, September 21, 1974; children: (first marriage) John Herbert, Louise; (third marriage) Julia Forrestel. *Education:* Amherst College, A.B. (summa cum laude), 1937; Columbia University, M.A., 1940. *Home address:* Roxbury Rd., Washington, Conn. 06793. *Office:* Whitney Book Shops, 61 Elm St., New Canaan, Conn. 06840.

CAREER: Bennett College, Millbrook, N.Y., instructor in social sciences, 1940-41; Office of Strategic Services, Washington, D.C., social science analyst, 1941-44; U.S. Embassy, Moscow, U.S.S.R., attache and chief of economic section, 1944-47; Associated Press of America (now Associated Press), staff correspondent in Moscow, 1947-53, foreign news analyst in New York City, 1953-59; Whitney Enterprises, Inc., New York City, president, 1966-68, chairman of board, 1966-73. Trustee of Julia A. Whitney Foundation. *Member:* Overseas Press Club (president, 1958-59), P.E.N., American Association for the Advancement of Slavic Studies, Phi Beta Kappa, Alpha Delta Phi, Thoroughbred of America, Turf and Field. *Awards, honors:* Litt.D. from Amherst College, 1972, and Assumption College, 1975.

WRITINGS: Has Russia Changed?, Foreign Policy Association-World Affairs Center, 1960; (author of introduction) *The Communist Blueprint for the Future: The Complete Texts of All Four Communist Manifestoes, 1848-1961,* Dutton, 1962; *Russia in My Life,* Reynal, 1962; (editor) Nikita Khrushchev, *Khrushchev Speaks: Selected Speeches, Articles, and Press Conferences, 1949-61,* University of Michigan Press, 1963; *Vasilisa the Beautiful* (juvenile), Macmillan, 1970; (editor) *The Young Russians: A Collection of Stories About Them* (juvenile), Macmillan, 1972.

Translator from the Russian: (And editor and author of introduction) *The New Writing in Russia,* University of Michigan Press, 1964; Aleksandr I. Solzhenitsyn, *First Circle,* Harper, 1968; *The Story of Prince Ivan, the Firebird, and the Gray Wolf* (juvenile), Scribner, 1968; *In a Certain Kingdom: Twelve Russian Fairy Tales* (juvenile), Macmillan, 1972; Solzhenitsyn, *The Nobel Lecture on Literature,* Harper, 1972; Solzhenitsyn, *The Gulag Archipelago, 1918-1956: An Experiment in Literary Investigation,* Harper, Volume I, 1974, Volume II, 1975; *Marko the Rich and Vasily the Unlucky* (juvenile), Macmillan, 1974; Vyacheslav Shishkov, *Children of the Street: Life in a Commune of Russia's Besprizorniki,* Strathcona, 1979. Also translator of *One Day in the Life of Ivan Denisovich,* by Solzhenitsyn, and of *Scarlet Sails,* by Alexander Green.

Contributor of articles to periodicals, including *Wall Street Journal, New York Times Magazine, Foreign Policy Bulletin,* and *New Republic.*

WORK IN PROGRESS: A translation from Russian of the autobiography of General Petro G. Grigorenko, publication by Norton expected in 1982.

SIDELIGHTS: "Readers of Solzhenitsyn in English should know that he is an extraordinarily difficult writer to translate and that *Gulag* is the most problematic work he has yet produced," wrote Strobe Talbott in *Harper's.* "Rendering *Gulag* into English must have been an unusually agonizing job for Thomas P. Whitney, the translator. . . . In fact, the vocabulary of *Gulag* sometimes perplexes Russians."

In a *Writer's Digest* interview, Whitney discussed some of the problems he faced while translating Solzhenitsyn's work. Apart from a single telephone call with a very bad connection from Solzhenitsyn, Whitney had no direct contact with the author. During the phone conversation, Whitney recalled, Solzhenitsyn emphasized that he wanted the translation to be published immediately and that he wanted it to be perfect. "You understand,

Mr. Whitney,'' said Solzhenitsyn, ''that there will only be *one* English translation of this work.''

The translation was a very difficult one, Whitney explained, because ''Solzhenitsyn sometimes makes up words; he makes new words out of roots that are established. You can usually figure out what he has done and why he has done it and how he has done it. . . . Since he lived in camps for eight years, he has done more than any other person to bring into the mainstream of the Russian language the language of the camps and the language of the jails and the language of the Russian underground. This adds a tremendous vividness to his expressiveness. And of course, it creates problems for the translator.''

Whitney also discussed the problems a translator faces in general. ''I think in general, translators do not get the recognition they deserve.'' He explained: ''All too often book reviews assign reviews on translations to competing translators. . . . The competing translator will run down the translation of the competitor, so that usually the best thing a translator can hope for in a review of his translation is not to get mentioned at all. Because in that case he knows that nobody even noticed it was a translation. If the work gets praised, he can understand, or anybody can understand by implication, that it's a good translation. Very rarely do any of the reviewers who cover translations mention, and in particular mention positively, the work of the translator.''

BIOGRAPHICAL/CRITICAL SOURCES: Saturday Review, April 28, 1962; *Writer's Digest*, July, 1974; *Harper's*, July, 1974.*

*   *   *

WHITTINGTON, Geoffrey   1938-

PERSONAL: Born September 21, 1938, in Warsop, England; son of Bruce and Dorothy Gwendoline (Gent) Whittington; married Joyce Enid Smith (a mathematician), September 7, 1963; children: Alan Geoffrey, Richard John. *Education:* London School of Economics and Political Science, London, B.Sc., 1959; Fitzwilliam College, Cambridge, Ph.D., 1971. *Office:* Department of Economics, University of Bristol, Alfred Marshall Building, 40 Berkeley Sq., Bristol BS8 1HY, England.

CAREER: Cambridge University, Fitzwilliam College, Cambridge, England, research officer in applied economics, 1962-72, fellow, 1966-72; University of Edinburgh, Edinburgh, Scotland, professor of accountancy and finance, 1972-75; University of Bristol, Bristol, England, professor of accounting and finance, 1975—. Member of Meade Committee on the Structure of Direct Taxation in the United Kingdom, 1975-77. *Member:* Institute of Chartered Accountants in England and Wales (fellow).

WRITINGS: (With Ajit Singh) *Growth, Profitability, and Valuation*, Cambridge University Press, 1968; *Prediction of Profitability and Other Studies of Company Behaviour*, Cambridge University Press, 1971; (with Geoffrey Meeks) *The Financing of Quoted Companies in the United Kingdom*, H.M.S.O., 1974; *The Theory of Inflation Accounting*, Cambridge University Press, 1981.

Contributor: Bryan Carsberg and Tony Hope, editors, *Current Issues in Accounting*, Philip Allan, 1978; Cedric Sandford and Chris Pond, editors, *Taxation and Social Policy*, Heinemann, 1980; Michael Bronwich and Anthony Hopwood, editors, *Accounting Research*, Pitman, 1981; Ronald Leach and Edward Stamp, editors, *British Accounting Standards: The First Ten Years*, Woodhead-Faulkner, 1981. Contributor to economic and business journals.

WORK IN PROGRESS: The Debate on Inflation Accounting, with David Tweedie, publication by Cambridge University Press expected in 1983.

*   *   *

WICKWIRE, Mary Botts   1935-

PERSONAL: Born February 13, 1935, in Carthage, Mo.; married Franklin B. Wickwire, June 14, 1957; children: Pamela M., Alan T. *Education:* Wellesley College, B.A., 1956; Yale University, M.A., 1957, Ph.D., 1963. *Home:* Bug Hill Rd., Ashfield, Mass. 01330. *Office:* Department of History, University of Massachusetts, Amherst, Mass. 01003.

CAREER: University of Massachusetts, Amherst, lecturer and instructor, 1961-72, assistant professor, 1972-73, associate professor of history, 1973—. *Member:* Conference on British Studies, Society of American Historians, List and Index Society. *Awards, honors:* American Philosophical Society grant, 1965-66.

WRITINGS—All with husband, Franklin B. Wickwire: *Cornwallis: The American Adventure*, Houghton, 1970 (published in England as *Cornwallis and the War of Independence*, Faber, 1971); *Cornwallis: The Imperial Years*, University of North Carolina Press, 1980.

WORK IN PROGRESS: A book on the treatment of aboriginal peoples by Western imperial powers.

SIDELIGHTS: Wickwire and her husband have written two books about Charles Lord Cornwallis, the British commander whose surrender at Yorktown in 1781 marked the end of the American Revolution. The first, *Cornwallis: The American Adventure*, details Cornwallis's life through the end of the Revolution and also examines the politics and personalities of the British Army in North America. The second, *Cornwallis: The Imperial Years*, covers Cornwallis's more successful but less familiar career as a governor in India and Ireland, cabinet minister in London, and diplomat in France.

Unlike most other biographies of the British commander, *Cornwallis: The American Adventure* sympathetically portrays him as a talented military commander whose loss at Yorktown was due mainly to the ineffective planning and indecisiveness of his superiors. ''Cornwallis emerges from this book as a soldier loved by his men, honored by his fellow officers, and devoted to his wife,'' said *Best Sellers*. The book also points out that as a member of the British Parliament, Cornwallis had opposed repressive English policies in America such as the Stamp Act and the Declaratory Act. Thomas Lask of the *New York Times* wrote that the authors made Cornwallis appear ''so attractive and so winning . . . that it would not take much more to make him an American hero.'' A *Spectator* critic, on the other hand, thought that ''most of the claims for Cornwallis are reasonable'' and praised the book's defense of Cornwallis as a ''serious academic effort.''

AVOCATIONAL INTERESTS: Tennis; raising, training, and exhibiting Rhodesian Ridgebacks.

BIOGRAPHICAL/CRITICAL SOURCES: Best Sellers, April 1, 1970; *New York Times Book Review*, May 3, 1970, July 6, 1980; *Virginia Quarterly Review*, summer, 1970; *New York Times*, July 4, 1970; *Spectator*, May 1, 1971; *Times Literary Supplement*, September 3, 1971.

*   *   *

WIECK, Fred D(ernburg)   1910-1973

OBITUARY NOTICE: Born in 1910 in Berlin, Germany; died

of a heart ailment, November 13, 1973, in Philadelphia, Pa. Editor. As a graduate of the University of Berlin Law School, Wieck immigrated to the United States in 1935 and was naturalized in 1942. After serving in the U.S. Army during World War II, he became associate editor of the University of Chicago Press and then editor and vice-president of the Henry Regnery Co. in Chicago. From 1954 to 1961 he was director of the University of Michigan Press, and in 1961 he was senior editor of special projects at Harcourt Brace & World (now Harcourt Brace Jovanovich). He held a similar position with Harper & Row from 1962 to 1967. At the time of his death Wieck was director of the University of Pennsylvania Press, a position he held since 1969. Publications he edited include the nine-volume *Complete Greek Tragedies* and the Richmond Lattimore translation of Homer's *Iliad* for the University of Chicago Press; Wieck also edited Lattimore's *Odyssey* translation and the works of Martin Heidegger for Harper. Obituaries and other sources: *New York Times,* November 18, 1973; *Publishers Weekly,* December 10, 1973.

*   *   *

WILDE, Oscar (Fingal O'Flahertie Wills)   1854-1900

BRIEF ENTRY: Born October 16, 1854, in Dublin, Ireland; died November 30, 1900, in Paris, France. Irish-born British playwright, essayist, poet, and novelist. Wilde, founder of the art-for-art's-sake movement, was known by his contemporaries as a brilliant eccentric whose flamboyant dress and behavior often made him the subject of caricature. Although married and the father of two sons, Wilde became involved in a homosexual relationship that ultimately ruined his career and brought about his imprisonment. Wilde's most famous poem, "The Ballad of Reading Gaol," published in *The Ballad of Reading Gaol, and Other Poems* (1898), was written during his confinement. Wilde's other well-known works include *The Picture of Dorian Gray* (1891), a Gothic novel about an aristocrat whose moral corruption is revealed only on a portrait of himself that he keeps hidden in an attic, and *The Importance of Being Earnest* (1899), a witty, light-hearted play that some critics regard as his masterpiece. Wilde wrote several other plays, including *Lady Windemere's Fan* (1893), *Salome* (1893), and *A Woman of No Importance* (1894). *Residence:* Paris, France. *Biographical/critical sources:* Alfred Douglas, *Oscar Wilde: A Summing-Up,* Verry, 1940; *College English,* October, 1956, April, 1964; *Saturday Review,* June 13, 1959; Frank Harris, *Oscar Wilde: His Life and Confessions,* reprint of revised edition, Michigan State University Press, 1959; S. Weintraub, *Literary Criticism,* University of Nebraska Press, 1969; *Twentieth-Century Literary Criticism,* Volume 1, Gale, 1978.

*   *   *

WILDER, Alec
See WILDER, Alexander Lafayette Chew

*   *   *

WILDER, Alexander Lafayette Chew   1907-1980
(Alec Wilder)

PERSONAL: Born February 16, 1907, in Rochester, N.Y.; died of lung cancer, December 24, 1980, in Gainesville, Fla.; buried in Avon, N.Y.; son of George (a bank president) and Lillian (Chew) Wilder. *Education:* Attended Eastman School of Music; studied with Herbert Inch and Edward Royce.

CAREER: Musical composer. Conductor of Alec Wilder Octet; host of National Public Radio (NPR) radio show. *Member:*

American Society of Composers, Authors and Publishers, Dramatists Guild. *Awards, honors:* Avon Foundation grant, 1968, and ASCAP-Deems Taylor award, 1974, both for *American Popular Song: The Great Innovators, 1900-1950;* honorary doctorate from the University of Rochester.

WRITINGS—All under name Alec Wilder: *Lullabies and Night Songs* (edited by William Engvick), Harper, 1965; *American Popular Song: The Great Innovators, 1900-1950* (edited by James T. Maher), Oxford University Press, 1972; *Letters I Never Mailed,* Little, Brown, 1975.

Composer for stage, films, television, and radio: "Thumbs Up" (play), first produced in New York City, at St. James Theater, December 27, 1934; "Peter and the Wolves," first produced in Warrenburg, N.Y., at Green Mansions, July 4, 1941; "Juke Box" (ballet), first produced in 1942; "Don't Look Now" (comedy), first produced in 1944; "A Piece of Orchestra," first produced in Rochester, N.Y., at Eastman Theater, November 20, 1947; "The Wind Blows Free" (opera), first produced in Suffern, N.Y., at Antrim Playhouse, August, 1950; "Sunday Excusion," first produced in 1952; "The Lowland Sea" (opera), first produced in Brooklyn, N.Y., at Brooklyn College, May 10, 1952; "See the Jaguar" (play), first produced in New York City, at Cort Theater, December 3, 1952; "Miss Chicken Little" (operetta for children), first produced in 1953; "Cumberland Fair," first produced in 1953; "The Opening," first produced in 1954; "Ellen" (opera), first produced in 1955; "The Long Way" (opera), first produced in Nyack, N.Y., at Nyack High School, June 3, 1955; "Hansel and Gretel," first broadcast by NBC-TV in 1958; "Kittiwake Island," first produced in Martinique, October 12, 1960; "The Sand Castle" (film), released in 1961; "Children's Plea for Peace," first produced in 1969. Also composer for "Albert Schweitzer" (film), "The Impossible Forest," "The Chuckendoose," "Racketty Packetty House," "Herman Ermine in Rabbit Town," "Pinocchio," and "Omnibus."

Instrumental compositions: "Concerto for Oboe and Strings," 1950; "Beginner's Luck," 1953; "Entertainment No. 1," Wilder Music, 1961; "Entertainment No. 2," Wilder Music; "Entertainment No. 3," Wilder Music; "Entertainment No. 4," Wilder Music; "Horn Sonata No. 3," Wilder Music; "Tuba Sonata No. 1," Mentor; "Brass Quintet No. 3," Wilder Music; "Flute Sonata No. 2," Wilder Music; "Wind Quintet No. 3," G. Schirmer; "Wind Quintet No. 4," Wilder Music; "Wind Quintet No. 6," Wilder Music; "Wind Quintet No. 10," Wilder Music; "Concerto," Wilder Music; "Trio," Wilder Music. Also composer of "Theme and Variations," "Air for Oboe," "Slow Dance," "Air for Bassoon," "Air for Flute," "Debutante's Diary," "Seldom the Sun," "Neurotic Goldfish," "Concerning Etchings," "She'll Be Seven in May," "Sea Fugue Mama," "Such a Tender Night," "Walking Home in the Spring," "Dance Man Buys a Farm," "Symphonic Piece," "Eight Songs for Voice and Orchestra," and "Bassoon Sonata No. 2."

Songs: "All the King's Horses," 1930; "It's So Peaceful in the Country," 1941; "Who Can I Turn To?," 1942; "I'll Be Around," 1943; "While We're Young," 1951. Also author of "Soft as Spring," "Lonely Night," "Milwaukee," "J. P. Dooley III," "Moon and Sand," "Goodbye, John," "Good for Nothin'," "Give Me Time," "Sing Our Song of Love," "Kalamazoo to Timbuktu," "Crazy in the Heart," "All the Cats Join In," "Stop That Dancin' Up There," and "At the Swing Shift Ball."

Contributor to magazines, including *Performing Arts Review.*

SIDELIGHTS: Wilder's musical career spanned five decades and ranged over various musical styles and settings. He wrote several hundred popular songs, some commissioned by performers such as Frank Sinatra and Bing Crosby. These songs feature unusual, lyrical melodies that blend musical elements of the classical and jazz styles. The unique blend of classical and jazz is reflected in Wilder's numerous other compositions, which include operas, choral works, orchestral and chamber music, and ballet and film scores. Wilder was particularly fond of chamber music and composed many works for small wind ensembles. While many of Wilder's popular songs became well-recognized standards, his concert music met with little acceptance from either jazz or classical musicians. Critics found that its elusive nature seemed to defy categorization, as did the individualistic Wilder himself, who continued to compose a variety of popular and concert music throughout his career.

In addition to his musical compositions, Wilder wrote three books, including the critically acclaimed *American Popular Song*. This 1972 book examines and analyzes the musical components of American popular songwriting from 1900 to 1950, exploring more than seven hundred songs. *American Popular Song* was recognized as definitive in its field; it brought Wilder a new role as host of a weekly radio series based on his book. The show's format allowed Wilder and his guests to discuss and perform the works of popular songwriters.

In 1975 Wilder published another book, *Letters I Never Mailed*, a collection of letters Wilder wrote over the course of nearly sixty years. The book forms a sort of diary addressed to relatives, friends, and notable colleagues in the musical and literary world. It affords readers some personal insight into the man who loved to ride on trains and who for fifty years lived out of three suitcases, usually at the Algonquin Hotel in New York City. Critics commended *Letters I Never Mailed* as a moving revelation of the life of a complex and fascinating artist.

BIOGRAPHICAL/CRITICAL SOURCES: John Tasker Howard, *Our American Music*, Crowell, 1946; *New Yorker*, September 4, 1971, April 29, 1972, July 9, 1973, February 17, 1975; *New York Times Book Review*, April 23, 1972, June 4, 1972; *Newsweek*, July 31, 1972; *Hi Fi*, August, 1972; *Times Literary Supplement*, October 27, 1972; Alec Wilder, *Letters I Never Mailed*, Little, Brown, 1975.

OBITUARIES: New York Times, December 25, 1980; *Newsweek*, January 5, 1981; *Time*, January 12, 1981.*

* * *

WILDING, Michael 1942-

PERSONAL: Born January 5, 1942, in Worcester, England; son of Richard (an iron molder) and Dorothy Mary (Bull) Wilding. *Education:* Lincoln College, Oxford, B.A., 1963, M.A., 1967. *Office:* Department of English, University of Sydney, Sydney, New South Wales 2006, Australia.

CAREER: Teacher at primary school in Spetchley, England, 1960; University of Sydney, Sydney, Australia, lecturer in English, 1962-66; University of Birmingham, Birmingham, England, assistant lecturer, 1967, lecturer in English, 1968; University of Sydney, senior lecturer, 1969-72, reader in English, 1972—. Director of Wild & Woolley Ltd. (publishers), 1974-79. Member of council of Literature Board of Australia, 1975-76. *Member:* Australian Society of Authors, Association for the Study of Australian Literature, Australian Universities Language and Literature Association, Poets Union, Sydney Filmmakers Cooperative. *Awards, honors:* Senior fellowship from Literature Board of Australia, 1978.

WRITINGS: Milton's Paradise Lost, Sydney University Press, 1969; (with Michael Green and Richard Hoggart) *Cultural Pol-*

icy in Great Britain, United Nations Educational, Scientific and Cultural Organization, 1970; *Aspects of the Dying Process* (stories), University of Queensland Press, 1972; *Living Together* (novel), University of Queensland Press, 1974; *The Short Story Embassy* (novel), Wild & Woolley, 1975; *The West Midland Underground* (stories), University of Queensland Press, 1975; *Scenic Drive* (novel), Wild & Woolley, 1976; *Marcus Clarke*, Oxford University Press, 1977; *The Phallic Forest* (stories), Wild & Woolley, 1978; *Political Fictions* (criticism), Routledge & Kegan Paul, 1980; *Pacific Highway* (novel), Hale & Iremonger, 1981.

Editor: (With Charles Higham) *Australians Abroad*, F. W. Cheshire, 1967; Henry James, *Three Tales*, Hicks Smith, 1967; *Marvell: Modern Judgements*, Macmillan, 1969; John Sheffield, *The Tragedy of Julius Caesar and Marcus Brutus*, Cornmarket, 1970; (with Shirley Cass, Ros Cheney, and David Malouf) *We Took Their Orders and Are Dead: An Anti-War Anthology*, Ure Smith, 1971; *The Portable Marcus Clarke*, University of Queensland Press, 1976; (with Stephen Knight) *The Radical Reader*, Wild & Woolley, Volume I, 1977, Volume II, 1981; *The Tabloid Story Pocket Book*, Wild & Woolley, 1978; William Lane, *The Workingman's Paradise*, Sydney University Press, 1980.

Author of "The Phallic Forest" (film), released by Sydney Filmmakers Co-op, 1972. General editor of "Australia and Pacific Writing Series," University of Queensland Press, 1972—. Contributor to magazines, including *Bachelor, Humanities Review, London Magazine, Nation Review, New Statesman, New Yorker*, and *Pacific Quarterly*. Editor of *Isis*, 1962, *Balcony*, 1965-66, *Tabloid Story*, 1972-75, and *Post-Modern Writing*, 1979—; Australian editor of *Stand*, 1971—.

WORK IN PROGRESS: Research on William Lane, 1861-1917, and New Australia, the communist settlement he established in Paraguay in 1893.

BIOGRAPHICAL/CRITICAL SOURCES: Southerly, Volume XXXIII, number 2, 1973; *Aspect*, spring, 1975; *Cleo*, June, 1975; Geoffrey Dutton, editor, *Literature of Australia*, revised edition, Penguin, 1976; *Caliban*, Volume 14, 1977; K. G. Hamilton, editor, *Studies in the Recent Australian Novel*, University of Queensland Press, 1978; *Waves*, Volume VII, number 4, 1979; *Pacific Quarterly*, Volume IV, number 4, 1979; *Kunapipi*, Volume I, number 2, 1980.

* * *

WILKERSON, Hugh 1939-

PERSONAL: Born March 27, 1939, in Columbia, S.C.; son of Hugh Lyon Clements (a physician) and Lily (Clark) Wilkerson. *Education:* Attended Haverford College, 1958-59; Boston University, B.S., 1961. *Office address:* P.O. Box 1771, Carlsbad, Calif. 92008.

CAREER: Free-lance motion picture editor and camera operator in Boston, Mass., and San Francisco, Calif., 1963-64; restaurant manager, 1965-68; Esalan Institute, Big Sur, Calif., motion picture editor and camera operator, 1969-70; free-lance photographer, 1970-75; builder and designer in California, 1975-77; real estate broker, 1977—. Real estate appraiser in California, 1980—.

WRITINGS: Tai Chi: A Way of Centering, Macmillan, 1970; *Life in the Peace Zone*, Macmillan, 1971.

WORK IN PROGRESS: A novel; short stories; a volume of poetry.

SIDELIGHTS: Wilkerson told *CA:* "My main interest has been in the exploration of lifestyles and how they affect people, why they choose certain ones, and what expectations are involved in those choices. Working from as broad a point of view as possible, I have sought to articulate my subjects' spiritual walk through examination of their daily actions and reactions to the circumstances of their daily existences.

"*Life in the Peace Zone,* a study of a contemporary American company town, explored the lives of several residents of Scotia, the home of Pacific Lumber Company in northern California. In pictures and text, this work revealed some of the effects of paternalistic, protective isolation in that structured environment on the attitudes and spiritual horizons of the inhabitants.

"Recently my attention has extended to include specific blocks to spiritual growth, especially addictions to alcohol and drugs. For the last six years I have been examining and internalizing considerable information on the life choices that precipitate and actualize the addictive personality, and the effects that continued, unfettered addiction may have on the individual and his intimates. I am of the opinion that arrestation of the practice of addiction through any means can lead to a total transformation of the person's outlook and spiritual health, leading, perhaps for the first time in his or her life, to a fully productive place in the mainstream of life.

"As a photographer, writer, and editor, I have worked in the area of journalistic nonfiction. My current work is a fictionalized account of one person's walk through a plethora of life crises, including the albatross of addiction, and that person's emergence into a new awakening to self, beginning with cessation of addictive practice and continuing on to spiritual, emotional, physical, and psychological growth, increasingly free of self-serving and obsessive preoccupations.

"Implicit in this work is the belief that there is an imperative abroad in the world today that the search for spiritual growth in every area of one's life is the only worthwhile, joyful activity; and that the quality of all one's relationships, most importantly with oneself, is dependent directly on the willingness and perseverance with which one pursues this."

*   *   *

WILKINS, Kathleen Sonia   1941-
(Kay S. Wilkins)

PERSONAL: Born December 28, 1941, in Conon Bridge, Scotland; came to the United States in 1967, naturalized citizen, 1978; daughter of Thomas Brewster and Sheila Margaret (Munro) Wilkins. *Education:* University of Southampton, B.A. (with honors), 1963, Ph.D., 1967. *Residence:* Cedar Grove, N.J. *Office:* Department of French, Montclair State College, Upper Montclair, N.J. 07043.

CAREER: State University of New York at Stony Brook, assistant professor of French, 1967-71; National University of Ireland, University College, Dublin, lecturer in French, 1971-72; Montclair State College, Upper Montclair, N.J., associate professor, 1972-80, professor of French, 1980—, coordinator of women's studies program, 1980—, president of faculty senate, 1980-82. *Member:* American Association of Teachers of French, American Society for Eighteenth-Century Studies, New Jersey Network for Women's Studies. *Awards, honors:* Awards from American Philosophical Society, 1974, for work on irrationalism in the eighteenth century, and 1976, for work on theories of children's education in the eighteenth century; grant from National Endowment for the Humanities, 1980, for work on a translation of the correspondence of Auguste Comte and John Stuart Mill.

WRITINGS: A Study of the Works of Claude Buffier, S.J., Institut et Musee Voltaire, 1969; (contributor) Ronald C. Ros-

bottom, editor, *Studies in Eighteenth-Century Culture,* Volume VI, University of Wisconsin Press, 1977; (under name Kay S. Wilkins) *Women's Education in the United States: A Guide to Information Sources,* Gale, 1979. Contributor to *Dictionnaire des journalistes francais, 1631-1787.* Contributor of articles and reviews to scholarly journals.

WORK IN PROGRESS: Research on concepts of virtue and educational theories of the eighteenth century.

SIDELIGHTS: Wilkins told *CA:* "My own interests in women's studies and research into different value systems for boys and girls promulgated in the eighteenth century led me to work on changing patterns in education for women in America. Most striking has been the tremendous attention given to this area in the last ten years, and I maintain a lively interest in changes and research trends. I am now working on links between ethical ideals set for women and men and the nature of society and political systems."

AVOCATIONAL INTERESTS: Reading, cinema, theatre, cards.

*   *   *

WILKINS, Kay S.
See WILKINS, Kathleen Sonia

*   *   *

WILKINS, Roy   1901-1981

PERSONAL: Born August 30, 1901, in St. Louis, Mo.; died of kidney failure, September 8, 1981, in New York, N.Y.; son of William D. (a minister) and Mayfield (Edmondson) Wilkins; married Aminda Ann Badeau (a social worker), September 15, 1929. *Education:* University of Minnesota, A.B., 1923. *Religion:* Protestant. *Home:* 147-15 Village Rd., Jamaica, N.Y. 11435. *Office:* National Association for the Advancement of Colored People, 1790 Broadway, New York, N.Y. 10019.

CAREER: Kansas City Call, Kansas City, Mo., managing editor, 1923-31; National Association for the Advancement of Colored People (NAACP), New York, N.Y., assistant executive secretary, 1931-49, editor of *Crisis* magazine, 1939-49, acting executive secretary, 1949-50, administrator of internal affairs, 1950-55, executive secretary, 1955-64, executive director, 1965-77, director emeritus, 1978—. Chairman of National Emergency Civil Rights Mobilization, 1949-50; chairman of American delegation to International Conference on Human Rights, Teheran, Iran, 1968; member of Presidential Leadership Conference on Civil Rights, 1968-78; affiliated with Freedom House, Muscular Dystrophy Association, and Friends of LBJ (Johnson Library).

AWARDS, HONORS: Outstanding achievement award from University of Minnesota, 1960; Spingarn Medal from NAACP, 1964; Freedom Award from Freedom House, 1967; Theodore Roosevelt Distinguished Service Medal, 1968; Presidential Medal of Freedom, 1969; honorary fellow of Hebrew University, 1972; Zale Award, 1973; Joseph Prize for Human Rights. Honorary degrees from numerous colleges and universities, including Lincoln University, 1958; Morgan State College, 1963; Manhattan College, Iona College, Howard University, Swarthmore College, Notre Dame University, and Middlebury College, all 1965; Fordham University and Tuskegee Institute, both 1966; Bucknell University and University of California, both 1968; Columbia University, 1969; Yeshiva University, 1972; Drake University and St. John's University, both 1975; Temple University, Villanova University, and Indiana State University, all 1977.

WRITINGS: (Contributor) Rayford W. Logan, editor, *What the Negro Wants,* University of North Carolina Press, 1944; *Talking It Over With Roy Wilkins: Selected Speeches and Writings,* compiled by wife, Aminda Wilkins, and Helen Solomon, M & B Publishing, 1977. Author of a weekly column in *Amsterdam News,* New York, N.Y., until 1970, and a column syndicated by the Register and Tribune Syndicate, 1969-80.

WORK IN PROGRESS: An autobiography, publication expected in 1982.

SIDELIGHTS: The grandson of a Mississippi slave, Wilkins served for more than sixty years as a speaker for racial equality. He grew up in an integrated neighborhood in St. Paul, Minnesota, and later attended the University of Minnesota. While in college he won an oratory contest for his speech protesting a lynching in Duluth, but it was not until he became a newspaper reporter in Kansas City, Missouri, that he experienced racial prejudice firsthand. Working for a black weekly, the *Kansas City Call,* Wilkins realized "the magnitude of racial bias in the U.S. . . . It was a slow accumulation of humiliations and grievances," Wilkins remembered. "Kansas City ate my heart out. It was a Jim Crow town through and through." At the *Call,* Wilkins urged an end to police brutality and encouraged blacks to exercise their strength at the polls to defeat white supremacist politicians.

In 1931 Wilkins began working for the organization that had made the abolition of lynching its primary goal, the National Association for the Advancement of Colored People (NAACP). In one of his first assignments he directed an investigation of blacks working on the southern Mississippi River levees, and his ensuing report, "Mississippi Slave Labor," brought about congressional action to improve wages and working conditions. Several years later Wilkins succceded W. E. B. Dubois as editor of the NAACP's *Crisis* magazine, where he led crusades against the poll tax and other forms of segregation. When NAACP Executive Secretary Walter White died in 1955, Wilkins was elected unanimously to the organization's top post. (The title was later changed to executive director.) He held the position for twenty-two years, during a time when forced integration of schools, protest marches, boycotts, sit-ins, and urban riots brought America's attention to its racial problems.

Wilkins's "crowning glory" in his career-long struggle for civil rights was the 1954 Supreme Court decision, *Brown* v. *Board of Education,* that declared segregation in public schools unconstitutional. The case had been argued before the Court by NAACP general counsel Thurgood Marshall, with Wilkins planning the case behind the scenes. Wilkins was also among the organizers of the celebrated March on Washington (August 28, 1963), and he worked personally with Presidents Kennedy and Johnson towards the passage of civil rights legislation. "Quiet confrontation," said Paul Delaney in the *New York Times,* was Wilkins's tactic.

As racial protests grew more militant during the 1960's, other groups stole attention from the NAACP. The Southern Christian Leadership Conference (SCLC) and Congress on Racial Equality (CORE) "furnish the noise," Wilkins explained at the time. The NAACP "pays the bills." The group's lawyers were particularly active, representing many of those arrested in the demonstrations and civil disturbances of the era. Later in the decade, when blacks rioted in the streets and called for separation from whites, Wilkins condemned the violence and warned of the dangers of a separate society. "Black power," he said, is "the father of hatred and the mother of violence. . . . In the quick, uncritical and highly emotional adoption it has received from some segments of a beleaguered people, [black power] can only mean black death. Even if it should

be enthroned briefly, the human spirit would die a little." Due to his nonmilitant approach, Wilkins was sometimes called an Uncle Tom. But, as Delaney noted, "Keeping his cool was one virtue that made Mr. Wilkins the pre-eminent civil rights leader of his day. . . . He kept his head when all about him were losing theirs."

Wilkins once explained the reasons for his approach: "The Negro has to be a superb diplomat and a great strategist. He has to parlay what actual power he has along with the good will of the white majority. He has to devise and pursue those philosophies and activities which will least alienate the white majority opinion. And that doesn't mean that the Negro has to indulge in bootlicking. But he must gain the sympathy of the large majority of the American public. He must also seek to make an identification with the American tradition."

Wilkins's last years with the NAACP were difficult ones. The link he shared with the nation's presidency was broken: he accused President Nixon of turning "back the clock" on "racial progress" and criticized President Ford's efforts to reduce the courts' power in school busing decisions as a "craven, cowardly, despicable retreat." Wilkins also battled within the NAACP, presiding over internal conflicts and resisting charges that he was incapable of leading the group in a rapidly changing world. In 1977, at the age of seventy-six, Wilkins retired and Benjamin Hooks was named the new executive director. After Wilkins's death in 1981, Hooks remembered his predecessor as "a towering figure in American history and during the time he headed the NAACP. It was during this crucial period that the association was faced with some of its most serious challenges and the whole landscape of the black condition in America was changed, radically, for the better."

AVOCATIONAL INTERESTS: Sports cars.

BIOGRAPHICAL/CRITICAL SOURCES: *Newsweek,* June 24, 1949, July 14, 1975, June 12, 1978; *Time,* August 30, 1963, July 12, 1976; George R. Metcalf, *Black Profiles,* McGraw, 1968; *Reader's Digest,* January, 1968; *New York Times Magazine,* September 28, 1969; Elton C. Fax, *Contemporary Black Leaders,* Dodd, 1970; *Ebony,* April, 1974; *American Teacher,* October, 1977.

OBITUARIES: *Detroit Free Press,* September 9, 1981; *New York Times,* September 9, 1981; *Washington Post,* September 9, 1981; *Newsweek,* September 21, 1981; *Time,* September 21, 1981.

—*Sketch by David Versical*

* * *

WILKINSON, John Thomas 1893-1980

OBITUARY NOTICE: Born December 10, 1893, in Hull, Yorkshire, England; died in November, 1980. Clergyman, educator, and author. A Methodist minister, Wilkinson was associated with the Hartley Victoria Theological College from 1946 to 1959. His writings include *Richard Baxter and Margaret Charlton, Principles of Biblical Interpretation,* and *William Clowes, 1780-1851.* (Date of death provide by daughter, Hettie M. Donnier.)

* * *

WILKINSON, Walter 1888-1970

OBITUARY NOTICE: Born in 1888 in Watford, England; died May 31, 1970, in Somerset, England. Puppeteer and author best known for his writings on puppetry. Wilkinson's books include *Puppets in Yorkshire, A Sussex Peepshow,* and *Puppets*

Through America. Obituaries and other sources: *AB Bookman's Weekly,* June 22, 1970; *The Author's and Writer's Who's Who,* 6th edition, Burke's Peerage, 1971.

*   *   *

WILLIAMS, Charles (Walter Stansby)   1886-1945

BRIEF ENTRY: Born September 20, 1886, in London, England; died May 15, 1945, in Oxford, England. British editor, poet, playwright, biographer, essayist, and novelist. Although Williams was employed as an editor at Oxford University Press during most of his writing career, he was able to write almost forty books and numerous other works. A devout Christian, Williams used the struggle between good and evil as the theme for most of his writings. Williams' work, admired by W. H. Auden, T. S. Eliot, and C. S. Lewis, became very popular in England in the 1930's. He is best known for his novels that are often described as supernatural or metaphysical thrillers. They include *War in Heaven* (1930), *The Place of the Lion* (1931), *The Greater Trumps* (1932), *Shadow of Ecstacy* (1933), *Descent Into Hell* (1937), and *All Hallows' Eve* (1945). *Biographical/critical sources: Atlantic Monthly,* November, 1949; John Heath-Stubbs, *Charles Williams,* Longmans, Green, 1955; A. M. Hadfield, *An Introduction to Charles Williams,* R. Hale, 1959; *Gordon Review,* winter, 1967; *Webster's New World Companion to English and American Literature,* World Publishing, 1973; *Twentieth-Century Literary Criticism,* Volume 1, Gale, 1978.

*   *   *

WILLIAMS, (George) Emlyn   1905-

PERSONAL: Born November 26, 1905, in Mostyn, Wales; married Molly O'Shann, 1935 (died, 1970); children: two. *Education:* Christ Church, Oxford, M.A., 1927. *Home:* 123 Dovehouse St., London S.W.3, England.

CAREER: Actor, director, and writer. Actor in stage productions, including "And So to Bed," 1927, "Man Overboard," 1932, "Othello," 1956, "A Month in the Country," 1965, and "Forty Years On," 1969; in motion pictures, including "Major Barbara," 1941, "Ivanhoe," 1952, "I Accuse!," 1958, "The L-Shaped Room," 1963, and "The Walking Stick," 1969; and in television productions, including "Every Picture Tells a Story," 1949. Actor in one-man shows from the works of Charles Dickens and Dylan Thomas. Director of stage productions, including "A Murder Has Been Arranged," 1930, "The Corn Is Green," 1938, "The Little Foxes," 1942, and "Beth," 1958. *Awards, honors:* New York Drama Critics Circle Award, 1941; LL.D., from University College of North Wales, Bangor, 1949; Commander of Order of the British Empire, 1962.

WRITINGS: George: An Early Autobiography, Hamish Hamilton, 1961, Random House, 1962; *Beyond Belief,* Hamish Hamilton, 1967, Random House, 1968; *Emlyn: An Early Autobiography, 1927-1935,* Bodley Head, 1973, Viking, 1974; *Headlong,* Heinemann, 1980, Viking, 1981.

Published plays: *A Murder Has Been Arranged: A Ghost Story* (first produced in London, 1930), Collins, 1930, Samuel French, 1931; *The Late Christopher Bean* (first produced in London, 1933; adapted from the play by Sidney Howard), Gollancz, 1933; *Night Must Fall* (first produced in London, 1936), Gollancz, 1935, Random House, 1936; *He Was Born Gay: A Romance* (first produced in London, 1937), Heinemann, 1937; *The Corn Is Green* (first produced in London, 1940), Heinemann, 1938, Random House, 1941.

The Light of Heart (first produced in London, 1940), Heinemann, 1940; *The Morning Star* (first produced in London, 1941), Heinemann, 1942; *A Month in the Country* (first produced in London, 1943; produced in Chicago, Ill., 1956; adapted from the play by Ivan Turgenev), Heinemann, 1943, Samuel French, 1957; *The Druid's Rest* (first produced in London, 1944), Heinemann, 1944; *The Wind of Heaven* (first produced in London, 1945; produced in Westport, Conn., 1945), Heinemann, 1945; *Spring 1600* (first produced in London, 1934), Heinemann, 1946; *Thinking Aloud: A Dramatic Sketch* (first produced in London, 1947; produced in New York City, 1975), Samuel French, 1946; *Trespass: A Ghost Story* (first produced in London, 1947), Heinemann, 1947; *Pepper and Sand: A Duologue* (first broadcast on radio in 1947), Deane, 1948; *Dear Evelyn* (first produced in Rutherglen, Scotland, 1948), Samuel French, c. 1949.

The Corn Is Green, With Two Other Plays (also contains "The Wind of Heaven" and "The Druid's Rest"; also see above), Pan, 1950; *Accolade* (first produced in London, 1950), Heinemann, 1951; *Readings From Dickens* (first produced as "Emlyn Williams as Charles Dickens," first produced in London, 1951; produced in New York City, 1952), Folio Society, 1953; *Someone Waiting* (first produced in Liverpool, England, 1953; produced in London, 1953; produced in New York City, 1956) Heinemann, 1954, Dramatists Play Service, 1956; "Vigil" (one-act; first produced in Oxford, England, 1925), anthologized in *The Second Book of One-Act Plays,* Heinemann, 1954; *Beth* (first produced in Brighton, England, 1958), Heinemann, 1959; *The Collected Plays,* (contains "The Corn Is Green," "He Was Born Gay," "The Light of Heart," and "Night Must Fall"; also see above), Random House, 1961; *The Master Builder* (first produced in London, 1964; adapted from the play by Henrik Ibsen), Theatre Arts Books, 1967.

Unpublished plays: "Full Moon", first produced in Oxford, 1927; "Glamour," first produced in London, 1928; "Port Said," first produced in London, 1931, revised edition produced as "Vessels Departing' in London, 1933; "Josephine" (adapted from the work by Herman Bahr), first produced in London, 1934; "Yesterday's Magic," (first produced in New York City, 1942; "Pen Don," first produced in Blackpool, England, 1943; "A Boy Growing Up," first produced in London, 1955; first produced in New York City, 1957.

Screenplays: "Friday the Thirteenth," 1933; "Evergreen," 1934; (author of additional dialogue; with Ian Dalrymple, Frank Wead, and Elizabeth Hill), "The Citadel" (adapted from the novel by A. J. Cronin), Metro-Goldwyn-Mayer, 1938; (author of dialogue; with A. R. Rawlinson and Bridget Boland), "This England," World, 1941.

Teleplays: "A Month in the Country," 1947; "Every Picture Tells a Story," 1949; "In Town Tonight," 1954; "A Blue Movie of My Own True Love," 1968; "The Power of Dawn," 1975.

Also author (and reader) of radio script "Emlyn" (adapted from own autobiography), 1974.

SIDELIGHTS: Williams was the writer and actor for the popular British productions of "Night Must Fall" and "The Corn Is Green" during the 1930's. In "Night Must Fall," he terrified London audiences with his chilling portrayal of a homicidal psychopath stalking an elderly woman and her young niece in a huge old home. "Suspense is faultlessly preserved as the play moves to a crisis of action," wrote Derek Verschoyle in *Spectator,* "but the interest of the audience is held less by the tension of the plot than by the skill with which the complexities of mind and motive in its central character are unravelled."

Verschoyle added that "in comparison with this play all other modern plays with murder as their theme ... seem in retrospect as flat as the proverbial pancake." When "Night Must Fall" was staged in New York City, critics there were similarly impressed. "When he is at his best," contended a reviewer for the *New York Times*, "as author and actor, Mr. Williams can be morbidly terrifying, and enough of *Night Must Fall* is just that. Definitely for the homicide squad."

"The Corn Is Green" concerns the efforts of a spinsterish schoolteacher to found a school for the children of Welsh miners in the late nineteenth century. In the original productions, Williams played Evans, an extremely intelligent older boy coaxed by the schoolteacher into competing for a scholarship to Oxford University. Evans eventually rejects the schoolteacher's guidance for the affections of a local harlot. After winning the scholarship, he learns of the harlot's pregnancy. He decides to marry the woman and abandon his hopes of further education. The schoolteacher, however, persuades Evans that his hope lies in improving himself, and she adopts his child.

Reviewers were impressed with "The Corn Is Green." "The simplicity of the story can be relied on to throw the spectator into a mood of acceptance of make-believe," declared James Agate, "from which he need make very occasional sorties to admire this bit of pathos pressed home but not too far home." Agate also praised Williams's "sense of wit and humour." Erik Johns wrote, "In the entire history of Wales [Williams] is the one solitary figure on the plane of first-rate dramatists to write a play in English that is essentially Welch in essence." He added that "Williams brought Wales to the stage most effectively in *The Corn Is Green*."

Williams enjoyed further popularity for his plays after World War II, such as "Trespass" and "Accolade," and his performances in stage productions and motion pictures. Perhaps his best known performances are his one-man shows from the works of Charles Dickens and Dylan Thomas. "I got the idea from Charles Dickens in 1951," Williams told the *Washington Post*. "I was reading his autobiography, and I suddenly thought I'll dress up as Dickens and do what he did—tell a story from one of his books." Williams's readings from Dickens were enormously successful, and he estimated in 1979 that he'd performed that show two thousand times. Williams began performing as Dylan Thomas after reading the poet's works at a benefit for the latter's widow and children. "The irony of it is that if [Thomas had] lived," noted Williams, "he almost certainly would have gone into the theater."

BIOGRAPHICAL/CRITICAL SOURCES: Spectator, June 7, 1935; *New York Times*, September 29, 1936, January 12, 1981; James Agate, *The Amazing Theatre*, Harrap, 1939; *Nation*, December 7, 1940, September 26, 1942; *New Yorker*, December 7, 1940, February 16, 1952, October 27, 1962, June 24, 1974; *New Republic*, December 9, 1940, September 28, 1942; *Commonweal*, May 1, 1942, October 2, 1942; *Time*, February 18, 1952, May 4, 1953; Walter Kerr, *The Theatre in Spite of Itself*, Simon & Schuster, 1963; *Washington Post*, August 21, 1979, February 24, 1981; *Contemporary Literary Criticism*, Volume 15, Gale, 1980; *Times Literary Supplement*, October 3, 1980; *Los Angeles Times Book Review*, March 15, 1981.

* * *

WILLIAMS, Francis   1903-1970

OBITUARY NOTICE: Born in 1903; died June 5, 1970, in Surrey, England. Historian and author. Williams was a historian of the trade union movement and was designated a Labour life-peer in 1962. His writings include *Nothing So Strange*.

Obituaries and other sources: *AB Bookman's Weekly*, June 22, 1970.

* * *

WILLIAMS, Joyce E(layne)   1937-

PERSONAL: Born February 4, 1937, in Rockdale, Tex.; daughter of Harry Lee (a laborer) and Essie Marie (Fergeson) Williams. *Education:* Mary Hardin-Baylor College (now University of Mary Hardin Baylor), B.A., 1958; Southern Methodist University, M.A., 1962; Washington University, St. Louis, Mo., Ph.D., 1971. *Home:* 1818 Teasley Lane, Apt. 802, Denton, Tex. 76201. *Office:* Department of Sociology, Texas Woman's University, Denton, Tex. 76204.

CAREER: Buckner Children's Home, Dallas, Tex., social case worker, 1958-62; Mary Hardin-Baylor College (now University of Mary Hardin Baylor), Belton, Tex., 1962-65, began as instructor, became assistant professor of sociology; Arlington State College, Arlington, Tex., instructor in sociology, 1965-67; Washington University, St. Louis, Mo., lecturer in sociology, 1967-69; University of Texas, Arlington, assistant professor, 1969-73, associate professor of sociology, 1973-74; Trinity University, San Antonio, Tex., assistant professor, 1974-75, associate professor of sociology, 1975-80; Texas Woman's University, Denton, associate professor of sociology and director of criminal justice program, 1980—. Member of visiting faculty at University of Texas, Austin, summer, 1977. Adviser to Como Community Betterment Council, 1969-74; member of board of directors of Tarrant County Legal Aid Foundation, 1972-75; member of Alamo Area Volunteer Advocate Program, 1974-80, Citizens United for the Rehabilitation of Errants and Community Education, both 1975—; member of planning and advisory committees of American Issues Forum, 1975; consultant to Southwest Center for Public Policy and Houston Area Women's Center.

MEMBER: American Sociological Association, Society for the Study of Social Problems, American Association of University Professors, National Organization for Women, Southwestern Social Science Association, Southwestern Sociological Association (member of executive committee, 1980—), Southern Sociological Association. *Awards, honors:* National Institute of Mental Health grant, 1976-79.

WRITINGS: Black Community Control: A Study of Transition in a Texas Ghetto, Praeger, 1973; (contributor) Jack Kinton, editor, *American Ethnic Revival*, Social Science and Sociological Resources, 1977; (contributor) Julian C. Bridges, editor, *Sociology: A Pragmatic Approach*, Hunter Publishing (Winston-Salem, N.C.), 1981; (with Karen A. Holmes) *The Second Assault: Rape and Public Attitudes*, Greenwood Press, 1981. Contributor of about a dozen articles and reviews to sociology journals. Associate editor of *Victimology: An International Journal*, 1980.

WORK IN PROGRESS: Contributing to *The Politics of Patriarchal Violence*, edited by Ruth Schwartz; a textbook on racial/ethnic minorities; research on faculty displacement in higher education, caused by tenure termination, unemployment, and underemployment.

SIDELIGHTS: Joyce Williams wrote: "Though the youngest child in a family of four, I was the first to finish high school. I have worked since the age of twelve and, no doubt, my early experience with poverty has shaped my professional interests as a humanistic sociologist. My major area of interest is inequality, particularly as it relates to poverty, racial/ethnic minorities, and women. I have been teaching for eighteen years and find that it is still a new and challenging experience; however, in my field some generations of students are certainly preferable to others as measured by their interest in social/political issues. I enjoy research and writing, although a full-time teaching load leaves all too little time for this. I have tried to research issues in which I have some personal and professional commitment, where I feel I can make some contribution to the alleviation of inequality of social problems. The subjects I choose to research and write about are an expression of my own values as well as of my sociological work.''

* * *

WILLIAMS, Russell J(ohn) 1944-

PERSONAL: Born January 10, 1944, in Whitehall, N.Y.; son of William J. and Eleanora A. (Engstrom) Williams; married Marsha J. Nowicki (a special educator), June 16, 1970; children: Amrys Orenda. *Education:* State University of New York College at Plattsburgh, B.S., 1965, M.S., 1968; State University of New York at Albany, D.Arts, 1979. *Residence:* Whitehall, N.Y. *Office:* Student Programs Office, New York State Senate, State Capitol, Room 500A, Albany, N.Y 12247.

CAREER: Chapman College, Orange, Calif., instructor in comparative social development for World Campus Afloat, 1969; State University of New York College at Plattsburgh, instructor in English, 1969-73, faculty member of Miner Institute for Man and His Environment, 1972-73; New York State Senate, Albany, director of student programs, 1979—. Co-founder of CLEAR (community environmental and recycling organization), 1970-73. *Member:* Modern Language Association of America, Associated Writing Programs, National Conference of State Legislatures. *Awards, honors:* Member of Bread Loaf Writers Conference, 1964.

WRITINGS: The Hole in Jocelyn's Forehead and Other Poems, State University of New York at Albany, 1979. Contributor of articles, poems, and reviews to magazines, including *Et Cetera, Best Sellers, Washout Review, Bitterroot, New Mexico Philatelist,* and *Colorado-North Review.*

WORK IN PROGRESS: A book of poems; stories.

SIDELIGHTS: Williams told *CA:* "I am the product of a rural childhood spent largely in the outdoors and in field and stream sports; I came alive artistically as a painter and pencil artist who profited by his background, and I awakened as a poet who benefited by the dynamic of his past and who understood vulnerability as a value: that and simple eyesight have become or are at the center of my vision.

"I am influenced by a curious science (only hinted at by Herbert Spencer's insightful observation, 'The truth is that those who have never entered upon scientific pursuits know not a tithe of the poetry by which they are surrounded'). Correspondingly, I read widely—and a good deal of what is wrongly called children's literature. I believe in basics. I believe in imagination. That is, the Sistine Chapel ceiling and the Apollo Man-on-the-Moon Project had more *qualities* in common than is ordinarily recognized, qualities of quest, imagination, and understanding. I want, I want my work to be, part of just such a human endeavor—conceptual, basic, and tactile all at once: man in place, mankind in space. If we cannot go there in our workaday lives, because perhaps we are washing dishes in the kitchen sink while the suds diminish around our wrists, still we can be prepared to understand the journey and the importance of our place in it, and we can send our ready imaginations. Ultimately, I believe it is only by investing ourselves (in one another) that we shall stave off the terror that is everywhere hungry and voluptuous around us.

"It is hinted to me that I say best in poetry what I am trying here to say in brief.''

* * *

WILLIE, Frederick
See LOVECRAFT, H(oward) P(hillips)

* * *

WILLOUGHBY, Charles Andrew 1892-1972

OBITUARY NOTICE: Military officer and author. A major general in the U.S. Army, Willoughby served as General Douglas MacArthur's chief of intelligence during World War II. Willoughby was one of the "Bataan Boys" who left the Philippines with the general in 1942; he remained MacArthur's confidant and companion for the next nine years. When President Truman fired MacArthur in 1951, Willoughby retired from the Army and, in collaboration with John Chamberlain, wrote *MacArthur, 1941-1951.* He also wrote *Shanghai Conspiracy.* Obituaries and other sources: *New York Times,* October 26, 1972; *Time,* November 6, 1972; *Newsweek,* November 6, 1972.

* * *

WILLY
See COLETTE, (Sidonie-Gabrielle)

* * *

WILLY, Colette
See COLETTE, (Sidonie-Gabrielle)

* * *

WILSON, Glenn Daniel 1942-

PERSONAL: Born December 29, 1942, in Christchurch, New Zealand; son of Daniel (an estate agent) and Dorothy (Williams) Wilson; married Judith Ann Holden (a medical illustrator), February 24, 1967; children: Kirsten Lee, Candice Lee. *Education:* University of Canterbury, B.A., 1965, M.A. (with first class honors), 1967; University of London, Ph.D., 1970. *Home:* 24 Dorchester Dr., London S.E.24, England. *Office:* Institute of Psychiatry, University of London, De Crespigny Park, London S.E.5, England.

CAREER: University of London, Institute of Psychiatry, London, England, lecturer in psychology, 1970-80, senior lecturer in psychology, 1981—. Visiting professor at California State University, Los Angeles, summers, 1971-72, 1974-75, Stanford University, summer, 1980, and San Francisco State University, summer, 1981. *Member:* British Psychological Society.

WRITINGS: (With D.K.B. Nias and P. M. Insel) *Manual for the Children's Attitude Scale,* Children's Studies, 1972; (editor) *The Psychology of Conservatism,* Academic Press, 1973; (with H. J. Eysenck) *The Experimental Study of Freudian Theories,* Methuen, 1973; (contributor) Peter Sainsbury and Norman Kreitman, editors, *Methods of Psychiatric Research,* Methuen, 1974; *Improve Your I.Q.,* Futura, 1974; *Manual for the Wilson-Patterson Attitude Inventory,* NFER Publishing, 1975; (with Eysenck) *Know Your Own Personality,* Temple Smith, 1975; (editor with Eysenck) *A Textbook of Human Psychology,* Medical & Technical Publishers, 1976; (with Nias) *Love's Mysteries: The Psychology of Sexual Attraction,* Open Books, 1976, published as *The Mystery of Love,* Quadrangle, 1977; (contributor) Thomas Blass, editor, *Personality Variables in Social Behavior*, Erlbaum, 1977; (with Diana Grylls) *Know Your Child's I.Q.*, Futura, 1977; (contributor) Harvey London and John Exner, editors, *Dimensions of Personality*, Wiley, 1978; *The Secrets of Sexual Fantasy*, Dent, 1978; (with Eysenck) *The Psychological Basis of Ideology*, MTP Press, 1978; (editor with Mark Cook) *Love and Attraction: An International Conference*, Pergamon, 1979; (with Eyseneck) *The Psychology of Sex*, Dent, 1979.

(With Chris Gosselin) *Sexual Variations: Fetishism, Sado-masochism, and Transvestism*, Faber, 1980, Simon & Schuster, 1981; *Love and Instinct*, Temple Smith, 1981; (with D. N. Cox) *A Non-Clinical Study of Pedophilia*, Pergamon, 1982. Contributor to *International Encyclopedia of Neurology, Psychiatry, Psychoanalysis, and Psychology* and *Encyclopaedia of Behaviour*. Contributor of articles and reviews to psychology journals. Book review editor of *Personality and Individual Differences*.

WORK IN PROGRESS: A book on psychology of drama and opera.

SIDELIGHTS: Wilson wrote: "I have a passionate interest in opera. I am a part-time professional singer (baritone) and opera director. I combine my interests by teaching a course on psychology of drama and opera. It is my belief that the world's great, evergreen operas (of which there are only a few dozen) have survived because they bear on the most fundamental human instincts and preoccupations. They thus comprise vital data for the understanding of human motivation and emotion."

* * *

WILSON, Jaye 1938-

PERSONAL: Birth-given name, Dorothy Jean Wilson; born October 3, 1938, in Memphis, Tenn.; daughter of Robert Louis and Frances (Sterling) Wilson; married Clovis James Walker, March 29, 1956 (divorced June 26, 1976); children: Clovis James, Jr., John Douglass. *Education:* Stephen F. Austin University, B.A., 1966; graduate study at Sam Houston University, 1973-74. *Home and office:* 5911 Fairgreen, San Antonio, Tex. 78242. *Agent:* Meredith Bernstein, Synapse Productions Ltd., 33 Riverside Dr., New York, N.Y. 10023.

CAREER: High school reading and English teacher in Beaumont, Tex., 1966-69; teacher of English and history at public schools in Madisonville, Tex., 1970-72; reading teacher at high school in Houston, Tex., 1975-78; high school English teacher in San Antonio, Tex., 1978-79; junior high school resource teacher in San Antonio, 1979-80; Spring South High School, Houston, teacher of English, 1980-81; writer. *Member:* National Education Association, Texas State Teachers Association, San Antonio Writers Guild.

WRITINGS: Houston Heat (novel), Fawcett, 1979; *Storm* (novel), Fawcett, 1982.

WORK IN PROGRESS: Plantation, a contemporary novel; *Bitterweed*, a novel set in East Texas in the 1940's and 1950's; a historical novel based on the loves of the Clovis and Frank families; a historical novel about a slave who rose to greatness in pre-Civil War East Texas.

SIDELIGHTS: Wilson commented: "To satisfy me, my writing must have two levels of justification—the venting of the creative urge and the indulging of a compulsion to examine and comment on 'underlying realities.' The most fascinating of these basic forces is suggested in the words 'power' and 'love.' I often concern myself with the clash of these two ideas which seem inevitably to destroy each other, yet magically restructure

again and again as in some wizard's grand illusion. Though the times, the characters, the conditions change, the pattern remains an eternal constant. This intrigues me.

"*Houston Heat,* for example, is a study on several levels. It is the struggle of an 'emerging woman' to find a place in the American power structure circa 1969. Jean Iversen is at once the character as well as all women of that time, and yet she is also the Jeanne D'Arc who dwells in everyone. Another character whose name suggests his attitudes is Bartel (*born* Bartleman), the 'complete mortal,' buried beneath the debris of a successful search for wealth, who, despite his talent and drive for accretion, is consummately unfulfilled. In a sense, he is power, she is love, and Joe Devereaux, all-American Joe, is the 'all of us' caught in the middle of these forces of consciousness. In all that I write I find variations of this basic pattern somewhat like the gathering of a storm, its rage, dissipation, and eventual forming anew whenever the winds meet again. The title of my next book, in fact, is *Storm.*"

AVOCATIONAL INTERESTS: Travel, art, music, swimming, fishing, horticulture.

BIOGRAPHICAL/CRITICAL SOURCES: Writer, July, 1979; *Austin Citizen*, August 3, 1979; *San Antonio Express News*, August 5, 1979; *Texas City Sun*, August 19, 1979; *Fort Worth Star Telegram*, August 19, 1979; *Houston Suburbia Reporter*, August 22, 1979; *Galveston News*, August 26, 1979; *Houston Chronicle*, August 26, 1979.

* * *

WINCHESTER, Clarence 1895-1981
(C. Tanner-Rutherford, Ornis)

OBITUARY NOTICE: Born March 17, 1895, in London, England; died March 15, 1981. Journalist, editor, and author. Well known in the aeronautical world, Winchester learned to fly in 1913 and at one time wrote on aeronautics for the *Daily Mail*. He was also a founding member of the original Institute of Aeronautical Engineers and an associate of the Royal Aeronautical Society. Winchester served as a periodical editor with Cassells and Amalgamated Press befor working as assistant editor on the *Daily Sketch*. While with Cassells he edited *Argosy, Cassell's Magazine, Storyteller, New*, and *Corner*. Winchester was also advisory editorial director of Crosby, Lockwood and Son Ltd. and correspondent on European affairs to the *Argonaut* of San Francisco. His own publications include *Aerial Photography, An Innocent in Hollywood, Three Men in a Plane*, and *A Great Rushing of Wings and Other Poems*. Obituaries and other sources: *London Times*, March 17, 1981.

* * *

WIND, Edgar 1900-1971

OBITUARY NOTICE: Born in 1900 in Berlin, Germany; died September 12, 1971, in London, England. Educator, art historian, and author. Considered an authority on the Renaissance, Wind was a noted lecturer throughout England and the United States and was elected a fellow of the American Academy of Arts and Sciences in 1951. Beginning in 1925, Wind was associated with several colleges and universities in the United States, including the University of North Carolina, New York University, the University of Chicago, and Smith College. In 1955 he became the first professor of art to be appointed by Oxford University. His many writings include *Bellini's Feast of the Gods, Pagan Mysteries in the Renaissance*, and *Michelangelo's Prophets and Sibyls*. A six-part lecture series he presented on the British Broadcasting Corp. (BBC) in 1960 was later published as a book entitled *Art and Anarchy.* Obituaries and other sources: *New York Times,* September 18, 1971; *AB Bookman's Weekly,* October 25, 1971.

* * *

WINSHIP, Laurence Leathe   1890-1975

OBITUARY NOTICE: Born February 19, 1890, in Somerville, Mass.; died after a long illness, in 1975, in Marlborough, Mass. Journalist and editor. Winship began his career in 1912 as a member of the staff of the *Boston Globe.* He later served the *Globe* as Sunday editor, managing editor, and editor, before retiring in 1965. His son Thomas succeeded him as editor. Winship came out of retirement in 1968 to cover the national political conventions for the newspaper. Obituaries and other sources: *Who's Who in America,* 38th edition, Marquis, 1974; *Time,* March 17, 1975.

* * *

WINSTON, Krishna   1944-

PERSONAL: Born June 7, 1944, in Greenfield, Mass.; daughter of Richard (a writer and translator) and Clara (a writer and translator; maiden name Brussel) Winston; married Donald Billingsley, August 28, 1976; children: Danielle Christina. *Education:* Attended University of Hamburg, 1963-64, 1965-66; Smith College, B.A. (summa cum laude), 1965; Yale University, M.Phil., 1969, Ph.D., 1974; attended University of Berlin, 1973-74. *Home:* 655 Bow Lane, Middletown, Conn. 06457. *Office:* Department of German Language and Literature, Wesleyan University, Middletown, Conn. 06457.

CAREER: Wesleyan University, Middletown, Conn., instructor, 1970-75, assistant professor, 1975-77, associate professor of German, 1977—. *Member:* International Arthur Schnitzler Research Association, Modern Language Association of America, American Association of Teachers of German (vice-president, 1976-78), Northeast Modern Language Association. *Awards, honors:* Grant from German Academic Exchange Service, for study in West Germany, 1973-74.

WRITINGS: Horvath Studies: Close Readings of Six Plays, Peter Lang, 1977; (contributor) Wolfgange Paulsen, editor, *Oesterreichische Gegenwart: Die moderne Literatur* (title means "The Austrian Present: Modern Literature and Its Relationship to Tradition"), Francke Verlag, 1980.

Translator: (Contributing translator) Peter Demetz and other editors, *The Disciplines of Criticism,* Yale University Press, 1968; Gunilla Bergsten, *Thomas Mann's "Doctor Faustus": The Sources and Structure of the Novel,* University of Chicago Press, 1969; (co-translator with father, Richard Winston) Erich Kahler, *The Orbit of Thomas Mann,* Princeton University Press, 1970; Tut Schlemmer, editor, *The Letters and Diaries of Oskar Schlemmer,* Wesleyan University Press, 1972; Manes Sperber, *Masks of Loneliness,* Macmillan, 1974; Heike Doutine, *German Requiem,* Scribner, 1975; Aniela Jaffe, *C. G. Jung: Word and Image,* Princeton University Press, 1978; Siegfried Lenz, *The Heritage,* Hill & Wang, 1981; (co-translator) Aldo Carotenuto, *Diary of a Secret Symmetry: Sabina Spielrein Between Jung and Freud,* Pantheon, 1982.

Contributor of articles, translations, and reviews to literature journals.

WORK IN PROGRESS: Translating the article "Man and Meaning" by Erich Neumann, for a collection for Princeton University Press; a monograph on Oedoen von Horvath, publication by Ungar expected in 1983.

SIDELIGHTS: Winston told *CA:* "In my career as a translator I follow in the footsteps of my parents, the noted translating team of Richard and Clara Winston, whose high standards and devotion to their craft I endeavor to emulate. I view translating as an important part of the attempt to mediate among cultures, and my teaching and scholarly activity also contribute to that effort.

"My scholarly interest in the Hungarian dramatist and novelist Oedoen von Horvath (1901-1938), who wrote in German, focuses chiefly on his brilliant portrayal of the petty-bourgeois mentality in Germany between the two world wars. Horvath captures through his characters' language the dangerous psychological state of persons whose patterns of response have been formed by the mass media and by an educational system which, intentionally or unintentionally, dulls the average citizen's critical faculties. Horvath and several of his contemporaries whose works I am also studying (Kurt Tucholsky, Erich Kaestner, Marieluise Fleisser, Irmgard Keun) offer a remarkably acute diagnosis of the sickness that produced fascism in Europe in the 1930's and produces reactionary movements in the Western democracies today."

* * *

WINSTONE, H(arry) V(ictor) F(rederick)   1926-

PERSONAL: Born August 3, 1926, in London, England; married Joan Marigold Cory (a pianist), December 20, 1947. *Education:* Attended University of London, 1943-44. *Politics:* "Old-fashioned liberal." *Religion:* "Protestant by birth, free-thinker by adoption." *Home:* 129 Fairacres, Bromley, Kent, England. *Agent:* Julian Bach Literary Agency, Inc., 747 Third Ave., New York, N.Y. 10017; and Campbell, Thompson & McLaughlin, 31 Newington Green, London N16 9PU, England.

CAREER: Express and Independent Newspapers, London, England, reporter, 1947-49; Comtel Bureau, London, England, reporter, 1950-52; DMA Editorial Design Ltd., London, joint managing director, 1952-65; free-lance writer, 1965—. *Member:* Royal Geographical Society (fellow).

WRITINGS: (With Zahra Freeth) *Kuwait: Prospect and Reality,* Allen & Unwin, 1972; *Captain Shakespear,* J. Cape, 1976; (with Freeth) *Explorers of Arabia,* Allen & Unwin, 1978; *Gertrude Bell,* J. Cape, 1978; (editor with Gerald de Gaury) *The Spirit of the East,* Quartet, 1979; (editor with de Gaury) *The Road to Kabul,* Quartet, 1981; *The Illicit Adventure,* J. Cape, 1981. Editor of *Potter's Gazette,* 1972-73, and *Ambassador: Journal of the Decorative Arts,* 1979-80.

SIDELIGHTS: The Illicit Adventure is a history of twentieth-century involvement of the "great powers" in Arab lands and Palestine. Winstone told *CA:* "I am not sure that it is healthy for a writer to allow himself to be forced into a 'specialist' corner, even though it is a shortcut to recognition. Publishers are liable to respond to their authors with a conditioned reflex— 'Oh, he's an expert on Arabs (or Jews or China or maritime history). What does he know about Russia, military intelligence, and the Berlin spy ring?'

"Aspiring writers should be warned to avoid labels. Those who already make a living by the pen will know the dangers. In the end you run out of variations on your chosen theme. However, I count myself fortunate in being involved in an area where political webs can seldom be unravelled in a hundred books (or as many years), and that attracted an imcomparably fascinating bunch of travelers, explorers, and Western agents over the past two centuries. The knowledge I have acquired so far takes me to about 1926. If I were to do my homework properly I would be about 126 years old when I arrived at an up-to-date account, which would probably be entitled "Semitic Colonies in Outer Space."'

*   *   *

WINTER, John F.   1913-

PERSONAL: Born July 30, 1913, in Piest'any, Czechoslovakia; came to the United States in 1939, naturalized citizen, 1946; son of Louis (a hotel owner) and Leona (Schauer) Winter; married Alice M. Kish; children: John L., Dorothy Winter Johnson. *Education:* Attended University of Brunn, 1931-33, University of Prague, 1933-34, and University of Vienna, 1936-37; Lafayette College, B.A. (summa cum laude), 1941; Princeton University, M.A., 1945, Ph.D., 1950. *Home:* 3412 Stettinius Ave., Cincinnati, Ohio 45208. *Office:* Department of Romance Languages, University of Cincinnati, Cincinnati, Ohio 45221.

CAREER: Lafayette College, Easton, Pa., fencing coach, 1939-41; teacher of French and Spanish at private preparatory schools in Warrenton, Va., 1941-42, and Lawrenceville, N.J., 1942-43; Princeton University, Princeton, N.J., instructor in French, 1945-46; Fordham University, New York, N.Y., instructor, 1946-48, assistant professor, 1948-58, associate professor of French, 1958-67, fencing coach, 1946-51; University of Cincinnati, Cincinnati, Ohio, professor of Romance languages, 1967—, director of graduate studies, 1967—, director of study tours to France, 1970—. Public speaker; fencing teacher at boys' camp in New London, N.H., 1940-44.

MEMBER: Modern Lauguage Association of America (chairman of Franco-German comparative litcrature group, 1960; chairman of sixteenth-century French literature section, 1971, and of its executive committee, 1972), American Association of Teachers of French, Renaissance Society of America, American Association of University Professors, History of Science Society, Societe des Professeurs Francais en Amerique, Midwest Modern Language Association, New York City Renaissance Club, Alliance Francaise of Cincinnati (member of council, 1967—), Phi Beta Kappa, Alpha Mu Gamma (vice-president, 1966—). *Awards, honors:* American Philosophical Society grants, 1961, 1965, 1969.

WRITINGS: Literary Criticism in the Seventies, University of Cincinnati Press, 1971; *The Renaissance in Literature and in the Arts,* University of Cincinnati Press, 1973; *Visual Variety and Spatial Grandeur,* University of North Carolina Press, 1974; (contributor) Alain Niderst, editor, *D'un art a l'autre* (title means "From One Art to Another"), Presses Universitaires de France, 1982. Contributor of articles and stories to magazines and newspapers in the United States, Germany, and Hungary.

WORK IN PROGRESS: French Imagery and the Universe, publication expected in 1983; "Concepts de la nature autout de 1500," to be included in *Histoire litteraire des langues europeennes* (title means "Literary History of European Languages").

SIDELIGHTS: Winter's languages include French, German, Spanish, Hungarian, Slovak, Czech, some other Slavic languages, and some Latin, Italian, and Greek.

Winter told *CA:* "I am vitally interested in relations between literature and art, as well as literary relations between France and classical antiquity on the one hand and France and contemporary European nations on the other." *Avocational inter-ests:* Music (playing cello and piano), sports (especially tennis and fencing).

*   *   *

WOHL, Robert   1936-

PERSONAL: Born February 13, 1936, in Butte, Mont.; son of Albert and Lani (Rowan) Wohl; married Monica Birgitta Lindros, July 4, 1966; children: Anna Maria. *Education:* Attended Dartmouth College, 1953-54; University of California, Los Angeles, A.B., 1957; graduate study at Harvard University, 1959-60, and Ecole des Sciences Politiques, 1960-61; Princeton University, Ph.D., 1963. *Home:* 16 Latimer Rd., Santa Monica, Calif. 90402. *Office:* Department of History, University of California, Los Angeles, Calif. 90024.

CAREER: University of Southern California, Los Angeles, instructor, 1961-63, assistant professor of history, 1963-64; University of California, Los Angeles, assistant professor, 1964-67, associate professor, 1967-69, professor of history, 1969—, chairman of department, 1970-73. *Member:* American Historical Association, Society for Italian Studies (member of advisory council, 1970-73).

AWARDS, HONORS: Woodrow Wilson fellowship, 1957-58; Ford Foundation fellowship, 1959-61; George Louis Beer Prize for European History from American Historical Association, 1967, for *French Communism in the Making;* Social Science Research Council fellowship, 1968-69; National Endowment for the Humanities senior fellowship, 1978-79; prize from Pacific Coast branch of American Historical Association, 1980, for *The Generation of 1914;* Guggenheim fellowship, 1981-82.

WRITINGS: French Communism in the Making, 1914-1924, Stanford University Press, 1966; *The Generation of 1914,* Harvard University Press, 1979.

WORK IN PROGRESS: A cultural history of World War I.

SIDELIGHTS: Robert Wohl commented: "For some years my primary interest has been the linkages and interactions between culture and politics in Europe during the period 1880-1945."

BIOGRAPHICAL/CRITICAL SOURCES: New York Review of Books, April 6, 1967, April 3, 1980; *New Republic,* November 3, 1979; *Times Literary Supplement,* May 16, 1980; *New York Times Book Review,* March 15, 1981.

*   *   *

WOLF, Arnold Veryl   1916-1975

OBITUARY NOTICE: Born December 3, 1916, in New York, N.Y.; died February 27, 1975. Physiologist and author. Instrumental in the development of the artificial kidney, Wolf was associated with the University of Illinois from 1952 until his death, at which time he was dean of the Medical Center's graduate college. His writings include *The Urinary Function of the Kidney, Thirst: Physiology of the Urge to Drink and Problems of Water Lack,* and *Aqueous Solutions and the Body Fluids: Their Concentrative Properties and Conversion Tables.* He co-wrote *An Introduction to Body Fluid Metabolism.* Obituaries and other sources: *AB Bookman's Weekly,* March 17, 1975; *Who's Who in America,* 39th edition, Marquis, 1976.

*   *   *

WOLFE, Randolph   1946-

PERSONAL: Born April 6, 1946, in Grosse Pointe Park, Mich.;

WOLFE

CONTEMPORARY AUTHORS • Volume 104

son of Bertrand (a clockmaker) and Rhula (Fischentraum) Wolfe; married Janine Funt (a filmmaker), May 15, 1980; children: Laszlo. *Education:* Educated in Michigan. *Home:* 221 Lewiston Rd., Grosse Pointe Farms, Mich. 48236.

CAREER: Writer. Worked as soundman for television productions for "Local Access," 1972-73; free-lance soundman and production assistant for recording contractors, 1973-80. *Member:* Great Lakes Writers Cooperative.

WRITINGS—Published by Lycanthrope: *Woods of Wayne* (nonfiction), 1974; *The Automobile: Boon or Bane?* (nonfiction), 1974; *What Are They Doing to the Air?* (nonfiction in verse form), 1975; *Evolution of the Detroit River: Being a Factual and Historial Analysis With Biological and Statistical Evidence* (nonfiction), 1977; *Still Clouds* (novel), 1978; *Beneath the Dawn* (novel), 1979; *Sound Careers: A Guide to Employment Opportunities in Audio Fields* (nonfiction), 1980.

WORK IN PROGRESS: A novel on pollution's effect on camping sites in southeast Michigan; a second collection of "fact-poems."

SIDELIGHTS: Wolfe told *CA:* "My writing reflects a variety of interests and skills. As a soundman for independently produced television productions in the Detroit area, I was able to discover a plethora of employment opportunities for budding audio workers. This resulted in *Sound Careers.* However, most of my writing is devoted to calling people's attention to pollution in the Detroit area. Factories are continuously poisoning our air. Because my writings are not readily available to the American public (my brother-in-law publishes through his mail-order Lycanthrope-World, Inc.), my findings have not yet annoyed the industrial magnates who are ruining life as we now know it. But I keep trying to spread the word on pollution and the benefits of clean, *breathable* air. I've done this in novels, poems, and standard nonfiction. *What Are They Doing to the Air?* is my favorite book."

*   *   *

WOLFE, Thomas (Clayton)   1900-1938

BRIEF ENTRY: Born October 3, 1900, in Asheville, N.C.; died of a tubercular infection of the brain, September 15, 1938, in Baltimore, Maryland; buried in Asheville, N.C. American novelist. Wolfe's ambition was to become a playwright, but because he was unable to have his works professionally produced he turned to writing fiction instead. His first novel, *Look Homeward, Angel* (1929), was enormously successful and established Wolfe's reputation as a major American novelist. The book, a fictionalized autobiography, was followed by another autobiographical novel, *Of Time and the River* (1935), which was also well received. Wolfe, a prolific writer, turned out as many as ten thousand words in a single day. At the time of his death Wolfe left an eight-foot pile of manuscript that his editors shaped into two novels, *The Web and the Rock* (1939) and *You Can't Go Home Again* (1940), and a collection of short stories, *The Hills Beyond* (1940). *Residence:* New York, N.Y. *Biographical/critical sources:* Richard Walser, *The Enigma of Thomas Wolfe: Biographical and Critical Selections,* Harvard University Press, 1953; *Cyclopedia of World Authors,* Harper, 1958; Richard S. Kennedy, *The Window of Memory: The Literary Career of Thomas Wolfe,* University of North Carolina Press, 1962; Andrew Turnbull, *Thomas Wolfe,* Scribner, 1967; Leslie A. Field, *Thomas Wolfe: Three Decades of Criticism,* New York University Press, 1968; *Twentieth-Century Literary Criticism,* Volume 4, Gale, 1981.

WOLNY, P.
   See JANECZKO, Paul B(ryan)

*   *   *

WOODFORD, Peggy   1937-

PERSONAL: Born September 19, 1937, in Assam, India; daughter of Ronald Curtis (an agriculturist) and Ruth (Laine) Woodford; married Walter Aylen (a lawyer), April 1, 1967; children: Alison, Frances, Imogen. *Education:* Attended St. Anne's College, Oxford, 1956-59. *Residence:* London, England. *Agent:* Murray Pollinger, 4 Garrick St., London W.C.2, England.

CAREER: British Broadcasting Corp. (BBC-TV), London, England, research and script assistant, 1961-63; College of Padworth, Reading, England, senior tutor in English, 1963-66; free-lance writer, 1966—. *Awards, honors:* Research scholarship from Italian government, 1960.

WRITINGS: *Abraham's Legacy* (novel), Deutsch, 1963; *Mozart: His Life and Times* (biography), Midas Books, 1977; *Rise of the Raj* (history; introduction by Rumer Godden), Humanities Press, 1978; *Schubert: His Life and Times* (biography), Midas Books, 1978; *New Stories Five,* Hutchinson, 1980.

Juvenile: *Mozart* (biography), illustrated by David Knight, J. Garnet Miller, 1964, Walck, 1966; *Schubert* (biography), illustrated by Barbara Brown, Walck, 1969; *Please Don't Go* (novel), Bodley Head, 1972, Dutton, 1973; *Blackwater War* (novel), Bodley Head, 1974, Farrar, Straus, 1975; (editor and contributor) *The Real Thing: Seven Stories of Love* (short stories), Bodley Head, 1977, published as *Looking for Love: Seven Uncommon Love Stories,* Doubleday, 1979; *See You Tomorrow* (novel), Bodley Head, 1979; (editor and contributor) *You Can't Keep Out the Darkness* (short stories), Bodley Head, 1980; (contributor) Susan Hill and Isabel Quigley, editors, *The Girl With a Voice,* Bodley Head, 1981.

WORK IN PROGRESS: *Charity and Gynaecology,* a volume of short stories, publication expected in 1982.

SIDELIGHTS: Peggy Woodford has definite ideas about the place of young adults in the realm of literature. Woodford told *CA* that she feels "strongly that fiction for teenagers should be adult in every way; the only consideration to be borne always in mind is that the theme and subject matter should appeal to and interest the adolescent."

Woodford's first novel, *Abraham's Legacy,* was written during a year of study in Rome on an Italian government scholarship. Her topic of research was "the Englishwoman in Italy in the eighteenth century." She then returned to London and got a job as a research and script assistant for BBC-TV. She worked most often with the late Paul Johnstone, who was connected with the "Chronicle" series.

Woodford next wrote biographies of the composers Mozart and Schubert. In general critical comment about her biographical methods, she is praised in her attempt to weave a background of the history and society in which the composers worked. The human rather than the artistic qualities of these men are stressed, an approach that disappointed some critics who thought the musical works should have received greater attention.

Among Woodford's novels are *Please Don't Go,* a story about teenage infatuation and first love, and *Backwater War,* a historical novel about the German occupation of the Channel Islands during World War II. In the latter book Woodford portrays the hardships endured by the Guernsey people. "To outline the simple structure of this novel does no sort of justice to the

528

layers of feeling and experience in it nor to its honesty,'' wrote Alasdair Maclean of the *Times Literary Supplement*. ''Miss Woodford is infallible, for example, on the psychology of an occupied countryside. She knows that war brutalizes civilians as well as soldiers and so far from turning her islanders into heroes she makes it clear that self-interest was rampant among them.''

Another book, *Looking for Love*, is a collection of short stories edited by Woodford, and she is a contributor as well. The stories center on different types of love, be it the love between parent and child, girl and boy, two friends, or the love of infatuation and hero-worship. *You Can't Keep Out the Darkness* is a companion volume to *Looking for Love*, and this time Woodford had another topic in mind. ''When I approached the contributors of *You Can't Keep Out the Darkness* they were aksed for stories on the theme of a young person's first awareness of good and evil. The resulting stories, and mine too I hope, have been a complete justification of my belief that 'teenage fiction' is adult fiction with the subject matter apt.''

BIOGRAPHICAL/CRITICAL SOURCES: Observer, November 26, 1972, March 30, 1975; *Times Literary Supplement*, December 8, 1972, April 4, 1975; *Washington Post Book World*, May 13, 1973; *New York Times Book Review*, December 28, 1975; *New Statesman*, October 14, 1977.

*   *   *

WOODRUFF, John Douglas   1897-1978

OBITUARY NOTICE: Born May 8, 1897, in Wimbledon, England; died in 1978 in England. Editor, historian, and author. Woodruff was editor of the Roman Catholic journal *The Tablet* for more than thirty years, and he was made a Commander of the Order of the British Empire in 1962. His many writings include *The Life and Times of Alfred the Great, Plato's American Republic,* and *Church and State in History.* Obituaries and other sources: *International Who's Who*, Europa, 1977; *AB Bookman's Weekly*, November 6, 1978.

*   *   *

WOODRUM, Lon   1901-

PERSONAL: Born December 8, 1901, in Fredric, Ill.; son of Sherman Thomas (a farmer) and Laura (Icenogle) Woodrum; married Ellene Fritchkorn (a teacher), July 17, 1960; children: Ruth, Paul, Riley, Robin. *Education:* Attended elementary school in Bonner Springs, Kan. *Home and office address:* Route 4, Box 111-E, De Funiak Springs, Fla. 32433.

CAREER: Ordained Methodist minister; field evangelist in U.S. and Canada, 1932-75; writer. Also worked as farmer and prospector. Lecturer at colleges and universities. Director of ''Little Church of the Fireside,'' on KFOX-Radio. *Awards, honors:* First prize from international fiction contest sponsored by Zondervan Publishing House, 1955, for *Eternity in Their Heart.*

WRITINGS: The Kingdom Beyond (essays), Beacon Hill, 1949; *Of Men and of Angels* (novel; Christian Herald Book Club selection), Zondervan, 1952; *If You Hear a Song* (novel), Zondervan, 1952; *Inherit the Earth* (novel), Zondervan, 1953; *Eternity in Their Heart* (novel), Zondervan, 1955; *Stumble Upon the Dark Mountain* (novel), Broadman, 1956; *Trumpets in the Morning* (novel), Zondervan, 1960; *The Rebellious Planet* (essays), Zondervan, 1965; *Right on With Love* (novel), Zondervan, 1971; *Love at Your Door* (poems), Word, Inc., 1977.

Work represented in anthologies, including *Masterpieces of Religious Verse* and *Principal Poets of the World*. Author of

''Meanderings,'' a newspaper column syndicated to weekly newspapers, 1940-50, and ''Chapel Rimes,'' a column in *Telescope-Messenger*, 1954-57. Contributor of poems and articles to magazines, including *Christianity Today, War Cry, Guideposts, Together, Christian Herald,* and *Christian Advocate.*

SIDELIGHTS: Woodrum wrote: ''Why does one write? Actually, he writes for his readers. If he doesn't he won't have any readers. Most of my stuff is meant to influence someone toward principles which I believe are valuable. I want to make people think, of course, but I also want to make them feel. What I want them to feel is that there's more in life than material values; there's goodness, justice, decency, redemption—yes, God. I feel the contemporary literary scene often is too engrossed in the flesh to be concerned about the spirit, even much of what passes for 'religious writing.'

''I've never had any specific 'habits' in my writing. When I wasn't doing something else I was thinking about writing. I did most of my work on the road, having traveled several million miles by train and plane in the U.S. and Canada. I have had about thirty books published, but I have written more books than that which were never published and doubtless never will be.

''Young writers often ask me how to write. I tell them it's simple: just write a word, then add some more words. The only problem is getting the words where they should be! My wife once said to me, 'I think I could be a writer.' 'You will not be one,' I assured her. 'Why?' 'Because a writer is one who *writes*. Which you don't.' *Writing*. That's the writer's biggest thing. However great his gifts, he'll have to sweat to produce. Actually, I wonder if it does any good to give advice to a young writer. If he's really a writer he won't need your encouragement to continue; if he isn't, your encouragement is wasted.

''Probably I was influenced by almost all the writers who wrote in English. And by those whose works were translated into English, especially the Russian novelists and the Frenchman Dumas. I liked a host of English poets. My favorite American poet is Edna St. Vincent Millay. Later I loved Jack London. I was influenced by writers with whom I greatly disagreed; such writers as Muggeridge, who was an unbeliever (later a believer). I found his style irresistible. I loathed his atheism but loved his way of saying *why* he was one. Much later I was deeply impressed by C. S. Lewis, and still am.

''I think the best compliment I've had was from Smilin' Ed McConnel of CBS-Radio (I wrote poetry for his hymn show): 'Woodrum writes a poem in order to say something; and he always says something.'''

BIOGRAPHICAL/CRITICAL SOURCES: De Funiak Springs Herald-Breeze (De Funiak Springs, Fla.), December 11, 1980.

*   *   *

WOODS, John E(dmund)   1938-

PERSONAL: Born July 21, 1938, in Aruba, Netherlands Antilles; son of Robert Edmund (an engineer) and Sarah Virginia Jean (Little) Woods; married Shirine Modarress, March, 1965 (divorced); married L. Paula Franke, September, 1970 (divorced); children: (first marriage) Jamile Sarah. *Education:* University of Texas, B.A. (magna cum laude), 1960; attended University of Cairo and American University of Cairo, 1960-61, and University of Tehran, 1964-69; Princeton University, M.A., 1965, Ph.D., 1974. *Home:* 5550 South Dorchester Ave., Chicago, Ill. 60637. *Office:* Department of History, University of Chicago, 5858 University Ave., Chicago, Ill. 60637.

CAREER: National University of Iran, Tehran, instructor in English language and literature, 1964-67; Iran-American Society, Tehran, assistant director of Academic Center, 1967-69; University of Chicago, Chicago, Ill., assistant professor, 1970-77, associate professor of Middle Eastern history and Near Eastern languages and civilizations, 1977—, associate director of Center for Middle Eastern Studies. Seminar director at Ecole Pratique des Hautes Etudes, 1976. Guest on radio and television programs.

MEMBER: Middle East Studies Association of North America, Society for Iranian Studies, Turkish Studies Association, American Institute for Iranian Studies (member of board of trustees), Phi Beta Kappa. *Awards, honors:* Fulbright fellow in Cairo, Egypt, 1960-61; Woodrow Wilson fellow, 1961-62; senior scholar of International Research and Exchanges Board in Tashkent, Soviet Union, 1979.

WRITINGS: (Translator) Seyed Mohamed Taqi Mostafavi, *Persian Architecture at a Glance,* Iranian Ministry of Culture, 1967; (editor with John C. Campbell, William R. Polk, and others) *The Middle East,* thirty-nine volumes, Arno, 1973; *The Aqquyunlu: Clan, Confederation, Empire—A Study in Fifteenth/Ninth Century Turko-Iranian Politics,* Bibliotheca Islamica, 1976; (editor) *Khunji-Isfahani's Tarikh-i 'Alam-ara-yi Amini: A Critical Edition and Commentary,* Bibliotheca Islamica, 1983. Contributor to academic journals.

WORK IN PROGRESS: A critical study of Timur (Tamerlane), publication by Princeton University Press expected in 1984; a detailed survey of Iranian political concepts transmitted in Islamic Fuerstenspiegel writing; a manual of Persian paleography and diplomatics.

SIDELIGHTS: John Woods wrote: "Current developments in the Middle East once again underscore the need in this country for a morally-committed cadre of professionals who are both broadly and deeply conversant with the traditions, cultures, and languages of this area as well as acutely aware of the significance of this knowledge for guiding our decision-making as Americans."

AVOCATIONAL INTERESTS: Running, travel (Venezuela, Iraq, Lebanon, Syria, Jordan, Egypt, Sudan, Libya, Tunisia, Morocco, Turkey, Afghanistan), counseling.

BIOGRAPHICAL/CRITICAL SOURCES: Michael Kammen, editor, *The Past Before Us,* Cornell University Press, 1980.

* * *

WOODSON, Thomas (Miller) 1931-

PERSONAL: Born April 24, 1931, in Hartford, Conn.; son of Jacob Tyree (a physician) and Lucy (a nurse; maiden name, Hodges) Woodson; married Nancy Potter (a teacher), January 19, 1963; children: Paula, Andrew, Sarah. *Education:* Yale University, B.A., 1953, M.A., 1956, Ph.D., 1963. *Home:* 3838 Kioka Ave., Columbus, Ohio 43220. *Office:* Department of English, Ohio State University, Columbus, Ohio 43210.

CAREER: Williams College, Williamstown, Mass., instructor in English, 1959-62; Yale University, New Haven, Conn., instructor in English, 1962-63; Ohio State University, Columbus, assistant professor of English, 1963-69; Yale University, visiting associate professor of English, 1969-70; Ohio State University, associate professor, 1969-74, professor of English, 1974—, chairman of department of comparative studies in the humanities, 1974-78. Fulbright lecturer at University of Pau, 1968-69. *Military service:* U.S. Army, 1953-55. *Member:* Modern Language Association of America (chairman of Division on Nineteenth-Century American Literature, 1978),

Hawthorne Society (member of advisory board, 1981), Phi Beta Kappa, Yale Elizabethan Club.

WRITINGS: Twentieth-Century Interpretations of the Fall of the House of Usher, Prentice-Hall, 1969; (editor) *The French and Italian Notebooks of Nathaniel Hawthorne,* Ohio State University Press, 1980. Contributor to literature journals.

WORK IN PROGRESS: Editing *Letters of Nathaniel Hawthorne* and *English Notebooks of Nathaniel Hawthorne,* publication by Ohio State University Press expected in 1983 and 1985, respectively.

* * *

WOOLF, (Adeline) Virginia 1882-1941

BRIEF ENTRY: Born January 25, 1882, in London, England; committed suicide by drowning, March 28, 1941, in Lewes, Sussex, England. English novelist, essayist, and critic. Acknowledged by many as the greatest woman novelist of the twentieth century, Virginia Woolf had, as the daughter of biographer and critic Sir Leslie Stephen, early exposure to such notable literary figures as Thomas Hardy and Alfred Tennyson. Such influence continued when, with her sister Vanessa Bell, Virginia was admitted to the famed "Bloomsburys," a group of intellectuals that included E. M. Forster, John Maynard Keynes, Lytton Strachey, and Leonard Woolf, whom Virginia later married. In 1917 the Woolfs founded the Hogarth Press, where they published the writings of Forster, Keynes, Gertrude Stein, T. S. Eliot, and Katherine Mansfield, and much of Virginia's own work as well. *Voyage Out* (1915), Virginia Woolf's first novel, was fairly traditional in style, but those that followed were increasingly unconventional. The characters in her most successful book, *To the Lighthouse* (1927), were drawn from her own life: two of them were based on her parents, and another, Lily Briscoe, the painter whose fear of ridicule nearly prevented her from realizing her artistic "vision," was a caricature of Virginia herself. Though sometimes criticized for her apparent inability to create memorable characters, Woolf was praised for her mastery of the stream of consciousness technique and for her skill in rendering her characters' interior monologues. Numbered among her other works are *Night and Day* (1919), *A Room of One's Own* (1929), and *The Waves* (1931). *Biographical/critical sources: Cyclopedia of World Authors,* Harper, 1958; *The Reader's Encyclopedia,* 2nd edition, Crowell, 1965; *Who's Who in Twentieth Century Literature,* Holt, 1976; *Twentieth-Century Literary Criticism,* Volume 1, Gale, 1978.

* * *

WOOLSON, Roland S., Jr. 1930(?)-1977

OBITUARY NOTICE: Born c. 1930; died after a long illness, June 30, 1977, in New York, N.Y. Editor. Woolson was engineering sciences editor in the Wiley-Interscience Division of John Wiley & Sons from 1971 until his death. Before joining Wiley, Woolson was science and engineering editor with Ronald Press, McGraw-Hill, and Macmillan. Obituaries and other sources: *Publishers Weekly,* July 11, 1977.

* * *

WORMALD, Francis 1904(?)-1972

OBITUARY NOTICE: Born c. 1904; died January 10, 1972, in England. Paleographer, liturgist, and author. A former president of the Society of Antiquaries, Wormald wrote primarily about the earliest known manuscripts. His books include *English Drawings of the Tenth and Eleventh Centuries* and *The*

Benedictional of St. Ethelwold. Obituaries and other sources: *AB Bookman's Weekly,* February 7, 1972.

* * *

WORMSER, Rene A(lbert) 1896-1981

OBITUARY NOTICE—See index for *CA* sketch: Born July 17, 1896, in Santa Barbara, Calif.; died July 14, 1981, in Greenwich, Conn. Attorney and author. A lawyer for over a half century, Wormser founded and was a senior partner of the law firm Wormser, Kiely, Allessandroni, Hyde & McCann. Specializing in estate planning, Wormser also taught at the University of Miami Law School and the Institute on Federal Taxation of New York University. He wrote several books in his field, including *Personal Estate Planning in a Changing World, Foundations: Their Power and Influence,* and *Wills That Made History.* Obituaries and other sources: *New York Times,* July 15, 1981.

* * *

WORSLEY, Dale 1948-

PERSONAL: Born November 3, 1948, in Baton Rouge, La.; son of Ashley C. (a chemical engineer) and Bess (Sheene) Worsley. *Education:* Attended Southwestern at Memphis, 1966-68 and 197-00-71. *Home:* 422 East Ninth St., No. 7, New York, N.Y. 10009. *Agent:* Ellen Levine Literary Agency, Inc., 370 Lexington Ave., New York, N.Y. 10017.

CAREER: U.S. Peace Corps, Washington, D.C., agricultural cooperative extension agent, English teacher, and contributing editor of *El Ecuador,* all in Ecuador, 1968-70; Mabou Mines (theater company), New York, N.Y., collaborator, 1970-72; Eads Hill (theater company), Memphis, Tenn., co-founder and co-director, 1972-73; Learning Place, Memphis, teacher of creative writing, 1973-74; Mabou Mines, collaborator, 1980-81. *Awards, honors:* Scholarship for Squaw Valley Community of Writers Conference, 1973; Creative Artists Public Service grant, 1979; Word Magic Award from National Federation of Community Broadcasters, 1980, for play, "Easy Daisy."

WRITINGS: Lives at Sea (nonfiction), Teachers and Writers Collaborative, 1980; *Focus Changes* (novel), Vanguard, 1981.

Plays: "Initial Survey" (one-act video play), released by Jack Frost and Dale Worsley in 1977; "Easy Daisy" (one-act), first broadcast by Australian Broadcasting Co., 1980. Also author of "The Comfort Cage" (one-act), 1980; "Laughing Stock" (one-act), 1981; and "Tiger Heaven" (one-act), 1981.

Contributor of articles and stories to magazines, including *Teachers and Writers.*

WORK IN PROGRESS: Keeper, a novel.

* * *

WORSWICK, Clark 1940-

PERSONAL: Born September 16, 1940, in Berkeley, Calif.; son of Wallace Burdette and Elizabeth (Benedict) Worswick; married Joan Mitchell (a teacher), September 19, 1970; children: Lucia, Nicholas. *Education:* Attended Visva Bharati, 1959, and Harvard University, 1966-70. *Home and office address:* Oak Summit Rd., Millbrook, N.Y. 12545.

CAREER: Worked as film director, 1960-75; Asia Society Gallery, guest director, 1975—. Guest director of Japan Society Gallery, 1978-79. *Awards, honors:* Indo-American fellowship from Smithsonian Institution, 1979.

WRITINGS: The Last Empire: Photographs of British India, Aperture, 1976, 3rd edition, 1979; *Imperial China: Photographs, 1850-1911,* Crown, 1978; *An Edwardian Observer,* Crown, 1978; *Japan: Photographs, 1854-1904,* Knopf, 1979; *Princely India,* Knopf, 1980; *The Camera and the Tribe,* Knopf, 1982.

Feature film scripts: "Changing Rains," 1965; "California," 1968; "Kotah," 1970; "Family Honor" (documentary), Cinerama/Abc Films, 1973.

WORK IN PROGRESS: The Nail, a novel.

SIDELIGHTS: Worswick wrote: "When I was eighteen I went to India to university. At a certain moment in time I calculated that I had traveled seventy thousand miles on Indian third-class trains—some sort of grotesque record, seeing the 'remains' of British India, archaeological sites, and tribal groups. Living in the Salvation Army hostels and the ashrams of the Maha Bodi society during the period I stayed in India affected me most as an artist; it was the last moment the 'white man' was held in (almost) universal esteem in Asia, the Middle East, and Africa. From the time I was eighteen until I was twenty-eight, over a ten-year period, I traveled more or less constantly in Asia, Africa, and the Middle East. I supported myself by doing free-lance photography and films.

"Somewhere along the way I discovered the work of nineteenth-century photographers working in the same areas I was working in, and I brought together a collection of work done in India during the nineteenth century that resulted in an exhibition and a book, *The Last Empire.* It has always amazed me that photography managed, at the penultimate moment in Asia and the Middle East, to document the way traditional cultures were before they were radically, irrevocably changed by the onslaught of the European industrial revolution. This change has been so complete that at this moment Tehran is very similar to Tokyo in looks, Bombay looks like Rio, etcetera."

* * *

WRIGHT, Alice E(dwards) 1905-1980

PERSONAL: Born March 27, 1905, in New Lebanon, Ohio; died August 14, 1980; daughter of John W. and Maud (Vaniman) Edwards; married Earl O. Wright, January 21, 1928 (died, October, 1949); children: Robert B., Richard J., David (deceased), Jane (deceased). *Education:* Ohio University, B.A., 1927; Kent State University, M.L.S., 1952. *Religion:* Episcopalian. *Home:* 7 North Park Pl., Apt. 31, Painesville, Ohio 44077. *Office:* Morley Library, 184 Phelps St., Painesville, Ohio 44077.

CAREER: Dayton Public Library, Dayton, Ohio, page, 1920-22; Akron Public Library, Akron, Ohio, assistant librarian, 1927-42; Office of Price Administration, Akron, supervisor, 1942-43; Akron Public Library, librarian at West Hill branch, 1951-59; Burbank Public Library, Burbank, Calif., librarian at North Glenoaks branch, 1959-60, young adult librarian, 1960-64; Morley Library, Painesville, Ohio, head librarian, 1964-76. Chairman of Painesville March of Dimes, 1967. *Member:* American Library Association, American Association of University Women, League of Women Voters of the United States, Ohio Library Association, Phi Mu, Daughters of American Colonists (past regent), Quota Club of Lake County (president, 1971-73), Ohio University Alumni Association (president, 1964).

WRITINGS: Library Clerical Workers and Pages, Shoe String, 1973. Contributor to library journals. Editor of *Contact.**

WRIGHT, Charles David 1932-1978

PERSONAL: Born June 2, 1932, in Marion, Ill.; died July 13, 1978; son of David (a pipefitter) and Minnie (Corgan) Wright; married Ruth Petty (a teacher), June 23, 1955; children: David Hugh, Vivian. *Education:* Wayne State University, B.A., 1953; University of Wisconsin (now University of Wisconsin—Madison), M.A., 1954; graduate study at University of Tuebingen, 1956; University of Iowa, Ph.D., 1963. *Residence:* Boise, Idaho.

CAREER: University of North Carolina, Chapel Hill, 1962-72, began as instructor, became associate professor of English; Boise State University, Boise, Idaho, professor of English, 1972-78. Member of summer staff at Pythagorean Institute of Art (Greece), 1969-72; past member of Orange County Executive Committee. *Military service:* U.S. Army, 1954-56. *Awards, honors:* Postdoctoral fellowship for cross-disciplinary studies from Society for Values in Higher Education, 1969-70; fellowship from National Endowment for the Arts.

WRITINGS: Early Rising (poems), University of North Carolina Press, 1968; *Clearing Away* (poems), Copper Canyon Press, 1981. Contributor of articles and reviews to literary journals and popular magazines, including *Harper's, Kenyon Review, Saturday Review, Atlantic Monthly,* and *New American Review.*

[Sketch verified by wife, Ruth P. Wright]

* * *

WRIGHT, Don(ald Conway) 1934-

PERSONAL: Born January 23, 1934, in Los Angeles, Calif.; son of Charles and Sally (Olberg) Wright; married Rita Rose Blondin, October 1, 1960 (died June, 1968); married Carolyn Ann Jay, February 5, 1969. *Education:* Attended public schools. *Home:* 6190 Moss Ranch Rd., Miami, Fla. 33156. *Office: Miami News,* 1 Herald Plaza, Miami, Fla. 33132.

CAREER: Miami News, Miami, Fla., copyboy and photographer, 1952-56, 1958-60, photo editor, 1960-63, political cartoonist, 1963—. Permanent exhibition of work displayed at University of Syracuse. *Military service:* U.S. Army, 1956-58. *Member:* American Association of Editorial Cartoonists, Sigma Delta Chi. *Awards, honors:* Pulitzer Prize for editorial cartooning, 1966 and 1980; Freedom Foundation award for editorial cartoon, 1966; named outstanding person in communications media by Young Democrats Clubs of America (Florida), 1966; Overseas Press Club award for best cartoon on foreign affairs, 1968; Grenville Clark Editorial Page Cartoon Award, 1970.

WRITINGS: Wright On!, Simon & Schuster, 1971.

SIDELIGHTS: Wright commented to a *Time* reporter that today's political cartoons are less vicious than in the past. "We don't seem to get cartoons with explosive impact any more, the kind that slams somebody right between the eyes with no subtlety at all." The *Time* reporter, however, observed: "[Wright] is too modest about his ability to slam. In fact, his work should satisfy the keenest appetite for cartoons that bludgeon." To illustrate, the reporter cited Wright's rough handling of Richard Nixon during the Watergate investigation and his lampoons of Lyndon Johnson during the Vietnam era.

A further example of Wright's skill was provided by Martin Schram in a *Newsday* review of *Wright On!,* Wright's collection of political cartoons. Schram pointed to the book's cover cartoon in which Spiro Agnew is caricatured with screws and bolts falling from his ear. "No caption needed," said Schram.

BIOGRAPHICAL/CRITICAL SOURCES: Newsday, July 24, 1971; *Time,* February 11, 1974; *Newsweek,* October 13, 1980.*

* * *

WRIGHT, Nancy Means

PERSONAL: Born in Glen Ridge, N.J.; daughter of Robert Thomas (in business) and Jessie (a teacher; maiden name, Thomson) Means; married Spencer Victor Wright (a teacher and tree farmer); children: Gary, Lesley, Donald, Catharine. *Education:* Vassar College, A.B.; Middlebury College, M.A., 1965; also attended Sorbonne, University of Paris. *Religion:* Unitarian-Universalist. *Home address:* R.D. 2, Middlebury, Vt. 05753. *Agent:* Jo Stewart, 201 East 66th St., Suite 18N, New York, N.Y. 10021.

CAREER: English teacher at private school in Garrison, Md.; head of language department at private academy in Andover, N.H.; Cornwall Crafts, Cornwall, Vt., owner and manager, 1973—. Part-time instructor at University of Vermont. Performer and play director with Middlebury Community Players; member of Middlebury Community Chorus; member of board of trustees of Vermont State Craft Center at Frog Hollow. *Member:* Poets and Writers, League of Vermont Writers (president, 1978-80; member of board of directors). *Awards, honors:* Bread Loaf Writers Conference scholar, 1959.

WRITINGS: The Losing (novel), Ace Books, 1972; *Down the Strings* (novel), Elsevier-Dutton, 1982. Contributor of stories, poems, articles, and reviews to magazines, including *Redbook, Seventeen, Yankee, Country Journal, American Craft,* and *Vermont Life.*

WORK IN PROGRESS: Green Grow the Lasses, a trilogy covering three generations of strong-minded Scottish-American women, 1912—, completion expected in 1984.

SIDELIGHTS: Nancy Wright told *CA:* "As a published writer I am a late bloomer, due to four children and twenty years of full-time teaching (English, French, and theatre); all my published writing has been since 1972, except for numerous poems. I am now running a craft and Early American furniture shop year-round and writing early in the morning (I manage to sit at my typewriter three hours daily). I also teach writing off and on at conferences and at a center for continuing education. All my money from writing is used for travel and research. A recent discovery in Scotland that my grandmother was illegitimate led to my projected trilogy, which will take as its theme the 'thistleness' of the Scot (or Scottish-American), her/his (and my own) struggle to remain earthbound in spite of ideal longings, and to somehow harmonize her/his divided nature."

* * *

WRIGHT, Sylvia 1917-1981

OBITUARY NOTICE—See index for *CA* sketch: Born January 21, 1917, in Berkeley, Calif.; died of cancer, May 9, 1981, in Cambridge, Mass. Editor and author. Wright worked for the publishing firm Farrar & Rinehart and was an editor with *Harper's Bazaar* magazine. She edited her father Austin Tappan Wright's novel, *Islandia,* in addition to publishing her own books. Her works include *Get Away From Me With Those Christmas Gifts* and *A Shark-Infested Rice Pudding.* Obituaries and other sources: *New York Times,* May 13, 1981.

WU, John C(hing) H(siung) 1899-
(Wu Ching-Hsiung)

PERSONAL: Born March 28, 1899, in Ningpo, China; son of Chia-ch'ang and Kwei-Yun (Yu) Wu; married Li Yuat'i, 1916 (died, 1959); married Agnes Chu Wen-yin, June 24, 1967; children: eleven. *Education:* Comparative Law School, Shanghai, China, LL.B., 1920; University of Michigan, J.D., 1921; also attended Harvard University, University of Paris, and University of Berlin. *Religion:* Roman Catholic. *Home:* 7 Chien-yeh Rd., Yang Ming Shan, Taipei, Taiwan.

CAREER: Writer. Served as president of Provisional Court in China in late 1920's; lecturer at Northwestern University Law School, beginning 1929; adviser to Shanghai Municipal Court in Shanghai, China, beginning 1931; vice-chairman of commission for drafting permanent Chinese constitution; Chinese minister to the Vatican, c. 1947; currently university professor in Taipei, Taiwan, and senior political adviser to president of Taiwan.

WRITINGS: Judicial Essays and Studies, Commercial Press, 1928; *The Art of Law and Other Essays Judicial and Literary,* Commercial Press, 1936; (editor with M.C. Liang) *Essays in Jurisprudence and Legal Philosophy,* School of Law, Soochow University, 1938; *Justice Holmes to Doctor Wu: An Intimate Correspondence, 1921-1932,* Central Book Co., 1947; *The Interior Carmel: The Threefold Way of Love,* Sheed, 1953; *Cases and Materials on Jurisprudence,* West Publishing, 1958; *Fountain of Justice: A Study in the Natural Law,* Sheed, 1955; *Chinese Humanism and Christian Spirituality: Essays of John C.H. Wu* (edited by Paul K. T. Sih), St. John's University Press, 1965; *Sun Yat-sen: The Man and His Ideas,* Commercial Press, 1971; *The Four Seasons of T'ang Poetry,* Tuttle, 1972; *The Golden Age of Zen,* Paragon, 1975.

Under name Wu Ching-Hsiung: *Beyond East and West* (autobiography), Sheed, 1951; *Ai ti k'o hsueh: The Science of Love, a Study in the Teachings of Therese of Lisieux* (in Chinese and English), [Taiwan], 1974; *Fa hsueh lun wen hsuan i chi: Essays on Legal and Political Philosophy* (in Chinese and English), [Taiwan], 1978.

In Chinese; under name Wu Ching-Hsiung: *Fa lu che hsueh yen chiu,* 1933; (editor) *Chung-hau min kuo liu fa li yu p'an chieh hui pien,* 1936; (editor) *Hsien hsing liu fa ch'uan shu,* 1937; (editor) *Yueh fa shih i,* 1937; (editor with Mao-shing Hua) *Fa hsueh wen hsiian,* two volumes, 1937; (with Kung-chueh Huang) *Chung-kuo chih hsien shih,* two volumes, 1937; (translator) Lao-tzu, *Tao teh ching,* St. John's University Press, 1961; *Chung hsi wen hua lun chi,* 1967; *Chung hsi wen hus chih pi chiao,* 1968; *Che hsueh yu wen hua,* 1971; (translator) *Sheng yung i i ch'u kao* (title means "Old Testament Psalms"), 1973; *Chiang tsung t'ung ti ching shen sheng huo,* 1975; *San min chu i yu Chung-hua wen hua,* 1978.

* * *

WU CHING-HSIUNG
See WU, John C(hing) H(siung)

* * *

WYMARK, Olwen Margaret 1932-

PERSONAL: Born February 14, 1932, in Oakland, Calif.; daughter of Philip W. (a professor of political science) and Barbara (Jacobs) Buck; married Patrick Wymark (an actor; died October 20, 1970), July 22, 1953; children: Jane, Rowan, Dominic, Tristram. *Education:* Attended Pomona College, 1949-

51, and University College, London, 1951-52. *Agent:* Harvey Unna and Stephen Durbridge Ltd., 14A Beaumont Mews, Marlybone High St., London W1N 4HE, England.

CAREER: Dramatist, 1966—. *Awards, honors:* Zagreb Festival Prize, 1967, for "Triple Image"; ATL New Play Prize, 1978, for "Find Me"; Italia Prize nomination, 1980, for "The Child."

WRITINGS—Plays: "Lunchtime Concert" (one-act), first produced in Glasgow, Scotland, at Citizens Theatre, 1966 (also see below); "Triple Image" (three one-act plays; contains "Coda," "Lunchtime Concert," and "The Inhabitants"), first produced in Glasgow at Citizens Theatre, 1967 (also see below); "The Gymnasium" (one-act), first produced in Manchester, England, at Stables Theatre, 1967, produced in London at Cockpit Theatre, 1971 (also see below); *Three Plays* (contains "Coda," "Lunchtime Concert," and "The Inhabitants"; also see above), Calder & Boyars, 1967; "The Technicians" (one-act), first produced in Leicester, England, at Pheonix Theatre, 1969, produced in London at King's Head Theatre, 1971 (also see below); "Stay Where You Are" (one-act), first produced in Edinburgh at Traverse Theatre, 1969, produced in London at Soho Poly Theatre, 1973 (also see below).

"Neither Here Nor There" (one-act), first produced in London at Soho Poly Theatre, 1971 (also see below); "Speak Now" (two-act), first produced in Edinburgh at Traverse Theatre, 1971; "The Committee" (one-act), first produced in London at Cockpit Theatre, 1971; "Jack the Giant Killer" (one-act), first produced in Sheffield, England, at Crucible Theatre, 1972 (also see below); *The Gymnasium and Other Plays* (contains "The Gymnasium," "Stay Where You Are," "Jack the Giant Killer," and "Neither Here Nor There"; also see above), Calder & Boyars, 1972; "Tales From Whitechapel" (one-act), first produced in London at Curtains Theatre, 1972; (with Brian Phelan) "Watch the Woman" (two-act), first produced in London at Cockpit Theatre, 1973; "The Inhabitants" (one-act), first produced in London at Unity Theatre, 1974 (also see above).

"The Twenty-Second Day" (one-act), first produced in London at Maximus Theatre, 1975 (also see below); "We Three" (one-act), first produced in London at Cockpit Theatre, 1977; "After Nature, Art" (one-act), first produced in London at Cockpit Theatre, 1977; "Find Me" (two-act), first produced in London, England, at Orange Tree Theatre, 1977, produced in Louisville, Ky., at Actors Theatre, 1979; "Loved" (two-act), first produced at Bush Theatre, 1979, produced in Syracuse, N.Y., at Syracuse Stage, April, 1979; "Please Shim Down on Me," first produced at Royal Court Theatre, 1980; "Best Friends," first produced at Richmond Theatre, 1981; "One Woman Plays" (adapted from three plays by Dario Fo and Franca Rame; first produced in London at National Theatre, 1981), published as *Female Parts,* Pluto Press, 1981.

Juvenile plays: "No Talking" (one-act), first produced in London at Arts Theatre, 1970; (with Daniel Henry) "Daniel's Epic" (one-act), first produced in London at Half Moon Theatre, 1972; "Chinig Chinich" (one-act), first produced in London at Arts Theatre, 1973; "The Bolting Sisters" (one-act), first produced in London at Arts Theatre, 1974; (collaborator) "Starters" (four-part play; contains "The Giant and the Dancing Fairies," "The Time Loop," "The Spellbound Jellybaby," "The Robbing of Elvis Parsley," and "I Spy"), first produced in London at Arts Theatre, 1975; (collaborator) "Three for All" (three one-acts; contains "Box Play," "Family Business," and "Extended Play"), first produced in London at Curtains Theatre, 1976.

Radio plays; broadcast by British Broadcasting Corp. (BBC): "The Ransom," 1956; "That Unexpected Country," 1957; "California Here We Come," 1957; "Stay Where You Are," 1972; "The Twenty-Second Day," 1973; "You Come Too," 1977; "Vivien the Block Buster," 1979; "Find Me," 1980; "The Child," 1980; "Best Friends," 1981.

Television plays for Crown Court series; broadcast by Granada-TV: "Mrs. Moresby's Scrapbook," 1973; "Vermin," 1974; "Marathon," 1975; "Mother Love," 1975; "Dead Drunk" 1975.

Work represented in anthologies, including *The Best Short Plays of 1972*, edited by Stanley Richards, Chilton, 1972; *The Best Short Plays of 1975*, edited by Richards, Chilton, 1975; and *Play Ten*, edited by Robin Rook, Arnold, 1977.

WORK IN PROGRESS: An untitled two-act stage farce about marriage and sexual confusion; an untitled hour-long teleplay for Thames-TV; a one-act play, written for the Actors Theatre in Louisville, about sex.

SIDELIGHTS: An American writer living and working in England, Olwen Wymark began receiving critical recognition in America around 1969. During that year, after seeing a production of "Triple Image," A. D. Coleman proclaimed in the *Village Voice* that the play was "a worthy debut for a playwright with much to say."

Following in the tradition of T. S. Eliot, Harold Pinter, and Noel Coward, Wymark writes, according to *Newsweek*'s Jack Kroll, to probe "the bad faith of comfy-cozy Western society, looking for the asp in aspidistra." Her play "Find Me," for instance, is a psychodrama that studies a couple and a disturbed child. "Loved," which some reviewers consider the stronger of the two plays, "is concerned," wrote Mel Gussow in the *New York Times*, "with vagrant dreams and bestial nightmares." Kroll called it "a metaphysical comedy of spiritual death."

Both the symbolism and the straightforwardness of Wymark's works have merited critical praise, particularly in "Loved." "Actually," commented Gussow, "'Loved' wears its symbolism like a signature on a designer scarf; no matter which way the wind blows, we never forget the label." Though, as Gussow pointed out, "bizarre things are stated in the most direct way," even the familiar becomes fantastic. Most notably, there is an episode in "Loved" in which Lawrence, the main character's husband, and the audience as well are terrified when they find his wife and her sister celebrating a peculiar pagan ritual. The horror continues until Lawrence understands that the sisters are cleaning a carpet.

Another play, "Coda," illustrates the ritual shared by a husband and wife who present each other with "symbols" of their married life: chain wheels and locks. On an even more bizarre level, a scene in the comedy "Lunchtime Concert" requires an effeminate bird-watcher to lecture an aging woman and a young man, an unusual pair of lovers, on the depravity of their relationship. "But gradually," Coleman explained, "his own perversions make themselves more and more obvious, until finally he empties out of his knapsack dozens of dead birds, into which he sinks his pen knife and his teeth."

Wymark told *CA:* "From the fifties until my husband died in 1970 I wrote plays because I wanted to; now I write them for a living. Although I have never written 'a commercial' play, I have to sell my work. Consequently I think my plays have become less obscure (and pretentious), and I find myself more drawn to comedy. The theatre is my first passion, but I love to write for radio and would like to write more for TV and would really like to write a film."

BIOGRAPHICAL/CRITICAL SOURCES: Village Voice, May 16, 1969; *New York Times*, April 28, 1979, June 8, 1979; *Newsweek*, May 7, 1979.

*   *   *

WYMER, Norman (George)   1911-

PERSONAL: Born in 1911 in England; married Jean Kinloch; children: two sons. *Education:* Attended Charterhouse. *Home:* 11 Grassmere Close, Felpham, Sussex, England.

CAREER: Associated with Odhams Press, 1929-31; *Evening News*, London, England, staff reporter, 1931-34; *Daily Telegraph*, London, correspondent, 1935-46; writer, 1946—. Literary adviser to Odhams Press, 1954; associated with overseas department of Longmans Group.

WRITINGS: English Country Crafts: A Survey of Their Development From Early Times to Present Day, Batsford, 1946; *A Breath of England* (travel), Lutterworth, 1948-51, Volume I: *The Southern Shires*, Volume II: *Wheatsheaf and Willow: The Eastern Shires*, Volume III: *Green Hills and Grey Spires: The West Midlands*, Volume IV: *Mere and Moorland: The Northern Counties; English Town Crafts; A Survey of Their Development From Early Times to the Present Day*, Batsford, 1949; *Sport in England: A History of Two Thousand Years of Games and Pastimes*, Harrap, 1949; *Companion Into Sussex* (travel), Methuen, 1950, Spurbooks, 1972; *Village Life*, foreword by H. J. Massingham, Harrap, 1951; *Rural Crafts*, self-illustrated, Oxford University Press, 1952; *Country Folk*, Odhams, 1953; *The Story of Winchester*, Staples, 1955; *The Times Guide to the Sky at Night*, illustrated by B. Weltman, Hamish Hamilton, 1966; *London Today* (travel), Longman, 1971.

Juveniles: *Look at Dogs*, illustrated by Constance Marshall, Hamish Hamilton, 1963; *With Mackenzie in Canada*, illustrated by Harry Tootbill, F. Muller, 1963; *Look at Radio*, illustrated by David Parry, Hamish Hamilton, 1964; *From Marconi to Telstar: The Story of Radio*, Longmans, Green, 1966; *Your Book of Television*, Faber, 1966.

"Behind the Scenes" series; published by Phoenix House, except as noted: *Behind the Scenes at London Airport*, illustrated by H. A. Johns, 1963, Dent, 1964; . . . *in an Ocean Liner*, illustrated by Johns, 1963, Dent, 1964; . . . *on an Oilfield*, 1964, Dent, 1964; . . . *in a Hospital*, illustrated by Laszlo Acs, 1965; . . . *in Parliament*, illustrated by Johns, 1966; . . . *in the Police*, Dent, 1970.

"It's Made Like This" series; all published by Baker, except as noted: *Glass*, 1964, Roy, 1969; *Roads*, 1964, Roy, 1969; *Pottery*, Roy, 1966; *Timber*, 1966.

Biographies: *Dr. Arnold of Rugby*, foreword by Sir Will Spens, R. Hale, 1953; *Father of Nobody's Children: A Portrait of Dr. Barnardo*, Hutchinson, 1954; *George Stephenson*, Oxford University Press, 1957; *Louis Braille*, Oxford University Press, 1957; *Medical Scientists and Doctors*, Oxford University Press, 1958; *The Man From the Cape*, Evans Bros., 1959; *Harry Ferguson*, Roy, 1961; *Yehudi Menuhin*, Phoenix House, 1961; *Gilbert and Sullivan*, Dutton, 1963.

Easy Readers: (Abridger) Archibald Joseph Cronin, *Hatter's Castle*, illustrated by James Cleaver, Longmans, Green, 1962; (abridger) Cronin, *The Citadel*, Longmans, Green, 1963; *Man Against Nature*, Longmans, Green, 1964; (abridger) Thor Heyerdahl, *The Kon-Tiki Expedition*, Longmans, Green, 1965; *The Woman in Grey and Other Pieces for Easy Reading*, University of London Press, 1971; *Oil*, Longman, 1972; (abridger) Ian Fleming, *For Your Eyes Only: Five James Bond Stories*, illustrated by John Holder, Longman, 1973; (abridger) Cronin,

The Stars Look Down, illustrated by Terrence Greer, Longman, 1973.

SIDELIGHTS: Norman Wymer is noted for supplying American newspapers with articles about life in England during World War II.

BIOGRAPHICAL/CRITICAL SOURCES: Guardian, March 24, 1961; *Times Literary Supplement*, May 19, 1961; *Best Sellers*, May 15, 1963; *New York Times Book Review*, September 29, 1963.*

Y

YANEY, George L(evings) 1930-

PERSONAL: Born October 30, 1930, in Teaneck, N.J.; son of Arthur J. (a chemist) and Frances (Levings) Yaney; married Ann Hinrichs, June 7, 1952; children: Brian, Dale, Carolyn, Tara. *Education:* Rensselaer Polytechnic Institute, B.Mgt.E., 1952; University of Colorado, M.A., 1956; Princeton University, Ph.D., 1961. *Office:* Department of History, University of Maryland, College Park, Md. 20742.

CAREER: College of Wooster, Wooster, Ohio, instructor in history, 1957-58; University of Maryland, College Park, assistant professor, 1960-67, associate professor, 1967-73, professor of history, 1973—. *Military service:* U.S. Marine Corps, 1952-54; became captain. *Member:* American Historical Association. *Awards, honors:* Grants for the Soviet Union from Inter-University Travel Grants Committee, 1965-66, and International Research and Exchanges Board, 1975, 1977; research fellow at Russian Research Institute, Harvard University, 1969-70; Fulbright grant for the Soviet Union, 1975, 1977.

WRITINGS: (Contributor) James Millar, editor, *The Soviet Rural Community: A Symposium,* University of Illinois Press, 1971; *The Systematization of Russian Government: The Evolution of Domestic Administration in Russia Under the Emperors, 1711-1905,* University of Illinois Press, 1973; *The Urge to Mobilize: Agrarian Reform in Russia, 1861-1930,* University of Illinois Press, 1982. Contributor to history and political science journals.

*   *   *

YASTRZEMSKI, Carl (Michael, Jr.) 1939-

PERSONAL: Born August 22, 1939, in Southhampton, N.Y.; son of Carl Michael (a farmer) and Hattie (Skonieczny) Yastrzemski; married Carolann Casper, January 30, 1960; children: Carl Michael, Mary Anne, Susanne. *Education:* Attended University of Notre Dame, 1957-58; Merrimack College, B.S., 1966. *Agent:* Eaton & Howard, Vance Sanders Inc., 24 Federal St., Boston, Mass. 02110. *Office:* Boston Red Sox, 24 Jersey St., Boston, Mass. 02215.

CAREER: Raleigh Capitals (Carolina League team), Raleigh, N.C., baseball player, 1959; Minneapolis Millers (American Association team), Minneapolis, Minn., baseball player, 1960; Boston Red Sox (American League team), Boston, Mass., baseball player, 1961—. *Awards, honors:* Named Most Valu-

able Player of Carolina League, 1959, and American League, 1967; member of American League All-Star Team, 1963, 1965-75.

WRITINGS: (With Al Hirshberg) *Yaz,* Viking, 1968; (with Hirshberg) *Batting,* Viking, 1972.

SIDELIGHTS: As Ted Williams's successor in left field for the Red Sox, Carl Yastrzemski had a lot to measure up to. For years, Boston fans booed him, whether he played badly or well. His performance was often less than brilliant, though, and many criticized his attitude. Even the 1967 season, when Yastrzemski won the triple crown and was named the American League's Most Valuable Player while leading the Red Sox to the pennant, stopped the booing only briefly, though it was a turning point in his career.

From that time on, Yastrzemski built a reputation as one of baseball's top outfielders and, in spite of a few prolonged slumps, a consistently strong hitter. He was the first American League player in history to get 3,000 hits and 400 home runs. In 1981 he ranked first among active players in games played, runs batted in, bases on balls, total bases, and extra base hits. Boston fans stopped booing him years ago; "now they give him a standing ovation when he pops up," said Johnny Pesky, who managed the Red Sox early in Yastrzemski's career. About the only achievement Yastrzemski has yet to gain in his long tenure with the Red Sox is a world championship—though he has played on two pennant-winning Boston teams, he has never been on the winning side in a World Series.

In his autobiography, *Yaz,* he told of his childhood on a Long Island potato farm, his signing with the Red Sox, and his career through the 1967 season, as well as much of his personal life. *Yaz* was less romanticized than many sports autobiographies, and Leonard Koppett of the *New York Times Book Review* called it "a simple, straightforward biography with flashes of surprising insight."

BIOGRAPHICAL/CRITICAL SOURCES: Carl Yastrzemski and Al Hirshberg, *Yaz,* Viking, 1968; *New York Times Book Review,* June 16, 1968; *New York Times,* March 21, 1972, October 8, 1975, August 20, 1979.*

*   *   *

YEADON, David 1942-

PERSONAL: Surname is pronounced Yeedon; born May 29,

1942, in Castleford, England; son of Claude Wade (a grocer) and Margaret Louise (Marchant) Yeadon; married Anne Coultish (a director of rehabilitation services and a writer), March 16, 1968. *Education:* Leeds University, B.City Planning, 1965. *Home and office:* 40 Fifth Ave., New York, N.Y. 10011.

CAREER: City planner in Wakefield, England, 1959-65; senior city planner in London, England, 1965-67; project coordinator for city of Tehran, Iran, 1968-70; associate city planner in Los Angeles, Calif., 1971-72; author and illustrator, 1972—. *Member:* Royal Town Planning Institute, Authors Guild.

WRITINGS: Exploring Small Towns in California, two volumes, Ward Ritchie, 1972; *Hidden Restaurants in California,* two volumes, Camaro, 1972; *Wine Tasting in California,* Camaro, 1973; *Sumptuous Indulgence on a Shoestring* (cookbook), Hawthorn, 1974; (with wife, Anne Yeadon) *Towards Independence,* American Federation for the Blind, 1974; *New York Book of Bars, Pubs, and Taverns,* Hawthorn, 1975; *Hidden Corners of New England,* Crowell, 1977; *Hidden Corners of the Mid-Atlantic States,* Crowell, 1977; *When the Earth Was Young: Songs of the American Indian,* Doubleday, 1978; *Nooks and Crannies: A Walking Tour Guide to New York City,* Scribner, 1979; *Backroad Journeys of the West Coast States,* Harper, 1979; (with A. Yeadon) *Living with Impaired Vision,* American Federation for the Blind, 1979; *Backroad Journeys of Southern Europe,* Harper, 1981; *Hidden Corners of Britain,* Allen & Unwin, 1981; *Offbeat England,* Penguin, 1982; *Island Retreats of America,* two volumes, Crown, 1982. Contributor of illustrated articles to numerous newspapers and periodicals, including *New York Times, Los Angeles Times, Cue,* and *America.* Also co-editor with A. Yeadon of eight self-study books on rehabilitation techniques for older blind individuals, Center for Independent Living, 1977-79.

SIDELIGHTS: The backroads of New York, of the West Coast states, of New England, and of the mid-Atlantic states are among the many that Yeadon has traveled. In his books as in his journeys, Yeadon downplays major sightseeing attractions and seeks out lesser-known neighborhoods and local landmarks. Typically, Yeadon discusses a place's architecture, its parks, its ethnic hold-outs, its markets, and its local museums. He sometimes peers into corners so obscure that they are unknown to many of their region's inhabitants.

For the more adventuresome visitor, Yeadon suggests unconventional activities such as traveling desert backroads, attending unusual fairs, visiting out-of-the-way lakes and valleys, discovering unique examples of folk architecture, and losing one's self on forest tracks. He looks at everything from mountain paths to cranberry festivals, and he discusses all types of attractions from uncommon front yards to resident recluses in desert hideouts. Yeadon chats with the inhabitants of backroad communities and collects their folklore to preserve their oral histories. "Much of the history is wonderful," said Dawn Druley West of the *Washington Post Book World;* for example, Yeadon recounts the time "during the gold rush . . . [when] Edwin Booth and Lola Montez were 'showered with gold dust after each tumultuous performance' at the theater in Downieville, Calif."

Yeadon's 1981 book, *Backroad Journeys of Southern Europe,* records his travels, totalling fifteen thousand miles, through southern France, Portugal, Spain, Italy, and southern Switzerland. "His book is studded with nuggets of history and quotations from other authors," a *New York Times* critic noted. "But many of his best passages concern small, unplanned-for adventures." The critic further remarked that Yeadon "writes expansively about food . . . markets and festivals, landscape and architecture, people and animals," and called *Backroad*

Journeys of Southern Europe "a remarkably sunny-natured book."

Yeadon told *CA:* "After ten years of professional practice, I put aside my city planning career and dabbled. At first an article, a few illustrations, and then came the aroma of that first check, disbelief at the gangling contract, all staples, folds, and formalities. How could anyone be so gullible to pay me for traveling America in a beat-up VW camper with very hazy notions of what I was doing? Not that they paid much at first. I made up the difference on the journey by selling pen sketches of lopsided gold towns and postcards of Victorian gothic fantasy architecture (six for a dollar, custom-backed by Anne in the back of the camper). It was supposed to be a short trip, a sabbatical from designing never-never new towns and solving the unsolvable, a chance to write about real places and people before cashing in the camper for a responsible expense-account-and-Cadillac career. Only it didn't happen that way.

"I never went back. I chose the backroads—thousands upon thousands of miles of them. I explored the hidden corners of America and even came into the big cities searching out the secrets of their nooks and crannies. Occasionally I'd digress for a book on budget gourmet cooking or on the songs of the American Indian. Anne and I collaborated on her work with the aging blind in New York and then set off again together on backroad odysseys of Britain and southern Europe. The books got longer, the illustrations better, and the themes clearer. Odd adventures and delights of discovery increased. We met wise people out there in quiet places, and they became both part of the book and our lives.

"In an era of mass travel on a global scale, many modern-day explorers overlook the riches of local environments and substitute superficial, fast-paced itineraries through exotic locations for the adventures and surprises of backroad travel closer to home. They miss a lot this way—the hidden places, the little legends, the heritage and the folklore of small communities, people living a quieter way of life reflecting more durable values.

"Future plans? Very vague, just as they should be. More of the same? It's never the same. Each book is a fresh experience, a bevy of new challenges and surprises.

"Yes, I'd like to build our home (an exercise in fantastitecture). I'd like to circle the earth, slowly and on the ground. I'd like to avoid predictability. I'd like to experiment with new writings and illustrations. Most of all, I'd like to keep alive."

AVOCATIONAL INTERESTS: Travel, adventure, illustration, photography, budget-gourmet cooking, reading and writing fiction, handmade homes.

BIOGRAPHICAL/CRITICAL SOURCES: Washington Post Book World, June 3, 1979; *World Literature Today,* summer, 1979; *New York Times,* August 16, 1981.

* * *

YEATS, William Butler   1865-1939

BRIEF ENTRY: Born June 13, 1865, in Sandymount, Ireland; died January 28, 1939, in Roquebrune, France; buried in Drumcliffe, Sligo, Ireland. Irish poet, playwright, and essayist. Yeats is generally considered one of the finest English-language poets of the twentieth century. Beginning with the late-romantic, Pre-Raphaelite verses in *The Wanderings of Oisin, and Other Poems* (1889), he sought to create a purely Irish literature, one that would revive Ireland's Celtic past and define its national culture. For the next twenty years, Yeats pursued a variety of styles and subjects. His early works are marked by sentimental and frequently abstract pronouncements on Ireland's past. In collections such as *The Green Helmet* (1910), however, Yeats courted the antithesis of the preceding works, producing less lyrical poems on contemporary issues. In the poems of the early 1920's, Yeats delved heavily into symbolism. The volumes *Later Poems* (1922) and *The Cat and the Moon and Certain Poems* (1924), while praised for their unique and highly-evolved style, were considered oblique by some readers. In 1925, Yeats wrote *A Vision,* an essay detailing his interest in mysticism and its subsequent symbolic function in his poetry. Though Yeats's reputation rests largely on his accomplishments as a poet, he was also influential in the development of Irish theatre. He helped J. M. Synge and Sean O'Casey establish the Irish Literary Theatre, which sparked a revival of verse-drama. Yeats's plays are usually prized for their poetry and criticized for their lack of characterization or content. His poems, especially those written after he was fifty years of age, are the ultimate achievement in his long career. In 1923, Yeats received the Nobel Prize for literature. *Biographical/critical sources: Cyclopedia of World Authors,* Harper, 1958; *Longman Companion to Twentieth Century Literature,* Longman, 1970; *Modern World Drama: An Encyclopedia,* Dutton, 1972; *Twentieth-Century Literary Criticism,* Volume 1, Gale, 1978.

* * *

YESENIN, Sergei Alexandrovich
    See ESENIN, Sergei (Alexandrovich)

* * *

YORICK, A. P.
    See TINDALL, William York

* * *

YOST, Charles W(oodruff) 1907-1981

OBITUARY NOTICE—See index for *CA* sketch: Born November 6, 1907, in Watertown, N.Y.; died of cancer, c. 1981, in Washington, D.C. Diplomat, lecturer, and author. Called the "Gray Ghost" because of his unobtrusive personality, Yost worked in the U.S. Foreign Service for more than thirty years. He held diplomatic posts in such countries as Thailand, Austria, and Greece, and served as an ambassador to Laos, Syria, and Morocco. In 1945 Yost was a member of the San Francisco conference that created the United Nations, and in 1969 he became the first career foreign service officer appointed U.S. ambassador to that international body. In recognition of Yost's diplomatic career, the Foreign Service conferred upon him the title of "career ambassador," its highest award. Yost also lectured at Columbia University's School of International Affairs. He wrote a number of books on foreign policy, including *The Insecurity of Nations: International Relations in the Twentieth Century, The Conduct and Misconduct of Foreign Affairs,* and *History and Memory.* Obituaries and other sources: *Time,* June 8, 1981.

* * *

YOUNG, Edgar Berryhill 1908-

PERSONAL: Born April 27, 1908, in Anderson, Ind.; son of Earl Edgar (a credit manager) and Irene Sherfey (Berryhill) Young; married Jane White, August 9, 1930; children: Robert Berryhill, John Barton, Peter Van Winkle. *Education:* DePauw University, A.B., 1929; graduate study at University of Pennsylvania, 1929-30, London School of Economics and Political Science, London, 1930-31, and American University, 1933-

34. *Religion:* United Church of Christ. *Home:* 60 Oak Ridge Ave., Summit, N.J. 07901.

CAREER: U.S. Employment Service, Washington, D.C., assistant to director, 1933-39; Bureau of the Budget, Washington, D.C., personnel director, 1939-45; Port of New York Authority, New York, N.Y., assistant to executive director, 1945-46; associate with John D. Rockefeller 3rd, 1946-73, consultant, 1973-78; writer, 1978—. Secretary of Lincoln Center for the Performing Arts, 1956-62, chairman of building committee, 1961-70, acting president of center, 1961, vice-president, 1961-65, director, 1961-81, director emeritus, 1981—; member of board of directors of Staten Island Rapid Transit Railway, 1947-62, and Arts Council of America, Inc., 1960-66. *Member:* Council on Foreign Relations, Japan Society (member of board of directors, 1972-78; vice-president, 1973-79), Asia Society, Phi Kappa Psi, University Club. *Awards, honors:* LL.D. from DePauw University, 1962.

WRITINGS: (Contributor) Donald B. Gooch, editor, *Theater and Main Street,* College of Design and Architecture, University of Michigan, 1963; *Lincoln Center: The Building of an Institution,* New York University Press, 1980. Contributor to academic journals and popular magazines, including *Arts and Society* and *Westsider.*

SIDELIGHTS: Young wrote: "In an era of increasing specialization, I have remained a generalist. My career focus, in public service and in private nonprofit institutions, has been in administration. I wrote *Lincoln Center* because I felt that the facts concerning the origin and development of this pioneer cultural center and the people involved in it should be a matter of historical record. I had been personally related to every facet of that development—organization, financial planning, fund raising, architectural planning, and actual construction. The complete documentation of the project was available to me. The published volume is an 'insider's' account, citing our problems, frustrations, and compromises, as well as our triumphs and satisfactions. Events are told as they were perceived at the time by those most intimately involved."

BIOGRAPHICAL/CRITICAL SOURCES: New York Times, December 14, 1961; *Newark News,* December 14, 1961, January 7, 1962, January 10, 1962, November 7, 1965; *Public Administration Review,* winter, 1962; *Anderson Daily Bulletin,* May 12, 1962, October 17, 1963; *Musical America,* September, 1962; *Indianapolis Star,* September 22, 1963.

* * *

YOUNG, Jock 1942-

PERSONAL: Born March 4, 1942, in Gorebridge, Scotland; son of Walter (a truck driver) and Margaret (Stewart) Young; children: Jesse. *Education:* London School of Economics and Political Science, B.Sc., 1965, M.Sc., Ph.D., 1972. *Politics:* Socialist. *Religion:* None. *Home:* 39 Parkholme Rd., London E.8, England. *Office:* Department of Social Science, Middlesex Polytechnic, Enfield College, Queensway, Enfield, Middlesex, England.

CAREER: Middlesex Polytechnic, Enfield, England, lecturer, 1967, senior lecturer, 1967-72, principal lecturer, 1972-78, reader in sociology, 1978—.

WRITINGS: The Drugtakers: The Social Meaning of Drug Use, MacGibbon & Kee, 1971; (with Ian R. Taylor and Paul Walton) *The New Criminology: For a Social Theory of Deviance,* Routledge & Kegan Paul, 1973; (with Victoria Greenwood) *Abortion in Demand,* Pluto Press, 1975; *Media as Myth,* Macmillan, 1982; *Contemporary Criminology Theory,* Routledge & Kegan

Paul, 1982; *Polytechnics in Transition*, D. C. Heath, 1982. Also author of *The Zookeepers of Deviancy*, 1970, and, with Mike Fitzgerald and Karen Margolis, *Know Your Own Society*, 1981.

Editor: (With Stanley Cohen) *The Manufacturer of News*, Constable, 1973, 2nd edition, 1981; (with Roy Victor Bailey) *Contemporary Social Problems in Britain*, Lexington Books, 1973; (with Taylor and Walton) *Critical Criminology*, Routledge & Kegan Paul, 1974. Also editor, with Bob Fine, of *Capitalism and the Rule of Law*, 1980.

SIDELIGHTS: Young told *CA:* ''My major perspective is a Marxist critique of both the Eastern and Western blocs that attempts to shed light on the problems of crime and the mass media. It aims at pointing to the possibility of a democratic control of crime and the development of a mass media which only reflects the needs and interests of people.''

Z

ZADE, Mirzo Tursun
See TURSUN-ZADE, Mirzo

* * *

ZAHLER, Helene S. 1911-1981

OBITUARY NOTICE: Born June 27, 1911, in Auburn, N.Y.; died in 1981 in New York, N.Y. Educator, historian, and author. A specialist in nineteenth-century American history, Zahler was an associate professor of history at Brooklyn College of the City University of New York until her retirement in 1977. She wrote *Eastern Workingmen and National Land Policy* and co-wrote *The United States in the Twentieth Century*. Obituaries and other sources: *AB Bookman's Weekly*, July 27, 1981.

* * *

ZOILUS
See LOVECRAFT, H(oward) P(hillips)

* * *

ZOLA, Emile 1840-1902

BRIEF ENTRY: Born April 2, 1840, in Paris, France; died of accidental asphyxiation, September 29, 1902, in Paris, France; buried in Pantheon, Rome, Italy. French novelist, critic, journalist, and playwright. The leader of the naturalist school, Zola has been called "the pioneer of modern sociological imagination." Around 1867, the writer turned against the romanticism of Hugo and developed determinism, a school suggesting that the lives of fictional characters are determined by their heredity and their environments. Zola was quick to point out that the naturalist school was not fatalistic since fate cannot be changed but environmental factors can. Zola adapted a scientific approach to writing; he observed and recorded reality without padding the story with imaginary creations. A series of twenty volumes, entitled *Les Rougon-Macquart,* traced the history of a single family and illustrated how environment and heredity determined an individual's life and how one family's congenital weaknesses debilitated society. Completed in 1893, the series is considered the chief monument of the French naturalist movement. *L'Assommoir* (1877; published in English as *Gervaise*) and *Germinal* (1855) are held to be the best novels in the Rougon series. Adapted into a dramatic production, the novel *Therese Raquin,* Zola's first major novel, brought naturalism to the theatre. In addition to his contribution to literature, Zola is remembered for the essay "J'accuse!" (title means "I Accuse"), which he wrote in defense of Captain Alfred Dreyfus, a Jewish army officer falsely accused of treason and sentenced to a life term on Devil's Island. Because of "J'accuse," the author was convicted of libel. He took refuge in England and returned to France after one year. His works include *La Confession de Claude* (1866; title means "Claude's Confession") and *La Roman experimental* (1880; title means "The Experimental Novel"). *Biographical/critical sources: Cyclopedia of World Authors,* Harper, 1958; *Twentieth-Century Literary Criticism,* Volume 1, Gale, 1978.

* * *

ZOOK, Deborah
See GREEN, Deborah

* * *

ZOPHY, Jonathan Walter 1945-

PERSONAL: Born September 5, 1945, in Milwaukee, Wis.; son of Walter Henry (a chemist) and Sarah (a nurse; maiden name, Jacobson) Zophy; married Angela Howard (a professor), April 10, 1971. *Education:* Michigan State University, B.A., 1967; Ohio State University, M.A., 1968, Ph.D., 1972. *Office:* Department of History, Carthage College, Kenosha, Wis. 53140.

CAREER: Lane College, Jackson, Tenn., associate professor of history, 1972-73; Carthage College, Kenosha, Wis., assistant professor, 1973-79, associate professor of history, 1979—. *Member:* American Historical Association, American Association of University Professors, American Society for Reformation Research, Sixteenth Century Studies Conference. *Awards, honors:* Grant from American Philosophical Society, 1973-74.

WRITINGS: (Editor with Lawrence Buck, and contributor) *The Social History of the Reformation,* Ohio State University Press, 1972; (contributor) J. A. Neuenschwander, editor, *Kenosha County in the Twentieth Century,* Kenosha Bicentennial Commission, 1976; *The Holy Roman Empire,* Greenwood Press, 1980. Contributor to history journals.

WORK IN PROGRESS: Reformation Diplomat: Christoph Kress of Nuremberg; The Joy of History, completion expected in 1984.

SIDELIGHTS: Zophy commented: "My historical writing has been inspired by the examples of the scholars who helped train me—people such as Harold Grimm, Clayton Roberts, and J. B. Harrison—and by a desire to obtain professional advancement and recognition. My first book was produced to honor Harold Grimm and to indicate some of the new directions that Reformation research was taking. *The Holy Roman Empire* was designed to help bridge the gap between scholars and specialists and to provide the first English-language reference work on the subject. I hope to do more creative writing in the future."

*   *   *

ZUBROWSKI, Bernard   1939-

PERSONAL: Born February 22, 1939, in Baltimore, Md.; son of Anthony and Catherine Zubrowski. *Education:* Loyola College, Baltimore, Md., B.S.; Boston College, M.S.T. *Home:* 46 Oliver St., Watertown, Mass. 02172. *Office:* Children's Museum, 300 Congress St., Boston, Mass.

CAREER: U.S. Peace Corps, Washington, D.C., served in Bangladesh, 1962-64; Children's Museum, Boston, Mass., bricoleur-in-residence, 1971—.

WRITINGS—For children: *Bubbles,* Little Brown, 1979; *Ball Point Pens,* Little, Brown, 1979; *Milk Carton Blocks,* Little, Brown, 1979; *Cake Chemistry,* Little, Brown, 1981; *Water Pumps,* Little, Brown, 1981; *Drinking Straw Structures,* Little, Brown, 1981.

WORK IN PROGRESS: Developing a series of programs, exhibits, and written materials to help children understand ancient and modern technology.

SIDELIGHTS: Zubrowski wrote: "I am interested in promoting among educators, parents, and the general public the idea that children's play is an important need in their understanding the world and becoming whole people.

"My unofficial title at the Children's Museum is 'bricoleur-in-residence.' Bricoleur is a French word indicating someone who was a combination inventor-handyman practicing a trade that was somewhere between an artist and scientist. The bricoleur was always collecting junk and transforming it into new objects or using it to repair something broken. The game of the bricoleur is to make do with what is at hand.

"I like to take everyday materials and transform them into objects of play. A ballpoint pen for me can become a whistle, a thermometer, or a pen that writes on water. Ivory dishwashing soap in a tray of water is an occasion for making visible air and water currents. In the design of these play objects for children I try to emphasize the aesthetic qualities of the object or phenomena, but at the same time present it in a context where basic science principles become exemplified. I feel strongly that education should be based on the positive qualities of people, and aesthetic curiosity is perhaps one of the noblest."